The Logic of
American
Politics

The Logic of
American
Politics

FOURTH EDITION

Samuel Kernell, Gary C. Jacobson, and Thad Kousser

University of California, San Diego

A Division of SAGE
Washington, D.C.

CQ Press
2300 N Street, NW, Suite 800
Washington, DC 20037

Phone: 202-729-1900; toll-free, 1-866-4CQ-PRESS (1-866-427-7737)

Web: www.cqpress.com

Cover design: Matthew Simmons, Myself Included Design
Interior design: Malcolm McGaughy
Maps: International Mapping Associates
Composition: BMWW

∞ The paper used in this publication exceeds the requirements of the American National Standard for Information Sciences—Permanence of Paper for Printed Library Materials, ANSI Z39.48-1992.

Printed and bound in the United States of America

12   11   10   09   08   1   2   3   4   5

Library of Congress Cataloging-in-Publication Data

Kernell, Samuel
    The logic of American politics / Samuel Kernell, Gary C. Jacobson,
      and Thad Kousser. — 4th ed.
    p. cm.
    Includes bibliographical references and index.
    ISBN 978-0-87289-604-8 (alk. paper)
    1. United States—Politics and government—Textbooks.   I. Jacobson, Gary C.
II. Kousser, Thad.   III. Title.

    JK276.K47 2008
    320.47301—dc22

                                                                    2008050644

To our wives—Dianne, Marty, and Kate

The following dedication to James Madison is from the oldest American government textbook we have found: William Alexander Duer's *Outlines of the Constitutional Jurisprudence of the United States*, published in 1833.

To you, Sir, as the surviving member of the august assembly that framed the Constitution, and of the illustrious triumvirate who, in vindicating it from the objections of its first assailants, succeeded in recommending it to the adoption of their country; to you, who, in discharging the highest duties of its administration, proved the stability and excellence of the Constitution, in war as well as in peace, and determined the experiment in favor of republican institutions and the right of self-government; to you, who in your retirement, raised a warning voice against those heresies in the construction of that Constitution which for a moment threatened to impair it; to you, Sir, as alone amongst the earliest and the latest of its defenders,—this brief exposition of the organization and principles of the National Government, intended especially for the instruction of our American youth, is most respectfully, and, in reference to your public services, most properly inscribed.

Columbia College, N.Y.
August 1st, 1833.

Brief Contents

Contents

logic.cqpress.com

logic.cqpress.com

logic.cqpress.com

Part II. The Institutions of Government

(Chapters 6–9)

logic.cqpress.com

Part IV. Conclusion

Chapter 15. The Prospects for Institutional Reform 696

Reference Material 726

Boxes, Tables, Figures, and Maps

Chapter 12. Political Parties

Chapter 13. Interest Groups

Chapter 14. The News Media

Preface

S ince this book's last edition went to press in June 2005 politics in Washington, D.C., and across the nation have changed dramatically. After President George W. Bush's reelection in 2004 and his party's renewed majorities in both the House of Representatives and the Senate, Republicans appeared poised to consolidate their control of the national government for a long, happy run in power. Republican leaders were forming support groups among the well-heeled K Street lobbyists, whom they actively discouraged from extending even token campaign support to congressional Democrats; Republicans occupied more local and state legislative offices than ever, promising seasoned recruits for future elections; and perhaps most importantly, Republicans had seized the "war on terror" issue and backed the Democrats into a corner. The Democratic Party couldn't find a way to oppose the administration's policies without appearing both unpatriotic and weak. Certainly, one would have reasonably thought, the Republican hegemony would endure past the third edition of *Logic*! Yet, as we go to press with the fourth edition shortly after the 2008 election, President Bush is limping out of office with 22 percent of the public approving his job performance. (Even the disgraced Richard Nixon's job performance rating was higher on that fateful August morning in 1974 when he boarded the helicopter to leave the White House for the last time.) Republican difficulties actually began in 2006 when the party narrowly lost control of Congress. But the full magnitude of the party's collapse occurred in the 2008 elections, when the Democrats won a lopsided majority in the House and a nearly filibuster-proof majority in the Senate.

With the election of Barack Obama, the 2008 election's significance extends well beyond the vagaries of party fortunes at the polls. The election of an African American as president represents the culmination of more than two centuries of political and moral conflict. In Chapter 4 we present the painful history of civil rights. This election makes that struggle even more poignant.

Amid such dramatic changes, it is easy to lose sight of the continuities of American politics. After a brief bout of mutual finger pointing, Republican politicians will regroup and provide a forceful counterpoint to the new administration. The difficulties of governing in a time of economic and international crises will challenge a unified Democratic government no less than they did (and undid) their Republican predecessors. And although a new group of politicians won control in 2008 chanting the mantra of "change," they occupy the same governmental offices as those they replace. These offices and the governing institutions they comprise are a powerful source of continuity, for they establish the authority, responsibilities, and constraints that shape any new regime regardless of its political aims.

Our overarching goal in *The Logic of American Politics* is to help students discern the rationale embedded in our extraordinary and complex array of American political institutions and practices. To accomplish this goal, we analyze political institutions and practices as (imperfect) solutions to problems facing people who need to act collectively. We highlight recurring obstacles to collective action in various contexts to illuminate the diverse institutional means that American politicians have created to overcome them. These obstacles include the conflict over values and interests, the difficulty of aggregating individual preferences into collective decisions, the need for coordination, and the threat of reneging implicit in every collective undertaking. Stable political communities strengthen their capacity to act collectively and reduce the costs of doing so by fashioning appropriate institutions. These institutions feature majority and plurality rule and procedures that convert votes into representation, delegate authority to agents, and permit some institutional actors to propose courses of action while allocating to others the right to veto proposals. Throughout the book we emphasize the strategic dimension of political action, from the Framers' trade-offs in crafting the Constitution to the efforts of contemporary officeholders to shape policy, so students can understand current institutions as the products of political conflicts, as well as the venues for resolving them.

New challenges pose fresh problems for collective action for which current institutions may seem inadequate. Yet, as the prolonged response to the September 11, 2001, attacks and more recently, the numerous tentative (albeit expensive) steps in remedying the mortgage crisis illustrate, reforms are not automatic or easy. The institutions created to deal with the challenges of collective action at one historical moment can continue to shape politics long after those challenges have receded. Therefore, we pay a good deal of attention to the historical development of political institutions, a narrative that reveals politicians and citizens grappling intellectually, as well as politically, with their collective action problems and discovering the institutional means to resolve them.

This book is the product of our nearly forty years of teaching American politics in a way that seeks to go beyond the basics. In addition to introducing students to the descriptive facts and fundamental principles, we have sought to help them cultivate an ability to analyze and understand American politics for themselves. None of us is closely associated with the rational choice school, yet over time our research and teaching have benefited from many of its insights, especially those familiarly referred to as "the new institutionalism." We have found these insights helpful in making sense of American politics in terms that students intuitively can grasp. Having absorbed these ideas into our own scholarly thinking, we employ them here to help students understand what the American political system looks like and why it has assumed its present shape.

Organization of the Book

Our emphasis on the primacy of institutions extends well beyond collecting and processing the preferences of citizens and politicians. In that institutions may structure the choices available to voters and their leaders, we view them as indispensable in explaining public opinion and the strategic behavior of the political organizations that seek to influence and mobilize these preferences. We therefore have adopted a somewhat unorthodox structure for the book. We cover the rules of the game and the formal institutions of government before discussing the "input" side of the political process—public opinion, elections, parties, and interest groups—because we emphasize the way rules and institutions structure the actions and choices of citizens and politicians alike.

The introductory chapter presents the concepts and ideas that form the framework for the subsequent chapters. The core concepts address problems of making and implementing collective choices. Along with traditional concepts that remain indispensable to understanding American politics—such as representation, majority rule, and separation of powers—we introduce students to a number of ideas from economics that political scientists have found increasingly useful for exploring American politics. These include the focal points of coordination, prisoner's dilemma, free-riding, tragedy of the commons, transaction costs, principal-agent relations, and public goods. Other concepts, with a more specialized and limited application in our discussion (such as negative agenda control), are presented later in the book, where they are most relevant.

The substantive chapters are arranged in four parts. Part I covers the foundational elements of American politics: the Constitution, federalism, civil rights, and civil liberties. The chapters that cover these topics give students an understanding of the political origins and development of the basic structure and rules of the national polity.

Part II examines the major formal institutions of national government: Congress, the presidency, the bureaucracy, and the federal judiciary. These chapters reveal how the politics and logic of their development have shaped their current organizational features, practices, and relations with one another.

Part III analyzes the institutions that link citizens with government officials, again in terms of their historical development, political logic, and present-day operations. Chapters in this section are devoted to public opinion; voting, campaigns, and elections; political parties; interest groups; and the news media.

The concluding chapter, found in Part IV, evaluates proposals to "reform" American government through the lens of our collective action framework. It begins by describing the obstacles that the Framers placed in the way of any potential changes to the system they designed. Then, the conclusion tells the story of four reform movements—the shift from caucus nominations to primary elections, the enactment of legislative term limits, efforts to increase voter turnout, and the failed move to give the president a line-item veto—viewed as attempts to solve collective action problems. The political fate of each movement, and the ultimate effect of each reform on the operations of government, has been driven by the same logic of American politics described throughout this book.

In elaborating on and reinforcing the themes of the text, we include several sets of boxes in every chapter. The "Logic of Politics" boxes explain the logical rationale or implications of some institutional feature presented in the text. In Chapter 7, "The Presidency," where the text presents the standard descriptive facts about the Constitution's provision for a presidential veto and the frequency with which it has been enlisted over the past two centuries, the adjacent "Logic of Politics" box compares those circumstances in which this "take it or leave it" choice confers real influence on the president in settings where a veto holds little promise for advancing the president's policy preferences. Another set of boxes, "Strategy and Choice," explores how politicians use institutions and respond to the incentives institutions provide in pursuing their personal or constituencies' interests. In Chapter 8, "The Bureaucracy," we learn that in building the B-1 bomber for the U.S. military, defense contractor Rockwell found it politically prudent to distribute its contracts with parts suppliers across hundreds of congressional districts—more than twice the dispersion involved in building commercial aircraft.

Rather than devote separate chapters to public policy, we incorporate policy issues throughout the book. "Politics to Policy" boxes, for example, explain how policies reflect the underlying political rationale of the institutions that produce them. In Chapter 11, "Voting, Campaigns, and Elections," we examine the politics behind the Bipartisan Campaign Reform Act of 2002 and trace out some of its consequences for subsequent elections.

Instructional Features

The Logic of American Politics includes special features designed to engage students' attention and to help them think analytically about the subject. Thematic questions at the beginning of each chapter preview important themes and set the tone for critical thinking. Each chapter then opens with a story that sets the scene, often dramatically, for the topic at hand. Chapter 14, "The News Media," for example, opens with a case study of the clergy sex abuse scandal and explores how citizens affected by the scandal used the Internet, which has changed the nature of news, to solve the collective ignorance created by the old, one-way news media. We include this case study to illustrate the chapter's broader theme that in the United States the vital civic function of informing the public is provided by private, profit-based, competitive businesses.

The introduction offers ideas and concepts that are employed throughout the text. They can be classified under two broad categories: collective action problems and institutional design concepts. Both sets of ideas have deeply informed each chapter's argument. Because this is an introduction to American politics, rather than to political theory, we have intentionally sublimated the analytic ideas in favor of enlisting them to explicate real politics. But be assured that these concepts and theoretical issues are never far beneath the surface of the narrative. To help the student reader spot these concepts when they occasionally break to the surface, we have highlighted these passages in bright blue text. In addition, important terms and concepts throughout the text appear in boldface the first time they are defined. These key terms are listed at the end of each chapter with page references to their explanations and are defined in a glossary at the back of the book. To encourage students to continue their studies of American politics beyond the pages of this volume, we have included annotated reading lists at the end of each chapter. We have also added review questions and exercises from our companion Web site to help students review chapter material, as well as remind them that additional study aids reside on the site.

Content created and updated by Scott MacKenzie of the University of California, San Diego, for the companion Web site (logic.cqpress.com) is rich in exercises and materials that go far beyond the text. Among them is a study guide that includes chapter summaries, learning objectives, and review questions with response boxes so students can e-mail answers directly to their professors. Students also will find interactive quizzes that offer results broken down into questions by type and by chapter section with the capability to e-mail results to instructors. The Web site sports a news blog, which is new to this edition. Not only do we post important news stories here that update topics covered in the text, but we also annotate each story to illustrate or extend themes of the book.

Exercises drawing on a wealth of information (such as *CQ's Politics in America*) permit students to explore how interest groups rate specific members of Congress, study declassified presidential primary source materials, or check out who is giving campaign contributions to whom. A section called "Explore" offers links and images so that students can observe Congress in action, listen in on White House conversations during the Cuban Missile Crisis, or compare today's tabloid journalism with the "yellow journalism" of the late nineteenth century.

The Web site is just one item in a valuable instructional package that accompanies the text. Instructor's resources (adopters should go to college.cqpress.com and click on "Ancillaries for Download") include a test bank, PowerPoint lecture slides, graphics from the book available in PowerPoint and PDF, and extra materials that professors can use throughout their courses, including additional tables and figures and a unique guide geared to teaching assistants for running class discussions. The test bank, written by Charles Anthony Smith of the University of California, Irvine, contains more than a thousand conceptual and factual questions, combining multiple-choice, fill-in-the-blank, short-answer, and essay formats. The extensive lecture materials were developed by Audrey Haynes of the University of Georgia.

An outstanding reference is offered to professors who adopt the text (subject to restrictions by the publisher): subscriptions to *CQ Weekly*, the same source on which political Washington relies for nonpartisan coverage and insightful analysis, are available.

Acknowledgments

Without the help and encouragement of department colleagues, friends, students, and the editorial staff at CQ Press, this book never would have been completed. The book also has benefited from the insightful and astute comments of colleagues at other institutions who took time from their busy schedules to review chapters. We are deeply obliged to everyone who has helped us along the way. In particular, the authors wish to thank Lawrence Baum, Lee Epstein, Rosalind Gold, Richard Hart, and Vickie Stangl for their assistance in procuring data for tables and figures and clarifying historical events.

Our colleagues and students at the University of California, San Diego, have contributed to every aspect of the book, often in ways they might not realize, for the way we think about politics is permeated by the intellectual atmosphere they have created and continue to sustain. Leigh Bradberry assisted us in revising those sections covering the judiciary and case law; her expertise and diligence in looking over our shoulder provided an education as well as assistance.

We are indebted to the executive director of the College Publishing Group of CQ Press, Brenda Carter, for her enthusiasm in taking up this project and bringing it to fruition. Charisse Kiino assumed development responsibilities for this edition, which regularly summoned her nonpareil skills as a diplomat, critic, dispatcher, coach, and booster. Allie McKay was instrumental in transmitting the manuscript and pulling together very useful transition guides for adopters. Anna Socrates cheerfully entered the ring with the authors to wrestle the prose into submission. Talia Greenberg searched diligently for photographs and cartoons and ushered the manuscript into print. That she gave all of our concerns prompt and careful attention is testament to her consummate professionalism. We also wish to thank Steve Pazdan, who oversaw the editing and production; Paul Pressau, who managed the typesetting and composition; Cynthia Richardson, who supervised the manufacturing of the book; Matthew Simmons, who designed the cover; Malcolm McGaughy for the new interior layout; Christopher O'Brien and Erin Snow for brochures, advertisements, and displays for the professional meetings; and Dwain Smith and Jerry Orvedahl, who worked with Scott MacKenzie on the Web site.

Listed below are colleagues across the country who have read and commented on the last three editions and given us an abundance of good advice, much of which we took in writing this revision. Equally essential, they kept us from making many embarrassing mistakes.

Danny M. Adkison, *Oklahoma State University*
E. Scott Adler, *University of Colorado*
Scott H. Ainsworth, *University of Georgia*
Richard Almeida, *Francis Marion University*
Ellen Andersen, *University of Vermont*
Ross K. Baker, *Rutgers University*
Lawrence A. Baum, *Ohio State University*
William T. Bianco, *Indiana University*
Sarah Binder, *Brookings Institution* and *George Washington University*
Christopher Bonneau, *University of Pittsburgh*
Michael Burton, *Ohio University*
Rosalee Clawson, *Purdue University*
Richard S. Conley, *University of Florida*
Michelle D. Deardorff, *Jackson State University*
John Domino, *Sam Houston State University*
Keith Dougherty, *University of Georgia*
Richard S. Fleisher, *Fordham University*

John Freemuth, *Boise State University*
John B. Gilmour, *College of William & Mary*
Lawrence L. Giventer, *California State University–Stanislaus*
Brad Gomez, *Florida State University*
Sanford Gordon, *New York University*
Paul Gronke, *Reed College*
Edward B. Hasecke, *Wittenberg University*
Valerie Heitshusen, *Georgetown University*
Richard Herrera, *Arizona State University*
Brian D. Humes, *University of Nebraska–Lincoln*
Jeffery Jenkins, *University of Virginia*
Paul E. Johnson, *University of Kansas*
Timothy Johnson, *University of Minnesota*
Joel Lefkowitz, *State University of New York–New Paltz*
Brad Lockerbie, *East Carolina University*
Amy Lauren Lovecraft, *University of Alaska–Fairbanks*
Forrest A. Maltzman, *George Washington University*
Wendy Martinek, *Binghamton University*
John McAdams, *Marquette University*
Madhavi McCall, *San Diego State University*
Scott R. Meinke, *Bucknell University*
Timothy Nokken, *Texas Tech University*
Bruce I. Oppenheimer, *Vanderbilt University*
Marvin Overby, *University of Missouri–Columbia*
Justin Phillips, *Columbia University*
Andrew J. Polsky, *Hunter College*
Jason Roberts, *University of Minnesota*
Beth Rosenson, *University of Florida*
Ronnee Schreiber, *San Diego State University*
Charles Shipan, *University of Michigan*
David Shock, *Kennesaw State University*
James D. Slack, *University of Alabama at Birmingham*
Brian Vargus, *Indiana University–Purdue University Indianapolis*
Charles E. Walcott, *Virginia Polytechnic Institute and State University*
Hanes Walton Jr., *University of Michigan*
Wendy Watson, *Southern Methodist University*
Christopher Weible, *University of Colorado–Denver*
Garry Young, *George Washington University*

Finally, our families. Dianne and Georgia Kernell, Marty and Karen Jacobson, and Kate, Will, and Kat Kousser also deserve our gratitude for putting up with what occasionally seemed an interminable drain on our time and attention. We are sure that they are as delighted as we are to have this revision finished.

A Note to Students

Plan of the Book

Our analysis of the logic of American politics begins in Chapter 1 with an introduction to the analytical concepts we draw on throughout the text. Although these concepts are straightforward and intuitive, we do not expect you to understand them fully until they have been applied in later chapters. The rest of the text is arranged in four main parts. Part I looks at the foundational elements of the political system that are especially relevant to understanding modern American politics. It begins with the constitutional system (Chapter 2, "The Constitution") and then moves on to the relations between the national government and the states (Chapter 3, "Federalism"), the evolution of civil rights and the definition of citizenship (Chapter 4, "Civil Rights"), and the establishment of civil liberties, such as freedom of speech and religion (Chapter 5, "Civil Liberties"). A recurring theme of Part I is *nationalization,* the gradual shift of authority from state and local governments to the national government.

Part II examines the four basic institutions of America's national government: Congress (Chapter 6), the presidency (Chapter 7), the bureaucracy (Chapter 8), and the federal judiciary (Chapter 9). The development of effective, resourceful institutions at the national level has made it possible for modern-day politicians to tackle problems that in an earlier time they would have been helpless to solve. We explain how all four institutions have evolved along the paths initiated and confined by the Constitution in response to the forces of nationalization and other social and economic changes.

Part III surveys the institutions that keep citizens informed about what their representatives are doing and enable them to influence their elected officials through voting and other forms of participation. Chapter 10, "Public Opinion," explores the nature of modern political communication by focusing on the ins and outs of mass public opinion. Chapter 11, "Voting, Campaigns, and Elections," examines the ways in which candidates' strategies and voters' preferences interact at the polls to produce national leaders and, on occasion, create mandates for policies. The Constitution mentions neither political parties nor interest groups, and the Framers were deeply suspicious of both. But they are vital to helping citizens make sense of politics and pursue political goals effectively. In Chapter 12, "Political Parties," and Chapter 13, "Interest Groups," we explain how and why parties and interest groups have flourished as intermediaries between citizens and government officials. President Woodrow Wilson once aptly observed that "news is the atmosphere of politics." Chapter 14 looks at the news media both as channels of communication from elected leaders to their constituents and as independent sources of information about their performance. The chapter also considers the implications of the rise of the Internet in coordinating the collective efforts of unorganized publics.

Part IV, which consists of Chapter 15, concludes our inquiry by reviewing the biases inherent in the institutions we have examined and considering how to evaluate proposals to reform current political arrangements.

Special Features

This book contains several special features designed to help you grasp the logic of American politics. At the outset of each chapter are questions that preview important themes and, we hope, will pique your curiosity. To help you more easily spot discussions of collective action problems and institutional design concepts, important passages and analytic points are highlighted in bold, blue text. Each chapter then opens with a story from the real world of politics that introduces one or more of the central issues to be explored. Within each chapter, thematic boxes labeled "Logic of Politics" consider more fully the logical rationale and implications of certain features of government design that are introduced in the core text. Another set of boxes, "Strategy and Choice," focuses on the sometimes imaginative ways politicians enlist institutions to advance their agendas and their constituents' goals. A third set of thematic boxes, "Politics to Policy," treats some of the public policy issues that have sprung forth from the political process. Additional boxes, tables, figures, photographs, and other visuals clarify and enliven the text. Since these features, including the substantive captions, play an integral role in the presentation and discussion, *you should read them with as much care as you do the text.* Key terms, another feature, appear in boldface when first explained and are summarized at the end of chapters. Definitions of these terms are listed in the glossary at the back of the book. Finally, to encourage you to pursue more information on topics you find particularly interesting, we have included annotated lists of suggested readings at the end of each chapter. We also feature review questions from the companion Web site to make it easier for you to study and review, as well as explore a wealth of online resources.

But more lies beyond the covers of this book. Be sure to check out the *Logic* Web site (logic.cqpress.com), where you will find chapter summaries and interactive quizzes that will give you a chance to test and extend your knowledge of the material. The site also posts current news stories from the nation's leading newspapers and discusses how the news follows and extends *Logic*'s analysis. The site also offers a wide variety of exercises, games, skill builders, images, and links to some of the best political and government sites on the Internet, along with a news blog that links current news stories to chapters in the book.

Politics, like every significant human endeavor, becomes more intriguing the more deeply it is explored and understood. Our book aims to give you not only a strong basic foundation for understanding political life in the present-day United States but also a glimpse of how intellectually enjoyable it can be to grapple with its puzzles and paradoxes.

The Logic of
American
Politics

The Logic of American Politics

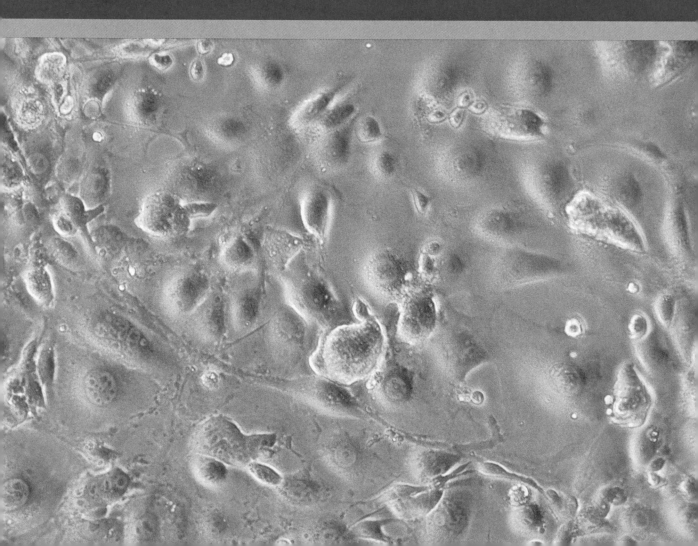

What good is politics in helping people solve their problems?

Do institutions matter? In a democracy, when a majority agrees on a course of action, how do the institutional arrangements really affect the majority's ability to do what it wants?

Are politicians the servants of the public, as they say in their campaign ads, or are they just self-serving? Why do we need them?

Since everyone dislikes auto pollution, and we know what causes it, why don't we just enact policies to end it?

O n August 9, 2001, President George W. Bush announced his policy on fed-eral funding of embryonic stem cell research to a national television audi-ence. Until recently few in Washington or across the country had even heard of stem cells, let alone considered them an issue requiring a presidential address to the nation. The subject was scientific, technical, and poorly understood by most Americans, including their elected representatives in Congress. Yet by the summer of 2001 these microscopic clusters of cells that many scientists were advancing as a source of potential miracle cures had become so contentious an issue that the presi-dent decided to justify his decision regarding future stem cell research to the Ameri-can public.*

Stem cells might be unfamiliar and technically challenging, but that did not stop people from adopting strong opinions about the issue. With near unanimity, the medical research community defended embryonic stem cell therapy as the best prospect for arresting and even reversing the effects of numerous devastating medical conditions including Alzheimer's, multiple sclerosis, Parkinson's, cancer, and severed

---

*Stem cells are unspecialized cells that are capable of replicating and developing into any human tissue. Medical researchers have found in nonhuman lab experiments that these cells can repair damaged tissue. Stem cells have been recovered from placentas, umbilical cords, aborted fetuses, cloning, and frozen surplus embryos created during *in vitro* procedures to help infertile couples have children. Cloned cells extracted from living embryos are the most versatile but also the most controversial since extracting them destroys the embryo. Another strain of research involves adult stem cells. Most scientists regard these cells as holding less promise either for research or therapy. Yet because this source does not require the destruc-tion of embryos, it is also less controversial and has attracted substantial federal support.

Embryonic stem cells as seen through a microscope.

spinal cords. Joining the scientists were patients, their families, and the myriad organizations promoting research on one or more of these disorders. Opposing this research and therapy were the predominantly Republican-leaning constituencies that had campaigned vigorously against abortion rights since the 1970s. Most outspoken were the leaders of fundamentalist Christian organizations and the Catholic Church.

The two sides advocated clear and unalterable opposing positions. Those in favor of stem cell research wanted a concerted federal program underwriting the development of hundreds of new strains of embryonic stem cell material; those opposed insisted on a federal law banning such research outright. At the time of his announcement, President Bush's options were limited to choices regarding federal financing: did the 1995 law banning federal support of research that would result in the death of a human embryo apply to embryonic stem cell research? The answer was unclear to government scientists at the National Institutes of Health, who in 1997 went to Congress for guidance. Alerted by these hearings, various constituencies concluded that embryonic stem cell research was either a godsend, offering potential cures for otherwise intractable diseases, or a godless technology that brazenly interfered with human life. Each side turned to the White House for support.

President Bush's decision steered carefully between the two. He announced that federal dollars would be available for research on the sixty or so embryonic stem cell collections that had already been developed, but that no federal money could go to new projects. Initially, this solution left many participants nonplussed. If the research was immoral, then it should be banned. If not, it should be actively pursued. Some pundits questioned the president's motives; others more directly condemned him for crass politics. Whether his accusers were justified, Bush's decision was undeniably political in seeking to reconcile conflicting interests and values that commanded significant support within the American public.* Bush tried to "split the difference," a solution that may be commonplace in, for example, negotiating budgets but not ordinarily attempted in conflicts between mutually exclusive moral stances.

Over the next few days research scientists and their supporters grew increasingly restive, especially after reports that only twenty-seven of the sixty available embryonic stem cell samples were suitable for research. Initially, leaders in the Christian political movement were muted in their criticism. "Not as bad" as he had feared, averred one prominent Christian right leader.[1] But after a few days this side had also decided that its moral views had been inadequately served by the president it had recently helped elect to office. Bush's effort to straddle the issue and minimally satisfy both sides appeared likely to fall apart. Democrats in Congress planned hearings to explore overturning the president's policy—hearings scheduled to begin on September 11, 2001.

The al Qaeda attacks only postponed the efforts by each side to secure the policy it thought it deserved. Beginning in 2002 conservatives in Congress proposed legislation each year to ban stem cell research. Meanwhile, supporters sought funds elsewhere, notably in California, where they successfully persuaded voters to commit

---

*A *Washington Post* survey taken several days after President Bush's televised address found 44 percent of the public opposing and 56 percent favoring federal aid to stem cell research.

$3 billion over a decade to underwrite stem cell research there. Leaders in other states, worried that they would suffer a "brain drain" and lose this potentially important biotechnology industry, adopted stem cell subsidies. Like most divisive political issues, stem cell policy has not been fully resolved. Politicians in Washington and the states continue to grope for a politically acceptable balance among their constituencies' competing demands.*

Inevitably, social choices breed conflict: conflicting interests, conflicting values, and conflicting ideas about whose values will be served and how best to allocate limited resources. Politics is how people try to manage such conflicts. But try as they may, politics does not always end in success. Resources are too scarce to satisfy the competing claimants, and values prove irreconcilable. And even when the configuration of interests might allow reconciliation, the political process may be deficient, failing to uncover participants' common interests or to ensure that the contending parties subsequently abide by their agreements. Under these circumstances, disagreement persists and disputants may even resort to force.† Successful politics does not always lead to happy endings. Yet politics allows us to live together and enjoy the fruits of social exchange. In fact, politics, like the air we breathe, is essential to our existence. Only when the air becomes foul—when politics fails and societies collapse into anarchy and civil war—do we grasp the significance of politics in sustaining our everyday lives as well as our plans for the future.

In more formal terms, **politics** is *the process through which individuals and groups reach agreement on a course of common, or collective,‡ action—even as they disagree on the intended goals of that action.* This definition covers a great variety of social relations. Parents and teenagers negotiate over use of a family car, bosses and employees haggle over working conditions and pay, and smugglers jockey over turf for conducting their illicit activities. Politics matters because each party needs to find a solution to its conflict or disagreement. A solution requires parties to cooperate, even when cooperation is costly and difficult to achieve.

Success at politics almost invariably requires **bargaining** and **compromise.** Where the issues are simple and the participants know and trust one another, bargaining, such as the prolonged exchange of proposals and counterproposals between teenagers and their parents, may be all that is needed for the group to reach a collective decision.

---

*In February 2005 Massachusetts governor Mitt Romney, a Republican, announced his opposition to use of cloning to create embryos for extracting stem cells but allowed that techniques that did not involve creating life to extract cells might be acceptable.

†In 1832 the Prussian general Carl von Clausewitz proclaimed famously that war is "politics by other means." Clausewitz wrote, "War is not merely an act of policy but a true political instrument, a continuation of political intercourse, carried on with other means." Carl von Clausewitz, *On War,* ed. and trans. Michael Howard and Peter Paret (Princeton: Princeton University Press, 1976), 87.

‡This text concentrates on politics in the American national government, but it also draws freely on examples from other settings because the logic embedded in political processes is not confined to matters related to government. Consequently, throughout the text we frequently refer to some generic "collectivity," whose members engage each other in reaching a "collective decision" either to engage in some "collective action" or produce some "collective good." We enlist these general terms whenever we offer a definition, observation, or conclusion that has a general application.

During the Great Depression, when millions of Americans were suddenly impoverished, many critics blamed unfettered capitalism. The National Association of Manufacturers, still a politically active industry association, posted billboards like this one around the country in an effort to bolster support for "private enterprise" by associating it with other fundamental preferences.

Although successful bargaining could lead to the discovery that the contending parties actually agree with each other or possibly to one side's capitulation (such as handing over the keys without any conditions attached), generally it ends in a compromise, or a settlement in which each side concedes some preferences to secure others.

Those who create government institutions (and the political scientists who study them) tend to regard **preferences** as "givens"—individuals and groups know what they want—that must be reconciled if they are to agree to some common course of action. Preferences may reflect the individual's economic situation, religious values, ethnic identity, or some other valued interest. We commonly associate preferences with some perception of self-interest, but they need not be so restrictive. Millions of Americans oppose capital punishment, but surely very few of those who do so expect to benefit personally from such a ban.

Reconciling preferences represents a fundamental problem of governance. In one of the most memorable and instructive statements justifying the new Constitution, James Madison, who played a dominant role in drafting the document and to whom we repeatedly turn for guidance throughout this book, explains that the new government must be devised to represent and reconcile society's many, diverse preferences that are "sown into the nature of man":

> A zeal for different opinions concerning religion, concerning government, and many other points . . . have, in turn, divided mankind into parties, inflamed them with mutual animosity, and rendered them much more disposed to vex and oppress each other than to co-operate for their common good. So strong is this propensity of mankind to fall into mutual animosities, that where no substantial occasion presents itself, the most frivolous and fanciful distinctions have been sufficient to kindle their unfriendly passions and excite their most violent conflicts.*

Certainly, Madison's observation appears no less true today than when he wrote it in 1787.

The Importance of Institutional Design

As participants and preferences multiply and as issues become more complex and divisive, unstructured negotiation rarely yields a collective decision all parties can accept. It may simply require too much time and effort. More crucially, it may expose each side to too great a risk that the other will not live up to its agreements. Fear of reneging may foster mutual suspicions and lead each side to conclude that "politics" will not work. When this occurs, war may become the preferred alternative. The conflict in the 1990s among Serbs, Croats, and Muslims in Bosnia followed such a dynamic. The collapse of Yugoslavia's communist government in 1990 resurrected ancient enmities among people who had lived peacefully as neighbors for decades. In the absence of effective political **institutions** they could count on to manage potential conflicts, ethnic and religious rivals became trapped in a spiral of mutual suspicion, fear, and hostility. Without a set of rules prescribing a political process for reaching and enforcing collective agreements, they were joining militias and killing one another with shocking brutality within a year. A decade and a half later, European and American forces still police the region as the former Yugoslav states, now separate national governments, strive to build institutions that can replace violence with politics.

Whether at war or simply at odds over the mundane matter of scheduling employee coffee breaks, the parties to a conflict will benefit from prior agreement on rules and procedures for negotiations. Indeed, this theme reappears throughout this book: a stable community, whether a club or a nation-state, endures by establishing rules and procedures for promoting successful collective action. In January 1999, when the Senate turned to the impeachment trial of President Bill Clinton, the stage was set for an escalation of the partisan rancor that had so marred the impeachment proceedings in the House of Representatives. Yet the Senate managed to perform its

---

*This passage is from Madison's *Federalist* No. 10, published initially in 1787 as a newspaper editorial supporting the Constitution's ratification. We shall examine this immensely insightful essay in Chapter 2; it is reprinted in its entirety in the Appendix.

constitutional responsibility expeditiously and with a surprising degree of decorum thanks to an early, closed-door meeting in which all hundred senators endorsed a resolution that laid out the trial's ground rules. More important, in their desire for partisan and institutional comity, senators gave their majority and minority leaders the right to reject any changes in these rules. Thus members on both sides of the partisan divide could proceed toward a decision without fear that the other side would resort to trickery to get the results it favored. That the Senate would find a way to manage its disagreements is not so surprising. Its leaders take pride in finding collegial ways of containing the potential conflicts that daily threaten to disrupt its business.

Reliance on rules and procedures to reconcile competing preferences is nothing new, of course. In an era of arbitrary kings and aristocrats, republican political theorists understood their value. In a 1656 treatise exploring how institutions might be constructed to allow conflicting interests to find solutions, the English political theorist James Harrington described two young girls who were arguing about how to share a single slice of cake. Suddenly one of the girls proposed a rule: " 'Divide,' said one to the other, 'and I will choose; or let me divide, and you shall choose.' " At this moment, Harrington stepped away from his story and seemingly shouted to the reader, "My God!" these "silly girls" have discovered the secret of republican institutions.* With that ingenious rule, both girls were able to pursue their self-interest (the largest possible slice of cake) and yet have the collective decision result in a division both could happily live with.[2]

Over a hundred years after Harrington's treatise, the Framers of the Constitution spent the entire summer of 1787 in Philadelphia debating what new rules and offices to create for their fledgling government. They were guided by their best guesses about how the alternatives they were contemplating would affect the interests of their states and the preferences of their constituencies (see Chapter 2). The result of their efforts, the Constitution, is a collection of rules fundamentally akin to the one discovered by the girls in Harrington's story. It was intended to reassure diverse interests that they would be better off under the proposed system than under the institutions they would replace under the Articles of Confederation.

The events in Philadelphia remind us that however lofty the goal that gives rise to reform, institutional design is a product of politics. As a result, institutions may confer advantages on some interests over others. Indeed, sometimes one side, enjoying a temporary advantage, will try to permanently implant its preferences in difficult-to-change rules and procedures. The present-day Department of Education, for example, arose from the former Department of Health, Education, and Welfare in 1977 after newly elected Jimmy Carter proposed this split as a reward for early support from teacher organizations who had long regarded a separate department as key to their ability to win increased federal funding for schools and teacher training. The history of this department bears out the wisdom of their strategy. Republican Ronald Reagan

---

*Actually, Harrington exclaimed, "Mon Dieu!" Note that the lowercase "republican" refers to a form of government, and not the (uppercase) Republican Party. The same case distinction applies to "democratic" and Democratic Party. Both of these forms of government are examined later in the chapter.

followed Carter into the White House with the full intention of returning the education bureaucracy to its former status. But before long the cabinet secretary he appointed to dismantle the department began championing it, as did many Republicans in Congress whose committees oversaw the department's activities and budgets. Nearly three decades later, the Department of Education is entrenched in Washington and helping President George W. Bush pursue his ambitious "No Child Left Behind" education reforms.

Constitutions and Governments

All organizations are governed by rules and procedures for making and enforcing decisions. Within colleges and universities, the student government, the faculty senate, staff associations, academic departments, and, of course, the university itself follow rules and procedures when transacting regular business. Although rules and procedures go by different names (for example, constitution, bylaw, charter), their purpose is the same: to guide an organization's members in making essentially political decisions—that is, decisions in which the participants initially disagree about what they would like the organization to do.

And what happens when the organization is a nation? Consider the problems: the number of participants is great, the many unsettled issues are complex, and each participant's performance in living up to agreements cannot be easily monitored. Yet, even with their conflicts, entire populations engage in politics every day. Their degree of success depends largely on whether they have developed constitutions and governments that work.

The **constitution** of a nation establishes its governing institutions and *the set of rules and procedures these institutions must (and must not) follow to reach and enforce collective agreements.* A constitution may be a highly formal legal document, such as that of the United States, or it may resemble Britain's unwritten constitution, an informal "understanding" based on centuries of precedents and laws. A **government,** then, consists of these institutions and the legally prescribed process for making and enforcing collective agreements. Governments may assume various forms, including a monarchy, a representative democracy, a theocracy (a government of religious leaders), or a dictatorship.

Power versus Authority

The simple observation that governments are composed of institutions actually says a great deal and implies even more. Government institutions consist of **offices** that confer on their occupants specific authority and responsibilities. Rules and procedures prescribing how an institution transacts business and what authority relations will link offices together. **Authority** is the acknowledged right to make a particular decision. Only presidents possess the "authority" to nominate federal judges. However, a majority of the Senate's membership retains sole authority to actually "confirm" these appointments and allow the nominees to take office.

Authority is distinguishable from **power,** a related but broader concept we enlist throughout the book. Power refers to an officeholder's actual influence with other officeholders, and as a consequence, over the government's actions. An office's authority will be an important ingredient in its occupant's power, but an officeholder's power includes the skill to deploy that authority when dealing with other officeholders and politicians. President Bush has the authority only to nominate a judge, but whether the Senate confirms his appointment may rest on Bush's persuasiveness with members of the Senate judiciary committee, his mobilization of key support groups to lobby undecided senators, and his ability to generate favorable publicity for his candidate and perhaps even unfavorable publicity for opponents.

Institutional Durability

Institutions are by no means immutable, but they tend to be stable and resist change for several reasons. First, with authority assigned to the office, not to the individual holding the office, established institutions persist well beyond the tenure of the individuals who occupy them. A university remains the same institution even though all of its students, professors, and administrators are eventually replaced. Institutions, therefore, contribute a fundamental continuity and orderliness to collective action. Second, the people who are affected by them make plans on the expectation that current arrangements will remain. Imagine how senior college students would react if, during their last semester, their college or university increased the required course units for a degree. Or consider the anxiety that the millions of workers approaching retirement must feel whenever politicians in Washington talk about changing Social Security.* Finally, even those who seek change typically find it hard to agree on a proposed alternative. Virtually everyone endorses some reform on national health care policy, but they disagree sharply over its direction. As a result, current arrangements, though preferred by few, if any, members of Congress, have undergone only minor changes.

Sometimes reform is undertaken to make institutions perform more efficiently. During the opening session of the First Congress in 1789, James Madison, while serving as a member of the House of Representatives from Virginia, observed that "in every step the difficulties arising from novelty are severely experienced. . . . Scarcely a day passes without some striking evidence of the delays and perplexities springing merely from the want of precedents." Then, more sanguinely, he predicted that "time will be a full remedy for this evil." And time has proven Madison right. By setting rules and following precedents, the House of Representatives has become a well-regulated machine, allowing members to concentrate on lawmaking.

On other occasions reforms enable institutions to accomplish new collective goals. In 1970 an executive reorganization plan consolidated components of five executive departments and agencies into a single independent agency, the Environmental Protection Agency, with a strong mandate and commensurate regulatory authority to protect

---

*Hence in his 2005 State of the Union address President George W. Bush sought emphatically to reassure the most anxious segment of the public approaching retirement—specifically, those over age fifty-five—that his sweeping reform proposal would not apply to them.

the environment. By coordinating their actions and centralizing authority, these formerly dispersed agencies could more effectively monitor and regulate polluting industries. Within agencies new tasks are added to old, until the work outstrips the capacity of existing structures; only then are new offices and procedures created. Before there was the modern White House Office, presidents relied informally on a handful of assistants loaned to them from the executive departments. In the late 1930s Congress, acceding to President Franklin Roosevelt's request, created a separate staff and designated six assistants to the president. Gradually, as presidents took on more responsibilities, the White House Office grew in number and complexity. Today its staff, composed of more than five hundred policy and political specialists, occupies two office buildings. Like rings within a tree, the history of the presidency can be seen in the layers of offices that have accumulated in response to successive demands and challenges. While the changes have been gradual, over time they transformed the office.

The Political System's Logic

The quality of democracy in modern America reflects the quality of its governing institutions. Embedded in these institutions are certain core values, such as the belief that those entrusted with important government authority must periodically stand before the citizenry in elections. Balanced against this ideal of popular rule is the equally fundamental belief that government must protect certain individual liberties even when a majority of the public insists otherwise. Throughout this text we will find politicians and citizens disagreeing on the precise meaning of these basic beliefs and values as they are applied or redefined to fit modern society.

Also embedded in these institutions—initially by the Framers in the Constitution and later by amendment and two centuries of political evolution—is a logic based on principles about how members of a community should engage one another politically to identify and pursue their common goals. Although the Framers did not use the vocabulary of modern political science, they intuitively discerned this logic and realized they must apply it correctly if the "American Experiment" were to succeed.* For us, too, this logic is essential for understanding the behavior of America's political institutions, the politicians who occupy them, and the citizens who monitor and respond to political actions. To that end, the concepts presented in the remainder of this chapter are the keys to "open up" America's political institutions to reveal their underlying logic. We begin with the problems (or one can think of them as puzzles) that confront all attempts at collective action. Many institutional arrangements have been devised over time to solve these problems. We examine here some that are especially important to America's political system and appear throughout the book.

---

*They were, after all, contemporaries of Isaac Newton and found in his theory of mechanics inspiration to search for similar natural laws to create a well-functioning polity. With Britain the only real-world model to guide them, which they tended to judge more as a model of what to avoid than to emulate, the Framers depended heavily on carefully reasoned ideas, which took them to Newtonian physics. Consequently, the terms "force," "counterweight," and "balance" were familiarly employed during debates at the Constitutional Convention and by both sides in the Constitution's subsequent ratification campaign.

Collective Action Problems

By virtue of their size and complexity, nations encounter special difficulties in conducting political business. In those nations where citizens participate in decisions through voting and other civic activities, still more complex issues arise. Virtually every contemplated collective action challenges participants to figure out what to do and how to do it. The former involves comparing preferences and finding some course of action that sufficient numbers of participants agree is preferable to proposed alternatives or doing nothing. The latter concerns implementation—not just the nuts and bolts of performing some task, but reassuring participants that everyone will share the costs (e.g., taxes) and otherwise live up to agreements.

These challenges to successful **collective action** (that is, the efforts of a group to reach and implement agreements) reappear throughout this book. Even when differences are in principle reconcilable, there is no guarantee that a solution will be discovered and implemented. Two fundamental barriers—coordination problems and prisoner's dilemmas—may block effective collective action. **Coordination** is perhaps the simplest to overcome: members of the group must decide individually what they want, what they are prepared to contribute to the collective enterprise, and how to coordinate their efforts with those of others. A **prisoner's dilemma** arises whenever individuals decide that even though they support some collective undertaking, they are personally better off pursuing an activity that rewards them individually despite undermining the collective effort. Prisoner's dilemmas pervade all of politics, from neighbors petitioning city hall for a stop sign to legislators collaborating to strike budget deals in Congress. These dilemmas especially interest us because the "solution"—that is, having everyone contribute to the collective undertaking—depends heavily on providing the kinds of incentives to individuals that governments are well suited to provide.

Coordination

A classical music performance offers an education in the costs of coordinating collective action. During a concert the members of a string quartet coordinate their individual performances by spending nearly as much time looking at each other as they do following their music. Volume, tempo, and ornamentation must all be executed precisely and in tandem. By the end of a successful concert, the effort required is evident on the triumphant musicians' perspiring faces. A symphony orchestra, by contrast, achieves comparable coordination, despite its greater numbers, by retaining one of its members to put aside the musical instrument and take up the conductor's baton. By focusing on the conductor, orchestra members are able to coordinate their playing and produce beautiful music. And at the end of the concert the conductor is the first one to mop a perspiring brow.

Coordination problems increase with the size of a group. Large groups trying to reach a shared goal might emulate the symphony in designating and following a leader. Members of the House of Representatives and the Senate configure procedures to enable Congress to decide policy for the hundreds of issues presented each session. But to achieve the same objective the 435-member House and the 100-member Senate proceed quite differently, following a logic reflecting the size of their organizations. The House delegates to a Rules Committee responsibility for scheduling the flow of legislation onto the floor and setting limits on deliberations and amendments. This important committee becomes the "leader" in setting the body's agenda. The entire House cedes this authority to a committee because coordination is vital to the chamber's success in identifying the most preferred legislation. By contrast, the smaller Senate has found that it can achieve comparable levels of coordination without having to surrender authority to a specialized committee. Rather, informal discussions among members and party leaders suffice.

When the number of participants desiring to coordinate is really large—say a state's voters—coordination may generally be unachievable. On some problems simple, self-enforcing rules—such as traffic staying to the right side of the street—might be all that is required. But when real decisions—those involving comparisons of preferences—are required, the task becomes daunting. It explains, after all, why a society's collective decisions are generally delegated to a small group of professionals, namely politicians, who engage one another in structured and presumably transparent settings, namely government, designed to facilitate their collective decisions. Yet, occasions do arise where citizens seek to coordinate their actions. A critical ingredient in their success lies in identifying a common **focal point** to target their energies toward a common purpose. Consider the dilemma faced by Democrats and Republicans in spring 2008 trying to settle upon a candidate best able to win the White House in the fall presidential election. With a half dozen candidates vigorously contesting each party's early presidential caucuses and primaries, the typical partisan voter faced the quandary of whom to support. Personal preferences for a particular candidate were less relevant than the need to settle upon one soon, hopefully the one with the best chance in November, before the intramural competition drained all of their resources and reputation. Once Mitt Romney demonstrated his unelectability and Mike Huckabee his narrow regional appeal, voters quickly turned to Sen. John McCain, whose campaign was unremarkable until the others faltered. Democrats in 2008 experienced greater difficulty in choosing between Barack Obama and Hillary Clinton than had any group of partisans in the past fifty years. With equal support and extraordinary fund-raising, neither candidate was able to emerge early as the focal point around which all partisans could rally.

Demonstrations and protests represent another kind of political activity that depends on massive coordination among individuals. Again a widely accepted focal point is critical. During the early 1960s Martin Luther King and his colleagues in the Southern Christian Leadership Conference had emerged as effective focal points in channeling demonstrations and protests throughout the South (see Chapter 4). They depended on like-minded individuals learning about their plans and joining in. A remarkable recent example of coordinated protest activity occurred in 2006 when a Los Angeles union and church organized a protest march against anti-immigrant legislation under consideration by the House of Representatives. The organizers targeted twenty thousand participants, but after they persuaded several Spanish-radio DJs to publicize the rally, over half a million protestors showed up. The size of the turnout

Renan Almedorez Coello,
"the Latino Howard Stern"

Humberto Luna

Eddie "Tweety Bird" Sotelo

These Los Angeles Spanish-language disk jockeys, among others, are credited with turning out nearly five hundred thousand demonstrators for an immigration reform rally in downtown L.A. in March 2006. A small union with modest resources initiated the event with little expectation of generating a large rally, until someone thought to appeal to these DJs. Even with the help of these radio personalities, few expected the crowd to reach over twenty thousand. Clearly, many L.A. Latino community members wanted to express their views on immigration. They just needed a little coordination.

amazed everyone, including the organizers and the quickly overwhelmed police force. Clearly, the protestors longed to express themselves and only needed guidance and encouragement and a place and time to show up.

Coordination problems essentially arise from uncertainty and insufficient information and may prevent collective undertakings even when a great majority agree on a course of action, such as the Democrats' desire to recapture the White House in the 2008 election. We now turn to potentially more problematic challenges to collective action—the problems of the prisoner's dilemma. Unlike coordination, where mutual ignorance prevents participants from identifying and working together for a common goal, "prisoner's dilemma" problems find participants privately calculating that they would be better off by not contributing to the collective action even when they wholeheartedly agree with its purpose. Where coordination problems frequently require no more than direction and information, prisoner's dilemmas generally necessitate monitoring and the threat of coercion.

The Prisoner's Dilemma

Since it was first formally introduced in the late 1950s, the "prisoner's dilemma" has become one of the most widely employed concepts in the social sciences. A casual Google search generated over half a million hits on this phrase, bringing up Web sites on subjects far afield from political science and economics (where systematic consideration of the concept originated), including psychiatry, evolutionary biology, and drama theory. The prisoner's dilemma depicts a specific tension in social relations, one long intuitively understood by political thinkers. Solving this dilemma fundamentally distinguishes political success and failure and is a cornerstone of our inquiry. What precisely is the prisoner's dilemma and why is it so important for the study of American politics?

The prisoner's dilemma arises whenever individuals, who ultimately would benefit from cooperating with each other, also have a powerful and irresistible incentive to break the agreement and exploit the other side. Only when each party is confident that the other will live up to an agreement can they successfully break out of the dilemma and work to their mutual advantage.

A simple example of how this works is the original exercise that gives the prisoner's dilemma its name. In the movie stills from the 1941 drama, *I Wake Up Screaming* (see photos), homicide detectives are subjecting screen legends Victor Mature and Betty Grable to the prisoner's dilemma. Specifically, each is being advised to confess and testify against the other, in return for a lighter prison sentence. The diagram on the next page maps out the likely prison term each faces. Deep down Mature and Grable know the police do not have enough evidence to convict them of murder but they might have to take the rap on a lesser gun possession charge. All they have to do is stick to their story (i.e., cooperate) and at worst, they will spend six months in jail. If both were to confess, each would get a five-year sentence. Each is offered a deal: in exchange for a full confession, the "squealer" will get off scott-free, while the "fall guy" or "sucker," convicted with the testimony, would likely receive a ten-year prison term. In the movie both suspects are isolated in their cell for a few days, with the detectives hinting that

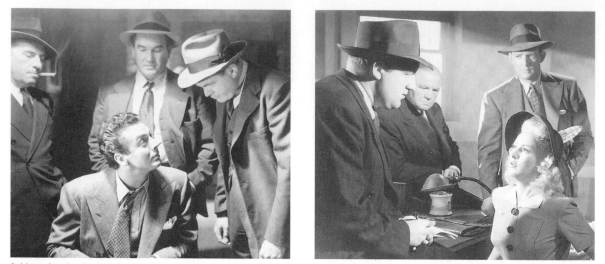

Subjected to the classic prisoner's dilemma interrogation, Victor Mature and Betty Grable turn out to have nothing to confess in this 1941 whodunnit *I Wake Up Screaming*. Since its introduction in the 1950s, thousands of articles have enlisted this metaphor to explore the fundamental conflict between what is rational behavior for each member of a group and what is in the best interest of the group as a whole.

their partner is "singing like a canary." As the days pass, each begins to recognize the other's character flaws and panics. If Mature squeals, Grable realizes, she must also in order to avoid a ten-year stretch. If, however, she has underestimated his virtues and he holds out, well, that would be unfortunate, but she gains some solace in knowing that her lone confession will be her "get-out-of-jail" card. Of course, Mature, stewing in his cell, reaches the same conclusion. Why this movie presents a genuine dilemma is that *in this setting* confessing offers the best outcome for each suspect, regardless of what the other individual does. So, Grable confesses. Mature, being no fool, does too. In the end they both cave in and spend the next five years in the slammer.*

		Victor Mature	
		Stays Silent	**Confesses**
Betty Grable	**Stays Silent**	6 months, 6 months	10 years, no jail
	Confesses	no jail, 10 years	5 years, 5 years

(Grable's sentence is listed first.)

So what does this dilemma have to do with American politics? Everything. Every successful political exchange must tacitly solve the prisoner's dilemma. Exchanges occur because each side recognizes that it will be better off with a collective outcome rather than trying to act alone. Had Mature and Grable somehow managed to stay silent, their

---

*For this reason police have traditionally objected to giving suspects early access to lawyers, who might help the otherwise isolated prisoners coordinate their plan. But this is a different story we will return to in Chapter 5. By the way, the movie offers a happy ending.

cooperation would have shaved all but six months from their five-year terms. And both knew this. Yet neither could be sure the other confederate would stay silent. To get something worthwhile, both sides must typically give up something of value in return. The moral: Unless participants in a collective decision can trust each other to abide by their commitments, they will not achieve a mutually profitable exchange.

How do the Matures and Grables shift the outcome from that quadrant, where neither cooperates, to the one where they both do? One solution involves making reneging and defection very expensive. In some settings this can be achieved informally. For example, politicians who repeatedly make campaign promises that they subsequently fail to act on lose credibility with voters, making them vulnerable to defeat in the next election. Once in office, reneging on an agreement will quickly damage a politician's reputation, and others will refuse to deal with her in the future. Where failure to live up to one's agreements imposes costs down the road, politicians will think twice before doing so.

Another common solution is to create institutions that help parties discover opportunities to profit through cooperation and most importantly, guarantee that agreements are honored. Here the government's coercive authority is useful. An anthropologist once reported that two tribes in a remote region of New Guinea lived in a state of continual warfare, to the point that many more men from both tribes had died in battle than from natural causes. The anthropologist summed up their dilemma: "In the absence of any central authority, they are condemned to fight forever . . . since for any group to cease defending itself would be suicidal." He added that these tribes might "welcome pacification." One day the distant government in Papua sent a ranger armed with a handgun to establish territorial boundaries between the tribes and rules governing their chance encounters. Suddenly, the decades-long warfare ended. Each side believed the ranger with his single sidearm presented sufficient force to punish any breaches of the peace agreements, and the now-peaceful neighbors began to use politics—not war—to solve their conflicts.[3] Members of a society must be able to engage one another politically. Without confidence that agreements will be enforced, the political process quickly unravels. Participants will balk at undertaking mutual obligations they suspect their bargaining partners will not honor.

In his 1651 treatise on the origin and purposes of government, *Leviathan,* political philosopher Thomas Hobbes examined the straits to which society is reduced when its government is unable to enforce collective obligations and agreements. (See box "Hobbes on Monarchs"). In a famous passage he warned that life would return to "a state of nature . . . solitary, poor, nasty, brutish and short."[4] The mortality rate of New Guinea tribesmen confirmed Hobbes's insight. They were not naturally bellicose; rather, these tribes simply could not trust each other. Thus enforcement succeeded in inducing cooperation, but not by flaunting overwhelming force or imposing a solution on the contending parties. The ranger's presence simply rendered any party's defection more costly than its compliance.

Hopefully, the relevance of the prisoner's dilemma to American politics is becoming clearer. Virtually every policy the government adopts represents a successful resolution of this dilemma. Constituencies and their representatives cooperate to achieve their separate goals—recall our definition of politics on page 5—because institutions have

Hobbes on Monarchs

In 1651 Thomas Hobbes argued in *Leviathan*, one of the most important books in political theory, that the English monarch was a necessary guarantor of collective agreements.[1] He proposed that since the king and his offspring derived their wealth directly from the population in taxes and labor, they would pursue the nation's welfare because it would enrich them as well. Even if the monarch were wicked and expropriated too much of the nation's wealth for himself, the citizenry was still better off with him wielding power arbitrarily than if no one had enforcement authority. Restated in the vocabulary of this text, Hobbes argued that monarchs offered a cost-effective means to collective action.

[1]Thomas Hobbes, *Leviathan, or The matter, forme, & power of a commonwealth ecclesiasticall and civill* (1651; reprint, Oxford: Clarendon Press, 1958).

developed to help diverse constituencies discover opportunities for mutual gain through cooperation and, just as importantly, deter them from reneging on their agreements. Like the ranger with a handgun in Papua, America's political institutions foster collective action by solving the prisoner's dilemma.

There are failures to be sure. Some issues simply do not offer mutual gains through cooperation. On these **zero sum** issues, one party's gain is the other's loss and politics may break down. The nation's stem cell policy appears to be such an issue. Abortion offers another instance of irreconcilable preferences seeking to control policy. Yet here too, American politics favors compromise so that even the losers on these issues can point to small or partial successes. Chapter 4 recounts the most intractable issue of all in American political history—the failure, despite repeated compromise attempts, to come up with a policy on slavery's extension into the territories during the 1850s. This issue was only resolved by the deadliest war of its time.

Even where each side can envision opportunities for mutual gains, American politics is not fail proof. Everyone agrees that in several decades the Social Security program will be unable to provide its current level of benefits for the next generation of retirees. Both Republican and Democratic politicians in Washington want to fix it, and from time to time one side will make an overture to the other. But all of the solutions are costly or unpopular, either requiring hefty new taxes or curtailing benefits. Both political parties worry that as soon as they offer a tough solution, the other side will seek to exploit it and score points in the next election. Until politicians figure out a way to cooperate and share the blame, Social Security reform will remain the proverbial "third rail" of politics: "Touch it and you are dead." *

FREE-RIDER PROBLEM. A form of the prisoner's dilemma that afflicts large groups is the **free-rider problem.** With each individual's contribution to the success of the collective activity quite small and inconsequential, each member will be tempted to free ride—that is, *to defect from the agreement by withholding a contribution to the group's undertaking while enjoying the benefits of the collective effort.* Of course, such a course of action is available to everyone, with the result that no one actually contributes to a collective enterprise all deem meritorious.

To better understand the critical role of group size to this particular form of prisoner's dilemma, let us return to the collective efforts of our quartet and symphony. Suppose a violinist is tempted to skip practice and party with friends the evening before a performance. When playing in a quartet, the violinist will face powerful incentives to fulfill obligations. If he performs poorly, his three colleagues will quickly notice and so too might the audience. After all, the other performers are cueing their playing in time with him. Since each musician's contribution is manifestly vital to the quartet's collective product, all are likely to stay home and practice. Now consider the decision of the would-be partygoer who is a member of the symphony. As one of twenty violinists in the orchestra, each performer's contribution adds only marginally to the collective product, certainly much less than do the contributions of members of the string quartet. This introduces an opportunity to free ride. The symphony musician might be tempted to spend the night on the town knowing that he could still bask in the orchestra's beautiful music.

The free-rider problem arises whenever citizens recognize that their small contribution to the collective enterprise will not affect its success or failure. And because contributing is somewhat costly, they decide not to make the effort. Even those citizens who enthusiastically support an enterprise realize that they (and others) can escape fulfilling their obligations. If many people react this way—and many do—and suspect their neighbors of doing so as well, too few people will contribute to collective endeavors and, thus, some may fail.

A good example of free riding is membership support of public television. Less than 10 percent of its regular viewers ever donate to their local PBS affiliate, which explains why the public television system requires an annual government subsidy to stay

---

*The third rail metaphor refers to the third rail of subway tracks, the one that carries the electricity.

in business. Given the logic of nonparticipation, why does anyone ever contribute to a collective enterprise? Clearly some people find some activities intrinsically rewarding, however minor their contribution. That said, most of the people, most of the time are inclined to free ride. If a collective effort is to succeed it must provide potential participants with a private inducement. A few PBS viewers donate to their local station because they want to express their support for public television (or perhaps their disgust with commercial television). But many others are lured into donating by the monthly program guide subscription, license-plate holders, coffee mugs, discount coupon books, and other direct benefits of membership.

In addition to providing an arena for a community to decide on its collective pursuits, government uses force in the form of laws to induce participation and prevent reneging. Immediately after the United States declared war on Japan after the attack on Pearl Harbor, thousands of patriotic young men rushed to the army and navy recruiters. In case they did not, however, Congress passed a draft law. Imagine how few people would pay income taxes if there were no Internal Revenue Service waiting in the wings. Governments also have a variety of other resources at their disposal to induce participation in collective undertakings. Almost every tax break in federal and state tax codes was enacted to encourage citizens to spend money to help achieve some real or imagined collective benefit.

THE TRAGEDY OF THE COMMONS. Another distinctive and important form of the prisoner's dilemma is the **tragedy of the commons.** It resembles free riding in that a large number of participants encourages each to renege on contributions to the public good. The difference is that the good already exists and will be destroyed if its exploitation is not brought under control. This dilemma takes its name from another instructive allegory. A number of herdsmen graze their cattle in a common pasture. Gradually they increase the size of their herds, destroying the pasture and with it their livelihood. In classic free-riding style, each herdsman reasons that adding a cow to the herd will increase his income and in itself have little impact on the future of the pasture. Of course, they all act accordingly and do so repeatedly. The end result is a disaster—eventually, overgrazing strips the pasture of its grass and the herdsmen go broke.

A real-world analogy is the collapse of the cod fishing industry off New England. Entire communities based their economies on fishing cod in nearby waters, but so many fishermen exploited this resource, without allowing nature to replenish it adequately, that they managed to wipe out the fishery on which their jobs depended.[5] Kansas wheat growers confront the same dilemma when they over-irrigate their fields even while recognizing that they are rapidly depleting the underground aquifer and, consequently, their long-term livelihood. In these and many other examples of overpopulation and pollution, participants find themselves racing toward ruin as they deplete natural resources. But the commons metaphor has broader applications. Every session of the House of Representatives finds its members introducing far more bills and resolutions than the chamber has time to consider. Naturally, each member would prefer to devote ample floor time to those issues important to his or her con-

Classic tragedy of the commons scene: Too many boats chasing too few fish, not because the skippers are greedy, but in the absence of an agreement, none can afford to stop fishing and surrender the harvest to the others. Here, in the mouth of the Egegik River in Bristol Bay, Alaska, the fleet competes for a limited and concentrated salmon fishery and manages to tangle its nets.

stituency. Yet if individuals' urges went unchecked, the session might well close with too little time to deliberate critical legislation.[6]

The trick to avoiding the tragedy of the commons lies in proper institutional design. As with free riding, the solution links the individual's personal interest to provision (in this instance, preservation) of the collective good. A decision to squander or conserve resources must affect personal welfare. Again, one solution is force—setting up regulations on use of a common resource and penalizing those who violate them. The House of Representatives strictly rations access to the floor with rules prescribing time limits to debates and germaneness of motions. But enforcement can be costly, and individuals will seek to exploit the collective good to the extent that they can get away with violating rules. This predicament has led to a novel solution—**privatize** the collective good—in many tragedy of the commons settings. Fence in the pasture and allocate sections to individual herdsmen. And, as is increasingly done in modern fishery management, grant commercial fishermen exclusive access to parts of the ocean, motivating them to harvest prudently and to keep "their" fishery healthy. Or, as with our PBS fans who might otherwise free ride, offer private inducements to get them to contribute. Once again, the solution to the collective action dilemma aligns personal gain with promotion of the collective good.

The Costs of Collective Action

Collective action offers a group benefits its members cannot achieve on their own. But participating in a collective enterprise also entails various costs. The key to successful collective action lies in designing a system that achieves the benefits of a collective effort while minimizing its costs. For example, the Senate, with its 100 members, efficiently accomplishes its business with fewer and less restrictive rules than those required for the much larger, 435-member House of Representatives.

Some of the costs associated with collective enterprises are not hard to spot. An obvious one is each person's monetary contribution to an enterprise—for example, tax payments funding road construction or staffing of a police department. Less obvious are the "overhead" costs of enforcing agreements such as the ranger's salary in New Guinea or the costs associated with the judicial system and the lawyers needed to ensure that those who enter into business agreements live up to their contracts. Overhead costs also include the government's effort to combat free riding. If people were not inclined to free ride, the federal government could disband the large bureaucracy that goes after tax cheats.

Two kinds of costs that are especially relevant for designing and evaluating institutions are **transaction costs** and **conformity costs.** Though they represent separate aspects of how a community tackles collective enterprises, they often involve a trade-off with one another. In creating institutions to achieve desirable collective goods, a society should collectively weigh the balance between members' private autonomy and the requirements for achieving the collective good.

Transaction Costs

Transaction costs are the time, effort, and resources required to make collective decisions. Consider a student activities committee that selects which band to bring to campus. First, do students want rock, hip-hop, or some other kind of music? Then, what bands are available, how good are they, and what do they charge? Of course, unsatisfactory answers to the second set of question might return the committee to the first. Once a decision has been made, the bands must be contacted, dates and prices negotiated, and a venue found. The time and effort spent researching available bands, debating preferences, and implementing decisions are all transaction costs of the collective good of campus entertainment.

Transaction costs can pose a formidable barrier to political agreements. These costs rise sharply as the number of participants whose preferences must be taken into account increases. In the absence of institutions for negotiating and implementing collective agreements, these costs might overwhelm the ability of participants to identify and to commit themselves to collective enterprises. With well-designed institutions, however, agreements have become easier to make. The student body of our example greatly reduced its transaction costs by authorizing a committee to make a collective choice for it. Other approaches to mitigating transaction costs involve streamlining rules and procedures. Before the Sixteenth Amendment creating a federal income tax

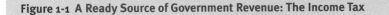

Figure 1-1 A Ready Source of Government Revenue: The Income Tax

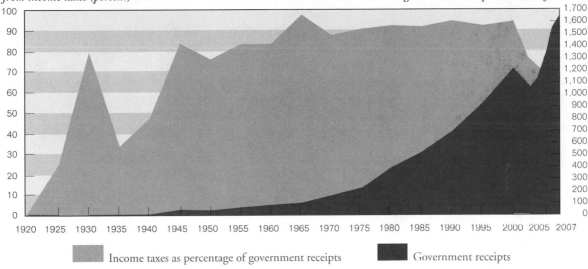

Total government receipts obtained from income taxes (percent)

Total government receipts (billions of dollars)

Income taxes as percentage of government receipts   Government receipts

Sources: U.S. Department of Commerce, Bureau of the Census, *Historical Statistics of the United States, Colonial Times to 1970* (White Plains, N.Y.: Kraus International Publications, 1989), Tables Y343–351, Y358–373. Additional data provided by U.S. Department of the Treasury, Bureau of Statistics, *Statistical Abstract of the United States* (Washington, D.C.: Government Printing Office, various years), Tables 358–361.

Note: Total government receipts do not include employment taxes, such as Social Security and Medicare.

was ratified in 1913, the government did not have a systematic method of taxing citizens. Without it, the nation would have inadequate revenue to finance the many federal programs to which Americans have become accustomed in the last half-century. Though enactment of the income tax undoubtedly required massive transaction costs, once legislators had established a dependable flow of revenue, they could finance new programs by doing little more than tinkering with the tax code. Raising taxes is still not easy, but it is far easier to adjust the tax code up or down than it was to raise revenue before there was a Sixteenth Amendment. Evidence of this can be found Figure 1-1. Over time, the income tax represents an ever larger share of government receipts. Reducing the transaction cost of raising federal revenue fueled the dramatic growth in federal policy and programs during the twentieth century.

Sometimes, though, high transaction costs are intentionally put in place to make some collective activities more, not less, difficult. Having fashioned a delicately balanced plan of government, the Framers were understandably uninterested in making it easy for some group down the road to rewrite the Constitution. Indeed, the prospect that their labors might soon be undone could have prevented them from reaching agreement in the first place. For future politicians the real possibility that the

In January 1798 Matthew Lyon, a member of Congress from Vermont known for his fiery temper, brawled with Roger Griswold from Connecticut in the chamber of the House of Representatives. The moral: transaction costs are real—and sometimes physical.

other side would rewrite the rules as soon as they got control of the government would return them to the uncertain world of the prisoner's dilemma and consequently have permanently undermined the nation's political stability. Without stable rules of the game each side faced a prisoner's dilemma. To address this dire prospect, the Framers ratcheted up the transaction costs of future constitutional change. A proposed amendment to the Constitution must be endorsed by two-thirds of the membership of both houses of Congress and ratified by three-fourths of the states.*

Conformity Costs

In negotiating a common course of action, parties advocating competing interests rarely discover that they want precisely the same thing. Politics invariably means compromise. Most of the time there are losers—parties whose preferences receive little accommodation but who must still contribute to a collective undertaking. To the extent

---

*Alternatively, two-thirds of the state legislatures can ask Congress to call a national convention to propose amendments, but this has never been done.

collective decisions obligate participants to do something they prefer
not to—and all resolutions of the
prisoner's dilemma involve this—we
refer to this necessity as a *conformity
cost*. Conformity costs range from an
ordinary task such as paying property taxes to extraordinary sacrifices
such as serving in Iraq away from
home and family. Rules that require
fishermen to stay at the dock during
a portion of the fishing season, rules
that make a citizen spend part of her
income to fund government programs that she opposes, and rules
that limit the time allotted a member of Congress for a floor speech all
impose conformity costs on individuals in order to achieve a collective
goal. Not surprisingly, members of a
community prefer minimum con-

The slogan "Don't Be Bullied" resonated with a majority of Irish voters, who rejected
a complex 287-page reform of the European Union's constitution that would have ceded
greater authority to the president of the European Union and was generally viewed as
eroding national sovereignty.

formity costs. But since collective goals never come effortlessly, governments continually weigh what kinds and how much costs its citizens are prepared to bear.

In that transaction and conformity costs generally entail a trade-off, such calculations tend to be complicated: those institutions that minimize transaction costs, making it easy for government to act, may do so by imposing excessive conformity costs.
An extreme case would be a dictator, who arbitrarily decides national policies (minimal transaction costs) by insisting that everyone do what he, not they, prefer (maximum conformity costs). At the opposite end of the continuum would be government
by consensus. The group does nothing unless everyone agrees to it. Of course, governments based on consensus often have a difficult time undertaking any collective enterprise although they expend great effort (exorbitant transaction costs) discovering this.

These extreme mixes of transaction and conformity costs might seem far-fetched
when referring to national governments, but for many of the Constitution's Framers
this was precisely the issue that brought them to Philadelphia. Chapter 2 examines
America's unhappy, precarious experience with government by consensus in the decade
following independence. The Articles of Confederation, the nation's first constitution,
allowed any state to block national action on important policies such as taxes. Moreover, the absence of enforcement authority fostered rampant free riding even when the
states could agree on a course of action. Consequently, even in a country with only
thirteen participating states—each with one vote in the Confederation Congress—the
transaction costs of consensus government proved impossibly difficult and prompted
all but one state, Rhode Island, to send delegates to a constitutional convention to create a more viable arrangement.

More commonly, governmental reform occurs within a narrow range of trade-offs between transaction and conformity costs. Rules, procedures, and resources are frequently changed to reduce transaction costs and make government more efficient and decisive. But sometimes the opposite scheme is adopted to prevent abuses. After the civil rights movement and the Vietnam War era, scandals uncovered widespread abuses by the FBI and CIA in spying on civil rights activists (including Martin Luther King) and antiwar leaders, Congress enacted procedures requiring judicial approval before these investigative agencies could undertake wiretaps and other forms of intrusive surveillance of citizens. Such reforms to prevent abuses were adopted with little opposition in Washington and represent a classic instance of increasing transaction costs as a way to hamstring action—in this instance, action taken against those who opposed current government policies. Over the objections of law enforcement officials, the government decided to preserve individuals' freedom of dissent (reduce conformity costs) by jacking up transaction costs on law enforcement officials. After September 11, 2001, the balance shifted back to reducing the transaction costs involved in going after potential terrorists (via the USA PATRIOT Act), and conformity costs increased.

Designing Institutions to Achieve Collective Action: The Framers' Toolkit

What constitutional arrangements best solve the problems and costs associated with collective action? It depends on what is being decided. If citizens fear that government might intrude too far into their private lives, they might want to add high transaction costs and require consensus to make collective decisions. This perhaps explains why those leaders who feared a shift in power from the states to the new national government clamored for a Bill of Rights to limit the ability of national majorities to demand religious and political conformity. (Their concerns resonated with the broader population and led to the quick adoption of the Bill of Rights as the first amendments to the new constitution.) If, by contrast, citizens greatly value quick and decisive action, as in defense against an imminent foreign threat, they may favor institutions that minimize transaction costs even at the risk of ceding more authority to leaders than they would normally deem prudent. Clearly, the delegates to the Constitutional Convention —many of them recent veterans with still fresh memories of the frustrating and nearly failed revolution—harbored both concerns and many variations in between.

In devising the several branches of the national government and its relations with the states, the Framers relied on design principles that instituted varying trade-offs between transaction and conformity costs to fit the purposes of the institutions they were creating. And they sought balance—keeping the branches in "their proper orbits"—so that none would gradually gain a permanent advantage over the others.

By intent, the Constitution provides only a general framework for government. As its institutions have evolved over the past two centuries, the Framers' design principles have shaped their subsequent development. These principles are just as useful for dissecting the internal organization of the modern House of Representatives as they are for studying the Framers' plan. Consequently, the Framers' toolkit presented below will inform our analyses throughout the text—especially, those chapters that delve into the logic of the governmental system.

Command

This refers to the authority of one actor to dictate the actions of another. Unlike the other design concepts, **command** authority gives its holder comprehensive control of those within the scope of its authority. Command cuts through both coordination and prisoner's dilemma problems by conferring the authority to impose a solution regardless of the preferences of others—a solution that invariably favors the authority's preferences over those who must comply with its edicts. So, while command certainly achieves efficiencies in reducing transaction costs, it does so by imposing potentially huge conformity costs on the community. For Hobbes (see box "Hobbes on Monarchs," page 18) monarchical command prevented society from deteriorating into anarchy.*

The Framers, and republican theorists before them, sought other institutional arrangements that would enable efficiency, yet minimize the conformity costs imposed by command. Consequently, "command" was rarely used in designing the Constitution. The only provision (Section 2, Article II) that comes close makes the president "the commander in chief of the army and navy." The military, then and now, is the one component of government designed to place a premium on conformity. Any squad member under enemy fire can appreciate the value of not having others in the unit calculating whether to cover for their buddies or to engage in free riding. Soldiers undergo intensive training to instill reflexive obedience to superiors' orders, subordinating their own well being to that of their unit. Each soldier's place within the hierarchy, or "command structure," is explicitly identified by his or her rank.

The work of government fundamentally differs from that of a squad in battle. Consequently, the president may be the supreme commander, but the Framers made sure any pretense of command authority ends there. Vivid evidence of their success appears in outgoing president Harry Truman's prediction about his successor, Army general Dwight Eisenhower: "He'll sit here, and he'll say, 'Do this! Do that!' And nothing will happen. Poor Ike—it won't be a bit like the Army. He'll find it very frustrating."† In Chapter 2 we will see the Framers opting repeatedly for institutional arrangements that would prevent any government official or institution from commanding compliance

---

*Moreover, Hobbes argued that in monarchies, the inherited right to rule was not just necessary but also salutary; monarchs had a long-term stake in their subjects' prosperity in order to maximize their own power and prosperity.

†According to most contemporary observers, Eisenhower's experiences in office bore out Truman's prediction. According to one description of Ike's sixth year in office, "The President still feels that when he has decided something, that *ought* to be the end of it . . . and when it bounces back undone or done wrong, he tends to react with shocked surprise." Richard E. Neustadt, *Presidential Power and the Modern Presidents* (New York: John Wiley and Sons, 1960), 10.

BORN TO COMMAND.

OF VETO MEMORY.

HAD I BEEN CONSULTED.

KING ANDREW THE FIRST.

Widely published in opposition Whig newspapers, this cartoon depicts President Andrew Jackson trampling on the Constitution and public works legislation. However imperiously Jackson dealt with the opposition-controlled Congress and the Supreme Court, whose decisions he selectively ignored, the veto in his left hand hardly sufficed to allow him "to rule" the country.

from the others. They largely achieved this goal by broadly distributing control over government decisions.

Veto

The **veto** embodies the right of an official or institution to say "no" to a proposal from another official or institution. Like command, the veto is unilateral, allowing its possessors to impose their views regardless of the preferences of others. Yet it is far less potent than command—and hence threatens fewer severe conformity costs—because of one critical difference: it is a "negative" or blocking action to preserve the status quo.* The veto confers little direct advantage in shifting government policy, but in Chapter 7 we find that a president's threat to use it may induce Congress to address the president's objections as it prepares legislation. Moreover, the blocking effects of the veto can be limited by providing those subject to a veto the means of circumventing it. After weighing the pros and cons of giving the president an absolute veto, the Framers backed off and added an override provision. With a two-thirds vote in each chamber, the House of Representatives and Senate can enact a vetoed bill without the president's endorsement. A policy that withstands the huge transaction costs entailed in mustering supermajorities in both chambers has demonstrated its merits and deserves enactment despite the president.†

The president's veto is the only explicit use of this instrument in the Constitution, but the Constitution implicitly creates other important veto relationships. Both the House of Representatives and the Senate must agree to identical legislation before it can proceed to the president's desk for his signature (or veto). In effect, then, each legislative chamber holds a veto over the legislation emanating from the other chamber. Yet another unnamed veto resides with the Supreme Court. Shortly after the new government was launched, the Supreme Court claimed the power of *judicial review,* asserting its author-

---

*In fact, many of the Constitution's Framers referred to the veto as a "negative."

†All state governors possess some form of veto over legislation; many of these vetoes differ significantly from the president's in allowing the governor to veto parts of bills and flexibility in appropriating expenditures less than those prescribed in the legislation.

ity to overturn public laws and executive actions it deemed unconstitutional. (We will discuss fully this important "discovered" authority in Chapters 2, 5, and 9.)

The greater the number of veto-holders, the higher the transaction costs in making new policy. Consequently, with its numerous veto-holders, the American political system deserves its reputation as being inherently conservative.

Agenda Control

This is the capacity to set the choices available to others. The choices might concern legislation, proposed regulations, or any other decision presented to a collectivity. For example, those voters who nominate candidates in primary elections set the agenda for all voters on Election Day. Effective **agenda control** involves both positive and negative authority. On the positive side an agenda setter can introduce a choice to the collectivity—a senator proposing an amendment to a bill under consideration, for example—which then decides to accept or reject it. Where everyone enjoys this right—when, say, any fellow senator can offer an amendment to any colleague's proposal—access to the agenda will be of little consequence in explaining collective decisions. Agenda control becomes consequential in settings where some members of the group exercise proposal power and others do not. The Constitution requires, for example, that tax bills originate in the House of Representatives, and so the House sets the Senate's agenda on this important topic.

Consider the advantage this right confers. The agenda setter can propose a course of action, while the others are limited to deciding between the proposal or the status quo (no action). The agenda controller thus *limits* the choices available to the collectivity. Unlike the Senate, where proposal rights are universal, the House has long been governed by rules that empower leaders to set the choices members will vote on. Leaders determine what, if any, amendments will be allowed, and limit the time available for debating alternatives. This procedural authority can have huge consequences. In fact, it probably led to that chamber's impeachment of President Bill Clinton in 1998. In late fall 1998 the Republican-controlled Judiciary Committee sent to the floor articles of impeachment against President Clinton. Republican floor leaders faced a potential problem. They favored impeaching the president as well, but they were fairly certain that a majority of members did not favor this drastic course. Republicans held only a nine-vote majority overall. Moreover, with Democrats appearing unified in opposing impeachment, four to six Republicans informed their leaders that they preferred a softer punishment—specifically, a resolution censuring President Clinton—to impeachment. Yet the Republican leadership's agenda control held a trump card that guaranteed their ultimate success. With the authority to decide which proposals would be available for the members to vote on, the leadership disallowed censure motions and forced Republican fence-sitters to decide between impeachment or no action. In the end the fence-sitters joined their colleagues, and on a nearly perfect party line vote, the House of Representatives impeached the president, even though a majority of the membership preferred censure.[7]

House members confer so much power on their leaders and knowingly bear heavy conformity costs, because in the absence of agenda control the transaction costs

"It's either this or a country run by lawyers."

Not just another lawyer joke. . . . Clearly the guards prefer the high conformity costs imposed by this hapless leviathan to the transaction costs of more democratic institutions.
© The New Yorker Collection 1997; Frank Cotham from cartoonbank.com. All Rights Reserved.

would be unmanageable. Without leaders orchestrating the chamber's decisions, the institution would be at the mercy of its 435 members, each like their colleagues in the smaller Senate, jealously protecting and exercising their right to offer any bill or amendment at any time. After a reform group in New York branded the majority leader of that state's Senate as an autocrat for not letting their favored proposals come to the floor, he responded "pure nonsense. . . . Talk to the C.E.O. of any company. If you want to act on something, and the company has 212 employees, what are you going to do, have a discussion and let 212 employees do whatever the agenda is? Is that what you do? So you have 212 different agendas. And that is just chaotic, doesn't work. That is Third-World-country stuff."[8]

Voting Rules

Any government that aspires to democracy must allow for diverse interests to be expressed in government policy. When members of a collectivity share decision-making authority, the outcomes are determined by some previously agreed-to voting rule. The most prominent option in classical democratic theory is **majority rule.** Normally this term refers to a **"simple majority,"** or one-half plus one.

Majority rule embodies the hallowed democratic principle of political equality. Equality requires that each citizen's vote carries the same weight and offers all citizens the same opportunity to participate in the nation's civic life. When all votes count the same, majority rule becomes an obvious principle: when disagreements arise, the more widely shared preference should prevail.

Yet majority rule offers no magic balance between transaction and conformity costs. It is just one possible constitutional rule midway between dictatorship and consensus. Governments controlled by popular majorities are less likely to engage in **tyranny**—that is, impose very high conformity costs—than are dictatorships, but this knowledge did not fully reassure the Constitution's Framers. Worried about tyranny by the majority, they carefully constructed institutions that would temper transient passions of majorities in the new government. Separation of powers with checks and balances—two concepts we will examine in detail in the next chapter—different term lengths for members of the House, Senate, president, and the federal judges, and explicit provision for states' rights all make it difficult for majorities to take charge of the new government.

Although majority rule figures prominently in the Constitution, it is explicitly required in only a few instances. A majority of the Electoral College is required to elect the president, although the winner may not necessarily receive a majority of the popular vote, as we saw in the contested presidential election of 2000 when Democratic candidate Al Gore received a half million more votes than George W. Bush but lost the election.[9] And a quorum, a majority of the membership of the House of Representatives, must be present before the House can conduct business. Much of what the government does requires action by Congress, which, the Framers seemed to assume, would conduct its business by majority vote.

Yet the Constitution permits or tacitly authorizes other voting rules. The Constitution leaves it to the states to specify rules electing members of Congress, and states almost always have preferred the **plurality** rule (the candidate receiving the most votes, regardless whether the plurality reaches a majority) in deciding winners. Elsewhere in the Constitution **supermajorities** of various amounts are required. If the president vetoes a bill passed by both houses of Congress, two-thirds of the House and of the Senate must vote to override the veto or the bill is defeated. And another example of steep transaction costs, three-quarters of the states must agree to any amendments to the Constitution.

Voting Rules of the United States Senate

Motion	Voting Rule
Unanimous consent to take up legislation out of turn	Unanimous agreement
Passage of ordinary bills and amendments	Simple majority of members present and voting
Rule 22 (cloture to set time limit on debate)	Three-fifths of the full Senate (normally 60 votes)
Veto override	Two-thirds

Delegation

When individuals or groups authorize someone to make and implement decisions for them, **delegation** occurs. Every time Americans go to the polls, they *delegate* to representatives the responsibility for making collective decisions for them. Similarly, members of the House of Representatives elect leaders empowered to orchestrate their chamber's business, thereby reducing coordination and other costs of collective action. The House also delegates the task of drafting legislation to standing committees, which are more manageable subsets of members. Delegation is a common method for controlling the transaction costs associated with decision making and implementation.

Social scientists who analyze delegation note that **principals,** those who possess decision-making authority, may delegate their authority to **agents,** who then exercise it on behalf of the principals. Every spring millions of Americans hire an agent—say, H & R Block—to fill out their tax forms for them and, they hope, save them some money. Similarly, the president (principal) appoints hundreds of staff members (agents) to monitor and promote the administration's interests within the bureaucracy and on Capitol Hill. We will use these terms to identify and illuminate a variety of important political relationships that involve some form of delegation.

Delegation is so pervasive because it addresses common collective action problems. It is indispensable whenever special expertise is required to make and carry out sound decisions. The vast and complex federal bureaucracy requires a full chapter (Chapter 8) to describe and explain—because Congress has pursued so many diverse public policies and delegated their implementation to agencies. A legislature could not possibly administer its policies directly without tying itself in knots. In the next chapter, we will examine the Continental Congress's failed attempts to directly supply Washington's army during the Revolutionary War. The predictable failure resulted in the chronically inadequate provision of essential supplies to the troops. The lesson was not lost on the participants, many of whom served as delegates to the Constitutional Convention in Philadelphia two decades later.

Beyond the need for technical expertise, majorities may sometimes find it desirable politically to delegate decisions. For example, the government allocates space on the frequency band to prevent radio or television stations from interfering with each other's signals. In 1934 Congress stopped allocating frequencies itself, leaving decisions instead to the five members of the Federal Communications Commission. Congress had learned early that assigning frequencies was difficult and politically unrewarding, as its decisions were regularly greeted with charges of favoritism or worse. Congress therefore delegated such decisions to a body of experts while retaining the authority to pass new laws that could override the commission's decisions. Thus Congress retains the ultimate authority to set the nation's technical broadcasting policies when it chooses to exercise it.

Finally, almost all enforcement authority—the key to solving prisoner's dilemmas of all types—involves delegation to a policing agent. It might be the IRS, Securities and Exchange Commission (SEC), the Equal Employment Opportunity Commission, or any of the hundreds of other federal, state, and local agencies that make sure that individuals abide by their collective agreements.

Delegation solves some problems for a collectivity, but it introduces others. A principal runs the risk that its agents will use their authority to serve their own rather than the principal's interest. The discrepancy between what a principal would ideally like its agents to do and what they actually do is called **agency loss.** Agency losses might arise "accidentally" by incompetence or the principal's failure to communicate goals clearly. Or losses might reflect the inherent differences between the goals of a principal and its agents. A principal wants its agents to be exceedingly diligent in protecting its interests while asking for very little in return. Agents, on the other hand, prefer to be generously compensated for minimal effort. The balance in most principal-agent relationships lies on a continuum between these extremes. Mild examples of agency loss include various forms of shirking, or "slacking off." Our agents in the legislature might attend to their own business rather than to the public's, nod off in committee meetings, or accept Super Bowl tickets or golf vacations from someone who wants a special favor. Citizens warily

Mechanics inspect grounded Southwest Airlines planes after revelations that managers at the Federal Aviation Administration, who had personal ties to Southwest executives, had overruled their agency's inspectors and allowed the airline's planes to continue flying despite missing periodic inspection deadlines.

appreciate the opportunities available to their agents in Washington to "feather their own nest." So voters are quick to respond to information, typically from opponents who covet the job, suggesting that the incumbent is not serving constituents well. Members of Congress who miss more than a few roll-call votes usually do so at their peril.

So how can a principal determine whether its agents are being faithful when it cannot observe or understand their actions? Car owners face a similar problem when an auto mechanic says the strange engine noise will require replacement of an obscure part costing a month's pay. How do owners know whether to trust the mechanic, especially since they know the mechanic's financial interest clashes with theirs? They could get a second opinion, investigate the mechanic's reputation, or learn more about cars and check for themselves, but all these solutions take time and energy. Governments employ all of these techniques and others to minimize agency loss. Whistleblower laws generously reward members of the bureaucracy who report instances of malfeasance. Or governments can create an agent who monitors the performance of other agents, and indeed, Congress has created about eighty inspector general offices within the federal bureaucracy to check and report to the president and Congress agency failures to perform their assigned duties faithfully and honestly. Delegation always entails a trade-off between the benefits of having the agent attend to decisions on the principal's behalf against the costs of agency loss and the effort required to monitor the agent's behavior.

A more virulent form of agency loss occurs when the agent turns its delegated authority against the principal. This possible scenario arises when principals provide agents with the coercive authority to ward off external threats or to discourage free riding. What prevents these agents—the police, the army, the IRS, the FBI, and many others—from exploiting their advantage not only to enrich but also entrench themselves by preventing challenges to their authority? Certainly many have. World history—indeed, current affairs—is rife with news of military takeovers, secret police, rigged elections, imprisoned opponents, ethnic cleansing, and national treasuries drained into Swiss bank accounts. Institutions created to minimize transaction costs may, as the trade-off indicates, impose unacceptably high conformity costs.

This risk raises another fundamental question: how much authority can citizens safely surrender in achieving their collective goals? When does delegation become abdication and invite tyranny? In Chapter 2 the Constitution's Framers struggle mightily with this conundrum. James Madison regarded this question as critical. "In framing a government," he wrote, "the great difficulty lies in this: you must first enable the government to control the governed; and in the next place oblige it to control itself." [10] How to design government to manage this "great difficulty" preoccupied the Framers of the Constitution, as it did the political philosophers who influenced them.

Representative Government

Modern democracies blend delegation with majority rule into what is known as **representative government.** Citizens limit their decisions to the selection of government officials who, acting as their agents, deliberate and commit the citizenry to collective enterprises. This form of democracy eliminates the massive confusion that would ensue if large communities tried to craft policies directly, and it frees most citizens from having to attend constantly to civic business. For a large group or society, representative government, through delegation, makes large-scale democracy possible. **Direct democracy,** in which citizens participate directly in collective decision making, is reserved primarily for small communities and organizations.*

Majority Rule versus the Republic

At the time of the adoption of the U.S. Constitution, the idea of majority rule was controversial. The ancient city-state of Athens, one of the few experiments with democracy known at the time, had ended ignominiously in mob rule and ultimately dictatorship. The eighteenth-century political theorists who influenced the Constitution's Framers endorsed a form of government called a **republic,** designed to allow

---

*Another approach to direct democracy that is adapted to a large electorate is the **referendum**. Nearly half the states allow the legislature to propose a change to the state's laws or constitution, which all the voters subsequently vote on. (An alternate and even purer form of direct democracy is the **initiative** which places a proposal on the ballot when the requisite number of registered voters have signed petitions to place the issue on an election ballot.

some degree of popular control and also avoid tyranny.[11] The Framers designed the new constitution to pose formidable transaction costs on collective action. The Framers especially favored some form of veto or "check" of one institution over another. In a republic, voters elect their representatives, but these representatives are constrained in following the majority's dictates by constitutional guarantees for minorities and by institutions and rules requiring exceptionally large majorities for certain decisions.

The notion of an independent, unelected judiciary also challenges the paramount democratic principle of majority rule, but presents no problem for the republican creed. By ratifying the Constitution and retaining the power to amend it, the people may choose to set up an institution independent of the others and unconcerned with short-term swings in public opinion to referee the political process and preserve the values on which the government is founded. In short, republican theorists, who had the allegiance of virtually everyone who attended the Constitutional Convention in 1787, *really* believed in the role of institutions in reaching and preserving agreements. And by making some collective decisions more difficult than others, the Framers consciously built in higher transaction costs, even if they did not use those terms.

Since the American experiment was launched over two hundred years ago, experience with majority rule throughout the world has proved it to be a viable approach to self-governance. Although constitutions written in the twentieth century—such as those in France and Germany—may still divide authority in ways that allow their countries to be referred to as republics, they have dispensed with the elaborate rules and institutions designed to constrain majority rule by ratcheting up transaction costs. Rather than separating the executive from the legislature, most of the world's modern democracies have fused them in **parliamentary government.** Many varieties of parliamentary government exist, but they all lodge decisive authority in a popularly elected legislature, whose actions are not subject to the same severe checks by executive and judicial vetoes. The legislature in turn elects a team of executives called a **cabinet,** one of whose members serves as the premier or prime minister (see Figure 1-2). This system promotes majority rule in the sense that the political party or coalition of parties that controls the legislature controls the executive. In effect parliamentary systems are able to forgo the higher transaction costs embedded in the U.S. Constitution's **separation of powers.** At the same time, as the majority gains the capacity to act on its preferences, those who disagree are obliged to accept the majority's preferences.

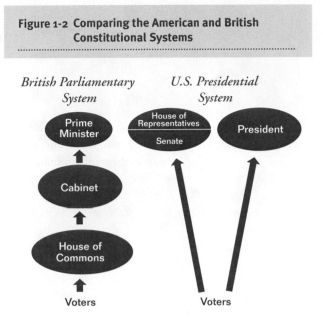

Figure 1-2 Comparing the American and British Constitutional Systems

In 1776 the Scottish economist Adam Smith laid the intellectual foundation for capitalism by declaring in his treatise *The Wealth of Nations* that the exchange of goods and services among private parties in an open marketplace generates a public good in the form of prosperity.

Politicians

Another innovation of representative government is elected **politicians.** These professionals specialize in discovering collective enterprises that unite citizens with different values and interests. These elected agents are sometimes called "public servants"—a euphemism they prefer because the self-effacing image tends to allay the public's fears of agency loss.

A much more apt term for a politician, however, is *entrepreneur.* Like entrepreneurs, politicians are deal-makers, but instead of putting together financial partnerships and other ventures, they assemble coalitions. A **coalition** is a combination of *unlike*-minded interests who nonetheless agree, for their own distinct reasons, to a common course of action. To win elections, politicians must succeed at building coalitions. Successful candidates persuade a plurality of voters to support them (a common action) by offering different constituencies their own reasons for doing so. For many Americans, the "ideal" politician is a dutiful, selfless public servant who abjures personal or political advantage in pursuit of the public good. But most citizens probably would not be satisfied with such a politician's performance. Where numerous competing interests are well represented and governing power is widely shared, the public is better served with politicians who are more dedicated to solving problems that satisfy the interests of their constituents than to pursuing their personal vision of the good society.

Throughout the book we will refer to the behavior of politicians as *strategic* when they subordinate their *sincere* preferences over what is best for their constituents in order to achieve results that stand a better chance of success. Every time a politician compromises, defers to a colleague, or decides not to resist certain defeat on an issue, she, knowingly or unknowingly, is behaving strategically. In distributing authority across institutions and by incorporating numerous preferences, the American political system essentially demands that its politicians behave strategically.

Citizens want their politicians to act as faithful agents—diligent custodians of their interests—and yet they fear that, once elected to office, politicians will pursue their own interests and neglect the concerns of the people who put them there. Such fears in the 1990s spawned a movement to limit the number of terms representatives can serve in Congress and in state legislatures. But a politician's responsiveness is linked to the desire to get reelected or to create a firm base for advancing to higher elective office. Thus the term-limit "solution" eliminates the one real device that democracy provides citizens for keeping their agents responsive.

The Work of Government

Given the variety of costs and risks associated with collective action, Americans weigh such undertakings carefully. Among other things, they calculate whether the prospective gains from a collective public effort are sufficiently greater than what they could achieve privately. The vast majority of these calculations favor private action, perhaps explaining why much of what Americans do and consume as individuals has little or nothing to do with government. Their homes, cars, clothes, food, and sources of entertainment fall into a realm called **private goods**—that is, things people buy and consume themselves in a marketplace that supplies these goods according to the demand for them.

What we will discuss in this book is the provision of **public goods,** which everyone participates in supplying—say, through tax dollars—and which anyone can freely consume, as much as he or she desires. Stated another way, the two distinguishing features of all public goods are that their costs are borne collectively and that no one can be excluded from their benefits. An example of a public good is a freeway, which, as its name implies, may be used by anyone. A toll road is a private good because its costs are met by the motorists who pay a fee (toll) for its use. A quintessential public good is national defense. However, in the early 1950s, at the beginning of the Cold War, some fearful homeowners took a "private goods approach" and installed backyard bomb shelters in the event of nuclear attack. They were eventually abandoned as just about everyone accepted the logic of relying on national defense—a public good—to protect them from nuclear assault.

Sometimes public goods are generated as a byproduct of people's private activities. Many such byproducts are undesirable and would more accurately be called "public bads," although they rarely are. Economists and political scientists call them **externalities.** Automobile pollution is a classic example of a negative externality, which is produced by motorists who act as free riders in serving their own interests over those of society at large. Motorists who profess to hate pollution and despise "polluters" rationalize that their own contribution to pollution (the externality) is minuscule and so will not appreciably affect air quality. Collectively, then, drivers gripe about this public bad even as they contribute to it.

Citizens frequently look to government to provide positive public goods: national defense, public order, a legal system, civil liberties, and public parks. They also count on government to prevent negative externalities by passing laws that control pollution, protect endangered species, and establish residential, commercial, and industrial zones. For these tasks, the government enjoys two important advantages: it has sufficient resources to undertake expensive projects, and it has coercive authority to prevent free riding. Many public goods simply could not be produced any other way. Some are too risky financially to attract private investment. What business could afford to build a multibillion-dollar supercollider to research nuclear fusion and, at the project's inception, expect to recover its costs within a period reasonable to shareholders? Other goods

POLITICS/POLICY

Fire Protection
From a Private to a Public Good

The history of fire protection in America offers a classic example of the evolution of private goods to a government responsibility. During the nation's colonial era, fire protection assumed the form of an insurance policy. Homeowners subscribed to a local protection service, mounted its identifying shield on the front of the house, and hoped that if they had a fire it would show up. Aside from the serious coordination problem of identifying the service provider during an emergency, this approach to fire protection was susceptible to a serious externality: when a neighbor's house burned to the ground because he failed to pay his premiums, the fire-protected house stood an excellent chance of catching fire as well.

In many small communities voluntary fire departments formed to turn fire protection into a public good. The coordination problems were resolved, and the service's responsiveness limited the spread of fires across structures. This arrangement worked reasonably well in towns and villages where everyone knew everyone else. Any "volunteer" who chronically slept through the fire bell might well have found his neighbors doing the same when the bell sounded for his house.

As communities grew and social controls on free riding weakened, voluntary fire protection gave way to government-run, professional fire protection. Typically governments created a special fire district with taxing authority and hired professional firefighters to supply this public good.

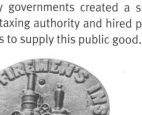

offer better value when converted from a private to a public good. The history of fire protection in America is one example (see box "Fire Protection: From a Private to a Public Good").

Because the consumption of public goods is disconnected from their production, consumers will be tempted to overuse or waste them. When Medi-Cal, California's health care program for the poor, treated eyeglasses as a public good, it soon discovered that its patients consumed almost twice as many pairs of glasses on average as the people who bought them in the private market. The solution, introducing a modest co-payment and partially privatizing consumption, promptly brought consumption rates in line with national averages. As we found earlier with the tragedy of the commons, one way to prevent a common resource from being overexploited is to tie the benefit of consuming a product to its cost—that is, to privatize it. In another variation, governments may regulate aspects of the consumption of private goods to achieve a public

POLITICS/POLICY

Evolution of Smoking from a Private to a Public Issue

An example of the government's intrusion into private behavior is the evolution of the nation's policy toward smoking (see chart). Before the 1980s lighting up a cigarette was regarded as a strictly private activity. There were externalities, to be sure, but as long as the smoke was believed to be no more than a nuisance, nonsmokers endured the fumes with resignation and no one seriously proposed a ban on smoking in public places. In the 1960s, as the externalities of smoking came to be regarded as serious—that is, costly to public health and budgets—the government undertook collective action by requiring health warning labels on cigarette packages. Today, the array of "public bads" associated with smoking—public health care costs, the carcinogenic properties of secondhand smoke, and teenage smoking—has transformed smoking into a prominent public policy issue.

	Discerned Externalities	Nature of Collective Action
1950s and earlier	Nuisance smoke	Voluntary "no smoking"
1960s	Carcinogenic	Package labeling
1970s	Greater scientific evidence and rising public health care costs	Advertising restrictions
1980s–1990s	Secondhand smoke	Smoke-free zones in indoor public facilities
1990s	Rising public health costs and teenage addiction	Settlement of lawsuit between tobacco industry and states' attorneys general to compensate states for public health costs of smoking; agreement to target teenagers for an antismoking message
2001	Smoke in public places	Community bans on smoking in public parks and other open-air places
2008	Secondhand smoke and smoke in public places	Thirty-four states and the District of Columbia enact smoking bans or partial smoking bans in restaurants and office buildings, and in southern California, even at the beach

good. Most kinds of pollution, for example, are created as byproducts of private activities, which means that the government, to protect the public from these byproducts, must intrude on private behavior. The government requires auto manufacturers to produce cleaner-burning engines, forces power plants to install scrubbers on smokestacks, mandates periodic auto emission inspections, and enacts smoking bans (see box "Evolution of Smoking from a Private to a Public Issue").

Another large class of goods and services has a "public good" aspect that justifies the collective provision of essentially private benefits. Earlier we examined a class of mixed policies where government privatizes the "commons" in order to conserve it. Federal and state tax codes are complicated because many of their provisions are not to raise revenue, but to motivate the public to engage in behavior that achieves some collective policy goal. There are tax deductions or credits for charitable contributions, for contributions to personal retirement accounts, for installing solar heating, for restoring historic homes, for investing in new equipment, and until recently, even for buying trucks and SUVs but only those that weighed more than two tons. Similarly, governments directly subsidize desirable private activities that citizens would not undertake in sufficient numbers without the subsidy. Farmers receive payments for growing corn, bankers for loaning students unsecured loans, and universities for scientific research.

In reality, most of the goods and services that governments provide cannot be easily sorted into either the private or the public bin. Public education is a classic example. A well-educated citizenry undeniably strengthens the civic and economic life of a society, but public education also bestows substantial *private* benefits on students and educators. The immediate beneficiary of a flu vaccination is the person who received it. But so too is everyone with whom he or she comes into contact, even if only by pushing the same elevator button. Because the work of modern governments typically belongs in this class of mixed goods, public policy is frequently referred to as **collective goods,** a term less restrictive than *public good.*

Mitigating "Popular Passions"

The Constitution's Framers, who assembled in Philadelphia during the summer of 1787, did not employ the modern vocabulary of collective action problems, such as prisoner's dilemma or externalities. Nor did they formally label and classify their institutional design mechanisms. Yet they were intimately preoccupied with the collective action issues that afflicted society and overwhelmed the capacity of the Articles of Confederation government to solve them. Perhaps most impressive about their deliberations is that, however much they disagreed on the design of the new government, they all understood that the nation's previous failures stemmed from politics and political institutions. Citizens and state governments engaged in rampant free riding and politicians failed to honor commitments because the institutions made cooperation risky. Americans were trapped in the same fundamental prisoner's dilemma that ensnared Victor Mature and Betty Grable. The Framers reformed, knowing that the survival of the republic was at stake.* To solve the nation's pervasive collective action problems, the Framers designed a new government that minimized conformity costs. Some delegates worried that the states were being reduced to minor administrative districts. Others, including James Madison, were far more concerned that passionate majorities might tyrannize minorities. The solution to both extremes lay in escalating

---

*Rival nations abroad realized that pitting states against one another in bidding for trade agreements would weaken and eventually destroy the new national government.

transaction costs so the new government could expeditiously solve the nation's problems but could not rapaciously usurp power. Separation of powers, staggered legislative terms, an unelected judiciary, limited national authority, and the other features explored in the chapters that follow, all effectively constrain majority rule. The result is arguably the most complex constitutional system in the world. The most appropriate place to begin our examination of *modern* American politics and apply the concepts presented here is at the reorganization of the entire government. In Chapter 2 we turn to the founding of the republic.

Nota Bene

This chapter presents two sets of concepts that our discussion will employ throughout the remainder of the book. The first distinguishes the various kinds of collective action problems that invariably arise both within society and within government whenever differently minded individuals attempt to work together. The second identifies simple institutional design principles that appear in all governmental organizations. For those chapters examining the several branches of government and federalism, problems of collective action and institutional design are naturally more prominent than in the political behavior chapters. Yet these issues arise in every chapter, and when they do, we will highlight the text (including the important topics located in the boxes!) to alert you that the concepts introduced here are being put to work.

Key Terms

logic.cqpress.com

agency loss, 32
agenda control, 29
agent, 31
authority, 9
bargaining, 5
cabinet, 35
coalition, 36
collective action, 12
collective goods, 40
command, 27
compromise, 5
conformity costs, 22
constitution, 9
coordination, 12
delegation, 31
direct democracy, 34
externalities, 37
focal point, 13
free-rider problem, 19
government, 9
initiative, 34
institution, 7
majority rule, 30
office, 9
parliamentary government, 35
plurality, 31
politician, 36
politics, 5
power, 10
preferences, 6
principal, 31
prisoner's dilemma, 12
private goods, 37
privatize, 21
public goods, 37
referendum, 34
representative government, 34

republic, 34
separation of powers, 35
simple majority, 30
supermajority, 31
tragedy of the commons, 20
transaction costs, 22
tyranny, 30
veto, 28
zero sum, 18

Suggested Readings

Safire, William. *Safire's New Political Dictionary.* New York: Ballantine Books, 1993. Arguably, Safire understands the American version of English better than any other modern popular writer. Fortunately, the former presidential speechwriter also has an especially keen eye for politics.

Shepsle, Kenneth A., and Mark S. Bonchek. *Analyzing Politics: Rationality, Behavior, and Institutions.* New York: Norton, 1997. This book, aimed at the undergraduate audience, elaborates on many of the rational choice concepts presented in this chapter.

Stanley, Harold W., and Richard G. Niemi. *Vital Statistics on American Politics, 2004–2005.* Washington, D.C.: CQ Press, 2005. If the text does not satisfy your appetite for tables and figures, this book, filled with well-organized data about American politics, will.

Tocqueville, Alexis de. *Democracy in America.* Many good paperback translations of Tocqueville are available, but beware of abridged versions in which, invariably, the lively asides and incidental observations are lost.

Review Questions

1. Why can't we solve our disputes through simple bargaining all the time? What factors undermine bargaining in different settings? What can people or governments do to help solve disputes despite these factors?

2. What sorts of institutions are commonly used to manage conflicts in societies? What are some examples of where these institutions have failed?

3. Discuss how the coordination and transaction costs for states changed when the national government moved from the Articles of Confederation to the Constitution.

4. What are principals and agents? When in your life have you been one or the other?

5. What are some examples of public and private goods that you have consumed today? How did you acquire them?

Exercises

Campus Constitutions

The authors argue that all organizations are governed by rules and procedures for making and enforcing decisions. Examine the rules and procedures of four different university organizations on your campus. (Note: make sure you include at least two organizations from outside your student government. If you would really like to suffer, read the rules for one school's academic senate: http://senate.ucla.edu/ Forms Docs/bylaws/toc.htm.) Compare and contrast the rules and procedures of the organizations, giving particular attention to the following areas:

- How are officials of the group selected?

- How are new members of the group added?

- How does the group reach a decision?

- Who has authority to spend money for the group?

- How can the rules or procedures of the group be changed (and how often has this been done)?

Group Grades

The professor of your large politics class has announced that she is considering assigning your class three group projects. Each member of the class would be assigned to one of the three projects, and all students in the group would be assigned the same grade for the project, regardless of the amount of work they put into the project. Use your readings for this chapter to construct a persuasive argument that the professor should or should not use this grading system for the class.

2

The Constitution

The Constitution has not changed much over the past two hundred years. Were the Framers really geniuses, or are Americans simply very lucky?

How can the United States call itself a democracy when so many features of its national political system are designed to frustrate majority rule?

Why is America's Constitution so complicated, where even the word "majority" has several meanings and can mean something different at different times?

Militarily, 1780 was a disastrous year for the American Revolution. Three years into the war the Continental Army, the revolutionary fighting force, teetered on total collapse. In May an entire garrison of five thousand men surrendered to the British at Charleston, South Carolina. In late summer, across the state in Camden, nearly nine hundred Continental soldiers were killed, and one thousand were taken prisoner in a single engagement. When the army regrouped, only seven hundred of the original four thousand men showed up. The fall brought no respite from the army's woes. Indeed, the young nation learned that one of its few illustrious military commanders, General Benedict Arnold, switched sides and became a byword for treason.

By the end of 1780, the American forces, under General George Washington, had shrunk from twenty-six thousand to fifteen thousand. New Year's Day 1781 saw even further deterioration in the army's situation; 1,300 mutinous Pennsylvania troops, camped in Princeton, New Jersey, demanded from Congress a year's back pay and immediate discharge. A congressional committee met the soldiers outside Philadelphia and agreed to some of their demands.

Although all these problems appeared to stem from unfit commanders or unwilling troops, the real problem was the fledgling national government, the Continental Congress. It simply was unable to act decisively or very rapidly because all decisions of consequence (such as taxes) required approval by all state governments. And it had virtually no administrative apparatus for implementing even those policies that enjoyed unanimous support. As a result, members of congressional committees sometimes found themselves deadlocked over how many uniforms the army needed. Long into

George Washington addresses delegates to the 1787 Constitutional Convention in this 1823 engraving from a book published by Huntington and Hopkins.

Countdown to the Constitution

Date	Event	Colonial Action
1750s		
	French and Indian War (1754–1763) drains the British treasury	Albany Congress calls for colonial unity (1754)
1760s		
	Stamp Act enacted by British Parliament (1765)	Stamp Act Congress attended by delegates from nine of the thirteen colonies (1765)
1770s		
	Tea Act (1773)	Boston Tea Party (1773)
	British adopt Coercive Acts to punish colonies (1774)	First Continental Congress rejects plan of union but adopts Declaration of American Rights denying Parliament's authority over internal colonial affairs (1774)
	Battles of Lexington and Concord (1775)	Second Continental Congress assumes role of revolutionary government (1775); adopts Declaration of Independence (1776)
	Thomas Paine's *Common Sense* (1776) published	Congress adopts Articles of Confederation as constitution for new government (1777)
1780s		
	British defeat Americans at Camden and Charleston (1780)	
	Hartford Convention (1781)	Articles of Confederation ratified (1781)
	British surrender at Yorktown (1781)	
	Shays's Rebellion (1786)	Constitutional Convention drafts blueprint for new government (1787)
	The Federalist (1787–1788) published	Constitution ratified (1789)

the war the army remained underfed, ill-clothed, poorly armed, unpaid (at least in currency of value), and despised by civilians uncompensated for requisitioned supplies. The troops struggled just to survive as a unit. Ultimately, of course, this depleted army had to confront the well-equipped British on the battlefield. During the winter of 1780, General Washington desperately exhorted Congress, "Where are the Men? Where are the provisions? Where are the Cloaths?"

The bitter irony was that many of the desperately needed provisions existed in ample supply. The war was causing shortages, but they were not severe enough to account for the deprivations hampering the army. Nor was the problem the strictly logistical exercise of keeping a traveling army supplied. Despite the difficulty of that task, British troops and their German mercenaries were reasonably well provisioned. Undermining the Revolution's cause was an epidemic of free riding by Americans—from political leaders to ordinary soldiers. States agreed to contribute money and supplies but failed to do so in a timely fashion, if at all. Contractors, paid with a currency that was losing about 10 percent of its value every month, sold the American army spoiled food, shoddy clothing, and poorly manufactured arms, and then shortchanged the

Continental Army even on these inferior provisions when the suppliers thought they could get away with it. Many recruits enlisted, received their requisitions, and then deserted with their new booty.

Although all of the politicians, merchants, and soldiers involved in the war effort may have been patriots, they were unprepared to shoulder the costs of serving the public good while their neighbors and colleagues conspicuously shirked the same duties. If, as we argued in Chapter 1, the enforcement of contracts and other collective agreements is the fundamental responsibility of government, then we must blame ineffective government for the free riding and other shirking that sap a community's will to

JOIN, or DIE.

In what is recognized as America's first political cartoon, Benjamin Franklin depicts the colonies as caught in a classic collective action dilemma. If united, the colonies represent a formidable force for England to reckon with. But if any colony attempts to free ride, the collective effort will survive no better than a dismembered snake.

achieve its collective goals. General Washington understood the problem and warned darkly that if the government did not soon take charge, "our Independence fails, [our government] will be annihilated, and we must once more return to the Government of Great Britain, and be made to kiss the rod preparing for our correction."[1] Over the next year Washington endured the government's ineptitude and avoided a catastrophic military defeat. Then, with time, the Revolution gained credibility abroad, which persuaded England's archrival, France, to loan Congress money to continue the war effort and, finally, to commit French naval and land forces to the battlefield. On October 17, 1781, the collaboration paid off with a decisive victory at Yorktown, Virginia, which ended the war.

The year 1783 brought a formal end to the hostilities and independence for the American colonies. But the young nation, still saddled with a government that could not act, was confronted with many of the same problems it had labored under during the war. Indeed, many observers feared that independence, won in war, would soon be lost in peace as the nation threatened to unravel into thirteen disputatious nations.

In the summer of 1787 fifty-five delegates from all the states except Rhode Island assembled in Philadelphia to consider revising the nation's constitution, known as the **Articles of Confederation.** (Content with the Articles, the citizens and politicians of Rhode Island feared correctly that their small state would lose influence under any reforms.) General Washington, presiding over this convention, and the twenty other delegates who had served under him in the field knew firsthand the failings of the current government. The rest of the delegates similarly drew on their varied governing experiences, some stretching back into the colonial era, as they worked together first to revise the Articles and then to formulate an entirely new constitution. How did these delegates use their experience and their familiarity with the new nation's struggle to solve the problems inherent in collective action? A closer look at the events leading up to the Constitutional Convention and the creative process it spawned will reveal the thinking that gave birth to America's constitutional system.

The Road to Independence

Geographically, America was well situated to be the first nation to break with monarchy and embrace republicanism; distance limited Britain's capacity to govern the colonies—a problem that gained painful significance during the Revolutionary War. Beginning early in the colonial era, Britain had ceded to Americans responsibility for managing their own domestic affairs, including taxation. The colonists enjoyed this **home rule,** and the British found it agreeable as well. After all, Britain's first concern was to control America's foreign commerce, thereby guaranteeing itself a market for British manufactured goods and a steady supply of cheap raw materials. Thus for more than a century before independence the colonists had routinely elected their own leaders and held them accountable for local policies and taxes. Breaking with Great Britain may have been emotionally wrenching for many Americans, but unfamiliarity with self-governance was not a factor in their hesitancy to seek independence.

A Legacy of Self-Governance

The first colonial representative assembly convened in Virginia in August 1619. By about 1650 all of the colonies had established elective assemblies, which eventually gained the authority to initiate laws and levy taxes. The British appointed governors, colonial councils, and judges in most colonies, and some of these officials vigorously resisted the expansion of local prerogatives. But because the elective assemblies paid their salaries and funded their offices, these officers of the Crown found that they, too, had to accommodate popular opinion. The colonial experience thus taught Americans that a popularly elected legislature in control of the purse strings could dominate other governmental institutions. The next generation of leaders recalled this important and enduring lesson as they convened in Philadelphia to revamp the new nation's constitutional system.

In addition to experience in self-governance, the state assemblies supplied the nation with another vital resource: elected politicians experienced in negotiating collective agreements. As the vanguard of the independence movement, these politicians provided the nation with an era of exceptional leadership.

Americans also entered independence well versed in constitution writing. A royal charter or contract between the Crown and a British company or business entrepreneur had provided the foundation for most colonies. Later, the colonists themselves wrote constitutions, which they periodically revised. When in 1776 and again in 1787 the nation's leaders confronted the task of designing new government institutions, a written constitution was, not surprisingly, the instrument of choice.

On March 5, 1770, British troops fired into a crowd of men and boys in Boston, killing five and wounding others. The massacre, depicted in this classic engraving by Paul Revere, gave the word tyranny new meaning. These and other events were instrumental in rousing colonial resistance to British rule on the eve of the American Revolution.

Home rule may have had its benefits for the American colonies, but as civic education it also shortchanged the nation in learning self-governance. In ruling its far-flung empire, which included the American colonies, Britain regulated all of its colonies' commerce, as well as provided them with military security by means of its navy, the world's largest. Thus the colonies prospered and managed their own domestic affairs while Britain dictated their foreign relations and bore the substantial costs of providing their security. Britain preferred to deal with the thirteen colonies individually rather than through some national assembly that might discover and give expression to collective interests that differed from those of Britain. As a result, instead of gradually assuming greater responsibility for their common destiny, America's colonial governments found few occasions to work together. Later, after the nation had declared its independence, politicians who had stridently resisted the Crown's incursions into their local authority would refuse to bear the costs of addressing their collective problems as a nation. With nationhood, the free ride on Britain would end.

Home rule experienced its first strains during Britain's war with France in the 1750s. Known in America as the French and Indian War and in Europe as the Seven Years' War, this lengthy, multicontinent conflict drained both Britain's treasury and its military resources. Searching for assistance, Britain in 1754 summoned delegates from each of the colonies to a conference in Albany, New York, to invite their collective assistance in defending the western frontier against the French military and its Indian allies. Because six of the thirteen colonies failed to send delegates, this would-be first national assembly failed even before it convened.

Yet the Albany Congress produced the first serious proposal for a national government. One of Pennsylvania's delegates, Benjamin Franklin, already renowned throughout the country as the man who had tamed lightning, proposed a "Plan of the Union" that would have created a national government. The plan called for an American army to provide for the colonies' defense, a popularly elected national legislature with the power to levy taxes, and an executive appointed by the British king. (On learning of Franklin's plan, King George III declared, "I am the colonies' legislature.") But none of the colonial assemblies could muster much enthusiasm for Franklin's ideas. Why should they share their tax base with some dubiously mandated new governmental entity? And why should they undertake Britain's burden of providing for the colonies' security and overseeing trade? For them, free riding made eminent sense as long as they could get away with it. And they did get away with it; another decade would pass before Britain tried to force Americans to contribute to their defense. Only then did Franklin's proposal make sense and attract interest.

Dismantling Home Rule

France's defeat in 1763 ended its aspirations for extensive colonization of America. The British, relishing their victory, had little idea, however, that the war would trigger events that would severely compromise Britain's claims in America over the next decade.

By the end of the war Britain was broke. With its citizenry already among the most heavily taxed in the world, the British government looked to the colonies to share in the empire's upkeep. At the time, the only British taxes on the colonies were duties on imports from outside the British Empire, designed less to raise revenue than to regulate commerce. To raise needed tax revenues, Britain had to assert its power to impose taxes. Moreover, to consolidate its power Britain began to violate home rule. Every revenue law the British government enacted during the decade after the French and Indian War contained provisions tightening its control over the internal affairs of the colonies.

The most aggressive challenge to home rule came in 1765 with passage of the Stamp Act.* This law imposed a tax on all printed materials, including legal documents, licenses, insurance papers, and land titles, as well as a variety of consumer goods, including newspapers and playing cards (proof of payment of the tax was the stamp affixed to the taxed document). The tax had long been familiar to the British public, but Americans greeted it as a personal affront. It inflamed American public opinion, not so much because of the money extracted but because of the instruments

---

*Earlier, the Sugar Act of 1764 had levied new duties on certain foreign imports and introduced new efforts to interdict Yankee smuggling to circumvent import duties. At the same time Parliament passed another inflammatory law, the Currency Act, which forbade the colonies from printing their own currency, thus requiring merchants to raise scarce hard cash to do business.

used to extract it. Americans had paid taxes before, but they had been self-imposed, levied by the colonial assemblies to provide local services. Thus the American response, "no taxation without representation," was not simply the rallying cry of a tax revolt. In fact, Americans were not genuinely interested in representation in the British Parliament. Rather, the colonists were asserting home rule. A more accurate rallying cry would have been, "No taxation by a government in which we want no part!"

The colonial assemblies passed resolutions demanding repeal of the tax, and most sent delegates to a national conference, the Stamp Act Congress, to craft a unified response. For the first time they united against Britain by agreeing unanimously on a resolution condemning the tax. They could not agree, however, on a course of action.

The organized resistance of ordinary citizens was more successful.* Throughout the colonies local groups confronted tax collectors and prevented them from performing their duties. Over the next decade these scenes were repeated as Britain imposed a half-dozen new tax and administrative laws designed to weaken the colonial assemblies. Americans countered by boycotting British products and forming protest organizations, such as the Sons of Liberty, the Daughters of Liberty, and the more militant Committees of Correspondence. Vigilantism and public demonstrations overshadowed assembly resolutions.

In this eighteenth-century satirical drawing by a British artist, Bostonians gleefully pour tea down the throat of a customs official, who has just been tarred and feathered. In the distance colonists dump tea into Boston Harbor, just as they did in 1773 at the Boston Tea Party. And, lest one British misdeed go unnoticed, a symbol of the hated Stamp Act, passed in 1765, appears on the tree.

Justly, the most famous of these demonstrations was the Boston Tea Party. No colony had chafed under Britain's new rules and import taxes more than Massachusetts, whose economy depended heavily on international trade and shipping. On a winter night in 1773 a group of patriots donned Indian dress and dumped 342 chests of tea owned by the East India Company into Boston harbor to protest a new tax on Americans' favorite non-alcoholic beverage. Britain responded with the Restraining Acts and Coercive Acts, which closed the port of Boston to all commerce, dissolved the Massachusetts assembly, decreed that British troops in Boston must be quartered in American homes, and ordered that Americans charged with protest crimes and British soldiers with crimes against the colonists be sent to England for trial. Colonists

---

*"Nothing else is talked of," wrote Sally Franklin to her father, Benjamin, in London. "The Dutch [Germans] talk of the stompt act the Negroes of the tamp, in short every body has something to say." Mary Beth Norton et al., *A People and a Nation: A History of the United States* (Boston: Houghton Mifflin, 1990), 117.

viewed these last provisions as ensuring serious punishment for the first group and lax punishment for the second.

The Continental Congresses

When colonists elsewhere witnessed Britain's heavy-handed policies in Massachusetts, they recognized their own vulnerability. Without hesitation, then, they answered the call of Boston resistance leader Samuel Adams to assemble in the fall of 1774 at Philadelphia for what became the First Continental Congress. Each colony sent its leading professionals, merchants, and planters. These men had mostly known one another only by reputation, but at this meeting they would form a nucleus of national leadership for the next decade. Among them were the future nation's first presidents: George Washington, John Adams, and Thomas Jefferson.

The Continental Congress promptly passed resolutions condemning British taxes and administrative decrees. When the idea of creating a national government was raised, Franklin's plan of union, the only existing proposal for unification, was introduced and briefly but inconclusively debated. The most significant actions of the First Continental Congress were adoption of a Declaration of American Rights, which essentially reasserted home rule, and endorsement of an agreement to ban all trade with Britain until it rescinded the despised taxes and regulations. To enforce the boycott against the prospect of massive free riding, Congress called for the formation of local elective "committees of observation" in every county, town, and hamlet in the country. Soon many of these newly formed organizations began imposing patriotic morality with investigations of "treasonable" conversations and public rebukes of more ordinary vices. Earlier import boycotts had been modestly successful—enough to alter British policy—but with the capacity to identify and sanction potential free riders, the new boycott won almost total compliance.

The eight thousand or so members of these local committees provided a base for the statewide conventions that sprang up throughout the colonies when the British prevented the colonial assemblies from meeting. Unhampered by local British authorities, these conventions quickly became de facto governments. (When some colonies' assemblies were enjoined from meeting, they would adjourn to a local tavern and resume doing business as an unofficial provincial convention.) They collected taxes, raised militias, passed "laws" forbidding the judiciary from enforcing British decrees, and selected delegates to the Second Continental Congress, which met in Philadelphia in May 1775.

By the time the Second Continental Congress gathered, war had broken out. Spontaneous bloody uprisings in the spring of 1775 at Lexington and Concord in Massachusetts had provoked the state conventions to mobilize local volunteer militias and disarm suspected British loyalists. Events demanded concerted action, and the Second Continental Congress responded by acting like a national government. Congress had no legal authority to conduct a war effort, but throughout the colonies patriots desperately required coordination, and it was the only national institution available.

Congress first instructed the conventions to reconstitute themselves as state governments based on republican principles. Using their former colonial governments as a model, most states adopted **bicameral** (two-chamber) **legislatures,** and all created a governorship. Accustomed to difficult relations with the royal governors, the states severely limited the terms and authority of these newly minted American executives. This antiexecutive bias would persist and influence deliberations at the Constitutional Convention a decade later.

Then, acting even more like a government, the Second Continental Congress issued the nation's first bonds and established a national currency. It also authorized delegate George Washington to expand the shrinking Massachusetts militia into a full-fledged national army. (As if his colleagues had needed a hint, Washington attended the convention in full military dress of his own design.)

The Declaration of Independence

During its first year's work of creating states and raising and financing an army, Congress did not consider the fundamental issue of separation from England. But it was discussed on street corners and in taverns throughout the nation. In January 1776 the pamphleteer Thomas Paine published *Common Sense,* which moved the independence issue to center stage. Within three months 120,000 copies had been sold, and Americans were talking about Paine's plainly stated, irresistible argument that only in the creation of an independent republic would the people find contentment.

The restless citizenry's anticipation that Congress would consider a resolution of separation was realized in June when Virginia delegate Richard Henry Lee called for creation of a new nation separate from Britain. Congress referred his proposal to a committee of delegates from every region with instructions to draft the proper resolution. One member of this committee was a thirty-three-year-old lawyer from Virginia, Thomas Jefferson. Asked to draft a statement because of "his peculiar felicity of expression," Jefferson modestly demurred. This prompted the always-direct John Adams of Massachusetts to protest, "You can write ten times better than I can." [2]

Jefferson's qualifications to articulate the rationale for independence extended well beyond his writing skills. Possessing aristocratic tastes but democratic values, he never wavered from an abiding confidence in the innate goodness and wisdom of common people. "State a moral case to a ploughman and a professor," he once challenged a friend. "The former will decide it as well, and often better than the latter, because he has not been led astray by artificial rules." * In the end, Jefferson agreed to draft the resolution of separation.

Jefferson concurred with the other delegates in many of the specific grievances itemized in the resolution he drafted, but for him the real rationale for throwing off British rule rested on the fundamental right of self-government. Such conviction produced this famous passage:

> We hold these truths to be self-evident, that all men are created equal, that they are endowed by their creator with certain unalienable Rights, that among these are Life, Liberty and the pursuit of Happiness. That to secure these rights, Governments are instituted among Men, deriving their just powers from the

---

*Whether drafting Virginia's first law guaranteeing religious freedom as a member of its House of Burgesses, revising Virginia's constitution, or founding the University of Virginia, Jefferson consistently engaged in activities liberating the inherent capacities of his fellow citizens. Joseph R. Conlin, *The Morrow Book of Quotations in American History* (New York: Morrow, 1984).

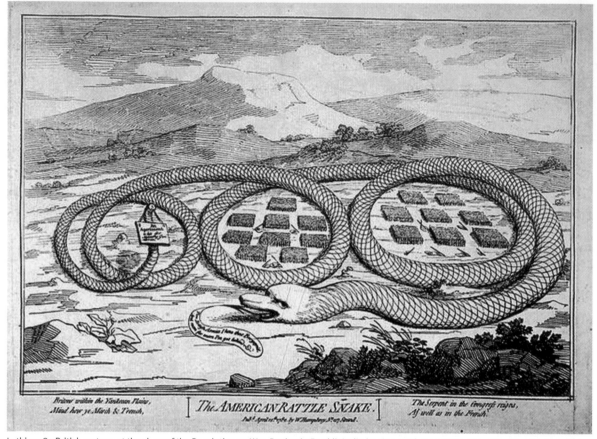

In this 1782 British cartoon at the close of the Revolutionary War, Benjamin Franklin's diminutive, garden-variety snake, struggling to stay whole (see page 47), has become through unity a voracious "American rattlesnake," eager to consume British armies. "Two British Armies I have thus Burgoyn'd, And room for more I've got behind," it boasts. A sign posted on its rattle advertises ominously to British readers, "An Apartment to Lett for Military Gentlemen."

consent of the governed. That whenever any form of government becomes destructive of these ends, it is the Right of the People to alter or abolish it, and to institute new Government. . . .

Jefferson's colleagues did not tamper with this centerpiece of the **Declaration of Independence,** but they did amend his list of grievances. Foreshadowing the future conflict over race, Jefferson's indictment of Britain for introducing slavery into the colonies offended the sensibilities of slave-owning southern delegates. Thus at their insistence this grievance was stricken from the final resolution.* (The full text of the Declaration of Independence appears in the Appendix.)

---

*Among the items deleted: "He [King George III] has waged cruel war against human nature itself, violating its most sacred rights of life and liberty in the persons of a distant people who never offended him, captivating them and carrying them into slavery in another hemisphere, or to incur miserable death in their transportation thither." In *Thomas Jefferson,* ed. Merrill D. Peterson (New York: Library of America, 1984), 21–22.

In a solemn ceremony on July 4, 1776, each member of the Second Continental Congress signed the document. Rebelling against a colonial power with a huge occupation army was a dangerous enterprise. The conclusion of the Declaration—"we mutually pledge to each other our lives, our Fortunes, and our sacred Honor"—was no mere rhetoric.

America's First Constitution: The Articles of Confederation

With the Declaration of Independence in hand, the delegates to the Second Continental Congress proceeded to "institute a new Government," as called for in the Declaration. Over the next several weeks they drafted and sent to the new states for ratification the nation's first constitution, the Articles of Confederation. Although not ratified until 1781, the Articles served as the nation's de facto constitution during the intervening war years.

As its name implies, the first American constitution created a **confederation,** a highly decentralized system in which the national government derives limited authority from the states rather than directly from citizens. Not only do the states select officials of the national government, but they also retain the authority to override that government's decisions.

The Articles transferred the form and functions of the Continental Congress to the new, permanent Congress, in which each state received one vote. Major laws required the endorsement of nine of the thirteen state delegations, while more fundamental changes, such as direct taxation, necessitated unanimous agreement to amend the Constitution. National authority was so restricted that the delegates saw little purpose for an executive branch or a judiciary. From time to time administrators might be required, but they could be hired as needed and directly supervised by the new Congress.

In adopting a confederation, the delegates sought to replicate the home rule they had lost in the 1760s. Clearly, after years of free riding under British rule, they were not yet willing to absorb the collective action costs associated with nationhood. Yet they also recognized that in declaring their independence they thrust upon themselves responsibility for supplying essential public goods—most important, defense and commercial markets—that Britain had provided under home rule. The same delegates who had pressed hardest for independence, knowing that it was likely to lead to war, were among those who most vigorously favored a confederation over a more centralized and powerful national government. Undoubtedly, the new nation's leaders still had a great deal to learn about the logic of collective action. But they would learn in time—the hard way. Their suspicion of national authority very nearly cost the fledgling nation its independence.

The Confederation at War

Faced with a war raging for over a year, the states, unwilling to give the national government sufficient authority to conduct the war, became chiefly responsible for recruiting troops and outfitting them for battle. The national military command, which answered to Congress, assumed responsibility for organizing the various state regiments into a single fighting force. In principle, Congress was assigned the role of coordinator. It would identify military requirements, assess the states, and channel their (voluntary) contributions to the army. Congress also was empowered to borrow money through bonds, but its lack of taxation authority made bonds a risky and expensive venture for the government, which had to offer high interest rates to attract investors.

The public's deep suspicion of government also prevented national officeholders from creating the administrative structures suitable for the new government's wartime responsibilities. John Adams even wanted to prevent Washington from appointing his own staff officers for fear that "there be too much Connection between them." Instead, he argued, Congress should select all officers so that these "officers are checks upon the General." Adams's appeal to the "proper Rule and Principle" stimulated serious debate, but he did not prevail in this instance. Adams was, however, more successful in other attempts to dilute executive powers.

The administrative vacuum sucked congressional committees into the daily affairs of requisitioning an army. These legislators struggled mightily, even heroically, to do their duty, but most were unskilled in administration and frequently unable to make timely decisions. In fact, the members of one committee expressed such a variety of views on the number of uniforms to be ordered that they were unable to come to a decision. The desperate plight of General Washington's army as the war continued attests to the naiveté and ineffectiveness of the confederation's structure. Thus the collective action problems described in Chapter 1 were evident in America's war effort: contagious levels of free riding and the reluctance of some states to contribute their fair share for fear that the other states would hold back (a classic prisoner's dilemma). Moreover, the undeveloped national administration provided fertile soil for equally debilitating free riding in the form of corruption.

Without the authority to play a more central role in administering the war, Congress responded to the quickly deteriorating military situation by decentralizing authority even further. Among other things, it passed resolutions instructing the states to supply their troops directly. Perhaps, some members reasoned, the states would be more forthcoming with support for their own sons in uniform. This scheme had the merit of converting a public good—military supplies that all state regiments could consume regardless of their state's contribution—into a more or less private good that linked the welfare of each state's troops to its legislature's effort. But the actual practice of thirteen states locating and supplying intermingled regiments scattered up and down the Atlantic seaboard presented a logistical nightmare. On hearing of it, General Washington caustically remarked that members of Congress "think it is but to say 'Presto begone,' and everything is done."

At the same time pressure mounted on various fronts, including within Congress itself, for Congress to assume greater authority to conduct the war.* Understandably, the

---

*Ten years later these advocates of congressional authority would form the core group of nationalists, led by James Madison and Alexander Hamilton, pressing the nation for a new constitution.

military commanders were the most outspoken in lobbying Congress and state governors for a "new plan of civil constitution." [3] General Washington advised Congress that an "entire new plan" providing it with the authority "adequate to all of the purposes of the war" must be instituted immediately. Washington's aide Alexander Hamilton, later one of the architects of the Constitution, showered members of Congress with correspondence urging them to grasp the emergency authority he claimed was inherent in the Articles. Without the "complete sovereignty" that could come only with an independent source of revenue, he argued, Congress would have neither the resources nor the credibility necessary to conduct the war. And, as the states' dismal performance had proved, if Congress did not take control, no one else could.*

The addition of the second major group—state officials—to the chorus for reform reveals the pervasiveness of frustration with the confederation. Although the confederation had sought to empower these officials above all others, many found themselves trapped in a classic prisoner's dilemma. They were prepared to sacrifice for the war, but only if they could be confident that the other states would also do their part. Moreover, many of their colleagues who had been outspoken champions of volunteerism were defeated in the 1780 elections by challengers calling for a strengthened national authority that could enforce agreements.

By the summer of 1780 some states were taking direct action. In August representatives of several New England states met and passed a resolution calling for investing Congress with "powers competent for the government." Several months later five northern states met at what is now known as the Hartford Convention to urge Congress to grant itself the power to tax. In a remarkable resolution the convention called for Congress to delegate to General Washington the authority "to induce . . . punctual compliance" from states that ignored their obligations to supply the army. The delegates realized that states would only cooperate (and end their prisoner's dilemma) under the threat of coercion.

Congress responded as best it could, but it labored under a constitution designed to frustrate national action. In 1781 Rhode Island, with less than 2 percent of the nation's population, vetoed a bill giving Congress the authority to levy taxes. Various administrative reforms were enacted but had to be watered down to win unanimous endorsement. Congress could not agree on how much independent authority to delegate to the executive offices it created. As a result, the offices had no authority, and their occupants served at the beck and call of the legislature's committees.

The tide turned after France, England's long-standing adversary, agreed to lend the Americans hard currency. By 1782 General Washington could write for the first time since the beginning of the war that his army was well fed, clothed, and armed. A reinvigorated American army and France's continued participation in the war presented Britain with the prospect of a far longer conflict. (France formally recognized American

---

*Hamilton also argued that Congress must delegate administration to "great officers of State—A secretary for foreign affairs—A President of War—A President of Marine—A Financier." In effect, he was calling for an autonomous national government with a legislature at its center and a separate executive branch.

independence and agreed to support the United States unilaterally in 1778.) In October 1781 British troops, under General Charles Cornwallis, suffered defeat at Yorktown, Virginia, and Britain sued for peace. Thus the United States had somehow survived a war with an occupying army. In the jubilation of victory, however, momentum for political reform was lost.

The Confederation's Troubled Peace

Shortly after signing the peace treaty with Britain, the nation lunged toward new perils—indeed, to the point that many Americans and even more Europeans wondered whether the hard-won independence might still be lost in national disintegration. By 1787 American leaders were openly speculating about the prospect of Britain reasserting its authority over the barely united and internally divided states.

THE WAR-TORN ECONOMY. After six years of war, the nation's debt was staggering. Congress owed Americans about $25 million and foreign governments another $10 million. The most urgent concern was the back pay owed the army. In the spring of 1783 General Washington learned of a conspiracy forming among disgruntled officers to march on Congress. Greatly alarmed, he wrote his former aide Alexander Hamilton, now a member of Congress, that the army should be paid and "disbanded without delay." The army is "a dangerous instrument to play with," he warned ominously. Prudently, Congress followed Washington's advice.

Creditors who had supplied the troops formed another long line. But Congress was more successful in ignoring these unarmed claimants, some of whom eventually received partial payment from the states. Abroad, debts to Britain negotiated in the peace settlement and loans from European governments and private interests all had to be repaid before normal commercial relations with these countries could resume. In the face of so much debt, the national currency plummeted to approximately one-tenth of its prewar value.

The complexities of governing by confederation compounded the problem. Congress held the debt, but the states controlled the purse strings. As it had during the war, Congress prescribed annual state contributions to reduce the debt over twenty-five years. But no one expressed confidence that the states, having proven so unreliable in war, would step forward in peace to accept fiscal responsibility for the nation. With no enforcement mechanism in place the states again individually confronted a classic prisoner's dilemma: No state would contribute its share of the revenue so long as it suspected one or more of the other states might not meet its obligations. Congress faced two tough choices. It could try to penalize those states that reneged or it could try to finance the debt on its own. The latter proved more feasible. Thus in the same bill that mapped long-term debt reduction Congress proposed a constitutional amendment giving the national government a source of direct revenue in the form of import duties. As in the past, however, the Articles' unanimous consent rule for amendments frustrated action. Unwilling to share the revenue from its already active port city of New York, the New York legislature killed this proposal.

TRADE BARRIERS AT HOME AND ABROAD. The nation's shaky finances were not helped by its trade problems, which also stemmed from the confederation's explicit reservation of all matters of commerce to the states. For example, Congress lacked the authority to negotiate credible trade agreements with other nations. European governments found this arrangement, in which trade agreements required the endorsement of each state's legislature, unwieldy. The national government also proved incapable of responding to discriminatory trade sanctions and other actions abroad. When the British and later the French closed their West Indies possessions to U.S. exports, the action threatened the fragile, war-torn economy that depended heavily on exports.

Economic relations among the states were nearly as unsatisfactory. States with international ports charged exporters from other states stiff user fees. New York victimized New Jersey; Virginia and South Carolina both extracted a toll from North Carolina. And each state minted its own currency. Some states, responding to political pressures from indebted farmers, inflated their currencies. Exchange rates fluctuated widely across states, rendering interstate commerce a speculative financial exercise.

To no one's surprise, many sectors of the economy clamored loudly for reform. The nation's creditors wanted a government able to pay its debts. Importers and the mercantile class desperately needed a sound currency and an end to capricious state policies toward other states' goods. The profits of southern tobacco and indigo growers depended wholly on open export markets, which only a national government could negotiate effectively. The need for a central authority that could create and manage a common market at home and implement a unified commercial policy abroad spurred diverse economic interests to call for a revision of the Articles of Confederation.

In the summer of 1786 Virginia made the first move, inviting delegates of other states to convene that fall at Annapolis, Maryland, to consider ways of strengthening the national government's role in commerce. Eight states named delegates, but when those from only five states showed up, the Annapolis convention adjourned after passing a resolution calling for another convention in Philadelphia nine months later. Thus the Annapolis convention earned a place in history by setting the stage for the Constitutional Convention in May 1787. Although the delegates had no reason to believe the next meeting would generate any better turnout, events during the intervening months galvanized interest in constitutional reform. **Shays's Rebellion** mobilized the states behind constitutional reform.

POPULAR DISCONTENT. In the economic depression that followed the Revolution, many small farmers lost their land and other assets. Markets were disrupted, credit became scarce, and personal debt mounted. The financial straits of small farmers spawned occasional demonstrations, but none so threatening as the one that erupted in the fall of 1786 in western Massachusetts, where taxes were especially onerous and the local courts unforgiving. Many farmers lost their land and possessions at the auction block, and some were even being hauled off to debtors' prison. The protest movement began with town meetings and petitions to the state legislature to suspend taxes and foreclosures. When their appeals failed to win much sympathy,

Despite their defeat, the protesting farmers led by Daniel Shays won a number of reforms from the Massachusetts state legislature, which lowered court costs and exempted household necessities and workmen's tools from the debt collection process. The unintended impact of Shays's Rebellion on national reform was far more dramatic. It demonstrated that the confederation could not perform the most basic function of government—keeping the peace.

these disaffected citizens found more aggressive ways to remonstrate their grievances. Under the leadership of Daniel Shays, a former captain in the Continental Army and a bankrupt farmer, an armed group composed mostly of farmers marched on the Massachusetts Supreme Court session in Springfield to demand that state judges stop prosecuting debtors. Shays's band was met by the state militia, but the confrontation ended peacefully after the magistrates adjourned the court.

In late January of 1787 Massachusetts erupted once more, this time with enough violence to convince the states to convene in Philadelphia. Having learned that Shays planned an assault on a government arsenal in Springfield, delegates from Massachusetts appealed to the national government to send funds and troops. Once again unable to muster compliance among the states, Congress could offer neither troops nor money. A similar appeal to neighboring states proved no more productive. Finally, the state organized a militia (in part with private donations) that intercepted and repulsed Shays's "army" of about a thousand farmers outside the arsenal. Over the next several weeks some of Shays's men were captured, others dispersed, and the rebellion ended.

Had it been an isolated incident, even this event might not have persuaded state leaders of the need for a stronger national government. But Shays's Rebellion coincided with a wave of popular uprisings sweeping across the country. The same winter, two hundred armed farmers in Pennsylvania had tried to reclaim neighbors' possessions that had been seized by tax collectors. On the same day as Shays's defeat, these farmers rescued a neighbor's cattle from a tax sale. Virginia protesters, following the example of the insurgents in Massachusetts, burned down public buildings. Their favorite targets were jails and courthouses where tax and debt records were kept.

State legislatures, either intimidated by threats of force or genuinely sympathetic with farmers' demands, started to cave in under the slightest pressure from these constituencies. At times, these bodies' knee-jerk responses caused them to behave in ways more in keeping with revolutionary tribunals than with deliberative republican legislatures respectful of property rights. Throughout the country they summarily overturned unpopular court decisions, altered property assessments, and issued quickly devalued paper money, which they then forced creditors to accept as full payment of farmers' debts. One scholar offered this assessment: "The economic and social instability engendered by the Revolution was finding political expression in the state legislatures at the very time they were larger, more representative, and more powerful than ever before in American history."[4] Observing all this, the troubled James Madison of Virginia wrote his friend Thomas Jefferson in Paris, where Jefferson was serving as the states' ambassador: "In our Governments the real power lies in the majority, and the invasion of private rights . . . chiefly [arises] . . . not from acts of Government contrary to the sense of its constituents, but from acts in which the Government is the mere instrument of the major number of the constituents."[5] Madison's discomfort with arbitrary majority action guided his efforts and those of like-minded delegates throughout the Constitutional Convention.

To many observers, Shays's Rebellion represented a wildfire threatening to sweep the country into anarchy.[6] No matter how persuasive Hamilton, the beloved Washington, or any of the other **nationalists** were in promoting the cause of constitutional reform, it was Daniel Shays who offered the most compelling reason for states to send delegates to the Philadelphia convention. Ultimately, the states took the first steps toward true unification not in response to their collective dilemma, but rather out of a more fundamental concern with self-preservation. When they assembled in Philadelphia the next spring, delegates from all states except Rhode Island showed up.

Drafting a New Constitution

In their deliberations the fifty-five youngish, well-educated white males who gathered in Philadelphia in 1787 drew on their shared experience of war and its aftermath, but they did not do so reflexively or out of narrowly construed self-interest. They also were highly conversant in the ideas and theories swirling "in the air" during the Enlightenment, as the dominant intellectual current of the eighteenth century was known. Influenced by recent advances in science, scholars—and even America's politicians—sought through careful reasoning to discern the "natural laws" that governed economics, politics, and morality. The impact of these ideas was not merely a matter of their novelty and intellectual appeal, but also in how they illuminated Americans' experiences.

Thus the Constitution that eventually arose out of the convention was grounded in theories of politics, economics, and even science that were attracting attention at the time throughout Europe. The delegates cited dozens of contemporary and ancient philosophers during floor deliberations, often quoting them in their original language of Latin or French. Of these thinkers, several deserve to be singled out because their ideas are clearly discernible in the Constitution.

Philosophical Influences

Heading any list of influential Enlightenment thinkers is the English philosopher John Locke (1632–1704), whose brilliant writings on political theory and design of government read in some places as if the Framers were his sole audience. In 1690 Locke vigorously defended the still-novel idea of **popular sovereignty**—that is, citizens' delegation of authority to their agents in government, with the ability to rescind that authority.[7] This argument clearly influenced Jefferson's words in the Declaration of Independence. Moreover, Locke stressed individual rights and the limited scope of government authority. If Locke's ideas strike the modern student as unexceptional, it is because they are so thoroughly embedded in the U.S. Constitution and governmental system that they are taken for granted.

During the same era another Englishman, Sir Isaac Newton (1642–1727), established the foundations of modern mechanics and physics. His discovery of the laws of physical relations (such as gravity) inspired the Framers to search for comparable laws governing social relations. Evidence of Newton's influence can be seen in the Framers' descriptions of their design proposals to each other and later to the nation. Concepts such as "force," "balance," and "fulcrum," and phrases such as "laws of politics" and "check power with power" that seemed borrowed from a physics textbook were bandied about with great familiarity.

Perhaps more than anyone else, the French philosopher Charles, Baron de Montesquieu (1689–1755) supplied the Framers with the nuts and bolts of a design of government, particularly his classification of governmental functions and forms as legislative, executive, and judicial. Like Locke, Montesquieu championed limited government—limited not only in the nature of its authority but also in the size of the political community it encompassed. Thus during and after the convention opponents of reform invoked Montesquieu's case for the superiority of small republics as a powerful counterargument to those who advocated empowering the national government.

Finally, the Scottish philosopher David Hume (1711–1776) treated politics as a competition among contending interests, in much the same way that his fellow countryman Adam Smith described competition in the marketplace of an emerging capitalist economy. An ocean away, James Madison adapted Hume's arguments to his own purposes, much as Jefferson did Locke's.

America's founding leaders, though politicians, often behaved as if they were philosophers, carefully studying and even writing treatises on government. The most important is James Madison's three-thousand-word essay "Vices of the Political System of the U. States," which he drafted in the spring of 1787 after extensive research on ancient and modern confederations. (Madison had Jefferson scour Paris bookstores for source materials.) Madison circulated copies of his manuscript among fellow Virginians who would be attending the Philadelphia convention to prepare them for the reform proposal he was writing. Madison's sophisticated understanding of politics is apparent in a passage attributing the confederation's failure not to a moral breakdown of the citizenry but to the classic prisoner's dilemma embedded in faulty institutions: "A distrust of the voluntary compliance of each other may prevent the compliance of any, although . . . [cooperation is] the latent disposition of all."

Getting Down to Business

Most of the delegates representing their states in Philadelphia probably were unaware of the grand scope of the enterprise on which they were about to embark. Some undoubtedly assumed that the convention would simply return to the Annapolis agenda that sought to resolve commercial disputes at home and coordinate the states' commercial policies abroad. Others anticipated minor reforms of the Articles and were prepared to take the positions dictated by their state legislatures. But at least a few, most notably James Madison, were planning—indeed, plotting with others of like mind—to scrap the Articles of Confederation altogether and start over.

Sensing his fellow Virginian's hidden agenda, war hero Patrick Henry announced he "smelt a rat" and refused to join the delegation to Philadelphia. The Delaware legislature was similarly suspicious and instructed its delegates to oppose any scheme that undermined the equality of the states. Another small state, the ever-independent Rhode Island, boycotted Philadelphia altogether.

The convention opened on a rainy Friday, May 25, 1787. By near universal acclamation, the delegates elected General Washington to preside over the deliberations, and the convention began on a harmonious note. Madison sat at the front, where he could easily participate in floor debates and record the arguments of his colleagues.* The convention agreed to keep the proceedings secret to allow a frank exchange of views and to facilitate compromise. This decision also meant keeping the window shutters closed during one of the hottest summers in Philadelphia's history.

The Virginia and New Jersey Plans

On the first day of substantive business Madison and his nationalist colleagues sprang their surprise. Edmund Randolph, also from Virginia, introduced Madison's blueprint for a new constitution. In this revised constitution Madison favored those institutional design features more closely resembling parliamentary systems than those of the future American republic. In the Virginia Plan, as it came to be known, Madison appears to have been more concerned with fashioning an active national government, even if it imposed high conformity costs on the states. The **Virginia Plan** dominated floor debate well into July. Although few of its provisions survived intact in the final draft of the Constitution, the Virginia Plan succeeded in shifting the deliberations from patching up the confederation to considering anew the requirements of a national union.

The centerpiece of the Virginia Plan was a bicameral national legislature. Members of the lower chamber would be apportioned among the states by population and directly elected by the citizenry. The lower chamber would, in turn, elect the members of the upper chamber from lists of nominees supplied by the state legislatures. It also would elect the officers of the proposed executive and judicial branches (see Figure 2-1). Madison's intent was clear: only representatives, whose direct election by the people gave them special legitimacy in formulating national policy, would control the selection of the other officers of government.

---

*Unable to fathom the purpose of certain provisions of the ancient constitutions he had examined in his preparation for the convention, Madison was determined not to leave future generations in the dark about the rationale of this new constitution. Thus he carefully recorded the business of the convention. *Notes on the Federal Convention,* were discovered among Madison's papers after his death in 1837. The federal government paid his widow, Dolley, $30,000 for the papers and published them three years later. This discussion closely follows Madison's *Notes.*

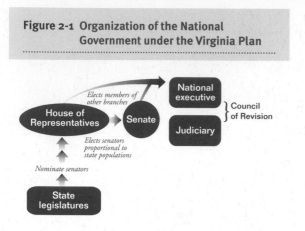

Figure 2-1 Organization of the National Government under the Virginia Plan

To solve the nation's collective action problems, the Virginia Plan also gave the national government enforcement authority. It could make whatever laws it deemed appropriate and veto any state laws it regarded as unfit. If a state failed to fulfill its legal obligations, the national government could summon military force against it. This provision proved to be a tactical mistake because it inflamed opposition. In the meantime, the nationalists realized belatedly that military force would never be needed because the national government could directly implement its own policies and would no longer depend on the cooperation of the states.

With the states reduced to the status of junior partners, the national legislature would assume a standing comparable to that of the British Parliament. Madison did provide one check on this legislative dynamo: a Council of Revision, composed of the executive and certain judges, which could veto legislation. Its members, however, would be elected by the legislature. Thus skeptical delegates reasonably questioned how effective such a check could be. In any event, Madison proposed allowing Congress to override a council veto.

After Madison achieved early success in some preliminary floor votes, opposition, mainly from two sources, to his radical reforms solidified. Delegates representing the less populous states were understandably upset. They could easily calculate that they (and their citizens) would have far less representation under the Virginia Plan than they presently enjoyed with equal state representation and the one-state veto rule. Another bloc (mostly from small states as well) wanted stronger safeguards of state sovereignty. For these states' rights delegates, continued state participation in the selection of national officeholders was as important an issue as how legislative seats were to be apportioned.

Both groups coalesced around an alternative proposed by New Jersey delegate William Paterson, known as the **New Jersey Plan.** This late, hastily drafted response to the Virginia Plan was not as thoroughly thought through as Madison's proposal. For example, it failed to propose the organization of the executive and judiciary. It satisfied the requirements of its **states' rights** supporters, however, by perpetuating the composition and selection of Congress as it functioned under the Articles of Confederation and continuing to give each state one vote. But the New Jersey Plan broke with the Articles by giving Congress the authority to force the states to comply with its tax requisitions. This plan also allowed a simple majority vote to enact national policy rather than the supermajority required in the Articles. The New Jersey Plan thus eliminated the most objectionable features of the confederation. But its retention of a seriously malapportioned Congress representing the states rather than the citizenry, did not come close to satisfying the demands of the nationalists.

Figure 2-2 Virginia Plan, New Jersey Plan, and Great Compromise

Virginia Plan

☆ Two-chamber legislature, representation based on state population

☆ Lower chamber of legislature elected by the citizenry; upper chamber, executive, and courts elected by the lower house

☆ Legislature can make any law and veto any state legislation

☆ Council of Revision (composed of executive and court) can veto legislation, but legislature can override by majority vote

New Jersey Plan

☆ Single-house chamber; equal representation for each state regardless of population

☆ Legislature has same power as under Articles, with added authority to levy taxes and regulate commerce; can exercise supremacy clause over state legislation

☆ Plural executive can be removed by legislature (on petition of a majority of states); courts appointed by executive

☆ Supreme Court hears appeals in limited number of cases

Great Compromise

☆ Two-chamber legislature, with lower chamber (House of Representatives) representation based on population and upper chamber (Senate) representation equal for every state

☆ Authority to levy taxes reserved to the lower chamber

Debate on the composition of Congress raged for weeks, with each side steadfastly and heatedly refusing to budge.* Stalemate loomed. As the meetings neared a Fourth of July recess, the delegates agreed to send the question of Congress—its selection and composition—to a committee with instructions to report out a recommendation after the break. Madison was not named to the committee.

The Great Compromise

The committee's solution was a Solomon-like compromise that split control of the legislature's two chambers between the large (House of Representatives) and small (Senate) states. The upper chamber, or Senate, would retain many of the features of Congress under the Articles of Confederation: each state legislature would send two senators to serve six-year terms. Madison's population-based, elective legislature became the House of Representatives. To sweeten the deal for the nationalists, who had rejected a similar compromise earlier in floor deliberations, the committee reserved to the House alone the authority to originate revenue legislation (see Figure 2-2).

The unanimous agreement rule that had hobbled the confederation Congress was gone, replaced by a rule that wholly ignored states as voting entities and instead empowered a majority of each chamber's membership to pass legislation. Moreover, the delegates agreed to a broad list of enumerated or expressed powers, contained in Article I, Section 8, of the Constitution, that extended the authority of the national legislature far

---

*Madison's allies did make one significant concession, accepting an amendment that gave the states sole authority to select the members of the upper house. Thus the Senate began to assume its ultimate form. But the delegates from small states pressed for more: equal state representation in both chambers.

The Large State, Small State Cleavage Reappears in Europe

Over the past several decades, the European Union (EU) has gradually expanded its collective efforts to solve common problems. Most recently, nearly all member states adopted a common currency, the Euro. As the EU has grown dramatically from the original six to twenty-seven members, leaders across Europe agreed that more formal—indeed, constitutional—arrangements were needed. Among all of the problems that arose over several years of deliberations, the one that proved the thorniest was the same that threatened the success of the Constitutional Convention—apportioning representation between the large and small states. With numerous small-state members but with the six largest states containing nearly three-quarters of the Union's population and an even greater share of its economic productivity, the stage was set again for impasse. The EU framers looked to the Philadelphia convention and weighed the creation of a bicameral legislature, with different repre-

sentational schemes like those for the House of Representatives and the Senate, but in the end decided on a mixed voting rule to accommodate both sides. Representation would be apportioned by population, but in order for legislation to pass it would have to receive both a majority of the votes (the large-state advantage) and support from at least fifteen country delegations that represented 65 percent of the EU's population.

beyond that available to Congress under the confederation. These powers included the authority to declare war, maintain an army and navy, and borrow money. Another item on the list of new powers stood out: the authority "to regulate Commerce with foreign Nations, and among the several States." This **commerce clause** greatly expanded the new Congress's—and, in turn, the national government's—sphere of action. And another clause in Section 8 further compounded its impact. The Framers closed the long list of explicit powers with the following general provision: Congress shall enjoy the authority "to make all Laws which shall be necessary and proper for carrying into Execution the foregoing Powers, and all other Powers vested by this Constitution in the Government of the United States." This critical provision, called the **necessary and**

proper clause, left the door open for a major expansion of Congress's legislative power and the nationalization of public policy during the twentieth century.*

Both defenders and critics of an activist federal government agree that all national policies affect interstate commerce in some way. Together these clauses have provided a rationale for enacting far-reaching national legislation, including federal laws against interstate kidnapping and bank robbery; regulations on agricultural production (covering even the growth of feed that never leaves the farm where it was grown); bans on racial and other discrimination in restaurants, hotels, and public transportation; laws against possession of guns near public schools; and thousands of other wide-ranging national policies.

The committee's proposal was adopted by a vote of 5–4, with the other states abstaining or absent. Opposition came uniformly from the nationalists who viewed the compromise as one-sided. Through the Senate a majority of the states could still prevail over national policy. But the nationalists also recognized that this was the best deal they could get. Because the preferences of the states' rights delegates were more closely aligned with those of the status quo, they could more credibly present the nationalist side with a take-it-or-leave-it proposition.

Now, more than two centuries later, the political logic of dividing representation in Congress between the citizens and the states no longer matches reality. The supremacy of the national government over the states was decided by the Civil War. Senators have been elected directly by the voters since adoption of the Seventeenth Amendment in 1913. Yet the Senate, the institution that embodied the initial logic of states' rights, persists. Indeed, as noted in Chapter 1, once in place an institution tends to survive long after the circumstances that fashioned it in a particular form have changed beyond all recognition. Although it is difficult today to justify a system in which, for example, citizens of Wyoming count for sixty-five times as much as citizens of California in one chamber of the national legislature, Americans are stuck with it. Yet, while still badly malapportioned, the modern Senate has become as attuned as the House of Representatives to changes in popular sentiments (see Chapter 6, Congress).

Because the compromise plan substantially strengthened the national government's capacity for action, most nationalists except Madison reconciled themselves to it—at least initially. The man who during his lifetime was called "the father of the Constitution" maintained that ultimately the nationalists would prevail by letting the country stew a while longer under the Articles. Eventually he was talked out of that idea, but he remained profoundly disillusioned. Then, perhaps literally overnight,

---

*Chapter 3, Federalism, traces the nationalization of public policy via the necessary and proper clause. In addition to listing what Congress can do, the Constitution lists what it—and the states—cannot do. Article I, Section 9, restricts Congress from granting titles of nobility, spending unappropriated funds, suspending the writ of *habeas corpus,* passing ex post facto laws, levying income taxes (the Sixteenth Amendment ratified in 1913 rescinded this provision), and taxing state exports. Section 10 imposes restrictions on states, prohibiting them from conducting foreign policy (through entering into treaties or alliances or conducting war), printing money, passing laws undermining contracts, and imposing tariffs or duties on trade.

Checks and Balances in the Constitution

The Framers feared that a concentration of power in any one group or branch of government would lead to tyranny—that is, one group would gain enough power to dominate the government and strip other groups of their basic rights. Thus they devised in the Constitution something of a political game in which each of the three branches of government has some capacity to limit, or trump, the power of the other two.

This system of *checks and balances* largely originated with the French philosopher Charles, Baron de Montesquieu (1689–1755), who argued that the concentration of government power could be effectively limited by locating the several functions of government—legislative, executive, and judicial—in separate and independent institutions. Notice in the diagram that rather than defining "separation of powers" according to these functions, the Constitution described separate institutions *sharing* power. All three branches possess legislative, executive, and judicial authority.

Checks on Executive Branch
- Congress passes legislation, controls the federal budget, can override a presidential veto, and can impeach and remove the president.
- The Senate confirms top executive branch appointments and ratifies treaties.

Checks on Legislative Branch
- The president can veto legislation.

Checks on Judicial Branch
- The president nominates Supreme Court and other federal judges.

Congress/
Legislative Branch

Checks on Judicial Branch
- Congress can impeach federal judges, set the size of the Supreme Court and the jurisdiction of lower courts, and determine judicial salaries and budgets.
- The Senate confirms all federal judges.

Checks on Executive Branch
- Courts can declare executive orders unconstitutional.

Checks on Legislative Branch
- Courts can declare laws unconstitutional.

President/Executive Branch

Supreme Court (and federal courts)/Judicial Branch

Madison scrapped the rest of the Virginia Plan and made what amounted to a 180-degree turn in his views on the proper relations among government institutions. A new, more strategic politician had emerged. Suddenly Madison expressed enthusiasm for a genuine separation of powers between the branches, with each side exercising **checks and balances** over the others. The reasoning behind his hurried reassessment might have gone something like this: if the state legislatures could corrupt the new Congress through their hold on the Senate, they also could corrupt the entire national government through Congress's power to select the officers of the other branches of government. The solution: insulate the executive and judicial branches and enlist them in containing any efforts by the states through the Senate to subvert national policy. Thus in early July, with the summer half over and the proceedings gathering momentum, Madison turned his attention to fashioning an independent executive and judiciary.

Designing the Executive Branch

Of all the delegates, Alexander Hamilton had shown the greatest enthusiasm for a strengthened, independent executive. His fixation on an executive elected for life, however, left him so far on the fringe that he enjoyed little influence on the rest of the delegates as they turned their attention to this institution. His eloquent speeches were "praised by everybody . . . [but] supported by none," reported one candid delegate.

The delegates' lack of enthusiasm for an active, authoritative presidency is understandable. They had just finished dividing legislative authority into two coequal chambers with representatives and senators to be elected for different terms and from different constituencies. With each chamber able to block intemperate policies arising from the other, the Framers could more safely invest in them broad authority to make policy. Once the delegates dismissed the idea of a plural executive as impractical, the presidency no longer contained the internal checks that would have it control its excessive impulses.

This posed a serious dilemma for the convention. Even a casual survey of world history would turn up a panoply of absolute monarchs and other tyrants. Such a list supplied ample examples of the techniques arbitrary executives employed to exploit the citizenry and preserve their power. Indeed, all of the delegates had lived under an arbitrary executive's thumb. They despised King George III and his agents, the vilified colonial governors, who chronically were at odds with the colonial legislature over who had what authority. After the revolution the new states had overreacted by creating weak governors. Based on his brief experience as Virginia's wartime governor, Jefferson dismissed the office as a "cipher," a nonentity. In the end the only acceptable model of the new American president was, in the words of one historian, "sitting there in front of them . . . dignified, silent, universally admired and respected . . . impartial, honored for his selfless devotion to the common good, not intervening in, but presiding over, their councils—a presider, a *president*. The executive was to be—George Washington." [8]

The presence of a real-life example of an ideal executive presiding over the convention kept in view the kind of leadership the delegates sought to institutionalize, yet it does not appear to have made their task any easier. In the end, Madison and Hamilton

The Framers, as do students of modern American government, considered how much military authority to grant the president and how Congress could constrain potential abuses of this authority. With Britain, Spain, and France controlling territories on America's borders, providing for the nation's security preoccupied the Framers. So, too, did an executive who might usurp power and turn the military against the other branches of government. Yet giving Congress both the "power of the purse and the sword" clearly violated the accepted guiding principle of checks and balances. In the end the Framers accepted the limits of institutional design and hoped to produce presidents in the mold of George Washington.

largely succeeded in fashioning an independent executive branch that might be incapable of abusing authority and might actually moderate excesses by an overreaching legislature. To achieve this, they designed several features. First, they limited the scope of presidential responsibilities and particularly the office's command authority. (The presidency of the twenty-first century might appear to belie their success. In Chapter 7 we will survey the evolution of the presidency and reconcile the modern with the early office.) Article II states, almost as an afterthought, that the president "shall take Care that the Laws be faithfully executed." Modern presidents sometimes assert that the **take care clause** allows them to undertake whatever actions the nation's well-being requires and is not expressly forbidden by the Constitution or public law. Yet, unlike Congress's expansive necessary and proper clause that bolsters their discretion in performing a long list of responsibilities, this mandate is not attached to any specific duty. Specifically, this new executive will appoint officers to fill vacancies in the executive department, receive and appoint ambassadors, negotiate treaties, serve as commander in chief of the army and navy, and periodically report to Congress on the state of the nation. The second design feature attached a legislative check, or veto, to each presidential duty. The Senate would confirm appointments and ratify any treaties (in this instance with a two-thirds vote) before they could take effect. Only Congress could declare war.

The third significant design feature was the **veto,** a negative action which would allow the executive to perform a "checking" function on the legislature. Unlike some constitutional executives, presidents cannot make policy or appropriate funds for programs, except as allowed in public laws. By requiring a supermajority vote of two-thirds of the members of each house to override a presidential veto, the Framers carved out an important role for the modern president in domestic legislation.

Over the next two centuries, the presidency became a much more consequential office, both in its duties and authority. But at least with respect to domestic policy, it has done so within a constitutional framework that has not changed. Most of the expansion has occurred through statutory provisions delegating policy responsibilities to the White House. If the Framers observed the president's role in domestic policy today, they might be shocked with what they found, but they would quickly recognize it as an extension of the office they envisioned.

One cannot be so confident that the Framers would come to the same assessment regarding the president's dominant role in foreign policy and national defense. Beginning with World War II the United States became a leader in international affairs. Whatever advantages its status conferred, it also entailed numerous—well over a hundred—military actions. None began with Congress declaring "war," although all of the large scale conflicts—Korea, Vietnam, both Iraq wars, among others—found Congress passing resolutions backing the president's actions that initiated the conflict. Some analysts argue that contemporary international affairs and modern military technology have eclipsed the Constitution's capacity to prescribe appropriate authority and responsibilities available to the executive and legislature in modern wartime. In part the Constitution's limited and general language regarding foreign affairs have contributed to this uncertainty. During the George W. Bush presidency, administration and congressional views on the constitutional prerogatives for these branches during wartime have at times diverged sharply. In Chapter 7 we will consider occasions during which White House officials have asserted that Congress has no role. Invariably the federal courts have had to resolve these constitutional disputes and have groped for answers along with the president and Congress. We take up these issues in detail later. The important point here is that the Constitution contains gaps—at times chasms—that have Americans more than two hundred years after the document was ratified asking fundamental questions about the appropriate role of Congress and the presidency. Much of the uncertainty occurs with subjects that Article II's creation of the presidency failed to resolve.

At the Constitutional Convention the delegates found that the only workable formula for agreement between the nationalists and states' rights advocates was to give both sides pretty much what they wanted, an approach that yielded the **Great Compromise,** and multiple routes for amending the Constitution. When the drafters turned to devising a procedure for electing the president, they returned to arduous committee deliberations and floor wrangling to find a compromise. This time Constitutional Convention politics produced arguably the most convoluted rules to be found in the Constitution: the workings of the **Electoral College.**

As a device, the Electoral College tries to mix state, congressional, and popular participation in the election process and in doing so has managed to confuse citizens for more than two hundred years. Each state is awarded as many electors as it has members of the House and Senate. The Constitution left it to the states to decide how electors are selected, but the Framers generally and correctly expected that the states would rely on statewide elections. If any candidate fails to receive an absolute majority (270) of the 538 votes in the Electoral College, the election is thrown into the House of Representatives, which chooses from among the three candidates who received the largest number of electoral votes. In making its selection, the House votes by state delegation; each state gets one vote, and a majority is required to elect a president (see Chapter 11 for more on the Electoral College). Until the Twelfth Amendment corrected the most egregious flaws of the Electoral College, votes for the president and the vice president were tallied side by side, resulting in a vice-presidential candidate almost winning the presidency in the election of 1800.

Designing the Judicial Branch

The convention spent comparatively little time designing the new federal judiciary, a somewhat surprising development given that the Constitution gives the Supreme Court final jurisdiction in resolving differences between the state and national levels of government. Armed with that jurisdiction and with the **supremacy clause** (Article VI), which declares that national laws take precedence over state laws when both properly discharge their governments' respective responsibilities, the Supreme Court emerged from the convention as a major, probably underappreciated, lever for expanding the scope of national policymaking.

States' rights advocates and nationalists did, however, spar over two lesser questions: who would appoint Supreme Court justices—the president or the Senate? And should a network of lower federal courts be created, or should state courts handle all cases until they reached the Supreme Court, the only federal court? The convention split the difference over appointments by giving the president appointment powers and the Senate confirmation powers, and they left it to some future Congress to decide whether the national government needed its own lower-level judiciary. The First Congress exercised this option almost immediately, creating a lower federal court system with the Judiciary Act of 1789.

An important issue never quite resolved by the Constitutional Convention was the extent of the Court's authority to overturn federal laws and executive actions as unconstitutional—a concept known as **judicial review.** Although the supremacy clause appears to establish the Court's authority to review state laws, there is no formal language extending this review authority to federal laws. Yet many of the Framers, including Hamilton, claimed that the Constitution implicitly provides for judicial review. Later in life Madison protested that he never would have agreed to a provision that allowed an unelected branch of government to have the final say in lawmaking. But in one of the great ironies of American history, Madison was a litigant in an early Supreme Court decision, *Marbury v. Madison* (1803), in which the Court laid claim to the authority to strike down any legislation it deemed unconstitutional.[9] In Chapter 9 we will return to this historic case and its profound effects on the development of the federal judiciary.

Substantive Issues

The remapping of federal-state responsibilities was largely intended to eliminate the collective action dilemmas that had discouraged voluntary compliance by the states under the Articles of Confederation. The Framers recognized that the states, to undertake joint activities successfully, had to surrender some of their autonomy to the national government to prevent any state from free riding or otherwise violating their collective agreements.

FOREIGN POLICY. Trade and foreign policy were at the top of the list of federal-state issues the Framers wanted the Constitution to solve. Shortly after the Revolutionary War, the states had found themselves engaged in cutthroat competition for foreign commerce. The Framers solved this dilemma by placing foreign policy under the administration of the president and giving Congress the explicit legislative authority to regulate commerce. As for common defense and security, the Framers placed those responsibilities squarely on the shoulders of the national government. The Constitution (Article I, Section 10) forbids any state from entering into a foreign alliance or treaty, maintaining a military during peacetime, or engaging in war unless invaded.

INTERSTATE COMMERCE. Relations among the states, a longtime source of friction, also figured prominently in the Framers' deliberations. As a result, Article I, Section 10, prohibits states from discriminating against each other in various ways. They may not enter into agreements without the consent of Congress, tax imports or exports entering local ports, print money not backed by gold or silver, or make laws prejudicial to citizens of other states.

The Framers balanced these concessions with important benefits for the states. The new national government would assume outstanding debts the states had incurred during the war, protect the states from invasion and insurrection, and guarantee that all states would be governed by republican institutions.

All these provisions of the Constitution are less well known than those creating and conferring powers on the several branches of government or the amendments known as the **Bill of Rights.** But the fact that Americans take them for granted reflects their success, not their irrelevance. With these provisions the Framers solved the most serious collective action dilemmas confronting the young nation, including trade. Taken together, the provisions to prevent states from interfering with commerce that crossed their borders established the essentials of a common market among the former colonies. As a result, the Constitution contributed vitally to the nation's

Why Women Were Left Out of the Constitution

Why is it that nowhere in the original Constitution or in the floor debates at Philadelphia are women mentioned? One reason is that the delegates to the Constitutional Convention, faced with the glaring deficiencies of the national government under the Articles of Confederation, were less concerned with individual rights than with making government more effective and establishing proper relations among the institutions they were creating. Early on, delegates agreed to allow the individual states to continue to decide which citizens should have the right to vote. Thus no one actually gained the right to vote in the Constitution.

Second, although it tacitly accepts franchise restrictions imposed by the states, the Constitution reads as though it was drafted to be as free of gen-

Susan B. Anthony

der bias as eighteenth-century usage allowed. Throughout, the words *persons* and *citizens,* not *men,* appear. Eligibility to serve as a member of Congress, for example, begins with the statement "No Person shall be a Representative. . . ." Elsewhere: "The Citizens of each State shall be entitled to all Privileges and Immunities of Citizens in the several States." A few passages of the Constitution use the pronoun *he* (in each instance, however, the masculine pronoun refers back to a gender-free noun), but until the twentieth century this referent was commonly employed and legally interpreted to include women. In this respect, then, women were not left out of the Constitution.

The third reason is that women's political rights simply had not yet become an issue. Absence of the

economic development during the next century, not only through its directives on interstate commerce but also through the other trade and business-related provisions in Article I. One such provision prevents the government from passing laws impairing the obligations of private contracts; others mandate that the national government create bankruptcy and patent laws.

SLAVERY. Throughout America's history the issue of race has never been far removed from politics. It certainly was present in Philadelphia, despite some delegates' best efforts to prevent a regional disagreement on slavery from thwarting the purpose of the convention. But how could delegates construct a government based on popular sovereignty and inalienable rights without addressing the fact that one-sixth of Americans were in bondage? They could not. Slavery figured importantly in many dele-

issue, however, did not mean that women remained apolitical during the Revolution and the subsequent crisis in governance or that they failed to protest other aspects of their inferior legal standing. The ample evidence in private correspondence indicates that many women followed politics carefully. A few even published monographs that received wide circulation. One of the most famous correspondents of either sex during this era was Abigail Adams, the wife of John Adams and the mother of John Quincy Adams. Her numerous letters to her husband and leaders, such as Thomas Jefferson, exhibit a candor and insight that make them compelling to modern readers as well. To her husband, who was away attending the Continental Congress, she wrote, "In the new code of laws which I suppose it will be necessary for you to make, I desire you would remember the ladies, and be more generous to them than your ancestors. Do not put such unlimited power in the hands of husbands. Remember, all men would be tyrants if they could." This passage often has been celebrated as one of the first expressions of women's political rights in America. But, in fact, Adams was addressing various civil laws that allowed husbands to confiscate their wives' property and made divorce all but impossible. Lack of a

woman's rights in marriage—not suffrage—was the grievance of these early feminists.

Not until publication of Sarah Grimké's *Letters on the Condition of Women and Equality of the Sexes* in 1838 and the Seneca Falls Convention declaration—"All men and women are created equal"—a decade later would women's suffrage be placed on the national political agenda. In 1869 Wyoming became the first state to add women to the voter rolls. Later in the nineteenth century, Susan B. Anthony of Massachusetts led a suffragist movement that claimed the right to vote under the Fourteenth Amendment and sought a constitutional suffrage amendment. In 1887 Congress defeated the proposal for the amendment, but the suffrage movement continued. President Woodrow Wilson (1913–1921) initially opposed the amendment, arguing that state action was more appropriate. But when protests grew into hunger strikes in 1918, he announced his support. The Nineteenth Amendment to the Constitution, guaranteeing women the right to vote, was ratified in 1920.

Source: Adapted from James Q. Wilson and John J. DiIulio Jr., *American Government: Institutions and Policies,* 7th ed. (Boston: Houghton Mifflin, 1998), 43.

gates' private calculations, especially those from the South. At several junctures, it broke to the surface.

The first effort to grapple with slavery was the most acrimonious and threatening. How should slaves be counted in allocating congressional representatives to the states? Madison had persuaded delegates to postpone this issue until they had finalized the design of the new Congress, but the issue soon loomed again. Trying to maximize their representation in the population-based House of Representatives, southern delegates insisted that slaves were undeniably people and should be included fully in any population count to determine representation. Northerners resisted this attempted power grab by arguing that because slaves did not enjoy the freedom to act as autonomous citizens, they should not be counted at all. In the end each side accepted a formula initially used to levy taxes under the Articles of Confederation, a plan that

STRATEGY AND CHOICE

Logrolling a Constitution

Many of the New England delegates who came to Philadelphia were frustrated by the nation's inability to conduct a coordinated commercial policy at home or abroad. Southerners, however, liked things pretty much the way they were, fearing that additional government controls might lead to taxes and regulations on their extensive agricultural exports to Europe. If the national government insisted, as in time it did, that a substantial share of exports must travel on U.S. ships, the Northeast (with its ports and shipping companies) would gain financially at the expense of southern producers. Consequently, the South had opposed giving the national government such commercial authority without the assent of two-thirds of

both houses of Congress. This large supermajority would have given the South, in effect, a veto over any objectionable policy, and as a result no commercial provision would have been adopted. Southerners also were committed to warding off an antislavery measure that most northerners and their state legislatures were on record as supporting.

Consider the range of policy options before the delegates. We can rank the policy preferences of any individual delegate or group of like-minded delegates. Although northern delegates preferred an antislavery policy, they desired a strong commercial policy even more. We can illustrate their preferences for various policy combinations by as-

signing letters to the alternatives: a strong commercial policy, C; no commercial policy, c; proslavery, S; and antislavery, s. Northern delegates most preferred a strong commercial policy coupled with antislavery, followed by a strong commercial provision and an allowance for slavery, and so on. Using letter combinations and the mathematical symbol for "is greater than," we can rank the northern delegates' preferences for possible policy combinations:

Northerners $Cs > CS > cs > cS$

The South, on the other hand, most wanted to maintain a proslavery policy and to defeat a commercial one. In floor debates at the convention, Southern delegates said they felt more strongly about maintaining slavery than about avoiding marginally more costly shipping. Using the same set of symbols, we can rank southern delegates' preferred policy combinations:

Southerners: cS > CS > cs > Cs

Note that the North's most preferred combination of constitutional provisions—strong commercial institutions and a ban on the slave trade—was the least preferred combination in the South. And, conversely, the South's most preferred position was the least desired in the North. With their sincere preferences so opposed, frustrations mounted, as did the temperature of the rhetoric. Finally, each side realized that it could not win its most preferred combination of policies, and a search for a compromise solution began. Look carefully and locate the compromise package that each side found comparatively more attractive, bearing in mind that failure to reach agreement on these issues might well have endangered the success of the convention and left thorny issues unresolved during the ratification process. The compromise solution, CS, was a policy that combined strong commercial language and a provision permitting slavery. It took a while for the delegates to find it, but they did.

This solution took the form of a classic logroll. Instead of finding separate compromise policies on each issue, the delegates engaged in vote trading. To win its most important preference, each side conceded to the other its least important choice.

Finding a solution and implementing it are separate exercises that may be equally susceptible to failure. After all, each side must give up something important to win a concession in return. It is a situation ripe with the possibility of reneging, an instance of the classic prisoner's dilemma that always threatens cooperation. (We found such a

situation in Chapter 1, where we discussed the classic prisoner's dilemma interrogation in the film *I Wake Up Screaming*.) And because delegates from each side appreciated the difficulty of having to return home and explain their agreement to an unpopular policy, the fear of reneging was real. New England delegates would have to justify writing slavery into the Constitution, while southerners would have to defend opening the door to dreaded commercial regulations.

To succeed, the logroll had to be consummated delicately and discreetly. In his record of the convention's proceeding, James Madison noted the careful language Charles Pinckney of South Carolina had used to signal to the other side that he and his southern colleagues were in agreement. "The true interest of the S[outhern] States is to have no regulation of commerce," said Pinckney, who then cited "the loss brought on the commerce of the Eastern States by the revolution" and the "liberal conduct [of those states] toward the views of South Carolina. . . ." Here, Madison inserted a footnote translating Pinckney's circumlocutions for future readers: by "liberal conduct," Pinckney "meant the permission to import slaves. An understanding on the two subjects of *navigation* and *slavery* had taken place between those parts of the Union. . . ."[1]

Logrolling is ubiquitous in all legislatures, whether they are constitutional conventions or student government committees. This form of strategic behavior is, in fact, essential for a society composed of many different and competing interests to transact its politics successfully. We will encounter numerous instances of it throughout this text. For a description of a less historic but no less curious logroll, see box "Porn for Corn" in Chapter 6.

1. Quoted in William Lee Miller, *The Business of May Next: James Madison and the Founding* (Charlottesville: University Press of Virginia, 1992), 135.

assigned states their financial obligations to the national government proportionate to population. Accordingly, the Constitution apportioned each state seats in the House of Representatives based on population totals in which each slave would count as three-fifths of a citizen.*

Later in the convention some southern delegates insisted on two guarantees for their "peculiar institution" as conditions for remaining at the convention and endorsing the Constitution in the ratification debates. One was the unrestricted right to continue importing slaves. The delegates from northern states, most of which had outlawed slavery, preferred to leave the issue to some future government. But in the end they conceded by writing into the Constitution a ban on regulation of the slave trade until 1808.† (A total ban on slave imports went into effect on January 1, 1808.) Late in the convention southerners introduced the Constitution's second slavery protection clause. It required northern states to return runaway slaves to their masters. After some delegates first resisted and then softened the language of the clause, the proposal passed.

Why did the delegations from the more numerous northern states cave in to the southerners? The handling of the slavery issue was likely another instance of intense private interests prevailing over more diffuse notions of the public good. Reporting to Jefferson in Paris, Madison wrote that "South Carolina and Georgia were inflexible on the point of slaves," implying that without the slave trade and fugitive provisions they would not have endorsed the Constitution. And since the southerners' preferences were secure under the Articles of Confederation, their threat to defect during the subsequent ratification campaign was credible. After launching anguished, caustic criticisms of southerners' demands during floor debates, the northerners cooled down and reassessed their situation. In the end, they conceded many of their antislavery provisions and adopted a more strategic posture that would allow them to gain something in exchange.

With neither side able to persuade the other to adopt its preferred position and yet with each effectively able to veto ratification, both sides began searching for a mutually acceptable alternative. Their first such attempt had produced the Great Compromise. This time the solution took the form of a **logroll**—a standard bargaining strategy in which two sides swap support for dissimilar policies. In the end, New England accommodated the South by agreeing to two provisions: Article I, Section 9, protecting the importation of slaves until at least 1808; and Article IV, Section 2, requiring that northern states return fugitive slaves. In return, southern delegates dropped their opposition

---

*The three-fifths rule had been devised under the Articles to resolve a sectional dispute over apportioning states' tax contributions according to population. At that time the northerners had a stake in recognizing the humanity of slaves—if slaves were people their numbers should be fully counted in apportioning tax obligations. Southerners had countered that, since they marketed slaves as property, slaves should be counted no more than any other property. After extended haggling, the groups agreed to add three-fifths of the number of slaves to a state's free population.

†The committee that drafted this language proposed that the ban on regulation end in 1800, but a coalition of New Englanders and southerners added eight years to the ban. Only Madison spoke out against extending the deadline. The delegates from Virginia, all of whom had owned slaves at one time or another, voted against extension.

on an altogether different issue that was dear to the commercial interests of the northern states. Article I, Section 8, allows Congress to regulate commerce and tax imports with a simple majority vote (see box "Logrolling a Constitution," page 76).

Amending the Constitution

In their efforts to provide a suitable means for amending the Constitution, the Framers broke new ground. (Amending the Articles of Confederation required the unanimous consent of the states, and the constitution creating the French republic in 1789 contained no amendment procedure whatsoever.) Perhaps the futility of trying to win unanimous consent for changing the Articles persuaded the Framers to find a more reasonable method for amending the Constitution, one that did not require a full convention like the Philadelphia convention. Yet, they did not want to place

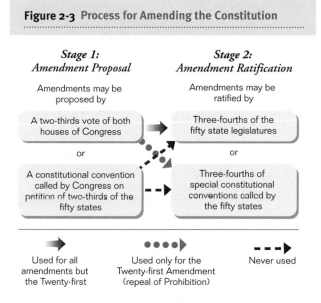

Figure 2-3 Process for Amending the Constitution

Stage 1: Amendment Proposal

Amendments may be proposed by

A two-thirds vote of both houses of Congress

or

A constitutional convention called by Congress on petition of two-thirds of the fifty states

Stage 2: Amendment Ratification

Amendments may be ratified by

Three-fourths of the fifty state legislatures

or

Three-fourths of special constitutional conventions called by the fifty states

→ Used for all amendments but the Twenty-first

•••• Used only for the Twenty-first Amendment (repeal of Prohibition)

- - -▶ Never used

the amendment option within easy reach of a popular majority. After all, some future majority frustrated by executive and judicial vetoes might try to change the Constitution rather than accommodate its opponents. So, again, the Framers solved the dilemma by imposing heavy transaction costs on changing the Constitution.

The concept of providing for future amendment of the Constitution proved less controversial than the amendment procedure itself. Intent on preserving their hard-won gains in the face of future amendment proposals, both the nationalists and states' rights advocates approached this matter warily. Delegates from small states insisted on endorsement of amendments by a large number of states, while the nationalists argued that the Constitution derived its legitimacy directly from the citizenry and that the citizens alone should approve any change. Unable to muster a majority for either position, the delegates again employed the formula of accepting parts of both proposals. As a result, the Constitution allows an amendment to be proposed either by a two-thirds vote of both houses of Congress or by an "application" from two-thirds of the states. Enactment occurs when three-fourths of the states, acting either through their state legislatures or in special conventions, accept the amendment (see Figure 2-3).

Since its ratification the Constitution has been amended twenty-seven times. In every instance Congress initiated the process, and in all but one case the state legislatures did the ratifying. (The Constitution and its amendments appear in the Appendix.) Six additional amendments—including the Equal Rights Amendment (see Chapter 4, Civil Rights)—were sent to the states but failed to win endorsement from a sufficient number. The paucity of near misses is deceiving, however. Each year dozens of amendments are proposed in Congress, but they fail to go any further either because they fail to attract the requisite two-thirds support in both chambers, or supporters foresee little chance of success in the states. During the 108th Congress (2003–2004), for example, members proposed amendments restricting marriage to a man and a woman; assuring "God" is included in the Pledge of Allegiance; and providing a mechanism for Congress to replenish its membership should more than a quarter of its members be killed, as in a terrorist attack.

The Fight for Ratification

The seventh and final article of the Constitution spells out an important procedure endorsed by delegates in the final days of the convention: "The Ratification of the Conventions of nine States, shall be sufficient for the Establishment of this Constitution between the States so ratifying the Same." Everyone knew that this deceptively straightforward provision was critical for the success of their enterprise. The delegates improvised by adapting the nine-state rule employed by the Articles for passing normal legislation, even though it was directed at the confederation's legislature and not the convention and that the Articles did not provide for amendment. And the ratification provision withdrew ratification authority from the state legislatures, which might have misgivings about surrendering autonomy, and gave it instead to elective special conventions. In sum, the delegates succeeded in a bit of legalistic legerdemain—appearing to conform to the requirements of the existing Constitution while breaking radically from it.

The Federalist and Antifederalist Debate

At the close of the convention, only three delegates refused to sign the Constitution. This consensus, however, is misleading; others who probably would have objected left early, and many prominent political leaders such as Virginians Patrick Henry and Richard Henry Lee had refused even to participate.

Over the next year every state but Rhode Island (it held out until 1790) elected delegates to state conventions that proceeded to dissect the Constitution and ponder its individual provisions. This was truly a time of national debate over the future of the country. As one observer noted, "Almost every American pen . . . [and] peasants and their wives in every part of the land" began "to dispute on politics and positively to determine upon our liberties." [10] On a lighter note, the *Boston Daily Advertiser,* responding to General Washington's call for public debate, admonished its readers: "Come on brother scribblers, 'tis idle to lag! The Convention has let the cat out of the bag." [11]

Delegates to the state conventions concentrated, predictably, on the concerns of their states and communities. Southern states carefully inspected each article for a northern avenue of attack on their "peculiar institution" of slavery. Finding none, all of the southern states except North Carolina lined up behind the Constitution. Constituencies and their delegates similarly aligned themselves for or against the Constitution according to its perceived impact on their pocketbooks. Small farmers, struck hard by declining markets and high property taxes after the war, had succeeded in gaining sympathetic majorities in many of the state legislatures. Thus they looked suspiciously on this attempt to shift fiscal policy to the national government.

Moreover, under pressure from small farmers, many state legislatures had printed cheap paper money (making it easier for the farmers to pay off their debts), overturned court decisions unfavorable to debt-laden farmers, and provided some with direct subsidies and relief. Thus these constituencies were reluctant to see their state legislatures subordinated to some more distant government that would assume control of critical activities such as currency and bankruptcy. The farmers failed to recognize, however, that the ascendancy of the national government would benefit them by shifting public finance away from property taxes and toward import duties. Some northeastern merchants who foresaw this shift lobbied their delegates to oppose ratification.

With the New York ratification narrowly divided, proratification forces staged a massive rally. The parade was graced by a "ship of state," an already well-developed metaphor. At the time, New Yorker Alexander Hamilton was widely regarded as one of the Constitution's most effective sponsors.

In the public campaign for ratification these issues tended to be reduced to the rhetoric of nationalism, voiced by the **Federalists,** versus the rhetoric of states' rights, voiced by the **Antifederalists.** The divisiveness characterizing the Philadelphia convention thus continued. But the labels given the two sides were confusing. Although they consistently distinguished the Constitution's supporters and opponents, the labels confused the positions of these camps on the issue of federalism. Many of those who opposed ratification were more protective of state prerogatives, as the term *federalist* implies, than were many of the prominent "Federalists." Appreciating the depth of state loyalties, Madison and his colleagues early on tactically maneuvered to neutralize this issue by claiming that the Constitution provided a true federal system, making those seeking ratification Federalists. Their success in expropriating this label put their opponents at a disadvantage in the public relations campaign. One disgruntled Antifederalist proposed that the labels be changed so that Madison and his crowd would be called the "Rats" (for proratification) and his side the "Antirats."

Although in the end the Federalists prevailed and are today revered as the nation's "Founders," the Antifederalists included a comparable number and quality of proven patriots. Foremost among them was Patrick Henry, who led his side's counterattack. With him were fellow Virginians Richard Henry Lee, George Mason, and a young James Monroe, who would become the nation's fifth president under the Constitution

TABLE 2-1

The First Ten Amendments to the Constitution: Bill of Rights

Amendment	Purpose
I	Guarantees freedom of religion, speech, assembly, and press, and the right of people to petition the government for redress of grievances
II	Protects the right of states to maintain a militia
III	Restricts quartering of troops in private homes
IV	Protects against "unreasonable searches and seizures"
V	Assures the right not to be deprived of "life, liberty, or property, without due process of law," including protections against double jeopardy, self-incrimination, and government seizure of property without just compensation
VI	Guarantees the right to a speedy and public trial by an impartial jury
VII	Assures the right to a jury trial in cases involving the common law (judge-made law originating in England)
VIII	Protects against excessive bail or cruel and unusual punishment
IX	Provides that people's rights are not restricted to those specified in Amendments I–VIII
X	Reiterates the Constitution's principle of federalism by providing that powers not granted to the national government are reserved to the states or to the people

he had opposed. Other famous outspoken opponents included Boston's Revolutionary War hero Samuel Adams and New York governor George Clinton.

In their opposition to the Constitution, the Antifederalists raised serious theoretical objections—ones that can still be heard more than two hundred years later. They argued that only local democracy, the kind found in small homogeneous communities, could approach true democracy. The United States, they asserted, already was too large and too diverse to be well ruled by a single set of laws. Turning their sights to the Constitution itself, the Antifederalists argued that a stronger national government must be accompanied by explicit safeguards against tyranny. Specifically, the Constitution needed a bill of rights—a familiar feature of most state constitutions. Some delegates to the convention proposed a bill of rights, but Madison and others had argued that it was unnecessary because the Constitution did not give the national government any powers that could be construed as invading the citizenry's rights. This argument, however, worked better at the convention than it did in the public campaign. The Antifederalists quickly realized they had identified a chink in the Constitution's armor and began pounding the issue hard. Even Madison's ally Jefferson wrote him from France insisting that individual rights were too important to be "left to inference." Suddenly on the defensive, Madison made a strategic capitulation and announced that at the convening of the First Congress under the new Constitution, he would introduce constitutional amendments providing a bill of rights. His strategy worked; the issue receded. In a sense, though, the Antifederalist strategy had worked as well. Madison kept his promise, and by 1791 the Constitution contained the Bill of Rights (see Table 2-1).

In June 1788 New Hampshire became the ninth and technically decisive state to ratify the Constitution. But Virginia and New York had still not voted, and until these two large, centrally located states became a part of the Union, no one gave the new government much chance of getting off the ground. But by the end of July both states had narrowly ratified the Constitution, and the new Union was a reality.

The Influence of *The Federalist*

Aside from eventually yielding a new constitution, the ratification debates fostered another national resource: eighty-five essays that were collected under the title *The Feder-*

alist. Published under the shared pseudonym Publius in 1787–1788, the essays were written by Alexander Hamilton (who wrote the majority), John Jay (who wrote five), and James Madison (who wrote the best). In one of history's interesting twists of fate, Hamilton initially recruited fellow New Yorker William Duer to join the Publius team. His submissions were judged inadequate, however, and Hamilton turned to Madison. Duer, a professor at Columbia University, later found his appropriate medium in a highly successful American government textbook in which he introduced students to the already famous *Federalist* essays, to which he almost contributed. (Duer wrote a heartfelt dedication in his textbook to Madison, which is reproduced on page vi.)

Because their immediate purpose was to influence the delegates to the New York convention, where ratification was in trouble, the *Federalist* essays first appeared in New York City newspapers. At one point Hamilton and Madison were cranking out four essays a week, prompting the Antifederalists to complain that by the time they had rebutted one argument in print, several others had appeared. Reprinted widely, the essays provided rhetorical ammunition to those supporting ratification.*

Whatever their role in the Constitution's ratification, *The Federalist Papers,* as they are also called, have profoundly affected the way Americans then and now have understood their government. A few years after their publication, Thomas Jefferson, describing the curriculum of the University of Virginia to its board of overseers, declared *The Federalist* to be indispensable reading for all undergraduates. It is "agreed by all," he explained, that these essays convey "the genuine meaning" of the Constitution.

The Theory Underlying the Constitution

Two of Madison's essays, *Federalist* No. 10 and *Federalist* No. 51, offer special insights into the theory underlying the Constitution. (For the full text of both essays, see the Appendix.) In different ways, each essay tackles the fundamental problem of self-governance, which Madison poses in a famous passage from *Federalist* No. 51:

> If men were angels, no government would be necessary. If angels were to govern men, neither external nor internal controls on government would be necessary. In framing a government which is to be administered by men over men, the great difficulty lies in this: you must first enable the government to control the governed; and in the next place oblige it to control itself.

The last goal is tricky. *Federalist* No. 10 tackles the problem by both exploring the likelihood that tyranny by the majority would arise within a democracy and identifying a solution. It is a powerful, cogent argument grounded in logic. *Federalist* No. 51 deals with the delegation problem of keeping the citizenry's agents (that is, government officeholders) honest. The solution lies in pitting politicians against one another

---

*Although they became famous, the *Federalist* essays, according to most historians, had a negligible impact on the outcome of the ratification process. Perhaps too many hard economic interests were in play for abstract arguments about the general welfare to do more than justify and dress up positions grounded firmly in self-interests. The New York convention shifted toward ratification only after New York City threatened to secede from the state if the vote went against ratification.

When James Madison was introduced with the accolade "Father of the Constitution," he frequently demurred, probably less from modesty than from disagreement with many of its provisions.

through the mutual vetoes embedded in the Constitution's separation of powers and checks and balances. This way, politicians can counteract each other's temptation to engage in mischief. Whatever their differences, these two essays can be read as following parallel paths—one at the societal level, the other at the governmental level—toward the same destination of a polity free from tyranny.

Federalist No. 10

Madison's first and most celebrated essay appeared in the November 24, 1787, issue of the *New York Daily Advertiser. Federalist* No. 10 responds to the strongest argument the Antifederalists could muster—that a "large Republic" cannot long survive. This essay borrows from the writings of David Hume, but over the course of a decade of legislative debate and correspondence Madison had honed his argument to fit the American case.[12] Indeed, Madison had made the argument before—at the Constitutional Convention when defending the Virginia Plan in a floor debate.

The major task Madison sets out for himself in *Federalist* No. 10 is to devise a republic in which a majority of citizens will be unable to tyrannize the minority. Madison wastes no time identifying the rotten apple. It is factions, which he describes as "mortal diseases under which popular governments have everywhere perished." He defines a **faction** as "a number of citizens, whether amounting to a majority or minority of the whole, who are united and actuated by some common impulse of passion, or of *interest,* adverse to the rights of other citizens, or to the permanent and aggregate interests of the community" (emphasis added). Madison's factions appear to have many of the attributes of modern-day interest groups and even political parties.

Madison then identifies two ways to eliminate factions, authoritarianism or conformism, neither of which he finds acceptable. Authoritarianism, a form of government that actively suppresses factions, is a remedy that would be worse than the disease. In a famous passage of *Federalist* No. 10 Madison offers an analogy: "Liberty is to faction what air is to fire, an aliment without which it instantly expires."

Conformism, the second solution, is, as Madison notes, "as impracticable as the first would be unwise." People cannot somehow be made to have the same goals, for "the latent causes of faction are . . . sown in the nature of man." Thus two individuals who are precisely alike in wealth, education, and other characteristics will nonetheless have different views on many issues. Even the "most frivolous and fanciful distinction" can "kindle their unfriendly passions," Madison observes, but most of the important political cleavages that divide a citizenry are predictably rooted in their life circumstances. In another famous passage the author anticipates by nearly a century Karl Marx's class-based analysis of politics under capitalism:

But the most common and durable source of faction has been the various and unequal distribution of property. Those who hold and those who are without property have ever formed distinct interests in society. . . . A landed interest, a manufacturing interest, a mercantile interest, a moneyed interest, with many lesser interests, grow up of necessity in civilized nations, and divide them into different classes, actuated by different sentiments and views.*

If the causes of faction cannot be removed without snuffing out liberty, then one must control their effects. Madison identifies two kinds of factions—those composed of a minority of the citizenry and those composed of a majority—that have to be controlled in different ways. During the late eighteenth century, the ubiquitous problem of factional tyranny occurred at the hands of the monarchy and aristocracy, a "minority" faction, for which democracy provides the remedy. A minority faction "may clog the administration, it may convulse the society; but it will be unable to execute and mask its violence under the forms of the Constitution." Democracy, however, introduces its own special brand of factional tyranny—that emanating from a self-interested majority. In Madison's era many people—especially those opposed to reform—ranted that majority rule equaled mob rule. Thus supporters of the new constitutional plan had to explain how a society could give government authority to a majority without fear that it would trample on minority rights. Madison explained: "To secure the public good and private rights against the danger of . . . a [majority] faction, and at the same time to preserve the spirit and the form of popular government, is then the great object to which our inquiries are directed."

Parting ways with some of the leading political philosophers of his era, Madison dismisses direct democracy as the solution:

> [T]here is nothing to check the inducements to sacrifice the weaker party or an obnoxious individual. Hence it is that such democracies have ever been spectacles of turbulence and contention; have ever been found incompatible with personal security or the rights of property; and have in general been as short in their lives as they have been violent in their deaths.

So much for town meetings.

Madison contends that the republican form of government, in which elected representatives are delegated responsibility for making governmental decisions, addresses the tyranny of the majority problem in two ways. First, representation dilutes the factious spirit. Madison does not trust politicians to be more virtuous than their constituents, but he recognizes that, to get elected, they will tend to moderate their views to appeal to a diverse constituency. Here Madison subtly introduces his *size principle,* on which the rest of the argument hinges: up to a point, the larger and more diverse the constituency, the more diluted is the influence of any particular faction on the preferences of the representative.

---

*In an earlier version of this passage, delivered at the convention in defense of the Virginia Plan, Madison had added that those who owned slaves and those who did not had distinct and antithetical interests. He may well have omitted this reference to slavery here because it had proven controversial with southern delegates. After all, this is a public argument intended to persuade readers to support adoption of the Constitution.

Sen. Robert Byrd, D-W.Va., has long argued that knowledge of the Constitution should be a key ingredient of every citizen's civic education. To that end, he discreetly inserted a provision in a 2005 appropriations bill mandating that every educational institution from primary school through college that receives federal funds be required to offer instruction on the Constitution. One critic of this idea from the Association of School Administrators appeared unwittingly to add credence to the senator's concerns when she incorrectly asserted that "the Tenth Amendment clearly states that education is a state's right."

A legislature composed of representatives elected from districts containing diverse factional interests is unlikely to allow a faction or a small coalition of them to so dominate the institution that it can deny rights to factions in the minority. This line of reasoning allows Madison to introduce a second distinct virtue of a republic. Unlike a direct democracy, it can advantageously encompass a large population and a large territory. As Madison argues,

> Extend the sphere, and you take in a greater variety of parties and interests; you make it less probable that a majority of the whole will have a common motive to invade the rights of other citizens; or if such a common motive exists, it will be more difficult for all who feel it to discover their own strength and to act in unison with each other.

In other words, their differences will pose a benign collective action problem. Any attempted collusion would confront such steep transaction costs that any efforts to engage in mischief would inevitably be frustrated.

What has Madison accomplished here? He has turned the Antifederalists' "small is beautiful" mantra on its head by pointing out that an encompassing national government would be less susceptible to the influence of factions than would state governments: "A rage for paper money, for an abolition of debts, for an equal division of property, or for any other improper or wicked project, would be less apt to pervade the whole body of the Union than a particular member of it. . . ." A geographically large republic would encompass dispersed, diverse population, thereby imposing serious transaction costs on their representatives in maintaining a majority coalition and minimizing the prospect of majority tyranny. Madison concludes: "In the extent and proper structure of the Union, therefore, we behold a republican remedy for the disease most incident to republican government."

Until the twentieth century, *Federalist* No. 10 attracted less attention than did some of its companion essays. Yet as the nation has grown in size and diversity, the essay has won new prominence for the prescience with which Madison explained how such growth strengthens the republic (see Map 2-1 on page 88). This Madisonian view of democracy often is referred to as **pluralism.** It welcomes society's numerous diverse interests and generally endorses the idea that those competing interests most affected by a public policy will have the greatest say in what the policy will be.

Federalist No. 51

By giving free expression to all of society's diversity, *Federalist* No. 10 offers an essentially organic solution to the danger of majority tyranny. *Federalist* No. 51, by contrast, takes a more mechanistic approach of separating government officers into different branches and giving them the authority to interfere with each other's actions. The authority of each branch must "be made commensurate to the danger of attack," Madison asserts. As for incentive: "Ambition must be made to counteract ambition. The interest of the man must be connected with the constitutional rights of the place." In other words, the Framers' efforts will have failed if future generations of politicians do not jealously defend the integrity of their offices. Here, then, is the rationale for separating governmental authority among several branches, with each having the authority to check the other.

Since popular election is the supreme basis for legitimacy and independence in a democracy, no constitutional contrivances can place appointive offices on an equal footing with elective offices. Madison explains:

> In republican government, the legislative authority necessarily predominates. The remedy for this inconvenience is to divide the legislature into different branches; and to render them, by different modes of election and different principles of action, as little connected with each other as the nature of their common functions and their common dependence on the society will admit.

Bicameralism is intended to weaken the legislature's capacity to act too quickly and impulsively, but even so it may not prevent the legislature from encroaching on the other branches. Madison offers the president's veto as a strong countervailing force and speculates that, by refusing to override the president's veto, the Senate might team up with the executive to keep the popularly elected House of Representatives in check. Madison even finds virtue in the considerable prerogatives reserved to the states: "In a compound republic of America, the power surrendered by the people is first divided between two distinct governments. . . . Hence a double security arises to the rights of the people. The different governments will control each other, at the same time that each will be controlled by itself."

Could this be the same James Madison who wanted to abandon the convention rather than agree to a Senate elected by the state legislatures, the same man who had wanted Congress to have an absolute veto over state actions? Madison's Virginia Plan had vested ultimate authority in a popularly elected, national legislature, and this model of a legislature became the House of Representatives. So why is he commending a Constitution that severely constrains this institution's influence over policy?

Madison probably was playing to his audience.[13] *Federalist* No. 51 seeks to reassure those fence-sitters listening to Antifederalist propaganda that the Constitution would take a giant step down the short path to tyranny. After all, the Antifederalists were presenting the specter of a powerful and remote national government and, within it, the possible emergence of a junta composed of unelected senators and an indirectly elected president bent on usurping the authority of the states, undermining the one popularly elected branch of government (the House of Representatives), and ultimately subjugating the citizenry. Madison is countering with a portrait of a weak, fragmented system that appears virtually incapable of purposive action, much less of hatching plots. He must have grimaced as he (anonymously) drafted the passage extolling the Constitution's checks on his House of Representatives.

Map 2-1 The Shape of America's Population

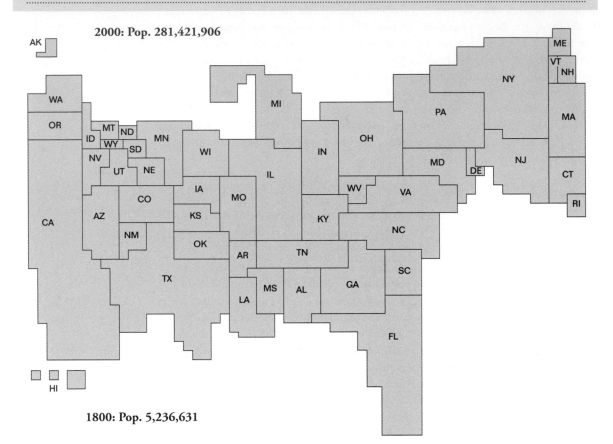

2000: Pop. 281,421,906

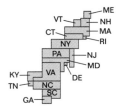

1800: Pop. 5,236,631

STATE POPULATION:

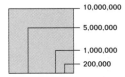

— 10,000,000

— 5,000,000

— 1,000,000

— 200,000

Sources: U.S. Census Bureau and the *New York Times*.

In James Madison's view, the little nation at the time of the Constitution's ratification supplied sufficient diversity of interests to reap the benefits of an "extended republic." The present-day American republic would appear to satisfy *Federalist* No. 10's requirements even better. Writing to a friend forty years later, however, Madison worried that America would outgrow the Constitution. Projecting the nation's current rate of growth, he estimated that by 1930 it would become too crowded and too polarized between "wealthy capitalists and indigent laborers." He predicted that the United States would require a different constitutional system, one that was more like Britain's with its strong executive. The nation's history corresponded closely to Madison's prediction, as shown in the timing of the Great Depression, the calls for radical reform, and, in Franklin Roosevelt, the rise of the modern presidency.

In summary, *Federalist* No. 10 conveys the theory of pluralism that guided the Constitution's chief architect; *Federalist* No. 51 explores how and why the governmental system that emerged from the political process in Philadelphia might actually work. Since these essays were written, Madison's insight into the operation of the Constitution has been largely borne out. As we shall see in Chapter 4, government policy sometimes fails to implement the preferences of national majorities for reasons he identifies in this famous essay.

Both the pluralism of competing interests and separated institutions have been judged less favorably by many modern students of American politics. With authority so fragmented, they argue, government cannot function effectively. And by adding a layer of institutional fragmentation on top of pluralism, the Framers simply overdid it. The result is an inherently conservative political process in which legitimate majorities are frequently frustrated by some minority faction that happens to control a critical lever of government. Furthermore, if the logic of *Federalist* No. 10 is correct, Americans do not need all of this constitutional architecture of checks and balances to get the job done.[14] Critics also point to the many other stable democracies throughout the world that function well with institutions designed to allow majorities to govern effectively. Would Madison have privately agreed with this critique? Probably so—after all, his Virginia Plan incorporated those checks and balances necessary to foster the healthy competition of factions and no more.

The Constitution: Born of Sweet Reason or Politics?

"America is a nation without a national government," one critic observed during the last days of the confederation, "and it is not a pretty sight." The Constitution was adopted to correct the problems inherent to localism. But rather than making a break with the past, as the nationalists had sought, the new Constitution simply veered in a somewhat more national direction. In the end, a century and a half of home rule, as well as the loyalty to state governments felt by those who had served successfully at that level, could not be denied. The new national government had to accommodate the states by allowing their participation in the selection of senators and reserving to them certain prerogatives and responsibilities.

It is deeply ironic that the kind of national pluralism Madison and his allies were trying to install already was at work at the convention, frustrating their success. Present were the contending interests that closely resembled the factions of *Federalist* No. 10. Large states competed with small over representation; the South pushed for constitutional protection for slaveholding, and the Northeast worked for favorable commercial regulations. The absence of a dominant majority faction meant intense bargaining resulting in shifting alliances that led to a novel, hybrid governmental system that is neither national nor confederative in nature. Many of the Constitution's provisions have no theoretical rationale; they are simply the hammered-out products of compromise. How does one justify the three-fifths rule, the malapportioned Senate, or the Byzantine procedures for electing a president, if not by explaining that each was born of political necessity? The Constitution is, in other words, a fine document arising not from the application of sweet reason but from politics. The document produced by the Constitutional Convention was a plan no delegate favored or could even have imagined on the opening day of the convention. It was, however, a plan that a substantial majority favored over the status quo and all could live with.

Despite their efforts, Madison and the nationalists won only a partial victory with the launching of the Constitution; the nation still added up to little more than a collection of states. Nevertheless, America's political development since 1787 has seen the realization of many of the goals that eluded the nationalists at the Philadelphia convention. For example, by building the Constitution on the consent of the governed rather than endorsement by the states, the nationalists successfully denied state governments any claim that they could ignore national policy. Over the next several decades, however, state politicians unhappy with national policy routinely threatened to secede or to "nullify" objectionable federal laws. But none of these threats became a full-fledged constitutional crisis until the eleven southern states seceded from the Union shortly after Abraham Lincoln was elected to the presidency in 1860. With the Union victory in 1865, this threat to nationhood ended conclusively. A central government capable of forcing compliance was finally achieved by war. Yet, as we shall see in Chapter 3, Federalism, the nationalization of government authority remained limited by modern standards. Nowhere is this more evident than in the domain of civil liberties, the subject of Chapter 5.

But what about Madison's other goal of building a national society that could prevent majority factions from tyrannizing local minorities? The two-hundred-year history of governance under the Constitution has been one of gradual nationalization—so gradual, in fact, that the nation only recently realized Madison's aspiration. In slavery, segregation, and the disenfranchisement of southern black citizens, Madison's worst dreams were realized, and nearly two hundred years would pass before these citizens would achieve equality in civic life. Chapter 4 surveys this inglorious history to illuminate the weaknesses and limitations of the constitutional system. As Madison correctly predicted, the U.S. Senate proved to be an institutional barrier to quelling the threat of state-level tyranny of the majority. More importantly, the history recounted in Chapter 4 illuminates why and how citizens and politicians would find it in their interest to extend rights to disenfranchised members of the society.

Key Terms

logic.cqpress.com

Suggested Readings

Dougherty, Keith. *Collective Action Under the Articles of Confederation.* New York: Cambridge University Press, 2001. Analyzes the Articles of Confederation and Shays's Rebellion with a keen eye toward identifying the historical circumstances that caused massive free riding to bring the young nation to a crisis.

Draper, Theodore. *A Struggle for Power: The American Revolution.* New York: Times Books, 1996. According to Draper, the Revolution represented the politics of self-interest rather than ideology. His account also examines the greater political context of the Revolution, in particular the long-standing conflict between the French and British.

Kernell, Samuel. *James Madison: The Theory and Practice of Republican Government.* Stanford: Stanford University Press, 2003. This collection of essays by leading students of modern American politics compares Madison's political science and leadership strategies with current concepts and ideas, including those presented in Chapter 1. (Kernell's essay was spawned by issues encountered in reconciling *Federalist* Nos. 10 and 51 while writing this chapter.)

Ketcham, Ralph. *James Madison: A Biography.* Charlottesville: University Press of Virginia, 1990. An authoritative and highly readable biography of America's first political scientist.

Miller, William Lee. *The Business of May Next: James Madison and the Founding.* Charlottesville: University Press of Virginia, 1992. An absorbing account of the politics leading up to and at the Constitutional Convention. This history served as the chief source of the account reported in this chapter.

Norton, Mary Beth. *Liberty's Daughters.* Boston: Little, Brown, 1980. A systematic and persuasive assessment of the considerable behind-the-scenes contribution of women during the Revolution and the impact of the war on the transformation of family relationships.

Riker, William. *The Strategy of Rhetoric.* New Haven: Yale University Press, 1996. A lively yet keenly analytical and systematic account of the Constitution's ratification as a political campaign.

Rossiter, Clinton. *1787: The Grand Convention.* New York: Macmillan, 1966. This classic portrayal of the Constitutional Convention remains the most readable and provocative treatment of the Framers at work in Philadelphia.

Wills, Garry. *Explaining America.* New York: Doubleday, 1981. An analysis of the logic and ideas of *The Federalist.* Few authors can match Wills's talent for rendering abstract concepts and ideas intelligible to the general audience.

Wood, Gordon S. *The Creation of the American Republic, 1776–1787.* New York: Norton, 1969. An indispensable intellectual history of the transformation of America from the Revolution through the adoption of the Constitution.

Review Questions

1. What steps were taken to construct a national government before the Articles of Confederation? What resulted from these steps?

2. How much experience did the colonists have in self-government prior to the Revolutionary War? In which issue areas did they have the most experience? And in which did they have the least? How did these experiences shape the institutions they designed in the Articles and under the Constitution?

3. How were decisions made under the Articles? What sorts of decisions were not made by the confederation? How did this system affect the war effort? How did it affect the conduct of the national and state governments once the war was over?

4. Why were small states suspicious of any plan to abandon the Articles?

5. What were the Virginia Plan and the New Jersey Plan? What sorts of states supported each plan and why? How did the Great Compromise attempt to satisfy both groups of states?

6. Why is the Electoral College so complicated?

7. How did the Framers balance the powers and independence of the executive and legislative branches?

8. Which issues were consciously left unresolved by the Framers? Why?

9. Why did Northern delegates compromise with Southern delegates on the issue of slavery?

10. What mechanisms for constitutional amendment were included in the Constitution? Why were multiple methods included?

11. According to James Madison, what are "factions"? What problems do they cause for government? How can they be eliminated? How can the effects of faction be minimized?

12. In *Federalist* No. 51, why did Madison argue that it was necessary to separate governmental authority among several branches?

Exercises

"Dead Wood" in the Living Document

The authors argue that the Constitution contains many carefully negotiated compromises and agreements. Yet if you look at a current copy of the U.S. Constitution (if your personal copy is in your other backpack, you can just turn to the Appendix in this book), you will notice that entire sections of the document are no longer in force. (In our copy these sections are indicated by [bracketed] text.) As you read through the Constitution, keep track of such sections and answer the following questions: When did each section become inoperative? What function did the section formerly serve? What section, if any, replaced it? Politically, what changed to allow the document to be altered from its original form? (Hint: many of these questions are answered in the endnotes.)

The Best-Laid Plans . . .

Assume that the Great Compromise never occurred and that the Constitution instead embodied the New Jersey Plan for determining representation in the House. Use the Census Bureau's estimates of state population for 2005 (www.census.gov/popest/states/NST-ann-est.html) to determine how many constituents each member would represent for each of the states. Comparing these estimates with the current distribution of House districts, can you determine which regions of the country would gain and lose the most representation?

Federalism

Is there a rationale for having some government services supplied locally, others by the states, and still others by the national government?

Despite the Framers' efforts to keep the national government out of the states' business, was it inevitable that so many policies once left to the states are now handled by the federal government?

When elected officials from the states challenge national authority, what determines who will have the final say over policy?

After endorsing California's landmark climate change legislation in the run-up to his reelection campaign in 2006, Governor Arnold Schwarzenegger took his state's battle against global warming on a world tour. When he signed the bill—which set a goal of cutting greenhouse gas emissions 25 percent by the year 2020—Schwarzenegger was joined by the premier of Canada's Manitoba province and lauded by Japan's consul general at elaborate signing ceremonies. He worked with British prime minister Tony Blair to create the framework for a trans-Atlantic market in carbon dioxide emissions, to assist British and Californian firms in cutting their pollution as efficiently as possible. Although the governor's spokesman emphasized that Schwarzenegger had not signed a treaty with the prime minister, Schwarzenegger looked every bit the head of state as he posed with Blair to announce the agreement.

He also played the role of the visiting dignitary in summer 2007 when he met with French president Nicolas Sarkozy to discuss fighting global warming. In Paris' Élysée Palace, the two talked about cooperating on climate change and how Sarkozy would, in Schwarzenegger's words, "put a new energy in the relationship between France and other countries, and our state." [1] In September of that year, Schwarzenegger opened a United Nations summit on global warming by boasting to international delegates that the states were taking the lead in American efforts to cut greenhouse gas emissions.

All of these actions raise an important question about American federalism: How could a state governor trot around the globe to meet with world leaders and tout a state approach to climate change that was fully at odds with national policy? After all,

Though he is a state governor, Arnold Schwarzenegger secured close relations with national leaders such as Britain's then–prime minister, Tony Blair, by championing his state's landmark policies to fight climate change.

the United States is the last major industrialized nation that has not signed the Kyoto Protocol, which aims to limit greenhouse emissions worldwide. President George W. Bush favors voluntary limits on American emissions, at least until developing nations like China and India agree to reduce their pollution. The president was noticeably absent from the governor's international meetings, even though both leaders are Republicans and Schwarzenegger campaigned for Bush in the 2004 presidential contest.

Yet while they may share the same party label, the president and the governor have different beliefs about environmental policy and represent different constituencies. President Bush's approach has won him allies in the coal mines of West Virginia and the automobile plants of Michigan, while Governor Schwarzenegger's position helped him secure reelection in a solidly Democratic state. When he followed his win with an international victory lap to publicize the global warming bill, Schwarzenegger was doing more than simply showing off his personal star power. He was demonstrating the independence that elected officials in the fifty American states often have to craft laws that are in line with what their voters want but at odds with federal policy.

In December 2007, though, federal officials demonstrated the limits of state independence when the Environmental Protection Agency (EPA) denied the federal waiver that California needed to implement key parts of its landmark law. At issue was whether states could act by themselves to limit automobile emissions. On the same day that President Bush signed a bill raising national fuel economy standards, EPA chief Stephen L. Johnson denied California's request to enact its own regulations. "The Bush Administration is moving forward with a clear national solution," Johnson argued, "not a confusing patchwork of state rules." One state should not act alone on an issue that "extends far beyond the borders of California." By exercising his federal administrative power, Johnson effectively preempted state action.

He also made a classic argument for nationalizing policy. Pollution and climate change are policy challenges that cross state borders. Exhaust from the tailpipe of a California car can cause smog in the Los Angeles basin, but the carbon emissions can also trap heat in the earth's atmosphere and affect the global climate. Since many people are affected by the car's emissions, not just its driver, the environmental damage done represents an **externality**, an effect felt by more people than just the one who chose to cause it. Because greenhouse gas emissions have national (and of course international) effects, Johnson argued, they should be combated by a consistent set of federal standards. Uniform laws also make compliance more straightforward for automakers and oil companies that want to sell the same products all across the country. Because the problems caused by carbon emissions are not limited to one state, and because any one solution might work better if applied consistently to all states, the EPA chief threw out California's regulations in favor of a national approach.

Just weeks later, California and fifteen other states responded by filing suit against the EPA, making a classic **states' rights** argument. Consistent backers of states' rights have a philosophical commitment to the decentralization of authority, and often find temporary allies when the federal government extends its reach. "They are ignoring the will of millions of people who want their government to take action in the fight against global warming," Governor Schwarzenegger charged.[2] If Californians want to be tougher on carbon emissions than the nation as a whole, why should the federal government stand in their way? Fifteen other states as varied as Arizona, Connecticut, Illinois, Maine, and Oregon wished to follow the Golden State's stricter standards, making it clear that the EPA was blocking tighter environmental protections across the country.

The idea that a policy with majority support in one state should be protected from national intervention, so long as it causes no harm to other states, has been at the heart of debates over federalism for all of American history. The idea of states' rights has been invoked by proponents of policies on both sides of the ideological spectrum. It is used as often to defend state gun control laws as it is to challenge the current federal preemption of many state abortion restrictions. Historically, states' rights arguments were wielded by the alcohol prohibition movement and, most shamefully, by defenders of slavery and the decades of state-sponsored racial segregation that soon followed slavery's abolition. Arguments about the legitimacy of states' rights come down to the debate over whether state or national majorities should govern, and how far courts should go to protect the rights of minorities.

States' rights arguments were even raised in the last round of major environmental legislation in the United States. When Congress passed the landmark Clean Air Act Amendments of 1970, it required states to put comprehensive pollution-control programs into place. While some challenged this approach as an infringement on state sovereignty, California's officials worried that it did not go far enough. They had passed their own, tougher standards in the 1960s, since California's smog problem was particularly severe. They lobbied Congress for an exemption to permit their more stringent regulations. The 1970 Amendments granted this states' right only to California. In 1977, Congress gave all states the option to adopt either the federal standards or the stricter California standards—but not to create their own. In both sessions, members of Congress from California and their environmentalist allies used states' right arguments to push for exemptions when they debated on the House floor.[3]

The location of those debates serves as a crucial reminder, though, that when state and federal interests collide on a states' right debate, the federal government decides who wins. When California filed suit to uphold its climate change law in 2008, it did so in federal court. Members of the state's U.S. House and Senate delegations held hearings to investigate the scientific basis of the EPA's decision. The campaign to save California's law focused on Washington, D.C., with Sen. Barbara Boxer replacing Governor Schwarzenegger as its champion. Even states' rights supporters today recognize that the federal government possesses the authority to determine what is and what is not a state right.

But just because the federal government has the final say over state's rights conflicts does not mean that the decision will always favor federal intervention. The federal judges and Supreme Court justices who often rule on states' rights issues are independent from the other branches of government, and often have jurisprudential reasons or policy motivations to side with the states. Members of Congress have dual roles that create conflicting incentives. Senator Boxer is a member of the federal government, but at the same time a representative of California voters and also a fierce

Map 3-1 The United States' Carbon Footprint

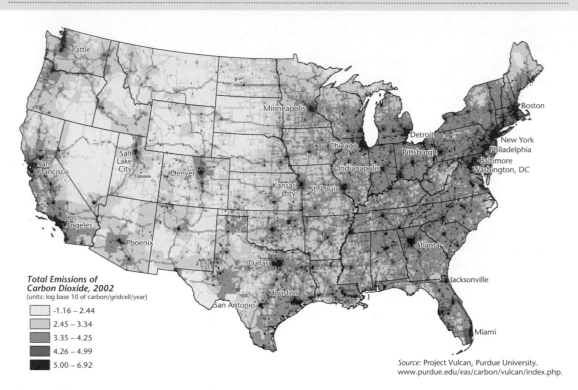

Total Emissions of Carbon Dioxide, 2002
(units: log base 10 of carbon/gridcell/year)

- -1.16 – 2.44
- 2.45 – 3.34
- 3.35 – 4.25
- 4.26 – 4.99
- 5.00 – 6.92

Source: Project Vulcan, Purdue University.
www.purdue.edu/eas/carbon/vulcan/index.php.

Note: This map displays America's "carbon footprint," the density of carbon dioxide emissions from sources such as power plants and automobiles as of 2002. While most carbon emissions come from urban areas, their impact on climate reaches throughout the country and indeed the world, a clear example of a negative externality that could be addressed by state or federal policies.

proponent of environmental regulations. In her congressional fight to reverse the EPA's decision, she will be aided by legislators from many other states whose leaders want to enact their own landmark climate change laws.

The fate of Schwarzenegger's carbon emission standards may be caught up in ideological fights and the rough-and-tumble of national partisan politics. But ultimately, it is a question of states' rights. The carbon emission controversy reminds us that the rules governing the interaction between state and federal governments in America are not fully settled: The structure of federalism is still being debated, with the highest policy stakes.

American-Style Federalism

In a federal system, the constitution divides authority between two or more distinct levels of government. For example, the system in the United States divides the national (federal) government and the states.* **Federalism** is a hybrid arrangement that mixes elements of a *confederation,* in which lower-level governments possess primary authority, and **unitary government,** in which the national government monopolizes constitutional authority, as shown in Figure 3-1.

Before adopting a federal system in the Constitution, the nation experienced first a unitary government and then a confederation. The decision by the distant British government to impose a central, unitary authority to tax and administer the subordinate colonies precipitated the American War of Independence. After the war, the citizens of the newly independent states reacted to the colonial experience by rejecting unitary authority in favor of a confederation in which smaller state governments held ultimate power. But because the Articles of Confederation failed to give the national government any enforcement authority, the individual states could, and did, ignore legislation from Congress that they did not like. Consequently, the national government accomplished little.

Across the world, unitary governments are far more common than federations and confederations combined. Under unitary systems, the lower-level governmental entities—such as counties and metropolitan districts in Britain and departments in France—are created by and ultimately dependent on the national government for authority and resources. Typically, the central government establishes national policies, raises money, and distributes it to the local units to carry these policies out. However deliberative and authoritative these subnational units may appear, they function largely as part of the administrative apparatus of the national government. A unitary government may decentralize its power by delegating some decisions and administration to a lower government entity, but even so the constitutional system remains unitary because the national government retains ultimate authority to alter or rescind this delegation.

Figure 3-1 Comparing Three Systems of Government

Unitary System

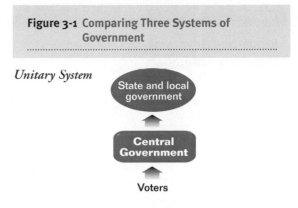

Authority is centralized with state and local governments administering authority delegated from central government. Examples: United Kingdom, France, and Japan

Federation

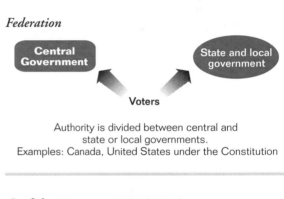

Authority is divided between central and state or local governments. Examples: Canada, United States under the Constitution

Confederation

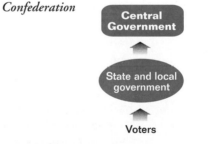

Authority held by independent states and delegated to central government by consensus agreements. Example: United States under the Articles of Confederation

---

*In this text and elsewhere, the terms *federal* and *national* are used interchangeably. This practice also characterized discussions leading to the formation of the Union. Any difference in usage was largely a matter of stress—that is, *federal* reflected the user's cognizance of the state elements also present in the national government. Hans Sperber and Travis Trittschuh, *American Political Terms* (Detroit: Wayne State University Press, 1962), 148–149.

TABLE 3-1	
Numerous Governments Comprise America's Federalism	
National	1
State	50
County	3,034
Municipal	19,429
Township and town	16,504
School district	13,506
Other special districts	35,052
Total	87,576

Source: Bureau of the Census, *Statistical Abstract of the United States: 2008* (Washington, D.C.: Government Printing Office, 2008), Table 414.

In a federal system, however, a government has constitutional relations across levels, interactions that satisfy three general conditions:

- The same people and territory are included in both levels of government.

- The nation's constitution protects units at each level of government from encroachment by the other units.

- Each unit is in a position to exert some leverage over the other(s).[4]

The second condition, independence, is critical because it sets the stage for the third condition, mutual influence. The lack of independence rendered the national government impotent under the Articles of Confederation. With the states commanding a veto over the most important national legislation, the national government lacked the resources and authority to act independently of the states.

Occasionally, observers of American federalism refer to local governments as if they were a separate level in a three-tiered federal system. This characterization is inaccurate. Local governments, which include thousands of counties, cities, and *special districts,* such as school districts, water boards, and port authorities, are established by the states (see Table 3-1). They are not mentioned anywhere in the Constitution. In providing a limited range of government services, local governing bodies may pass laws, worry each year about balancing their budgets, generate revenue through taxes and fees, and spend public money through their own agencies, but these bodies do not exercise independent, constitutional authority. In a famous decision, Judge John F. Dillon concluded "that the great weight of authority denies *in toto* the existence, in the absence of special constitutional provisions, of any inherent right of local self-government which is beyond [state] legislative control." Dillon's Rule made it clear that local governments are mere "creatures of the state."[5]

State officials can and often do exercise their power to intervene in local affairs. They may determine matters as fundamental as the governing structures of cities, counties, and special districts, their taxation powers, and even their geographic boundaries. They can wield authority over local issues that are important to voters statewide, as New York's state legislature did in early 2008 when its members halted New York City mayor Michael Bloomberg's plan to charge an $8 toll to drivers entering Manhattan during rush hours. State officials, such as the Alabama legislature in its 1880 session, can also intervene in areas as trivial as "prohibiting the sale, giving away, or otherwise disposing of, spirituous, vinous, or malt liquors within two and one-half miles of the Forest Home (Methodist) church, in Butler county."

Even when metropolitan areas are ceded great discretion to decide local policies through state home-rule provisions, they remain the legal creations of states, which retain the authority to rescind or preempt local ordinances. Whereas the relations between the state and national governments are premised on separate constitutional authority and qualify as "federal," those between state and local governments are not and therefore can best be classified as "unitary."[6]

Evolving Definitions of Federalism

The three defining features of federalism, listed above, leave room for different kinds of relations between state and national governments. Two distinct forms of American federalism have been identified: dual and shared. **Dual federalism** is perhaps the simplest possible arrangement, leaving the states and

New York City Mayor Michael Bloomberg's plan to charge a steep toll on all commuters entering Manhattan needed approval from the state legislature, just as many local government policies do. As this cartoon shows, his commuter tax was not well received by state legislators meeting in Albany.

the national government to preside over mutually exclusive "spheres of sovereignty." James Madison described this arrangement (and the intent of the Framers of the Constitution) in *Federalist* No. 45: "The powers delegated by the proposed Constitution to the Federal Government are few and defined. Those which are to remain to the State Governments are numerous and indefinite." For example, foreign policy and national defense are purely national concerns; matters that "in the ordinary course of affairs, concern the lives" of the citizens are the responsibility of the individual states.

A second conception, called **shared** (or "cooperative") **federalism,** recognizes that the national and state governments jointly supply services to the citizenry. While each level of government has exclusive authority over some policy realms, state and federal powers intersect over many of the most important functions. Figure 3-2 gives examples of these areas of exclusive and shared authority.

Throughout American history, the nation's practices better resemble the overlapping arrangements of shared federalism rather than the neat divisions of dual federalism. In the early years of the nationhood, states exercised national authority on important matters. In the Civil War the Union forces assembled to put down the Confederacy were recruited and initially provisioned by the states. Only after the men joined the ranks of other states' enlistees did the federal government assume control.

Soon after that war, however, **nationalization** shifted the "indefinite" authority Madison assigned to state governments to the national side. Today, in fact, the national government has a hand in almost all policies that "concern the lives" of the citizenry. The most important expansions of national power are described later in this chapter. These include the New Deal policies of the 1930s and the Great Society programs of

Figure 3-2 The Constitutional Basis for "Dual" and "Shared" Federalism

National Government

Exclusive Powers

★ Coin money
★ Regulate interstate and foreign commerce
★ Tax imports and exports
★ Make treaties
★ Make all laws "necessary and proper" to fulfill responsibilities
★ Make war
★ Regulate postal system

Powers Denied

★ Tax state exports
★ Change state boundaries
★ Impose religious tests
★ Pass laws in conflict with the Bill of Rights

State Governments

Exclusive Powers

★ Run elections
★ Regulate intrastate commerce
★ Establish republican forms of state and local governments
★ Protect public health, safety, and morals
★ All powers not delegated to the national government or denied to the states by the Constitution

Powers Denied

★ Tax imports and exports
★ Coin money
★ Enter into treaties
★ Impair obligation of contracts
★ Enter compacts with other states without congressional consent

Shared Authority

★ Tax
★ Borrow money
★ Charter banks and corporations
★ Take property (eminent domain)
★ Enforce laws and administer a judiciary

Source: Adapted from Lee Epstein and Thomas G. Walker, *Constitutional Law for a Changing America: Short Course,* 4th ed. (Washington, D.C.: CQ Press, 2009), Table III-1.

the 1960s, through which the federal government redesigned more limited state and local pension, welfare, and health care programs by providing most of the funding for them, designing a basic framework for each state to work through, and opening up eligibility to all qualifying Americans. In the past decade, the testing and funding provisions of the "No Child Left Behind" Act have sharply increased federal authority over the way local schools operate. The trend toward nationalization has not been entirely a one-way street. Both the Nixon and Reagan administrations pushed for a "New Federalism" by giving states more control over the implementation of some federal programs and grants, and Bill Clinton worked with Congress to increase state control over other federal policies through the "Devolution Revolution" of the 1990s. Yet these exceptions to the rule of ever-increasing federal power have occurred only with the willing agreement of federal leaders.

Overall, then, the United States has moved from Madison's dual federalism to a shared federalism in which federal officials generally decide how authority over intersecting state and federal policy areas should be divided. Indeed, the modern ascendancy of the national government surely would have amazed all (and horrified most) of the delegates to the Constitutional Convention. After all, protecting the states from encroachment by a stronger national government was, in the words of one nationalist delegate, "the favorite object of the Convention." All but a handful of the states' rights delegates were satisfied with the final product, and most of them later publicly advocated the Constitution's ratification. So why have their efforts to partition federal and state responsibilities into separate, self-contained spheres been so thoroughly eclipsed?

Part of the answer is that modern policy challenges and a political consensus that "the government" should provide more services and solve more problems than the Founders anticipated has made a joint, cooperative strategy across states and levels of government necessary. Pollution does not honor state boundaries; neither does unemployment, inflation, crime, greenhouse gases, methamphetamines, or irresponsible mortgage lenders. Then there is the Internet, which knows no boundaries whatsoever. National disasters such as Hurricane Katrina affect areas far beyond the reach of floodwaters and require responses on a scale that no single state can provide. The increasing complexity of policy dilemmas and growing interrelationship between American states have driven the move toward nationalization.

But political logic in tandem with the rules that govern the boundaries of American federalism are just as important in explaining the increasing involvement of the federal government in matters that "in the ordinary course of affairs, concern the lives" of Americans. Federal officials have many incentives to increase federal power. Presidents are often rewarded when they bring state or regional policies into line with what their national constituency desires. Members of Congress can claim political credit when they work through the federal government to help their districts, and often draw on the immense national tax base to do so. When either logic leads to an expansion of federal authority that the states resist, the critical question becomes: Who gets to decide whether this expansion is legitimate? As the next section shows, the Constitution opened the door to nationalization by granting the federal government ultimate power to determine (within certain bounds) the extent of its authority over the states.

Federalism and the Constitution

In countering Antifederalist alarms about an overly powerful national government, Madison cited two kinds of protections in the Constitution: first, the "structure of the Federal Government," referring mostly to the Senate; and second, explicit rules reserving important prerogatives to the states. Neither has proved an effective barrier to national action.

Transformation of the Senate

In the nineteenth century the equal representation of states regardless of population, combined with the selection of senators by state legislatures, gave the Senate the motive and the means to defend state prerogatives against national encroachment. The history of slavery reveals just how effective the institution was in this task. At first, some state legislatures were so possessive of the Senate and its members that they would pass resolutions instructing their senators how to vote on particular issues. Senators who failed to comply were asked to resign, and some did.[7] Even after this practice died out in the

1840s, most senators continued to regard themselves as agents of the state party organizations that controlled the state legislatures and elected them.

The real *coup de grâce* for the Senate as the bulwark of federalism came with ratification in 1913 of the Seventeenth Amendment, which mandated direct, popular election of senators. Amid persistent, widespread, and sometimes well-founded charges that senators bribed legislators to buy seats (and instances when divided state legislatures failed to agree on a nominee, leaving the state without representation for an extended period), a public consensus formed against indirect election of senators. Public pressure mounted to such an extent that more than three-quarters of state legislatures surrendered control and turned Senate selection over to popular election. The amendment, however, while targeting dysfunctional political practices, also knocked out an important prop of federalism. Today, the Senate is a central pillar of the national government. Senators may, incidentally, protect states' interests as they serve those of their constituents, but there are no guarantees. In fact, major extensions of federal authority have originated on the floor of the Senate, where more than a few of that chamber's members have cultivated a national constituency with an eye toward future presidential campaigns. Both Barack Obama and John McCain burnished their national credentials and launched their bids for the White House from the Senate.[8]

Constitutional Provisions Governing Federalism

The Constitution gives the national government at least as much responsibility for overseeing the integrity of the states as it does the states for overseeing the integrity of the national government. All but the original thirteen states entered the Union by an act of Congress; the national government defined the boundaries of territories, oversaw their administration, and eventually ushered them into the Union. Moreover, Article IV of the Constitution obliges the federal government to ensure that all states adhere to republican principles. While Congress may create new states, it cannot destroy an established state—say, by dividing it in half—without its consent. For their part, two-thirds of the states may petition Congress to convene a special constitutional convention to propose amendments. In these seldom invoked provisions, the Constitution enlists each level of government to keep the other in check.

Language distinguishing the authority and responsibilities of the states from those of the national government runs throughout the Constitution. In partitioning responsibilities, the Framers worked within a structure of dual federalism. Thus in three major sections of the Constitution they attempted to specify boundaries between the two levels of government. By understanding what these provisions sought but largely failed to do, we can better appreciate how America's governmental system has yielded to nationalizing forces.

THE SUPREMACY CLAUSE. The provision of the Constitution with the most profound implication for modern American federalism is the so-called supremacy clause in Article VI: "This Constitution, and the Laws of the United States which shall be made in Pursuance thereof [that is, in keeping with the principles of the Constitution] . . . shall be the supreme Law of the Land." Although this clause appears to give the national government license to do whatever it wants, the text actually contains an important qualifier: the national government enjoys supremacy, but only insofar as its policies conform to a Constitution that prohibits certain kinds of federal activities.[9] This qualifier restricted national authority throughout most of the nineteenth century. The original intent was simply to have the national government prevail over states when both governments were acting in a constitutionally correct manner. Thus the supremacy clause was framed to avoid impasses over jurisdiction rather than to cede authority to the national government. Over the next two hundred years, however, the sphere of legitimate national action expanded, allowing national policy to enter domains once occupied only by the states. Wherever the national government carved out new authority, it automatically became supreme.

THE POWERS OF CONGRESS. Article I, Section 8 lists the powers reserved to Congress. But these provisions have as much to do with federalism—that is, creating jurisdictional boundaries between the states and the national government—as they do with parceling out authority among Congress, the president, and the Supreme Court. After protracted deliberations in which many possibilities were considered, the Framers finally agreed to list in the Constitution a dozen or so **enumerated powers** that should be in the domain of the national government—specific authority that would enable the government to address problems the states had not grappled with effectively under the Articles of Confederation. One example: even Antifederalists conceded that a national postal system made better sense than trying to stitch together thirteen individual state systems.

Recognizing that contingencies requiring a national response might arise in the future, the Framers added to Section 8 what is now known as the **elastic clause.** It allows Congress to "make all Laws which shall be necessary and proper for carrying into Execution the foregoing Powers."[10]

The Constitution's Provisions for Federalism

Article I, Section 8, Commerce Clause
The Congress shall have Power . . . To regulate Commerce with foreign Nations, and among the several States, and with the Indian Tribes; . . .

Article I, Section 8, Elastic Clause
The Congress shall have Power . . . To make all Laws which shall be necessary and proper for carrying into Execution the foregoing Powers, and all other Powers vested by this Constitution in the Government of the United States, or in any Department or Officer thereof.

Article IV, Section 3, Admission of New States
New States may be admitted by the Congress into this Union; but no new State shall be formed or erected within the Jurisdiction of any other State; nor any State be formed by the Junction of two or more States, or Parts of States, without the Consent of the Legislatures of the States concerned as well as of the Congress.

Article IV, Section 4, Enforcement of Republican Form of Government
The United States shall guarantee to every State in this Union a Republican Form of Government, and shall protect each of them against Invasion; and on Application of the Legislature, or of the Executive (when the Legislature cannot be convened) against domestic Violence.

Article VI, Supremacy Clause
This Constitution, and the Laws of the United States which shall be made in Pursuance thereof; and all Treaties made, or which shall be made, under the Authority of the United States, shall be the supreme Law of the Land; and the Judges in every State shall be bound thereby, any Thing in the Constitution or Laws of any State to the Contrary notwithstanding.

Tenth Amendment
The powers not delegated to the United States by the Constitution, nor prohibited by it to the States, are reserved to the States respectively, or to the people.

This open-ended provision, whose interpretation later would undermine the restrictive purpose of the carefully worded list of enumerated powers, apparently escaped the attention of many of the delegates, since the convention accepted it with little debate. Later, the Antifederalists detected in it an opening for broad national authority, as did the generations of national officeholders who followed them. As the variety of economic transactions that directly involve interstate commerce has grown sharply over the past two centuries, so too has the sphere of policy over which the national government can claim some jurisdiction. Moreover, laws governing a broad variety of social relations that are only incidentally economic—such as racial discrimination in access to public accommodations and possession of handguns near public schools—have invoked the commerce clause to justify federal involvement in these longtime state responsibilities.

THE TENTH AMENDMENT. In the ratification debates Madison answered Antifederalist charges of impending tyranny by promising that once the new government was in place, he would immediately introduce a bill of rights (see Chapter 2). In view of the controversy surrounding federal power in the ratification debates, it is not surprising that many members of the First Congress insisted that the first ten constitutional amendments include protections for the states as well as for individual citizens.

The **Tenth Amendment** offers the most explicit endorsement of federalism to be found in the Constitution: "The powers not delegated to the United States by the Constitution, nor prohibited by it to the States, are reserved to the States respectively, or to the people." Yet, despite its plain language, the Tenth Amendment has failed to fend off federal authority. The powerful combination of the supremacy and the elastic clauses reduces the Tenth Amendment to little more than a truism: those powers not taken by the national government *do* belong to the states. About all that it offers critics of nationalization is lip service to the principle of states' rights.

Interpreting the Constitution's Provisions

The sweeping language with which the Constitution variously endorses national power and states' rights has given politicians easy openings to interpret the Constitution according to their own political objectives. Thus the Framers envisioned a Supreme Court that would referee jurisdictional disputes among the states and between states and the national government. Among the thousands of judicial decisions that have grappled with the appropriate roles of the national and state governments, one early Supreme Court ruling stands out for protecting the national government from incursions by the states. In 1816 Congress created a national bank that proved unpopular with many state-level politicians who preferred the state-chartered banks over which they exercised control. To nip this federal meddling into what it viewed as a state matter, Maryland levied a heavy tax on all nonstate-chartered banks. James McCulloch, an agent for the national bank in Baltimore, refused to pay the tax, and the two sides went to court. The historic decision *McCulloch v. Maryland* (1819) brought together the supremacy and elastic clauses and moved them to the forefront of constitutional interpretation.[11] Writing for the Court, Chief Justice John Marshall declared that because the national bank assisted Congress in performing several of its responsibilities enumerated in Article I, Section 8—namely borrowing money, levying taxes, and issuing a national currency—the elastic clause gave the national government the implicit authority to create the bank. In one of the most famous passages in Supreme Court opinion, Marshall enunciated this definitive constitutional doctrine:

> Let the end be legitimate, let it be within the scope of the Constitution, and all means which are appropriate, which are plainly adapted to that end, which are not prohibited, but consistent with the letter and spirit of the Constitution, are constitutional.

Marshall iced the cake by removing the young national government from the purview of the states. Because "the power to tax involves the power to destroy," the supremacy clause implicitly exempts the federal government from state taxes.

Five years later, in 1824, the Marshall Court handed down another decision that must have appeared far less significant to contemporaries than it came to be regarded in the twentieth century. In settling a dispute between New Jersey and New York over each state's efforts to give a favored steam company a monopoly over shipping on the Hudson River, the Court held in *Gibbons v. Ogden* that neither state could control such a concession.[12] Only Congress possessed the authority to regulate interstate commerce.

In combination, these two cases created powerful precedents that would allow future national policy to develop free of the constraints of state prerogatives. Once the Court in *Gibbons* had sanctioned federal authority to regulate commerce, the supremacy clause gave the national government the authority to preempt the states in virtually all policies involving interstate commerce. Many traditional tasks of states, such as providing for public safety, enforcing fair advertising laws, and overseeing waste disposal, would slip easily into federal control via the commerce clause.

Congress is not the only branch of the federal government that has gained authority over policy areas once ruled by the states; the Supreme Court has also given itself the power to overrule state laws that it sees as inimical to the Bill of Rights or to a less explicit notion of "justice." Prior to the Civil War, the Bill of Rights was understood as applying only to the federal and not to state governments. The post-war passage of the Fourteenth Amendment, though, allowed later courts to use its due process clause (see Chapter 5) as a basis for striking down state laws that violated various explicit and implicit federal rights. The 1925 *Gitlow v. New York* ruling held that states could not abridge the free speech rights of their residents, while *Near v. Minnesota* (1931) applied the First Amendment's protections of a free press to the states. The door to intervention by the federal judiciary was opened more broadly by the 1937 *Palko v. Connecticut* decision, which held that states could not violate rights without which "neither liberty nor justice would exist." Based on this rationale, the Court held that a state prohibition on the use of contraceptives violated the inherent right to privacy of its residents (*Griswold v. Connecticut,* 1965), and then ruled that states could not impose strict limits on abortions like the Texas law struck down in *Roe v. Wade* (1973). These cases demonstrate that the federal judiciary has often been as aggressive as Congress in expanding national authority over the states.

The Saturday Press

Vol. I, No. 4   Minneapolis, Minn., Oct. 15, 1927   Price 5 Cents

A Direct Challenge to Police Chief Brunskill

In the *Near v. Minnesota* case, the U.S. Supreme Court held that the federal Constitution's First Amendment also preserved the freedom of the press from state incursion. Jay M. Near was the publisher of the *Saturday Press,* which accused Minneapolis' police chief and mayor of working with gangs that held a "deadly grip" on the city.

As national politicians sought over the years to expand their authority and responsibilities, they discovered that the wall between the federal government and the states was not as impregnable as most of the Framers had apparently supposed. The Constitution's provisions and language leave ample room for a variety of federal-state relations. Thus nationalization of public policy reshaped federalism largely unfettered by constitutional constraints and without triggering a constitutional crisis. Nationalization did not just happen, however. As many problems outgrew state borders, pressure usually built for a greater national role. But whether the federal government actually assumed responsibility remained—and still is—a political decision, reflecting as much the competition of interests as any objective rationale for national action. The build-up of antislavery sentiment in the northern states, which led to Abraham Lincoln's election in 1860, the South's secession, and the Civil War, remains the nation's most bitter and tragic conflict involving federalism. Yet while the war was nominally triggered by a dispute over the bounds of federal authority to abolish slavery, it should be seen as a larger political and moral clash that broke down into military conflict rather than a battle over the principles of federalism.

The Logic of Nationalization

The forces favoring nationalization are many and varied. They can be simply classified, however, according to whether they address a collective action problem or whether they are purely political interests that shift policy to Washington. Perhaps the best way to demonstrate how both collective action dilemmas and purely political strategies can push policy to the national level is with a simple hypothetical situation. Consider the decisions of a small farming community trying to upgrade its local roads (see box "Nationalization as a Road-Building Game"). After a bitter winter, the farmers' driveways and neighborhood roads are in disrepair. Moreover, new markets for their crops are opening up nearby, but access will require construction of a new road.

How will these sixteen farmers approach their road improvement and construction decisions? For the driveways, we can assume the farmers have always maintained their own and that this policy will not change. Each driveway represents a quintessential private good: the one person who benefits also bears full responsibility for its provision.

The neighborhood roads (A–D) qualify as public goods, at least for the local residents. The issue is whether those who use them will contribute to their maintenance. Because the number of users is small, informal negotiations will likely reveal who favors and who opposes the voluntary project. This said, there is no guarantee that each neighborhood will maintain its road. That decision will depend on the cost of the project in relation to each farmer's perceived benefit. In fact, in this hypothetical community some farmers (shaded) announce early in the discussion that the roads are not so bad and they prefer to skip the expense and ordeal of resurfacing this year. The other farmers want to make the repairs, and over the course of the conversation, each reveals a willingness to pay up to a third of the total road improvement cost. If each neighborhood organizes itself purely as a voluntary cooperative in which farmers who wish to repair their roads work together to do so, A and B will be improved even though farmers 1 and 8 do not contribute and get their roads graded for nothing. In collective action terms, these farmers "free ride," receiving the benefits of the road repairs funded by their neighbors without paying any of the costs.* Meanwhile, farmer 9 is not prepared to bear the full cost of regrading road C, nor are farmers 13 and 14 willing to split the cost for road D. These roads, then, will not be improved.

For these small-scale collective activities, informal negotiations and voluntary compliance yield a fairly successful final outcome. The roads were regraded in those neighborhoods where three of the four farmers wanted to do so and unchanged where demand fell short. Overall, thirteen of the sixteen farmers benefited in some fashion (seven by not having to pay for something they did not want). Only farmers 9, 13, and 14 found their preferences frustrated by their neighbors' choices.

Of course, farmers 2–7 may not have liked the fact that they paid more than their fair share of the costs for regrading roads that farmers 1 and 8 enjoyed for nothing. To solve this free-riding problem, the neighborhoods might organize themselves as governments—let's call them states—rather than as voluntary associations. A clear majority of three farmers in each state would still need to vote to regrade a road, but if they did, all four farms in a state would pay for the improvement. Under

---

*Farmers 2–7 do not have to worry about free riding from one of their neighbors who endorsed the repair; everyone understands that if any one of them drops out the project will become too costly for the others and it will falter. But as long as three of the four farmers in any neighborhood participate, the road will be built.

LOGIC OF POLITICS

Nationalization as a Road-Building Game

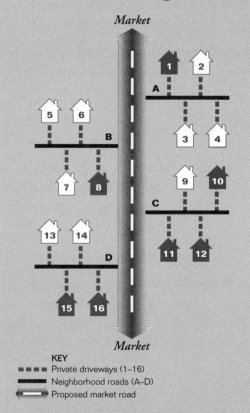

KEY
- ▬ ▬ ▬ ▬ Private driveways (1–16)
- ▬▬▬ Neighborhood roads (A–D)
- ◀▭▭ Proposed market road

Building hypothetical roads and lighthouses is a favorite pastime of political scientists and economists. Such "games" allow the players to isolate the essential features of a problem and inspect how they relate to one another. Here the problem (described fully in the text) is one of replicating the forces of nationalization as they influence the road improvement choices of a hypothetical farming community.

this arrangement, the same state roads (A and B) would be built, farmers 2–7 would be happy to see their contributions drop from a third to a quarter of the construction costs, and farmers 1 and 8 would be angry at having to contribute anything at all. Moving the decision about whether or not to repair a road from the private sphere into public government, then, helped to solve the free rider problem but imposed conformity costs on the two farmers who were in the voting minority in their states.

What would be gained and lost if a second change in governmental structure is made, shifting authority from the four states to a single "national" government? When states hold power, a state road is repaired only when a majority of farmers in the state are willing to pay for it, which avoids the inefficiency of supplying a good for which there is little demand. By keeping road improvement decisions local, the farmers also avoid the substantial transaction costs entailed in making decisions at a higher level of government. If, by contrast, the decision whether to regrade all four state roads was made at the national level, all sixteen farmers would have to pay the costs of holding an election. A slim nine-to-seven majority would favor the package of repairing all four state roads. Now, five more farmers (10–12, 15, 16) would be disgruntled at having to pay for unwanted road repairs, while only three (9, 13, 14) would be made happier. Importantly, the farmers from states A and B, who provided most of the votes in favor of the national package of state road repairs, would be no better off than they were when each state decided for itself, because they never drive on roads C and D. The lesson of this exercise for federalism is clear: state jurisdiction over public goods that fall within state borders offers real advantages.

But once the public good encompasses the larger community, the logic for local control (that is, states' rights) disappears. Consider the third road-building decision facing this hypothetical farming community: whether to build a road to the new markets for its crops. Each farmer figures that the profits gained by access to these markets would well exceed his or her one-sixteenth share of the cost of road construction. If the states tackled the decision to build a road to the market one state at a time, they might find it hard to coordinate on the timing of construction or fail to make each state's portion of the road transition seamlessly into the next state's road. (Indeed, during the nineteenth century, railroad lines in different European countries were built at different widths, requiring passengers to switch trains at national borders.) Constructing a road to the market in a piecemeal fashion would face real obstacles.

Entrusting the national government with the responsibility to build the market road would help overcome obstacles, without bringing any of the new problems that federalizing the state roads created. Since farmers from every state potentially benefit from using the entire market road, a majority vote in favor of building it would indicate that no portion of the new road would go to waste. Making the decision through a national government, rather than through private action, eliminates the free rider problem by ensuring that every farmer is taxed equally to pay a fair share of the costs. In this example, a national government could provide a national public good efficiently, while solving some coordination and collective action problems.

When a policy question straddles state borders, as issues like transportation, interstate commerce, and pollution often do, a national government can provide rational solutions to it. But when a policy affects only those within a single state, granting the national government authority over it can lead to inefficient outcomes that place heavy burdens on some states. And if states set up a national governing structure to build a market road, that government may be tempted to expand its power—at the expense of some states—by assuming control over state roads.

As we will see in the next section, the history of American federalism has followed a course resembling that of the hypothetical farmers. Both the logic of collective action and the opportunities for political advantage have at times shifted policy from the states to Washington. States have often resisted nationalization, and there have been important instances when federal officials have found it advantageous to shift power back to states. Yet the overall trend has been toward an expansion of federal authority, with Congress and the Supreme Court having the last word on turf wars between federal and state governments. The lesson of the road-building farmers is that by giving the national government the authority and resources to nationalize policy when it is essential, the states may open the door to national action even when it is not.

The Paths to Nationalization

Throughout the first half of the nineteenth century, the United States remained a nation of segmented communities whose commercial intercourse required minimal coordination across states. But just as the arrival of distant markets caused our hypothetical farmers to expand their concerns from local potholes to a new market road, so too did the United States shift its attention from strictly state and local matters to national problems and solutions. With growth, industrialization, urbanization, and the development of national transportation and communication systems, the nation's appetite grew for public goods that outstripped the scope and resources of local communities and states.[13] In the early 1870s, for example, the farm states tried in vain to prohibit the railroads from engaging in rate discrimination and exorbitant charges. They finally turned to Washington for regulation, and in 1887 Congress obliged by passing the Interstate Commerce Act. A similar process spurred the federal government to enforce national food safety standards, enact antimonopoly laws, and undertake numerous other services.

The nationalization of public policy, which altered America's federal-state relations, was propelled by a rationale, or logic, that grew out of the requirements of collective action. Played out historically, the logic of collective action has assumed several forms. First, as with the farmers' decision to build the market road, Americans have at times decided collectively to adopt policies of such magnitude and scope that they outstripped the resources of states. The result has been a historic movement of large blocks of domestic policy from the state capitals to Washington. We soon will examine two important historical instances of this movement: Franklin Roosevelt's New Deal and Lyndon Johnson's War on Poverty.

Second, states have solicited federal intervention when they could not solve their problems by working together individually. Considering that the U.S. mainland is

One major step toward nationalization that literally connected states was the building of the Interstate Highway System, now 46,837 miles long. Promoted by President Dwight D. Eisenhower in the 1950s, this massive public works project allowed people and products to move much more quickly within and across states, yet also imposed sharp costs on the small towns—such as the one pictured above, on the old U.S. Route 1 between Washington, D.C., and Baltimore—that withered when they were bypassed by the new highways. Because decisions were made at the federal level, small-town residents who might have been able to influence their local or state governments had little say in the national policy.

carved into forty-eight separate state jurisdictions, one can easily imagine a great variety of issues arising that require states' cooperation. And yet the Constitution prohibits formal interstate agreements (Article I, Section 10) in the absence of the national government's consent. Voluntary cooperation, by definition, holds the potential for reneging, particularly when serious, costly commitments are required. For that reason, following the 1906 San Francisco earthquake, which overwhelmed the capacity of California's state government to respond to $500 million in property damage and assist over 250,000 homeless residents, the states welcomed a national insurance policy against such disasters even though it meant surrendering control of disaster relief to federal agencies.

Finally, the political considerations that inspired the farmers to assign authority over the market road to a hypothetical "national" government have also been at work in the actual American government, where national majorities have insisted on federal involvement in what were formerly state and local matters. Sometimes mere expediency is at work as a national majority finds it easier to succeed in Washington than in each of the states. Similarly, companies with business around the country sometimes lobby for national regulations simply so that they do not have to deal with fifty different states' policies. On other occasions, the cause has been just and noble, as the history of civil rights policy in America shows. In asserting its authority to protect the rights of African Americans—from the Civil War in the 1860s to the civil rights laws a century later—the national government breached the separation of national from state spheres of control. Although the impact of civil rights on federalism has been profound, it is a subject with broad implications for all Americans and warrants separate consideration (see Chapter 4).

Historic Transfers of Policy to Washington

President Franklin Roosevelt's New Deal, enacted in the 1930s, and President Lyndon Johnson's Great Society program, realized in the mid-1960s, represented two equally historic shifts toward nationalization. In addition to broadening the scope of federal responsibilities, these watershed programs followed the election of large national majorities to Congress from the president's party, with an apparent mandate to create a broad new array of collective goods.

Roosevelt's New Deal was a comprehensive set of economic regulations and relief programs intended to fight the Great Depression (1929–1940). The innovation of the New Deal stemmed less from the form of its policies than from their size and scope. During Roosevelt's first two terms (1933–1941), he and the huge Democratic majorities in Congress established economic management as one of the national government's primary responsibilities. Federal policy took two basic forms: regulating and financing (and with it, prescribing) state action. Despite the continuing debate between present-day Republicans and Democrats over the proper division of federal and state responsibilities, no one has seriously proposed dismantling the framework of economic management constructed by the New Deal.

At the outset of the Depression, 40 percent unemployment rates were not uncommon in many communities. The states, responsible for welfare programs, had to reduce services to fend off insolvency. In the process, they also had to abandon people in need of help.* When the Roosevelt administration's offer to fund 90 percent of the costs for relief and new make-work programs finally came, the principle of federalism did not prevent state leaders from cheerfully accepting the help. All forty-eight states quickly signed up for the Works Progress Administration, Old Age Assistance, Civilian Conservation Corps, Social Security, and other federally sponsored public assistance programs. During these Depression years the dramatic growth in federal spending, coupled with corresponding reductions in funds at the state and local levels, provided evidence of the sharp shift from state to federal responsibility for social programs (see Figure 3-3).

To justify its unprecedented intervention in the economy, the Roosevelt administration invoked the commerce clause. Although demands for national regulation of

---

*Unlike the federal government, most state governments are forbidden by their constitutions from enacting annual budgets that incur deficits. But while they may have to balance their budgets, most states can and do frequently borrow billions of dollars to build schools, roads, parks, dams, hospitals, canals, railroads, and other vital parts of their infrastructures.

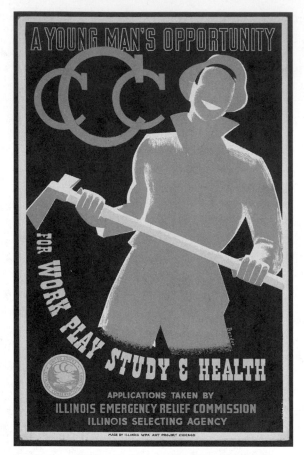

Franklin Roosevelt's New Deal included federal sponsorship of the Civilian Conservation Corps, which offered jobs to unemployed citizens in every state.

the economy began modestly in the late nineteenth century, they reached a new level of intensity with the onset of the Great Depression. FDR's New Deal introduced regulations that touched virtually every aspect of the nation's economic life, from how securities were sold on Wall Street to the amount of feed corn a Kansas farmer could grow for his livestock. At first, a conservative Supreme Court resisted. Narrowly interpreting the commerce clause to include only direct trade across the states, the Court ruled that federal workplace policies such as child labor restrictions were unconstitutional because they regulated intrastate commerce, an area left to the states. Under great political pressure, however, the Court eventually relented by extending its interpretation of the commerce clause to include intrastate commerce that indirectly affected commerce across state lines.

Was the nationalization of authority over commerce and responsibility for welfare programs that occurred during the Depression inevitable? Perhaps if a different president had been elected in 1932, or if Congress has been unwilling to go along with Roosevelt's New Deal proposals, welfare and pensions might have remained entirely a state responsibility. Under different political circumstances, the Supreme Court could have resisted the pressure to expand its interpretation of the commerce clause. On the other hand, the scale of the economic devastation that the Depression wreaked may have made political upheaval a certainty and left only the federal government with the resources and flexibility to respond. Either way, the New Deal was certainly a critical juncture that set the United States further down the path of nationalization.

Another great wave of nationalization of domestic policy occurred in the mid-1960s. Elected in 1964 in an even larger landslide than FDR's 1932 victory, Lyndon Johnson and the overwhelmingly Democratic Congress launched a War on Poverty as part of its Great Society agenda. In 1964–1965 Congress passed more than a hundred new programs that would be carried out by states but funded (and controlled) through federal grants, spending over $5 billion. The largest of these were Medicaid (which provides health insurance to low-income families, senior citizens in nursing homes, and disabled Americans) and Aid to Families with Dependent Children (the welfare program now known as Temporary Aid to Needy Families). Other traditional state and local responsibilities such as school funding, teacher training, urban renewal, and public housing became important federal responsibilities. As with the New Deal, these grants subsidized state programs that implemented national goals.

But all these grants came with strings attached. To qualify for funding, state and local authorities had to follow detailed programmatic guidelines prescribing how funds were to be spent. These strings greatly expand the federal government's power, even over services that are still funded mostly by state and local governments, such as schools. Because states now rely on the federal education grants that were created during the Great Society era, they have been forced to accept federal policy dictates such as the No Child Left Behind testing requirements in order to keep federal funds flowing (see box "No Child Left Behind: The Test of a Standardized Education Policy"). Without paying all of the costs of education, the federal government can still exert much control over it. Even while grant programs transfer money from the national to state governments, they often transfer authority back to Washington, D.C.

Nationalization — The Solution to States' Collective Dilemmas

When modern state governments encountered the same collective action dilemmas that prompted their eighteenth-century counterparts to send delegates to Philadelphia, they solved these dilemmas in the same way—by shifting responsibility from the state to federal authorities. Every kind of collective action problem introduced in Chapter 1, from simple coordination to the prisoner's dilemma, has frustrated state action at one time or another and repeatedly required states to turn to Washington for help.

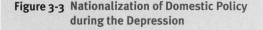

Figure 3-3 **Nationalization of Domestic Policy during the Depression**

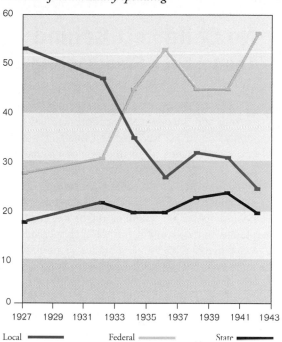

Percent of nonmilitary spending

Local ▬▬▬   Federal ▬▬▬   State ▬▬▬

Source: John Joseph Wallis, "The Political Economy of New Deal Fiscal Federalism," *Economic Inquiry* 29 (July 1991): 511.

Note: About half of the increase in federal spending in this figure took the form of direct financial support to indigent citizens.

COORDINATION PROBLEMS. A nation composed of fifty states inevitably faces coordination problems—some dramatic, some rather mundane. Even when the states agree to cooperate, thereby allowing each to deal more effectively with a common responsibility, they may have difficulty figuring out precisely how to work together. For example, until 1986, the principle that each state administers its own driver's license laws appeared unassailable. But after heavy lobbying by state officials, Congress passed the Commercial Motor Vehicle Safety Act, which standardized state driver's licenses for interstate truckers and created a bureau within the Department of Transportation to centralize traffic violation records. What prompted federal intervention was the practice common among truckers of obtaining licenses in several states to maintain a valid license regardless of the number of traffic tickets accumulated. Centralized record keeping offered a far simpler solution to state coordination than requiring each

No Child Left Behind
The Test of a Standardized Education Policy

The 2001 reauthorization of the 1965 Elementary and Secondary Education Act, now commonly known as "No Child Left Behind," teaches two clear lessons about the ironies of American politics and federalism. When President Bush signed this act after it passed with strong bipartisan majorities in both houses of Congress, it appeared to be the culmination of his campaign pledge to be a uniter, rather than a divider in Washington, D.C. Today, it stands as perhaps his most controversial domestic policy initiative and has drawn fire from members of both parties in Congress. And while the inspiration for the act came from the education reforms that President Bush helped to pass when he was the governor of Texas, the extension of one state's approach to all the others led to the most far-reaching exercise of federal power over state and local schools in American history.

On his second day in office, President Bush began assembling the bipartisan coalition that he would need to pass No Child Left Behind by inviting Democratic senator Edward Kennedy to the

state to update its records with those from every other state. Disgruntled truckers pointed to the new law as another example of interference by "heavy-handed Washington bureaucrats," but in fact it precisely fulfilled the states' request.

Even when the need for coordination is evident, there is no guarantee that the states will agree to shift this responsibility to Washington. In addition to the transaction costs of conforming to national standards, state politicians, like the farmers in the example on page 109, may worry that surrendering authority for one accepted purpose might lead the federal government to undertake less desirable policies. Such considerations are holding up agreement in Congress to strengthen national regulation of

White House. Surprisingly, the longtime liberal from Massachusetts and the Republican president found common ground in their shared goals of increasing funding for schools and narrowing the achievement gap between white and minority students. The act that they drafted together in 2001 provided billions of dollars more in federal aid to schools, but attached many strings to these funds.

Chief among the hundreds of new federal directives in the 1,000-page bill was the requirement that states administer standardized math and reading tests to all of their students, starting in third grade. Each state could develop its own tests, but the federal government got to decide what happened when a school registered consistently low scores: financial sanctions would kick in, and students would be allowed to transfer. The new act traded the carrot of funding for the stick of sanctions and federal control. With the final vote coming just weeks after the September 11, 2001, terrorist attacks, members of Congress from both parties backed the compromise that Senator Kennedy and President Bush reached and passed No Child Left Behind by 381–41 in the House and by 87–10 in the Senate.

Soon after the act went into effect, though, it drew criticism from both sides of the aisle. Over the next few fiscal years, Democrats like Kennedy were disappointed that the amount of federal aid to schools did not grow as quickly as they antici-

pated. Teachers and parents worried that schools were turning into test-taking factories, focusing all of their attention on math and reading and simply "teaching to the test." Many states protested that the national regulations did not give them the flexibility to deal with their unique challenges. Arizona and Virginia have asked for more time to teach English to students with limited proficiency before testing them in English. Utah's rural school districts have struggled to find teachers with college degrees in the subjects that they teach, as the act requires. Connecticut has filed a lawsuit charging that the federal government must provide more funding to go along with the new directives.

With so many of their states in open rebellion against the national policy, fifty Republican members of Congress introduced legislation in 2007 that would have let states opt out of the No Child Left Behind testing requirements, without losing their federal funding. The bipartisan consensus now seems against the act, but it is unclear whether it will be made more flexible, given more funding, or ultimately abandoned.

Sources: Sam Dillon, "Battle Grows over Renewing Landmark Education Law," *New York Times,* April 7, 2007; Peter Baker, "An Unlikely Partnership Left Behind," *Washington Post,* November 5, 2007.

electrical transmission across the country. Every state exercises some regulatory control over its electricity industry. In an earlier era, when most utilities were local monopolies with in-state generation and transmission, state-level policy made sense. Today, however, power flows through an extensive continental grid; residents of one state consume electricity from dozens of sources throughout the region. As the massive blackout on August 13, 2003, demonstrated, state regulation no longer works. The question still being deliberated in Congress and the states is, can regulatory coordination be delegated to the Federal Energy Regulatory Commission (FERC) without surrendering state control over rates? (Even several years after the blackouts of the

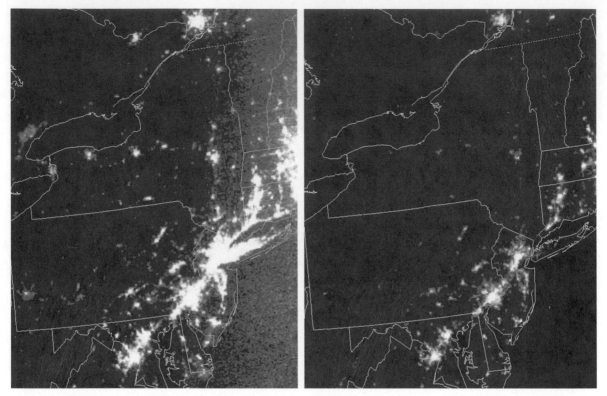

Not long ago, the transmission lines that constitute the nation's "power grid" mostly transmitted electricity from a generator to a local market. Consequently, regulatory oversight belonged predominantly to the states. But with deregulation of utility rates in the early 1990s electricity started chasing prices across state lines, and fragmented state regulation prevented the construction of new high-power transmission lines to keep pace with demand. In August 2003 a minor power outage in Ohio cascaded into a blackout across the East Coast.

Midwest and East Coast, members of Congress from the South and Northwest still have not agreed to new federal authority for fear that their cheap local electricity would chase market prices and drive up their local costs.)

RENEGING AND SHIRKING. In the nation's early years, states agreed to a course of common action but then failed to honor their commitments. The Constitution and national laws solve many of these dilemmas by authorizing the federal government to take direct action in raising resources and administering policy. However, in certain situations national responsibility and jurisdiction is either undecided or allows the states a prominent role. Movements to reduce pollution and conserve natural resources, among the most pervasive and thorny challenges to effective collective action in recent years, have inspired innovative approaches enlisting federalism as a solution. Both problems qualify as tragedies of the commons, introduced in Chapter 1. No one wants to breathe polluted air, but without some mechanism to arrange and enforce agreements, everyone continues to pollute under the assumption that doing otherwise will not by itself clean up the atmosphere (that is, promote the public good or lead to the betterment of the "commons"). Because pollution knows no borders, unilateral action by one state may be washed away by the acid rain created by another. Coordinated national policies are necessary to solve this collective action problem, and the Clean Air Act Amendments passed by Congress and signed by President Nixon in 1970 provide one example. By establishing national enforcement mechanisms, the legislation brought the states together into a common framework to control environmental damage (though it exempted California, as mentioned in this chapter's introduction).

CUTTHROAT COMPETITION. Under the Articles of Confederation each state was free to conduct its own international trade policy. This arrangement allowed foreign governments and merchants to exploit competition among the states to negotiate profitable trade agreements. The losers were American producers and the states, which found themselves in a classic prisoner's dilemma. Their best strategy would have been first to agree among themselves on a single rate (to form a kind of cartel) and then to negotiate with Britain from a united front. But this approach would have required that none of the states break rank when the British offered to reward the first "defector" with an especially lucrative, sweetheart deal. Not wanting to be played for the sucker, all states underbid each other, or engaged in **cutthroat competition.** Searching for a solution, both nationalists and advocates of states' rights readily agreed at the Constitutional Convention that the states were best served by the national government assuming control in foreign affairs, including trade.

At various times cutthroat competition has prompted state officials to lobby Washington to prevent bidding wars. When the national government defended a 1937 federal minimum wage law before the Supreme Court, it reminded the justices that rather than usurping state prerogatives, Washington was actually serving the states: "State legislators . . . over a period of time have realized that no state, acting alone, could require labor standards substantially higher than those obtained in other states whose producers and manufacturers competed in the interstate market." [14]

Environmental regulation is another area in which the national government has taken action. To lure new business, states sometimes are tempted to relax their environmental standards to give them a competitive edge over their neighbors. Thus one state's strong environmental policies may expose it to other states' gamesmanship. As much as state officials like to complain about the policies of the Environmental Protection Agency, the presence of national standards insulates environmental protection from cutthroat competition.

Competition among states can take other forms as well. Companies considering relocating facilities will strategically select two or three "finalist" sites in different states and then sit back and let them bid against one another by offering tax breaks or special services. Although the states generally would be better off if they could avoid this competition, none can afford to do so. Each state will raise its bid until the costs of subsidizing a new company through property improvements and reduced taxes exceed the expected economic benefits. States also face incentives to engage in a **race to the bottom** in social services by cutting back on things like the size of the monthly check a state pays to welfare recipients, so that it will not become a "welfare magnet"

Cutthroat competition between the states has even touched the entertainment industry, with many states offering tax incentives to lure tele-vision and film crews away from Hollywood. In 2008, the television show *Ugly Betty* moved its production from Los Angeles to New York after a new state law there offered producers a 30 percent refund on their expenses via a tax credit. That same year the state of Georgia took out an ad in the entertainment magazine *Variety* offering a 30 percent tax incentive to any production that moved to the Peach State.

which attracts the low-income residents of its neighbors. There remains much debate over whether or not states do indeed race toward the bottom,[15] but the incentives that a decentralized welfare policy creates to do so might harm society's most vulnerable.

Whether pitting the states against one another in a bidding war is a good thing depends wholly on whose interests are being served. By one recent estimate cities and states are paying about $40 billion annually in direct compensation, special services, and tax exemptions to lure and retain large employers.[16] Corporate executives seeking attractive concessions would understandably view any agreement among the states to avoid competition as unwelcome collusion. Alternatively, one could argue that these bidding wars represent a market mechanism establishing the true price of a project and hence promote efficiency.

Moreover, competition between states and performance comparisons may allow politicians across the country to discover which innovative solutions to common policy challenges actually work. The idea—that one state can experiment and, if successful, that other states and the national government may replicate it—presents a compelling justification for competitive federalism. Many state policy innovations have spread across the country. What is less certain is that the innovations which have been copied are always the most successful ones. In response to negative public opinion after Texas rated poorly in many national rankings of primary and secondary school test scores, politicians, including then governor George W. Bush, made the state's low educational scores a political issue. During the next several years, educational expenditures increased significantly across Texas, as did, eventually, its test scores and national ranking. After he was elected president, Bush applied some parts of the Texas plan on a national scale through the "No Child Left Behind" legislation (see the Politics/Policy box on pages 116–117). Opponents of this approach to education and critics of competitive federalism in general might ask how we know which parts of President Bush's plan improved test scores, and whether we can be sure that the nation copied a state's successful innovations rather than its failures.

The Political Logic of Nationalization

As in the farm road grading exercise, promoters of a policy will sometimes try to shift it from the states to the national government because either they expect more sympathetic treatment in Washington or they find it easier than lobbying fifty state governments. National campaigns for legislation banning automatic weapons and handguns, regulating hazardous waste disposal, and mandating special education programs in public schools are instances in which "state" issues have been strategically shifted to Washington.

If a cause enjoys widespread national support, lobbying Congress is far more efficient than lobbying fifty state legislatures. After all, a single federal law can change a policy in all fifty states. In 1980 a mother whose teenage daughter was killed by a drunk driver formed Mothers Against Drunk Driving (MADD), which quickly mushroomed into a national organization with thousands of members. Initially, MADD pressed state legislatures for stiffer laws and higher drinking ages. And although all proclaimed their enthusiasm for removing drunks from the highways, those states with lower drinking ages had a financial interest in maintaining the status quo. Such states profited from underage customers who visited from neighboring states with higher legal drinking ages. As a result, variations in the states' drinking ages perversely encouraged some young people to take to the highways in search of alcohol.

In 1984 MADD took its case to Congress.[17] Few politicians proved willing to defend federalism against the movement to reduce drunk driving. In 1985 Congress passed legislation that instituted a simple, effective way to regulate drinking age laws. If a state failed to raise its drinking age to twenty-one in 1986, it would lose 5 percent of its federal highway funds. Failure to do so in 1987 would trigger a 10 percent deduction. All the states got the message and promptly raised the drinking age by 1988. They also brought suit in the Supreme Court, claiming extortion and federal intrusion into strictly state jurisdictions. The Court sided with the national government.[18]

Even those who do not desire national action sometimes invite it to avoid burdensome and varied regulations from each of the states. In recent years many state attorneys general have charged the airlines with practicing illegal "bait and switch" advertising when they run local newspaper promotions for steeply discounted fares that

Despite his outspoken opposition to the intrusion of the federal government into longtime state domains, President Ronald Reagan did not hesitate to sign the popular legislation requiring states to change the drinking age to twenty-one to qualify for full federal highway funding. The thrilled onlooker is Candy Lightner, who in reaction to her twelve-year-old's death in a DUI accident founded Mothers Against Drunk Driving, or MADD, and lobbied aggressively for the legislation.

few customers find available. The airlines, however, have successfully evaded state prosecution by persuading the Department of Transportation to assert its preemptive federal authority to regulate airline rates and advertising. Thus even businesses wanting to remain free of any government regulation may prefer to deal with one federal agency rather than having to fend off regulation attempts from fifty states.*

Perhaps the most compelling strategic reason for a group to prefer national over state policy is that the national arena may be the only place in which it can hope to prevail, especially when a policy is opposed in the community where it would need to be enforced. This situation characterized civil rights in the South during the 1960s, but virtually any domain of public policy where the state and national governments share responsibility is subject to this political maneuver. After increasing its majorities in both the House and Senate in the 2004 elections, Republicans opened the 109th Congress by promptly passing a law that moved most class-action lawsuits from state to federal court jurisdictions. Some state courts had earned reputations for favoring plaintiffs, which aggrieved Republican-supporting business groups and endeared them to Democratic-supporting trial lawyers' associations.

Perhaps no area of national policy has so thoroughly been reshaped by this dynamic than the extension of environmental protections at the expense of state and local constituencies. Protection of environmental resources can be costly—directly or indirectly—in lost jobs and business. Either way, local residents typically pay the bulk of the costs. Idaho ranchers worry that the reintroduction of wolves in the nearby national parks will endanger their sheep. The Navajos' coal-burning, electricity-generating plant in Arizona may blanket the Grand Canyon in dense fog, but they prefer the profits gained from selling electricity to a national market. The lumber industry in northern California and Oregon believes jobs will be imperiled if it must curtail the harvest of old-growth forest to protect the endangered spotted owl.

The rest of the country, by comparison, bears little of these costs. It can "afford" the appropriate environmental measures far better than can those whose livelihoods

---

*Similarly, major software companies, including Microsoft and AOL, assembled in 2004 to respond to Utah's recently enacted law requiring any company loading cookies and other software onto a personal computer via the Internet to first obtain permission from the computer owner. With several other states poised to pass similar legislation, the software firms feared patchwork regulations would hamstring their capacity to innovate in this area. John Schwartz and Saul Hansell, "The Latest High-Tech Legal Issue: Rooting Out the Spy in Your Computer," *New York Times,* April 26, 2004.

are adversely affected by them. Restoring the original ecology of Yellowstone National Park, maintaining a smoke-free Grand Canyon, and protecting an endangered owl are all desirable and essentially free public goods. Thus conflicts arising over the environment frequently pit local resource users (such as ranchers and developers) who bear the costs of environmental regulation against nationally organized environmental constituencies that do not.

Sometimes the reverse political process occurs as groups that lose at the national level seek smaller victories in those states where they enjoy majority support. A dramatic example is California's $3 billion initiative to fund stem cell research after President Bush's executive order limited federal support of this research. California's innovation in this area has now been replicated by stem cell research funds in many other states. Similarly, social conservatives, frustrated in their efforts to restrict abortion rights and validate school prayer at the national level, have lobbied state legislatures and sponsored petition drives to put these issues on state ballots. Table 3-2 shows the success of antiabortion groups in winning restrictive state laws since legalization of abortion in the Supreme Court's 1973 *Roe v. Wade* decision (see Chapter 5). Similarly, gun-control groups, unable to persuade Congress to adopt tougher handgun laws, have taken their campaign to the legislatures of sympathetic states. By 2007, twenty-eight states had passed laws mandating safety devices or other methods of keeping firearms away from children in order to prevent accidents. States that have passed even more stringent gun control laws may see them struck down, though, in the wake of the controversial 2008 *District of Columbia v. Heller* Supreme Court decision that overturned Washington, D.C.'s handgun ban on the grounds that it violated the Second Amendment's right to keep and bear arms.[19]

As James Madison emphasized in *Federalist* No. 10, states and the national government combine the citizenry's preferences into different groupings, with the result that the two levels of government may adopt different, even opposite, policies to address the same problem. Although Madison was prepared to take his chances with national majorities, whose decisions, he believed, would be moderated by the collective preferences of a broad, diverse nation, he also knew what we learned in the farm road building exercise and our discussion of federal environmental policy: that national majorities will at times impose costs on local constituencies. Thus federalism presents opportunities for two kinds of majorities—state and national—to pursue their interests in competition with each other. For better or worse, national majorities have the institutional resources to nationalize many policy questions that once were the exclusive domain of state majorities.

Modern Federalism

Entering the twenty-first century, the national government's primacy in setting domestic policy is secure, even in domains that once belonged exclusively to the states. Whether through outright takeover of a function or by selective financial inducements, Washington can pretty much dictate state policy when its policymakers are so

TABLE 3-2

Abortion-Rights Foes Secure State-Level Restrictions

Type of Policy	Explanation	Total Number of States
Abortion-specific informed consent	Prohibits abortion without the pregnant woman's "informed consent," which requires that she receive anti-abortion lectures or materials approved by the state.[a]	20
Anti-abortion memorial	Requests that Congress ban abortion	25
Clinic violence	Prohibits violence toward or harassment of abortion clinics and workers	9
Conscience clause	Allows physicians not to provide abortions if they are opposed to abortion	36
Fetal disposal	Regulates disposal of aborted fetuses	11
Fetal experimentation	Prohibits experiments using material from aborted fetuses and bans abortions for the purpose of experimentation	30
Feticide	Outlaws killing of a fetus	10
Gag rules	Prohibit those working in state-run health care facilities from presenting abortion as an option to patients	18
Hospitals only	Stipulates that abortions only may be performed in hospitals	26
Insurance restrictions and bans	Permits restricted access only or prohibits insurance companies from including abortion in their health coverage	15
Mandatory counseling	Requires physicians to read a counseling "script" to any patient seeking an abortion	30
Medicaid ban	Eliminates federal funding of abortions	34
No wrongful life/wrongful birth policy	Prohibits lawsuits in which a person argues that he or she should not have been born (wrongful life) or parents allege that had they been informed correctly, they would have had an abortion (wrongful birth)	8
Parental consent or notification	Requires minors to obtain consent for an abortion from parents or the courts, or that a minor's parents be notified before an abortion is performed	44
Physician only	Stipulates that only licensed physicians may perform abortions	45
Post-viability	Establishes when viability occurs and regulates abortions after viability	30
Post-viability care	Requires postabortion care for a viable fetus	30
Public facilities	Bans the use of public facilities in performing abortions	6
Refusal clause	Allows physicians not to provide abortions if they are opposed to abortion	47
Reporting requirement	Stipulates that all abortions be reported to a state agency	20
Right to life	Makes it illegal to kill a fetus in the womb unless certain conditions are met and/or requires the physician to give any fetus born alive during an abortion a chance to live	12
Spousal consent	Requires the husband's consent for an abortion	9
TRAP (Targeted Restrictions on Abortion Providers) laws	Restrictions on facilities that perform abortions	33
Waiting period	Specifies a period that must pass between the request for an abortion and the time the procedure is performed	26

Sources: Adapted from Deborah R. McFarlane and Kenneth J. Meier, *The Politics of Fertility Control: Family Planning and Abortion Policies in the American States* (New York, N.Y.: Chatham House, 2001), 94–95; and from Melody Rose, *Safe, Legal, and Unavailable?* (Washington, D.C.: CQ Press, 2007), 103–104.

a. "Informed consent" has a different meaning for other medical procedures.

inclined. Some observers find recent Supreme Court decisions beginning to fence in the federal government's ability to dictate policy. Even so, the shift has been modest and easily circumvented by an alternative strategy of financial inducements.

The National Government's Advantage in the Courts

Indicative of how far nationalization has shifted the balance of power, today's constitutional litigation over federalism typically concerns direct efforts by the federal government to regulate the activities of state and local governments and their employees. In *Garcia v. San Antonio Metropolitan Transit Authority* (1985) the Supreme Court approved the application of federal wage-and-hour laws to state and local employees. Writing for the majority, Justice Harry Blackmun dismissed the Tenth Amendment as too ambiguous to guide federal-state relations. But this was no great matter, he added, because the proper relations between the states and the national government were protected in other ways. The states' "sovereign interests," he wrote, "are more properly protected by procedural safeguards inherent in the structure of the federal system than by judicially created limitation on federal power." Because members of Congress come from the states, the majority opinion concluded, "the political process ensures that laws that unduly burden the States will not be promulgated."[20] Such an argument may have befitted federalism during the days when senators really were agents of their state legislatures, but, at the time of *Garcia v. San Antonio*, the Court had little basis for expecting the states' interests to win a sympathetic audience in Washington. Indeed, this decision illustrates just how much over the years the Supreme Court favored the national government in refereeing federal-state relations.

In recent years the Supreme Court has begun to take a more circumspect view of federal authority and has sought to preserve some semblance of state independence in federal-state relations. For example, in *United States v. Lopez* (1995) the Court narrowly decided in favor of a student who had been caught carrying a handgun onto campus in violation of the federal Gun-Free School Zones Act of 1990.* For the first time in many years the Court held that some "empirical connection" needed to be established between a law's provisions and its actual effect on interstate *commerce* before the national government could make policy that would supersede state policy in the traditional domains of state jurisdiction.[21] The Court first applied the *Lopez* rationale in 2000, when it overturned the 1994 Violence Against Women Act allowing female victims of gender-motivated violence to sue their attackers in federal court. Writing for a narrow majority, then–chief justice William H. Rehnquist argued that Congress had exceeded its commerce clause authority by intruding into state control of law enforcement. Unpersuaded by Congress's concerted effort to show that violence affected interstate commerce, Rehnquist responded, "Simply because Congress may conclude that a particular activity substantially affects interstate commerce does not necessarily make it so."[22] After applying this precedent in several decisions, however, the Court in 2005 rejected the *Lopez*-based argument that California's and nine other states' laws protecting

---

*The Gun-Free School Zones Act established a zone around public schools in which anyone caught having a gun was charged with a federal felony. *United States v. Lopez,* 514 U.S. 549 (1995).

Mitt Romney and an Ambitious Governor's Dilemma

When he was elected governor of Massachusetts—one of the nation's most Democratic states—in 2002, Republican Mitt Romney had to decide how much he would adapt his policy positions in order to represent the left-leaning voters in his state. The devout Mormon faced especially tough choices on controversial social issues.

When he ran for governor, Romney made it clear that despite his personal beliefs, he supported keeping abortion legal in order to ensure that the procedure would be performed safely. He drew the ire of the National Rifle Association (NRA) for his support of Massachusetts' tight gun-control laws and his pledge not to loosen them if elected. Indeed, a candidate who opposed abortion rights and gun control would have had little chance of being elected in the Bay State. As governor, Romney signed a universal health care plan and implemented same-sex marriage after the state Supreme Court ruled that gay and lesbian couples could not be denied the right to wed.

By making these difficult decisions, Romney succeeded in representing the views of the voters who sent him to Massachusetts' highest office. But when

As governor of Massachusetts, one of the nation's most liberal states, Mitt Romney took moderate positions on issues such as immigration and gay rights. When he ran for the Republican presidential nomination, he first came under fire for these positions and then was accused of flip-flopping as he moved toward the right.

he set his sights on the White House, Governor Romney's liberal record on social issues presented a huge challenge to his new campaign. The voters that he now needed to impress, Republicans across the country in the 2008 presidential primaries, were much more conservative than the Massachusetts electorate. As it became clear that John McCain would capture most moderate Republicans, Romney sought to reestablish his conservative credentials. He urged Congress to amend the Constitution to ban gay marriage. He toured a gun show with representatives of the NRA. On the nation's most incendiary social issue, abortion, he described himself as pro-life and argued that states should be able to pass their own abortion laws.

There are many reasons why Romney's presidential campaign did not ultimately succeed, but surely the positions he took as Massachusetts governor created obstacles that he was not able to overcome with Republican primary voters. He faced the same dilemma that many ambitious governors do in a federal system: How far can you go to represent a state constituency, if these positions are likely to alienate voters nationwide?

Sources: Joan Vennochi, "Romney's Liberal Shadow," *Boston Globe,* June 17, 2007; Scott Helman, "Romney Retreats on Gun Control: Ex-Governor Woos Republican Votes," *Boston Globe,* January 14, 2007; Associated Press, "Mitt Romney Says He Opposes Abortion: Switch Has Some Critics Asking Whether He Has a Philosophical Core," *The Associated Press,* February 7, 2007.

the noncommercial cultivation of marijuana for personal, medical use prevent the federal government from enforcing national anti-drug laws. However heartening recent small victories may be for defenders of states' rights, the medical marijuana decision reminds us that they have not seriously undermined the extensive authority nationalization has thrust on the federal government.

Preemption Legislation

Today the clearest and most unequivocal expression of nationalization's impact on public policy appears in the growth of **preemption legislation**—federal laws that assert the national government's prerogative to control public policy in a particular field. Preemption owes its existence to the supremacy clause and its frequent use to the nationalizing forces described earlier. Over the 150 years prior to the New Deal, Congress enacted 83 laws that in some way substituted federal policy for that of the states. From 1933 to 1969, 123 such statutes were adopted, and since 1969 twice that number.[23] If preemption were all that had changed federal-state relations, modern American federalism might still be described as dual. The national government's "sphere of sovereignty" would merely have grown at the expense of the states'. But preemption accounts for only a small part of the impact of nationalization on federal-state relations. Generally, the jurisdictions of the states have been not so much curtailed as the national government has joined with the states in formulating policy. The result is the shared federalism described earlier in this chapter.

A cursory examination of trends in government growth during the twentieth century might raise the question of whether the impact of nationalization on reshaping modern federalism has been overstated here. Today states and localities employ more workers than ever before, their largest increases occurring since the nationalizing thrust of the New Deal (see Figure 3-4). Paradoxically, state governments have grown because of, rather than despite, nationalization. Just as the New Deal grafted national policy onto state administrations, much federal domestic policy continues to be implemented through the states instead of directly through the federal bureaucracy.

The national government has developed two ways—the carrot and the stick—to induce cooperation from the constitutionally independent states. The carrot consists of financial inducements, usually in the form of grants to states. The stick is regulation and mandates. Since the 1980s, chronic federal budget deficits have led national politicians to rely more heavily on the stick to achieve their policy objectives, and, thus, pass the costs on to the states.

The Carrot: Federal Grants to the States

Although federal aid dates back to the Articles of Confederation, when the national government doled out public lands to the states, only during the last half-century have federal **grants-in-aid** become an important feature of intergovernmental relations. By one count, a mere handful of these programs that provide money to a state for a specific purpose existed before the New Deal; today they number in the hundreds. Typically these grants amount to more than just inducements for states to provide services that they otherwise might not be disposed to offer or could not afford.

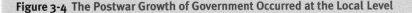

Figure 3-4 The Postwar Growth of Government Occurred at the Local Level

Number of public civilian employees (millions)

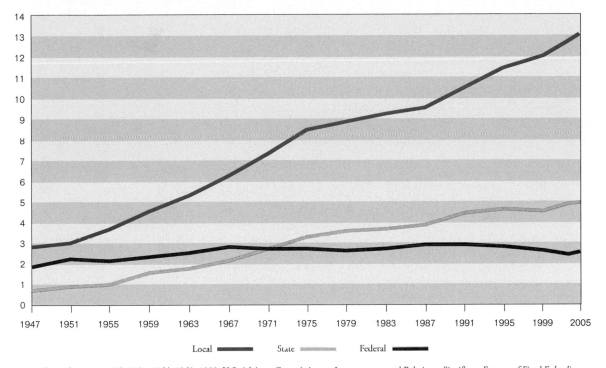

Local ▬▬▬ State ▬▬▬ Federal ▬▬▬

Sources: For 1949, 1952, 1954, 1959, 1964, 1969–1988: U.S. Advisory Commission on Intergovernmental Relations, *Significant Features of Fiscal Federalism, 1990,* vol. 2 (Washington, D.C.: U.S. Advisory Commission on Intergovernmental Relations, 1990), 177; for 1989–1992: *1994,* 151; for other years: U.S. Bureau of the Census, *Historical Statistics of the United States,* Series Y189–198 (Washington, D.C.: U.S. Government Printing Office, 1975), 1100; Bureau of the Census, *Statistical Abstract of the United States: 2000* (Washington, D.C.: Government Printing Office, 2000), Tables 524 and 525; *Statistical Abstract of the United States: 2004* (Washington, D.C.: Government Printing Office, 2004), Table 453; Bureau of the Census, *Statistical Abstract of the United States, 2008* (Washington, D.C.: Government Printing Office, 2008), Table 448.

Rather, they give the national government opportunities to define these "state" programs with great specificity.

The exact structure of a grant can have an enormous impact on how much control the federal government exercises over the scope of state programs and even over the ideological direction in which policy is likely to move. Though it may seem like a bureaucratic detail, the difference between a **block grant** and a **matching grant** is crucial. When the federal government makes a block grant, it gives each state or local government an exact amount of money to spend for some purpose. If the state wants to do more in the policy area, it can, but the state's government must pay all the costs of this program expansion by itself. If state officials do not place a high priority on the policy area, they are free to spend less than the block grant, but all of the savings will stay in the federal treasury. States thus have little incentive to control their costs below

One type of federal policy expansion that generates little ideological debate is spending to help build water projects such as the Central Arizona Project, pictured above. Federal money has built massive dams and canals in the western states, helped to restore the Florida Everglades, eased the navigation of the Mississippi and many other rivers, and cleaned up environmental damage across the nation. These projects have broad bipartisan support, and the first time that Republicans and Democrats came together to override a veto during George W. Bush's presidency was in November 2007, when they overrode his veto of a $23 billion water project bill.

the level of the block grant, and a huge disincentive to spend above it. They generally spend exactly as much as the block grant gives them, which effectively lets the federal government set state spending levels.

The logic and consequences of a matching grant work differently. With a matching grant, the federal government promises to provide matching funds, usually between one and two dollars, for every dollar that a state spends in some area. These blank checks, not surprisingly, often lead to major program expansions. A matching grant creates a "moral hazard," a situation in which people or groups behave differently, and often take more risks, when they do not have to pay all the costs of their actions.

Consider the logic of Medicaid, the state health insurance program funded through federal matching grants. States are required to cover some of their poorest residents and provide a minimum number of health care services through Medicaid, but can choose to insure more people or pay for more services if they want. When a state's budget is flush and its leaders decide to expand Medicaid, a state that receives a $2-to-$1 federal match[24] can cover an extra $300 million of services and spend only $100 million, because the federal government will pay the other $200 million. Its residents receive a lot of benefit, while its taxpayers assume little financial risk. This makes Medicaid expansion a relatively easy decision for state lawmakers. But when the state faces a budget crunch, the matching rate makes Medicaid cuts a bad deal. In order to save $100 million in state spending, state officials would have to trim Medicaid services by $300 million, leaving $200 million of federal grants on the table. This ensures a lot of pain for little gain, and explains why state and federal Medicaid spending has grown steeply over the past few decades. When states are not forced to pay the full costs of a new program, they take advantage of their blank checks to spend more and more federal money.

Of course, national lawmakers have long realized the implications of this moral hazard for the growth of government. The Democratic-controlled Congresses that created and expanded Medicaid and welfare programs funded them through matching grants because they knew this financial arrangement would spur even the most conservative and cash-strapped states to spend freely on social services. When Republicans took control of Congress in 1994, they wanted to remove this moral hazard in order to restrain state and federal spending. After trying and failing to shift Medicaid to a block grant program in 1995, the Newt Gingrich led Congress succeeded in block granting the Temporary Aid to Needy Families program as part of a 1996 welfare reform deal with Bill Clinton. The ideological stakes of these battles over funding formulas were clear; both sides knew that government would grow more quickly under matching grants than block grants. These episodes illustrate once again that in fights over federalism, each combatant is usually more concerned with a policy goal than with shaping the proper relationship between national and state governments.

The Stick: Unfunded Mandates

Until the 1960s the only federal regulations applied to the states were those governing the routine reporting and accounting for grants.* Since then, Washington has relied increasingly on rules to pursue policy objectives. Not only are states required to administer policies they might object to, but, adding insult to injury, the federal government may not even compensate the states for the costs of administration. One of the most controversial examples is the Education for All Handicapped Children Act of 1975, which requires states and school districts to offer prescribed, and in many cases costly, levels of special education for children with disabilities without providing more than a fraction of the funds needed to finance these mandated programs. Many school districts, as a consequence, find themselves strapped for resources and must curtail existing instructional programs to satisfy this federal mandate.

The national government uses four basic methods to prescribe state policy and supervise its administration: cross-cutting requirements, crossover sanctions, direct orders, and partial preemption. The states have challenged each before the Supreme Court and lost. Taken together, these methods allow the national government to create new state responsibilities, stipulate eligibility requirements, and monitor the implementation and enforcement of these requirements. In many areas of social policy, such as welfare and medical care for the indigent, the states have acted as little more than extensions of the federal bureaucracy. States regained some control in the late 1990s, when federal policy was changed to give them some flexibility in experimenting with different programs.

---

*The one exception was the Hatch Act (1940), which sought to clean up corruption by preventing federal and state employees from engaging in a variety of partisan political activities.

The welfare reform law of 1996 restructured the federal/state partnership for providing assistance to very low-income families with a new block grant for Temporary Aid to Needy Families. States gained spending flexibility within federal guidelines designed to move families off of welfare more quickly and require parents to spend more time working or taking part in job-training programs. The federal government gained control over welfare spending levels but relinquished authority over the details of policy implementation.

Cross-cutting requirements are statutes that apply certain rules and guidelines to a broad array of federally subsidized state programs. Since the 1960s this device has been used widely to enforce civil rights laws. For example, the failure of any state to follow federal guidelines that prohibit discriminatory employment practices can result in prosecution of state officials as well as loss of grants. Another prominent area of cross-cutting requirements is the environment. All state programs that include major construction and changes in land use must file environmental impact statements with the federal government.

Crossover sanctions are stipulations that a state, to remain eligible for full federal funding for one program, must adhere to the guidelines of an unrelated program. One example, mentioned earlier, is Congress's stipulation tying federal highway funds to state adoption of a minimum drinking age of twenty-one. Similarly, the Education for All Handicapped Children Act requires that a school district develop special education programs meeting federal guidelines to remain eligible for a broad variety of previously created grants-in-aid programs, including school construction and teacher-training subsidies.

National politicians frequently use crossover sanctions to influence state policies beyond their jurisdiction. In 1994 Sen. Patrick Leahy, D-Vt., proposed legislation banning the sale of soft drinks on public school campuses, and Sen. Dianne Feinstein, D-Calif., introduced a bill requiring that all students caught entering school with a handgun be suspended for a minimum of one year. Both bills provided for a cutoff in school aid funds if the districts failed to comply.

Direct orders are requirements that can be enforced by legal and civil penalties. The Clean Water Act, for example, bans ocean dumping of sewage sludge. In 1996, when the city of San Diego resisted a multibillion-dollar investment in a sophisticated sewage treatment facility that would alleviate the problem, the EPA brought suit in federal court to impose punitive financial penalties on the city.

Certain federal laws allow the states to administer joint federal-state programs so long as they conform to federal guidelines—a practice known as *partial preemption*. If a state agency fails to follow the instructions of federal agencies, the state might lose control of the program altogether; alternatively, federal grants might be suspended via crossover regulations. Good examples of partial preemption regulations are state air pollution policies. Public law and the EPA set minimally acceptable standards, but enforcement of these standards rests mostly with state agencies.

Hardly any area of state policy is unaffected by federal regulations of one kind or another. A close look at the major federal laws listed in Table 3-3 reveals several

TABLE 3-3

Examples of Major Unfunded Mandates

Public Law	Kind of Mandate
Civil Rights Act of 1964 (Title VI) Prevented discrimination on the basis of race, color, or national origin in federally assisted programs.	Cross-cutting
Age Discrimination in Employment Act (1967) Prevented discrimination on the basis of age in federally assisted programs.	Cross-cutting
Clean Air Act Amendments (1970) Established national air quality and emissions standards.	Cross-cutting, crossover sanctions, partial preemption
Occupational Safety and Health Act (1970) Set standards for safe and healthful working conditions.	Partial preemption
Endangered Species Act (1973) Protected and conserved endangered and threatened animal and plant species.	Cross-cutting, partial preemption
Fair Labor Standards Act Amendments (1974) Extended federal minimum wage and overtime pay protections to state and local government employees.	Direct order
Education for All Handicapped Children Act (1975) Provided free, appropriate public education to all handicapped children.	Crossover sanctions
Hazardous and Solid Waste Amendments (1984) Reauthorized and strengthened scope and enforcement of the Resource Conservation and Recovery Act of 1976; established program to regulate underground storage tanks for petroleum and hazardous substances; required annual EPA inspections of state and locally operated hazardous waste sites.	Partial preemption
Asbestos Hazard Emergency Response Act (1986) Directed school districts to inspect for asbestos hazards and take the necessary actions to protect health and the environment; required state review and approval of local management response plans.	Direct order
Americans with Disabilities Act (1990) Established comprehensive national standards to prohibit discrimination in public services and accommodations and to promote handicapped access to public buildings and transportation.	Cross-cutting, direct order
Clean Air Act Amendments (1990) Imposed strict new deadlines and requirements dealing with urban smog, municipal incinerators, and toxic emissions; enacted program for controlling acid rain.	Partial preemption
National Voter Registration Act (1993) Required states to provide all eligible citizens the chance to register to vote when they apply for renewal of their driver's license.	Direct order
Ban on Internet sales tax (rider on 1998 appropriations law) Placed a three-year moratorium on state sales taxes on Internet commerce and created a commission of state and industry representatives to recommend permanent policy.	Direct order
No Child Left Behind Act (2001) Established standards for performance of schools with frequent standardized testing required and prescribed levels of credentialed instructors.	Crossover sanction
Help America Vote Act (2003) Established standards and partially financed changes in voting procedures.	Direct order
Fair Minimum Wage Act (2007) Increased the federal minimum wage from $5.15 to $7.25 per hour by 2009.	Direct order
Internet Tax Freedom Act Amendments (2007) Extended the moratorium on states charging sales tax on Internet purchases until 2001.	Direct order

Sources: Advisory Commission on Intergovernmental Relations and various issues of *Congressional Quarterly Weekly Report* and *CQ Weekly.*

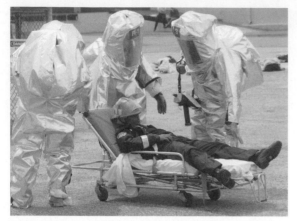

One new expansion of federal aid that has been popular across the states is increased funding for "first responders" after the September 11 terrorist attacks. Far away from Ground Zero or the Pentagon, emergency workers and medical personnel have received more training, equipment, and grants. The first responders pictured above are training in a federal facility in Anniston, Alabama.

interesting trends and characteristics. First, although federal grants were plentiful before the 1970s, few regulatory policies were in place. Second, since the 1970s the more coercive forms of regulation—direct orders and partial preemption—have been favored. Finally, the content of the policies reveals the political processes that produced them. Federal regulation of the states is concentrated on civil rights and the environment—the two sectors in which national majorities are likely to be at odds with state majorities. The same policy disagreements also may explain why coercion is such a favored policy instrument today. Regulatory statutes compel states to administer policies they would spurn if federal regulations did not legally require their compliance.

When members of Congress pass a law that obligates the states to provide particular services, they are yielding to a temptation all politicians share: the desire to respond to some citizens' demands without being held responsible for the costs. In forcing the states to pay for a program, members are imposing costs for which they will not be held accountable. Like the grants process, mandates deprive state political representatives of their rightful decision-making authority. Of greater concern to fiscal conservatives, unfunded mandates increase government spending. In 1995 President Bill Clinton and the Republican Congress agreed to rein in future temptations to "spend" the states' revenues. The result was the Unfunded Mandates Reform Act, which required that new federal laws pay for the programs and regulations they imposed on the states. A 1998 study, however, found that the law was exerting minimal constraint on mandates.[25] Perhaps the temptation to respond to demands for services while avoiding costs overwhelms the ideologies of even conservative politicians. In any event, Congress has continued to enact preemptive and mandate legislation.

Federalism: A Byproduct of National Policy

No feature of American government has been more dramatically transformed during the twentieth century than federal-state relations. Some of the most important contributions to this development have come through sudden bursts of national policymaking in which the federal government has assumed jurisdiction over and responsibility for large sectors of public policy once reserved to the states. President Roosevelt's New Deal response to the Depression and President Johnson's Great Society initiatives against poverty in America are two notable examples. It is instructive that both occurred when the Democratic Party controlled the White House and enjoyed the largest majorities in Congress ever seen in the twentieth century. In other instances, changes in federal-state relations have occurred more gradually and inconspicuously as interest groups and constituencies have pressed for national action after failing to win in the states. On still other occasions, the states themselves have invited federal participation to tap federal funding or to institute federal oversight and sanctioning authority to solve their own collective action problems.

The nationalization of public policy that proceeded from these causes did not arise from some grand design. Rather, it occurred as politicians sought solutions to problems and responded to the demands of their constituencies. No one had a stake in trying to rationalize intergovernmental relations or wrest authority away from the states. In this sense, then, the condition of modern federalism has had little to do with responses to collective action dilemmas and much to do with the interplay of political interests. And if the behavior of recent presidents and Congresses is any indication, federal-state relations will continue to evolve in this way.

In Chapter 4 we turn to a series of national decisions that even more dramatically refashioned federalism in America. The issue is civil rights for African Americans. The Civil War, Reconstruction, and the civil rights movement of the 1960s all required vigorous national action against entrenched state policies instituting slavery and, later, segregation. Southerners, recognizing that their positions on slavery and segregation were untenable, nevertheless sought to rationalize and defend their policies from the higher ground of federalism. The Confederacy's only president, Jefferson Davis, went to his grave steadfastly maintaining that the South's secession was not about slavery but about states' rights. Nearly a century later, Alabama governor George Wallace used the same rhetoric when confronted by federal officers seeking to enforce national laws and court orders. Because of the South's experience with civil rights, federalism came to be viewed as a hollow ruse that could be brushed aside without serious consideration whenever national action appeared necessary.

logic.cqpress.com

Key Terms

block grant, 129

cutthroat competition, 119

dual federalism, 101

elastic clause, 105

enumerated powers, 105

externality, 96

federalism, 99

grants-in-aid, 128

matching grant, 129

nationalization, 101

preemption legislation, 128

race to the bottom, 119

shared federalism, 101

states' right, 96

Tenth Amendment, 106

unitary government, 99

Suggested Readings

Beer, Samuel H. *To Make a Nation: The Rediscovery of American Federalism.* Cambridge: Belknap Press of Harvard University Press, 1993. Beer reviews the history of American federalism, its roots in traditional republican theory, and its modern evolution.

Campbell, Ballard C. *The Growth of American Government: Governance from the Cleveland Era to the Present.* Bloomington: Indiana University Press, 1995. Another historical survey of nationalization that focuses almost exclusively on the national government.

Kettl, Donald H. *System under Stress: Homeland Security and American Politics, Second Edition.* Washington, D.C.: CQ Press, 2007. This balanced look at federal, state, and local responses to the September 11, 2001, attacks examines the system-wide failures that led to the disaster—such as poor coordination among the nation's intelligence agencies—and assessing the consequences for the bureaucracy.

Lowry, William R. *The Dimensions of Federalism: State Governments and Pollution Control Policies.* Durham: Duke University Press, 1992. A study of shared federalism in water pollution policy that finds a stronger state presence than is commonly assumed.

Peterson, Paul E., Barry G. Rabe, and Kenneth K. Wong. *When Federalism Works.* Washington, D.C.: Brookings, 1986. A thorough and authoritative study of modern federalism in America.

Skowronek, Stephen. *Building a New American State: The Expansion of National Administrative Capacities, 1877–1920.* New York: Cambridge University Press, 1982. A modern classic on the institutional conflicts involved in shifting the center of public policy from the states to Washington.

Wiebe, Robert H. *The Search for Order, 1877–1920.* New York: Hill and Wang, 1967. An authoritative, well-written historical survey of the nationalization of American life.

Review Questions

1. What are the main differences between unitary, confederal, and federal governments? Which type of government is most common?

2. Most of the Framers felt that the Constitution adequately protected the states against encroachment by the national government. How then did proponents of nationalization succeed in expanding the power of the national government?

3. When states encounter problems that cross state borders, why don't they just make formal agreements with each other to solve the problems? What happens in the absence of such arrangements?

4. Why would national majorities sometimes find it easier to work through the national government than through state governments? What are some examples of policy areas in which this strategy has been used?

5. What factors facilitated the expansion of national powers in the New Deal and Great Society programs?

6. What are the three main types of collective action problems faced by state governments? Give an example of each.

7. What sorts of groups find it more efficient to lobby for policy changes at the national level? What sorts of groups might prefer to do it at the state level?

8. How did the Supreme Court's decisions in *McCulloch v. Maryland* and *Gibbons v. Ogden* help pave the way for the expansionist role of the national government over a century later?

9. What are unfunded mandates? What four general forms can these mandates take? Why does the federal government increasingly rely on these mandates?

Exercises

The Invisible Amendment?

In this chapter the authors argue that the supremacy and elastic clauses have reduced the Tenth Amendment to "little more than a truism." Go to the FindLaw LawCrawler search engine (http://lawcrawler.findlaw.com) and search for the keyword "Tenth Amendment" (in quotes) under the category "U.S. Government Sites." How many sites do you find? What kind of sites do they appear to be? Then do the same searches for the First, Second, Fourth, Fifth, Ninth, and Fourteenth Amendments. Then do a full-text search for the Tenth Amendment in FindLaw's database of First Circuit Court decisions (http://findLaw.com/casecode/courts/1st.html). Repeat for the other amendments.

It Depends on What the Definition of "Exclusive" Is. . . .

Refer to Figure 3-2 in your text. Take note of the "exclusive" powers of state governments. Then go to Louisiana State University's master listing of U.S. federal government agencies (www.lib. lsu.edu/gov/fedgov.html). Try to locate at least one federal agency involved in each of the exclusive state powers. Then go to a state government's Web site (see Yahoo's master listing of all state government Web sites at http://dir.yahoo.com/government/u_s__government) and try to find examples of states performing a power exclusively given to the national government.

CHAPTER

4

Civil Rights

How could a nation that embraced the Declaration of Independence's creed that "all men are created equal" condone slavery?

Why would a majority in society ever seek to extend and protect the rights of its minorities in the face of huge costs—even those imposed by a tragic civil war?

Does America's constitutional system impede or promote the cause of civil rights?

Are "civil rights" generic, or do we define them differently across groups according to issues for which they seek protection?

A ll nineteen hijackers who coordinated, commandeered, and launched, the September 11, 2001, attacks were Middle Eastern males. In the subsequent investigations, authorities found that other terrorist cell members implicated in the assaults were also Middle Eastern.

For the next five months, as federal agencies issued reports and advisories about terrorist threats, their communiqués frequently included mug shots of Arab suspects, who allegedly were in the United States. Unavoidably, perhaps, government officials and ordinary citizens alike began to regard male Arab strangers with suspicion. This wariness took on more specificity as the Justice Department systematically interviewed twelve hundred male, Middle Eastern visa holders in the United States; then– Attorney General John Ashcroft unveiled new procedures to expedite expulsion hearings for people who had overstayed or violated their visas; some pilots and flight crews refused to fly with suspicious-looking passengers (including, in one case, Rep. Darrell Issa, R-Calif., and, in another, a member of President George W. Bush's secret service). Critics of these measures charged discrimination and **racial profiling** (identifying suspects solely on the basis of race or ethnicity), starting a national debate over how government and airline officials should prevent the next terrorist attack, which nearly everyone thought was imminent.

One national survey taken soon after September 11 found that 58 percent of the public endorsed more intensive security checks for Arabs, while two-thirds supported "random stops" of people of Middle Eastern descent.[1] Arab American support groups and some local American Civil Liberties Union (ACLU) chapters opened "hotlines"

President Lyndon B. Johnson and Rev. Martin Luther King Jr. meet in the cabinet room of the White House, March 18, 1966.

Shortly after the attack on Pearl Harbor, President Franklin Roosevelt began issuing executive orders that placed restrictions on Japanese Americans living on the West Coast. Eventually, more than 110,000 Japanese Americans—including native-born U.S. citizens—were removed to internment camps throughout the nation. The internees were given little time to dispose of their homes, businesses, or other property, causing financial ruin for many.

for registering discrimination complaints. Civil liberties watchdogs argued that only a tiny fraction of individuals posed a threat, therefore treating with suspicion everyone who fit the Middle Eastern profile constituted discrimination. The reaction to September 11 recalled the internment of Japanese Americans that took place nearly sixty years earlier. After Japan bombed Pearl Harbor in 1941, the same fear of imminent attack—fueled by government alerts, air-raid drills, and other civil defense activities—gripped the nation. Within months government officials spawned the plan, now recognized as clearly unwarranted, to deport thousands of West Coast Japanese Americans to internment camps for the duration of World War II.

The Transportation Department recalled this misguided relocation as it dealt with the September 11 crisis. To counteract reports of overbearing airport screening, the department issued rules for airport and other security personnel that sought to balance protecting the public's right to security with preventing civil rights violations. Reminding officials about the illegality of discrimination, the department prohibited screeners from giving people special attention based solely on their "race, color, national origin, religion, sex, or ancestry." Arab-looking males who spoke no English were to be screened no differently than other passengers, including, for example, the elderly non-Arab women whose knitting needles were suddenly seized by security guards.[2]

Critics of the policy countered that because dozens of known terrorists fit the same distinctive gender and ethnic profile, public officials are justified in using this information to identify hard-to-find suspects. One nationally prominent civil libertarian condoned racial profiling as "entirely appropriate," repeating former Supreme Court justice Robert Jackson's declaration that "the Constitution is not a suicide pact." In any event, observed one leading civil rights lawyer, it was expecting too much to ask screeners who must "make on the spot decisions about whom to detain and whom to question [to] disregard ethnicity."[3]

The ongoing racial profiling debate will not be resolved any time soon. If for no other reason, it is notable for our consideration simply because it is still taking place. Remarkably not long ago a racial profiling policy would have failed to generate this intense civic discussion. The controversy reminds us that civil rights apply to everyone. For many years, the term *civil rights* referred almost exclusively to the privileges of

African Americans and the history of civil rights in the United States concerned the emancipation of African Americans—first from slavery and then, in the twentieth century, from segregation. The legacy concerns the rights of everyone.

Shortly before September 11, in fact, racial profiling was already a familiar news item. Police departments from New Jersey to Los Angeles were under investigation for stopping black motorists without cause. By the end of summer 2001, nine states had banned such practices. And in August the Bush administration's Justice Department

After a 1978 incident and subsequent lawsuit in which state troopers used their firearms to apprehend four minority motorists on the New Jersey Turnpike, that state's law enforcement practices have come under intense scrutiny for racial profiling by both private rights groups and the Department of Justice.

had launched a national investigation into the pervasiveness of racial profiling. Despite the apprehension of another attack, concerns with racial or ethnic profiling have continued to generate protective laws and enforcement. By the beginning of 2005 twenty states had enacted some form of antiprofiling laws, and in 2003 the Justice Department issued guidelines for all federal officials to limit the influence of racial and ethnic information in searching for suspected terrorists.

The new federal laws, administrative practices, and agencies to secure the rights of African Americans became available to enforce the rights of "new" claimants. Voting rights laws authorizing Justice Department intervention against discriminatory practices in the 1960s were summoned by Hispanic voters fearing arbitrary rules, such as challenges of citizenship, that would disenfranchise them in the 2004 presidential election. The civil rights struggle of African Americans ends with all Americans changing their view of their own rights and privileges. In this respect, the debate over how closely airport screeners should consider the ethnicity and gender of passengers reflects prior debates over the civil rights of African Americans.

What Are Civil Rights?

Throughout the nation's history, Americans have applied the terms **civil rights** and **civil liberties** to a variety of rights and privileges. Although they have sometimes been used interchangeably, *rights* and *liberties* do offer useful distinctions for organizing our discussion in this and the next chapter. We classify as civil liberties the Constitution's protections *from* government power, meaning the government *may not* take these freedoms—including the freedoms of speech, liberty, and the right to privacy—away. Typically, violations of these liberties occur when some government agency, at any level, oversteps its authority. Civil rights, on the other hand, represent those protections *by* government power, or things government must secure on behalf of its citizens. The crucial difference is that civil rights require governments to act, whereas civil liberties are well served when government does nothing.[4]

In colonial times civil rights equaled "civic" rights—protections against arbitrary action by the distant British crown. Although the term *civil rights* was not commonly used until the late 1760s, when colonial Americans rallied to the slogan "No taxation without representation," the colonists were clearly seeking these rights, including the right to vote and have their views represented in the British Parliament. Thomas Jefferson's eloquent statement in the Declaration of Independence that all governments must defer to humanity's "unalienable Rights" of "Life, Liberty and the pursuit of Happiness" gave the Revolutionary War its moral certitude.

Once they had gained their independence and established republican institutions, Americans turned from seeking protection from an arbitrary and distant government to looking for it from one another. In *Federalist* No. 10 James Madison explored whether a majority of citizens could use government authority to strip adversaries of their rights and thereby gain a permanent advantage. This prospect bothered leaders on both sides of the Constitution's ratification issue. For Madison and the other nationalists, the pluralism of large republic provided the best insurance against such factionally inspired tyranny; as the number and diversity of groups increased, the likelihood that any one group could impose its will on another decreased. But Patrick Henry and others opposing ratification insisted on a bill of rights to further deter the new national government from usurping power. Along with voting (an issue the Constitution resolved by allowing the states to set voting requirements), virtually everyone's list of freedoms included freedom of speech, free assembly, and a free press.

Modern-day "civil rights" encompass much more than these "civic" rights of political expression and participation. They also include safeguards against any effort by government and dominant groups in a community to subjugate another group and take unfair, mostly economic, advantage of it. Before the American Civil War, southern governments teamed up with white slave owners to configure state laws and institutions to legalize and preserve slavery. (In most southern states, for example, it was illegal for slave masters to free their slaves.) Many decades later, segregation in the South, also regulated by the states, dominated virtually all interpersonal contact between the races. Civil rights, then, also include the rights of individuals in their relations with one another: to live free from bondage and intimidation, to enter into contracts and own property, to have access to businesses that serve the public, and to enjoy equal educational opportunities.

The Civil Rights of African Americans

In December 1997 Bill Lann Lee, a second-generation Chinese American, opened his acceptance statement as President Bill Clinton's acting assistant attorney general for civil rights by describing his post as "haunted by the ghosts of slavery, the Civil War, Jim Crow." He then proceeded to cite modern instances of racial, ethnic, and religious discrimination.[5] Indeed, as Lee knew and the history books describe, African Americans have been engaged in a two-hundred-year struggle for civil rights, spanning slavery to full citizenship. As we will see in this chapter and the next, the results have redefined the rights and liberties of *all* Americans.

The history of black civil rights provided a laboratory to test James Madison's ideas on democracy in America, laid out in his *Federalist* essays. Dominant white majorities throughout the South instituted slavery—and later segregation—to gain a permanent advantage over the black minority. And what is the solution to such tyranny? As Madison argued in *Federalist* No. 10, a diverse national community would be less inclined than state-level majorities to engage in tyranny and more likely to halt it.

The history of black civil rights follows Madison's script in another respect. The effort to secure civil rights rested less on making formal rules—which Madison noted had little impact on intemperate majorities—and more on configuring politics to allow society's competing interests to check one another. This chapter, as did Madison, recognizes civil rights in America as products of the political process. But the abuses of slavery and segregation endured for almost two centuries before the national majority struck out against local tyranny. The effect of institutions on democracy explain this disturbing situation. For one thing, the Framers rejected a national veto over all state laws, as Madison had repeatedly proposed. Public policy, such as public safety and regulation of elections, was left to state control, allowing slavery to flourish within the South.

African Americans faced two major obstacles in securing rights. First, the Constitution reserves important authority for the states, such as the power to determine voting eligibility. It also separates powers among the three branches of government, making it difficult for national majorities to control the federal government to the extent required to strike against tyranny in the states.

Madison's observation that government is controlled by "men" and not "angels" sums up the second obstacle to obtaining civil rights for African Americans. People do not engage in costly behavior without some expected return. Madison, recognizing that citizens and politicians alike act most forcefully when they have a personal stake in the outcome, believed that tyranny could best be avoided by empowering every faction to look out for its own interests. But what of a faction without the capacity to defend itself? This predicament is central to the nation's long ordeal over civil rights for African Americans. Indeed, politics based on self-interest in a fragmented constitutional system largely explains why it took so long to eradicate slavery, segregation, and other discrimination. Instead, the real question is why the civil rights of America's black population were ever addressed at all.

The Politics of Black Civil Rights

The efforts to seek civil rights for African Americans took different forms at different times. Notably, in 1787 Benjamin Franklin convened an abolition society meeting in his home and invited delegates to the Constitutional Convention to attend. Throughout

Do not look at the Negro.

His earthly problems are ended.

Instead, look at the seven WHITE children who gaze at this gruesome spectacle.

Is it horror or gloating on the face of the neatly dressed seven-year-old girl on the right?

Is the tiny four-year-old on the left old enough, one wonders, to comprehend the barbarism her elders have perpetrated?

Rubin Stacy, the Negro, who was lynched at Fort Lauderdale, Florida, on July 19, 1935, for "threatening and frightening a white woman," suffered PHYSICAL torture for a few short hours. But what psychological havoc was being wrought in the minds of the white children? Into what kinds of citizens

Between 1882 and 1950, 4,729 lynchings were reported in the United States. African Americans were the victims in about three-quarters of the cases. This 1930s NAACP poster graphically featured this tyrannical practice designed to intimidate the entire black population.

the antebellum era and during the Civil War, a small but persistent abolitionist movement forced the nation to face the discrepancy between the ideal of "Life, Liberty and the pursuit of Happiness" and the enslavement of 10 percent of its population. Emancipation shifted the issue from fundamental "life and liberty" rights to those of full citizenship.* Several years later the Fifteenth Amendment granted former slaves the right to vote,† but another century would pass before most could safely exercise this right. With civic rights secured, the dominant issue again shifted, this time to equal opportunity in the marketplace—particularly in education, employment, and housing.

By and large, national majorities have over the decades consistently favored the civil rights for African Americans, but only twice did they strike out forcefully against discrimination. The first time was Reconstruction after the Civil War; the second was the national attack on segregation in the 1960s. Why were rights advanced at these particular moments in American history and not at others? A look at the successes and failures will answer this question and illuminate the conditions under which national majorities are able to dictate national policy.

The Height of Slavery: 1808–1865

Late in 1807, with the Constitution's prohibition against the federal government's regulation of the slave trade about to expire, Congress passed a law ending the importation of slaves. Southern representatives in Congress, not yet aware that the rise of "King Cotton" would soon dictate a slave-centered, plantation economy, did not vigorously contest the new law. In fact, some probably anticipated that the restricted supply of new slaves might drive up the market value of their human property. Thus the nation took this first step toward eradicating slavery with deceptive ease. It would never be easy again.

---

*As late as 1858 Abraham Lincoln, in his famous Senate race debates in Illinois with Stephen Douglas, distinguished between citizenship rights based on equality and fundamental rights. He protected his flank by stating there was "no purpose to introduce political and social equality between the white and black races." But then, in one of the most progressive statements made by any elected officeholder of the time, he asserted: "There is no reason in the world why the negro is not entitled to all the natural rights enumerated in the Declaration of Independence. . . . I hold that he is as much entitled to these as the white man." Donald G. Nieman, *Promises to Keep: African-Americans and the Constitutional Order, 1776 to the Present* (New York: Oxford University Press, 1991), 43.

†This achievement stemmed in part from the Senate's insistence that the former Confederate states ratify the amendment as a condition of their reentry into the Union.

Over the next decade slavery remained a side issue only because the northern and southern states carefully maintained regional balance in the Senate, thereby preserving the South's veto over national policy. This balance required matching states' entry— one slave state with one free state—into the Union. As we learned earlier, institutions created to achieve one goal can over time come to serve other purposes. Where equal apportionment of the Senate reassured small states that their interests would not be ignored in the new national government, by the 1820s this same rule guaranteed the South a veto over policy curtailing slavery. Many northern politicians found the practice objectionable, but did not press for its eradication against intransigent southerners for fear of fracturing fragile regional party alliances. Indeed, the North hoped that slavery would eventually wither away.

THE MISSOURI COMPROMISE. Then in 1819 the citizens of Missouri, most of whom had emigrated from the slave states of Kentucky and Tennessee, petitioned Congress for admission as a slave state. Instead of shriveling up, slavery threatened to expand beyond its southern borders, upset the balance, and ignite the nation. "Like a fire bell in the night," wrote a retired Thomas Jefferson, the political conflagration he foresaw "awakened and filled me with terror."[6]

After months of debate in Washington and throughout the country, Congress enacted the Missouri Compromise in 1820. The plan matched Missouri's entry as a slave state with Maine's as a free state, thereby maintaining the balance in the Senate between free and slave states. Moreover, the South agreed to accept Missouri's southern border as the northern boundary beyond which slavery could not extend in the future (see Map 4-1). The boundary at latitude 36°30' stretched to the end of the Louisiana Territory, where Spain's possessions began. Once again, slavery appeared to be fenced in. The compromise itself was a classic "political" solution—one that was not entirely satisfactory to either side but that allowed agreement on a national policy applicable to the foreseeable future.

For the next decade or so this compromise worked. It began to unravel, however, as territories applying for statehood were not conveniently paired off as slave and free states. Gradually southern senators realized that, under the current formula, their ability to block national policy was doomed as more free than slave states joined the Union with continued westward expansion. Thus they began searching for an effective alternative to their Senate veto that would ensure continuation of the institution of slavery.

Meanwhile, the containment strategy also was losing favor in the North, where a small but highly vocal group of abolitionists had never accepted the compromise. More broadly, the abolitionist movement, under the banner of the Liberty Party, reminded the nation of its hypocrisy in condoning slavery. Although few voters endorsed its outright eradication, they were angry about slavery's territorial expansion.*

---

*After its recent war with Mexico, the United States had annexed territory in the Southwest, almost all of it falling into the slavery zone. Moreover, California was petitioning for statehood, and southerners were proposing that the 36°30' line be projected to the Pacific Ocean and California be split into one slave and one free state.

Map 4-1 The Missouri Compromise and the State of the Union, 1820

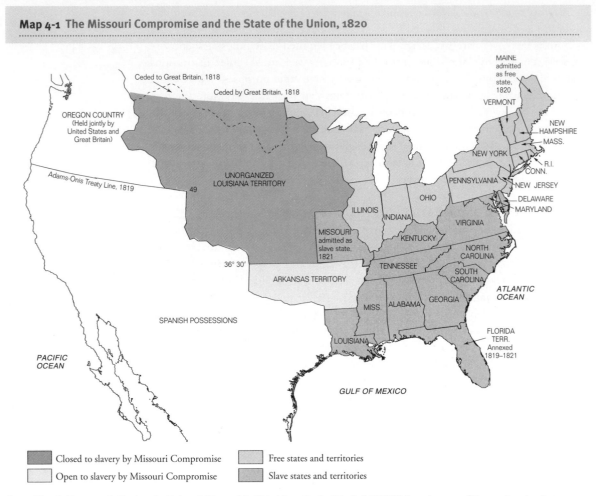

Ceded to Great Britain, 1818

Ceded by Great Britain, 1818

MAINE admitted as free state, 1820

VERMONT

OREGON COUNTRY (Held jointly by United States and Great Britain)

NEW HAMPSHIRE

MASS.

NEW YORK

Adams-Onis Treaty Line, 1819

UNORGANIZED LOUISIANA TERRITORY

49

R.I.

CONN.

PENNSYLVANIA

NEW JERSEY

OHIO

DELAWARE

MARYLAND

ILLINOIS

INDIANA

VIRGINIA

MISSOURI admitted as slave state, 1821

KENTUCKY

36° 30'

NORTH CAROLINA

ARKANSAS TERRITORY

TENNESSEE

SOUTH CAROLINA

ATLANTIC OCEAN

SPANISH POSSESSIONS

MISS.

ALABAMA

GEORGIA

FLORIDA TERR. Annexed 1819–1821

LOUISIANA

PACIFIC OCEAN

GULF OF MEXICO

Closed to slavery by Missouri Compromise

Open to slavery by Missouri Compromise

Free states and territories

Slave states and territories

Source: Mary B. Norton et al., *People and a Nation: A History of the United States,* 2 vols., 5th ed. © 1999 Wadsworth, a part of Cengage Learning, Inc. Reproduced by permission.

THE WILMOT PROVISO AND THE COMPROMISE OF 1850. In 1846 David Wilmot, a Democratic representative from Pennsylvania, introduced a bill that would have gutted the compromise by banning slavery in the recently acquired territories. Wilmot denied any "squeamish sensitivities" or "morbid sympathy for the slave." Rather, he professed devotion to "the rights of white freemen . . . [and] white free labor."[7] Simply put, slave labor depressed wages for free, white workers. The Wilmot Proviso was introduced twice and passed the House of Representatives both times, but it made no headway in the evenly divided Senate. Still, the failure of Wilmot's proposal eventually led significant numbers of northern whites to recognize they had a stake in containing slavery.

By 1848 Wilmot's allies joined the abolitionists in the new antislavery Free Soil Party. Its election slate that year was headed by presidential candidate Martin Van

Buren, who already had served one term as president, as a Democrat, in 1836. His 1848 campaign revolved around a single issue: opposition to the extension of slavery on behalf of "free labor." The Free Soil Party managed to scare the two major political parties, the Democrats and the Whigs, by winning 10 percent of the national popular vote and finishing second in several states. Six years later the Free Soil Party joined a broader coalition against slavery's extension that called itself the Republican Party.

In 1850, the Missouri Compromise buckled under the weight of southern and northern grievances. Southerners had complained that runaway slaves who reached the North via the "Underground Railroad"—a network of abolitionists who hid slaves and provided them with transportation northward—were not being returned to their owners. At the same time, northerners were repulsed by slave auctions in Washington, D.C., "within the shadow of the Capitol." But the compromise finally collapsed when California applied in 1849 for admission to the Union as a free state. If the South agreed to admit California, it would lose its ability to block legislation in the Senate. Ultimately the South did agree, but only in return for passage of the **Fugitive Slave Law** compelling northerners to honor southerners' property claims to slaves. Moreover, the new Compromise of 1850, introduced by aging Whig senator Henry Clay of Kentucky, allowed the residents of the territories to decide for themselves whether to apply for statehood as a slave or free state.

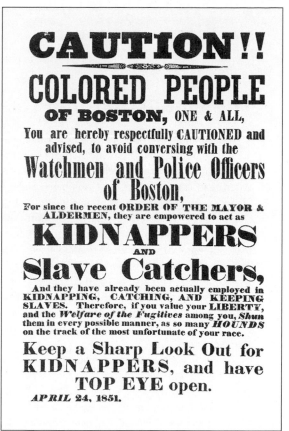

The Fugitive Slave Law of 1850 forced law enforcement authorities in both the North and South to act as slaveholders' agents in seizing and returning their "property." As this broadside warned, even free African Americans were in danger of being seized and sent into slavery as unscrupulous law enforcement officials colluded with slaveholders in making bogus claims that these free citizens were actually runaway slaves.

DRED SCOTT GALVANIZES THE NORTH. The

South may have lost its Senate veto, but a few years later it would unexpectedly acquire a new one. In 1857 the Supreme Court delivered one of its most unfortunate decisions in *Dred Scott v. Sandford.*[8] With every justice writing a separate opinion, a 7–2 majority of the Court concurred that the federal government could not prevent slavery in the territories. The Herculean effort to legislate mutually acceptable policy over the previous half-century was undone in a single decision by the nine unelected justices. The mostly southern majority argued that the Constitution's Framers had never intended African Americans to be citizens. Consequently, African Americans enjoyed "no rights which a white man was bound to respect," and any federal law that interfered with the right of an individual to his property, including slaves, was unconstitutional. Sympathetic lower-court judges appeared ready to extend the logic of this argument and rule that *state* laws banning slavery also were

The Emancipation Proclamation

Emancipation of the slaves was born of war rather than politics, but its planning and implementation were nonetheless highly strategic. When read carefully, President Abraham Lincoln's Emancipation Proclamation, issued in the fall of 1862, appears to have been composed more with an eye to encouraging southern defections from the Confederacy than to emancipating slaves. Lincoln announced that slaves would be freed in those states that persisted with the rebellion. Slavery was to remain intact in the border states that had stayed in the Union, and even in those sections of the Confederacy that had fallen under Union control.

This policy exposed the president to the criticism that he had failed to free the slaves where he could and freed them where he could not. But by mapping emancipation this way, he prevented it from becoming politically divisive among the Union states (a few still allowed slave ownership), while simultaneously trying to drive a wedge into the Confederacy. Moreover, the rebel states might have to deal with slaves asserting their freedom. Not until the 1864 presidential campaign did Lin-

coln openly endorse the universal abolition of slavery.

In 1863 David Gilmour Blythe depicted a homespun Lincoln (his rail-splitter's maul is in the foreground) at work in his study writing the Emancipation Proclamation. Pushed to one side, unheeded, are the states' rights theories of John C. Calhoun and John Randolph. Instead, Lincoln rests his hand on the Holy Bible and heeds Andrew Jackson's call: "The Union Must & Shall Be Preserved."

unconstitutional. The specter of the whole nation being opened to slave-holding by judicial fiat galvanized the North. Campaigning vigorously on the slogan "Free Soil, Free Labor, Free Men," Republican candidate Abraham Lincoln won the 1860 presidential election. So too did so many fellow Republican congressional candidates that this young party took majority control of the House of Representatives and, in alliance with splinter parties, formed a narrow antislavery majority in the Senate. For the first time in American history, the president and a majority of both houses of Congress were aligned against slavery's extension.

Recognizing that the seemingly insurmountable transaction costs to effective majority action had finally and suddenly been swept away, the South did not wait to contest new antislavery policy in Congress. Once president-elect Lincoln announced that the national government would no longer tolerate "the minority [the South] over the majority," the southern states seceded with South Carolina the first to proclaim its independence on December 20, 1860. By June 1861 ten more states had left the Union and established a new, confederation-style government. On April 12, 1861, the "Confederates" fired on Fort Sumter, a federal garrison in Charleston harbor. The American Civil War had begun, a war that would claim more than six hundred thousand American soldiers dead and many thousands more maimed for life.

Thus the first half-century of racial politics in the United States closely followed Madison's prediction of tyranny in the states unconstrained by national majorities. In the South white majorities enlisted state authority to preserve slavery. They were aided and abetted by their agents in the Senate who, as Madison had warned, succeeded in frustrating national action. Only the decisive 1860 Republican electoral victory and the secession of the slave states from the Union gave the national majority sufficient control over government to enforce its preferences. Along the way, strategic politicians, like Wilmot and Lincoln, transformed a losing issue into a winning one by focusing narrowly on the territories and the interests of northern whites more concerned about their own welfare than that of slaves. In the end, this appeal enabled these politicians to win control of the government and eventually eradicate slavery (see box "The Emancipation Proclamation").

Reconstruction: 1865–1877

In the five-year period from 1865 to 1870, slaves were formally emancipated (Thirteenth Amendment), granted citizenship (Fourteenth Amendment), and guaranteed the right to vote (Fifteenth Amendment). At the close of the Civil War, however, only a handful of Union states gave black citizens equal access to the ballot box. Some subjected African Americans to special criteria—such as proof of property ownership and literacy—that effectively disenfranchised most of them. Other northern states simply barred African Americans from voting.* For most states, then, freeing slaves and granting them full-fledged citizenship were two different things, and the latter was regarded as radical even by abolitionists. Militant abolitionist newspaper publisher William Lloyd Garrison concluded that, "according to the laws of development and progress," the franchise "is not practical." † So how did the Fifteenth Amendment manage to clear, with remarkable alacrity, the formidable hurdles of the amendment process?

The ability to count is invaluable to a politician. Shortly after the war ended in 1865, House Republican leader Thaddeus Stevens of Pennsylvania calculated the

---

*Of the eleven referendum votes held from 1865 through 1869 in eight northern states on constitutional changes to provide African Americans with the ballot, only those in Iowa and Minnesota in 1868 succeeded. The white voters of Illinois, Indiana, Pennsylvania, and New Jersey never voted on the issue, which may have indicated a higher intensity of racial prejudice in those states than in Connecticut, New York, and Ohio, where equal suffrage was defeated. La Wanda and John H. Cox, "Negro Suffrage and Republican Politics: The Problem of Motivation in Reconstruction Historiography," *Journal of Southern History* 33 (August 1967): 318–319.

†Another enemy of slavery who conceded that freedmen could not be transformed instantly into full citizens was Republican senator Charles Sumner of Massachusetts, who before the war had earned his abolitionist credentials the hard way by being severely caned by an enraged southern member from the House after a floor speech denouncing slavery.

probable partisan makeup of Congress after the South returned to the Union. Taking into account that African Americans now counted as full rather than three-fifths citizens for apportioning congressional seats across the states, Stevens estimated that the South would gain thirteen seats over its prewar level. Moreover, with southern legislatures busily enacting laws, called **black codes,** that effectively prevented former slaves from voting (and thus from supporting the party of Lincoln), Stevens rightly suspected that all thirteen seats would be added to the Democratic column. Southerners, he noted, "with their kindred Copperheads [Democrats] of the North, would always elect the President [as well as] control Congress."[9]

The outlook was bleak for the Republican Party. Even as Andrew Johnson of Tennessee, Lincoln's Democratic successor in the White House, planned for the South's rapid readmission to the Union, congressional Republicans were staring at possible defeat in the next national election. The Republican response was Reconstruction; whereby under the watchful eye of federal troops, the South would be transformed from a slave society into a free one in which African Americans would fully enjoy the privileges of citizenship. At least that was the plan.

THE FOURTEENTH AND FIFTEENTH AMENDMENTS. The Republicans' foray into political and social reconstruction began with the Fourteenth Amendment. It opens with a straightforward definition of citizenship that encompasses former slaves: "All persons born or naturalized in the United States, and subject to the jurisdiction thereof, are citizens of the United States and of the State wherein they reside." It then declares that no state shall "deprive any person of life, liberty, or property, without the *due process* of law; nor deny to any person within its jurisdiction the *equal protection* of the laws" (emphasis added). (Chapter 5 examines the full impact of the due process and equal protection clauses on the liberties of all Americans.)

Section 2 of the Fourteenth Amendment turns to the immediate business of Reconstruction. It reaffirms the constitutional prescription of apportioning seats in the House of Representatives according to a state's population, but then makes an exception: if a state fails to allow black males to vote in federal and state elections, the number of seats allocated to it will be reduced proportionately. A purely political calculation dictated the provision of additional seats only where the Republican Party stood a fighting chance of winning. The amendment was intended to protect two constituencies: African Americans in the South and the Republican majority in Washington, D.C. After the war, as before, civil rights rode on the shoulders of partisan, self-interested politics.

But how did this skillfully crafted amendment gain the necessary support when new legislatures in the South were rejecting it by nearly unanimous majorities? The Republicans in Congress, enjoying veto-proof majorities and a recent landslide victory in the 1866 midterm elections, devised an ingenious plan to foil southern opposition. The First Reconstruction Act of 1867 disbanded the governments of the southern states (with the exception of Tennessee, which already had been readmitted to the Union), thereby voiding their votes against the amendment. It then replaced the state governments with five military districts, headed by generals and administered by more than twenty thousand northern troops. To ensure ratification once the state governments were reinstituted, the law bluntly extended the vote to all freedmen and withheld it from the white, rebel ex-soldiers. In Louisiana, where the racial composition of the adult male population was roughly evenly split, black voter registration soon doubled that of whites.* Then, putting one last nail in the Confederacy's coffin, Congress made readmission to the Union contingent on a state's ratification of the Fourteenth Amendment.

The narrow partisan purpose of Reconstruction is evident in what the Republican policy omitted. Abolitionists and black leaders pressed Congress for land reform and a degree of economic independence for slaves from their former masters. Instead, all that the freed slaves got from Congress was the ballot. Republican cabinet secretary Gideon Welles concluded cynically, "It is evident that intense partisanship rather than philanthropy is the root of the movement." [10]

Two years later congressional Republicans sought to make the black franchise inviolable by passing and sending to the states the Fifteenth Amendment. Quickly ratified, it simply states, "The right of citizens of the United States to vote shall not be denied or abridged by the United States or by any State on account of race, color, or previous condition of servitude."

RIGHTS LOST: THE FAILURE OF RECONSTRUCTION. Despite these efforts, Reconstruction's advancement of black civil rights proved temporary. Relying heavily on black support, Republicans dominated southern state legislatures for a few years, but white Democrats seized control of Tennessee and Virginia as early as 1869, and by 1877 all of the former Confederate states had reverted to white Democratic control. Once this happened, Reconstruction was doomed, and African Americans saw their newly acquired status as freed men and women slide back to near servitude.

Power slipped away from African Americans during these years for several reasons. Vigilante violence as a political resource erupted in the late 1860s. Murderous white rioters in New Orleans, Memphis, and other southern cities targeted politically active African Americans and their white allies. In the countryside, the Ku Klux Klan, a secret society of white supremacist men, perfected intimidation through selective brutality.

Meanwhile, northern politicians' commitment to Reconstruction was waning. After many Republicans went down to defeat in the 1874 midterm congressional elections, apparently because of an economic recession, the new Democratic majority in the House of Representatives refused to appropriate funds to support the military forces that remained in the South. Northern constituents wanted their sons returned home. Congress passed additional laws to protect the freed slaves, but without serious enforcement provisions, they offered African Americans in the distant South little real support. With the rise of the Ku Klux Klan, accompanied by the rapid demobilization of the occupying Union Army, the trajectory of southern politics became clear.

---

*Similarly, in Alabama there were approximately twenty thousand more white than black men but forty thousand more black voters. C. Vann Woodward, *The Burden of Southern History* (Baton Rouge: Louisiana State University Press, 1968), 98–99.

Originally titled *The Clansmen*, *The Birth of a Nation* is recognized both as one of the most important films in the development of American cinema and one of the most racist. D. W. Griffith's 1915 film was the first to use natural settings, night photography, original music, panning shots, moving cameras, and dozens of other innovations. It remains shocking today in part because it looks like a documentary. The blatant racism that depicted freed slaves as villains and the Ku Klux Klan as the salvation of humanity reveals the state of the nation's attitude toward African Americans at the time. It became a blockbuster hit, but not without severe criticism. President Woodrow Wilson described it as "like writing history with lightning. And my only regret is that it is all terribly true." Stung by the criticism, Griffith followed it with *Intolerance*, on the effects of bigotry and inhumanity. Though less famous, many critics consider it his greatest achievement.

Killed by the same short-term partisan considerations that gave birth to it, Reconstruction officially ended with the 1876 presidential election. The Democratic candidate, Samuel Tilden, came within one vote of an Electoral College majority, but in the disputed states of Florida and Louisiana both parties produced their own favorable vote counts. As a result, the election was thrown into the House of Representatives, where a Republican pledge to end Reconstruction induced southerners to break ranks and support the Republican candidate, Rutherford B. Hayes. In 1877 federal troops pulled out of the South, leaving African Americans at the mercy of their former masters.[11]

During the early post–Civil War years, therefore, the Constitution presented fewer barriers to majority rule than in any other period in American history. The Republican majority in Congress and the White House opted for a middle course of political reform. Rather than undertaking a massive social and economic reconstruction of the South, they limited Reconstruction to making the South Republican, thereby realizing the party's goal of remaining the nation's majority party and satisfying the interests of their constituents. Even so, local interests in northern congressional districts soon rose against this limited reconstruction. Twenty thousand war-weary northern soldiers remained in the South, and the government continued to assess high wartime taxes nationwide to achieve in the South what few white citizens anywhere would have tolerated in their own communities—the creation of a sizable black electorate. In the North voters no longer wanted to sacrifice to solve distant problems and the Republican majority soon lost the will to act. Full citizenship for African Americans would wait one hundred years for the emergence of northern politicians whose constituencies favored intervention in race relations in the South.

The Jim Crow Era and Segregation: 1877–1933

In the 1890s **Jim Crow laws** (named after a popular minstrel show character of the era) were adopted throughout the South to disenfranchise black citizens and physically separate African Americans and whites. These laws institutionalized **segregation** of African Americans and whites in their access to schools, hospitals, prisons, public parks, restrooms, housing, and public conveyances. Indeed, hardly any government service or social interaction between the races was unaffected.

But to secure segregation the southern states had to prevent black citizens from voting, and so they did. By the end of the century all southern states constructed a maze of electoral laws that systematically excluded African Americans from civic life. One common device, the **white primary,** excluded African Americans from voting in primary elections. Because winning the Democratic primary in the solidly Democratic South was tantamount to winning the general election, this law effectively disenfranchised southern black voters. Another effective barrier was the **poll tax** levied on all registered voters, which typically had to be paid months before the election.

Perhaps the most notorious and effective legal barrier was the **literacy test.** Local white registrars would require prospective black voters to read and interpret arcane passages of the state's constitution. Few could satisfy the registrars' rigorous demands, and by 1910 less than 10 percent of black males were voting in the South. These restrictive laws also caught many poor and illiterate whites. Most states, however, provided **grandfather clauses,** which exempted from these registration requirements those whose grandfathers had voted before the Civil War.

Without the backing of the Supreme Court, the southern state legislatures would have found it harder to strip away black civil rights. The Court generally upheld segregation and disenfranchisement laws against challenges. Conversely, when federal laws extending rights to African Americans were challenged, the Court summarily overturned them. The Court based these decisions on a tortuously narrow reading of the Fourteenth and Fifteenth Amendments. Consider this passage from the Fourteenth Amendment: "No State shall make or enforce any law which shall abridge the privileges or immunities of citizens of the United States." The Supreme Court interpreted this clause to mean only that states could not abridge privileges conferred explicitly by

Until federal laws in the 1960s banned segregation in public accommodations, the doctrine "separate but equal" pervaded every aspect of social contact between the races throughout the South. The policy differed little from South Africa's dismantled apartheid system.

the Constitution to the national government, such as unrestricted interstate travel and open navigation of rivers. The justices excluded state laws from the Bill of Rights' guarantees. Decades later, the Supreme Court would reject this interpretation of the Fourteenth Amendment and rediscover the broad national guarantees this clause provides.*

The *coup de grâce* came in 1896 when the Supreme Court, ruling in *Plessy v. Ferguson,* declared the South's Jim Crow laws and systematic segregation constitutional.[12] The case arose when shoemaker Homer Plessy, who was seven-eighths white (but still black, according to law), appealed his conviction for having violated Louisiana's segregation law by sitting in a "whites only" railroad car. The Court argued that the Fourteenth Amendment's guarantee of equal protection of the law referred only to "political" equality. If African Americans were socially inferior to whites, the Court reasoned, laws such as Louisiana's could reflect that inferiority so long as political equality was not compromised. The Court then ruled that government-enforced segregation of the races was constitutional as long as the facilities for African Americans and whites were equal. And apparently they were, the Court reasoned; after all, whites were prohibited from sitting in the black passenger car. With that ruling, the Court established nationally the **separate but equal doctrine,** which officially sanctioned segregation throughout the South for the next half-century. Dissenting justice John Marshall Harlan vigorously attacked the majority's reasoning in language that would provide a foundation for overturning the "separate but equal" doctrine a half-century later. Appearances of equality were a sham, he argued, "every one knows that the statute in question had its origin in the purpose, not so much to exclude white persons from railroad cars occupied by blacks, as to exclude colored people from coaches occupied by or assigned to white persons." †

---

*Similarly, interpreting the Fifteenth Amendment, the Supreme Court held that state laws denying voting rights to African Americans were permissible unless they could be shown to be motivated by race. By applying the poll tax or literacy test to everyone, or even claiming to, the southern legislatures could satisfy the Court.

†Why did a mostly Republican-appointed Supreme Court interpret the Fourteenth and Fifteenth Amendments in ways that negated Reconstruction? C. Vann Woodward reasonably conjectures that as Republican politicians reoriented their party toward rapidly emerging business constituencies, black civil rights became a low priority. See Woodward, *Reunion and Reaction: The Compromise of 1877 and the End of Reconstruction* (Boston: Little, Brown, 1966), 22–50.

Democratic Party Sponsorship of Civil Rights: 1933–1940s

From 1929 until 1933 the Republican Party presided over the worst depression in American history. Among the many victims of the economic hard times was the party itself. The Great Depression ended Republican dominance in national politics for the next fifty years. Ironically, while the rest of the nation was abandoning the Republican incumbent, Herbert Hoover, in favor of Democrat Franklin Roosevelt, most black voters were sticking with their party's ticket in the presidential election of 1932, despite being hit harder by the Great Depression than any other group of Americans. (By 1936, however, three-quarters of African Americans supported Roosevelt's reelection.) Today, the appeal of mostly liberal Democratic politicians to black voters appears quite natural, requiring no special explanation. This partnership took nearly three decades to establish.

Both future partners first had to break enduring ties that pulled in opposing directions. The loyalty of black voters to the Republican Party grew out of emancipation and Reconstruction, and Democratic politicians had done nothing in the intervening years to prompt African Americans to question their partisanship. But their loyalty was rooted more in habit than reward and thus was susceptible to a Democratic appeal. For Democratic politicians, taking up the cause of African Americans was fraught with risk. Ever since its return to the Union, the South had provided the Democratic Party with the electoral base it needed to compete nationally. Northern Democratic members of Congress had long depended on the automatic victories of their southern colleagues to win majority control of Congress. Democratic presidential candidates could count on the South's large bloc of electoral votes; all they had to do was ignore segregation, just as their counterparts before the war had disregarded slavery.

THE NEW DEAL. Neither Franklin Roosevelt's winning electoral campaign in 1932 nor his "New Deal" to pull the nation out of the Depression overtly championed the cause of African Americans. Both did, however, alter political circumstances in a way that prompted black Americans and Democratic politicians to contemplate their mutual interests. When pressed, Roosevelt refused to battle southern Democratic senators for passage of popular antilynching legislation, privately citing his need for friendly relations with southern Democrats to enact his emergency economic policies.* Yet the New Deal's evenhanded treatment of the black community appealed to black voters. Many of its programs offered African Americans government assistance for the first time since Reconstruction. (Other programs, however, such as Social Security, excluded many low-income occupations that were disproportionately black.) Federal authorities investigated racial discrimination in relief aid distribution, especially prevalent in the South, and largely rooted it out. Roosevelt also appointed more than one hundred black administrators, some to prominent posts. Finally, the Justice Department rejuvenated its long-dormant civil liberties division.

---

*While President Roosevelt had been reluctant to back federal antilynching and anti–poll tax legislation, many congressional Democrats introduced and championed hundreds of bills targeted at these and other civil rights issues. (The legislation repeatedly passed in the House of Representatives but, just as in the antebellum era, failed in the Senate, where the South held a greater share of the membership.)

Eleanor Roosevelt's civil rights activism worked to the advantage of the president. FDR was able to woo African American voters, many of whom had voted Republican (the party of Lincoln) in the 1932 election, without alienating southern Democrats in Congress whose support was essential to sustain his New Deal programs. In serving as her husband's de facto envoy to the black community, the first lady often conveyed her messages through public speeches, here to a black college in Florida. Seated is Mary McLeod Bethune, president of the college and director of Negro affairs for the National Youth Administration, a New Deal federal agency.

Following the White House initiative, congressional Democrats added nondiscrimination language to a score of public laws creating federal programs. In 1941 Roosevelt issued an executive order banning employment discrimination in federal agencies, and he established the Committee on Fair Employment Practices to enforce nondiscrimination in defense-related industries. These measures, requiring that African Americans be treated as ordinary citizens, represented a major breakthrough for America's civil rights policy.

AFRICAN AMERICANS AND THE NEW DEAL COALITION. During the Roosevelt years, Democratic politicians continued to woo black voters, but from a sufficient distance to allow the Democratic Party to maintain its southern alliance. Nonetheless, hindsight reveals that subtle changes were under way in the political landscape, leading up to political realignment and the Democratic Party's embrace of black voters. In Washington twenty years of nearly uninterrupted Democratic control of both the presidency and Congress replenished the Supreme Court and lower federal judiciary with judges more sympathetic to civil rights claims. This laid the groundwork for an era of active judicial intervention against state laws enforcing segregation, particularly in public education.

More importantly, African Americans gradually shifted their party loyalties from the "party of Lincoln" to the "party of Roosevelt." The political transformation could not have been timed more propitiously for the Democratic Party for hundreds of thousands of these potential new Democrats were migrating from the South, where they could not vote, to northern and midwestern cities, where solicitous Democratic political organizations eagerly registered and ushered them to the polls. The resulting demographic transformation of America's cities, recorded in Table 4-1, reflect the cumulative effects of several distinct forces.* For a century black sharecroppers and tenant farmers had been one of the least mobile population groups in the nation. But World War II (1939–1945) sent many young black males from the segregated Deep South into the armed services, where they were stationed in less racist, or at least less intimidating, communities. Other southern African Americans were lured north by relatively high-paying jobs in

---

*In Detroit, for example, the black population doubled from 8 percent in 1930 to 16 percent in 1950 and to 44 percent by 1970. Although Detroit had the most dramatic growth in black population, every major urban center throughout the nation experienced a similar trend. Edward G. Carmines and James A. Stimson, *Issue Evolution: Race and the Transformation of American Politics* (Princeton: Princeton University Press, 1989), Table 4-1.

wartime industry. Still others followed after the war as farm mechanization rendered labor-intensive farming obsolete. Migration transformed these black citizens from political nonentities into pivotal voters.

Politicians seeking to win elections needed to adapt their appeals to their new constituents. Democratic state party conventions outside the South quickly adopted the civil rights cause on a variety of policy fronts. Invariably, many of these stances were unpopular with white voters, and not all state conventions wrote such planks into their platforms. Yet as early as the 1940s (see Figure 4-1) numerous state Democratic conventions ardently advocated civil rights.

Not until the growing Democratic commitment to civil rights received national expression from Congress and the presidency, where the electoral and governing coalition between northern and southern Democrats had prevented real advances in civil rights, would the fortunes of African Americans improve. The first crack in this coalition came in 1948, when Democratic president Harry Truman openly courted the black vote for reelection, even at the risk of alienating the South. A faltering, strike-plagued economy appeared to doom the unpopular president to electoral defeat. Desperately searching for a winning campaign plan, Truman's advisers proposed a novel strategy for the Democratic Party: "Unless there are real and new efforts . . . to help the Negro," stated one strategy memo, "the Negro bloc, which, certainly in Illinois and probably in New York and Ohio, *does* hold the balance of power, will go Republican." This strategy prompted President Truman in the 1948 election year to issue an executive order integrating the armed services and introduce legislation making Roosevelt's Committee on Fair Employment Practices a permanent agency. Truman's most important action was sponsoring a comprehensive civil rights bill, the first since the end of Reconstruction, that finally made racial lynching a federal crime, provided federal guarantees for voting rights, and prohibited employment and housing discrimination.*

At the Democratic Party's national convention in the summer of 1948, liberal northern Democrats pressed fellow delegates to adopt a strong civil rights platform. Southern delegates were outraged and bolted from the meeting. In the fall these "Dixiecrats," as they were called, ran their own candidate, Strom Thurmond, under the States' Rights Party banner and pulled several southern states' electoral votes away

TABLE 4-1					
The Road to Political Power: African Americans Migrate North					
	1930	1940	1950	1960	1970
All 12 SMSAs	7.6	9.0	13.7	21.4	30.8
New York	4.9	6.9	9.8	14.7	23.4
Los Angeles–Long Beach	5.0	6.0	9.8	15.3	21.2
Chicago	7.1	8.3	14.1	23.6	34.4
Philadelphia	11.4	13.1	18.3	26.7	34.4
Detroit	7.8	9.3	16.4	29.2	44.0
San Francisco–Oakland	4.9	4.9	11.8	21.1	32.7
Boston	2.9	3.3	12.3	9.8	18.2
Pittsburgh	8.3	9.3	18.0	16.8	27.0
St. Louis	11.5	13.4	5.3	28.8	41.3
Washington, D.C.	27.3	28.5	35.4	54.8	72.3
Cleveland	8.1	9.7	16.3	28.9	39.0
Baltimore	17.7	19.4	23.8	35.0	47.0

Source: Adapted from Leo F. Schnore, Carolyn D. Andre, and Harry Sharp, "Black Suburbanization, 1930–1970," *The Changing Face of the Suburbs,* ed. Barry Schwartz (Chicago: University of Chicago Press, 1976), 80. The figures were transposed to yield data on black percentages.

Note: Table shows the percentage of African Americans in central cities of the twelve largest Standard Metropolitan Statistical Areas (SMSAs).

---

*The legislation, predictably, died in the Senate, where southern members prevented it from coming to a vote.

Figure 4-1 Attention to Civil Rights in Non-Southern State Party Platforms, 1920–1965

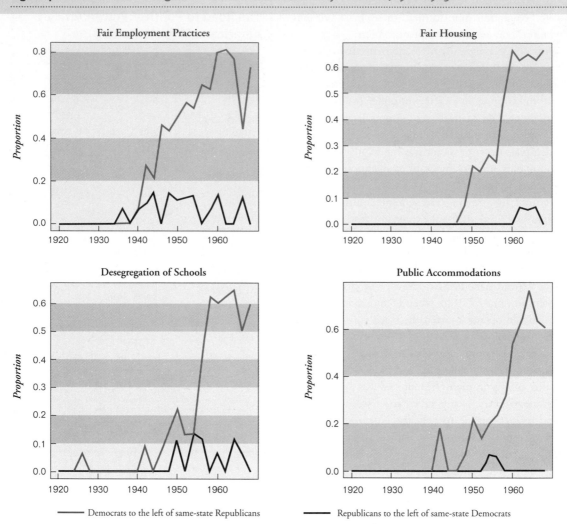

Democrats to the left of same-state Republicans

Republicans to the left of same-state Democrats

Source: Adapted from Figure 5 of Brian D. Feinstein and Eric Schickler, "Platforms and Partners: The Civil Rights Realignment Reconsidered," *Studies in American Development* 22, no. 1 (March 2008): 12.

from the Democratic ticket (see Map 4-2). The defection reminded national Democrats that the South could be taken for granted only so long as the party left segregation alone. Despite losing this traditional stronghold, Truman won reelection.

The Truman administration's unsuccessful 1948 attempts to enact a civil rights law, like the defeat of the Wilmot Proviso a century earlier, presaged a later victory by identifying a political rationale for northern politicians to attack southern tyranny. With the New Deal, the Democratic Party attracted activist liberals and union leaders who were ideologically committed to civil rights. Like Republican abolitionists one

Map 4-2 Truman Wins Presidency in 1948 Despite Dixiecrat Defection

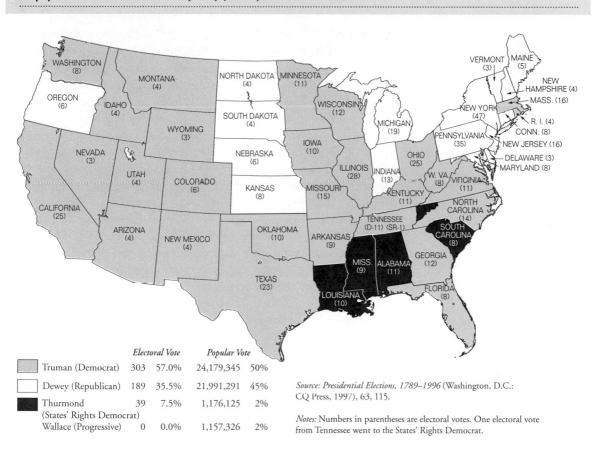

		Electoral Vote		Popular Vote	
	Truman (Democrat)	303	57.0%	24,179,345	50%
	Dewey (Republican)	189	35.5%	21,991,291	45%
	Thurmond (States' Rights Democrat)	39	7.5%	1,176,125	2%
	Wallace (Progressive)	0	0.0%	1,157,326	2%

Source: Presidential Elections, 1789–1996 (Washington, D.C.: CQ Press, 1997), 63, 115.

Notes: Numbers in parentheses are electoral votes. One electoral vote from Tennessee went to the States' Rights Democrat.

hundred years earlier, their efforts made these activists important to their party, more than their numbers alone would attest.[13] But not until Democratic presidential candidates realized that the black vote might offset the potential southern losses did the party's politicians have a collective stake in advancing civil rights. Similarly, not until northern congressional Democrats discovered that speaking out against southern segregation won them the votes of the recent southern black migrants did a congressional majority committed to breaking up segregation coalesce.

Emergence of a Civil Rights Coalition: 1940s–1950s

The 1950s saw only modest advances in civil rights, but a new coalition—requiring renewed support for civil rights from the Republican Party and profound shifts within the Democratic Party, whose leaders historically had been hostile to the cause of African Americans—set the stage for success. Two landmark events of the 1950s stand out: the historic *Brown v. Board of Education of Topeka* decision and the Civil Rights

Act of 1957.[14] Although important, both events proved more influential in identifying the issues and cleavages for the next decade than in yielding real gains in civil rights.

THE NAACP'S LITIGATION STRATEGY. In 1909 the National Association for the Advancement of Colored People (NAACP) began to represent black defendants throughout the South and to use the federal judiciary to challenge the legal structure of segregation. Although southern opposition in the Senate blocked legislative solutions, a decade of Roosevelt judicial appointments had recast the Supreme Court and many federal district and appeals courts with judges more sympathetic to the southern blacks' cause. One of its most important landmark victories during these early years came in 1944, when the NAACP persuaded the Supreme Court in *Smith v. Allwright* to throw out white primary laws.[15] The Court ruled that because race was the explicit criterion for discrimination, such laws violated the Fifteenth Amendment.

Nowhere in the South, however, was the electoral potential of the black vote close to being realized. Long-standing Supreme Court doctrine requiring that plaintiffs prove a law's discriminatory *intent* rather than simply demonstrate a bias in its *effect* frustrated the NAACP's efforts to dismantle other racial barriers. For example, in trying to eradicate the poll tax, which also disenfranchised poor whites, the NAACP could not satisfy the Court's tough requirements.

In the 1940s the NAACP launched a second line of attack against Jim Crow laws, this time targeting segregated public education. Since *Plessy v. Ferguson* in 1896, the federal judiciary had upheld segregation in the South, but the "separate but equal" doctrine proved to be an easy target. The soft underbelly of segregation was the word "equal." Nowhere in the South did the separate facilities for African Americans equal those for whites.

The NAACP targeted the most blatant disparities. Since many states did not provide black graduate and professional schools and black residents were shut out of both public and private white facilities, the NAACP had a relatively easy time convincing the Court of the inequality of separating the races in education. In *Sweatt v. Painter* (1950) the Court unanimously agreed that the University of Texas could not stave off desegregation at its law school by instantly creating a black-only facility.[16] Then the NAACP successfully attacked segregated schools where separate facilities existed but were patently unequal in the education offered students. Less conspicuous forms of inequality were taken on next. In a 1950 decision the Court accepted the argument that intangible factors such as faculty reputation and alumni prestige contributed to educational inequality.

***BROWN* TRUMPS *PLESSY*.** Having established that "separate but equal" *could* be unconstitutional, the NAACP directly attacked *Plessy*. The opportunity came in 1950 when Oliver Brown, an assistant pastor from Topeka, Kansas, violated local segregation laws when he tried to enroll his daughter, Linda, in a white neighborhood public school. Representing the NAACP, future Supreme Court justice Thurgood Marshall took up Brown's case, which four years later brought the pivotal Supreme Court ruling in *Brown v. Board of Education of Topeka*. Writing for a unanimous Court, Chief Jus-

At least symbolically, Labor Day 1957 was a watershed event in school integration. Elizabeth Eckford, textbooks in arm, and eight other black students were escorted through a hostile crowd into Little Rock's Central High School. The jeering student behind Eckford, Hazel Bryan, would later rue this moment when she became "the poster child for the hate generation, trapped in the image captured in the photograph." Later Bryan contacted Eckford to apologize, and subsequently they jointly participated in local racial tolerance workshops. The second photo was taken at the same site and by the same photographer on the fortieth anniversary of this historic moment.

tice Earl Warren argued that education is the foundation of good citizenship and thus constitutes "a right which must be made available to all on equal terms." Stipulating that racial segregation "generates a feeling of inferiority as to [black children's] status in the community that may affect their hearts and minds in a way unlikely ever to be undone," Warren concluded, "separate educational facilities are inherently unequal." With this 1954 ruling, *Plessy,* the principal legal prop of Jim Crow, crumbled.

The *Brown* decision, argued as a class-action suit on behalf of all citizens similarly denied access to white public schools, had broad legal ramifications. The next year the Court empowered lower federal courts to hear segregation cases and oversee the desegregation of public schools with "all deliberate speed."[17] Hundreds of school desegregation cases were filed in the federal courts in the decade after *Brown.*

Yet even this flurry of litigation did not end segregation. Efforts to implement *Brown* encountered all of the problems associated with enforcing judicial rulings. The decision was met by massive resistance across the South. Acting as if the nation were still governed by the Articles of Confederation, some state legislatures boldly asserted that public education lay beyond the national government's jurisdiction and that they would ignore the Court's "illegal" decision. When this bluff failed, state politicians devised more imaginative blocking tactics. In Virginia public schools were closed and "private" ones, created with state financing, opened in the vain hope that the new schools would be exempt from the *Brown* ruling. When these and other legal tricks were exhausted, state officials simply defied black parents and federal marshals sent to implement a desegregation ruling. The Supreme Court itself intervened in 1957, ordering the city of Little Rock, Arkansas, to enroll black students in all-white Central High School. When Arkansas governor Orval Faubus and school officials failed to comply, President Dwight Eisenhower sent in U.S. Army troops to escort black students to their new school.

The last bulwark of segregation's defense was tokenism—perhaps the most successful dilatory tactic of all. A school district would admit a handful of black students and then rush to federal court claiming compliance. The result would be another round of litigation during which further desegregation would be suspended. Civil rights lawyers may have won many cases during this era, but their clients had little success in gaining access to "whites-only" schools. In 1962, eight years after *Brown,* less than one-half of 1 percent of black students in the South were actually attending desegregated schools.

THE 1957 CIVIL RIGHTS ACT: REHEARSAL FOR THE 1960s. The year 1957 was ripe with political opportunity for the Democrats. With Republican two-term president Dwight Eisenhower ineligible for reelection in 1960, the Senate was full of ambitious Democrats grooming themselves for a presidential bid. John Kennedy of Massachusetts, Stuart Symington of Missouri, and Hubert Humphrey of Minnesota would later declare their candidacies and campaign actively in the 1960 presidential primaries. Other, less-daring Senate colleagues could barely contain their aspirations for the top spot. Among them was Democratic majority leader Lyndon Johnson from Texas.

Daring or not, all would-be Democratic candidates had to appeal to a national constituency that now included substantial numbers of black voters in the large, vote-rich industrial states. For Johnson, a southerner, this requirement posed a serious problem. How could this Texan establish his credentials with African Americans and therefore be taken seriously by the northern Democratic Party leaders who controlled the nomination?

Johnson's vehicle into the national arena was the 1957 Civil Rights Act, which he introduced. This modest law allowed African Americans who felt their right to vote had been denied because of race to sue their state in federal court. But the prospect of expensive litigation and the provision that defendants—say, a local voter registrar—would be entitled to jury trials proved such formidable barriers that the NAACP and similar civil rights organizations filed suits designed only to establish widespread voting discrimination. To no one's surprise, few, if indeed any, black citizens gained the vote by virtue of this limited law.

The significance of Johnson's strategic sponsorship of the 1957 Civil Rights Act, then, lay more in what it represented politically than in any real gains it produced for African Americans. Southern senators, who wanted to boost Johnson's presidential bid over those of northern liberals Humphrey and Kennedy, strategically refrained from vigorous opposition and, in a few cases, abstained in the final floor vote. This message was reinforced by the passage of another, slightly less anemic, voting rights bill in the spring of 1960, only weeks before many of these senators headed for the Democratic presidential nominating convention. Although Johnson lost the Democratic presidential nomination to Kennedy, he won the consolation prize—the vice-presidential nomination. And ever mindful of the black vote, Johnson and his colleagues oversaw enactment of yet another minority voting rights law during the summer before the 1960 presidential election.

With passage of the Civil Rights Act of 1957, the first civil rights law since Reconstruction, Democratic congressional leaders committed themselves to passing civil rights legislation. This and other early civil rights laws represented a transition, not so much for African Americans seeking full citizenship as for the Democratic Party.

Kennedy's narrow victory in 1960 reminded Democrats once again that winning the presidency without the South was virtually impossible. Even majority control of Congress would be jeopardized if more southern politicians decided—as a few in fact had—to disassociate themselves from northern Democrats and change parties. But even if the party accepted these risks and championed civil rights, they still lacked sufficient votes to enact the kinds of policies necessary to dismantle segregation. To jettison the party's southern wing by embracing civil rights and then fail to deliver on its commitment to the cause would constitute political suicide.

Yet during the 1960s Democratic presidents Kennedy and Johnson and their congressional colleagues broke with the South and committed the nation to an activist civil rights policy before it was politically expedient to do so. Why? Because doing nothing suddenly became the riskier strategy. A civil rights movement based on demonstrations and protest was generating a groundswell of support throughout the nation that the Democratic Party, which controlled Congress and the presidency, could not ignore. Failure to deal with this issue would have jeopardized the political relations of many Democratic politicians with their core supporters. Then, in the 1964 election, an event rarer than Halley's comet occurred: the emergence of a *dominant* governing coalition in Washington. Not only did Democrats retain the presidency, but they also greatly enlarged their majorities in both chambers of Congress. Like a comet, this coalition did not last long, but while present it burned brightly. The result was half a decade of legislation followed by vigorous enforcement of laws dismantling segregation and voting discrimination. Finally, the national government had decided to finish the project of Reconstruction and assume responsibility for every citizen's civil rights.

The Civil Rights Movement: 1960s

Before the early 1960s, the civil rights movement, led by the NAACP, followed a strategy designed more to influence judges than politicians. This strategy had garnered some impressive court victories, but judicial successes had not translated into real gains in civil rights. Entering the 1960s, the civil rights movement took a new course—public protests directed against segregation and the authorities who administered it. Ultimately, the protests sought to influence public opinion and, in turn, Congress and the president.

Rosa Parks, whose refusal to move to the back of a city bus in December 1955 touched off the historic Montgomery, Alabama, bus boycott, is fingerprinted by Montgomery deputy sheriff D. H. Lackey. Her courageous act and subsequent arrest triggered massive demonstrations in the city and a boycott of local public transportation and white businesses. These events led eventually to the dismantling of local segregation policies and stimulated other acts of civil disobedience elsewhere.

This new course began in December 1955, when a black seamstress, Rosa Parks, boarded a city bus in Montgomery, Alabama. When Parks refused to surrender her seat to a white patron and move to the back of the vehicle, as the law required, she launched the historic Montgomery bus boycott, which became the model for later boycotts. In 1960 the first "sit-in" was held when several black college students in Greensboro, North Carolina, occupied seats in a local restaurant reserved for whites and refused to move until they were served or arrested.

Shifting strategy from litigation to mass demonstrations introduced collective action problems that had to be solved for the civil rights movement to succeed. Who would lead the movement in this new direction? Could the NAACP, an organization of lawyers—many of them white, nonsouthern volunteers—be expected to engage in, much less organize massive civil disobedience? Disenfranchised black southerners did not have politicians—professionals in the art of solving collective action problems—to inspire and organize efforts to bring down Jim Crow through confrontation.

Ironically, segregation itself supplied the leaders who would press for its dissolution. Segregation in the South separated the races in all aspects of social organization: schools, churches, entertainment, hospitals, and professions; even cemeteries were segregated. Two largely parallel social groups coexisted in every community. Some black professionals—such as public school teachers—worked under the supervision of white-controlled institutions and would suffer serious repercussions if they challenged segregation. Other black professionals, however, served an exclusively black clientele and were fairly well insulated from white retribution: shop owners, morticians, and especially preachers—the latter were already well versed in organizing congregations and enjoyed credibility among those they would ask to make sacrifices. With control of scarce resources—skill at organizing, and the trust of their congregations—and largely exempt of the potentially severe white reprisals, it is not surprising that black southern preachers participated in planning and coordinating demonstrations. Hundreds of them mobilized their congregations and coordinated with colleagues from other communities to generate large, effective demonstrations. The most important of these leaders, Rev. Martin Luther King Jr., was a Methodist minister. His organization, which during the next decade spearheaded demonstrations throughout the South, was appropriately named the Southern Christian Leadership Conference (SCLC).

King's strategy of nonviolent resistance may have been inspired by the Indian leader Mahatma Gandhi (1869–1948), but his political pragmatism was a page out of James Madison's playbook. Ultimately, King reasoned, rights would be won not in the courts through cogent argument but in legislatures through direct engagement with opponents whose interests were at stake. "Needless fighting in lower courts," King argued, is "exactly what the white man wants the Negro to do. Then he can draw out the fight."[18] If African Americans were to realize their rights, he knew they would have to claim them.

The first serious hurdle for the protest strategy was finding leaders who could bear the heavy transaction costs and personal risks and who possessed the communication and organizational skills to mobilize a population inexperienced in expressing their grievances. The second problem, just as formidable, concerned the movement's followers. Specifically, would ordinary African Americans agree to demonstrate in the streets, boycott public transportation and white businesses, and confront local registrars bent on denying them their right to vote? Many of these activities violated state and local segregation laws; participants would face a legal system administered by unsympathetic officials. More importantly, the vast majority of black southerners worked for white employers who would actively discourage participation. With these disincentives, many (perhaps too many) of those sympathetic with this new strategy might instead free ride.[19] What would become of the civil rights movement if insufficient numbers answered the call to action?

The scene is Jackson, Mississippi, where the local lunch crowd is drenching lunch counter demonstrators with mustard and ketchup. Such demonstrations occurred throughout the South in the 1960s. Most of the participants were local black and northern white college students.

History showed otherwise. Demonstrations began in earnest in 1960, and over the next six years almost 2,500 were held, with many receiving national news coverage.[20] In retrospect, the success of the movement is easy to understand. In addition to the nationally prominent clergy in SCLC headquarters, ministers with the professional and rhetorical skills to mobilize direct action ran most of the eighty-five local chapters throughout the South. Moreover, these local leaders enjoyed exceptional credibility with those whom they needed to motivate. When King and other SCLC leaders endorsed a boycott or some other action, the local chapters served as a focal point to coordinate a joint action. Without the organizational efforts of these local leaders, the movement would not have enjoyed such broad-based support.

The pivotal protest of spring 1963 in Birmingham, Alabama, forced the Democratic Party to commit to an aggressive civil rights policy and led directly to passage of the landmark Civil Rights Act of 1964.

THE BIRMINGHAM DEMONSTRATION. In early 1963 President Kennedy pleaded for patience from King and other leaders, arguing that Congress should enact his less-controversial social programs before tackling segregation. Civil rights leaders suspected that Kennedy's real motivation was to keep the South in the Democratic column in the upcoming 1964 election. King and the other leaders had their own strategic reasons for impatience; demonstrations were turning violent, and events were only

Major Events in the Civil Rights Movement, 1955–1968

December 1955	African Americans in Montgomery, Alabama, begin boycott of city buses in protest of segregated seating.
September 1, 1957	Central High School in Little Rock, Arkansas, engulfed in turmoil as the governor calls out Arkansas National Guard to prevent enrollment of nine black students. President Dwight Eisenhower forced to send in federal troops to restore order.
February 1, 1960	Wave of "sit-ins" touched off across the South by four students in Greensboro, North Carolina, who are refused service at a segregated lunch counter.
May 4, 1961	"Freedom rides" begin as African Americans try to occupy "whites only" sections of interstate buses. U.S. marshals ultimately are called in to settle violent reaction to black efforts.
September 30, 1962	Federal troops are used to quell a fifteen-hour uprising by University of Mississippi students protesting the enrollment of a single black student, James Meredith. Two students are killed. (Televised live across the nation.)
April 1963	Demonstrations begin in Birmingham, Alabama. Local authorities use fire hoses and police dogs to disperse demonstrators.
August 28, 1963	March on Washington by more than two hundred thousand African Americans and whites. Rev. Martin Luther King Jr. delivers his "I Have A Dream" speech, and "We Shall Overcome" becomes the anthem of the civil rights movement.
September 1963	Demonstrations begin in St. Augustine, Florida, to protest the arrest and detention of seven students. African Americans boycott several northern schools in protest of de facto segregation. Four black children are killed in bombing of Birmingham, Alabama, church.
June 1964	Three civil rights workers, two white and one black, working to register black voters are killed in Mississippi. Murderers include sheriff's deputies.
July 1964	First in a wave of ghetto riots breaks out in New York City's Harlem.
January 1965	King organizes protest marches in Selma, Alabama. Marches end in violent attacks by police.
August 11, 1965	Ghetto riots erupt in Watts section of Los Angeles. Four thousand rioters are arrested; thirty-four are killed.
June 6, 1966	James Meredith suffers gunshot wound in march across Mississippi.
Summers 1966 and 1967	Riots and violent demonstrations occur in cities across the nation.
April 4, 1968	Martin Luther King Jr. assassinated in Memphis, Tennessee.

partially under their control. To keep the movement directed toward civil disobedience and peaceful protest, SCLC leaders needed to start producing results.

The selection of Birmingham as a protest venue reflected the broad strategic purpose of the demonstrations. Birmingham's segregation was no worse than in many other cities throughout the Deep South. But Birmingham had a notoriously intolerant local police chief, Eugene "Bull" Connor, known for rough treatment of civil rights demonstrators. He would provide a graphic display of the institutional violence that enforced segregation. As the nation watched on network television, Connor arrested and jailed two thousand marchers for not having a parade permit. The local law enforcement officers then resorted to police dogs and fire hoses to disperse peaceful demonstrators, including children barely old enough to go to school.

The Birmingham demonstrations succeeded when the city's business community agreed to negotiate with the protesters. But more important, the protesters created a national crisis that President Kennedy could not ignore. For years the monthly Gallup Poll had asked its national sample of respondents to name the most important problem facing the country. Until the 1955 Montgomery bus boycott, civil rights never figured prominently in responses to this query. From April to July 1963, however, the percentage of respondents mentioning civil rights shot up from 10 to nearly 50 percent.

Suddenly, continued accommodation of southern Democrats imposed significant political costs on Kennedy. Failure to act might irreparably damage his reputation among black voters who might well provide a margin of victory in a reelection bid. These events, orchestrated by the civil rights movement, turned the president into a reluctant champion of its cause. Shortly after a televised address to the nation unveiling the new

Protestors parading down the streets of Birmingham, Alabama, in 1963 were bent on focusing national attention on their cause. The local police proved quite accommodating in demonstrating to the horror of television viewers throughout the nation the brutality with which segregation was enforced.

civil rights legislation, Kennedy invited movement leaders to the White House to plan a legislative strategy. The president explained to the group the bind he and the Democratic Party were in:

> This is a very serious fight. The Vice-President [Lyndon Johnson] and I know what it will mean if we fail. I have just seen a new poll—national approval of the administration has fallen from 60 to 47 percent. We're in this up to the neck. The worst trouble of all would be to lose the fight in the Congress. We'll have enough trouble if we win; but, if we win, we can deal with those. A good many programs I care about may go down the drain as a result of this—we may go down the drain as a result of this—so we are putting a lot on the line.[21]

Democrats were about to commit to a strong civil rights program without having the means to succeed.[22]

THE DEMOCRATIC PARTY'S COMMITMENT TO CIVIL RIGHTS. On June 11, 1963, President Kennedy addressed the nation, proclaiming his full support for the aspirations of African Americans and announcing a major revision of the civil

For years Georgia senator Richard Russell (right) and other southerners had blocked civil rights legislation with the threat of a filibuster. New president Lyndon Johnson (left), however, was not deterred in his push for civil rights legislation. Here, two weeks after President John Kennedy's assassination, Johnson warns his Senate mentor to stand aside or be run down.

rights bill then before Congress. The courts would no longer determine violations; for the first time federal agencies could independently identify discrimination and impose remedies. Although this new proposal was far weaker than the sweeping civil rights reforms King and his colleagues had requested, they accepted it as a solid step in the right direction.

Five months later Kennedy was assassinated, and Vice President Johnson succeeded to the presidency. At the time, a strengthened version of the legislation, which had passed the House of Representatives on a bipartisan vote, was predictably stalled in the Senate. Southern senators did not have enough votes to defeat the legislation outright, but they were prepared to filibuster* it indefinitely.

Within a few days of assuming the presidency, Johnson addressed a joint session of Congress and a nationwide television audience to announce that a strong civil rights law would be the nation's memorial to the fallen president. This proclamation set the stage for a struggle in Washington. The outcome would make 1964 a year of historic successes for both civil rights and the Democratic Party.

---

*The filibuster, allowing a minority of the Senate membership to delay floor consideration of legislation, is discussed more fully in Chapter 6.

POLITICS/POLICY

The 1964 Civil Rights Act and Integration of Public Schools

One of the most effective provisions of the 1964 Civil Rights Act authorized the Department of Health, Education, and Welfare to withhold federal grants from school districts that failed to integrate their schools. No longer could southern school boards hide behind token desegregation and endless visits to the federal courts. The effects were quick and dramatic: within a year more black children were admitted to formerly all-white schools than in the entire decade after the 1954 *Brown v. Board of Education of Topeka* decision. Within ten years over 90 percent of black children in the South were attending integrated schools.

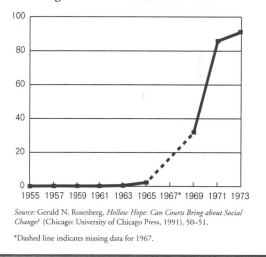

Percentage of All Southern Black Schoolchildren Attending School with Whites, 1955–1973

Source: Gerald N. Rosenberg, *Hollow Hope: Can Courts Bring about Social Change?* (Chicago: University of Chicago Press, 1991), 50–51.

*Dashed line indicates missing data for 1967.

THE 1964 CIVIL RIGHTS ACT. Once Johnson persuaded Senate Republicans to join northern Democrats in breaking the southern filibuster, the Senate promptly passed the Civil Rights Act of 1964. This law, which was substantially stronger than the legislation President Kennedy introduced, authorized the national government to end segregation in public education and public accommodations (see box "The 1964 Civil Rights Act and Integration of Public Schools").

The Democratic administration's high-profile sponsorship of the civil rights law put forth civil rights as a decisive campaign issue in the 1964 presidential election. The Republican Party in Congress traditionally had been more supportive of civil rights than the Democrats, but in 1964 it began to veer sharply away from its long-standing support. At their national convention Republicans chose Barry Goldwater of Arizona as their presidential candidate, one of the few senators outside the South to oppose the 1964 civil rights bill. When the Democrats convened to nominate the incumbent president Johnson, they underlined the party differences on this issue by seating delegates who challenged segregationist Democrats and by selecting as Johnson's running mate Sen. Hubert Humphrey, a longtime vocal proponent of civil rights.

Map 4-3 The Key to Unlocking Black Voting Rights: Vigilant Administration of Civil Rights Laws

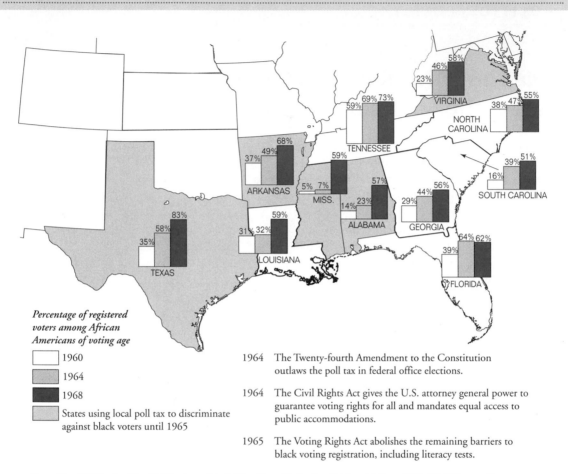

Percentage of registered
voters among African
Americans of voting age

☐ 1960

▨ 1964

■ 1968

▨ States using local poll tax to discriminate
against black voters until 1965

1964 The Twenty-fourth Amendment to the Constitution
outlaws the poll tax in federal office elections.

1964 The Civil Rights Act gives the U.S. attorney general power to
guarantee voting rights for all and mandates equal access to
public accommodations.

1965 The Voting Rights Act abolishes the remaining barriers to
black voting registration, including literacy tests.

Source: Harold W. Stanley, *Voter Mobilization and the Politics of Race: The South and Universal Suffrage, 1952–1984* (Westport, Conn.:
Praeger, 1987), 97. Copyright © 1987 by Harold W. Stanley. Reproduced with permission from Greenwood Publishing Group. All rights reserved.

The outcome of the election was the largest presidential landslide in history. The
Democrats also racked up huge majorities in the congressional elections. Goldwater
won only five states in the Deep South and his home state of Arizona. With over
95 percent of black voters preferring Johnson, the Democratic and Republican Parties
swapped constituencies in the South.[23] When the new Congress convened in 1965,
northern Democrats dominated both chambers. Even some border states elected
Democrats who were moderate supporters of civil rights and who were prepared to
support national policies that would dismantle segregation. Finally, the sheer magnitude of the Democratic victory swamped the Constitution's separation-of-powers barrier to collective action. With the severe transaction costs of policymaking swept away,

the Washington cognoscenti and ordinary voters alike sensed that the Johnson land-slide would bring about an onslaught of civil rights legislation.

THE VOTING RIGHTS ACT OF 1965. Every civil rights law enacted since 1957 addressed voting rights, but throughout much of the South black registration remained at low levels. Only 7 percent of eligible black citizens in Mississippi were registered in 1964; in Alabama the figure was 20 percent. Each of these civil rights laws had the same fatal flaw: they required individuals to prove discrimination in court. Black leaders thus pressed the White House to authorize federal agencies to guarantee the right to vote by taking over voter registration or directly supervising local officials, just as the 1964 Civil Rights Act authorized government action against segregation in education and public accommodations.

Responding to their pleas, President Johnson asked King and other leaders to "give the nation a chance to catch its breath" on civil rights. After all, African Americans would be well served, Johnson argued, by his Great Society programs in employment, education, and health care. But for movement leaders, Johnson's request asked too much. King and his colleagues knew that not since Reconstruction had such large, sympathetic majorities controlled both houses of Congress, yet from recent experience, they also knew precisely what was needed to spur legislative action.

The spring 1965 demonstrations in Selma, Alabama, closely paralleled the 1963 Birmingham actions. Brutal local law enforcement—attack dogs, club-wielding police on horseback, and liberal use of powerful fire hoses—yielded vivid television images of the official violence that enforced segregation. Civil rights leaders again succeeded when President Johnson went on prime-time television to introduce new civil rights legislation.

Ignoring the outcry of southern senators, Congress passed and the president promptly signed the Voting Rights Act of 1965. The law was aggressive—its drafters knew that virtually everyone added to the registration rolls would soon be voting Democratic. Its main provision authorized the Department of Justice to suspend restrictive electoral tests in southern states that had a history of low black turnout. In these states the Justice Department could (and did) send federal officers into uncooperative communities to register voters directly. The states also had to obtain clearance from the Justice Department before changing their election laws. While the Antifederalist Patrick Henry might have turned over in his grave at the thought of the Voting Rights Act and federal registrars entering his home state of Virginia, the policy was perfectly consistent with Madison's proposed national veto over objectionable state laws.

Few laws have ever achieved their goals more dramatically or quickly. Registration soared, yielding dramatic effects. For the first time southern politicians paid attention to their newly registered black constituents. In 1970, when several southern senators polled their colleagues about opposing an extension of the voting rights law, they found little enthusiasm. Democratic conservative Herman Talmadge of Georgia begged off: "Look, fellows, I was the principal speaker at the NAACP conference in my state last year." And South Carolina Democrat Ernest Hollings was direct: "I'm not going home to my state and explain a filibuster to black voters."[24] Moreover, Table 4-2 traces a new class of

The Emergence of Black Politicians: A Result of the Surge in Black Voting

Office	1970	1980	1990	2002
Members of Congress and state officials	179	365	465	671
City and county officials	715	2,807	4,481	5,749
Judges, sheriffs, and other law enforcement officers	213	528	769	1,081
Boards of education	362	1,214	1,655	1,969
Total	1,469	4,914	7,370	9,470

Source: Information supplied by the Joint Center for Political and Economic Studies, Washington, D.C.

politicians emerging to represent this large, rapidly growing, and residentially concentrated constituency. From 1970 to 2002, the number of black elected officials at all levels of government grew from 1,469 to 9,470. Many of these men and women won office by appealing in part to white voters. In a real sense these many local officeholders paved the way for Barack Obama's success.

The 1965 Voting Rights Act was, then, a culminating achievement of the civil rights movement of the 1960s. (For summaries of the 1965 law and other federal civil rights acts, see box "Key Provisions of Federal Civil Rights Legislation.") During the second half of the decade events began to change the way African Americans and whites looked at civil rights. In the summer of 1965 a two-week riot, in which thirty-four people were killed, exploded in the black neighborhood of Watts in Los Angeles. Over the next few summers similar riots would erupt in other cities. Late in 1965 the Vietnam War began to replace civil rights demonstrations on television news, and the vocal opposition of some civil rights leaders to the war sapped support in Washington. The next year Congress defeated a fair housing bill. (A somewhat weaker law was passed two years later, however.) Then, in 1968, King was assassinated in Memphis after leading a march supporting striking sanitation workers (see box "Major Events in the Civil Rights Movement, 1955–1968" on page 166). Riots erupted in cities throughout the nation. Shortly thereafter, "law and order" replaced civil rights as the mantra of political campaigns throughout the United States.

The Era of Remedial Action: The 1970s to the Present

The civil rights movement may have lost momentum, but the advances continued. Over the next thirty years, legislation (including the Fair Housing Act of 1968) shifted the responsibility for identifying and eradicating abuses from injured individuals and the courts to the federal bureaucracy. This redelegation of principal enforcement authority to the Department of Health, Education, and Welfare (HEW) made it much easier for federal agencies to administer civil rights policy. Rather than having to investigate and prove a specific discriminatory act that prevented African Americans from enjoying their rights, the government could focus instead on the "outcome" of local practices. The underrepresentation of African Americans on voter registration rolls and in apartment rentals, schools, employment, and the like was enough to establish a reasonable suspicion of discrimination, which the government could then remedy.

In the 1980s and 1990s civil rights enforcement moved beyond the South to include all government and private actions that yielded indicators of discrimination. A favorite target of federal investigators was schools. In fact, when these officials searched for evidence of discrimination in black versus white enrollment figures, they netted many schools outside the South where **de facto segregation** was in play. In these cases,

Key Provisions of Federal Civil Rights Legislation

Civil Rights Act, 1957

Established U.S. Commission on Civil Rights to investigate the status of civil rights in the country. Made it a federal crime to attempt to prevent a person from voting.

Civil Rights Act, 1960

Increased sanctions against abridging or denying the right to vote. Permitted federal government to appoint "referees," under the jurisdiction of the courts, to register voters denied the right to vote by a pattern or practice of discrimination.

Civil Rights Act, 1964

Voting: By equating a sixth-grade education with literacy, the act made it more difficult to disenfranchise African Americans through literacy tests.

Public accommodations: Barred discrimination on basis of race, color, religion, or nationality in restaurants, service stations, theaters, transportation, and hotels with five rooms or more. Empowered attorney general to initiate suits.

Schools: Authorized attorney general to bring suit against segregated schools. Also permitted federal government to withhold funds from segregated schools.

Employment: Barred discrimination on the basis of race, color, religion, nationality, or sex in a range of employment practices. Established Equal Employment Opportunity Commission to enforce this provision.

Voting Rights Act, 1965

Permitted appointment, under Civil Service Commission, of voting examiners in place of local registrars in all areas where less than 50 percent of those eligible to vote actually voted in the 1964 presidential election. Use of literacy tests and similar mechanisms suspended.

Age Discrimination Act, 1967

Prevented employment discrimination based on age for workers forty to sixty-five years old. Later amended to prevent mandatory retirement.

Fair Housing Act, 1968

Outlawed refusal to rent or sell housing on grounds of race or religion, but exempted citizens who rented or sold their homes without using a real estate agent.

Rehabilitation Act of 1973

Instituted affirmative action programs for employers to hire "qualified handicapped individuals" and barred discrimination solely on the basis of a disability.

Civil Rights Restoration Act, 1988

Applied anti–sex discrimination standards to all institutions' programs if the institution received federal funding.

Civil Rights Act of 1991

Gave victims of intentional discrimination based on sex, religion, or disability the right to sue for monetary damages. (Victims of racial discrimination had had this right since a Reconstruction-era law.)

the segregation was not mandated by law (**de jure segregation**), as it was in the South, but arose as a byproduct of former discriminatory housing laws that kept neighborhood schools segregated.* When the courts, the Department of Justice, and HEW decided jointly to force school districts to bus students to sometimes distant schools for the sake of integration, the measure produced waves of public protests. Indeed, busing proved to be one of the most contentious civil rights policies of the modern era, with public opinion surveys in the 1970s and 1980s showing it to be nearly consistently the national policy most upsetting to Americans.

---

*Until the Supreme Court ruled them illegal in 1968, *restrictive covenants* were commonly embedded in property deeds, preventing owners from selling the property to Jews and African Americans. *Jones v. Alfred H. Mayer Co.,* 392 U.S. 409 (1968).

In an effort to rectify the legacy of residential segregation for public education, during the 1970s the federal bureaucracy and courts adopted a policy of busing students to schools outside of their neighborhoods to achieve racial integration. For the next two decades school busing scored at or near the top of the list of policies most upsetting to the American public. As busing has declined in recent years as the judicially preferred remedy, so too has its status as a political issue.

Note that the government found straightforward solutions for redressing discrimination in voting rights and schools: it enrolled black voters and redirected students to new schools. But what about past discrimination in employment? The government could not simply tell its own agencies or private businesses to hire an equal number of minorities. Instead, it resorted to **affirmative action,** a policy that requires any employers or government agencies that have practiced past discrimination to compensate minorities and women by giving them special consideration in their selection for employment and education. Affirmative action is most controversial when applied to government contracting, university admission rules to increase minority enrollments, and employment policies to promote minority presence and advancement in business and the professions. Early affirmative action efforts in the 1970s, rejected by both the federal courts and the American public, involved the use of **quotas**— that is, setting aside a certain share of admissions, government contracts, and jobs for those who suffered from past discrimination. In the most famous of these cases, *Regents of the University of California v. Bakke* (1978), the Supreme Court decided that, while creating a special admission pool for minority students might serve the laudable goals of attaining a diverse student body, the university medical school's approach violated the equal protection rights of white applicants.[25]

During the intervening decades the Supreme Court has decided numerous affirmative action cases without resolving the issue of preferential treatment beyond outlawing quotas. Virtually all of the tough cases that have reached the Court have been decided by a single vote, with the balance teetering in favor of or opposition to affirmative action according to the changing membership of the Court (see Chapter 9). Where in 1987 the Court ruled that sex could be considered along with other criteria in promotion decisions, and apparently could be done even without evidence of past discrimination, by 1995 it was prescribing "narrowly tailored" standards designed to achieve a "compelling government interest."[26]

The most recent decisions find the Court still grappling to identify acceptable avenues for favoring some applicants over others without using quotas. In 2003 it decided a pair of long-anticipated University of Michigan cases that had received apparently contradictory rulings at the appeals level. In the end the Court mirrored the legal confusion over affirmative action. It ruled that undergraduate admissions at Michigan went too far by giving an extra point to minority applicants (roughly equivalent to a full point on an applicant's high school grade point average), while the law school program passed muster because it merely took race into account. This latter ruling was narrowly decided (5–4) and vigorously argued by the dissenting minority. The decision promises to settle the issue only until the next case arrives.[27]

The judiciary's collective ambivalence with affirmative action policy reflects national attitudes. Congress has been chary to take on the issue, perhaps recognizing the political problems they might face with the electorate were they to do so. Opinion surveys convey a public that mostly favors the principle of "affirmative action" while disapproving of almost every specific approach for achieving it. One national survey taken during the Court's deliberation of the Michigan cases found public opinion mostly running strongly against preferential treatment. When asked, "As you may know, the U.S. Supreme Court will be deciding whether public universities can use race as one of the factors in admissions to increase diversity in the student body. Do you favor or oppose this practice?" 65 percent registered opposition and 26 percent support. Yet the same survey offered some endorsement of the Court's eventual decision. When asked if affirmative action were permissible to overcome past discrimination as long as it did not involve "rigid" quotas, 49 percent agreed compared to 43 percent, who said the policy should be terminated.

Beginning with passage of Proposition 209 by California voters in 1996, the political battle over affirmative action opened on a second front—the states. In a vote of 54–46 percent, Californians added language to the state's constitution banning the use of "race, sex, color, ethnicity or national origin as a criterion for either discriminating against, or granting preferential treatment to, any individual or group in the operation of the State's system of public employment, public education or public contracting." Unsurprisingly, those opposed to the proposition immediately went to court, but over the next five years most challenges were turned back, and 209's provisions changed the state's university admissions and hiring practices. In 1999 a similar referendum passed in Washington State, and in 2006 in the aftermath of the Supreme Court rulings, Michigan voters banned affirmative action and effectively undid the permissible affirmative action in the Court's decision. That same year the Florida legislature banned racial preference in university admissions. Among civil rights groups and their opponents, debate over the value and constitutionality of affirmative action continues today. Voters in five other states attempted to get similar measures on the ballot in November 2008, but in the end, enough signatures were gathered in only two states: Nebraska and Colorado. The measure passed in Nebraska but was narrowly defeated in Colorado.

The Legacy of the Civil Rights Movement

Although race remained a prominent civil rights issue in the 1970s, the civil rights movement branched out to include women, the elderly, the disabled, homosexuals, and virtually every ethnic minority. The new directions of civil rights over the past several decades owe their progress, however, to African Americans' two-hundred-year struggle for civil rights. It paved the way politically for these new efforts, both in honing the techniques of demonstrations and protest and in creating a receptive audience in the news media and American public opinion. But most important, the black civil rights movement built a foundation of federal laws, judicial precedents, and administrative regulations that could be easily extended to other groups.

Equal Rights for Women: The Right to Vote

Long before abolitionists took up the cause of slavery, early feminists, later calling themselves **suffragists,** were campaigning for the vote. (Many early suffragists also were active in movements for prison reform, public education, temperance, and above all, abolition of slavery.) These women viewed their cause as inextricably linked to full citizenship for African Americans in the "rising tide of prodemocratic sentiment."* Yet, despite their efforts, "sex" was excluded from the Fifteenth Amendment. Except for local school board elections and liquor referenda in twenty states, women did not obtain the franchise until 1869, when the territory of Wyoming passed the first women's suffrage law.[28] In 1919, nearly a century after women organized and began promoting their cause, Congress sent the Nineteenth Amendment extending the right to vote to all women. The next year the amendment was ratified by the states.

Women, unlike African Americans, experienced little delay in implementing the right to vote. Although registration rates varied across states, women's rates approached three-quarters of men's within a decade after ratification. Over the next decade or so women were voting regularly at a rate only slightly below that of men.

From the late 1840s to the late 1860s, voting rights for African Americans and women tracked very different courses. Ironically, slaves had been liberated and handed the vote, while women, despite needing to traverse a much shorter distance, had progressed little toward gaining the franchise. (On two other issues—allowing inheritance and access to public education—the movement successfully revised many state laws.) Trying to account for the torpid pace of women's suffrage is risky. Even in an era before opinion polls regularly measured public sentiment, a comparison of the histories of black and women's rights movements suggests political circumstances that extended voting rights for one group but not the other.

First, unlike the black vote, which contemporaries agreed would go directly to the Republicans, the women's vote appeared to confer little advantage to either party. Republicans found the black votes in the South particularly attractive since the former rebel states, poised to reenter the Union, would form a Democratic majority in Washington. Suffrage leaders Elizabeth Cady Stanton and Susan B. Anthony actively lobbied to include women in the Fourteenth Amendment and probably expected to succeed.[29] As Stanton famously declared, black suffrage opened the "constitutional door" and the suffragists intended to "avail [themselves] of the strong arm and the blue uniform of the black soldier to walk in by his side."† Their expectations were dashed when Republican leaders explicitly limited the amendment to male citizens.

---

*During the colonial era, single property-owning women in New Jersey could vote. See Alexander Keyssar, *The Right to Vote* (New York: Basic Books, 2000); Judith Apter Klinghoffer and Lois Elkis, "The Petticoat Electors: Women's Suffrage in New Jersey, 1776–1807," *Journal of the Early Republic* 12 (1992): 159–193.

†See Ellen Carol Dubois, "Outgrowing the Compact of the Fathers: Equal Rights, Women's Suffrage, and the United States Constitution, 1820–1878," *The Journal of American History* 74, no. 3 (December 1987): 836–862, at 845.

Claiming that including women would have endangered ratification, Republican politicians clearly viewed women's suffrage to be a costly issue.*

Without a compelling political advantage to be gained, few politicians—particularly the Republican majority in Congress framing the amendment—were prepared to absorb the heavy political costs of extending the vote to women. This is consistent with the history of suffrage. Enthusiasm for women's suffrage appears to have been concentrated among the urban, upper-middle class. Various other women's groups either opposed or ignored the issue. Unlike the black vote—desperately needed by Republicans if they hoped to retain control of Congress and the presidency after the rebel states were readmitted into the Union—the women's vote, especially given the narrow support base for this reform, conferred little political advantage to Republicans.†

Having lost out in the Reconstruction amendments, the women's movement set out to build national support. Yet, with only women remaining on the outside of the polling booth (at least formally), the movement no longer could cast its appeal in terms of universal suffrage. Now, women's suffrage became a women's issue and gave rise to two widely circulated and seemingly incompatible lines of arguments. Some proponents struck a conservative note. The more conservative line queried the inconsistency of denying women the vote when so many ill-informed and illiterate immigrant men were voting. The southern variant of this argument had the white women's vote diluting any chance of African Americans winning elections. At the other end of the ideological continuum, recasting the women's vote as a women's issue connected with a broader feminist platform. Denial of the franchise was simply emblematic of women's subjugation, a condition entrenched in the traditional family structure. Prominent women's issues today found their origins in the arguments of many late nineteenth-century suffragists. These strongly held, incompatible views invariably competed for leadership of the movement. Whether these organizational weaknesses reflected or contributed to the failure of women's suffrage to win public support is difficult to say. As long as these fissures persisted the women's movement continued to attract supporters for various causes all along the ideological spectrum—including vocal pacifism during World War I—and it took nearly four decades to achieve the Nineteenth Amendment. Gradually, public support for women's suffrage increased, first in Wyoming in 1869 and over the next several decades in other, mostly western states. By 1919, fifteen states provided for women's voting in at least some elections.

---

*In one particularly heated exchange, Frederick Douglass—a former slave who had been present at the first national suffrage conference at Seneca Falls in 1848—argued that until white women were "dragged from their houses and hung upon lamp-posts" only then would they have "an urgency to obtain the ballot equal to our own." Susan B. Anthony gave the withering response: "if you will not give the whole loaf of suffrage to the entire people, give it to the most intelligent first." Mari Jo Buhle and Paul Buhle, *The Concise History of Woman Suffrage* (University of Illinois Press, 1978), 258.

†Ironically, the difference in the partisan advantage between black and female vote extensions might well explain the historical differences in the success of these groups in exercising their newly won franchise. The reemergent Democratic Party throughout the South later systematically stripped the vote from ex-slaves with literacy tests, white primary laws, and poll taxes. Threatening no one, other than saloon proprietors, women exercised their franchise largely unhindered. Indeed, both political parties took credit for their newly won right and appealed for their support.

Victoria Claflin Woodhull was one of the most outspoken feminists of the late nineteenth century. The first woman to declare herself a candidate for the presidency, she also ran a brokerage firm and published a Marxist-tinged newspaper. In her 1871 keynote address to the National Woman Suffrage Association, Woodhull admitted her ultimate goal was the overthrow of the government, by treason if necessary. Her subsequent announcement that she practiced as well as preached free love lent credibility to opponents' claims that female suffrage would be the first step toward some brave new world.

Congress renewed consideration repeatedly from the mid-1880s until 1919, when with President Woodrow Wilson's strong endorsement, two-thirds of both the House and Senate sent the Nineteenth Amendment to the states for ratification.

The Modern History of Civil Rights

The modern extension of subsequent civil rights guarantees to women clearly followed the civil rights movement. In fact, sex discrimination—although through a political miscalculation—was included in the 1964 Civil Rights Act. Initially the legislation included language that covered discrimination based only on religion, national origin, and race. Southern opponents proposed and voted to add sex to this list, certain that it would decrease overall support for and ultimately defeat the civil rights bill. This strategy of weighing the legislation down with controversial provisions backfired, however, when Congress accepted their amendment and proceeded to pass the legislation.

The surprising legislative victory did not lead to immediate enforcement, however, even though the 1964 law created an enforcement mechanism—the new Equal Employment Opportunity Commission (EEOC)—authorized to investigate and file suits against racial discrimination in the workplace. With one early EEOC commissioner calling the sex discrimination policy "a fluke," the commission initially balked at enforcing the employment discrimination protections for women. But the agency revised its orientation after a successful political campaign focused national attention on employment discrimination against women.

The National Organization for Women (NOW) was formed in 1966 in direct reaction to the EEOC's refusal to enforce this provision. Organized along the same lines as the NAACP, NOW initially pursued a litigation strategy with mixed success. To establish a stronger legal foundation, NOW and other women's rights organizations dusted off the Equal Rights Amendment (ERA), which had been introduced in Congress in 1923 and every year thereafter with little fanfare and poor prospects. The amendment gave Congress the authority to implement the following statement: "Equality of rights under the law shall not be denied or abridged by the United States or by any State on account of sex."

Using many of the same tactics honed by the civil rights movement—demonstrations, televised appeals, Washington rallies, and intense lobbying—NOW and other feminist organizations won over a sympathetic public. The mostly male members of Congress were not far behind. After languishing for years, the ERA was sent to the states in 1972, and within the first year twenty-two of the required thirty-eight states voted for ratification. But then the amendment hit a brick wall with the abortion issue (discussed more fully in Chapter 5).[30] Thus instead of pitting men against women, as the Nineteenth Amendment had done earlier in the century, the ERA divided feminist and antiabortion women's groups. What began as an uncontroversial endorsement of women's rights—after all, the amendment's wording simply asserts that women enjoy the same rights as men—ended in strident, contentious rhetoric between opposing camps.* On June 30, 1982, the timetable for ratification expired, and the ERA became history.

Feminists may have lost the battle over the ERA, but they appear to have won the war. During the decades since the failed ERA campaign, national civil rights policy in areas of special concern to women has advanced steadily. In 1972 Congress enacted Title IX of the Higher Education Act, which prohibits funding for schools and universities that discriminate against women, including the size of their intercollegiate sports programs. When the Supreme Court in 1984 limited the law's coverage of private groups, ruling that it prohibited discrimination only in those programs of a private organization that directly benefited from federal funding, Congress responded by passing, over President Ronald Reagan's veto, a law that overturned the Court's decision.[31] And to send a message to the conservative Court, the Democratic majorities deliberately titled the new law the Restoration of Civil Rights Act of 1988.

Most significant developments in civil rights policy on employment practices have occurred during the past two decades, reflecting women's increasing presence in the workforce. However measured—whether by percentage of women in the workplace, or numbers of working mothers, or the share of women who are their families' primary breadwinner—the numbers indicate dramatic growth in women's workforce participation.

As employment issues increased, working women and their legal advocates discovered that the Civil Rights Act of 1964—just as some critics of the ERA had argued—offered ample legal protections for their discrimination claims. Though drafted principally to eradicate racial discrimination, the language of Title VII of that law is unequivocal in its provisions against sex discrimination in the workplace: "[it is] an unlawful employment practice for an employer . . . to discriminate against any individual with respect to his compensation, term, conditions, or privileges of employment, because of such individual's race, color, religion, sex, or national origin." During the last twenty years, as the Supreme Court has considered the merits of women's lawsuits charging sexual harassment by male supervisors, the Court has relied heavily on the 1964 provision to find that sexual harassment violates the federal civil rights law.

Congress further strengthened employment discrimination claims on various fronts. The Pregnancy Discrimination Act (1978) and the Family and Medical Leave Act (1993) prevent unfair firing and demotion during absences for childbirth and family medical emergencies. The Civil Rights Act of 1991 required employers to show that

---

*Public support waned. By 1981 less than half of all voters still endorsed the amendment in those states where it had not yet been ratified. Gallup Poll cited in Jane Mansbridge, *Why We Lost the ERA* (Chicago: University of Chicago Press, 1986), 214.

unequal hiring and compensation practices did not reflect gender discrimination and gave victims the right to sue for damages. In recent years gender has replaced race at the top of the civil rights agenda. The courts, Congress, federal agencies, and state legislatures devote a significant amount of time to policies governing relations between the sexes in the workplace. Today, claims of sexual discrimination in hiring, pregnancy discrimination in retention and advancement, and harassment in the workplace constitute more than one-third of all complaints presented to the EEOC.[32]

Rights for Hispanics

According to the U.S. Census Bureau, in 2007 the Hispanic population increased by 3.3 percent over the previous year's estimates and now totals 15.1 percent of the U.S. population.* Over the years Hispanics have experienced many of the same civil rights injustices endured by African Americans. As "national origin" became a protected rights category and as the Hispanic population has grown rapidly, so have the number of discrimination complaints. In many respects, Hispanics have successfully enlisted the legal, administrative, and judicial structures constructed to protect African Americans. Yet their civil rights concerns are also distinctive. The 2000 census figures indicate that about four in ten Hispanics are foreign-born, with most arriving from Mexico and Central America. Many lack the language skills to exercise their civic responsibilities in English. This introduces special civil rights issues associated with language and citizenship. Recognizing this problem early on, Congress passed the 1970 extension of the Voting Rights Act of 1965, requiring that ballots also be available in Spanish in those constituencies where at least 5 percent of the population is Hispanic.

Other recent government actions concerning language have been less accommodating, however. Whether from discrimination or the expressed difficulty of administering multilingual applications, a few states have adopted English-only laws mandating that most state business be conducted in English. When an applicant for an Alabama driver's license challenged the state's English-only law as a civil rights violation, a narrowly divided Supreme Court in *Alexander v. Sandoval* (2001) ruled that an individual could not challenge Alabama's regulation that all driver's license tests and applications be written in English. The 1964 Civil Rights Act allowed individual suits only in cases of "intentional discrimination." The law, according to the majority opinion, left to federal enforcement agencies the determination whether English-only rules had an inherently discriminatory outcome. The decision, in effect, turned this class of civil rights complaints away from the courts and to political and administrative institutions, and stimulated Hispanic efforts to influence national policy.

Illegal, or undocumented, aliens, who constitute a significant share of the Hispanic population, enjoy fewer civil rights protections than do legal aliens, who in turn enjoy

---

*African Americans and Asians by comparison comprise 13.6 and 5 percent of the population, respectively. "U.S. Hispanic Population Surpasses 45 Million, Now 15 Percent of Total," U.S. Bureau of the Census Population Division, May 2008.

This individual from Los Angeles is one of four thousand Hispanics preparing to say the Pledge of Allegiance and complete the naturalization process. This is a critical juncture for the emergence of the Hispanic community as a powerful constituency that comparatively few members complete. In California, for example, less than one third of Hispanic residents who have lived in the United States more than ten years become citizens. This compares to nearly 80 percent citizenship for immigrants from Vietnam, the Philippines, and China. Perhaps coming to the United States from nearby Mexico dissuades many from taking up citizenship. Once citizens, however, Hispanics vote at rates comparable to native whites, controlling for their social and economic status.

less access to government than do citizens. (Moreover, some government entitlements are limited to citizens only. The welfare reform law of 1996, for example, requires citizenship as a condition for obtaining food stamps and certain welfare benefits.) Besides having limited rights claims, illegal aliens are unlikely to exercise those rights when doing so may draw attention to their illegal status and lead to their deportation. Moreover, some states and the federal government have sought to make illegal aliens ineligible for various social services. In 1994 California voters overwhelmingly passed Proposition 187, a referendum denying government services to most undocumented residents. Much of the law's provisions were gutted by a federal court in 1998, but it stimulated other states to enact similar legislation. The figures in Table 4-3 show that immigrant access to state services is one of the most active new areas of state legislation over the past several years.*

---

*Not all of the bills tallied in Table 4-3 are restrictive. A Connecticut law explicitly allows illegal residents to attend the state's universities at the resident tuition fees.

TABLE 4-3

The Profusion of State Laws on Immigration in Absence of National Immigration Reform

Main Topics	2005 Number of Laws	2005 Number of States	2006 Number of Laws	2006 Number of States	2007 Number of Laws	2007 Number of States	2008 Number of Laws	2008 Number of States
Education	3	3	22	17	3	3	12	8
Employment	5	5	29	20	14	9	18	12
Identification/driver's license	11	10	40	30	6	5	30	15
Law enforcement	3	3	16	9	8	6	10	8
Legal services	2	2	3	3	5	5	2	2
Omnibus	0	0	1	1	1	1	2	2
Public benefits	5	5	33	19	10	7	11	10
Human trafficking	9	9	18	13	13	9	4	4
Voting	0	0	0	0	6	6	1	1
Miscellaneous					6	6	28	17
Total laws	38		162		72		118	

Source: Annual Reports of National Council of State Legislatures.

The extent to which Hispanics succeed in having their complaints addressed by political and bureaucratic institutions may depend on their ability to maximize a fundamental political resource—the right to vote. One of every four foreign-born Hispanics is a naturalized citizen.* When this number is added to the 60 percent who are native-born, it means that about seven in ten Hispanics in the United States are citizens. Although the courts in recent years have tended to include aliens under federal civil liberties protections described in the next chapter, citizenship alone confers the right to vote. Therefore, population numbers alone overstate the Hispanic community's potential political power. Another potential source of vote dilution comes out of voter identification laws adopted by six states in 2007 (see Table 4-3). Indiana's law requires voters to show polling place officials photo identification. In 2008 the Supreme Court accepted this requirement as a justifiable protection against potential voter fraud. The 2008 election will be the first to test whether it interferes with voting in general and depresses Hispanic voter turnout in particular, as many Hispanics may not have driver's licenses.

Despite the obstacles facing illegal aliens and other Hispanics, the long-term prognosis for Hispanic civic gains is bright. The population is growing rapidly (see Map 4-4), as are naturalization rates. Moreover, the population as a whole is quite young, with about 40 percent of Hispanics below voting age. As these young people, most of whom are native-born citizens, become eligible to vote, Hispanic electoral power is bound to surge. Finally, with the Hispanic population concentrated residentially, it ensures that a sizable number of officeholders elected by both political parties will

---

*To be eligible for naturalization, immigrants must have permanent resident visas for five years, or if married to a U.S. citizen, have lived in the country for three years.

Map 4-4 High Concentration of U.S. Hispanics: A Guarantee of Political Influence

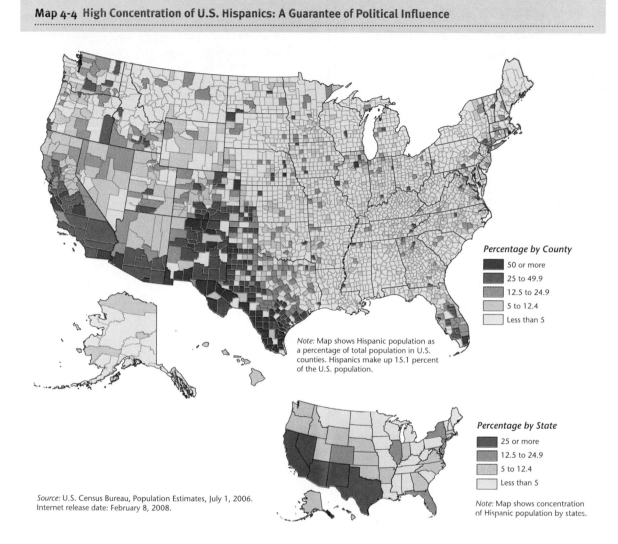

Percentage by County

- 50 or more
- 25 to 49.9
- 12.5 to 24.9
- 5 to 12.4
- Less than 5

Note: Map shows Hispanic population as a percentage of total population in U.S. counties. Hispanics make up 15.1 percent of the U.S. population.

Percentage by State

- 25 or more
- 12.5 to 24.9
- 5 to 12.4
- Less than 5

Note: Map shows concentration of Hispanic population by states.

Source: U.S. Census Bureau, Population Estimates, July 1, 2006. Internet release date: February 8, 2008.

come from their ranks. Indeed, from 1996 to 2007 the number of elected Hispanic officials increased from 3,743 to 5,129 (see Table 4-4). In 2004 more than 25 percent of the California state legislature membership were Hispanic.

Growing numbers and concentration also mean that other politicians will find that they can ill afford to ignore this constituency. The practice of both major-party presidential candidates appealing to voters in 2008 with extensive Spanish-language advertising suggests that in the future the special civil rights claims of Hispanics will find a prominent place on the national agenda.* And just as many of the civil rights gains of

---

*12 and 5 percent of the delegates attending the 2008 Democratic and Republican national conventions, respectively, were Hispanic.

TABLE 4-4

The Emergence of Hispanic Elected Officials: A Result of Growing Numbers

Level of Office	1996	2004	2007
Federal	17	22	26
Statewide officials (including governor)	6	10	6
State legislators	156	221	238
County officials	358	474	512
Municipal officials	1,295	1,585	1,640
Judicial/law enforcement officials	546	638	685
School board/education officials	1,240	1,723	1,847
Special district officials	125	180	175
Total	3,743	4,853	5,129

Source: The National Association of Latino Elected and Appointed Officials (NALEO) Educational Fund.

Hispanics have piggybacked on the success of the black civil rights movement, so too will the policy achievements of Hispanics serve the interests of other similarly situated immigrant groups.

Gay Rights

The favorable "rights" climate generally has encouraged other groups to come forward, particularly the gay community. But civil rights protections directed to homosexuals remain a murky area of national policy. In part, this reflects the recent emergence of gay rights as a prominent national issue. Moreover, many claims of the gay community do not fit neatly into the statutory provisions or judicial precedents created during the civil rights era that subsequently formed the basis for civil rights protection of other groups. Gay rights has thus far failed to attract the levels of popular support that propelled civil rights advances for African Americans, Hispanics, and women.

Where some observers foresee recent Supreme Court decisions as establishing a beachhead for a gay rights movement, the gains are modest at best. As recently as 1986 the Court had ruled state antisodomy laws to be constitutional. Recently, however, in *Lawrence v. Texas* (2003) the Court reversed this decision citing individuals' privacy protections. Some states have extended both job and "hate crime" protections to gays and lesbians. (A recent addition to the repertoire of civil rights defenses, the **hate crime** designation refers to those provisions of the criminal code that make illegal—or stiffen penalties for—violence directed against individuals, property, or organizations solely because of the victims' race, gender, national origin, or sexual orientation.) Other states, however, have sought explicitly to exclude sexual orientation as a protected category. The issue came to the Supreme Court after Colorado voters passed a state constitutional amendment striking down any state and local antidiscrimination laws that stiffened penalties for hate crimes directed at homosexuals. In 1996 the Supreme Court struck down the Colorado amendment as unconstitutionally denying homosexuals equal protection. The Court did not actually confer any specific rights to homosexuals, but, in *Romer v. Evans* it did keep this group eligible for positive protections if state and local jurisdictions deemed them appropriate. Both of these cases dealt with state and local laws.[33] Although state governments and not Washington remain the battlegrounds of the civil rights movement, this soon may change with the emergence of gay marriage on the gay rights agenda.

This controversial issue had been brewing in state and federal courts and in state legislative deliberations for over a decade before it burst into the national news early in 2004. The Massachusetts Supreme Court laid the groundwork late in 2003, when it ruled that a state law banning gay marriages violated Massachusetts's constitution. In 2008, the California Supreme Court ruled that the state's ban on same-sex marriage violated the state constitution's equal protection provisions.

These sudden, mostly judicial changes in long established policy were bound to trigger a reaction. Within weeks of the California decision, sponsors of an initiative to amend the California constitution to define marriage as the union of one man and one woman qualified for the 2008 election ballot. To the surprise of many, California voters—long thought of as among the most progressive in the country—passed the initiative by a margin of 52 percent to 48 percent. That same day, voters in Arizona and Florida also passed state

Published in The New Yorker, July 26, 2004.

"There's nothing wrong with our marriage, but the spectre of gay marriage has hopelessly eroded the institution."

constitutional amendments banning gay marriage. Only Massachusetts and Connecticut—again via state supreme court decisions—sanction same-sex marriages. Eight states provide for some form of civil union between same sex partners. More than half of the states have passed laws or amended their constitution to ban gay marriages outright.

No national law provides explicitly for civil rights protections for this group. In 1995 Congress voted down legislation that would have incorporated sexual preference into existing employment rights laws. The next year it passed the Defense of Marriage Act, which not only rejects same-sex marriages but allows states to ignore homosexual unions sanctioned in other states. By one count, over a thousand federal rights and benefits are available to married couples, including Social Security survivor's benefits, Medicaid eligibility, and estate tax exemptions or reductions.[34] In 2004 President Bush proposed a constitutional amendment limiting marriage to heterosexual couples, while leaving the states the option to fashion alternative civil union laws.*

Rights of the Disabled

The advances in civil rights over the past half-century have been extraordinary in both the kinds of privileges encompassed and the variety of groups that have sought civil rights protections. For example, in addition to the rights of Hispanics, women, and

---

*Vermont is the only state to have a civil union law on its books. Passed in 2000, about 85 percent of the unions have been for out-of-state couples. Most states have refused to recognize this novel legal relationship, which means among other things that couples must return to Vermont to get divorced, for which state residency (for six months) is required.

Map 4-5 States Banning Gay Marriage

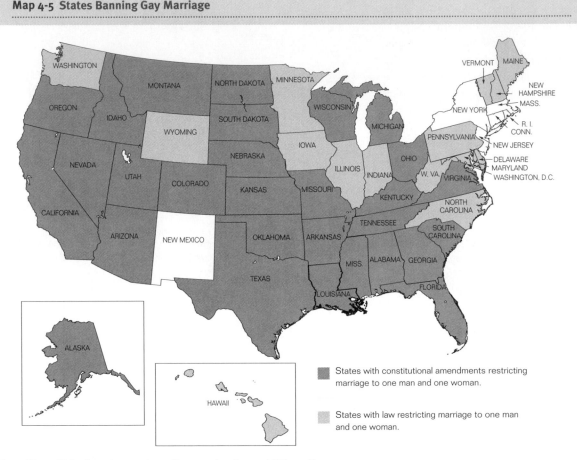

States with constitutional amendments restricting marriage to one man and one woman.

States with law restricting marriage to one man and one woman.

Source: Human Rights Campaign, www.hrc.org/documents/marriage_prohibitions.pdf.

gays, the rights claims of the disabled have become important terrain in civil rights policymaking. Passage in 1990 of the Americans with Disabilities Act, which bars discrimination in employment, transportation, public accommodations, and telecommunications against people with physical and mental disabilities, set in motion legal and political processes that are still defining who the disabled are and the rights claims available to them. In large part the evolving policy reflects the broad, ambiguous definition of *disabled* contained in the law: "a physical or mental impairment that substantially limits one or more of the major life activities." The ambiguous qualifier "substantially" opens the door to every point of view and continual litigation.

Two recent cases illustrate the problems courts confront in implementing this landmark civil rights law. In 1999 the Supreme Court ruled that an airline with a policy of hiring only pilots with naturally occurring 20-20 vision could reject two pilots who needed corrective lenses to achieve such vision. Because their vision was correctable, the Court said, the pilots were not really disabled after all, and therefore the law did not apply to them. In 2001, however, the Court decided that Casey Martin, a golfer with an atrophied leg, could use a golf cart on the PGA tour despite a rule forbidding one. Walking, the Court decided, was not a "fundamental" part of the competition. With dozens of contradictory judgments arising every year in the lower federal court system, national policy on the rights of the disabled in employment practices threatens to become more rather than less muddled.[35]

Challenging Tyranny

This historical survey of civil rights in America reveals courageous men and women advocating for their fellow citizens who were suffering injustice. But this history also reveals that these efforts did not suffice. True to James Madison's observation in *Federalist* No. 10, the cause of civil rights is advanced only when a large national majority fully takes control of the federal government and challenges tyranny in the states. The politicians who assembled these broad national coalitions were keen political strategists. Abraham Lincoln and the Republican Party rode into office advocating "Free Soil, Free Labor, Free Men," not eradication of slavery. Nonetheless, their political success allowed them to conduct a costly and bloody war to preserve the Union and abolish slavery.

From the 1880s through the 1950s neither party could muster a majority even within their party, much less the government, on behalf of civil rights for African Americans. Consequently, the cause languished, and generations of African Americans were doomed to lives marred by segregation's shameful regimen. Then, in the 1960s, the Democratic Party rode the crest of public opinion generated by the civil rights movement. The 1964 election gave Democrats the presidency and huge majorities in both chambers of Congress. They enacted strong new civil rights policies and enforced them. Advances in civil rights since those years rest on a firm foundation of laws and institutions created in response to these historic events.

What does the difficult history of the civil rights movement say about the operation of America's political system? The struggle for civil rights has seriously tested the politics of self-interest. Yet all of the strategic politicians who worked to advance black civil rights offer a more confident depiction of political ambition than the one James Madison presented in *Federalist* No. 51. Whereas Madison viewed competing ambitions as performing a limited, but vital, service of neutralizing politicians who might be inclined to serve themselves more than their constituencies, the history of civil rights portrays these same vote-seeking politicians as transforming moral justice into public policy. David Wilmot, Abraham Lincoln, Lyndon Johnson, and others assembled coalitions of self-interested constituencies behind policies that have rapidly evolved to secure the civil rights of all Americans.

logic.cqpress.com

Key Terms

affirmative action, 174

black codes, 150

civil liberties, 141

civil rights, 141

de facto segregation, 172

de jure segregation, 173

Fugitive Slave Law, 147

grandfather clauses, 153

hate crime, 184

Jim Crow laws, 153

literacy test, 153

poll tax, 153

quotas, 174

racial profiling, 139

segregation, 153

separate but equal doctrine, 154

suffragists, 176

white primary, 153

Suggested Readings

Anderson, Kristi. *After Suffrage.* Chicago: University of Chicago Press, 1996. Anderson assembles all of the available voting and registration data in providing a detailed and varied history of the entry of women into American politics.

Branch, Taylor. *Parting the Waters: America in the King Years, 1954–1963.* New York: Simon and Schuster, 1988; and *Pillar of Fire: America in the King Years, 1963–65.* New York: Simon and Schuster, 1998. These two installments of Branch's detailed political history of civil rights offer a wealth of instruction to students of politics and history alike.

Carmines, Edward G., and James A. Stimson. *Issue Evolution: Race and the Transformation of American Politics.* Princeton: Princeton University Press, 1989. Although these scholars use sophisticated statistical techniques, they offer an accessible and convincing account of the evolution of the Democratic Party among politicians and citizens as the party of civil rights.

Garrow, David J. *Bearing the Cross: Martin Luther King Jr. and the Southern Christian Leadership Conference.* New York: Morrow, 1986. An absorbing account of the rise of King from the Montgomery bus boycott to his assassination in 1968.

Keyssar, Alexander. *The Right to Vote.* New York: Basic Books, 2000. This highly readable history of the extension of voting rights in America has emerged as the authoritative source on the subject.

Oates, Stephen B. *With Malice Toward None: The Life of Abraham Lincoln.* New York: New American Library–Dutton, 1978. Our favorite Lincoln biography has two great virtues: Lincoln is shown to be a masterful politician, and the gradual emergence of emancipation as a wartime issue is described clearly.

Review Questions

1. More Americans were killed in the Civil War than in any other war in American history. What did the South expect to gain from the war? The North?

2. What features of government did the southern states employ to prevent the eradication of slavery? What steps were necessary to remove the obstacles to emancipation?

3. How and why did the readmission of the southern states after the Civil War threaten the Republican Party's grip on power? How was Reconstruction tailored to help ensure that Republicans remained in power?

4. What benefits did Reconstruction produce for former slaves? For northern whites? What benefits and which groups did Reconstruction "leave out" and why?

5. What party did most African Americans support prior to the 1930s and why? Why did this change after the 1930s and what was responsible for the change?

6. How did the civil rights demonstrations of the 1960s change the political calculations of Democratic politicians? How were the demonstrations planned strategically to increase pressure on politicians?

7. What challenges and opportunities do Hispanics face in their current civil rights efforts? How do these challenges differ from those blacks faced in their civil rights campaigns?

8. How has the Supreme Court responded to efforts to use affirmative action in college admissions? What accounts for the current state of affirmative action jurisprudence?

9. Why did the Equal Rights Amendment fail to be ratified despite its initial popularity?

10. How does the campaign for gay rights differ from prior civil rights campaigns?

Exercises

The Changing Face of [Your County Name Here]
Go to the Historical United States Census Data Browser at http://fisher.lib.virginia.edu/collections/stats/histcensus. Select the 1860 census from the menu bar on the left side of the page. Use the menus to select the total number of slaveholders, slaves, white persons, and "free colored persons." After you've browsed the information for all states, select your state from the list and use the "view counties" option at the lower left to view the specific information for your county. Then go back to the main menu and repeat the applicable searches for 1900, 1930, and 1970. How have the demographics of your county changed over time?

Building on the Roots
This chapter makes the argument that the black civil rights movement has paved the way for other societal groups to assert their own civil rights. Go to the following groups' Web sites and see how they frame their agenda in terms of "civil rights."

- Webplace Search Page (http://search.aarp.org)
- National Organization for Women search page (http://now.org/search/search.cgi)
- National Gay and Lesbian Task Force Press Releases Simple Search (http://thetaskforce.org/search.cfm)
- Disability Rights Education and Defense Fund site search (http://dredf.org/search/search.pl)

Do an Internet search for "bill of rights." Note the different types of groups that are pursuing or have acquired their own "bill of rights."

5

Civil Liberties

Has the existence of a formal Bill of Rights really secured the freedoms of Americans?

Does the Supreme Court's primacy in this area of public policy imply that democracy requires an institution of unelected judges for its protection? What other ways of protecting civil liberties might there be?

What roles, if any, do Congress, the president, and the states play in defining civil liberties?

Since the Bill of Rights does not mention "right of privacy," how can the Supreme Court deem it to be a fundamental constitutional right?

"A 24-Hour-a-Day Centralized System of Surveillance"

Approximately five thousand surveillance cameras in public schools, public housing developments, metro stations, public parks, and streets keep watch over Washington, D.C., residents. While some locals and the American Civil Liberties Union (ACLU) oppose any surveillance cameras, Mayor Adrian Fenty boosted the cameras' capabilities with a centralized monitoring facility that connects the vast majority of the cameras into a single network. With more cameras to be added by the end of 2008, opponents have criticized the absence of specific rules to safeguard citizen privacy and prevent misuse of surveillance footage. In June 2008, the D.C. Council passed legislation mandating the same rules that apply to the police department's surveillance system, but the mayor resisted, announcing his own emergency rules until he and the Council can reach agreement. In the post–September 11 climate, cameras—and the privacy rights debate that accompanies them—will likely remain fixtures in major American cities such as Washington, D.C., New York, Chicago, and Philadelphia.

"Keeping It 'In the Family': California's Expansive Use of DNA to Solve Crime"

In 2004, California voters passed Proposition 69 requiring the state to take DNA samples from all convicted felons. The samples are put into a database, which is then searched for a direct match to any DNA taken from a crime scene. In spring 2008,

Police officers monitor twenty-two screens of the Washington, D.C., surveillance system, believed to be the most extensive in the country.

Attorney General Jerry Brown announced a controversial new policy in which law enforcement would search for criminals using *partial* DNA matches. If a partial match is found, the sample is then further analyzed to determine if a male relative of the convicted felon could be a match, which could then make the relative a suspect in the crime. Many civil liberties groups objected to this new policy as "genetic surveillance," amounting to an unreasonable search under the Fourth Amendment and an unwarranted violation of the individual's privacy. Moreover, beginning in 2009 California will collect DNA samples of everyone *arrested* on felony charges whether eventually convicted or not. If the charges are subsequently dropped or the individual is found not guilty, he or she may petition a court for removal of their DNA from the database, but there is no right to appeal. A federal court turned aside an early challenge to this law by the ACLU on the grounds that litigation was premature. Undoubtedly, legal battles will follow once the state implements the new policies.

"University Reprimands Student/Employee for Reading a Book about the KKK, Then Changes Its Mind"

In late 2007, Keith Sampson, a student at Indiana University–Purdue University Indianapolis (IUPUI) who was also employed as a janitor, was reprimanded by the university for racial harassment against black coworkers. Sampson was further warned that "any future substantiated conduct of a similar nature could result in serious disciplinary action." Ironically, the harassing conduct at issue was his reading a book—available from the university's own library—entitled *Notre Dame vs. the Klan: How the Fighting Irish Defeated the Ku Klux Klan*. After the ACLU and other groups raised, among other issues, "freedom of speech" concerns—the courts have long equated consuming ideas as equivalent to expressing them—and the national news media took notice, the university's response and tone slowly began to change. First, IUPUI's office "clarified" its reprimand saying that Sampson could read scholarly books during break times and that the reprimand letter meant only to address his "conduct" (although reading the book was the only "conduct" raised in the initial letter). Later, the chancellor wrote the university's *mea culpa* letter, expressing regret, and affirming its "longstanding commitment" to "the principles of freedom of expression." Later, during summer 2008, approximately a week after a *Wall Street Journal* editorial lambasted the university, IUPUI formally apologized to Sampson.

"Fighting Eminent Domain with the First Amendment"

In a major 2005 case the Supreme Court ruled that the Constitution's Fifth Amendment "takings" clause (see page 239) did not prevent government entities from forcing property owners to sell their property for public use (popularly referred to as "eminent domain"). That decision has emboldened many cities to take over and redevelop run-down areas. Many times property owners put up a fight. Jim Roos, who manages property in a targeted area in St. Louis, Missouri, protested with a two-story mural proclaiming "End Eminent Domain Abuse." When the city tried to force him to remove the sign, under an ordinance banning signs of a certain size without permits, Roos filed a lawsuit asserting not only his private property rights, but also his First Amendment freedom of speech. The city has countersued to force Roos to remove the sign, claiming that the problem is not the *content* of the message, but the *size* of the mural.

Nationalization of Civil Liberties

Civil liberties claims—of all kinds—dominate today's newspaper headlines and lead television evening news programs, and for good reason. Occasionally an established freedom is being abridged. Arguably more common, however, a policy change expands personal liberties and extends established freedoms into new domains. Everyone prefers freedom to tyranny, but an expansion of civil liberties is often controversial. As the above cases illustrate, civil liberties claims frequently run up against the ardent preferences of a majority of the citizenry, the nation's legitimate security needs, or even the rights claims of others.

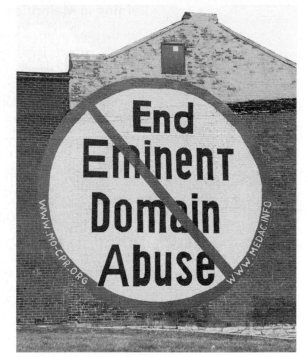

Is it art or simply "a two-story piece of graffiti"?

Civil liberties, though, have not always been so prominent in the nation's news and policy deliberations. At the end of the nineteenth century readers might have had to scour newspapers for more than a month to discover claims invoking such constitutionally established privileges as freedom of the press, speech, and religion. Many modern-day civil liberty assertions would have struck the nineteenth-century public as bizarre. If and when gay marriages, physician-assisted suicides, and abortions occurred in nineteenth-century America, they were clandestine, and ultimately criminal, enterprises.

Civil liberties have emerged as a major part of the national policy agenda for a variety of reasons. New technologies and modern lifestyles are partly responsible for the entry of individual liberties into the public arena. Technological advances in every field from communications to medicine challenge established principles. The *principle* of free expression was not an issue in 1996 when Congress passed the Communications Decency Act allowing censorship of the Internet, or in 1997 when the Supreme Court struck it down as unconstitutional.[1] The *real* issue was how existing standards of free expression applied to this new medium in which juveniles could easily access sexually explicit language and images. Other civil liberties issues are responses to cultural changes bringing freer expression in lifestyle, art, and politics.

Reining in Majorities

Over the past century, determination of national civil liberties policy has shifted from nearly the exclusive jurisdiction of states and communities to Washington. Previously, defendants' rights amounted to little more than what the local police and sheriff would allow. In many states local judges, prosecutors, and legal associations agreed that exclusively white (and mostly older) male jurors satisfied their standards of impartiality and that an attorney for indigent defendants represented an unneeded luxury. Local ministers tendered prayers to school principals, who handed them to teachers and students for morning recitations. Eventually, though, the national government assumed jurisdiction over defendants' rights and school prayer. With a new, expansive interpretation of the Constitution, the courts applied the Bill of Rights to state and local policies as well as national policy.

The histories of civil rights and civil liberties have much in common. Indeed, the constitutional amendments conferring full citizenship to recently freed slaves would later provide a rationale for the national government to enter the civil liberties arena. In both histories the judiciary played a pivotal role in denying or accepting the claims of an individual or group's rights over the objections of some local or national majority. But in other important respects, the history of civil liberties proceeds down a different path. As discussed in Chapter 4 the greatest advances in civil rights occurred when a national majority took up a minority's cause; so long as the national government continued silent, slavery and segregation were secure. The federal judiciary struck the first blows against segregation, but the rights of African Americans did not substantially improve until congressional majorities joined presidents prepared to stake their party's electoral fortunes on intervening directly against segregation and black disenfranchisement. In the end, civil rights required the sustained efforts of a national majority exerting the full force of the federal government. By contrast, advances in national civil liberties policy have frequently involved reining in majorities that assert their prerogatives over the objections of individuals and groups who did not wish to conform to prevailing social norms and rules. National policy protecting flag-burning demonstrators from incarceration, barring communal prayer at public school graduations, and preventing juries from hearing confessions from defendants before they were read their rights are just a few examples where recent civil liberties policy has frustrated the preferences of local and even national majorities.

The Bill of Rights Checks Majority Rule

Where the history of civil rights emphasizes the capacity of majorities to control policy, the history of civil liberties reminds us that the United States is a republic whose institutions are designed to temper the fleeting passions of majorities. The Framers well understood that civil liberties policy would at times check majority preferences; the First Amendment to the Bill of Rights intentionally begins with the emphatic and revealing language "Congress shall make no law," and covers six different areas of personal and political liberty. Unlike civil rights, civil liberties are a domain in which national majorities will be constrained in fixing national policy. This opening phrase also invited the Supreme Court to eventually define civil liberties, in part since the judiciary was designed to be insulated from popular pressures. Recognizing this fact, James Madison predicted that the courts "will consider themselves in a peculiar manner the guardians of [civil liberties]: they will be an impenetrable bulwark against every assumption of power in the legislative or executive; they will be naturally led to resist every encroachment upon rights." [2]

The Bill of Rights (see box "The Bill of Rights") was designed to limit the capacity of the government to impose conformity costs on those individuals and minorities whose views differ from those of the majority. By insisting that these first ten amendments be placed in the Constitution, the Antifederalist critics of ratification sought assurance that these rights could not be easily removed or abridged. Only if the majority was overwhelming and enduring, could it absorb the high transaction costs required to modify these rights via a constitutional amendment. Thus the Supreme Court's authority to veto Congress and state governments on these policies places civil liberties under the protective purview of an institution intentionally insulated from the "popular passions" of the majority.

The generally clear and unequivocal language of the Bill of Rights also provides government officials with little latitude to relax its proscriptions. Yet no amendment has ever been judged absolute, and some are downright ambiguous. What precisely does the First Amendment clause "Congress shall make no law respecting an establishment of religion" really mean? Its narrow construction is unambiguous. Congress cannot "establish" a particular faith as the "official" religion of the country. Beyond that, the clause offers little guidance and has even fostered opposing interpretations of the relationship between church and state. Does it prevent a moment of silent prayer in public schools? Does it deny government transportation and textbook subsidies for children attending private, church-sponsored schools? Similarly, what does the Eighth Amendment's prohibition of "cruel and unusual" punishment mean, and of greater practical significance, who decides? Are the justices of the Supreme Court endowed with special insight on appropriate punishment? If not, should states' citizens decide the matter in their criminal statutes, as is largely the case today? If so, what did the Framers have in mind when they employed this language in the national Constitution?

Sometimes ambiguity arises from two or more clearly worded Constitutional provisions that are directly opposed to each other. An example of a particularly thorny conundrum concerns how unregulated press reportage (a First Amendment right) undermines a criminal defendant's Sixth Amendment right to an impartial jury. Which value should prevail when press coverage introduces highly incriminating or biased information and opinions before the trial?

Other constitutional responsibilities, especially those concerning the country's collective security, may bring official actions into conflict with individual rights. The preamble to the Constitution charges the national government to "provide for the common defence," and Article II designates the president as "Commander in Chief." Does this presidential responsibility allow the government to restrict freedom of the press during times of war, as President Abraham Lincoln claimed, or to eavesdrop on defendant-attorney conversations, as the George W. Bush administration announced

The Bill of Rights

Amendment I

Congress shall make no law respecting an establishment of religion, or prohibiting the free exercise thereof; or abridging the freedom of speech, or of the press; or the right of the people peacefully to assemble, and to petition the Government for a redress of grievances.

Amendment II

A well regulated Militia, being necessary to the security of a free State, the right of the people to keep and bear Arms, shall not be infringed.

Amendment III

No Soldier shall, in time of peace be quartered in any house, without the consent of the Owner, nor in time of war, but in a manner to be prescribed by law.

Amendment IV

The right of the people to be secure in their persons, houses, papers, and effects, against unreasonable searches and seizures, shall not be violated, and no Warrants shall issue, but upon probable cause, supported by Oath or affirmation, and particularly describing the place to be searched, and the persons or things to be seized.

Amendment V

No person shall be held to answer for a capital, or otherwise infamous crime, unless on a presentment or indictment of a Grand Jury, except in cases arising in the land or naval forces, or in the Militia, when in actual service in time of War or public danger; nor shall any person be subject for the same offence to be twice put in jeopardy of life or limb; nor shall be compelled in any criminal case to be a witness against himself, nor be deprived of life, liberty, or property, without due process of law; nor shall private property be taken for public use, without just compensation.

Amendment VI

In all criminal prosecutions, the accused shall enjoy the right to a speedy and public trial, by an impartial jury of the State and district wherein the crime shall have been committed, which district shall have been previously ascertained by law, and to be informed of the nature and cause of the accusation; to be confronted with the witnesses against him; to have compulsory process for obtaining witnesses in his favor, and to have the Assistance of Counsel for his defence.

Amendment VII

In Suits at common law, where the value in controversy shall exceed twenty dollars, the right of trial by jury shall be preserved, and no fact tried by a jury, shall be otherwise re-examined in any Court of the United States, than according to the rules of the common law.

Amendment VIII

Excessive bail shall not be required, nor excessive fines imposed, nor cruel and unusual punishments inflicted.

Amendment IX

The enumeration in the Constitution, of certain rights, shall not be construed to deny or disparage others retained by the people.

Amendment X

The powers not delegated to the United States by the Constitution, nor prohibited by it to the States, are reserved to the States respectively, or to the people.

in the aftermath of the September 11 attacks? Whether liberties are competing with one another or with other parts of the Constitution, the Bill of Rights represents a Pandora's box of unanswered policy questions.

The absolute language of the Bill of Rights notwithstanding, civil liberties policy is essentially a line-drawing or boundary-setting activity separating what government actions are and are not permissible. At times all three branches of government, in grappling with an issue, disagree over the meaning of the Bill of Rights. In a series of rulings beginning in 1990 the Supreme Court started a protracted disagreement over a new standard for whether state and local laws impinged on protected religious practices. In *Employment Division v. Smith* the Court ruled that otherwise valid, neutral laws of general applicability (such as drug laws) that incidentally impinge on a particular religious practice do not violate the First Amendment's free exercise clause.[3] Seeking to blunt the impact of the decision, religious organizations of every persuasion that had been exempt from a wide variety of laws, ranging from antidrug statutes to zoning restrictions, lobbied Congress to enact a blanket law that would effectively exempt them from local regulations.

In 1993 Congress passed the Religious Freedom Restoration Act, which voided any law or regulation that "substantially burdened" religious practices if it could not be shown to serve a "compelling government interest . . . by the least restrictive means." In signing the new law, President Bill Clinton noted that it effectively reversed the Court's 1990 decision and in his judgment was "far more consistent with the intent of the Founders than [was] the Supreme Court." Four years later the Court ruled that Congress had overstepped its constitutional authority in applying the new law to the states (as opposed to the federal government), and struck down the act to that extent. The Court majority reminded Congress and the president that "[t]he power to interpret a case or controversy remains in the Judiciary."[4] Congress promptly reopened hearings and in 2000 enacted legislation making it harder for local governments to enforce zoning decisions against religious organizations. Although by the close of its 2008 session the Supreme Court had not stepped back into this exchange of policy views, it did decide *not* to review two appeals by churches against local regulations that appeared to violate the revised federal law.* In this long, tit-for-tat exchange, the Supreme Court stressed the Constitution's prohibition of religious establishment by the federal government; Congress and the president emphasized religious freedom.

The result, a rare demonstration of these institutions squaring off against each other, contrasted with their usual practice of jointly defining current liberties and rights. The conflict also reconfirmed how the Constitution's language has permitted the modern Supreme Court to carve out a large role in formulating civil liberties policy. The judiciary's move to the forefront of civil liberties policy created a revolution in rights and liberties, an important theme of this chapter.

Writing Rights and Liberties into the Constitution

The Constitution, as it emerged from the 1787 Philadelphia Convention, did not seriously address civil liberties. Late in the convention George Mason of Virginia had

---

*In 2006, the Court did unanimously uphold application of the Religious Freedom Restoration Act against the *federal* government. *Gonzales v. O Centro Espirita Beneficiente Uniao Do Vegetal,* 546 U.S. 418 (2006).

proposed prefacing the document with a bill of rights (many state constitutions already had one), but most delegates were skeptical about the need for such an addition.[5] (Mason subsequently cited this omission as the reason he turned against the Constitution's ratification.) The delegates reasoned that the solution to tyranny lay in correctly designed institutions that balanced interests through competition. Some delegates also feared that a list of rights in the Constitution might imply that the federal government had the authority to restrict the freedoms not expressly protected. Alexander Hamilton posed the question famously in *Federalist* No. 84: "Why declare that things shall not be done which there is no power to do? Why, for instance, should it be said that the liberty of the press shall not be restrained, when no power is given by which restrictions may be imposed?"

Mason was not the only advocate of a federal bill of rights. Throughout the ratifying process Antifederalists rallied opposition by arguing vigorously that the new constitutional plan flirted with tyranny by omitting explicit protections for the citizenry. Recognizing a chink in their armor, Madison and fellow supporters of the Constitution conceded the point and agreed that after its ratification they would introduce at the first session of the new Congress the amendments required for a bill of rights.

The Constitution actually acquired civil liberties protections in several steps over a long period of time. The first step was inclusion of the Bill of Rights, which insulated citizens from interference by the federal government in a variety of areas. The second, taken more than seventy-five years later, after the Civil War, was ratification of the Fourteenth Amendment, which gave the national government the authority to protect the rights of former slaves. And in a third step, which has occurred over the twentieth century and into the twenty-first, the Supreme Court has interpreted the Fourteenth Amendment to apply the Bill of Rights to the actions of state and local governments. Judicial scholars commonly refer to this process as **incorporation**—that is, bringing state laws and practices under Bill of Rights protections by applying the Fourteenth Amendment to the states. Thus, the nationalization of civil liberties has not only altered the balance of power between Washington and the states, but it has also dramatically expanded the range of protections offered by the Bill of Rights. The federal judiciary now plays an increasing role in this area of public policy.

The First Ten Amendments

In June 1789 James Madison, elected to the First Congress as a representative from Virginia, followed through on his earlier commitment to a bill of rights by introducing seventeen constitutional amendments. His letters indicate that he may even have been persuaded of the merit of having these government proscriptions stated explicitly. Writing to his friend Thomas Jefferson, Madison conjectured that constitutionally guaranteed rights "acquire by degrees the character of fundamental maxims of free Governments, and as they become incorporated with the national sentiment, counteract the impulses of interest and passion."[6]

Madison may have been won over to the Bill of Rights, but he steadfastly believed that the states and not the national government provided the most fertile soil for tyranny. Acting on that belief, one of the amendments he submitted to the First Congress limited state authority. It read: "No state shall infringe the right of trial by jury in criminal cases, nor the right of conscience, nor the freedom of speech or of the press." States' rights advocates, however, were suspicious. Madison's effort to restrain the states smacked of another "nationalist" ruse, and they struck it from the list of amendments sent to the states for ratification. Two years then passed before the required three-quarters of the states ratified the Bill of Rights. Although the Antifederalists lost the ratification fight, they salvaged a major political concession in the Bill of Rights, their chief legacy to future generations of Americans.

In 1833 states' righters secured a victory in a landmark Supreme Court decision that governed the Court's posture and removed civil liberties from the national agenda for nearly a century. *Barron v. Baltimore* concerned road repairs made by the city of Baltimore that caused a buildup of gravel and sand in the area of John Barron's wharf, impeding access of deep-bottomed vessels.[7] Barron sued the city of Baltimore for violating his constitutionally guaranteed property rights. Pointing out that the Fifth Amendment forbade the public "taking" of private property without "just compensation," Barron argued that this provision applied to the states as well as the federal government and, therefore, Baltimore owed him money.

The Supreme Court ruled unanimously against Barron, holding that the Bill of Rights restrained only the actions of the national government. The whole thrust of the Bill of Rights, the justices reasoned, was directed exclusively at federal power. In short, the federal courts could not alleviate the excesses of state and local governments. Handed down in an era of limited federal responsibilities, the ruling rendered the Bill of Rights virtually meaningless, for most citizens' quarrels were with their state governments. If a state's residents wanted the rights that Barron claimed, they should amend their state constitution, suggested the Court. The other option—to amend the U.S. Constitution to apply the Bill of Rights to the states—was left unsaid. Yet achievements on the civil liberties front continued, and instead of serving as the last word on the subject, *Barron* today is a historical relic, illustrating how Americans once regarded their rights and federal-state relations. Reflecting the low salience of civil liberties in the nation's civic discourse, an introductory American government textbook written ten years after *Barron* devoted fewer than 5 of its 332 pages to the Bill of Rights.[8]

Incorporation via the Fourteenth Amendment

Among the several constitutional amendments proposed during Reconstruction was the Fourteenth—a text crammed with now-familiar phrases (see box "Fourteenth Amendment: Section 1"). Although the amendment, passed in 1868, was intended initially to protect former slaves by explicitly declaring that rights of citizenship were not subject to state controls, over time its sweeping language led other groups to seek its umbrella protections. Yet nearly a half-century of jurisprudence passed before the Supreme Court began to interpret the Fourteenth Amendment language as requiring the states to adhere to the national government's Bill of Rights protections.[9] One of the great ironies of American history is that while this amendment failed to achieve its

Fourteenth Amendment

Section 1

All persons born or naturalized in the United States and subject to the jurisdiction thereof, are citizens of the United States and of the State wherein they reside. No State shall make or enforce any law which shall abridge the *privileges or immunities* of citizens of the United States; nor shall any State deprive any person of life, liberty, or property, without *due process of law*; nor deny to any person within its jurisdiction the *equal protection of the laws* [emphasis added].

immediate objective, a century later it extended the rights and liberties of all citizens in directions unimaginable to its authors.

The first sentence of the amendment provides for a unified national citizenship and thereby directly contradicts the Court's assertion in *Barron* that state citizenship and national citizenship are separate affiliations. The second sentence, in articulating both the **due process clause** and the **equal protection clause,** states flatly that *all* persons enjoy the same civil liberties and rights, which the states cannot deny "without due process of law" (that is, without following reasonable, legally established procedures), and which the states must apply equally to everyone. To the modern reader this language seems plainly to say that states cannot violate the Bill of Rights, but in 1868 this broad interpretation of the Fourteenth Amendment continued to elude most readers—at least those on the Supreme Court.

In 1873 the Court rejected its first opportunity to incorporate the Bill of Rights into the Fourteenth Amendment. In the *Slaughterhouse Cases* a group of disgruntled butchers sued to invalidate a New Orleans ordinance that gave a single company a monopoly over all slaughterhouse business.[10] They based their appeal on the Fourteenth Amendment, arguing that the monopoly denied them the "privileges and immunities" (that is, the constitutionally protected rights) of citizens. The Court did not agree. By a 5–4 decision it ruled that the monopoly did not violate the Fourteenth Amendment because the amendment was intended to protect black citizens. Moreover, broad application of the amendment to state policy would "fetter and degrade the State governments by subjecting them to the control of Congress." With that decision, the Court effectively short-circuited any future development of the **privileges and immunities clause;** subsequently lawyers trying to persuade the Court that the Fourteenth Amendment applied to the states targeted the due process provision that this decision did not address. Although plaintiffs in these cases consistently lost their arguments as well, most justices agreed that the due process clause might be construed to protect certain unspecified "fundamental rights."[11]

Some twenty-five years into the twentieth century the Court gingerly began to incorporate into the Fourteenth Amendment those provisions of the Bill of Rights dealing with personal freedoms.* Only gradually, about the same time it was relinquishing its custodianship of laissez-faire capitalism, did the Supreme Court assume guardianship of civil liberties by applying piecemeal the various provisions of the Bill of Rights to state laws and practices (Table 5-1 shows the growth in the civil liberties docket of

---

*Throughout the nineteenth century litigants mostly contested property rights, not personal liberties. As a result, little case law on the subject accumulated.

TABLE 5-1

The Supreme Court's Civil Liberties Cases: A Major Share of Decisions

	Civil Liberties Cases per Term			Civil Liberties Cases per Term	
	No.	%		No.	%
1946	33	24	1977	47	35
1947	40	35	1978	49	37
1948	31	26	1979	63	45
1949	25	27	1980	41	32
1950	20	21	1981	47	32
1951	30	33	1982	54	35
1952	30	28	1983	66	43
1953	20	19	1984	62	44
1954	27	29	1985	69	45
1955	19	19	1986	69	45
1956	36	30	1987	56	39
1957	49	39	1988	59	42
1958	37	31	1989	61	47
1959	26	23	1990	40	35
1960	53	41	1991	38	35
1961	30	30	1992	40	36
1962	33	26	1993	35	40
1963	31	24	1994	30	36
1964	30	28	1995	28	37
1965	32	31	1996	30	37
1966	40	36	1997	31	35
1967	53	43	1998	23	29
1968	40	36	1999	39	53
1969	39	36	2000	32	44
1970	52	42	2001	31	40
1971	62	42	2002	25	34
1972	62	41	2003	34	47
1973	53	36	2004	32	42
1974	43	31	2005	34	46
1975	61	40	2006	26	37
1976	55	38			

Source: Adapted from Lee Epstein et al., *The Supreme Court Compendium: Data, Decisions, and Developments,* 4th ed. (Washington, D.C.: CQ Press, 2008), Table 2-11 and Table 3-8. Updates provided by Lee Epstein.

Notes: In the table the term *civil liberties* encompasses the following issue areas: criminal procedure, First Amendment, due process, privacy, and attorneys. For 1995–2006, the totals on which the percentages are based do not include interstate relations cases. From 1946–1994, the Court heard fifty-five such cases, or an average of about one per term.

the Court). Through this process, called **selective incorporation,** civil liberties have been gradually "nationalized" (see Table 5-2). The Supreme Court first incorporated a provision of the Bill of Rights into the Fourteenth Amendment's due process clause in 1897, when it selected for incorporation the Fifth Amendment's ban on taking private property without compensation.

TABLE 5-2

Cases Incorporating Provisions of the Bill of Rights into the Due Process Clause of the Fourteenth Amendment

Constitutional Provision	Case	Year
First Amendment		
Freedom of speech and press	*Gitlow v. New York*	1925
Freedom of assembly	*DeJonge v. Oregon*	1937
Freedom of petition	*Hague v. CIO*	1939
Free exercise of religion	*Cantwell v. Connecticut*	1940
Establishment of religion	*Everson v. Board of Education*	1947
Fourth Amendment		
Unreasonable search and seizure	*Wolf v. Colorado*	1949
Exclusionary rule	*Mapp v. Ohio*	1961
Fifth Amendment		
Payment of compensation for the taking of private property	*Chicago, Burlington and Quincy R. Co. v. Chicago*	1897
Self-incrimination	*Malloy v. Hogan*	1964
Double jeopardy	*Benton v. Maryland*	1969
When jeopardy attaches	*Crist v. Bretz*	1978
Sixth Amendment		
Public trial	*In re Oliver*	1948
Due notice	*Cole v. Arkansas*	1948
Right to counsel (felonies)	*Gideon v. Wainwright*	1963
Confrontation and cross-examination of adverse witnesses	*Pointer v. Texas*	1965
Speedy trial	*Klopfer v. North Carolina*	1967
Compulsory process to obtain witnesses	*Washington v. Texas*	1967
Jury trial	*Duncan v. Louisiana*	1968
Right to counsel (misdemeanor when jail is possible)	*Argersinger v. Hamlin*	1972
Eighth Amendment		
Cruel and unusual punishment	*Louisiana ex rel. Francis v. Resweber*	1947
Ninth Amendment		
Privacy[a]	*Griswold v. Connecticut*	1965

Source: Adapted from Lee Epstein and Thomas G. Walker, *Constitutional Law for a Changing America: Rights, Liberties, and Justice,* 6th ed. (Washington, D.C.: CQ Press, 2007), Table 3-1.

a. The word *privacy* does not appear in the Ninth Amendment nor anywhere in the text of the Constitution. In *Griswold* several members of the Court viewed the Ninth Amendment as guaranteeing (and incorporating) that right.

From the 1920s through the 1940s the Court took up the First Amendment freedoms (speech, press, and religion), which remain the rights most carefully protected. At first, the justices viewed criminal rights as a special class for which incorporation did not apply.* But then, in the 1960s, the Court also covered most of the provisions of the Fourth, Fifth, and Sixth Amendments through the due process and equal protection clauses. Today, a third wave of advances in civil liberties may be forming as judges and politicians explore the right to privacy.

The Supreme Court's post-1925 incorporation decisions have served as precedents in guiding lower federal and state courts and, by offering new opportunities for litigation, have generated the dramatic growth in the civil liberties docket of the Court. Yet incorporation has occurred incrementally, case by case. Indeed, some provisions of the Bill of Rights are still not applied to the states: the Second Amendment right to keep and bear arms, the Third Amendment prohibition against quartering soldiers, the Fifth Amendment provisions concerning grand jury hearings, the Seventh Amendment right to a jury trial in civil cases, and the Eighth Amendment right against excessive bail and fines. The states retain broad discretion in regulating these areas. Nonetheless, the accumulated precedents mean that Madison's vision of the national government as the ultimate guarantor of individual rights has largely been realized.

Judicial Interpretation

The incorporation of Bill of Rights provisions into the Fourteenth Amendment was a

---

*Palko v. Connecticut, 302 U.S. 319 (1937). At the same time, the Court also refused to assume federal jurisdiction over a double jeopardy case, finding that protection against double jeopardy was not as fundamental to "liberty" and "justice" as were the First Amendment guarantees.

historic development in civil liberties, comparable to adoption of the Bill of Rights itself. As we have seen, incorporation occurred not through legislative mandate or the amendment process but through judicial interpretation. Once this was done, the Supreme Court could turn to the more substantive issue of whether particular state policies violated constitutional protections and, if so, what the remedies should be.

Supreme Court justices agree that as jurists they are obligated to interpret the Constitution as objectively as possible. Yet on any particular ruling they frequently disagree—sometimes sharply—over what an "objective" interpretation prescribes. A literalist, finding no language in the Constitution that protects burning of the U.S. flag, might conclude that the Bill of Rights does not defend this act. Another justice might view flag burning as a kind of political expression sufficiently close to speech and deserving of First Amendment protection.

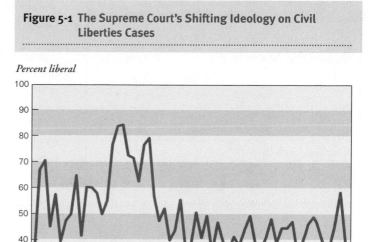

Figure 5-1 The Supreme Court's Shifting Ideology on Civil Liberties Cases

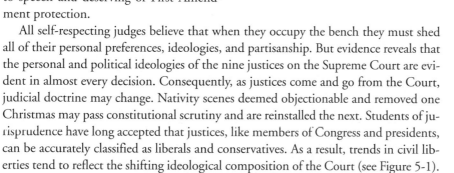

Percent liberal

Source: Adapted from Lee Epstein et al., *The Supreme Court Compendium: Data, Decisions, and Developments,* 4th ed. (Washington, D.C.: CQ Press, 2008), Table 3-8.

All self-respecting judges believe that when they occupy the bench they must shed all of their personal preferences, ideologies, and partisanship. But evidence reveals that the personal and political ideologies of the nine justices on the Supreme Court are evident in almost every decision. Consequently, as justices come and go from the Court, judicial doctrine may change. Nativity scenes deemed objectionable and removed one Christmas may pass constitutional scrutiny and are reinstalled the next. Students of jurisprudence have long accepted that justices, like members of Congress and presidents, can be accurately classified as liberals and conservatives. As a result, trends in civil liberties tend to reflect the shifting ideological composition of the Court (see Figure 5-1).

The reality that justices do follow their ideological beliefs has the advantage of predictability, much appreciated by presidents who, in nominating these life-tenure officeholders, seek candidates who would continue to implement the president's political views, as if they were dutiful delegates, long after the president leaves office. By selecting and confirming nominees whose political values agree with their own, the White House and the Senate can seek to influence the course of judicial policy. Far from undermining democratic responsibility, judicial ideology allows elected officeholders to keep the judiciary from straying too far from the majority opinion in the nation.

For example, the Supreme Court shifted in a conservative direction shortly after Republican Richard Nixon, elected president in 1968, started filling Court vacancies,

TABLE 5-3

Americans' Great Tolerance of Unpopular Speech

	Should be allowed to speak (percent)	Should be allowed to teach in a college (percent)	His or her book should be allowed in your library (percent)
An admitted communist			
1954	28	6	29
1976	56	44	58
1985	59	46	59
1996	66	60	67
2002	71	62	71
2004	70	66	71
A person who believes African Americans are genetically inferior			
1976	62	42	62
1985	57	44	62
1996	62	48	66
2002	64	53	67
2004	63	47	66
Someone against all churches and religion			
1954	38	12	37
1976	65	42	61
1985	66	47	62
1996	74	58	71
2002	78	75	75
Homosexual			
1976	64	54	57
1985	69	60	57
1996	83	77	71
2002	85	80	77
2004	84	88	75

Source: General Social Survey, National Opinion Research Center, University of Chicago, various years.

and the trend continued even after he left office. Until Democratic president Bill Clinton made his first appointment in 1993, every justice was a Republican nominee. Chapter 9 examines this and other control mechanisms available to the elected branches to keep judicial policy from diverging sharply and potentially creating a constitutional crisis. Nowhere is this danger greater than in the delicate area of civil liberties, with its often polarizing effects on public opinion and its reliance on the Supreme Court to set national policy.

Freedom of Speech

> **Amendment I:** *Congress shall make no law . . . abridging the freedom of speech.*

Freedom of speech is essential to representative government and the exercise of individual autonomy. But what exactly constitutes legitimate expression? And how does one balance free speech against other rights and claims?

When the issue is free speech, Americans do not always practice what they preach. Almost all survey respondents endorse the Constitution's Bill of Rights, but when they are pinned down with specific, hypothetical examples, their tolerance for freedom of speech depends on who is doing the speaking and where. In a 1996 survey, 83 percent of national respondents believed homosexuals should be allowed to speak in their communities, but only 62 percent were willing to extend this right to "an avowed racist" (see Table 5-3). Less than half were prepared to allow a racist to teach in a college. The general trend clearly points to Americans becoming ever more tolerant of political minorities across various forms of expression.*

---

*John L. Sullivan, James E. Piereson, and George E. Marcus, *Political Tolerance and American Democracy* (Chicago: University of Chicago Press, 1982). The authors of the survey caution, however, that the trend toward increased tolerance may not be nearly so great when one takes into account that public opinion toward groups changes over time. Communists, for example, seem less despised now that the Cold War is over. When respondents were first asked to identify groups they most disdained, researchers found that respondents registered levels of intolerance comparable to those directed at "communists" in the 1950s.

Free Expression and National Security

Throughout the early years of the twentieth century, the Supreme Court rejected arguments for nationalizing free speech guarantees through the Fourteenth Amendment and continued to leave protection of free expression up to the state governments. Typical of the Court's posture during this era was a 1922 judgment in which it declared, as baldly as possible, that the "Constitution of the United States imposes upon the states no obligation to confer upon those within their jurisdiction either the right of free speech or the right of silence." * By the end of World War I in 1918, more than thirty states had enacted sedition laws aimed at pacifists, socialists, and communists—laws that forbade the advocacy of violence or other "unlawful" means to change the government.

The Court did, however, seek to define the degree to which *federal* legislation must protect free speech. That opportunity arose in the 1919 case of *Schenck v. United States.*[12] In mailings to men eligible for the military draft, Charles Schenck, general secretary of the Socialist Party in Philadelphia, argued that World War I was immoral; he urged draftees to resist. Schenck was convicted under the Espionage Act of 1917 for attempting to foment disloyalty and mutiny in the armed forces during time of war. Writing for a unanimous Court, Justice Oliver Wendell Holmes declared,

> The most stringent protection of free speech would not protect a man in falsely shouting fire in a theater and causing panic. . . . The question in every case is whether the words used are in such circumstances and are of such a nature as to create a *clear and present danger* that they will bring about the substantive evils that Congress has a right to prevent [emphasis added].

When the government is unable to show that particular words demonstrate a "clear and present danger," the words are protected. The federal judiciary widely adopted Holmes's **clear and present danger test** to distinguish protected from unprotected expression. But the test did not ensure decisions that favored individual freedom. In Schenck's case, the Court ruled that his circulars did in fact constitute a legitimate danger, and affirmed his jail sentence.

In 1925 the Court finally applied the First Amendment protections to the states.[13] The case was brought to the Court by Benjamin Gitlow, the leader of a radical faction of the Socialist Party who was arrested in New York City at the height of the Red Scare. Charged with advocating "criminal anarchy" through organized labor strikes, Gitlow was found guilty in a New York State court. In its review of his case, the Supreme Court ruled that states could not interfere with the "fundamental personal rights and 'liberties' " contained in the First Amendment. The Court thus established the Fourteenth Amendment's jurisdiction over the states, at least when it came to free speech. But, moving cautiously, the Court continued: "the State cannot reasonably be

---

Prudential Insurance Co. v. Cheek, 259 U.S. 530 (1922), quoted in Richard C. Cortner, *The Supreme Court and the Second Bill of Rights* (Madison: University of Wisconsin Press, 1981), 57. The Court's refusal to incorporate free expression occurred in the context of a "Red Scare" spurred by fear of the 1917 Bolshevik Revolution in Russia and the creation of the Comintern, whose avowed purpose was to destroy capitalism.

POLITICS/POLICY

When War Erupts, Borders Tighten

After the al Qaeda attacks of September 11, 2001, U.S. government agencies proposed and implemented a number of policies tightening entrance requirements and other regulations for noncitizens. Border officials at checkpoints from Canada to Mexico so tightened inspection rules that businesses complained they were jeopardizing commerce, and visa applications from Middle Eastern males were processed so thoroughly that few if any had been approved within six months of the attacks. FBI and local law enforcement officers, seeking information about potential terrorist threats, conducted "voluntary" interviews of Middle Eastern visitors. And early in 2002 the Immigration and Naturalization Service (which later became part of the Department of Homeland Security) announced new procedures for tracking the whereabouts and length of stay of foreign visitors on student visas. To finance these and many other border security measures, President George W. Bush requested an additional $11 billion in his 2003 budget. Almost all of these policies imposed personal costs on citizens and foreign visitors alike, causing some to claim that their civil liberties had been violated. In addition, the Intelligence Reform and Terrorism Prevention Act of 2004 added new burdens to ordinary travel, such as requiring all Americans to have a passport when flying between the United States and Canada, Mexico, Bermuda, or the Caribbean.

Congress has tightened immigration restrictions, prompting claims of civil liberties violations, whenever America has gone to war or feared terrorism. Restrictions of this kind first appeared in 1798, when Congress, expecting war with France, passed the Alien Enemy Act, authorizing the deportation of "alien enemy males of 14 years and upward." World War I witnessed the Entry and Departure Controls Act (1918), which allowed the president to deport or bar from entry any noncitizen "whose presence was deemed contrary to public safety." Two decades later, with Europe at war and the United States soon to be, Congress authorized the fingerprinting and registration of all noncitizens. More than a half-century after that, in response to the first bombing of the World Trade Center in 1993, Congress passed a law allowing deportation of any alien who was a member of a terrorist organization and who had entered the country unlawfully, "regardless of the duration of his or her presence in the United States."

Source: "Civil Liberties vs. Threats to Society through U.S. History," *New York Times,* November 10, 2001.

After working on the first-ever feature-length movie, *The Birth of a Nation,* Robert Goldstein (center) produced a patriotic melodrama starring Jack Cosgrove and Adda Gleason (shown here) titled *The Spirit of '76.* Unfortunately, his timing was terrible; a month earlier the United States had entered World War I allied with Britain, which Goldstein had cast as the nation's murderous archvillain. When the censor board instructed him to expunge the objectionable scenes, he apparently agreed but then did not. In a revealingly titled federal court case, *United States v. The Spirit of '76,* the judge upheld his conviction and ten-year prison sentence for violating the Espionage Act. He served three years and later emigrated to Germany.

required to measure the danger from every such utterance in the nice balance of a jeweler's scale. A single revolutionary spark may kindle a fire that, smoldering for a time, may burst into a sweeping and destructive conflagration." So Gitlow went to prison.

Even during World War II and the conflicts that followed, the Court persisted in giving the government the benefit of the doubt during times of crisis (see box "When War Erupts, Borders Tighten"). During the Korean War (1951–1953) the Court upheld the Alien Registration Act of 1940 by affirming the conviction of eleven top members of the American Communist Party for having advocated the violent overthrow of the government. After all, the government could not idly watch traitors hatch a rebellion, the Court argued. Indeed, Chief Justice Fred Vinson, in *Dennis v.*

United States, proposed a new **clear and probable danger test** for the courts to enlist in free expression cases: "In each case [the courts] must ask whether the gravity of the 'evil,' discounted by its probability, justifies such invasion of free speech as is necessary to avoid the danger."[14]

The evolution of the Supreme Court's thinking on the relationship of national security to free speech is important in two respects. First, it strikes at the ability of government officials to block opposition. That one does not find American officials invoking national security to suppress opposition parties and candidates is testimony to the strength of the nation's First Amendment protections. Second, this jurisprudence provides a rationale for liberalizing freedom of speech standards in nonsecurity cases. If speech does not constitute a danger to public safety, why inhibit it?

In 1969 the Supreme Court ruled that freedom of speech allowed high school students in Des Moines, Iowa, to wear black armbands to school to express their opposition to the Vietnam War.[15] War protesters also began burning and otherwise desecrating the American flag. Court decisions protecting these highly unpopular acts soon followed. The defendant in *Texas v. Johnson* (1989) was a protester who burned an American flag outside of the 1984 Republican National Convention in Dallas, Texas.[16] Justice William Brennan, writing for the Court in a 5–4 decision, held that "if there is a bedrock principle underlying the First Amendment, it is that the Government may not prohibit the expression of an idea simply because society finds the idea itself offensive or disagreeable." The Court deemed the burning of the flag to be an expression of a political idea and thus was constitutionally sanctioned.

Shortly after the *Texas v. Johnson* decision, public opinion polls found that two-thirds of the American public favored a constitutional amendment protecting the flag. In response, Congress promptly enacted the Flag Protection Act of 1989, which, in less than a year, the Supreme Court struck down as unconstitutional.[17] The issue did not die, however. In a national survey conducted in July 1998, 79 percent of respondents said flag burning should be illegal; only 17 percent said it should be a protected right. Such figures have inspired elected officials to submit annually—and, at least in the House of Representatives, to pass—resolutions calling for a constitutional amendment prohibiting flag burning. On each occasion, the measure has failed in the Senate by a few votes.

After the 2001 al Qaeda attacks in New York and Washington, protection for personal freedoms appeared poised for retrenchment. Early public opinion polls showed respondents less protective of press criticism of the government's antiterrorist efforts and more willing to allow government monitoring of religious activities than before.[18] However, in contrast to past wars that gave rise to national censorship boards and other organized efforts to stifle dissent, demands for conformity have been notably absent since September 11. In late March 2003, protest groups in more than 2,400 communities across the country coordinated demonstrations opposing the attack on Iraq.[19] Some arrests were made, as was to be expected when tens of thousands of agitated individuals were cordoned off into limited space, but nothing resembling the bloody protests and police riots of the Vietnam era occurred.[20]

Hate Speech

In 1969 the Court overturned the conviction of a Ku Klux Klan leader under an Ohio law that prohibited the advocacy of violence as a means to political reform.[21] The Klan head had maintained that "the nigger should be returned to Africa, the Jew returned to Israel" and, at a cross-burning rally, had called for "vengeance" against African Americans and Jews. Yet the Court let him off, holding that speech that endorses "lawless action" cannot be punished unless such action is "imminent." In 1977 the Court also supported the right of the National Socialist Party, modeled on Adolf Hitler's Nazi Party, to parade through a predominantly Jewish community in Skokie, Illinois, while wearing full Nazi regalia.[22] Some observers found the federal government's defense of the free speech rights of the Ku Klux Klan and the National Socialist Party to be a perversion, since these groups intended to intimidate fellow citizens. But others saw in the controversial decisions a commitment to civil liberties, even for marginal and offensive groups that offend the majority's values or interests.

Sexually Explicit Expression

The First Amendment does not protect **obscenity,** whether expressed verbally, graphically, on the Internet, or on the conventional written page. The Supreme Court and law enforcement, however, have had problems defining obscenity and drafting objective standards that enable judges and police to distinguish the merely pornographic (sexually explicit) from the truly obscene. Until the 1950s obscenity was pretty much what local city officials, public librarians, postmasters, and movie censors said it was. In the meantime, the Supreme Court was adhering to an 1870s doctrine that designated as obscene any material inappropriate for children. Such a doctrine, however, required a variety of officials—from librarians to movie censors and even to beat cops—to judge what constituted obscenity. In one famous case in the 1930s censorship found its way into a U.S. Post Office where a diligent postal official charged with enforcing the Comstock Act, which banned obscene material from the U.S. mail, presumably read and seized copies of James Joyce's novel *Ulysses,* claiming it contained "obscene" passages.

Despite these restrictive rules and practices, pornography flourished by the 1950s. Those charged with enforcing communities' moral codes were losing the war. Yet civil libertarians, including lawyers in the ACLU, were not happy either; obscenity policy allowed local officials to catch and prosecute the producers and consumers of pornography. Against this contentious backdrop, the Supreme Court reviewed obscenity policy in 1957 and issued new doctrine in *Roth v. United States.*[23] The majority ruled that a work was obscene if it was "utterly without redeeming social importance" and, "to the average person, applying contemporary **community standards,** the dominant theme of the material, taken as a whole, appeals to prurient interests." With this language, the Court tried to thread its way between the conservative forces calling for tight local regulation of loose morals and the libertarians who sought to banish the concept of "obscenity" from jurisprudence. But every key word in the passage is ambiguous and subject to lenient or restrictive interpretation. Who decides the tastes of the "average person"? Which community's "standards"—a town's, a state's, or the nation's—should be applied? How much obscene material may a work contain before it "dominates" the work's theme? And how does one begin to define "prurient" in a way that would offer clear guidelines to those charged with enforcing obscenity laws?

Only as the Court answered these questions in later rulings did the full extent of the libertarian victory become clear. One of the most important follow-up decisions defined "community standards" as national standards, which is itself so vague that almost nothing could be deemed obscene.[24] Answers or not, these rulings propelled all federal, state, and local efforts to define and regulate pornography into federal court.

During the early 1970s an increasingly conservative Supreme Court began retrenching the "anything goes" doctrine of the 1960s. The reasons for the change in judicial policy came out of the changing political forces in Washington. Within five months of his inauguration in 1969, Republican Richard Nixon had made the first of the four Supreme Court appointments that would become available over the next two years. By 1973 the reconstituted Court was ready to formulate clearer and more stringent doctrine (and perhaps lighten its caseload). In the case of *Miller v. California* the Court shifted primary authority for obscenity policy back to the state—and, implicitly, to local—governments.[25] It reformulated the standard for obscenity: governments could ban and otherwise regulate those materials "which, taken as a whole, appeal to the prurient interest in sex, which portray sexual conduct in a patently offensive way, and which, taken as a whole, do not have serious literary, artistic, political or scientific value."

In the years since *Miller* many commentators, including members of the Court, have argued that this test still fails to offer adequate guidelines. Indeed, it remains unclear whether it improves upon Justice Potter Stewart's 1964 "I know it when I see it" definition of obscenity.[26] Yet returning the issue to the state level has greatly strengthened local authorities' hands in regulating a variety of sex purveyors such as massage parlors, topless bars, and pornographic book and video stores. And delegation to the states helped the Court clear its docket. Since adoption of *Miller* as its prevailing doctrine, the Court has decided less than a quarter of its obscenity cases in favor of First Amendment claims.[27]

Overall, then, the Court has struggled for decades to define obscenity in a way that balances individual liberty with prevailing norms of public decency and fosters consistent administration. This task might be impossible, especially with the onslaught of new media, such as the Internet. How can local standards apply when anyone can go to the local library and instantaneously call up a pornographic video from Copenhagen? The problem of the Internet has played out over the last decade in a back-and-forth between Congress and the Court. In 1996, Congress passed the Communications Decency Act, criminalizing the "indecent" and "patently offensive" online transmission of sexual materials accessible by children. However, in 1997, the Court struck it down, finding that in trying to protect youngsters from obscenity, the "vaguely worded" law would stifle adult access to protected speech.[28] In an attempt to remedy these deficiencies, Congress and President Clinton responded in 1998 with the Child Online Protection Act, which required Web sites to request some form of adult identification, such as a credit card, before offering their obscene or merely pornographic products. However, in a 5–4 ruling in 2004, the Supreme Court upheld a lower federal court's decision to issue a preliminary injunction barring enforcement of the act until after trial on the merits. The Supreme Court agreed that the government had not met its burden of showing that the requirements of the act were the least restrictive and most effective means of protecting children (compared to other options such as such as filtering and blocking software installed by adults on home computers). The Supreme Court expressly declined to address other arguments about the constitutionality of the act in general, and instead sent the case back to the district court for trial.*

Despite these rebukes to Congress, the Court upheld the Children's Internet Protection Act of 2000, which, among other things, cut federal funding for public libraries that failed to implement Internet-filtering technology. The Supreme Court found this version more acceptable by a surprisingly clear-cut, 6–3 majority.† Some justices reasoned that the censorship was modest in that libraries could remove the filter at the request of adult patrons. Moreover, libraries were not forced to participate; only if they accepted federal subsidies for their Internet services would the law apply. Still, given the ubiquity of the Internet, the constant concern of protecting children, and the primacy given to First Amendment rights by the Court, this negotiation between Congress and the Court likely will continue.‡

Freedom of the Press

Amendment I: *Congress shall make no law . . . abridging the freedom . . . of the press.*

An independent press is indispensable in maintaining a representative democracy. Without reliable information about the performance of officeholders, citizens would be hard-pressed to monitor their elected agents. Without the news media, politicians would find it difficult to communicate with their constituents and to keep an eye on each other. The role of the news media is so critical, in fact, we devote a full chapter to this "fourth branch" of government (see Chapter 14). The laws and judicial policy

---

*The Third Circuit in July 2008 affirmed the district court's most recent finding that the government failed to meet its burden, but in addition, the lower court and the Third Circuit also held that the act was unconstitutional because while the government has a compelling interest in protecting children, the provisions of the act were not *narrowly tailored* to that interest and certain provisions were impermissibly overbroad and vague. It is likely that the Department of Justice will appeal this decision to the United States Supreme Court, giving the Court another opportunity to judge Congress in this area.

†*United States v. American Library Association,* 539 U.S. 194 (2003).

‡Other recent examples of this negotiation are the cases of *Ashcroft v. Free Speech Coalition,* 535 U.S. 234 (2002), and *United States v. Williams,* 553 U.S. ___ (2008). In the first case, the Court struck down provisions of the Child Pornography Prevention Act of 1996 that included in the definition of child pornography computer-generated or virtual images of children (as opposed to actual images of real children). However, in the latter case, the Court upheld a provision of the PROTECT Act (passed in response to the adverse decision in *Free Speech Coalition*) that criminalized the offer to provide (e.g., to advertise or promote) child pornography, even if the images offered were computer-generated and thus not actually child pornography.

This was the scene in the crowded courtroom after the jury found Dr. Samuel Sheppard guilty of second-degree murder. Reporters and photographers mingled with court officials and attorneys trying to obtain pictures and statements. Dr. Richard Sheppard, brother of the convicted osteopath, is at left (in profile), and chief defense attorney William J. Corrigan can be seen at right facing the camera.

regulating the modern news media reflect the sweeping language of the First Amendment. We will take up the privacy of news sources, government censorship, and publication of classified information in Chapter 14. Here we consider conflicts between press freedom and individuals' privacy and defendant rights.

The Sixth Amendment guarantees that "the accused shall enjoy the right to . . . an impartial jury of the State." The importance of an impartial jury is obvious. As for a public trial, the history of the concept has less to do with prosecuting criminals than with preventing law enforcement officials from meting out arbitrary justice. By exposing the judicial process to public scrutiny, and by implication, the press, the Framers intended to keep police, judges, and prosecutors in check.

In one famous trial, however, public scrutiny led to public chaos that threatened the defendant's right to a fair hearing. In 1954 Ohio osteopath Samuel Sheppard (whose case inspired the long-running television series and movie *The Fugitive*) was convicted of murdering his wife. His trial attracted almost as much news coverage as the O. J. Simpson trial some forty years later. Yet the Simpson trial, however tumultuous, was a model of judicial and press decorum compared with the Sheppard proceedings. The testimony of witnesses could not be heard at times because of the din from a courtroom packed with reporters. Moreover, the jurors, who were not sequestered, were exposed to the media circus throughout the trial. Order was eventually restored but only years after Sheppard's imprisonment: in 1966 the Supreme

Court found that the "carnival atmosphere" surrounding the trial had undermined Sheppard's right to a fair day in court, and it reversed his conviction.[29]

Does the *Sheppard* case require a uniform ban on the press in trials involving sensitive issues or famous defendants? Apparently not. In 1982 the Supreme Court overturned a Massachusetts law that excluded the public from trials of sex crimes involving victims under the age of eighteen.[30] Although it conceded the value of protecting an underage victim, the majority argued that the victim's welfare did not justify the mandatory exclusion of the public. Rather, the question of public access should be decided on a case-by-case basis.

A similar strain of judicial reasoning crops up in libel doctrine. (This covers both written—**libel**—and spoken—**slander**—forms of false and malicious information that damages another person's reputation.) Civil litigation involving private citizens follows well-established standards of what constitutes libel and appropriate monetary damages, but when one party is a newspaper and the other a public figure—such as a politician, televangelist, or movie star—an altogether different doctrine kicks in. Simply stated, public figures largely forfeit legal recourse to protect their reputation. The injured party must prove that the news media acted with "malice" by knowingly publishing a false story that harmed the individual's reputation. This test raises the bar of proof so high that politicians stand little chance of winning in court.[31] Presumably, because the press is free from any real threat of being sued for knowingly spreading falsehoods about a public figure, it will feel less constrained in seeking the truth, even when public officials might find the truth embarrassing.

Freedom of Religion

Amendment I: *Congress shall make no law respecting an establishment of religion, or prohibiting the free exercise thereof.*

Although the First Amendment is best known for its free speech guarantees, it actually begins with freedom of religion. Many of the early colonies designated official churches, which believers and nonbelievers alike were forced to attend and support with their taxes (a practice that continued in some states even after Independence). And yet by the Revolution, America already was home to a great variety of religious denominations. In *Federalist* No. 10 Madison identified religious conflict as one of the issues bound to generate factional struggle.* In fact, Virginia's religious fights gave Madison the insight that factional conflict could provide a solid foundation for democracy. One of Madison's favorite observations on this score came from Voltaire: "If one religion only were allowed in England, the government would possibly be

---

*In private correspondence with Jefferson, Madison stated precisely the same argument in favor of religious diversity that he later would offer for factions. By letting a thousand denominations bloom, he reasoned, none would attract sufficient popular support to dominate the others.

arbitrary; if there were but two, the people would cut each other's throats; but, as there are such a multitude, they all live happy and in peace."[32]

The religious freedom provision of the First Amendment prohibits Congress from passing any legislation "respecting an *establishment* of religion, or prohibiting the *free exercise* thereof" (emphasis added). But like the rest of the amendment, the **establishment of religion clause** and the **free exercise clause** at first applied only to actions of the federal government. In fact, some states retained laws discriminating against particular religions for years after the Bill of Rights was added to the Constitution.

Madison and Jefferson both subscribed to the frequently stated view that the First Amendment erects "a wall of separation" between church and state.* But theirs was merely one interpretation. Separation is not mentioned in the Constitution itself, and it has not been followed consistently by Congress or the Court. Nor can it be in many instances. Indeed, the Court has argued that tensions between the free exercise and establishment clauses may allow government to support religious institutions in various ways.

Establishment

Because the national government rarely had occasion to subsidize religious institutions or their ancillary activities during the nineteenth century, the first real establishment of religion decision did not come until 1899, when the Supreme Court allowed the federal government to subsidize a Catholic hospital that was open to all patients.[33] In 1947 the Supreme Court applied the due process clause to the establishment provision and thereby placed the states under the same restraints as those limiting the federal government.[34] As the Court entered this field of state policy, it found some states subsidizing parochial schools and others offering religious training in public schools. A 1960 survey of school districts revealed that 77 percent of schools in the South and 68 percent in the East were conducting Bible readings.[35] And throughout the nation most students accompanied the Pledge of Allegiance to the American flag with a prayer.

THE *LEMON* TEST. Over the years, most of the controversial policies triggering establishment arguments have concerned the various ways states have subsidized private schools. Tuition grants, textbooks, and school buses have all had their day in court. The most far-reaching of these cases was *Lemon v. Kurtzman* (1971), in which the Court specified three conditions every state law must satisfy to avoid running afoul of the establishment prohibition:[36]

1. The statute in question "must have a secular legislative purpose," such as remedial education.

2. The statute's "primary effect must be one that neither advances nor inhibits religion."

3. The statute must not foster "an excessive government entanglement with religion."

---

*Jefferson referred to a "wall of separation" between church and state in an 1802 letter written to the Danbury Baptist Association.

Inspired by Cecile B. DeMille's 1956 film *The Ten Commandments,* the Fraternal Order of Eagles placed about 200 of these granite structures at courthouses and other governmental buildings around the country. After four decades, these mostly ignored monoliths suddenly fueled controversy across the country as communities responded to a lower federal court ruling that the monument was unconstitutional. In Texas, the ruling was ignored, landing this Austin, Texas, monument in a Supreme Court case. The Supreme Court, in a fractured 4–1–4 decision (Justice Breyer concurred in the judgment but did not join the Court's opinion, and six of the justices wrote their own concurring or dissenting opinions), upheld the monument, but left little clear guidance in future establishment clause cases; the Court plurality explicitly did not apply the *Lemon* test, and instead relied on the "nature of the monument and our Nation's history." On the same day the Texas decision was handed down, the Court held 5–4 in a different case that displays of the Ten Commandments in county courthouses violated the establishment clause. Ironically, a marble statue of Moses holding these tablets adorns the facade of the U.S. Supreme Court building.

If any of these conditions are violated, the policy fails the ***Lemon* test**. The Court was trying mightily to construct clear doctrine, but with highly subjective criteria such as "primary" and "excessive" it succeeded better perhaps in describing how justices thought these issues through than in identifying to the states those policies that would satisfy the Court's interpretation of the "establishment" clause.

The problems inherent in applying *Lemon* soon became evident in the highly inconsistent decisions that followed its adoption. For example, sometimes the federal courts applied the test to dismantle nativity scenes on public property; at other times judges enlisted the same guidelines to approve official displays of nativity scenes as a celebration of the historic origins of Christmas.[37] The Supreme Court viewed prayers at school football games and convocation exercises as clear violations of the Constitution, but had no problem with the devotions that begin each day's business in

After Joshua Davey declared his intention to major in "pastoral ministries" at a small Pentecostal college in Washington, a state agency yanked his $2,500 scholarship in accordance with the state's strict policy of separation of church and state. By the time the case had wended its way to the U.S. Supreme Court, Davey had graduated and enrolled in Harvard Law School. *Locke v. Davey* clearly changed his life; when asked about it, he observed: "You can look at the law as a ministry, too."

Congress. In the judgment of one constitutional scholar, the vague, three-pronged *Lemon* test inspired judges to engage in reasoning "that would glaze the minds of medieval scholastics."[38]

TESTING A POLICY'S "NEUTRALITY." By the 1990s the *Lemon* test was fading from establishment decisions as the justices increasingly tested a policy's "neutrality." They used the **neutrality test** not so much to prevent favoritism among religious groups as to root out policies that preferred religious groups generally over nonreligious groups engaged in a similar activity. Tax credits for religious school tuition were permissible if they also were available for secular, private instruction. Religious organizations could meet on public school property as long as they observed the same access rules governing any other school club.

In 1994 the Supreme Court applied the emerging neutrality doctrine in *Board of Education of Kiryas Joel Village School District v. Grumet.*[39] A sect of Orthodox Jews in upstate New York persuaded the state legislature to carve out a new, publicly financed school district that would include only their community. Since students from that district who had no special needs already attended a private religious school, the new district would offer only special education classes for the community's disabled children. The Court ruled, however, that creation of this school district breached the rule of neutrality and was thus unconstitutional: "the district's creation ran uniquely counter to state practice, following the lines of a religious community where the customary and neutral principles would not have dictated the same result." Since then the Court has followed its neutrality rule in permitting public funding of mandated special education courses in parochial schools; in allowing state subsidies for some instructional materials in private schools, such as school computers and library resources; and in upholding as constitutional a school voucher program that allowed thousands of Cleveland, Ohio, students to attend religious schools.[40] This last decision in 2002 rekindled a hot political issue championed by President George W. Bush in the 2000 election but left out of his No Child Left Behind legislation in order to garner support for his educational reforms. Now that the Court has removed this legal issue, vouchers may find renewed interest in Washington and many state capitals as a way of exposing public education to the discipline of market forces—that is, giving students and their parents the freedom to choose schools.

Just as the neutrality standard appeared to allow a host of subsidies for religious education, a 2004 Supreme Court decision made a critical distinction between funding religious institutions for their secular activities and funding religious training. The issue involved a college student in Washington State who received a state scholarship to help finance his undergraduate education. After he declared his intention to major in religious studies designed to train him to become a minister, however, the state withdrew the scholarship. This was standard practice in thirty-seven states at the time, and in a 7–2 opinion the Court found the state's decision to appropriately apply separation of church and state.[41]

Although the Court continues to sustain the neutrality standard as the governing establishment doctrine, some question whether it has achieved the intended result. Critics charge that the Court has dismantled the chief barrier to expanded public subsidies for church-sponsored education, which some states have been eager to provide. Voters witnessed its door-opening effect when Republican candidate George W. Bush proposed during the 2000 campaign to federally fund "faith-based" social service programs. Bush couched his plan, which even won a tepid endorsement from his Democratic opponent, Al Gore, on the principle of neutrality, saying that the initiative would permit federal grants to church-affiliated social services and standardize eligibility requirements for all recipients.* A few years ago the prevailing *Lemon* test would have cast such a shadow over the constitutionality of such a policy that it probably would not have been seriously promoted by the president or deliberated by Congress.[42]

School Prayer and Bible Reading

None of the establishment issues has aroused more enduring enmity among religious conservatives than the Supreme Court doctrine banning prayer and Bible readings in public schools. This issue is, arguably, the only real wall separating church and state not yet breached by the Supreme Court. In *Engel v. Vitale* (1962) the Court ruled the following New York State–composed prayer unconstitutional: "Almighty God, we acknowledge our dependence on Thee, and we beg thy blessings upon us, our parents, our teachers, and our country."[43] The next year it invalidated Bible readings in public schools.[44]

Over the years these decisions and the later ones that bolstered them have angered many Americans. Indeed, neither a majority of the public nor those politicians who periodically ask for their votes have ever been won over to the Supreme Court's point of view (see Figure 5-2). Congress has periodically considered a constitutional amendment allowing school prayer, most recently in 1998. Each time, however, proponents have attracted majority support in Congress but have failed to win the two-thirds support necessary to send an amendment to the states.[45]

In the absence of a national policy alternative, states have continued to pass laws trying to circumvent or accommodate the federal courts, but with no success. In 1985, for example, the Court ruled unconstitutional an Alabama state law that mandated a moment of silence at the beginning of the school day.[46] Seven years later it

---

*Proving more controversial than screening of recipients was a Bush administration proposal in 2005 to allow religious organizations to base employment decisions on religion and for those employed to administer the federally subsidized programs.

Figure 5-2 Americans' Disagreement with the Supreme Court on School Prayer

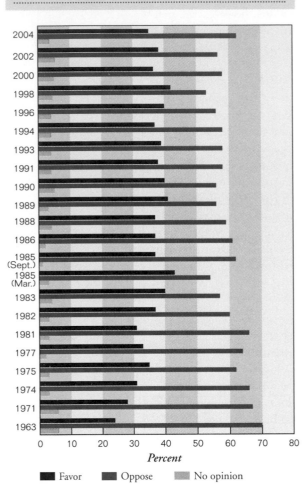

Percent

■ Favor   ■ Oppose   ▨ No opinion

Source: Harold W. Stanley and Richard G. Niemi, *Vital Statistics on American Politics, 2007–2008* (Washington, D.C.: CQ Press, 2008), Table 3-13.

Note: Question on school prayer: "The U.S. Supreme Court has ruled that no state or local government may require the reading of the Lord's Prayer or Bible verses in public schools. What are your views on this—do you approve or disapprove of the Court ruling?" Sources of data: 1963, 1971—Gallup Poll (1972), 1837; 1981, 1985 (September)—ABC News/*Washington Post* survey; 1974–1977, 1982–1985 (March), 1986–2002—General Social Survey, National Opinion Research Center, University of Chicago.

found invocation and benediction prayers at graduation equally objectionable.[47] Moreover, in a throwback to the days of school desegregation in the 1950s and early 1960s, many local school districts throughout the South have simply ignored the federal courts' instructions on school prayer. Three years after the 1963 unequivocal banning of Bible reading, one study revealed that only one Tennessee school official of the 121 interviewed even bothered to claim compliance with the Court decision.[48] In 1997 a federal district judge found school prayers to pervade school life in Alabama despite the federal courts' efforts to forbid these practices. When the judge appointed a "monitor" to ferret out classroom violations of his order to end prayers, the Alabama governor denounced his action as tantamount to employing "secret police." Nearly 500 of the 636 students in the affected district, as well as students in other states, protested the judge's ban by walking out of class.[49] This is just one example of the judiciary's inability to enforce its own decisions, which is discussed more fully in Chapter 9.

Until recently school prayer seemed to be an exception to the rule that the Court's policy decisions do not stray far beyond the bounds of citizen opinion. In 2001, however, a federal appeals court turned away a challenge to a Virginia law permitting a moment of silence at the start of each class day in the state's high schools. And later in the year, the Supreme Court refused to review the decision, thereby letting it stand as state policy. So although it is safe to assume that these issues will remain contentious and that the judiciary will revisit them frequently, the courts might have found a way to accommodate the states and public opinion without seriously undermining the establishment clause.

Free Exercise

The case law delineating the free exercise doctrine is relatively clear and simple when compared with the tortured history of religious establishment cases. The doctrine's incorporation into the Fourteenth Amendment began on a spring day in 1938, when the Cantwells, a family of Jehovah's Witnesses, drove into New Haven, Connecticut, to proselytize their faith and solicit donations. Jehovah's Witnesses believe that each member of the church, as one of its ministers, is obligated to spread the gospel of salvation. Some local residents, however, objected to the Witnesses' intrusion on their privacy and called the police, who arrested the Cantwells for soliciting money door-to-door without a permit.

Ruling on this case in 1940, the Supreme Court decided for the first time that First Amendment protections of free exercise of religion were incorporated in the "fundamental concept of liberty embodied" in the Fourteenth Amendment. Connecticut's regulation of financial solicitation by religious groups, the Court ruled, represented an unconstitutional "censoring" of religion.*

What makes many free exercise cases difficult is that rarely is a particular religious practice specifically targeted by a law. Instead, many generally applicable laws—laws that are passed to solve some general societal

About fifty students gathered outside Sardis (Mississippi) High School in November 1997 to pray and chant, "We want prayer!" They walked out of class in support of fellow students seeking school prayer in Alabama after a federal court restricted moments of silent prayer in public schools.

problem, and are applied to everyone—interfere with some group's religious practice (such as rules requiring compulsory education up to a certain age). For years, when the Court was confronted with these situations, it generally asked whether the government had a compelling interest and then attempted to balance that interest against the degree of infringement on the individual's free exercise of religion.

This all changed with the Court's decision in *Employment Division v. Smith* (1990), involving two Native American church members who were dismissed from their drug counseling jobs for ingesting peyote (a hallucinogenic derived from cactus) as part of a religious ceremony.[50] When the state of Oregon denied their request for unemployment benefits, the church members sued the state for infringing on their free exercise of religion. In a surprising 5–4 decision authored by Justice Antonin Scalia, the Court ruled that otherwise valid, neutral laws of general applicability that incidentally impinge on a particular religious practice do not violate the First Amendment's free exercise clause, period; no compelling governmental interest need be shown. As discussed earlier in the chapter, Congress responded by passing the Religious Freedom Restoration Act, part of which has been upheld by the Court, and part of which has been found unconstitutional.

Cantwell v. Connecticut, 310 U.S. 296 (1940). The Court concluded that, "in spite of the probability of excesses and abuses, [religious] liberties are, in the long view, essential to enlightened opinion and right conduct on the part of citizens of a democracy." See Cortner, *The Supreme Court and the Second Bill of Rights,* 99–108, for a thoughtful review of this case.

Still, as the Court reiterated in 1993, if a law is *not* neutral (in other words, if the law targets a specific religious practice) "it is unvalid unless it is justified by a compelling interest and is narrowly tailored to advance that interest."[51] As a result, the Court struck down a Hialeah, Florida, city ordinance after determining that the real purpose of the law was to stop the animal sacrifice performed by a Santeria church as part of a religious rite.

Both the free exercise and establishment issues spark competing rights claims that require careful balancing from courts. The problems are rooted in the language of the First Amendment. Does "free exercise" extend to behavior that imposes costs on the larger community—whether it be drug use, proselytizing, or disregard of local zoning ordinances? Does the prohibition against establishing a state religion cover moments of silence, church-sponsored school clubs, or overtly religious Christmas displays? As the Supreme Court's wavering decisions reveal so clearly, there is no single "correct" answer to the questions raised by the First Amendment's guarantee of religious freedom. The courts, politicians, and public, then, have ample room to decide for themselves and thus disagree.

Criminal Rights

"The history of liberty," remarked Supreme Court Justice Felix Frankfurter, "has largely been the observance of procedural safeguards."[52] Nowhere is this insight more applicable than to criminal rights. In fact, an article on world affairs in today's newspaper is highly likely to confirm Frankfurter's comment. Leaders in nondemocratic societies often throw their adversaries in prison on trumped-up criminal charges as an easy way of quelling the opposition.

But procedural safeguards remove the criminal process from politics and protect the individual citizen from the raw power of the state. The Framers had firsthand experience in this area: Britain had employed criminal statutes and prosecutions in its attempts to tighten its political control over the colonies. The wary drafters of the Bill of Rights carefully and systematically constructed barriers to arbitrary law enforcement.

Public safety and law enforcement are quintessentially state and local responsibilities. This fact probably explains why the Bill of Rights provisions in Table 5-4 were among the last to be incorporated into the Fourteenth Amendment and applied to all levels of government. Until the 1960s the Supreme Court applied the Fourteenth Amendment's due process clause to defendants only in egregious instances of state misconduct, such as a 1936 case in which a suspect was tortured to near death before he confessed.[53] Clearly, for a long time a majority of the Court wanted to avoid overseeing the state criminal justice system. Even when it did accept the argument that a particular constitutional provision applied to the states, the Court hesitated to impose the rules and standards used in federal criminal cases.

The public has disapproved of the incorporation of criminal rights into the Fourteenth Amendment; law-abiding citizens and their representatives tend to sympathize

TABLE 5-4

The American Criminal Justice System

Stage	Governing Amendment[a]
Reported or suspected crime ↓	
Investigation by law enforcement officials ↓	Fourth Amendment search and seizure rights Fifth Amendment self-incrimination clause
Arrest ↓	Sixth Amendment right to counsel clause
Booking ↓	
Decision to prosecute ↓	
Pretrial hearings (initial appearances, bail hearing, preliminary hearing, arraignment) ↓	Fifth Amendment grand jury clause Sixth Amendment notification clause Eighth Amendment bail clause
Trial ↓	Fifth Amendment self-incrimination clause Sixth Amendment speedy and public trial, jury, confrontation, and compulsory process clauses
Sentencing ↓	Eighth Amendment cruel and unusual punishment clause
Appeals, postconviction stages	Fifth Amendment double jeopardy clause

Source: Lee Epstein and Thomas G. Walker, *Constitutional Law for a Changing America: A Short Course,* 4th ed. (Washington, D.C.: CQ Press, 2009), Table VI-1, 558.

a. The right to due process of law is in effect throughout the process.

more with the victims of crime than with the accused. When a national survey asked Americans in 1972 whether the courts treat criminals "too harshly" or "not harshly enough," two-thirds said the latter. By 1994 this figure had risen to 85 percent, but perhaps reflecting the effects of more restrictive decisions in recent years and longer sentences, it dropped to 78 percent in 1996 and again to 67 percent in 2002.[54] Today criminal rights remain one of the most controversial aspects of modern civil liberties policy.

Elected officeholders have responded to these opinions and controversies by paying closer attention to the legal opinions of the men and women they are appointing and confirming to the federal judiciary. Although criminal rights have not been

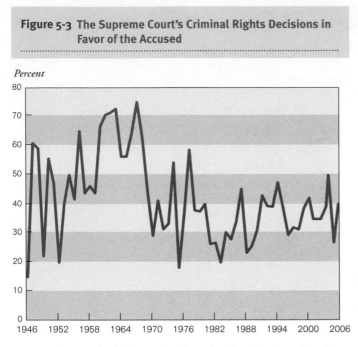

Figure 5-3 The Supreme Court's Criminal Rights Decisions in Favor of the Accused

Percent

Source: Lee Epstein et al., *The Supreme Court Compendium: Data, Decisions, and Developments,* 4th ed. (Washington, D.C.: CQ Press, 2008), Table 3-8.

"unincorporated" or sharply curtailed, vigilant recruitment appears to have brought criminal rights court rulings into closer alignment with the preferences of the American public. As a consequence, Supreme Court decisions have on average become less supportive of criminal rights than they were during the 1960s, when major policy changes occurred in this field (see Figure 5-3). After the September 11 attacks led first to a sweeping new law, the USA PATRIOT Act of 2001, and shortly thereafter to numerous arrests and detentions of suspected terrorists and "enemy combatants," the federal judiciary initially looked away from most of the administration's practices to which it would clearly have objected in normal criminal cases. Since then, the courts have become increasingly circumspect. Since these decisions apply only to criminal rights in a national security context, we take them up separately after reviewing the established case law.

Fourth Amendment: Illegal Searches and Seizures

Amendment IV: *The right of the people to be secure in their persons, houses, papers, and effects, against unreasonable searches and seizures, shall not be violated, and no Warrants shall issue, but upon probable cause, supported by Oath or affirmation, and particularly describing the place to be searched, and the persons or things to be seized.*

The Fourth Amendment is quite specific and detailed. At times efforts to determine what constitutes illegal searches and seizures and what remedies are available to defendants when police and prosecutors go too far have occupied much of the Supreme Court's time. Attempts to answer these two questions have generated two distinct sets of legal doctrine that continue to evolve with the changing ideological disposition of the Supreme Court and the ever-growing capacity of technology to unobtrusively monitor our behavior.

For centuries the principle was commonly asserted and eventually accepted that unless the police convinced a judge to give them a search warrant, the home was indeed a "castle" from which ordinary citizens could escape government intrusion. Indeed, colonists' vivid memories of British official intrusions at the advent of the Revolution probably guaranteed the Fourth Amendment's place in the Bill of Rights. Until recently the Supreme Court followed this principle—almost literally. The Court deemed out of bounds only police investigations that violated an individual's private *physical space*. Accordingly the Court ruled that phone wiretaps performed without search warrants were legal and that any evidence obtained in this way could be introduced in a trial. The first real limitations on search and seizure "beyond the domicile" came not from the judiciary but from Congress, which, in setting up rules and administrative structures for regulating broadcast and telephone communications (the Federal Communications Act of 1934), added language proscribing most police use of wiretaps.

Not until 1967 did the Supreme Court start expanding the domain of privacy and limiting police use of technology to conduct warrantless searches. Following accepted procedures, FBI agents placed a listening device outside the phone booth used by a suspected bookie, Charles Katz. They were rewarded with incriminating evidence that helped convict Katz. The case did not end there, however, because his lawyers challenged the wiretap, arguing that a telephone booth is a "constitutionally protected area." In *Katz v. United States* the Court agreed, breaking new legal ground in two respects.[55] First, the Court did not limit protections to discovery of physical evidence, and second, it indicated that even searches not involving "physical penetration" of an individual's space might be illegal.

Some have interpreted the *Katz* decision to say that whether the listening device is inside or outside the phone booth does not really matter. But in shattering the pane of glass, the Court opened a vast realm of possibilities, as reflected in the thousands of legal challenges and dozens of Supreme Court decisions that *Katz* spawned. For example, in 2001 the Court ruled that police cannot use a thermal imaging device to perform a blanket sweep of neighborhoods to look for basement marijuana fields.[56] This and other recent decisions have helped to clarify the Court's approach to search and seizure cases. The Court generally allows police searches and seizure of evidence without a warrant under the following circumstances:

- during a valid arrest (after all, the police must be sure those they arrest do not remain armed);
- when searching to ensure that evidence is not lost;
- when searching with the consent of the suspect;
- when the search occurs in "hot pursuit" of a suspect in the act of committing a crime;
- when seizing evidence that is in plain view; and
- when searching places other than residences that the Court has decided merit low protection (such as automobiles).[57]

Still, even the conservative-leaning Roberts Court has protected defendants' Fourth Amendment rights in two recent decisions. In one, the Court ruled unanimously that passengers in automobiles (in addition to the driver) are "seized" for Fourth Amendment purposes during a traffic stop, and can thus challenge the stop; in another, a closely divided Court strengthened Fourth Amendment protections for occupants who share their residences with others.[58]

One of the most difficult questions the Court has faced is what should be done with illegally obtained, incriminating evidence? The Court grappled with this question as early as 1914, when it decided that such material must be excluded from consideration by the trial judge and jury. But as late as 1949 the Court resisted incorporating this **exclusionary rule,** reasoning that if police act improperly, the accused person could complain to police superiors or file a private lawsuit (the main recourse provided by British law). Not until the early 1960s did an increasingly liberal Supreme Court, under the leadership of Chief Justice Earl Warren, turn to incorporation of criminal rights. In *Mapp v. Ohio* (1961) the Court finally extended the exclusionary policy to the states.[59] Unlike its decisions on obscenity or religious establishment, the Court's ruling on the exclusionary rule was clear and simple: improperly obtained evidence could not be admitted at any trial.

The Court majority must have believed it created an absolute standard. Over the next few years it and lower federal courts unflinchingly threw out improperly acquired evidence, no matter how incriminating. The public was outraged. But as membership on the Court became more Republican and more conservative, the seemingly absolute standard set down in *Mapp* became more ambiguous and flexible. In two 1984 cases the Court ruled that if law enforcement officers made a "good faith" effort to abide by established procedures, the evidence retrieved could still be introduced,[60] and in 2006, the Court ruled in a 5–4 decision that the exclusionary rule does not apply to evidence obtained after police failed to follow properly the "knock and announce" rule required by the Fourth Amendment.[61] The Court has also ruled that improperly acquired evidence is admissible if one could reasonably assume it would have been discovered anyway. (In the case on which this ruling was based, the evidence was the body of the murder victim, lying exposed in a field.[62])

Fifth Amendment: Self-Incrimination

> **Amendment V:** *No person . . . shall be compelled . . . to be a witness against himself.*

This protection applies not only to testimony in a trial but also to any statement made by a defendant awaiting trial. The principle against self-incrimination has been a bedrock of American jurisprudence. Only if granted immunity from prosecution, based on requested testimony, can an individual be legally compelled to testify. But what happens when defendants claim they were coerced or tricked into confessing?

Law enforcement officials have always preferred obtaining confessions to preparing for trials. The alternative, gathering evidence and building a case, can be time consuming and risky. As late as the 1960s, many police departments throughout the nation routinely induced confessions by beatings, threats, and severe deprivations. Moreover, "tricks of the trade," including placing codefendants in a prisoner's dilemma situation, induced some of the accused—even some who were innocent—to confess.

<table>
<tr><td>

PD 47
Rev. 8/73

METROPOLITAN POLICE DEPARTMENT

WARNING AS TO YOUR RIGHTS

You are under arrest. Before we ask you any questions, you must understand what your rights are.

You have the right to remain silent. You are not required to say anything to us at any time or to answer any questions. Anything you say can be used against you in court.

You have the right to talk to a lawyer for advice before we question you and to have him with you during questioning.

If you cannot afford a lawyer and want one, a lawyer will be provided for you.

If you want to answer questions now without a lawyer present you will still have the right to stop answering at any time. You also have the right to stop answering at any time until you talk to a lawyer.

</td><td>

WAIVER

1. Have you read or had read to you the warning as to your rights? _____

2. Do you understand these rights? _____

3. Do you wish to answer any questions? _____

4. Are you willing to answer questions without having an attorney present? _____

5. Signature of defendant on line below.

_____

6. Time _____   Date _____

7. Signature of Officer _____

8. Signature of Witness _____

</td></tr>
</table>

Reading this statement, or one very much like it, is standard operating procedure for police and sheriffs all across the country when making arrests.

In 1964 the Supreme Court took the first step toward eradicating these abuses by applying the Fifth Amendment to the states.[63] It followed that decision with a controversial ruling two years later in *Miranda v. Arizona,* aimed at protecting suspects from self-incrimination during the critical time between arrest and arraignment.[64] In the *Miranda* case the Warren Court held that police custody is inherently threatening and that confessions obtained during that period can be admitted as evidence only if suspects have been advised of their constitutional right to remain silent. Moreover, defendants must be warned that what they say can be used against them in a trial, informed that they have a right to have a lawyer present for any statements (and that the state will provide an attorney if they cannot afford one), and told of the right to end the interrogation at any time.

In 1968, as part of a more encompassing crime law, Congress enacted legislation that sought to overturn *Miranda* by permitting all demonstrably voluntary confessions. Lawmakers intended the provision to return the judiciary's focus *to* the nature of the confession and *away* from strict adherence to the ***Miranda* rule**. For the next three decades, attorneys general and local prosecutors did not enforce this provision of the law, perhaps believing it to be unconstitutional. Then in 2000 a case involving the provision finally reached the Supreme Court. Arguing that the *Miranda* rule was a fundamental "constitutional principle," the Court held that Congress did not have the authority to change the *Miranda* decision.[65]

Sixth Amendment: Right to Counsel and Impartial Jury of Peers

> **Amendment VI:** *In all criminal prosecutions, the accused shall . . . have the Assistance of Counsel for his defence.*

Defendants in any American courtroom can take comfort in the Sixth Amendment assurances that they are entitled to "a speedy and public trial, by an impartial jury of the State and district wherein the crime shall have been committed," a "compulsory process for obtaining witnesses in [their] favor," and "the Assistance of Counsel." The protections offered in this amendment have been subject to little controversy.

In 1932 the Supreme Court partially applied the Sixth Amendment to the states when it required them to provide all indigent defendants in capital cases (that is, those potentially involving the death penalty) with a lawyer. Full incorporation, however, had to wait until 1963, when Clarence Earl Gideon won one of the most famous decisions in Court history.[66] Gideon, a drifter, was accused of breaking into a pool hall. Unable to afford a lawyer, he asked the Florida trial judge for representation, but was turned down, convicted, and promptly sent to prison. There he became an inspiration for "prison lawyers" everywhere.

With classic David-versus-Goliath determination, Gideon researched the law and sent to the Supreme Court a handwritten petition claiming that his five-year prison sentence was unconstitutional because he had been too poor to hire an attorney and, as a result, had been required to defend himself.

Upon taking his case, the Court assigned Gideon a first-class attorney (and future Supreme Court justice), Abe Fortas, who successfully argued that Gideon's constitutional right to counsel had been denied. Indeed, the decision in *Gideon v. Wainwright* decreed that anyone charged with a felony must be offered legal representation. Later the Court expanded eligibility to include any defendant whose conviction might result in incarceration.[67]

In many conviction appeals the Sixth Amendment claim has turned from the availability of counsel to the adequacy of the defense that court-appointed attorneys provide. The appeals courts are reluctant to become closely involved with this part of the process, lest they find themselves asked to second-guess the defense whenever a guilty verdict occurs. Nonetheless, beginning with a 1984 case, the Court has prescribed that "counsel has a duty to make reasonable investigations or to make a reasonable decision that makes particular investigations unnecessary."[68] Evidence that the defense failed to perform at a minimal competence level offered the defendant grounds to request retrial. Generally, cases involving the death penalty have received the most careful appellate review.[69]

As for the Sixth Amendment's reference to juries and their procedures, the federal courts have largely allowed the states to determine jury size and whether unanimous agreement is required for conviction. However, the courts have concentrated on whether juries are adequately composed of the defendant's peers. Unrepresentative juries can arise in two ways: the pool of potential jurors is itself unrepresentative or the selection process is biased. Until the 1960s African Americans in the South were effectively excluded from juries because jury pools were drawn from voter registration lists (see Chapter 4). When federal registrars signed up black voters, however, this discrimination was automatically dismantled.

Potential jurors may be rejected from service either for "cause" (arising from suspected prejudice) or as the target of a peremptory challenge. The latter, a pervasive practice in state and local courts, allows attorneys on both sides to reject a certain number of individuals without having to establish cause. Lawyers, seeking the most sympathetic jury possible, routinely exempt certain types of people depending on the nature of the case and the personal characteristics of the defendant. They may not, however, use their challenges to eliminate jurors on the basis of race or sex.

Eighth Amendment: "Cruel and Unusual" Punishment

Amendment VIII: *Excessive bail shall not be required, nor excessive fines imposed, nor cruel and unusual punishments inflicted.*

The federal judiciary has been reluctant to define the Eighth Amendment's highly subjective phrase **"cruel and unusual,"** a reticence reflected by the Supreme Court in 2004 when it upheld the California "three-strikes" law, which sharply stiffens sentences for three-time offenders.[70] Instead, it has largely limited application of this amendment to death penalty cases. Until the 1970s the federal judiciary rarely intruded in state sentencing laws despite numerous opportunities to do so. Then, in 1972, the Supreme Court issued a stunning 5–4 decision in *Furman v. Georgia*.[71] The legal arm of the National Association for the Advancement of Colored People convincingly argued that the Georgia law allowing juries to determine whether to mete out the death penalty to a convicted murderer had led to large racial disparities in sentencing. African Americans convicted of murdering whites were far more likely to receive the death penalty than were whites convicted of the same crime. A close inspection of the 243-page decision, the longest in Court history, reveals that the majority declaration of the death penalty as "cruel and unusual" was not nearly so secure as it first appeared. Only three justices maintained that the death penalty inherently violates the Bill of Rights. The others who joined the majority took a narrow approach, citing discriminatory practices rather than questioning the death penalty itself as cruel and unusual.

Immediately the federal government and thirty-five states redrafted laws to deal with the Court's objection to Georgia's sentencing procedures. Some states tried to eliminate discrimination by mandating that certain heinous crimes carry an automatic death penalty. But these laws were later rejected under the Eighth Amendment as inherently arbitrary and because they did not allow consideration of mitigating circumstances in sentencing. The solution was found in a new Georgia statute that separated the conviction from the sentencing stage of the trial, allowing juries to weigh the particular crime and defendant and any mitigating and aggravating circumstances. In 1976 the 7–2 majority in *Gregg v. Georgia* proclaimed the new Georgia statute to be a "model" law, and the death penalty ceased to constitute cruel and unusual punishment.[72] Indeed, the Georgia solution appears to have become an acceptable option for the state governments that rewrote sentencing procedures shortly after the *Gregg* decision and for the prosecutors, judges, and juries that implement them. Numerous defendant appeals of faulty trial and sentencing procedures failed to win favor with the Court during the intervening years. However, in 2003 the Court rejected state laws authorizing judges to mete out the death penalty, holding that only juries can do so in deliberations separate from those establishing guilt.[73]

A second area of review with potentially greater impact on the use of the death penalty concerns the defendant's competency and, hence, capital-level responsibility for the crime. In a series of recent decisions addressing mental retardation and age, the Court has ruled that the death penalty for incompetent defendants violates the Eighth Amendment's ban on cruel and unusual punishment. After more than a decade of standing on a ruling that left it up to the states to determine whether mental retardation should preclude the death penalty, the Supreme Court in 2002 struck down a Virginia sentence of a murder defendant with an IQ of 59.[74] The Court reasoned against its past position by noting that since its previous ruling, fewer states subject mentally retarded defendants to the death penalty, and even among the minority that do, few enforce it. Moreover, recent state legislative actions against the death penalty in retardation cases have involved lopsided majorities. Hence, the majority ruled a consensus had emerged that such executions represent cruel and unusual punishment. In other words, the Court dealt with the ambiguity of this phrase by striving not for some absolute stance—say, the prevailing meaning of the phrase at the time of ratification of the Bill of Rights—but rather by becoming the arbiter of national opinion as reflected in state laws.

In two 2008 death penalty decisions, the Court again gravitated toward a national consensus among states. In one case, the Court held that Kentucky's lethal injection protocol—which administers three drugs in three phases—did not violate the Eighth Amendment's ban on cruel and unusual punishment. As Chief Justice John G. Roberts noted, there is a "broad consensus" among thirty states and the federal government not just for lethal injection, but for the specific three-drug combination.[75] In addition, in a tragic case involving the rape of an eight-year-old child by her stepfather, the Court held, 5–4, that the Eighth Amendment prohibited imposing the death penalty in a case in which a child was raped, but not murdered. The Court noted that only six states authorize the death penalty for child rape, and referenced the similar "national consensus" against executing mentally retarded offenders and juveniles.[76]

More than 1,100 death sentences have been carried out since reinstatement of the death penalty in 1976. At the beginning of 2008, over three thousand inmates were sitting on death row. About 80 percent of all executions have been carried out in the South, with over four hundred executions in Texas alone, far surpassing its neighbors and, for that matter, the rest of the world.[77] Both the escalation of executions in the mid-1990s and more recently the equally sharp decline (see Figure 5-4) have tracked trends in public opinion favoring capital punishment. Where in 1993 national survey respondents preferred the death penalty for murderers over life imprisonment by a two-to-one margin, a 2005 survey found the public evenly divided on this question. Nonetheless, acceptance of capital punishment appears well established both among the public and on the bench.

Time has shown that the rights of the accused are not always easy to appreciate or enforce. Criminal rights almost always trigger precarious balancing between the defendant's interest in fair treatment and the community's interest in punishing the guilty and maintaining social order. When a court frees a guilty person because of some technical glitch in the criminal justice system—such as from an improperly

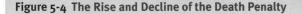

Figure 5-4 The Rise and Decline of the Death Penalty

Number of executions

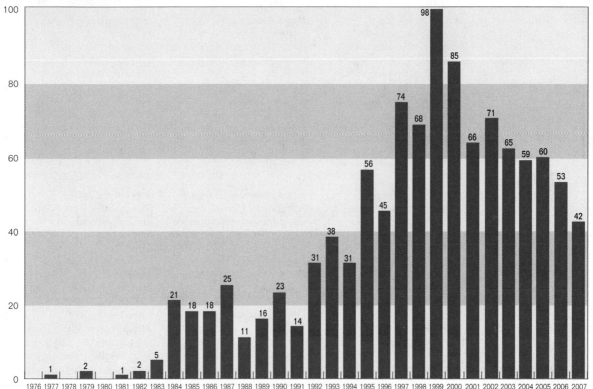

Source: Used with permission from the Death Penalty Information Center, 2008.

filled-out search warrant or an untimely prosecution—controversy erupts. Perhaps the role of legal technicalities as much as the other thorny issues described in this section account for the delayed incorporation of criminal rights (see Table 5-5). By the late 1940s the Supreme Court had applied to the states the entire First Amendment—as well as the Fourth Amendment (without mandating the exclusionary rule)—but it hesitated until the 1960s to nationalize the remainder of the Bill of Rights.

Criminal Rights and National Security

In contrast to First Amendment rights, criminal rights protections have, since September 11, been sharply reduced for anyone suspected of involvement in terrorism or alliance with Afghanistan's Taliban regime. In fall 2001, Congress enacted the USA PATRIOT Act, a comprehensive law designed to strengthen the government's hand in investigating and prosecuting domestic terrorists. Among its nine hundred provisions

TABLE 5-5

The Meandering Path of Criminal Rights

	Early	1960s and 1970s	Recent Developments
Search and seizure (Fourth Amendment)	*Wolf v. Colorado* (1949): Fourth Amendment applies to states but exclusionary rule not mandated.	**Mapp v. Ohio** (1961): Improperly obtained evidence cannot be introduced at trial.	*United States v. Leon* (1984): Exclusionary rule not constitutionally protected but a means to deter police illegality. Allows good faith and inevitable discovery exceptions.
Non–self-incrimination (Fifth Amendment)	*Brown v. Mississippi* (1936): Outlaws confessions extracted by torture.	**Miranda v. Arizona** (1966): Officers must inform suspects of their rights before interrogation.	*Illinois v. Perkins* (1990): For confessions heard by undercover police, the Court rules: "*Miranda* forbids coercion, not strategic deception."
Right to lawyer (Sixth Amendment)	*Betts v. Brady* (1942): Denies right to lawyer in state prosecutions where special circumstances do not apply.	**Gideon v. Wainwright** (1963): Reverses *Betts*, guaranteeing all defendants charged with a felony a lawyer at trial.	*Ross v. Moffitt* (1974): Right to counsel is not required for discretionary appeals after conviction.
Double jeopardy (Fifth Amendment)		*Benton v. Maryland* (1969): Forbids state reindictment of acquitted defendant.	*Heath v. Alabama* (1985): Double jeopardy does not apply across levels of government.
Capital punishment (Eighth Amendment)	*Louisiana ex rel. Francis v. Resweber* (1947): Death penalty not inherently "cruel and unusual" punishment.	**Furman v. Georgia** (1972): "Arbitrary" sentencing process disallows death penalty.	*Baze v. Rees* (2008): Kentucky's lethal injection protocol (used by almost thirty other states) does not violate the Eighth Amendment.

Note: Cases in **bold** discussed in text.

the act relaxed constraints on surveillance activities and dismantled a formidable firewall separating criminal from national security investigations.* It also gave the government more latitude in seizing suspects and their assets and in conducting prosecutions and deportations. Lawmakers from both parties who drafted the legislation were well aware of the implications of these changes for civil liberties and their potential for abuse. These individuals carefully included language prohibiting any use of this new authority against individuals exercising their First Amendment freedoms (for example, by expressing dissent or practicing a religion), and they added sunset clauses specifying that many of the law's provisions would expire in 2005. After extending the deadline for renewal, and after adding a few new provisions intended to better protect civil liberties, Congress in 2006 voted to renew the PATRIOT Act.

---

*No longer, for example, would a member of the FBI's criminal investigation division need to go to federal court to share information with a colleague in the FBI's domestic security division.

Congress and President Bush versus the Supreme Court
The Battle over Prisoners' Rights at Guantánamo Bay

The following cases, executive actions, and laws illustrate the back-and-forth among the three branches of government over the rights of prisoners at Guantánamo Bay, Cuba, as well as the role of the courts in determining those rights.

The Supreme Court:
On June 28, 2004, in *Rasul v. Bush,* the Supreme Court held that United States courts had jurisdiction to hear habeas corpus petitions filed by noncitizen prisoners held at Guantánamo Bay, Cuba. Thus, despite the fact that the prison was not on U.S. soil, foreign nationals captured abroad and held there had the right to challenge the legality of their detentions in court. The decision was 6–3, with Justice O'Connor still on the Court and in the majority, and Justices Scalia, Thomas, and Rehnquist dissenting.

The Executive Branch's Response:
Just a little over a week after the Court's decision in *Rasul,* on July 7, 2004, Deputy Secretary of Defense Paul Wolfowitz issued an Order Establishing Combatant Status Review Tribunals. The order stated that these special military tribunals (and implicitly, *not* federal courts) would review a detainee's status as an "enemy combatant." During this process, detainees could be assigned a "personal representative" who was a military officer, but could not have an attorney represent them.

Congress and the President's Response:
On December 30, 2005, President Bush signed into law the Detainee Treatment Act of 2005 (DTA), which stripped United States courts of jurisdiction to hear habeas corpus petitions filed on behalf of alien (noncitizen) detainees at Guantánamo Bay.

The Supreme Court's Response:
On June 29, 2006, in *Hamdan v. Rumsfeld,* the Court ruled that the DTA did not apply retroactively to *pending* habeas petitions filed by Guantánamo detainees such as Hamdan. This decision, issued after Justice O'Connor left the Court and the death of Chief Justice Rehnquist, was 5–3, with Chief Justice Roberts abstaining and Justices Scalia, Thomas, and Alito dissenting.

Congress and the President's Response:
On October 17, 2006 (just weeks before the 2006 midterm election that shifted control of Congress to the Democrats), President Bush signed into law the Military Commissions Act of 2006 (MCA). In the MCA, Congress stripped jurisdiction from United States courts to hear a habeas corpus petition from any alien detainee either determined to be an enemy combatant or awaiting an enemy combatant determination.

The Supreme Court's Response:
On June 12, 2008, the Court ruled in *Boumediene v. Bush* that alien detainees designated as enemy combatants at Guantánamo Bay had the constitutional right to seek habeas corpus review, and that certain provisions of the MCA operated as unconstitutional suspensions of the writ of habeas corpus. The decision was 5–4, written by the swing vote Justice Kennedy, with Justices Scalia, Thomas, Alito, and Roberts dissenting. Recognizing the significant separation-of-powers battle embedded in the case, Justice Kennedy wrote that "few exercises of judicial power are as legitimate or as necessary as the responsibility to hear challenges to the authority of the Executive to imprison a person."[1]

---

1. *Boumediene v. Bush,* 553 U.S. ___ (2008), Slip Opinion at 69.

Because the PATRIOT Act altered for these special cases many criminal procedures established by Supreme Court constitutional case law, court challenges to the act were inevitable. This wave of litigation has provoked a modern separation of powers battle between the president, Congress, and the Court. While in earlier cases involving wiretapping and the seizure of assets the Supreme Court deferred to the judgment of the president and Congress, in cases of individuals' physical imprisonment the Court's decisions have not been favorable to the Bush administration and the formerly Republican-controlled Congress. In 2004 the Court's first ruling concerning detainees imprisoned at Guantánamo Bay held that despite the prison's location on foreign soil, federal courts have jurisdiction to hear habeas corpus petitions (petitions essentially alleging that one is being held in violation of the Constitution or other federal law) brought by prisoners held there.[78] Congress—then controlled by the Republicans—responded by enacting laws removing from federal courts' jurisdiction the authority to hear such petitions.[79] However, the Court's most recent decision in June 2008 held that portions of such acts are unconstitutional, and ruled again that prisoners at Guantánamo Bay—even those who are foreigners and not American citizens—have the right to petition federal courts for habeas relief.[80]

If Congress were still under firm Republican control, we might expect a quick legislative response in yet another attempt to override the Court's determination that United States courts do have jurisdiction over these cases. However, with the election of Barack Obama in 2008 and Democrats firmly controlling Congress, the prospect is dim for a law undoing the Court's decision. In the end, one could conclude that when a national security crisis initially appears, the Court may defer to the president's need for latitude in capturing, holding, and prosecuting criminal suspects. However, as the immediate threat passes, the pendulum may swing back toward the constitutionally based procedural protections for criminal defendants.

Privacy

A right to privacy, unlike other civil liberties, is not explicitly stated in the Bill of Rights or elsewhere in the Constitution. Indeed, although an implicit "right of privacy" had been postulated by legal jurists as early as the 1890s, the Supreme Court did not explicitly recognize its existence until 1965.

But how could the Court "recognize" as constitutional a right that is nowhere mentioned in the Constitution? In 1965 the Court reasoned in *Griswold v. Connecticut* that Americans' guaranteed rights are not limited to those specifically identified in the Constitution.[81] Indeed, the Ninth Amendment says as much: "The enumeration in the Constitution, of certain rights, shall not be construed to deny or disparage others retained by the people." This amendment opened the door to unstated rights. Moreover, a reasonable reading of other amendments invites privacy into the Constitution's protected liberties. After all, what does the Constitution's guarantee of "liberty" mean if not privacy from state surveillance? Other explicit rights such as freedom of speech and assembly and the prohibitions against self-incrimination and unreasonable search and seizure require some measure of privacy if they are to be secure. These explicitly guaranteed rights form **penumbras,** or implicit zones of protected privacy rights on which the existence of explicit rights depends. For example, freedom of speech and a free press must include not only an individual's right to engage in these activities but also the right to distribute, receive, and read others' views. Without these other rights, the specific rights would be insecure.

Once identified, the right to privacy became subject to all the complexities of interpretation and enforcement associated with other civil liberties. But the overriding question was: in the absence of constitutional standards, what actions and practices are so personal or private that they should be shielded from interference by the government and other third parties? The massive online databases maintained by employers, credit agencies, health providers, insurance companies, credit card companies, and banks are highly intrusive of privacy. So why are the courts not flooded with suits charging the people who control these databases with invasion of privacy? Perhaps the long-standing judicial doctrine that information loses its privacy privilege once conveyed to third parties has discouraged claims. Or perhaps this area of civil liberties has simply failed to attract the kinds of group sponsorship typically needed to make strong cases and sustain them through the judicial system. Whatever the reason, when federal independent prosecutor Kenneth Starr investigating President Bill Clinton sought in 1998 to subpoena the records of bookstore purchases made by former White House intern Monica Lewinsky, no privacy policy prevented him from doing so. Similarly, during hearings on Judge Robert Bork's nomination to the Supreme Court in 1987, journalists obtained and published the nominee's video rental records to see if he might have rented movies with sexually explicit content. Bork had no recourse. Over the next few years, as immigration offices, airport security services, and public facilities vulnerable to terrorism install new kinds of surveillance and identification technology, as in Washington, D.C., in the opening vignette, one can be sure that the courts will examine these mostly unexplored domains of privacy rights.[82]

Childbearing Choices

The Supreme Court's attentiveness to privacy claims has largely been confined to an important but narrow domain of public policy: reproductive rights. In extending privacy in childbearing choices, the courts began not with abortion but with access to contraceptives. In 1961 Estelle Griswold, executive director of the Planned Parenthood League of Connecticut, opened a Planned Parenthood clinic, which dispensed contraceptives. Three days after the clinic opened, Griswold was arrested for violating an 1879 Connecticut law prohibiting the use of contraceptives. After losing her case in the state courts, the defendant appealed her test case in federal court. Not only did she win, but the Supreme Court decision, *Griswold v. Connecticut,* laid precedents that emboldened feminist and reproductive freedom groups to pursue abortion rights.

In 1972 Justice William Brennan's argument in *Eisenstadt v. Baird* bolstered the efforts of such groups: "if the right of privacy means anything, it is the right of the individual, married or single, to be free from unwanted governmental intrusion into matters so fundamentally affecting a person as the decision to bear or beget a child." [83] One year later, in the landmark abortion rights decision *Roe v. Wade,* a Court majority ruled: "the right of privacy, whether it be founded in the Fourteenth Amendment's concept of liberty . . . or . . . in the Ninth Amendment's reservation of rights to the people, is broad enough to encompass a woman's decision whether or not to terminate her pregnancy." *

Abortion rights in America did not begin with this historic and controversial decision; many states permitted abortion until the late nineteenth century. Moreover, in the ten years leading up to the *Roe* decision, eighteen states either relaxed or repealed their statutes prohibiting abortion. Thus the Court's nationalization in 1973 of a woman's right to terminate her pregnancy ended abortion's varying legality across the states.

This said, *Roe v. Wade* did not completely remove the states from abortion rights policy. This decision established that a woman's decision to end her pregnancy belongs within the protected sphere of privacy, but it did not wholly exempt abortion from government regulation. Rather, the Court ruled that in the interest of the mother's health and the "potential" life of the fetus, state governments could regulate abortions from the end of the first trimester of pregnancy to fetus viability (months four through six). Within the final trimester the states could forbid all abortions except those required "for the preservation of the life or health of the mother." In 1992 the Court backed away from the first trimester standard and substituted a more ambiguous "undue burden" criterion: states could impose certain regulations on both the women who seek abortions and the doctors who perform them.[84] Waiting periods, counseling sessions, and parental consent were deemed constitutional as long as they did not place an undue burden on the abortion right.

Abortion politics remains the subject of an intense political debate that takes many forms—confrontational demonstrations by the anti-abortion movement, platform fights at presidential nominating conventions, and legislation both extending and voiding the *Roe* decision. Dozens of new state laws adjusting the boundaries of this privacy right (see Table 3-2, page 124) have been enacted and amended over the past decade. In 2003 Congress passed the Partial-Birth Abortion Ban Act, which prohibits very late stage abortions. The Supreme Court accepted the law's limitations in a 5–4 ruling.[85] Although *Roe v. Wade* has yet to be overturned, the controversy over abortion will continue to overshadow politics at all levels, whether reproductive rights remain largely a federal concern or are returned entirely to the states.

In 2000 one statistic estimated late-term abortions (typically after the fifth month of pregnancy) at about 2,200 that year. Early-term abortions—about 90 percent occur within the first nine weeks of pregnancy—have emerged as a common form of birth control.† Thirty-five years after *Roe,* abortion remains controversial. Every con-

---

*But as Justice Byron White wrote in his dissent from the *Roe* decision, "the upshot is that the people and the legislatures of the fifty states are constitutionally disentitled to weigh the relative importance of the continued existence and development of the fetus, on the one hand, against a spectrum of possible impacts on the mother, on the other hand." *Roe v. Wade,* 410 U.S. 113 (1973).

†These figures include use of medical abortions (RU-486). This procedure approved late in 2000 is now used in about a fifth of all early-term abortions.

gressional and presidential candidate must declare his or her position on a woman's right to terminate a pregnancy. Confirmation hearings of federal judges invariably raise this issue as well, although the nominees dissimulate to avoid being pinned down in some future decision and for some, to improve their chances for confirmation. Despite controversy, abortion is now established as a common form of birth control in America. In Figure 5-5, the annual number of abortions has begun to decline, although the reasons are not altogether clear. It may simply reflect the decline of pregnancies among young, unmarried women over the same period.

Other Life Choices

In *Griswold, Roe,* and related cases, the Supreme Court enlisted various constitutional penumbras and the Ninth Amendment—stating that the rights listed in the first eight amendments should not be construed as the only ones available to the citizenry—to broadly protect citizens against government intrusion into their private lives. Once reticent to rely on privacy rights to overturn state and federal laws, the Supreme Court has begun applying these rights more confidently.

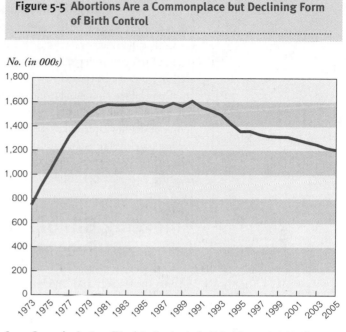

Figure 5-5 Abortions Are a Commonplace but Declining Form of Birth Control

No. (in 000s)

Source: Guttmacher Institute, "Trends in Abortion in the United States, 1973–2005" (New York: Guttmacher Institute, 2008); www.guttmacher.org/presentations/trends.pdf.

Note: By the end of 1970, four states had repealed their antiabortion laws and eleven states had reformed them. The data for 1983, 1986, 1989, 1990, 1993, 1994, 1997, 1998, 2001, 2002, and 2003 are estimates from interpolations of numbers of abortions.

A good example of this trend is its reversal of past stances on sodomy laws. In 1986 the Court turned away a suit challenging a Georgia law prohibiting homosexual acts between consenting adults, but in 2003 it reversed this position, noting that over the intervening years a consensus against such laws had emerged. As with capital punishment, it measured this consensus with a canvass of state laws; in 1986 half of the states had antisodomy laws on their books, although many had not enforced them in some time. By 2003 only thirteen retained such laws.

Recently another privacy claim has emerged: the right to die. Unlike the sodomy cases, the Court continues to defer to the states on this issue, which arose in the 1970s over the removal of life-sustaining technology for patients in a vegetative state. In 1990 the Supreme Court rejected the right to die—even the removal of life support equipment—as a fundamental privacy right.[86] The states, the Court declared, could largely determine the level of commitment and kinds of evidence required before family members were given authority to halt medical treatment. In 1994 the right to die took a new turn as Oregon's voters narrowly approved a ballot initiative, the Death with Dignity Act, allowing terminally ill patients, under proper safeguards, to obtain a physician's prescription to end their lives. In 2001, the law was challenged by then–attorney general John Ashcroft, who determined that using controlled substances to assist in committing suicide was not a "legitimate medical purpose" under the federal Controlled Substances Act (CSA), so that any physician who prescribed or dispensed such substances under the Oregon act would be in violation of federal law. However, in 2006, in a decision that was as much a victory for states' rights as it was for advocates of physician-assisted suicide, the Supreme Court held that the attorney general did not have the authority to make such a determination, which meant that those acting under the Oregon law were not in violation of the CSA.* Through 2007, 341 ill individuals have enlisted the law in Oregon to commit suicide. While similar ballot measures have failed in other states, voters in Washington State approved a right to die measure in November 2008 by a substantial margin of 59 percent to 41 percent.

Emerging Bill of Rights Issues: Guns and Property

Against this backdrop of an expanding universe of civil liberties, two provisions of the Bill of Rights, the Second Amendment's right to bear arms and the Fifth Amendment's "takings" clause, have received comparatively scant judicial scrutiny. But the active efforts of organized groups and a core of sympathetic, conservative justices on the Supreme Court seem to be changing this situation.

The Right to Bear Arms

Easily the most ambiguous language in the Bill of Rights is the Second Amendment's provision that "[a] well regulated Militia, being necessary to the security of a free State, the right of the people to keep and bear Arms, shall not be infringed." When representatives debated this amendment in Congress, the Revolutionary War was still very much on their minds. Most historians and judicial scholars who have read the congressional deliberations agree that those who sent this amendment to the states clearly meant to secure the right of local militias to bear arms. (These militias were composed of local, private citizens who organized against Britain and later were occasionally called into action during local emergencies.)

While the Court for years arguably read the amendment as guaranteeing this right of citizens only in their capacity as soldiers in their state militias, a number of resourceful interest groups and many vocal individuals have opposed this collective, or *group right,* interpretation. Instead, the National Rifle Association (NRA), the Second Amendment Foundation, and others have vigorously advanced the belief that the amendment guarantees an *individual right* to own a gun. Besides lobbying Congress and every state legislature, they have waged public information campaigns and, in-

---

Gonzales v. Oregon, 546 U.S. 243 (2006). The majority opinion rejected such a "radical shift of authority from the States to the Federal Government to define general standards of medical practice in every locality."

creasingly, have cultivated cases to challenge the narrow interpretation of the "bear arms" amendment. Although for years judicial opinion appeared entrenched in favor of a collective right, this opinion had rarely been tested in actual decisions—perhaps fewer than six cases in the history of the Republic. Until recently, the last word from the Court was back in 1939 in *United States v. Miller,* when the justices upheld registration of a sawed-off shotgun, using a rationale that seemed to deny an individual right.[87]

However, this line of interpretation would change in June 2008, when the Supreme Court issued its most important Second Amendment ruling to date: *District of Columbia v. Heller.* In a bitterly divided 5–4 opinion split predictably along conservative-liberal lines, the majority explicitly adopted the *individual* right interpretation of the Second Amendment. To do so it rejected the long-standing interpretation that the phrase "to keep and bear Arms" was limited to weapons used in military service.* Specifically, the Court held that Washington, D.C.'s absolute prohibition of handguns used for self-defense in the home was unconstitutional under the Second Amendment. The Court was clear, however, that the right to own a gun—like the First Amendment right of free speech—is not unlimited.

The recent Supreme Court decision changes doctrine in finding in the Constitution's language the right of individuals to possess firearms. Yet it left in place a panoply of federal and state permit laws that screen applicants and regulate weapons. The extent of the limits will soon be tested. Within days of the ruling pro-gun individuals and organizations in San Francisco and Chicago filed suits challenging those cities' strict gun laws.† Notably, the lawsuit in San Francisco filed by the NRA alleges that the city's ban on handguns in public housing violates the Second Amendment right of "responsible, law-abiding" Americans to keep firearms in their dwellings for self-defense—language taken almost directly from Justice Scalia's majority opinion buttressing the rights of "law-abiding, responsible citizens to use arms in defense of hearth and home." It appears initially that pro-gun plaintiffs will follow cues from the majority opinion by focusing on gun laws that apply to the home, self-defense in the home, and/or self-defense generally.

The "Takings" Clause

Along with bans on self-incrimination and double jeopardy, the Fifth Amendment contains a provision on property rights: "private property [shall not] be taken for public use, without just compensation." After the Supreme Court applied this provision, known as the **takings clause,** to state policy, the body of law on the clause seemed to be settled.[88] After all, state, city, and county governments are typically the ones doing the taking for projects arguably for the good of greater public. After acquiring private property and compensating its owners, governments construct roads, expand waterways, build baseball parks, and provide citizens with other collective goods. In recent years, however, the argument over what constitutes a "taking" of one's property has taken an interesting turn as various federal and state environmental policies have imposed severe regulations

---

District of Columbia v. Heller, 554 U.S. ___ (2008).
†See Jesse McKinley, "Challenges to Bans on Handguns Begin," *New York Times,* June 28, 2008.

Interest Groups Take on the Courts
Solving Collective Action Problems

Courts make civil liberties policy as they respond to individual citizens who claim in a legal proceeding that their rights have been violated. From a Florida prison cell, Clarence Gideon (see pages 225–226) wrote the Supreme Court a personal letter arguing that the Constitution guaranteed him a right to legal representation in his defense against state criminal charges of theft. The timing of his appeal could not have

been more fortuitous, since at the time Chief Justice Earl Warren was looking for a case that would allow him to propose to his colleagues extension of the Sixth Amendment's right to counsel to state criminal trials. So Gideon's petition found a Court poised to come to his rescue.

Yet this famous, frequently recounted textbook case was unusual and conceals as much as it reveals about making civil liberties policy. Nor-

Anthony Palazzolo

on the development of wetlands and other private property. Frequently these regulations, designed to stop development that might threaten endangered wildlife, prevent owners from developing their property in any way, whether for personal or commercial purposes, and so owners have charged that these regulations amount to an unconstitutional "taking" of their property without just compensation. Increasingly, organized groups of owners have challenged these environmental regulations and won. In 2001,

mally litigation is a time-consuming process conducted by lawyers who charge by the hour. Taking one's case all the way to the Supreme Court is a luxury few people can afford even if the case has merit and appeals judges are willing to consider it. As a consequence, the seeds of civil liberties cases—violations of established rights and claims of new rights—commonly are found in police departments and criminal trials without any judge taking notice. In this respect, civil liberties litigation presents citizens with a classic collective action question: who among them will assume the costs of supplying a new collective good?

The answer of course lies in finding someone who is sufficiently resourceful and interested in the outcome to justify paying the high transaction costs of litigation required to plead a case with an uncertain result. One such set of actors is the wide array of interest group organizations that use federal courts to try to change public policy. In Chapter 4 we encountered a prominent example of this kind of interest group in the National Association for the Advancement of Colored People, which took up the case of an elementary school student in Kansas whose parents objected to her being sent to a distant, segregated school. The result, of course, was the historic decision to overturn segregation in *Brown v. Board of Education of Topeka* (1954).

Today dozens of organizations across the political spectrum sponsor cases that will allow them to influence civil liberties policy. Since litigation is costly, these groups search selectively for those cases that will give them the best chance to achieve their policy goals. One such group that recently won a surprising victory, the Pacific Legal Foundation (PLF) of Sacramento, California, looks for cases to defend property rights, and in 2001 it found a good one in *Palazzolo v. Rhode Island*.

Rhode Island resident Anthony Palazzolo owned eighteen acres of beachfront property, on which he had long planned to build houses or a beach club. The Rhode Island coastal commission, created in the early 1970s, ruled that because his property had been designated as protected wetlands, it could not be developed. Palazzolo sued the state when it refused to compensate him for the greatly diminished value of his property.

After losing an appeal in the Rhode Island Supreme Court, Palazzolo's lawyers approached PLF with hat in hand. Their client's finances were exhausted, and yet his lawyers thought they had a strong case for appeal. After examining Palazzolo's claims, the state's case, and previous courts' opinions, PLF agreed and took over the case. Palazzolo, as it happened, lucked out twice—first, when PLF decided to sponsor him, and subsequently, when the Supreme Court ruled in his favor. In winning the case, the Pacific Legal Foundation scored a victory for property owners everywhere: they now have a decision they can invoke if they believe the government has violated the constitutional protections to which they are entitled under the "takings" clause.

for example, the Supreme Court ruled that even an owner who had purchased property after a regulation had gone into effect might still claim to have been deprived reasonable use. However, in a recent and controversial Fifth Amendment takings clause case, property owners were not so lucky. In *Kelo v. City of New London*,[89] the Court held that a city's decision to take property for *economic development* (as opposed to taking property, for example, to construct a road that clearly is a public good to be used by all) did in fact satisfy the "public use" requirement of the Fifth Amendment, thus forcing owners in an area targeted for redevelopment to sell their homes in exchange for just compensation. The 5–4 decision included vigorous dissenting opinions, so future changes in the composition of the Court could lead to a revisiting of this hot-button issue. (For information on how other organizations have tried to change civil liberties policy, see box "Interest Groups Take on the Courts: Solving Collective Action Problems.")

Assessing Civil Liberties as Public Policy

At first, the nationalization of civil liberties in the Bill of Rights was not a popular idea. Madison's proposal to amend the Constitution to apply them directly to the states was handily defeated in Congress as those members sympathetic with the Antifederalists, who had insisted that civic freedoms be written into the Constitution, explicitly rejected the idea of extending them to the states.

Only during the twentieth century, and gradually by incorporation, has the Bill of Rights come to be accepted as *national* policy that applies to every level of government. Yet states still formulate the rules that implement many of the rights guaranteed. For example, the Supreme Court allows states to determine the size of juries and level of agreement required to convict in state courts. Similarly, the states are free to decide the legality of physician-assisted suicide and have plenty of room to regulate the availability of abortions.

Civil liberties policy has developed on another front as well, one equally unimagined by its eighteenth-century sponsors. The members of Congress who drafted and deliberated these liberties and the state legislators who ratified them probably had in mind essentially "civic" rights: the right to dissent, to organize opposition, and, in extreme instances, to resist—essential bulwarks against the impulses of any intemperate majorities and tyrannical government officials. As we have seen, these rights have been broadened, in some instances dramatically, to create personal spheres of expression and privacy. This evolution is evident in modern case law on search and seizure, unconventional religious practices, nude dancing, the right to die, abortion, guns and property, and many other issues reviewed in this chapter.

Americans, however, do not see eye-to-eye on these matters. In fact, modern civil liberties number among the most divisive and unsettled issues facing the nation. None is more contentious than abortion rights. In the years since the 1973 *Roe v. Wade* decision, the issue has surfaced at every level of government from neighborhood rallies and demonstrations to restrictive amendments in annual appropriations legislation in Congress. At times the intensity of disagreement even spills over into violence directed at the physicians who perform abortions and their clinics. Abortion, together with the other conflicting civil liberties issues on the modern scene—flag burning, school prayer, and assisted suicide, to mention a few—reminds us of the inherent fractious nature of public policy when it collides with personal behavior.

The modern Supreme Court's preeminent role in deciding these policies contributes to their controversy. Once, these issues resided exclusively in the political arena—that is, with state and local governments and with Congress. But as the Supreme Court carved out a larger role in these policies, its insulation from public opinion exposed its decisions to criticism and second-guessing. And, of course, its insulation has allowed it at times to issue highly unpopular decisions, such as its stance on flag burning and, during the 1960s, its restrictions on established law enforcement practices.

How does the image of a small number of unelected, life-tenured justices deciding public policy comport with the principles of democracy? Those who insist that majority rule must prevail in a democracy cannot justify the Court's having any role at all other than duties delegated to it by the democratic (that is, elected) branches of government. Others, however, may accept the authority of a national community to impose limits on itself and future majorities in making certain decisions. The elaborate rules to amend the Constitution are a prime example. Other limits can be found in the Bill of Rights. It removes various personal prerogatives and private behavior from casual government intrusion. The First Amendment opens with "Congress shall make no law . . . ," and the list of proscriptions continues throughout the ten amendments. Madison recognized at the outset that the Supreme Court was well designed to enforce these antimajoritarian rules. The Court's unelected, life-tenured members are well insulated from the "popular passions" that can run roughshod over personal freedoms. Moreover, the explicit prohibitions to congressional action create space for the Court to enter as the Constitution's guardian.

If a national majority wants to ban flag burning, it can wait for new justices to be appointed and hope they are sympathetic with its position, or it can try to pass a constitutional amendment. Both avenues promise a lengthy delay and high transaction costs for the majority with little guarantee of success.

Finally, still others may point out that the majority is not as frustrated in exerting its preferences as it might appear. Supreme Court justices are subject to many of the same social and civic influences as are ordinary citizens, and as these circumstances change, so might justices' opinions—in tandem with those of the citizenry. Two weeks after the September 11 attacks, Justice Sandra Day O'Connor observed without alarm, "We are likely to experience more restrictions on our personal freedom than has ever been the case in our country." [90] That these heightened restrictions may occur and be sanctioned in future judicial policy reflects not so much the compromise of principle in the face of reality as the fact that judicial doctrine includes provisions for balancing these elements. The phrase "compelling government interest," for example, allows evidence to inform doctrine and hence opens the way for doctrine to change with conditions.

Moreover, even though federal judges may not be elected, voters' preferences do not go unheard. Court policy rarely deviates far from public opinion. In sum, the Constitution provides many safeguards to ensure that this institution stays on track with national majorities—and the political branches of government that serve them—and to limit the Court's influence when it fails to do so. Civil liberties policy may consume much of the caseload of today's Supreme Court, but the nine-member Court acts knowing that its words are rarely the last.

Given the absolute language of the Bill of Rights, someone who is unfamiliar with the modern history of civil liberties policy might assume that it is settled policy. As we have seen here, however, civil liberties seem to be constantly changing. When judges come and go, they permit Court ideology to be brought into closer alignment with partisan control of the rest of the government. To the extent that citizens disagree on many of these civil liberties issues, so, too, will their elected officeholders and, in turn, the judges these politicians appoint. Other, more direct influences on the Court can be found in the efforts of organized interests as they sponsor clients and submit "friend of the court" briefs. And finally, ever-changing technology throws into question (and sometimes into confusion) civil liberties policies based on old realities. All of these forces guarantee that civil liberties policy, far from settled, as the Framers might have envisioned, will be continuously revisited and frequently revised.

logic.cqpress.com

Key Terms

Suggested Readings

Carter, Stephen L. *The Culture of Disbelief: How American Law and Politics Trivialize Religious Devotion.* New York: Basic Books, 1993. A thoughtful argument against prevailing Supreme Court doctrine on the separation of church and state.

Epstein, Lee, and Thomas G. Walker. *Constitutional Law for a Changing America: Rights, Liberties, and Justice.* 6th ed. Washington, D.C.: CQ Press, 2007. A massive, comprehensive examination of the issues and Supreme Court opinions that define modern civil liberties policy. The authors retain a lively, pedagogic style.

Garrow, David J. *Liberty and Sexuality: The Right to Privacy and the Making of* Roe v. Wade. New York: Macmillan, 1994. A thorough, well-written survey of the circumstances and legal proceedings that culminated in this famous decision.

Hentoff, Nat. *Free Speech for Me . . . But Not for Thee: How the American Left and Right Relentlessly Censor Each Other.* New York: Harper Perennial, 1992. A highly original account of how political groups gain a political advantage through censorship.

Irons, Peter. *The Courage of Their Convictions.* New York: Free Press, 1988. Six case studies, including interviews with defendants who took their cases to the Supreme Court.

Lewis, Anthony. *Freedom for the Thought That We Hate: A Biography of the First Amendment.* New York: Basic Books, 2007. Although on balance Lewis is more comfortable with established free speech doctrine that embraces the marketplace metaphor, he does not consider it sacrosanct. Might hate speech and libel doctrines, among others, impose real cost on society? Once again, Lewis poses serious questions in a style and language appropriate for a general audience.

Maltzman, Forrest, James F. Spriggs II, and Paul J. Wahlbeck. *Crafting Law on the Supreme Court: The Collegial Game.* New York: Cambridge University Press, 2000. A revealing, behind-the-scenes account of how justices act strategically when crafting majority opinions.

Marshall, Thomas. *Public Opinion and the Supreme Court.* New York: Unwin/Hyman, 1989. An authoritative assessment of the extent to which judicial liberties and rights policies correspond to the opinions of the American public.

Review Questions

1. Through what individual steps did the Constitution acquire civil liberties protections?

2. How has individual liberty been elevated from a private local matter into a prominent national policy issue?

3. How has the role of national government differed in the development of civil rights policy versus that of civil liberties?

4. How did the Bill of Rights come to apply to states?

5. Which parts of the Bill of Rights currently apply to states?

6. Why do governments tend to restrict speech and other liberties more during wartime than in peacetime? How have these restrictions varied over time?

7. How has the Internet changed the way obscenity is regulated?

8. What is the Court's current position on prayer in school? Is this position supported by the public? How is it enforced?

9. What is the Court's current stance on capital punishment? What have been some past Court objections to executions, and how have states attempted to address these issues? How do executions vary by state and region?

10. How supportive has the public been about the incorporation of criminal rights into the Fourteenth Amendment? How has the level of incorporation altered with changes in the Court's membership?

11. What rights do citizens have against police searches and seizures of their property? How broad are these rights?

12. What is the constitutional basis for the right to privacy? Does privacy receive as much protection as do other rights?

13. Who is granted the right to "bear arms" by the Second Amendment? Has the Court's answer to this question changed over time?

14. Do the states still have a role in defining civil liberties?

Exercises

Spy Hunting?

In 1999 former British spy Richard Tomlinson was accused of posting a list that named British undercover intelligence officers worldwide (http://kimsoft. com/1997/m16list.htm). What do you think would have happened if an American agent had tried to publish a list of American agents in the Middle East after the September 11 attacks? Now that Tomlinson's list is on the Internet, what can be done to prevent the information from falling into the "wrong" hands?

The Japanese American Detentions of World War II

Go to the Smithsonian's interactive exhibit on America's internment of Japanese during World War II (http://americanhistory.si.edu/perfectunion/ experience). In viewing the site, take care to note the military and constitutional justifications for the action. What forms of resistance did the government's policy provoke? How did the Supreme Court view the internments in the 1940s? How does it view the internments in retrospect? What parallels are there between the situation of Japanese Americans following the Pearl Harbor attacks and Arab Americans following the September 11 attacks?

Fundamentally Different Fundamental Rights

How does the Bill of Rights of the United States compare with those of other governments? Read the Hong Kong Bill of Rights (www.oefre.unibe.ch/law/ icl/hk05000_.html), the New Zealand Bill of Rights (www.justice.govt.nz/lac/pubs/1991/legislative_ change/appendix_c.html), and the California Declaration of Rights (www.leginfo.ca.gov/.const/ .article_1). What freedoms are present in all three documents? Which document seems to grant the broadest freedoms? Which places the most limitations on the granted freedoms? What are the other important differences between the documents?

CHAPTER

6

Congress

Why do members of the House and Senate follow complex, arcane rules and precedents in processing legislation even when such devices keep majorities from getting their way?

Why do members of Congress show such a strong inclination to be individually responsive but collectively irresponsible?

Congressional incumbents rarely lose elections. Why then are they obsessed with the electoral implications of nearly everything they do?

How could a change in party control of the Senate have profound political consequences without any change at all in Senate membership?

In 2006, Democrats won majorities in both the House of Representatives and the Senate, taking full control of Congress for the first time since 1994.* That was the year that Republicans had ended an even longer period of Democratic dominance, after winning control of both chambers for the first time since 1952. The two historic midterm victories share a number of notable features. Both represented a popular repudiation of a president who shared the majority party's label, Democrat Bill Clinton in 1994 and Republican George W. Bush in 2006; the electorate's unhappiness with a president not on the ballot was taken out on his fellow partisans who were on the ballot. In both instances, the House minority leader—Newt Gingrich in 1994, Nancy Pelosi in 2006—effectively exploited the administration's unpopularity, organizing vigorous national fund-raising efforts and recruiting strong candidates for races in competitive districts. Both were rewarded with elevation to Speaker of the House after their party's respective victories.

In both years, the winning party had campaigned on a specific agenda of popular legislative proposals, the Republicans with their "Contract with America" in 1994 and the Democrats with their "100-Hour Agenda" in 2006, which they pledged to enact in the first few months of the new Congress. Both winning parties had also promised

---

*Republicans held majorities in the House during this entire period. The Senate was tied, 50–50, after the 2000 election, but in May 2001 Vermont senator James Jeffords left the Republican Party to become an independent, giving control to the Democrats until Republicans won it back in the 2002 midterm election.

Nancy Pelosi, elected Speaker of the House at the beginning of the 110th Congress, is the first woman to hold the position, which places her second in the line of presidential succession after the vice president. Here she shares the historic moment with her grandchildren.

More than three hundred Republicans stepped up to sign the Contract with America during the 1994 midterm election campaign. Although it is history and its architect, Newt Gingrich, has left Congress, the contract, together with the Republican class of 1994 it helped to elect, demonstrated that a minority opposition party in Congress can present a coherent alternative to the president's policies. The fact that this opposition effort was the first to succeed is a reminder of how hard it is for political parties in America to commit their members to a course of action.

to reverse the course set by the unpopular incumbent president. Republicans would undo Clinton's tax increases and slash domestic social programs he supported, dismantling whole cabinet-level departments in the process. Democrats sought to force Bush to change course in Iraq, wind down the war, and set a timetable for the withdrawal of U.S. forces.

After both the 1994 and 2006 elections, the eager new majorities soon found their ambitions thwarted by institutional realities. In both instances, the victorious party kept its promise to deliver quickly on its flagship agenda items—but only in the House, where the rules allow the majority party to work its will regardless of the minority's sentiments. Senate rules give minority parties much more leverage, so proposals solidly opposed by the Senate minority went no further. And even measures that passed both houses were subject to veto by a president disinclined to follow the dictates of an opposition-controlled Congress. Most of the legislation implementing the Contract with America died in the Senate; those initiatives from the Democrats' 100-Hour Agenda that did become law had to be altered significantly to meet objections by Republican senators and President Bush. The federal government did not shrink during Clinton's last six years in office, and Bush increased rather than decreased the U.S. military presence in Iraq after the Democrats took over in 2007. Still, both new majorities did achieve important changes in the direction of national policy, if only by denying the president's legislative wish list. What do these events say about Congress?

- The House and Senate occupy the center stage in national policymaking, although their power over legislation is not unalloyed, for the Constitution gives a share of legislative authority to the president.

- Electoral politics influences almost everything members of Congress do, collectively and individually.

- The majority party, through its leaders, directs and sometimes dominates the action in the House and Senate.

- The rules and organizational structures the House and Senate adopt have a deliberate and crucial effect on both the distribution of power and policymaking in Congress.

- It is always far easier to stop things from happening in Congress than to make things happen.

This chapter explores each of these themes while explaining how and why the House and Senate operate as they do. It also looks at how these institutions have evolved in response to the changing motives and opportunities, personal and political, of the politicians elected to them. Any such discussion must be prefaced, however, by a review of the constitutional design of Congress and the extensive powers granted it by the Framers.

Congress in the Constitution

The basic structure of Congress is the product of the Great Compromise at the Constitutional Convention, described in Chapter 2. Balancing the demands of the large states for national representation against those of the small states for protection of states' rights, the Framers established in the Constitution a House of Representatives, with seats allocated by population and members elected by the citizenry, and a Senate composed of two members from each state chosen by the state legislature. Bicameralism (two houses) also resolved another dispute. Delegates to the convention disagreed about the appropriate degree of popular influence on government. But, using the bicameral structure, they were able to devise a mixed solution. Representatives would be "popularly" chosen in biennial elections held in even-numbered years. The two-year term was a compromise between the annual elections advocated by many delegates and the three-year term proposed by James Madison. Broad suffrage—the qualification for voting was to be the same as for the "most numerous Branch of the State Legislature" (Article I, Section 2)—and short tenure were intended to keep the House as close as possible to the people.

The Senate, by contrast, would be much more insulated from transient shifts in the public mood. Senators would be chosen by state legislatures, not directly by the voters.

Washington's city planner, the young Frenchman Pierre L'Enfant, consulted the Constitution before placing the Capitol on the highest hill in the city. From 1825 to 1856 the Capitol lacked a large dome—the original low wooden dome is depicted here—causing L'Enfant to describe it as "a pedestal waiting for a monument."

The term of office was set at six years, another compromise; terms ranging from three to nine years had been proposed. Continuity was ensured by the requirement that one-third of the Senate's membership stand for election every two years. The Senate could thus act as a stable, dispassionate counterweight to the more popular and radical House, protecting the new government from the dangerous volatility thought to be characteristic of democracies. As James Madison put it in *Federalist* No. 62, "The necessity of the Senate is . . . indicated by the propensity of all single and numerous assemblies to yield to the impulse of sudden and violent passions, and to be seduced by factious leaders into intemperate and pernicious resolutions." The Senate also incorporated remnants of state sovereignty into the new national government.

Qualifications for office also reflected the Framers' concept of the Senate as the more "mature" of the two chambers (*senate* is derived from the Latin *senex,* old man). The minimum age for representatives was set at twenty-five years; for senators, thirty years. Representatives had to be citizens for at least seven years; senators, for nine years. Both were required to reside in the state they represented. Representatives do not have to live in the districts they serve, but in practice they almost always do. These are the only qualifications for office specified in the Constitution. The property-holding and religious qualifications included in many state constitutions were explicitly rejected, as was a proposal to forbid a member's reelection to office after serving a term. The Articles of Confederation had included a reelection restriction, but the Framers thought it had weakened Congress by depriving it of some of its ablest members.

Powers of Congress

As we saw in Chapter 2, the Constitution established a truly national government by giving Congress broad power over crucial economic matters. Article I, Section 8, authorizes Congress to impose taxes, coin and borrow money, regulate interstate and foreign commerce, and spend money for the "common Defence" and "general Welfare." Tacked on at the end of this list of specific powers is a residual clause authorizing Congress "to make all Laws which shall be necessary and proper for carrying into Execution the foregoing Powers, and all other Powers vested by this Constitution in the Government of the United States, or in any Department or Officer thereof." Accepted by many delegates as an afterthought, this **necessary and proper clause**—often known as the elastic clause because it "stretched" the powers of Congress—has proved to be the single most extensive grant of power in the Constitution, giving lawmakers authority over many different spheres of public policy (see Chapter 3). Indeed, it was under this authority that Congress banned discrimination in public accommodations and housing in the 1960s (see Chapter 4).

Congress was given significant authority in foreign affairs as well. Although the president is designated commander in chief of the armed forces, only Congress may declare war, raise and finance an army and navy, and call out the state militias "to execute the Laws of the Union, suppress Insurrections and repel Invasions" (Article I, Section 8). The Senate was granted some special powers over foreign relations. In its "advice and consent" capacity, the Senate ratifies treaties and confirms presidential appointments of ambassadors.

The Senate also approves presidentially appointed Supreme Court justices and top executive branch officials. These powers reveal that, in part, the Framers viewed the Senate as an advisory council to the executive, modeled on the upper chambers of some state legislatures. But they also reflect the Framers' belief that the more "aristocratic" and insulated of the two houses would keep a steadier eye on the nation's long-term interests.

In distributing power between the House and the Senate, the delegates sought a proper balance of authority. One bone of contention was the power to raise and spend money. Some delegates wanted to give the House, as the chamber closer to the people, the exclusive authority to enact legislation to raise or spend money; the Senate would be allowed to vote on House bills but not amend them. The final compromise required merely that bills raising revenue originate in the House, with the Senate having an unrestricted right to amend them. The House was given no special mandate to initiate spending bills, but it has assumed that right by custom as an extension of its special authority over revenue bills.

Despite its many legislative powers, Congress does not have exclusive authority over legislation. The president may recommend new laws and, in emergencies, call Congress into special session. Most important, the president has the power to veto laws passed by Congress, killing them unless two-thirds of each chamber votes to override the veto.

The Electoral System

Two other choices made by the Framers of the Constitution have profoundly affected the electoral politics of Congress. First, members of Congress and presidents are elected separately. In parliamentary systems like those found in most European countries, government authority rests with the legislature, which chooses the chief executive (called the prime minister or premier). Thus voters' choices for legislators depend mainly on voter preferences for leader of the executive branch. In the United States, voters are presented separate choices for senator, representative, and president.

Second, members of Congress are elected from states and congressional districts by plurality vote—that is, whoever gets the most votes wins.* Some parliamentary systems employ **proportional representation,** which gives a party a share of seats in the legislature matching the share of the votes it wins on Election Day. For example, if a party's share of votes entitles it to eighty-five seats, the first eighty-five candidates on the party's slate go to parliament. The voters, then, choose among parties, not individual candidates, and candidates need not have local connections. Party leaders under this system are very powerful because they control parliamentary careers by deciding who goes on the list and in what order.

American legislators are elected from territorial units, not party lists. Parties do matter in congressional elections, and with rare exceptions, only major party nominees have any chance of winning (see Chapter 12). In the past two decades only one member of Congress, Rep. Bernard Sanders, I-Vt., was not at least initially elected as a Republican or Democrat. But the parties do not control nominations. Almost all congressional nominees are now chosen by voters in primary elections—preliminary contests in which voters select the parties' nominees. Candidates thus get their party's nomination directly from voters, not from party activists or leaders.

Congressional Districts

After the first census in 1790, each state was allotted one House seat for every thirty-three thousand inhabitants, for a total of 105 seats. Until the twentieth century the House grew as population increased and new states joined the Union. Total membership was finally fixed at its current ceiling of 435 in 1911 when House leaders concluded that further growth would impede the House's work. Since 1911, states have both lost as well as gained seats to reflect population shifts between the decennial (ten-year) censuses. Changes in the sizes of state delegations to the House since World War II illustrate vividly the major population movements in the United States (see Map 6-1). States in the West and South have gained at the expense of the large industrial states in the Northeast and Midwest.

Federal law may apportion House seats among states after each census, but each state draws the lines that divide its territory into the requisite number of districts. In 1964 the Supreme Court ruled in *Wesberry v. Sanders* that districts must have equal populations.[1] In *Thornburg v. Gingles* (1986) the Court ruled that district lines may not dilute minority representation, but neither may they be drawn with race as the predominant consideration.[2] Within these limits states can draw districts pretty much as they please. If one party controls both the legislature and governorship, it may attempt to draw district lines that favor its own candidates. The idea is to concentrate the opposition party's voters in a small number of districts that the party wins by large margins, thus "wasting" many of its votes, while creating as many districts as possible

---

*In the past, some states elected some or all of their U.S. representatives in statewide "at-large" districts. A 1986 Supreme Court decision, *Davis v. Bandemer,* ended the practice by requiring that districts have equal populations. One state, Georgia, requires an absolute majority of votes to win general elections to Congress. If no candidate wins such a majority, a runoff election is held between the top two finishers.

Map 6-1 Apportionment's Winners and Losers

Since 1950, the South and West have been gaining House seats at the expense of the Northeast and Midwest

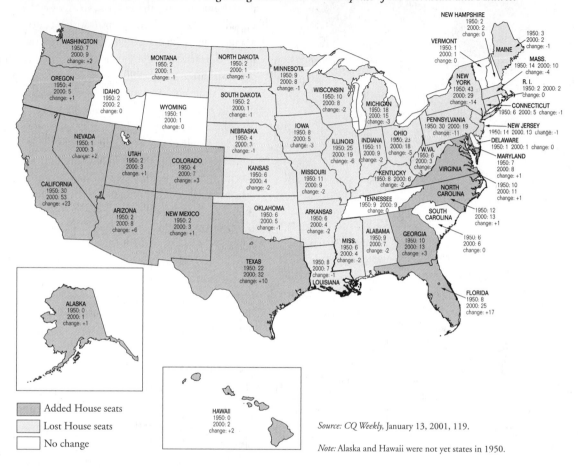

Added House seats

Lost House seats

No change

Source: CQ Weekly, January 13, 2001, 119.

Note: Alaska and Hawaii were not yet states in 1950.

where one's own party has a secure, though not overwhelming, majority. Called **gerrymandering,** these tactics sometimes produce bizarrely shaped districts (see box "The Original Gerrymander").

The constitutionality of partisan gerrymanders has been challenged in court, but so far without success. In *Davis v. Bandemer* (1986) the Supreme Court held that a gerrymander would be unconstitutional if it were too strongly biased against a party's candidates, but as yet no districting scheme has run afoul of this vague standard.[3] In 2004 the justices rejected a Democratic challenge to a gerrymander that had in 2002 raised the Republicans' advantage from 11–10 to 12–7 in Pennsylvania (*Vieth v. Jubelirer*)[4] and let stand a Texas redistricting that cost the Democrats six House seats in 2004 (see box "Partisan Redistricting, Texas-Style").

The Original Gerrymander

T he practice of "gerrymandering"—the extensive manipulation of the shape of a legislative district to benefit a certain incumbent or party—is probably as old as the Republic, but the name originated in 1812. That year, the Massachusetts legislature carved out of Essex County a district that historian John Fiske said had a "dragonlike contour." When the painter Gilbert Stuart saw the misshapen district, he penciled in a head, wings, and claws and exclaimed, "That will do for a salamander!" Editor Benjamin Russell replied, "Better say a Gerrymander"—after Elbridge Gerry, then governor of Massachusetts.

RACIAL GERRYMANDERING. The Court's 1986 *Thornburg* decision, requiring that legislative district lines not discriminate, even unintentionally, against racial minorities, was widely interpreted as directing mapmakers to design districts in which racial and ethnic minorities constituted a majority of voters wherever residence patterns made this feasible.[5] Attempts to conform to this decision after the 1990 census inspired some artistry that would have made Massachusetts governor Elbridge Gerry, from whom the gerrymander got its name, proud (see box "The Original Gerrymander"). For example, North Carolina legislators carved out two majority black districts (First and Twelfth) that eventually came before the Court (see Map 6-2). In 1993 the Court decided that such irregular districts went too far[6] and in 1995 that districts could not be drawn solely to benefit one race.[7] Thus the North Carolina districts (along with thirty-four districts in four other states) had to be redrawn. Modified twice before receiving final court approval, the districts had some of their rough edges smoothed off but retained all the earmarks of a painstaking gerrymander.

Unequal Representation in the Senate

The fifty Senate constituencies—entire states—may not change boundaries with each census, but they vary greatly in size of population. Sen. Dianne Feinstein, D-Calif., represents more than thirty-seven million people, while Sen. Michael Enzi, R-Wyo., has fewer constituents (523,000) than does the average U.S. representative (699,000). The nine largest states are home to 51 percent of the total U.S. population, while the smallest twenty-six states, with 52 percent of Senate seats, hold only 18 percent of the population. Unequal representation in the Senate sometimes matters politically. For example, Republicans held a Senate majority between 1981 and 1987 even though their candidates had received overall a smaller percentage of the popular vote than Democrats because Republican candidates won so many of the smaller states.[8]

Until 1913 senators were chosen by state legislatures. Most Americans had long since concluded that this method of selection was undemocratic and corrupting (between 1890 and 1905 charges of bribery shadowed Senate elections in seven different states).[9] But it took the reforming spirit of Progressivism at its peak to convince

STRATEGY AND CHOICE

Partisan Redistricting, Texas-Style

If there were any doubt that the practice of partisan gerrymandering is alive, well, and effective, recent events in Texas would lay it to rest. Texas has been growing increasingly Republican in its voting habits for several decades, but Democrats held onto a majority of the state's U.S. House delegation up through the 2002 elections by careful gerrymanders aimed at protecting the party's incumbents.[1] Thus even though the Democratic candidate had won no more than 44 percent of the Texas vote in presidential elections going back to 1980, and Republicans had won every statewide office in 2002, the Democrats still held a seventeen-to-fifteen-seat majority in the state's House delegation.

House Majority Leader Tom DeLay, a Texas Republican looking to strengthen his party's narrow majority, found this situation intolerable and saw an opportunity to change it when Republicans won both chambers of the state legislature in 2002. At his behest, the Republican governor proposed during the 2003 legislative session a new redistricting that would do maximum damage to incumbent Democrats. With nothing in federal or Texas law standing in the way of redrawing the districts a second time in a decade, the beleaguered Democratic minority in the Texas House fled en masse to Ardmore, Oklahoma, just before a scheduled May vote on the plan to wait out the few days until it was too late to act in the regular session of the legislature. By leaving the state, they denied the legislature a quorum while avoiding arrest under a Texas statute aimed at preventing just this ploy.[2]

Not to be thwarted, DeLay then got the governor to call a special session of the legislature on June 30 to redraw the districts. This time, eleven Democratic state senators moved to Albuquerque, New Mexico, again denying the Republicans a quorum throughout this second legislative session. They held out until September 2, when one of their ranks capitulated and returned home. The governor then called a third session, which began on September 15; the legislature finally enacted the Republican gerrymander on October 13. The new map thoroughly dismantled several Democrats' districts, giving them largely unfamiliar, more conservative constituencies, or forcing them to move by placing them in districts with other Democrats, or, in two cases, pitting them against incumbent Republicans in redrawn, overwhelmingly Republican districts.[3]

DeLay and the Texas lawmakers did not overestimate the stakes. Prior to the redistricting, Republicans held fifteen of Texas's thirty-two House seats. After the new map was enacted, one Democrat—Ralph T. Hall—switched to the Republican Party, another retired, another was defeated in a primary, and four were defeated in the general election. Only one targeted Democrat managed to survive. After the election, Republicans held twenty-one Texas seats, their six-seat gain more than offsetting their net loss of three seats elsewhere in the 2004 congressional elections. DeLay's exploitation of the strategic opportunity offered by Texas politics and districting rules thus helped solidify Republican control of the House for the 109th Congress (2005–2006). Care to try your hand at gerrymandering?

---

1. The post-2000 redistricting was done by a three-judge panel that, aiming to protect current incumbents by preserving their constituencies as far as feasible, in effect perpetuated the effects of the Democrats' post-1900 partisan gerrymander.

2. DeLay sought help from federal agencies to track the missing Democrats, a move that earned him a formal admonishment from the House Ethics Committee.

3. Seth McKee and Daron R. Shaw, "Redistricting in Texas: Institutionalizing Republican Ascendancy," manuscript, University of Texas, May 2004.

Map 6-2 Acceptable and Unacceptable Gerrymanders

North Carolina, 1991, 1998, 2001

1991 version (rejected by the Supreme Court)

1998 version (accepted by the Supreme Court)

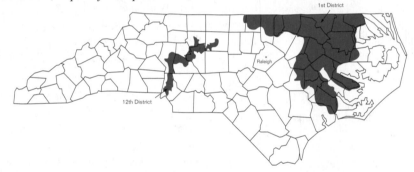

After the 2000 census (2001)

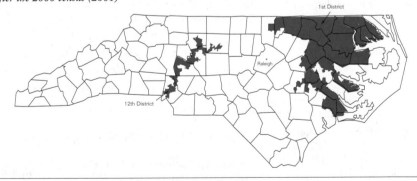

Sources: Congressional Districts in the 1990s: A Portrait of America (Washington, D.C.: Congressional Quarterly, 1993), 548; *Congressional Staff Directory* (Washington, D.C.: CQ Press, 1999); *CQ's Politics in America 2004* (Washington, D.C.: CQ Press, 2003), 741.

Note: North Carolina's First and Twelfth Districts were drawn to give the state its first black representatives in ninety-three years. First elected in 1992, the two black representatives were subsequently reelected; after the First District representative retired in 2003, she was replaced by another African American.

senators to agree to a constitutional amendment (the Seventeenth) providing for popular election.[10] As it turned out, they had little to fear from the change; senators have been about as successful in winning reelection as they had been in persuading state legislatures to return them to office.*

Congress and Electoral Politics

The modern Congress is organized to serve the goals of its members. A primary goal for most of them is to keep their jobs. And since voters have the final say in their hiring and firing, a career in Congress depends on members winning the voters' endorsement at regular intervals. Winning regular reelection is essential to everything else members want to achieve in office. Electoral imperatives thus shape all important aspects of congressional life.

Candidate-Centered versus Party-Centered Electoral Politics

The post–World War II era of Democratic majorities in Congress coincided with the emergence of a candidate-centered pattern of electoral politics. Similarly, the Republican takeover of Congress in the 1994 midterm elections followed and reflected a modest resurgence of party-centered electoral politics. Neither connection was accidental. During their era of dominance, congressional Democrats thrived on, and thus sought to encourage, a kind of electoral politics in which candidates operated largely as independent political entrepreneurs. Republican leaders, unable to win House majorities by playing the game this way (Republicans did manage to control the Senate from 1981 through 1986), sought in 1994 to have their candidates run more as a party team, emphasizing national issues and a common program of action. The strategy succeeded beyond their expectations. Thus in triumph the Republican majority, owing their new-found control to party-centered electoral politics, immediately moved to alter the House and the Senate, long shaped by the Democrats' candidate-centered electoral politics, to suit their own electoral and policy goals.

During the long period of Democratic majorities, members of both parties had won election to Congress, and stayed there, largely because of their own efforts. Most "recruited" themselves, organized their own campaigns, and raised their own campaign money. Party organizations and **political action committees** (PACs)—organizations that raise and distribute money for campaigns (see Chapter 13)—were ready to help, but not until campaigns had shown promise. "Promise" usually meant the candidate had won the primary election, gained some favorable media attention, and raised a substantial amount of start-up money—most of which often came from the candidate's own pockets.

---

*A remaining democratic anomaly is the absence of representation of any kind, in the Senate or the House, for the more than half-million Americans who live in Washington, D.C. Citizens living in the nation's capital do get to vote for three presidential electors, however. They also elect a nonvoting delegate to the House of Representatives (Eleanor Holmes Norton during the 110th Congress).

Rahm Emanuel, chair of the Democratic Congressional Campaign Committee, and Chuck Schumer, chair of the Democratic Senatorial Campaign Committee, celebrate their party's victory in the 2006 elections. Their candidate recruitment and fund-raising efforts effectively exploited the prevailing pro-Democratic national climate, helping to deliver control of Congress to the Democrats.

Although congressional candidates ran under party labels for national offices, most congressional campaigns were personal and centered on local interests and values. National issues that did enter the campaign were given a local spin. Campaigns for reelection dwelled on the services, projects, and locally popular programs the incumbent delivered to constituents, making it possible for members to separate their electoral fates from those of their party's other candidates.[11] For example, between 1972 and 1992 House Democrats won victories in 45 percent of the districts that delivered majorities to Republican candidates in presidential elections (Republicans won in 12 percent of the much smaller number of districts that delivered majorities to Democratic presidential candidates).[12]

The local component of congressional elections had not always been so dominant. During much of the nineteenth century, party-line voting was far more common than it is now. Voters based their choices on the top of the ticket—the presidential candidates in presidential election years—and on the parties' platforms. Congressional candidates' fates were decided by national trends they could do little personally to shape or control. Changes in the laws regulating elections and parties around the turn of the century weakened parties and encouraged **ticket-splitting**—that is, voting for candidates of different parties for different offices.[13] The most important of these changes were the introduction of primary elections for choosing the parties' nominees and the secret ballot (see Chapter 12). Still, party conflicts over national policy, most notably the political battles over President Franklin Roosevelt's New Deal, continued to inject a strong national component into congressional elections until the 1950s. As the New Deal controversies faded, however, the party coalitions built around them fractured under the stress of divisive new issues, most prominently civil rights, the Vietnam War, and social issues such as abortion and the environment. Party lines became blurred and party loyalty among voters declined.

The Advantages of Incumbency

Congressional incumbents both exploited and abetted the loosening of party ties. The decline in party loyalty among voters offered incumbents a chance to win votes that once would have gone routinely to the other party's candidate. Members could ex-

Figure 6-1 Consistent Success of House Incumbents

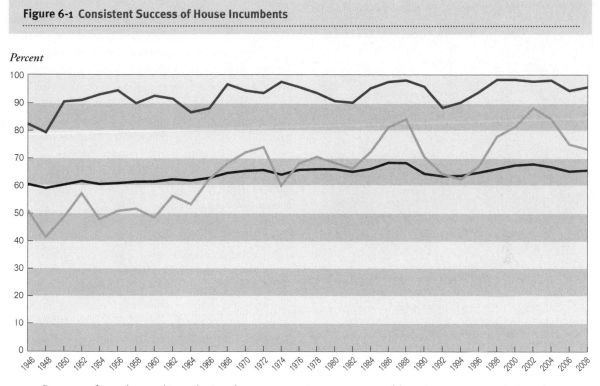

Percent

——— Percentage of incumbents seeking reelection who won ——— Average percentage of the major-party vote won by incumbents
——— Percentage of incumbents winning more than 60 percent of vote

Source: Compiled by the authors.

pand their electoral base by emphasizing individual character, legislative performance, and constituency services, encouraging voters to use such criteria in deciding how to vote.[14] Realizing that the growth of candidate-centered electoral politics worked to the advantage of incumbents willing to build a personal following, members of Congress voted themselves greater resources for servicing their states and districts—that is, higher allowances for staff, travel, local offices, and communication. These allowances are now worth more than $1.2 million per legislator in the House and up to three times as much per senator, depending on the population of the state represented.[15]

Electoral data demonstrate the success of these efforts. The average share of votes won by House incumbents increased from 61 percent in the 1940s and 1950s to 68 percent in the 1980s before retreating a bit to 64 percent in the 1990s. The average share was 65 percent in 2006 (see Figure 6-1). The proportion of incumbents winning more than 60 percent of the vote grew even more steeply, from as low as 41 percent in 1948 to as high as 88 percent in 2002. Incumbent reelection rates also have generally been higher since the mid-1960s, although some years, notably in the early 1990s, have been exceptions. Even before the 1960s House incumbents were winning

Until the 1890s, Americans voted with paper ballots supplied by party workers or printed in newspaper advertisements. The voter simply took the ballot to the voting desk and publicly submitted it. On this 1876 ballot for the Republican ticket of Rutherford B. Hayes and his vice-presidential running mate, William Wheeler, the voter voted for all Republicans from president down to the lowly register of deeds. Because this method of voting made ticket-splitting so difficult, the success of congressional candidates was tied to the fortunes of their party's presidential candidate.

reelection very consistently; their overall success rate since World War II exceeds 92 percent. Even in a year like 1994, with a strong electoral tide running against one of the parties, incumbency remained a potent advantage. Republican candidates won 71 percent (22 of 31) of the contests for open House seats (those without an incumbent running) that had been held by Democrats but only 15 percent (34 of 225) of the seats defended by Democratic incumbents. In 2006, with the electoral tide running in the opposite direction, Democrats won 36 percent (8 of 22) of open Republican seats but only 10 percent (22 of 210) of seats held by Republican incumbents.

The remarkable wins/losses record for incumbents raises an important question: if incumbency is so advantageous and if members of Congress win reelection so consistently, usually by comfortable margins, why do electoral worries do so much to shape congressional life? The answer is that the incumbency advantage does not accrue automatically to officeholders; it stems from diligent use of the many resources that come with holding office. Incumbents win reelection consistently because they work so hard at it, and they work hard because so much of their electoral fate is in their own hands.[16]

One purpose of hard work is to discourage potential opponents. In a candidate-centered system of electoral politics, ambitious, talented people rarely challenge incumbents if they see no chance of winning; and contributors decline to waste money on hopeless causes. Obscure, underfinanced challengers simply cannot compete. The most successful incumbents win easy reelection by making themselves appear so invincible that no qualified opponent is willing to take them on.[17] But an image of invincibility is not invincible; it is vulnerable to unexpected events, such as the House bank scandal in 1992 or strong national partisan tides as in 1994 or 2006. These events demonstrate why members of Congress—even those with long records of past electoral success—are right to worry about reelection.

The revelation in April 1992 that 350 past and current members of the House had written some twenty thousand overdrafts on their House bank checking accounts between July 1988 and October 1991 provoked a storm of outrage from the press and public that contributed to the largest turnover of membership in fifty years. Even members who wrote no bad checks suffered in the fallout.[18] The strength of the Republican tide in 1994 also surprised nearly everyone on Capitol Hill, as Republicans succeeded in turning long-simmering public anger over the Clinton administration, stagnant incomes, declining public services, high crime rates, continuing budget deficits, high taxes, and congressional malfeasance against Democratic candidates for both national and local offices. Thirty-four Democratic House incumbents, including Speaker Thomas Foley of Washington, were defeated. Republicans suffered in turn in 2006 through widespread disaffection with President Bush and the Iraq War and from ethics scandals besetting some congressional Republicans. Members of Congress, then, inhabit a world fraught with far more electoral uncertainty than their wins/losses record would lead one to believe. An easy victory against feeble opposition in one election carries no guarantee of success against a talented and well-financed challenger in the next.

CONSTITUENT SERVICE. Recognizing that they hold their jobs at the sufferance of sometimes-fickle electorates, members of Congress are highly responsive to their constituencies. Decisions on legislative issues are shaped by the potential need to explain and defend them in future campaigns.[19] Most members also spend a great deal of time back home, keeping in touch and staying visible. They solicit and process **casework,** requests from constituents for information and help in dealing with government agencies. A lost Social Security check? A bureaucratic mix-up over veterans' benefits? A representative or senator is ready to help. Some requests—and services—go well beyond the expected. One constituent tried to get his senator to intercede with the head of the state university's board of regents to raise the C grade his son received in a political science course.[20] The senator did not comply, but electoral logic makes it hard to resist almost any opportunity to please people back home.

VULNERABLE SENATORS. Although senators engage in many of the same constituency-building activities as representatives, they have not been as successful in keeping their jobs. Since 1946 their overall rate of reelection, 79 percent, has left them three times more likely to lose their seats than House incumbents. But because senators face reelection only one-third as often, tenure in office tends to even out between the chambers. Overall, though, Senate election outcomes are more variable than House outcomes; in the post-war era, incumbent reelection rates have been as low as 55 percent (1980) and as high as 97 percent (1990). Even when Senate incumbents do win, their margins of victory tend to be narrower than those of representatives. Why do Senate incumbents win less consistently and typically by narrower margins? First, because states (other than the seven with only one representative) are more populous and diverse than congressional districts, most senators are unable to develop the kinds of personal ties to constituents that many representatives cultivate. Second, states are more likely than congressional districts to have balanced party competition; few states are securely in either party's pocket. Third, Senate races attract a larger proportion of experienced, politically talented, well-financed challengers. Fourth, states usually fit media markets—formed by cities and their suburbs reached by local TV and radio stations and newspapers—better than House districts, making it easier for challengers to get out their messages. Senators receive far more attention from the news media than representatives, but so do their opponents. Representatives may be largely ignored by journalists, but this vacuum leaves them freer to shape the information that does reach constituents. And finally, senators are more readily associated with controversial and divisive issues, and they do not have the pressure of a two-year election cycle to keep them attuned to the folks back home. All these things contribute to making senators more vulnerable than representatives to defeat by challengers.

National Politics in Congressional Elections

The modest resurgence of party-centered campaigning since 1994 has strengthened the national component of congressional election politics, but even during the heyday of locally focused, candidate-centered elections, national forces continued to have a palpable effect on electoral fates. Congressional candidates are still better off if their party's presidential candidate wins. Winners may have shorter **presidential coattails**— the common metaphor for the capacity of a successful presidential candidate to pull the party's other candidates into office—than they once did, but coattail effects remain significant.[21]

In midterm elections the president's party almost always loses congressional seats, but the size of its losses depends in part on the performances of the national economy and the president. Losses tend to be fewer when the economy is booming and the president is popular, greater when the economy or the administration's popularity sags. Thus, for example, congressional Democrats suffered in 1994 from, among other things, Bill Clinton's low job approval ratings and voters' doubts about the economy. In 1998, by contrast, Clinton's approval rating stood nearly twenty points higher than it had in 1994 and the economy was in its best shape since the 1960s. As a result, the Democrats broke precedent by actually gaining House seats. Similarly, George W. Bush's leadership in the war on terrorism produced high approval ratings in 2002 that helped his party achieve small gains in the House and Senate; with Bush's ratings 25 points lower in 2006, Democrats picked up enough seats to take control of both chambers.*

As the 1994 and 2006 elections showed so dramatically, members of Congress cannot always dissociate themselves from their party's fate, so they retain a personal stake in their party's public image as well as the public standing of the president. Nor can they separate themselves from Congress itself, though incumbents frequently try to do so. Individual members remain far more popular than Congress collectively (see Figure 6-8, page 308), but they still suffer at the ballot box when the public's normally

---

*Clinton's 66 percent job approval rating in 1998 was the highest for any president at a midterm election since the Gallup Poll began measuring the percentage more than fifty years ago; Bush, with 63 percent approving, came in second (matched by Ronald Reagan in 1986). Partly as a consequence, the 1998 and 2002 midterm elections were only the second and third since the Civil War in which the president's party gained House seats (the other was the 1934 contest). By 2006, Bush's approval rating had fallen to 38 percent, and Democrats picked up thirty-one House seats and six Senate seats. Gary C. Jacobson, "Referendum: The 2006 Midterm Congressional Elections," *Political Science Quarterly* 122 (Spring 2007): 1–24.

mild hostility toward Congress becomes intense, as it did in 1992 in response to the House bank scandal. In 1994, when Republicans managed to transform hostility to Congress into hostility to the party controlling it, Democrats lost their majority. Similarly, disdain for the Republican-controlled Congress also contributed to the Democrats' success in 2006. But individual members cannot do much about such sentiments by themselves, so they concentrate on activities such as casework, by which their individual efforts can make a difference.

Representation versus Responsibility

Different electoral processes produce different forms of representation. In a party-centered electoral process, for example, legislators represent citizens by carrying out the policies promised by the party (or parties in multiparty systems) winning a majority of seats. Legislators know they will be held responsible by voters for their party's performance in governing, so ensuring the success of their party and the government takes top priority.

The candidate-centered electoral process that flourished during the long period of Democratic control and has ebbed only moderately since then gives members of Congress far more incentive to be individually *responsive* than collectively *responsible*. This imbalance is a primary source of Congress's collective action problems. For example, electoral logic induces members to promote narrowly targeted programs, projects, or tax breaks for constituents without worrying about the impacts of such measures on spending or revenues. Recipients notice and appreciate such specific and identifiable benefits and show their gratitude at election time. Because the benefits come at the expense of general revenues (money supplied by the taxes that everyone pays), no one's share of the cost of any specific project or tax break is large enough to notice. Thus it makes political sense for members of Congress to pursue local or group benefits that are paid for nationally even if the costs clearly outweigh the benefits. Conversely, no obvious payoff arises from opposing any particular local or group benefit because the savings are spread so thinly among taxpayers that no one notices.

The pursuit of reelection therefore makes *logrolling*—a legislative practice in which members of Congress offer reciprocal support to each other's vote-gaining projects or tax breaks—an attractive strategy (see Chapter 2). But this situation creates a classic prisoner's dilemma. When everyone follows such an individually productive strategy, all may end up in worse shape politically when shackled with collective blame for the overall consequences. Spending rises, revenues fall, the deficit grows, government programs proliferate, and the opposition attacks the logrolling coalition—in practice, the majority party—for wastefulness and incompetence. Individual responsiveness leads to collective irresponsibility.

Democratic candidates suffered across the board in 1994 as voters turned against the aggregate consequences of collective irresponsibility: a government they perceived as too big, too expensive, and too inept. To demonstrate that they were different, the newly elected Republican majority invited voters to hold them collectively accountable for delivering on the Republican "Contract with America," with its basic promise

The Rock and Roll Hall of Fame in Cleveland, Ohio, was a recipient of Congress's pork barrel largesse. The fiscal 2004 budget earmarked $200,000 for its "Rockin' the Schools" program.

to shrink government, cut taxes, and change how the government operates. They stuck together on the contract, but after losing a standoff over the budget in late 1995 to President Clinton, they broke ranks on issues such as repealing the ban on assault weapons, weakening protection of endangered species, and raising the minimum wage. In 1996 it was their Democratic opponents, bolstered by independent campaigns mounted by labor unions and other activists, who sought to inject national issues into the campaign, while endangered Republicans strove to show their independence from House Speaker Newt Gingrich.[22] Thus a noticeable shift away from the candidate-centered toward a more party-centered electoral politics was evident in 1994 (for the Republicans) and 1996 (for the Democrats). By 1997, however, congressional Republicans were showing renewed interest in the particularistic politics of **pork barrel legislation**—measures earmarking projects for individual members' districts*—that had served the Democrats so well for so long. And with a budget surplus in 2000, "Republicans and Democrats . . . joined hands in a spending spree on roads, courthouses, schools, rivers, runways, and research that . . . left even some veteran staff members amazed."[23] According to the Congressional Research Service, between 1994 and 2005 the total number of designated projects grew from 4,126 to 12,852 with their estimated cost rising from $23.2 to $63.8 billion.

The same logic that encourages logrolling makes members of Congress hesitate to impose direct costs on identifiable groups to produce greater, but more diffuse, benefits for all citizens. For example, laws designed to clean up the environment for everyone impose direct costs on industrial firms, such as the expenses incurred in installing antipollution equipment. The cost of compliance is clear to every firm affected, but the benefit of any firm's investment is diffused across so many people that few are likely to know of it. Members of Congress, then, fear retaliation from the losers without a compensating increase in support from the winners. Congressional majorities have found ways to get around this problem. One tactic is to delegate authority to bureaucratic agencies or state governments, letting them take the heat (see Chapter 8).

---

*According to the *C-SPAN Congressional Dictionary,* " 'pork barrel' came into use as a political term in the post–Civil War era. It comes from the plantation practice of distributing rations of salt pork to slaves from wooden barrels. When used to describe a bill, it implies the legislation is loaded with special projects for members of Congress to distribute to their constituents back home as an act of largesse, courtesy of the federal taxpayer."

POLITICS/POLICY

Surprising Success
The Tax Reform Act of 1986

Although its instinct is to do the opposite, Congress sometimes can find a way to enact policies that impose costs on specific groups to produce benefits shared by many people. For example, the Tax Reform Act of 1986 eliminated a host of special tax favors to reduce tax rates for everyone. Although the law was a popular idea pushed by Republican president Ronald Reagan and embraced by Democrats who did not want their party left defending "special interests," its success nonetheless depended heavily on the procedural strategies of congressional leaders. The package was assembled behind closed doors without recorded votes so no member could be blamed personally for eliminating any particular tax break. It then came to the floor of the House under a modified closed rule that allowed only three specific amendments to be offered (see section "Making Laws" for an explanation of closed rules). Some powerful members whose support was deemed essential received special concessions in the form of breaks for specific taxpayers in their states or districts—with support for the bill set as the minimum price for any concession. Among other taxpayers, sports facilities in New Jersey (the Meadowlands complex), Miami (Joe Robbie Stadium), and New Orleans (the Superdome) received special treatment.

In the Senate, which does not use closed rules, the bill's principal sponsor, Sen. Bob Packwood, a Republican from Oregon, won agreement that amendments on the floor had to be revenue neutral—that is, any change producing a tax benefit to some group had to be offset by increased taxes on another group. This agreement prevented the kind of logrolling among proponents of special tax breaks that would have unraveled the package.

Members of both houses had to go on record as for or against a substantial cut in taxes for a large majority of taxpayers. Because members were given no opportunity to do any behind-the-scenes favors for the myriad special interest groups that traditionally have feasted at tax-writing time, they could not be blamed for not doing the favors. By agreeing to tie their own hands, then, members were able to solve the acute collective action problem that tax bills always present. In the end, the bill's success took most seasoned observers of Congress by surprise, illustrating how uncommon such an outcome is.

Sources: R. Douglas Arnold, *The Logic of Congressional Action* (New Haven: Yale University Press, 1990), chap. 8; Jeffrey H. Birnbaum and Alan S. Murray, *Showdown at Gucci Gulch: Lawmakers, Lobbyists, and the Unlikely Triumph of Tax Reform* (New York: Vintage, 1988).

Another is for legislative leaders to frame the lawmaker's choice in a way that highlights credit for the general benefits while minimizing individual responsibility for the specific costs.

More broadly, the trick is to make the electoral payoffs from disregarding special interests to benefit a broader public outweigh the costs. One essential ingredient is that the issue be important (or potentially important if an opponent raises it in a future election campaign) to many voters. A challenge for legislative leaders is to frame the decision on an issue in a way that forces members to put themselves on the record for or against the issue's general benefits without having an opportunity to amend or modify the policy to serve narrower interests. Meeting this challenge requires skillful manipulation of congressional procedures. In addition, leaders may have to buy off the most powerful potential opponents with special concessions or side deals (see box "Surprising Success: The Tax Reform Act of 1986," page 265, which describes a classic example of successful execution of the strategy described here).

Who Serves in Congress?

The people who win seats in the Senate and House are by no means "representative" of the American people in any demographic sense. Almost all members have graduated from college; 41 percent have law degrees. Next to law, business is the most common prior occupation. A large majority are professionals of one kind or another; only a handful have blue-collar backgrounds. Most have served in lower elected offices. The true vocation of the average member is, in fact, politics.

Women and racial minorities continue to be under-represented in Congress, though their numbers have been increasing (see Figures 6-2 and 6-3). In 1961 only three African Americans and twenty women held House or Senate seats; by 1981 the number of black members had grown to seventeen, while only one more woman had been added. Growth continued to be slow until 1992, when the number of African Americans and Hispanics in the House increased sharply after the 1982 Voting Rights Act amendments had been interpreted to require states to maximize the number of "majority-minority" districts when drawing new district lines. The 1992 election also saw women candidates and campaign donors mobilized in unprecedented numbers in response to an event widely publicized in 1991: the insensitive handling by an all-male Senate committee of sexual harassment charges made by college professor Anita Hill against Supreme Court nominee Clarence Thomas. Women also represented a change from politics as usual in a year when that was what most voters wanted.

After the 2006 elections the Senate included sixteen women, one African American, three Hispanics, and two Asian Americans; the House, seventy-one women, forty African Americans, twenty-three Hispanics, and four Asian Americans. Despite a sharp increase in diversity in the 1990s, Congress remains overwhelmingly white and male because white males still predominate in the lower-level public offices and private careers that are the most common stepping stones to Congress. As women and minorities continue, albeit slowly, to assume a larger share of state and local offices and professional careers in law and business, their representation in Congress will continue to rise as well.

The gender and racial makeup of Congress makes a difference. For example, black members led the fight for sanctions punishing South Africa for its apartheid system in the 1980s. And the influx of women has made Congress far more attentive to issues of sex discrimination and sexual harassment.[24]

Figure 6-2 Women in Congress: Higher Numbers but Still Underrepresented

Number

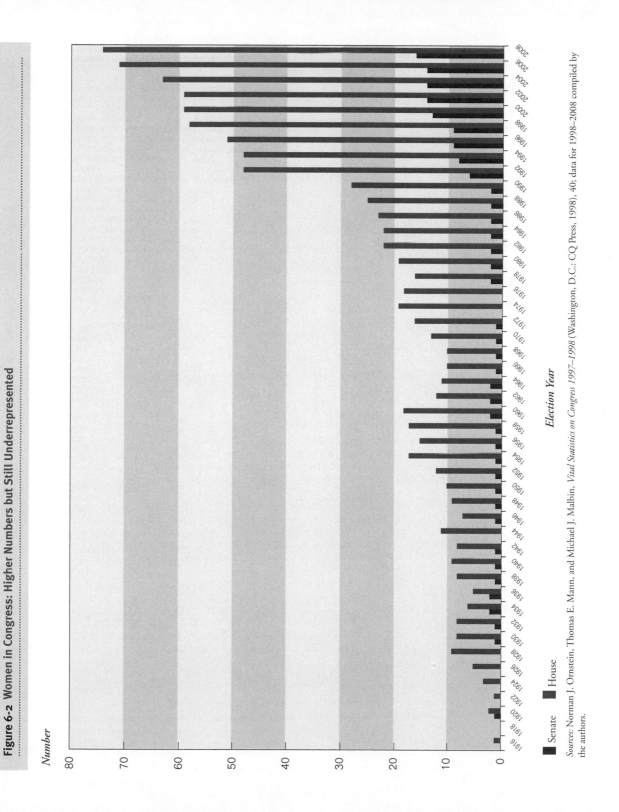

Election Year

■ Senate   ■ House

Sources: Norman J. Ornstein, Thomas E. Mann, and Michael J. Malbin, *Vital Statistics on Congress 1997–1998* (Washington, D.C.: CQ Press, 1998), 40; data for 1998–2008 compiled by the authors.

Figure 6-3 Congress Has Grown More Diverse but Has Yet to Mirror the Electorate

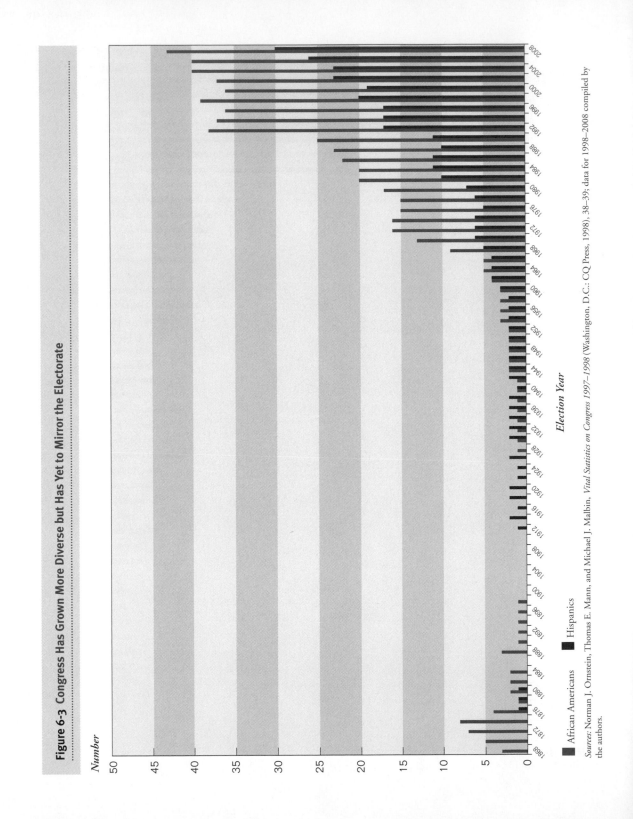

Number

Election Year

■ African Americans   ■ Hispanics

Sources: Norman J. Ornstein, Thomas E. Mann, and Michael J. Malbin, *Vital Statistics on Congress 1997–1998* (Washington, D.C.: CQ Press, 1998), 38–39; data for 1998–2008 compiled by the authors.

The Basic Problems of Legislative Organization

The Constitution established a basic framework for a national legislature, but today's Congress is the product of more than two centuries of institutional development. Although the House and Senate have evolved into highly complex institutions with remarkably elaborate and arcane rules, procedures, and customs, a logic underlies this sometimes bewildering complexity. To understand how Congress reflects the diverse and conflicting needs and intentions of its members, one must understand what representatives and senators want to accomplish and what obstacles they have to overcome to achieve their goals.

The delegates in Philadelphia created and empowered a national legislature—on paper at least; it was up to members of Congress to make the words into an institutional reality. To exercise the powers conferred on them by the Constitution, the House and Senate had to solve some basic problems: how to acquire information, how to coordinate action, how to resolve conflicts, and how to get members to work for common as well as personal goals. As these problems have become more acute over the years, members of Congress have scrambled to adapt the institution to cope with them more effectively while recognizing that every solution raises problems of its own. The challenges that spurred members to develop the modern Congress fall into two classes: problems besetting the House and Senate as organizations and problems arising from the competing individual and collective needs of members.

In 2007 Rep. Louise Slaughter, D-N.Y., became chair of the House Rules Committee, the most powerful committee in Congress. A Kentucky coal miner's daughter and strong feminist, Slaughter acquired this key position after twenty years of service, illustrating the continuing importance of seniority as well as the growing clout of women in Congress.

The Need for Information

Legislation is only as effective as the quality of knowledge underlying its inception. For example, a legislator cannot regulate the stock market sensibly without knowing how the market works or attack environmental pollution effectively without knowing how pollution is produced. As the United States has become more and more complex—socially, economically, and technologically—and the activities of the federal government have expanded, the informational demands on Congress have grown enormously.

Congress has responded with a solution common to the problem of performing complex social tasks efficiently: division of labor and specialization. The division of labor has given rise to the committee and subcommittee systems, large personal and committee staffs, and specialized research agencies that characterize the modern Congress. Specialists are able to develop a deeper understanding of their domains. By becoming specialists themselves or by drawing on the knowledge of other specialists, members of Congress can make better-informed decisions, and Congress, in turn, becomes a more effective institution. To provide the chamber with expertise, members must invest a lot of time and effort in mastering an area of specialization (as we learned earlier, public goods are more attractive in their consumption than in their production). Congress compensates members who master an area of specialization and supply specialized information with enhanced influence in their area of expertise. For example, unparalleled mastery of health care issues has made Rep. Henry A. Waxman, D-Calif., the most influential House Democrat by far in this important policy area. One problem, however, is that specialists may dominate policymaking in their domains, shutting out the broader viewpoints of other members. Thus the efficiencies gained by a division of labor are paid for by diminished participation in policymaking outside one's specialty.

Coordination Problems

As noted in Chapter 1, any group of people trying to act in concert faces coordination problems. Coordination becomes more difficult—and necessary—the greater the group's workload and the more elaborate its division of labor. As the volume and complexity of Congress's work have grown, so has its need for traffic management: dividing up the work, directing the flow of bills through the legislative process, scheduling debates and votes on the floor. Coordination problems of this kind usually are solved by a group giving one or several of its members the authority to coordinate—that is, take on the role of "traffic cop." In Congress party leaders serve this function; but procedures also shape policy. Control over the agenda—deciding what gets voted on when—is a powerful legislative weapon. For example, a majority of House members probably would have preferred to censure rather than impeach Bill Clinton, but the Republican House leaders refused to allow a vote on censure, leaving a vote for impeachment as the only alternative to letting the president off completely. (Had they allowed a vote on censure, Clinton probably would have avoided impeachment and trial in the Senate.) Members thus sacrifice a measure of their autonomy in return for the gains in efficiency that come from delegating agenda control to party leaders.

Resolving Conflicts

Legislation is not passed until the majorities in both houses agree to its passage. The rich pluralism of American society guarantees that resolving conflicts is a fundamental task of any institution that reflects America's diversity. Agreement requires successful politicking: getting people who are pursuing divergent, even conflicting, ends to take a common course of action. Even when there is a consensus on ends, Congress often must resolve disagreements about means. During the 108th Congress (2003–2004), for example, almost all members agreed that a major overhaul of intelligence gathering was needed to combat terrorist threats, but leaders had to reconcile competing ideas about what should replace the current system in order to reform intelligence.

Many of Congress's rules, customs, and procedures are aimed at resolving or deflecting conflicts so it can get on with the business of legislating. For example, when representatives speak on the floor of the House, all remarks are officially addressed to the Speaker, making it less likely that debates will degenerate into personal confrontations. More substantively, members delegate the task of building legislative coalitions to party leaders, who hold such positions by virtue of their demonstrated skills at negotiating legislative deals. The political parties in Congress themselves serve as ready-made coalitions. Party members agree on matters often enough to adopt a common label and to cooperate routinely on many—but by no means all—of the matters that come before the House and Senate. The presence of ready-made coalitions resolves many conflicts in advance, reducing the transaction costs of negotiating agreements on legislation. The price, however, is loss of autonomy to the party and of authority to leaders: individual members incur greater conformity costs because they cannot always do what is politically best for themselves rather than their party.

Collective Action

Everyone who wins a seat in the House or Senate wants to belong to a well-informed, effective legislature capable of fulfilling its constitutional mandate. Moreover, senators and representatives run under party labels and so have a stake in their party's reputation. But all of them have personal interests as well: winning reelection or advancing to higher office by pleasing constituents, enacting pet policies, and attaining influence and respect in Washington. The problem is that what members do to pursue individual goals—tax breaks for local firms, special projects for their constituents—may undermine the reputation of their party or of Congress as a whole. The tension between individual and collective political welfare—the standard prisoner's dilemma—pervades congressional life. Congress has responded to the problem by developing devices such as the committee system that give members individual incentives to work for collectively beneficial ends. As noted, members who contribute to Congress's performance by becoming well informed about issues in their subcommittee's jurisdiction are rewarded with preeminent influence over policy in that area. Others listen to them, and they are given a chance to take personal credit for particular pieces of legislation.[25]

Transaction Costs

In trying to meet its many challenges, Congress must cope with another pressing problem: high transaction costs. These costs, as noted in Chapter 1, are literally the price of doing politics—the time, effort, and bargaining resources (favors to be exchanged) that go into negotiating agreements on action in the absence of agreement on the purposes of the action. Because many of the transaction costs involved in building legislative coalitions are unavoidable—such as the conflicts to be ironed out, compromises to be arranged, and favors to be traded—Congress has organized itself to reduce other transaction costs. One way is the use of fixed rules to automate decisions. For example, the **seniority rule,** by routinely allocating first choice in committee chairs, offices, and committee assignments to majority party members who have served longest, reduces the time and energy members would otherwise put into competing for these valued positions. Another way is to follow precedent; battles over legislative turf, for example, are minimized by strict adherence to precedent in assigning bills to House committees.

The House-Senate conference committee that met in October 2004 to consider S. 2845, the National Intelligence Reform Act, faced intense political pressure to act swiftly on the September 11 Commission's recommendations for a drastic overhaul of the nation's fifteen intelligence services. It also faced strong disagreements over the form the overhaul should take. Negotiations dragged on until December 5, when the conference finally achieved a compromise agreement that was quickly endorsed by both chambers and signed by the president.

The pressing need to reduce transaction costs explains, then, why Congress does its work within an elaborate structure of rules and precedents. Absent these devices, transaction costs can be high. A recent example was the Senate's struggle to reach agreement on procedures for Bill Clinton's impeachment trial. Presidential impeachment trials (fortunately) occur so rarely that few usable rules or precedents were available. Like any attempt to reduce transaction costs, following precedent or seniority can have its own downside, for it inevitably increases the power of some members at the expense of others. Rules are never politically neutral.

Time Pressures

The pressure to avoid unnecessary transaction costs is intensified by the ticking clock—both within the one-year session of Congress and over the two-year tenure of each Congress. The chief source of Congress's authority is its power of the purse over government revenue raising and spending. But if it fails to enact a federal budget in some form each year (or session), large portions of the federal government have to shut down, as happened in late 1995 when the Republican Congress and Democratic president played a high-stakes game of chicken over the budget. As budgets have grown larger, broader in scope, and, in recent years, more hotly contested, Congress often has found it difficult to enact them on schedule. Thus it has continued to tinker with the budgetary process. Other legislation has to pass through all the hurdles (outlined later in this chapter) within the two-year life of a Congress. Bills in the pipeline but not enacted by the end of the second session of one Congress must be reintroduced in the next Congress.

The organization and rules of the House and Senate have evolved over two centuries through the accumulation of solutions deliberately chosen to overcome the pressing challenges just described (as well as, of course, to serve the immediate political needs of the majority then in power).[26] Because its membership substantially exceeds that of the Senate, the House experiences organizational problems more acutely than does the Senate. Senators can get away with looser organization and retain more individual autonomy and equality simply because there are fewer of them. Their counterparts in the House, to solve their coordination problems, have to follow stricter rules of procedure and tolerate greater control by leaders.

Organizing Congress

To preserve the House and Senate as the powerful legislative bodies envisioned in the Constitution, members of Congress have had to devise means to overcome the formidable barriers to effective collective action discussed in the previous section. The crucial institutional structures they have created to exercise, and therefore preserve, Congress's power in the federal system are the party and committee systems.

The Parties

Decisions in the House and Senate are made (with a few important exceptions) by majority vote. Majorities not only enact bills but also set rules, establish procedures, choose leaders, and decide how to organize their respective houses. This reality creates powerful incentives for members of Congress to join and maintain durable coalitions—that is, political parties (for a broader analysis of the logic of party formation, see Chapter 12). What individual members give up in freedom to go their own way is more than made up for by what they can gain by cooperating with one another.

Parties do not arise through spontaneous, voluntary cooperation, however. Like other coalitions, political parties are formed when people recognize it is in their best interests to cooperate despite their disagreements. Party coalitions are assembled and maintained by party leaders. But leaders cannot lead without effective means to resolve conflicts, coordinate action, and induce members to cooperate when they are tempted to do otherwise. Members, in turn, must sacrifice independence by conceding some authority to party leaders. Yet as we noted in Chapter 1, when a group delegates authority to a leader to achieve coordination and reduce transaction costs, it risks incurring conformity costs and agency losses.

Members of Congress, aware of the risks, relinquish autonomy only so far as necessary, which accounts for the notable differences in the evolution of party leadership between the House and Senate as well as the changes over time in the power of House and Senate leaders.[27]

DEVELOPMENT OF CONGRESSIONAL PARTIES. Parties began to form in the first session of the First Congress. A majority of members in the House favored the program for national economic development proposed by Alexander Hamilton, President George Washington's secretary of the Treasury, and worked together under his leadership to enact it. James Madison, a member of the House, and Thomas Jefferson, the secretary of state, led the opposition to what they saw as an unwarranted expansion of federal activity. Recognizing the obvious—that, to prevail, they needed more votes in Congress—Madison's followers sought to increase their numbers by recruiting and electing like-minded men to the House.

These "factions" soon had names—Hamilton's Federalists and Jefferson's Republicans (later called Democratic-Republicans and then Democrats—and party competition was under way. (See Chapter 12 for a fuller account of these developments.)

When the House and Senate divided into parties, congressional and party leadership merged. Formal leadership was established more quickly and more powerfully in the House because, as the larger and busier body (the Senate's legislative role was decidedly secondary in the early Congresses), its collective action problems were more acute. Elected by the reigning majority, the **Speaker of the House** became the majority's leader and agent. Speakers were given the authority to appoint committees, make rules, and manage the legislative process on the majority party's behalf.

SPEAKER OF THE HOUSE. Centralized authority reached its peak under Thomas Brackett "Czar" Reed, a Republican from Maine, who served as Speaker in the Fifty-first (1889–1890), Fifty-fourth (1895–1896), and Fifty-fifth (1897–1898) Congresses. Reed appointed all committees and committee chairs, exercised unlimited power of recognition (that is, decided who would speak on the floor of the House), and imposed new rules that made it much more difficult for a minority to prevent action through endless procedural delays. He also chaired the Rules Committee, which controlled the flow of legislation from the other committees to the floor of the House.

Although denounced by his opponents as a tyrant, Reed could not have amassed so much power without the full support of the Republican House majority. They were willing to delegate so much authority for two reasons. First, disagreements within the Republican Party were, at the time, muted; no important faction thought its interests could be threatened by a powerful leader allied with a competing faction. Second, service in the House had not yet become a career. The average member served only two terms. Indeed, in some places the local party organizations that controlled nominations enforced a two-term limit so that more of the party's stalwarts could enjoy the honor of serving in Congress. Without long-term career prospects and accustomed to party discipline, most members had little reason to object to strong leadership.

But once these conditions no longer held, the House revolted. Republican Speaker Joseph Cannon of Illinois (served 1903–1911) made the mistake of offending the progressive faction of the Republican Party that had emerged since Reed's day; he denied its members committee chairs and opposed the policies of the progressive Republican president, Theodore Roosevelt. In response, the Republican insurgents, with their Democratic allies, voted in 1910 to strip the Speaker of his power to appoint committees and chairs, forced him off the powerful Rules Committee, and limited his power of recognition. The increasingly career-oriented membership filled the power vacuum with a more decentralized and impersonal leadership structure, making seniority the criterion for selecting committee chairs. By weakening the Speaker, House members in effect chose to tolerate higher transaction costs to reduce their conformity costs.

The degree of consensus within a party continues to affect how much authority party members are willing to delegate to party leaders. In the 1970s, for example, the Democrats strengthened the hands of the Speaker. He was given the authority to nominate all the Democratic members of the Rules Committee and to appoint temporary committees and special legislative task forces to deal with complex or controversial bills. At the same time, the Democratic Caucus (the organization of all House Democrats) reasserted its authority over committee organization, appointments, rules, and chairs. Once committee chairs became subject to election by secret ballot in the caucus, they lost much of the autonomy they had enjoyed since the New Deal.

Joseph Cannon was the last of a generation of powerful Speakers of the House of Representatives. During his tenure as Speaker of the House, "Uncle Joe" swatted many an opponent. Too many of his victims were fellow Republicans, however, and in 1910 thirty-six of them joined with Democrats in the historic revolt that dismantled the strong Speaker system and decentralized House administration.

Democrats could afford to strengthen their party's capacity to act collectively because the ideological distinctiveness of southern Democrats had been undermined by the in-migration of northerners, industrial development, the movement of conservative whites from the Democratic into the Republican camp, and the Voting Rights Act of 1965, which brought black voters into southern Democratic electorates. A more cohesive Democratic Party saw smaller potential conformity costs in centralizing authority and faced an assertive Republican president, Ronald Reagan, and from 1981 through 1986 a Republican-controlled Senate. By the 1990s congressional Democrats were more unified than they had been in decades.[28]

Republicans granted even more authority to their leaders when they took over the House in 1995. Unified by the party's Contract with America, House Republicans made Newt Gingrich the most powerful Speaker since Cannon. At his behest, the Republican Conference (the Republican counterpart of the Democratic Caucus) ignored seniority in appointing committee chairs, ratifying without dissent the slate proposed by Gingrich. The Speaker also had a strong say in all the committee assignments, which he used to reward loyal junior members, and was given control of the House Administration Committee, which supervises management of the nonlegislative business of the House. The new majority party also adopted a rule limiting committee chairs to three two-year terms, reducing anyone's opportunity to build an independent committee domain. House Republicans gave their leader an unusually strong hand to overcome their coordination and other collective action problems because they believed that keeping their promise to act on every item in the Contract with America within one hundred days of taking office was crucial to their and their party's future electoral fates.

By 1997, however, House Republicans' unity had frayed badly, and one faction mounted a quickly aborted attempt to depose the Speaker. Gingrich hung on until Republican members, angry at the party's losses in the 1998 midterm election, forced him to resign—a pointed reminder that party leaders, as the majority's agents, are subject to dismissal if they do not satisfy their principals. Gingrich's eventual replacement, Dennis Hastert of Illinois, assisted by the hard-line tactics of Tom DeLay, first as majority whip, then as majority leader, was able to maintain a high level of party unity, notably keeping his narrow but overwhelmingly conservative House majority together in support of the George W. Bush administration's legislative proposals. Leading the Democrats in opposition to the Bush administration during her first year as Speaker in 2007, Nancy Pelosi presided over the most unified Democratic team in at least fifty years. In sum, Congress is subject to what political scientists have labeled **conditional party government,** meaning that the degree of authority delegated to and exercised by congressional party leaders varies with—is *conditioned by*—the extent of election-driven ideological consensus among members.[29]

Increased Partisanship

The decline and resurgence of congressional partisanship since the 1950s is evident in Figure 6-4. In both the House and Senate the proportion of "party unity" votes—those on which the party majorities took opposite positions—fell off in the late 1960s and early 1970s, when the parties were beset by internal divisions, then increased through the 1980s and 1990s as the party coalitions became more homogeneous. The proportion of representatives and senators of both parties who voted with their party's majority on these party unity votes also dipped before rebounding to their highest levels in a half-century during the Clinton administration. The House vote on the impeachment of Bill Clinton in December 1998 epitomized this trend; 98 percent of House Republicans voted for at least one article of impeachment, while 98 percent of House Democrats voted against all four articles. Despite the bipartisan support for President George W. Bush's response to the al Qaeda attacks of September 11, 2001, party unity on votes that split the parties reached their highest levels in the postwar era in both houses during his administration.

As the congressional parties became more unified, they also became more polarized along ideological lines. The ideological gap between the two parties in both houses of

Figure 6-4 Rising Party Unity in Congress

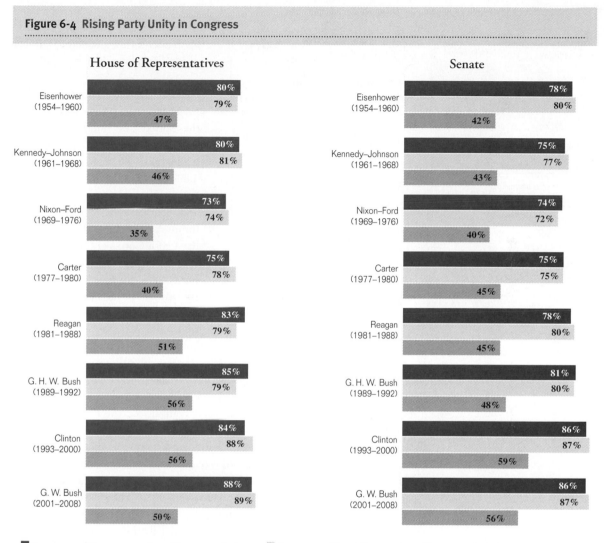

House of Representatives

Eisenhower (1954–1960): 80%, 79%, 47%

Kennedy–Johnson (1961–1968): 80%, 81%, 46%

Nixon–Ford (1969–1976): 73%, 74%, 35%

Carter (1977–1980): 75%, 78%, 40%

Reagan (1981–1988): 83%, 79%, 51%

G. H. W. Bush (1989–1992): 85%, 79%, 56%

Clinton (1993–2000): 84%, 88%, 56%

G. W. Bush (2001–2008): 88%, 89%, 50%

Senate

Eisenhower (1954–1960): 78%, 80%, 42%

Kennedy–Johnson (1961–1968): 75%, 77%, 43%

Nixon–Ford (1969–1976): 74%, 72%, 40%

Carter (1977–1980): 75%, 75%, 45%

Reagan (1981–1988): 78%, 80%, 45%

G. H. W. Bush (1989–1992): 81%, 80%, 48%

Clinton (1993–2000): 86%, 87%, 59%

G. W. Bush (2001–2008): 86%, 87%, 56%

■ Percentage of Democrats voting with party majority   Percentage of Republicans voting with party majority
Percentage of party unity votes

Sources: Norman J. Ornstein, Thomas E. Mann, and Michael J. Malbin, *Vital Statistics on Congress 1997–1998* (Washington, D.C.: CQ Press, 1998), 210–213. Data for 1999–2000 are from *CQ Weekly,* January 6, 2001, 56, 67; data for 2001 are from *CQ Weekly,* January 12, 2002, 114, 142; data for 2001–2007 are from *CQ Weekly,* January 14, 2008, 148.

Note: Party unity votes are those votes on which party majorities took opposite positions.

Congress has widened appreciably since the 1970s (see Figure 6-5). Republicans grew, on average, steadily more conservative. Democrats became more liberal as their party's conservative southern members were gradually replaced in Congress by Republicans, leaving the remaining southern Democrats ideologically more similar to other congressional Democrats. Ideological polarization thus helped to internally unite the parties,

CONGRESSIONAL CHESS MATCH

separate them from each other, and strengthen party leaders. It also made life harder for the dwindling number of ideologically moderate members.

PARTY ORGANIZATION. The majority party in the House is led by the Speaker of the House, whose chief assistants are the **majority leader** and the majority whip (see Table 6-1 for a list of major party offices and organizations in the House and Senate). The structure of the minority party, the Republicans in the 110th Congress (2007–2008), is similar to that of the majority party but without the Speaker; the **minority leader** is its head. The party whips head up the whip organization—the members who form the communication network connecting leaders with other members—whose purpose is to help solve the party's coordination problems. (The term **whip** comes from Great Britain, where the "whipper-in" keeps the hounds together in a pack during a foxhunt.) In addition to these official party committees, the Rules Committee is, in effect, an instrument of the majority party.

Party members give House party leaders resources for inducing members to cooperate when they are tempted to go their own way as free riders (for example, by breaking ranks on roll-call votes to enhance their own electoral fortunes at the expense of their party's collective reputation for effective governance). These resources mainly take the form of favors the leaders may grant or withhold. For example, party leaders have a strong voice in all committee assignments (officially the province of the Steering Committees), and they set the legislative agenda. Because a place on the agenda is a scarce resource, scheduling decisions determine the fates of many bills. Leaders also choose how much of their own time, energy, and organizational resources to devote to each legislative proposal. They also control access to pork, routinely using earmarked projects to win support of wavering members.[30] And they can help with reelection campaigns, especially the fund-raising component. Party leaders are therefore in a position to make it easier (or more difficult) for members to attain positions of influence, shape policy, and win reelection.

House party leaders are members' agents, however—not their bosses. They do not hire and fire party members; voters do, and so voters come first. Members, then, choose the style of leadership they believe will best serve their goals. Party leaders, who are elected or reelected to their positions at the beginning of every Congress, are

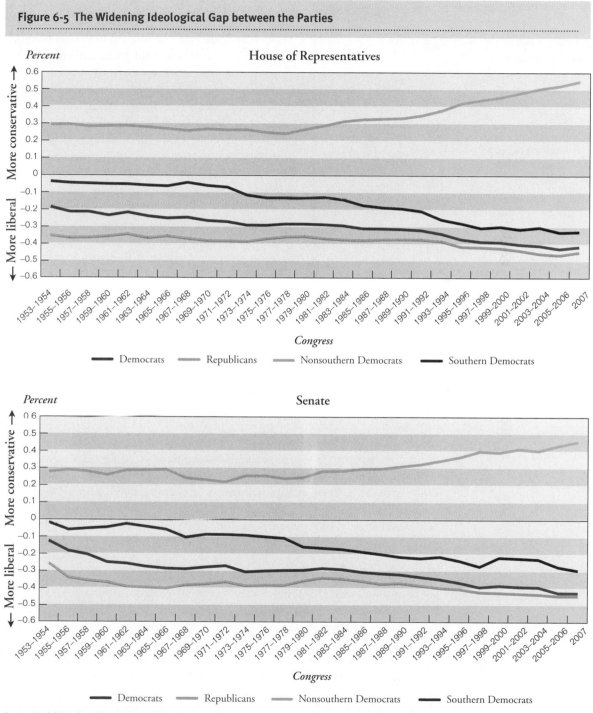

Figure 6-5 The Widening Ideological Gap between the Parties

Percent House of Representatives

Democrats   Republicans   Nonsouthern Democrats   Southern Democrats

Percent Senate

Democrats   Republicans   Nonsouthern Democrats   Southern Democrats

Sources: Keith T. Poole and Howard Rosenthal, *Congress: A Political-Economic History of Roll Call Voting* (New York: Oxford University Press, 1997). We thank Keith T. Poole for data updated through 2007.

TABLE 6-1	
Party Committees and Leaders in Congress	
Democrats	Republicans
House of Representatives	
Speaker	
Majority Leader	Minority Leader
Majority Whip	Minority Whip
Caucus (all Democrats)	Conference (all
Steering Committee	Republicans)
Policy Committee	Steering Committee
Democratic Congressional	Policy Committee
Campaign Committee	National Republican
	Congressional Committee
Senate	
President Pro Tempore	
Majority Leader	Minority Leader
Assistant Majority Leader	Assistant Minority Leader
(Whip)	(Whip)
Conference (all Democrats)	Conference (all
Policy Committee	Republicans)
Steering and Outreach	Policy Committee
Committee	National Republican
Democratic Senatorial	Senatorial Committee
Campaign Commitee	

Note: Table covers the 110th Congress (2007–2008).

thoroughly, if informally, screened. They are members who have been around for a long time and whose styles, abilities, and flaws are well known. In the pre-Gingrich decades when Democrats held a majority of seats, they chose leaders, such as Thomas "Tip" O'Neill of Massachusetts (majority leader from 1973 to 1977), who were experts on procedure rather than policy and who cared more about building successful coalitions than about achieving specific legislative goals. But when the Republicans took over the majority in 1995, Speaker Gingrich, as we saw earlier, pursued—with the full support of Republican members—a legislative agenda much more policy and ideologically focused than those undertaken by the Democratic Speakers before him.

For the minority party in the House, legislative leadership is normally less crucial because the party's legislative role has usually been modest. When the party balance is very close, minority leaders can sometimes influence legislation by forming alliances with more moderate members of the majority party, although this has happened infrequently in the most recent Congresses. When the majority enjoys a wider margin, minority leaders choose between two strategic options: cooperating with the majority, and thus exerting some influence but getting little credit, or opposing and attacking the majority to position their party for future electoral battles. The minority's dilemma is sharpened when a president of their party sits in the White House, because the president has to cut deals with the majority to accomplish anything at all. As former minority whip, Gingrich managed to lead Republicans to majority status by abandoning a strategy of accommodation in favor of harsh partisan confrontation. Subsequently, Democratic minority leaders Richard Gephardt and then Nancy Pelosi sought to retake the House (and win the Speakership) through energetic campaigning and fund-raising in behalf of Democratic candidates, an effort crowned with success in 2006.

PARTIES AND PARTY LEADERS IN THE SENATE. Over the years the Senate has been slower than the House to develop formal leadership positions, and senators have never delegated as much authority to their leaders as have representatives. Senators initially saw themselves as ambassadors from sovereign states, and as such could accept no less than equal rights with one another. In the years since, they have retained wide freedom of individual action because, with its smaller size, the Senate is able to get by without elaborate procedural shackles.*

---

*The Senate began with twenty-six members and did not reach one hundred until 1959; the House already had exceeded one hundred members by 1793.

Under the Constitution, the vice president is the presiding officer of the Senate. The designated **president pro tempore** presides when the vice president is absent. But neither office has a real leadership role—after all, the vice president, who seldom presides, is not chosen by the Senate, and the president pro tempore, as the Latin term suggests, is formally a temporary position. In fact, in the first few Congresses a new president pro tempore was elected every time the vice president was away. In practice, no one led the Senate during the pre–Civil War period.

Parties formed in the Senate almost from the start, but party members were little inclined to delegate authority. The party caucuses did not take full control of committee appointments until 1846, after which they avoided intraparty conflicts over committee control by resorting to a strict seniority rule. Not until the end of the nineteenth century did senators concede the means to enforce party discipline—on procedural matters only—to party leaders. The positions of majority leader and minority leader were not formalized until 1913.

President pro tempore is now, by tradition, the majority member with the greatest Senate seniority. In the 106th Congress (1999–2000), ninety-six-year-old Strom Thurmond, a South Carolina Republican first elected to the Senate in 1954, filled the position. In the 110th Congress, the office went to Democrat Robert Byrd of West Virginia, a comparatively youthful eighty-nine, pictured here (left) being sworn in for his ninth Senate term. West Virginia's other senator, Jay Rockefeller, holds the Bible; Vice President Dick Cheney looks on. Byrd is third in line of presidential succession after the vice president (now Joe Biden) and House Speaker Nancy Pelosi.

The power and influence exerted by Senate leaders have depended largely on their personal political skills and the extent of intraparty divisions. Lyndon Johnson, who led the Senate Democrats from 1953 until resigning to become vice president in 1961, exercised extraordinary influence over the Senate through skillful persuasion and manipulation. The resources at his disposal were no greater than those of other Senate leaders, but he used them to greater effect. Although no majority leader has since matched Johnson's fire or authority, others, such as Bob Dole, a Kansas Republican (served 1985–1987, 1995–1996), and George Mitchell, a Maine Democrat (served 1989–1995), have been skillful and effective majority leaders.

Party leadership in the Senate is more collegial and less formal than in the House. The minority party has greater influence in the Senate because so much of that body's business is conducted under **unanimous consent agreements** negotiated by party leaders. These agreements, which can be killed by a single objection, might govern, for example, the order in which bills are considered and the length of debate allotted to them. However, the majority party in the Senate is still at a considerable advantage because its leader strongly shapes, if not fully controls, the Senate's agenda. Hence the switch in party control in January 2007 portended more than simply a reshuffling of

Although intense partisan rivals, Democrat Harry Reid, Senate major-ity leader (left), and Republican Mitch McConnell, Senate minority leader, conferred regularly on procedural matters during the 110th Congress (2007–2008). The Senate's rules make it easy for a dis-gruntled minority to block action, so Reid has to accommodate McConnell, just as Reid had to be accommodated when Republicans held the majority in the previous Congress.

offices. But unanimous consent agreements serve as only the most extreme examples of the general rule: the ca-pacity of House and Senate party leaders to lead depends largely on the willingness of party members to follow.

OTHER GROUPS IN CONGRESS. Although par-ties are by far the most important of Congress's coali-tions, members have formed dozens of other groups. Some are explicitly ideological (Republican Study Com-mittee, Progressive Caucus, New Democratic Coalition, Blue Dog Coalition). Others are based on demograph-ics (Congressional Black Caucus, Hispanic Caucus, Asian Pacific American Caucus, Caucus for Women's Is-sues). Bipartisan groups form around shared regional interests (Northeast-Midwest Coalition, Western Cau-cus, Appalachian Caucus) and economic concerns (Steel Caucus, Automotive Caucus, Wine Caucus, Biotech-nology Caucus). Other groups focus on specific issues (Pro-Life Caucus, Pro-Choice Caucus, Human Rights Caucus). No fewer than twenty-nine foreign countries enjoyed the attention of a congressional caucus in the 110th Congress.

Such groups give members better access to informa-tion and allies on issues that are of special concern to them (or their constituents) and that do not fit neatly into regular party or committee categories. The groups reflect the value of ready-made alliances in a system where suc-cess depends on building majority coalitions.

The Committee Systems

The committee systems of the House and Senate are the second organizational pillar upholding the institutional power of Congress in the federal system. Although com-mittee power has at times been used to frustrate party majorities and leaders, commit-tees are ultimately subject to the majority party, and the committee and party systems are closely integrated and mutually dependent. House committees, like House party leaders, are more powerful than their counterparts in the Senate, again reflecting the need for tighter organization in the larger body.

EVOLUTION OF CONGRESSIONAL COMMITTEES. The first Congresses delegated authority to committees sparingly. Instead, the House would turn itself into a Committee of the Whole (sitting as a committee, the House operates under a more flexible set of rules), frame a piece of legislation, elect a temporary committee to draft the bill, then debate and amend the bill line-by-line. After reassuming its guise as the House, it would vote on final passage.

From the start, this process was intolerably cumbersome. One early member, Fisher Ames of Massachusetts, likened it to trying to make a delicate etching with an elephant's foot.[31] Thus the House began to delegate more and more work to permanent committees. Ten were in place by 1809, twenty-eight by 1825. Transaction costs were further reduced by having committee members appointed by the Speaker rather than elected. As the Speaker emerged as leader of the majority party, appointments became partisan affairs, and choice committee assignments became rewards for party loyalty and bargaining chips in campaigns for the Speakership.

The Senate was slower to set up permanent committees. Despite their smaller numbers and lighter workload, senators also found they were spending too much time on electing a new committee to draft each bill, and the Senate began to accumulate **standing committees**—those that exist from one Congress to the next unless they are explicitly disbanded. The initial twelve were established in 1816; by 1841 there were twenty-two. The Senate also was slower to delegate legislative action to committees and has never gone as far in this direction as the House. After the Senate's parties assumed the right to make committee assignments, seniority became the criterion for selecting committee chairs: the office was awarded to the majority party member with the longest term of service on the committee. Reducing transaction and conformity costs, the seniority rule avoided two unwelcome alternatives: election, which would have led to divisive, time-consuming intraparty squabbles, and appointment by party leaders, which would have given the leaders more power than senators thought desirable or necessary.

TYPES OF COMMITTEES. The standing committees of the House and Senate embody Congress's division of legislative labor. Standing committees have fixed jurisdictions (that is, they always deal with the same legislative topics) and stable memberships, both of which facilitate specialization. Once appointed, a member in good standing cannot be forced off a standing committee unless his or her party suffers large electoral losses. Party ratios on committees generally match party ratios in the House and Senate. A House party with a narrow overall majority usually gives itself somewhat larger committee majorities, and it always accords itself extra seats on the most important committees. The job security associated with standing committees gives committee members both the motive and the opportunity to become knowledgeable about policy issues under their committee's jurisdiction. Expertise brings influence—other members defer to the judgment of committee experts they trust—and therefore a chance to make a real difference in at least one area of national policy.

Although committee membership is generally stable, changes occur when legislators seize the opportunity to move up to the committees deemed more important and desirable than the others. At the top of the heap in both chambers are the money committees—the Ways and Means and the Appropriations Committees in the House, the Finance and the Appropriations Committees in the Senate—because their activities are so central to Congress's main source of power in the federal system, its control over the budget. The House and Senate Budget Committees share some of this prestige. Seats on the Senate Foreign Relations and Judiciary Committees also are in demand because of the Senate's special authority over treaties and diplomatic and judicial appointments. In the House the powerful Rules Committee, which controls the flow of legislation from committees to the floor, is especially attractive. Among the least desirable committees are those dealing with the internal administration of Congress, particularly its members' ethics; many members feel uncomfortable sitting in judgment on their colleagues.

COMMITTEE ASSIGNMENTS. Assignments to committees are made by party committees under the firm control of senior party leaders and are ratified by the party membership. Members pursue committee assignments that allow them to serve special constituent interests as well as their own policy and power goals. For example, the Agriculture Committees attract members from farm states, and the Armed Services Committees attract members from regions with large military installations.

Because party leaders want to keep their followers in office, they are responsive to arguments that a particular assignment will help a member win reelection. Moreover, when members are assigned to the committees that best serve their personal and political interests, they will take committee work more seriously, making a larger contribution to their party's overall performance. The danger is that committees may become stacked with members whose views do not represent those of their party's majority. By and large, party leaders have managed to avoid this problem by judicious distribution of assignments, especially to the committees whose jurisdictions are most important to the party. A party's committee members are, like party leaders, the party's agents, and party majorities use their ultimate control over committee assignments to keep their agents responsive to the party's desires.[32]

Most committees are divided into subcommittees, many of which also have fixed jurisdictions and stable memberships. Like full committees, subcommittees encourage specialization and, at the same time, reward members who develop expertise with special influence over their own small pieces of legislative turf. Both committees and, in the Senate, subcommittees come with staffs of experts to help members do their work. Most committee staffers report to committee and subcommittee chairs; the ranking minority committee members control a much smaller set of staff assistants.

In addition to the standing committees, Congress also forms special, select, joint, ad hoc, and conference committees. In theory, most **special committees** and **select committees** (the terms are interchangeable) are appointed to deal with specific problems and then disappear. A good example was the House's Select Committee on U.S. National Security and Military/Commercial Concerns with the People's Republic of China, appointed in 1998 to investigate technology transfers to China and disbanded a year later after issuing a 1,016-page report detailing the loss of military secrets to that country and recommending steps to stop it. However, some special and select committees sometimes last through many Congresses—for example, the Senate's Special Committee on Aging has been around since 1961.

JOINT COMMITTEES. These are permanent committees composed of members from both chambers; the committee leaderships rotate between the chambers at the

TABLE 6-2

The Committees of the 110th Congress

	Party Ratio	Number of Subcommittees		Party Ratio	Number of Subcommittees
House of Representatives			Appropriations	15D : 14R	12
Standing Committees			Armed Services	13D : 12R	6
Agriculture	25D : 21R	6	Banking, Housing, and		
Appropriations	37D : 29R	11	Urban Affairs	11D : 10R	5
Armed Services	34D : 28R	7	Budget	12D : 11R	—
Budget	22D : 17R	—	Commerce, Science,		
Education and Labor	27D : 22R	5	and Transportation	12D : 11R	7
Energy and Commerce	31D : 26R	6	Energy and Natural Resources	12D : 11R	4
Financial Services	37D : 33R	5	Environment and Public Works	10D : 9R	6
Foreign Affairs	27D : 23R	7	Finance	11D : 10R	5
Homeland Security	19D : 15R	6	Foreign Relations	11D : 10R	7
House Administration	6D : 3R	2	Health, Education, Labor,		
Judiciary	23D : 17R	5	and Pensions	11D : 10R	3
Oversight and Government			Homeland Security and		
Reform	23D : 18R	7	Governmental Affairs	9D : 8R	5
Resources	27D : 22R	5	Indian Affairs	8D : 7R	—
Rules	9D : 4R	2	Judiciary	10D : 9R	7
Science	24D : 20R	4	Rules and Administration	10D : 9R	—
Small Business	18D : 15R	5	Small Business and		
Standards of Official Conduct	5D : 5R	—	Entrepreneurship	10D : 9R	—
Transportation and			Veterans' Affairs	8D : 7R	—
Infrastructure	41D : 34R	6			
Veterans' Affairs	16D : 13R	4	*Special and Select Committees*		
Ways and Means	24D : 17R	6	Select Committee on Ethics	3D : 3R	—
			Select Committee on Intelligence	8D : 7R	—
Select Committees			Special Committee on Aging	11D : 10R	—
Permanent Select Committee					
on Intelligence	12D : 9R	4	**Joint Committees**		
Select Committee on Energy			Joint Economic Committee	12D : 8R	—
Independence and			Joint Committee on the		
Global Warming	9D : 6R	—	Library of Congress	6D : 4R	—
			Joint Committee on Printing	6D : 4R	—
Senate			Joint Committee on Taxation	6D : 4R	—
Standing Committees					
Agriculture, Nutrition,					
and Forestry	11D : 10R	5			

beginning of each newly elected Congress. Joint committees gather information and oversee executive agencies but do not report legislation. One joint committee (Library) oversees the Library of Congress, the Botanical Garden, and public statuary; another (Printing) oversees the Government Printing Office and the arrangement and style of the *Congressional Record,* which publishes all of the speeches and debates on the floors of the House and Senate. In the House the Speaker occasionally appoints **ad hoc committees** to handle bills that are particularly sensitive (congressional pay raise legislation, for example). **Conference committees** are appointed to resolve differences between the House and Senate versions of bills (see section "Making Laws" in this chapter). The committees of the 110th Congress are listed in Table 6-2.

Segregationist representative Howard W. Smith, D-Va. (left), became notorious for using his powers as chair of the House Rules Committee to block civil rights legislation during the 1950s. One of his tactics was simply to go home to his Virginia farm when a civil rights bill came to the committee, which could only meet at his call. Committee chairs lost such dictatorial powers in the reforms of the 1970s.

COMMITTEE POWER. A century ago House committees were dominated by the Speaker, who appointed committee members and chairs. The revolt against Speaker Cannon in 1910 effectively transferred control over committees to committee chairs, who, under the altered rules, owed their positions to seniority, not loyalty to their party or its leaders. By the 1950s both chambers were run by a handful of powerful committee chairs who could safely ignore the wishes of party majorities. Conservative southern Democrats, continually reelected from one-party strongholds, chaired the most powerful committees and cooperated with Republicans to thwart policies supported by a majority of Democrats, especially in the area of civil rights. The most notorious example was Howard W. Smith, a segregationist Virginia Democrat who used his position as chair of the House Rules Committee during the 1950s to stop civil rights bills. The rules allowed chairs to run committees like dictators, and some of them did.

In 1959 frustrated younger liberals formed the Democratic Study Group (DSG) to take on the conservative Democrats, hoping that they could make up in numbers what they lacked in institutional clout. Over the next decade the DSG grew large enough to take over and revitalize the Democratic Caucus. The most important changes occurred after the 1974 election, when the public reaction to the Watergate scandal brought seventy-four new Democrats, eager for action and disdainful of seniority, into the House. At their instigation, the Democratic Caucus adopted a rule that forbade any individual from chairing more than one committee or subcommittee; this way, many more members could enjoy this privilege. Committee members and the caucus, rather than chairs, assumed control over committee rules, budgets, and subcommittee organization. Committee nominations were transferred from Democrats on the Ways and Means Committee, who had held this authority since the revolt against Cannon, to the caucus's own new Steering and Policy Committee.*

The caucus itself elected committee chairs by secret ballot (secrecy removed the threat of retaliation). In 1975 the caucus actually deposed three committee chairs, all elderly southern conservatives, underlining the new reality that the party's majority, not seniority, would now have the final say in who runs committees.

These changes produced a more fragmented and decentralized committee system in which fully half of the Democrats in the House chaired a committee or subcommittee. Although members benefited individually, they found it more difficult to act collectively. The simultaneous strengthening of the Speaker's authority, described ear-

---

*The Steering and Policy Committee was subsequently split into a Steering Committee, which retained the authority to make committee assignments, and a separate Policy Committee.

lier, logically complemented these changes. The party leaders may have found the task of coordination more difficult, but they also were given more tools (for example, control of nominations to the Rules Committee) to carry it out. The net effect was a strengthened party capacity for collective action and a decline in the power of conservative Democrats.

The new Republican majority that took over the House in 1995 revised committee rules to ensure that the legislative agenda outlined in its Contract with America would move swiftly to enactment. The new rules gave committee chairs greater control over subcommittees by authorizing them to appoint all subcommittee chairs and control the work of the majority's committee staff. But committee chairs themselves now had to report to the Speaker and were limited to three consecutive terms (six years) as chair. All these changes gave the Republican majority more control over its committees than any House majority had exercised since the early years of the twentieth century. Returning to power after 2006, Democratic leaders kept the term limits and tighter controls over committee assignments but generally followed seniority in choosing committee chairs.[33]

JURISDICTION. In the House, does international trade policy fall within the jurisdiction of the Energy and Commerce Committee or Foreign Affairs Committee? Should education programs for veterans be handled in the Senate by Veterans' Affairs or by Health, Education, Labor, and Pensions? Where does something like homeland defense, which affects virtually every aspect of American life—transportation, energy infrastructure, international trade, the administration of justice, national defense— fit? Moreover, such technical issues are overlaid with political agendas. Committees and subcommittees compete for jurisdiction over important policy areas, but the supply of legislative turf is always insufficient to meet the demand. Thus it is not surprising that the House and Senate have altered the number and jurisdictions of their committees from time to time; nor is it surprising that such changes have been highly contentious.

Within Congress, the constant pressure to multiply standing committees and subcommittees arises out of the increasing complexity, volume, and scope of legislative business and members' desires to serve as committee and subcommittee chairs, especially now that Congress is populated by career politicians seeking their own pieces of the action. Inactive committees are hard to kill off. For example, the Senate maintained a Committee on Revolutionary Claims (requests for payment of bills incurred during the American Revolution) until 1920, when it pruned its standing committees back from seventy-four to thirty-four. Many of the disbanded committees had not met in years, but their chairs clung to them because committees came with staff and office space. The cutbacks were achieved only by giving individual senators their own clerks and offices.

Since the 1920s the House and Senate have trimmed their committee systems several times, notably in the Legislative Reorganization Act of 1946, which sharply reduced the number of standing committees in both chambers (from thirty-three to fifteen in the Senate, from forty-eight to nineteen in the House). The act also rearranged committee jurisdictions to reduce the overlap and confusion and to make the House and Senate systems more similar. Reductions were achieved by consolidation, however, so many former committees simply became subcommittees. The most recent committee changes occurred in 1995, when the victorious House Republicans abolished three standing committees and made other modest alterations in committee jurisdictions.

The political problem with trying to distribute committee jurisdictions more sensibly is that changes redistribute power and upset long-established relationships among committee members, administrative agencies, and interest groups. Nevertheless, Congress must rationalize jurisdictions occasionally, or the emergence of new issues will lead to turf battles, overlapping jurisdictions, uneven workloads, and confusion. For example, homeland security policy is so multifaceted that by one count, eighty-eight congressional committees and subcommittees, which included as members every member of the Senate and all but twenty representatives, held jurisdiction over one or more of its components.[34] Outsiders (and a few insiders) advocated the creation of new committees in both houses to handle the new Department of Homeland Security's nominations, budget, and legislation and to oversee its operation. As one former deputy defense secretary put it, "If they don't create a separate oversight committee in the House and Senate, there's never going to be a functioning department. You can't create a new department if all the elements of the new department keep going back to their old bosses."[35] But members of Congress relinquish jurisdiction over important matters with great reluctance, and homeland security was no exception. Congress established the new department in 2002, but the House and Senate did not form new standing committees on homeland security until 2005. Powerful leaders of existing committees resisted giving up jurisdiction and not only out of pure self-interest, for they could plausibly argue that the deep fund of experience and expertise, both of members and staff, regarding the department's diverse component agencies (see Chapter 8) held by their old committee overseers might be lost if a new committee took full jurisdiction over them. The result could be enfeebled congressional oversight.[36]

Party leaders sometimes cope with the problem of multiple jurisdictions by using **multiple referrals**—that is, sending bills, in whole or piece by piece, to several committees at the same time or in sequence. For example, a banking reform bill introduced in the House in the 102nd Congress (1991–1992) went first to Banking, Finance, and Urban Affairs, then to Energy and Commerce, then to Agriculture, then to Judiciary, and finally to Ways and Means.[37] In the 108th Congress (2003–2004) 21 percent of all bills and 25 percent of major bills were subject to multiple referrals.[38]

THE MONEY COMMITTEES. The "power of the purse" has inspired the most contentious jurisdictional fights. In the earliest years of government, revenue and spending bills were handled by Ways and Means in the House and Finance in the Senate. Then, during the 1860s, the spending power was transferred to a separate Appropriations Committee in each house to help deal with the extraordinary financial demands of the Civil War. Other committees in both houses later broke the Appropriations Committees' monopoly on spending, and by 1900 authority over national finances was spread among nearly twenty House and Senate committees. In the House this devolution of authority was not such a great impediment to action when powerful Speakers dominated the chamber, but a few years after the revolt against Cannon the Republican House majority underlined its commitment to parsimony by restoring the Appropriations Committee's monopoly. The Senate followed suit in 1922.

Since then, legislative spending has been a two-step process in each chamber. In the first step the committee with jurisdiction over a program *authorizes* expenditures for it, and in the second the Appropriations Committee *appropriates* the money—that is, writes a bill designating that specific sums be spent on

R&B musician John Legend and actress Kerry Washington testify before a House Appropriations Committee hearing on "Funding for the Arts" in 2008, providing a livelier spectacle—and getting more media attention—than the more typical parade of bureaucrats requesting funding for their agencies' programs.

authorized programs. The sums appropriated need not and often do not match the amounts authorized because more spending may be authorized than the appropriators, concerned with the total size of the budget, are willing to appropriate. For some important programs expenditures take the form of **entitlements,** which designate specific classes of people who are entitled to a legally defined benefit. Social Security and Medicare payments and military pensions are examples. Congress must spend whatever it takes to cover those who are eligible for entitlements—unless it changes the eligibility standards or the amounts to which the eligible are entitled.

After 1921 the money committees took on the institutional task of protecting congressional majorities from the collective damage that the pursuit of individual electoral goals threatened to impose. In the House the powerful Appropriations Committee used its authority to keep members' desires for locally popular projects (such as dams, highways, and harbor improvements) and programs (such as housing, urban renewal, and police equipment) from pushing up taxes or deficits to politically intolerable levels. Tax legislation emerging from Ways and Means was routinely deemed ineligible for amendment to prevent a scramble for revenue-draining tax breaks for local firms or well-connected interests.

BUDGET REFORM. By the early 1970s the ability of the money committees to enforce collective self-control had been seriously eroded. The committee reforms weakened committee leaders, and a move toward congressional "openness"—doing more business in public—made it harder for individual members to resist the temptation to promote locally popular projects of dubious worth. At about the same time, President

Richard Nixon used his authority to impound—refuse to spend—some of the funds authorized and appropriated by Congress to subvert the spending priorities of its Democratic majorities. In 1972, for example, he refused to spend $9 billion in clean-water funds and terminated many agricultural programs.[39] Nixon even impounded appropriations passed over his veto. His actions posed fundamental challenges to the House and Senate as institutions as well as to their Democratic majorities.

Congress responded with the Budget and Impoundment Control Act of 1974. The act subjected presidential impoundment authority to strict congressional control. More important, it revamped Congress's budgetary process with the goal of making impoundment unnecessary. Among other things, the act established a Budget Committee in each chamber to oversee the coordination of taxing and spending policies. It also instituted procedures and timetables for setting budget targets, supervising the committees' decisions on revenues and spending, and reconciling the tax and spending bills enacted by Congress with the targets. The system was designed to compel members to vote on explicit levels of taxation, expenditures, and deficits, thereby taking direct responsibility for the fiscal consequences of the many separate decisions made during a session.

Despite Congress's good intentions, the reformed budget process proved entirely incapable of preventing the huge budget deficits produced by budget politics during the Reagan and Bush administrations of the 1980s and early 1990s. Orderly budgeting fell victim to the intense partisan conflict between the Republican presidents and congressional Democrats over budget priorities. Presidents Ronald Reagan and George H. W. Bush sought to keep taxes low, congressional Democrats to protect popular domestic spending programs. Since both low taxes and spending for popular programs proved politically irresistible, the budget was left unbalanced. No amount of reform, then, could have prevented the massive budget deficits of the 1980s and early 1990s because nothing can force Congress to follow the rules it makes for itself. Procedures are chosen to produce desired outcomes; when the rules stand in the way of desired outcomes, members can always find ways around them.[40]

Attempts to reduce the deficit by procedural devices failed repeatedly until both sides developed the political will to support a precarious agreement. The negotiations that produced the Budget Enforcement Act of 1990, a package of tax increases and program cuts designed to reduce the projected deficit by some $500 billion over five years, exemplified budgeting under divided government. It consisted of improvised deals worked out in charged, high-level negotiations between the president and congressional leaders. Congress and the administration, both under Democratic control after the 1992 elections, made further inroads into the deficit in 1993 with another round of tax increases and spending cuts intended to reduce the deficit by another $500 billion between 1994 and 1998.

Still, the budget did not come into balance, requiring yet another round of budget confrontations and negotiations, stretching from 1995 to 1997—and this time between a Republican Congress and a Democratic president. The agreement became possible when the booming economy produced a bonanza of tax revenues, making it much easier to accommodate the desires of both sides. By 1998 the economy had pro-

Figure 6-6 Expanding Congressional Staff

Number of employees

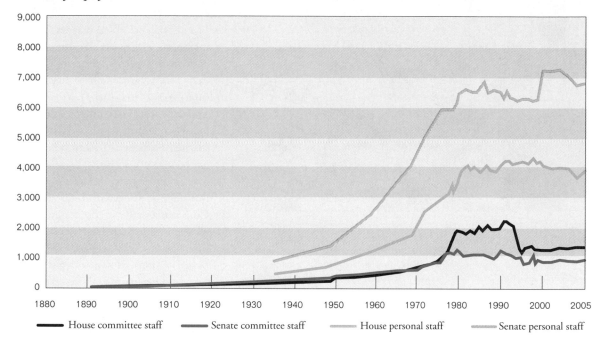

| House committee staff | Senate committee staff | House personal staff | Senate personal staff |

Sources: Norman J. Ornstein, Thomas E. Mann, and Michael J. Malbin, *Vital Statistics on Congress 2001–2002* (Washington, D.C.: American Enterprise Institute, 2002), Tables 5-2 and 5-5; for 2002–2005, from Norman J. Ornstein, personal communication.

duced so much in new tax revenues that the budget was in surplus, and budget politics turned, temporarily, to the happier task of choosing among tax cuts, additional spending for government programs, or paying down the national debt. But a slowing economy put the squeeze on resources in 2001, and revenues were further reduced by major tax cuts enacted at the behest of the George W. Bush administration. As spending rose with the cost of homeland security and the wars in Afghanistan and Iraq, deficits returned as a major problem, reviving contentious partisan conflicts over budget priorities. In budgeting, politics continues to dominate process, and the formal budget rules control the action only insofar as they do not prevent congressional majorities from doing what they want.

Congressional Staff and Support Groups

In addition to relying heavily on its committee system, Congress has sought to cope with its expanding workload by adding staff (see Figure 6-6) and specialized research agencies. Staff doubled between the mid-1950s and the late 1970s (with most of the growth in personal staff); the numbers then remained stable until 1995, when House Republicans reduced House committee staffs by 30 percent. The cuts, however, left

Members of Congress pursue job security by trying to show constituents they are responsive, accessible, and effective—in other words, that they are good agents. Thus when Republicans took over the House in 1995, they cut congressional committee staffs by one-third but rejected a proposal to reduce members' personal staff assistants—the people who answer the mail, perform casework, and otherwise help members keep in touch with constituents. Copyright, cartoon by *The Birmingham News*, 1998.

them with much larger committee staffs than they had had when House Republicans were in the minority; the staffers who lost their jobs were all on Democrats' payrolls.

Personal staff assistants manage members' offices in Washington and back in the state or district. They also draft bills, suggest policy, prepare position papers, write press releases, handle casework for constituents, deal with lobbyists, and negotiate with other staff on their boss's behalf. Almost any political or legislative chore short of casting formal votes in committee or on the floor can be delegated to staff assistants. Committee staffs are deeply involved in all legislative activities; they organize hearings and investigations, research policy options, attend to legislative details, and negotiate with legislators, lobbyists, and executive branch officials on behalf of the party faction on the committee that employs them.

Members receive additional help in gathering and processing information from several specialized congressional agencies. The Government Accountability Office (GAO) audits and investigates federal programs and expenditures, probing for waste, fraud, and inefficiency. The Congressional Research Service (CRS) gives Congress access to a highly professional team of researchers. The Congressional Budget Office (CBO), created as part of the 1974 budget reforms, provides Congress with the economic expertise it needs to make informed fiscal decisions and to hold its own in conflicts with the president's Office of Management and Budget (see Chapter 7). Among its tasks are economic forecasting and economic policy analysis. Although CBO was mainly designed to serve the collective institutional needs of Congress, it also serves members individually; it will, on request, provide analyses to let members know how various budget alternatives would affect their home states and districts.

By using the expert advisers within committee staff and congressional support agencies, members of Congress do not have to take the word of experts from the executive branch or interest groups, who cannot always be expected to impart unbiased information. Although officially bipartisan, the support agencies are the most valuable to the majority party in Congress when the other party controls the executive branch. Indeed, it was no accident that a Democratic Congress created CBO and initiated a major expansion of CRS during the Nixon administration or that Republicans replaced the CBO director when they took control of Congress in 1995.

Making Laws

Congress's rules and structures—the parties and committee systems—are designed to enable majorities to make laws. At every stage of the many routine hurdles a bill must clear to become law, individual and collective (usually partisan) political interests shape the action (see Figure 6-7). The lawmaking process presents opponents of a bill with many opportunities to sidetrack or kill the legislation. It is considerably easier, then, for members to stop bills than to pass them. Although Congress quickly bypasses regular legislative procedures in emergencies,* and party leaders now regularly circumvent normal procedures when trying to enact important and controversial bills, an examination of these procedures completes the picture of how ordinary legislative politics is supposed to work.[41]

Introducing Legislation

Only members may submit legislation to the House or Senate. Many proposals originate outside Congress—from the executive branch, interest groups, constituents—but they must have a congressional sponsor to enter the legislative process. The process itself is largely routine and routinely political. Some bills carry (informally) their authors' names; the Immigration Reform Act of 1986 is known as the Simpson-Mazzoli law after its chief sponsors, Republican Alan Simpson of Wyoming in the Senate and Democrat Romano Mazzoli of Kentucky in the House. The Bipartisan Campaign Reform Act of 2002 is informally known as the Shays-Meehan Act after Reps. Christopher Shays, R-Conn., and Martin Meehan, D-Mass. Even whole programs may be named after their authors. For example, the government helps college students finance their educations through Pell grants, named after Democrat Claiborne Pell of Rhode Island, who championed the

---

*For example, within three days of the attacks of September 11, 2001, Congress passed a joint resolution (PL 107-40) authorizing the president "to use all necessary and appropriate force against the nations, organizations, or people that he determines planned, authorized, committed, or aided the terrorist attacks." Congress also passed a major antiterrorism bill (PL 107-56) on October 25, a little more than a month after President Bush had requested it.

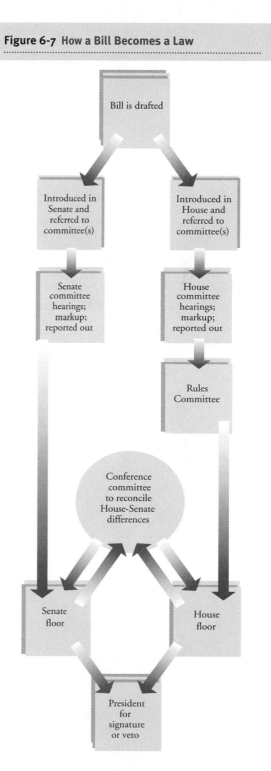

Figure 6-7 How a Bill Becomes a Law

Bill is drafted

Introduced in Senate and referred to committee(s)

Introduced in House and referred to committee(s)

Senate committee hearings; markup; reported out

House committee hearings; markup; reported out

Rules Committee

Conference committee to reconcile House-Senate differences

Senate floor

House floor

President for signature or veto

program when he was in the Senate. Personal credit for what is, after all, a collective act of Congress (one vote is never sufficient and rarely necessary to accomplish anything) is a valuable commodity. Proponents of bills try to line up cosponsors both to build support (by sharing credit) and to display it (increasing the chances for legislative action). Most important bills are introduced in the House and Senate at the same time so the chambers can work on them simultaneously.

The parties and the president (with the cooperation of congressional friends) also use legislative proposals to stake out political positions and to make political statements. Republican presidents Reagan and George H. W. Bush regularly submitted proposals they knew were "dead on arrival" to establish a record that their party could run on in the future. Members of Congress routinely do the same.

Assignment to Committee

After a bill is introduced, it is assigned a number (preceded by *H.R.* in the House, *S.* in the Senate) and referred to a committee. Even the number assigned can make a political point. In 2007 Democrats gave top billing to items in their promised "100-Hour Agenda"; *H.R. 1* was assigned to a bill adopting some recommendations from the 9/11 Commission, *H.R. 2* to a bill increasing the federal minimum wage, and *H.R. 3* to a bill expanding funding for research on embryonic stem cells. Most bills are routinely assigned to the appropriate committee; complex bills are sometimes referred to several committees, and controversial bills are occasionally handled by temporary ad hoc committees appointed for that single purpose. The Speaker makes the nonroutine decisions in the House, manipulating the committee process to ensure more friendly or expeditious treatment of legislation important to the majority party. In the Senate party leaders negotiate agreements to settle disputed referrals.

Once a bill has been referred to a committee, the most common thing that happens next is: nothing. Most bills die of neglect—and are meant to—in committee. Many more bills are introduced than members have time to deal with—roughly ten thousand in a typical two-year Congress. Some bills are introduced "by request," meaning the introducer was doing someone—a constituent or campaign contributor—a favor by offering the bill but has no further interest in its fate. Bills introduced by the minority party to score political points or embarrass the majority are deliberately buried. Like party leaders, committee chairs and their allies strive to avoid situations in which their party colleagues might have to cast potentially embarrassing votes. If the committee decides on further action, the bill may be taken up directly by the full committee, but more commonly it is referred to the appropriate subcommittee.

Hearings

Once the subcommittee decides to act, it (or the full committee) may hold hearings, inviting interested people—from executive agencies, from interest groups, from academia, from almost anywhere—to testify in person or in writing about the issue at stake and proposals to deal with it. In a typical recent two-year Congress, the Senate held about 1,200 hearings; the House, about 2,300. Hearings may be orchestrated to make a record for (or against) a particular proposal, to evaluate how a program is working, or simply to generate publicity—for committee members as well as issues. Committees can investigate almost anything, including the White House or Congress itself. The White House is especially likely to be targeted when controlled by the congressional majority's rival party (see box "Congressional Investigations"). Senate committees also hold hearings to evaluate judicial, diplomatic, and senior administrative appointments.

Hearings also provide a formal occasion for Congress to monitor the administration of the laws and programs it enacts. The heaviest duty falls on the Appropriations subcommittees in the House, for government agencies have to justify their budget requests to these panels every year. Congress often is criticized for shirking its duty to oversee the administration of laws. After all, if carried out, comprehensive oversight would be a tedious, time-consuming, politically unrewarding chore. Instead, members of Congress set up administrative procedures that give affected interests an opportunity to protest damaging bureaucratic policies and decisions. In this way, members can confine their oversight to those areas of administration where the political stakes are demonstrably high. Members operate more like firefighters than police, waiting for fire alarms to go off before taking action rather than patrolling the streets looking for crime.[42] By relying on people affected by administrative decisions to alert it to problems, Congress, in effect, puts a big bumper sticker on bureaucrats that says, "How am I driving? Call 1-800-Congress" (see Chapter 8).

Reporting a Bill

If the subcommittee decides to act on a bill (and often it does not), it marks it up—that is, edits it line by line—and reports it to the full committee. The full committee then accepts, rejects, or amends the bill. With the exception of important and controversial bills, committees usually defer to subcommittees; otherwise, they lose the benefits of a division of labor.

Much of the coalition building that produces successful legislation takes place as subcommittees and committees work out the details of bills. No one wants to waste time on a bill that has no chance of passing—unless political points could be scored, such as when a Republican Congress sent Democratic president Bill Clinton a measure banning partial-birth abortion he was certain to veto. If a bill cannot attract solid support from at least the majority party committee members (and perhaps minority party members as well), its chances on the House or Senate floor are slim indeed. But if amendments, compromises, and deals can build a strong committee coalition for a bill, its chances on the floor are very good. The committee system, then, also divides the labor of coalition building.

The written report that accompanies every bill reported out of committee is the most important source of information on legislation for members of Congress not on the committee and for other people in government, including the agencies and courts that have to implement and interpret the law once it is passed. These reports summarize the bill's purposes, major provisions, and changes from existing law. They also summarize the arguments for and against the bill.

Congressional Investigations

Under divided government, the party controlling Congress has to share lawmaking power with the party controlling the White House, and the party's more ambitious legislative goals are likely to be frustrated. But divided government does not impair Congress's powers of oversight—the authority to hold hearings and investigations, issue subpoenas compelling testimony from individuals in and out of the executive branch, and generally pry into any matter that catches a members' eye. Indeed, under divided government the use of this authority becomes more attractive for both partisan and institutional reasons: to embarrass the rival party by exposing its supposed misgovernment, and to assert Congress's authority as a branch of government coequal to the executive branch that the rival party controls.

During the 2006 campaign, Democrats had criticized the Republican Congress for lax oversight of the Bush administration. With their members' electoral fates linked by shared party label to the public's evaluation of the president and his policies, the Republican leaders' reluctance to draw attention to the administration's shortcomings is understandable. As one Republican House member candidly observed, "Our party controls the levers of government. We're not about to go out and look beneath a bunch of rocks to try to cause heartburn."[1] But protecting the administration led to accusations that the Republican Congress had given up its constitutional status as a coequal branch of government. Democrats could thus claim the constitutional high road while pursuing investigations that promised significant partisan payoffs.

After the 2006 elections, recognizing that the president and Senate Republicans would limit what they could accomplish legislatively, the victorious Democrats immediately initiated a series of investigations targeting the administration and its officials. Some initial targets for investigation, listed below, reflect the Democrats' pent-up demand for "accountability" in the executive branch and illustrate the range of their ambitions in this domain. In the first one hundred days, the House alone held at least one hundred hearings, far more than Republicans had held at a similar point in the previous Congress. Few of these hearings and investigations would lead to legislation, at least during the 110th Congress, but Democrats hoped they would expose the administration's alleged misgovernment and become grist for election campaigns in 2008. The administration fought back through assertions of executive privilege (see Chapter 7) and stalling in response to committees' demands for documents.

Senate Investigations

Armed Services Committee probes allegations of mistreatment of suspects at Guantánamo prison.

Finance Committee investigates extravagant expenses by the head of the Smithsonian Institution.

Select Committee on Intelligence conducts hearing on administration officials' leak to selected reporters identifying Valerie Plame as a CIA operative.

Judiciary Committee launches extensive hearings into the Justice Department's firing of eight U.S. attorneys in the previous fall.

Judiciary Committee investigates White House pressure on Justice Department officials in 2004 to reauthorize secret wiretaps.

Senate's homeland security oversight committee conducts hearings on administration handling of offers of foreign aid after Hurricane Katrina.

Senate's agriculture committee conducts hearings on the on the Food and Drug Administration's investigation of contaminated pet food.

House Investigations

House Oversight and Government Reform Committee questions General Services Administration officials about pre-election briefings of government administrators encouraging them to find opportunities to assist Republican congressional candidates.

Judiciary Committee questions FBI officials on widespread abuse of "national security" and "exigent circumstances" anti-terrorism authority to obtain phone records and engage in surveillance without a judicial order in over two thousand instances where citizens were suspected of other crimes.

Judiciary Committee launches extensive hearings into the Justice Department's firing of eight U.S. attorneys in the previous fall.

House votes to authorize subpoena of Secretary of State Condoleezza Rice and other administration officials to answer questions from the oversight committee on her knowledge about the claim that Iraq sought to import uranium from Niger for its nuclear weapons program.

---

1. Zachary Roth, "Investi-gate," *Washington Monthly,* June 2006.

At a hearing before the House Oversight and Government Reform Committee in June 2007, newly elected Democratic representative Paul Hodes of New Hampshire questions the way the Pentagon used information to influence Americans' views of the Iraq War. Advocating legislation intended to prevent behind-the-scenes efforts by the Bush administration to manipulate public opinion, Hodes said, "I hope it inspires the Pentagon to tell the truth."

Scheduling Debate

When a committee agrees to report a bill to the floor, the bill is put on the House or Senate calendar—a list of bills scheduled for action. Each chamber has different calendars for different types of bills. In the House noncontroversial bills are put on the Consent Calendar (public bills) or Private Calendar (bills concerning individuals) to be passed without debate. Such bills also may be dealt with expeditiously under a suspension of the rules, which waives almost all of the formalities to allow swift action. Most legislation passed by the House follows one of these routes.

Controversial or important bills are placed on the Union Calendar (money bills) or House Calendar (other public bills). The committee reporting such bills must ask the Rules Committee for a **rule,** a resolution that specifies when and how long a bill will be debated and under what procedures. The rule may permit amendments—changes in wording—from the floor (**open rule**), only certain amendments (**restricted rule**), or no amendments (**closed rule**). A rule may also specify the order in which amendments are considered, thereby stacking the deck to favor particular outcomes. Majority party leaders use restricted or closed rules to keep unwanted amendments off the agenda, both to protect their party's members from casting embarrassing votes and to keep legislative packages from unraveling. Closed rules help to solve the majority's prisoner's dilemmas; many proposals that would not be enacted piece by piece because different members would defect on different sections can pass if they are voted on as packages. As partisan competition became more intense during the 1980s, Democratic House leaders used restricted or closed rules to maintain control of the floor agenda. Republicans objected strenuously but, after taking over in 1995, resorted to restrictive rules themselves to prevent Democrats from hindering the Republicans' promised speedy action on proposals set forth in the Contract with America (see Table 6-3). Democrats did the same to ensure enactment of their "100-Hour Agenda" after taking over in 2007.

If the Rules Committee holds hearings on a rule, interested members may express their views on the legislation. After hearings, a bill may be granted a rule or it may be denied a rule entirely, at least until the originating committee has revised it to the Rules Committee's satisfaction. Once the Rules Committee grants a rule, it must be adopted by a majority vote on the floor. When floor action on a bill is constrained by its rule, a House majority has, in fact, consciously chosen to constrain itself. Sometimes the House kills a bill by voting against the rule rather than against the bill itself. In 1994, for example, the House rejected a rule for a bill to elevate the Environmental Protection Agency to cabinet status because the bill did not require the new department to consider the economic costs and benefits of new environmental regulations. The House's action killed the legislation.

In 2001 Republican House leaders tried to kill a campaign finance reform bill they strongly opposed by proposing a rule so unacceptable to the bill's proponents that they joined in voting the rule down. When the Republican leaders refused to act further on the bill, its supporters eventually got it out of Rules through a **discharge petition,** which brings a bill directly to the floor without committee approval when signed by a majority of House members (218). This discharge petition was a rare success; since

1967, only twelve such petitions have received the required 218 votes.*

The Senate has no equivalent of the House Rules Committee or, indeed, any rules limiting debate or amendments. Thus the leaders of both parties routinely negotiate unanimous consent agreements to arrange for the orderly consideration of legislation. Unanimous consent agreements are similar to a rule from the House Rules Committee in that they limit time for debate, determine which amendments are allowable, and provide for waivers of standard Senate procedures.

Without a unanimous consent agreement, there is no limit on how long senators can talk or on how many amendments they can offer. Individuals or small groups can even **filibuster**— hold the floor making endless speeches so that no action can be taken on the bill or anything else—to try to kill bills that the majority would otherwise enact. And breaking a filibuster is difficult. Under Senate rules an extraordinary three-fifths majority of the Senate membership (sixty votes) is required to invoke **cloture,** which allows a maximum of thirty additional hours of debate on a bill before a vote must be taken.

TABLE 6-3

The Growth of Restrictive Rules in the U.S. House

Congress	Total Rules Granted	Open Rules		Restrictive Rules	
		Number	Percent	Number	Percent
95th, 1977–1978	211	179	85	32	15
96th, 1979–1980	214	161	75	53	25
97th, 1981–1982	120	90	75	30	25
98th, 1983–1984	155	105	68	50	32
99th, 1985–1986	115	65	57	50	43
100th, 1987–1988	123	66	54	57	46
101st, 1989–1990	104	47	45	57	55
102nd, 1991–1992	109	37	34	72	66
103rd, 1993–1994	104	31	30	73	70
104th, 1995–1996	151	86	57	65	43
105th, 1997–1998	142	72	51	70	49
106th, 1999–2000	184	93	51	91	49
107th, 2001–2002	112	41	37	71	63
108th, 2003–2004	128	33	26	95	74
109th, 2005–2006	138	22	16	116	84

Source: Roger H. Davidson and Walter J. Oleszek, *Congress and Its Members,* 11th ed. (Washington, D.C.: CQ Press, 2008).

Note: Democrats claim that Republicans misclassified rules in the 104th–106th Congresses, thereby overstating the frequency of open rules.

Conservative southern senators used filibusters most notoriously in their rearguard action against civil rights laws a generation ago, but senators of all ideological persuasions now use the tactic. In fact, filibustering has become much more common in recent years, rising from an average of only one filibuster per Congress in the 1950s to more than thirty-two per Congress in the 106th–108th Congresses (1999–2004). Senate Republicans, then in the minority, used it to kill a number of Bill Clinton's initiatives during the 103rd Congress (1993–1994), including his economic stimulus package, a proposal to raise fees for grazing cattle on federal lands, a package of campaign finance reforms, a bill to bar members of Congress from accepting gifts from lobbyists, and a bill to forbid employers from permanently replacing workers who go

---

*Ultimate success is even rarer for discharged bills. Since 1910, when the procedure was first instituted, only three bills brought to the House floor via discharge have become law: once in 1931, once in 1960, and again in 2002, when Congress passed the Shays-Meehan campaign finance reforms.

The longest speech in the history of the Senate was made by Strom Thurmond of South Carolina. Thurmond, a Democrat who later became a Republican, spoke for twenty-four hours and eighteen minutes during a filibuster against passage of the Civil Rights Act of 1957. This display of stamina was no fluke; in 2002 at the age of ninety-nine Strom Thurmond finally decided to retire from the Senate.

on strike for higher pay. After 1994 Senate Democrats found new affection for the tactic; an average of fifty-six cloture votes were taken in the 106th through the 108th Congresses, of which only about 43 percent were successful.[43]

Even the threat of a filibuster can stop action on legislation because Senate leaders dislike wasting time on bills not likely to pass. With filibustering now so routine—more than half of the major legislation considered by the Senate in recent Congresses has been subject to filibusters and other delaying tactics[44]—the new reality is that the support of sixty senators is needed to pass any controversial piece of legislation except the budget resolution, which is protected by a special rule.

In addition to permitting filibusters, the rules allow individual members to tie the Senate up in knots by refusing to concur with unanimous consent agreements aimed at facilitating the chamber's work. Senators, then, must depend on mutual restraint and bipartisan cooperation to get their work done. When cooperation breaks down, the Senate is immobilized. Senators thus buy lower conformity costs at the price of higher transaction costs.

Debate and Amendment

In the House the time for debate is divided equally between the proponents and opponents of a bill. Each side's time is controlled by a floor manager, typically the committee or subcommittee chair and the opposing ranking member. If amendments to a bill are allowed under the rule, they must be germane (pertinent) to the purpose of the bill; extraneous proposals, known as **riders,** are not allowed. Debate on amendments usually is restricted to five minutes for each side. The House often debates bills as a Committee of the Whole because, acting in the guise of a committee, the House is less encumbered by formal procedures. For example, for the Committee of the Whole, a **quorum**—the number of members who must be present for the House to act officially—is 100 rather than the usual majority of 218, and a member chosen by the Speaker wields the gavel. The House must revert back to itself, however, to vote on legislation.

Floor debates do not change many minds because, jaded by experience, politicians are rarely swayed by one another's eloquence. Debates are for public consumption: to make arguments that members will use to justify their votes to constituents and others; to shape public perceptions through the media; to guide administrators and courts

STRATEGY AND CHOICE

The "Nuclear Option"

During the first George W. Bush administration (2001–2004), the minority Senate Democrats used the filibuster to block confirmation votes on ten of the president's 229 nominees to the federal bench on the grounds that they were too extreme or too biased to qualify for the lifetime appointment. They were also retaliating for the Republicans' refusal to allow votes on a considerably larger number of Bill Clinton's judicial nominees in the previous administration. The threat of tit-for-tat vengeance escalated when Bush began his second administration in 2005 by resubmitting seven of the blocked nominees and Senate Republicans, led by Majority Leader Bill Frist, R-Tenn., threatened to change the Senate's rules to ban filibustering on judicial nominations, a move dubbed the "nuclear option" because it would escalate partisan conflict to total war. "One way or another, the filibuster of judicial nominees must end," said Frist, calling the practice "a formula for tyranny of the minority."[1] His side, always sensitive to rhetoric, took to calling the rules change the "constitutional option." The Democrats' leader, Sen. Harry Reid, D-Nev., threatened reprisal in no uncertain terms: "If they decide, for whatever reason, to do this, . . . they will rue the day they did it because we will do whatever we can to strike back."[2] This was not an idle threat, because by simply withholding unanimous consent for bypassing the Senate's many cumbersome formal rules, Democrats could effectively bring all Senate floor action to a screeching halt whenever they chose to do so.

At stake was not only the fate of current nominees, but more importantly, that of future Supreme Court appointments anticipated during Bush's second term. Democrats wanted to retain the capacity to block changes that would build a Court majority to overturn *Roe v. Wade,* while Republicans wanted to set aside any such impediment, allowing the president to stack the federal judiciary with conservatives from top to bottom.

The ensuing high-stakes game of chicken involved a complicated mix of short- and long-term considerations. Republicans had to balance their desire to guarantee the president's appointees an up-or-down vote against both the short-term partisan fallout, likely to be heavy but with a relatively short half-life (although they could make the majority's life miserable for a while, Democrats could not block Senate action indefinitely), and the longer-term prospect that a future Democratic majority would retaliate in kind, perhaps eliminating the filibuster entirely. As always, uncertainty bolstered the status quo, and a number of Senate Republicans were less than enthusiastic about going nuclear. A showdown was averted at the last minute on May 23, 2005, when seven Republicans and seven Democratic moderates ignored their party leaders to cut a deal that allowed a vote on at least three of the judges while preserving the right to filibuster.

1. Helen Dewar and Mike Allen, "GOP May Target Use of Filibuster," *Washington Post,* December 12, 2004, A1.
2. Ibid.

when they apply and interpret the legislation; to stake out partisan positions; to show off. More important, formal floor debates serve to legitimize policy. Whatever deals and compromises went into building a legislative coalition, whatever the real purposes of its supporters, they have to make a case that the proposed action will serve the public interest. The opposition has equal time to argue against the action. Occasionally public justification assumes historic proportions, such as in 1991 when ninety-four senators and more than three hundred representatives took the floor to explain their positions on U.S. intervention in the Persian Gulf.

Floor action does more to shape legislation in the Senate than in the House. Because unanimous consent is required to limit Senate debate (except when cloture is used to end a filibuster), members are free to spend as much time as they like debating a bill. Unlike in the House, few conflicts are resolved in Senate committees or subcommittees; senators do much more legislating on the floor, offering amendments or complete alternatives to the bill reported by the committee. Senate amendments need not even be germane; important bills are sometimes passed as amendments—or riders—to completely unrelated bills. For example, in 1994 when the Senate passed a bill elevating the Environmental Protection Agency to cabinet status—the same bill the House killed by voting down the rule—it also inserted into the text an amendment that would have reauthorized the 1974 Safe Drinking Water Act. Unrestrained floor debate is the fullest expression of the Senate's individualistic, participatory ethos. It also provides a prominent forum for the articulation of any social interest that catches the fancy of even one senator.

The Vote

Members of Congress are ever alert to the political implications of votes on important bills. The fate of legislation often is decided by a series of votes rather than a single vote. For example, opponents of a measure may propose "killer" amendments, which, if passed, would make the bill unacceptable to an otherwise supportive majority; in 2002 House Republican leaders tried to kill campaign finance reform with this tactic. In addition, opponents may move to recommit the bill—that is, to send it back to committee for modification or burial—before the final vote. And on occasion, members may try to straddle an issue by voting for killer amendments or to recommit but then voting for the bill on final passage when these moves fail. Sophisticated observers have little trouble picking out the decisive vote and discerning a member's true position, but inattentive constituents may be fooled.

How do members of Congress decide how to vote? Political scientist John Kingdon sought to find out by asking them. They revealed that, along with their own views, the opinions of constituents and the advice of knowledgeable and trusted colleagues have the strongest influence on their decisions. Often members are aware of what their constituents want without anyone having to tell them. At other times they rely on letters, phone calls, faxes, e-mails, text messages, editorials, and polls to get a sense of what people think. Even on issues on which constituency opinion is unformed, members try to anticipate how constituents would react if they were to think about the issue. The idea is to cast an *explainable vote,* one that can be defended publicly if it is brought up by a challenger in some future campaign. Not every vote has to please the people who hire and fire members of Congress, but too many "bad" votes can expose a member to the charge of being out of touch with the folks back home.[45]

In general, members have reason to listen to anyone who can supply them with essential information: political information about how constituents and other supporters will view their actions and technical information about what the legislation will do. They also have reason to weigh the views of anyone who can help or hinder them in winning reelection, advancing their careers in Washington, and having an impact on policy. Constituents' views count the most because they have the most direct control over members' careers, but the views of interest groups, campaign contributors, and party leaders also shape decisions, especially on issues of little concern to constituents.

Most constituents know and care little about most of the issues on which members vote. The minority of the public that does pay attention varies from issue to issue. The relevant constituency opinions are those held by people who care, pay attention, and are not securely in the other party's camp, for their support will be affected by how the member handles the issue. In other words, the politically relevant interests on most issues are special interests. For that reason, in Congress intense minorities often prevail over apathetic majorities. One example: opponents of gun control, led by the National Rifle Association, have stopped or weakened gun control legislation many times over the years despite widespread public support for stronger regulation of firearms.

Trusted colleagues strongly influence voting decisions because legislators cannot possibly inform themselves adequately about all the matters that require a vote. They depend instead on the expertise of others, most often members of committees (usually from their own party) with jurisdiction over the bills outside their own specialties. Members say that lobbyists, executive branch officials, party leaders, congressional staff, and the news media influence their decisions much less than do constituents and colleagues. Groups representing special interests are deeply involved in congressional policymaking, but their direct influence is not strongly felt at this point in the legislative process; effective groups work through constituents and colleagues (see Chapter 13).

How influential is the president when the votes are finally cast? Occasionally presidents have been able to win against the odds by persuading wavering members of their party to stick with the team or by cutting special deals with pivotal members. For example, in 1993 President Clinton's successful appeals to party loyalty were crucial to his razor-thin budget victories (218–216 in the House, 51–50 in the Senate, where Vice President Al Gore's vote broke a tie); no Republican in either chamber would support the budget because it included tax increases. Essential, too, were the bargains made to modify the bill to satisfy reluctant Democrats.[46] On most votes, however, the administration's wishes are by no means paramount.

The same is true of the wishes of party leaders. Senate leaders exert little formal influence at this or any other stage of the legislative process. House leaders use their much more formidable powers at earlier stages and through control of the agenda. The majority party's leaders may, if they wish, do much to frame the choices that House members face. But their job is to construct legislative packages that party members are comfortable supporting. If they are successful, no persuasion is necessary. If they fail, few members are likely to put party loyalty ahead of constituents' views except under the most intense pressure and on the party's most important bills.

House members use this electronic voting device to record their votes on matters coming to the floor. Despite the technology for instant voting, the process is sometimes delayed for hours as the majority's leaders work to bring party dissidents back into the fold to avoid defeat.

In the House unrecorded voice votes may be cast, but at the request of at least twenty members a recorded **roll-call vote** is taken. When voting by roll-call, members insert a small plastic card into one of the more than forty stations scattered about the House floor and press a button for "yea," "nay," or "present" (indicating they were on the floor for the vote but did not take a side). Senators simply announce their votes when their names are called from the roll of members rather than record them by machine. Senators may also take unrecorded voice votes, but as a matter of senatorial courtesy a recorded roll-call vote is taken if any senator requests it.

In Conference

Once passed, a bill is sent to the other chamber for consideration (if some version has not already been passed there). If the second chamber passes the bill unchanged, it is sent to the White House for the president's signature or veto. Routine legislation usually follows this route, but controversial bills often pass the House and Senate in different versions, so that the two bodies have to reconcile the differences in the versions before the bill can leave Congress.

This reconciliation is the job of a conference committee. Party leaders in each house appoint a conference delegation that includes members of both parties, usually from among the standing committee members most actively involved for and against the legislation (if a conference committee is not appointed, as sometimes happens, the bill dies). The size of the delegation depends on the complexity of the legislation. The House delegation to the conference handling the 1,300-page Clean Air Act amendments of 1990 consisted of 130 representatives from eight different committees. The Senate got by with a delegation of nine from two committees. But the relative size of the delegations is not important, for each chamber votes as a separate unit in conference, and a bill is not reported out of conference to the House and Senate until it receives the approval of majorities of both delegations.

Conference committees are supposed to reconcile differences in the two versions of a bill without adding or subtracting from the legislation. In practice, however, they occasionally do both. Conference committees generally exercise the widest discretion when the two versions are most discrepant (see box "Porn for Corn" for an amusing example of conference maneuvering—and of how politics is done).

Once conferees reach agreement on a bill, they report the details to each chamber. A conference report is privileged—that is, it can be considered on the floor at any time without going through the usual scheduling process. The divisions of opinion in conference committees normally reflect the divisions in the chambers they represent, so majorities assembled in conference can usually be reproduced on the House and Senate floors. If both chambers approve the report, the bill is sent to the president.

STRATEGY AND CHOICE

Porn for Corn

The conference committee charged with working out differences between the House and Senate versions of the fiscal 1992 appropriations bill for the Interior Department faced a typical problem and came up with a classical solution. The House had voted to increase the very low fees stock raisers pay to graze their animals on public land by more than 400 percent over a four-year period. The Senate, which overrepresents sparsely populated western states, opposed this provision.

In the meantime, the Senate had, in its Interior Department Appropriations bill, adopted language proposed by Republican senator Jesse Helms of North Carolina forbidding the National Endowment for the Arts (NEA) from spending federal money "to promote, disseminate, or produce materials that depict in a patently offensive way sexual or excretory activities or organs." Majorities in both chambers probably opposed censoring NEA grants, but they also realized it was politically risky to go on record as permitting tax-

payers' money to fund anything that might smack of pornography.

The conference committee struck a bargain: the House delegation would vote to drop the grazing fee increase if the Senate delegation would vote to drop Helms's provision—an exchange of "porn for corn," as it was quickly labeled. The conference bargain held on the floors of the House and Senate. Helms tried to put the restrictions back in the appropriations bill, but western conservatives feared the resurrection of the grazing fee increase if they broke the deal and refused to go along with him.[1]

"Porn for corn" is a definitive example of doing politics: conservative western ranching interests made common cause with the liberal urban arts community though they scarcely shared common purposes.

---

1. Phillip A. Davis, "After Sound, Fury on Interior Bill Signifies Nothing New," *Congressional Quarterly Weekly Report,* November 2, 1991, 3196.

Sometimes one or both chambers balks and sends the conferees back to work, perhaps with instructions about what to change. If differences cannot be reconciled, the bill dies. This outcome is unusual, however; when a proposal has attracted enough support to make it this far and members face a choice to take it or leave it, they usually take it. This situation strengthens the hands of the committees that originally reported the legislation because the conference delegates are normally drawn from these committees and the conference gives them a chance to have the last word.

To the President

Upon receiving a bill from Congress, the president has the choice of signing the bill into law; ignoring the bill, with the result that it becomes law in ten days (not counting Sundays); or vetoing the bill (see Chapter 7 for more information on the veto process). If Congress adjourns before the ten days are up, the bill fails because it was subject to a **pocket veto** (the president, metaphorically, stuck it in a pocket and forgot about it). When presidents veto a bill, they usually send a statement to Congress, and therefore to all Americans, that explains why they took such action.

Congressional override of a presidential veto requires a two-thirds vote in each chamber. If the override succeeds, the bill becomes law. Success is rare, however, because presidents usually can muster enough support from members of their own party in at least one chamber to sustain a veto. When a head count tells presidents that an override is possible, they hesitate to use the veto because the override would expose their political weakness. Of the 480 regular vetoes cast between 1945 and 2008, only 48 were overridden. Presidents also exercised 310 pocket vetoes, none of which could be overridden, over the same period.[47]

Presidents often prevail without having to resort to a veto because members of Congress are reluctant to invest time and effort in legislation that will die on the president's desk. The exception is when congressional majorities want to stake out a position on a prominent issue to score political points. The veto, then, is a major weapon in the presidential arsenal; presidents can threaten to kill any legislative proposal they find unsatisfactory, usually leaving Congress with no choice but to cut presidents in on deals.

A Bias against Action

Emerging from this review of the process and politics of ordinary congressional lawmaking is one central point: it is far easier to kill a bill than to pass one. Proponents of legislation have to win a sustained sequence of victories—in subcommittee, in committee, in Rules (in the House), in conference, on the floors of both chambers (repeatedly), and in the White House—to succeed. To do this supporters of a bill have to assemble not one but several majority coalitions. Opponents need win only once to keep a bill from going forward. The process imposes high transaction costs, conferring a strong bias in favor of the status quo.

UNORTHODOX LAWMAKING. The majority party can easily find its legislative agenda frustrated by the minority party when ordinary legislative procedures are followed. As party divisions in Congress intensified and minority obstruction became more common over the past three decades, majority party leaders have improvised unorthodox procedures to enact legislation. In the House, these include designing complex special rules to structure debate and amendment to minimize the minority's influence; bypassing or overriding committees to draft bills directly; rewriting legislation in conference committee after it has passed the floor; and combining separate bills into huge omnibus packages that leave members the choice of accepting all or getting nothing. In the Senate, the minority party has probably contributed most to deviations from orthodoxy through the unbridled use of the filibuster, compelling leaders to negotiate supermajority coalitions of at least sixty votes to act on controversial issues. Majority Senate leaders have responded with procedural strategies designed to minimize the damage. In dealing with important and controversial legislation, unorthodox procedures have in fact become the congressional norm.[48]

Unorthodox lawmaking requires a heavy investment of leaders' resources—time, energy, and favors—reflecting the high transaction costs incurred in getting Congress to act collectively on issues that provoke strong disagreement. Only a limited number of measures can receive such treatment, thus enhancing the status-quo bias of legislative politics. Proposals that fall along the wayside can always be revived and reintroduced in the next Congress, however. Indeed, it is not at all unusual for many years to elapse between the initial introduction of a major piece of legislation and its final enactment. Proposals for national health insurance have been on the congressional agenda for more than sixty years (only Medicare, applying exclusively to the elderly, has passed so far). Defeats are rarely final, but neither are most victories; the game is by no means over when a law is enacted. The real impact of legislation depends on how it is implemented by administrators and interpreted by the courts (see Chapters 8 and 9). And laws always are subject to revision or repeal by a later Congress. That victories or defeats almost always are partial, and conceivably temporary, contributes a great deal to making politics—cooperation in the face of disagreement—possible. Politicians recognize that taking half a loaf now does not mean they cannot go for a larger share in the future.

Evaluating Congress

Americans hold contradictory views about their national legislature. In the abstract, most people approve of the Constitution's institutional arrangements. Any proposals for change advanced by constitutional scholars and reformers are ignored by virtually everyone else. And Americans generally like their own representatives and senators. Most members receive high approval ratings from constituents, and most win reelection even when the public professes to be thoroughly fed up with national politics and the politicians of one or both parties. But Congress as it operates and its members as a class are rarely appreciated. Sometimes large majorities of Americans assign their Congress a failing grade (see Figure 6-8). The low points in congressional approval occurred in the early 1990s and in 2006 and coincided with unusually high turnover in congressional seats.

The public's general disdain for Congress reflects the low repute garnered by politicians as a class. Habitual contempt for politicians arises from the nature of politics itself. Americans use politics as a vehicle for social decisions even when they share no consensus about the best course of action. Politics, then, inevitably requires compromises and trades, the results of which leave no one fully satisfied. The alternative to compromise—stalemate—is often equally scorned by a public more inclined to view legislative gridlock as a product of partisan bickering than of intractable conflicts among legitimate values, interests, and beliefs. In reality, Congress's difficulty in deciding on a budget, reforming the health care system, or dealing with an array of social problems (poverty, crime, education, job loss) reflects the absence of any public consensus on what should be done about these issues. The only consensus is that national leaders, when failing to act, have failed to do their job.

Figure 6-8 Americans' Contradictory Views: Praise for Incumbents but Disdain for Congress

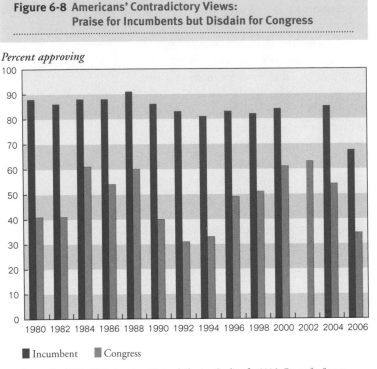

Percent approving

■ Incumbent ■ Congress

Sources: For 1980–2004, American National Election Studies; for 2006, Center for Survey Research (Indiana) Study.

Note: Question about incumbent not asked in 2002.

Congress's poor reputation also arises from the very nature of pluralism. In pluralist politics, adamant minorities frequently defeat apathetic majorities because the minorities invest more of their political resources—votes, money, persuasive efforts—in getting their way. Indeed, the ability of pluralist systems to weigh the intensity of preferences as well as to count heads is viewed as a major advantage because it means that groups tend to win when they care most and lose when they care least. But it also means that "special interests" often win out over general interests, leaving members of Congress perpetually open to the charge of violating the public trust.[49]

Congress's reputation also suffers from recurrent ethics scandals, including those involving such powerful leaders as Democratic Speaker Jim Wright (forced to resign in 1989 over a shady book deal), Republican Speaker Newt Gingrich (fined and reprimanded in 1997 for lying to the House Ethics Committee), Ways and Means chair Dan Rostenkowski (jailed for mail fraud in 1996), Senate Finance Committee chair Bob Packwood (resigned in 1995 to avoid expulsion for sexual harassment), Republican House majority leader Tom DeLay (resigned in 2006 under indictment for violating campaign finance laws), and Sen. Ted Stevens (indicted for accepting bribes in 2008). More broadly, the House bank overdraft scandal of 1992 and the publicity that followed about other congressional perks—gyms, beauty parlors, and limousines—fueled widespread scorn for Congress and helped Republicans overthrow forty years of Democratic rule in 1994, and diverse scandals, several involving members' relationships with convicted lobbyist Jack Abramoff, helped Democrats to victory in 2006.

All of these sources of public disdain for members of Congress represent conditions to be coped with rather than problems that can be solved. Senators and representatives cannot avoid making political deals, representing conflicted publics, or paying special attention to intensely held views. And not all of them will resist the many opportunities for corruption that come with the job. Thus members of Congress as a class are never likely to be revered by the public for any length of time.

Still, approval of Congress does vary in response to how it seems to be doing its job. The public prefers bipartisan agreement to partisan bickering, cooperation with the president over conflict between the branches, and, most of all, successful government policies. For example, in early 1998, on the heels of the 1997 balanced budget agreement between Clinton and the Republican Congress and against a background of a booming stock market and unemployment and inflation rates down to levels not seen since the 1960s, public approval of Congress in the Gallup Poll reached 57 percent, up nearly thirty points from its low in 1992. But when Congress engaged in a highly partisan battle over impeaching Clinton for perjury and obstruction of justice in his attempt to cover up his sexual dalliance with a White House intern, its level of public approval fell sharply. In recent years, intense partisan conflict has been far more common than bipartisan cooperation, so most of the public has found fault with Congress most of the time.

Evaluations of Congress became dramatically more positive in the wake of the al Qaeda attacks on the United States in September 2001. The approval rating reached a record high of 84 percent a month after planes hit the World Trade Center and the Pentagon. With Congress itself under apparent biological attack from anthrax disseminated through the mail (its source was later found to be domestic and unrelated to the September 11 attacks) and displaying bipartisan resolve in supporting the Bush administration's initial proposals to combat terrorism, Congress-bashing went suddenly out of fashion. The distinction in the public mind between Congress as a revered constitutional invention and as a bunch of politicians doing the messy and often unsightly work of politics dissolved for a brief time, and Congress was included in the surge of patriotic affection for the symbols of American democracy the attacks had inspired (see Chapter 10). Soon, however, the public's view of Congress resumed its normal shape; within a year approval of Congress had fallen below 50 percent, and by the 2006 midterm election was down to 25 percent. Public regard for Congress rose briefly after the Democrats' takeover but slumped back down into the low 20s amid economic turmoil and political stalemate during the final year of the George W. Bush administration.

Despite all its faults, perceived or real, the U.S. Congress remains the most powerful and independent legislature in the world. It has retained its power and independence for both constitutional and institutional reasons. The Constitution not only granted the House and Senate extensive legislative powers, but also provided the basis for electoral independence from the executive. Congress's formal legislative powers and electoral independence would have been of little avail, however, had members not created effective institutional devices for acquiring information, coordinating action, managing conflict, and discouraging free riding. By developing the party and committee systems and securing the assistance of numerous staff and specialized research agencies, members of Congress have given themselves the organizational means to carry out, and thus to retain, their constitutional mandate. But their task is rarely easy or the way smooth, for the Madisonian system that Congress epitomizes erects formidable barriers to collective action, and the range and complexity of contemporary political conflicts continually test Congress's fundamental ability to do politics successfully.

logic.cqpress.com

Key Terms

ad hoc committee, 285

casework, 261

closed rule, 298

cloture, 299

conditional party government, 276

conference committee, 285

discharge petition, 298

entitlement, 289

filibuster, 299

gerrymandering, 253

joint committee, 284

majority leader, 278

minority leader, 278

multiple referral, 288

necessary and proper clause, 251

open rule, 298

pocket veto, 306

political action committee, 257

pork barrel legislation, 264

president pro tempore, 281

presidential coattails, 262

proportional representation, 252

quorum, 300

restricted rule, 298

rider, 300

roll-call vote, 304

rule, 298

select committee, 284

seniority rule, 271

Speaker of the House, 274

special committee, 284

standing committee, 283

ticket-splitting, 258

unanimous consent agreement, 281

whip, 278

Suggested Readings

Arnold, R. Douglas. *The Logic of Congressional Action.* New Haven: Yale University Press, 1990. Explains how congressional leaders can manipulate the rules to overcome electorally induced free riding when they want to enact policies that impose short-term or concentrated costs to achieve longer-term or diffuse benefits.

Cox, Gary W., and Mathew D. McCubbins. *Legislative Leviathan: Party Government in the House.* Berkeley: University of California Press, 1993. Lucid explanation of the logic that undergirds the House party organizations; makes a strong case that congressional parties are more powerful than most observers have assumed.

Davidson, Roger H., Walter J. Oleszek, and Frances E. Lee. *Congress and Its Members.* 11th ed. Washington, D.C.: CQ Press, 2008. Thorough, authoritative text that is especially good at explaining rules and procedures.

Dodd, Lawrence D., and Bruce I. Oppenheimer. *Congress Reconsidered.* 8th ed. Washington, D.C.: CQ Press, 2005. Offers historical and theoretical perspectives on congressional change and an up-to-date discussion of the contemporary Congress.

Fenno, Richard F., Jr. *Home Style: House Members in Their Districts.* Boston: Little, Brown, 1978. Fenno's close personal observation of House members' interactions with their constituents produces a wealth of insights about how representation actually works.

Jacobson, Gary C. *The Politics of Congressional Elections.* 7th ed. New York: Longman, 2009. A comprehensive look at congressional elections.

Mayhew, David R. *Congress: The Electoral Connection.* New Haven: Yale University Press, 1974. Classic analysis of how electoral incentives shape almost every aspect of congressional organization and behavior.

Rohde, David W. *Parties and Leaders in the Postreform House.* Chicago: University of Chicago Press, 1991. Explains the decline and resurgence of party unity in the House over the past several decades, paying special attention to how the reforms of the 1970s fostered greater partisanship.

Sinclair, Barbara. *Unorthodox Lawmaking: New Legislative Processes in the U.S. Congress.* 3rd ed. Washington, D.C.: CQ Press, 2007. Explains how and why Congress has increasingly ignored its own standard legislative procedures to get its work accomplished.

Review Questions

1. How do the differences between the House and the Senate reflect the competing interests of small and large states?

2. How does the electoral system established by the Constitution differ from that of other parliamentary democracies?

3. What constraints are placed on states when they draw districts for congressional elections? How can parties give their members an advantage through districting?

4. How has the role of political parties in congressional elections changed over time? How did congressional incumbents help change this role? How did the 1994 and 2006 elections change the prevailing pattern of electoral competition?

5. Why do members of Congress worry about reelection when incumbents are so consistently successful at winning another term? Why do incumbents work so hard to appear invulnerable?

6. What impact do national forces have on a member's chances for reelection?

7. What is the difference between a member being responsive and a member being responsible? How does the method of election help foster one behavior over the other?

8. Why is it so difficult for Congress to put the interest of the public above special interests?

What strategies can members use to overcome these difficulties?

9. Why did the Tax Reform Act of 1986 pass when other similar attempts had failed in the past?

10. Why weren't members of Congress allowed the chance to vote on censuring President Bill Clinton?

11. What are the different types of committees used in Congress and why might they matter?

12. Why does the House have stricter rules and greater leadership control than does the Senate? How do these differences affect the day-to-day operation of the chambers?

13. If members are elected by majorities from their districts, why do interest groups sometimes prevail, even in conflicts with majority opinion?

Exercises

Good Districts Make Good Neighbors

The president, your two state senators, your state's governor, and your district's member of Congress all represent you in government. Are all five politicians members of the same party? Do they appear to be similar ideologically? Use the Census Bureau's address search feature (go to www.census.gov, click on American FactFinder in the navigation bar, and then look for the button "Address Search") to look up available 2000 census data for your home and/or school address. Then compare the demographics of your congressional district (about the eighth item down on the list of results) with those of your state (the top item on the list) and with those of the country as a whole (www.census.gov/census2000/states/us.html). How similar are the characteristics of the three groups? How well might they explain any differences in the characteristics of the members elected from those districts? Which district do you think best "represents" you as a voter?

It's Good to Be the Incumbent

Go to the Federal Election Commission's Summary Report Search site (www.fec.gov/finance/disclosure/srssea.shtml). Select your state and congressional district. Compare the contributions to candidates running for office in your district in 2008. If the race had an incumbent, did he or she receive more contributions than did the challenger? By what amount or percentage? Where did each candidate get most of his or her money: donations from indi-viduals, other committees, or personal funds? How much cash on hand did each candidate still have at the end of the campaign? Who won the election? Go to the FEC's 2008 House campaign summaries. Based on the contributions to candidates in your state, in how many cases did the candidate with less cash on hand lose the general election? (See general election results at http://cnn.com/ELECTION/2008.) Did close fund-raising totals seem to translate into close election outcomes?

The Presidency

What happened historically to transform the president from the "chief clerk" of the government (Abraham Lincoln's job description) to a formidable politician whose preferences must be taken into account?

All modern presidents seek the public's support for their policies. But does their ability to sway public opinion really help them in dealing with other politicians in Washington, and if so, how?

Does the growth of the "institutional presidency" risk transforming America's executive into an isolated, imperial office?

In the aftermath of the Abu Ghraib prisoner abuse scandal and continuing controversy over the use of waterboarding and other extraordinary interrogation techniques to extract information from terrorist suspects, a group of Democratic and Republican senators introduced the Detainee Treatment Act in 2005. Facing a certain George W. Bush veto, Senate leaders incorporated the bill as a rider in the 2006 appropriations legislation. Following serious negotiation between the Senate sponsors and the White House, the two sides eventually compromised on language that the senators viewed as satisfying their objective to clean up interrogation methods. In December President Bush signed the legislation into law. The sponsors' elation over striking a deal was cut short when the president issued the following statement when he signed the bill:

> The executive branch shall construe . . . the Act, relating to detainees, in a manner consistent with the constitutional authority of the President to supervise the unitary executive branch and as Commander in Chief and consistent with the constitutional limitations on the judicial power . . . which will assist in achieving the shared objective of the Congress and the President . . . of protecting the American people from further terrorist attacks.

What does this statement mean, and why did it disturb Senate sponsors enough to call a press conference to condemn it? On its face, the statement reads like a truism. Presidents need not announce that they will abide by the Constitution in implementing a new law. But Bush's statement signaled something quite different to legislators,

President George W. Bush signs into law the "Departments of Labor, Health and Human Services, and Education, and Related Agencies Appropriations Act, 2006" from the family ranch in Crawford, Texas, on December 30, 2005. This was the same day he signed the Detainee Treatment Act.

pundits, and political scientists. With the references to the president's commander-in-chief responsibilities and the "unitary executive," President Bush informed Congress that he would follow the new limitations on interrogation to the extent he saw fit.

President Bush similarly claimed **unitary executive** prerogatives in **signing statements** attached to nearly a hundred bills during his first term. In each instance, he asserted his right to modify implementation or to ignore altogether provisions of the new law that encroached on his constitutional prerogatives as "the chief executive" or as commander in chief. In the past, presidents have occasionally questioned a bill's provisions during signing ceremonies. In some instances, they cited contradictory implications within the bill or between one of its provisions and current law. Infrequently, presidents have averred that they might not enforce the new law based on constitutional objections, usually concerning federalism or civil liberties issues. Rarely, if ever, have presidents objected to bills they signed for encroaching on their executive authority. In sum, although Bush's statements were not altogether unprecedented in raising constitutional issues, they arguably constitute the strongest effort by a president to unilaterally expand the power of the office.

So, when and where did this unitary executive notion originate? Until President Bush invoked it as if it were established doctrine, few politicians and presidential scholars had heard of this novel doctrine. It was not President Bush's brainchild. For the past several decades a small group of legal scholars, many of them working at conservative think tanks, had constructed a case for the unitary executive. According to the unitary executive argument, the Framers gave presidents far more command authority than past presidents and those who deal with them realized. With respect to administration, the unitary executive holds that presidents may remove all subordinates in the executive branch; they may also direct these subordinates to take a particular action; and finally, they can veto any objectionable actions, including those mandated by Congress. If the unitary executive doctrine were to prevail, the president presumably could rescind any of the thousands of specific mandates, requirements, and obligations that federal law places on the heads of federal departments and agencies.

A long-standing devotee of this mostly academic exercise was Vice President Dick Cheney, who as a young man had served as President Gerald Ford's White House chief of staff at a time when Congress appeared determined to weaken the presidency in the wake of the Watergate scandal. Another outspoken proponent of the unitary executive sits on the Supreme Court.* In a 1988 ruling that upheld the insulation of special prosecutors from presidential removal, Justice Antonin Scalia alone dissented. His opinion became scripture for the proponents of a unitary executive in the Bush administration:

> The Constitution provides, "The executive Power shall be vested in a President of the United States." . . . This does not mean *some* of the executive power, but *all* of the executive power. . . . It is not for us to determine, and we have never presumed to determine, how much of the purely executive powers of government must be within the full control of the President. The Constitution prescribes that they *all* are.[1]

Scalia's argument may appear to clarify the issues by moving all gray areas of jurisdiction to the president's side of the ledger, but it actually introduces great uncertainty over the scope of the president's command authority. Does all executive power refer to that authority specifically conferred by the Constitution and public laws or does it mean all decisions that are executive in nature? In 1974, President Richard Nixon decided that some appropriations already signed into law no longer squared with his policy to fight inflation by reducing government spending. So, he *impounded* previously appropriated money by instructing the Treasury Department to withhold funds from the agencies responsible for implementing the programs. Disbursement of appropriated funds is quintessentially an executive action, but it is also a policy decision the Constitution explicitly delegates to Congress. Can the president legally withhold funds? Members of Congress howled in protest and the agencies in line to receive the funds went to various federal district courts to force the president to release impounded funds. Before the president relented, several federal district courts ruled for the plaintiffs in lawsuits challenging President Nixon's actions. Congress subsequently enacted the Budget and Impoundment Act of 1974 severely limiting the president's power to freeze spending without congressional consent. Does Scalia's opinion imply that the courts and Congress had trespassed into the executive's domain?

Against this notion are stacked a mountain of long-standing federal statutes and judicial rulings imposing obligations on agency heads that would appear to insulate them from presidential intrusion. Federal laws generally provide fixed terms for heads of independent agencies such as the Federal Reserve and the Food and Drug Administration (described in Chapter 8). Numerous other laws stipulate that an agency head or some other officer must report to Congress or even take specified actions if certain conditions or circumstances arise. The $700 billion financial bailout legislation enacted to remedy the credit crisis in the fall of 2008 stipulated that the Treasury Department create and implement limits on corporate executives' compensation and

---

*In 2006 Scalia was joined by Samuel Alito, a colleague who had previously espoused the unitary executive doctrine in opinions while serving as a legal counsel in the Department of Justice.

establish transparent criteria for hiring outside firms to purchase banks' mortgage assets. The legislation also mandated periodic reports to Congress and funded the bailout in stages that required congressional votes.[2] Beyond the capacity for congressional oversight, numerous laws give states and private groups standing in federal courts to challenge administrative decisions, including those taken under direction of the president.

Note that President Bush's statement on the Detainee Treatment Act quoted at the beginning of the chapter also cited his commander-in-chief responsibilities as giving him authority to intervene in administrative decisions. With the nation engaged in ground wars in Iraq and Afghanistan and confronting a terrorist threat globally, this claim could potentially lead to an even more expansive view of presidential authority. One of the more controversial statements (among the many) issued from the Justice Department's Office of Legal Counsel during the Bush presidency was a 2002 opinion that "*Any* effort by Congress to regulate the interrogation of battlefield detainees would violate the Constitution's sole vesting of the Commander-in-Chief authority in the President." In effect, where the president finds a compelling military reason for a course of action, no laws or treaties can prevent him from pursuing it. Opinions like this one, though on shaky legal and constitutional grounds, buttressed Bush's dismissal of the Detainee Treatment Act in the signing statement.*

After more than two centuries of governance under the Constitution, we are still arguing over which institution has the power to make national policy. And President Bush's frequent signing statements asserting the unitary executive remind us that these are not inconsequential, pedantic, scholarly debates. Nor do they concern some narrow band of discretion falling in the interstices between the branches' otherwise clearly defined jurisdictions. Rather, Congress and the president continue to contest a broad swath of government authority.

The persistence of this conflict does not arise from contradictory language in the Constitution. Rather, it reflects the Constitution's silence on key aspects of separation of powers. Chapter 2 noted that the Constitution is a relatively brief blueprint for a national government; wisely, the Framers intentionally left it "incomplete" for future officeholders to fashion and refashion according to national needs. Consider, for instance, how different the modern presidency would have looked had the Constitution limited the presidential staff to two assistants or the army to several thousand troops, as one delegate at the Constitutional Convention actually proposed.†

Nowhere is the Constitution's ambiguity more apparent than in the authority relations between Congress and the presidency. Great, even cataclysmic, historic battles

---

*In a case examined more fully in Chapter 9 a federal appeals court rejected the "sole vesting" notion in ruling in 2008 that the navy must suspend submarine exercises off the Pacific coast because it failed to follow a Marine Mammal Protection Act's requirement that it first assess the effects of the naval exercises on whale migration. In its decision, the court rejected the president's exemption of the navy from this regulation based on his commander-in-chief authority. In November 2008 the Supreme Court ruled in favor of the navy.

†Chapter 9 documents an early resolution to arguably the most serious lacuna in constitutional prescription, judicial review. The Constitution at best only implies it, and contemporaries argued at length over whether the Supreme Court could rule laws and executive actions as unconstitutional.

have been waged in this undefined region. After the Civil War the Republican Congress passed the 1867 Tenure of Office Act to prevent unsympathetic president Andrew Johnson from ending Reconstruction by removing key administration officials without Senate "confirmation." When President Johnson defied Congress and dismissed his war secretary, the House of Representatives quickly impeached the president and the Senate came within a single vote of removing him from office. In the modern era Congress still seeks to extend its authority into the executive domain. Earmarks (see Chapter 6) specify in detail how funds must be spent to accomplish the broad policy goals of a piece of legislation. Dozens of laws include a legislative veto, allowing either or both chambers of Congress to rescind some executive decision (such as a new regulation) by passing a concurrent resolution that is not subject to a veto.*

At the same time, institutional and political divisions of the legislature frequently give presidents an opportunity to stake out policies that opponents in Congress will have a hard time reversing. And if Congress manages to pass a bill altering course, the president may still be able to block it with his veto. Even on appropriations, where Congress appears to enjoy the upper hand—since at the end of the day the president has to sign a bill or shut down the unfunded agencies or programs—the president may still succeed in committing the nation to a policy, effectively obliging Congress to support it. After the Democratic majority took control of Congress in 2007, it sought through a variety of measures to wind down the war in Iraq. After several false starts, Congress finally agreed to attach a rider to a supplemental funding bill for the Iraq War that tied funding to a timetable for withdrawal. Bush promptly vetoed it and demanded a bill with no strings attached. As the date approached when current funds were projected to be depleted, the Democratic Congress and Republican president engaged in a game of chicken. To outsiders Congress appeared to hold the upper hand; if it did nothing, the American military would grind to a halt. Washington's political cognoscenti knew from experience that this prospect would, in fact, force Congress to back down in the face of withering criticism that its inaction would hamstring the ability of troops in the battlefield to defend themselves. Shortly, after a failed veto override attempt, Congress capitulated and gave the president the funds he requested. This case illustrates a broader implication of the unitary executive. Where presidents can change a policy unilaterally, they gain the opportunity to exercise agenda control over Congress's choices. Although unanticipated by the Framers, who sought to have Congress set the president's agenda by having it present bills to the president for his up or down "vote" (that is, the veto), the president's capacity to take the initiative is embedded in the institutional design of the executive and legislative branches.

When presidents try to extend their influence through unilateral actions, opponents are quick to charge that the chief executive is trying to turn the office into an **imperial presidency,** an elected monarch with a retinue of aides to do his bidding. Rarely is this

---

*As noted in Chapter 8, inclusion of the "legislative veto" arises when Congress is delegating new authority to the executive branch but worries that the administration might implement it in a way that Congress opposes. The legislative veto is a favorite presidential target in signing statements, but presidents generally abide by legislative vetoes out of concern that ignoring them might prompt Congress from passing a law removing the authority altogether.

label fair. The expectations of the American people and government officials for modern presidents exceed the explicit authority delegated to the presidency in the Constitution.

As if the job were not hard enough, President Bush appeared to go out of his way to inflame opposition to his policies. Instead of seeking to influence policy through politics—such as compromising and finding common ground with members of Congress—or vetoing the bill in order to negotiate one more to his liking, President Bush repeatedly fired off his unitary executive broadside by signing the bill but singling out objectionable provisions he might not implement. Paradoxically, President Bush pressed his unilateral authority hardest during periods in which he did not need it—when his party controlled both houses of Congress. In 2005 Bush announced that he had the authority to create military commissions to try terrorist suspects being detained in Guantánamo Bay, Cuba. After the Supreme Court rejected his claim of inherent authority to set up new procedures for trying terrorists, he turned to Congress. It responded with the Military Commissions Act of 2006, which created judicial procedures that closely followed the president's preferences.

After the Democratic takeover of both the House and Senate in the 2006 midterm elections, President Bush toned down his rhetoric somewhat. Toward the end of his administration in October 2008, he appeared relieved at the signing of a bitterly contested $700 billion bailout of financial institutions in an effort to stave off a severe economic recession. He made no reference to reserving unitary authority in his signing statement despite the presence of provisions that introduced some of the strictest accountability requirements and congressional oversight procedures of any legislation enacted during his presidency. As his presidency closed, Bush appeared to have gained little advantage from invoking the doctrine. Many of the procedures he propagated unilaterally for detecting terrorists and bringing them to trial were overturned by the courts. Moreover, he rarely followed through on his signing statement threats.* He succeeded mainly in galvanizing his opponents. By the end of his second term, he left the office with few allies in Washington or supporters in the country.

---

*One clear instance occurred in 2008, when citing the unitary executive, Bush instructed the secretary of homeland security to withhold a congressionally mandated report on the number of complaints filed by citizens who felt that some action by the department had violated their civil rights. See Charlie Savage, "Administration to Bypass Reporting Law," *New York Times,* October 25, 2008.

The unitary executive doctrine is unlikely to be accepted any time soon as representing the true meaning of Article II of the Constitution. It contradicts virtually everything we know about the Framers' priorities from the deliberations in Philadelphia and during the subsequent ratification debates. No president has ever come close to actually wielding the kind of authority the doctrine claims. In the early days of the Republic the presidency was a small, diminutive institution. With notable exceptions—George Washington, Andrew Jackson, Abraham Lincoln, and perhaps one or two others, reflecting the personal prestige of the president or the crisis times in which they served—presidents rarely involved themselves with public policy formation or administration of the executive branch. In the historical survey below, the vigorous, problem-solving institution envisioned in "unitary executive" theory does not appear on the national scene until the early twentieth century.

The Historical Presidency

The trick in designing an energetic presidency lies in avoiding a Napoleon, an ambitious individual who would use the temporary advantages conferred by a national crisis to permanently alter the constitutional order. By rejecting a plural office, the Framers accepted the proposition that, unlike the bicameral legislature, the executive would contain none of the internal checks provided by institutional design (described in *Federalist* No. 51) or factions (*Federalist* No. 10). The convention delegates finally solved the dilemma by giving the executive enough resources for coordinating national responses during emergencies but insufficient authority to usurp the Constitution. They achieved this objective—at least to the satisfaction of the majority that enacted Article II—by withholding certain executive powers, such as broad and easily invoked emergency powers that executives in other presidential systems have sometimes employed to get the upper hand over their political opponents. Leadership gravitates toward the office during moments of national urgency, but it does not involve suspension of the constitutional prerogatives belonging to the other institutions, and it is expected to dissipate as the crisis recedes.

During the Republic's first century, presidents typically assumed a small role as a governmental actor. Their accomplishments were mostly limited to their responses to wars, rebellions, and other national crises. In fact, early presidents played a larger role in conferring benefits to their political parties.

On a day-to-day basis, filling vacancies in a growing federal bureaucracy consumed most of nineteenth-century presidents' time. Throughout the century, all federal employees—from the secretary of state to the postmaster in Cody, Wyoming—were appointed directly by the president or one of his agents. Large chunks of presidents' daily calendars were devoted to interviewing job seekers, listening to their party sponsors, and signing appointment letters. And because party colleagues in Congress and national party committees expected their nominees to be appointed, presidents could derive little political advantage from the appointment authority. Rather, it was a thankless task, befitting a clerk. "For every appointment," President Grover Cleveland

Introduced by their member of Congress in return for past political support, job seekers, hats in hand, approach the president for positions in his administration.

observed ruefully, "I make one ingrate and ten enemies." Presidents took special care, however, in naming their cabinets. After all, these department heads represented important factions and interests within the president's party that had to be served if he hoped to win renomination and election and enjoy his party's full support in Congress.

The Era of Cabinet Government

Nineteenth-century Congress routed all matters related to administration and policy through the appropriate department secretary. When a president had a question about a policy, needed clarification on complaints or rumors about an agency head's performance, or sought advice on whether to sign or veto a bill, he consulted his cabinet. Indeed, the nineteenth-century department heads composing the cabinet routinely performed much of the work now carried out by the president's staff. There is not much evidence of the unitary executive in the daily routines of this era's presidents.

Clearly, a strong cabinet did not necessarily make for a strong president. Cabinet appointees, who were resourceful, independent, and frequently ambitious politicians, could not be expected to subordinate their own welfare to that of their titular leader. An adviser to President Warren G. Harding may have only slightly exaggerated a basic truth in remarking, "The members of the cabinet are the president's natural enemies."[3] Thus, a pattern of intersecting interests characterized president-cabinet relations: presidents selected their department heads for their political assets, such as their influence with a particular wing of a political party in Congress or with the electorate (see box "Lincoln and His Cabinet"). Those who joined the cabinet, however, were likely to pursue their own political and policy objectives and, perhaps incidentally, the president's (if indeed he harbored any). The result was a partnership based not on loyalty but on reciprocity: cabinet members helped the president achieve his limited political goals, and, through the cabinet appointment, he afforded them opportunities to pursue their agendas.

The modern cabinet has lost much of its luster as an attractive office—that is, one with real political clout. Control over policy and even of department personnel has gravitated to the Oval Office. Consequently, whereas ambitious politicians in the nineteenth century saw a cabinet post as a stepping stone to the White House, modern politicians are more likely to view a stint in the cabinet as a suitable terminus to a career in public service.

STRATEGY AND CHOICE

Lincoln and His Cabinet

Upon taking office in 1861, Republican president Abraham Lincoln confronted a nation threatening to dissolve. He also had to contend with a weak, young Republican Party composed of politicians who only recently had coalesced for the sole purpose of defeating the majority Democratic Party. To keep the party coalition together, Lincoln filled his cabinet with Republican leaders, even some of his rivals for the presidency.[1] Secretary of the Treasury Salmon Chase and Secretary of State William Seward, Lincoln's principal rivals for the presidential nomination, strongly disliked each other, but their support within the party and Congress kept both in Lincoln's cabinet.

Other cabinet officials of lesser stature but with impeccable political credentials were Pennsylvania's corrupt party boss and senator Simon Cameron, who was forced to resign the post of secretary of war, and Maryland Republican Party leader Montgomery Blair, who oversaw the patronage-rich Post Office Department. Blair's presence in the cabinet proved critical as he muscled the Maryland state legislature to defeat narrowly a motion calling for Maryland to secede from the Union.

Perhaps the most formidable cabinet member of all was the brusque Edwin Stanton, Cameron's replacement as secretary of war and a leader of

the "war Republicans" in Congress. At times this gave him a veto over policy. "Stanton and I have an understanding," Lincoln wrote a friend. "If I send an order to him which cannot be consistently granted, he is to refuse it. This he sometimes does."[2] Thus by surrendering control over large blocks of the executive branch to these self-interested, strong-willed politicians, President Lincoln succeeded in keeping the fragile Republican majority in Congress behind the unpopular Civil War.

---

1. David Herbert Donald, "Lincoln, The Politician," in *Lincoln Reconsidered: Essays on the Civil War Era* (New York: Random House, 1956).

2. David Herbert Donald, *Lincoln* (London: Jonathan Cape, 1995), 334.

Parties and Elections

For nineteenth-century politicians the political party that controlled the presidency was their paramount concern. Any particular individual could perform the duties of the nineteenth-century presidency—namely, signing appointment letters to the several hundred thousand patronage offices presented to him. Presidential elections were the focal point for the national parties' efforts; after all, whichever party captured the

TABLE 7-1

Nineteenth-Century Newspaper Coverage of Presidents: Heavy Only in Presidential Election Years

Election Year	Percentage of Political News Devoted to	
	President	Congress
1824 (presidential)	43	57
1830 (midterm)	40	60
1840 (presidential)	98	2
1850 (midterm)	16	84
1860 (presidential)	76	24
1870 (midterm)	19	81
1876 (presidential)	70	30

Source: Samuel Kernell and Gary C. Jacobson, "Congress and the Presidency as News in the Nineteenth Century," *Journal of Politics* 49 (November 1987), 1016–1035.

Note: Percentages based on total column inches devoted to Congress (including members and committees) and the president (including cabinet and presidential candidates) by daily newspapers in Cleveland, Ohio, 1824–1876.

presidency won control of federal patronage. Moreover, in this patronage era before election reforms allowed voters privacy and the opportunity to easily vote separately for the different offices, the party that won a state's presidential contest almost invariably gained control of all the other state and local offices on the ticket. (For an example of the nineteenth-century, party-supplied ballot, see page 260.) As a result, the political party that carried the presidency almost always took control of Congress as well.

Presidential candidates were the engines that pulled the party trains. A look at the coverage of the president and Congress by daily newspapers in Cleveland, Ohio, from 1824 to 1876 reveals just how specialized the president's role was during this era (see Table 7-1). In total coverage (measured in column inches) presidents (or presidential candidates) moved to center stage in presidential election years and receded into the background during midterm election years, when they were not on the ballot. In 1840, 98 percent of all stories were centered on the president, and only 2 percent dealt with Congress. Ten years later, in a midterm election year, nearly the opposite was true. Unlike today, when presidents dominate the television network evening news, in the nineteenth century they received little media coverage outside of presidential election campaigns. Congress, not the government's chief clerk, held the spotlight.

At the national party nominating conventions, presidential candidates usually were valued a great deal more for their widespread popular appeal and willingness to distribute patronage according to party guidelines than for their policy pronouncements.* As a result, candidates with little experience in government frequently enjoyed an advantage over established politicians who might be associated with a particular faction of the party or who, as officeholders, had taken controversial positions on divisive national issues. National military heroes—Andrew Jackson, Zachary Taylor, and Ulysses S. Grant, and a number of generals who were nominated but lost—made fine presidential candidates. But for most of those who won, leadership ended on Election Day when their glorified "clerkship" began.

What, then, does the nineteenth-century presidency say about the modern presidency? If the Constitution thrusts command authority on the office, the first century's occupants failed to notice. President Bush's assertion of the office's unfettered constitutional mandate to run the government is about as alien from nineteenth-century practice as one can imagine.

---

*There were, however, a few "litmus test" issues such as the tariff, and during moments of national crisis the president's policy preferences would suddenly matter a great deal—consider Lincoln's position on slavery in the territories in 1860.

Yet the nineteenth-century experience is not wholly divorced from the circumstances in which modern presidents find themselves. Even then, the singular character of the office gave presidents a competitive advantage over other national politicians in attracting the public's attention. Their capacity to serve as a focal point coordinating the efforts of state parties during national elections and occasionally in mobilizing the nation for war offers a glimmer of national leadership that would occur early in the next century.

Arrival of the Modern Presidency

By any measure the national government grew enormously during the twentieth century. Hundreds of government functions once left exclusively to the states and local communities are now administered in Washington. Many other activities that resided beyond the scope of any government are now the routine concerns of some federal agency. Rules and crop subsidies administered by the U.S. Department of Agriculture (USDA) enter into farmers' decisions about how much of which crops to plant; the Occupational Safety and Health Administration regulates the working conditions of farm hands (concerning everything from the availability of toilets to exposure to unsafe chemicals); the Securities and Exchange Commission regulates the farm commodities markets, which establish the prices farmers will be paid for their crops; and a USDA agency inspects food processing and distribution facilities. Many other sectors of the economy involve a similar federal government presence.

Throughout the early twentieth century but especially in responding to the Great Depression and America's entry into the two world wars, presidents assumed administrative responsibilities unimagined a decade earlier. With additional responsibilities, these chief executives generally gained broad discretion in deciding how specifically to implement and administer policies to achieve mandated objectives. Most of the presidents during this era enthusiastically accepted their new role. By the late 1930s the presidency as an organization received a major make-over by designers who believed that only the office's antiquated staffing arrangements prevented presidents from assuming their rightful place as the CEO of the national government.

The Modern Presidency

The following sections assess the president's modern responsibilities against the backdrop of his constitutional authority. Although every aspect of the office's modern development has occurred in tandem, we will for purposes of discussion consider the modern presidency's leadership in three spheres: in international affairs as commander in chief and head of state, as chief executive officer, and as chief legislator. Taken together, these separate responsibilities do not fully account for the forceful character of the presidency that emerged during the mid-twentieth century. Unlike Congress's authority, which is firmly grounded in the Constitution's explicit Article I provisions, much of the presidency's authority remains, as we have already discussed, more ambiguous and contentious. Much of it arises through statutory delegations where changes in law and budgets could erode or even revoke authority presidents take for granted. As a result, presidents are not guaranteed successful leadership. It rests in the final analysis on their skills as politicians, a topic we return to at the conclusion of the chapter.

The President as Commander in Chief and Head of State

With several major European powers occupying territory bordering the United States, and frequently at war with each other, national security and foreign affairs were special concerns of delegates to the Constitutional Convention. The young nation's dismal record in international relations under the Articles of Confederation moved all but the most fearful delegates to charge the presidency with this responsibility. On the home front, the domestic uprising in 1786 by disgruntled Massachusetts farmers, led by Daniel Shays, and the contagion of unrest that it spawned in the other colonies, exposed the Confederation's inability to provide national security.

THE COMMANDER IN CHIEF. The Constitution declares the president to be **commander in chief** of the nation's armed forces. The notion of putting the military under the control of a single individual was difficult for the Framers. One troubled convention delegate proposed limiting the military to no more than five thousand troops, provoking General George Washington to quip sarcastically that the Constitution also should limit invading armies to three thousand.[4] His point made, the Framers settled on a different kind of check on the president's powers as commander in chief: only Congress can declare war.

History and recent experience alike demonstrate that Congress's war declaration authority does not resolve the problem of a president taking the nation into war. Presidents often commit troops and engage in hostilities and then go to Congress for authority to continue. Presidents acting in this sequence can set Congress's agenda for a choice to continue the conflict or desist in such a way that places the legislature in a severe bind. Calls to pull back are branded as abandoning the troops in the field. Even when America's invasion of Iraq was found to have been based on faulty evidence and the conflict was going badly, the Democratic-controlled Congress in 2007 could not collectively bring itself to cut off, or even curtail, funding for the troops.

American history is replete with instances of the president's ability to make the first move and thereby frame Congress's choice to either accept or reject the president's actions, so that in reality the legislature has little choice but to ratify the president's actions. Within six months of the Confederate firing on Fort Sumter in 1861, President Abraham Lincoln suspended the writ of *habeas corpus* that prevented the Union Army from detaining civilians suspected of spying or even just publicly opposing the war effort. He did not consult Congress before acting. Lincoln also approved a naval blockade of southern ports, extended voluntary military enlistment to three years, increased the size of the army and navy, and authorized the purchase of materials, all without congressional sanction or even appropriation. Later, Lincoln justified his actions to Congress by relying exclusively on his authority as commander in chief: "The executive found the duty of employing the war power, in defense of the government, forced upon him. Whether strictly legal or not," he added, these measures "were ventured upon . . . trusting, then as now, that Congress would readily ratify them."[5]

The idea that presidents have the military at their disposal—at least in the short run—remains unchallenged. And Congress's authority to declare war is, in most respects, a hollow check. Neither the Korean War (1950–1953) nor the Vietnam War, which began over a decade later, was ever formally declared.

In 1973, Congress sought to carve out new authority for itself by approving the **War Powers Act** over President Nixon's veto. The law requires the president to inform Congress within forty-eight hours of committing troops abroad in a military action. Moreover, the operation must end within sixty days unless Congress approves an extension. But neither the law's constitutionality nor its effectiveness in limiting the president's military authority has ever been tested. Presidents have continued to commit the military without informing Congress—witness Ronald Reagan's 1983 invasion of Grenada, George H. W. Bush's 1992 deployment of U.S. troops to Somalia as part of a United Nations peacekeeping force, and Bill Clinton's commitment of American forces in the North Atlantic Treaty Organization's 1999 action against Yugoslavia. In fact, since 1989 U.S. armed forces have been almost continuously engaged somewhere in the world (see Figure 7-1). Although members of Congress may question presidents' policies, Congress as an institution has not challenged presidential authority to order an extended military engagement without a declaration of war.* After all, does Congress really want to unwittingly strengthen the resolve of the nation's enemies and further endanger troops in combat, as opponents of such a policy would claim?

When President Bush landed on the aircraft carrier USS *Abraham Lincoln* to greet sailors returning from the Middle East, his arrival was chronicled by all the major broadcast and cable outlets and print media photographers. Widely proclaimed by admirers and critics alike as the "mother of all photo opportunities," cable news networks devoted the rest of the day's airtime to replaying the magnificently choreographed images.

HEAD OF STATE. The Confederation government, consisting of little more than a legislature, also found it difficult to transact foreign affairs. Even routine duties, such as responding to communications from foreign governments, proved to be an ordeal. To promote commerce, the states tried to fill this vacuum, but European merchants and governments were able to pit one state against another in a ruinous competition for markets and trade. The Framers discerned that a single executive would enjoy an inherent advantage over Congress in conducting foreign policy. With some misgivings,

---

*As a result, Congress sometimes finds itself presented with a presidential *fait accompli*. In 1907, for example, a startled Congress learned that President Theodore Roosevelt had sent the entire U.S. fleet on a two-year world cruise intended to impress other nations, especially Japan, with the U.S. resolve to play an active role in world affairs.

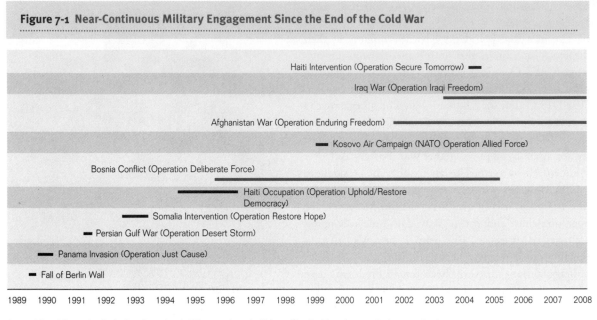

Figure 7-1 Near-Continuous Military Engagement Since the End of the Cold War

Sources: Adapted from a timeline by Dow Jones, Inc. (1999); www.pbs.org/wgbh/pages/frontline/shows/pentagon/etc/cronagon.html.

Notes: End of conflict demarked by end of casualties. Colored bars indicate that military personnel and/or peacekeeping forces are still deployed.

then, they provided the president with broader authority to transact diplomatic affairs than they found desirable on the domestic front.

From the outset, President George Washington interpreted the Constitution's provision "to receive Ambassadors and other public Ministers" to mean that he alone could decide whether the United States would recognize a new government and, accordingly, "receive" its ambassadors. The howls of protest in Congress that greeted this interpretation were echoed in the Capitol a century and a half later when President Harry Truman recognized the state of Israel.

The most important constitutional limitation on the president's leadership in foreign affairs is the requirement that a two-thirds majority of the Senate ratify treaties. At times, the Senate has rebuffed a president's leadership by rejecting a treaty negotiated by the White House. Perhaps the most famous exercise of the Senate's ratification authority occurred at the close of World War I, when that chamber rejected the peace treaty that contained provisions for President Woodrow Wilson's brainchild, the League of Nations. Overall, however, this reservation of authority has proven less consequential than the Framers probably assumed.

To sidestep treaty rejections, presidents sometimes negotiate **executive agreements,** which are exempt from Senate ratification. Unlike treaties, which require ratification from two-thirds of the Senate membership, executive agreements are simply statements of understanding between the administration and a foreign government. They are frequently employed to implement a broader agreement contained in a treaty, but also occasionally to achieve in practice a policy to which Congress would never agree or would rather keep private. During the Vietnam War, Congress discovered that President Lyndon Johnson created a number of executive agreements tendering foreign aid funds to countries that kept token forces in Vietnam.[6] However, executive agreements cannot supersede U.S. law. Congress can pass laws that remove these agreements, and the courts may judge them to violate the Constitution or existing law and void them. But in most instances executive agreements remain "in force" as long as the parties find their interests well served by them. Because they can be changed easily, executive agreements, not treaties, constitute the primary instruments for conducting relations with other countries.

By giving the president full discretion to decide when to stop working through the UN and to invade Iraq, Congress assumed a measure of responsibility for the war's outcome.

The President as Chief Executive

The Framers' deep ambivalence about the kind of executive they wanted is reflected in Article II's rambling provisions for the office. Compared with Article I's detailed development of the structure and powers of Congress, Article II's description of the executive is long on generalities and short on details. It begins by stating, "The executive Power shall be vested in a President of the United States of America." But instead of proceeding to define this power, the article abruptly shifts to a lengthy description of the means of election, qualifications for office, succession procedure, and compensation requirements.

Not until Section 2 does the Constitution confer any real administrative authority. It states that the president may appoint the officers of government "by and with the Advice and Consent of the Senate"—that is, by a majority confirmation vote. Yet, not content with this check on the president's discretion, the Framers immediately qualified this authority by adding, "but the Congress may by Law vest the Appointment of such inferior Officers, as they think proper, in the President alone, in the Courts of Law, or in the Heads of Departments." On the subject of direct administrative authority, Section 2 is more revealing in what it leaves unsaid about the president's administrative powers. At the outset, Section 2 declares simply that from time to time the president may "require the Opinion, in writing, of the principal Officer in each of the executive Departments." Then, as if fully addressing the president's appointment and administrative authority, the Constitution, in Section 3, admonishes the president to "take Care that the Laws be faithfully executed."

But where does the Constitution enumerate the administrative tools presidents need to carry out this mandate? Conspicuously missing is any provision for executive

Contemplating the shock that his successor, General Dwight Eisenhower, would experience in the Oval Office, President Harry Truman remarked, "He'll sit here and he'll say, 'Do this! Do that!' And nothing will happen. Poor Ike—it won't be a bit like the Army. He'll find it very frustrating."

departments or their administrative heads, who later would constitute the president's cabinet. Perhaps the Framers should be applauded for leaving the structure and work of administrative departments wholly to the discretion of future Congresses, to be determined in pace with the nationalization of public policy. This omission, however, obviated any serious consideration of the president's administrative controls. Had the Framers actually created at least some of the easily anticipated "inferior officers" alluded to in the Constitution, more explicit and stronger checks on the executive might have emerged as well. The Framers could have given the president the authority to propose budgets, oversee spending, supervise personnel, and even countermand administrative decisions. These were, after all, among the familiar routine duties of eighteenth-century executives, just as they are for present-day senior administrators, including the president. Instead, in allowing Congress to create the executive branch, the Framers also gave that body the prerogative to establish and subsequently modify what, if any, role the president would play as chief executive.

EXECUTIVE PRIVILEGE. Congress "intruded" on presidents' executive discretion in another important way—by challenging what has come to be called **executive privilege.** This term refers to the president's right to withhold information from Congress and the courts. On this matter the Constitution is silent. When presidents assert this right—and they have done so since George Washington—they argue that it is necessary to maintain separation of powers among the branches of government. In the early years of the Republic, when Presidents Washington, Jefferson, Madison, and Monroe confronted congressional requests for information, they defined executive privilege narrowly, asserting it only when they thought secrecy would serve the national interest.

In the modern era, presidents facing opposition-controlled Congresses—or, worse, special prosecutors who might try to indict them for some crime—have defined executive privilege broadly and invoked it frequently. The only Supreme Court ruling to test the existence and extent of this asserted right came during the Watergate investigations, in which President Nixon claimed executive privilege to avoid surrendering to a prosecutor what eventually proved to be hugely incriminating evidence—secret Oval Office tape recordings. In *United States v. Nixon* (1974) the Court held that the president could not use this privilege to impede criminal investigations. In 1982 President Reagan sought to broaden executive privilege to include any "deliberative processes of the executive branch," even in agencies far removed from the White House and where the president was not personally involved.[7] Reagan eventually backed down in the face of congressional opposition, but twenty years later George W. Bush drew similar opposition for withholding politically charged documents about the role of industry executives in formulating the administration's energy policy. Invoking open meetings laws, Congress's Government Accountability Office joined the Sierra Club in a lawsuit to force President Bush to release the records of these meetings. However, the courts disagreed: first, the Supreme Court rejected the plaintiffs' demands for records in order to press their suit, and in 2005 the U.S. Court of Appeals unanimously rejected the plaintiff's argument as threatening to violate the Constitution's separation of powers.

EXECUTIVE ORDERS. Until the twentieth century, presidents found themselves ill-equipped to intrude into administrative practices and thus rarely did so. Instead, Congress exercised oversight of the bureaucracy by assigning its committees and subcommittees jurisdictions that matched those of the federal departments. Presidents stayed in the background and, except during national crises when they acted on their authority as commander in chief, seldom contested congressional control over the executive departments. To the degree the presidents of that era sought to influence policy, they generally did so informally through their political appointees who ran agencies and departments. They also, on occasion, issued formal instructions called **executive orders.** An executive order has the force of law until the president or a successor retracts it, Congress nullifies it, or a federal court rules it violates either the Constitution or some federal law. The government did not begin retaining and cataloguing executive orders by publishing and assigning them consecutive numbers until 1907; by spring 2008 presidents had issued over 13,500 executive orders.

The vast majority of executive orders arise from the authority and responsibilities explicitly delegated to the president by law. Most frequently they are enlisted to establish executive branch agencies, modify administrative rules or actions, change decision-making procedures, and give substance and force to statutes (see box "Presidents Making Policy: Executive Orders Address a Variety of Issues"). For example, the Pendleton Act of 1883 inaugurated the civil service system for federal employees by converting about 10 percent of the federal workforce from political patronage positions to merit appointments based on examinations (see Chapter 8). This law also authorized the president to issue executive orders extending the civil service system to other classes of workers. Over the next half-century, presidents signed executive orders that shifted hundreds of thousands of employees from political patronage positions into the civil service system.

A much smaller class of executive orders is based not on some explicit congressional delegation but on presidents' assertions of authority implicit in the Constitution's mandate that the president "take Care that the Laws be faithfully executed." Not until the twentieth century did presidents begin seriously to entertain the notion that this **"take care" clause** might give them more authority than their predecessors had claimed. Early-twentieth-century president Theodore Roosevelt was the first to subscribe to this expansive view of the office. "The most important factor in getting the right spirit in my administration," wrote Roosevelt, reflecting on his term, "was my insistence upon the theory that the executive power was limited only by specific

Presidents Making Policy
Executive Orders Address a Variety of Issues

September 1997   Directed federal agencies to use existing programs to help communities refurbish waterfronts and improve water quality in selected rivers.

February 1998   Applied the patient's "bill of rights" to all federal health programs.

Created a White House council to coordinate efforts to fix the Y2K (year 2000) problem.

May 1998   Extended federal workforce affirmative action guidelines to cover sexual orientation.

June 1998   Directed federal agencies to avoid any action that would degrade the condition of coral reef ecosystems within U.S. waters.

November 2002   Delegated to attorney general authority to detain undocumented Caribbean aliens at Guantánamo Bay until admission is decided.

March 2003   Confiscated blocked funds held in U.S. banks by Iraqi banks and government agencies for eventual disbursement to Iraqi people.

June 2004   Directed the Small Business Administration and the Veterans Affairs and Commerce Departments to create centers for faith-based initiatives to expand participation of religious organizations in their grants programs.

April 2006   Blocked property of persons in connection with the conflict in Sudan's Darfur region.

July 2007   Interpreted the Geneva Conventions Common Article 3 as applied to a program of detention and interrogation operated by the CIA.

February 2008   Improved the coordination and effectiveness of youth programs.

Note: All executive orders are listed in the following government Web site: www.archives.gov/federal-register/executive-orders/.

restrictions and prohibitions appearing in the Constitution or imposed by Congress in its constitutional powers."[8]

This doctrine bears some resemblance to the general authority extended to Congress by the "necessary and proper" clause (Article I, Section 8)—an "elastic" authority Congress invoked frequently during the twentieth century to broaden its sphere of action (see Chapter 2). The big difference, however, is that Congress's authority is explicitly stated ("The Congress shall have Power . . ."), whereas the admonition to the president to "take Care" sounds more like a job description. In lawsuits challenging presidents' broad use of executive orders, federal courts have at times interpreted this authority as clearly justifying a president's action; at other times they have rejected presidential claims. In 2001 President Bush relied on his inherent authority when he issued an uncontroversial order creating the White House Office of Homeland Security, which would "develop and coordinate the implementation of a comprehensive national strategy to secure the United States from terrorist threats or attacks."

The President as Administrator

Given the conspicuous absence from the Constitution of any real administrative authority for the president, it was by no means obvious that the growth of the national government would enhance the president's control over public policy. Congress could have kept the president at bay, as it often did in the nineteenth century, by insisting that executive agencies report directly to congressional oversight committees. But as the obligations of government mounted, oversight began to tax Congress's time and resources and interfere with its ability to deliberate new policy. So instead of excluding the chief executive from administration, Congress found its interests best served by delegating to the White House a sizable share of administration and, necessarily, the policy discretion that goes with it. The fact that the same political party generally controlled the legislative and executive branches made it easier for Congress to transfer administration to the president. Given the scale of growth in the number and variety of federal programs during the twentieth century, Congress really had no practical alternative. The rise of presidential leadership has, as a consequence, tracked the growth of the national government.

DELEGATION. By delegating to the president and the appointed executive branch the discretion to decide how best to implement and adjust policy to achieve its objectives, Congress shares a substantial amount of its lawmaking powers with the president. As early as 1950, a survey found that over 1,100 public laws delegated discretionary authority to the White House.[9] If such a survey were undertaken today, the number would, of course, be far larger. As indispensable as the presidency is for administering the panoply of government programs, the president is a tricky agent for Congress to delegate to. The presidency is a constitutional office largely insulated from congressional control; the veto alone provides presidents with a powerful lever to resist congressional efforts to tightly prescribe how to administer programs. Moreover, with presidents separately elected and frequently representing a different political party than the one that controls Congress, presidents may have little stake in serving as dutiful agents. "Let anyone make the laws of the country, if I can construe them," President William Howard Taft once remarked.[10] A legislature that delegates too much discretion to a president may find it difficult to regain control.

In writing public laws and fine-tuning them through the legislative language that accompanies annual appropriations, Congress can choose to delegate more or less rulemaking authority to the president. If it opts for too little, it freezes policy until the next act of Congress and may leave rigid programs that fail to respond to changing conditions. If, however, Congress delegates too much discretion to the executive, it may surrender control over important implementation decisions that could alter the intent of the legislation. In 1980 Congress erred in that direction when it passed the Paperwork Reduction Act, designed, as its name implies, to reduce the forms clogging the federal government and irritating citizens. Soon after entering office, President

Ronald Reagan, acting on his delegated power to implement the law, enlisted it to block congressionally mandated regulations he did not like. When the U.S. Department of Health and Human Services proposed a survey of Americans' sexual practices to better understand and combat the AIDS epidemic, Reagan invoked the act to stop the department from printing the surveys.

At times, Congress delegates not from programmatic necessity but to gain political advantage. When legislators agree on the goals of a bill but disagree on its specifics, they may deliberately swathe its intent in vague language—thereby delegating broad authority to the executive branch—to secure majority support. At other times, members of Congress may find political advantage in delegating to the president broad responsibility for policies that might have politically unattractive outcomes. In such instances, legislators "pass the buck" and hope to avoid blame. In the 1970s, for example, the principle that endangered species should be protected aroused far less controversy than any particular plan to achieve it. To avoid negative repercussions, Congress delegated to the U.S. Fish and Wildlife Service the discretion to establish criteria for classifying species as "endangered" and "threatened." Years later, when the service listed the northern spotted owl as a threatened species and limited the logging industry's access to Oregon's old-growth forests, the industry vented its anger at the agency and President George H. W. Bush—not Congress. Not only did members of Congress escape retribution, but they also won some credit for subsequently softening the economic blow by passing a law that permitted timber companies to harvest fallen trees.

As we have noted, as attractive as delegation may be, it always entails costs of one form or another. One must monitor agents' performance to ensure that they are vigorously pursuing prescribed tasks. Another cost occurs when agents use their delegated discretion to shift policy in an undesirable direction. These costs can be high when the agent is the president. Congress does not hire, nor can it easily fire, this agent. And because of the threat of a veto, Congress might find its hands tied when trying to alter how a policy is administered or to rein in a president determined to take a program in a direction different from the one Congress intended.

BUDGETING. Presidents carry out one of their most important "clerical" tasks when they formulate and send to Congress the annual budget for all federal programs. Yet budgeting also offers them an opportunity to set the spending priorities of the federal government. In fact, this authority exists because Congress long ago insisted that presidents assume responsibility for the government's bookkeeping. Until the 1920s, agencies sent their budget requests directly to the House Appropriations Committee, which held hearings, determined appropriations, and passed them on to the chamber for a vote and then over to the Senate for its consideration. During this process, no one formally solicited the president's views. But when the flow of department and agency budgets began to congest the legislative process, Congress in 1921 passed the Budget and Accounting Act, which gave the president responsibility for compiling budgets from the executive departments and submitting them to lawmakers as a single package. With this act Congress found itself strengthening the president's role in national policymaking.

The president's annual budget, submitted to Congress on the first Monday in February, represents months of assembling and negotiating requests from the agencies to bring them into conformity with the White House's policy goals and proposed spending ceiling. Some years, the president's budget has sailed through Congress with minimal changes. Other years, Congress has ignored the president's proposals and written a wholly "congressional" budget, daring the chief executive to veto it. As we will see later in the chapter, presidential and congressional budgets can differ so much that compromise becomes a test of political will.

The president's budget provides Congress with valuable technical and political information. Running into hundreds of pages, it supplies congressional committees with economic forecasts, projected tax revenues, baseline spending estimates for each department broken down by program, and other essential information for devising spending and taxation legislation. Politically the budget represents the president's "opening bid" in negotiations over how much the government should spend on particular programs and where the revenue will come from. From the early 1980s until the late 1990s, annual deficits forced politicians in both branches to concentrate on spending cuts or tax increases, unpalatable either to the beneficiaries of retrenched programs or to taxpayers. When the president made the first move in his budget, Congress could shed some of the political costs associated with trimming popular programs. In 1997, however, President Bill Clinton turned the tables on Congress. He sent to Capitol Hill a budget that targeted savings on Medicare but shied away from identifying cuts to achieve the savings. The Republican-controlled budget committees first denounced and later pleaded with administration officials to pinpoint where they would like the cuts to be made. The president had effectively passed the buck. Congress, facing the next deadline on the budget calendar, was forced to increase premiums and reduce benefits to bring the program's finances into conformity with the blueprint for balancing the budget.

CENTRALIZED ADMINISTRATION. Through delegation, Congress has "pushed" work—and, with it, considerable discretionary authority—toward the presidency. Presidents have tried to pull control over policy into the White House as well. Their efforts may take the form of unilateral assertions of authority, but as we found with President George W. Bush's experience, these moves may meet with mixed and temporary success since they are based solely on claims that Congress and the courts might later reject. Or the president might try to reroute the flow of information within the executive branch or between it and Congress to make sure that his preferences are inserted in others' decisions. The rest of this section describes how three presidents, decades apart, tried to extend their authority by centralizing administration.

Congress rapidly rejected these presidential efforts to centralize power by passing sweeping legislation that prohibited anyone from interfering in communication between federal employees and Capitol Hill. Given this principal's need to ferret out problems within the bureaucracy that agency heads might try to conceal, legislators do, from time to time, reinforce the free flow of information from the bureaucracy, most recently in the Whistleblower Protection Act (1989), which protects employees who report waste and corruption to Congress.

Theodore Roosevelt, who succeeded assassinated president William McKinley in 1901 and then went on to win the 1904 election, dedicated himself to refashioning the executive branch and exerting control over administration. In 1902 he issued an executive order prohibiting all federal employees from communicating with Congress, "either directly or indirectly, individually or through associations, to solicit an increase of pay or to influence or to attempt to influence in their own interest any other legislation." His handpicked successor, William Howard Taft, extended the so-called **gag rule** to cover "congressional action of any kind" and barred workers from responding to congressional requests for information except as authorized by their department heads.[11] Moreover, these choices placed the president at the forefront of efforts to propose future policy changes.

In 1939 Franklin Roosevelt approached the same goal but somewhat differently and with greater success. Citing his statutory responsibility to prepare the annual budget, the president, through an executive order, required that all department communications to Congress that could affect future budgets first be cleared as consistent with the president's policy by the Bureau of the Budget (today's Office of Management and Budget, or OMB). Unlike the gag rule, Roosevelt's order has endured, and today **central clearance** is a standard procedure for agency officials heading to Capitol Hill to give testimony.[12] The clearance procedure has strengthened the president's hand in national policy, but not because it prevents agencies from communicating to Congress their policy differences with the president. (In fact, Congress can easily probe agency representatives when they testify at congressional hearings.) Rather, it stops officials from casually expropriating the president's endorsement for their legislative initiatives. Central clearance also alerts the White House early to attempted end runs in which an agency might seek more money and statutory authority than the president favors.*

In the third and more recent case, the president enlisted the mechanisms of central clearance for quite a different purpose. Elected in 1980 on a promise "to get the government off the backs of business," President Reagan, upon entering office, issued an executive order instructing all federal agencies to submit any new regulations or rules to OMB for a cost-benefit analysis. The reduced heft of the *Federal Register*, which lists proposed regulations, offers evidence of his success at curbing new rules; between 1980 and 1987 it shrank from eighty-seven thousand pages a year to fewer than fifty thousand.[13] Angered by this mechanism to block enforcement of various laws, the Democratic-controlled House voted to cut off funding for the OMB agency that administered regulatory reviews. The Senate entertained legislation to reorganize this presidential agency and subject the officer who administered oversight to Senate confirmation. After negotiations, Congress and the White House informally agreed that OMB would relax its clearance rules and Congress would withhold legislative action.

---

*Yet Congress may curb even this administrative prerogative. For example, in 1982, during a Republican administration, House Democrats pushed a law through Congress that prevented OMB from revising or delaying submissions of certain mandated agency reports to Congress. Morton Rosenberg, "Congress's Prerogative over Agencies and Agency Decisionmakers: The Rise and Demise of the Reagan Administration's Theory of the Unitary Executive," *George Washington Law Review* 57 (January 1989).

In these cases, the farther the presidents reached, the stronger the resistance from those whose own prerogatives were invaded by the innovation. The gag rule lasted less than a decade, and although both forms of central clearance introduced by Franklin Roosevelt and Ronald Reagan have become accepted procedure, they are exercised within negotiated bounds and are subject to numerous legislated exceptions. Congress has signaled clearly that a president who seeks to extract too much control from these practices is likely to lose them.

The President as Legislator

The Constitution gives presidents only a modest role in the legislative arena. They may call Congress into special session (little used, since the modern Congress is nearly always in session) and, most important, veto laws passed by Congress. Presidents also arc called on to report "from time to time" to the legislative branch on the state of the Union. Yet modern presidents, acting on the expectations of the public, the media, their parties, and even Congress, try to direct American policy by establishing a legislative agenda and doing everything they can to persuade lawmakers to pass it.

The adage coined by President Franklin Roosevelt that "the president proposes, Congress disposes" aptly describes an important aspect of modern presidential leadership—one that the Framers did not envision when they placed the president at the end of the legislative process. However, the growth in the president's administrative duties, accompanied by congressional delegations of discretion, has ensured that Congress will give a chief executive's legislative proposals serious consideration. As noted above, Congress begins deliberating the all-important annual budget only after the president has submitted spending and taxation proposals for the next fiscal year, with planned expenditures broken down for each federal agency. More generally, lawmakers expect the president to advise them about problems with current policy and administration and to recommend adjustments to improve performance. Presidents—and their appointees who administer federal agencies—enjoy an informational advantage, inherent in all delegation, that may also give them an advantage when proposing legislation. At times, presidents can improve their chances of legislative success by selectively withholding information from legislators who prefer some policy they oppose. In a variety of ways, modern presidents' central role in administration assures them a major role in the legislative process. Consequently, about 90 percent of presidents' initiatives are considered by some congressional committee or subcommittee.[14]

This does not mean, however, that presidents have an easy time with Congress. Some years a president submits a budget and it is accepted with only minor tinkering. At other times Congress mostly ignores the president's proposal. In 1984 a prominent Democratic chair of a House budget committee tersely pronounced Republican Ronald Reagan's budget to be "DOA" ("dead on arrival"). Whether presidents can take advantage of their formal agenda-setting opportunities to shape public policy depends on Congress's receptivity to their recommendations.

In assembling support for their legislation, presidents begin with their party allies in Congress. These men and women will want their party leader to succeed, but this does not mean they will bow before the president's wishes. Members of Congress must, after all, attend to the interests of their constituents. Presidents cultivate the support of fellow partisans in Congress in many ways designed to strengthen members' standing back home. These include advocating spending on programs and public works (such as highways and water treatment plants) for a district or state, appointing a member's congressional aide as an agency head, and visiting a lawmaker's district to generate local enthusiasm and financing for the next reelection campaign. (President Bill Clinton's prowess as a party fund-raiser is described in Chapter 12; see box "The President as Party Coordinator.") Moreover, politicians in the White House and the two chambers of Congress follow the dictates of different electoral calendars. Consequently presidents routinely confer with their party's congressional leaders to determine which issues and stances attract support and to decide when to schedule presidential initiatives. The president's fellow partisans in Congress, conversely, do what they can to support their leader. Their shared party label might cause voters' assessments of the president's success to affect their own fortunes in the next election.

Mutual accommodation requires effort, but the incentives for partisans in Congress and the White House to cooperate are powerful. In President Clinton's last year in office, Democrats supported his publicly stated position in roll-call votes 89 percent of the time in the Senate and 73 percent in the House. Impressive statistics, to be sure, but during his first year in office, Clinton's successor, George W. Bush, managed to do even better, enjoying fellow Republican support at 94 percent and 86 percent in the Senate and House, respectively.

None of these incentives to cooperate is present in the president's relations with legislators from the opposition party. Indeed, opposition partisans in Congress correctly recognize that the president's legislative success might very well debit their vote count in the next election. Although no one wants to be perceived by voters as blocking the chief executive's initiatives for narrow partisan advantage, opposition party members have a stake in defeating the administration when they disagree with its policies and in co-opting credit for passage of those initiatives with which they agree. As a consequence, opposition members' roll-call votes on average line up with the president's position less than half the time.

UNIFIED VERSUS DIVIDED PARTY CONTROL OF GOVERNMENT. One implication of the shared political stakes of fellow partisans in Congress and the presidency is that when presidents find their party in majority control of the House and the Senate, they have excellent prospects for passing their legislative agenda. Twice during the twentieth century presidents enjoyed huge majorities in both chambers. The legislative floodgates opened and a broad array of new social policies poured out of Congress. The first set of programs, known as the New Deal, occurred in the early 1930s as President Franklin Roosevelt and congressional Democrats sought to ameliorate the Great Depression. The second, which we have already encountered in Chapter 4, was Lyndon Johnson's Great Society policies during the mid-1960s.

Conversely, during **divided government,** when the party in opposition to the president's controls either or both legislative chambers, the president confronts majorities with different policy preferences and a political stake in making him look bad to voters. In this situation, neither side is willing to compromise, and in the resulting **gridlock** the government accomplishes little and may even come to a halt. This chapter later examines a classic case of gridlock, the budget confrontation between President Clinton and the Republican Congress that briefly padlocked most federal agencies in the fall of 1995.

For most of American history, party control was unified across the legislative and presidential branches. The winning presidential candidate customarily pulled his party's congressional candidates into office on his electoral coattails. Table 7-2 shows that during the last seventy-seven years, however, unified party control has been the exception rather than the rule. Of the thirty-two Congresses since the end of World War II, nineteen have experienced divided party control. (Chapter 12, Political Parties, considers the various causes for this development.) Only for the first of President Clinton's four Congresses did Democrats enjoy unified control. President George W. Bush began with unified Republican government and took advantage of it to keep his campaign promise of a tax cut. Immediately thereafter, however, Sen. James Jeffords switched from Republican to independent, and the Senate's razor-thin Republican majority (based on the vice president's authority to break tie votes) flipped to an equally narrow Democratic majority (see Chapter 6). For the remainder of the decade almost every combination of party control of these branches occurred. In 2002 Republicans solidified their power, then lost control of the Senate. In 2008 it was the Democrats' turn to unify party control of government.

And how do modern presidents deal with an opposition Congress? As relations with Congress become uncooperative, presidents necessarily rely more heavily on their constitutional and other unilateral resources. Vetoes and threats to veto may become a critical asset in forcing the legislature to pay attention to the president's preferences. All presidents have at times responded to an opposition Congress by pulling decisions into the White House; this includes heavy reliance on executive orders, centralized administration, and broad assertions of executive privilege.

TABLE 7-2

The Growth of Divided Government, 1928–2008

Election Year	President	House of Representatives	Senate
1928	R (Hoover)	R	R
1930	R (Hoover)	D	R
1932	D (Roosevelt)	D	D
1934	D (Roosevelt)	D	D
1936	D (Roosevelt)	D	D
1938	D (Roosevelt)	D	D
1940	D (Roosevelt)	D	D
1942	D (Roosevelt)	D	D
1944	D (Roosevelt)	D	D
1946	D (Truman)	R	R
1948	D (Truman)	D	D
1950	D (Truman)	D	D
1952	R (Eisenhower)	R	R
1954	R (Eisenhower)	D	D
1956	R (Eisenhower)	D	D
1958	R (Eisenhower)	D	D
1960	D (Kennedy)	D	D
1962	D (Kennedy)	D	D
1964	D (Johnson)	D	D
1966	D (Johnson)	D	D
1968	R (Nixon)	D	D
1970	R (Nixon)	D	D
1972	R (Nixon)	D	D
1974	R (Ford)	D	D
1976	D (Carter)	D	D
1978	D (Carter)	D	D
1980	R (Reagan)	D	R
1982	R (Reagan)	D	R
1984	R (Reagan)	D	R
1986	R (Reagan)	D	D
1988	R (G. H. W. Bush)	D	D
1990	R (G. H. W. Bush)	D	D
1992	D (Clinton)	D	D
1994	D (Clinton)	R	R
1996	D (Clinton)	R	R
1998	D (Clinton)	R	R
2000	R (G. W. Bush)	R	D*
2002	R (G. W. Bush)	R	R
2004	R (G. W. Bush)	R	R
2006	R (G. W. Bush)	D	D**
2008	D (Obama)	D	D

Source: Harold W. Stanley and Richard G. Niemi, *Vital Statistics on American Politics, 2007–2008* (Washington, D.C.: CQ Press, 2007).

Note: Blue type indicates divided government.

*Democrats gained control of the Senate after Vermont senator James Jeffords switched from Republican to independent (voting with the Democrats) in May 2001, breaking the 50–50 tie left by the 2000 elections.
**The Senate had 49 Democrats, 49 Republicans and two independents.

Figure 7-2 Presidential Use of the Veto

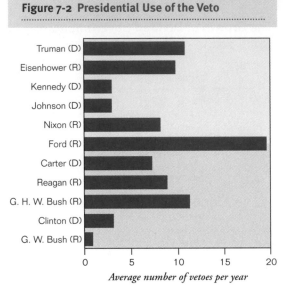

Average number of vetoes per year

Sources: Various issues of *CQ Almanac, CQ Weekly.*

Moreover, presidents carefully screen appointees to head federal agencies to ensure that they delegate discretion to administrators who will remain loyal and responsive in the face of interest groups' entreaties and opposition party pressure in Congress.

THE VETO. Perhaps the president's most formidable tool in dealing with Congress is the veto. The Framers, ever alert to opportunities to introduce "checks and balances," were already familiar with the concept of an executive veto, exercised by most state governors. Unlike the president's administrative powers in Article II, Section 2, the veto authority is defined quite precisely by the Constitution. (See section "Making Laws" in Chapter 6, where the place of the veto in the legislative process is described in detail.) Over the past half-century, presidents have averaged fewer than ten vetoes a year. The record belongs to Republican president Gerald Ford. Although he served less than one full term (from August 1974 until January 1977), Ford vetoed sixty-six bills (see Figure 7-2). In the 1976 election he campaigned on his veto record, claiming that only a Republican in the White House would stand between hard-earned taxpayer dollars and the "spendthrift" Democratic Congress. Only twelve of Ford's vetoes were overridden, even though the Democrats commanded large majorities in both the House and the Senate. Thus Ford won many of the battles, but he lost the war—the election.

The Framers frequently referred to the veto as a "negative"—an appropriate characterization of this inherently conservative instrument. The veto allows presidents to block Congress, but it does not permit them to substitute their own policy preferences. Moreover, unlike most negotiating settings where each side must agree to a joint outcome, Congress acts first. That vetoes are reactive—a response to "take it or leave it" proposals from Congress—limits a president's ability to shape policy. Later in this chapter we will see how modern presidents frequently try (with some success) to get Congress to anticipate a possible veto as it drafts new legislation (see box "The Brief Life of the Line-Item Veto").

Especially when dealing with an opposition Congress, presidents often enlist their veto authority. The veto offers presidents a clear, self-enforcing means of asserting their preferences. Moreover, as Alexis de Tocqueville first observed in 1836, the public nature of the veto—frequently boosted by accompanying messages—enhances it as "a sort of appeal to the people," which modern presidents have not been shy about invoking whenever they discern public backing for their stands.[15] Earlier we noted that the Framers carefully tailored the president's veto authority to achieve a couple of seemingly contradictory goals: to install a check capable of stalling legislative abuses

The Brief Life of the Line-Item Veto

Presidents confronted with omnibus legislation containing numerous unrelated parts must decide whether to sign or veto the entire bill. Frequently, thanks to logrolling, such legislation includes tax breaks or spending measures that benefit one or more narrow constituencies. In 1996 the Republican Congress, seeking to restrain these special-interest expenses, enacted the Line Item Veto Act. The act allowed the president, within five days of signing a bill into law, to reject spending provisions and tax breaks that affected less than a hundred persons or entities. Congress can repass these provisions with a simple majority vote, but the president can veto them as well, requiring Congress to override with a two-thirds vote.

In 1997, the first year the **line-item veto** was in effect, President Clinton used it to strike eighty-two items out of eleven bills. He claimed he saved the nation about $1 billion by eliminating narrow tax breaks, a special provision to help New York finance its Medicaid program, and local military construction projects. In June 1998 the Supreme Court, in a 6–3 decision, struck down the line-item veto as violating the Constitution's separation of powers doctrine. The Court reasoned that the Line Item Veto Act authorized the president to change a law passed by Congress into one whose text had not been voted on by either house of Congress or presented to the president. Thus the majority opinion ruled that the law was unconstitutional. Today some form of the line-item veto remains an important instrument of budgetary control for forty-three of the states' fifty governors.

Source: Andrew Taylor, "Few in Congress Grieve as Justices Give Line-Item Veto the Ax," *CQ Weekly,* June 27, 1998.

while continuing to deny the executive the unilateral authority that, throughout history, had proven so injurious to the welfare of ordinary citizens. The veto, with its strong but exclusively negative quality, seemed to meet both objectives. The Framers failed to appreciate fully how a skilled politician in the White House could use the threat of this endgame option to manipulate Congress's expectations about the likely result of alternative legislative packages, and thereby insert his policy preferences into legislation at an early stage of the process.

The record of presidential-congressional relations under modern divided party control of government indicates that the Framers were only partly correct. The veto certainly does not allow presidents to dictate policy, but it does normally require Congress to take into account the president's preferences as legislation is written. Lawmakers need concede only the minimum number of provisions necessary to present the president with a bill more attractive to the administration than the status quo, or the current policy. Whether the veto offers the president great or little influence over public policy often depends on how close the White House's priorities are to the status quo

The Veto Game

The veto game begins with the president and Congress at odds over a change in government policy (the status quo). If the two sides can agree on a change, a new policy will be created. If they continue to disagree and the president vetoes Congress's preferred policy, there is no change and the status quo prevails. (It is assumed the congressional majority is too small to muster the two-thirds support needed for a veto override.) Within this context, three scenarios are possible:

Scenario 1: The president and Congress have sharply different policy preferences.

This scenario depicts the simplest situation— and the only one that might actually end in a veto. Congress passes legislation changing the status quo. The president prefers the status quo, refuses to compromise, and simply vetoes the new legislation Congress has passed.

Anticipating this outcome, Congress may not even bother to create the legislation. When President Ronald Reagan (1981–1989) announced early in his first term that he would welcome legislation weakening certain provisions of the Clean Air Act, environmentalists in Congress knew that any attempt to strengthen the law during his tenure was doomed to failure. For the next eight years, then, the House Commerce subcommittee dealing with the environment occasionally held hearings but did not take action. The president's tacit veto trumped any real efforts to strengthen policy.

Scenario 2: Congress favors a more drastic change in policy than does the president.

In Scenario 2 both Congress and the president want a change in the status quo, with Congress favoring a greater change than does the president. If Congress passes a law incorporating its preferences, the president will veto the bill since the administration favors the status quo more than the change Congress advocates. Nevertheless, Congress does not have to capitulate and precisely meet presidential demands. It only has to alter the original legislation enough to make the proposed policy marginally more attractive to the president than the status quo. Since the president's policy preferences are better served by signing than vetoing, the bill will become law.

When President George H. W. Bush (1989–1993) announced he would welcome a modest

compared with those of Congress. (To understand how the "take it or leave it" option allows Congress to ignore the president's veto on some occasions but not others, see box "The Veto Game.")

Presidents might be the last to vote, and then only to accept or reject a piece of legislation, but this does not mean that they will passively await the choice Congress presents them. Facing an opposition Congress, modern chief executives do all they can to break out of the Constitution's "take it or leave it" bind. Here presidents find the threat to veto legislation useful. How, short of constitutional amendment, might presidents achieve this objective? They can commit in advance to veto a bill if it fails to include or omit certain provisions. To be effective, a veto threat must be credible— that is, presidents must convince those they wish to persuade that they are not bluff-

strengthening of the Clean Air laws, he shifted the game from Scenario 1 to Scenario 2. By stipulating early the provisions the bill would have to contain to win his signature, including a ceiling of $20 billion in new federal obligations, he was trying to signal precisely where the compromise should be. The Democrats immediately went to work on new legislation, but they did not confine themselves to the changes the president had proposed. After all, they only had to provide him with a bill that he found marginally more attractive than current policy. In the end, the Democratic House and Senate passed a stronger bill than the president had wanted, and Bush reportedly spent almost the full ten days vacillating between a veto and a signature. Finally Bush pronounced the legislation barely acceptable and signed into law the 1990 revision of the Clean Air Act. The president's temporizing and carping reflect how well congressional Democrats squeezed all they could from the president.

Scenario 3: The president favors a more drastic policy change than does Congress.

In Scenario 3 the president and Congress swap places. The president favors a greater policy change than does Congress. Congress wants to change public policy as well, but by far less than does the president. Thus Congress can confidently pass its preferred legislation and expect the president to sign it since the bill goes further in meeting the president's goal than does the status quo. In this situation the veto is worthless; Congress's preferences are enacted into policy.

In 1983 President Reagan sent Congress a budget calling for a 10 percent increase in defense spending. The Democratic-controlled House agreed to only a 4 percent increase. When asked about the lower figure at a news conference, the president hinted that he might have to veto such a bill. The Democrats, however, quickly turned the tables. On hearing of Reagan's comment, a Democratic leader retorted that the president had better be careful, for the next time the House might just lower the increase to 2 percent! President Reagan grudgingly signed the 4 percent increase.

More often than not, presidents who find themselves in this position are liberals promoting new social programs. Perhaps this finding accounts for the comparatively infrequent use of the veto by Democratic presidents (see Figure 7-2).

These simple illustrations of veto policies reveal much about the role of the veto in presidential leadership. In the first instance, the veto allows the president to single-handedly preserve the status quo. In the second, it prescribes the kind of compromise that allows both sides to agree. In the third, the veto proves worthless in pushing Congress where it does not want to go.

ing and will actually follow through if Congress does not accommodate them. This strategy requires that the threat be explicit and leave presidents little wiggle room. Moreover, it must be public—the more public the better—so that presidents will incur political embarrassment by backing down. Ronald Reagan is famous for his "make my day" and "line drawn in the sand" announcements in which he insisted that Congress give him legislation that reflected his preferences or suffer a veto. Of course, such announcements may be costly, so presidents do not issue them casually. Bravado stands against popular bills can backfire immediately in an adverse public response. And tying one's own hands to gain credibility entails risks. Presidents cannot change their minds without hurting themselves politically. Even so, modern presidents threaten vetoes frequently. President Clinton averaged fifty-five threats per year during the six years (1995–2000) that Republicans controlled the House and Senate during his administration.* Similarly, in his last Congress, a contentious two years with Democratic majorities in both the House and Senate, President Bush issued numerous threats.

MOBILIZING PUBLIC OPINION. Until the early twentieth century, presidents routinely satisfied their constitutional obligation (Article II, Section 3) to report on the state of the Union by conveying their messages to Congress by courier. There, an officer of Congress read the presidential communiqué inaudibly to an inattentive audience more interested in socializing after a long adjournment. Today, however, sophisticated broadcast communications have transformed the **State of the Union address** into a televised "prime-time" opportunity for presidents to mold public opinion and steer the legislative agenda on Capitol Hill. The influence presidents derive from this event depends in large part on the susceptibility of politicians in Washington to the political breezes presidents can stir up in the country.

The nationally televised State of the Union address is today simply the most prominent instance of a strategy of **going public**—that is, engaging in intensive public relations to promote the president's policies to the voters and thereby induce cooperation from other elected officeholders in Washington. Presidents and members of Congress share constituencies. If presidents can win the public's backing for themselves and their policies, opponents in Congress may fear voters' reprisals in the next election. Understanding this reality, popular presidents frequently exploit their ability to grab the public's attention and generate favorable news coverage for their legislative initiatives. If they succeed in rallying public support for their policies, they may force the accommodation of a Congress otherwise indifferent or opposed to the president's ideas.

Evidence suggests that presidents view going public as a viable alternative to negotiating with the opposition on Capitol Hill. As a Clinton aide explained to reporters who were complaining about the heavy travel schedule: "Clinton has come to believe that if he keeps his approval ratings up and sells his message as he did during the campaign, there will be greater acceptability for his program. . . . The idea is that you have to sell it as if in a campaign." [16] Immediately after Senator Jeffords's defection in 2001 cost Republicans control of the Senate, reporters asked President Bush's chief of staff, Andrew Card, how the president would respond. Card replied that Bush might have to switch strategies and "use the bully pulpit a little more . . . to get [his legislation] moving." † (Originating with President Theodore Roosevelt's characterization of the

---

*The Clinton average represents the combined tally from several sources: *CQ Weekly,* OMB's "Statements of Administration Purpose," and AP wire stories. One study over a longer time frame found that 90 percent of presidents' veto threats extracted concessions from Congress. Charles Cameron, *Veto Bargaining* (New York: Cambridge University Press, 2000), 188.

†Card added, "This experience is one that obviously we wish we didn't have to live through." Other Bush advisers elaborated that the president might travel to states of vulnerable Democratic senators to pressure them to back his policies. "When you have a coalition-style government," explained one aide, "you have to use the bully pulpit to change the terms of the battlefield." Dana Milbank and Amy Goldstein, "Bush to Pursue Unaltered Agenda," *Washington Post,* May 26, 2001.

This image of the president (here, Franklin Roosevelt) delivering the State of the Union address to a joint session of Congress has been a familiar scene ever since Woodrow Wilson (1913–1921) reintroduced the long-abandoned practice of presidents personally appearing before Congress to fulfill their constitutional duty.

presidency, "bully pulpit" refers to the advantageous position afforded the office for rallying public support.)

Perhaps at no time did governing and campaigning so meld together as in early 1999, when the Senate deliberated President Clinton's removal from office. With the charged impeachment proceedings serving as an uninviting backdrop for the annual State of the Union address, many members of Congress publicly and privately advised Clinton to cancel or postpone the event. Ignoring this advice and Republicans' chilly reception in the audience, Clinton delivered a critically acclaimed speech. Then, instead of dutifully retreating to the White House to await the Senate's verdict, he immediately took his legislative program on the road. During the next three weeks he logged nineteen separate appearances outside Washington. By going public at this unlikely moment, Clinton drew the contrast between his attentiveness to the "business of the American people" and the Republican Senate's preoccupation with the impeachment trial, which a majority of the public opposed.

All modern presidents devote much of their time to cultivating the support of key constituencies through appearances at various assemblies and conferences. In this fashion, presidents can reassure receptive audiences that their interests are being heeded by the White House. In March 1983 President Ronald Reagan's description of Soviet communism as the "focus of evil in the modern world" won an enthusiastic response from his audience of evangelical preachers, but foreign and domestic critics were not nearly so enthralled, pointing out, among other things, that the speech would have a polarizing effect on arms control negotiations.

In the aftermath of reelection President Bush used his 2005 State of the Union address to launch a "Sixty Stops in Sixty Days" blitzkrieg around the country to build a grassroots campaign for a massive overhaul of Social Security. His appearances were accompanied by extensive television advertising by the Republican National Committee and business groups supporting his privatization proposal, as well as by various groups opposed to his reforms. In pursuing this strategy Bush outdid Clinton by engaging Congress with unprecedented levels of travel to telegenic settings, speeches to appreciative audiences, and targeted television commercials.

If asked to name a president whose addresses drew a warm response from the American public, many would think first of Franklin Roosevelt, whose nationally broadcast radio addresses, known as "Fireside Chats," rallied the American public during the Depression and World War II. Others might recall John Kennedy's speeches and live press conferences. Of recent presidents, Reagan and Clinton scored well in public relations. From this list of specialists in presidential rhetoric, we might conclude that nothing much has changed over the past half-century. An examination of the number of times

Figure 7-3 Presidential Addresses: Going Public More Often

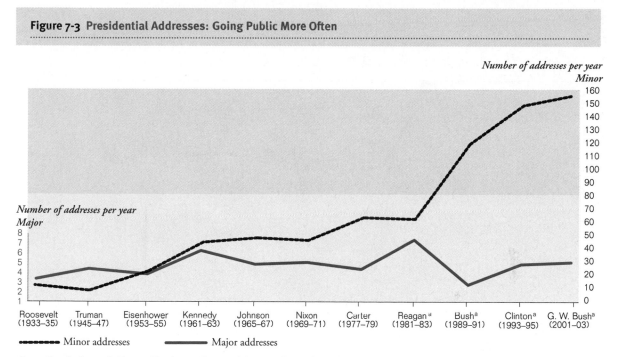

Number of addresses per year
Minor

Number of addresses per year
Major

●●●●●●●● Minor addresses ━━━━━ Major addresses

Sources: Data for Roosevelt, Truman, Eisenhower, Nixon, and Carter are from William W. Lammers, "Presidential Attention-Focusing Activities," in *The President and the American Public,* ed. Doris A. Graber (Philadelphia: Institute for the Study of Human Issues, 1982), Table 6-1, 152. Data for Kennedy, Johnson, Reagan, G. H. W. Bush, Clinton, and G. W. Bush are from *Public Papers of the Presidents* series. See also Samuel Kernell, "The Presidency and the People: The Modern Paradox," in *The Presidency and the Political System,* ed. Michael Nelson (Washington, D.C.: CQ Press, 1984), 242.

Note: Data reflect yearly averages. To eliminate public activities inspired by concerns of reelection rather than governing, only the first three years have been tabulated. For this reason, Gerald Ford's record of public activities during his two and one-half years of office has been ignored.

   a. Includes television addresses only.

presidents have gone public, however, reveals a different picture. We can easily discern the steady growth in public relations undertaken by the White House in the rising number of presidential speeches and days devoted to political travel.

Today presidents spend a great deal of their time, energy, and staff taking their messages directly to the American people. Though appearing on prime-time television is the most dramatic way of going public, presidents rely on this method sparingly, holding their major television addresses in check (see Figure 7-3). They know they will lose the public's attention if they go to this well too often. During the energy crisis of the late 1970s Jimmy Carter informed a consultant that he was about to give yet another nationally televised speech—the fifth!—on the crisis and the need to conserve energy. Backed with polling data, the consultant dissuaded him from doing so, arguing that the public had stopped paying attention to him.*

---

   *Several decades earlier, Franklin Roosevelt had made a similar point in private correspondence: "The public psychology . . . [cannot] be attuned for long periods of time to the highest note on the scale. . . . People tire of seeing the same name, day after day, in the important headlines of the papers and the same voice, night after night, over the radio." Douglass Cater, "How a President Helps Form Public Opinion," *New York Times Magazine,* February 26, 1961, 12.

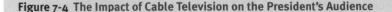

Figure 7-4 The Impact of Cable Television on the President's Audience

Percent of households watching State of the Union address

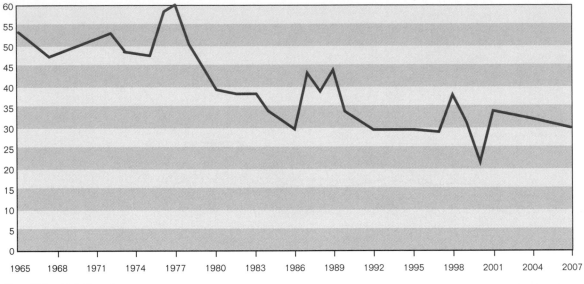

Source: Nielsen Media Research.

Note: Data reflect Nielsen ratings for State of the Union addresses delivered from 1965 through 2007.

Since the Carter years, the continued growth of cable and satellite service has eroded presidents' capacity to enlist television to go public. In the 1960s, when viewers had few choices other than NBC, CBS, and ABC, these networks would agree to suspend commercial programming and broadcast the president's address. They even used the same camera feeds; consequently viewers had little recourse other than the apparently drastic alternative of turning off the television, which as audience ratings suggest, very few did. Since 1970 the proportion of American households that subscribe to cable and satellite television has grown from 7 percent to nearly 90 percent, and the number of cable channels has multiplied dramatically. Viewers have more alternatives to watching a presidential speech than ever before. Now, of course, they need only reach for the remote to choose among dozens of viewing options. Figure 7-4 illustrates one result of this proliferation of choices—a sharp reduction in the share of households that tune into the president's annual State of the Union address.*

---

*Aware that when viewers change channels, they often do not return for the rest of the evening, the big three television networks have increasingly balked at surrendering airtime to presidents for national addresses. The first instances of outright refusal occurred in the 1980s, when President Reagan encountered network resistance to his request for airtime on two separate occasions. In June 1992 the networks denied President George H. W. Bush a time slot for an evening press conference, and six of President Clinton's appearances (through January 1998) failed to attract full network coverage.

Mindful of the limitations of television, presidents communicate with voters in other ways. They take their messages to the public through appearances at graduation exercises, union conferences, and conventions held by trade and professional associations, where they can address the concerns of particular constituencies. Figure 7-3 reveals that these less visible, minor addresses have provided increasingly attractive vehicles for presidential communication: Reagan, Carter, and Nixon used them, on average, four times more often than did Truman, Roosevelt, and Hoover. George H. W. Bush managed to double the already high frequency of these targeted addresses; during his first three years in office he made, on average, a minor address every three days. Clinton did Bush one better: he delivered a minor address nearly every other day during his first three years in office. George W. Bush began his term with a barrage of public speeches, probably to gain the public's acceptance after a delayed, litigated election victory despite receiving fewer popular votes nationally. He was campaigning for his education reform proposals in Florida during the September 11, 2001, terrorist attacks. Abruptly his schedule of minor addresses to targeted constituencies yielded to national appeals for unity in combating terrorism at home and in Afghanistan. But within several months the president resumed his public relations strategy, and by the end of his third year he had far eclipsed President Clinton's record of appearances.

Presidential foreign and domestic travel, typically undertaken for different political purposes, has increased significantly in the past half-century (see Figure 7-5). President Dwight Eisenhower's 1959 "goodwill tour" around the world is generally recognized as the first international presidential travel for which favorable publicity appeared to be the primary consideration. Subsequent presidents have favored the idea as well. Presidents Carter and George H. W. Bush, who enjoyed their greatest policy successes in foreign affairs, traveled extensively. By the end of his third year in office, Bush was so conspicuously absent due to overseas travel that his critics—especially his opponent in the next election, Bill Clinton—found a large segment of the public agreeing with them that the president was not paying enough attention to solving the economic recession at home. Under pressure to focus on domestic issues, Bush postponed a trip to Asia in late 1991, saying that he had stayed home to keep tabs on the Democratic Congress.

Clinton had a special reason for his heavy travel schedule around the country: with third-party candidate Ross Perot in the race Clinton had won the 1992 election with just 43 percent of the popular vote. By the 1996 election Clinton had averaged a visit to California, with its fifty-four electoral votes, every six weeks. Just as a precarious victory had motivated Clinton to travel, it also spurred his successor, George W. Bush, who eked out an Electoral College (and Supreme Court) victory despite winning half a million fewer popular votes than did his Democratic opponent, Al Gore. Much of his frenetic travel schedule in 2002 was directed at raising record-shattering campaign contributions (see box "The President as Party Coordinator" in Chapter 12) for Republican Senate candidates. By the end of his third year, President Bush logged nearly a third of his days in office traveling somewhere in the United States or abroad.

Everything we have considered thus far about the emergence of the modern presidency implies vastly more work and activity than was envisioned by the Framers. As

Figure 7-5 Going Public Involves More Presidential Travel

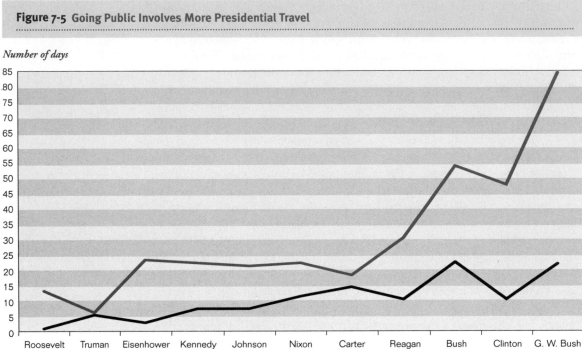

Number of days

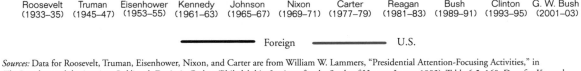

Sources: Data for Roosevelt, Truman, Eisenhower, Nixon, and Carter are from William W. Lammers, "Presidential Attention-Focusing Activities," in *The President and the American Public*, ed. Doris A. Graber (Philadelphia: Institute for the Study of Human Issues, 1982), Table 6-5, 160. Data for Kennedy, Johnson, Reagan, G. H. W. Bush, Clinton, and G. W. Bush are from *Public Papers of the Presidents* series. See also Samuel Kernell, "The Presidency and the People: The Modern Paradox," in *The Presidency and the Political System*, ed. Michael Nelson (Washington, D.C.: CQ Press, 1984), 244.

Note: Data reflect yearly averages. To eliminate public activities inspired by concerns of reelection rather than governing, only the first three years have been tabulated. For this reason, Gerald Ford's record of public activities during his two and one-half years of office has been ignored.

government programs have grown, Congress has delegated to the chief executive significant responsibility for managing the large bureaucracy and ample discretion for adapting policy to changing circumstances. Modern presidents aspire to be more than administrators, of course, and whether in lobbying Congress or in communicating to the public, they depend heavily on staff to help them do their work. Consequently, the emergence of modern presidential leadership has been accompanied by the steady development of a larger, more complex staffing system.

The Institutional Presidency

As an organization the presidency began modestly. When President Washington summoned his secretary to help him with correspondence, Thomas Jefferson walked through the door with pen and paper, in perhaps a classic instance of quality over quantity. By the early 1800s the number of staff working in and around the White

House was fewer than a dozen, two or three of whom were clerks who spent most of their time copying letters, receiving visitors, and running errands.[17] When Franklin Roosevelt entered the White House more than 130 years later, the president's staff had grown to about fifty, most "detailed" over from another government agency to lend the White House a hand.* Despite the heavier workload associated with overseeing the executive branch departments, the presidency as an institution remained an informal working group whose tasks were personally and daily managed by the president.

In 1937 the President's Committee on Administrative Management, also known as the Brownlow Committee, concluded in its detailed analysis of the state of the presidency that "the president needs help." Likening the president to the chief executive officer of a large corporation, Louis Brownlow, one of a new breed of progressive public administration reformers, called for the creation of an organization dedicated to helping the occupant of the Oval Office. If the president was like the CEO of a major corporation, Brownlow claimed, then he required the same kinds of authority, expertise, information, and staffing afforded modern executives in the business world.

The recommendations in the Brownlow report ignored the fact that the Constitution fails to provide the presidency with the kind of authority it would need to command the executive branch. The chief executive's constitutional predicament was not lost on Congress, however. When a delighted President Roosevelt forwarded Brownlow's recommendations to Capitol Hill for enactment, he was rebuffed. Congress, still angry over FDR's ill-fated attempt to pack the Supreme Court (described in Chapter 9), refused to act on the report. Not until two years later, with most of the world preparing for war, did Congress agree to a reduced form of the Brownlow proposal.

Thus the institutional presidency was born and christened the **Executive Office of the President** (EOP). At first it housed five "new" presidential agencies, two of which were and remain significant assets: the Bureau of the Budget (the present-day **Office of Management and Budget,** or OMB), which Roosevelt moved from the Treasury Department by executive order, and the **White House Office,** the president's personal staff system.[18] The White House Office was vital to FDR, who frequently bemoaned his inability to elicit advice from and give orders to the departments except through the cabinet secretaries. In frustration, he sometimes compared himself to "a power plant with no transmission lines." His enlarged staff would help him transact daily business with the cabinet departments. The Brownlow report called for six loyal "Assistants to the President," who would perform their duties with "a passion for anonymity." When President Roosevelt read this phrase, he reportedly chuckled and averred that such an animal does not exist in Washington. What began as six "senior" aides (albeit assisted by a couple of dozen clerks) now approaches four hundred.

EXECUTIVE OFFICE OF THE PRESIDENT. Over the years the Executive Office of the President (EOP) has housed those agencies the president or Congress would like

---

*And, at least in a few instances, to keep tabs and report back to the agency what the president was doing. The FBI and War Department were large contributors to the president's staff before the White House had its own.

to keep in the shadow of the White House. Typically, the dozen or so agencies that make up the modern EOP work much more closely with the president and the White House Office staff than they do with each other. In performing classic staff functions, these agencies gather information—either from the departments from within the executive branch (**National Security Council**, or NSC) or from the broader policy environment (Council of Economic Advisers and Council on Environmental Quality)—or they help to maintain the organization itself (Office of the Vice President and Office of Administration). With no programs to administer, the presidential bureaucracy does not require a field staff outside of Washington.

The most important of the presidential agencies is the OMB. Staffed by accountants, economists, and tax lawyers, OMB creates the annual federal budget, monitors agency performance, compiles recommendations from the departments on **enrolled bills** (bills that have been passed in identical form by both houses of Congress and presented to the president for his signature), and performs central clearance over agencies' communications with Congress.

Another important agency within EOP is the NSC. Its statutory responsibility appears modest: to compile reports and advice from the State and Defense Departments and the Joint Chiefs of Staff and to keep the president well informed on international affairs. Yet the national security adviser, who heads this presidential agency, has at times assumed a role in conducting foreign policy that is close to that traditionally associated with the secretary of state. The president's OMB director and national security adviser spend as much time working with the president as do any cabinet heads or other staff advisers.

WHITE HOUSE OFFICE. The White House Office has grown in both numbers and complexity. What began as a small, informal group of aides has evolved into a large, compartmentalized, multilayered bureaucracy. Richard Nixon assembled the largest single staff at almost 660. It probably would have continued to grow had the Watergate scandal that drove Nixon from office not sent some Nixon aides to federal prison and turned the size of the White House staff into a campaign issue. Moreover, Congresses since then, most controlled by opposition parties, have reined in staff growth through budgets and legislative language limiting the president's ability to borrow staff from other agencies. The present-day White House staff has leveled off at about four hundred.

In its early years the organization of the White House varied according to the working styles of the presidents. In the last two decades, however, the president's staff has coalesced into a small bureaucracy whose organizational structure transcends administrations and whose offices are occupied by policy and political specialists. Presidents Franklin Roosevelt and Harry Truman favored a collegial management style in which they personally supervised their staffs. Roosevelt resisted the notion of fixed staff assignments; instead, he fostered competition by giving aides duplicate tasks or projects. Aware that the president might already have been briefed on a subject, or soon would be, FDR's aides undertook their assignments with special diligence, not to be outdone. This management technique represented an ingenious solution to the problem inher-

ent in a principal's dependence on an agent for information and advice. Truman preferred more cooperative relations among his staff. He conducted a meeting each
morning with ten to twelve of his "senior" staff to receive
reports and give out assignments. Later presidents tried
to emulate FDR's and Truman's collegial management
styles but typically with less success.

Perhaps reflecting his military background, President
Eisenhower introduced a more orderly and hierarchical
organization to the White House. His assistants had
fixed routines, job titles, and middle-level supervisors.
On top, running the day-to-day activities of this still
small (about two hundred) and only partially formed
bureaucracy, was a chief of staff. Democratic critics derided this new approach to staffing as one that would
render the president overly reliant on his agents' judgment and policy preferences. Ike's successors, John F.
Kennedy and Lyndon Johnson, reverted to the informal,
president-run staff structure. But Richard Nixon, who
had served eight years as Eisenhower's vice president in
close proximity to Eisenhower's staff, reinstated the formal chief-of-staff model. For years, then, these alternative styles, or models, of staff organization were enlisted
according to the president's party affiliation.

When Democrat Jimmy Carter assumed office, the
pattern continued, but only for a while. Carter, perhaps uncharacteristically for a former submarine commander, returned to the Democratic collegial, president-

H. R. Haldeman, chief of staff to President Richard Nixon, became
entangled in the presidentially directed Watergate cover-up. After
federal indictment in 1973, his boss asked him to resign his White
House post, which he dutifully did. Haldeman subsequently served a
brief prison term over this affair. In retirement he reflected on "the
lessons of Watergate" in numerous public interviews and a memoir.

administered staff organization. But he immediately ran into problems. After coming
under heavy criticism, even from Democrats, for being disorganized and failing to
formulate a consistent legislative program, Carter sacked five of his cabinet secretaries
who did not get along with the staff and reorganized the White House with clear lines
of authority flowing from a strong chief of staff.

Carter's successors have not looked back. The chief of staff has become a fixture in
the White House. More broadly, specialists performing specific routine tasks have replaced yesterday's agents who depended on their president for assignments. Reflecting
the more sophisticated division of labor, office and job titles have become attached to
names, and organization charts are routinely issued to new staff members.

With its clear organizational lines, fixed assignments, and loyal and enthusiastic
employees, the White House staff system should run like a well-tuned engine. The
facts, however, belie the expectations. Every recent president has experienced serious
staffing problems that have erupted into public controversy, if not scandal. Many
aides are motivated as much by interest in advancing a particular cause or policy
agenda as by a desire to serve the president. This tendency is reinforced by outside

President Dwight Eisenhower's passion for golf, when combined with his limited number of legislative initiatives, left him exposed to criticism that he installed Sherman Adams as his chief of staff so that he could devote himself to his favorite game.

pressures as key constituencies lobby for one of their own to be on the staff. "Everyone in the White House has a constituency," complained senior Reagan aide Michael Deaver.[19] In 1978 a Carter aide who sided with his Jewish constituency's opposition to the sale of reconnaissance jets to Saudi Arabia called a press conference and resigned in protest.[20] More often, staff will discreetly "leak" to the press information supporting their preferences. (The strategy of White House leaks is taken up more fully in Chapter 14.)

Most of the president's staff arrives at the White House fresh from the presidential campaign. They not only typically come to Washington lacking the experience that will serve them best in their new positions, but they also come from a setting—the campaign—that actually rewards behavior that may be counterproductive once the candidate becomes president. Rather than seek compromise on a controversial policy with members of Congress, campaign aides in the White House might wrongly advise their president to stand firm on constituency commitments and appeal for public support, even when reasonable accommodations are available.

Staff members also might view their positions at the White House as way stations to lucrative careers. Some may therefore have a greater stake in the outcomes of decisions and making their mark on policy than in respecting the integrity of the organization's procedures designed to inform presidents and advance the presidential agenda. As staff members compete with others inside and outside the White House for influence, the tenets of orderly organization can crumble. Consequently, the staff has often been largely reconstituted by the end of a four-year term.

Presidents as Strategic Actors

Through delegation and the successful assertion of authority, modern presidents are thoroughly enmeshed in the administration of the government's vast bureaucracy. Aided by an elaborate presidential staffing system, their day-to-day activities fully realize the Constitution's job description: "The executive Power shall be vested in a President of the United States." The modern presidency enjoys far more responsibility and authority, a much bigger and more expert staffing system, and a greater capacity to speak to the public than the Framers could possibly have imagined. Yet presidents still do not sit at the controls and pull the levers of government. The fundamental dilemma facing U.S. presidents remains: they have too little authority to satisfy the expectations for their performance. George W. Bush's flirtation with the unitary executive—a doctrine that could have endowed him with stronger command authority—ended ignominiously as he became unpopular in the nation and ignored in the Congress. Recent events proved the doctrine to be a chimera as fleeting as the power derived from politics.

In part this dilemma reflects the intractability of many of the problems modern presidents must deal with. After the September 11 attacks showed how easily commercial aircraft could be turned into weapons, the president and Congress responded with a series of public laws, executive orders, and administrative regulations costing billions of dollars, yet subsequent inspections of aviation security found that the new systems were far from achieving a safe commercial aviation system. The disparity between expectations and performance reflects the reality of politics. The presidency remains tethered to its limited constitutional mandate, and the Constitution intentionally tilted power relations among the branches toward Congress, as befitting a democracy. Particularly in an era of divided party control of government, presidents rarely find other politicians in Washington rushing to fulfill their requests. Except for moments of national crisis, presidential success remains problematic and depends today as in the past on the president's talent as a politician.

Abraham Lincoln, whom historians generally rank as America's greatest president, frequently referred to his job as "chief clerk." Everyone, he complained, needed him to do something for them, among them job seekers wanting patronage appointments, generals seeking more troops and supplies, and members of Congress requesting his endorsement—or at least his signature—for their pet legislation. In his classic treatise *Presidential Power and the Modern Presidents,* Richard E. Neustadt argues persuasively that despite sharp expansion of statutory authority and the dramatic growth in the institutional resources presented in this chapter, the modern presidency still confronts a dilemma of leadership.[21] The demands of the office continue to exceed the resources available to incumbents to meet them. As a consequence, whether a new president will emerge a leader and actually shape national policy or recede into the more passive routines of clerkship remains uncertain and, for every president, a problem to be resolved. Whether a chief executive succeeds in converting his "clerkship" responsibilities into real leadership has less to do with the authority of the modern office than with the president's political skill. Whether the politician in the White House recognizes the opportunities offered by this setting and is able to take full advantage of them is an altogether different matter. It is fitting, then, that we close our consideration of this most important office by assessing the skill factor that can make all the difference between success and failure. The following two case studies consider presidents in similar situations but with far different outcomes.

In the 1990s two presidents found themselves at loggerheads with an opposition-controlled Congress over the next year's budget. Eventually the critical moment arrived when each president had to decide whether to negotiate with Congress or to confront it. Either way, the president would navigate a political minefield sown by the opposition party. In the first case the president's plan went awry and veered sharply toward failure. In the second it took an arduous path leading to success. Both presidents controlled the same constitutional leverage—the threat to veto unacceptable legislation—but exercised it with far different consequences for both national policy and their political careers.

Failure

In the late fall of 1990 President George H. W. Bush sat uncomfortably in front of a teleprompter, waiting to deliver a prime-time appeal to the American people. Facing a mounting budget deficit that would soon trigger harsh cuts across government services, he was unveiling a deficit-reduction plan of increased taxes and reduced spending that more closely resembled the preferences of congressional Democrats than those of his fellow Republicans. Ironically, Bush worked hard to reach this unenviable position. To get budget negotiations moving he had to sacrifice his earlier promise to American voters to hold the line on taxes. Indeed, the Democrats insisted that the president retract his 1988 campaign slogan "Read my lips, no new taxes" before they would sit down with him to talk about raising taxes. For months he refrained from publicly criticizing the Democratic Congress lest he drive its members away from the bargaining table. Facing this predicament, Bush delivered his television address, feigning enthusiasm for the budget compromise. No wonder his appeal was brief and tepid, without impact on the country or Congress.

In negotiating a budget compromise with congressional Democrats, Bush largely ignored congressional Republicans; they were an inflexible minority uncommitted to the plan and fearful that in the upcoming congressional election they, as members of the president's party, would be held responsible for the tax increases. With congressional Republicans in open revolt, President Bush faced a dilemma. He could apply the prevailing law to automatically reduce the deficit with severe across-the-board cuts in discretionary spending, or he could negotiate for stronger Democratic support. He opted for the latter, probably fearing that he would be blamed for sudden reductions in popular federal programs.

By all objective indicators, Bush's strategy failed. The president's approval rating dropped from the mid-seventies to the mid-fifties in the weeks leading up to the midterm congressional elections. When the voters had their say, the Democrats added nine seats to their House majority. As for President Bush, his about-face on taxes later haunted him in his losing reelection campaign against Bill Clinton.

Success

Five years later congressional leaders contemplating another budget deal with the president remembered Bush's failure. This time, however, Congress was controlled by Republicans and a Democrat, Bill Clinton, occupied the White House. Congressional Republicans, led by House Speaker Newt Gingrich and Senate Majority Leader Bob Dole, declared they would make President Clinton accommodate them just as congressional Democrats had "worked over" President Bush.

Having campaigned in 1988 on the slogan "Read my lips, no new taxes," President George H. W. Bush was hunted down by reporters in 1990 after he conceded a tax increase in negotiations with congressional Democrats. When reporters caught the president jogging one morning and baited him with his contradiction, he yelled, "Read my hips." In the national news story that followed, the president's response was reported as an expression of his disregard for his promises.

Nothing about President Clinton's first two years in office suggested he could stand up to pressure. His all-too-frequent willingness to compromise forced even loyal staffers to wonder what he stood for.[22] Confronting the newly installed Republican Congress in early 1995, Clinton appeared clearly overmatched. By fall, a Republican budget axing many favored Democratic programs reached the final stages of congressional passage. President Clinton failed to moderate the deep cuts in social spending and failed to stave off a massive tax cut that favored wealthier constituents. As they approached the endgame, Republican leaders believed they could trump any threat of a presidential veto: they attached their spending and revenue legislation to a debt-ceiling bill the federal government needed to meet its payroll and entitlement obligations. The president would have to accept the whole package or shut down the government.

Clinton made his decision and vetoed the Republican budget. "If America has to close down access to education, to a clean environment, to affordable health care, to keep our government open," Clinton asserted, "then the price is too high." He

Little did these self-satisfied Republican congressional leaders suspect when they passed their 1996 appropriations legislation that within a matter of weeks they would be bearing the brunt of the public's blame for shutting down the government. They thought they had cornered Democratic president Bill Clinton with a "take it or leave it" bill that he could not politically afford to refuse, but they had underestimated the ability of modern presidents to shape public perceptions. As a consequence, the popular standing of Senate Majority Leader Bob Dole (seated left) would never equal its level at the time of this photo, and Clinton would soundly defeat him in the next year's presidential election.

then added, "Yes to balancing the budget. No to the cuts." One White House aide confided to a reporter that the president was "prepared to fight all winter" on this issue. Two days later eight hundred thousand federal workers were sent home. They would not return to their jobs for six days.

Media polls immediately detected that public opinion had swung to the president's side. When asked whether the president should have vetoed the budget, 56 percent of respondents in a *Wall Street Journal* poll said yes, and only 36 percent said no. By comparison, Gingrich and Dole received 33 percent and 30 percent approval ratings, respectively.*

After weeks of fruitless negotiations and posturing by both sides—with Clinton characterizing congressional Republicans as bullies and their budget strategy as "an exercise of raw, naked power"—the government shut down again. By mid-January both sides were facing the specter of government default on its debts. A weary Speaker Gingrich conceded to a reporter that the president and his team "were tougher than I thought they would be. . . . They have less flexibility than I thought they would have. Our strategy failed." Over the next few weeks, Republican leaders backed off a seven-year balanced budget commitment and more than half of the tax cuts they had passed three months earlier. By February Republican and Democratic negotiators agreed to fund the government for the next year at reduced levels. They eliminated a few programs and achieved mutually acceptable savings by broadly scaling back discretionary domestic spending.

Politically, Clinton and the Democrats won a significant victory. The president reestablished his presence in Washington and recaptured the attention of the American public. His approval rating, instead of plunging after each government shutdown, rebounded to a level that made reelection in 1996 conceivable. Meanwhile, Republi-

---

*The president's arguments were repeated in national television commercials sponsored by the Democratic National Committee, which had budgeted $1 million a week for ads that ran through early 1996. Dennis Farney, "Clinton Seems to Have Emerged in Good Shape from the Blame Game over the Budget Impasse," *Wall Street Journal,* November 21, 1995.

can leaders Gingrich and Dole saw their fortunes sink.

The differences between Bush's and Clinton's performances were subtle but consequential. Each threatened the veto; each sought the support of the American public. Clinton managed to extract full advantage from these assets, while Bush enlisted them ineptly. The starkly different outcomes of these two political struggles remind us that despite the accoutrements of power, the presidency gives its occupants no more than an opportunity to make a difference. Whether presidents succeed or fail depends on luck—that is, things beyond their control, such as the actions and preferences of others—and on their skill as politicians. We began with the Constitution and, despite the two centuries of dramatic evolution chronicled here, that is where we end. The Framers, in their deep-seated ambivalence toward an independent executive, mandated that presidents be *leaders* yet gave them the tools to be no more than *clerks*.

Using the pen with which President Lyndon Johnson had signed the Medicare law In 1965, President Bill Clinton vetoed the congressional budget bill on December 6, 1995, and announced to the network cameras, "Today I am vetoing the biggest Medicare and Medicaid cuts in history, deep cuts in education, a rollback in environmental protection, and a tax increase on working families. With this veto, the extreme Republican effort to balance the budget through wrongheaded cuts and misplaced priorities is over."

logic.cqpress.com

Key Terms

central clearance, 336

commander in chief, 326

divided government, 338

enrolled bill, 352

executive agreement, 328

Executive Office of the President, 351

executive order, 331

executive privilege, 330

gag rule, 336

going public, 344

gridlock, 339

imperial presidency, 319

line-item veto, 341

National Security Council, 352

Office of Management and Budget, 351

signing statements, 316

State of the Union address, 344

"take care" clause, 331

unitary executive, 316

War Powers Act, 327

White House Office, 351

Suggested Readings

Cameron, Charles. *Veto Bargaining.* New York: Cambridge University Press, 2000. This book offers a sophisticated consideration of the veto and veto threats as bargaining instruments in presidents' efforts to influence an opposition-controlled Congress.

Cohen, Jeffrey. *The Presidency in the Era of 24-Hour News.* Princeton: Princeton University Press, 2008. Although based on sophisticated statistical techniques, the research reported in this book is full of insights on the effects of the transformation of the news industry on modern presidential communications.

Goldsmith, Jack. *The Terror Presidency* New York: W. W. Norton, 2007. This first-person account by John Yoo's successor in the Justice Department's Office of Legal Counsel tells a fascinating story of politics within the Bush administration while laying out intelligibly the serious issues presented in the administration's concept of the unitary executive.

Kernell, Samuel. *Going Public: New Strategies of Presidential Leadership.* 3rd ed. Washington, D.C.: CQ Press, 1997. The author develops more fully the argument summarized here that modern presidents are more inclined than were their predecessors to engage in public relations in seeking influence in Washington.

Neustadt, Richard E. *Presidential Power and the Modern Presidents: The Politics of Power from Roosevelt to Reagan.* 4th ed. New York: Free Press, 1990. This volume is *the* classic statement of the leadership predicament confronted by all presidents. Originally published in 1961 and in print ever since, the book is a touchstone for anyone aspiring to understand the American presidency.

Woodward, Bob. *The Agenda: Inside the Clinton White House.* New York: Simon and Schuster, 1994. A lively and apparently accurate portrayal of life inside the early Clinton White House. It is not a pretty picture.

Review Questions

1. What are the powers granted to the president in the Constitution? What are the nonconstitutional sources of presidential power? When were these sources of power first tapped?

2. What are executive orders? Executive agreements? What are the president's alternatives to using them?

3. How did the presidency of the 1800s differ from that of today? In particular, how did the president's interactions with his party and his cabinet change over time?

4. What are the trade-offs between the collegial and chief-of-staff models of presidential staff organization? Which model seems to have predominated with recent presidents?

5. What is "going public"? What specific tools or resources are available to the president when he chooses to use this strategy?

6. How has the rise of cable and satellite television affected the president's ability to communicate with the public?

7. Why don't members of Congress go public as often as the president does? Why doesn't the president use this tactic on every issue?

Exercises

Now You See Him . . .
The *New York Times* has put up a massive archive of its news coverage over the past 150 years. Your challenge, should you choose to accept it, is to find *two consecutive weekdays* in the last thirty years (no fair using Saturdays or Sundays) in which the president is *not* mentioned in the paper. (*Note:* use the advanced archives search at www.nytimes.com/ref/membercenter/nytarchive.html or http://pqasb.pqarchiver.com/nytimes/advancedsearch.html and specify the dates you want. You don't have to pay for the documents you find, just look at the results—the titles of the articles. You can find a list of presidents here: http://clerk.house.gov/art_history/house_history/presVP.html.) Then repeat the search for the Speaker of the House (you can find a list of all Speakers here: http://clerk.house.gov/art_history/house_history/speakers.html) on those two days, and compare the volume of coverage.

Now You Don't
Repeat the same searches as above, except this time select your dates from the first thirty years of the archive: 1851–1881. How do the results differ from your recent search?

The Bureaucracy

Who controls the bureaucracy? The president? Congress? The courts? No one?

Why do efforts to make government agencies more accountable lead to the proliferation of red tape?

How can the government grow while the bureaucracy shrinks?

Why has it been so hard to coordinate intelligence activities aimed at preventing terrorist attacks?

T he deadly al Qaeda terrorist assaults of September 11, 2001, on New York City and Washington, D.C., stand as a tragic failure of government to deliver the most basic of all public goods—protection from foreign attack. In the catastrophe's aftermath, questions about what went wrong and how to prevent further assaults leapt to the top of the political agenda. The ensuing investigations exposed deep shortcomings in the government institutions charged with gathering and analyzing intelligence about threats and with responding to them. Field agents of the Federal Bureau of Investigation (FBI) suspected that al Qaeda terrorists were getting flight training in the United States, but their reports never reached top FBI officials. Other organizations, including the Central Intelligence Agency (CIA), the State Department, and the National Security Agency (NSA) had acquired various items of information about suspicious people and activities but did not share their data with each other. The alleged mastermind of the attacks, Mohammed Atta, obtained a visa to enter the United States from the State Department even though another agency had tied him to al Qaeda months earlier. The NSA, which eavesdrops on electronic communications, and the CIA had learned independently of two other future hijackers' al Qaeda connections but did not inform one another or the immigration officials who could have denied them entry. The government, it turned out, had gathered enormous quantities of data on possible threats, but the coordination and communication among the diverse agencies doing the gathering was so poor that no agency or person was in a position to piece together the entire picture.

Severe coordination problems also arose in the government's reaction to the attacks. The president's order, relayed through Vice President Dick Cheney, to shoot down

Testifying before the commission investigating the September 11, 2001, al Qaeda assaults on New York and Washington, D.C., Condoleezza Rice, national security adviser to President George W. Bush during his first term (2001–2004), insisted that "there was no silver bullet that could have prevented the 9/11 attacks." Rice served as Bush's secretary of state during his second term.

hijacked airliners came after the planes had already crashed and never reached the air force pilots who had scrambled to intercept them. The heroic efforts of "first responders"— police, firefighters, paramedics— were hampered by confused lines of authority, breakdowns in communication, poor planning, and insufficient resources. When thought turned to the countless other ways terrorists might attack the United States—underlined by the appearance of deadly anthrax spores in letters mailed to media figures and political leaders shortly after September 11—it was clear that government agencies at all levels were woefully unprepared either to prevent or cope with what might happen next.

The individual and collective shortcomings of government agencies charged with protecting Americans from terrorists, so painfully exposed in 2001, made bureaucratic reform a political imperative. But, as we shall see, the quest for better coordinated and more effective responses to terrorist threats has proven enormously challenging, not only because so many points of vulnerability demand attention, but also because the basic structure of the American political system works against it. As one journalist put it, "The U.S. government was just not designed with terrorism in mind."[1]

The roots of the **bureaucracy**—that diverse collection of departments, agencies, bureaus, commissions, and other units of the executive branch that carry out national policies—are found in the Constitution, which authorizes Congress to make laws and the president to see that they are faithfully executed. Congress creates executive branch agencies with authority to implement the laws it passes, and presidents necessarily delegate their executive chores to numerous subordinate agents. In the nation's earliest years these agents delivered the mail, collected customs duties (taxes on imported goods) and excise taxes (on alcohol and luxuries), prosecuted violations of federal laws, and managed relations with foreign nations. Surely the Framers did not envision anything like today's 157,000-member Department of Homeland Security (DHS) or the rest of the federal establishment, comprising some 2,000 departments, bureaus, agencies, and commissions, which employ some 2.7 million nonmilitary personnel. But the modern bureaucracy mirrors in a very direct way the pluralistic nature of American politics and society. Every new agency has been brought into being by a unique configuration of political demands and forces. Reflected in each agency's mandate and organization is the attempt of a successful policy coalition to preserve its victory through institutional design. The remarkable variety of arrangements adopted to administer government policies is largely a product of the endless search by Congress and the White House for ways to maximize the potential political benefits and minimize the potential political costs each time they decide to exercise and delegate their authority. The end product is the extravagantly diverse collection of entities that now compose the federal bureaucracy. It is scarcely surprising, then, that institutions with such diverse origins and purposes defy easy coordination or reorganization even in the face of a disaster on the scale of September 11.

The Development of the Federal Bureaucracy

The Framers viewed the executive as the necessary source of "energy" in government, but questions of administration received remarkably little attention at the Constitutional Convention, and the Constitution itself said little about how the executive branch was to be organized. As we saw in Chapter 7, it did authorize the president, with the advice and consent of the Senate, to appoint ambassadors, Supreme Court justices, heads of departments, and other senior executive branch officials. Congress was left with the task of establishing executive departments and determining how they would be staffed.

From the beginning, Congress was wary of delegating too much power to the executive. The colonial experience with the king's governors and other royal officials was too fresh. But members of Congress also knew that delegation was unavoidable; the Continental Congress's attempt to make all administrative decisions through congressional committees had proven quite impractical. Delegate John Adams, for one, "found himself working eighteen-hour days just to keep up with the business of the 90 committees on which he served." [2]

Modest Beginnings: The Dilemma of Delegation

With these experiences in mind, the First Congress began its work on the executive branch by reestablishing the departments that had existed under the Articles of Confederation: Treasury, Foreign Affairs (quickly renamed State after Congress decided to assign the department some domestic duties), and War. Congress also authorized the hiring of an attorney general to give the president and department heads legal advice. The larger departments were soon subdivided into more specialized offices, later called bureaus. For example, by 1801 the Treasury Department was dividing its work among units headed by a commissioner of revenue, who supervised tax collection; a purveyor in charge of buying military supplies; and an auditor who, among other duties, oversaw the operation of lighthouses. The Treasury Department also included a General Land Office to deal with the sale of public lands.[3]

Congress readily agreed that each executive department should be headed by a single official responsible for its operations. There was far less consensus, however, about whether department heads were accountable to Congress or to the president. As noted earlier, presidents appointed senior officials, but appointments were subject to senatorial approval (see Chapter 7). Could presidents, then, dismiss officials without the consent of the Senate? The First Congress gave the president the sole right of removal, but only narrowly; Vice President John Adams cast the tie-breaking vote in the Senate.[4] The issue came up again during the Jackson administration (1829–1837) and later during Reconstruction (1865–1877) before it was finally settled in the president's favor: officials held their jobs at the pleasure of the chief executive. Nonetheless, many lower-level federal jobs such as local postmaster were, by the time of the Adams administration (1797–1801), effectively controlled by Congress. When the president turned to members of Congress for advice on appointments in their states and districts, they had quickly come to expect that it would be followed.

The dismissal controversy was one of many instances in which Congress faced the familiar dilemmas of delegation. The advantages of delegating authority to a unified executive that could energetically and efficiently implement laws were clear. But so was a potential drawback: executives might also pursue ends contrary to those desired by congressional majorities. Recognizing this drawback, Congress leveraged its authority to establish executive branch agencies and set their annual budgets as a way to balance the president's power.

The executive struggled with the same dilemma. Even the skimpy government of the Federalist period (1789–1801) was too large to be managed by the president and his cabinet secretaries without delegating authority to subordinate officials. Thus the executive also faced a standard principal–agent problem: how to ensure that agents acting ostensibly on its behalf would faithfully carry out official policies. As the nation has grown and the range of federal activities expanded, so has the challenge of keeping appointed officials responsive to elected officials, just as elected officials are, in their turn, supposed to be responsive to the citizenry. As we will see in this chapter, the various ways in which the government has tried to meet this challenge have had enduring consequences for the modern bureaucracy.

The Federalist Years: A Reliance on Respectability

For many decades the federal government had few responsibilities, and so it was small. In fact, George Washington (1789–1797) had so few staff that he occasionally called on his cabinet chiefs to take dictation, making them secretaries in a less exalted sense.[5] Yet Washington and his successors still had to deal with the problem of delegation, heightened during the Republic's early days by long distances and primitive communications between the nation's capital and the states and cities where federal policies were administered.

During this period most federal government workers, laboring far from their bosses in the capital, were occupied with delivering the mail and collecting duties and taxes. The potential for corruption was considerable. President Washington believed that popular support for the young national government depended on honest and competent administration. Thus he sought to appoint civil servants of character and ability who were respected by their communities—in other words, men of superior education, means, family, and local reputation. The problem of delegation was to be met, in the first place, by choosing the right sort of people as agents. Other techniques also were used to ensure honest administration. Officials sometimes were required to post bonds of money or property that they would forfeit if they failed to perform their duties. Customs and alcohol tax collectors received a share of the proceeds from the sale of goods they seized from smugglers, giving them a financial incentive to detect and thwart smuggling. Heavy fines were imposed for giving or taking bribes.[6]

President Washington's efforts to establish an honest, competent federal civil service largely succeeded. Although presidents remained free to dismiss officials at will, an informal custom of tenure during good behavior emerged and remained in place until the 1820s. Indeed, it was not uncommon for officials to pass positions on to their sons or nephews.[7] This practice, consistent with Federalist notions of government by respectable gentlemen, was contrary, however, to the democratic spirit that eclipsed Federalist views during the early decades of the nineteenth century.

Democratization of the Civil Service: The Spoils System

The most prominent spokesman for this democratic spirit, President Andrew Jackson, argued that public offices held as, in effect, private property would "divert government from its legitimate ends and make it an engine for the support of the few at the expense of the many." Moreover, "the duties of all public officers are, or at least admit of being made, so plain and simple that men of intelligence may readily qualify themselves for their performance."[8] In other words, when it comes to governing, "no experience is necessary." Jackson thus advocated **rotation in office;** an official would serve in a position for a short, fixed period, then move on to something else, perhaps in government, but more often returning to private life. The Jacksonian idea was to democratize the civil service along with the rest of the political system.

The democratic ideal of rotation in office meshed with the practical need of party organizations to reward the activists they relied on to mobilize the expanding mass electorate (see Chapter 12). Who better deserved appointment to public office than the men who had proved their mettle by helping their political party to triumph? Debating this issue in 1835, Sen. William Marcy, a New York Democrat, assured himself a place in the history books by celebrating "the rule, that to the victor belong the spoils of the enemy,"[9] and giving the **spoils system**—the practice of the winning party dispensing government jobs—its name. Once government jobs became a primary resource for maintaining party machines, members of Congress developed an even keener interest in influencing appointments to federal offices in their states and districts.

Ironically, rotation in office and the spoils system, meant to democratize administration, led instead to its bureaucratization. Bureaucratic organization arises when

President Andrew Jackson's campaign to democratize public administration led to the distribution of government jobs to loyal party workers. This depiction of Jackson astride a gluttonous hog makes it clear that the "spoils system," as this practice came to be called, was by no means universally celebrated.

leaders try to solve the huge problems of coordination and delegation raised by many forms of large-scale collective action. Max Weber, the German sociologist, delineated more than a century ago the characteristic features of bureaucratic institutions[10]:

- a *hierarchical structure* of authority in which commands flow downward and information flows upward (for coordination and control)

- a *division of labor* (to reap the advantages of specialization in taking on complex tasks)

- a consistent set of *abstract rules* regarding what is to be done and who is to do it (for coordination among specialists, control over subordinates, and uniformity of action in each position regardless of who holds it)

- *impersonality,* treating everyone in the same category equally regardless of who they are as individuals (for consistency and impartiality)

- a *career system,* with appointment and advancement by demonstrated merit, and often considerable job security (to create incentives for loyal and effective performance)

- *specified goals* toward which the collective action is aimed (unlike, for example, economic markets, in which individuals and firms have goals—making money—but the market as a whole does not).

The model bureaucracy is, in short, a purposive machine with interchangeable human parts designed to facilitate collective action (coordinating relevant actors, discouraging free riding, and enforcing cooperative agreements) while enabling principals to control agents. Centralized control is exercised over large numbers of people performing complex social tasks, greatly amplifying the power of whoever sits at the apex of the hierarchical pyramid. The classic example is an army, with its clear chain of command from the five-star general at the top down to the lowliest private at the bottom. Most modern business corporations, government agencies, and even spiritual enterprises such as the Roman Catholic Church also have organized themselves bureaucratically for more effective central control over collective pursuits. But whatever its advantages, bureaucratic organization imposes heavy conformity costs on both bureaucrats and the people they deal with in return for reducing transaction costs and agency losses (see Chapter 1).

American bureaucracies, like American political parties, arose more from expedience than from conscious design. The Jacksonian Democrats had no intention of erecting new bureaucratic structures, but the spoils system created administrative problems that begged for bureaucratic solutions. With its widespread rotation in office, the spoils system was fraught with the dangers of incompetence and corruption. Jackson, no less than Washington, sought honest, efficient government, recognizing that the continued success of his party depended on delivering it. Jobs thus became more specialized and clearly defined so that novices could quickly master and perform them. Administrative jurisdictions and responsibilities were spelled out in greater detail to avoid confusion and conflict among people who would be in office only for a short time. Hierarchies became more formal and elaborate, with new procedures designed to monitor and control agents who had no long-term stake in how they performed their jobs. Officials kept meticulous records of their actions, which were subject to audit by a separate set of specialists. Government became more impersonal.[11]

The complex arrangements needed to ensure control quickly bred the kind of **red tape**—labyrinthine procedures, layers of paperwork (in quadruplicate!), demands for strict adherence to form—for which bureaucracies are legendary. In 1836, for example, the House Ways and Means Committee blamed the Treasury Department's excessive workload on an accounting system that required the concurrence of no fewer than five officers—the treasurer, the auditor, the comptroller, a secretary, and the registrar—for all receipts of funds and expenditures. "The result of the reciprocal checks here established," the committee noted, "is that no money can be received or paid out without the agency of these five separate offices, involving the labor of one or more clerks in each."[12] When senior officials place the desire to monitor agents ahead of efficiency (in this case by arranging for them to monitor each other), chronic bureaucratic sluggishness is the inevitable result.

Civil Service Reform

Under Jackson, the federal administration did not become fully bureaucratized in the Weberian sense; rotation in office precluded the development of government service as a career with job security and advancement based on merit. Only after the Civil War (1861–1865) were calls from citizens and reformers to adopt this additional component of bureaucracy finally heard. The emerging industrial economy raised administrative problems that a civil service composed of short-term amateurs was poorly suited to address. More important, financial scandals, particularly during Ulysses S. Grant's administration (1869–1877), fueled attacks on the spoils system and prompted political support for civil service reform.[13] Perhaps the most dramatic incident was the exposure of the Whiskey Ring (see box "The Whiskey Ring"). Civil service reformers also exploited their pivotal positions as leaders of a swing constituency in an era of close two-party electoral competition.

Defenders of the old system did not give up easily, however, and reforms that protected officials from political firing and imposed merit criteria for hiring and advancement were extended gradually. The most compelling argument for reform was the assassination of President James Garfield in 1881 by a demented job seeker incensed at having lost a chance for a patronage appointment. The ensuing revulsion against the spoils system led in 1883 to passage of the Pendleton Act, the basis of the modern civil service. The act itself put only 10 percent of federal jobs under the merit system,

The Whiskey Ring

During the Grant administration, a group of revenue officials, all political appointees, conspired with distillers to evade taxes on distilleries on a massive scale. The conspirators, dubbed the "Whiskey Ring," included General John McDonald, collector of internal revenue in St. Louis, the initial center of the conspiracy, as well as collectors and their subordinates in Chicago, Milwaukee, and San Francisco. Other co-conspirators were the chief clerk of the internal revenue division of the Treasury Department in Washington and General Orville Babcock, President Grant's private secretary.

A small group of honest officials led by Secretary of the Treasury Benjamin Bristow exposed the conspiracy in May 1875. When the dust settled, forty-seven distillers, sixty rectifiers (who set the alcohol content of distilled spirits), ten wholesale dealers, and eighty-six of the Treasury Department's field agents were facing indictment. In all, 230 indictments were handed down. Of these, about a hundred defendants pleaded guilty, twenty were convicted, and a dozen fled the country. Babcock was acquitted with the help of Grant, who mistakenly thought he was innocent and made a deposition in his behalf for his trial. Grant later named Babcock inspector of lighthouses. Meanwhile, Bristow was forced from Grant's cabinet.

Source: Leonard D. White, *The Republican Era: A Study in Administrative History, 1869–1901* (New York: Macmillan, 1958), 372–374.

but it authorized the president to extend coverage by executive order. Presidents from Grover Cleveland onward did exactly that, although, ironically, for the crassest of partisan motives. Each president about to relinquish office to the opposition party extended civil service protection to thousands of his own patronage appointees. By the time Franklin Roosevelt became president in 1933, 80 percent of federal workers were included in the merit system.[14]

The merit system bred its own set of agency problems, however. Rotation in office may have left the government short on experience and efficiency, but it had kept officials in close touch with ordinary citizens and responsive to the elected politicians who appointed them. Some proponents of a professional civil service naively thought it would turn government agencies into efficient, politically neutral tools subject only to the will of policymakers in Congress and the White House. Career bureaucrats, however, inevitably develop their own personal and institutional interests, and the rules designed to protect them from political retaliation make it difficult to punish them for shirking or incompetence. They become the reigning experts in their bureau's procedures and policy domains, magnifying the problems of hidden action (principals unable to observe what agents are doing) and hidden information (agents knowing things that principals do not) inherent in principal–agent relationships (see section "Delegation" in Chapter 1). Moreover, they can easily develop perspectives quite different from people outside of government. Organized into unions, bureaucrats form a potent political force. These problems are compounded by a Constitution that compels Congress and the president to share, and compete for, control over administration; the agents can play their multiple principals against one another. The political attempts to come to terms with these problems are responsible for much of the complexity and diversity of the administrative units added to the federal government over the past century.

On July 2, 1881, Charles Guiteau, upset at being rejected for a patronage appointment, assassinated Republican president James A. Garfield in a Washington train station. Garfield died on September 19, 1881. The public uproar over the incident galvanized support in Congress for civil service reform.

An Expanding Government

Despite dramatic changes in *how* the government operated after Jackson, *what* it did changed very little. The number of federal officials grew along with the population, but they continued to perform the same limited set of tasks assigned during the Federalist period: collecting duties and taxes, delivering the mail, disposing of public lands in the West, granting patents, managing relations with foreign nations and Native Americans, and maintaining a small army and navy. The federal establishment began small and stayed that way for decades because most Americans wanted it that way. Cheap, limited government was part of the democratic creed professed by disciples of Thomas Jefferson and Jackson, and any attempts to expand the federal domain met firm resistance in Congress.

After the Civil War, however, the federal government began expanding its activities and personnel, and that trend, with a few exceptions, has continued to the present day. As Figure 8-1 reveals, federal employment grew steadily but not very steeply (except during World War I) from the 1870s until the New Deal period (1933–1941), when the rate of growth began to increase. World War II produced a dramatic surge in the size of the federal workforce that was only partially reversed afterward. Until 1990, the number of civil servants continued to trend upward, but since then, it has fallen steadily. As a proportion of the population, the federal workforce has actually been shrinking since the 1950s (see Figure 8-2). The federal government has not been shrinking in any other sense, however; politicians have found many ways to expand the government's activities without expanding its workforce.

Government could only grow if Congress and the president were willing to delegate authority to new agencies. Historically, the most common reasons for delegating authority have been to handle large-scale administrative tasks, to exploit expertise, to

Figure 8-1 Changes in Federal Civilian Employment

Number of federal civilian employees (1,000s)

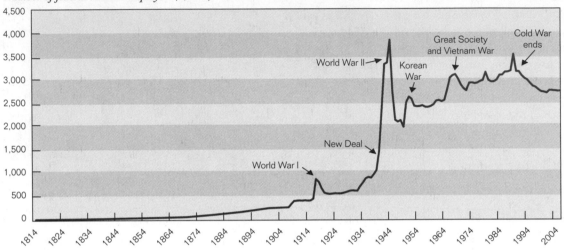

Sources: Harold W. Stanley and Richard G. Neimi, *Vital Statistics on American Politics, 1999–2000* (Washington, D.C.: CQ Press, 2000), 259–256; data for 1999–2007 from U.S. Office of Personnel Management, Federal Civilian Workforce Statistics, Employment and Trends, bimonthly release.

Figure 8-2 Federal Civilian Employment Per Capita

Federal employees per 1,000 population

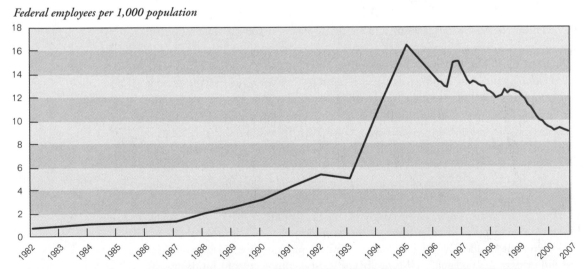

Sources: 1921–1961: Calculated by authors from Harold W. Stanley and Richard G. Neimi, *Vital Statistics on American Politics, 1999–2000* (Washington, D.C.: CQ Press, 2000), 259–260 and 355; 1962–2007: Executive Office of the President, Office of Management and Budget, *Budget of the United States Fiscal Year 2009,* Historical Tables, 335.

avoid blame for unpopular decisions, to make credible commitments to stable policy, or to deal with crises demanding swift, coordinated action. Varying goals have inspired varying degrees of delegation as well as different organizational strategies for limiting potential agency losses (see Chapter 1). Political battles arising from conflicting goals within Congress and between Capitol Hill and the White House have also done much to shape and reshape bureaucratic institutions.

The Cabinet

Agencies that rise to the department level and gain a seat in the president's cabinet receive no special powers or privileges. Presidents can and do invite whomever they wish to serve in their cabinets, regardless of whether they head a department. For example, John P. Walters, director of the Office of National Drug Control Policy, and Susan C. Schwab, U.S. Trade Representative, enjoyed cabinet-level status during the second George W. Bush administration (2005–2008). Over the years, however, political entrepreneurs have fought vigorously to confer departmental status on the agencies that administer policies affecting their constituents. They do this in part for a leg up in the competition for scarce resources and in part for symbolic recognition of the political centrality of their concerns. Each addition to the roster of cabinet-level agencies represents and helps to sustain the political triumph of a particular coalition. The history of the cabinet thus provides a concise, if incomplete, picture of the succession of social and economic interests that have become powerful enough to command this level of political recognition (see Table 8-1).

THE EARLIEST DEPARTMENTS. Until 1849, Treasury, State, Navy, and War stood alone as cabinet-level departments. They were joined that year by the Department of the Interior, whose creation represented a major political victory for members of Congress from the western states. These westerners wanted the government to pay more attention to their constituents' concerns: public lands, natural resources, and Native American affairs. The department's creation provided symbolic as well as practical acknowledgment of the continental expansion of the United States.

The Department of Justice achieved cabinet status in 1870 after Congress, in response to the Civil War, Reconstruction, and the problems created by the growth of

TABLE 8-1

Origin of Cabinet-Level Departments

1789	War, State, and Treasury (The attorney general, a part-time appointee, sat in on cabinet meetings as well.)
1798	Navy (split off from War)
1849	Interior
1870	Justice (Office of the Attorney General was established in 1789 and elevated to department status in 1870.)
1889	Agriculture (established in 1862 but not elevated to cabinet status until 1889)
1903	Labor (established as the Bureau of Labor in Interior in 1884; achieved cabinet status as the Department of Labor and Commerce in 1903; split from Commerce in 1913)
1903	Commerce (established as part of the Department of Labor and Commerce; split from Labor in 1913)
1947	Defense (combined War, Navy, and new Air Force Departments; initially called the National Military Establishment; renamed Defense in 1949)
1965	Housing and Urban Development
1966	Transportation
1977	Energy
1979	Health and Human Services (formerly Health, Education, and Welfare, 1953–1979)
1979	Education (established as a free-standing subcabinet department in 1867; placed in Interior a year later; eventually ended up in Health, Education, and Welfare, from which it split when it was raised to cabinet status)
1988	Veterans Affairs
2002	Homeland Security

Source: Compiled by the authors.

One of the original four cabinet-level departments, the Treasury Department includes the Bureau of Engraving and Printing, which literally prints money. Here, Treasury Secretary Henry Paulson inspects a sheet of new $20 bills, the first to bear his signature.

industry, expanded the government's role in law enforcement. Among other things, the department took over all of the government's legal work, thereby ending the expensive practice of letting each department hire its own lawyers and allowing the ruling party to centralize the processing of patronage appointments of judges, U.S. attorneys, and U.S. marshals. The head of the Justice Department, the attorney general, has been a key political figure in most administrations.[15]

CLIENTELE AGENCIES. The Departments of Agriculture (1889), Labor (1903), and Commerce (1903) represented a new type of government agency altogether. Unlike the existing departments, which served general social purposes, each of the new departments was established to serve the particular **clientele** indicated by its title: farmers, labor unions, and business. In seeking cabinet-level status, these constituencies were represented by sophisticated interest groups, which lobbied intensely on behalf of their clients (organized labor successfully insisted on the separation of "its" department from Commerce in 1913). In granting their wishes and supporting department budgets, members of Congress could claim credit for the continuing flow of benefits they provided to an important set of constituents.

The demand for such clientele agencies reflected the emerging national market economy and the Industrial Revolution's legacy of increasingly distinct economic interests. With the advent of the new industrial economy, information became a valuable resource. Thus in their early years all three departments devoted an important part of their work to gathering and disseminating the kinds of technical information needed by their clients. The Department of Agriculture helped farmers by sponsoring experiments; collecting, testing, and distributing new plants and seed varieties; and gathering crop and market statistics. Labor settled industrial disputes and looked out for workers' welfare, but also conducted economic research through its Bureau of Labor Statistics. Commerce sought to make American business more prosperous and competitive internationally by, among other activities, gathering and publishing commercially useful data. The Census Bureau, which, besides counting heads every ten years, produces detailed information on the domestic economy and foreign trade, came under its jurisdiction.

THE MILITARY ESTABLISH-MENT. The Department of Defense (1947) was a legacy of the Second World War and the emergence of the United States as an international superpower. Until World War II the United States had maintained a modest military establishment, except in times of war. Indeed, until the twentieth century state militias were the main sources of trained soldiers for wartime duties; the colonial experience had convinced Americans that large standing armies were tools of oppression. In 1796 the American army numbered 3,300, climbing to only 16,200 by the eve of the Civil War. During the war it expanded to more than 1 million, but a few years

In the summer of 1997 federal workers moved into Washington's newest federal building, the largest to be built in half a century. According to one estimate, it contains as much space as a 150-story skyscraper. With great irony (and perhaps some hypocrisy), the new structure was named after Ronald Reagan, a politician who bashed the bureaucracy with special zeal.

later it was back under 25,000. The army grew to 3.7 million during World War I but fell to 214,000 in 1920 and to 135,000 by 1932. Shifts in naval strength were less dramatic but followed a similar pattern.[16]

The enormous military machine assembled to fight World War II—8.3 million soldiers, a 2,800-ship navy, an air corps of 2.4 million personnel and 80,000 planes—also quickly shrank after 1945, but it remained much larger than in the prewar period. With the onset of the Cold War, it was expected to remain large indefinitely.[17] For U.S. military and civilian leaders, World War II was instructive: only with a unified command of all military forces could the government coordinate the land, sea, and air operations essential for modern warfare. In 1947 Congress, acting on this knowledge despite considerable resistance (the navy in particular resented losing full-fledged departmental status), combined the army, navy, and air force into a single cabinet-level National Military Establishment, headquartered in a five-sided building in northern Virginia, across the Potomac River from Washington, D.C. The department was renamed Defense two years later (to avoid the unfortunate acronym NME, "enemy"). From then on, the Pentagon became the symbol of the large, expensive military responsibilities assumed by the United States as a world power.[18]

EXTENSION OF THE FEDERAL DOMAIN. Established in 1979, the Department of Health and Human Services (HHS) embodies another major transformation in the government's role. HHS, like its predecessor, the Department of Health, Education, and Welfare (HEW), is an umbrella department containing numerous social welfare agencies and programs that have their roots in the New Deal and its aftermath.

The establishment of HEW in 1953 by a Republican administration and Congress was a pivotal political statement: the Republicans had finally accepted the legitimacy of the federal government's expanded role in providing for the economic welfare of Americans; their party would not repeal the New Deal but only manage it more efficiently. The creation of HEW also was a Republican ploy to reduce the autonomy of officials appointed by the Democrats during the New Deal.

The next three departments also consolidated expansions of the federal domain while making pointed political statements. The Department of Housing and Urban Development (HUD) embodied the commitments of the Kennedy and Johnson administrations to reviving inner-city neighborhoods and solving urban housing problems. HUD also was linked to the civil rights movement. President John F. Kennedy campaigned for the department in part so he could appoint Robert C. Weaver as its head, thereby seating the first African American in the cabinet. It was President Lyndon Johnson, however, who finally made the appointment after he convinced Congress to authorize HUD in 1965.

The new Department of Transportation became home to all the agencies established piecemeal over the years to promote different forms of transportation: highways, air carriers, railroads, sea transport, and later, urban mass transit. These agencies often had worked at cross purposes—for example, the agency responsible for locating new highways would labor in ignorance of the plans of the agency responsible for locating new airports. President Johnson proposed the department's creation in 1966 to improve coordination of plans and policies for the various interlocking transportation modes. Congress agreed, but only after carefully limiting the department's authority over federal spending for transportation projects. Members were not about to reduce their own influence over a domain so rich in "pork."

The Department of Energy embodied another effort to coordinate policy, this time for types of energy (coal, oil, natural gas, atomic, hydroelectric, geothermal, solar). Its establishment in 1977 was President Jimmy Carter's political response to the energy shortages of the early 1970s and a declaration of his administration's commitment to assuring the nation of adequate supplies of the energy essential to modern American life.

THE SYMBOLISM OF CABINET STATUS. The creation of the Departments of Education in 1979 and Veterans Affairs in 1988 was almost entirely symbolic. By pushing through the legislation that established a cabinet-level Department of Education, Carter kept his promise to the teachers' groups whose support had been crucial to his bid for the White House. The elevation of the Veterans Administration to the Department of Veterans Affairs and to cabinet status was, among other things, a belated symbolic bow to veterans of the long, contentious Vietnam War as well as an effort by the Republican Reagan administration to woo the veteran vote. Neither department came with much in the way of new programs. Education took over programs and bureaus from HEW and other agencies; Veterans Affairs continued to do what it had done as an independent executive agency. Symbolism, then, played a major role in the creation of both departments. Proponents of the departments also hoped that cabinet status would strengthen each department's interests in the battle for government's limited resources, including the president's attention. But symbolism has its drawbacks. Until George W. Bush made education a centerpiece of his 2000 presidential campaign, Republican leaders had regularly sought to dismantle the Department of Education out of hostility to its largely Democratic clientele.

THE DEPARTMENT OF HOMELAND SECURITY. The terrorist attacks of September 11, 2001, inspired the latest addition to the cabinet, the Department of Homeland Security (DHS). President Bush's initial response to the manifest failures of the agencies responsible for preventing such horrors was an executive order establishing a White House Office of Homeland Security, to be headed by former Pennsylvania governor Tom Ridge and charged with coordinating domestic preparedness and counterterrorism among some fifty federal agencies. Despite widespread recognition that an office lacking an independent budget or statutory authority would not be able to overcome congressional and bureaucratic resistance to any sweeping redistribution of authority and resources, the president resisted congressional pressure to create a new cabinet-level department until his staff could work out, in secret, a detailed plan for the department that satisfied the administration's ambitions. The result was a motion, unveiled on June 6, 2002, that was immediately recognized as the most far-reaching government reorganization since the formation of the Department of Defense more than fifty years earlier.

The DHS combined twenty-two agencies having at that time more than 180,000 employees and budgets totaling more than $33 billion, with most resources taken from eight of the existing cabinet departments (see Table 8-2). The diverse agencies that were absorbed into DHS reflect the wide range of potential terrorist targets. They included, for example, the Coast Guard and Transportation Security Administration (both from the Department of Transportation), the Immigration and Naturalization Service (from the Department of Justice), the Animal and Plant Inspection Service (from the Department of Agriculture), the Nuclear Incident Response Team (from the Department of Energy), the Federal Computer Incident Response Center (from the General Services Administration), and the Secret Service and Customs Service (both from Department of the Treasury). DHS did not, however, absorb any of the major agencies dealing with intelligence (the FBI, CIA, or NSA) whose lapses of analysis and coordination were the focus of the post–September 11 investigations; they were eventually covered by a later round of institutional reform (see box "Rationalizing Intelligence" on page 408).

As is the case with all bureaucratic agencies, the structure and authority of DHS reflect its political origins. Experts had for years recommended reorganizing the government to better address the emerging terrorist threat, but congressional and bureaucratic resistance prevented any change until the need for it was so shockingly demonstrated. The attacks had put the United States on a war footing, and the president's constitutional primacy in defense matters, backed by the public's focus on terrorism, forced Congress to concede unprecedented, sweeping authority over the organization of a cabinet-level agency. Most significantly, the administration won the

TABLE 8-2

Nearly Two Dozen Agencies Move to Homeland Security

Agency Moved To ⟶	Border and Transportation Security	Emergency Preparedness and Response	Science and Technology	Information Analysis and Infrastructure Protection
Justice	Immigration and Naturalization Service Office of Domestic Preparedness	Domestic emergency support team National Domestic Preparedness Office (FBI)		National Infrastructure Protection Center
Treasury	U.S. Customs Service Federal Law Enforcement Training Center			
Agriculture			Plum Island Animal Disease Center	
Transportation	Transportation Security Administration			
General Services Administration	Federal Protective Service			Federal Computer Incident Response Center
Health and Human Services		Chemical, biological, radiological, and nuclear response assets		
Energy		Nuclear Incident Response Team	Lawrence Livermore National Laboratory Environmental Measurements Laboratory	National Infrastructure Simulation and Analysis Center Energy Security Program
Defense			National Bio-Weapons Defense Analysis Center	National Communications System
Commerce		Integrated Hazard Information System		Critical Infrastructure Assurance Office
Independent agencies		Federal Emergency Management Agency		
Other	The Coast Guard (from Transportation), the Animal and Plant Health Inspection Service (from Agriculture), and the Secret Service (from Treasury) report directly to the department secretary.			

Source: White House, reprinted in *CQ Weekly,* November 16, 2002, 3002.

authority to write its own personnel rules for the department and, if it chose, to ig-nore protections previously enjoyed under collective bargaining agreements by the many unionized employees in affected agencies. In wartime, the president's national security rationale for reducing transaction costs in managing homeland security policy trumped Congress's normal reluctance to risk higher conformity costs and agency losses by broad delegations of authority to the president.

The DHS is now second only to Defense in number of personnel, although other departments have much larger budgets, notably Treasury, which pays the interest on the public debt, and HHS, which administers the Medicare program (see Table 8-3). Altogether, the executive branch departments account for about 63 percent of the civilian government workforce and about 78 percent of the more than $2.2 trillion the federal government spends annually. The rest is accounted for by a host of agencies that, for a variety of calculated political reasons, have been placed outside the mainline departments.

Non-Cabinet Agencies

The expansion of the federal government has not been confined to cabinet-level executive departments. Since the Civil War, Congress and the president have created an additional set of administrative bodies to make and carry out national policy. Most fall into one of three general categories: independent executive agencies, regulatory commissions, and government corporations.

INDEPENDENT EXECUTIVE AGENCIES. Executive agencies are placed outside departments for one of several reasons, all political. Presidents promoting new initiatives that demand quick action may want to avoid placing bureaucratic layers between them and the responsible agency. For example, President Kennedy kept his cherished Peace Corps out of the stodgy and unsympathetic State Department. When the Soviet Union launched its space vehicle *Sputnik* in 1957, the National Aeronautics and Space Administration (NASA), established in 1958, was the administrative response. Its status as an independent executive agency reflected both the space program's urgency and the politicians' desire to keep it in civilian hands. NASA proved to be a brilliant organizational success, fulfilling President Kennedy's audacious dream of landing a man on the moon by 1969. Agencies also may report directly to the president to enhance the agency's prestige; the Environmental Protection Agency (EPA), a candidate for cabinet status during the Clinton administration, is an example. In keeping with the president's role as commander in chief, the directors of National Intelligence, U.S. Arms Control and Disarmament Agency, and Selective Service System all report directly to the president. Their independent status is intended, in part, to keep important defense-related activities—intelligence gathering, arms control negotiations, and the draft—under predominantly civilian control.

TABLE 8-3		

Projected Cabinet Department Staff and Budget Outlays: 2009 Budget

Department	Personnel (thousands)	Budget (billion dollars)
Agriculture	91.1	94.8
Commerce	53.9	9.2
Defense	677.2	651.2
Education	4.2	63.5
Energy	16.1	23.3
Health and Human Services	60.8	738.7
Homeland Security	166.2	44.3
Housing and Urban Development	9.5	45.6
Interior	68.6	10.2
Justice	115.8	26.5
Labor	16.8	54.2
State	32.2	22.1
Transportation	55.5	71.1
Treasury	109.6	547.8
Veterans Affairs	253.4	91.8

Source: U.S. Office of Management and Budget, *Analytical Perspectives, Budget of the United States Government, Fiscal Year 2009*, 340, 365.

The independent executive agencies, as organizations, look much like the divisions within regular executive departments. They typically are headed by presidential appointees, subject to Senate approval, who serve "at the pleasure of the president"—meaning the president can dismiss them at any time. One example is the Social Security Administration, which has a budget larger than any cabinet-level department except HHS ($692.8 billion in 2008) and was part of HHS until 1995. The Veterans Administration was an independent executive agency before it was elevated to the Department of Veterans Affairs in 1988. The United States Information Agency was also independent until 1997, when Republican Jesse Helms of North Carolina, chair of the Senate Foreign Relations Committee, insisted that, for economy's sake, it be put under the State Department.

INDEPENDENT REGULATORY COMMISSIONS. Unlike the independent executive agencies, independent regulatory commissions are designed to maintain their independence from the president and the executive departments. Congress adopted the commission form of administration to cope with new problems of delegation. The emergence after the Civil War of an industrial economy with a national market gave rise to economic dislocations and disputes on a scale too wide to be managed, as in the past, by local authorities. As a result, the railroads and the steel, oil, and banking industries became targets for national regulation. But Congress could not and did not want to do the regulating itself; the issues were too many, too technical, too dynamic, and too fraught with political conflict. The regulatory commission represents Congress's attempt to hedge against the potential political costs of delegation by restricting the influence of presidents and party politics on regulatory decisions. Table 8-4 lists the most important independent regulatory commissions.

Typically, independent regulatory commissions are run by boards of commissioners (usually five in number) who conduct their decision making by majority rule rather than by single directors. The commissioners are appointed by the president, with the consent of the Senate, to serve fixed, staggered terms of no fewer than five years. Terms are staggered so presidents cannot stack the deck in their favor by new appointments; terms of five or more years ensure that service exceeds any single presidential term. In most cases the president cannot dismiss appointees without cause—evidence of some sort of malfeasance—and therefore cannot simply replace commissioners whose decisions are displeasing. Appointments are bipartisan, with no party permitted to have more than a one-vote majority. In theory, this keeps presidents from stacking the agency with their own partisans, but in practice, they always can find someone in the other party who shares their regulatory goals.

On occasion Congress does give the president greater than normal authority over regulatory bodies. Some agencies are governed by commissioners who serve at the president's pleasure. Other regulatory agencies, such as the Food and Drug Administration and the Occupational Safety and Health Administration, are ordinary bureaus housed in executive departments and subject to the normal executive authority. Congress is not without means for keeping these agencies at least as responsive to it as to the president, but sometimes Congress chooses not to use the tools at its disposal.

A major reason for delegating authority to an independent agency is to avoid direct responsibility for unpopular decisions. In 1887 Congress set up the now-defunct Interstate Commerce Commission to regulate the railroads in part because any decision made about shipping rates would likely anger some politically potent interest. The Postal Rate Commission takes the heat for increases in postage rates. The most striking case, however, is the Federal Reserve Board, which makes decisions of enormous consequence for the entire economy (see box "Insulating the Fed"). In this case and in others, the agency's independence helps to insulate the president and Congress from the political fallout from unpopular decisions, explaining why both have been willing to accept this form of administration.

Over the years, the government's regulatory reach expanded in roughly three waves. The first, which swept in during the late nineteenth and early twentieth centuries as government sought to cope with a rapidly expanding national market economy, was regulation of the railroads (Interstate Commerce Commission), trusts (Federal Trade Commission), and monetary system (Federal Reserve System). The second, also economic in focus, occurred during the 1930s as part of the Franklin D. Roosevelt administration's response to the Great Depression. The government assumed responsibility for, among other things, the integrity of the banking system (Federal Deposit Insurance Corporation), the stock market (Securities and Exchange Commission), and labor relations (National Labor Relations Board). The third wave occurred during the 1960s and 1970s as a growing network of activist organizations lobbied successfully for federal protection of consumers (Consumer Product Safety Commission), motorists (National Transportation Safety Board), the environment (Environmental Protection Agency, Nuclear Regulatory Commission), and civil rights (Equal Employment Opportunity Commission).

The third wave did the most to expand the scope of regulation (see Figure 8-3). The dramatic growth in regulation during the 1970s, as measured by the number of

TABLE 8-4

Independent Regulatory Commissions

Agency	Year Established	Term of Service	Service at President's Discretion?
Federal Reserve System (Fed)	1913	14	No
Federal Trade Commission (FTC)	1914	7	No
Federal Deposit Insurance Corporation (FDIC)	1933	6	No
Federal Communications Commission (FCC)	1934	7	No
Securities and Exchange Commission (SEC)	1934	5	Yes
National Labor Relations Board (NLRB)	1935	5	No
Federal Maritime Commission (FMC)	1961	5	No
Equal Employment Opportunity Commission (EEOC)	1965	5	Yes
National Transportation Safety Board (NTSB)	1966	5	Yes
Postal Rate Commission (PRC)	1970	6	No
Consumer Product Safety Commission (CPSC)	1972	7	No
Commodity Futures Trading Commission (CFTC)	1975	5	No
Federal Election Commission (FEC)	1975	6	No
Nuclear Regulatory Commission (NRC)	1975	5	No

Source: Compiled by the authors.

LOGIC OF POLITICS

Insulating the Fed

Sometimes the task given an independent regulatory commission is such a hot potato that members of Congress, the president, and even lobbyists maintain a hands-off policy. When the task is the sensitive one of setting a nation's economic course, the logic of insulating the commission from political pressures makes imminent sense. The Federal Reserve System, popularly known as the Fed, is the most independent and powerful of the regulatory commissions. Its main responsibility is to make monetary policy.

The decisions handed down by the Fed influence the country's supply of credit and level of interest rates, which in turn affect the rates of inflation, unemployment, and economic growth. During periods of economic recession and high unemployment, the Fed buys securities from banks, increasing the banks' reserves so that they have more money to make loans. Interest rates then fall, stimulating investment that leads to faster economic growth and job formation. This makes everyone happy. When a booming economy and low unemployment bring (or sometimes

Alan Greenspan (right) congratulates his successor, Ben Bernanke.

pages in the *Federal Register* (which publishes all new administrative rules that have the force of law), was followed by a drop in the 1980s after the deregulation of the transportation and telecommunications sectors and the 1981 arrival of the Reagan administration, which was ideologically hostile to regulation. The Clinton administration clearly was not, and regulatory activity expanded once again during the 1990s before leveling off during the more anti-regulatory George W. Bush administration.

Variations in the structure, duties, and procedures of independent regulatory agencies, as with all other government agencies, stem from the politics of their creation. Agencies embody the objectives, strategies, and uncertainties of the coalitions that bring them into being. Because the parties making up these coalitions have different objectives, agencies often are given potentially incompatible missions. For example,

even threaten) inflation, the Fed puts on the brakes by selling securities, which reduces the supply of money banks can lend, thereby raising interest rates. Profits fall, investment declines, the economy slows, and some people may lose their jobs. This does not make everyone happy.

Members of the Fed's board of governors are appointed by the president, with the Senate's approval, to a single fourteen-year term; they can be removed only for cause (evidence of wrong-doing). The board's chair, who dominates its deliberations and is appointed for a renewable four-year term, is one of the most influential people in government. During the long economic expansion and stock market boom of the 1990s, the financial community scrutinized Chairman Alan Greenspan's every comment for omens about the future of interest rates, and every hint of an increase brought a sharp (but often temporary) drop in the price of stocks and bonds. When the economy later slowed after September 11, 2001, and stock prices tumbled, the Fed began reducing interest rates in an effort to stave off recession, cutting them eleven times in 2001 alone. In 2004, as signs of economic recovery set off inflation worries, the Fed began raising rates again. Rising interest rates contributed to a crisis in the housing market, forcing up mortgage costs while the price of houses was falling. Large financial institutions lost billions of dollars when many homeowners, especially those with variable-rate mortgages, could no longer meet their mortgage payments on houses now worth less than what they owed on them. It was left to Ben Bernanke, Greenspan's successor appointed in 2006, to deal with the financial fallout of the housing meltdown in 2008 by pumping $540 billion in loans into the money market funds in an attempt to unfreeze the credit market.

Presidents sometimes complain about the Fed's decisions, but they do not really desire greater control over the Fed because they do not want responsibility for its decisions. Neither does Congress, which even allows the Fed to finance itself through its own investments. Politically insulated, the Fed is left alone to take the heat for the painful steps sometimes needed to protect the nation's economy. Nonetheless, the Fed is usually careful to accommodate the fiscal policies of the president and Congress. Even when the president and Congress are genuinely unhappy with the Fed's actions, they dare not do much beyond grumbling about it because any real action to curb the Fed might spook the financial markets.

Source: Jeffrey E. Cohen, *Politics and Economic Policy in the United States* (Boston: Houghton Mifflin, 1997), 215–221.

the Interstate Commerce Commission was supposed not only to regulate railroads in the public interest but also to ensure they remained profitable. Interests opposed to regulation sometimes lose the battle over creating an agency but win the war by strangling it with "fragmented authority, labyrinthine procedures, mechanisms of political intervention, and other structures that subvert the bureaucracy's performance and open it up to attack." [19] In other words, unresolved political conflicts may be built into an agency's structure, where they will continue to play themselves out in a new venue.

INDEPENDENT GOVERNMENT CORPORATIONS. When Congress puts the government in the business of delivering the kinds of services usually provided by private corporations, it sometimes imitates the corporate form of administration as

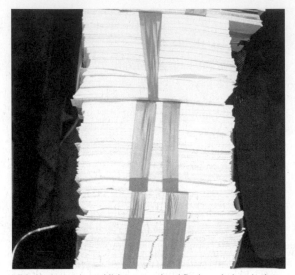

All federal agencies publish proposed and final regulations in the *Federal Register*. In 2007 it contained more than seventy-four thousand pages.

well. Like private corporations, government corporations are typically run by a chief executive officer, or CEO, under the supervision of a board of directors or commissioners and chosen in the same manner as members of regulatory commissions. Government corporations can buy and sell property, lend and borrow money, and sue or be sued like any other business. Congress, however, may put any constraints it chooses on their organization or activities.

Besides the U.S. Postal Service, the most important of the government corporations are the Tennessee Valley Authority (TVA) and the National Railroad Passenger Corporation, or Amtrak. The TVA was created in 1933, during the New Deal, to develop electric power, water transportation, and agriculture in the Tennessee Valley area, which at the time was poor and economically backward. Amtrak, launched in 1970, represents Congress's effort to maintain intercity rail passenger service, which had been dying out for want of investment and from competition from air, bus, and auto travel. The U.S. Postal Service actually predates the Constitution; it was established in 1777 by the Second Continental Congress. Known then as the Post Office Department, it was for much of its history the largest government agency delivering the most familiar government service. It also was a major source of congressional patronage during the heyday of patronage-based party politics in the latter decades of the nineteenth century (see Chapter 12). But politics did not promote efficiency or innovation in the postal service, and by the post–World War II economic expansion, the system's inadequacies had become quite evident. The agency was radically reorganized as a government corporation in 1970.

INDIRECT ADMINISTRATION. Over the past sixty years federal spending in real (inflation-adjusted) dollars has increased by 500 percent, and federal programs and activities have mushroomed. Yet the federal workforce has scarcely grown at all (see Figure 8-1, page 372; in fact, as a proportion of the population (and total labor force) it has been falling for more than fifty years (see Figure 8-2, page 372). How can this be? The answer, as we saw in Chapter 3, is that many federal policies and programs are administered by someone else: state governments, private contractors, and grant recipients. State governments administer such major social welfare programs as Medicaid and Temporary Assistance for Needy Families. State and local agencies also carry out some of the federal government's regulatory work, such as enforcing air pollution rules and occupational health and safety standards. By delegating administrative duties to state and local government agencies, Congress can add programs, which voters like, without increasing the federal bureaucracy, which voters do not like.

The federal government also provides grants to private nonprofit organizations and to state and local governments to implement programs. For example, the Depart-

Figure 8-3 The Growth of Federal Regulation

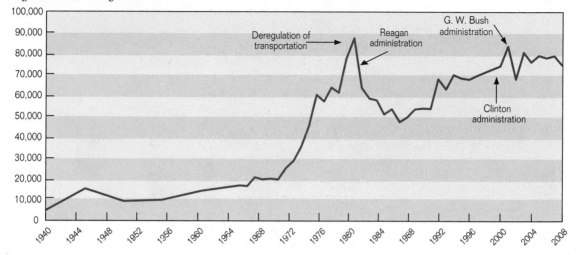

Pages in the Federal Register

Sources: Harold W. Stanley and Richard G. Neimi, *Vital Statistics on American Politics, 2003–2004* (Washington, D.C.: CQ Press, 2003), 266; data for 2003–2007 compiled by author from the *Federal Register* for that year.

ment of Education's programs for Indian education, special education, library construction, vocational education, and adult education are all carried out by nonfederal organizations funded by grants dispensed by the department. Nonfederal institutions, including universities, research laboratories, and think tanks, administer more than 80 percent of the federal government's scientific research funds.[20] The government also contracts with private companies for a countless variety of goods and services. The Department of Energy, for example, uses contractors to operate nuclear weapons plants; NASA uses contractors to load the space shuttle and to pick up its reusable engines after liftoff.[21] Contracts and grants thus provide another way for the federal government to take on more tasks without hiring more personnel. For politicians, the payoff can be significant. They can claim credit for reducing the size of the federal bureaucracy without reducing popular programs and services.

Indirect administration is not without political risks to principals. During investigations in 2004 into the abuse of prisoners held by the American military at Abu Ghraib prison outside of Baghdad, Iraq, senior members of Congress discovered that the accused abusers included some private contractors hired by the Defense Department to conduct interrogations.[22] Later, the activities of a private firm handling security for the State Department created another political stir symptomatic of the problems created by the administration's extensive use of private contractors in Iraq (see box "Outsourcing the War in Iraq").

LOGIC OF POLITICS

Outsourcing the War in Iraq

On September 16, 2007, guards employed by Blackwater USA, a private firm hired by the State Department to provide armed security for its employees in Iraq, opened fire in a Baghdad square, killing seventeen civilians and wounding eighteen others. The guards claimed they had been fired on and were simply defending themselves; Iraqi witnesses said the action had been unprovoked. An FBI investigation found no evidence of an attack on the guards and determined that at least fourteen of the seventeen deaths were entirely unjustified.[1] The Iraqi government was outraged and moved to ban Blackwater from operating in the country but quickly lifted the ban when the United States made it clear that, without Blackwater's services, American diplomats could not leave the heavily protected "Green Zone." The State Department did not try to justify the guards' action, but it did defend its use of private firms to provide its security. The U.S. ambassador to Iraq, Ryan Crocker, testifying before a Senate committee on the issue, put it this way:

Plainclothes contractors working for Blackwater USA have taken an active part in firefights during the Iraq War. Here they join U.S. troops in defending a position in Najaf against militias loyal to Muqtada Al Sadr, a prominent opponent of the U.S. occupation.

Because much of the government's work is performed by someone other than federal bureaucrats, a head count of federal personnel drastically understates the government's true size. According to one authoritative estimate, in 2005, in addition to the federal civilian workforce of 1.9 million, full-time equivalents of 7.6 million employees worked under federal contracts, 2.9 million held jobs created by federal grants, 767,000 worked for the Post Office, and 1.44 million served in the armed forces, for a total federal workforce of 14.6 million.[23] Add the estimated 4.6 million in state and local positions created by federal mandates, and the total reaches 19 million.[24]

"There is simply no way at all that the State Department's Bureau of Diplomatic Security could ever have enough full-time personnel to staff the security function in Iraq. There is no alternative except through contracts." [2]

The same could be said of the entire American effort in Iraq. The estimated 160,000 employees working for private contractors in Iraq in 2007 actually outnumbered the American military personnel there. In addition to providing security, they performed such vital functions as transporting food, fuel, and ammunition for the U.S. forces. Proponents claim that outsourcing such services saves money; its critics argue that the savings are mythical but the costs in lost accountability are real. [3] The Blackwater incident, the Abu Ghraib prison scandal, and criminal investigations into alleged corruption in multibillion-dollar procurement contracts highlight the problems inherent in delegating key functions on this scale under chaotic conditions. Monitoring agents is always problematic, but all the more so when the people responsible for the monitoring are in short supply and distracted by more pressing duties. As Shay D. Assad, the director of defense procurement and acquisition policy, put it, "in a combat environment, we didn't have checks and balances we should have in place, so people who don't have ethics and integrity are going to be able to get away with things." [4]

The broader issue of how to prevent massive agency losses has become increasingly acute as the total spent by the government through contracts and grants has grown to more than $500 billion per year. For example, when the Pentagon more than doubled the volume of goods and services it purchased from the private sector between 2001 and 2006, it found itself without the staff and expertise needed to oversee the contracts and had to hire private companies to do the supervisory work. "In some instances, businesses that had won multibillion-dollar contracts were later awarded additional contracts to supervise their own performance." [5] This is obviously not a recipe for effective control of agents.

---

1. David Johnston and John M. Broder, "FBI Says Guards Killed 14 Iraqis without Cause," *New York Times*, November 13, 2007, A1.

2. Peter Grier and Gordon Lubold, "Private Security in Iraq: Whose Rules?" *Christian Science Monitor*, September 20, 2007, at www.csmonitor.com/2007/0920/p01s05-wome.html, accessed December 21, 2007.

3. Peter W. Singer, "Sure. He's Got Guns for Hire. But They're Just Not Worth It," *Washington Post*, October 7, 2007, archived at www.brookings.edu/opinions/2007/1007militarycontractors.aspx, accessed December 21, 2007.

4. Eric Schmitt and Ginger Thompson, "$6 Billion in Contracts Reviewed, Pentagon Says," *New York Times*, September 21, 2007, A1, at www.nytimes.com/2007/09/21/washington/21contract.html?pagewanted=print, accessed December 21, 2007.

5. Josh Rogin, "The Hidden Cost of a Buying Spree," *CQ Weekly*, July 23, 2007, 2168.

Bureaucracy in Action

Who are the bureaucrats? The people who staff the myriad federal agencies by and large contradict the stereotypical image of "bureaucrat" prevalent in American popular culture. Accused variously of being inordinately "inflexible, rule-bound, cautious, impersonal, haughty, fearful, deceptive, alienated, or secretive," the reality disclosed by empirical research suggests, if anything, the contrary. [25] Moreover, the federal civil service mirrors the American population far more accurately than, say, Congress. Thirty percent are minorities, matching the overall population; 45 percent are women. Their range of skills matches that of workers in the private sector, as does their dedication to their jobs. Their views on most public or personal issues are indistinguishable from those of other citizens—except that they place a higher value on civic participation and commitment to democratic values. Contrary to popular belief, civil servants generally perform their jobs as well or better than people doing the same work in the private sector. Most, in fact, want to be good "agents," responsive to elected officials and supportive of the missions assigned to their agencies.[26] The federal bureaucracy displays numerous and sometimes severe shortcomings, to be sure, but these cannot be fairly blamed on the civil servants staffing the institutions.

Bureaucratic Culture and Autonomy

In theory, bureaucratic agencies are subject to the authority of Congress, the president, and the courts, but bureaucrats are by no means always kept on a short leash; some agencies operate with substantial autonomy, while others are carefully monitored by their multiple principals. The ability of agencies to expand their autonomy—that is, to use their discretionary authority as they think best—depends on a variety of circumstances, not the least of which are the political skills of individual bureaucrats.

It is neither surprising nor necessarily a bad thing that government agencies strive for autonomy. During long service in agencies, people develop a strong sense of what their agency is supposed do and how it is supposed to do it—that is, they absorb its **bureaucratic culture.** Political scientist James Q. Wilson defines an organization's culture as its "persistent, patterned way of thinking about the central tasks of and human relationships within [the] organization. Culture is to an organization what personality is to an individual. Like human culture generally, it is passed on from one generation to the next. It changes slowly, if at all."[27]

Bureaucrats imbued with their agency's culture come to dislike interference from outsiders ignorant of the problems, practices, and political environment the bureaucrats know so intimately. They also tend to value their agency's programs and services more highly than outsiders might and thus seek the resources and the freedom to carry out their missions in the way they believe is best. On the whole, then, there is nothing undesirable about having agencies staffed with people who have a strong sense of professionalism and confidence that their work is important and that they know best how to do it. A nation would not want its military officers, for example, to think any other way. The problem is that the very conditions that give an agency high morale and a strong sense of mission may encourage it to seek independence from political control.

The development of distinctive bureaucratic cultures and missions also inhibits cooperation between agencies. The FBI's traditional mission, for example, has been to catch and punish lawbreakers, so it has come to value the kind of information that can be used to convict criminals in public court. The CIA is charged with secretly monitoring potential foreign enemies and thwarting their plots, so it resists any release of information that might eventually expose its informers or methods. The two agencies also operate under very different sets of legal constraints imposed by Congress in response to actual or imaginable abuses of power. Hence even after September 11 the

FBI and CIA have remained reluctant to share information, and getting them to cooperate in other ways has remained difficult.

For similar reasons, the integration of the DHS's disparate bureaucratic components, each imbued with its distinctive bureaucratic culture, into an institution capable of coping with the huge range of tasks needing coordinated attention if the United States were to be made secure from terrorist attack has proven a daunting task. The legislation creating DHS provided for a year of transition to get the department up and running, but the process has taken years to complete. Experts on mergers and acquisitions from the private sector—people who had overseen huge corporate acquisi-

The U.S. Forest Service, which maintains the nation's 152 national forests, enjoys a reputation for professionalism and independence. The agency has achieved this standing despite the fact that 90 percent of its revenue traditionally comes from logging permits. A less professional organization might favor logging and forget conservation. Controlled burns, as shown here, are routinely employed by the U.S. Forest Service to maintain healthy forest lands and prevent massive fires that would endanger nearby private property.

tions at General Electric, Hewlett-Packard, and Lockheed Martin—had to be solicited for advice, for no one else had experience with reorganization on such a grand scale.[28]

Bureaucrats as Politicians

As partisans of their agencies and missions, bureaucrats are necessarily politicians. Indeed, the Weberian notion of civil servants who act as neutral instruments for implementing the policies chosen by their elected superiors has never taken hold in the United States. Agency officials operate in a world of competition for scarce resources, often intense conflicts among interests and values, and multiple bosses (principals). Scholars have proposed a variety of motives, in addition to the desire for autonomy, that might account for bureaucratic behavior. These motives include a quest for larger budgets, more subordinates, and greater authority; the chance to do some good; a preference for a stable, predictable environment; and the opportunity for career security and advancement. But whatever the goals, they can be achieved only through politics: mobilizing supporters, gathering allies, negotiating mutually beneficial deals with other politicians, keeping in touch with people whose cooperation is needed, and adapting to the realities of power.

The political environment of most government agencies is occupied by the House and Senate members of the subcommittees handling agencies' authorizing statutes and budgets, the committee and subcommittee staff, the political appointees who head agencies, the White House (especially its Office of Management and Budget), the interest groups affected by agency activities, and the federal courts. Occasionally,

The National Aeronautics and Space Administration (NASA) runs the U.S. space program, an expensive enterprise ($17.3 billion in 2008) that has no direct impact on the lives of most Americans. To win support, NASA encourages the public to share in the excitement of space exploration by offering spectacular pictures and detailed information on Web sites devoted to each of its missions. The Mars *Pathfinder* mission's rover returned this panorama of the Martian landscape in 1997. Ten years later, NASA announced plans to put a person on Mars by 2037.

the news media and the broader public also show up on the radar screen. Bureaucrats' most important political relationship is usually the one with Congress, as it controls the organization, authority, budgets, and staffing—in fact, the very existence—of departments and bureaus. Although presidential appointees rarely stay in their agencies more than a few years, members of Congress and senior committee staff are in for the long haul, as are the interest groups that play an important role in Congress's political environment. Keeping Congress happy often means keeping interest groups happy.

Politically astute bureaucrats carefully cultivate members of Congress and their staffs. The principle is simple, though following it is sometimes far from simple: do things that help members to achieve their goals and avoid doing things that have the opposite effect. Along the way, establish a reputation for competence and frugality. No one whose job relies on voters is going to defend bureaucratic ineptitude or malfeasance.[29] Keeping in touch, usually through congressional staff, also is crucial. Politicians and bureaucrats live in an uncertain, ever-changing world. Good information is a scarce and therefore valuable commodity (see Chapter 6). Information about their own activities is one political resource bureaucrats have in abundance. A regular exchange of intelligence helps both sides anticipate consequences and reduces the incidence of unpleasant surprises. Shrewd bureaucrats are responsive to informal suggestions as well as legislative mandates; they can take a hint. In short, bureaucrats prosper by convincing their congressional principals that they are good and faithful agents— never an easy task where hidden action and hidden information abound.

The survival of bureaucrats, like that of other politicians, also depends on having an appreciative constituency. Some agencies acquire organized constituencies at the moment of birth—the interests who lobbied them into existence. Others have to organize supporters themselves. An early secretary of commerce, for example, helped to found the U.S. Chamber of Commerce. Many of the groups that now lobby on behalf of programs for the physically disabled, mentally ill, and other disadvantaged people were brought into being through the efforts of government officials in social service agencies (for other examples, see Chapter 13).[30] Agencies that service politically feeble clienteles—such as the Bureau of Prisons (federal criminals) and the Agency for International Development (foreign countries)—inevitably suffer in the struggle for political attention and resources. Government agencies also try to cultivate broad public support, and most have public relations offices devoted to publicizing their activities.

Savvy bureaucrats design and manage their programs in ways that enhance political support in Congress. If feasible, programs produce widely distributed local benefits even when their main purpose is to generate diffuse national benefits. For example, defense spending buys a diffuse national good—protection from potential enemy nations—but also helps the local economies where the money is spent. Aware of this aspect of military procurement, Pentagon officials protect weapons programs by making sure weapons components are produced in as many states and districts as possible (see box "How to Build a [Military] Airplane").

Bureaucrats also target benefits to key members of Congress. For example, from 1965 through 1974 a disproportionate share of grants for water and sewer facilities under a program administered by HUD went to the districts' subcommittee members that dealt with the program and to those of conservatives who otherwise might have voted against it.[31] To sweeten such deals, bureaucrats make sure members of Congress take credit when local projects or grants are announced. They also try to stay in close touch with the organized interests active in their policy domains to anticipate and possibly head off political problems (see box "A Politically Untouchable Bureaucrat: J. Edgar Hoover of the FBI"). The interest groups, for their part, naturally want to maintain cordial relations with "their" agencies as well.

Bureaucratic Infighting

Agencies with different missions, clienteles, skills, and ideologies compete for influence, authority over policy, control of implementation, and resources. The most striking recent example was the bitter infighting between the State and Defense Departments over guidance of policy toward the war in Iraq (see box "State and Defense at War"). Bureaucratic infighting also takes place within organizations. Many military professionals, for example, were unenthusiastic about the nation-building role they were assigned in Iraq. The armed forces are organized, equipped, and trained to fight wars, not to police cities, manage public works, or install democratic institutions. Thus they did not share their civilian bosses' ambition to control the process of rebuilding Iraq. Indeed, strong disagreements between civilian and military leaders in the Defense Department are routine. Former defense secretary Donald Rumsfeld had to overcome considerable resistance to develop a war-fighting strategy in Iraq that relied more on speed, technology, coordinated air support, and special forces units than on large numbers of heavily armed soldiers on the ground. The strategy's initial success

STRATEGY AND CHOICE

How to Build a (Military) Airplane

National defense is a public good. Yet, as much as voters value it, candidates cannot get much electoral edge simply by supporting it. All politicians endorse national defense, but none can credibly claim great personal credit for providing it. So in order to use defense to gain a competitive advantage over future opponents, members of Congress focus on the thousands of separable activities that contribute to the nation's defense—mostly by protecting their district's and state's military facilities and defense contractors. The Pentagon and those companies that build the nation's weapons systems understand this strategy. To entice congressional support for their weapons programs, the military bureaucracy and its prime defense contractors—Boeing, Lockheed Martin, Raytheon, and others—spread as much of the subcontracting for a weapon's supplies and components as broadly as possible. In a real sense, a military weapon is the physical embodiment of a political coalition.

The B-1 Bomber was assembled in this Palmdale, California, plant, but with components manufactured in forty-eight other states.

When California-based defense contractor Rockwell started production of the B-1 bomber in the 1970s, the plane had already experienced enough serious cost overruns, technical snags, and congressional rumblings to result in the project's cancellation. Rockwell saw the project through to successful production, however, by making this new bomber politically attractive to as many of those who would decide its future as pos-

sible. In one manifestation of this strategy, Rockwell spent only 29 percent of the bomber's development and production budget in California; it distributed the rest to hundreds of subcontractors scattered across forty-eight other states. By comparison, when McDonnell Douglas built a passenger jet, the MD-80, to be sold to airlines rather than the government, it did not have to build political support and was free to subcontract strictly according to financial and technical considerations. Consequently, this prime contractor spent 57 percent of its production allowance in-house and paid the remainder to subcontractors in fewer than half as many states.

Source: Kenneth R. Mayer, *The Political Economy of Defense Contracting* (New Haven: Yale University Press, 1991), 158–174.

STRATEGY AND CHOICE
....

A Politically Untouchable Bureaucrat
J. Edgar Hoover of the FBI

The career of J. Edgar Hoover, director of the Federal Bureau of Investigation (FBI) from 1924 until his death in 1972, reveals just how much power and independence a politically astute bureaucrat can amass. Officially the FBI is a subunit of the Justice Department. Its director is subordinate to the attorney general and serves at the pleasure of the president. How then did Hoover manage to hold onto his job for forty-eight years even though his conflicts with the various attorneys general and the eight different presidents under whom he served would have ended in the firing of anyone else?

Taking over an agency notorious for its corruption, political favoritism, and incompetence, Hoover turned it into a professional, disciplined, technologically advanced, and efficient anticrime force—and then did everything he could to make sure the public would always see it as such. One of his innovations, the famous "Ten Most-Wanted List," still generates news reports of FBI triumphs whenever suspects on the list are captured. Hoover also cooperated with the journalists and radio, movie, and television producers who made FBI agents the heroes of their stories. He remained wary, however, of the crime-fighting activities—enforcing drug laws and attacking organized crime—in which the bureau might not succeed and which might invite corruption. Indeed, for years Hoover denied that organized crime even existed.

Hoover also cultivated and served two clienteles. First, the FBI served local police departments, which consulted, among other things, its Central Fingerprint Repository and National Automobile Altered Number File. Second, the bureau fueled and championed the cause of people who thought the United States was swarming with subversives bent on destroying the American way of life. In the eyes of many Americans, any criticism of Hoover or the FBI carried the taint of disloyalty. Hoover also used the bureau to gather highly personal information about politically prominent individuals who might cross him. That way, the information could be selectively shared with those in power and leaked to cooperative members of Congress or friendly reporters.

Although presidents from Franklin D. Roosevelt to Richard Nixon would have happily fired Hoover, the potential political cost was never worth the potential political gains. So, they had to live with him. Hoover used his autonomy to run the FBI like a personal fiefdom, and he illegally harassed organizations and leaders he found politically objectionable, keeping a separate set of secret records on the projects so that his and the FBI's lawbreaking would not be discovered. In the early 1960s, although formally under the supervision of Robert F. Kennedy (at right in photo), the attorney general and brother of President John F. Kennedy (left), Hoover ran his agency without much regard for the wishes of either Kennedy. Threatening to leak embarrassing information on civil rights leader Martin Luther King Jr., Hoover "persuaded" the Kennedys to authorize phone wiretaps on King, which unleashed massive FBI surveillance of the civil rights leader. Hoover's attempt to discredit King was probably his most egregious abuse of power.

Source: Jack H. Knott and Gary J. Miller, *Reforming Bureaucracy: The Politics of Institutional Choice* (Englewood Cliffs, N.J.: Prentice Hall, 1987), 190–192.

favored the civilian defense intellectuals around Rumsfeld, who wanted to restructure the military for twenty-first century warfare as they envisioned it, in their struggles with military professionals, who defended the force configurations and war-fighting doctrines that formed part of their bureaucratic cultures. Later developments in Iraq forced both sides to reconsider what kind of military would be best suited to the tasks it was likely to face in the future.

Who Controls the Bureaucracy?

The more things elected representatives want the government to do, the more discretionary authority they must give to administrators. The proliferation of government agencies and programs during the New Deal and afterward has led critics to charge that Congress has abdicated its authority to the president, to an out-of-control bureaucracy, or to the clients the agencies serve.[32] The charges deserve to be taken seriously. Congress, in fact, has delegated a wide range of tasks, often with only the vaguest guidelines on how authority is to be exercised. In 1914, for example, Congress authorized the Federal Trade Commission to enforce laws against "unfair methods of competition . . . and unfair or deceptive acts or practices" without defining what these methods, acts, or practices were. At times, government agencies and programs have served private interests almost exclusively; the history of the Department of Agriculture is littered with examples. Regulatory commissions have sometimes served as the handmaidens of the interests they are supposed to regulate in the public interest. Until the mid-1970s, for example, the Civil Aeronautics Board fought valiantly to protect the major airlines from competition. Congress often pays little attention to what its bureaucratic agents are doing, as administrative oversight is not a high priority (see Chapter 6). However, congressional majorities have found many ways in which to delegate authority without abdicating control. Legislators are fully aware of principal–agent dilemmas (though they do not think of them in those terms) and have strategies to cope with them.

Methods of Congressional Control

Congress operates from a position of overwhelming strength in its relationship to administrative agencies. It creates and empowers them by ordinary legislation, and it can eliminate or change them in the same way. Most agencies require new budget appropriations every year to continue functioning. Congress also has a say in who is appointed to head departments and bureaus. Indeed, some programs are set up with the explicit understanding that a particular individual will or, in some cases, will not be chosen to run it. Any president who wants an agency to thrive will choose appointees who can get on well with the agency's handlers in Congress. Bureaucratic agents recognize that, at some level, the very existence of their agency (and jobs) depends on at least the toleration of their congressional principals even when the principals seem to be paying no attention to what they are doing.

LOGIC OF POLITICS

State and Defense at War

Both the State and Defense Departments perform tasks that are integral to the conduct of U.S. foreign policy, but they have very different assignments. State conducts diplomacy, managing the United States' political relationships with other nations and international bodies. Defense prepares to fight and win wars. Friction easily arises when each department, in pursuing its tasks, makes the other's work more difficult. For example, the most effective course of military action may require ignoring the sensitivities of friendly or neutral foreign governments; conversely, maintaining international support for American foreign policy may require limiting military options and increasing risks to combatants. During the George W. Bush administration, the endemic conflicts between State and Defense were intensified by ideological differences between the political appointees the president chose to lead each department. These divisions became more acute when attention turned to Iraq after the Taliban regime in Afghanistan had fallen. Secretary Donald Rumsfeld and his hawkish staff of defense intellectuals believed that removing Saddam Hussein's regime was essential to American national security, and therefore it was in the United States' best interest to use military force to achieve this end without delay, and, if necessary, without international backing. Secretary Colin Powell's State Department was more cautious, more doubtful about the need for immediate action, and more concerned with developing international backing for the use of military force to overthrow the Iraqi dictator.

In all such conflicts, the president ultimately decides who prevails. Diplomacy did so for a time. Powell and the president persuaded the UN Security Council to demand, under threat of war, that Iraq permit weapons inspectors to renew their investigations. Iraq's partial compliance was sufficient to keep the council from authorizing the military action against Hussein's regime; countries opposed to using force included nations usually considered the United States' closest friends, including Canada, Chile, France, Germany, Mexico, and Turkey. When diplomacy failed, the president chose nonetheless to make war on Iraq allied with a "coalition of the willing," of which only Great Britain supplied significant military resources.

Bush's decision to wage a preemptive war opposed by most of America's traditional allies represented a triumph for civilian leadership of the Defense Department—namely, the group of defense intellectuals surrounding Rumsfeld. As one embittered State Department officer put it, "I just wake up in the morning and tell myself, 'There's been a military coup,' and then it all makes sense."[1] The ascendancy of Defense reflected, in part, wartime realities, but also the president's own preferences. In wartime even more than peacetime, the president has the power to settle policy arguments among his appointees and their agencies; indeed, often only he can settle them. After 9/11 gave George W. Bush's presidency its mission—defending the United States against terrorists and, by extension, anyone else who might threaten the U.S. homeland, directly or indirectly—the president proved more willing to risk action than inaction, more willing to alienate friendly nations than to accept the constraints of collective international action. It is not surprising, then, that influence over foreign policy shifted from State to Defense. When the president's cabinet was reorganized after the 2004 election, Powell departed and Rumsfeld stayed on until he was replaced by Robert Gates after the 2006 elections.

1. "Diplomats on the Defensive," *Los Angeles Times,* May 8, 2003.

Colin Powell and Donald Rumsfeld flanking their boss—and referee.

In May of 2007, former assistant attorney general James B. Comey testified that in 2004 the White House had pressured him and hospitalized attorney general John Ashcroft to approve continued wiretaps, circumventing judicial approval. When the Senate Judiciary Committee inquired about this in 2004 and invited Ashcroft and Comey to testify, the Justice Department responded that neither man "would be in a position to provide any new information." Three years later, with the committee now controlled by the opposition Democrats, Comey recounted this incident before the same committee. Not surprisingly, the Democrats who took control of the House and Senate after the 2006 elections proved much more eager to investigate the activities of the Bush administration than had the Republicans when they were in control.

Congress uses a variety of methods to keep its bureaucratic agents in line. Among them are:

- **Hearings and investigations,** in which bureaucrats are called before subcommittees to explain and defend their decisions, and outsiders are sometimes invited to criticize them. Most agencies must testify annually about their activities before the House Appropriations subcommittee that has jurisdiction over their budgets.

- **Mandatory reports,** in which Congress requires executive agencies, even the president, to report on programs. For example, under an anti-drug bill passed in 1986 the president is required to submit a report every March 1 on whether certain nations where illegal narcotics are produced or transshipped have "cooperated fully" with U.S. efforts to stem the drug traffic. Countries not certified as cooperating face a cutoff in U.S. aid.

- **Legislative vetoes,** which allow one or both houses of Congress (sometimes even individual House and Senate committees) to veto by majority vote an agency's policy proposals. Although the Supreme Court in 1983 declared the legislative veto unconstitutional because it violates the separation of powers, Congress continues to enact legislative vetoes, and agencies continue to send decisions to Congress for prior approval, knowing that Congress has other sanctions at its disposal if they do not.[33]

- **Committee and conference reports,** which often instruct agencies how Congress expects them to use their "discretion." Though not legally binding, bureaucrats ignore such instructions at their peril.

- **Inspectors general,** with independent offices (outside the normal bureaucratic chain of command) in virtually every agency, who audit agency books and investigate activities on Congress's behalf.

- The **Government Accountability Office,** with a staff of more than five thousand, which audits programs and agencies and reports to Congress on their performance.

Congress can also guard against agency losses by putting a time limit on delegations of authority. For example, the expanded wiretap and surveillance authority included in the USA PATRIOT Act's broad grant of new powers to investigate and detain suspected terrorists enacted after September 11 was set to expire automatically by the end of 2005 unless Congress extended it. As former House majority leader

Dick Armey explained, "We gave the Justice Department a huge increase in power" but with an expiration date "on the theory that would make them more responsive to oversight." [34] Congress extended the act's authority, slightly modified, in 2006.

A variety of *procedural devices* also are available to Congress for monitoring and controlling bureaucrats. Congress may not have the capacity to specify *what* bureaucrats are to do, but it can tell them *how* they have to do it. The broadest procedural requirements are found in the Administrative Procedure Act (APA) of 1946, which covers all rulemaking by government agencies unless an agency's legislative authorization specifies otherwise.

Congress normally regulates by delegating broad grants of authority to regulatory agencies and letting them fill in the details by making rules. These rules have the force of law, just as if Congress itself had enacted them. When an agency wants to make a rule, it first must give public notice in the *Federal Register,* outlining the proposed rule, disclosing the data and analysis on which it is based, and inviting written comments from the public. Public hearings may be held as well. The agency then responds to public comments in compiling the rulemaking record, which will be needed to justify the agency's decision if it is challenged in federal court.

These procedures serve several purposes. For one thing, they make rulemaking a public act, observable by members of Congress and anyone else who may be interested. They also give members of Congress—and agency officials—advance notice of the political fallout that any particular regulation would produce, allowing them to avoid political trouble. When the Federal Trade Commission proposed rules in 1982 requiring more complete disclosure of funeral costs and used car defects, undertakers and used car dealers protested loudly. Members of Congress, who were quickly reminded just how many undertakers and used car dealers they had in their districts and how influential they were, forced the agency to back down.[35] In other words, the APA sets up a fire alarm mechanism that alerts members of Congress when delegated authority is being exercised in a way that might hurt them politically. In effect, it recruits interested outsiders to monitor the activities of bureaucratic agents on Congress's behalf.

When it chooses, Congress can fine-tune procedures to guarantee a desired balance of interests in regulatory policymaking. For example, the National Environmental Policy Act of 1969 requires federal agencies, as well as many other public and private entities, to consider what effects all major undertakings (construction projects, landfills, dredging schemes, and so forth) might have on the environment and to prepare environmental impact statements specifying the environmental effects of proposed projects and their alternatives. The act also gives private citizens legal **standing** to bring suit in federal court to challenge the adequacy of impact statements and, indirectly, the proposals they were intended to justify. Standing enables environmental groups and their lawyers to enforce compliance through the courts, ensuring that environmental interests will not be ignored.

How, then, do we reconcile this picture with news clips of members of Congress portraying themselves as enthusiastic bureaucracy bashers on the principle that "no politician ever lost votes by denouncing the bureaucracy"? [36] They are, in fact, the principal architects of the bureaucracy, and its design generally suits the political purposes of the congressional coalitions that create and sustain its various components. It is no accident that the division of responsibilities among agencies in the executive branch tends to mirror the division of legislative turf in the congressional committee and subcommittee systems. This is not to say, however, that Congress has exclusive control over the administration of agencies. The president and the federal courts also have a major say, and Congress itself is subject to pressure from interest groups, the media, and constituents on how it deals with administrative issues. Moreover, the fragmented political system can give agencies considerable room to maneuver in pursuit of their own ends.

The President and the Bureaucracy

The president, who as the chief executive is charged by the Constitution with seeing that the laws are faithfully executed, sits officially atop the bureaucratic hierarchies of the executive branch. The heads of departments and other executive agencies and their immediate subordinates—the undersecretaries, assistant secretaries, and bureau chiefs—serve at the president's pleasure, as do members of some of the governing boards, commissions, foundations, institutes, and public corporations that make up the rest of the executive branch. With their duty to implement laws, power to appoint senior government officials, and other congressionally conferred grants of authority, presidents have enormous administrative responsibilities. The institutional realities, however, impose formidable barriers to presidential influence—let alone control—over the sprawling federal bureaucracy.

THE POWER OF APPOINTMENT. Presidents pursue their policy goals by appointing senior officials loyal to them and their ideas. For example, Ronald Reagan's appointment in 1981 of conservatives Anne Gorsuch Burford to head the Environmental Protection Agency and Michael Connolly as general counsel to the Equal Employment Opportunity Commission resulted in sharp reductions in these agencies' regulatory activities.[37] Congress, however, may not be content to sit on the sidelines, and presidents may find their influence diluted. Indeed, if enough members of Congress oppose the objectives of the president's appointees, they can force the agency back into line. Both Burford and Connolly eventually resigned under heavy congressional and public criticism for failure to carry out their agencies' mandates.

SENATORIAL APPROVAL. Presidential appointments require Senate approval, and senators make the most of their authority. Rarely does the full Senate reject a nominee, but it is not unusual for an appointment to be withdrawn after an unfavorable committee vote or, earlier, after unfavorable publicity during a hearing on the appointment. In 1993 President Clinton had to withdraw his first two nominations for attorney general, corporate lawyer Zoë Baird and then federal judge Kimba Wood, when the media reported that both had employed illegal immigrants for household duties. Bernard Kerik, President George W. Bush's nominee to replace Tom Ridge as head the Department of Homeland Security, withdrew from consideration after running into a similar controversy in December 2004. Many nominations are not even made because presidents anticipate Senate opposition and decide the fight is not worth the political resources it would take to win. Senators also use the approval process to extract promises from appointees about what they will or will not do in office, further limiting administrative discretion. Seeking Senate approval in 2007, Michael Mukasey, George W. Bush's nominee to replace attorney general Alberto Gonzales, who had resigned after months of harsh criticism for politicizing the Justice Department and for his role in setting the administration's policies on torture and surveillance, had to promise that he would resign if asked by the White House to vio-

Michael Mukasey, nominated to replace attorney general Alberto Gonzales in 2007, was grilled by Senate Judiciary Committee Democrats about his views on torture, surveillance, and executive power. His answers satisfied six of the Senate's fifty-one Democrats, enough, when combined with unanimous Republican support, to win confirmation.

late the law or the constitution. His confirmation was nearly derailed when he ducked the question of whether the technique of simulated drowning called "waterboarding" used to interrogate suspected terrorists constituted torture, but after declaring that he personally found the procedure "repugnant," he was confirmed on a 53-40 vote.[38] For a new technique that the Senate has employed to control presidential appointments made during Senate recesses, see box "Thwarting Recess Appointments."

In addition to the Senate, the president may have to satisfy the clientele groups that care intensely about who heads "their" agency or risk alienating them and weakening the agency. Thus the secretary of labor requires the nod of the AFL-CIO, at least if the president is a Democrat; the chair of the Federal Reserve Board must measure up on Wall Street; and the head of the National Institutes of Health needs the respect of the academic and research communities. Clientele groups of the president also may benefit from the appointments process, because presidents often use appointments as symbolic payoffs to important factions in their party's electoral coalition. In 1993 Bill Clinton took extraordinary pains to assemble an administration that "looked like America," insisting on racial, gender, and geographic diversity. Eight years later George W. Bush also sought a diverse administration, not only by carefully choosing his cabinet—including Colin Powell, the first black secretary of state—but also by making sure that his party's various ideological factions were acknowledged and represented. In making appointments for any reason, however, the president also must weigh competence; policy expertise may not be essential, but no president wants to be embarrassed by appointees too ignorant or unskilled to manage their agencies' business. The danger was vividly illustrated by the damage to George W. Bush's public

LOGIC OF POLITICS

Thwarting Recess Appointments

The Constitution allows the president to make temporary appointments of officials normally requiring Senate confirmation without Senate approval while the Senate is in recess (Article II, Section 2). Recess appointments expire at the end of the Senate's next session, and thus may last for as long as nearly two years. Presidents have sometimes used this authority to appoint officials the Senate has refused to ratify. Bill Clinton, for example, used recess appointments to make Bill Lan Lee the assistant attorney general for Civil Rights and James Hormel the ambassador to Luxembourg. The Senate had balked at Lee's appointment because of his strong support of affirmative action and at Hormel's because he was openly gay. George W. Bush's recess appointments included the blunt and controversial John Bolton as ambassador to the United Nations and Sam Fox as ambassador to Belgium. Bolton's nomination had been derailed by a Senate filibuster. The appointment of Fox, who contributed $50,000 to the Swift Boat Veterans and POWs for Truth that had broadcast ads attacking John Kerry's war record during the 2004 presidential campaign, made little headway in getting approval from the Senate Foreign Relations Committee, of which Kerry was a leading member. Altogether, Clinton made 139 recess appointments, Bush (through 2006), 167.[1]

In 2007, Senate Democrats took steps to prevent Bush from making any more recess appointments (which would have lasted until the end of his term) by remaining in pro forma session throughout the customary two-week Thanksgiving and five-week Christmas breaks. As long as a member officially gavels the Senate open and then gavels it closed at least once every four days—a process that takes only a few seconds—the Senate is formally in session and no recess appointments can

be made. Majority Leader Harry Reid organized a lineup of Democratic volunteers, mostly from states near the capitol, to show up to perform this duty as necessary during the holiday breaks. There were some individual payoffs for providing this particular (for Democrats) collective good: the first volunteer, freshman senator James Webb of Virginia, reaped "a minor media bonanza. . . CNN carried the brief session live then broadcast a post-session interview with Webb."[2] Whether this innovation becomes the normal practice when Congress and the White House are controlled by different parties, it will certainly remain as part of the arsenal available to the Congress in its enduring struggle with the president for influence over administrative matters.

1. Henry B. Hogue, "Recess Appointments: Frequently Asked Questions," Congressional Research Service, January 16, 2007, at www.senate.gov/reference/resources/pdf/RS21308.pdf.

2. Paul Kane, "The Fastest Gavel in the Senate," *New York Times,* December 31, 2007, A13.

James Webb

standing inflicted by the slow and inept response of the Federal Emergency Management Agency (FEMA) to Hurricane Katrina's devastation of New Orleans 2005. George W Bush was indirectly blamed for the failure of FEMA head Michael Brown, a Bush crony, to coordinate an effective response to Hurricanes Katrina and Rita.

Some presidents, notably Ronald Reagan and George W. Bush, have tried to ignore other criteria in order to stack their administrations with personal or ideological loyalists, but with incomplete success. Sheer numbers pose a serious problem. Because presidents are responsible for filling more than four thousand positions, they must rely on the advice of others and an imperfect screening process to fill most of the slots. They also must accept the fact that most appointees will be total strangers to them. In short, the president, as principal, can make only limited use of the power of appointment to guard against political losses.

Once appointed, even initially loyal officials tend, as Richard Nixon's chief domestic aide famously put it, to "go off and marry the natives," becoming agents of their departments or bureaus instead of the president. Political appointees typically serve short terms—about two years—and often are unfamiliar with the rules, programs, and political relationships of the organizations they lead. To avoid disastrous mistakes, let alone to achieve anything positive, they need the candid advice and active cooperation of permanent civil servants. In return, they can offer effective advocacy of their agency's interests in the battles waged over programs and resources within both the administration and Congress.[39] In doing so, they may come to identify with the success of their agency rather than with that of the president, and thus pursue more programs and larger budgets—or defend programs and budgets from cuts—without regard for how their agency fits into the administration's overall program. Department and bureau heads also wield powers delegated directly to them by Congress, allowing them to bypass the president and further promote their independence from the president and their dependence on Congress.

MECHANISMS FOR PRESIDENTIAL SUPERVISION. In an attempt to gain some control over the far-flung activities of the federal bureaucracy, presidents have built up their own supervisory bureaucracy in the Executive Office of the President (analyzed more fully in Chapter 7). The president's primary control instrument is the Office of Management and Budget (OMB), which oversees agency budgets and rulemaking and assembles the annual budget for all government agencies that the president is required to submit annually to Congress. The budget process allows presidents to emphasize their own priorities and policy goals. When Congress ignores presidents' recommendations—which it frequently does—presidents may use the veto to nudge that recalcitrant legislative body closer to their own budget preferences, as President Bush did with considerable success after the Democrats took control of Congress in 2007 (see Chapter 7).

For bureaucrats, favorable treatment in the president's budget is worth pursuing—so they have an incentive to keep the White House happy. But this inherently political relationship works two ways: the White House is much more likely to get its way if it can persuade political appointees and permanent civil servants that their best interests are served by doing what it wants. Because presidents do not hold undisputed authority over the executive branch, bargaining or indirect manipulation through mobilized interest groups or congressional allies is often more effective than issuing orders.[40]

By constitutional design, presidents enjoy special authority over agencies involved in diplomacy and national defense, and this authority is greatly magnified in times of national crisis. Moreover, public support for presidents is highest in such moments, so opposition to presidential demands carries unusually high political risks. President George W. Bush, like his predecessors, did not hesitate to use this institutional and popular wartime advantage to assert control over policy and institutions. Congress quickly complied with the president's request for legislation authorizing him "to use all necessary and appropriate force against the nations, organizations, or people that he determines planned, authorized, committed, or aided the terrorist attacks on the United States that occurred September 11, 2001."[41] He also won an extraordinary degree of authority to shape and run the DHS as he saw fit and a remarkably free hand on almost every aspect of the Iraq War. Pushing the limit, the administration had demanded total discretion in deciding how to spend $60 billion of the $78.5 billion supplemental appropriation for the war. Secretary of Defense Rumsfeld said flatly that "whatever is put forward by the Congress by way of money will be expended in a way that the president decides it should be expended."[42] Congress refused to go that far but agreed to give the president full discretion to allocate $15.7 billion of the total appropriated. Even after the Democrats assumed control of Congress in 2007 on promises to end the war in Iraq, Bush got his way on funding for the war by reframing the issue as one of supporting American troops rather than financing an unpopular war. The Bush administration also sought to extend the broad authority enjoyed by the president in his role as commander in chief to other executive functions, renewing the struggle with Congress for control of the bureaucracy that has been part of American politics since the first Congress.

The Courts and the Bureaucracy

The third main branch of government, the judiciary, also shares authority over the bureaucracy. The United States inherited the English common law principle that the government, no less than individual citizens, is bound by law. Under this principle, a dispute between the government and a private individual over whether the government is acting according to law—that is, a statute duly passed by Congress and signed by the president—comes before the courts as a normal lawsuit. The judge treats the government as any other party to a lawsuit, granting it no special status whatsoever. This tradition has strongly influenced the development of American administrative law. Judicial review of administrative decisions is taken for granted; regulatory commissions and agencies have, from the beginning, been constrained by the courts' defense of individual rights.

Expansion of the government's regulatory activities, particularly during the New Deal, put a host of bureaucratic agencies in the business of making rules and applying them—that is, agencies were authorized to make general rules, just like a legislature, and to adjudicate individual cases under them, just like a court. Federal courts maintained appellate jurisdiction over both sets of activities, hearing appeals on rules as well as their enforcement, and court decisions gradually imposed a set of procedural standards that Congress eventually codified in the Administrative Procedure Act of 1946 (APA.)

Under the APA, any agency dealing with individual cases like a court must act like a court—that is, it must hold hearings conducted by neutral referees (now called administrative law judges). Parties may be represented by counsel, with written and oral testimony and opportunities for cross-examination. Decisions handed down by the agency must be issued in writing and justified on the evidence in the record. Those decisions that violate these procedures can be challenged and overturned in federal court. An agency that wants its judgments sustained must carefully follow the rules of administrative due process.

Over the years the federal courts have come to interpret the APA as requiring almost as much procedural care in making rules as in deciding cases. Courts have elaborated on and formalized the APA's notice and hearings requirements and now insist on a comprehensive, written justification backed by a complete record of all information and analysis that went into an agency's decision. The APA allows courts to invalidate rules only if they are "arbitrary and capricious," which would seem to give agencies wide latitude. Yet in the 1960s and 1970s the courts used judicial review "to create and impose on agencies a huge body of administrative law which was so complex and demanding that it allowed judges to strike down new agency rules whenever they pleased."[43] The courts were particularly interested in highly contentious, highly technical areas of regulation: the environment, health, and safety. Soon regulatory agencies adapted, however, by overwhelming the courts with reams of data and analysis, both to convince the judges they had made the most scientifically defensible choice and to make it more difficult for judges lacking technical expertise to say otherwise. The courts have since backed off a bit, but they still play a major role in shaping regulatory decisions.

Congress may, of course, rewrite the law if the courts invalidate rules that solid House and Senate majorities want to see implemented, and it may also alter the courts' jurisdiction over administrative matters. Yet any change must negotiate the usual congressional obstacle course, which, as we saw in Chapter 6, is by no means easy, particularly if the president prefers the courts' position. Congress does rectify both judicial and administrative decisions it does not like, but only under major provocation.

Iron Triangles, Captured Agencies, and Issue Networks

The politics of program administration gives agency staff, members of Congress, and organized interest groups powerful incentives to form mutually beneficial alliances to manage policy in their areas of specialization. When successful, these alliances become **iron triangles:** narrowly focused subgovernments controlling policy in their domains, out of sight or oversight of the full Congress, the president, and the public at large. The classic examples operated in the areas of agriculture, water, and public works, where the active players enjoyed concentrated benefits—projects benefiting private interest groups, budgets and programs for administrators, and electoral support for congressional sponsors from grateful beneficiaries.[44] The broader public, excluded from the process, paid the diffuse costs.

Similarly, the politics of regulation allows the regulators to be "captured" by the very interests they are supposed to regulate. Once Congress establishes a regulatory agency in response to some threat to public welfare—whether it be railroad monopolies, dangerous or quack medicines, or impure processed food—the agency's dealings are with the very industries it should be regulating. Because industries have an enormous economic stake in how they are regulated, they become the primary source of political pressure on the regulators. Ironically, the regulated sectors also are the primary repository of the expertise—information and personnel—agencies need. Add to this the routine legislative mandate that the agency maintain the economic health of the industries it regulates, and the story is complete: regulators become the allies, if not agents, of the sector they regulate. At times, for example, the Food and Drug Administration (FDA) catered to drug companies; the Interstate Commerce Commission (ICC) ended up at the beck and call of established firms in the trucking industry; and the Civil Aeronautics Board (CAB), as noted earlier, protected the major airlines from competition.

In reality, iron triangles and captured agencies survive only as long as the costs they impose on everyone are small enough to avoid attracting serious attention from political entrepreneurs in Congress or the White House who may be scouting for popular issues to champion. For example, the CAB and the ICC no longer exist; the former was abolished in 1985, and ten years later the latter, by then more than one hundred years old, was finally put to rest. The marketplace now governs the sectors they once regulated. In the early 1960s one congressional coalition forced the FDA to impose much tougher standards for proving the safety and efficacy of new drugs. The 1990s, however, saw another coalition compel it to ease up again on the ground that delays in approval of new drugs also hurt the public health.

Members of Congress learned from these experiences and designed new regulatory procedures to prevent the capture of agencies such as the Environmental Protection Agency (EPA) (see the discussion of "standing" earlier in this chapter). The proliferation of self-proclaimed public interest groups in the 1960s also changed the political environments of many agencies, leaving them no option but to negotiate a far more complex, open, and conflict-ridden configuration of political forces (see Chapter 13). Thus scholars now talk of policy domains shaped by **issue networks**—amorphous, ever-changing sets of politicians, lobbyists, academic and think-tank experts, and public interest entrepreneurs such as Ralph Nader—rather than iron triangles.[45]

Agencies adapted. The Department of Agriculture now pays attention to nutrition and other consumer concerns as well as to the needs of agribusiness. Today's EPA considers the economic as well as environmental effects of its decisions. But agencies do not always find it easy to adapt because new missions may go against the culture of an agency. For example, the U.S. Army Corps of Engineers, which for two centuries had been damming rivers, dredging harbors, and draining wetlands, was not eager to make cleaning up toxic wastes and protecting threatened ecosystems a high priority. But when the political environment changes, government agencies have little choice but to change as well.

Bureaucratic Reform: A Hardy Perennial

Every modern president has viewed the federal bureaucracy as a problem that needs fixing. The Clinton administration's effort focused on improving the delivery of bureaucratic services. Vice President Al Gore headed the administration's National Performance Review, which sought ways to "cast aside red tape," encourage entrepreneurial administration that "put customers first," decentralize authority to "empower those who work on the front lines," and in general, produce "better government for less" with a reduced workforce.[46] Not to be outdone, the Republican House freshmen elected in 1994 sought not merely to reinvent government but also to disinvent it. House Republicans proposed abolishing the Departments of Commerce, Energy, Education, and Housing and Urban Development, terminating many of their programs and bureaus and distributing the remainder to other departments. The George W. Bush administration tried another tack, proposing in 2001 to shrink government and increase efficiency by expanding "competitive sourcing" (letting firms in the private sector bid against government agencies for contracts to deliver government services) to include jobs currently performed by 425,000 civil servants, about one-fourth of the total federal workforce.

Both the Republican and Democratic initiatives were imbued with political logic. Making government work like a business that depends on keeping customers happy has obvious appeal. So does getting rid of obsolete, wasteful programs and agencies and using competition to increase efficiency. Yet despite some success in improving the performance of several agencies and reducing the number of federal employees, the Clinton administration's goal of an efficient, customer-friendly bureaucracy remained largely unfilled. And House Republicans, though slashing some agency budgets and terminating a few programs, failed to eliminate any major agency, let alone whole cabinet departments. By 2003 the Bush administration's target for competitive sourcing had been reduced to 103,000 jobs in the face of congressional resistance and new, post-9/11 realities.[47] The fact is that the federal bureaucracy is hard to reform and still harder to prune because its actions and structure have a political logic of their own.

The Logic of Red Tape

Red tape does not flourish by accident. It proliferates because it helps principals control and monitor their agents (the goal of the APA) and helps agents demonstrate to their principals that they are doing their jobs correctly. Many rules and procedures are adopted to ensure fair or at least equal treatment of each citizen by preventing unaccountable, arbitrary behavior. For example, federal agencies procuring goods and services from the private sector are bound by an elaborate set of requirements imposed on them by Congress.

Even after the Federal Acquisition Streamlining Act of 1994 simplified the rules, especially for relatively small purchases, the *Federal Acquisition Regulation,* which spells them out, still runs to more than five thousand pages. Bureaucrats have a strong incentive to follow the rules, for there is only one safe answer—"I followed the rules"—

when a member of Congress asks pointedly why a favorite constituent did not get the contract.[48] By the same logic, bureaucrats like to have rules to follow. Detailed procedures protect as well as constrain bureaucrats, so red tape is frequently self-imposed.

Empowering bureaucrats on the front lines of service delivery may increase efficiency and even customer satisfaction, but it also may make it easier for bureaucrats to go astray. Each time an agency does so, Congress tends to write more elaborate procedures and add another layer of inspectors and auditors to keep it from happening again. Thus *red tape often springs directly from Congress's desire to control administration.* As a result, although Congress rails against red tape in general, it views with suspicion attempts to reduce the controls that generate it. Successful efforts at easing controls could reduce congressional ability to monitor and influence administration, a risk congressional majorities have been reluctant to accept, especially when the other party holds the White House.

Reformers seeking bureaucratic efficiency may also run into several other problems. Efficiency stems from using resources in a maximally productive way, so any assessment of efficiency must be based on measures of output. The output of many agencies defies measurement, however. Diplomats in the State Department are supposed to pursue the long-term security and economic interests of the nation. How do we measure their "productivity" in this endeavor? Complicating matters even more, agencies sometimes are assigned conflicting objectives. Is the IRS supposed to maximize tax compliance, requiring tough enforcement, or customer service, requiring flexible, sympathetic enforcement? Effective enforcement and effective customer service are not the same thing.

Because an agency's degree of success in accomplishing its vaguely defined ends is often impossible to measure, bureaucrats focus instead on outputs that can be measured: reports completed, cases processed, meetings held, regulations drafted, contracts properly concluded, forms filled out and filed. These means become the ends because they produce observable outputs for which bureaucrats can be held accountable. The result is yet more red tape. The notorious bureaucratic focus on process rather than product arises from the reality that, unlike private businesses, government agencies have no "bottom line" to measure the success or failure of their enterprise.

The Bureaucratic Reward System

Conflicting goals and the lack of a bottom line hardly inspire the creative, "entrepreneurial" government envisioned by the Clinton/Gore National Performance Review. Entrepreneurs take risks proportionate to prospective rewards. Civil servants, by contrast, seldom profit personally from their attempts to make agencies more productive or customer-friendly. And if bold new approaches end in failure, they can count on being blasted in the media and in Congress. Bureaucrats are famously cautious for a good reason: a mistake is much more likely than a routine action to set off a fire alarm in Congress. If an alarm does sound and the routine was followed, the routine, rather than the bureaucrat, gets the blame.

The merit system rewards conscientious, long-term service; it does not encourage entrepreneurial risk taking. Congress could, of course, decide to give agency managers more authority to hire, promote, reward, redeploy, or fire staff personnel on the basis of their performance. But doing so would mean reducing the civil service protections put in place for well-considered political reasons: to avoid a partisan spoils system and to preserve congressional influence over administration.

The Clinton and Bush administrations' plans for reforming government inevitably included proposals to reduce bureaucratic waste and improve policy coordination by consolidating overlapping agencies and programs. Every president since Franklin Roosevelt has sought to do the same. And of course, it is easy to find examples of duplication, confused lines of authority, and conflict among the government's multifarious activities. Basic scientific research, for example, is funded by the National Science Foundation; the National Institutes of Health; the Departments of Energy, Agriculture, and Defense; and NASA. The National Park Service, the Forest Service, the Bureau of Land Management, and the U.S. Fish and Wildlife Service all manage public campgrounds. Responsibility for developing water resources is spread over five separate agencies. The government has programs to keep tobacco farming profitable and to discourage smoking. One agency subsidizes the lumber industry by building logging roads into national forests; another tries to curb it to protect endangered species. And the list could go on.

This duplication would all seem senseless if government pursued a coherent set of interrelated goals, but it does not. Government pursues overlapping, conflicting, or disconnected goals in response to the diverse demands Americans place on it. Each agency and each program reflect the coalition of forces that brought it into being and that now form its political environment. Different coalitions want different things and design different administrative institutions to get them.

In short, then, the problem of bureaucracy is not bureaucracy but politics. It is not impossible to reform, reinvent, streamline, or shrink the administrative leviathan, but it is impossible to do so without changing power relationships among interests and institutions. Deregulating the bureaucracy and empowering frontline bureaucrats would make agencies more efficient, but it also would make them less accountable to elected officials. Consolidating and rationalizing bureaucratic authority would reduce duplication, confusion, and expense, but it also would create losers whose interests or values would no longer enjoy undivided institutional attention. It took a national trauma on the scale of September 11 to overcome the instinctual defense of bureaucratic turf that usually prevents the consolidation and rationalization of bureaucratic authority. And the DHS continues to confront problems of communication and coordination raised by its component bureaucracies' conflicting missions, cultures, personnel rules, constituencies, and computer systems, as well as by the competing demands placed on it by rival congressional committees, the White House, and state and local government agencies. Despite the enactment of the National Intelligence Reform Act, the gathering and sharing of information among intelligence agencies remains problematic. Everyone acknowledges the need for greater coordination but wants it to be on their own terms; "the *what* of coordination is one thing; the *how* is quite another."[49] Even under the exigencies of the war on terrorism, the "how" will be determined by power politics (see box "Rationalizing Intelligence").

Rationalizing Intelligence

In July 2004 the bipartisan commission appointed to investigate the September 11 terrorist attacks published a scathing critique of the "failures of imagination, policy, capabilities and management" that allowed the disaster to occur and recommended, among other things, sweeping reforms in the nation's intelligence operations. The commission proposed that all agencies responsible for foreign, defense, and domestic intelligence (the CIA, FBI, NSA, and twelve other less prominent agencies) be placed under a single national intelligence director who would report directly to the president. The director would oversee a new national counterterrorism center responsible for analyzing threats and setting priorities for clandestine intelligence gathering in the United States and abroad. Recognizing that redistributing bureaucratic authority required redistributing congressional authority, the commission also called on Congress to radically overhaul how it oversees counterterrorism activities, consolidating into a single committee in each chamber the oversight authority now scattered among dozens of committees and subcommittees.

Although no one argued that the commission had misdiagnosed the problem, its solution was predictably resisted by people in both the agencies and Congress who would lose power and turf if it were adopted. The Pentagon, CIA, DHS secretary Tom Ridge, and some members of Congress immediately expressed opposition. Critics argued that the office would simply create another bureaucratic layer, adding to delay and bureaucratic conflict. The issue was instantly politicized as Democratic presidential challenger John Kerry called for immediate implementation of the report. President George W. Bush at first declined to endorse any of the commission's recommendations but soon recognized that doing nothing was politically infeasible and promised quick action to address at least some of the problems identified.

Congressional leaders promised hearings on intelligence reorganization but nothing more. The commissioners, meanwhile, fully aware of the strong opposition their proposal would provoke, kept up the pressure on Congress and the president to act by taking their case to the country. In December 2004 Congress finally passed and the president signed the National Intelligence Reform Act, which provided for a cabinet-level director of national intelligence (DNI), charged with coordinating all fifteen segments of the intelligence community and acting as the principal intelligence advisor to the president. The director of central intelligence, formerly the government's senior intelligence officer, became director of the Central Intelligence Agency, in theory subordinate to the DNI. Resistance by key members of the House, including the chair of the Armed Services Committee, limited the DNI's authority over military intelligence activities and control over intelligence budgets. Defense secretary Donald Rumsfeld used this opening to expand the military's intelligence activities in competition rather than coordination with the CIA and other spy agencies. Coordination improved after Robert M. Gates took over as defense secretary in 2007, but critics believe that DNI needs stronger legal authority to have any chance of solving the coordination problems exposed by September 11. After passage of the act, the commissioners turned to the even harder task of persuading Congress to reorganize its intelligence oversight mechanisms, the effort was at best a work-in-progress more than four years later.

Sources: Articles on the commission's report in the *Los Angeles Times,* July 23, 2004; "Bush Signs Intelligence Reform Bill," *Washington Post,* December 18, 2004, A01; Tim Starks, "New Players, New Hope for Intelligence Comity," *CQ Weekly,* March 26, 2007, 880–881; Tim Roemer, "How to Fix Intelligence Oversight," *Washington Post,* December 20, 2007, A29.

logic.cqpress.com

Key Terms

bureaucracy, 364

bureaucratic culture, 388

clientele, 374

committee and conference reports, 396

Federal Register, 382

Government Accountability Office, 396

hearings and investigations, 396

inspectors general, 396

iron triangle, 403

issue network, 404

legislative veto, 396

mandatory reports, 396

red tape, 369

rotation in office, 367

spoils system, 367

standing, 397

Suggested Readings

Downs, Anthony. *Inside Bureaucracy.* Boston: Little Brown, 1967. The theory of bureaucracy from a nontechnical but "economic" perspective.

Gormley, William T., Jr., and Steven J. Balla. *Bureaucracy and Democracy: Accountability and Performance.* 5th ed. Washington, D.C.: CQ Press, 2008. The factors that ultimately lead to bureaucratic successes and shortcomings, with a focus on accountability.

Light, Paul C. *Thickening Government: Federal Hierarchy and the Diffusion of Accountability.* Washington, D.C.: Brookings, 1995. How and why bureaucratic layers have multiplied and how this affects accountability and effectiveness.

Seidman, Harold. *Politics, Position, and Power: The Dynamics of Federal Organization.* 5th ed. New York: Oxford University Press, 1998. How politics shapes bureaucratic organizations and practices.

Shapiro, Martin. *Who Guards the Guardians? Judicial Control of Administration.* Athens: University of Georgia Press, 1988. A lucid and informative account of court–agency relations since the New Deal.

Skowronek, Stephen. *Building a New American State: The Expansion of National Administrative Capacities, 1877–1920.* Cambridge: Cambridge University Press, 1982. Classic account of the development of the modern American bureaucracy, focusing on the civil service, the army, and agencies regulating the economy.

Waterman, Richard W. *Presidential Influence and the Administrative State.* Knoxville: University of Tennessee Press, 1989. Case studies from the Nixon, Carter, and Reagan administrations of presidential efforts to implement policies via the bureaucracy.

Wilson, James Q. *Bureaucracy: What Government Agencies Do and Why They Do It.* New York: Basic Books, 1989. If you read only one book on the bureaucracy, it should be this one.

Review Questions

1. Why is a bureaucracy necessary? What are the general characteristics of bureaucracies as set forth by Max Weber?

2. What powers does the president have over the bureaucracy? What powers does Congress have over the bureaucracy? Why would political actors ever choose to exercise less control over a bureaucratic actor?

3. How were members of the bureaucracy selected in George Washington's time? In Andrew Jackson's time? In George W. Bush's time? How do the ways in which bureaucrats get their jobs relate to their performance once in office?

4. How can the rules or procedures Congress establishes for bureaucratic agencies affect how those bureaucracies do their jobs?

5. If everybody hates "red tape," why does it still flourish? Why might bureaucrats themselves prefer to have detailed rules governing some of their actions?

Exercises

Consult the Oracle

Head to the CFR (Code of Federal Regulations) Web site (www.gpoaccess.gov/cfr/index.html) to see how the national government "regulates" zebras, diapers, ashtrays, and pork. The amount of regulation may surprise you. Then check in with congressional oversight committees and learn how specific laws are implemented.

Someone to Watch over Me

Go to the House Committee Hearing Schedules and Oversight Plans page at http://thomas.loc.gov/home/hcomso.html. Review the oversight plans of five different committees. How many cases can you find in which the committees are holding hearings to examine the implementation of a specific law?

Stringing Us Along?

In this chapter the authors note the power of procedural devices to help control the bureaucracy. One of the tools they identify is the Administrative Procedure Act of 1946, which requires all proposed rule changes to be published in the *Federal Register*. Search the *Federal Register* for proposed rules involving string (go to www.gpoaccess.gov/fr/advanced.html and use the "proposed rule" checkbox). How long are the periods of public comment for these rule changes? Pick two cases and find out the outcome of the process.

Finally, visit one of several federal agencies, from the Department of Commerce to the Postal Service, through this chapter's companion Web site page, or peruse data compiled by various divisions of the federal bureaucracy.

CHAPTER

9

The Federal Judiciary

EQUAL·JUSTICE·UNDER·LAW

Should nine unelected justices have the authority to nullify state and national laws enacted by elected representatives?

Is the judiciary truly, as Alexander Hamilton argued in *The Federalist*, "the least dangerous branch" of government?

If the Supreme Court "guards" the Constitution, then who guards the guardians?

Since all federal judges are appointed for life and are independent of one another, how can the federal judiciary be expected to dispense justice consistently and equitably?

In what ways is the judiciary susceptible to the same pressures of politics and national opinion that affect the elected branches?

By 1800 the national leaders who led the nation through the Revolution and adoption of the Constitution divided into two warring camps: the ruling Federalist Party, led by John Adams and Alexander Hamilton, who advocated a vigorous national government; and the Democratic-Republican opposition, led by Thomas Jefferson and James Madison, who favored less federal activity. Once allies, these two groups now despised and feared one another. Each believed that the future of the Republic rested on its party's victory in the presidential election of 1800. Consequently that year's electoral campaign was one of the bitterest in American history.

Both sides indulged in negative campaigning, but the Federalists excelled at it; they attacked Jefferson as the devil incarnate. In political pamphlets and letters to the editor the Federalists called Jefferson an "infidel" and "atheist," a darling of the French Revolution who favored the use of the guillotine, a proponent of majority rule (and thus apt to destroy the republican Constitution), a philanderer, and—perhaps the ultimate insult for a politician—a "philosopher." The author of one pamphlet added that Jefferson was not even a very good philosopher—barely adequate for a college professor but certainly not for a president. The attack finally dredged the bottom in charging that Jefferson had written a "textbook" on American government that promoted abstract ideas and "hooted at experience."

Toward the end of the campaign both sides sensed that Jefferson could not be stopped, but neither anticipated the magnitude of the Democratic-Republican victory. Not only did the party walk away with the Electoral College vote, but it also took control of Congress. It was not clear who had been elected president, however,

The Supreme Court of the United States, Washington, D.C.

because of a quirk in the Constitution's rules that caused votes cast for a party's vice-presidential candidate to be counted as if they were cast for the presidential candidate. As a result, when Jefferson and his running mate, Aaron Burr, ended up with the same number of electoral votes, they found themselves tied for the presidency. The apparent tie triggered a constitutional provision requiring the election to be decided by the House of Representatives, still controlled by the outgoing Federalists.*

During the weeks between the election and the House vote, rumors of conspiracies swirled across the nation. Would the Federalist Congress ignore the Constitution's technical glitch and ratify Jefferson's victory, or would it exploit the opportunity to deny the White House to this so-called free-thinking radical? One scenario had the Federalists contriving a tie vote in the House, thus taking the presidential election beyond circumstances anticipated by the Constitution. Another had President Adams stepping down at the end of his term and Secretary of State John Marshall assuming caretaker control of the executive branch until a new presidential election could be called.† And yet another option, which clearly lay within the Constitution's provisions and was perhaps more seriously considered, had the Federalists electing Burr president as the lesser of two evils.‡ None of these options appeared feasible, however. Thus, after weeks of strategizing and perhaps a little soul searching, the Federalist Congress ratified the nation's choice, and Jefferson became the third president of the United States.

Had power not transferred peacefully in this first real test of the new Republic, the election of 1800 might have weakened the Constitution permanently. Failure here would have put the Constitution's integrity in doubt and left future politicians with a prisoner's dilemma of deciding whether to abide by the rules or reneging before the other side could. But the Federalists did not capitulate altogether. Their risky fallback strategy triggered a different kind of constitutional crisis with the unanticipated outcome of reconfiguring power among the branches of government, in particular the Supreme Court.

Setting the Stage for Judicial Review

As they prepared to leave office, the Federalists passed the Judiciary Act of 1801. The law, designed to protect the Constitution against perceived Democratic-Republican

---

*The Twelfth Amendment corrected this problem in 1804.

†Evidently Marshall seriously considered his elevation. He reportedly promoted it as "legal" among colleagues, and one biographer spotted Marshall's pen in anonymous newspaper endorsements of this option. On hearing of this plot, Virginia's Democratic-Republican governor and future president, James Monroe, warned vaguely that force would be enlisted to remove Marshall, Virginian or not. Donald O. Dewey, *Marshall versus Jefferson: The Political Background of* Marbury v. Madison (New York: Knopf, 1970), 42–43.

‡In the end, though, Burr proved to be Jefferson's ideal running mate; he scared many Federalists even more than did the radical from Monticello. Burr later took up dueling and assumed imperial aspirations—raising "soldier of fortune" armies to seize western territories from the French and create his own country.

schemes, sharply increased the number of district and appeals courts and conveniently created new judgeships for aspiring Federalists.* The partisan purpose of this last-minute reform was evident in the provision that shrank the size of the Supreme Court from six members to five. Intended to take effect after President Adams filled the current chief justice's vacancy and a sitting member left the Court, this feature of the law would have denied the new Democratic-Republican administration the right to appoint a justice for a long time, if ever. Moreover, President Adams nominated and the Senate quickly confirmed outgoing secretary of state John Marshall as the new chief justice.

At this point, the story turns from the grand drama of contending partisan armies to a soap opera about the personal foibles and ambitions of politicians. President Adams needed help processing the flurry of last-minute Federalist judicial appointments and so asked his new chief justice to stay on briefly as secretary of state. According to Jefferson, Adams was still signing appointment commissions at nine o'clock the evening before his departure from office. Apparently, in the rush, Marshall left on his desk a stack of signed and sealed justice of the peace commissions for the District of Columbia, five-year positions created to reward loyal Federalists. The next day Marshall, as chief justice of the United States, delivered the oath of office to the new president, his archrival, Thomas Jefferson.

Later, on discovering or being advised (the lore is inconsistent on this point) that some of the commissions had not been delivered but were lying around the office, Jefferson ordered that they be withdrawn. These commissions were the least of the Federalists' worries, however.

After the inauguration the Democratic-Republicans derided the judiciary as a "hospital of decayed politicians" and made clear their intention to repeal the Judiciary Act as soon as their Congress opened the following December. In a letter Jefferson expressed his party's sentiment: the Federalists "retired into the Judiciary as a strong hold . . . and from that battery all the works for republicanism are to be beaten down and erased by fraudulent use of the constitution."[1] In his message to the new Congress, Jefferson's intent was also clear: "The judiciary system of the United States, and especially that portion of it recently erected, will of course present itself to the contemplation of Congress." Indeed, in private, and apparently unbeknownst to Jefferson, some nervous Federalist politicians were urging their recently appointed judges to ignore the new Congress until the Marshall Court could come to their rescue. The convening of Congress promised an epic partisan battle in which the Democratic-Republicans controlled the presidency and (narrowly) both chambers of Congress, while the Federalists directed the federal judiciary.

But could Congress legally abolish courts and thereby remove life-tenured judges? More precisely, could Democratic-Republicans in Congress somehow be prevented from eliminating the Federalist-created judgeships? With repeal of the Judiciary Act imminent, Federalist politicians urged Marshall to defend the party's bulwark by voiding any such repeal legislation. This strategy presupposed, of course, that the Supreme Court possessed the authority, known as **judicial review,** to rule acts of Congress

---

*Article III of the Constitution gives Congress the power to establish lower federal courts.

unconstitutional. Judicial review appears to have been implicitly provided in Article III of the Constitution, debated at the Constitutional Convention with some Framers assuming that the final wording of Article III included it but others—most notably, James Madison—arguing that it did not, and brought up again, more hotly, at various states' ratifying conventions. Nearly everyone appears to have accepted that the Constitution's supremacy clause (Article VI) allows the Supreme Court to exercise judicial review and veto *state* laws that trespassed on federal jurisdiction or violated the Constitution. But whether this unelected branch enjoyed authority comparable to the veto power of Congress and the president was altogether different—could the Supreme Court declare an act of Congress unconstitutional?

On February 3, 1802, by a 16–15 vote, the Senate repealed the Judiciary Act and eliminated the Federalist judgeships. All but one Democratic-Republican voted for repeal, and all Federalists voted against it. The House passed the repeal bill a month later, with only a single Democratic-Republican holdout, and Jefferson promptly signed it into law.* The Supreme Court had already decided that it would not or could not resist repeal, but Jefferson and his allies did not learn this until the Court's next session, in 1803.

On March 2, 1803, the long-anticipated showdown over the repeal of the Judiciary Act ended badly for the Federalists as the Court ruled in *Stuart v. Laird* that Congress had the authority under Article III to reorganize the judiciary.[2] The Federalist barricade had been dismantled; the Democratic-Republican victory was complete. The Federalist Party would never again win control of the presidency or either chamber of Congress. Chief Justice Marshall had not caved in, however. The young Constitution had survived the election of 1800, the partisan confrontation surrounding the Judiciary Act, the Federalists' late-night machinations on the eve of Jefferson's inauguration, and the Democratic-Republicans' resolute resistance. As important as the peaceful, albeit difficult, transfer of government control was for the nation's future, it was followed by a comparably significant, and eventually better known, judicial event. Six days before the *Stuart* decision, the Marshall Court delivered another ruling that at the time was largely ignored as a toothless partisan maneuver. Subsequently, however, the *Marbury v. Madison* decision would come to be appreciated for establishing the Court's "coequal" status among the branches of the American government.

William Marbury and several other Federalists who had been denied their eleventh hour justice of the peace commissions nearly two years earlier appealed to the Supreme Court for redress. They asked the Court to issue a **writ of mandamus,** a judicial instruction to a government officer—in this instance Secretary of State James Madison—to perform his duty and deliver the commissions. Based on the facts of the case, *Marbury v. Madison* did not seem the ideal vehicle for establishing "new" authority for the Court: the issue bordered on the trivial, and Chief Justice Marshall was himself deeply entangled in the dispute. His oversight as secretary of state, after all, had caused

---

*To avoid colliding immediately with the Court, Congress then suspended the Court's schedule for the next thirteen months. This move not only eased the dismantling of the eliminated courts but also prevented the Court from continuing the partisan battle while Congress was out of session.

the problem in the first place. Moreover, a casual inspection of Marshall's options suggests that *Marbury* was a terrible case for a weak Court to face because it presented an apparent no-win situation. On the one hand, if the Court decided in favor of Marbury and ordered Madison to deliver the commissions, Marshall could reasonably assume that its decision would be ignored. (No administration official had even bothered to appear before the Court to defend Jefferson's decision to withdraw the commissions.) There was even talk in the Democratic-Republican press of impeaching the justices if they decided in Marbury's favor. Such a ruling, then, jeopardized the long-term health of the federal judiciary. On the other hand, if Marshall ruled against Marbury, the Court would appear to be kowtowing to the Democratic-Republicans and confirming the judiciary's subordinate position. Faced with this dilemma, Marshall found an ideal solution that not only extricated the Court from its predicament but also established an important principle for the future.

In ruling on the case, Marshall asked three questions: First, does Marbury have a right to the commission? Second, do the laws of the United States afford him a remedy? Third, is the appropriate remedy a writ of mandamus issued by the Supreme Court? Marshall's affirmative answer to the first two questions boded well for Marbury. However, Marshall answered "no" to the third question, concluding that the Supreme Court did not have jurisdiction to hear the case.

John Marshall (1755–1835) had never sat on the bench before his installation on the Supreme Court. Moreover, his legal education was limited to reading Blackstone's *Commentaries* with his father and to three months of lectures by George Wythe at the College of William and Mary in 1780. Marshall's formidable powers of reasoning and leadership in unifying his colleagues behind unanimous decisions were complemented by an amiable disposition and "some little propensity for indolence."

While dismissal by a court for lack of jurisdiction was nothing novel, Marshall's *reasoning* would have far-reaching consequences for the balance of power between the Court and Congress. Marshall's argument was as follows: Article III of the Constitution explicitly lists cases that are within the Supreme Court's original jurisdiction,* and a writ of mandamus is not one of them. Article III of the Constitution does not give Congress the power to *add* to the Court's original jurisdiction. Because the Judiciary Act attempted to add a writ of mandamus to the Court's original jurisdiction, the act conflicts with the Constitution. In such a conflict, either the Constitution is superior to ordinary laws or it is on the same level as ordinary laws (and therefore may be altered when the legislature desires to change it). If the Constitution is not superior, then it would be a meaningless check on the powers of government. If, however, the Constitution is superior to

---

*Cases of original jurisdiction are those that can be brought directly to the Supreme Court, without going to some lower court first.

ordinary laws, "then a legislative act contrary to the constitution is not law." Marshall then delivered the conclusion that solidified the Court's power of judicial review: because the Constitution is the supreme law of the land, acts of Congress that conflict with the Constitution are unconstitutional and, thus, void. In one of his most famous statements, Marshall wrote: "It is emphatically the province and duty of the judicial department *to say what the law is.*"[3] By refusing to hear the case, Marshall backed away from a confrontation he could not win and simultaneously asserted new judicial authority.

Marbury v. Madison did not immediately strengthen the Court's power in its relations with the president or Congress. After all, Marshall's ruling did not require that the other political actors do anything to affirm the Court's new-found authority. It required only that the Court refuse to act in Marbury's behalf. The *Marbury* decision is a testament to Marshall's strategic political skills, as Jefferson and the Democratic-Republicans remained confident that the Federalist bench had at last been tamed.*

However, the Court's ruling in *Marbury* proved to be one of the most important Supreme Court decisions in its history. It provided a precedent that the other branches' actors did not repudiate (after all, the Court upheld Secretary of State Madison's action) and a rationale for the Court's broad authority to declare acts of Congress (and of the president) unconstitutional. This expansive vision of judicial review remained untested for nearly half a century, until the Court decided to enlist it in the infamous *Dred Scott* case. However, the Court's success in overturning key parts of the Missouri Compromise of 1820 had little to do with the other branches' acquiescence to its claimed authority and a lot to do with a sympathetic president in office and a Congress so riddled with internal disagreement that it could not nullify the ruling.

Over time, however, the other branches affirmed the Court's power of judicial review. When in 1895 the Supreme Court declared unconstitutional a federal law that taxed income derived from property, Congress implicitly conceded the Court's authority and turned to the laborious amendment process, eventually passing the Sixteenth Amendment.[4] Eighty years later another case testing and affirming judicial review arose. In *United States v. Nixon* (see page 330) the Supreme Court rejected President Richard M. Nixon's claim that the Watergate tapes were protected by executive privilege, and ordered him to surrender the tapes to a special prosecutor. President Nixon largely complied, notwithstanding a mysterious eighteen-minute gap during a critical Oval Office conversation. Whether his compliance reflected heartfelt acceptance of the Court's power of review or recognition that balking would lead quickly to impeachment does not matter. The Supreme Court prevailed in asserting judicial review over actions of the executive.

---

*Although the Supreme Court left *Marbury* alone for much of the nineteenth century, there is evidence that early on it was accepted as legal dogma. *Marbury* was cited numerous times by lower courts and in lawyers' arguments. Whenever Jefferson encountered these citations, he objected. As late as 1823 he griped to one of his Supreme Court appointees, "This case of Marbury and Madison is continually cited by bench & bar, as if it were settled law, without any animadversion on its being *merely* an obiter dissertation by the Chief Justice." Letter from Jefferson to Justice William Johnson, June 12, 1823, cited in Dewey, *Marshall versus Jefferson,* 145 (emphasis added).

While the discussion on separation of powers later in the chapter makes clear that Congress and the president nevertheless sometimes refuse to abide by the Court's decisions, their general acknowledgment of the Court's power of judicial review has enhanced the Court's power vis-à-vis Congress and the president to a level that was not foreseen in 1803 when *Marbury v. Madison* was decided.

Three Eras of the Court's Judicial Review

The Supreme Court's exercise of judicial review has varied substantially across different decades. Between 1790 and 1860, portions of only two federal laws had been declared unconstitutional. The frequency with which the Court struck down acts of Congress and presidential executive orders remained low throughout the late nineteenth century, but as Table 9-1 shows, it surged during the 1920s and 1930s. The exercise of judicial review then receded to nineteenth-century levels over the next two decades, but in the 1960s an activist Court once again scrutinized federal and state laws alike. This ebb and flow of the Court's intrusion into the decisions of Congress and the president have marked the three eras in the modern Court's development.

In each of these three eras, the most important cases that came before the Court embodied particular unresolved questions about the interpretation of the Constitution. These questions first concerned nation-state authority, then government regulation of the economy, and finally civil rights and liberties. As the controversy surrounding each issue developed, the federal judiciary confronted an upwelling of cases in which it asserted its preferences over those of other national, as well as state, officials.

TABLE 9-1

The Supreme Court's Willingness to Declare State and Federal Laws Unconstitutional

Years	Federal	State and Local
1790–1799	0	0
1800–1809	1	1
1810–1819	0	7
1820–1829	0	8
1830–1839	0	3
1840–1849	0	10
1850–1859	1	7
1860–1869	4	24
1870–1879	7	36
1880–1889	4	46
1890–1899	5	36
1900–1909	9	40
1910–1919	6	119
1920–1929	15	139
1930–1939	13	92
1940–1949	2	61
1950–1959	5	66
1960–1969	16	151
1970–1979	20	195
1980–1989	16	164
1990–1999	23	62
2000–2005	13	26
Total	160	1,293

Source: Lawrence Baum, *The Supreme Court,* 9th ed. (Washington, D.C.: CQ Press, 2007), Table 5-2, 165; and Table 5-3, 168.

Note: Table shows the number of federal and state and local laws declared unconstitutional by the Supreme Court. The Court has always been more willing to exercise judicial review over the states than to apply the doctrine in striking down federal laws.

Nation versus State

During the first and least active of these issue eras (from the Founding to the Civil War), the judiciary's most significant cases probed the unresolved jurisdictional boundaries between the national and state governments. Under Marshall's leadership, the Court favored national authority when it conflicted with states' rights. Reasoning that the national government had been approved directly by the citizenry in special ratification conventions, Marshall maintained that the national government's legitimacy was both independent of and superior to that of the individual states and concluded that the power of judicial review applied to the actions of state governments. As the following cases illustrate, sometimes the Court sided with the federal government, while at other times the Court favored states' rights.

***McCULLOCH V. MARYLAND* AND NATIONAL SUPREMACY.** One of Marshall's historic decisions on national supremacy came in 1819 in *McCulloch v. Maryland,* a case that was, like *Marbury,* rooted in party conflict.[5] When in power, the Federalist Party created a nationally chartered bank and appointed party members to administer it. Showing their displeasure, several Democratic-Republican–controlled state governments, including Maryland's, sought to tax the national bank out of existence. In the *McCulloch* decision, Chief Justice Marshall, speaking for the Court, issued the famous declaration that "the power to tax involves the power to destroy." Thus, state taxation of federal property or its activities was unconstitutional. But first Marshall dealt with an even more fundamental issue. The state argued that in the absence of any provision in the Constitution explicitly authorizing Congress to charter a national bank, the national government had exceeded its authority. Marshall responded that the necessary and proper clause (Article I, Section 8) gave Congress a broad mandate to use "all means which are appropriate" to carry out any of its explicitly enumerated powers, as long as the means are plainly adapted to achieve such enumerated power(s) and not otherwise constitutionally prohibited. In *McCulloch,* the enumerated powers at issue included the power to levy and collect taxes, borrow money, and regulate commerce. Because the establishment of a national bank was an appropriate means plainly adapted to such enumerated powers, the Court rejected Maryland's argument that Congress had overstepped its constitutional bounds. The practical result in the case was that federal authority trumped state authority. In *Dred Scott,* decided thirty-eight years later, that result was reversed.

***DRED SCOTT V. SANDFORD* AND STATES' RIGHTS.** Despite its Federalist leanings, the Marshall Court could not permanently establish the explicit powers of the state and national governments. Marshall died in July 1835, and at the end of that year President Andrew Jackson selected Roger B. Taney to serve as the next chief justice. Jackson favored Taney largely because of his advocacy of states' rights, and, true to his reputation, Chief Justice Taney led the Court away from the national supremacy doctrine Marshall crafted. Taney's effort culminated in *Dred Scott v. Sandford* (1857), which, as we found in Chapter 4, brought the nation to the brink of a civil war by claiming that African Americans were not citizens under the Constitution.[6] In addition to ruling that escaped slaves in the North had to be returned to their owners, Taney's majority opinion held that federal laws outlawing slavery north of the Mason–Dixon line (for example, as set in the Missouri Compromise) unconstitutionally infringed on settlers' territorial rights to self-government and private property.*

---

*The opinion in *Dred Scott v. Sandford* was only the second time the Court had overruled an act of Congress. Considering that in the first instance, *Marbury,* the Court had merely asserted its authority but did so in such a way as to avoid reversing the president's action, the *Dred Scott* decision may represent the real, if inauspicious, beginning of judicial review of acts of Congress.

The overwhelming public outcry against Taney's reasoning left the Court—an unelected branch of government—seriously discredited. *Dred Scott v. Sandford* took on issues that were too important and divisive to be settled by judicial fiat. In the end, after politics failed, the enduring problems of states' rights and slavery could only be settled by war rather than by legislation or litigation. The defeat of the Confederacy in the Civil War signaled a decisive triumph for federal over state government.

After the Civil War, the Fourteenth and Fifteenth Amendments were ratified, and Congress passed laws that committed the Court to review state laws that ran counter to national statutes. The Court was not bound to support the federal government in every dispute, but it was obliged to devote more attention than ever before to policies emanating from the lower levels of government. Thus after 1860 the decisions striking down state and local laws increased markedly (see Table 9-1). Oliver Wendell Holmes Jr., one of the most distinguished Supreme Court justices of the early twentieth century, observed, "I do not think the United States would come to an end if we lost our power to declare an Act of Congress void. I do think the union would be imperiled if we could not make that declaration as to the laws of the several States."[7]

Regulating the National Economy

The major issue during the second era of judicial review, from the end of the Civil War to the 1930s, was the government's regulation of the economy. Although the Civil War had settled the supremacy issue in favor of the national government, the actual scope of government powers at both levels remained uncertain. With the rapid industrial expansion after the war, Washington, D.C., and state capitals alike came under increasing pressure to regulate monopolies and to provide new services to the citizenry. Most such demands were brushed aside, but some, such as the call to regulate the railroads, proved politically irresistible. Invariably, whenever a state or, infrequently, the national government enacted a regulatory policy, it quickly found its way onto the docket of an unsympathetic Court.

THE PRIMACY OF PROPERTY RIGHTS. By the late nineteenth century, a constitutional tradition had developed that shielded business from economic regulation. The Framers considered the right to private property to be fundamental, and equated it with liberty. Indeed, it was the economic problems caused by the Articles of Confederation—namely, its failure to prevent state raids on property rights—that brought the delegates together in Philadelphia in the first place. Marshall shared the Framers' commitment to property, and during hard economic times the Court vigilantly protected the integrity of contracts against state efforts to annul them on behalf of debtors. Marshall wrote in one decision, "the people of the United States . . . have manifested a determination to shield themselves and their property from the effects of those sudden and strong passions to which men are exposed."[8]

After the Civil War the Court generally maintained its historical sympathy for property rights. The Fourteenth Amendment was adopted in 1868 to protect newly freed slaves from the repressive actions of the former Confederate states. The amendment said, in part, that no state shall "deprive any person of life, liberty, or property, without

Figure 9-1 Changing Caseload of the Supreme Court by Decade

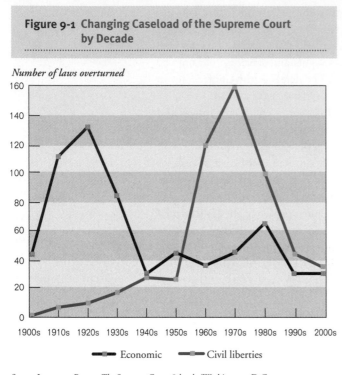

Number of laws overturned

Source: Lawrence Baum, *The Supreme Court*, 9th ed. (Washington, D.C.: CQ Press, 2007), Figure 5-1, 176.

Note: Figure shows the number of economic and civil liberties laws (federal, state, and local) overturned by the Supreme Court by decade. Civil liberties category does not include laws supportive of civil liberties.

due process of law." As we saw in Chapter 4, the nineteenth-century Supreme Court discovered little basis in the due process clause to shield African Americans from disfranchisement and segregation. It did, however, find ample justification for protecting railroads and other businesses from regulation. To invoke the due process clause, the Court defined corporations as "persons."

The Supreme Court did not deliver a pro-business decision in every case, however. It consistently upheld state prohibitions against the sale of alcohol and occasionally affirmed state regulation of business when the public interest was at stake.[9] But this last criterion, "public interest," is ambiguous, and it prevented the Court from settling on a consistent doctrine. Consequently the states continued to test the boundaries of permissible regulation, and the early-twentieth-century federal courts were inundated with these cases.

The Court's track record in work hour regulation is one example. In *Lochner v. New York* (1905) the Court struck down a New York law restricting the work hours of bakers to a maximum of ten hours a day or sixty hours a week.[10] Laws "limiting the hours in which grown and intelligent men may labor to earn their living," the majority declared, "are mere meddlesome interferences with the rights of the individual." Three years later, however, the Court upheld an Oregon statute limiting the workday of female workers.[11]

During the 1920s the Supreme Court became decidedly more conservative on economic issues and with unprecedented vigor struck down laws regulating business in state after state. Figure 9-1 shows a steady rise in the number of economic measures overturned under the due process clause, reaching a peak of 133 from 1920 to 1929.[12] These decisions won the Court the enmity of many elected officials who found that the justices obstructed their efforts to respond to the demands and needs of their constituents.

After the great stock market crash of 1929, the nation plummeted into a deep economic depression. State and federal governments responded with numerous emergency economic reforms, many of which the Court narrowly affirmed. Yet, as the Great Depression lingered on and the government intervened more substantially in the economy, the Court majority consistently ruled against regulation. From 1934 to 1937 the Court, still made up of justices who had been appointed before the Depression, struck down twelve statutes enacted during President Franklin D. Roosevelt's first term. These included laws creating emergency relief programs, controlling the production of coal and basic agricultural commodities, regulating child labor, and providing mortgage relief, especially to farmers.

A NATIONAL CONSENSUS AND THE COURT'S ABOUT-FACE. Earlier, the Civil War had ended slavery and rendered moot the *Dred Scott* decision. In this era of economic turmoil, resolution of the impasse required a direct confrontation between the Supreme Court and the elected branches of government. Shortly after his landslide reelection in 1936, President Roosevelt proposed a plan for revamping the judiciary. Part of it was the famous (or infamous) **Court-packing plan.** Ostensibly the plan proposed to alleviate the backlog of cases on the Court's docket by allowing the president, among other things, to appoint an additional Supreme Court justice for every sitting justice over the age of seventy. With the opportunity to name as many as six new justices to the high bench, Roosevelt

Congressional attempts to curb child labor by taxing the items produced were repeatedly rebuffed by the Supreme Court in the early twentieth century.

could ensure himself a Court majority sympathetic to his New Deal programs. Public reaction to the idea was generally negative, and the legislation failed in Congress, despite its lopsided Democratic majorities. Ultimately, however, victory went to Roosevelt. With a 5–4 decision in a case about regulating wage and working conditions in Washington State, the Court began to uphold the same type of economic regulations it had been rejecting for the past two years.[13]

The Court's about-face started when one justice began to favor federal economic assistance. Justice Owen Roberts's famed "switch in time that saved nine" allowed the Court to bend to the emerging national consensus that recovery required the government's active management of the economy. In the years after the Court-packing crisis, President Roosevelt sealed the Court's retreat from economic policy by filling vacant seats on the bench with appointees who were committed to the New Deal. He had many opportunities: between 1937 and 1941, seven members of the Court either died or retired. Only Roberts and Harlan Fiske Stone, whom Roosevelt raised to chief justice, remained. The justices, now more in tune with the elected branches' thinking about the government's role in the economy, began to pay attention to a different set of issues—civil rights and civil liberties. In the end, the dramatic conversion of the Supreme Court's agenda—from protecting capitalism against the New Deal to taking up the cause of civil rights and liberties—came not through institutional reform, as might have been expected. Rather, it resulted from the replacement of retirees with a new generation of jurists in closer agreement with the president and Congress. Below we will see that the power to appoint like-minded judges is an important tool with

which presidents influence the federal judiciary's policies, and that even for the *unelected* branch politics matters.

The Rise of Civil Rights and Civil Liberties

The third era of judicial review began in earnest in the 1940s. During this period the Court's concern was the relationship between the individual and government. We surveyed the broad scope of this new direction in Chapters 4 and 5; here we are interested in why the Supreme Court went in this particular direction.

A number of historical reasons for this development have been proposed, and all of them may be true. For example, the rise of totalitarian regimes in Europe and the horrors of World War II may have caused jurists to reflect more critically on the preservation of personal freedoms in the United States. Black troops returning from the war expected their lives to be better than before, and they were joined in their search for a better life by the large numbers of African Americans who had migrated from the South to Northern industrial cities. There, they created a community that no longer would allow the nation to ignore segregation in the South and racial discrimination elsewhere. Before winning victories in Congress, civil rights proponents found a Supreme Court willing to support their cause.

A Fourth Era? The Court as Chief Referee

The three eras reviewed here are historic not only because they led to major changes in the country but also because they represent periods of sharp disagreement between the Court and the elected branches. Once the Court left the policy domain of economic regulation, a field in which much of the consequential and politically contested public policy continues to reside, it removed a major source of friction between it and the elected branches. Certainly during the modern era, relations between the judiciary and the elective branches have not erupted into constitutional confrontations that led to efforts to reconstitute the Court. The present-day judicial and elective branches continue to adjust to each other's decisions, but their actions and reactions occur on a much narrower field of policy, on the periphery of those issues that most concern Congress and the president. As a result, although the Supreme Court still engages in judicial review, as indicated in Table 9-1 by the comparatively large number of federal and state laws invalidated, these instances of judicial assertiveness do not threaten or disrupt relations between the judiciary and the elected branches.

The current Court may be tentatively ushering in a fourth era, one that finds it increasingly limiting the federal government's ability to impose policy and administrative restrictions on the states (see Chapter 3). These kinds of decisions reflect another aspect of its modern role that is grounded in judicial review: the Court serves as the political system's chief referee. In the 1970s federal courts overturned extensive presidential use of impoundment (delaying or withholding budgeted expenditures), and these rulings, in turn, spurred the president and Congress to reform the way budgets are formulated and implemented. In 1998 the Court struck down Congress's attempt to give the president a line-item veto (see Chapter 7). In 2001 it unanimously rejected an appeals court ruling that Congress delegated too much regulatory discretion to the Environmental Protection Agency (EPA) and, in effect, unconstitutionally abdicated its authority. And in 2008 the Court rejected President George W. Bush's executive order that Texas must retry a Mexican citizen convicted in a death penalty case because he had not been given the opportunity to consult with the Mexican consulate, as required by the World Court. Without explicit authorization by public law, the president's authority was insufficient to act alone. In these and other cases the Supreme Court acted as a disinterested third party applying the rulebook—that is, the Constitution—to keep those officeholders who compete over public policy in their proper constitutional orbits.

Finally, and perhaps the most pervasive source of its influence on national policy, the modern Supreme Court and the rest of the federal judiciary are intimately involved in the administration of national policy. A much greater share of the judicial branch's caseload involves overseeing the bureaucracy's performance in relation to its statutory responsibilities. Whenever the EPA issues a new pollution standard, there is a fair chance that an affected party will sue the agency, claiming that it exceeded its authority. The Court must determine whether the agency conformed substantively and procedurally to its statutory responsibilities and guidelines. In many other cases, the Court simply decides what the law says. Bankruptcy law protects retirement funds from liens by creditors. Does this include 401(k) savings accounts that can be withdrawn at any time but with a penalty before the individual reaches a certain age? Yes, the Court answered in 2005. Then, for the next session, it considered whether Social Security disability payments were similarly protected.[14] By one count the Court delivered 374 decisions interpreting public laws from 1986 through 1990—a large share of the caseload for an institution that normally issues about one hundred decisions each year. At times, the Court will even recommend changes in the law that will produce the intended results and resolve conflicting laws and ambiguous delegations of authority to the bureaucracy.[15]

In many instances the modern federal judiciary acts as an extension of the bureaucracy. When the federal government believed that software giant Microsoft violated antitrust laws, it could not, unlike governments in many other countries, directly penalize the company. Antitrust laws required that the government sue Microsoft; have a judge and jury decide if the charges were true; and, if so, formulate an appropriate penalty. On many other occasions public laws place the federal courts at the end of the administrative process to hear appeals from private parties who argue that an agency's administrative regulation or other action exceeded its authority. So although judicial review elevated the Supreme Court to as close to a "coequal branch" as can be

POLITICS/POLICY

....

The Court as a Reluctant Constitutional Referee

Adopting a constitutional referee role does not let the federal judiciary avoid having to make tough judgment calls and balancing claims from each of the different branches. The boundaries defining the jurisdictions of the states and the several branches of the national government are frequently unclear and sometimes contradictory. A recent example of the courts proceeding gingerly in reviewing the president's executive authority, especially the office's commander-in-chief prerogatives, occurred in a 2007 lawsuit filed by a coalition of environmentalist groups to stop the U.S. Navy's training exercises that involved mid-frequency active sonar ("MFA sonar"). There is some evidence that the high-intensity sound confuses and hence endangers whales and thereby violates both the National Environmental Protection Act

("NEPA") and the Coastal Zone Management Act ("CZMA"). In early 2008 a California federal district court agreed with this reasoning and issued a preliminary injunction against the exercises. But it

found among national judiciaries around the world, it is Congress's delegation of oversight across a broad range of national policy that ensures the Court's active participation in governance.

The Structure of the Federal Judiciary

The United States has several hundred federal courts, but only the Supreme Court is explicitly mentioned in the Constitution's Article III. The Framers knew more would be needed, but unable to agree whether to create a separate federal judiciary or have

also allowed the navy to carry out its remaining training exercises, *provided* that it followed specific mitigation measures.

However, less than two weeks later, President George W. Bush tried to compensate for the loss by issuing an executive order exempting the navy's use of MFA sonar from the CZMA. Concurrently, the Council on Environmental Quality (CEQ)—an executive branch agency—temporarily exempted the navy from the NEPA requirements

at issue. The environmental litigants went back to the district court, which once again ruled in their favor. Although the court's opinion found President Bush's action "constitutionally suspect," it skirted a presidential challenge and instead upheld its injunction *solely* by judging CEQ's decision invalid. In such a situation it is always easier to question the bureaucracy's decisions than those of the president. The district court's decision illustrates the established practice of "constitutional avoidance" (avoiding a constitutional question when a case can be decided on other grounds).

As a result, the Ninth Circuit dodged a confrontation with the White House when reviewing the case on the navy's appeal. Although upholding the injunction, the appeals court relaxed the most stringent mitigation measures imposed by the district court in ways that were more favorable to the navy. Thus, the Ninth Circuit slightly tipped the scales back in favor of the navy and the interests of national security. The Supreme Court accepted the government's appeal and heard oral arguments in October 2008. The next month the Court ruled, 5–4, in favor of the navy.

the state courts oversee the initial trials and lower-level appeals, they agreed to defer the decision and let Congress create "inferior" courts as necessary. Congress promptly did so in the Judiciary Act of 1789. Of the various types of courts Congress has created over the years, those of most interest here are **constitutional courts,** which are vested with the general judicial authority outlined in Article III.* These lower-level courts, designed to handle litigation, exercise the same power of judicial review available to

---

*The nonconstitutional courts are classified as legislative courts. They are created by Congress under Article I and fulfill some special purpose; their judges are appointed by the president for fixed terms. Examples are the U.S. Court of Military Appeals, the U.S. Tax Court, and bankruptcy courts.

the Supreme Court. In this sense the entire federal judiciary serves as agents of the Supreme Court. The lower federal courts weigh the merits of a case against prescribed Supreme Court doctrine and presumably arrive at approximately the same decision the Supreme Court would have rendered had it heard the case.

As we have seen, Congress delegates work to specialized committees and sizable staffs to deal with the myriad issues and policies it handles. Similarly, the modern presidency includes a large retinue of highly specialized White House staff and an Office of Management and Budget (OMB) to monitor the hundreds of executive branch agencies. As with these other institutions, the Supreme Court's effectiveness also rests on delegation—in this case, on persuading the lower federal judiciary, by the strength of its opinions, to implement its policies.

Jurisdiction of the Federal Courts

As almost every American law school student immediately learns, federal courts are courts of *limited* jurisdiction. The precise scope of federal court jurisdiction is not, in fact, so simple, which accounts for the semester-long law school courses devoted to this subject. Generally speaking, federal courts are authorized to hear two types of cases: those concerning "federal questions," and those involving citizens of different states. Among other things, federal question jurisdiction includes questions of U.S. constitutional law, such as the various civil liberties claims reviewed in Chapter 5. Or, more commonly, this jurisdiction involves the judiciary interpreting and applying federal statutes in criminal and civil cases. For example, the Justice Department successfully sued Microsoft in federal court for engaging in monopolistic practices. The second major type of federal jurisdiction concerns cases where states or citizens of different states sue each other. The reasoning here is that a citizen of State A who is sued by a citizen of State B in State B might not be treated fairly by a court in State B.*

Jurisdictional questions can be complicated by the fact that state courts also have jurisdiction over federal civil claims, unless Congress has given federal courts *exclusive* jurisdiction over certain kinds of federal cases (which it has the authority to do, and often does). However, defendants in such a case can invoke "removal jurisdiction" to transfer a case filed in state court to federal court if the case could have been filed in federal court to begin with. Therefore, as a practical matter, the vast majority of cases that can be heard in federal court usually will be heard in federal court instead of state court. In addition, a criminal defendant who has been convicted under a state criminal law in state court, but who feels that his federal constitutional rights have been violated, can appeal his case to the U.S. Supreme Court—although the defendant is generally required to first "exhaust" his appeals through the state court system. For example, the defendant in the seminal case of *Miranda v. Arizona,* after losing his appeal to the Supreme Court of Arizona, successfully appealed to the U.S. Supreme Court, which determined that the defendant's Fifth Amendment rights against self-incrimination

---

*Federal statutory law also imposes the requirement that the amount at issue between citizens of different states must be more than $75,000.

had been violated.* Finally, federal courts also have jurisdiction under federal law to hear *habeas corpus* petitions. Although a discussion of the complicated topic of *habeas corpus* is beyond the scope of this chapter, the basic idea is that a criminal defendant in state court may file an action in federal court, alleging that the state's incarceration violates the Constitution or other federal law.

The Supreme Court's Delegation

The federal judiciary is organized as a three-layered pyramid. At its base are ninety-four **district courts** staffed by approximately 642 active judges.† Every state has at least one district court, and the three largest states—California, New York, and Texas—have four. District courts are trial-level courts, and (with some exceptions) most cases in the federal system must start there. If one of the parties is not satisfied with the outcome of a case at the district court level, they must appeal their case to one of the U.S. Courts of Appeals. There are currently thirteen **courts of appeals,** administered by approximately 167 active judges. Eleven separate geographic regions, or "circuits," cover the fifty states; a twelfth is assigned to the District of Columbia (see Map 9-1). The thirteenth, called the U.S. Court of Appeals for the Federal Circuit, has a nationwide jurisdiction and deals mostly with specialized federal law such as patent and trademark law. Usually sitting as three-judge panels, courts of appeals review district court decisions.

The Supreme Court is the court of final appeal. Under its appellate jurisdiction, the Court may hear cases appealed from the lower federal courts or directly from the highest state courts when an important constitutional question is in dispute. Through these channels, the Court receives the bulk of its work. Article III also gives the Court original trial court jurisdiction in all cases "affecting Ambassadors, other public Ministers and Consuls, and those in which a State shall be Party." This constitutional quirk required the Supreme Court in 1998 to hear a dispute between New York and New Jersey over which state "owned" Ellis Island, which is located at the mouth of the Hudson River. Original jurisdiction cases always have accounted for a small part of the Court's work—only about 160 cases in two hundred years.

The Supreme Court depends heavily on the lower courts behaving like loyal agents in deciding thousands of cases annually. The Court's lofty position at the apex of this pyramid of federal courts suggests a command over the subordinate courts' policies that in fact does not exist. Contrary to the clean lines of authority implied by the organizational structure, the judicial system is anything but a tightly supervised hierarchy. Rather, it is a decentralized organization, physically dispersed across the nation and administered at every level by independent, life-tenured judges. Unlike the presidency, which delegates oversight of the bureaucracy to OMB, or the House and Senate, which delegate responsibility for drafting legislation to committees, the Supreme Court wields few administrative controls over the lower courts. Thus, successful implementation of

---

*In addition, occasionally a crime will violate both state and federal law, exposing the defendant to the brunt of both judicial systems in separate trials.

†The most recent figure is for 2005. In addition, 292 senior judges preside over a reduced caseload.

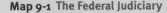

Map 9-1 The Federal Judiciary

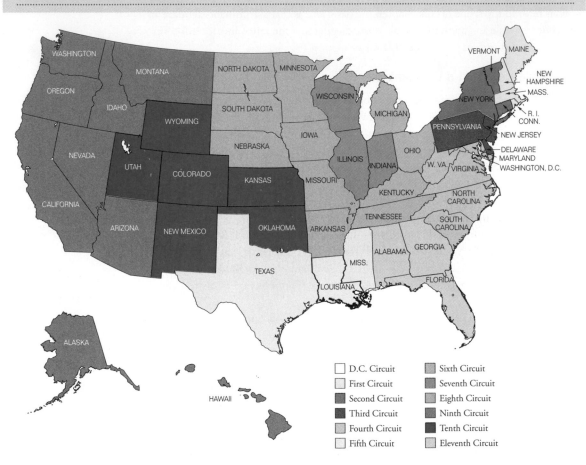

the Supreme Court's policies is not guaranteed and depends greatly on the degree to which the justices concur in a course of action and on how clearly they communicate it to their colleagues throughout the judiciary.

The Limits of Internal Control

If the Supreme Court truly sat atop a hierarchical organization, it would enjoy a far different relationship with the district and appeals courts. Like the CEO of a major corporation or a cabinet secretary, it would routinely supervise and give orders to its subordinate agents. Motivated by the knowledge that making the wrong choice might result in an unfavorable merit review, demotion, or even dismissal, subordinates would defer to their principal and seek guidance. None of these techniques to keep subordinates on the right track is available to the Supreme Court in steering decisions from the district and appellate courts. Instead, the life tenure of judges, which insulates the judiciary from the other branches, also insulates judges from each other.

Only Congress can remove a federal judge, and then only for serious offenses—not for incompetence or policy disagreement with the Supreme Court. Moreover, the Supreme Court cannot distribute the caseload to the lower courts; the distribution of cases depends on geographical jurisdictions created by Congress and, to some extent, litigants' choice of courts.

The Supreme Court also may have difficulty enforcing implementation of its decisions in the lower courts. Outright resistance to Supreme Court decisions by lower-court judges is unusual but does occur. Declaring that the Court "erred," an Alabama federal judge in 1983 upheld prayer in the public schools, in spite of the Court's prohibition of the practice.[16] In a capital punishment case in 1993 an appellate judge kept granting a stay of execution despite the Supreme Court's rejection of the defendant's appeal. When a lower court disregards a directive, the Court has several options available. It may hear the case a second time, rebuke the lower-court judge, issue a writ of mandamus ordering the lower-court judge to take a specified action, or assign the case to a different court. Because all such alternatives are costly in terms of the time and monitoring required, they illustrate the limits of Supreme Court control, though they also ensure that the Court will ultimately prevail if it feels sufficiently strongly on an issue.

More commonly, policy differences occur when lower-court judges take advantage of ambiguities arising from the particular facts of a case or in the language of Supreme Court doctrine to avoid complying with the higher court's preferences. This is precisely what happened in the aftermath of *Brown v. Board of Education*.[17] When the Court ordered public schools to desegregate with "all deliberate speed" instead of setting a deadline, it unwittingly invited segregationist federal judges throughout the South to move at a snail's pace.

Yet the Supreme Court is not helpless. It can reverse lower-court decisions when it disagrees; even the threat of reversal often deters deviations from Court doctrine. After all, a reversal represents a "defeat" for a judge, and those who suffer frequent reversals may damage their reputations. A record of reversals also alerts judges higher up to scrutinize their judgments carefully for incompetence or noncompliance with established precedents. Fearing reversal, most judges strategically temper their rulings to sufficiently conform with established doctrine, and thus to withstand litigants' efforts to persuade an appeals court or the Supreme Court to review the rulings.

Nonetheless, reversal remains an imperfect sanction. Some judges may be willing to risk a few reversals to defend strongly held views and to force other courts to reconsider current policy. In addition, given the Supreme Court's ability to control the number of

TABLE 9-2		
The Federal Judiciary: Number of Judges		
Court	Circuit	District
D.C. Circuit	12	15
1st	6	29
2nd	13	62
3rd	14	61
4th	15	55
5th	17	84
6th	16	63
7th	11	47
8th	11	42
9th	28	113
10th	12	40
11th	12	69
Federal Circuit	12	—

Note: Current as of May 2005, including vacancies.

cases it hears on appeal—a very small percentage of all cases actually appealed—most circuit court judges realize that the probability of the Court reviewing their decisions is very low. However, a circuit court, like the liberal Ninth Circuit Court of Appeals in the west, can press its luck a bit too much. From 2000 to 2004 the Supreme Court overturned the Ninth Circuit's judgments at about twice the rate of the other appeals courts, and nearly half of these reversals brought a frequently divided Supreme Court into unanimous agreement. As a result, the present Supreme Court monitors this wayward delegate closely. About one-third of all cases the Court reviews originate in this circuit, again about twice the share one would expect.

Judicial Decision Making

The pyramid shape of the court system accurately portrays the realities of the modern federal judiciary, at each level of which the caseload continues to mount. As alluded to above, the huge docket of the judicial branch means that the risk of reversal may not be so great. In fiscal year 2007, over 325,000 new cases were filed in the federal district courts, and over 58,000 new cases were filed in the circuit courts of appeals. The Supreme Court, in contrast, decides fewer than 100 cases annually, or about 1 percent of the appeals it receives. For example, in the 2006 term, 8,857 cases were filed in the Supreme Court, but only 78 cases were argued.[18] These numbers reveal that the intermediate, appeals level of the judiciary, not the Supreme Court, oversees the district courts' compliance with prevailing doctrine. As long as the appeals courts' judgments agree with the policies of the Supreme Court, the latter is free to act as a "general staff or selective formulator of policies."[19]

Selecting Cases

In 1925, when the number of appeals began to grow at an alarming rate, the Supreme Court persuaded Congress to change the rules granting access to a hearing by the Court. Over the years these rules have been strengthened in favor of giving the Court greater discretion to choose the cases it reviews. Instead of having a right to "their day in court," litigants must file a **writ of certiorari** requesting that the Court order a lower court to send it the records of the trial in question. With this device, the Supreme Court gained control over its caseload since the vast majority of the cases arrive by this route. Indeed, the Court has managed to cut in half the number of cases it hears annually, despite a six-fold increase in the number of requests.

Discretionary control over its caseload solved only part of the Court's problem, however. From the eight thousand or so *certiorari* requests it receives each year, how does the Court decide which one hundred (or fewer) to review? In small, intimate work settings members need not delegate agenda control in order to coordinate their decisions. The Supreme Court's **rule of four** provides that when four justices support hearing a case the *certiorari* petition is granted.[20] With so many cases, the absence of extensive delegation of case selection—say to some central clerk staff supervised by the chief justice—the rule of four protects the prerogatives of individual justices but at a cost to each member of having to cull through a mountain of petitions. Unlike congressional and presidential staffs numbering in the thousands, the Supreme Court is not served by a large bureaucracy to help it sort through that mountain and find cases that satisfy its criteria. Each justice is permitted to hire up to four clerks, usually graduates of the country's most prestigious law schools, who spend a year or two at the Court. To deal with the petitions, the clerks form a "cert pool" to review them and make recommenda-

This 1885 *Puck* magazine cartoon calls for Congress to relieve the Supreme Court's congested docket. Relief would come later with reforms giving the Court the writ of *certiorari*.

tions to the justices. Because the opportunity to hear cases is limited, justices take a hard, strategic look at each one before promoting it to their colleagues. Do the facts of the case allow the Court to arrive at a "clean" decision that will guide the lower courts? More important, will the justice's preference stand a chance of garnering the five votes necessary to win if the case is heard on its merits? If not, a justice who otherwise would want to hear a case will pass on it for fear of allowing the majority to establish even more firmly a policy he or she opposes.[21] Thus deciding whether to hear a case is itself a major decision—and one fraught with political strategy. After all, as Chief Justice William Rehnquist acknowledged, "There is an ideological division on the Court, and each of us has some cases we would like to see granted, and on the contrary some of the other members would not like to see them granted."[22] And because justices want to weigh in on cases in which they think the lower courts have made an error, cases granted *certiorari* have a good chance of being overturned; in a typical year almost two-thirds are.

RESOLVING LOWER-COURT DISAGREEMENTS. Recognizing that the Court has a strong stake in maintaining standards and coherence within this highly decentralized organization, justices look for cases they can use to resolve ambiguities and conflicting lower-court decisions. In recent years the Supreme Court stayed clear of affirmative action cases. Finally in 2003, with the Eleventh Circuit Court of Appeals deciding firmly against racial preferences—and in doing so concurring with a prior opinion of the Fifth Circuit—and with the Ninth Circuit just as firmly endorsing such quotas, the Court had no choice but to come up with a more consistent policy. As we found in Chapter 4, it did so by accepting racial criteria for admissions to promote

Chief Justice William Rehnquist, who served as a law clerk for Justice Robert Jackson (served 1941–1954), meets with his clerks to discuss pending cases.

diversity while continuing to reject quotas. In this and on numerous other issues contradictory policies reflecting different ideological preferences of judges percolate up the judicial pyramid.

Sometimes, however, the source of policy disarray is the Court itself, which highlights the significance of crafting doctrine carefully. In 2004 the Court ruled unconstitutional a Washington State law requiring judges to sentence defendants strictly according to guidelines that score the defendant's leadership role in the crime, past criminal record, and other criteria. Immediately sentencing throughout the federal judiciary was thrown into disarray, because the state law closely resembled the federal mandatory sentencing law. One federal district judge in Manhattan suspended all sentencing until the Court addressed the federal law. Another colleague in the same building started issuing two sentences—one if the Court upholds mandatory sentencing, another if not. Yet other judges decided simply to ignore the mandatory guidelines altogether. As the different appeals courts came up with their own interim solution, the law designed to standardize sentencing across the country began having the opposite effect, much to the disgust of members of Congress. To resolve the mess it unwittingly created, the Court took up an appeal in an expedited hearing and early in 2005 overturned mandatory sentencing while prescribing that judges continue to use the congressional sentencing rules as guidelines.[23]

TAKING CUES FROM OTHERS. In selecting cases for resolution, the justices economize by paying close attention to what others tell them. In addition to hearing from the plaintiff (or prosecutor in criminal cases) and defendant, the Court allows interested groups not party to the litigation—interest groups, businesses, and government agencies, among others—to submit *amicus curiae* (friend of the court) briefs arguing that a *certiorari* petition should be granted or denied. Just as interest groups testify before Congress in hearings, business, government, nonprofits, and other interest groups "testify" before the Supreme Court in these briefs. Of all the interested parties, the most important and prolific is the federal government itself. Through the office of the **solicitor general** the administration lets the Court know which cases it thinks are important.

The anecdotal record has long acknowledged that the presence of *amicus curiae* briefs from prestigious sources increases a case's chances of being accepted by the Court. One systematic analysis of the Supreme Court's decision to grant or reject *certiorari* found that the solicitor general—the chief attorney for the United States government—supported a hearing in about half of the cases the Court accepted.[24] And in controversial cases—defined as those cases in which lower courts disagreed or *amicus curiae* briefs had been filed on both sides of the issue—the Court's decision to hear a case followed the solicitor general's recommendation more than 95 percent of the time.

At first glance, these figures appear to indicate that the solicitor general dictates the Court's agenda. A more subtle process is probably at work, however. In looking for cases they hope will persuade the Court to adopt a doctrine to their liking, the government and interest groups tend to promote those cases they think will attract the Court. In this way, they actually help the Court separate wheat from chaff and identify those decisions that most deserve the Court's attention. In lieu of an extensive bureaucracy to process nearly eight thousand cases, the Court has informally and effectively delegated some of this work to outside agents. When they sound an alarm, the Court pays attention. (And were they to abuse this influence by overly calling attention to cases they would like the Court to hear, but do not really require its attention, they would find their legal briefs carrying less weight with the Court.)

Doctrine: Policymaking by the Court

Congress passes laws, courts make doctrine. Both are public policy, but they take very different forms. A public law typically assigns responsibility and appropriates money to a federal agency to achieve certain stated policy goals. A judicial policy decision, by contrast, typically states a rule or doctrine. In rendering decisions the Court prescribes guidelines for district and appeals judges to apply when trying similar cases. These guidelines are considered **judicial doctrine** that lower-court judges carefully weigh. Not only does judicial doctrine make their jobs easier, it also provides valuable information for estimating how far lower courts can diverge from the Supreme Court's preferences before being reviewed and overturned.

Judicial doctrine assumes two forms: procedural and substantive. **Procedural doctrine** governs the specific ways in which the lower courts should do their work. **Substantive doctrine,** more akin to policymaking, guides judges on which party in a case should prevail. Sometimes the two doctrines clash, such as when the Court decides to change current policy—for example, a search and seizure doctrine—but altering a policy requires the Court to repudiate existing methods or procedures that the lower courts have dutifully followed.

PROCEDURAL DOCTRINE. Like the managers of other decentralized organizations, the Supreme Court has sought to exercise control and to cope with its ever-growing caseload by establishing standard operating procedures prescribing how lower federal courts should decide cases. The most important such doctrine, ***stare decisis***

(Latin for "let the decision stand"), directs the lower courts, as well as the Supreme Court itself, to follow established precedent in deciding current cases. Generally precedents are earlier decisions, such as *Griswold v. Connecticut,* that establish a new substantive doctrine—in this case, the implicit right of privacy (see Chapter 5). Especially at the appellate stages of a case, the plaintiff's and the defendant's lawyers invoke precedents that support their positions. To the extent that they follow *stare decisis,* the lower courts find it easier to extend the Supreme Court's preferences. This, in turn, frees the Court to monitor closely those decisions that fail to follow precedent or are otherwise unresolved.

Even when followed conscientiously, *stare decisis* cannot strictly determine the outcome of many cases; new and unusual circumstances arise for which existing doctrine offers little guidance. Or the doctrine may be ambiguous, perhaps reflecting uncertainty or disagreement among members of the Court over what the policy should be. Or, as happens frequently, the facts of a case may bring two doctrines into conflict. The ability to interpret doctrine and apply precedents to specific cases is an important skill. Among other things, a judge must decide whether a specific precedent applies to a particular case. Some judges develop strong reputations for writing convincing opinions that influence the way other judges think about comparable cases—that is, their opinions assume value as precedent.

Other procedural doctrines identify who may initiate cases in federal court and under what circumstances. Only litigants who are directly and adversely affected by the disputed action have the right, or **standing,** that is, sufficient personal stake in the outcome to bring the case to court. Similarly, the Court long established the principle that the judiciary would not rule on moot (otherwise resolved) or hypothetical issues. Do presidents have the authority to impound appropriated funds? The only way to find out is for a president to impound money and have someone file suit. Though at times highly inconvenient to other actors, this doctrine prevents the judiciary from becoming embroiled in hypothetical issues. But in the federal sentencing debacle, this doctrine trapped the Court into deciding a state-level case emphatically while remaining mute on virtually identical circumstances in federal sentencing rules. Yet another important procedural doctrine establishes a boundary of federalism within the judiciary: only those cases in the state courts that raise a constitutional question at the outset—such as a civil liberty protected by the Bill of Rights—may be appealed to the federal judiciary after a loss in the state courts.

SUBSTANTIVE DOCTRINE. As the Supreme Court selects and decides cases, it is less interested in simply "seeing justice done" in a particular instance than in identifying standards and general characteristics of cases that will allow a decision to be applied to government policy as well as to future cases. In the *Miranda* decision discussed in Chapter 5, the Court set out clear police procedures for protecting defendants against self-incrimination. Today thousands of local law enforcement jurisdictions follow the *Miranda* guidelines as a standard operating procedure when making an arrest.

Some issues lend themselves better than others to this form of policymaking. One issue that did not was obscenity. The Supreme Court agonized for years over how to define obscenity, one of the few kinds of speech that does not enjoy First Amendment protection. As noted in Chapter 5, the effort led one exasperated justice to exclaim, "I know it when I see it!" As a result these cases continued to be decided inconsistently across the nation's state and federal district courts and required the appeals courts and Supreme Court to devote considerable attention to reconciling decisions and clearly defining obscenity.

Although the ideology of judges matters most at the higher levels where doctrine is made, current doctrine often leaves judges with abundant discretion in the lower courts. Aside from the conventional liberal-conservative distinction that applies to many cases, judgments also vary according to the way a judge views his or her role on the bench. A judge who in the absence of a clear violation of the Constitution or established doctrine will defer to the policies emanating from the elected branches, is commonly described as exercising judicial **restraint.** Those who change doctrine to conform with their view of the Constitution in a changing society are exercising judicial **activism.** In mod-

After inflaming white southerners with the Court's ruling in *Brown v. Board of Education* in 1954 and other groups throughout the country with liberal civil liberties rulings, Chief Justice Earl Warren became a target of a grassroots impeachment campaign. In this 1963 photo he accepts impeachment literature while passing picketers. No Supreme Court justice has ever been removed by impeachment.

ern political debate, the term "activist" has often been used pejoratively to describe a judge who seeks to substitute his or her policy views for that of the legislature. The Warren Court during the 1960s was widely regarded as activist in that it reopened and changed doctrine in many areas of civil rights and civil liberties. During this era activism and liberalism were used more or less interchangeably in the news media to describe judges and their decisions. However, in the present era, with most of the activist views of the Warren Court solidified as established policy, activism is just as likely to be found among judges favoring a conservative policy agenda. Thus, the term "activist" can apply to either a conservative or a liberal justice. A good example is district court rulings disputing long-established doctrine that the Second Amendment's clause concerning the right to bear arms applied to militias and not individual citizens.

Deciding Doctrine

Every Supreme Court decision contains two elements essential to creating doctrine. The first is the vote that decides the case in favor of one of the parties. The second is the opinion, a statement or set of statements in which the majority explains the rationale for its decision in a way that creates doctrine (that is, makes policy) and the minority, if there is one, articulates why it dissents.

The Politics of Opinion Writing

Every Supreme Court justice would like the Court to adopt his or her preferences as its policy. Generally members' preferences differ, so only occasionally will five or more justices immediately hit upon a majority opinion. More commonly, members' deliberations involve efforts to persuade each other and negotiate a ruling on which a majority can agree. Because it takes a majority to create a policy, this setting is ripe with opportunity for strategic behavior. A skilled judge will search for a position that will attract majority support while minimally compromising his or her sincere policy preferences. Unlike mark-up sessions in congressional committees, the process of making collective decisions on the Court occurs behind closed doors, and justices rarely talk about how they engage one another politically as they search for a majority.

Sometimes, however, we do catch a glimpse of the process and find judges undertaking the kinds of political exchanges familiar to all other political actors examined in this text. Consider the example of Justice William Brennan who, just before his retirement in 1990, wrote the majority opinion in *Pennsylvania v. Muniz*. In this case the state had used videotaped footage of a police of-

ficer stopping a suspected drunk driver. When the officer asked the driver his name and address, the defendant's slurred speech gave him away as inebriated. The officer then asked what year he had turned six years old. Clearly drunk, the defendant could not do the simple addition to give the correct answer. The question for the Court was, did this video evidence violate the defendant's right of protection against self-incrimination since the officer had interrogated him without first advising him of his *Miranda* rights (see Chapter 5)?

The Court ruled yes and no. The "routine booking questions" were admissible but not the "trick" question about age that might have been intended to stump the defendant and prove he was drunk. Only one justice, Thurgood Marshall, wrote a dissent opposing any use of the videotape, while four justices joined in a separate concurring opinion, which held that all information on the tape was permissible. This latter group fell only one vote shy of the majority needed to significantly modify the *Miranda* rule. Anticipating this, Brennan engaged in a sharp bit of Court politics. In a note to Marshall, Brennan acknowledged that he, too, opposed all use of the videotape, but then went on to explain that "I made the strategic judgment to concede the existence

A unanimous Court decision, simply because it is less likely to be reversed in the future, creates more compelling precedent than does a case decided by a 5–4 vote. After the justices express their views on a case and vote tentatively on the outcome in a private conference, the chief justice (if voting with the majority) assigns one of the majority the task of drafting an opinion.* The task is not insignificant; the author of an opinion voices the majority position and, in doing so, strongly influences the shape of that judicial policy.

---

*If the chief justice is in the minority, the most senior associate justice in the majority assigns the opinion.

of an exception to *Miranda* [for the routine booking questions]... [and] to use my control over the opinion to define the exception as narrowly as possible."

In a subsequent note to Marshall, he described his rationale for this maneuver: "I fully understand your wanting to take me to task for recognizing an exception to *Miranda,* though I still firmly believe that this was the strategically proper move here. If Sandra [Day O'Connor] had gotten her hands on this issue, who knows what would have been left of *Miranda.*" (O'Connor apparently had expressed interest in relaxing the *Miranda* standard even more.) To avoid opening the door wide to the possibility that police might use deception to get evidence before reading the *Miranda* rules, Brennan found that he needed to open it a *little.* His success can be seen in the failure of this case to lead to a major alteration of policy on police procedures.

Source: Forrest Maltzman, James F. Spriggs II, and Paul J. Wahlbeck, *Crafting Law on the Supreme Court* (New York: Cambridge University Press, 2000).

The cast of characters: among the justices O'Connor is seated at far right, Brennan is at far left, and Marshall is two seats to his right in this 1986 file photo.

Once the majority opinion is drafted, it often undergoes prolonged internal bargaining as the writer tries to persuade the other justices that its legal arguments are correct (for a behind-the-scenes look at the opinion writing process, see box "The Politics of Opinion Writing," page 438). The author of the opinion generally writes to maintain the decision's core support as well as appeal to dissenters who might be converted. In 1954 Chief Justice Earl Warren used his considerable powers of persuasion to coax reluctant justices to abandon their disparate, and strongly held, positions on school desegregation and forge a unanimous opinion against segregation in *Brown v. Board of Education.*

Figure 9-2 Number of Dissenting and Concurring Opinions

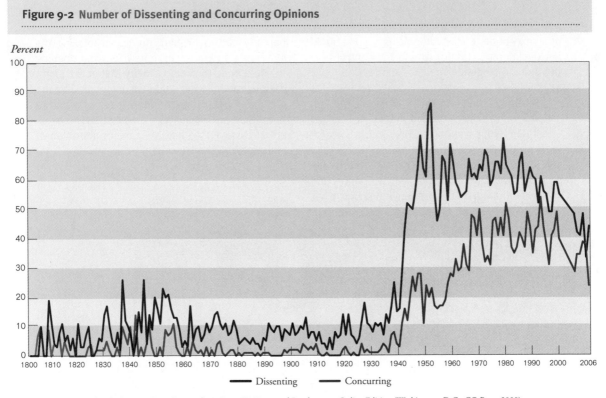

Source: Lee Epstein et al., *The Supreme Court Compendium: Data, Decisions, and Developments*, Online Edition (Washington, D.C.: CQ Press, 2008), Table 3-2, 211–215, and Table 3-3.

Successful persuasion has its costs, however. Generally, to persuade colleagues to maintain or shift their positions, the drafter must change the opinion's language and perhaps blur its message, allowing each member of the majority to find language in the opinion with which he or she can agree. Thus reluctant justices joined Warren's opinion in *Brown* on the condition that he not specify a time schedule for school desegregation. The consequences, we found in Chapter 4, were considerable. The failure to set a deadline allowed southern school boards to delay by first resisting and then engaging in token desegregation and tying up enforcement with litigation. The price of broad support among the justices may be vague, imperfectly enforced doctrine.

The prevalence of closely divided decisions—containing numerous opinions—is a modern development (see Figure 9-2). The rationale on which an opinion is based may be more consequential for future cases than for the decision itself. Because all justices wish to influence future decisions, each has an interest in opinion writing. A justice who disagrees with the majority of the Court may elect to explain why in a **dissenting opinion.** A justice who has unique reasons for supporting the majority may choose to write a **concurring opinion.** Concurring and dissenting opinions allow justices to provide their interpretations of what the majority opinion means. Although only the majority opinion counts as the Court's final decision in any given case, dissenting and concurring opinions may nonetheless influence reactions to the majority's position, by lower-court judges or by a future Supreme Court revisiting the policy.

Until passage of the Judiciary Act of 1925, which gave the Supreme Court greater control over its caseload, the Court decided far more cases than it considers today. Obligated to review many lower-court decisions with which it agreed, the Court before 1925 produced a large number of unanimous opinions. As the Supreme Court has freed itself to focus on cases that contain important, unresolved policy issues, the proportion of controversial cases has risen dramatically, and thus there are higher numbers of concurring and dissenting opinions.

Two other influences contributed to this rise in opinion writing. First, the Court stopped contesting the authority of Congress and the president to regulate economic activity and began applying the Bill of Rights to state—not just federal—actions. That the justices would not march in unison toward this new body of judicial doctrine is not surprising. The second influence has been the somewhat regular alternation of party control of the White House—a pattern largely absent in the late nineteenth and early twentieth centuries. An important result of this political development has been an ideologically more heterogeneous Supreme Court.

The Supreme Court's Place in the Separation of Powers

Judicial review seems to give the Court the last word on much of public policy. But we have found throughout our discussion, both here and in the earlier chapters on civil rights and civil liberties, that this is not necessarily so. Even when the Court's members agree on a decision and solve their internal compliance problem, the high court still faces formidable obstacles when its policy preferences differ sharply from those of Congress and the president. When the elected branches have decided on a course of action—whether dramatic, such as Roosevelt's New Deal Court-packing plan, or more modest in scope and intensity of sentiment, such as Congress's Religious Freedom Restoration Act, on which the Court rendered back-and-forth decisions (see Chapter 5)—they usually prevail.

Absence of Judicial Enforcement

In 1974 President Richard Nixon refused to release Oval Office recordings of private conversations to the special prosecutor investigating the variety of misdeeds known as the Watergate scandal. When the two sides went to court, the Supreme Court, by an 8–0 vote, rejected Nixon's claim of executive privilege and instructed him to turn over the tapes to the special prosecutor, which he did.[25] The contents of the tapes led directly to his resignation. At this point the Court's role largely ended. Had Nixon defied the Court—and the press speculated that he might—Congress would have taken the next step and decided whether his refusal constituted grounds for impeachment and removal from office.

The absence of enforcement authority has allowed Congress and the president at times to ignore Supreme Court rulings. As President Andrew Jackson famously remarked on learning that the Court had ruled his policies regarding removing Cherokee Indians from their land unconstitutional,[26] "They made their decision. Now, let them enforce it." Jackson ignored the decision and forced the Cherokee to give up their lands in return for land west of the Mississippi River. Many died on the trek later known as the Trail of Tears. The Court's inability to enforce its decisions is strikingly apparent in the failure of *Immigration and Naturalization Service v. Chadha* (1983) to end legislative practices that Congress and presidents have long found useful. In *Chadha* the Court declared the one-house legislative veto unconstitutional (see Chapter 8), upsetting procedures established by Congress and the executive branch.[27] The case itself concerned a minor issue, the deportation of a man who had overstayed his student visa, but its implications were potentially far-reaching for policymaking. The legislative veto dates back to 1932, when Congress and the president agreed to provisions that since then have been included in more than two hundred public laws, including the War Powers Act. These provisions allow either one or both houses of Congress to pass a resolution to reject an agency's action. Although *Chadha* technically voided this mechanism, the executive departments still abide by these legislative vetoes. And Congress and presidents have good reasons for favoring this approach that allows Congress to delegate lawmaking discretion to the executive branch without surrendering ultimate control. A bureaucrat is free to design a policy within broad guidelines, but if it drifts too far away from the legislature's intent, Congress can rescind it by passing a resolution. Presidents realize that Congress is more willing to relax control when it knows it can easily reassert its preferences if it disagrees with the bureaucracy's implementation of a policy. By continuing to honor these statutory provisions, designed to create more flexible principal-agency relations, the elected branches have colluded informally to "overrule" the Supreme Court's verdict on the unconstitutionality of the legislative veto.[28]

Constitutional and Statutory Control

Several provisions of the Constitution equip Congress and the president with the power to rein in the Supreme Court when they disagree with its decisions. Article III allows Congress to set the jurisdiction of the Court and to create lower courts. The Constitution is silent on the size of the Supreme Court, which means the Framers implicitly gave this authority to Congress. During the nineteenth century, Congress did, in fact, add to and subtract from the number of justices, but since 1869 the number has been set at nine. At times, when one of the political parties has captured control of the White House and Congress, it has expanded the size of the lower judiciary as a way of creating vacancies that can be filled with sympathetic judges.[29] The net effect of this practice is to bring the judiciary into closer alignment with changes in national opinion.

When all else fails, Congress may move to amend the Constitution (Article V). The Fourteenth Amendment's declaration that "all persons born or naturalized in the United States . . . are citizens of the United States" was designed to invalidate the Court's claim in *Dred Scott v. Sandford* that African Americans cannot be U.S. citizens. After repeated failures to persuade the Supreme Court that the Constitution does not forbid an income tax, Congress sent to the states the Sixteenth Amendment legalizing the personal income tax once and for all. The states ratified it in 1913.

The historical rarity of congressional attempts to amend the Constitution does not mean they are altogether irrelevant to the relations between the elected branches and the judiciary. The recurrence of these attempts reminds justices that they cannot long impose a radically different interpretation of the Constitution without triggering a reaction from the elected branches. In 1937 President Roosevelt lost the Court-packing battle but won the war in preventing the Supreme Court from overturning any more of his New Deal economic recovery policies. The conservatives on the Court confronted the stark reality of the superior authority of the elected branches, and so they nimbly began undoing precedents they had asserted only a few years before. Shortly thereafter, the Four Horsemen—the apocalyptic nickname given to the conservative justices who voted in unison against Roosevelt's policies—left the bench and were replaced by justices sympathetic to New Deal economic policies.

Legislative responses to disagreeable Supreme Court interpretations to public laws are, by contrast, straightforward and routine. One study found that from 1967 through 1990 Congress averaged a dozen new laws a year explicitly designed to reverse or modify a federal court ruling. Moreover, about half of all Supreme Court decisions that involved interpretation of federal law became the specific subject of congressional hearings. And another study found that from 1954 through 1990 Congress passed new laws to reverse 41 of 569 Supreme Court decisions voiding state or federal laws in some way.[30]

One area in which congressional oversight has been especially rigorous is civil rights. In 1980 the Supreme Court ruled on violations of the 1965 Voting Rights Act. To obtain a ruling on whether the electoral rules diluted the political impact of a racial minority, the plaintiff had to demonstrate that the laws not only had an adverse "effect" but also were enacted with the "intent" to discriminate.[31] Because some of the local laws in question had been on the statute books for a half-century or more, proving intent was sometimes impossible. In 1982, when Congress renewed the Voting Rights Act for another seven years, it added language stating that plaintiffs need only demonstrate vote dilution to challenge local electoral laws. In 1991, with the enactment of new civil rights laws, Congress overrode nine Supreme Court decisions.

Department of Justice

The federal government, represented primarily by the Department of Justice, is by far the most frequent and most important litigant in the federal court system. Indeed, the structure of the department parallels that of the federal courts, giving it the power (and efficiency) to press for legal action at all levels of the federal court system. The head of the department, the **attorney general** of the United States, can select cases and choose to file in courts where the Justice Department is most likely to win and create precedent for its legal position on an issue.

The department includes the U.S. attorneys, one for each of the ninety-four federal judicial districts. Presidential appointment and department supervision guarantee that U.S. attorneys serve as dutiful agents as they choose cases and enlist the court system to implement administration policy. In 1996, after a number of black churches

By the time Attorney General Alberto Gonzales appeared before the Senate Judiciary Committee in July 2007 for yet another grilling, he looked haggard. If so, he had good reason to be. The Senate's hearings commenced five months earlier with sworn testimony and sympathetic questioning of fired U.S. attorneys Carol Lamm, David Iglesias, John McKay, and H. E. "Bud" Cummins (and others). The intervening months had produced a steady flow of damaging Senate revelations, unflattering news coverage, and weakening support among Senate Republicans.

had been firebombed, President Bill Clinton announced a special effort to find and prosecute the culprits. Over the next six months, several cases were prosecuted in federal court. Conversely, in the same year when California passed an initiative intended to legalize the use of marijuana for medicinal purposes, the U.S. attorneys stayed clear of prosecution, despite the Justice Department's warning that possession of marijuana remained a federal crime. In January 1998 the Clinton administration changed its policy. It moved in federal court to shut down the California marijuana clubs where members met to use the drug for purportedly medical purposes.[32]

These and other instances of Justice Department litigation acting as an instrument of administration policy reflect a level of responsiveness from U.S. attorneys, uncharacteristic of other government agencies. U.S. attorneys depend on the attorney general and the White House for their job security. The capacity of these officials to embarrass the administration by investigating and filing criminal charges and civil suits against other government officials led Franklin Roosevelt, and all of his successors, to resist efforts to insulate U.S. attorneys with civil service protections. Most recently, U.S. attorneys were subject to directives and inquiries about current cases from the administration and even Republican senators, with some apparently motivated by concern with their party's success in the 2006 midterm election. After a review by the Justice Department and the White House staff—including President Bush's chief political consultant, Karl Rove—eight U.S. attorneys were dismissed and replaced with Bush administration loyalists. When the new Democratic-controlled 110th Congress launched an inquiry into the firings in 2007, Attorney General Alberto Gonzales appeared both incompetent and sycophantic to the White House staff. In the end even many normally stalwart congressional Republicans abandoned Gonzales, and he eventually resigned. Many of the same administration officials entangled in the attorneys' hiring and firing also have a say in the recruitment of federal judges. But these appointments have two key differences: nominees for judgeships must be confirmed by the Senate and once in office, judges cannot be removed except by impeachment. As a result when a U.S. attorney stands before a federal judge, these officials will reflect very different concerns about White House preferences, even in those instances where both were appointed at the same time by the same president.

Judicial Recruitment

The Constitution provides that all federal judges shall be nominated by the president with the "Advice and Consent" of the Senate (Article II, Section 2). Traditionally the president has deferred on district court nominations to the preferences of the senators from the state in which the court is located. Appointments to the courts of appeals and Supreme Court, however, tend to be more presidential and less collegially reliant on the Senate's "advice" than are lower-court appointments. In fact, judicial nominations represent the veto game in reverse (see box "Senate Confirmation: Another Kind of Veto Game," page 450). The president nominates, and the Senate accepts or rejects. As with the legislative veto, this shared responsibility provides politicians in these institutions with their best chance to influence the policies flowing from the federal judiciary. Moreover, it guarantees that the president and Senate will carefully consider the nominee's political views. From the earliest days of the Republic, the president and Congress have appreciated the merits of appointing like-minded colleagues to the federal judiciary. As we saw in the opening of this chapter, the outgoing Federalists understood this as early as the 1790s, when they stuffed as many of their partisans as possible into this branch before vacating the presidency and Congress. Two hundred years later, so too did George H. W. Bush and Bill Clinton, each of whom appointed members of their own parties 90 percent of the time (see Figure 9-3).

In picking judicial nominees, presidents and Senate sponsors also have a stake in selecting individuals with strong professional credentials. Most nominees, for example, are practicing attorneys or sitting judges. Other things being equal, quality appointees will more effectively represent the president's views on the high bench. Moreover, less than stellar résumés may open the way for senatorial and other opponents who can claim to disapprove of the nominee not because they disagree with his or her views but because of a desire to appoint only the best-qualified candidates with impeccable records. When Justice Abe Fortas resigned from the Court in 1969, Richard Nixon nominated southerner Clement Haynsworth to replace him. Although Haynsworth was judicially well qualified, the Senate rejected him because he had participated in cases in which he may have had a financial interest. In early 1970 Nixon selected another southerner, G. Harrold Carswell. Senate Democrats successfully attacked Carswell's lackluster career in his state's court system. There should be room for mediocre justices, argued Sen. Roman Hruska of Nebraska, Carswell's exasperated Republican

Figure 9-3 Presidential Imprint on the Federal Bench

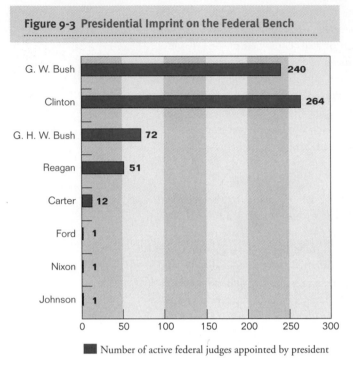

Number of active federal judges appointed by president

Source: Personal correspondence with Alliance for Justice, July 2008.

supporter, because "all Americans, even the mediocre members of society, deserve to be represented" on the Court. But this argument failed to persuade the majority of the Senate. In 2005 President George W. Bush's Supreme Court nominee, Harriet Meirs, knew she was in trouble when both liberal Democrats and conservative Republicans found some of her positions on issues troubling. Within a month of careful scrutiny her intellectual credentials and experience for the position had been effectively impugned, and the president withdrew her nomination.

PRESIDENTIAL APPOINTMENTS. Historically nominations to the district courts have concerned the senators from the state where the court is located more than the president. Consequently modern presidents delegate the task to those senators in a practice known as **senatorial courtesy**—one of the last vestiges of the patronage era of American politics. Because the courtesy of such appointment power is extended only to senators of the president's party, this practice largely explains why every administration's nominations are so heavily skewed in favor of judges from that party.

Presidents traditionally have taken greater personal interest and enjoyed more discretion in filling vacancies to the appeals courts. Senatorial courtesy has never formally applied to these appointments, probably reflecting the greater policy importance of these judges as well as the impracticality of vetting a nominee with all of the senators from those states encompassed by the court. Nine western states, for example, fall within the jurisdiction of the Ninth Circuit Court of Appeals.[33] Presidents have generally relied on the Department of Justice to screen candidates for the courts of appeals. President Jimmy Carter, however, departed from this tradition, creating a U.S. circuit judge nominating commission with panels in each circuit designed to recruit judicial nominees from a broader spectrum of the population. Although the nominating commission ostensibly aimed at removing politics from the selection process, "merit" hardly seemed to be the defining characteristic of the commission's selections: 82 percent of Carter's appointments at this level were Democrats of a markedly liberal bent.[34] President Ronald Reagan dismantled the commission and returned control of the selection process to the Justice Department.

Nominees to the Supreme Court, the highest federal tribunal, receive the full attention of the president, the Senate, and the many constituencies whose interests are af-

In this 1956 photo President Dwight Eisenhower congratulates his Supreme Court nominee William Brennan. Looking to fill a vacancy with a Catholic, Eisenhower later complained that Brennan was too liberal and that he regretted his choice. Brennan went on to serve on the Court for thirty-four years and participate in about twelve hundred cases, mostly voting with a liberal majority to expand civil liberties doctrine. This photo of a conservative president with his liberal judge should serve to remind any president to pay careful attention to appointments to these lifetime offices.

fected by judicial decisions. A president's impact on the composition of the Court depends on the frequency with which vacancies arise—something over which the president typically has no control. During the first three years of the Nixon administration, four vacancies occurred, but none during Jimmy Carter's four years in the White House. President Reagan made four appointments, and George H. W. Bush, Clinton, and George W. Bush made two each.

When a vacancy occurs, the president enlists several criteria in choosing a nominee. Understandably, in appointing an individual to a lifetime position of such importance, presidents try to guess how the nominee will vote on the controversial issues of the day—especially those that concern the president's supporters. Yet predicting a future justice's votes has at times proved to be a highly unreliable science. One never knows how the particulars of a case will affect a justice's thinking. Also, suddenly insulated from political pressure, elected officeholders who join the Court may shed political positions that had more to do with their roles as representatives than with their sincere preferences.

"It is a war," California Supreme Court justice Janice Rogers Brown warned her conservative Catholic audience at its annual retreat to mourn the confirmation defeat of their hero, Robert Bork (see page 449). "These are perilous times for people of faith." For Brown, who has labeled FDR's New Deal "the triumph of our socialist revolution," her speech was less notable for its content than its timing—during a partisan imbroglio in the Senate where Republicans were trying to label her Democratic opponents as radicals. Her appointment to the appeals court was confirmed in June 2005 by a highly partisan vote.

One way of reducing uncertainty is to select nominees from the president's party—and, in fact, more than 90 percent of all nominees to the Supreme Court have shared the president's party affiliation. Another is to interview potential nominees carefully and subject their work to intensive examination. Sandra Day O'Connor, for example, was interviewed twice by administration officials and once by President Reagan before her nomination was announced.

Presidents also may regard a vacancy as an opportunity to reward a political ally or personal associate. President Franklin Roosevelt appointed Alabama senator Hugo Black to the Court in recognition of Black's strong support for the New Deal and the Court-packing plan. Few anticipated that this Alabama politician, who had once belonged to the Ku Klux Klan, would become one of the Supreme Court's most ardent civil libertarians. But perhaps the most famous example of all of a justice surprising the appointing president occurred in President Dwight Eisenhower's nomination of Earl Warren, the governor of California, to serve as chief justice, reportedly as a reward for the crucial support Warren's delegation provided for Eisenhower's nomination at the 1952 Republican convention. Eisenhower later regretted his choice of Warren as well as that of another justice, William Brennan, both of whom proved too activist and liberal for Eisenhower's taste. Asked if he had made any mistakes as president, Eisenhower, it is widely reported, responded, "Yes, two, and they are both sitting on the Supreme Court." [35]

Presidents also may use appointments to buttress and build political alliances. Historically an appointee's region of origin was an important criterion. More recently presidents have focused on the religion, sex, and race of nominees in an effort to build support with constituencies who might reward having one of their own appointed to the Supreme Court. Just as Louis Brandeis broke the anti-Semitic barrier to the Court earlier in the century, Thurgood Marshall was the first African American on the Court, and Sandra Day O'Connor the first woman. That O'Connor was a conservative appointed by a Republican (Reagan) suggests that presidents can make these symbolic gestures to constituencies without jeopardizing their policy goals.

SENATE CONFIRMATION. Once the president has named someone to fill a judicial vacancy, the Senate Judiciary Committee schedules confirmation hearings so that it can make a recommendation to the full chamber. When the same party controls the presidency and Senate, these nominations sail through the chamber with only cursory examination. But when the opposition controls the Senate, as has happened in about half of the Congresses over the past half-century, the process of scrutinizing the nominee often becomes highly political and slows to a crawl as the opposition majority becomes—to use its characterization—"highly deliberative." Although only eight Supreme Court nominees have been rejected (or withdrew their doomed nominations) during the twentieth century, five of these have occurred since 1964, when Republican presidents tried to get judicial conservatives past a Senate controlled by Democrats.

Toward the end of a president's first term the opposition-controlled Senate becomes so deliberative that nothing much happens until the senators learn the identity of the next president. In 1996, a presidential election year, the Republican Senate set a record in confirming none of President Clinton's nominees for the appellate court and only seventeen for the district court. Two years later, with the president facing possible removal from office, the Senate confirmation process halted once more. In fact, not until mid-June 1999 did Senate confirmation hearings resume, and then only after President Clinton and Senate Judiciary Committee Republicans cut a political deal. In the past, the election of a new president normally has thawed the freeze on Senate confirmations, but perhaps as retribution for the Republican majority's treatment of Clinton, George W. Bush's nominations mostly languished during his first term. The cumulative effect of divided government during the Clinton and Bush administrations was to saddle the federal judiciary with vacancies, which meant a burdensome caseload for many sitting judges. Politically, the cadre of chronically pending appointments festered party divisions as interest groups mobilized their force for and against Clinton's and then Bush's nominees. With the increased number of Republican senators after the 2004 election, the issue came to a head. In danger of losing any opportunity to filibuster objectionable nominations, the Democrats in the Senate agreed to let some of Bush's blocked appointees be confirmed by the Republican majority. As a result the number of vacancies had shrunk to forty-four by June 2005, less than half the number during the period when the opposition party controlled the Senate. During the summer of 2008 with President Bush's tenure nearing an end and little prospect of confirmation by the Democratic-controlled Senate, the president nominated only one judge to fill one of the forty-seven vacancies on the federal district and appeals courts.

The president's announcement of a nominee usually triggers responses from a variety of interest groups whose policy preferences will be affected by who sits on the bench. Consequently, civil rights activists and corporate lobbyists alike seek to influence the Senate's decision. The height of interest group activity came in 1987, during the confirmation battle over Supreme Court nominee Robert Bork. Liberal interest groups, convinced that Bork would make the Court more conservative, campaigned heavily against his confirmation, supplementing personal lobbying of senators with direct mailings, newspaper advertisements, and press conferences. This effort cost an estimated $12–$15 million, an unprecedented amount to influence a Senate confirmation. These liberal organizations overwhelmed Bork's poorly organized conservative supporters. Largely because of their efforts, Bork's nomination was defeated, 58–42.

LOGIC OF POLITICS

Senate Confirmation
Another Kind of Veto Game

Under the Constitution the president nominates candidates to the federal judiciary, and the Senate confirms or rejects them. This sequence reverses the veto game described in Chapter 7 in which Congress proposes legislation and the president either endorses or vetoes it. In this game it is the Senate that confronts a "take it or leave it" decision that limits its opportunity to shape the result. When the White House and Senate are controlled by the same political party, the two sides cooperate informally to identify candidates both can support. As a consequence, nominees rarely encounter difficulty or delay in confirmation. Under divided government, however, the opposition party's rejection of the president's candidates—either outright or by inaction—has become increasingly commonplace as the Senate has tried to insinuate its preferences into judicial nominations. How, then, can compromise occur when divided government threatens to stall the nomination process?

President Bill Clinton's dealings with the Republican Senate demonstrated two possible solutions.

Clinton accommodated the Senate by nominating moderate judges whose views were acceptable to its conservative majority. An alternative solution was to assemble a "package" of nominees that would allow Republicans to identify some appointments in exchange for confirmations of others. President Clinton had been reluctant to do this, however, largely because Republicans wanted conservative jurists, who were bound to stir up heated opposition from some of Clinton's core constituencies.

Nonetheless, in 1999 Sen. Orrin Hatch, R-Utah, chair of the Senate Judiciary Committee, persuaded the president to negotiate such a deal. Entering mid-June with seventy-two vacancies in the federal judiciary and forty-two Clinton nominations awaiting Senate action, Hatch's committee had yet to conduct its first confirmation hearing for 1999. In the meantime, Hatch was promoting Republican Ted Stewart, conservative head of Utah's Department of Natural Resources, for a vacancy to the federal district court in Salt Lake City. With a wink and a nod, Hatch suggested that were Clinton to nomi-

The confirmation "veto" offers an opposition-controlled Senate more influence than the generally small number of rejected nominees would indicate. Presidents, calculating the prospects of defeat of a nominee, usually forgo the battle and potential embarrassment of defeat and opt for someone whom the administration and the Senate find acceptable. Whatever the Senate's indirect influence, one can reasonably conclude that partisanship and ideology represent primary considerations in nomination and confirmation of federal judges. Because judges do in fact make policy, it is fitting that the president and Congress take their ideology into account and understandable that they would prefer judges who agree with their own political views. Indeed, with some exceptions, the judges appointed by Democratic presidents tend to

nate Stewart, the committee would go to work processing the president's pending nominees.

For nearly two months President Clinton had hesitated. If he agreed, the Senate might clear dozens of pending nominees. But then he would lose the opportunity to fill the Utah vacancy with someone who shared his views on environmental policy. Worse, the president might anger environmentalists who adamantly opposed Stewart's nomination and had been publicly pressuring Clinton to reject Hatch's overture. Clearly the Stewart nomination would be costly, and the president had to be sure he would get something in return. But could he assume that Hatch would, or even could, safely usher many of his nominees to their seats on the federal bench?

The deal with Hatch represented a political minefield. How many pending nominees would Republicans allow through the committee in exchange for Stewart? Once Stewart's name was sent up, would Hatch, who had urged the president's removal during the impeachment trial earlier in the year, renege and play the president as a sucker? A successful deal required the president and Hatch to navigate around a potential prisoner's dilemma. Beyond this, Clinton had to wonder about the fate of his nominees on the Senate floor even with the committee's endorsement. Republican Senate majority leader

Trent Lott already had groused that Hatch's committee had been too generous with Clinton's nominations over the years. Would Stewart sail through confirmation while the Republican Senate (perhaps with Hatch's private complicity) refused to bring the president's nominees to a vote?

In mid-June the president decided time was running out and he had to make a move. In a phone conversation Hatch and Clinton agreed to proceed in small, cautious steps that would allow each to avoid a potential double cross. The president discreetly initiated the routine FBI check and submitted Stewart to the American Bar Association for its assessment. In return, the Senate Judiciary Committee on June 17 held its first hearing on eight of Clinton's judicial nominees. Two weeks later the deal finished up when the president announced his intent to nominate Stewart, and Hatch announced his committee's goal to clear for a Senate vote at least ten of Clinton's pending nominees.

During the 107th Congress (2001–2002) the tables were turned as Republican president George W. Bush sent judicial nominations to an unresponsive Democratic Senate. That the two sides failed to achieve a compromise of the kind just described is testament to the difficulty of solving this class of prisoner's dilemmas.

vote in a liberal direction, and those appointed by Republican presidents tend to be conservative.[36]

This observation implies that the party that wins the White House receives, if the opportunity arises, the chance to shape the policies of the Supreme Court. And because Supreme Court justices serve for life, presidents' imprints may continue long after they have left office. When one party dominates the presidency, the cumulative impact on judicial policy can be great. As Republicans returned to the White House in 1953 for the first time in two decades, they encountered a Supreme Court wholly appointed by Democrats Roosevelt and Truman. But by the time President Eisenhower had left office in 1961, Republican appointees constituted a majority of the membership. Since 1969,

Toles © 2000 The Buffalo News. Reprinted by permission of Universal Press Syndicate. All rights reserved.

however, Democratic presidents have appointed only two justices—Clinton's appointments of Stephen Breyer and Ruth Bader Ginsburg. With Republican presidents making most of the appointments over the past several decades, the Supreme Court has shifted in a distinctly more conservative direction.

A variety of evidence reveals the indirect impact of presidents on the direction of policy coming out of the judiciary. In Table 9-3 we see decisions in which President Bush's two appointees in 2006—Chief Justice John Roberts and Justice Samuel Alito—voted together and swung the majority in their direction. All of these decisions sided with the administration. More systematic evidence of presidential influence over the past half-century can be seen in Figure 9-4. One commonly accepted metric of the Court's ideology is the ideological scoring of the nine justices' median (tie-breaking) member. In Figure 9-4 these median ratings are plotted. Just as expected, the Court gradually shifts with the political tides in the elective branches. Although conservative radio talk-show hosts still relish a good Court-bashing, the fact is that since the 1970s the Supreme Court has assumed a more conservative posture on many policy issues.

The Federal Judiciary in National Policymaking

The question that arose in Chapter 5 rears its perplexing head again here: how appropriate is it that unelected, life-tenured judges can decide on the constitutionality of acts of Congress? This arrangement does violate the democratic principle of majority rule, but it met the Framers' broader concerns that they create a balanced political system in which competing interests check one another. Majorities, we saw in *Federalist* No. 10, are just as capable of exploiting their control of government to pursue their own interests and take advantage of the powerless as are kings and other unelected rulers. Through the Constitution's separation of powers and checks and balances, the Framers appear to have planned for the judiciary to be part of the Constitution's balancing act.

But who is to guard the guardian? Does not this seemingly absolute authority violate the republican principle of balance as much as it does the democratic principle of

TABLE 9-3

President Bush's Appointments Create a Conservative Tilt on the Supreme Court

Ruth Bader Ginsburg	John Paul Stevens	David Souter	Stephen Breyer	Anthony Kennedy	John G. Roberts Jr.	Samuel Alito	Antonin Scalia	Clarence Thomas

Prominent 5–4 Decisions in 2007 and 2008 in Which Bush Appointees Shifted the Balance of Power on the Court

Decision	Summary
Hein v. Freedom from Religion Foundation	Ruled that ordinary taxpayers cannot challenge a White House initiative that helps religious charities get a share of federal money.
Morse v. Frederick	Tightened limits on student speech, ruling schools may prohibit student expression that can be interpreted as advocating drug use.
Federal Election Commission v. Wisconsin Right to Life	Restricted a key advertising provision in federal campaign finance reforms in a ruling that will allow issue advertisements in the final days of federal elections.
National Association of Home Builders v. Defenders of Wildlife; EPA v. Defenders of Wildlife	Sided with developers and the Bush administration in a case that involved the intersection of two environmental laws, the Clean Water Act and the Endangered Species Act, and how federal and state agencies can handle competing laws.
District of Columbia v. Heller	Held that the right "to keep and bear Arms" in the Second Amendment is an individual right not limited to service in a militia, and struck down Washington D.C.'s absolute ban on handguns.
Gonzales v. Carhart; Gonzales v. Planned Parenthood	Upheld the nationwide ban on partial-birth abortions, saying the law that went into effect in 2003 does not violate a woman's constitutional right to an abortion.
Parents Involved in Community Schools v. Seattle School District No. 1; Meredith v. Jefferson County Board of Education	Restricted the ability of public school systems to use race-based systems for making primary and secondary school assignments, striking down voluntary admissions policies in Seattle, Washington, and Louisville, Kentucky.

Source: For 2007 session, "Split Decisions: Environmental, Sentencing Divides," *Wall Street Journal* online, June 25, 2007, available at http://online.wsj.com/public/resources/documents/info-scotusdiary-061002.html.

Note: Bush appointees marked in blue.

majority rule? This chapter has identified several sources of limitations on the absoluteness of judicial review. They are found in other provisions of the Constitution, in the internal, organizational weakness of the federal judiciary, and in the various subtle ways Congress and the president can redirect judicial doctrine. Together they prevent the Court from long straying too far from national opinion.

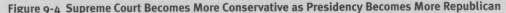

Figure 9-4 Supreme Court Becomes More Conservative as Presidency Becomes More Republican

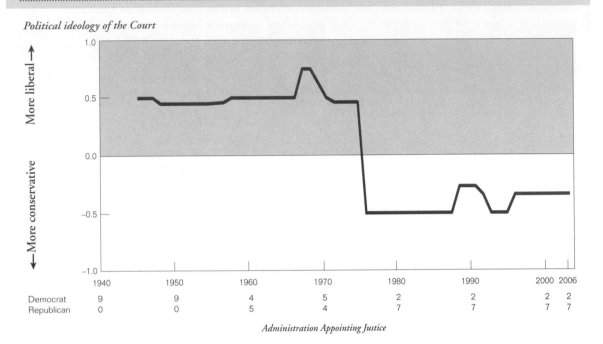

Political ideology of the Court

Administration Appointing Justice	1940	1950	1960	1970	1980	1990	2000	2006
Democrat	9	9	4	5	2	2	2	2
Republican	0	0	5	4	7	7	7	7

Source: Lee Epstein et al., *The Supreme Court Compendium: Data, Decisions, and Developments,* Online Edition (Washington, D.C.: CQ Press, 2008), Table 6-2.

Note: Figure depicts the political ideology of the median justice on the U.S. Supreme Court, 1941–2006.

The constitutional amendment process offers one certain way to countermand the Court's ruling of unconstitutionality, but the process is difficult and thus rarely employed. The Constitution also empowers Congress to alter the size (and therefore the ideological complexion) of the Court as well as change its jurisdiction, but these ploys have been attempted even less frequently. Perhaps the rarity with which Congress has resorted to these difficult constitutional remedies reflects its ability to achieve adequate responsiveness through easier and less controversial means.

To enforce its policies, the judiciary depends on the compliance of other institutions. In the face of concerted opposition—whether from school districts bent on segregation or Congress and presidents wanting to preserve a legislative veto—the Court may have a difficult time changing public policy. Moreover, Congress can effectively nullify an adverse judicial decision by writing a new public law that addresses the Court's concern or achieves the same goal in a somewhat different way. The Supreme Court may rule that Congress cannot order local sheriffs to administer federal gun control procedures, but the ruling does not prevent Congress from tying such compliance to the eligibility of states and their communities for federal grants. Finally, the facts that presidents appoint justices and that Congress may expand the number of district courts allow the elected branches to pull a straying Court back into the mainstream of opinion.

As for judicial review and the long shadow cast by *Marbury v. Madison,* they have allowed the modern Supreme Court to stake out a large role in those areas of public policy, such as the Bill of Rights, in which the Constitution seems to give it special license to intervene. The doctrine of judicial review has worked because it does not foreclose effective responses from the other branches. Moreover, the Court's decisions, just like those emanating from the other branches, come and often go; rarely are they final.

In fact, on close inspection, the federal judiciary appears to lack the kinds of internal resources that would allow it to be a powerful, autonomous policymaker. The limited veto authority offered by judicial review, the huge caseload, the lack of enforcement authority, and even the life tenure of its members reveal it to be an organization ill designed to formulate and implement public policy. This is the way it should be in a democracy.

logic.cqpress.com

Key Terms

activism, 437

amicus curiae, 434

attorney general, 443

concurring opinion, 440

constitutional courts, 427

court of appeals, 429

Court-packing plan, 423

dissenting opinion, 440

district courts, 429

judicial doctrine, 435

judicial review, 415

procedural doctrine, 435

restraint, 437

rule of four, 432

senatorial courtesy, 446

solicitor general, 434

standing, 436

stare decisis, 435

substantive doctrine, 435

writ of certiorari, 432

writ of mandamus, 416

Suggested Readings

Baum, Lawrence. *The Supreme Court.* 8th ed. Washington, D.C.: CQ Press, 2004. An up-to-date introduction to all facets of the Court's structure and procedures, including a thorough discussion of judicial recruitment and approaches to decision making.

Brest, Paul, and Sanford Levinson. *Processes of Constitutional Decisionmaking.* 3rd ed. Boston: Little, Brown, 1992. A detailed introduction to the structure and function of the federal court system emphasizing the important policymaking opportunities enjoyed by lower-court judges.

Epstein, Lee, and Jack Knight. *The Choices Justices Make.* Washington, D.C.: CQ Press, 1997. A fine demonstration of the value of thinking strategically about the judiciary.

McCloskey, Robert, and Sanford Levinson, eds. *The American Supreme Court.* 2nd ed. Chicago: University of Chicago Press, 1994. A comprehensive historical account of the development of the Supreme Court as a political branch of government.

Rosenberg, Gerald N. *The Hollow Hope: Can Courts Bring about Social Change?* Chicago: University of Chicago Press, 1991. One of the few books to carefully examine the effects of Court decisions on public policy.

Toobin, Jeffrey. *The Nine: Inside the Secret World of the Supreme Court.* New York: Random House, 2007. A highly readable account of recent politics on the Supreme Court including "insider" stories on decision making among the nine distinct personalities on the bench.

Woodward, Bob, and Scott Armstrong. *The Brethren: Inside the Supreme Court.* New York: Simon and Schuster, 1979. Not only highly readable, but generally regarded as an accurate fly-on-the-wall report of the inner workings of the Supreme Court.

Review Questions

1. How does the Supreme Court's ability to delegate tasks compare with those of the other branches?

2. Why is the judiciary regarded as the "least dangerous" branch of government?

3. What features of the Court make it appear undemocratic?

4. How does the Court enforce its decisions on lower courts? On the executive and legislative branches?

5. Which cases appealed to the Supreme Court are most likely to be taken up by the justices? What factors can increase a case's likelihood of being granted *certiorari?*

6. How do executive branch attorneys influence the Court's agenda?

7. What significance is attached to unanimous decisions by the Court? Why are such decisions less common today than during the nineteenth century?

8. How does the membership of the Court affect its decisions? How is membership of the Court determined?

Exercises

It's Not Just a Job

Look up the biographies of current members of the Supreme Court (http://straylight.law.cornell.edu/supct/justices/fullcourt.html). Prior to their appointment to the Court, were the justices ever appointed to the bench by a president? If so, were the two presidents who appointed them of the same party? Have any of the justices ever worked in the private sector? Which justices have also served as prosecuting attorneys? Compare their biographies with those of a random sample of nine eighteenth- or nineteenth-century justices (http://straylight.law.cornell.edu/supct/cases/judges.htm).

Coalitions of the Court

Find the Court's opinions from the current session (http://supremecourtus.gov/opinions/opinions.html). Pick ten cases and determine whether each justice supported or dissented from the opinion in each case. Then determine which justices were most likely to agree or disagree on a given case. Were justices appointed by presidents of the same party (http://supremecourtus.gov/about/biographiescurrent.pdf) more likely to vote together than were those appointed by presidents of the opposing party? Were there exceptions?

10

Public Opinion

MISSION ACCOMPLISHED

Do policy advocates try so hard to move public opinion because people's views are so easy to manipulate or because they are so difficult to manipulate?

How can stable and coherent public opinion arise from a population that often is uninformed about basic political facts and lacks consistent political views?

How accurately can we predict Americans' political views by knowing their age, race, sex, religion, or education?

Polls often present conflicting evidence about the public's opinions on political issues. When can we believe polling results?

To what extent does public opinion determine public policy?

O n March 19, 2003, the George W. Bush administration began a "preemptive" war to drive Saddam Hussein from power in Iraq, evidently with the solid backing of the American people. In polls taken earlier in the year, about two-thirds of the public consistently approved of using military action to oust the dicta-tor; once the war started, approval of the action jumped another ten percentage points. Support for war reflected the widespread belief that Hussein secretly pos-sessed weapons of mass destruction (WMDs), contradicting his claims and violating United Nations (UN) resolutions. Nearly 80 percent of the U.S. population thought he had such weapons, and nearly half were convinced that he had been personally in-volved in the September 11, 2001, attacks on New York and Washington, D.C.[1] These beliefs did not arise in a vacuum. They were encouraged by the president and members of his administration, who claimed that solid intelligence proved that Iraq had the weapons and repeatedly linked Hussein with al Qaeda and other terrorist or-ganizations in public statements justifying the war.[2]

The president leveraged public support for the war into a virtual blank check from Congress to decide if and when the United States would invade Iraq. Many Democrats went against their better judgment to back what one called "the largest grant of presidential authority ever given by a Congress" because they feared the pub-lic's wrath if they did not.[3] Although many backed the war, Americans on the whole were not eager for it. Large majorities preferred a diplomatic solution if at all possi-ble, and support for military action was much lower if it were to be taken without strong international support. Most wanted to allow the United Nations' weapons

President George W. Bush flashes a "thumbs-up" after declaring the end of major combat in Iraq on May 1, 2003.

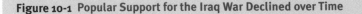

Figure 10-1 Popular Support for the Iraq War Declined over Time

Percent supporting war

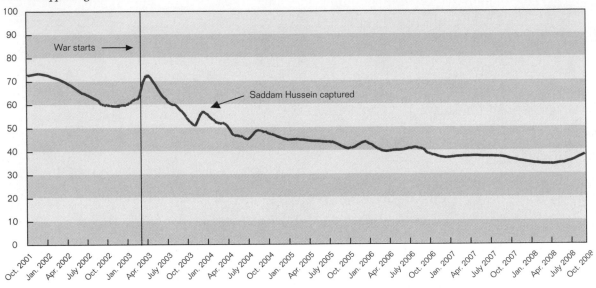

Sources: CBS News/*New York Times,* ABC News/*Washington Post,* NBC News/*Wall Street Journal, Los Angeles Times,* Gallup, Pew Center for the People and Press, *Newsweek,* CNN/*Time,* Fox News, Quinnipiac College, National Annenberg Election Study, Knowledge Networks, and Democracy Corps polls reported at www.pollintreport.com, at the polling company's Web site, or archived at the Roper Center for Public Opinion Research.

Note: The trend is estimated by lowess smoothing of responses in 865 polls to more than twenty differently worded questions designed to register support for the war.

inspectors all the time they needed to complete their investigations before embarking on a full-scale U.S. invasion of Iraq.[4] Partly in response to such sentiments, Colin Powell, the popular secretary of state, was dispatched to the UN to make the case against Hussein. Although he failed to persuade the Security Council, Powell did succeed in shoring up domestic support for military action by detailing intelligence reports suggesting that Iraq was hiding chemical and biological weapons, as well as a program for developing nuclear weapons, from UN inspectors.

Public support for invading Iraq grew after the war began (if only out of support for U.S. troops in harm's way) and escalated after the initial military phase ended quickly and successfully (see Figure 10-1).[5] When the president celebrated by landing on an aircraft carrier to greet sailors returning from the Middle East, addressing them from the deck backed by a huge banner reading a triumphant, if premature, "Mission Accomplished," polls indicated that about 75 percent of the public approved of his handling of Iraq and 70 percent approved of his overall job performance.[6] But conditions in Iraq then took a turn for the worse: The collapse of Hussein's regime provoked widespread looting and destruction. Conflicting Iraqi groups, many openly hostile to the U.S. occupation, struggled to fill the power vacuum left by his fall. Remnants of the regime and radicals from abroad began sustained urban guerrilla warfare targeting American troops, reconstruction workers, and Iraqis cooperating with the occupation. Moreover,

Figure 10-2 Partisanship Increasingly Affected Support for the Iraq War

Percent supporting war

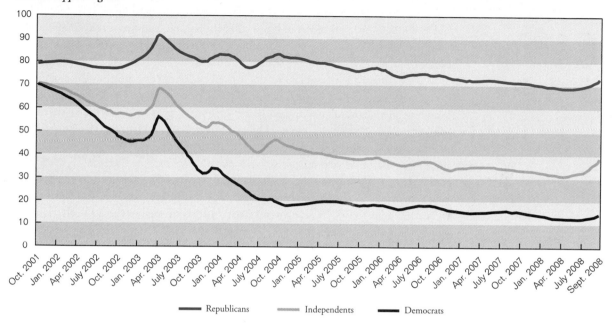

Sources: CBS News/*New York Times,* ABC News/*Washington Post,* NBC News/*Wall Street Journal, Los Angeles Times,* Gallup, Pew Center for the People and Press, *Newsweek,* CNN/*Time,* Quinnipiac College, and National Annenberg Election Study at the polling company's Web site, or archived at the Roper Center for Public Opinion Research.

Note: Trends are estimated by lowess smoothing of responses in 675 polls to seven differently worded questions designed to register support for the war.

months of searching turned up no WMDs and little evidence of a serious effort to produce them. And Hussein's regime was found to have had only the most tenuous relations with al Qaeda and no evident involvement in the September 11 attacks at all.

As American casualties mounted, and with little visible progress toward a stable and democratic Iraq, public support for the war and the president began to erode. Although the capture of Hussein in December 2003 briefly revived both, continuing problems, punctuated by the revelations of abuse of American-held Iraqi prisoners at Abu Ghraib and the growing realization that the administration's primary justifications for the war did not stand up, renewed the downward trend. By the Iraq War's first anniversary, approval of the president and the war had fallen slightly below 50 percent, and instead of an electoral asset, "Mission Accomplished" became a potential liability to the president's reelection effort.

The decline in public support for the war was limited, however, by the public's partisanship, misperceptions, and satisfaction that the war had at least deposed a murderous dictator. Republicans continued to back the war by wide margins; Democrats and, to a lesser degree, independents, accounted for most of the decline (see Figure 10-2).[7] Even after officials abandoned the search for WMDs as futile, half the public still believed that they existed; and despite the 9/11 Commission's finding that no direct evidence linked Hussein to the September 11 attacks, about 40 percent of the population continued to believe that he was personally involved in the attacks.[8] These misconceptions were considerably more prevalent among Republicans than Democrats, and they helped limit the damage to the president's standing with the public. As late as 2008, 63 percent of Republicans still believed Iraq had possessed WMDs at the time the United States went to war, and 39 percent thought Saddam Hussein had been personally involved the September 11 attacks.[9]

With ordinary Democrats increasingly doubtful about the administration's justifications for the war, it became a powerfully polarizing issue in the 2004 presidential campaign. The candidates engaged in an intense struggle to shape the views of uncommitted swing voters on the wisdom of the war, the president's strategy for waging it, and which candidate would best deal with its troublesome consequences. Views on the war ended up having a decisive influence on the vote; an Election Day exit poll found that 88 percent of voters who thought that invading Iraq was worth the cost voted for Bush, while 84 percent who believed it was not voted for the Democratic candidate, John Kerry.[10] The war remained a hotly contested in the 2006 elections, in which more than 80 percent of war supporters voted for Republican House candidates, and more than 80 percent its opponents voted for Democrats,[11] and its overall unpopularity cost the Republicans control of Congress. Yet despite growing public discontent with the war, President Bush chose to send additional troops to Iraq rather than wind down U.S. involvement and frustrated all attempts by the Democratic Congress to change the direction of American policy. The unpopular war was expected to be a major bone of contention in the 2008 election, but the "surge" eventually produced a sharp decline in American casualties, making the war less salient (if no more popular), and by Election Day the economic crisis that had come to a head in late 2008 overshadowed it and everything else (see Chapters 11 and 12).

What Is Public Opinion?

Political leaders' attention to public opinion regarding the war in Iraq, the effort that went into probing it (through countless polls) and shaping it (through public statements and projected images), the way it shifted in response to changing conditions, the way it varied across groups, and its electoral significance all attest to the importance—and complexity—of public opinion's role in American politics. To understand this role, we must first consider an elementary question: What is public opinion? The simplest definition, proposed more than thirty years ago by the eminent political scientist V. O. Key Jr., is that **public opinion** consists of "those opinions held by private persons which governments find it prudent to heed."[12] According to this definition, every government, democratic or otherwise, has to pay attention to public opinion in some fashion. Democracies differ from other forms of government in terms of which private persons governments find it prudent to heed (potential voters and those who can sway potential voters) and the main reason it is prudent to do so (an election is coming). In the United States basic constitutional guarantees—regular elections, broad suffrage, freedom of speech and press, freedom to form and join political organizations—allow citizens to express their views freely and compel government leaders to take the public's opinions into account if they want to keep their jobs. These guarantees also make it both possible and essential for political leaders and policy advocates to try to shape and mobilize public opinion on behalf of their causes.

The origins of these guarantees predate the Constitution, and American public opinion has from the beginning been treated as a political force to be alternatively shaped, mollified, or exploited. The object of the *Federalist* was to sway educated public opinion in favor of the Constitution, but national ratification was secured only when its proponents bowed to the widespread public demand that a bill of rights be added (see Chapter 2). In the first years of the Republic, leaders of the nascent parties

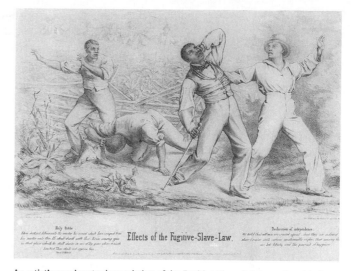

Effects of the Fugitive-Slave-Law.

An artist's passionate denunciation of the Fugitive Slave Act shows four black men being shot down by a white posse, with captions citing *Deuteronomy* ("Thou shalt not deliver unto the master his servant which has escaped from his master unto thee . . . ") and the Declaration of Independence ("We hold that all men are created equal . . .") to underline the evil and injustice of the law and the "institution" it was designed to sustain.

quickly established newspapers to promote themselves and their policy proposals and to attack the ideas and character of their opponents. The highly partisan press they created continued to give form and voice to public opinion throughout the nineteenth century. Ever mindful of the public's concerns, ambitious politicians routinely sought to squeeze political advantage from whatever issue excited the people, be it hysteria about the supposed machinations of secret societies, which led to brief success for the Anti-Masonic Party in the 1830s, or hostility to Irish Catholic immigrants, which did the same for the American or "Know-Nothing" Party in the 1850s (see Chapter 12).

The leaders of movements dedicated to the abolition of slavery, prohibition of alcoholic beverages, suffrage for women, and the end of the spoils system (see Chapters 8, 12, and 13) labored mightily to mold public opinion (through pamphlets, speeches, demonstrations, sermons, editorials, magazines, novels, and plays) and then to serve as agents for its political expression. Any incident that inflamed public sentiment was fair game for exploitation. Enforcement of the Fugitive Slave Act, for example, led to incidents that regularly outraged northern communities, helping abolitionists to win converts and silence opponents. Then, as now, interest group entrepreneurs sought to mobilize public opinion as a weapon in the policy wars, threatening electoral retaliation against leaders who refused to support their cause.

Modern efforts to measure, shape, and exploit public opinion have spawned two linked industries: scientific polling and public relations. The first is devoted to sounding out the public on an endless array of issues, and the other to marketing ideas, policies, and politicians. Before the advent of scientific polling, politicians gauged public opinion haphazardly, relying on information supplied by editorials, pamphleteers, local leaders, spokespersons for social causes, party activists, and sometimes even less-conventional sources. According to one member of Congress who served in the 1930s, "This might sound odd, but myself and many other members of Congress that I knew, used to get a lot of ideas on how the general public felt by reading the walls in bathrooms in towns and cities that we were in." [13] Self-selected, perhaps angry, with axes to grind, such sources were of doubtful reliability. Even open expressions of public sentiments, such as marches, rallies, and riots, could not be taken at face value because they said nothing about the views of the majority that had stayed home. Not until well into the twentieth century was **scientific polling** developed as a tool for systematically investigating the opinions of ordinary people.

Measuring Public Opinion

The basic techniques developed to measure public opinion accurately are simple in concept but often difficult to carry out in practice: Select a random sample of the population of interest, ask the people in the sample some appropriate questions about their views, and count up their answers. The larger the sample, the more closely the sample's answers will approximate the answers the pollster would get if the entire population could be asked. As the sample gets larger, however, the rate of improvement in accuracy declines; it makes little sense to use a sample size larger than 1,200–1,500 people. With numbers in this range, researchers can be confident that, nineteen times out of twenty, the sample's division on a typical question will fall within three percentage points of the entire population's division. For example, if 45 percent of the respondents in a poll of 1,500 people say they approve of the president's job performance, chances are nineteen in twenty that the actual level of approval throughout the whole U.S. population falls somewhere between 42 percent and 48 percent. Strange as it may seem, a sample of 1,500 mirrors a population of 250 million just as accurately as it would a population of 10,000.

A truly random sample of any population is rarely feasible, however, because there is no single directory where everyone is conveniently listed and so can be given a perfectly equal chance of being selected, which is what strict random sampling requires. Most polls are conducted over the phone using random-digit dialing and so they do not reach the 6 percent of the population without telephones of any kind. Moreover, people who use only cell phones—about 14 percent—are sometimes omitted because they require drawing a separate sample, which adds to the expense. Not everyone selected is willing to answer questions, and people who refuse differ systematically from the people who answer the pollster's questions (on average, refusers have less money, education, and political knowledge). Methods have been developed to adjust for these problems—most often, weighing the responses of people in underrepresented demographic categories more heavily than those in overrepresented categories—but they work imperfectly, so no poll is completely free of the biases they introduce.

Straw Polls

Newspapers and magazines had taken "straw polls" for a hundred years before the advent of scientific polling. The term refers to tossing straws in the air to see which way the wind is blowing. The *Harrisburg Pennsylvanian* sponsored the first known newspaper poll in 1824, correctly predicting that Andrew Jackson would win the popular vote in the presidential election. The polling techniques varied, but all allowed respondents to select themselves to be participants in the poll. Sometimes readers were invited to clip facsimile ballots from the paper, fill them out, and send them in, or they were mailed postcards that they were asked to complete and return.

The *Literary Digest,* a popular magazine, had used the postcard method successfully to forecast the presidential winner in every election from 1920 to 1932. In 1936, it again sent out ten million postcard ballots to names and addresses taken from telephone books, voter registration lists, club rosters, and lists of automobile owners and mail order customers. The returned cards split 57 percent for Alf Landon, the Republican candidate, to 43 percent for Franklin Roosevelt, the Democratic president running for a second term. On Election Day Roosevelt defeated Landon, 62 percent to 38 percent, winning every state but Maine and Vermont.

How did the *Literary Digest* get it so wrong? First, their sample was badly biased for an election that, unlike the previous contests, divided the electorate strongly along economic lines. During the Great Depression, telephones and cars were luxuries that many Americans could not afford; those who could afford them were far more likely to favor Landon and the Republican Party. Second, the respondents selected themselves. Only 22 percent of those who were sent the postcard ballot responded. The kinds of people who respond to mail surveys are not typical; they tend to have more education, more money, and more ardent political views. Finally, the postcards were sent out too early (September) to pick up any late-breaking trends. Meanwhile the fledgling Gallup Poll, following more sophisticated sampling principles and drawing on a much smaller sample, accurately predicted Roosevelt's landslide victory.

Modern professional polls avoid the pitfalls of straw polling, but nonscientific sampling is still common. The White House reports mail counts ("the mail is running 5 to 1 in favor of the president's position"); members of Congress claim to know the public mind from responses to questionnaires inserted into their newsletters; CNN invites watchers to call a 900 number (at $.50 a call) to register their views on issues and reports the results. In all such polls, the respondents select themselves. The samples are therefore subject to severe bias, and the results are completely unreliable as measures of public opinion.

Another potential problem with interpreting polls lies in the questions, which respondents may not always understand or may answer incorrectly—by, for example, offering an instant opinion on an issue they have never thought about before. Even the most carefully designed question is subject to some measurement error because the fit between the words and concepts used in questions and how people actually think about issues is never perfect. Properly conducted polls with well-designed questions are nonetheless far less subject to distortion than any other method of measuring public opinion (see box "Straw Polls," which describes some pitfalls of alternative techniques for measuring public opinion).

From modest beginnings in the 1930s, opinion polling has grown into a vast industry producing an endless stream of information about the public's views on almost any conceivable matter. Every president since Jimmy Carter (1977–1981) has had an in-house pollster taking regular readings of the public's pulse. In just one year, 1993, the Clinton administration spent nearly $2 million to monitor public opinion, taking three or four polls and conducting three or four focus groups (described in Chapter 11) every month.[14] Bill Clinton's successor, George W. Bush, who claimed to disdain polls, nonetheless maintained access to an estimated $1 million worth of public opinion research annually.[15] Even a leader who has no intention of yielding to public opinion needs to learn how people are thinking in order to persuade them to follow.

Efforts to shape and channel public opinion have grown apace. As presidents have become more reliant on grassroots public support for winning policy battles, the line between campaigning and governing has blurred. Early in 1997, when campaign-weary news reporters asked Clinton's press secretary why the president maintained such a heavy travel schedule even after winning reelection, he replied, "Campaigns are about framing a choice for the American people. . . . When you are responsible for governing you have to use the same tools of public persuasion to advance your program, to build public support for the direction you are attempting to lead."[16] George W. Bush followed suit, crisscrossing the country to, in his words, "gin up support" for his ten-year, $1.6 trillion tax cut in 2001 and repeating this tactic in 2005 in an unsuccessful attempt to rally a skeptical public behind his proposal to privatize part of Social Security.

The president has no monopoly on the "tools of public persuasion." Virtually all large modern institutions—government agencies, political parties, corporations, universities, foundations, religious bodies, and so on—employ public relations specialists whose job is to present the organization in the best possible light. Interest and advocacy groups of all kinds issue reports and exposés, publish newsletters and magazines, jostle for space on the op-ed pages of newspapers, and promote their causes through ads in the mass media. Back in 1994, opponents of Clinton's health care proposals spent a reported $60 million on television commercials alone.[17] More recently, groups both opposing and supporting Bush's proposed changes in Social Security sought to sway the public to their side with expensive mass advertising campaigns.

Institutions also promote the *expression* of public opinion. Pollsters articulate public opinion by the very process of measuring it. A 1997 survey on issues raised by the threat of global warming discovered that 60 percent of Americans were apparently willing to pay an additional $.25 per gallon for gasoline to reduce hydrocarbon emissions, a level of support that came as a surprise to people on both sides of the policy debates.[18] Policy advocates routinely take polls hoping to demonstrate that the people are on their side, and they do not always resist the temptation to choose questions that will elicit the "right" responses, a subject discussed later in the chapter. Organized efforts to mobilize citizens to write, call, protest, or otherwise express their views to political leaders also are common. The banking industry, for example, got many of its customers to protest vigorously when in 1998 the Federal Deposit Insurance Corporation (FDIC) proposed a regulation requiring banks to monitor their customers' transactions and report to federal agents any activity that might indicate money laundering. More than two hundred thousand comments arrived by e-mail, virtually all of them opposing the regulation, and the FDIC quickly backed down.[19] Firms specializing in organizing or, according to their critics, counterfeiting outpourings of "grassroots" sentiment are now available for hire by anyone.

Modern techniques for molding or measuring public opinion have contributed to the nationalization of American politics. Earlier strategies for gauging and shaping opinion depended on institutions such as newspapers and party organizations whose primary focus was local. The relevant publics were those of specific cities, towns, counties, and, to a lesser extent, states; national opinion emerged only as an aggregate of diversely measured local opinions. The advent of scientific polling has made it possible to measure and therefore to treat public opinion as a national phenomenon. National polls probe issues of national concern, raising their visibility in the minds of politicians, the news media, and the public alike. Organized efforts to shape public opinion have taken on national dimensions as well. To be sure, politicians who hold their jobs by the grace of local electorates maintain an abiding interest in local opinion (ask any member of Congress), but the institutional forces that shape local opinion have themselves become national in scope.

Finally, albeit unintentionally, the work to measure and shape public opinion has helped individual citizens to act collectively. Individual expressions of opinion to influence public policy are subject to the standard free-rider problem, because it is exceedingly unlikely that any single person's message will make a difference. But polls and mobilization campaigns can produce collective expressions of opinion that politicians ignore at their peril.

The Origins of Public Opinion

Public opinion attracts all this attention because of its effect on political behavior, most notably voting, which is the main, sometimes the only, political act of the great majority of ordinary citizens. Like the vote, public opinion has its political effect as an aggregate phenomenon, but also like the vote, it is no more than the sum of its individual parts. To make sense of public opinion, we need to understand the basis of individual opinions.

Attitudes

Where do the individual opinions that collectively constitute public opinion originate? Most scholars who study public opinion believe that expressed opinions reflect underlying attitudes. Basically, an **attitude** is "an organized and consistent manner of thinking, feeling, and reacting with regard to people, groups, social issues, or, more generally, any event in one's environment."[20] An attitude thus combines feelings, beliefs, thoughts, and predispositions to react in a certain way. For example, a person's attitude toward the Republican Party might include feelings ("I trust the Republicans"), beliefs ("the Republican Party is against high taxes"), and an inclination to answer "Republican" to a pollster's question about which party handles the economy better. When invited to state opinions or cast votes, people respond in ways that express the underlying attitudes evoked by the choices they face.

Individuals differ widely in the attitudes they bring to bear on political choices. Some people have an elaborate set of informed, organized, internally consistent attitudes that allow them to understand, evaluate, and respond to almost any political phenomenon that catches their attention. Such people are unusual, however. Most people have more loosely structured sets of political attitudes, not necessarily consistent with one another or well informed by facts and concepts. And some people's attitudes are so rudimentary that they offer little guidance in making sense of or responding to political phenomena. People also differ in how strongly they hold attitudes. Some are intensely partisan—the "rock-ribbed Republicans" and "yellow-dog Democrats" (who would vote for a yellow dog if it were a Democrat) of political lore (for further discussions of partisan attitudes, see Chapters 11 and 12). Others maintain attitudes that are far more tentative and open to modification by new information or ideas. Individuals thus vary widely in how they form opinions and make political choices, and the forces that shape public opinion work in different ways on different people.

Ideologies

Elaborately organized sets of political attitudes often take the form of political **ideologies.** In theory, ideologies promote consistency among political attitudes by connecting them to something greater, a more general principle or set of principles. In practice, ideologies often combine attitudes linked more by coalitional politics than by principle. The ideological labels commonly used in American politics are liberal and conservative. Over time, the meanings of these labels change, reflecting shifts in the clusters of issue positions adopted by rival sets of political leaders, who, like other people centrally involved in politics, routinely use ideological categories to simplify the complexities of political life.

In American politics today, **liberals** typically favor using government to reduce economic inequalities, champion the rights of disadvantaged groups such as racial minorities and women, and tolerate a more diverse range of social behaviors. They prefer a smaller defense establishment and usually are less willing to use military force in international politics. They believe that the rich should be taxed at higher rates to finance social welfare programs. **Conservatives** distrust government and have greater faith in private enterprise and free markets, but they are more willing to use government to enforce traditional moral standards. They favor a larger military and more assertive pursuit of national self-interest. Conservatives advocate lower taxes, particularly on investment income, to stimulate growth and to restrict the government's capacity to finance social welfare programs. But these two sets of attitudes are by no means the only logical ways to combine political views. For example, some people are libertarians, who prefer to minimize government regulation of both social and economic behavior and oppose any military involvement except direct defense of U.S. territory. But these two standard combinations approximate current party alliances, with most liberals in the Democratic Party and most conservatives in the Republican Party.

Although *liberal* and *conservative* are used constantly in public discussions of politics and are familiar to everyone active in politics, these terms do not guide the political thinking of most citizens, nor do the opinions most people express fall neatly into one ideological category or the other. When asked to place themselves on a scale from very liberal to very conservative, about half the people classify themselves as liberals or conservatives; of the rest, about a quarter locate themselves in the middle and another quarter do not place themselves at all.[21] Those who do locate themselves on the scale tend to take positions on issues that are consistent with their chosen location, but a substantial minority takes positions inconsistent with it. About half the adult population can apply the terms *liberal* and *conservative* correctly to political issues and figures, but only about one in five uses these terms spontaneously to explain their own opinions on parties and candidates.[22] Ideological labels may be indispensable to politicians and pundits, but most citizens get by without them and feel no obligation to be consistently liberal or conservative.

Adopting a liberal or conservative pattern is not the only way people organize their political attitudes. Some studies suggest that a person's political attitudes reflect a small number of **core values,** such as individualism, support for equal opportunity, moral traditionalism, or opposition to big government. A favorable attitude toward Republicans might reflect the values of individualism and opposition to big government. Attitudes that arise from the same core value will be in harmony, but because most people maintain more than one, attitudes also can conflict.[23] Psychologists have found that people are uncomfortable holding inconsistent attitudes and tend to modify one attitude or the other to reduce inconsistency when they become aware of it, mitigating, in the technical jargon, cognitive dissonance. Often, however, people remain blissfully unaware of inconsistencies among their attitudes, keeping them in separate mental compartments so they are not brought to mind at the same time by political figures and events. A citizen who dislikes "big government" but favors stricter regulation to protect consumers, workers, and the environment is by no means unusual.

Partisanship

For most Americans, the political attitude that shapes opinions and organizes other political attitudes most consistently is their disposition toward the political parties. A large majority of Americans are willing to identify themselves as Republicans or Democrats and respond to political questions accordingly. Party identification is subject to varying interpretations, but they are complementary rather than mutually exclusive. The researchers who developed the concept in the 1950s viewed party identification as a psychological phenomenon. People who were willing to label themselves Democrats or Republicans identified with the party in the same way they might have identified with a region or an ethnic or religious group: "I'm a New Yorker, an Irish Catholic, and a Democrat." The party preference was, literally, an element of an individual's personal identity, either rooted in powerful personal experiences (best exemplified by the millions who became Democrats during the Great Depression) or learned, along with similar identifications, from family and neighborhood. So interpreted, identification with a party was thought to establish an enduring orientation

Families often pass on partisan identities to their children, just as they pass on religious and ethnic identities or a passion for the hometown sports teams. Usually the process is informal and unconscious, but such products as this T-shirt and button are available to parents who do not want to leave anything to chance.

toward the political world. Voters might defect if they had strong enough reactions to particular candidates, issues, or events that ran counter to their party identification. But once these short-term forces were no longer present, the influence of party identification would reassert itself and they would return to their partisan moorings. For most citizens, only quite powerful and unusual experiences would inspire permanent shifts of party allegiance.[24]

Another interpretation emphasizes the practical rather than psychological aspects of party identification. People think of themselves as Democrats or Republicans because they have found, through past experience, that their party's politicians are more likely than those of the other party to produce preferred results. Past experience is a more useful criterion than future promises or expectations because it is more certain. Party cues are recognized as imperfect, and people who are persuaded that a candidate of the other party would deal more effectively with their concerns vote for that candidate. If cumulative experience suggests that politicians of the preferred party are no longer predictably superior in this respect, the party preference naturally decays.[25] According to this interpretation, partisanship can change gradually in strength or direction without the psychological upheaval associated with revising one's personal identity.

But, again, these interpretations are not mutually exclusive. A party might be just a shorthand cue for some voters, but a source of personal identity for others. Cumulative practical experience with leaders and policies might well strengthen or weaken an individual's sense of psychological identification with a party. Conversely, gut feelings about the parties may simply be the brain's efficient way of storing the results of cumulative experiences, providing a shortcut to action (deciding how to vote or to evaluate political actors and events) without further cognitive effort. However interpreted, party remains for a large majority of voters a default cue: unless there is a compelling reason to do otherwise, Americans interpret political phenomena in ways that favor the preferred party. For example, after George W. Bush was finally awarded Florida's electoral votes and thus the presidency in December 2000, 85 percent of self-identified Republicans thought that he had won fair and square, 11 percent that he had won on a technicality, and 3 percent that he had stolen the election. However, among self-identified Democrats, only 18 percent thought that he had won fair and square, 49 percent that he had won on a technicality, and 31 percent that he had stolen the election.[26] Reactions to Bill Clinton's impeachment in 1998 also were sharply partisan: nearly two-thirds of self-identified Republicans wanted him impeached and convicted, while about 85 percent of Democrats did not.[27]

Such partisan discrepancies are not exceptional; indeed, responses to political actors and events have become increasingly polarized along party lines over the past thirty years. Reactions to George W. Bush are illustrative. Bush entered the White House in 2001 with the widest partisan difference in job approval of any newly

> ### Figure 10-3 Partisan Attitudes Strongly Influenced Evaluations of George W. Bush's Performance as President

Percent approving (monthly averages)

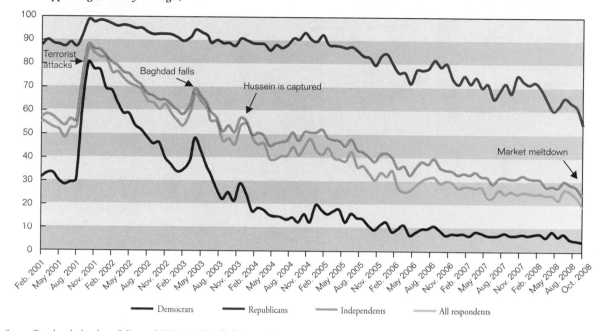

Democrats ——— Republicans ——— Independents ——— All respondents

Sources: Four hundred and ten Gallup and CBS News/*New York Times* polls, February 4, 2001, to October 13, 2008.

elected president since polling began more than fifty years ago (in no small part because of the partisan battles over the Florida vote count). Democrats rallied to his side in the upsurge of national solidarity inspired by the terrorist attacks of September 11, 2001 (see Figure 10-3), but the gap soon began to widen again. Among Republicans, Bush's approval rating stayed very high, while among Democrats it began a steady decline, briefly interrupted by reactions to the successful military phase of the Iraq War in April 2003 and capture of Saddam Hussein in December 2003. By the fall of 2004, the gap between the parties' identifiers had widened to an average of more than seventy-nine percentage points, an all-time high. Similar differences appeared in the distribution of responses to questions on almost anything having to do with the Bush administration and its policies, but most notably the Iraq War. The nearly sixty-percentage-point partisan difference in backing for the Iraq War (see Figure 10-2) was more than twice as large as any recorded in any poll on the Korean, Vietnam, or first Gulf Wars.

Party identification, like other attitudes, affects beliefs as well as opinions. Attitudes introduce bias into perceptions and interpretations of political information because people tend to pay more attention and give more credence to information that confirms

rather than challenges their beliefs. For example, a 2004 study found that Republicans outnumbered Democrats in conservative radio commentator Rush Limbaugh's audience more than seven to one, while Democrats outnumbered Republicans among viewers of Michael Moore's anti–George W. Bush documentary *Fahrenheit 9/11* by more than five to one.[28] And although post-war searches of Iraq turned up neither WMDs nor evidence that Hussein had been involved in terrorist attacks against the United States, millions of Americans continued to believe the contrary because it neatly fit their view of the dictator. Not surprisingly, Republicans, backing the war and the Bush administration, were much more likely than Democrats to express these beliefs.[29] In general, the more ambiguous the situation, the more prior attitudes such as party identification shape beliefs; the Florida vote count is a classic example, for to this day no one can conclusively say who really won.

Acquiring Opinions

Where do the attitudes that underlie political opinions come from? In one way or another, attitudes derive from the practical experience of growing up and living in the social and political world. The menu of possibilities is set by families, schools, friends, opinion leaders of all kinds, and the mass media. People adopt the values and beliefs that pay off in some way—for example, confirming identity with a group, pleasing others important to them, making the world comprehensible, or validating material or psychological aspirations. Children who grow up in families that talk about politics adopt political beliefs and values, just as they adopt other beliefs and values imparted by the people who raise them and whose approval they value. Schools reward the learning of political knowledge and values through the study of the Declaration of Independence and the Constitution or the conduct of classroom elections; they also teach politics informally through the way teachers and other school officials resolve conflicts and exercise authority. Later, peer groups—friends, fellow students, coworkers—become sources of political ideas and information and of incentives for paying attention to them. The news media supply a steady stream of information and commentary designed to shape people's thinking about politics. Books, movies, and television shows convey political ideas and values in ways that engage people's emotions as well as their intellects. Movie offerings run the gamut from the idealistic *Mr. Smith*

Goes to Washington to the cynical *JFK, Primary Colors,* and *Wag the Dog.* **Political socialization,** as the process of acquiring political attitudes is known, takes place during childhood and young adulthood, but new experiences can alter attitudes at any stage of life. People who are out of work for the first time, or run the bureaucratic maze of paperwork and regulations necessary to start a small business, or see how much the government takes out of their first paycheck, or try to keep a toxic waste incinerator out of their neighborhood may well revise their attitudes toward government and politics in light of their new experiences. When political attitudes do not "work," when they no longer seem to give adequate guidance for understanding and acting, we change them.

Although attitudes are certainly influenced by personal experiences, they are by no means dominated by them. For example, most people base evaluations of the president's economic performance on their beliefs about the national economy, not on their own family's economic fortunes. Large majorities say the health care system is in crisis even though their own medical arrangements are satisfactory. The perception that public schools are failing or crime is rampant creates a potent political issue even when most people are satisfied

In 1998 "wag the dog" entered America's political lexicon after a movie by that title told the story of a president who succeeded in deflecting public attention from a sex scandal by staging a mock war in Albania. The movie's uncanny similarities to the situation President Bill Clinton found himself in a year later—war in Kosovo (Albania's neighbor) and a White House sex scandal—left him defending his policies as critics and news reporters repeatedly invoked the movie's title. In this scene from *Wag the Dog,* actor Dustin Hoffman, in the role of producer of the mock war, envisions a scene from his political pageant.

with their own local schools or feel safe in their neighborhoods. Indeed, when people rely solely on their own circumstances to make political judgments, it often is because they are unaware of what is happening more broadly and so have no other information to go on. Because politics is primarily about the provision of collective goods, and ordinary citizens can achieve political ends only through collective action, it is logical that political opinions would reflect attitudes arising more from collective than from personal experiences. For example, people can be unemployed for any number of reasons, but whatever the reason, their economic future is brighter when unemployment stands at 5 percent rather than 10 percent, and it therefore makes sense to use national rather than personal unemployment to judge the president's management of the economy.

Widely shared experiences give rise to the political ideas and opinions that are advanced by the various agents of political socialization. The experiences of slavery, segregation, and continuing racial prejudice have given many African Americans a view of politics that leads them to express greater support for government programs aimed at integrating schools, workplaces, and neighborhoods than is typical among whites. Millions of working people who were helped by Franklin Roosevelt's New Deal during the Great Depression developed an abiding loyalty to the Democratic Party. Some experiences fix political thinking for generations; it took a hundred years for white

After nearly five decades away from their country, Cuban exiles have never forgotten their homeland or abandoned public rallies as a means of reminding the American public and politicians of their cause. Here, they toss a giant sculpture of Fidel Castro's head into a garbage truck in a mock burial ceremony held in 2006. The sculpture was originally intended for display in New York's Central Park, but the Miami Cubans convinced the artist who created it to let them destroy it instead.

southerners to move beyond political attitudes forged in the Civil War and Reconstruction. Collective political attitudes and beliefs of this sort are grounded in experience, but not necessarily direct experience. Rather, they arise from how families, politicians, journalists, historians, storytellers, songwriters, moviemakers, and artists interpret events. Such interpretations offer socially based cues to "appropriate" attitudes for people who identify with a group but have not themselves shared its formative experiences. Conflicting attitudes arising from competing versions of experience underlie much of the diversity of political opinions both within and between social groups.

Information

Generally, people tend to develop more complex, richly informed attitudes only when the payoff is greater than the cost of doing so. Individuals raised among politically active people, or who spend more years in school where they are exposed to political concepts and information, or whose jobs put them in touch with political affairs on a regular basis, are more likely to develop elaborate and well-informed political views, because they can do so without conscious effort. Most people, however, live in social settings where political ideas, events, and personalities are far down on the list of things their families and peers talk or care about, so they have neither the opportunity nor the incentive to develop informed, sophisticated political attitudes on their own. Because people are "cognitive misers," reluctant to pay the cost of acquiring information that has no practical payoff, the opinions they express on issues often appear to be both uninformed and unstable.

Numerous polls have found the public to be surprisingly ignorant of basic political facts, concepts, and issues. A sampling of questions illustrating typical levels of public information on political matters is shown in the box "The Public's Political Knowledge." The percentages listed reveal that large majorities know some basic facts about the presidency and can identify major political figures such as the vice president and their state's governor. Smaller majorities know something about government institutions, such as the Supreme Court's authority to rule on the constitutionality of legislation or the president's power to appoint federal judges, and they understand basic political facts such as which party is more conservative. But more detailed policy questions and lower-level political figures go unnoticed by most of the public. In 2007, for example, only about one American in five could identify Robert Gates as secretary of defense, and only one in seven could identify Harry Reid as majority leader of the Senate.

The box also reveals that knowledge of political facts varies with the availability of free information about them. One source of free information on items in the list is the basic high school civics course. But people are most aware of leaders and events on the front page and the nightly television news. Less newsworthy figures and issues go largely unrecognized. The difference in recognition of Newt Gingrich (60 percent) and his successor Dennis Hastert (10 percent) during their respective terms as Speaker of the House is instructive. Although both held the same formal position, Gingrich, as point man for the Republican "revolution" initiated in 1994, figured more prominently in the news, so more people could identify him. Nancy Pelosi, celebrated as the first woman ever to hold that position, was much better known than Hastert but not so well known as Gingrich.

Ignorance does not necessarily prevent people from expressing opinions; pollsters can get as many as one-third of the people they interview to offer opinions on entirely imaginary issues.[30] Uninformed opinions are not very stable, however. The same person asked the same question at different times may well give different answers. When a sample of citizens was asked in both January and June of 1980 whether the United States should take a more cooperative or more confrontational stance toward the Soviet Union, only 45 percent gave the same answer both times, even though 30 percent would be expected to do so if they simply answered randomly both times.[31]

Answers may be affected by even ostensibly minor changes in question wording. Public support for the Iraq War, for example, varied systematically according to how polls questioned it (see Figure 10-4). People asked whether the United States "had made the right decision" in going to war were consistently the most supportive, whereas those asked whether "the result was worth the cost in American lives" were consistently the least supportive. The difference averaged about ten percentage points

The Public's Political Knowledge

- 95 percent knew the length of the president's term (1989)
- 89 percent knew the meaning of "veto" (1989)
- 84 percent identified Dick Cheney as the vice president (2004)
- 78 percent knew the Republicans are the more conservative party (2004)
- 76 percent knew the Supreme Court decides if laws are constitutional (2006)
- 76 percent knew the Democrats had a majority in the House of Representatives (2007)
- 75 percent knew it took a two-thirds vote to override a presidential veto (2006)
- 73 percent identified the governor of their state (1989)
- 71 percent knew the president nominated federal judges (2006)
- 62 percent knew Tony Blair was prime minister of Great Britain (2004)
- 60 percent could identify Newt Gingrich as Speaker of the House (1998)
- 60 percent knew which party had a majority in the Senate (2004)
- 57 percent knew what an economic recession is (1989)
- 52 percent knew each state has two U.S. senators (1978)
- 52 percent knew what the Fifth Amendment is (1989)

- 49 percent could identify Nancy Pelosi as Speaker of the House (2007)
- 46 percent knew that the first ten amendments are called the Bill of Rights (1989)
- 36 percent could identify Vladimir Putin as president of Russia (2007)
- 30 percent knew that the term of a U.S. representative is two years (1978)
- 25 percent could identify both senators from their state (1989)
- 25 percent knew that the term of U.S. senators is six years (1991)
- 21 percent could identify Robert Gates as Secretary of Defense (2007)
- 20 percent could name two First Amendment rights (1989)
- 15 percent could identify Harry Reid as Majority Leader of the Senate (2007)
- 10 percent could identify Dennis Hastert as Speaker of the House (2004)
- 2 percent could name two Fifth Amendment rights (1989)

Sources: 2004 entries are from the American National Election Studies; 2006 data are from the 2006 Congressional Election Survey of the Center on Congress of Indiana University; 2007 data are from the Pew Research Center for the People and Press; other entries are from Michael X. Delli Carpini and Scott Keeter, *What Americans Know About Politics and Why It Matters* (New Haven: Yale University Press, 1996).

(and more than fifteen points during 2003 and 2004 when the war was still relatively popular).[32]

Because wording can influence responses, poll questions are sometimes formulated to elicit maximum support for the views advocated by their sponsors. But even legitimate pollsters need to be careful about how their choice of words affects results—one reason why they asked so many different questions in probing public support for the

Figure 10-4 Popular Support for the Iraq War Depended on How the Question Was Asked

Percent offering supportive answer

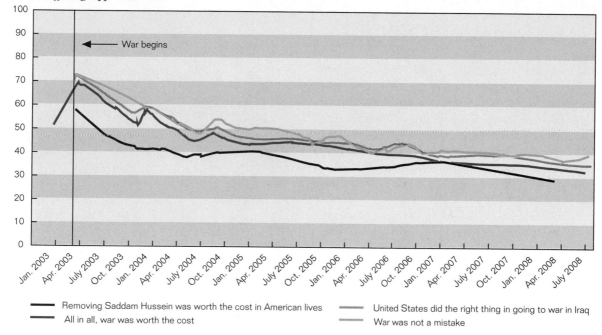

Removing Saddam Hussein was worth the cost in American lives

All in all, war was worth the cost

United States did the right thing in going to war in Iraq

War was not a mistake

Source: CBS News/*New York Times* poll, the Gallup Poll, NBC News/*Wall Street Journal* poll, Pew Research Center for the People and the Press poll, *Newsweek* poll, ABC News/*Washington Post* poll, *Los Angeles Times* poll, *Time*/CNN poll, and Knowledge Network poll, reported at http://pollingreport.com/iraq.htm, August 18, 2008, and the National Annenberg election survey, reported at http://annenberg publicpolicycenter.org/naes/, August 18, 2004.

Note: Trends are estimated by lowess smoothing of responses.

Iraq War. Sophisticated users of polling data recognize that polls always provide a *mediated* take on public opinion and pay close attention to the details of sampling and question wording when interpreting them.

Framing

Social scientists have argued for years about whether unstable survey responses mean that many people's expressed opinions are not anchored in relevant attitudes or that survey questions are too crude to gauge attitudes accurately.[33] Although there are elements of truth in both views, the most important source of instability in a person's expressed opinions is probably **ambivalence.** Particular issues may evoke attitudes and beliefs that pull in opposite directions. When that happens, the response to a pollster's questions depends on which considerations come to mind first and seem most weighty. And that depends on the context: recent events, reference to particularly potent symbols or images (such as the mention of American lives or Saddam Hussein in questions about the Iraq War), or questions that have come earlier in the survey.

Framing Bill Clinton

Allegations of sexual and financial improprieties plagued President Bill Clinton throughout his administration, and the public came to take a dim view of his honesty and morals. Yet as controversy intensified in January 1998 with published accusations of sexual involvement with a White House intern, Clinton's Gallup Poll job approval rating reached 69 percent, the highest level of his administration, and stayed near that mark for months afterward. Many Americans evidently made a sharp distinction between Clinton as a person—they maintained serious doubts about his morals—and his policies—they rewarded him for a robust economy, a balanced federal budget, and declining rates of crime, welfare dependency, and unwed motherhood. In doing so, they ignored the frame presented by the news media's obsessive coverage of the scandal (as well as of earlier allegations of campaign finance improprieties), responding instead to conditions in which they had a more direct personal stake: jobs, inflation, and crime.[1]

Clinton's continuing high level of public approval through 1998 and into 1999 did not stop the Republicans in Congress from trying to remove him from office via impeachment, but it did prevent them from succeeding. With large majorities of Democratic and independent voters opposed to the Republican effort, Democrats in Congress found it politically easy to oppose impeachment and block conviction. Congressional Republicans faced a more difficult choice: heeding the two-thirds of the general public who opposed impeachment, or heeding the two-thirds of Republican voters (and three-quarters of Republican activists) who wanted Clinton removed. All but a handful sided with their core partisan supporters.

1. John R. Zaller, "Monica Lewinsky's Contribution to Political Science," *PS: Political Science and Politics* 31 (June 1998): 182–189.

Some people might believe the poor deserve government help, but they also might detest welfare cheats. Thus these people might well respond differently if asked about their views on "government programs to help the poor" rather than "welfare programs" (see box "Public Opinion and Welfare Reform," page 492). They also might respond differently depending on whether earlier questions brought to mind hungry kids or welfare queens. Or they might respond differently depending on whether last night's TV documentary focused on homeless families or welfare scams. In other words, their responses are shaped by the considerations most recently brought to their attention because they think of them first.[34] The context frames the question, and the frame determines which attitudes govern the response.

Framing explains how both the mass media and political campaigns can affect people's expressed political opinions. The messages sent by the media and the candidates do not have to change underlying attitudes to change expressed opinions. All they have to do is frame the issue in a way that draws out one response rather than the other. For example, one experimental study found that tolerance for public rallies by the white supremacist Ku Klux Klan was significantly lower when framed by a television news story as a public order issue than when it was framed as a free speech issue.[35] Other studies have shown that the content of TV news programs affects the standards people use to evaluate presidents; people who have watched stories about a particular problem give greater weight to the president's performance on *that* problem when forming their overall evaluation of his performance.[36] Simply by covering some issues and ignoring others, the news media help to define the political agenda (see Chapter 1), influencing which considerations are in the foreground when citizens make political judgments; in technical terms, they **prime** their audience to use particular frames in responding to political phenomena. Election campaigns, as we see in the next chapter, do not set out to change people's political views but to bring to the forefront attitudes that favor their candidates. In the 2008 presidential campaign, John McCain sought to make national security and foreign policy the central issues, because voters gave him and his party superior marks in these domains. Barack Obama sought to convince Americans that their vote should be about the economy and the failures of the Bush administration, frames that strongly favored the Democratic side.

From this perspective, we can understand why the answers to pollsters' questions about the value of invading Iraq seem inconsistent. Different questions evoked different frames, putting different beliefs and attitudes into play. Americans responded more positively when asked about the rightness of the decision, bringing to mind U.S. intentions and perhaps the evil of Hussein's regime, than when reminded of the deaths of American soldiers and Iraq's post-war chaos.

Is Public Opinion Meaningful?

If large segments of the public are politically ignorant, hold inconsistent views, and can be manipulated by varying the words or context of questions, how can public opinion play its assigned role in democratic politics, which is to guide and constrain elected agents? The answer is that, despite the deficiencies uncovered by survey research, public opinion continues to play a crucial and effective part in American politics because a variety of formal and informal political institutions give it shape and force. And public opinion is meaningful because, although individual opinions may be badly informed and unstable, **aggregate public opinion**—the sum of all individual opinions—is both stable and coherent.

Stability of Aggregate Public Opinion

The evidence for the stability of aggregate public opinion is impressive. When there is no obvious reason to expect significant change, the distribution of opinion tends to be highly stable. One study examined more than a thousand policy questions asked in identical form at least twice in surveys conducted between 1935 and 1990. In a majority of cases there was no appreciable change in the distribution of public responses between surveys, and nearly half of the changes that did occur were modest. On some questions, aggregate public opinion has not changed significantly for several decades. Figure 10-5 illustrates the stability of aggregate public opinion on whether the government is spending too little on health care.

More important, when substantial changes in the distribution of public opinion occur, they reflect intelligible historical trends or responses to changed conditions.[37] For example, the public's expressed willingness to vote for presidential candidates without regard to race, religion, and sex has grown steadily over the past several decades as public policy and public sentiment turned against discrimination on these dimensions, although Mormons face some lingering prejudices, and atheists and homosexuals need not apply (see Figure 10-6). Support for greater spending on national defense rose in the late 1970s and early 1980s, responding to crises in Iran and Afghanistan and President Ronald Reagan's leadership on the issue, but then declined once the government had increased military spending. Shrinking defense budgets during the 1990s eventually led to greater public support for higher defense spending, even before the terrorist attacks of September 11, 2001. But by 2004, after a large increase in the defense budget and amid growing disillusion with the Iraq War, public opinion had turned against higher defense spending once again (see Figure 10-7). In aggregate, then, public opinion appears both consistent and intelligible.[38]

Other studies have detected broad cyclical changes in public opinion across a range of issues, with opinion swinging back and forth between liberal and conservative "moods." The inevitable shortcomings of both the liberal and conservative approaches to government eventually make the opposition's ideas more attractive. Experience with conservative policies moves public opinion in a liberal direction, while experience with liberal policies makes the public more conservative.[39] For example, the liberal expansion of the welfare state in the 1960s under Lyndon Johnson eventually led to the conservative tax revolts of the late 1970s and early 1980s and the election of Reagan, a conservative Republican, as president. The growing economic inequalities produced by the policies of Reagan and his successor, George H. W. Bush, revived, at least temporarily, public support for government programs to improve the economic well-being of the less affluent, helping to elect Bill Clinton. Changes in mood bring about changes in policy, as candidates more in tune with the new mood win office and many of the holdovers adapt to survive. After Reagan's victory in 1980, congressional Democrats had to adapt to stay in office and they did—by joining Republicans to cut income taxes and social welfare spending.

Figure 10-5 Public Opinion on Health Care Spending: Too Low

Percent saying "too little"

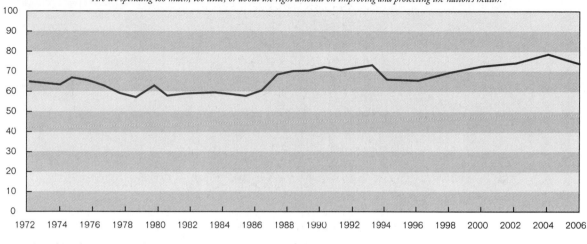

Are we spending too much, too little, or about the right amount on improving and protecting the nation's health?

Source: General Social Survey, National Opinion Research Center, University of Chicago.

Percent who would vote for person in the category

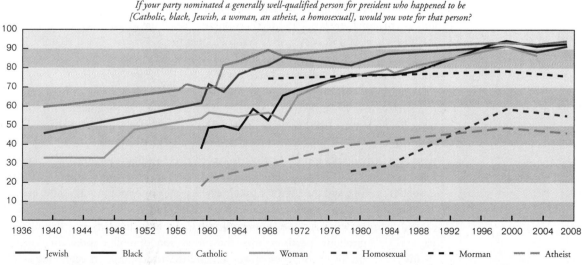

If your party nominated a generally well-qualified person for president who happened to be [Catholic, black, Jewish, a woman, an atheist, a homosexual], would you vote for that person?

Jewish — Black — Catholic — Woman — Homosexual — Morman — Atheist

Source: www.gallup.com/poll/4729/Presidency.aspx, accessed April 28, 2008.

Figure 10-7 Public Opinion on Defense Spending, 1960–2006

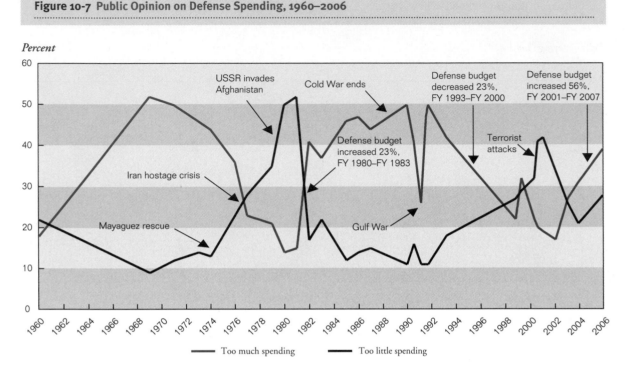

Percent

Sources: Harold W. Stanley and Richard Niemi, *Vital Statistics on American Politics, 1999–2000* (Washington, D.C.: CQ Press, 2000), Table 3-22; data for 2004 and 2006 from www.ropercenter.uconn.edu, August 8, 2008.

Aggregate opinion also varies in coherent ways over the shorter term. The president's level of public approval varies from month to month with economic conditions and international events. The two Bush presidencies offer striking examples. The senior Bush's level of approval in the Gallup Poll reached what was then a record 83 percent in early 1991 in appreciation of his skillful handling of the Gulf War, but continuing high unemployment and slow economic growth over the next eighteen months, along with Bush's seeming inattention to the problem, brought it down to 32 percent. George W. Bush's approval ratings had been stuck in the low 50s for months until the September 2001 terrorist attacks. His forceful response to the crisis and the strong upsurge of national unity provoked by the attacks rallied virtually all Americans to his side, driving his approval ratings to record levels—up to a remarkable 92 percent in one national poll. It thereafter began a steady decline, briefly interrupted by the triumphant early days of the Iraq War and Hussein's capture eleven months later, eventually dipping below 30 percent as disillusion with the Iraq War and bad economic news sapped the president's support among all but Republican loyalists (see Figure 10-3, page 471). **Aggregate partisanship**—the proportion of poll respondents labeling themselves Republicans or Democrats—also shifts with changes in economic conditions, political events, and presidential approval. Popular presidents presiding over growing economies and successful foreign policies enhance their party's strength among voters; failed policies, foreign and domestic, undermine it.[40] As a whole, then, public opinion does not move erratically or unintelligibly. When it is not stable, its movements can usually be explained by real-world events and circumstances.

Opinion Leadership

How can stable and coherent public opinion arise from unstable and incoherent individual opinions? Part of the answer lies in the aggregation process itself. When survey responses are added together, **measurement errors** (from the mismatch of survey questions with the attitudes they are supposed to measure) and random individual changes tend to cancel one another out; therefore, the average remains the same if circumstances remain the same. The more important part of the answer lies in the division of labor between the minority of the public that is attentive and informed and the much larger majority that is neither. A small segment of the public forms opinions by paying close attention to political events and issues. The uninformed and inattentive majority routinely free rides when forming opinions by taking cues from members of this attentive segment. In aggregate, public opinion is given rationality and coherence by these **opinion leaders**.[41]

Opinion leadership arises naturally as people respond to different incentives. The widespread ignorance of political facts and issues does not mean that most Americans are dunces. Indeed, in an important sense political ignorance is rational. It takes time and energy to become informed. Political issues and processes often are exceedingly complicated, and even the most devoted student of politics cannot hope to master them all. Most citizens, on most political questions, receive no tangible payoff from becoming better informed. People are unlikely to improve either U.S. policy or their own lives by developing a better understanding of the Israeli-Palestinian conflict. The same goes for health care policy. Better information holds no promise of a better outcome because the views of any single individual are so unlikely to be decisive. It makes sense to gather information about options when we get to make the decision (what kind of car to buy), but not when our influence on the choice is effectively nil (what kind of helicopters the Marines should buy).

Suppose we do want to participate in politics, if only in a small way, by voting or by responding to a public opinion poll. Or suppose friends are discussing politics. To join in, we need to adopt some positions on the issues. But how do we know which side of an issue to favor, and why, without investing the time and effort to learn about it? If we are like most people, we rationally free ride on the efforts of others, following the cues given by people we consider informed and whose biases we know. They may be people we know personally—friends, relatives, or coworkers who pay special attention to politics; community activists; or leaders in our places of worship. They may be public figures—political leaders, TV or radio personalities, and newspaper columnists. Organizations such as the Sierra Club, the Roman Catholic Church, and the National Organization for Women also may be sources of cues. Thus instead of learning about an endless variety of complicated political issues, all we have to learn is whose attitudes reliably match or contradict our own and then follow their cues.

The popularity among young adult viewers of Jon Stewart's nightly parody of TV network news, *The Daily Show with Jon Stewart* on the Comedy Central cable channel, has made the comedian a genuine if reluctant opinion leader. The ironic finding by a poll taken during the 2004 presidential campaign that Stewart's viewers were better informed than people who watched only regular network or cable news programs or read newspapers is no doubt more the result of self-selection in his audience than of his program's raw informational content.

Their biases need not match ours for the cues to be useful; sometimes we can determine what we are for by noting who is against it, and vice versa. In effect, we avoid incurring information costs by delegating opinion formation to (we hope) reliable agents chosen for that purpose.

Cognitive shortcuts of this sort are available because interested people and groups have a stake in gathering and disseminating political information. Some folks find politics as fascinating as others do baseball and enjoy being recognized by friends as political mavens. But most people who traffic in political information do so to pursue their power and policy goals more effectively. The activities and biases of information specialists usually reflect their institutional roles. Tobacco company officials need to know everything that is said about the dangers of second-hand smoke to counter these claims and defend corporate profits. The American Cancer Society's staff seeks out and publicizes information emphasizing the damage tobacco does to the nation's health and health care budgets. Officials at the Center for Responsive Politics, a public interest lobby, investigate and publicize campaign contributions from political action committees (PACs) to justify its proposals to reform the campaign finance system. Newspaper columnists and radio talk show hosts are paid to express opinions on political issues. Professional politicians and those with political ambitions also need to master issues and be prepared to discuss them. A pluralist political system breeds—and depends on—opinion leaders of many kinds.

The sources of opinion leadership differ from issue to issue, as does the audience for policy. Many political issues go unnoticed except by distinct **issue publics**—subsets of the population who are better informed than everyone else about an issue because it touches them more directly and personally. Farmers pay attention to farm programs; retired people (and their doctors) keep tabs on Medicare policy; research scientists monitor National Science Foundation budgets and rules. Citizens committed to a moral cause, such as protecting animal rights, banning abortion, or protecting civil liberties, form issue publics for policies affecting their cause. Most policy domains are of concern only to issue publics, so it is usually their opinions, not mass opinion, that matter to politicians. Together, opinion leaders and issue publics are the main conduits of public opinion in a pluralist political system. They apply most of the routine pressures felt by government officials engaged in the day-to-day making of public policy on the countless matters dealt with by the federal government. By the same token, their interest makes them the targets of most organized attempts to sway and mobilize public opinion for political ends.

Aggregate public opinion, then, is given its coherence and focus by opinion leaders, typically based in institutions, whose knowledge, ideas, proposals, and debates define the positions and options from which ordinary citizens, acting logically as cognitive misers, adopt their ex-

"Never mind what the voters are saying. What are the pollsters saying?"

pressed views. This conclusion does not mean that public opinion is routinely manipulated by self-serving elites (although there is no shortage of attempts to do so); pluralist competition usually denies any particular opinion leader a monopoly. Opinion leaders maintain their leadership status only if people choose to follow them. Even though the news media focused on the scandals plaguing Bill Clinton during his second term as president, the public proved quite capable of ignoring the "scandal" frame in evaluating his performance as president (see box "Framing Bill Clinton," page 478).

The aggregate stability of popular views reveals that, in an often confused and poorly articulated way, people do have a real basis for the opinions they express. They do not respond to opinion leaders randomly but in ways that are consistent with the values and notions about politics they have accumulated during their lives. Cognitive shortcuts would be of no value if they did not bring people somewhere near the destination they would have reached by taking the longer path.[42] Agents can be fired; opinion leaders, therefore, lead by expressing the political sentiments of those who follow them. This is why politicians, who are fully aware of how fickle and poorly informed people's expressed opinions may be, still think twice about going against the polls. Aggregate opinion is meaningful, and aggregates are what count when a politician is running for reelection or trying to get a bill passed.

For this reason, public opinion, at least as measured by polls, is regularly if not invariably found to influence public policy. One recent summary concluded that public opinion significantly affected public policy in three-quarters of the fifty-two possible instances examined in thirty separate research studies; the more prominent the issue, the more likely public opinion was to be influential.[43]

The Content of Public Opinion

Political opinions reflect people's underlying values and beliefs about how the world works. This fact is no less true of second- or third-hand opinions—those derived, respectively, from one other person or from an opinion leader through another person—than of original opinions, which are formed through personal experience. This is because core values and beliefs influence people's choice of cue-givers (recall who listens to Rush Limbaugh and who to Michael Moore). Americans share a broad consensus on basic political values that puts real limits on what is politically possible. Yet within these bounds, Americans find plenty on which to disagree. Consensus on the basics makes politics—defined here as reaching agreement on a course of common, or collective, action despite disagreement on the purposes of the action—*possible;* disagreement within this general consensus makes politics *necessary.*

Consensus on the System

Opinion polls find that almost every American supports the institutional underpinnings of modern democracy: the right of every citizen to vote; the freedom to speak, write, and work with others for political goals; the right to due process and equal treatment by courts and other government agencies. Although each of these principles was once controversial (see Chapters 4 and 11), opposition to them has now virtually disappeared from public life. Large majorities also favor a capitalist economy, defined as one in which businesses are privately owned, free markets allocate goods, people choose their own occupations, and incomes depend on the market value of services rendered. No one with serious aspirations to political leadership attacks democracy or free enterprise.

When it comes to the practical application of these abstract values, however, consensus breaks down. When a poll taken in 1940 asked a sample of Americans, "Do you believe in freedom of speech?" 97 percent said yes. When those who answered yes were asked, "Do you believe in it to the extent of allowing fascists and communists to hold meetings and express their views in the community?" 76 percent said no. In 1940, the year these questions were posed, war was raging in Europe, and both fascism and communism loomed as serious threats. But even in calmer times, many people who say they favor First Amendment rights would deny them to people with unpopular views. Polls taken in the mid-1970s found 82 percent agreeing that "nobody has the right to tell another person what he should or should not read," but also 50 percent agreeing that "books that preach the overthrow of the government should be banned from the library."[44] A 2007 survey found Americans were divided on the question of whether "freedom of speech should . . . extend to groups that are sympathetic to terrorists," with 50 percent saying it should, and 45 percent saying it should not.[45] When the abstract value of free expression comes up against the more tangible matters of national security or social order, free expression does not always come out on top. It is therefore important to note that free speech and other democratic values find stronger support among the minority of Americans who specialize in politics; those

Conservatives who tune into Rush Limbaugh's radio broadcasts and liberals who attend Michael Moore's movies and lectures receive continuing confirmation of their worldviews as well as cues about the "appropriate" slant to adopt on new or unfamiliar public issues. Professional opinion leaders such as the two pictured here mainly "preach to the choir," but in doing so they contribute form and focus to mass public opinion.

who play the political game are more supportive of its rules.[46] When the George W. Bush administration proposed "Operation TIPS," a program to recruit transportation workers, utility crews, letter carriers, and other private citizens to report suspicious activities to the government as part of the war on terrorism, members of Congress from both parties objected and quickly passed a law killing the program.

Other basic political values are also hedged. Large majorities say they favor free enterprise and dislike government meddling in the economy, but majorities just as large back laws regulating businesses in order to protect the environment or the health and safety of workers and consumers. Again, people who pay more attention to politics are more likely to recognize the implications of one position for another and to offer more consistent sets of opinions. But almost everyone holds political values and beliefs that clash. Forced to choose, people have to consider trade-offs; sometimes political conflict and compromise even occur right in our own heads.

At one level, the values of democracy and capitalism are not compatible. Democracy treats people as equals and permits majorities to rule. Capitalism extols liberty, not equality. It distributes its rewards unequally and leaves crucial economic decisions (what products to produce, what jobs to offer, where to build factories) in the hands of individuals and private corporations, whose goals are profits. The fear that democracy

Majorities of Americans value free enterprise, job opportunities, cheap and abundant energy, and an unobtrusive government, but majorities also value clean air and water, the continued survival of wild creatures in their natural environments, and some measure of protection from market risks. The tension among such competing values—symbolized here by endangered polar bears on the Arctic National Wildlife Refuge, a fragile environment holding substantial oil deposits—creates personal as well as political dilemmas, especially when the price of gasoline skyrockets.

would bring economic ruin by allowing popular majorities to despoil the wealthy minority was a central motive behind the Constitution's elaborate avoidance of direct popular rule. But the fear proved to be groundless because Americans have come to make sharp distinctions about the kinds of equality they consider appropriate. Just about everyone favors political equality. Support for equal opportunity is at least as strong: statements such as "everyone in America should have an equal right to get ahead" and "children should have equal education opportunities" are accepted almost without dissent when posed in opinion polls.[47] Americans also support equal pay for equal work and generally oppose discrimination against any class of persons (women, racial minorities, and homosexuals) in the workplace.

Very little popular support exists, however, for mandating equal outcomes. Asked whether, under a fair economic system, all people would earn about the same or people with more ability would earn higher salaries, 7 percent chose the first option, 78 percent the second.[48] Nor is there much support for affirmative action programs intended to remedy past discrimination against women or racial minorities by putting them first in line for jobs and school admissions. When asked whether "ability determined by test scores" or special treatment "to make up for past discrimination" should govern decisions on jobs and college admission, overwhelming majorities choose test score ability (although vaguer forms of affirmative action are generally supported—question wording is highly consequential in this area).[49] The result is that Americans, renowned since Alexis de Tocqueville's day for their egalitarian social and political values, tolerate huge—and growing—differences in wealth and well-being among individuals and groups.

Politicians: A Suspect Class

Americans approve overwhelmingly of the U.S. political system and its symbols; pride in the Constitution and the flag are nearly universal. They are normally far less pleased, however, with the people they elect to run the system. Criticizing the government is a national pastime with a pedigree longer than baseball's, but the public's distrust of government and its practitioners deepened markedly over the last half of the twentieth century. Figure 10-8 traces the public's varying cynicism about government through a set of questions that have been asked repeatedly in the biennial American National Election Studies and occasionally in other surveys. Far more than in the 1950s and 1960s, Americans in recent years have been inclined to believe that public officials are crooked and that the government wastes tax money, cannot be trusted to do what is right, is run by a few big interests for their own benefit, and does not care about ordinary people.

The most common explanation for these trends is that the conflicts over civil rights and the Vietnam War in the 1960s, followed closely by the Watergate scandal that drove a president from office (note the sharp drops in 1974), led to a more critical press and a disillusioned public. Confidence revived somewhat with the economy in 1984, but later problems, including a stagnant economy during the George H. W. Bush administration (1989–1993), large federal budget deficits, assorted political scandals, high crime rates, and a pervasive sense that the United States was moving in the wrong direction, kept public distrust of government high.

One result was widespread public support for measures to curb politicians: term limits for legislators, constitutional amendments compelling Congress to balance the budget, national referenda in which voters would be allowed a direct say in making laws by putting them on a national ballot. A large part of the appeal of Ross Perot, who won 19 percent of the vote as an independent presidential candidate in 1992, was his image as a champion of political reforms intended to make elected officials more accountable to ordinary people. Any popular sentiment as widespread as this is bound to find political sponsors. Indeed, part of the Republicans' strategy for taking control of Congress in the 1994 elections was a promise to act on constitutional amendments to impose term limits and a balanced budget. In Figure 10-8 three of the confidence measurements reached their lowest points in 1994, evidence of the anger at government that Republicans both fanned and exploited to win Congress.

Confidence in government rebounded with the booming economy and balanced federal budget during the second Clinton administration but still remained far below what it was in the 1950s. This trend continued through the first year of George W. Bush's presidency until the al Qaeda attacks on the United States effectively reframed

Figure 10-8 Americans' Varying Cynicism about Government

Percent

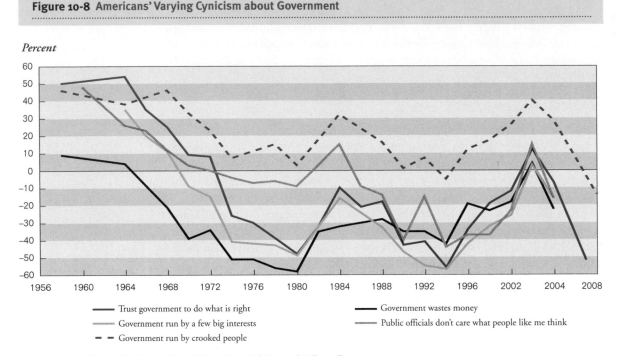

Trust government to do what is right

Government run by a few big interests

Government run by crooked people

Government wastes money

Public officials don't care what people like me think

Sources: American National Election Studies, CBS News/*New York Times* and Gallup polls.

Note: The entries are the percentage of respondents expressing confidence in government minus the percentage expressing a lack of confidence in government on each question. The questions are:

1. How much of the time do you think you can trust the government in Washington to do what is right—just about always, most of the time, or only some of the time? ("Always" or "most of the time" minus "some" or "none of the time.")
2. Do you think that people in government waste a lot of money we pay in taxes, waste some of it, or don't waste very much of it? ("Some" or "not much" minus "a lot.")
3. Would you say that the government is pretty much run by a few big interests looking out for themselves or that it is run for the benefit of all? ("Benefit of all" minus "a few big interests.")
4. Please tell me if you agree or disagree with this statement: Public officials don't care what people like me think. ("Disagree" minus "agree.")
5. Do you think that quite a few of the people running the government are crooked, not very many are, or do you think hardly any of them are crooked? ("Hardly any" or "not many" minus "quite a few.")

the issue. The events of September 11, 2001, and their aftermath had an immediate and dramatic effect on how Americans responded to polling questions about their government and its leaders. Not only did Bush's approval rating shoot to record highs, but so did approval of Congress (84 percent in one poll, topping the previous high of 57 percent) and congressional leaders. The proportion of respondents who said they trusted the government in Washington to do what is right "almost always" or "most of the time," which had been below 45 percent in every poll since the Watergate scandal in 1974 and had fallen as low as 18 percent in the early 1990s, jumped to 56 percent. The sharp rise in expressed support for government and its leaders reflected a radical change in the context in which people thought about these questions. Under deadly attack from shadowy foreign enemies, Americans rallied behind their government as the defender and institutional embodiment of American democracy. For a time, politicians and other government officials enjoyed the kind of broad public support normally reserved for such national symbols as the flag and the Constitution. Moreover, the attacks were a forceful reminder of the need for a government capable of organizing and sustaining collective action in pursuit of that most fundamental of public goods, security from foreign attack. In this context, the ordinary annoyances and frustrations people associate with government and politics became decidedly secondary. This mood did not, however, survive the reemergence of politics as usual and the increasingly bitter partisan differences provoked by the Iraq War and other Bush administration decisions. By 2008, amid deep public discontent with the war, the economy and overall direction of the country, cynicism again dominated Americans' views of their elected leaders.

Public Opinion on Issues

Popular agreement on the fundamentals of representative democracy does not translate into agreement on every important policy area. In each of three broad domains—the economy, societal morality, and foreign policy—the central issues have consistently generated wide divisions of opinion. It is crucial to understand how these differences split the public because these factions form the raw material from which political leaders try to construct majority coalitions. When the public is divided in different ways on different issues and lacks consensus on which are most important, strategies for assembling and maintaining party coalitions become more difficult to conceive and execute.

ECONOMIC ISSUES. Although Americans believe fundamentally in capitalism, almost no one believes that private businesses should be completely unregulated or that the things people value should be allocated exclusively by an unfettered free market. Political conflict occurs over how far the government should go in regulating business and redressing market-driven economic and social inequalities. Historically the trend has been toward an ever-larger government role in managing economic affairs, with notable expansions in the 1930s under Franklin Roosevelt's New Deal policies, in the 1960s with Lyndon Johnson's Great Society programs, and in the 1970s with new laws to protect consumers and the environment (see Chapter 8). Today, government action to enhance economic welfare usually enjoys broad public support. At the same time, people are less than enthusiastic about paying the costs of "big government" in the form of higher taxes and greater bureaucratic regulation. Programs that serve the middle class attract the most support; programs that serve the poor are on shakier political footing.

More specifically, large majorities typically support stable or increased government spending for programs that serve (or will eventually serve) nearly everyone: Social Security (pensions for the disabled or retired), Medicare (medical care for retirees), and unemployment insurance (cash for people laid off from jobs). Social Security is so popular that politicians call it "the third rail of American politics—touch it and you are dead" (referring to the high-voltage rail from which subway trains draw their power). George W. Bush's 2005 campaign to whip up support for reforming the

POLITICS/POLICY

Public Opinion and Welfare Reform

The public is broadly supportive of major social spending programs—except those that evoke the wrong frames. Consider the public's responses to the following question: "Should spending on the following programs increase, decrease, or stay the same?"

	Increase	Stay the Same	Decrease
Social Security (2004)	53%	38%	7%
Improving and protecting health (1993)	74	18	8
Public schools (2000)	76	18	5
Welfare (2004)	12	42	44
Aid to poor people (2004)	42	38	18
Food stamps (2000)	16	51	33
Solving problem of the homeless (1996)	58	31	11
Aid to college students (1996)	53	38	9
Research on AIDS (2000)	51	39	9

Note: Percentages may not add to one hundred due to rounding.

Only a tiny minority wants the government to spend less on Social Security, health, the public schools, college loans, the homeless, and AIDS research than it is now doing. Programs whose names evoke the wrong symbols, however, enjoy much less support. Here, for example, 44 percent would reduce spending on "welfare," and only 12 percent would increase it, although 42 percent would increase spending on "aid to poor people"—overlooking the fact that welfare *is* aid to poor people. This is a clear example of framing. Most Americans think government should help the poor, but the word "welfare" conjures up images, however unfair, of lazy people living off the sweat of the taxpayers. Charity is a virtue, but so is self-reliance, and poverty issues can be framed in terms of either one.

Images and frames do matter. In 1996 the Republican Congress sent Bill Clinton a welfare reform bill that cut back on federal assistance to poor people. Among other things, the bill imposed a time limit on welfare eligibility for the first time since the adoption of the original assistance program in the 1930s. It also slashed the food stamp program, which apparently shares welfare's negative connotations (see the entry for food stamps in the table). Most congressional Democrats opposed the bill, but, facing reelection, Clinton signed it anyway because it was widely supported by a public that had applauded his previous campaign promise to "end welfare as we know it."

Sources: 1993 data are from the General Social Survey, reported by Robert S. Erikson and Kent L. Tedin in *American Public Opinion*, 5th ed. (Boston: Allyn and Bacon, 1995), 89; 1996, 2000, and 2004 data are from the 1996, 2000, and 2004 American National Election Studies.

program implicitly acknowledged the danger; the president spent months traveling the country telling audiences that Social Security needed a major overhaul to remain fiscally sound without mentioning that, absent major tax increases that Bush had ruled out, the overhaul would have to include substantial cuts in promised future benefits. Other individual government programs designed to improve health and welfare also command broad support—with a few revealing exceptions (see box "Public

Opinion and Welfare Reform," which lists some typical poll results and illustrates how such opinions can affect major policy decisions).

By and large, Americans seem to support a wide range of economic and social welfare policies that commonly are classified as liberal. But when it comes to principles, as opposed to programs, Americans are much more likely to think of themselves as conservatives. Majorities also agree with conservative politicians who say that taxes are too high, that the government wastes a lot of money, that bureaucrats are too meddlesome, and that people ought to take care of themselves rather than depend on government handouts.

SOCIAL AND MORAL ISSUES. Politics is about the distribution of goods, which can be moral as well as material. The great struggles to abolish slavery, achieve votes for women, prohibit alcohol, and end racial segregation were driven largely by moral rather than economic considerations. Today social and moral issues produce some of the most heated political controversies. Questions about abortion, religion in public life, and the rights of women, ethnic and racial minorities, immigrants, and homosexuals make up an important part of the political agenda. These issues raise conflicting considerations that are difficult to reconcile, not only between opposed groups but also for individuals in their own minds.

In modern times abortion is the best-known example. Since the Supreme Court handed down its *Roe v. Wade* ruling in 1973, thereby overturning state laws making abortions illegal, the abortion issue has become a defining one for a whole political generation. Groups with starkly opposing positions have dominated the public debate. At one extreme are those who want the law to forbid abortion as murder; at the other are those who object to any restriction on a woman's right to abort. Neither of these positions commands a majority, although more favor no restriction (40 percent in 2000) than favor a total ban (11 percent).[50] For most people, the answer is, "It depends."

Aggregate public opinion on abortion is both highly consistent and acutely sensitive to how the issue is framed. Figure 10-9 shows the trends in responses to one set of questions posed regularly in polls since 1965. After an initial increase in support for legalized abortion (coinciding with *Roe v. Wade*), aggregate opinion has changed little. Large majorities think abortion should be legal if the pregnancy resulted from rape or would endanger the woman's health or if there is a strong chance of serious birth defects. The public is much more evenly split on whether abortion for financial or family reasons should be legal. Other ways of wording the questions produce a similar spread.

Unlike the activists on both sides, most Americans are torn on the issue. Majorities agree that "abortion is murder" (62 percent) and "morally wrong" (61 percent), but they also think that a woman should be allowed to have an abortion if she wants to and her doctor agrees to it (61 percent), and oppose a constitutional amendment outlawing abortions (70 percent). Perhaps the best expression of the average person's view is summed up by an option offered by one poll on the issue: "I personally feel that abortion is morally wrong, but I also feel that whether or not to have an abortion is a decision that has to be made by every woman for herself"; 78 percent agreed.[51]

Abortion is the kind of issue that defies political resolution because the wide disagreement on values leaves little space for agreement on action. It generates intense

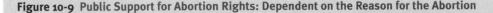

Figure 10-9 Public Support for Abortion Rights: Dependent on the Reason for the Abortion

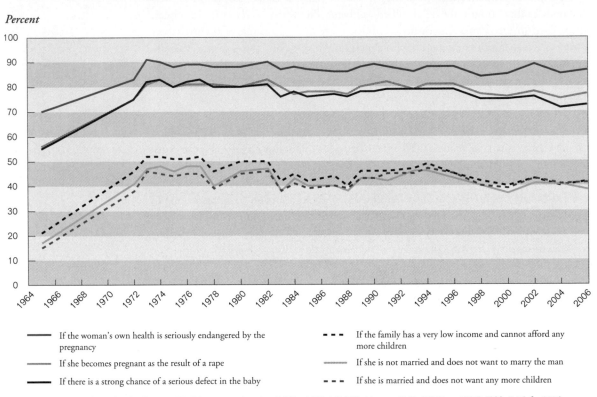

Percent

	If the woman's own health is seriously endangered by the pregnancy		If the family has a very low income and cannot afford any more children
If she becomes pregnant as the result of a rape		If she is not married and does not want to marry the man
If there is a strong chance of a serious defect in the baby		If she is married and does not want any more children

Source: Harold W. Stanley and Richard Niemi, *Vital Statistics on American Politics, 2003–2004* (Washington, D.C.: CQ Press, 2003), Table 3-16; for 2006, General Social Survey.

feelings among minorities on both sides who tolerate nothing less than full support for their position. Intense feelings are, moreover, far more prevalent among political activists (some of whom are activists *because* of their intense feelings), and they are most common among the minority that would forbid abortion entirely. Ordinary citizens are much less certain about how the issue should be resolved and remain uncomfortable with either extreme. Thus exploitation of the issue politically is a delicate undertaking. In running for president in 2008, John McCain had to maintain a firm "pro-life" position to attract support from conservative Christians, many of whom were Republicans primarily because the party was committed to banning abortion, without leading uncommitted moderates to worry that "choice" would immediately be threatened if he were to win.

Americans take conservative positions on most other social issues, but in practice their views are often balanced by considerable respect for individual freedom. Formal prayer in public schools, banned by Supreme Court decisions in the early 1960s, receives widespread public support. Likewise, large majorities take strong "law and order" positions, favoring capital punishment for murderers and opposing the legalization of drugs such as marijuana and cocaine. In 1999, two-thirds favored a constitutional amendment that would permit Congress to outlaw burning the American flag as a form of political protest.[52] Few support unrestricted access to pornography. Social conservatism grew during the 1990s as problems of crime, drug abuse, single-parent families, and welfare dependency became the focus of political attention. Yet the public remains leery about using government to impose traditional moral standards on private citizens. Most people (about 80 percent) believe that homosexuality is immoral, but a majority (57 percent) thinks homosexual relations between consenting adults

The abstract ideal of equal rights is widely shared by Americans, but its application is often vigorously disputed. Here, supporters and opponents of gay marriage mount competing demonstrations outside the California Supreme Court, which was hearing arguments in March 2008 on the constitutionality of a voter initiative that banned gay marriage. The supreme court overturned the ban, prompting yet another initiative, this one a constitutional amendment, on the 2008 California ballot. It passed narrowly, 52–48.

should be legal. Majorities oppose gay marriage, but most Americans support some form of legal recognition for gay couples.[53]

FOREIGN POLICY. During the 2004, 2006, and to a lesser extent 2008 election campaigns, foreign policy, particularly regarding the wars in Iraq and Afghanistan, shared the spotlight with the national economy. In light of the war's controversial justification and growing cost in American life and treasure, this was not at all surprising. But it was unusual. Except when Americans are dying overseas, foreign policy issues tend to be remote from everyday experience, and few people pay sustained attention to foreign affairs. In such relatively quiet times, public opinion on foreign policy is particularly responsive to opinion leadership. The president is the most important opinion leader on foreign policy, but presidential influence varies according to whether other opinion leaders—rival politicians, foreign policy experts, and news commentators—agree or disagree with the White House.[54] Since World War II large majorities have supported an active international role for the United States, but backing for particular policies has been much more variable.

Until the breakup of the Soviet Union at the end of 1991, the Cold War conflict between the United States and the Soviet Union framed both public and elite thinking on foreign affairs. The avowed U.S. objective of "containing" the Soviet Union to prevent the expansion of communism enjoyed broad public acceptance, but the public did not agree on all of the actions taken in the name of containment. Both the Korean

Antiwar protesters, depicted here, were a vocal if ineffective minority at the onset of the Iraq War. In the months after Baghdad had fallen, the war's main justifications (that Iraq was stockpiling weapons of mass destruction and that Saddam Hussein was plotting with al Qaeda terrorists) could not be confirmed, and a much broader segment of the public, especially Democrats and independents, came to doubt the war's wisdom and necessity.

and Vietnam Wars lost popular support as casualties mounted.[55] Later, majorities opposed proposals by the Reagan and Bush administrations to give military assistance to the Nicaraguan contras in their civil war against the avowedly socialist Sandinista government. In all of these cases, public divisions reflected in a direct way the divisions among opinion leaders. In general, opinion on whether to take a tougher or more conciliatory approach to dealing with the Soviets varied with U.S. perceptions of Soviet behavior. Events like the Soviet invasion of Afghanistan in 1979 to prop up a threatened communist regime made a tougher line more popular, whereas arms control agreements and summit meetings between the United States and the Soviet Union during the Cold War years made conciliation more popular.[56]

National leaders reached no new consensus on a guiding framework for U.S. foreign policy during the post–Cold War era of the 1990s, and so neither did the public. The war against Iraq to liberate Kuwait in 1991 attracted widespread public support even before its stunning success because Iraq's invasion threatened the U.S. economy (by putting the Persian Gulf oil supply at risk) and America's closest ally in the region, Israel. But the Clinton administration had great difficulty building popular support for policies aimed at resolving conflicts in Somalia, Bosnia, Haiti, and Kosovo, partly because the administration itself was vague about what was at stake for the nation in these conflicts and partly because other opinion leaders opposed the administration's policies.

Drift and division on foreign policy issues ended almost instantly with the assaults on the World Trade Center and the Pentagon. Foreign policy issues became, tragically, anything but remote. The Bush administration moved immediately to direct virtually all its foreign policy resources to mounting a multifaceted war on terrorism. Leaders in both parties overwhelmingly supported the administration's initial actions, and so did the public; in October 2001 polls, nine of ten Americans said they backed the ongoing military action against the terrorist organizations and the Taliban government in

Afghanistan. A large majority was even willing to accept several thousand U.S. casualties if that was what it took to succeed.[57] With the United States itself in harm's way, little opinion leadership was at first necessary; indeed, any leader who did not support a vigorous, conspicuous response would have been badly out of step with mass opinion. But after the apparent rout of the Taliban in Afghanistan with the fall of Kandahar and the Battle of Tora Bora in December 2001, the administration's shift of focus to Iraq was not so uniformly applauded and, as already noted, became less popular over time as citizens and leaders divided increasingly along party lines over the wisdom of the invasion. Rather than sharing consensus, the public has become divided not only over Iraq, but also over the legitimacy of preemptive wars and the value of working with allies or the UN. Few contest the necessity of combating terrorism to protect the U.S. homeland, but there is no agreement on how best to accomplish this goal.

Effects of Background on Public Opinion

People's opinions on specific issues reflect the knowledge, beliefs, and values they have acquired over their lifetimes. The public's various points of view often represent differences in background, education, and life experiences. When polling data are analyzed, these differences show up in the way opinions vary with demographic characteristics such as race, ethnicity, gender, income, education, region, religion, and age. Politicians pay close attention to group differences because they determine feasible coalition-building strategies.

Race and Ethnicity

The sharpest differences of opinion between major groups in U.S. politics occur between African Americans and whites, and the biggest gap is on issues related to race. Unlike in the past, a large majority of white Americans now reject segregation and support equal opportunity for all races, but they disagree with African Americans on what, if anything, should be done about the lingering effects of racial discrimination. A 2003 survey asked respondents if they favored or opposed "affirmative action programs for racial minorities." Seventy percent of African Americans but only 44 percent of non-Hispanic whites said they supported such programs. In the same survey, 49 percent of African Americans but only 22 percent of whites thought that race should be taken into account in college admissions to promote "diversity."[58] African Americans also are more likely than whites to favor greater government action to provide jobs, health care, and other government services. But they are less supportive of defense spending and foreign wars; according to a February 2008 Gallup Poll, 87 percent thought the Iraq War had been a mistake (see Figure 10-4, page 477).[59] Finally, 44 percent of African Americans oppose the death penalty for murder, compared with only 16 percent of whites.

These contrasting views reflect the profoundly different perceptions and life experiences of African Americans and whites in American society. African Americans, along with numerous other minority groups—Hispanics, Native Americans, and Asian Americans of diverse national origins—share a history of discrimination based

Just because an issue is especially important to a particular ethnic group does not guarantee that the group will express a consensus on it. Here, Hispanic protesters opposed to bilingual education support a Colorado initiative that would require students not fluent in English to be enrolled in an English immersion program unless parents explicitly request bilingual education. Other Hispanic leaders advocate bilingual education as a way of keeping native Spanish-speaking children from falling behind academically.

on race; many have experienced discrimination firsthand. Whites tend to think that legal equality has now been achieved and that any special effort to overcome the effects of past discrimination is unfair. African Americans also tend to have lower incomes than whites and so are typically more favorably disposed toward government efforts to improve economic welfare. Their greater propensity to oppose the death penalty reflects skepticism, based on bitter historical experience, about the fairness of the criminal justice system toward black defendants.

On all of these issues, the views of African Americans are closer to the positions taken by the Democratic Party, and African Americans vote overwhelmingly Democratic. As a result, they are a crucial part of the Democratic coalition. Only twice since World War II has the Democratic presidential candidate won more of the white vote than the Republican candidate (Lyndon Johnson in 1964 and Bill Clinton in 1996); every other Democratic victory (Harry Truman in 1948, John Kennedy in 1960, Jimmy Carter in 1976, and Bill Clinton in 1992) has depended on huge majorities among African Americans to offset narrower Republican majorities among whites. African Americans also gave Al Gore his popular plurality in 2000, awarding him more than 90 percent of their votes.* Barack Obama, the first African American to run for president on a major party ticket, won an even larger share of African American voters, 95 percent in the national exit poll; equally important for his election, he inspired extraordinarily high turnout among black voters.

Other minority groups show distinctive patterns of issue opinion and voting behavior, but in most instances these patterns reflect the group's economic status rather than particularly ethnic views. Hispanics tend to have lower incomes and so favor more extensive government services and the Democratic Party; Asian Americans tend to have higher incomes and so are economically more conservative and more Republi-

---

* According to *American National Election Study, 2000,* Gore won 91 percent of the black vote; the Election Day exit polls put the figure at 90 percent.

can than Hispanics. But there are enormous differences within these broad categories in the ethnic backgrounds and economic status of subgroups. Hispanics include Cuban Americans, Puerto Ricans, Mexican Americans, immigrants from the nations of Central America, and people whose roots in the Southwest go back centuries. Asian Americans include people of Korean, Japanese, Chinese, Vietnamese, Philippine, and Laotian extraction, some further divided into different eras of immigration and regions of origin.

Generalizing about group opinions is risky, although one pattern seems to hold: ethnic minorities do express strong and distinctive political views on issues directly affecting their groups. Cuban Americans are deeply concerned about U.S. policy toward Cuba. Opposed to any softening of the official U.S. hostility toward Cuba's communist government, Cuban Americans favor Republicans, who generally take a harder line against the dictatorship. Mexican Americans are far more likely than other groups to oppose the denial of public education and health care to undocumented immigrants, a view that brings them closer to the Democrats. These differences show up in party identification (see Figure 10-10) and were especially important in making Florida, with a large Cuban American population and where Mexican Americans have formed the fastest-growing segment of the population, a highly competitive swing state in recent presidential elections.

Figure 10-10 **The Party Affiliation of Hispanic Voters Depends on Their Country of Origin**

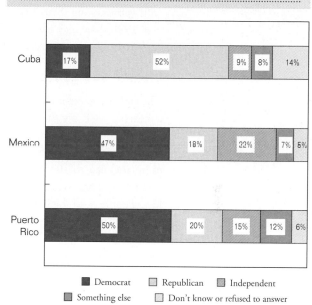

Sources: Data from Pew Hispanic Center/Kaiser Family Foundation, "The 2004 National Survey of Latinos: Politics and Civic Participation," reanalyzed by the authors.

Gender

On most kinds of issues, the sexes think alike, but on some things they do not. Women are consistently less inclined than men to support the use of violence in foreign and domestic policy. For example, they are more likely to oppose military involvement in foreign conflicts, to support arms control negotiations, and to back gun control, and less likely to demand the death penalty for murderers.* The differences between the sexes on such issues can be quite large, twenty percentage points or more. By smaller margins, women have more favorable attitudes toward social welfare spending and regulations designed to protect the environment, consumers, and children.[60] The reasons for these differences are still a matter of debate. What is known is that they have created a "gender gap" in recent electoral politics, with women more supportive than men of the Democratic Party and its candidates, and men more

---

* In April 2003, 53 percent of men compared to only 41 percent of women favored preemptive war against counties that might attack the United States. See CBS News/*New York Times* poll, April 11–13, 2003, at http://cbsnews.com/sections/opinion/polls/main 500160.shtml, May 30, 2003.

supportive of Republicans. In 2008 Barack Obama's support ran about seven percentage points higher among women than among men; unmarried women are especially likely to favor Democrats and account for most of the difference between the sexes.[61]

It is interesting to note that women and men do not differ much on sex-related issues. Both show high levels of support for women and men having an equal role in society and politics; the sexes do not differ in distribution of opinions on abortion.

Income and Education

The politicians who designed the Constitution thought the most enduring political conflicts would pit the poor against the rich. Surveys find abundant evidence that opinions differ among income classes, but the differences are modest compared with those found in most other modern industrial nations. People with lower incomes are more inclined to support spending on government services helpful to people like them: Social Security, student loans, food stamps, child care, and help for the homeless. People with higher incomes are notably less enthusiastic about government spending on social programs or taxing higher incomes at higher rates. Economic self-interest easily explains these differences: people getting more of the benefits tend to see greater merit in social programs than do those paying more of the costs.

On noneconomic issues, however, higher income groups tend to be more liberal than lower income groups. This difference has less to do with income than it does with education. People in higher income groups tend to have more years of formal education, and the more education people have, the more likely they are to take the liberal side on issues such as abortion, homosexual rights, equality of the sexes, freedom of speech, and minority rights.

Religion

Religion has played an important role in American political life since the founding of the first colonies. A large majority of Americans profess a religious affiliation, and more people belong to religious groups than to any other kind of organization. Religious beliefs shape values, including many of the values people pursue through political action. The movements to abolish slavery, prohibit alcohol, extend civil rights to African Americans, end the war in Vietnam, and ban abortion have all been strongly imbued with religious ideals.

Differences in religious beliefs often underlie differences in political opinions. Not surprisingly, religious beliefs influence opinions on more social issues than economic issues. People who are secular (no religious preference), Jewish, or members of one of what scholars call the mainline Protestant denominations, such as Episcopalians, Presbyterians, and Congregationalists, tend to be more liberal on social issues. Evangelical Protestants, such as Southern Baptists and Pentecostals, tend to be very conservative. Roman Catholics, who form the largest single denomination, fall in between, but only on average; a wide variety of social views are supported by various organizations within the Catholic Church. Regardless of religious affiliation, the more active people are in religious life, the more socially conservative they are likely to be.

Beginning with the Reagan administration, the Republican Party has made a concerted effort to win the support of evangelical Protestants and other religious conservatives, with a good deal of success. Although the country as a whole was split down the middle between Bush and Gore in 2000, white voters of the religious right went for Bush, 80 percent to 18 percent.[62] Aware of this fact, Bush's 2004 reelection campaign made a special effort to organize get-out-the-vote drives through their churches. Christian conservatives have become so large and active an element in the Republican coalition that they now dominate the party organization in many states. The risk for the party is that their prominence may alienate affluent and educated social liberals who would otherwise be attracted by Republican economic policies.

Other Demographic Divisions

Other demographic divisions of opinion are worth noting. Younger voters tend to be more liberal than their elders on social and economic issues; they are, for example, much more supportive of gay marriage. City dwellers are more liberal than residents of suburbs, small towns, or rural areas. People living near the coasts or in the upper Midwest tend to be more liberal than people living in the South, the plains, or the mountain states, particularly on cultural issues. The red state–blue state division made so much of in the 2000 and 2004 elections reflects this culturally based regional divide. White southerners once stood out starkly from the rest of the population in their opposition to racial integration, but the gap has almost entirely disappeared.

Religion and politics came together explosively in 2005 when conservative Christian leaders such as James Dobson, president of Focus on the Family, pictured here, reacted to the judicial decisions that allowed Terri Schiavo (a Florida woman who had been in a persistent vegetative state for fifteen years) to die by demanding that Congress curb judicial independence. Dobson classed the black-robed judges with the white-robed Ku Klux Klan as ones who "did great wrong to civil rights and to morality" and referred to the anticipated future Supreme Court nomination battle as "World War Three."

Differences of opinion among major social groups constitute the raw material of electoral politics. Candidates and parties trying to win elections have no choice but to piece together coalitions out of the material at hand. The more affluent voters tend to be economic conservatives but social liberals; voters with more modest incomes combine economic liberalism with social conservatism. Social issues have given Republicans a wedge to split the Democratic coalition by appealing to the social conservatism of voters who, on economic issues, think like Democrats. And Democrats have countered by using issues such as abortion rights and gun control to woo highly educated voters (particularly women) whose economic interests place them closer to the Republicans. Because there are more voters with modest than with ample incomes, Democratic candidates usually like campaigns to focus on economic issues, while Republican candidates want to talk about "family values" and law and order.

Map 10-1 Presidential Election Results, 2008

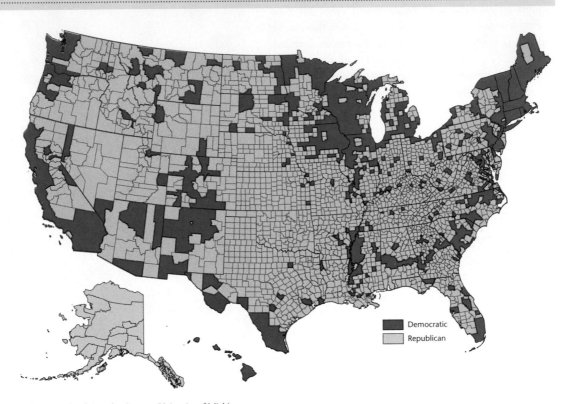

Source: Center for the Study of Complex Systems, University of Michigan.

Public Opinion: A Vital Component of American Politics

The vast network of organizations engaged in measuring or trying to influence public opinion attests to its crucial influence in American politics. But the complexity of the network also underlines the reality that public opinion's influence is rarely simple or unmediated. Individual opinions become public opinion only when aggregated, and organizations and leaders do the aggregating. Polling organizations reveal and express public opinion even as they measure it. Politicians and other policy advocates give it shape, focus, and force through their efforts to persuade and activate citizens to support their causes. The mass media report and interpret the collective political experiences that become the material basis for individual opinions. Opinion leaders provide the cues that the rationally ignorant majority uses as shortcuts to forming its opinion.

Individual opinions, although rooted in personal values and experiences, are both shaped by and expressed through leaders and institutions.

Leaders and institutions do not, however, control public opinion. People choose which leaders to follow and which messages to heed according to the values and beliefs they accumulate over a lifetime. Their assessments of parties, issues, candidates, and other political phenomena, derived from personal observations and life experiences as well as from families and friends, retain a strong practical component, reflecting real interests and needs. For most people, basic political orientations, whether reflections of ideologies, a few core values, or simple party preferences, are quite resistant to change. The raw individual material that goes into the construction of public opinion is not particularly malleable, and neither, therefore, is aggregate opinion. Candidates, policy advocates, and anyone else whose political goals require public support (or at least acquiescence) have little choice but to work within the formidable if often hazy constraints imposed by public attitudes. They succeed, if at all, by framing the choice favorably rather than by changing minds. This is clearest in the electoral context, which is the subject of the next chapter.

logic.cqpress.com

Key Terms

aggregate partisanship, 482

aggregate public opinion, 480

ambivalence, 477

attitude, 467

cognitive shortcut, 484

conservative, 468

core values, 469

framing, 479

ideology, 468

issue publics, 484

liberal, 468

measurement error, 483

opinion leader, 483

political socialization, 473

prime, 479

public opinion, 462

scientific polling, 464

Suggested Readings

Asher, Herbert. *Polling and the Public: What Every Citizen Should Know.* 7th ed. Washington, D.C.: CQ Press, 2007. A nontechnical primer for citizens who wish to become smarter, more critical consumers of polls and the media stories that report them.

Brody, Richard R. *Assessing the President: The Media, Elite Opinion, and Public Support.* Stanford: Stanford University Press, 1991. The public's rating of the president is shaped by the economy, international crises, political scandal, the news media, and politicians.

Clawson, Rosalee A., and Zoe M. Oxley. *Public Opinion: Democratic Ideals, Democratic Practice.* Washington D.C.: CQ Press, 2008. This introduction to public opinion links normative theory to empirical research.

Norrander, Barbara, and Clyde Wilcox. *Understanding Public Opinion.* 2nd ed. Washington, D.C.: CQ Press, 2002. These essays highlight the diversity of approaches to explaining public opinion.

Page, Benjamin I., and Robert Y. Shapiro. *The Rational Public.* Chicago: University of Chicago Press, 1992. Mass public opinion responds in reasonable ways to national political events and experiences.

Sniderman, Paul M., and Edward G. Carmines. *Reaching Beyond Race.* Cambridge: Harvard University Press, 1997. A cleverly designed survey using computer-assisted telephone interviews examines what white Americans say about race when they face no risk of appearing racist.

Stimson, James A. *Public Opinion in America: Moods, Cycles, and Swings.* 2nd ed. Boulder, Colo.: Westview Press, 1999. Broad trends in public opinion on a wide range of policy issues, or public "moods," both shape and reflect broad trends in national policy. At the most general level, government policies do respond to public preferences.

Zaller, John. *Nature and Origins of Mass Opinion.* New York: Cambridge University Press, 1992. Four simple axioms about how people respond to political information generate a rich variety of models of how public opinion shifts in response to events and to elite persuasion.

Review Questions

1. How did popular support for the war in Iraq change over time? How did the changes for Republicans, Democrats, and independents differ?

2. In 1936 the *Literary Digest* ran a "straw poll" that mistakenly predicted that Franklin Roosevelt would be defeated in his reelection attempt. What factors undermine the accuracy of such polls? What factors can undermine the accuracy of even "scientific" polling?

3. How have modern techniques for molding and measuring public opinion contributed to the nationalization of American politics?

4. Do voters think in terms of ideologies? Are voters' attitudes generally consistent? If not, what explains the inconsistency?

5. Given the mechanisms through which politicians and the media can influence it, does public opinion really matter?

6. Since aggregate opinion is simply the combination of all individual opinions, how can it be more stable and coherent than individual opinion?

7. Who are opinion leaders? Why might typical individuals rely on the statements or positions of these opinion leaders in forming their own opinions? What are the limits on how much these opinion leaders can control public opinion?

8. In which areas does the American public agree or disagree on basic political values and policies? How does this agreement or disagreement make politics possible or necessary?

9. In what areas do men and women differ most in their opinions? Where do they differ the least?

Exercises

My Mind's Made Up?

Using information from the National Election Studies (www.electionstudies.org/), present an argument for whether or not aggregate public opinion has been stable in the following policy areas. Then present a reasoned argument for why changes might or might not have occurred.

- Power of the federal government
- Government services and spending
- Favoring desegregation or segregation
- Aid to African Americans/minorities
- Government seeing to fair treatment in jobs
- Equal role for women
- School prayer
- United States should not concern itself with world problems
- Military spending
- Have economic policies of federal government made things better or worse?

Who Uses Ideology?

In this chapter the authors argue that ideology does not guide the political thinking of most citizens. To test this notion, use the advanced search tool of Google's massive archive of discussion forum posts (http://groups-beta.google.com/advanced_search) to perform the following keyword searches. (*Note:* You should probably limit your searches to political forums, or forums containing the word "politics.") How many messages does each search return? When you look over the posts, do people seem to be using the terms in the same ways?

- Ideology (or ideological)
- Conservative
- Liberal
- Republican
- Democrat (or Democratic)
- Left-wing
- Right-wing
- Fascist
- Anarchist
- Congress

"Ethical" Polling

The American Association for Public Opinion Research (AAPOR) has published a Code of Professional Ethics and Practices (www.aapor.org/aapor codeofethics?s=code%20of%20professional%20 ethics), as well as a listing of the best practices for polling (www.aapor.org/bestpractices?s=best%20 practices). Read over these documents, as well as the survey practices that AAPOR condemns (www. aapor.org/surveypracticesthataaporcondemns). Then see if you can find any news organizations or polls online that appear to violate AAPOR guidelines.

Voting, Campaigns, and Elections

If Americans cherish the right to vote, why do so many neglect to exercise it?

Why is political party identification, which many Americans discount, still the best single predictor of how people will vote?

If attentive and informed voters are likely to be turned off by negative advertisements, why do campaigns pour so much money into running them?

Is the reform of the campaign finance system really working?

D uring the 2008 presidential campaign, the administration of Republican president George W. Bush came under withering criticism for excessive "spending, the conduct of the war in Iraq for years, the growth in the size of government, . . . laying a $10 trillion debt on future generation of America, owing $500 billion to China, . . . failure to enforce and moderize the regulatory agencies that were designed for the 1930s, . . . [and] failure to address the issue of climate change seriously."[1] The critic in this case was not, however, the Democratic candidate, Sen. Barack Obama of Illinois, but the Republican candidate, Sen. John McCain of Arizona. Obama was even more scathing in denouncing what he depicted as the failures of the Bush administration, basing his candidacy on the promise of comprehensive, if not always precisely defined, "change" in national politics and policies.

The spectacle of both presidential candidates running against the incumbent administration, while historically unique, was only one of the unusual features of the 2008 presidential election. For the first time since 1952, neither candidate was a sitting president or vice president (otherwise, McCain's criticism of his own party's administration would have been inconceivable). Both parties had lively (and lengthy) primary election seasons. The Democrats' choice quickly narrowed down to two candidates, either of whom would represent a historical first: Hillary Clinton would be the first woman, or Barack Obama would be the first African American, to win a major party presidential nomination. Obama won a surprising (and narrow) victory through superior organization and a strong appeal to younger voters. In the Republican contest, John McCain began the primary season mired in third place in the polls

President-elect Barack Obama and Vice President–elect Joe Biden, along with their wives Michelle Obama and Jill Biden, celebrate Obama's historic victory at an election-night party in Chicago's Grant Park attended by an estimated quarter of a million people.

but managed to pull off a remarkable come-from-behind victory to become, at 72, the oldest first-time presidential nominee (for more details, see Chapter 12). He then chose a young, charismatic, and largely unknown woman, Alaska governor Sarah Palin, as his vice presidential running mate—only the second woman ever to be nominated for the office.

The nation McCain and Obama sought to lead was deeply unhappy with its current regime. George W. Bush's approval ratings languished in the mid-20s, the lowest of his presidency. An overwhelming majority of Americans were dissatisfied with the direction of the country.[2] The ongoing war in Iraq was a factor, but the main source of such widespread dissatisfaction was the economic crisis, triggered by the steep decline in housing prices that began in late 2006. The turmoil eventually spread to the credit and stock markets, wiping out major financial institutions and reducing Americans' wealth by trillions of dollars. By fall 2008, economists were virtually unanimous in predicting a deep recession, perhaps the worst since the Great Depression of the 1930s.

The economy came to dominate electoral politics, to the great advantage of Obama and other Democratic candidates. In every election, each side tries to persuade voters that the issues that the public thinks it handles better than its rival are the issues that should determine their votes. The Democratic Party's customary advantage on economic issues was even greater than usual under the conditions prevailing in 2008. Republicans generally get higher marks on national security issues, and, with his military background and Senate experience, McCain was ideally suited to a campaign that emphasized defense and foreign policy issues. He had strongly supported Bush's controversial decision announced in early 2007 to send thousands of additional American troops to Iraq to try to reverse the deteriorating situation there. The "surge" eventually did succeed by the standard that American voters care most about: monthly American combat deaths dropped by nearly 75 percent between 2007 and the summer of 2008. The McCain campaign hoped to use the progress in Iraq following the "surge," which Obama had opposed, to underline the risks voters would be taking in electing someone as young and inexperienced as Obama. But the economic crisis forced McCain to focus instead on economic issues, which were not his strong suit. It also made it harder for McCain to avoid partisan association with the Bush administration, and therefore to counter Obama's most potent theme, that a McCain presidency would be equivalent to a third Bush term.

Behind in the polls, McCain sought to enliven his campaign and shore up support among his party's social conservatives by choosing Palin as his running mate. The strategy initially seemed to work, and for a brief time after the Republican convention he led Obama in the national polls. But Palin's questionable preparation for the job became an issue—undermining Republican criticism of Obama on the same grounds—and she became a polarizing figure, embraced by social conservatives but not by independents or Democrats, most notably the Democratic women who had supported Hillary Clinton in the primaries.

Presidential elections are as much about candidates as about issues, and so the personal characteristics of the candidates were a central focus of both campaigns. The

Long lines at the polls were common in the 2008 primary and general elections as a result of the intense effort by the presidential campaigns— particularly Barack Obama's—to register new voters and get them to the polls. Here, Virginia voters wait to vote in the February 12, 2008, primary. The Virginia primary winners, Democrat Obama and Republican John McCain, went on to win their party's nominations.

McCain campaign emphasized his heroism as a prisoner of war in Vietnam and his image as a patriotic man of honor and an independent-minded maverick—not an orthodox Republican or follower of Bush. It also sought to raise doubts about Obama's character and associations, attacking him for empty eloquence, "palling around with terrorists," and embracing socialism. The idea was to raise enough uncertainty about Obama that voters would see him as too risky a choice, regardless of what they thought of McCain's Republican associations. Obama was careful always to praise McCain's wartime heroism while portraying him as unaware and out of touch with the economic struggles of ordinary Americans. Obama's main goal, however, was to convince voters, the vast majority of whom knew nothing about him at the start of the campaign season, that he was qualified to be president. He sought to do so by displaying a mastery of the issues and their connections to voters' lives and by projecting a steady, calm, and disciplined image through the lengthy primary and general election season as voters were getting to know him. The three presidential debates were crucial to this effort, for they put Obama in a straight match-up with the far more seasoned McCain, giving Obama the opportunity to appear equally "presidential."

Obama largely succeeded and was, according to all of the national polls, the consensus winner of all three debates.[3]

In the end, voters opted for change over experience. The twin burdens of Bush's unpopularity and the economic meltdown left McCain few options for a winning strategy. He had to hope Obama would falter, making mistakes and reinforcing the doubts the McCain campaign tried to raise about his character and qualifications. But Obama kept his focus and avoided mistakes, mounted the best organized and financed presidential campaign in history, and won a larger share of the popular vote than any Democrat since Lyndon Johnson in 1964, 52.6 percent to McCain's 46.1.* His margin in the Electoral College was even larger, 365 to 173. The political climate was as toxic for Republican House and Senate candidates as for McCain, and Democrats augmented their congressional majorities with an additional six seats in the Senate and twenty-one seats in the House. A time of change, to be led by the first African American president, was clearly at hand.

As the example of 2008 shows, elections forge the main link between public opinion and government action in the United States. They not only prompt elected officials to take voters' views into account when they make policy choices but also provide a reason for citizens to form opinions on issues and candidates. For candidates, public opinion serves as the raw material of electoral politics. As we saw in Chapter 10, Americans are divided on a broad range of political issues. Often, the divisions do not form consistent patterns; different groups come together on different issues. The challenge for each candidate is to find ways to persuade voters of disparate and often conflicting views to agree on a common action, which is to vote for the candidate. Building coalitions—getting people to agree on an action in the absence of agreement on the purposes of the action—is what pluralist politics is all about, and it is as fundamental to electoral politics as it is to governing. The challenge for voters is to figure out which candidates will best serve their interests and represent their values. The way voters and candidates attempt to meet these challenges is the subject of this chapter. To begin, however, we need to examine the logic of elections and their historical development in the United States.

The Logic of Elections

Democracy in America is representative democracy. James Madison, in defending the Constitution in *Federalist* No. 10, adopted the term *republic* to emphasize the distinction between democracy as eighteenth century Americans saw it and the proposed new system:

> The two great points of difference between a democracy and a republic are: first, the delegation of the government, in the latter, to a small number of citizens elected by the rest; secondly, the greater number of citizens, and greater sphere of country, over which the latter may be extended.

---

*The results for the 2008 elections are tentative as of November 10, 2008, pending a complete count of ballots.

The sheer size of the new nation made self-government by direct democracy impossible (imagine the transaction costs). If the American people were to govern themselves at all, they would have to do it indirectly through the delegation of their authority to a small number of representative agents. But delegation raised the unavoidable danger, immediately acknowledged by Madison, that these agents might use their authority to serve themselves rather than the people they are supposed to represent: "Men of fractious tempers, of local prejudices, or of sinister designs, may, by intrigue, by corruption, or by other means, first obtain the suffrages [votes], and then betray the interests of the people."

As noted in Chapter 1, any delegation of authority raises the possibility of agency loss. Whenever we engage someone to act on our behalf, we face the risk that they will put their interests ahead of ours. Worse, it is often difficult to tell whether they are faithful agents because we cannot see what they do or know why they are doing it. The problem of delegation has no perfect solutions. One effective, if *imperfect,* solution adopted by representative democracies is to hold regular, free, competitive elections. Elections ameliorate the delegation problem in several ways. First, they give ordinary citizens a say in who represents them. Second, the prospect of future elections gives officeholders who want to keep (or improve) their jobs a motive to be responsive agents. And third, elections provide powerful incentives for the small set of citizens who want to replace the current officeholders to keep a close eye on representatives and to tell everyone else about any misconduct they detect.

Elections do not guarantee faithful representation; indeed, many Americans today do not feel faithfully represented (see Figure 10-8, page 490), even though the United States holds more elections for more public offices than any other nation in the world. But the absence of regular, free, competitive elections does make it unlikely that ordinary citizens will be faithfully represented. Competitive elections in which virtually all adult citizens are eligible to vote are the defining feature of modern democratic governments.

The Right to Vote

The practice of selecting leaders by ballot arrived in North America with the first settlers from England. So, too, did the practice of limiting suffrage. Every colony imposed a property qualification for voting, and many denied the franchise to Catholics, Jews, Native Americans, and freed black slaves. No colony allowed women to vote.

Many of these restrictions survived the Revolution intact; only about half of the free adult male population was eligible to vote at the time the Constitution was adopted. The story since that time has been the progressive, if sometimes frustratingly slow, extension of the franchise to virtually all adult citizens (defined as people who have celebrated their eighteenth birthdays) not in prisons or mental institutions. Every expansion of suffrage had to overcome both philosophical objections and resistance rooted in the mundane calculations of political advantage. The triumph of (nearly) universal adult suffrage reflects the powerful appeal of democratic ideas, combined

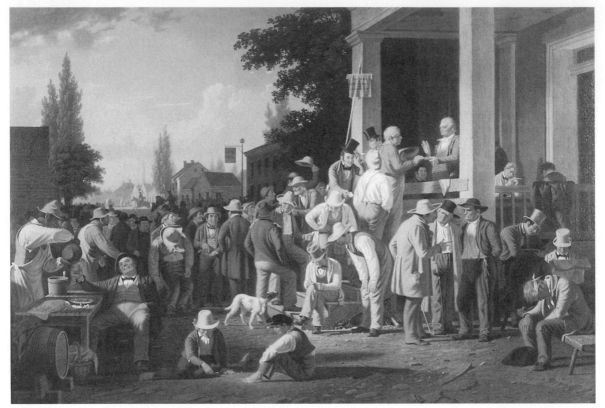

Nineteenth-century itinerant American artist George Caleb Bingham sometimes depicted local campaign scenes. In fact, Bingham was as much politician as painter. An ardent supporter of Whig candidate William Henry Harrison in the 1840 presidential election, Bingham gave speeches and painted banners. He also was elected to the Missouri legislature (on his second attempt) and later served as state treasurer. In *County Election* citizens line up to declare their votes publicly. Although the painting offers a stylized image of democracy in early America, the inebriated voter toward the end of the line being helped to the poll serves as a reminder that this painter-politician also had the sensibilities of a realist, to be expected of someone who once had been narrowly defeated for election.

with profound social changes, the struggles of dedicated activists, and the perpetual scramble of politicians for votes.

Wider Suffrage for Men

The property qualifications and voting restrictions brought over from England in colonial times reflected the basic social realities there. Most adults were poor, illiterate, and dependent; they were servants, tenants, hired hands, or paupers. Members of the upper-class minority—a well born, prosperous, and educated elite—took for granted their right to govern. They were not about to risk the existing social order, which served them so well, by extending voting rights to people whose interests might be better served by changing it. The trip across the Atlantic took some of the bite out of the property qualifications. Land was easier to acquire and far more evenly distributed in the colonies than in England, so a larger proportion of adult males qualified to vote. In the more fluid colonial communities, property restrictions often were enforced laxly if at all. By the revolutionary period any "respectable" man—meaning white, Protestant, and gainfully employed—was, in practice, allowed to vote in many places.[4]

The Revolutionary War exerted a powerful influence on the demands to enlarge the franchise. The rallying cry against England of "no taxation without representation," initially a demand for home rule, also implied that anyone who paid taxes should have the right to vote. Men who risked their lives in the fight for independence felt entitled to full political citizenship regardless of wealth. More important and more long-lasting, the ringing pronouncements in the Declaration of Independence that "all men are created equal" and enjoy unalienable rights to "Life, Liberty, and the pursuit of Happiness" and that governments derive "their just powers from the consent of the governed" left little ground for denying voting rights to any citizen.

Still, universal suffrage for (white) men was not fully achieved until the 1840s in the wake of the triumph of Jacksonian democracy. The rear guard defense of suffrage restrictions rested on traditional arguments: people without a stake in the social order should not have a voice in governing it. If every man were allowed to vote, the votes of those dependent on the wealthy for their livelihoods—employees, tenant farmers, servants, and apprentices—would be controlled by their patrons, enhancing the power of the rich. If, to avoid such untoward influence, a secret ballot were used, the more numerous poor might support unscrupulous demagogues promoting schemes to redistribute wealth. The argument for limiting suffrage boiled down to this: only the independent and virtuous were fit to govern, and the best evidence of independence and virtue was being a property-holding, white, Protestant male.

Gradually, however, this view lost ground to the argument for political equality implicit in the Declaration of Independence, and opposition to universal male suffrage became a political liability. The more democratic the electorate, the more politically suicidal it was to oppose more democracy. The French observer Alexis de Tocqueville noted with his usual clarity:

> There is no more invariable rule in the history of society: the further electoral rights are extended, the greater is the need of extending them; for after each concession the strength of the democracy increases, and its demands increase with its strength. . . . Concession follows concession, and no stop can be made short of universal suffrage.[5]

Suffrage for Women

As Tocqueville correctly observed, the democratic logic that justified giving the vote to all white men did not stop there; it also nurtured demands that all adult citizens, regardless of race or sex, be eligible to vote. For more than a century, race, sex, and the institution of slavery interacted to complicate suffrage politics. The women's suffrage movement grew directly out of the antislavery movement, sharing its underlying ideals and some of its activists. Suffragists felt betrayed when the Civil War amendments (formally, if not in practice) enfranchised the newly freed black men but not white or black women. The largely successful effort by white southerners to purge blacks from the electorate after the end of Reconstruction (see Chapter 4) raised a major barrier to giving women the vote. Southern whites opposed any action that

SHALL WOMEN VOTE?
No, They Might Disturb the Existing Order of Things

The campaign to give women the right to vote was fueled by the hope that their presence in the electorate would improve the moral tone of political life. This 1909 cartoon, captioned "Shall Women Vote? No, they might disturb the existing order of things," suggests that the existing order was thoroughly corrupt and thus ought to be disturbed.

might focus national attention on repressive local electoral practices. As one Mississippi senator candidly put it in the 1880s, "We are not afraid to maul a black man over the head if he dares to vote but we can't treat women, even black women, that way. No, we'll allow no woman suffrage. It may be right, but we won't have it."[6]

The resistance to women's suffrage was gradually overcome by a combination of social change—the expansion of education for both sexes, the entry of women into the workforce outside the home—and political need. Western territories (later states) were the first to grant women the right to vote, not because places like Wyoming and Utah were hotbeds of radical democracy but because women were expected to vote for "family values" in raw frontier communities. The campaign for suffrage sometimes took on nativist overtones, proposing to use women's votes to uphold Anglo-Saxon civilization; indeed, many suffragists did not object to the literacy tests, poll taxes, and other devices designed to keep the "wrong" sorts of people out of the electorate. As women's suffrage grew at the state and local levels, politicians competing for women's votes naturally supported further expansion. Once party politicians sensed an irresistible trend, they scrambled to make sure their side was not stigmatized for standing in the way. Only southern Democrats held out to the bitter end; the defense of white supremacy trumped everything else.[7] The Nineteenth Amendment to the Constitution, adopted in 1920, finally guaranteed women everywhere the right to vote.

Suffrage for African Americans, Young Americans

Despite ratification of the Civil War amendments, the effective extension of the vote to blacks and other minorities came much later, again as a result of social changes and the political incentives they produced. The story, crowned by the landmark Voting Rights Act of 1965, is told in Chapter 4.

The most recent expansion of voting rights—the Twenty-sixth Amendment (1971), which lowered the voting age of citizens to eighteen years—also was a political move, one provoked by the Vietnam War. The idea appealed to antiwar activists because young people were so prominent in their movement. Politicians who supported the war also endorsed the amendment because it enfranchised the troops fighting in Vietnam, most of whom were under the age of twenty-one. The movement echoed the logic advanced after the Revolutionary War that those who risk their lives on the battlefield ought to have a voice in governing the nation they are defending.

Consider, though, what consequences did *not* ensue from the formal expansions of suffrage. The propertyless did not despoil the propertied; hence the conformity cost most dreaded by defenders of limited suffrage never materialized. Votes for women did not immediately transform electoral politics in any measurable way: no distinctive pattern of women's voting was evident until the 1980s, following a steep increase in the proportion of single working women in the electorate. The only discernible consequence of granting eighteen-year-olds the right to vote has been a decline in the percentage of those eligible who turn out to vote. The Fourteenth and Fifteenth Amendments did not prevent a century of racial discrimination at the polls. Only the Voting Rights Act quickly and effectively achieved its goals of increasing African American voting in states practicing discrimination. The democratic idea has yet to reach its logical limits, however. Some activists have proposed enfranchising children and noncitizen residents, even those illegally in the United States.[8] In contemporary America, "no taxation without representation" implies a remarkably inclusive franchise.

Who Uses the Right to Vote?

Most Americans agree that the right to vote is the very essence of democracy. On Memorial Day and other holidays the nation honors the soldiers who have fought and died for that privilege. If the right to vote is so valuable, then, why do millions of Americans choose not to exercise it?

It might seem paradoxical that many people who think that the right to vote is worth dying for do not bother to go to the polls. But this reality is not paradoxical at all: it is inherent in the logic of elections. The benefits of elections—in both the broad sense of maintaining democratic accountability and in the narrower sense of electing a preferred candidate—are collective benefits. People enjoy these payoffs even if they have not helped to produce them by voting. It makes perfect sense for citizens to insist on the right to vote, for it gives leaders a reason to care about people's interests, opinions, and values. But it makes equal sense not to bother voting if the only purpose in voting is to influence leaders. After all, the likelihood that any single vote will influence anyone or anything is minute. Totaled up, votes are decisive; individually, they count for next to nothing. Why then spend the time and energy required to go to the polls if individual participation, or its absence, makes no difference in the outcome of the election? The real question is not so much why millions of Americans do not vote, but why millions of Americans forgo free riding and *do* vote.

The same logic applies to gathering information about the competing candidates and parties if a person chooses to vote. There is no point in investing time, energy, or money in becoming better informed about electoral options because the payoff for casting the "right" vote—for the candidate who would, in the voter's view, do the best job—is for all practical purposes nil. If there is no real chance that a vote will be decisive, it is of no consequence whether the vote is right or wrong. Ignorance, like abstention from voting, is rational.

Followed to its logical conclusion, this idea would lead to the collapse of electoral politics and thus to the collapse of democracy: no voters, no accountability, no consent of the governed. In practice, however, these free-rider problems are overcome, but they are overcome quite imperfectly and in ways that have important consequences for how American democracy actually works.

The share of eligible voters who go to the polls has varied widely over American history (turnout patterns are traced in Chapter 12). The most important change in the past half-century was the sharp decline in voter turnout between 1968 and 1972. Since then, an average of only about 58 percent of the eligible electorate has bothered to register and vote in presidential elections; even the hotly contested 2008 race inspired a turnout of only about 61 percent.[9] Variations in turnout pose the questions we address in this section: who votes, why, and to what effect? Why did turnout rates fall after the 1960s, and does it matter?

Individual Factors Affecting Turnout

A great deal of research has gone into figuring out who votes, who does not, and why. The state of the art in this endeavor is represented by the work of political scientists Steven J. Rosenstone and John Mark Hansen; their findings are partially summarized in Table 11-1.[10] The entries in the table indicate the difference a particular factor makes in the likelihood of voting (with the effect of the rest held constant). For example, other things being equal, turnout in midterm elections (when people vote for senators and representatives but not the president) is twenty-seven percentage points higher for the most educated as compared with the least educated. In presidential elections turnout among the oldest citizens is twenty-nine points higher than it is among the youngest citizens.

Age and education have the strongest influence on voting, but many other things affect turnout as well. African Americans and Hispanics are less likely to vote (taking all other factors into account), as are people who live in southern states or states bordering the south. People with deeper roots in their communities (longer-time residents, homeowners, church members, and people with jobs) are more likely to go to the polls, as are individuals with greater confidence in their own ability to understand and engage in politics (internal efficacy, as it is known in political science) and in their ability to influence the decisions of government (external efficacy). Turnout also is higher among people with stronger partisan views and electoral preferences and those who live in areas with active parties and competitive campaigns. Finally, turnout is higher where legal barriers to registration are lower.

Why is sex missing from this list of influences on voting? Other things being equal, the voting rates for men and women are about the same. Also absent are measures of trust in government and beliefs about government responsiveness; the cynical and distrusting are as likely to vote as everyone else. This point contradicts a popular explanation for the decline in participation—that it results from the dramatic increase in public cynicism and mistrust since 1960.[11]

The explanation for these patterns is straightforward. Voting and other forms of political participation, such as contributing money or time to campaigns, writing letters to elected officials, and attending political meetings, incur costs but produce benefits. People participate when they can meet the costs and appreciate the benefits. Those with money, education, experience, free time, and self-confidence find it easier to meet the costs; those with a greater psychological stake in politics—from a concern with issues, a sense of obligation to carry out their duties as citizens, or a strong interest

---

TABLE 11-1

Influences on Voter Turnout

	Presidential Elections	Midterm Elections
Demographic Characteristics		
Income	15.8	4.6
Education	16.6	27.0
Age	29.0	25.7
African American	−4.4	−8.5
Mexican American and Puerto Rican	−5.7	−9.3
Lives in southern state	−16.3	−9.8
Lives in border state	−6.1	−8.4
Social Involvement		
Years in community	10.7	23.3
Church attendance	15.1	10.2
Homeowner	7.5	5.5
Currently employed	2.1	
Psychological Characteristics		
Internal efficacy	2.9	
External efficacy	10.6	8.2
Evaluation of Parties and Candidates		
Strength of party identification	10.6	17.5
Affect for a party	11.4	
Cares which party wins presidential election	6.4	
Cares which party wins congressional elections		20.7
Affect for a presidential candidate	5.6	
Mobilization by Parties and Campaigns		
Contacted by a party	7.8	10.4
Close presidential election	3.0	
Gubernatorial election	5.0	
Open House seat		3.7
Unopposed House seat		−4.0
Toss-up House election		6.0
Legal Organization of Elections		
Voter registration closing date	−5.6	
Literacy test (African Americans)	−16.0	
Poll tax (African Americans)	−10.2	
Periodic registration (African Americans)	−11.6	
Voting Rights Act (African Americans)	26.4	
Voting Rights Act (whites)	19.5	

Source: Steven J. Rosenstone and John Mark Hansen, *Mobilization, Participation, and Democracy in America* (New York: Macmillan, 1993), 130–131. Copyright © 1993 by Macmillan Publishing Company. Reprinted by permission of Pearson Education, Inc.

Notes: Data for presidential elections cover 1956 through 1988; data for midterm elections cover 1974 through 1986. *Table entries are the differences in turnout rates between the highest and lowest values taken by each variable, controlling for the effects of the other variables.* For income, it is the difference between people in the highest (top 4 percent) and lowest (bottom 16 percent) of five income groups; for education, it is the difference between people with some college and people with no more that an eighth-grade education. For age, it is the difference between the oldest and youngest citizens. Party affect is measured by the absolute value of the sum of positive comments about the first party and negative comments about the second minus the sum of positive comments about the second party and negative comments about the first (responses to questions about what respondents liked and disliked about the parties); affect toward presidential candidates is measured equivalently. The voter registration closing date indicates the number of days prior to the election that one can last register to vote. Voting Rights Act is coded 1 if respondent lived in a state covered by the Voting Rights Act in 1986 or 1972; 0 otherwise.

The elderly vote. Free time, a distaste for taxes, and dependence on government retirement programs render the elderly a highly vigilant, issue-oriented electorate whom politicians approach with some fear and great care.

in parties or candidates—receive greater benefits (also mainly psychological) from participation. Voting, therefore, is rational for the millions of individuals who derive personal satisfaction from going to the polls. Expressing themselves through voting outweighs the typically modest cost of casting a ballot.

Institutional Factors Affecting Turnout

Differences in participation cannot be explained completely by individual differences in resources and psychological involvement, however. The institutional context—for example, variations in registration laws—affects turnout equally. The more onerous the registration requirement, the higher is the cost of voting. In the decades after the Civil War southern states adopted devices such as poll taxes, literacy tests, and the requirement that voters reregister periodically to discourage African Americans from voting. In many cases, these practices also discouraged poor whites from participating as well. But after the Voting Rights Act of 1965 banned literacy tests and authorized the Justice Department to oversee voter registration in states with a history of flagrant racial discrimination, voting among African Americans (and whites, too) increased sharply. Still, the effects of old practices linger on. Even with the end of formal and informal restrictions on voting and the advent of two-party competition in their region, southerners are notably less likely to vote than are Americans who reside elsewhere.

Social circumstances also play a crucial part in stimulating turnout. Social connections create personal incentives to participate when, for example, coworkers take note of who is performing their citizen's duty to vote (and who is wearing the "I voted" sticker). These connections also provide plenty of free information through casual conversation touching on politics. Even more significant, however, are the deliberate efforts of political activists of all kinds to get people to vote. Often, people participate because they are asked, a fact that has never been a secret to politicians. The desire to win elections has inspired extensive efforts by candidates, parties, interest groups, and other campaigners to get their potentially free-riding supporters to show up at the polls. The massive and effective turnout efforts mounted by the Obama campaign in 2008 are a case in point.

The assorted demographic and institutional influences on voting produce an elec-torate in which wealthy, well-educated, older white people are overrepresented and the poor, uneducated, young, and nonwhite are underrepresented. Unequal resources are only part of the reason. The other is that people with social advantages are more likely to be mobilized by parties, interest groups, and campaign organizations. Politi-cal leaders deploy their scarce resources efficiently, targeting the people who are cheapest to reach and likeliest to respond. In other words, they go after people like themselves (educated and relatively affluent), people already organized and identified by membership in voluntary associations, and people whose social characteristics already incline them to participate. "Thus," in the words of Rosenstone and Hansen, "the pressures that political leaders face to use their own resources most effectively build a class bias into their efforts to mobilize."[12]

Variations in Turnout over Time

If these factors explain variations in participation among individuals, what accounts for variations in turnout over time? More specifically, why did turnout decline from an average of about 68 percent in 1952–1968 to about 58 percent since then? (See Figure 12-3, page 573.) The decline has been especially puzzling to scholars because voter registration laws have been eased and educational attainment has risen—two trends that should have increased turnout. But they have not done so because their ef-fects have been more than offset by contrary trends. Rosenstone and Hansen's analysis of the forces contributing to changes in turnout is summarized in Table 11-2.

Easier registration and increased formal education have had a positive effect on turnout, but other changes have had the opposite effect. For example, extending the franchise to eighteen-year-olds reduced the turnout percentage by enlarging the pool of eligible voters with the age group least inclined to vote—citizens younger than twenty-five. Turnout also has declined because fewer people have deep community roots, feel politically efficacious, or feel strongly about parties and candidates.

The major reasons for the decline, however, are institutional: a decline in **mobiliza-tion** by parties, candidates, and groups such as labor unions. Fewer people are voting in part because fewer people are being mobilized—that is, being asked to vote by neigh-borhood activists working for parties or candidates. Most candidates and parties have replaced labor-intensive door-to-door campaigns with money-intensive television and direct-mail campaigns. Moreover, because media campaigns are so expensive, parties and others concentrate scarce resources on the tightest races, thereby reducing attempts to mobilize voters in less-competitive races. The fading of the civil rights movement di-minished efforts to get African Americans to register and vote. The decline of the labor movement eroded the unions' traditional grassroots campaigning, though in recent elections labor leaders have sought, with some success, to reverse this trend. When the competing presidential campaigns invested heavily in grassroots activities to get out the vote in 2004 and 2008, turnout rose significantly. In short, turnout is directly affected by the activities of political entrepreneurs pursuing offices or policies. When their goals

TABLE 11-2

Sources of the Decline in Voter Turnout between the 1960s and 1980s

Change	Effect on Percentage Change in Turnout between 1960s and 1980s	Percentage of Total Decline in Turnout
Easing of voter registration laws	+1.8	
Increased formal education	+2.8	
A younger electorate	−2.7	17
Weakened social involvement	−1.4	9
Declining feelings of political efficacy	−1.4	9
Weakened attachment to and evaluation of political parties and their candidates	−1.7	11
Decline in mobilization	−8.7	54
Net change in voter turnout	**−11.3**	**100**

Source: Steven J. Rosenstone and John Mark Hansen, *Mobilization, Participation, and Democracy in America* (New York: Macmillan, 1993), 215. Copyright © 1993 by Macmillan Publishing Company. Reprinted by permission of Pearson Education, Inc.

Note: The first column lists the net contribution of each change in electoral conditions to changes in the turnout rate between the 1960s and 1980s; the second column indicates the proportion of the total change in turnout over this period accounted for by each factor.

and tactics change, so does the level of electoral participation.[13]

The decline in voting turnout after the 1960s was much more pronounced among those whose participation is most dependent on outside stimulation: the poorest and least-educated citizens. In general, the smaller the electorate, the greater is its upper-class bias. Logically, a biased electorate should produce biased policy because politicians naturally cater to the people whose votes control their futures. In confronting a budget deficit in the 1980s, for example, Congress was more willing to cut social welfare programs benefiting poor people (food stamps, job training programs, and aid to families with dependent children) than to cut social welfare programs benefiting the politically active middle class (Social Security and Medicare). Even so, the systematic evidence suggests that the policy preferences of voters and nonvoters are usually not very different and that few, if any, election results would change if every eligible person voted.[14] Such evidence has not, however, kept policies designed to raise turnout from provoking partisan squabbles (see box "The Motor Voter Law").

How Do Voters Decide?

Casting a vote is making a prediction about the future—that electing one candidate will produce a better outcome in some relevant sense than electing another candidate. To make such a prediction, a voter has to choose the standards for "better" and "relevant" and then determine which candidate best meets the standards. These choices are made under conditions of considerable uncertainty, and because the likelihood of casting a decisive vote is so tiny, people find it makes little sense to put much effort into acquiring information that might reduce uncertainty. Thus they economize by using simple cues as cognitive shortcuts and by relying heavily, if selectively, on the free information delivered by the news media, campaign advertising, opinion leaders, and their own experience to inform their predictions.

Past Performance and Incumbency

One way to predict the future is to look at the past. Voters may treat an election as a referendum on the incumbent's or majority party's performance in office. Has the

LOGIC OF POLITICS

The Motor Voter Law

Tens of millions of eligible Americans do not bother to vote in national elections. This rampant free riding inspires chronic editorial hand-wringing and numerous projects for boosting turnout. Any attempt to raise turnout through legislation, however, automatically becomes a partisan issue. Politicians believe, despite evidence to the contrary, that higher turnout favors Democrats.[1]

The National Voter Registration Act of 1993, popularly known as the motor voter law, is a case in point. Enacted over Republican opposition, the law requires states to allow citizens to register to vote when applying for or renewing their drivers' licenses, to register by mail, or to receive mail registration forms and assistance in filling them out at state welfare offices. It also forbids states to purge voters from the rolls for failing to vote. The purpose of the bill is to increase turnout by making registration easy—in other words, by reducing the cost to the citizen.

Republicans attacked the proposal in Congress and later in the courts as, in the words of Republican senator Paul Coverdell of Georgia, "a classic example of a bully government placing an extreme financial burden on our states."[2] Their real concern, however, was not the unfunded mandate (see Chapter 8), but the prospect of hordes of new Democratic voters. Ironically, the law's effect so far has favored Republicans; the regions with the largest increases in registration under the law have been Republican strongholds in the South and West.

The motor voter law added millions to the voter rolls, and analysts suggest that it has the potential to increase turnout by as much as ten percentage points.[3] But voting participation was actually lower in the presidential (1996 and 2000) and midterm (1998) elections held after the law took effect than in the two comparable elections immediately before (1992 and 1994). Many of the new registrants apparently did not immediately begin voting, indicating that the cost of registering was not what was keeping them from the polls. The large increases in turnout for 2004 and 2008, especially among young voters, may have been facilitated by the law, but intensive registration campaigns and strong feelings aroused by the competing presidential candidates probably had more to do with it.

1. Benjamin Highton and Raymond E. Wolfinger, "The Political Implications of Higher Turnout" (paper presented at the annual meeting of the American Political Science Association, Boston, September 3–6, 1998).

2. Alan Greenblatt, "Court Rejects 'Motor Voter' Case, But the Battle Isn't Over," *Congressional Quarterly Weekly Report*, January 27, 1996, 232.

3. Benjamin Highton and Raymond E. Wolfinger, "Estimating the Effects of the National Voter Registration Act of 1993," *Political Behavior* 20 (June 1998): 79–94.

current agent done an adequate job of serving the voters' values and interests? One simple rule is to vote for incumbents who have performed well. The question then becomes, performance on what? The answer depends on the office, the circumstances, and what the voter considers important. Presidents seeking reelection often are held accountable for the national economy—the rates of inflation, unemployment, and economic growth. Economic problems probably cost Jimmy Carter and George H. W. Bush their jobs, while a strong economy contributed to Ronald Reagan's reelection in 1984 and to Bill Clinton's in 1996. The question famously posed by Reagan captures this standard: "Are you better off now than you were four years ago?" Presidents also may be reviewed for their conduct of foreign policy. Dwight Eisenhower's success in ending the war in Korea helped ensure his reelection in 1956; Carter's inability to obtain the release of the U.S. diplomats held hostage by Iran damaged his reelection chances in 1980. George W. Bush's reelection hinged in good part on how voters weighed his response to the September 11, 2001, attacks, particularly his decision to invade Iraq. The performance of representatives and senators, by contrast, is often measured by their success in providing services and projects for their states and districts or in casting acceptable votes in Congress (see Chapter 6). But some voters hold the president's party as a whole responsible, casting their congressional votes according to how well they think the administration has governed. Many of the voters who were upset with President Clinton in 1994 took it out on Democratic candidates for Congress. Similarly, many voters unhappy with President Bush and the Iraq War took it out on congressional Republicans in 2006.

Assessing the Issues and Policy Options

How can voters assess performance efficiently? Personal experience supplies a good deal of politically relevant information. Looking for a job, shopping at the supermarket, or trying to get a mortgage to buy a house teaches people about unemployment, inflation, and interest rates. Taking out a student loan or applying for veterans' benefits teaches something about government programs. Millions of retired Americans are keenly aware of the size of their monthly Social Security checks. The threat of a military draft certainly raised the political consciousness of college-age Americans during the Vietnam War. Those without direct experience with certain issues learn about them through the news media. For example, crime became a bigger public issue in the 1990s than it had been a decade earlier—even though the crime rate had actually declined—because of the greater emphasis the news media put on it. And, of course, Americans needed no direct personal experience of terrorist attacks and the Iraq War for these events to shape their judgments of George W. Bush's fitness for reelection in 2004.

Another strategy for predicting which candidate will be the more satisfactory agent is to compare the future policy options they represent. By the positions they take on issues, by their overall ideological stances, or by their party affiliations, candidates offer choices among alternative national policies. Which policy positions matter? The answer depends on the voters and current circumstances. For voters with strong views on abortion, any difference between candidates on this issue may be enough to settle their choice. **Single-issue voters** also coalesce around causes such as gun control (its most adamant opponents) and environmental protection (its most adamant proponents).

Instead of a single issue, other voters may consider bundles of issues, choosing between, say, the expectations of lower taxes and more generous social spending. The times also may determine which issues become important to voters. Civil rights became critical in the 1964 election when the Republican candidate, Sen. Barry Goldwater of Arizona, voted against the Civil Rights Act of 1964. What to do about Vietnam dominated voter opinion while American soldiers were fighting there. Similarly, the wisdom of invading Iraq was central to voters' deliberations in 2004. Iraq was expected to be the central issue again in 2008, but with the collapse of housing prices, frozen credit markets, a plummeting stock market and a looming recession, the economy overwhelmed all other issues.

Voter Cues and Shortcuts

The news media and the campaigns supply plenty of free information about candidates' positions on the issues and policy promises.

Endorsements by well-known interest groups give voters cheap and reliable cues about the policy inclinations of candidates. Here, Vice President Dick Cheney accepts the gift of a fancy flintlock rifle from leaders of the National Rifle Association (President Kayne Robinson, right, and Vice President Wayne LaPierre, left), an unmistakable signal to voters on either side of the gun control issue that the 2004 Bush-Cheney ticket stood with the NRA against greater regulation of firearms.

But voters cannot take the information at face value, for candidates have an incentive to misrepresent themselves to win votes. Voters can deal with this problem by taking cues from opinion leaders (see Chapter 10). In electoral politics, opinion leadership is often formalized through endorsements from organizations and individuals. A candidate supported by the National Abortion and Reproductive Rights Action League, the Reverend Jesse Jackson, and the Sierra Club is certain to have rather different policy objectives from one endorsed by the Christian Coalition, the National Rifle Association, and the National Taxpayers Union.

Voters also make predictions based on the candidates' personal characteristics. One set of personal considerations includes qualities such as competence, experience, honesty, knowledge, and leadership skills. Another set includes characteristics such as sex, race, ethnicity, age, and place of residence. The rationale for such criteria is straightforward. Voters cannot anticipate all the problems and issues that will come up after the election, nor can they easily monitor the behavior of their elected officials. Much of what these agents do is out of public sight, and much of the information they act on is unknown to their constituents. Under these circumstances, using personal criteria makes a great deal of sense. A candidate's demographic features give voters clues about his or her personal values. Voters feel that people who are like them in some tangible way are more likely to think and act as they would in the same circumstances. As an African American, Barack Obama faced the challenge of convincing a majority of voters that, although he may not look like them, he nonetheless understood their needs and values and would thus be an effective agent for them. A candidate's competence and character give clues about how far he or she can be trusted to do the right thing even when no one is watching.

The most important information shortcut voters use to make predictions is the **party label.** A large majority of voters continue to take their cues from the parties, even though popular attitudes toward parties as institutions tend to range from indifference to outright hostility.[15] The party label provides useful information for both **performance voting** (voting for the party in control, or "in-party," when one thinks the government is performing well; voting for the "outs" when one thinks the party in charge is performing poorly) and **issue voting** (the typical positions of Republicans and Democrats differ in predictable ways on many issues). Most voters drastically simplify their electoral evaluations and decisions by developing a consistent bias in favor of the candidates of one of the major parties, making party label the most influential "endorsement" of all.

The Power of Party Identification

As the best single predictor of the vote in federal elections, **party identification** is a central focus of modern electoral research (see Chapter 10). Since the 1950s a biennial survey, the American National Election Study, has asked scientifically selected samples of the American public a set of questions probing the strength and direction of their partisanship. Respondents are first asked, "Generally speaking, do you usually think of yourself as a Republican, a Democrat, an independent, or what?" Those who answer "Democrat" or "Republican" are then asked, "Would you call yourself a strong Democrat (Republican) or a not very strong Democrat (Republican)?" Those who answer "independent" or something else are then asked, "Do you think of yourself as closer to the Republican Party or the Democratic Party?" Answers to these questions locate respondents on a seven-point scale: strong Democrats, weak Democrats, independents leaning Democratic, pure independents, independents leaning Republican, weak Republicans, and strong Republicans. This scale serves as the standard measure of party identification.

Party identification has proven to be a strong predictor of the vote in any election in which candidates run under party labels. In 2004, for example, about 97 percent of the strong partisans voted for their own party's presidential candidate; weaker partisans were less loyal, and pure independents split their votes nearly evenly between the two major-party candidates. In general, the weaker a survey respondent's partisanship, the more likely he or she was to vote for a minor-party candidate (see Figure 11-1).

The connection between party identification and vote choice varies over time but is always quite powerful. Figure 11-2 shows that in elections from 1952 through 2004,

Figure 11-1 Party Identification: A Strong Predictor of the Presidential Vote

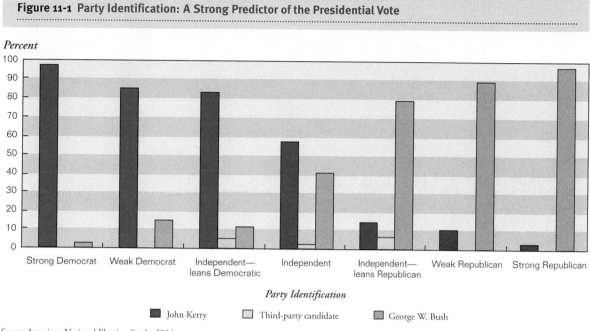

Source: American National Election Study, 2004.

Figure 11-2 Partisan Voting in Presidential Elections

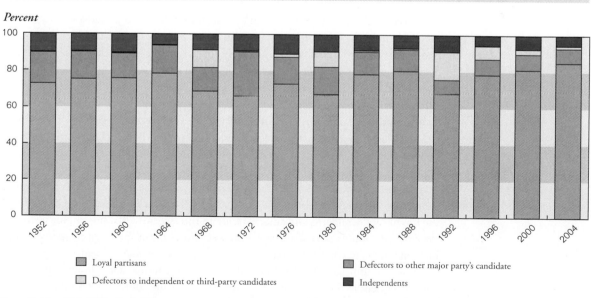

Source: American National Election Studies.

typically about three-quarters of presidential voters were self-identified partisans supporting their party's candidate. Their portion of the electorate has been growing since the 1970s, and in 2004 it reached 85 percent, its highest level yet (comparable data for 2008 are not yet available). The proportion defecting to the opposing party's candidate ranged from 7.6 percent to 24.1 percent, and the proportion voting for independent or third-party candidates varied from less than 1 percent to 15.3 percent. Usually, less than 10 percent are pure independents who claim to favor neither party. Still, there are enough independents and partisan defectors to keep party identification alone from determining who wins or loses presidential elections.

Election Campaigns

If voters are short of information and uncertain about their choices, the candidates and their allies are only too happy to help them out. Experienced campaigners are fully aware of voters' reliance on free information and cognitive shortcuts, and they concoct strategies for winning votes accordingly. Each campaign emphasizes selected facts and cues aimed at getting at least a plurality of voters to the polls. The choice among strategic options depends on what the candidate and campaign staff believe will work in *this* contest in *this* year with *this* electorate. Campaigns are intensely pragmatic, opportunistic affairs, highly variable because they must adapt to circumstances that are highly variable—the office in question, whether the contest is a primary or general election, and current political events and issues. Nonetheless, all competitive campaigns have features in common because they face many of the same challenges.

The Basic Necessities: Candidates and Messages

The basic necessities of any campaign are a candidate, a message, and a way to inform voters about both. A **candidate** is a person who can be portrayed as sufficiently qualified and trustworthy for the job. Achieving this status is not as simple as it sounds. Members of the House of Representatives often run unopposed because no one is willing to take them on in the primary or general election. Even more often, members run against candidates so lacking in political experience, talent, temperament, or background that voters do not consider them seriously as viable choices. Sometimes, although less frequently, senators are equally lucky: Sen. Bob Dole of Kansas, for example, was opposed in 1986 by a candidate who reportedly abhorred advertising and large crowds.[16] Guess who won?

Because potential candidates think strategically, the quality of House and Senate candidates varies with their prospects for success. The smaller the chances of winning, the less likely the talented and ambitious are to run (see box "To Run or Not to Run"). Presidential contests usually attract plenty of political talent, but even the pool of presidential candidates may be affected by expectations: when President George H. W. Bush seemed unbeatable in 1991 after the Gulf War triumph, some prominent Democratic presidential prospects decided not to run, leaving room for Arkansas governor Bill Clinton, a relative unknown, to move to the front of the pack.

STRATEGY AND CHOICE

To Run or Not to Run

Variations in the quality of House and Senate candidates reflect the rational strategies of people interested in successful political careers. Politically ambitious people with the skills, resources, and experience to be effective candidates hesitate to try to move up the political ladder unless they are likely to succeed, for defeat will stall, and may effectively end, a career in electoral politics. Unless conditions are promising—say, the incumbent is in political trouble or the seat is open—the strongest potential candidates will stay out of the race and leave the field to weaker candidates for whom defeat will be less costly to their already unpromising careers.

As politicians decide to run or not to run, they also gauge the national partisan breezes. A strong economy, the absence of party scandal, or a president who enjoys the public's support might tilt the election toward the president's fellow party members, while the opposite conditions will shift the political winds toward the out-party's candidates. Because quality candidates have career investments to protect, more will come forward when national conditions are favorable to their side. Moreover, because the presence of quality candidates greatly affects the election outcome, their anticipated responses will tend to reinforce and magnify the effect of national conditions on congressional elections. The figure shows how differences in challenger quality affect election results. Note that the party with the most quality challengers for the House tended to gain a larger share of seats.

Entering fall 2001 Democratic and Republican Party officials were busy trying to entice quality candidates to run in the 2002 midterm elections. With economic indicators pointing mostly toward recession, Democrats were optimistic that they might take back control of the House and strengthen their grip on the Senate. "On Labor Day, we had them exactly where we wanted them," recalled the director of the Democratic Senate Campaign Committee. "We were talking Social Security. It was nirvana." Then on September 11 the terrorist attacks on the World Trade Center and the Pentagon totally changed the national agenda. Suddenly potential challengers in both parties found it unseemly to tout their partisan aspirations for political office. At the same time, many of the mostly Republican incumbents who had been leaning toward retirement announced that they would do their

Challenger Quality: A Factor in Party Success

In House elections the party with the most quality challengers has tended to win a larger share of House seats.

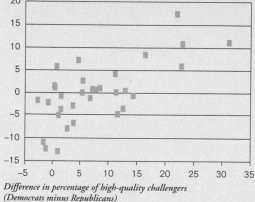

Change in percentage of House seats won by Democrats

Difference in percentage of high-quality challengers (Democrats minus Republicans)

Source: Data compiled by the authors.
Note: Datapoints represent House elections from 1946 through 2008.

patriotic duty and serve another term. Knowledgeable observers from both political parties concluded that the terrorist attacks and subsequent events deterred many quality Democratic candidates and limited the party's prospects in the 2002 elections.

The political climate in 2006 was far different. The unpopularity of the Bush administration and the Iraq War were apparent well before the election (see Chapter 10), encouraging vigorous Democratic challenges and discouraging potentially strong Republican candidates from taking on Democratic incumbents. Anticipating a favorable national tide, Democratic operatives, candidates, and contributors positioned themselves to exploit it. As a result the Democrats picked up thirty Republican seats while losing none of their own.[1] Effectively exploiting similarly favorable national conditions in 2008, the Democrats picked up another twenty-one House seats.

1. Gary C. Jacobson, "Referendum: the 2006 Midterm Congressional Elections," *Political Science Quarterly* 122 (Spring 2007): 1–24.

GETTING OUT THE MESSAGE. The **message** is the answer to the voter's question: why should I vote for this candidate rather than another? It tells voters why, *in their terms,* this particular candidate is their best choice. Messages are shaped by candidates' theories about the political beliefs, perceptions, values, and responses of different segments of the electorate. Uncertainty is so pervasive and good information about voters so valuable that campaigns invest heavily in research—if they can afford it.

Presidential campaigns can afford it, and they employ the full range of research techniques. They run hundreds of opinion surveys and conduct numerous **focus group** sessions in which a small number of ordinary citizens are observed as they talk with each other about political candidates, issues, and events. Presidential campaigns use focus groups to test their general themes as well as the specific advertisements promoting those themes. They monitor the effects of campaign ads and events with daily tracking polls that sample citizens' views on a continuing basis to measure changes in responses. In 1988 there was nothing accidental about the Bush campaign's relentless attacks on the Democratic opponent, Michael Dukakis, for being "soft on crime." Nor was it simple intuition in 1992 that made Clinton's campaign manager, James Carville, put up the now-famous sign reminding himself and the rest of the staff of their campaign's most powerful theme: "it's the economy, stupid." Nor was there anything mysterious about Clinton in 1996 endlessly repeating the vow to protect "Medicare, Medicaid, education, and the environment" or about George W. Bush choosing to define himself as a "compassionate conservative" in 2000 and the nation's shield against terrorism in 2004, or in Barack Obama's effort to tie John McCain to Bush's unpopular legacy in 2008. In each case the campaign's research told it that these messages were winners.

These examples illustrate something else about campaign messages: they are chosen opportunistically. Slow economic growth during the administration of George H. W. Bush handed the Clinton campaign in 1992 a powerful, ready-made theme, and the campaign really would have been stupid not to make the most of it. Clinton's questionable candor about his draft record, experimentation with marijuana, and alleged extramarital adventures handed the Bush campaign its central message: Bill Clinton was too untrustworthy to be president. Bob Dole took advantage of the aura of scandal permeating the first Clinton administration to make the point again in 1996. By embracing "compassionate conservativism," the younger Bush sought to attract moderate swing voters weary of the Democratic administration but repelled by the hardline conservatism displayed by congressional Republicans. Bush also vowed repeatedly to "uphold the honor and dignity of the office" of president, a not-so-subtle appeal to voters disgusted by Clinton's behavior. Imagine how different the 2004 campaigns would have been had the terrorist attacks of September 2001 never occurred or how different the 2008 campaigns would have been had the economy been booming and had Bush been popular.

The same opportunistic strategy is applied to congressional races. The House bank scandal (Chapter 6) gave House challengers a powerful message for their 1992 campaigns: vote the self-serving deadbeats out of office. The controversial hearings in 1991 over the nomination of Clarence Thomas to the Supreme Court provided another stick. Anita Hill's accusations that Thomas sexually harassed her were handled clumsily by a committee of middle-aged men, who, many women thought, "just didn't get it." The result was that a candidate's sex became an important shorthand cue for many congressional voters in 1992, who thus elected nineteen additional women to the House (for a total at the time of forty-seven) and four to the Senate (for a total of six). Candidates work hard to convey the message that they do "get it," that they understand and care about the concerns of their fellow citizens. Like other job seekers, candidates prepare glowing résumés highlighting their credentials, experience, and accomplishments. But they also try to show that, regardless of their backgrounds, they share some common ground with voters of all sorts. Patrician Yale graduate George Bush Sr. advertised his fondness for pork rinds and bass fishing to connect with ordinary folks during his campaign in 1988. Clinton's impromptu saxophone jams showed that he could be just one of the gang. It is a robust appetite for votes, not food, that leads candidates to eat bagels and lox at a corner deli in a Jewish neighborhood in the morning, black-eyed peas at an African American church at lunch, and green chili enchi-

Professional campaign strategists are an integral part of every serious national campaign and often continue to provide political advice to the winner. None has been more successful in this role than Karl Rove (shown here with John McCain during the 2004 campaign), hailed as a political genius for his strategic and tactical planning of Bush's successful campaigns in 2000 and 2004 but loathed in some (Democratic) quarters for alleged duplicity and dirty tricks. Rove served as an adviser to John McCain in 2008 despite having orchestrated a characteristically take-no-prisoners campaign against him in the 2000 Republican presidential primaries.

ladas at a Mexican American fiesta in the evening. The implicit message is empathy: "Though I may not be one of you, I appreciate your culture and understand your special needs and concerns, so I can serve effectively as your agent."

Actions intended to symbolize a candidate's concerns do not always work as planned, however. In 1972 the Democratic candidate, Sen. George McGovern of South Dakota, displayed his ignorance rather than appreciation of Jewish culture when he ordered milk to go with his kosher hot dog while campaigning in a Jewish neighborhood in Queens, New York. Handed a tamale while campaigning among Mexican American voters in San Antonio in 1976, Gerald Ford took a vigorous bite out of the inedible cornhusk wrapper, a gaffe that made all the network news broadcasts. During the 1988 presidential campaign, Michael Dukakis reaped widespread ridicule, not enhanced credentials on defense issues, when news broadcasts showed him peering out dolefully from under an ill-fitting helmet while riding on an army tank.[17] In all three instances, the action conveyed a message quite opposite to the one intended. Campaign advisers may want to display their candidates as all things to all people, but the human material often proves recalcitrant.

Acquiring and maintaining a public image appropriate to the office sought is a particular challenge for presidential candidates, who are subject to intense scrutiny by both their opponents and the news media over many months of campaigning. Most presidential primaries now take place so early in the election year—forty-one states had selected convention delegates for one or both parties by the end of February 2008—that

Despite the potential for embarrassment, candidates find it hard to resist donning unusual costumes as they pursue media attention while campaigning around the country. In 1988, Democratic presidential aspirant Michael Dukakis sought to burnish his credentials as a prospective commander in chief by donning a helmet and riding in the machine gunner's spot in an army tank. Unfortunately for him, the event produced visuals that had the opposite effect, making Dukakis the butt of countless jokes and cartoons.

campaigns begin shortly after the mid-term election, if not earlier. In years with crowded primary fields (at one time eight Democrats and seven Republicans were officially in the race for the 2008 nominations) aspirants have to fight for attention and to make sure that they, rather than their opponents or skeptical reporters, shape their public images. Candidates blessed with famous names (in 2000, George W. Bush, governor of Texas and son of a former president, and Elizabeth Dole, holder of cabinet positions in the Reagan and George H. W. Bush administrations, president of the Red Cross, and wife of the 1996 Republican candidate, Bob Dole; in 2008, Hillary Clinton) and ample money (in 2000 Bush, in 2004 Howard Dean and John Kerry, and Barack Obama, Hillary Clinton, and Mitt Romney in 2008) enjoy a distinct advantage in these endeavors, but front-runners also become all the other candidates' favorite targets, and the candidate with the most money doesn't always win the nomination, as Dean learned in 2004 and Romney learned in 2008.

Televised debates are another special challenge for presidential candidates trying to convey the message that they are right for the job. For clear front-runners, especially those not fully comfortable in front of television cameras, the risks of damaging missteps during a debate outweigh the potential gains from winning it. But the media and public now expect debates, so there is no graceful way to avoid them. For challengers and candidates behind in the polls, the nationally televised debates offer a chance to share equal billing with the leader and to make up lost ground before the largest audiences of the campaign. Independent candidate Ross Perot, for example, made the most of his opportunity in 1992, stealing the first debate from Bush and Clinton with his folksy style, populist rhetoric, and handmade charts, thereby giving his candidacy a major boost.[18] Usually, however, independent and minor-party candidates are excluded; Ralph Nader and Pat Buchanan protested vigorously but fruitlessly when they were kept out of the debates in 2000 on the ground that their support in preelection polls was too low to make them viable candidates and thus eligible to participate. Only Obama and McCain shared the debate stage in 2008; Obama, looking younger and calmer than his better-known opponent, was the consensus winner of all three of their debates, giving his candidacy an important boost.

Debates demand considerable preparation—cramming and rehearsal—as much to prevent embarrassing lapses in knowledge and misstatements as to score points. Predictably, the leading candidates focus on avoiding mistakes and tend to stick with their tried-and-true campaign themes while deflecting their opponents' efforts to shake things up. Running behind in 1996, Bob Dole went on the attack, charging Clinton with destroying Americans' faith in their government: "[Y]ou have thirty-some in your administration who have been investigated or in jail or whatever, and you've got an ethical problem. . . . I'm not talking about private, we're talking about public ethics."[19] Clinton countered with a neat (and no doubt prepared) variation on the "Medicare, Medicaid, education, and the environment" theme, declaring loftily that "no attack ever created a job or educated

Campaigning for Congress in 1938 in Crossville, Tennessee, Walter Faulkner followed the standard practice of his day: passing through towns and hamlets, attracting an audience with loudspeakers attached to his car, and "pressing the flesh." Photograph by Dorothea Lange from her Farm Security Administration series.

a child or helped a family make ends meet. No insult ever cleaned up a toxic waste dump or helped an elderly person."[20] In 2008, McCain was primed to counter Obama's argument that a McCain administration would equal a third Bush administration: "I am not President Bush," he said during their third debate. "If you want to run against President Bush, you should have run four years ago."

In 2000 the George W. Bush campaign initially seemed reluctant to schedule debates, feeding speculation that Bush's advisers feared embarrassment: with his limited knowledge of national and international issues and a propensity to trip over the English language, Bush might show to disadvantage against the experienced and thoroughly informed Al Gore. As it turned out, they need not have worried. Gore had trouble finding the middle ground between appearing too overbearing and seeming too passive. Voters found him more articulate and better informed, but Bush appeared more likeable. More important, in the eyes of Republicans and enough independents, if by no means all voters, Bush seemed sufficiently knowledgeable and coherent to qualify for the presidency. In other words, the Bush campaign won the "expectations game" played out in the media prior to the debates by keeping expectations low enough so that Bush's performance could be seen as "surprisingly" effective. The Republican vice presidential candidate in 2008, Sarah Palin, similarly benefited from low

In 2008, the presidential choice was not only between the candidates' competing policies, ideologies, and party labels, but also between generations. John McCain, at 72, was a full twenty-five years older than 47-year-old Barack Obama.

expectations by appearing lively and coherent in her debate with Democrat Joe Biden after her disastrous interview with Katie Couric on the CBS evening news.

Debates rarely cover new campaign ground, but they remain popular among the press and public because they show the presidential candidates up close under sustained pressure. They may also help frame the choice in clear terms for voters. In 2004, for example, the candidates' differences on the wisdom of the decision to invade Iraq came out starkly in the debates: repeatedly, Bush defended his choice as an integral part of the war on terrorism, while Kerry attacked it as a dangerous and unnecessary distraction from it. In 2008, the debates underlined the generational and temperamental contrasts between the two presidential aspirants as well as their stark differences on plans to deal with the economic crisis. Candidates for the House and Senate occasionally participate in debates, but incumbents often duck debates to deny their obscure opponents free publicity and the opportunity to upstage them.

NEGATIVE CAMPAIGNING. Campaign messages emphasizing one candidate's personal suitability for the job invite rebuttals from the other side. **Negative campaigning,** pointed personal criticism of the other candidate, is thus a normal if sometimes ugly component of the electoral process—and an effective one. As one Democratic consultant explained: "People say they hate negative campaigning. But it works. They hate it and remember it at the same time. The problem with positive is that you have to run it again and again to make it stick. With negative, the poll numbers will move in three or four days."[21] Campaign professionals distinguish between accurate comparative ads that highlight differences between the candidates (fair) and strictly personal attacks of dubious accuracy or relevance (unfair), although voters may not always appreciate the distinction. Negative ads exploit voters' uncertainty inherent in the delegation of authority to powerful agents. Research suggests that negative ads do inform people about the candidates but also make them less enthusiastic about voting for any particular candidate.[22]

As negative campaigns have proved effective, candidates have sought to erect defenses against them. In 1988 Bush campaign adviser Lee Atwater created a series of attack ads that succeeded in branding Dukakis, who began the campaign unfamiliar to most voters, as a far-out liberal, soft on crime and weak on defense. Four years later, Clinton's strategists, determined to prevent a similar fate for their candidate, organized a rapid response team that blanketed the news media with forceful rebuttals of every charge made by Bush or his supporters, often on the same day charges were made. They also replied swiftly to negative television ads. For example, within forty-eight hours of the broadcast of a spot criticizing Clinton for his tax record while governor of Arkansas, the Clinton campaign produced, tested with a focus group, revised, and aired its own spot that included some text from the Bush ad with "UNTRUE" stamped across it.[23] The idea was to counter negative messages before they could sink in. The wisdom of this strategy was apparent in 2004, when John Kerry was evidently hurt by his slow reaction to charges from a group calling itself the "Swift Boat Vets and POWs for Truth" that had mounted an independent campaign harshly assailing his Vietnam service. In 2008, the McCain campaign's attempt to portray Obama as someone who, as Sarah Palin put it in her stump speech, "pals around with terrorists" was forcefully countered by the Obama campaign (and by Obama himself during the third debate), and most Americans came to regard the charge as unfair.[24]

Negative or not, campaign ads are rarely subtle, for their targets are the rationally ignorant, marginally involved voters who have not already made up their minds—not the informed political sophisticates or the confirmed partisans for whom the information provided by campaigns is superfluous. As one campaign consultant put it:

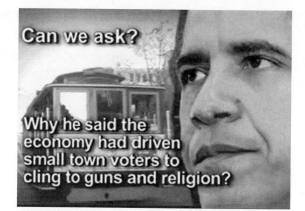

Can we ask? Why he said the economy had driven small town voters to cling to guns and religion?

Negative campaign ads are a staple, if often deplored, component of presidential campaigns. The most effective ones take advantage of a candidate's mistakes. Here, the Republican National Committee reminds voters of a statement Barack Obama made at a fundraiser in San Francisco to underline its claim that he is an elitist who looks down on ordinary middle Americans. Notice the cable car in the background to remind voters of the connection to San Francisco, a city known for its social liberalism.

> The voters have a lot more important things on their minds than political campaigns. . . . Most of the people we are trying to reach with our message don't think about [campaigns] at all until late October. They don't read all the news magazines, the *Wall Street Journal,* and two local dailies. They don't watch CNN and C-SPAN. They watch "Wheel of Fortune," and they think about politics and campaigns less than five minutes a week.[25]

Simplicity, repetition, exaggeration, and symbolism (images of home, hearth, neighborhood, and flag) are therefore the staples of political advertising.

In the end a successful campaign comes down to several basics. Its goal is to win a majority of votes, not every vote. Planners begin by using past voting records, polling, and telephone or door-to-door canvassing to figure out who is certain to support the candidate, who is up for grabs, and who is certain to support the opponent. The central clue here, at least for general elections, is the voter's party identification. The campaign is designed to appeal to the first two groups but especially to the second— particularly if, as is usually the case, the first does not amount to a majority. Campaign staffs find out where the swing voters live, what they care about, and what their mood and concerns are this year. Then campaign strategists frame the choice—establish what the election is about—in a way that underlines the candidate's strengths and plays down his or her weaknesses. In doing so, they develop a simple, coherent campaign theme that explains both why the candidate should be elected and why the opponent should not. Finally, they repeat the theme ad nauseam to reach the crucial late-deciding voters who pay almost no attention to politics. None of these things, however, can be accomplished without money.

The Other Necessity: Campaign Money

No matter how qualified the candidate is or how powerful the message, neither will count for much if voters never hear about them. Thus the third requirement of a competitive campaign is an effective way to communicate with voters. For most of America's history, party organizations and newspapers were the chief conduits for political propaganda. Parties organized marches, rallies, and picnics; supplied the speakers; did the door-to-door canvassing of potential voters; and distributed pamphlets, broadsides, and posters bearing the campaign message. The campaign itself was a team affair, agitating for the election of all of the party's candidates, although the spotlight usually was on the top of the ticket.

After World War II, however, patronage-based party organizations declined and television gained popularity as a campaign medium (see Chapter 12). As a result, parties gradually lost their central role in campaigns, to the point that today campaigns are largely the province of individual candidates and their personal organizations. Candidates assemble their own campaign teams, raise the funds, hire the consultants and technical specialists, and design and execute their own individual campaign strategies, sometimes with the help of their national or local party organizations but often without it.

All of these activities cost money. Modern campaigns for federal office are unavoidably expensive. There is simply no way for most candidates to organize and plan a campaign, do research, develop and package a message, and get that message out to potential voters on the cheap. Genuine electoral competition that gives voters a choice of agents and gives the winners an incentive to remain faithful (lest they be replaced) requires that candidates raise and spend money—lots of it. In 2006, for example, the 120 House candidates in highly competitive elections—defined as races in which the winner received 55 percent or less of the major-party vote—spent on average more than $2.25 million each. Senate candidates in competitive races typically spend much more, although the total varies with the size of the state's population. In 2004 Democratic minority leader Tom Daschle, D-S.D., spent nearly $20 million losing to challenger John Thune, who spent $14 million; their combined spending reached a record $86 per voter. The most expensive single Senate race so far was in New York in 2000, when, between them, Hillary Rodham Clinton, and Rick Lazio spent $69 million. Presidential campaigns are in a class by themselves, with total expenditures exceeding $1 billion in 2004 and $2 billion in 2008.

REGULATING CAMPAIGN MONEY. Taxpayers partially finance presidential campaigns, but a great deal of the money spent on them, and all of the money spent on House and Senate elections, comes from private sources. Privately financed elections inevitably raise two related problems for American democracy. First, democracy demands political equality: one person, one vote. But because money is distributed unequally, its role in electoral politics threatens democratic equality. Second, privately financed elections raise the suspicion that elected officials will serve as agents of their contributors rather than of their constituents. The dilemma, then, is that mean-

Sens. John McCain, R-Ariz. (left), and Russell Feingold, D-Wis. (right), were the chief sponsors of the Bipartisan Campaign Reform Act of 2002. Trent Lott, R-Miss. (center), had opposed the law, but after the 2004 campaigns, in which 80 percent of the money spent independently by the so-called "527" groups (see box, page 539) went to help Democrats, he joined the reformers' drive to expand it to include new restrictions on such organizations. Many Republicans remained unhappy with the legislation and thus with its main Republican sponsor. But McCain used his sponsorship as evidence for his maverick ways in 2008, a year when Republican orthodoxy would have been a hard sell.

ingful elections require money, but the pursuit of money can subvert the very purpose of elections.

Efforts to resolve this dilemma through regulation have enjoyed only limited success. Prior to the 1970s, campaign money was effectively unregulated. Congress had, from time to time, passed limits on contributions and spending, but the limits were easily circumvented and never enforced. This casual attitude toward campaign money faded with the spread of candidate-centered campaigns and the rise of broadcast campaigning, both of which quickly drove up costs. Higher costs accelerated not only the demand for campaign money but also the fear that the winners would favor contributors over constituents.

Congress's response was the Federal Election Campaign Act of 1971 (FECA), extensively amended in 1974. FECA provided partial public funding for presidential campaigns and required full public reporting of and strict limits on all contributions and expenditures in federal elections. It also established a Federal Election Commission to enforce the law and to collect and publish detailed information on campaign contributions and expenditures. The Supreme Court, in *Buckley v. Valeo* (1976), upheld the reporting requirements and contribution limits (to prevent "corruption or the appearance of corruption") but rejected spending limits on the ground that they interfered with political speech protected by the First Amendment.[26] Presidential candidates, however, could be required to abide by spending limits as a condition of receiving public funds for their campaigns. Also in *Buckley* the Court overturned, again on First Amendment grounds, ceilings on how much of their own money candidates could spend on their campaigns and on how much anyone could spend to agitate for or against candidates independently of candidates' campaigns.

Concerned that spending limits were choking off traditional local party activity in federal elections, Congress liberalized FECA in 1979, amending the act to allow unrestricted contributions and spending for state and local party-building and get-out-the-vote activities. A 1996 Court decision gave party organizations the right to unfettered independent spending as well.[27] Funds for these activities were commonly called **soft money,** as contrasted with the "hard money" raised and spent under FECA's limitations. When the unregulated soft money contributions to party committees ballooned, soft money became the favorite target of campaign finance reformers, and in March 2002 Congress passed the Bipartisan Campaign Reform Act (BCRA), which among other reforms prohibits parties from raising or spending soft party money for federal candidates. Aided by the high emotions generated by the presidential race, the parties countered in 2004 by raising vastly increased sums of hard money, and many former soft money donors redirected their contributions to so-called 527 committees (named after the section of the tax code dealing with them), which together spent $405 million on independent campaigns for—or, more often, against—the presidential candidates (see box "Soft Money Finds a New Home").

Broadly speaking, campaign finance operates through two parallel systems. Money going directly to candidates or parties is subject to limits on the size of contributions and full public disclosure of sources.* Presidential candidates who accept public funds also must observe spending limits. (Both Obama and McCain refused public funds for their primary campaigns in order to avoid FECA's spending limits; McCain accepted the funds and limits for the general election but Obama did not, and Obama's prodigious Internet fund-raising operation gave him a clear financial advantage in the final weeks of the campaign.) But in the other system, money raised and spent outside of the parties' and candidates' campaigns under the guise of issue advocacy is lightly regulated and not subject to limits (BCRA's attempt to restrict issue advocacy by unions, corporations, and other such entities just before elections was rejected by the Supreme Court in 2007 as an infringement on free speech). In practice, this means that any citizen who wants to invest any amount of money in campaign activities can find a legal way to do so.

---

*In congressional elections individuals may give no more than $2,000 per candidate per campaign, with primary, runoff, and general election campaigns treated as separate campaigns. Nonparty political action committees are limited to $5,000 per candidate per campaign. Parties may give no more than $5,000 to a House candidate and $17,500 to a Senate candidate. The $2,000 individual contribution limit also applies to presidential primary candidates; presidential candidates who accept public funds for the general election may not accept any other direct contribution to their campaigns. Contributions from foreign sources are illegal in all federal elections.

POLITICS/POLICY

Soft Money Finds a New Home

The story of how campaign finance reform led to the flood of "soft money" in presidential election campaigns, and how reforms aimed at stemming the flood merely rechanneled it, exemplify the partisan conflicts, dilemmas, and unanticipated consequences that vex campaign finance policy. With their party in debt after the 1968 election, congressional Democrats embraced reform proposals that would limit campaign spending and finance presidential campaigns with public funds. Republican opposition to these reforms collapsed in the wake of the Watergate scandal, in which campaign finance abuses had figured prominently. After Richard Nixon resigned in August 1974 to avoid impeachment, his successor, Gerald Ford, who like Nixon opposed public financing of campaigns, reluctantly agreed to sign the Federal Election Campaign Act (FECA) amendments, conceding that "the times demand this legislation."

Use of the new system in the 1976 elections exposed an unanticipated problem. To meet spending limits, the presidential campaigns focused on mass media advertising to take advantage of its efficiencies and maintained tight central control of all other campaign activity to avoid violating the law. State and local parties had little chance to participate, and the absence of the familiar paraphernalia of grassroots campaigns— bumper stickers, lapel buttons, yard signs—was widely noted and lamented. To preserve a role for local parties and grassroots activists in presidential campaigns, Congress in 1979 amended FECA to permit state and local parties to raise and spend money on party building, voter registration, and get-out-the-vote activities. No limits were placed on contributions or expenditures for these purposes, and, until the law was amended again in 1988, the sums involved did not even have to be reported to the Federal Election Commission. These funds were nicknamed "soft money" to distinguish them from the tightly regulated "hard money" governed by the public funding system.

Permissive interpretations by the Federal Election Commission and the federal courts of what constituted "party building" allowed presidential candidates to raise and spend unlimited sums under the legal fiction that they were merely helping to fertilize the grassroots. Consequently, presidential campaign finance became almost as wide open as it had been before the reforms of the 1970s. For years, partisan disagreements kept Congress from reforming the system, but finally in 2002, scandals surrounding the collapse of energy giant Enron, a generous donor of both hard and soft campaign money to both parties, induced majorities in both houses to pass the Bipartisan Campaign Reform Act (BCRA) despite strong opposition from Republican leaders. Among other things, BCRA banned soft money contributions to the parties, completely depriving them of this source of funds.

But soft money did not disappear. Tax-exempt groups organized under regulations in section 527 of the revenue code can raise unlimited money to spend on voter mobilization, issue advocacy, and almost any other campaign activity as long as they refrain from expressly advocating the election or defeat of a federal candidate and do not coordinate their activities with parties or candidates. In response to BCRA, most large soft money donors shifted to supporting 527 committees, whose financial participation in federal elections jumped from $151 million in 2002 to $405 million in 2004. More than fifty individuals and organizations contributed at least $1 million to such groups; financier George Soros led the way, with $24 million in donations to several anti-Bush, pro-Kerry 527s. Because of Soros and several other generous liberal multimillionaires, four out of every five 527 dollars went to help Democrats in 2004. The partisan balance was more even in 2006 and 2008, when 527 committees invested $429 and $374 million, respectively, in federal and state campaigns.

Sources: Dollar Politics, 3rd ed. (Washington, D.C.: Congressional Quarterly, 1982), 8–24; Frank J. Sorauf, *Inside Campaign Finance* (New Haven: Yale University Press, 1992), 147–150; Steve Weissman and Ruth Hassan, "BCRA and the 527 Groups," in *The Election after Reform: Money, Politics, and the Bipartisan Campaign Reform Act,* ed. Michael Malbin (Rowman and Littlefield, 2006); www.opensecrets.org/527s/index.php.

THE FLOW OF CAMPAIGN MONEY. Although the proponents of the original FECA had hoped to rein in the cost of campaigns, the flow of campaign money has continued to outpace inflation. Total funding from all sources for the general election campaigns for president rose from $453 million in 1996 to $676 million in 2000, to $1.262 billion in 2004 and will top $2 billion when the final figures for 2008 are in. Spending in House and Senate campaigns also has continued to grow since FECA took effect, rising by averages of about 9 percent in House elections, 12 percent in Senate elections (in inflation-adjusted dollars) from one election year to the next. In 2006 the average House campaign spent $953,000 and the average Senate campaign about $7.9 million. Both supply and demand have driven campaign spending up. The supply of contributions continues to grow because the stakes represented by elections are so great. Decisions made by the federal government affect every aspect of American economic and social life, so there is no shortage of incentives for trying to influence who gets elected and what the winners do in office. In recent elections, tights battle for majority control of Congress has also stimulated heavier investment in campaigns. And demand is continually keeping pace with supply. Candidates' appetites for campaign funds continue to grow because the cost of developing an effective message and getting it out to voters continues to climb.

House and Senate spending averages mask the huge variation in the amounts available to individual congressional candidates. Some candidates raise and spend millions, while others have to make do with almost nothing. The differences result from strategic choices made by contributors and candidates. Congressional candidates in search of campaign money can tap four basic sources: individuals, political action committees (PACs) (discussed in detail in Chapter 13), their own pocketbooks, and party organizations. House candidates typically receive about 55 percent of their funds from private individuals and get about 35 percent from PACs; another 7–8 percent comes out of their own pockets. Senate candidates raise relatively more from individuals (about 60 percent) and less from PACs (about 20 percent). Direct party contributions amount to only about 1 percent of candidates' funds, but the parties also help out with significant amounts of **coordinated** and especially **independent** campaign spending. Party committees make coordinated expenditures in behalf of candidates for activities such as polling, producing ads, and conducting research on the opposition; the totals are, however, limited by law.* Independent expenditures are not limited and go for campaign activities (mainly advertising) that are not supposed to be coordinated in any way with the candidate's campaign; such expenditures grew explosively in 2004 after BCRA closed the parties' soft money loophole, reaching totals of $158 million in House contests and $62 million in Senate contests in 2006, far more than in any previous election.

All types of contributors, with the possible exception of the candidates themselves, distribute their funds strategically. They avoid wasting resources on hopeless candidacies, preferring instead to put their money behind their favorites in races they expect

---

*In 2004 coordinated party expenditures were limited to $74,620 in House races; limits for Senate races depend on the state's population and ranged up to $1,944,896 (California).

to be close, where campaigning and therefore campaign spending might make a difference. Contributors also favor likely winners whose help they might need after the election. In practice, then, congressional incumbents, usually safe—or, at worst, in tight races for reelection—have the least trouble raising campaign funds. How much they actually acquire depends in good part on how much they think they need; the safer they feel, the less they raise and spend.

Challengers to incumbents, however, have a great deal of trouble raising money unless they can make a persuasive case to contributors that they have a serious chance of winning. But few challengers manage to do so in any election year. Because races tend to be closer when the advantages of incumbency do not apply, candidates for

Cartoon by Khalil Bendib.

open seats are usually in a much better position to raise funds. Contributors correctly see open contests as their best opportunity for taking a seat from the other party. As a result, average campaign spending varies sharply according to the kind of candidate (see Figure 11-3). Incumbents typically outspend challengers by a wide margin, while candidates for open seats are sometimes even better financed than incumbents.*

Does it matter how much candidates are able to raise and spend? It matters only to the degree that a lack of money prevents candidates from getting their messages out to voters. Campaign money has little to do with the results of general elections for president, and this was true even before public funding guaranteed that major-party candidates would have well-funded campaigns. The presidential candidates' campaigns always are at least adequately financed, and huge sums of additional money are now spent by party organizations and independent committees on the candidates' behalf. Add to this the abundant free information the media transmit about presidential candidates, and the balance of resources makes little difference. What matters is how voters respond to the competing campaign messages.

Campaign money does matter in presidential primaries, in which rationally ignorant voters cannot rely on party labels as default cues and so need to know something about the candidates. Well-known candidates have a leg up, but lesser-known contenders, to have any chance at all, need to get the attention of voters, which almost always requires spending substantial sums of money. Held at the beginning of the primary season (in 2008, January), the Iowa caucuses and New Hampshire primary once gave unknowns such as Jimmy Carter (1976) and Bill Clinton (1992) an opportunity to parlay relatively inexpensive early successes into fund-raising bonanzas for later

---

*The same differences in spending among types of candidates hold for Senate elections, but variations in state populations and states holding elections (only two-thirds of the states hold Senate elections in any given election year, with the same set repeating only at six-year intervals) make year-to-year comparisons of the kind presented in Figure 11-3 less informative.

Figure 11-3 Incumbent versus Challenger: Campaign Spending in Contested House Elections

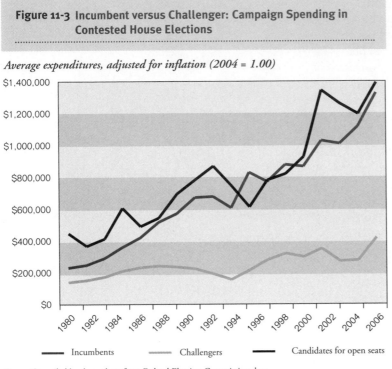

Average expenditures, adjusted for inflation (2004 = 1.00)

——— Incumbents ——— Challengers ——— Candidates for open seats

Source: Compiled by the authors from Federal Election Commission data.

primaries (see Chapter 12). But with so many states now holding primaries in February, candidates have little time to exploit unexpected success and cannot compete effectively without raising a great deal of money before the election year begins.

In House and Senate races, money—specifically, the lack of it—is frequently decisive. Typically half of Senate incumbents and 70–80 percent of House incumbents win by default because their opponents spend too little money to make a race of it. In a candidate-centered electoral system, voters tend to reject candidates they know nothing about and support those they recognize. In the elections held from 1980 through 2004 an average of 92 percent of House voters and 96 percent of Senate voters recognized the incumbent's name. Awareness of the challengers was much less common; over the same period only 54 percent recognized the House challenger's name and 77 percent the Senate challenger's name. Challengers who do not improve substantially on these averages have no chance of winning, and few can do so without heavy campaign spending. But campaign spending has little effect on awareness of incumbents because voters already are familiar with them before the campaign begins.[28]

Campaign money, then, is much more important to challengers (and obscure candidates of any kind) than it is to incumbents or other well-known candidates. In House elections the more challengers spend, the more likely they are to win, but few spend enough to be competitive (see Figure 11-4). In elections from 1984 through 2006, a majority (54 percent) of challengers spent less than $100,000, and every single one of them lost. As spending increases, so does the likelihood of winning. Curiously, though, the opposite appears true for incumbents. They are much more likely to spend at high levels, yet the higher their spending, the more likely they are to lose (see Figure 11-5).

This surprising fact is a byproduct of the strategies pursued by contributors and candidates. The more threatened incumbents feel, the more they raise and spend, but the additional effort does not fully offset the threat that provokes it. For incumbents, then, spending lavishly is a sign of electoral weakness that is ultimately registered at

Figure 11-4 Increasing Returns: Challenger Spending in House Elections

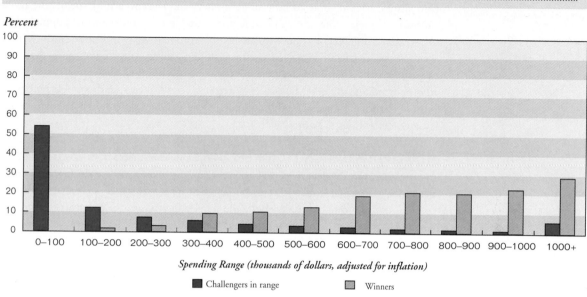

Source: Compiled by the authors from Federal Election Commission data, 1984–2006.

Figure 11-5 Heavy Campaign Spending: The Sign of a Weak Incumbent

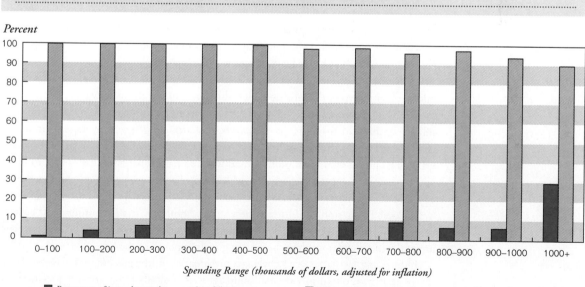

Source: Compiled by the authors from Federal Election Commission data, 1984–2006.

the polls. For challengers, higher spending is a sign, as well as a source, of electoral strength. Challengers with better prospects (attractive candidates with potentially effective messages) are able to raise more money; and the more they spend, the more professional their campaigns, the more voters they reach, and the more support they attract. Challengers do not have to outspend incumbents to win. Indeed, only 30 percent of the successful House challengers in the past decade spent more than the incumbents they defeated; on average, they spent $466,000 less. They simply have to spend enough to make their case. When both candidates spend enough money to mount full-scale campaigns, the content of the campaigns, not the balance of resources, determines the outcome.

HOW ARE CAMPAIGN FUNDS SPENT? Once candidates have raised campaign money, they have to decide how to spend it, unless, like many congressional incumbents, they face such feeble opposition that they are free to stash it away for some future contest. No one is certain about the most effective way to use scarce campaign resources. The most commonly expressed view is that "half the money spent on campaigns is wasted. The trouble is, we don't know which half."

Because a fundamental goal of every campaign is to reach voters with the candidate's message, it is no surprise that a detailed study of spending in the 1992 House and Senate campaigns found that the largest expense was advertising, with television and radio ads leading the way (see Figure 11-6). Senate campaigns made heavier use of broadcast advertising, while House campaigns used more "persuasion mail." The reason is efficiency. Media markets in large metropolitan areas may include as many as thirty House districts (Greater New York). Thus House candidates opting for broadcast advertising have to pay for a station's entire audience, not just that fraction living in the target district. Mailings, by contrast, can be targeted precisely to district residents. Still, House campaigners with enough money often use television even where it is inefficient because it is the only way to reach many potential voters and avoids the risk of campaign brochures being tossed out as "junk mail."

Only a small proportion of funds is spent on traditional campaigning—speeches, rallies, soliciting votes door-to-door, and shaking hands at the factory gate. Yet these activities remain a major part of every campaign because candidates hope to extend their impact far beyond the immediate audience by attracting news coverage. Campaigns display considerable imagination in coming up with gimmicks that will gain free media exposure; indeed, campaign professionals work so hard for it that they prefer to call it "earned" media. One particularly brave House challenger even traveled with a large pig to underline his opposition to the incumbent's "pork barrel politics" (see Chapter 6). What local TV station could resist the visuals? Another tactic is running paid ads designed to provoke controversy. The ensuing news coverage then spreads the message to an audience much larger than the one originally exposed to the ad.

In pursuing favorable news coverage, presidential campaigns are in a class by themselves. Indeed, modern presidential campaigns are basically made-for-TV productions. Candidates tolerate grueling travel schedules, participate in countless carefully staged events, and compose pithy "sound bites"—short comments designed to be excerpted for

Figure 11-6 House and Senate Campaign Expenses

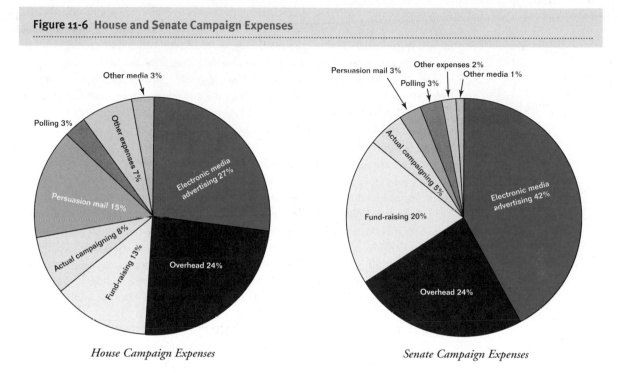

House Campaign Expenses *Senate Campaign Expenses*

Source: Based on data reported by Dwight Morris and Murielle E. Gamache in *Handbook of Campaign Spending: Money in the 1992 Congressional Races* (Washington, D.C.: Congressional Quarterly, 1994), Table 1-3, 8; and Table 1-6, 12.

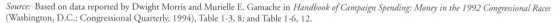

broadcast, such as George H. W. Bush's "read my lips, no new taxes" promise in 1988—to get their messages on the news and out to the voters. The celebratory post-convention bus tour taken by the Clintons and Gores in 1992 is a successful example; it brought out large, exuberant crowds, generating a good deal of positive media coverage both nationally and in the states visited. Presidential candidates also exploit soft news and entertainment shows. In recent elections, both parties' candidates have made multiple appearances on television's talk and comedy shows, chatting with Oprah Winfrey and Regis Philbin, joking with David Letterman and Jay Leno, trading stories with Larry King. In 2008, Sarah Palin went on *Saturday Night Live* to joke with Tina Fey, who had been parodying her in the comedy show's sketches, while John McCain went on Letterman's show to stop the needling Letterman had been giving him for having canceled an appearance a few weeks earlier. The campaigns took these events seriously, for these shows reach audiences who do not otherwise pay much attention to political news.

When it comes to media coverage, the rich get richer and the poor get ignored. The best-funded campaigns (for president or hotly contested Senate seats) get the most attention from the news media. Poorly funded candidates may be desperate for news coverage because they cannot afford to buy airtime, yet the very fact of their poverty makes them look like sure losers and therefore not worth covering. Campaigns that must depend on the news media to get their messages out invariably fail.

A large share of congressional campaign funds pays for expenses not directly connected to reaching voters (see Figure 11-6). For example, nearly a quarter of the money spent in 1992 went into overhead—staff salaries, office and furniture rental, computers and other equipment, telephone calls, travel, legal and accounting services, and the like. Fund-raising was another major expense, particularly for Senate candidates, who spend 20 percent of their money on just raising more money. Because of their larger constituencies, Senate candidates usually have to raise bigger sums than House candidates do, but FECA contribution limits compel them to raise it in the same-size chunks.

Incumbents and nonincumbents have somewhat different spending patterns. Often, weak opposition leaves incumbents free to spend relatively less on reaching voters or not to spend the money at all. Nonincumbents spend about two-thirds of their funds on activities designed to reach voters directly; incumbents spend a little less than half of their funds for such purposes. In 1992 House incumbents actually gave away 6 percent of their campaign money, sometimes to local charities but mostly to their parties and to other candidates. Members aspiring to leadership positions now routinely cultivate support by passing on campaign money to less-secure colleagues or to their party's campaign committees; some even form their own PACs for this purpose.

WHERE ARE PRESIDENTIAL CAMPAIGN FUNDS SPENT? Presidential candidates invest heavily in television advertising, the most efficient way to reach an electorate of more than one hundred million people. In recent elections the campaigns have together spent hundreds of millions of dollars on television time. Decisions about where to spend the money are dominated by the design of the Electoral College (see box "The Electoral College: Where the Big States Hold the Cards"), which encourages a strategy of focusing on states with large numbers of electoral votes rather than the national electorate. Whoever wins the most popular votes in a state, except for Maine and Nebraska, gets all of its electoral votes no matter how narrow the margin of victory.* The object of a presidential campaign, then, is to piece together enough state victories to win at least 270 electoral votes.

The usual strategy is twofold: (1) to concentrate on states that polls indicate could go either way and that are populous enough to be worth winning, and (2) to ignore states that are locked up by either side. For example, in 2008 as in the previous two presidential elections, the campaigns focused on the so-called battleground states that could not be taken for granted by either party. The close national divisions and fluctuating party fortunes revealed by pre-election surveys were echoed in many states, and the number that polling data indicated were in play remained high, with between thirteen and eighteen considered closely contested in various analyses published during fall 2008. Both candidates invested heavily in the largest of these states—Florida (27 electoral votes), Pennsylvania (21), Ohio (20), and initially Michigan (17) (the McCain campaign gave up on Michigan in late September)—and they also campaigned

---

*In Maine and Nebraska the electoral vote can be divided if one congressional district votes for a candidate who loses statewide.

The Electoral College
Where the Big States Hold the Cards

The Constitution's formula for allocating electoral votes to each state is simple: number of senators + number of representatives = number of votes in Electoral College. This formula heavily favors the populous states, which not only have a lot of electoral votes, but, following a rule adopted by all states except Nebraska and Maine, award all their state's electoral votes to the candidate receiving the most votes. This winner-take-all rule means that California with its fifty-five electoral votes, Texas with thirty-four, New York with thirty-one, and Florida with twenty-seven largely decide the winner. Based on the 2000 census, the ten most populous states in the nation control 256 out of the 270 electoral votes needed to elect a president. By contrast, the thirteen least populous states have only forty-six electoral votes—fewer than those held by the largest state, California.

White House hopefuls plan their campaign stops accordingly, heavily criss-crossing the vote-rich states, often at the expense of the vote-poor ones. Whether conservative or liberal, presidential candidates can ill-afford to avoid addressing the problems of these large, highly urban states.

An ongoing criticism of the Electoral College system is that a candidate can win a plurality of the popular vote nationally but still not be elected because of failure to gain a majority in the Elec-toral College. This happened to presidential candidates Andrew Jackson in 1824, Samuel J. Tilden in 1876, Grover Cleveland in 1888, and Al Gore in 2000. Jackson and Cleveland succeeded, however, in their next runs for the office. More typically, the electoral vote merely exaggerates the margin of victory of the winner of the popular vote. In 1992, for example, Bill Clinton won 43.3 percent of the popular vote but 68.7 percent of the electoral vote; Barack Obama won 52.6 percent of the popular vote but 67.7 percent of the electoral vote in 2008. The 2000 and 2004 elections, however, proved exceptions to the rule. In 2000, George W. Bush's share of the popular vote (47.8 percent) nearly equaled his slice of the electoral vote (50.4 percent); the two figures were equally close in 2004, when Bush won 50.7 percent of the popular vote and 53.2 percent of the electoral vote.

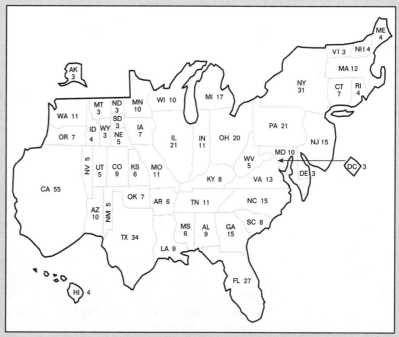

The States in Proportion to Their Electoral Votes 2001–2010

intensively in the medium-sized swing states, including Virginia (13) North Carolina (15), Missouri (11), Indiana (11) Wiconsin (10), Minnesota (10), and Colorado (9). As the tide moved in Obama's direction late in the campaign, McCain focused on holding states won by Bush in 2004 (Florida, North Carolina, Virginia, Ohio), while Obama campaigned to move these states and several other Bush states (Missouri, Colorado, West Virginia, Indiana) into the Democratic camp. Campaign resources, including visits from the presidential and vice presidential candidates were, as always, heavily concentrated in the potential swing states. States not on the battleground list were generally ignored; had they depended on the campaigns for information, California's sixteen million registered voters would scarcely have known a presidential election was taking place. Obama succeeded in turning nine states from red to blue (Colorado, Florida, Indiana, Iowa, Nevada, New Mexico, North Carolina, Ohio, and Virginia) while holding all of the states won by John Kerry in 2004.

Money and Elections: Policy Issues

Perhaps now it is clearer why the dilemma noted at the beginning of this discussion of campaign money is so thorny. Elections are supposed to keep agents responsive by making them compete with other would-be agents for the votes needed to win and hold their jobs. This does not mean that every election must be hard fought, but it does require agents to anticipate serious competition if they serve their constituents poorly. Serious electoral competition is expensive, though, because informing voters about alternatives is so expensive. These costs are met by gathering large sums of money from people and groups whose values and interests may differ from those of voters. This practice raises the suspicion that elected officials will be more responsive to contributors than to voters, undermining the purpose of elections and, eventually, democracy. The evidence for the claim that campaign money buys influence and that elected officials ignore voters to please donors is actually quite tenuous (see Chapter 13). But no one denies that money buys **access,** or a politician's ear.

Still, the news media and self-proclaimed public interest lobbies have convinced most Americans that campaign donations buy, in addition to White House hospitality and golf dates with congressional leaders, specific policy favors. The democratic dilemma posed by the campaign finance system has grown more acute with the rise in campaign spending, and major changes in the system are proposed in Congress after every election. In 2002, nearly three decades after the adoption of FECA, reformers succeeded in enacting BCRA, but it did little to resolve the fundamental problems. Some popular reform proposals are based on a misunderstanding of electoral politics. For example, most Americans are convinced that campaigns have become too expensive and would like to impose ceilings on campaign spending. But if the goal is competitive elections, the greater problem is that a large number of campaigns are too poorly funded to give voters even a modestly informed choice. Moreover, unless the spending limits are quite high, they will help incumbents at the expense of challengers (see Figures 11-4 and 11-5, page 543).

Another reform suggested would democratize congressional campaign finance by forbidding large donations and banning PACs, forcing candidates to finance their campaigns with small contributions from private individuals. This reform runs aground on a standard free-rider problem, however. Because a candidate's victory benefits all who desire it whether or not they contribute to the campaign, and because no single small contribution will affect the outcome or buy access to the victor, it is impossible for most candidates to raise enough money in small donations to conduct a competitive campaign. Recognizing this fact, reformers have proposed a standard solution: financing campaigns with tax dollars. In their view, elections untainted by special-interest contributions are a public good that citizens should compel themselves to purchase just as they pay for national defense. The precedent is the system for financing presidential campaigns (ignoring, for the moment, independent spending and the candidates' option to stay out of the system).

For many who support the idea, publicly financed congressional elections have another advantage: candidates could be required to accept spending limits in return for public funds for their campaigns. But again, unless the limits are high enough, this scheme would hurt challengers, reducing electoral competition. Yet if every campaign gets enough money to be truly competitive, the system will be expensive, with tens of millions of tax dollars spent on many candidates who have no serious prospects of winning. Moreover, any method of public finance would have to accommodate primary elections and third-party or independent candidacies. So far, the idea of extending public funding to congressional candidates has made little headway because the public does not support the move. Opponents have succeeded in characterizing public funds as "welfare for politicians," a frame that combines two widely unpopular referents.

Financier George Soros, one of the world's richest men, contributed more than $23 million to seven different 527 committees dedicated to defeating George W. Bush in the 2004 election. Soros and other wealthy liberals helped keep the Democrats in the financial game but inevitably drew criticism for trying to "buy" the election. Even if contributions to 527 committees were to be brought under the FEC's limits, Soros could still, under First Amendment protection, spend all he wanted on his own independent campaigns for or against parties or candidates. Soros contributed another $4.9 million to pro-Democratic 527s in 2008.

The ultimate barrier to a more egalitarian campaign finance system, however, is the First Amendment as currently interpreted by the Supreme Court. Even if campaigns were fully funded by tax dollars and private contributions to candidates prohibited, people and organizations would remain free to spend all the money they could gather on independent campaigns supporting or attacking candidates. Moreover, we can be certain that many of the people and groups who now send dollars to candidates would merely redirect their funds into independent campaigns if the law closed off other avenues of participation. The dramatic increase in money going to 527 organizations after BCRA banned soft party money is an indication of what to expect. Because no one believes that the justices will change their minds anytime soon, some reformers, including former representative Richard Gephardt of Missouri, then the Democratic House minority leader, proposed in 1997 amending the Constitution to allow Congress to impose "reasonable" spending limits on everyone. The amendment went nowhere that year or since, but the idea is likely to be around as long as the campaign finance impasse remains.

Despite widespread agreement among politically active people that the campaign finance system is flawed in one way or another, fundamental changes are unlikely because there is no consensus on what would count as an improvement or how to achieve it. Even reining in soft money, a minor change, took an extraordinary effort. Larger changes likely will come only in the form of ever more inventive campaign finance practices. But this is not necessarily a bad thing: if the campaign finance system is far from egalitarian, it is remarkably pluralistic. People espousing a wide variety of interests and values take part in financing campaigns, and no single point of view predominates. Promising candidates with potentially effective messages usually can find financial allies, and therefore elected officials can anticipate electoral trouble if they get out of touch or out of line with the people who elected them. Money is important because candidates need it to reach voters, but the voters still have the last word.

The Logic of Elections Revisited

Despite all the problems with U.S. elections, they work remarkably well to preserve American democracy. Regular, free, competitive elections guard the nation against the dangers that inevitably arise when citizens delegate authority to governments. Elections allow citizens, as principals, to pick their agents and to fire and replace those whose performance falls short. The threat of replacement provides elected officials with a powerful incentive to listen to their constituents. Elections also create incentives for entrepreneurs and organizations to solve the free-rider and coordination problems that beset citizens acting as collective principals. Aspiring leaders and their political allies compete for votes by keeping an eye on officials and informing citizens about their shortcomings, paying the information costs that individual citizens would not rationally pay. Similarly, by getting out the vote on Election Day they turn citizens who might otherwise rationally abstain from casting a ballot into voters. They also bear much of the cost, through polling and focus groups, of keeping track of what citizens want from their agents in government, again making up for the lack of rational incentives for individual political expression. But all of these activities cost money, and the campaign finance system presents its own set of agency problems that are not easily solved.

Elections also induce candidates and campaigns to help solve the massive coordination problem faced by millions of voters trying to act collectively to control or replace their agents. By offering competing frames for a voting decision, they clarify and focus the electoral choice to the point where rationally ignorant voters can manage it. Candidates' opportunistic choice of issues puts voters' concerns on the agenda and helps make election results intelligible: in 2008, for example, a crucial issue really *was* the appropriate strategy for invigorating the economy. When candidates form relatively stable coalitions with other would-be leaders—that is, combine into political parties— they narrow the choices to a manageable number, often as few as two. Indeed, party labels simplify voters' choices across offices and over a series of elections. They also allow voters to hold elected officials collectively responsible for their performance in office. In other words, elections create strong links between public opinion and government action. But they do so only because politically ambitious people have found that it serves their own purposes to engage in the activities that forge the links. One durable institutional byproduct of political ambition pursued under American electoral rules, the party system, is the subject of the next chapter.

Key Terms

access, 548

candidate, 528

coordinated spending, 540

focus group, 530

independent spending, 540

issue voting, 526

message, 530

mobilization, 521

negative campaigning, 534

open seat, 541

party identification, 526

party label, 526

performance voting, 526

single-issue voters, 524

soft money, 538

Suggested Readings

Abramson, Paul R., John H. Aldrich, and David W. Rohde. *Change and Continuity in the 2004 and 2006 Elections.* Washington, D.C.: CQ Press, 2007. The 2004 and 2006 elections provide the context for exploring basic voter behavior and post–World War II political patterns.

Campbell, Angus, Philip E. Converse, Warren E. Miller, and Donald E. Stokes. *The American Voter.* Chicago: University of Chicago Press, 1976. First published in 1960, this seminal survey-based study of American voting behavior presents the classic psychological theory of party identification. It is still essential reading for every student of American politics.

Downs, Anthony. *An Economic Theory of Democracy.* New York: Harper and Row, 1957. The seminal theoretical work explaining how electoral and party politics reflects rational strategies of candidates and voters.

Fiorina, Morris P. *Retrospective Voting in American National Elections.* New Haven: Yale University Press, 1981. Survey-based study supporting the Downsian theory of party identification as a running tally of positive and negative experiences with the parties' performance in government.

Lupia, Arthur, and Mathew D. McCubbins. *The Democratic Dilemma: Can Citizens Learn What They Need To Know?* New York: Cambridge University Press, 1998. The answer, according to the theory and experimental evidence reported in this book, is a clear yes; despite "rational ignorance," people use freely available cues to make reasoned choices among candidates.

Miller, Warren E., and J. Merrill Shanks. *The New American Voter.* Cambridge: Harvard University Press, 1996. Sequel to *The American Voter,* with an emphasis on generational changes in patterns of turnout and partisanship since the New Deal.

Niemi, Richard G., and Herbert F. Weisberg. *Controversies in Voting Behavior.* 4th ed. Washington, D.C.:

CQ Press, 2001. Sixteen important journal articles that collectively give the reader a good feel for contemporary debates on voter behavior, from voter turnout to campaigns to the party system.

Popkin, Samuel L. *The Reasoning Voter: Communication and Persuasion in Presidential Campaigns.* 2nd ed. Chicago: University of Chicago Press, 1994. How voters use "gut reasoning" and information shortcuts to decide how to vote in primary and general elections for president.

Rosenstone, Steven J., and John Mark Hansen. *Mobilization, Participation, and Democracy in America.* New York: Macmillan, 1993. The most prominent and intractable question in American politics is why voting turnout has declined over the last thirty years. Rosenstone and Hansen offer the closest thing we have to an answer that is actually supported by evidence.

Review Questions

1. What are the potential problems with delegating authority to representatives in government? How do elections help reduce these risks?

2. Why did those in favor of restricting suffrage link it to property ownership? Why did the elite fear giving those without property the vote?

3. What benefits do people get from voting? Which of these benefits do they still receive if they personally do not vote?

4. What factors explain the decline in voter turnout since the 1960s? Why is this decline surprising?

5. Voting, in effect, makes voters choose between a future governed by candidate A and one governed by candidate B. Most voters can't predict the future. What tools allow voters to make these predictions of future performance?

6. What are the basic requirements for mounting a successful election campaign?

7. Why do so many members of Congress run unopposed? What factors make strong challengers more likely or less likely to enter the race?

8. What are the main differences between modern campaigns and those of the patronage-based party organizations of the past? Why are campaigns more expensive now?

9. Where does the money required to finance these modern campaigns come from? What are the legal limitations on campaign spending? How has the passage of bans on "soft money" changed these limitations?

10. What are the four basic sources of congressional campaign money? How is the money spent?

11. Why do congressional incumbents who spend more money actually appear to be more likely to lose their elections?

12. What "free" means of communicating with voters are available to candidates? What must candidates do to take advantage of them?

13. Where do candidates spend their advertising dollars?

Exercises

Such Kind, Giving Individuals

The Federal Election Commission (FEC) keeps records of donations from all individuals who contribute at least $200 directly to a candidate. Go to www.fec.gov/finance/disclosure/advindsea.shtml and perform the following searches of FEC databases, noting patterns of contributions:

- Donors from your zip code

- Donors from the Beverly Hills (90210) zip code

- Donors with your last name
- Donors with your parents' occupations
- Donors who are also employed by your employer or your parents' employers
- Donors who star in your favorite television series
- Donors who work for Enron, WorldCom, or Halliburton

Who Am I? Why Am I Here?

Go to the House of Representatives' home page (www.house.gov/house/MemberWWW.shtml), select the Web site of your member of Congress, and find that member's biography. Before running for Congress, what (if any) prior elected office had your member held? What is his or her demographic information (religion, age, marital status, occupation, and so on)? Then consult the Census Bureau's Web sites to find out the demographics of your congressional district (http://factfinder.census.gov/servlet/ DTGeoSearchByListServlet?ds_name=DEC_2000_ PL_U&state=dt&mt_name=DEC_2000_PL_U_ PL003&_lang=en&_ts=47086070086%20). Finally, consult http://cnn.com/ELECTION/2008/ to see what information is available about the challenger in this race and the incumbent's margin of victory in the prior election. If you were the incumbent, what information might make you nervous heading into the next campaign? What information will likely help the incumbent?

Has Your Vote Been Rocked Today?

Go to the Census Bureau's statistics on demographics and voter behavior (www.census.gov/population/ www/socdemo/voting/tabs00.html). Take note of your own state of residence, ethnic or racial origin, and age. Then go to the detailed file (www.census. gov/population/socdemo/voting/proj00/tabA.txt) and scroll down the list until you have found the line that matches your demographic information. Compare this information with the averages at the beginning of the document. Based on this information, are you more or less likely than average to register? To vote? Then look at the historical voting and registration characteristics of people like you since 1964 (www. census.gov/population/socdemo/ voting/history/htab01.txt). How have the rates of voting and registration changed among your peers over this time? How do you think this change affects the political influence of people sharing your demographics?

Political Parties

Why does a nation as diverse as the United States sustain only two major parties?

If the first generation of leaders elected under the Constitution rejected political parties on principle, why did they create them anyway?

Today national party conventions merely certify the winners of primary elections instead of choosing the presidential nominees, as they did in the past. So why do the parties continue to hold these gatherings?

Ninety percent of Americans claim they always vote for the person best suited for the job, regardless of party. How can it be, then, that political parties are as healthy as ever?

R unning for president in 2000, George W. Bush promised a bipartisan approach to governing that would end the fierce partisan bickering typical of the Clinton years. "I have no stake in the bitter arguments of the last few years," he said in his acceptance speech at the Republican National Convention. "I want to change the tone of Washington to one of civility and respect." Rhetorically, Bush sought to align himself with the disdain for parties and partisanship that is part of American popular culture. More than 90 percent of Americans claim they always vote for the candidate they think best suited for the office, regardless of party.[1] A majority believes that "parties do more to confuse the issues than to provide a clear choice on the issues."[2] Only 38 percent favor continuing the current two-party system rather than having candidates run as individuals without party labels (28 percent) or forming new parties that could effectively challenge the Democrats and Republicans (34 percent). Among potential swing voters (self-described independents, including those leaning toward one of the parties), only 25 percent want to maintain the two-party system.[3] Majorities consistently say they prefer that control of government be divided between the parties rather than monopolized by one party.[4]

Some political scientists and other observers have concluded from such responses that parties no longer matter much to voters.[5] Yet in 2000 the same electorate supposedly so hostile or indifferent to parties cast the most consistent party-line vote for president recorded in the entire forty-eight-year history of the American National Election Study, and party loyalty was also unusually high in House and Senate elections. Moreover, after the elections, when attention turned to the disputed presidential vote count

National conventions display party politics in its most colorful and distilled form. Here, John McCain and Sarah Palin are greeted with unrestrained enthusiasm by delegates to the 2008 Republican National Convention.

557

in Florida, ordinary Americans, no less than politicians and activists, responded in a decidedly partisan fashion, and not only in the heat of the moment; even four years later, when Bush was running for reelection, 91 percent of Republicans, but only 18 percent of Democrats, believed that he had won the 2000 election legitimately.[6]

The public had good reason to view the conflict through partisan lenses. Once the battle over the disputed votes began in Florida, the fight *was* nakedly partisan, shifting the odds overwhelmingly in Bush's favor because his party controlled all the institutions where the ultimate decision might possibly be made. To be sure, Florida's attorney general and many local election officials were Democrats, and Democratic appointees dominated the Florida Supreme Court, where Al Gore won some initial skirmishes. But Florida secretary of state Katherine Harris (the official responsible for election administration) was a Republican activist, and Bush could count on his brother, Republican governor Jeb Bush, as well as Republican legislative majorities, if Florida's legislature chose the state's electors (which it threatened to do if the vote counts were not completed in time to certify an official slate). Had the dispute moved to Congress for resolution, Republicans would have had the votes to award the election to Bush. And the U.S. Supreme Court had the authority to trump the Florida court, as it indeed did, when five Supreme Court justices—all conservative Republican appointees—preemptively terminated the recount, making certain that Bush received Florida's decisive electoral votes.

Entering the White House on the heels of the most partisan (and disputed) election in living memory, Bush's pledge to be "a uniter, not a divider" proved ephemeral. Despite the huge upsurge in national unity that followed the September 11 attacks, the election that returned Bush to the White House in 2004 turned out to be even more intensely partisan than the one that first put him there (see Chapter 11). By the end of Bush's second term as president in 2008, partisan divisions in Washington were far wider than they were before he took office, and Americans' assessments of his administration were the most polarized along party lines ever recorded (see Chapter 10). Both presidential candidates in 2008, Barack Obama and John McCain, presented themselves as leaders who would bridge the partisan divide, but party-line voting was almost as high as in 2000 and 2004.

Clearly, reports of the parties' demise have been greatly exaggerated. Indeed, anyone who looks at how people vote, who wins elections, and how the nation is governed would have to conclude that the two major parties rarely have been healthier. A large majority of voters are willing to identify themselves as Republicans or Democrats, and, of these partisans, a large majority vote loyally for their party's candidates. Rarely does a candidate win state or federal office without a major-party nomination; as of 2008 all of the fifty state governors and all but two of the 535 members of Congress were either Democrats or Republicans.* Moreover, party remains the central organizing instrument in government (see Chapter 6).

---

* Two independents served in the 110th Congress (2007–2008)—Sen. Bernard Sanders of Vermont and Sen. Joseph Lieberman of Connecticut. Lieberman was a Democrat until he lost the 2006 primary and had to run for reelection as an independent. Of the 7,382 citizens serving in state legislatures after the 2006 elections, only 21 (0.3 percent) were neither Democrats nor Republicans.

The wide gap between people's opinions about and behavior toward political parties has deep roots in American history. None of the politicians who designed the Constitution or initially sought to govern under it thought parties were a good idea—including the very people who unwittingly created them. Even in their heyday in the latter part of the nineteenth century, parties never lacked articulate critics or public scorn. Still, parties began to develop soon after the founding of the nation and, in one guise or another, have formed an integral part of the institutional machinery of American politics ever since. The chief reason for their longevity is that the institutions created by the Constitution make the payoffs for using parties—to candidates, voters, and elected officeholders—too attractive to forgo. American political parties represent the continuing triumph of pure political expedience.

Although expedience explains the existence of the parties, the activities that maintain them contribute to successful democratic politics in unforeseen ways. Indeed, the unintended consequences of party work are so important that most political scientists agree with E. E. Schattschneider, who said that "Political parties created democracy and that modern democracy is unthinkable save in terms of parties." [7] Parties recruit and train leaders, foster political participation, and teach new citizens democratic habits and practices. Beyond that, they knit citizens and leaders together in electoral and policy coalitions and allow citizens to hold their elected agents collectively responsible for what the government does. They also help to channel and constrain political conflicts, promoting their peaceful resolution. Finally, parties organize the activities of government, facilitating the collective action necessary to translate public preferences into public policy (see Chapters 6 and 7). In short, political parties make mass democracy possible.

This chapter examines the origin and development of national parties in the United States and explains what parties are, why and how they were invented, and how they have evolved. Parties, as we shall see, are the products of a compelling political logic, emerging from the strategic acts of politicians and citizens pursuing their political goals within the framework of institutions established by the Constitution.

Scholars have proposed a variety of formal definitions of **political party.** Two of the most prominent stand in clear contrast to one another (except in their conventional sexism). Edmund Burke, an eighteenth-century British politician and political philosopher, defined a party as "a body of men united for promoting by their joint endeavors the national interest, upon some particular principle in which they are all agreed." [8] Anthony Downs, in his modern classic *An Economic Theory of Democracy,* defined a party as "a team of men seeking to control the governing apparatus by gaining office in a duly constituted election." [9] Although rhetorical references to principle are a staple of party politics, the American parties have displayed a shared appetite for public office a good deal more consistently than they have for the pursuit of shared principles.

The Constitution's Unwanted Offspring

The Constitution contains no mention of political parties. During the nation's founding, parties were widely considered to be dangerous to good government and public

No One Wanted to Party

In the early years of the United States, conventional wisdom inveighed against political parties. Benjamin Franklin spoke out against the "infinite mutual abuse of parties, tearing to pieces the best of characters."[1] In *Federalist* No. 10 James Madison called them a species of "faction," which, by definition, holds intentions "adverse to the rights of other citizens, or to the permanent and aggregate interests of the community." George Washington used his Farewell Address to "warn . . . in the most solemn manner against the baneful effects of the Spirit of Party, generally,"[2] and his successor, John Adams, averred that "a division of the republic into two great parties . . . is to be dreaded as the greatest political evil under our Constitution."[3] Even Thomas Jefferson once declared, "If I could not get to heaven but with a party, I would not go there at all."[4]

1. Richard Hofstadter, "The Idea of a Party System," in *After the Constitution: Party Conflict in the New Republic,* ed. Lance Banning (Belmont, Calif.: Wadsworth, 1989), 20.

2. Nobel E. Cunningham, ed., *The Making of the American Party System: 1789 to 1809* (Englewood Cliffs, N.J.: Prentice Hall, 1965), 16.

3. Hofstadter, "Idea of a Party System," 20.

4. Richard Hofstadter, *The Idea of a Party System: The Rise of Legitimate Opposition in the United States, 1780–1840* (Berkeley: University of California Press, 1970), 123.

order, especially in republics (see box "No One Wanted to Party"). In such an intellectual climate, no self-respecting leader would openly set out to organize a political party.

The pervasive fear of parties reflected both historical experience and widely held eighteenth-century social beliefs. Factional conflict brought to mind the bloody religious and political wars of England's past and the internal strife that destroyed the republics in ancient Greece and Rome, and later, the city-states of Renaissance Italy. Society was viewed ideally as a harmonious whole, its different parts sharing common interests that all wise and honest authorities would dutifully promote. (Pluralism, though implicit in James Madison's defense of the Constitution in *The Federalist,* was not yet on the intellectual horizon.) People in authority saw themselves as agents acting on behalf of the whole community; any organized opposition was therefore misguided at best, treasonous at worst. Accepting the same perspective, rivals justified their opposition by imagining that those in power were betrayers of the community's trust. When the leaders of the new government took the steps that led to the creation of the first political parties, they did not expect or want party competition to become a permanent feature of American politics. Rather, their aim was to have the common good—their version, naturally—prevail and their opponents consigned to oblivion. The first parties were created as temporary expedients.

Expedient they were, but temporary they were not. Disdained by almost all, parties nonetheless flourished. The First Amendment's guarantees of freedom to speak, write, and assemble ensured that party activities would be legal. Beyond that, the framework of institutions established by the Constitution created powerful incentives for undertaking the activities that created and sustained parties. The design of the Constitution also had a profound effect on the *kind* of parties that developed. The party system has changed in important ways over the years as political entrepreneurs have adapted parties to new purposes and opportunities, but the basic features that reflect the constitutional system have reappeared in every period.

Incentives for Party Building

The political incentives that spawned parties are transparent. In any system where collective choices are made by voting, organization pays. When action requires winning

Congressional party leaders recognize that their words and actions send signals to voters and create issues that affect the success of all candidates who share the party label. Here, the Democratic leaders of the Senate and House, Harry Reid and Nancy Pelosi, sign a 2007 comprehensive energy bill intended to deal with the steeply rising costs of energy by promoting conservation and alternative fuels.

majorities on a continuing basis in multiple settings, organization is absolutely essential. The Constitution's provisions for enacting laws and electing leaders therefore put a huge premium on building majority alliances across institutions and electoral units. Parties grew out of the efforts of political entrepreneurs to build such alliances and to coordinate the collective activity necessary to gain control of and use the machinery of government.

TO BUILD STABLE LEGISLATIVE AND ELECTORAL ALLIANCES. The first American parties appeared in Congress when leaders with opposing visions of the nation's future began competing for legislative votes. Passing legislation requires majority support in the House and Senate. Any leader wanting to get Congress to act has to identify enough supporters to make up a majority, arrange a common course of action, and then get supporters to show up and vote. To control policy consistently, then, legislative leaders found it advantageous to cultivate a stable group of supporters, forming durable alliances that sharply reduced the transaction costs of negotiating a winning coalition on each new proposal. Since lawmaking powers are shared by three institutions—the presidency, the House, and the Senate—the value of alliances that cross institutional boundaries was also obvious.

Given the diversity of American society, it is impossible for stable alliances of any appreciable size to be built solely on shared interests or values. Rather, alliances are, by necessity, coalitions: participants have to agree to cooperate on action even though they have different, even conflicting reasons for doing so. Holding diverse coalitions together takes continuing political effort, for participants cooperate only as long as it serves their purposes. The sustained organizational effort needed to keep legislative coalitions working in harmony produces legislative parties.

Organized competition for votes in Congress leads directly to organized competition for votes in congressional elections. Coalitions vying for majority status need to recruit like-minded candidates and work to elect them; successful legislative alliances in Washington depend on successful electoral alliances in the states and districts. The organizational work required to negotiate and maintain electoral alliances expands legislative parties into electoral parties.

The presidential selection rules also offer powerful incentives for building electoral alliances across districts and states. The Constitution assigns selection of the president to the Electoral College or, if no candidate wins a majority of electors, to the House of Representatives. Many early observers expected the House to make the choice most of the time, believing that sectional jealousies would keep a majority of electors from uniting behind a single candidate. In fact, sectional rivalries and the competing ambitions of the larger states were constant sources of political friction. The incentives embodied in the rules for selecting the president provide a powerful counterweight to sectionalism, however. If an alliance can recruit and elect people pledged to one candidate in enough states, it can win the presidency. The alternative is to stack the House of Representatives with enough supporters to make the alliance's choice prevail should no candidate win a majority in the Electoral College. In either case, the problem is to sustain cooperation among numerous politicians, often with competing purposes and interests, across great distances. To the degree that the effort succeeds, the result is a national party organization.

TO MOBILIZE VOTERS. No matter how well organized, electoral alliances fail if they cannot get enough people to vote for their candidates. The competition for votes motivates alliance leaders to attract voters and get them to the polls on Election Day. In the early days of the Republic, electioneering followed traditional forms. The custom of political deference to one's "betters" had by no means died with the Revolution. The natural agents of a harmonious society were thought to be its most prominent and successful members, and a community's interests were assumed to be safest in the hands of those with superior breeding, education, and experience in public affairs. Restrictions on suffrage were common (see Chapter 11). Those who could vote made their preferences known orally and in public, a practice that encouraged deference to the local gentry. The elections themselves were decided largely on a personal basis; contests, if they arose, were between individuals backed by their personal followers. In such circumstances, open pursuit of political office was thought to be unseemly, and campaigns had to be conducted on the sly, through friends and allies. This is not to say that election campaigns were unknown; after all, the techniques of soliciting support and rounding up votes had been known for centuries because elections had been held for centuries. But they were techniques designed for small communities with even smaller electorates that, for the most part, took their cues from local worthies.

After the adoption of the Constitution, property and other qualifications for (white male) voting were progressively reduced or eliminated, and the egalitarian spirit of the frontier gradually eclipsed the habits of deference, even in the older states. As the size of the electorate increased, so did the task of identifying and attracting supporters and getting them to show up at

"Get out the vote" drives, conducted here using Spanish-language campaign literature, are among the oldest party strategies in America. At election time the national Democratic Party organizes these drives among those core supporters who chronically turn out to vote in low numbers—among them, Hispanics and African Americans.

the polls. Whoever could win over these new voters would enjoy a distinct political advantage. The networks of leaders and activists assembled to mobilize electoral support became the first party organizations.

TO DEVELOP NEW ELECTORAL TECHNIQUES. Once organized, electoral parties initiated new relationships between voters and elected leaders. The personal appeals and services that candidates had used to win the support of their neighbors since colonial times did not disappear, but they were, by themselves, inadequate for reaching a much larger, dispersed, and anonymous electorate. Party organizers turned to mass communications—newspapers, pamphlets, public letters, and printed speeches—designed to excite voters with emotional appeals on issues. The temptation to press hot buttons was irresistible when campaigns sought to persuade politically unsophisticated and uninvolved people that they had a stake in the election and a compelling reason to vote. Anyone trying to mobilize citizens to vote also has to overcome the electorate's tendency to free ride, for a party's victory is a collective good that people get to enjoy whether or not they vote (see Chapter 11). Since the beginning, then, much of the work of campaigns has been aimed at overcoming, by one means or another, the free-rider problem.

TO USE PARTY LABELS AND ENFORCE COLLECTIVE RESPONSIBILITY.
Voters need a way to distinguish among candidates, and party labels offer a serviceable shorthand cue that keeps voting decisions cheap and simple—as long as the labels are

informative. The more accurately a candidate's party label predicts what he or she will do in office, the more useful it is to voters and the more voters will rely on party cues in making their choices. In addition, the more voters rely on party cues, the more valuable party labels are to candidates. Would-be leaders adopt one of the existing political identities to benefit from the electorate's cue-taking habits. Local candidates join national party alliances even though local political divisions may have no logical relation to the issues that national parties fight about.

Once they have adopted the party label, however, politicians have a personal stake in maintaining the value of their party's "brand name," which may impose conformity costs by requiring the subordination of their own views and ambitions to the party's welfare and reputation. Party labels allow voters to reward or punish elected officials as a group for their performance in office. If voters do not like what the government is doing and want to "throw the rascals out," they have an easy way to identify the rascals: they are members of the majority party. The threat of collective punishment gives the majority party a strong incentive to govern in ways that please voters. Parties, then, developed into three-part systems connecting (1) the *party in government,* an alliance of current officeholders cooperating to shape public policy; (2) the *party organization,* dedicated to electing the party's candidates; and (3) the *party in the electorate,* composed of those voters who identify with the party and regularly vote for its nominees.[10]

Basic Features of the Party System

Parties emerged, then, not because anyone thought they were a good idea but because the institutional structures and processes established by the Constitution made them too useful to forgo. Their obvious value to elected leaders competing for political goods, to candidates competing for office, and to voters in search of cognitive shortcuts to voting decisions guaranteed that parties' practical virtues would be rediscovered by every political generation. Parties have not always taken the same form, to be sure; there is more than one way to arrange for collective action in American politics. But certain features reappear in every historical party system because they reflect the basic constitutional structure of American government. These features include competition between two major parties made up of decentralized, fragmented party coalitions that are maintained by professional politicians.

TWO-PARTY COMPETITION. During the first few Congresses, national leaders gradually divided into two major camps, initiating a pattern of two-party competition that has continued, with a few temporary exceptions, to this day. Americans tend to think of a **two-party system** as normal, but most modern democracies have more than two parties (see Figure 12-1). It is, in fact, remarkable that a people continually divided by region, religion, race, and ethnicity, not to mention social beliefs and economic interests, could fit into as few as two major political camps. But this pattern has continued for a compelling reason. In any election where a single winner is chosen by plurality vote (whoever gets the most votes wins), there is a strong tendency for serious competitors to be reduced to two because people tend to vote strategically. If their favorite party's candidate has no chance to win, they turn to the less objection-

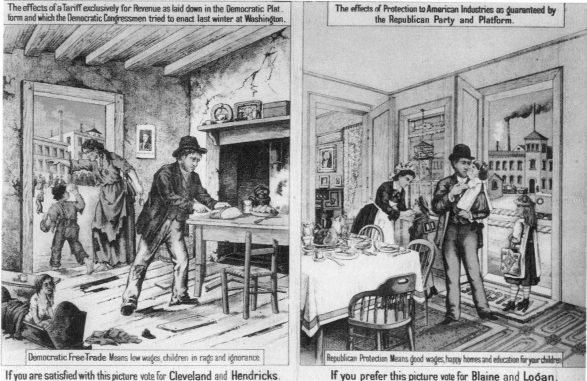

The effects of a Tariff exclusively for Revenue as laid down in the Democratic Platform and which the Democratic Congressmen tried to enact last winter at Washington.

The effects of Protection to American Industries as guaranteed by the Republican Party and Platform.

Democratic Free-Trade Means low wages, children in rags and ignorance.

Republican Protection Means good wages, happy homes and education for your children.

If you are satisfied with this picture vote for **Cleveland** and **Hendricks**.

If you prefer this picture vote for **Blaine** and **Logan**.

This 1884 Republican poster explains to voters why they should vote Republican. High tariffs supported working families because they kept products made by cheap foreign labor out of the country. With protection, the factories hum (compare smokestacks), food is on the table, and mom does not yell at the kids. Note also the prominence given party labels during the nineteenth century.

able of the major-party candidates who does have a chance to win (see box "Third-Party Blues"). This tendency is so strong that scholars have given it the status of a law, known as Duverger's law, named after the French political scientist who articulated it.[11] Office seekers, aware of this pattern, usually join one of the two competitive parties rather than pursuing office as independents or third-party nominees.

This logic is sufficiently compelling that, at most, only an election or two is required after the disruption of old party alliances and the appearance of new party coalitions for voters to narrow the viable choices down to two. In horseracing terms, to survive, a party must win or place; a third place show is no better than out of the money. Competition for survival, not to mention victory, puts strong pressure on party leaders to assemble broad coalitions, extending the party's hand to the voters ready to give up on their first choice. Any idea promoted by a third party that proves to be popular with voters is subject to poaching by one, or sometimes both, of the established parties. Thus incentives to expand electoral coalitions also help to reduce the number of parties to two.

Elections in the United States have almost always been winner-take-all affairs, so the rules have continually worked to reduce the viable options to two. An alternative kind of

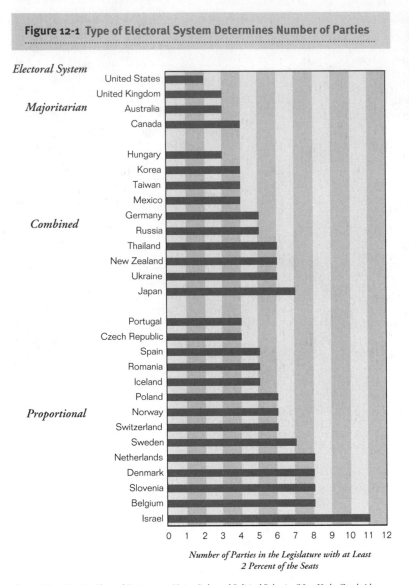

Figure 12-1 Type of Electoral System Determines Number of Parties

Number of Parties in the Legislature with at Least 2 Percent of the Seats

Sources: Pippa Norris, *Electoral Engineering: Voting Rules and Political Behavior* (New York: Cambridge University Press, 2004), 87; and *The Europa World Year Book 2004* (London: Europa Publications, 2004).

electoral system—**proportional representation,** under which a party receives legislative seats in proportion to its share of votes—is used in many European democracies. This system helps to preserve smaller parties because votes for their candidates are not wasted (hence the proportional systems listed in Figure 12-1 produce an average of 6.5 legislative parties), but it has never been tried in the United States on any significant scale. Once two-party competition was in place, both parties had a stake in preserving electoral rules that discriminate against third parties. State legislatures controlled by the major parties, for example, erected legal hurdles to getting on the ballot and banned **fusion tickets,** which allow minor parties to boost their votes by nominating candidates also nominated by major parties.

Strictly speaking, the winner-take-all logic applies only within a given electoral unit (a single congressional district or state, for example); it does not require that the same two parties face each other in every electoral unit. But for purposes of electing a president, the entire United States works as a single electoral unit. The contest for the presidency became so central to electoral politics that it shaped party competition for lesser offices as well.

DECENTRALIZED, FRAGMENTED PARTY COALITIONS. Another reason the two-party pattern endures is that federalism fragments the political system. Historically, national parties have been assembled from diverse state and local political factions concerned chiefly with the vibrant politics of their states, counties, or cities. The decentralized policy-making system allowed these local parties to work together to elect national leaders while going their own way on matters closer to home. National leaders could maintain diverse, unwieldy coalitions because many of the factions

LOGIC OF POLITICS

Third-Party Blues

Third-party and independent candidates have a hard time with the winner-take-all electoral system. Even with considerable popular backing, these candidates may get few votes if their supporters believe they cannot win and vote instead for one of the major-party candidates. For example, many voters who preferred independent Ross Perot in 1992 but believed—correctly—that he could not win, voted for Bill Clinton or George H. W. Bush in an effort to keep their least favorite candidate from winning. By arguing that "a vote for Perot is a vote for Bush," the Clinton campaign attracted Perot supporters whose top priority was replacing Bush. The Republicans made a variation of this pitch—"a vote for Perot is a vote for Clinton"—to voters who preferred Perot to Bush but Bush to Clinton. Only voters whose disdain for both major-party candidates exceeded their desire to elect the lesser of two evils stuck with Perot. In 1992 a surprising 19 percent of the voters did so, but Perot's vote dropped to 8 percent in 1996, and his successor as the Reform Party candidate, Pat Buchanan, won less than 1 percent in 2000.

In the end, then, only those third parties (or independent candidates) that manage to supplant one of the two reigning parties as a viable option in voters' minds gain rather than lose support from strategic voters. The last time this occurred on a national scale was 1856, when the Republicans surged ahead of the Whigs, who were fatally split over the slavery issue.

Third-party and independent candidates can be influential despite their electoral futility, however. Ralph Nader, candidate of the Green Party in 2000, gave

George W. Bush the presidency. Had he not been on the ballot in Florida, any plausible redistribution of the ninety-seven thousand votes he received would have given the state to Al Gore (most of Nader's support came from liberals who preferred Gore to Bush). Nader immediately became the exemplar of the dangers of "wasting" a vote, and when he ran again in 2004 his national vote total dropped from 2,882,995 (2.74 percent) to 443,830 (0.37 percent) and he was not a factor. Nor was he a factor in 2008, winning only 0.54 percent.

Even when independent and third-party candidates do not affect the outcome, the policies and ideas they promote may survive them through adoption by one, sometimes both, of the major parties. For example, many of the regulatory innovations sought by the Populist Party in the 1890s became part of the Democrats' New Deal after 1932. George Wallace's 1968 campaign theme of law and order soon found its way into many Republican campaigns. And the legislative term limits advocated by Perot ended up in the Republicans' 1994 "Contract with America." Third-party movements thus contribute to the evolution of the major-party coalitions even as the winner-take-all electoral system takes its inevitable toll.

From the 1940s to the 1970s the Democratic Party balanced northern presidential nominees with southern vice-presidential nominations to appeal to the divergent political views of Democratic voters in these regions, especially on the race issue. Despite the sometimes bitter relations between the candidates and their staffs, in 1960 Massachusetts-born John Kennedy was compelled to team up with Texan Lyndon Johnson to strengthen his bid for the South. An August 1960 campaign stop in Amarillo, Texas, was one of their few joint appearances. In fact, most of the time these candidates ran separate campaigns in different parts of the country, with little coordination between them. At the bottom of the photo is Lyndon Johnson's wife, Lady Bird Johnson.

within them had little contact with one another except when choosing the party's presidential candidate. Indeed, since the beginning the major parties have been diverse, unwieldy coalitions, ready to fly apart unless carefully maintained. Skillful management and the compelling need to hold these factions together for any chance at office have usually, but by no means always, kept the parties from self-destructing.

PROFESSIONAL POLITICIANS. At the time the Constitution was adopted, political leadership was the prerogative of successful and prominent men who viewed service in public office as a temporary duty that fell to members of their class. As organization became essential to winning public office, political power flowed into the hands of people with the skills to build networks of party workers, manage alliances of local leaders, and mobilize voters on Election Day. Personal wealth, education, and status were still advantages, but they no longer were essential. Of those attracted to party politics, many were ambitious people who latched onto the party as a vehicle for personal advancement; opportunism made no small contribution to the emergence of political parties.

Eventually the variety and frequency of elections generated by the multilayered federal system made party management a full-time job in many places. To maintain the electoral machinery, party managers had to attract resources and reward the efforts of party workers. Thus **patronage**—jobs, offices, government contracts, business licenses, and so forth—grew in importance. By the 1840s, when they were fully developed, parties had become ends in themselves to the thousands of local politicos who depended on them, one way or another, for their livelihood. That dependence ended in the late nineteenth and early twentieth centuries, however, when reforms largely destroyed the patronage-based party organizations. Today, full-time professionals manage the parties, and the activists are mainly amateurs who volunteer their time.

The Development and Evolution of the Party Systems

The historical development of parties (see Figure 12-2) reveals how they were shaped by politicians' strategic reactions to the opportunities and challenges posed by the

Figure 12-2 American Political Parties

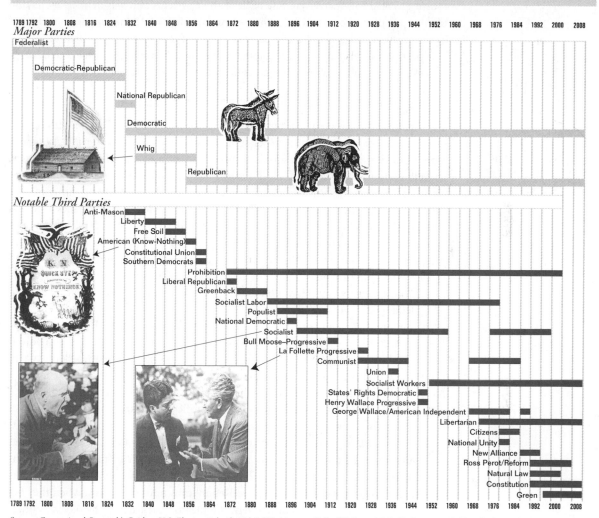

Sources: Congressional Quarterly's Guide to U.S. Elections, 5th ed., Vol. 1 (Washington, D.C.: CQ Press, 2006). Updates provided by Rhodes Cook.

Note: Throughout U.S. history there have been more than 1,500 political parties. For this chart Congressional Quarterly editors have selected those parties that achieved national significance during presidential election years. The spaces between the rules on this chart indicate the election year only. For example, the Constitutional Union Party and the Southern Democrats were in existence for the 1860 election only and were gone by 1864. Similarly, the Green Party first fielded a presidential candidate in 1996.

Constitution. Scholars have identified a sequence of five (possibly now six) distinct historical party systems. Each system derives its special characteristics from its era's society, economy, and technology, as well as the goals and tactics of political leaders. But common strategic responses to ongoing institutional incentives unite them all.

The first party system (1790–1824) illustrates the logic that led to the creation of national parties. Institutional innovation in the second party system (1824–1860) set parties on their basic organizational course. The full flowering and then decline of party machines under Progressive assault characterized the third (1860–1894) and fourth (1894–1932) party systems. Each of these systems also was defined by its distinctive pair of rival coalitions, but the coalitional nature of American parties is clearest in the creation and erosion of the party coalitions of the fifth party system (1932–?). The party coalitions have changed enough since the 1950s to suggest that a sixth party system is now in place, although there is no consensus on its date of origin.

The First Party System: The Origin of American Parties

The American party system was born in the first few Congresses as leaders with opposing views on national political issues sought to have their views prevail. Alexander Hamilton, secretary of the Treasury in George Washington's administration, proposed an ambitious and controversial set of measures designed to foster economic development and to give propertied interests—financiers, wealthy merchants, and manufacturers—a stake in the new Republic. Other prominent leaders, notably James Madison and Thomas Jefferson, who saw no constitutional basis for the federal government doing any such thing, opposed Hamilton's program. They thought Hamilton's ideas favored New England over other regions and threatened the well-being of the small farmers and tradesmen who made up a majority of the citizenry. The two sides also disagreed on foreign policy: Hamilton and his allies wanted strong ties with England, while Jefferson's group leaned toward France.

Hamilton's pursuit of votes in Congress led him to create what was, in effect, a legislative party. Although he was not a member of Congress, "Hamilton was involved much in the manner of a modern floor leader, caucusing with members, trying to round up votes, and helping to schedule legislation."[12] His ambitious effort to enact his proposals led him to cultivate a stable group of allies known as the "Federalists." The name derived from its earlier support for ratification of the Constitution and its endorsement of a strong national government.

Members of Congress who opposed Hamilton's policies gradually coalesced under the leadership of Jefferson and Madison. Protesting the alleged aristocratic pretensions (or intentions) of Hamilton's group, they styled themselves as Republicans. Members of this party also were called Democratic-Republicans until the 1820s, when they became known simply as Democrats. Today, the Democratic Party is the oldest political party in the world.

As the Federalists continued to roll up legislative victories, the Democratic-Republicans realized they needed more votes in Congress if they were to prevail. That meant getting more like-minded people into Congress, which meant recruiting and electing candidates. Because senators were chosen by state legislatures, the Democratic-Republican national leaders began to pay attention to state elections as well. The Federalists recognized the same realities and reached the same conclusions. The two groups began to compete in elections.

The presidential election required the parties' attention as well, for the Federalists—Hamilton, acting in Washington's name, and John Adams as Washington's successor—had demonstrated the importance of controlling the presidency as well as

Congress. The Constitution had left it up to the states to decide how to select their presidential electors. A number of selection procedures were tried—most commonly popular election, selection by the state legislature, or some combination of the two. In 1800, for example, five of the sixteen states chose electors by popular vote, and state legislatures made the choice in the others. The Framers expected the electors to be prominent local men who would deliberate with others from their states before deciding how to cast their votes.[13]

Challenging Adams for the presidency in 1800, Jefferson and his Democratic-Republican allies realized that these deliberations could be circumvented if they recruited and elected a majority of electors pledged to support Jefferson (see Chapter 9). By reaching out to local political leaders who were potential electors and to the growing mass of voters who chose the electors and state legislators, Jefferson successfully patched together an alliance of state and local factions, which led to a historic victory for his Democratic-Republicans and the ousting of the Federalists. In another innovative maneuver intended to rally voters to their cause, the Democratic-Republicans wedded organization to a controversial issue. They attacked the Alien and Sedition Acts, enacted by the Federalists in 1798 to stifle political criticism, as a frontal assault on republican government itself.* Their tactics were adapted to an expanding electorate:

> Party spokesmen . . . exploited every available agency of mass communication: official papers such as petitions against governmental measures, public circular letters from congressmen to their constituents, newspapers, pamphlets, handbills, private letters which circulated among leading figures, and personal contacts and word-of-mouth communications.[14]

It is no accident that the Democratic-Republicans did the innovating: the history of party building is largely a story of the "outs" finding new ways to become the "ins." The losers then imitate successful innovations. The Federalists tried with uneven success to duplicate the Democratic-Republicans' organizational efforts. They were hampered, however, by their nostalgia for deferential politics—the feeling that "better" people like them were by right the natural leaders—which left them uncomfortable making popular appeals to an increasingly egalitarian electorate.

With the designation of competing slates of electors pledged to support specific presidential candidates, the candidates replaced individual electors as the objects of the voters' decisions. The practice of pledging therefore went a long way toward democratizing the choice of president. In doing so, it strengthened the president's hand within the constitutional system as an executive chosen by the people and beholden to them, not other politicians.

The first parties were by no means the elaborate national organizations that emerged a generation later. One eminent historian has characterized them as "loose

---

* The Sedition Act, for example, imposed fines and imprisonment on anyone convicted of publishing "any false, scandalous and malicious writing" bringing the president, Congress, or U.S. government into disrepute. Ten editors and publishers—all Democratic-Republican supporters of Jefferson—were convicted under the statute; on becoming president, Jefferson pardoned them all. See Jeffrey B. Morris and Richard B. Morris, *Encyclopedia of American History,* 7th ed. (New York: HarperCollins, 1996), 147.

collections of provincial interests. . . . Highly local, evolving from rivalries within towns and cities, counties and states, they appealed to an electorate without firmly anchored, hereditary loyalties."[15] Both parties' coalitions were unstable, lacking even uniform names. In fact, any loyalty felt by politicians or voters did not extend much beyond the immediate issue or election.

When their pro-British leanings put them on the wrong side in the War of 1812, the Federalists faded as a national force. In the aftermath of the party's collapse, politicians and informed observers hoped that party competition—and therefore parties—would disappear. The idea that organized opposition would or should be a permanent part of American national politics was still unorthodox. Nevertheless, the first parties accurately presaged future developments.

The Second Party System: Organizational Innovation

By the second decade of the nineteenth century the Democratic-Republicans had eclipsed the Federalists nearly everywhere. James Monroe crushed the Federalists' last presidential nominee in 1816 and was reelected without significant opposition in 1820. The Monroe years were so lacking in party conflict that the period was dubbed the Era of Good Feelings. But the end of party conflict did not mean the end of political conflict; it only meant that political battles were fought within the remaining party. Without the need for unity to win national elections, party networks fell apart. Personal and factional squabbles reemerged to replace party conflict in most states. One immediate consequence was a dramatic falloff in voter participation in presidential elections: turnout among eligible voters dropped from more than 40 percent in 1812 to less than 10 percent in 1820—eloquent testimony to the parties' crucial role in mobilizing voters (see Figure 12-3).

Party competition revived with a fight for the presidency. Under the first party system, the parties' congressional **caucuses** (members assembled with their allies to make party decisions) nominated presidential candidates—a natural development because electoral competition began as an extension of party competition in Congress. This method became a problem, however, when the Federalists dissolved, leaving almost everyone in Congress a nominal Democratic-Republican. With one party so dominant, whoever picked its nominee effectively picked the president. The caucus, then, could have its way as long as there was a general consensus among its members on the nominee, as in the case of Monroe. Without a consensus, the caucus lost influence and legitimacy.

In 1824, after Monroe, no fewer than five serious candidates—all of them Democratic-Republicans—sought the presidency. The congressional caucus nominated William Crawford, who came in third in the electoral vote and dead last in the popular vote. Andrew Jackson, hero of the Battle of New Orleans in the War of 1812, won the most popular and electoral votes but a majority of neither. John Quincy Adams came in second, and House Speaker Henry Clay came in third in popular votes but fourth in the Electoral College. (The remaining candidate, John C. Calhoun, withdrew early and was elected vice president instead.) Because no candidate received a majority of electors, the election was thrown into the House of Representatives. There, Clay gave his support to Adams, who, upon taking office, made Clay his secre-

Figure 12-3 Voter Turnout in Presidential and Midterm Elections, 1789–2008

Percent of eligible electorate voting

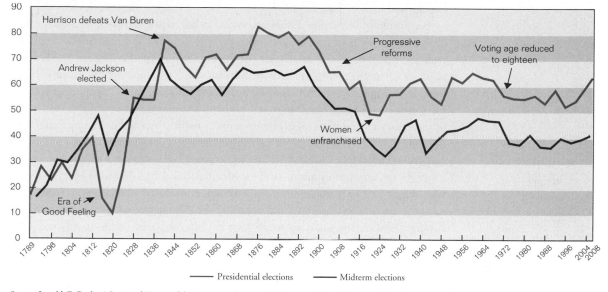

Presidential elections —— Midterm elections

Sources: Jerrold G. Rusk, *A Statistical History of the American Electorate* (Washington, D.C.: CQ Press, 2001), Tables 3-3 and 3-5. Data for 1998–2004 are from Michael P. McDonald, "Turnout Tables," http://elections.gmu.edu/voter_turnout.htm, May 26, 2008; data for 2008 are McDonald's preliminary estimate of 64.1 percent reported November 5, 2008, at www.realclearpolitics.com/news/ap/politics/2008/Nov/05/voter_turnout_best_in_generations_maybe_a_century.html.

tary of state—and, hence, the heir apparent to the White House, since Adams was the fourth president in a row who had previously served as secretary of state.

Jackson's supporters were outraged that a "corrupt bargain" had denied "Old Hickory" his rightful place in the White House. In the midst of that outrage a shrewd New York politician, Martin Van Buren, recognized the opportunity to build a new political coalition. Believing that a national party along the lines of the old Jeffersonian coalition would have the best chance of containing the most explosive issues of the day, particularly slavery, Van Buren put the case for such a party like this:

> Political combinations between inhabitants of the different states are unavoidable & the most natural & beneficial to the country is that between the planters of the South and the plain Republicans of the north. The country has once flourished under a party thus constituted & may again. It would take longer than our lives (even if it were practicable) to create new party feelings. . . . If the old ones are suppressed, geographical divisions founded on local interests or, what is worse prejudices between free and slave holding states will inevitably take their place.[16]

With Jackson as the focal point, Van Buren assembled a political network that became the Democratic Party. Central committees set up in Washington and Nashville, Jackson's hometown, promoted the formation of state organizations, which in turn promoted Jackson clubs or committees in towns and counties. Aided by a nationwide chain of newspapers established to support the cause, Van Buren and Jackson used this organizational pyramid to spread propaganda that kept Jackson and the "wrong" done him in the public consciousness. Local politicians, recognizing Jackson's popularity as a vehicle for their own ambitions, rallied voters with meetings, marches, barbecues, and hickory pole raisings.[17]

Supporters of President Adams had no choice but to put together a network of their own. Adams detested parties and had sought during his administration to build a coalition that incorporated all factions of the old Democratic-Republican and Federalist Parties. He did nothing himself to cultivate electoral allies. Yet his backers, in the process of nominating electors and candidates for other offices and working to get people to vote for them, created what amounted to an Adams party. As one historian has put it, "just by standing for reelection Adams brought a national party into being."[18]

NATIONAL CONVENTIONS. Jackson's smashing victory in 1828 was, among other things, a powerful lesson in the value of political organization. The 1832 election, which he also won handily, featured the first **national party conventions.*** The national convention was promoted as a more democratic alternative to the discredited congressional caucus, allowing much broader popular participation in making presidential nominations. But it also was an eminently practical device for solving problems of conflict and coordination that stand in the path to the White House. The convention was the occasion for assembling, and later refurbishing, the national party coalition. It provided a forum for doing the politicking that convinced diverse party factions to agree to rally behind a single presidential ticket—without necessarily agreeing on anything else. It also was a giant pep rally, firing up the party troops for the contest to come.

The Democrats held a national convention again in 1836, this time to nominate Van Buren as Jackson's successor. Meanwhile, Jackson's leading opponents, including Henry Clay and Daniel Webster, organized themselves as the Whig Party, a name borrowed from British political history that had come to symbolize opposition to royal tyranny, which "King Andrew" Jackson's opponents were fond of alleging. A fractious coalition promoting national development but united primarily by their hostility to Jackson, the Whigs did not hold a national convention but instead attempted to divide and conquer by running three regional candidates. Their plan was to combine their strength behind the strongest candidate in the Electoral College or, failing that, to throw the election into the House.

When that strategy flopped in 1836, the Whigs turned to a ploy that won the party its only two presidential victories: nominating a popular military hero without known political coloration and obscuring party divisions by not writing a platform. The Whig nominee in 1840 was William Henry Harrison, hero of the Battle of Tippecanoe (fought against a confederation of Native American tribes in 1811) and extolled as a

---

* Actually, the Anti-Masonic Party (see box "The Anti-Masonic Party," page 577) had held a convention in 1831, and Jackson's loosely organized opponents, calling themselves National Republicans, had convened a small national gathering that year as well. But the Democratic convention that met in Baltimore to renominate Jackson in 1832 is considered the original full-scale national party convention.

rough-hewn man of the people. He defeated Van Buren in a contest that moved party competition to an entirely new level—but whether higher or lower is still a matter of debate.

The 1840 campaign extended organized two-party competition to every state in the nation, framing not only the contest for president but also competition for offices at all levels of government. Competition inspired unprecedented efforts to involve and mobilize ordinary voters, turning political campaigns into the most exciting spectacles the era offered. As one historian of the period observed:

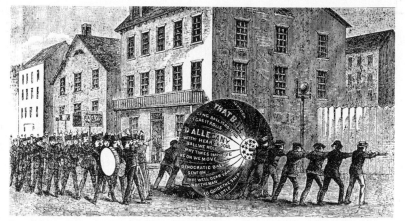

One of the most spectacular campaign gimmicks was the great ball stitched together for Whig William Henry Harrison's presidential campaign in 1840. Made in Allegheny County, Maryland, of buckskin and carrying a long, rhymed message, the ball was rolled through the state by costumed mountain boys. The gimmick originated the phrase "keep the ball rolling."

> Those tens of thousands of men and women who attended the mammoth Whig festival at Nashville in 1840; those untold millions who carried torches, donned uniforms, chanted slogans, or cheered themselves hoarse at innumerable parades and rallies; those puffed-up canvassers of wards, servers of rum, and distributors of largess; and all those simple folk who whipped themselves into a fury of excitement and anxiety as each election day approached, were thrilling to a grand dramatic experience, even a cathartic experience. There was no spectacle, no contest, in America that could match an election campaign.[19]

In effect, the parties solved the problem of free riding endemic to mass electorates by making participation exciting and fun. One sign of their success was a dramatic increase in turnout (see Figure 12-3, page 573). In 1824 only 27 percent of the eligible electorate (adult white males) bothered to vote in the presidential election. When Jackson was elected in 1828, turnout rose to 55 percent, and it stayed at about that level for the next two presidential contests. In 1840 fully 78 percent of the eligible voters took part. More striking evidence of the crucial role of parties—and party competition—in making mass democracy a reality could scarcely be imagined.

Participation in the hoopla surrounding the presidential contest bred strong feelings of party loyalty among many voters. The emotional ties and bonds of loyalty developed in the heat of battle became powerful forces to keep the parties intact even when the inevitable strains that beset such diverse coalitions threatened to break them up.

THE SPOILS SYSTEM. Parties on the rise always attract opportunists. The politicians who flocked to Jackson's banner or joined his Whig opponents were not, for the most part, altruists; rather, they carried on the party work because they were ambitious for an office or other favors. These motives are neither surprising nor appalling.

Parties pursue a collective good: victory for their candidates and policies. All who prefer the winner benefit from the party's victory whether or not they contribute to it. Thus, without some prospect of private reward for party activists, as well, the free-rider problem would have left parties stillborn. The men who worked to elect Jackson or Harrison took as their right the spoils of victory—mainly government jobs but also contracts to supply goods and services to the government or special projects from which they might profit.

The pursuit of political spoils, which came to be known as the spoils system (see Chapter 8), intensified party competition and put a heavy premium on winning. For better or worse, party entrepreneurs proved themselves willing to rise above principle if that was the price of winning. On the positive side, putting victory ahead of principle made parties open and inclusive. For a time, broad national coalitions helped manage the dangerous intersectional conflict over slavery and other divisive issues. The high stakes also inspired imaginative efforts to mobilize the first mass electorate in history. On the negative side, the desire to win contributed to corruption, moral myopia regarding slavery, and public cynicism about the honesty and motives of politicians. In either case, the Democrats and Whigs of the second party system set the pattern for the future: every successful American party has cared more about winning elections than about furthering a consistent set of principles.

Indeed, principled conflict is often a threat to party coalitions. Established party politicians put unity first because their careers depend on it, but voters have no such stake and may care very deeply about the positions a party takes on controversial issues. The Whigs and the Democrats built coalitions around differences on economic policy. The Whigs favored a national bank, high tariffs to protect U.S. manufacturers, and federally sponsored public works; the Democrats rejected the bank and the activist economic role it implied and advocated low tariffs to benefit farmers. Both parties had northern and southern wings and so were badly split by the slavery issue. Leaders tried to keep slavery off the political agenda, but, as feelings intensified, this proved impossible. When the extension of slavery became the dominant national issue, the coalitions that formed the second party system fell apart. For the first and only time in U.S. history, a third party emerged to supplant one of the two dominant parties.

The Third Party System: Entrepreneurial Politics

The Republican Party, organized in 1854 as a coalition of antislavery forces, is unusual only in the success of its challenge to the two-party establishment. Third parties have arisen time and again, but most have failed to attract enough of a following to become more than obscure refuges for the disaffected. On a few occasions, however, third parties have managed to shake up the system, leaving notable traces in party politics long after they have disappeared. The Anti-Masonic Party and the American (Know-Nothing) Party (see boxes "The Anti-Masonic Party" and "The American [Know-Nothing] Party") are examples from the pre–Civil War era. Both sprouted in periods of economic distress and social crisis, originating as anti-parties—movements of "the people" against corrupt and compromising party regulars. As soon as they showed a capacity to win elections, however, they attracted opportunists seeking to jump-start

The Anti-Masonic Party

The Anti-Masonic Party arose during the late 1820s in western New York during a period of disconcertingly rapid social and economic change. The Masons were a secret fraternal organization with a largely upper-class membership. Charges that a Mason had kidnapped and murdered a local dissident who had revealed the order's secrets and then used political clout to cover up the crime provoked a frenzy of public outrage. Agitators denouncing the Masons as a monstrous elite conspiracy against republican government found a ready audience among poor farmers. The movement also attracted religious enthusiasts eager to join a crusade against sin as manifested in slavery, intemperance, and urban life. For a time in the early 1830s, the Anti-Masons formed the primary opposition to the Democrats in parts of New England and the mid-Atlantic states. In 1831 the party held the first national convention, nominating William Wirt for president. Wirt won only a single state (Vermont), but the party managed to elect two governors and win fifty-three House seats.

The party was so successful in achieving its initial purpose of destroying Freemasonry that it soon lost its main rallying point. In New York, for example, the number of Masonic lodges dropped from 506 to 48 in six years. Most of its leaders and adherents eventually joined the Whigs, with profound consequences for that party. As one scholar observed,

> Antimasonry left Whigs a legacy of egalitarianism and evangelism. Antimasonic leaders . . . were much more willing to rabblerouse and organize lower class voters than patrician National Republicans had been. . . . Antimasonic voters among the Whigs remained moralistic crusaders susceptible to isms, and they imparted to Whiggery a Sabbatarian, protemperance, and antislavery spirit in the North that shaped national and state campaigns and often did more than economic issues to define the Whigs.[1]

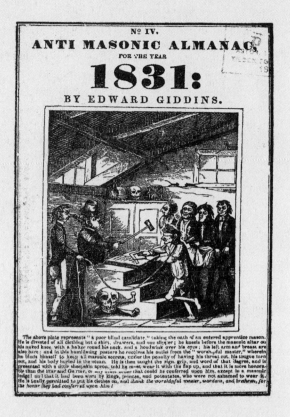

1. Michael F. Holt, *Political Parties and American Political Development from the Age of Jackson to the Age of Lincoln* (Baton Rouge: Louisiana State University Press, 1992), 111.

political careers. For some ambitious men, the protest party was a way station to a position of leadership in a major party. Anti-Masons joined the Whigs; Know-Nothings joined the Republicans.

The Republican Party was organized in opposition to the Kansas-Nebraska Act (1854), which overturned limits on the extension of slavery to the territories enacted

The American (Know-Nothing) Party

The American Party began life as the Order of the Star Spangled Banner, organized in 1849 in New York. Its members, sworn to secrecy, replied to inquiries about its rituals and aims by saying, "I know nothing about it." The Know-Nothings, as they came to be called, were united by their hostility to immigrants—especially Roman Catholics—and to the reigning Democrat and Whig politicians who refused to nominate only native-born American Protestants for public office. They initially entered politics by secretly backing sympathetic candidates of the major parties. Then, in 1855, they went public as the American Party.

The party grew rapidly by fanning anti-Catholic bigotry among native Protestants, making immigrants scapegoats for the economic and social dislocations of the time. (In the cartoon Irish and German immigrants are "stealing" the ballot box and with it American elections.) It also picked up factions of the Whig coalition as it fell apart over the slavery issue. The party appealed to people disgusted with the corruption and compromises of the regular party politicians. In the mid-1850s Know-Nothings won governorships in California, Connecticut, Delaware, Kentucky, Massachusetts, New Hampshire, and Rhode Island, and elected five senators and forty-three members of the House.

For a brief time, the Know-Nothings outstripped the Republican Party in the contest to replace the moribund Whigs as the Democrats' major opposition. But they, too, soon split over slavery. In 1856 the party chose former president Millard Fillmore, signer of the notorious Fugitive Slave Law, as its presiden-

tial nominee, pleasing the southerners but alienating northerners, many of whom defected to the Republican candidate, John C. Fremont. Fremont finished second to the victorious Democrat, James Buchanan. Fillmore came in third with 21 percent of the popular vote—the most ever for a third-party presidential candidate, but still third. Within a short time most of the northern Know-Nothings—leaders as well as followers—had been absorbed by the Republican Party, which in return took on an anti-Catholic, nativist tinge in many states. Although Abraham Lincoln opposed Know-Nothingism, he owed his nomination in 1860 to former Know-Nothings in the Republican Party who hated his chief rival, William Seward, even more than they did him.

Source: Michael F. Holt, *Political Parties and American Political Development from the Age of Jackson to the Age of Lincoln* (Baton Rouge: Louisiana State University Press, 1992), 123–125.

earlier in the Missouri Compromise of 1820 and the Compromise of 1850. It drew leaders and followers from two earlier antislavery parties, as well as the Know-Nothings, antislavery Whigs, and dissident Democrats. Its adopted name laid claim to the mantles of both the Jeffersonian Republicans and the National Republicans who had backed Adams against Jackson.

Although founded on the slavery issue, the Republican Party was by no means a single-issue party. It also appealed to business and commercial interests (elements of the old Whig coalition) by promising a protective tariff and a transcontinental railway and to farmers by promising free land for homesteading. On only its second try the party elected a president, Abraham Lincoln. His victory over divided opposition in 1860 triggered the South's secession from the Union and then the Civil War, from which the Republicans emerged as the party of victory and union. For the next generation the party sought to retain its ascendancy by appealing variously to patriotism, national expansion, and laissez-faire capitalism and by distributing pensions to Civil War veterans and protective tariffs to manufacturers.

The end of Reconstruction in 1876 restored local control to white southern politicians (see Chapter 4) and left the newly revived Democratic Party an equal competitor for national power. Democrats benefited from overwhelming majorities in the South, where whites despised the Republicans as the party of the enemy and African Americans were largely disenfranchised. The Democrats also had pockets of strength in the West, in the border states (heavily settled by southerners), and among immigrant groups in urban northern areas (especially German Lutherans and Irish Catholics).

PARTY MACHINES. Party organizations reached their peak of development during the third party system. Patronage—jobs, contracts, development rights, zoning favors—generated by the rapid growth of industrial cities provided the capital; party entrepreneurs provided the management. The classic **party machines** were built on simple principles of exchange: party politicians provided favors and services to people throughout the year in return for their votes on Election Day. They found an eager market for their offerings among the growing population of poor immigrants whose basic needs—shelter, food, fuel, jobs, and help in adapting to a new and bewildering country—were far more pressing than any concern for party programs or ideologies. One such party politician was George Washington Plunkitt, who, thanks to such exchanges, thrived during the heyday of New York City's Tammany Hall Democratic machine at the turn of the century (see box "The Wisdom of George Washington Plunkitt").*

The late nineteenth-century party machines represented the culmination of trends reaching back to the Jacksonian era. Politics had become a full-time profession for thousands of individuals. Those who took it up were mostly "men of slender social distinction, whose training came not from the countinghouse or the university, but from the street gang, the saloon, the fire department, the political club."[20] Winning local elections was the paramount goal of party professionals; issues, programs, and candidates (national as well as local) mattered only insofar as they could help or hinder that goal. National parties were contentious alliances of local party organizations competing for patronage. Votes were sought wherever they were available by whatever means worked.

---

* The most powerful Democratic faction in New York City for nearly a century was commonly referred to as "Tammany Hall." The name reflected its origins in the Society of Saint Tammany, named after a legendary Delaware Indian chief. Founded in 1789 as a patriotic fraternal and charitable club, it had become by the 1840s the club of choice for leading Democratic politicians, and by the 1860s "membership in Tammany and leadership of the Democratic organization were so parallel as to be interchangeable." Tammany Hall was the "wigwam" where the club met. See Arthur Mann, "Introduction," in *Plunkitt of Tammany Hall,* ed. William L. Riordan (New York: Dutton, 1963), xii–xiii.

The Wisdom of George Washington Plunkitt

There's only one way to hold a district: you must study human nature and act accordin'. . . .

To learn real human nature, you have to go among the people, see them and be seen. I know every man, woman, and child in the Fifteenth District, except them that's been born this summer—and I know some of them, too. I know what they like and what they don't like, what they are strong at and what they are weak in, and I reach them by approachin' at the right side.

For instance, here's how I gather in the young men. I hear of a young feller that's proud of his voice, thinks he can sing fine. I ask him to come around to Washington Hall and join our Glee Club. He comes and sings, and he's a follower of Plunkitt for life. Another young feller gains a reputation as a baseball player in a vacant lot. I bring him into our baseball club. That fixes him. You'll find him workin' for my ticket at the polls next election day. . . . I rope them all in by givin' them opportunities to show themselves off. I don't trouble them with political arguments. I just study human nature and act accordin'. . . .

* * *

What tells in holdin' your grip on your district is to go right down among the poor families and help them in the different ways they need help. I've got a regular system for this. If there's a fire in Ninth, Tenth, or Eleventh Avenue, for example, any hour of the day or night, I'm usually there with some of my election district captains as soon as the fire engines. If a family is burned out I don't ask whether they are Republicans or Democrats, and I don't refer them to the Charity Organization Society, which would investigate their case in a month or two and decide they were worthy of help about the time they are dead from starvation. I just get quarters for them, buy

George Washington Plunkitt dispensing advice from the New York County Courthouse bootblack stand.

clothes for them if their clothes were burned up, and fix them up until they get things runnin' again. It's philanthropy, but it's politics, too—mighty good politics. Who can tell how many votes one of these fires brings me? The poor are the most grateful people in the world, and let me tell you, they have more friends in their neighborhoods than the rich have in theirs.

* * *

Another thing, I can always get a job for a deservin' man. I make it a point to keep track of jobs, and it seldom happens that I don't have a few up my sleeve ready for use. I know every big employer in the district and the whole city for that matter, and they ain't in the habit of saying no to me when I ask them for a job.

Source: William L. Riordan, ed., *Plunkitt of Tammany Hall: A Series of Very Plain Talks on Very Practical Politics* (New York: Dutton, 1963), 25–28.

THE PROGRESSIVE ATTACK. Party machines were regularly attacked as corrupt and inefficient and party politicians as incapable of imagining, let alone implementing, solutions to the many problems created by the growth of large industry and national markets. Reformers, working almost entirely from within the two-party system, sought to destroy the party machines by depriving party leaders of the capacity to reward followers. Eventually, they succeeded. The most important changes were introduced during what is now called the **Progressive Era**—the decades just before and after the turn of the twentieth century, overlapping the end of the third party system and the beginning of the fourth. The most important reforms were the civil service, the Australian ballot, and primary elections.

After passage of the Pendleton Act in 1883, reformers began to replace the spoils system with a civil service system in most jurisdictions. Under the spoils system, the winning party filled appointive government jobs with its faithful workers, firing everyone who had not worked for the ticket. The civil service system turned government jobs into professional careers. Appointment and advancement depended on merit (typically, performance on a competitive examination), not political pull, and civil servants could not be fired except "for cause"—failing to do their jobs or committing crimes (see Chapter 8). As more government jobs were brought under civil service, the rewards for party work shrank, reducing the number of party workers.

Another reform associated with the Progressive Era was the secret ballot. Prior to the 1890s each party produced its own ballots (listing only its candidates), which were handed to voters outside the polling place (see Chapter 7). Because party ballots were readily distinguishable, voters could not keep their choices to themselves or easily vote a **split ticket**—that is, vote for candidates of different parties for different offices—for this required manipulating several ballots. The system invited corruption and intimidation; party workers could monitor voters and reward or punish them accordingly. Thus between 1888 and 1896, 90 percent of the states adopted the **Australian ballot,** named for its country of origin. The new type of ballot, still in use today, was prepared by the government, listed candidates from all parties, and was marked in the privacy of a voting booth. This change made it much more difficult for parties to exchange favors for votes because it left no (legal) way for the party to know if voters had kept their side of the bargain.

With adoption of the Australian ballot, the government became involved in party nominations, for someone had to determine officially which parties and names would be listed on the government-produced ballot. Laws were passed to regulate party nominating conventions and, later, to allow a party's voters to nominate candidates through **primary elections.** Strong party machines were still able to dominate primaries, but as party organizations were weakened by other changes, primaries deprived them of a crucial political resource: the ability to control access to elective public office by controlling nominations.

Progressives advocated, and in many places achieved, other reforms intended to detach local politics from national politics on the ground that "there is no Republican or Democratic way to pave a street" (forgetting that Democrats and Republicans may have different priorities in deciding whose streets to pave or who gets the paving contract). At the local level, elections were made officially "nonpartisan" and held separately from federal elections. States also adopted laws requiring would-be voters to register before Election Day (to reduce the possibilities of fraud) and to pass literacy tests (unlike the old party-produced ballots, the Australian ballot could be used only by literate voters). Professional city managers were hired to run cities like business corporations, and urban services were "taken out of politics" by putting them under the

SAMPLE BALLOT - BEXAR COUNTY (BOLETA DE MUESTRA) - (CONDADO DE BEXAR)
Joint General and Special Election (Elección Conjunto General y Especial)
Tuesday, November 4, 2008 (Martes 4 de Noviembre de 2008)

INSTRUCTIONS NOTE: 1. Vote for the candidate of your choice in each race by darkening in the oval provided to the left of the name of the candidate. 2. You may cast a straight-party vote (that is, cast a vote for all the nominees of one party) by darkening in the oval provided to the left of the name of the party. If you cast a straight-party vote for all the nominees of one party and also cast a vote for an opponent of one of that party's nominees, your vote for the opponent will be counted as well as your vote for all the other nominees of the party for which the straight-party vote was cast. 3. You may vote for a write-in candidate by writing in the name of the candidate on the line provided and darkening in the oval provided to the left of the line. 4. Use only the marker provided.
NOTA DE INSTRUCCIÓN: 1. (Vota por el candidato de su preferencia en cada carrera llenando completamente el espacio ovalado a la izquierda del nombre del candidato. 2. Usted podrá votar por todos los candidatos de un solo partido político (es decir, votar por todos los candidatos nombrados del mismo partido político) llenando completamente el espacio ovalado a la izquierda del nombre de dicho partido político. Si usted vota por un solo partido político ("straight-ticket") y también vota por el contrincante de uno de los candidatos de dicho partido político, se computara su voto por el contrincante tanto como su voto por todos los demás candidatos del partido político de su preferencia. 3. Usted podrá votar por inserción escrita escribiendo el nombre del candidato en la línea provista y llenando completamente el espacio ovalado a la izquierda de la línea. 4. Solamente use el marcador provisto.)

Straight Party
(Partido Completo)
- REPUBLICAN PARTY (REP) (Partido Republicano)
- DEMOCRATIC PARTY (DEM) (Partido Demócrata)
- LIBERTARIAN PARTY (LIB) (Partido Libertario)

Federal
(Federal)

President and Vice-President
(Presidente y Vice Presidente)
- John McCain / Sarah Palin (REP)
- Barack Obama / Joe Biden (DEM)
- Bob Barr / Wayne A. Root(LIB)
- Write-in(Voto Escrito)

United States Senator
(Senador de los Estados Unidos)
- John Cornyn (REP)
- Richard J. (Rick) Noriega (DEM)
- Yvonne Adams Schick (LIB)

United States Representative, District 20 (Representante de los Estados Unidos, Distrito Núm. 20)
- Robert Litoff (REP)
- Charles A. Gonzalez (DEM)
- Michael Idrogo (LIB)

United States Representative, District 21 (Representante de los Estados Unidos, Distrito Núm. 21)
- Lamar Smith (REP)
- James Arthur Strohm (LIB)

United States Representative, District 23 (Representante de los Estados Unidos, Distrito Núm. 23)
- Lyle Larson (REP)
- Ciro D. Rodriguez (DEM)
- Lani Connolly (LIB)

United States Representative, District 28 (Representante de los Estados Unidos, Distrito Núm. 28)
- Jim Fish (REP)
- Henry Cuellar (DEM)
- Ross Lynn Leone (LIB)

State (Estado)

Railroad Commissioner
(Comisionado de Ferrocarriles)
- Michael L. Williams (REP)
- Mark Thompson (DEM)
- David Floyd (LIB)

Chief Justice, Supreme Court
(Juez Presidente, Corte Suprema)
- Wallace B. Jefferson (REP)
- Jim Jordan (DEM)
- Tom Oxford (LIB)

Justice, Supreme Court, Place 7 (Juez, Corte Suprema, Lugar Núm. 7)
- Dale Wainwright(REP)
- Sam Houston (DEM)
- David G. Smith (LIB)

Justice, Supreme Court, Place 8 (Juez, Corte Suprema, Lugar Núm. 8)
- Phil Johnson (REP)
- Linda Reyna Yanez (DEM)
- Drew Shirley (LIB)

Judge, Court of Criminal Appeals, Place 3 (Juez, Corte de Apelaciones Criminales, Lugar Núm. 3)
- Tom Price (REP)
- Susan Strawn (DEM)
- Matthew E. Eilers (LIB)

Judge, Court of Criminal Appeals, Place 4 (Juez, Corte de Apelaciones Criminales, Lugar Núm. 4)
- Paul Womack (REP)
- J.R. Molina (DEM)
- Dave Howard (LIB)

Judge, Court of Criminal Appeals, Place 9 (Juez, Corte de Apelaciones Criminales, Lugar Núm. 9)
- Cathy Cochran (REP)
- William Bryan Strange, III (LIB)

State Senator, District 21 (Senador Estatal, Distrito Núm. 21)
- Louis H. Bruni (REP)
- Judith Zaffirini (DEM)
- Barry L. Allison (LIB)

State Senator, District 26 (Senador Estatal, Distrito Núm. 26)
- Leticia Van de Putte (DEM)
- Steve Lopez (LIB)

State Representative, District 116 (Representante Estatal, Distrito Núm. 116)
- Trey Martinez Fischer (DEM)
- William T. Armstrong (LIB)

State Representative, District 117 (Representante Estatal, Distrito Núm. 117)
- John V. Garza (REP)
- David McQuade Leibowitz (DEM)

State Representative, District 118 (Representante Estatal, Distrito Núm. 118)
- Don Green (REP)
- Joe Farias (DEM)
- James L. Thompson (LIB)

State Representative, District 119 (Representante Estatal, Distrito Núm. 119)
- Roland Gutierrez (DEM)

State Representative, District 120 (Representante Estatal, Distrito Núm. 120)
- Ruth Jones McClendon (DEM)

State Representative, District 121 (Representante Estatal, Distrito Núm. 121)
- Joe Straus (REP)
- Arthur M. Thomas IV (LIB)

State Representative, District 122 (Representante Estatal, Distrito Núm. 122)
- Frank J. Corte, Jr. (REP)
- Frances Carnot (DEM)
- Sally Baynton (LIB)

State Representative, District 123 (Representante Estatal, Distrito Núm. 123)
- Mike Villarreal (DEM)

State Representative, District 124 (Representante Estatal, Distrito Núm. 124)
- José Menéndez (DEM)

State Representative, District 125 (Representante Estatal, Distrito Núm. 125)
- Joaquin Castro (DEM)

Chief Justice, 4th Court of Appeals District (Juez Presidente, Corte de Apelaciones, Distrito Núm. 4)
- Ann Comerio (REP)
- Catherine Stone (DEM)

District Judge, 37th Judicial District (Juez del Distrito, Distrito Judicial Núm. 37)
- David Berchelmann (REP)
- Amber Liddell Alwais (DEM)

District Judge, 57th Judicial District (Juez del Distrito, Distrito Judicial Núm. 57)
- Joe F. Brown, Jr. (REP)
- Antonia (Toni) Arteaga (DEM)

District Judge, 73rd Judicial District (Juez del Distrito, Distrito Judicial Núm. 73)
- Andy Mireles (DEM)

District Judge, 131st Judicial District (Juez del Distrito, Distrito Judicial Núm. 131)
- John D. Gabriel (DEM)

District Judge, 166th Judicial District (Juez del Distrito, Distrito Judicial Núm. 166)
- Martha Tanner (DEM)

District Judge, 175th Judicial District (Juez del Distrito, Distrito Judicial Núm. 175)
- Mary Roman (DEM)

District Judge, 379th Judicial District (Juez del Distrito, Distrito Judicial Núm. 379)
- Bert Richardson (REP)
- Ron Rangel (DEM)

District Judge, 386th Judicial District (Juez del Distrito, Distrito Judicial Núm. 386)
- Laura Parker (REP)

District Judge, 399th Judicial District (Juez del Distrito, Distrito Judicial Núm. 399)
- Juanita Vasquez-Gardner (REP)

District Judge, 407th Judicial District (Juez del Distrito, Distrito Judicial Núm. 407)
- Karen Pozza (DEM)

District Judge, 408th Judicial District (Juez del Distrito, Distrito Judicial Núm. 408)
- Larry Noll (DEM)

County (Condado)

Sheriff (Sherife)
- Dennis J. McKnight(REP)
- Amadeo Ortiz (DEM)

County Tax Assessor-Collector (Asesor-Colector de Impuestos del Condado)
- Sylvia Romo (DEM)

County Commissioner, Precinct No. 1 (Comisionado del Condado, Precinto Núm. 1)
- Sergio "Chico" Rodriguez (DEM)

County Commissioner, Precinct No. 3 (Comisionado del Condado, Precinto Núm. 3)
- Kevin A. Wolff (REP)
- Chip Haass (DEM)
- Jeff Carruthers (LIB)
- Timothy E. Ferry (IND)
- Write-in(Voto Escrito)

Justice of the Peace, Precinct No. 1, Place 1 (Juez de Paz, Precinto Núm. 1, Lugar Núm. 1)
- Monica Lisa Caballero (DEM)

Justice of the Peace, Precinct No. 2, Place 1 (Juez de Paz, Precinto Núm. 2, Lugar Núm. 1)
- Marcia S. Weiner (REP)
- Steve Walker (DEM)

Constable, Precinct No. 1 (Condestable, Precinto Núm. 1)
- Ruben C. Tejeda (DEM)

Constable, Precinct No. 2 (Condestable, Precinto Núm. 2)
- Johnny Bustos (REP)
- Val Flores (DEM)

Constable, Precinct No. 3 (Condestable, Precinto Núm. 3)
- Mark Vojvodich (REP)
- Edward (Ed) Coleman (DEM)

Constable, Precinct No. 4 (Condestable, Precinto Núm. 4)
- Robert 'Mike' Blount (DEM)

control of independent boards. At the national level a constitutional amendment, ratified in 1913, took the choice of U.S. senators from the state legislatures and gave it to the voters, eliminating the party politics that had governed the selection of senators.

Although ostensibly aimed at rooting out corruption and cleaning up electoral politics, progressive reforms also were designed to enhance the political clout of the "right" kind of people—educated middle- and upper-middle-class folks like the reformers themselves—at the expense of poor urban immigrants and their leaders "of slender social distinction." Stricter voter registration laws discriminated against the poor and uneducated. Literacy tests had the same effect and were used widely in the South to disenfranchise African Americans and sometimes poor whites.

Progressive reforms were adopted to varying degrees in almost every state. And on the whole they worked, weakening or destroying party machines and preventing their resurrection. Where the progressive agenda was most fully achieved, parties became little more than empty shells, existing mainly to help the state government administer elections. Until recently, for example, official party organizations in California were not even allowed to endorse candidates in primary elections.

Vigorous party organizations did survive, though, in some places, often for many years. For example, a tightly controlled Democratic machine ran Chicago until the 1970s. Over the long run, however, progressive reforms deprived state and local party organizations—the basic building blocks of national parties—of much of their political power.

THE CONSEQUENCES OF PROGRESSIVE REFORMS. These changes had several important consequences for electoral politics. First, turnout declined. Tighter registration laws, the Australian ballot, and literacy tests discouraged voting. With fewer jobs and favors to reward the party workers, fewer people were willing to do the work that wedded voters to the party and brought them to the polls. According to Figure 12-3, from the Civil War to the 1890s about 80 percent of the eligible electorate voted in presidential elections. By the 1910s turnout had fallen to around 60 percent. It fell further when women were enfranchised in 1920 and the number of eligible voters doubled. It has not risen much above 60 percent in any election year since. Many women initially ignored politics as "men's business," and women's turnout levels—which today surpass men's—took a half-century to pull even. Turnout declined most among poor and uneducated people, the very citizens most dependent on parties for incentives to vote. (For more on turnout, see Chapter 11.)

The reforms also began to shift the focus of electoral politics from parties to candidates. When party organizations controlled nominations and voters chose between whole party tickets, political careers were

President Franklin Roosevelt and his allies assembled the Democrats' New Deal coalition from remarkably diverse segments of American society. In this 1936 photo Roosevelt chats with members of one group served by New Deal policies, North Dakota farmers who have received drought relief grants.

bound tightly to parties. With the advent of the Australian ballot and primary elections, these bonds weakened. Candidates could win nominations with or without the party's blessing by appealing directly to voters; they could campaign separately from the party's team because voters could now split their tickets more easily. The full flowering of candidate-centered electoral politics had to await the development of new communication technologies—mainly television and computerized direct mail—but the seeds were planted by the progressive reforms.

By altering the incentives to perform party work, reforms also contributed to changes in the demographics and goals of party organizations. Traditional party organizations were built on material incentives attractive to working-class people; consequently, parties concentrated on winning elections to keep the material benefits flowing. As their resource base shrank, patronage-based parties were supplanted by party organizations made up of middle-class people inspired by nonmaterial incentives—devotion to a particular candidate, issue, or ideology—people for whom a party victory was often less important than the success of their preferred candidate or issue positions.

Paradoxically, the Progressive Era left the Republicans and Democrats organizationally weaker but more entrenched than ever in the political system. Once considered private groups, parties were now treated by the law in many states as essentially public entities charged with managing elections. Regulations tended to privilege the two major parties and discriminate against new parties and independent candidates.

Moreover, the advent of primary elections encouraged dissidents to work within the established parties because outsiders could now compete for control of the party's machinery and name. Why should malcontents buck the long odds against winning under a new party label when they could convert an established party to their cause? No new party came close to challenging either of the major parties in the twentieth century, but those parties suffered some convulsive changes as the result of challenges from within.

The Fourth Party System: Republican Ascendancy

From the end of Reconstruction in 1876 until 1894, the third American party system settled into place, and the Republicans and Democrats competed on nearly even terms. In 1896 the Democrats reacted to a severe economic downturn by adopting the platform of the People's Party, or Populists, a party of agrarian protest against high railroad rates and the gold standard, whose first presidential candidate had won five states in 1892. The Democrats nominated for president William Jennings Bryan, a candidate with strong Populist sympathies. Bryan and the Democrats proposed, among other economic innovations, to make silver as well as gold a monetary standard. The silver standard would increase the money supply, easing interest rates and therefore the pressure on debtors, which included most farmers and westerners. The Republican campaign persuaded many urban workers that the Democrats' proposals threatened their livelihoods ("sound" money backed by gold was the backbone of the financial system that sustained the industrial economy) and so converted them into Republicans. The reaction to the agrarian takeover of the Democrats left the Republicans with a clear national majority for the next generation; the new alignment is commonly designated the fourth party system.

The Republican Party ultimately lost its ascendancy to the Great Depression. Having taken credit for the prosperity of the 1920s with policies highly favorable to financial institutions and industrial corporations, the Republicans and their president, Herbert Hoover, were saddled with the blame for the economic devastation and high unemployment that followed the 1929 stock market crash. Franklin Roosevelt, the Democratic candidate, defeated Hoover in the 1932 election. Roosevelt's New Deal solidified a new coalition of interests that gave the Democrats a popular majority. Despite the coalition's slow demise since the 1960s, the Democratic Party has retained that majority—sometimes barely—to this day.

The Fifth Party System: The New Deal Coalition

Nothing illustrates the diversity of American party coalitions more strikingly than does the **New Deal coalition,** which brought together Democrats of every conceivable background. It united white southern segregationists with northern African Americans (few southern African Americans could vote), progressive intellectuals with machine politicians, union members and their families with the poorest farmers, Roman Catholics with Southern Baptists. These diverse groups agreed on only one thing—electing Democrats—while having very different reasons for wanting to do so.

Some were attracted by Roosevelt's New Deal policies, which, in tackling the Depression's devastation, radically expanded the federal government's responsibility for, and authority over, the economic and social welfare of all Americans. The Wagner Act of 1935, known as organized labor's "bill of rights," cemented union support. Public works programs pulled in poor and unemployed citizens, including northern African Americans (who until then favored the party of Lincoln), and provided patronage for urban machines. Farm programs appealed to distressed rural voters. Progressive intellectuals applauded the federal government's expanded role in attending to the economic welfare of citizens. The adoption of the Social Security and unemployment insurance systems earned the gratitude of working people whose economic insecurity had been so painfully exposed by the Depression.

Other groups were part of the Democratic coalition by tradition. Conservative southern whites were still expressing political identities forged in the Civil War. Roman Catholics, already disproportionately Democratic (a tinge of anti-Catholic nativism was a legacy of the Republicans' Know-Nothing heritage), had become overwhelmingly so in 1928, when the party chose Al Smith, the first of their faith to be nominated for president by a major party. They remained in part because the Democrats kept their pledge to repeal Prohibition. As a movement, Prohibitionism was largely Protestant, with clear anti-Catholic and anti-immigrant overtones. Jews in the cities of the East and Midwest also had supported Smith, in reaction to the rural and small-town Protestant bigotry his candidacy had provoked, and stayed with the Democrats under Roosevelt, an early and staunch enemy of Nazi Germany.

The opposing Republican coalition was a smaller, inverted image of the Democratic coalition: business and professional people, upper-income white Protestants, residents of smaller towns and cities in the Northeast and Midwest, and ideological conservatives. It was united by what it opposed: Roosevelt's New Deal programs and the greatly enlarged federal bureaucracy they engendered (see Chapter 8), which Republicans excoriated as unconstitutional, unwise, and un-American.

EROSION OF THE NEW DEAL COALITION. The complexities of coalition politics aside, national electoral competition during the New Deal period was organized around a single question: are you for or against the New Deal? As long as that was the question, the New Deal alignment held. But when new issues became the focus of electoral politics, the Democratic coalition began to unravel. The Republicans enabled new issues to shape electoral politics by finally recognizing that the major New Deal programs were there to stay; a party in search of a national majority cannot cling forever to losing positions. When they finally regained the White House in 1952 (using the old Whig ploy of nominating a military hero, General Dwight Eisenhower), it was not on a promise to repeal the New Deal but to administer its programs more frugally. Once that question was settled, other issues could come to the fore.

The first and most important of these issues was civil rights for African Americans (discussed in detail in Chapter 4). As the Democrats became the party of civil rights, white southerners began to depart. At about the same time, the war in Vietnam also split the Democrats, largely along the fault lines of class. The party machine politicians and labor leaders whose blue-collar constituents supplied most of the soldiers generally supported the war, as did most southern Democrats. Opposition was led by liberal intellectuals and was most conspicuous on elite university campuses. New controversies over the bounds of acceptable social behavior deepened the split as sexual freedom, pornography, abortion, women's rights, and gay rights became the stuff of politics.

Traditional Democratic constituencies also were divided over new economic initiatives. The Great Society programs enacted during Lyndon Johnson's presidency (1963–1969) lacked the broad appeal of the New Deal. The major New Deal programs—Social Security, unemployment insurance, and Medicare (a New Deal–type program, although not enacted until 1965)—serve politically active majorities. Great Society programs—housing subsidies, school nutrition programs, Head Start, food stamps, and Medicaid—serve a politically apathetic minority: the poor. For many working-class and middle-class Democrats, the New Deal was for "us," but the Great Society's War on Poverty was for "them." The costs of these programs weighed more heavily as economic growth slowed in the 1970s, increasing opposition to taxes. A new issue—environmental protection—also posed dilemmas for Democrats, pitting blue-collar jobs (or recreation activities) against the aesthetic and health benefits sought by middle-class environmentalists.

The Republicans, although less diverse than their rivals, could not avoid some serious divisions of their own. The conservative and moderate wings struggled for dominance from the New Deal period until the 1980s. Conservatives took over the national party in 1964, nominating one of their own, Sen. Barry Goldwater of Arizona, for president. Goldwater's vote against the Civil Rights Act of 1964 endeared him to southern segregationists but alienated moderates in his own party, as did his hostility to the core New Deal programs. His overwhelming defeat left the party temporarily in tatters. It quickly recovered, however, by taking advantage of the deep divisions within the old Democratic coalition to win five of the next six presidential elections.

Republican candidates since Richard Nixon have built winning coalitions by combining affluent economic conservatives with middle-class and working-class social conservatives, particularly from what is called the Christian Right. To attract economic conservatives, the Republicans declared war on taxation, regulation, and welfare; to win over social conservatives, they offered law and order, patriotism (opposition to the Vietnam War left Democrats vulnerable here), and "traditional family values," defined to mean a ban on abortion, promotion of prayer in public schools, and heightened concern for the civil rights of white males. But this coalition is not much more united than its Democratic counterpart. Many affluent economic conservatives are not attracted to the Christian Right's social agenda, and many social conservatives of modest means remain reluctant to expose themselves to the mercies of an unfettered free market.

CHANGING THE RULES. Divisions within the parties' electoral coalitions during the 1960s were played out in intraparty battles that reshaped the parties as organizations. One major result was the progressive-style reform of presidential nominations. The Democrats' nominating practices had fallen into disrepute because many southern

Battles between Vietnam War demonstrators and the Chicago police outside the 1968 Democratic national convention caused a revolt in the convention, culminating in the removal of the Chicago mayor, Richard J. Daley, as a delegate. Not only did the last of the party machine mayors depart, but the turmoil also stimulated the party to install reforms that have dramatically altered the way the political parties nominate their presidential candidates.

delegations were discriminating against black voters just recently activated by the civil rights movement. It was the Vietnam War, however, that triggered wholesale reform. When those Democrats opposed to American involvement in Vietnam sought to nominate an antiwar candidate in 1968, they found the diverse, arcane state procedures for selecting delegates to the national nominating convention a formidable barrier. Only fifteen states held primary elections, and in some of them support in primaries did not translate into convention delegates. Presidential primaries were merely venues for candidates to show party bosses how electable they were. Because party leaders chose the delegates in most states, leaders from the larger states dominated the convention. In Pennsylvania, for example, the antiwar candidate, Sen. Eugene McCarthy, won 72 percent of the primary votes, but Vice President Hubert Humphrey got 80 percent of Pennsylvania's convention delegates.

In 1968 the convention was still the quadrennial coming together of diverse and fractious state party organizations that it had been since the 1830s. Most party regulars were, by habit, loyal to their president, Lyndon Johnson, and his anointed successor, Vice President Humphrey. Meeting in Chicago, the Democrats nominated Humphrey while antiwar protests filled the streets outside the convention hall. When the demonstrations got out of hand, they were violently suppressed by the Chicago police on the orders of Mayor Richard J. Daley, boss of the strongest surviving party machine and a major Humphrey backer. The party's internal divisions, dramatized by the riots and exposed to the world on national television, doomed the Democratic ticket and led to the election of Richard Nixon as president.

PRIMARY ELECTIONS AND CAUCUSES. To repair the Democratic coalition and restore the convention's legitimacy, a party commission (the McGovern-Fraser Commission) drew up a new set of criteria specifying that convention delegations had to be chosen in a process that was "open, timely, and representative." The state parties could comply in one of two ways. They could hold a primary election, the outcome of which would determine at least 90 percent of the state's delegation. Or they could hold local party caucuses open to all Democrats, who would select delegates to a meeting at the county, congressional district, or state level. These delegates would in turn elect delegates to the national convention. The easiest option was the primary, and most state parties have adopted it. In 2008 Democratic primaries were held in thirty-seven states; the rest selected delegates via caucuses.

In another change, the winner-take-all method of allocating delegates went out the window. Instead of awarding all of a state's delegates to the top vote getter, the new rules allocated delegates proportionately to candidates according to the share of votes they received in the primary or the caucus. To meet the "representativeness" standard, delegations had to include more minorities, women, and young adults. Because most elected officeholders were white males over thirty, these rules meant that many of them could no longer attend the convention.

The Democrats' delegate selection rules created a whole new ball game. Previously the party's supreme plum, its presidential nomination, had been conferred by party leaders, who sought to pick a winner who would be obligated to them and therefore send presidential favors their way. Moreover, they wanted a candidate who would help the whole party ticket on Election Day. Now the nomination goes to the candidate who can best mobilize support in primary elections. If party leaders are to exercise any influence in this process, they must do it by delivering endorsements and electoral resources to their favorite before and during the primary season.

The new process may be "fairer," as intended, but it has threatened other party goals, namely winning and governing. In some years, the candidate who most excites the activist minority who show up for primary elections (turnout is typically 20 to 30 percent of eligible voters) was not even the best vote-getter among Democrats generally, let alone the broader electorate. For example, Sen. George McGovern, the 1972 nominee, was the choice of antiwar Democrats but no one else; he won only 38 percent of the general election vote, the worst showing for a Democrat since the New Deal realignment.

The system also allows outsiders with tenuous links to other Democratic leaders to compete. Jimmy Carter, an obscure one-term governor of Georgia, won the nomination and then the White House in 1976 but found it nearly impossible to work effectively with his party in Congress. Carter's lack of experience in the ways of Washington, and his lack of political ties to its movers and shakers, clearly handicapped his administration (see Chapter 7).[21] Responding to such problems, the Democrats altered their rules several more times to give party regulars more influence in the selection process. Prominent elected officials—governors, senators, and representatives—are now automatically among the convention delegates. These so-called **superdelegates** accounted for 823, or 19 percent of the 4,257 votes at the Democrats' 2008 convention. Because Barack Obama led Hillary Clinton by only 137 votes among delegates allocated through the primaries and caucuses, the superdelegates effectively determined the choice of candidate for the first time. Most of them sided with Obama after the final primaries in June, assuring him of the nomination. Had they instead handed the nomination to Clinton, they would have outraged Obama supporters and split the party badly, a potential downside evidently not contemplated when the party added superdelegates to the mix.

The nomination process enables the parties to solve the coordination problem posed by competing presidential aspirants. Sometimes party elites do the coordinating; if they can reach broad agreement on which candidate to support, they can be decisive, as the nomination of George W. Bush in 2000 illustrated. Bush initially faced a crowded field of twelve candidates, but by the beginning of the delegate selection process (the Iowa caucuses on January 24), six had dropped out, and by early February only Sen. John McCain remained a serious rival. Bush swept away the competition by persuading the Republican Party establishment, elected officials and campaign donors alike, that his candidacy offered the best chance of returning the White House to Republican control. Bush was acceptable to all factions of the party, from affluent "country club" Republicans to religious conservatives, emerging as the consensus solution to the party's problem of coordinating Republican opposition to Democratic nominee Al Gore.

Leaders are not the only partisans who can coordinate the choice of presidential nominee. In 2004 it was the Democrats who attended the Iowa caucuses on January 19 who effectively organized the nomination of Bush's opponent. Prior to the caucuses, Democrats across the country were divided on whom they wanted to challenge the president, with six candidates getting significant support in polls; Vermont governor Howard Dean led but was preferred by only a quarter of Democratic voters. By giving John Kerry the nod over Dean and the other candidates (with 37 percent of the vote), Iowa Democrats signaled their belief that he was the party's strongest prospect to defeat Bush. Kerry got an immediate boost in the national polls, which was reinforced by his victory in New Hampshire eight days later. By mid-February, Kerry had become the Democrats' consensus favorite and had locked up the nomination.

John McCain performed a similar feat in 2008. His revival in national preference polls after a long decline throughout 2007 that had him running in third place just before the primary season (Figure 12-4a) suggests that Republican voters had reservations about his candidacy but, after auditioning the rest of the field, decided that he best fit the role after all. His national support soared after his performance in the January primaries in New Hampshire, Michigan, South Carolina, and Florida, and he subsequently sewed up the nomination by winning 61 percent of the delegates at stake in the primaries held in twenty-one states on February 5. McCain benefited from party rules in most states with Republican primaries that allocate delegates as winner-take-all, either statewide or by congressional districts. For example, McCain won 42 percent of the vote in the California primary to former Massachusetts governor Mitt Romney's 34 percent, but took 96 percent of the delegates to Romney's 4 percent.

Democratic voters had a much more difficult time settling on their candidate in 2008 (Figure 12-4b). Hillary Clinton led in national polls for all of 2007 but could not add to her numbers. Barack Obama's early victories in Iowa and South Carolina transformed the contest into a two-person race with him as the leading candidate, but

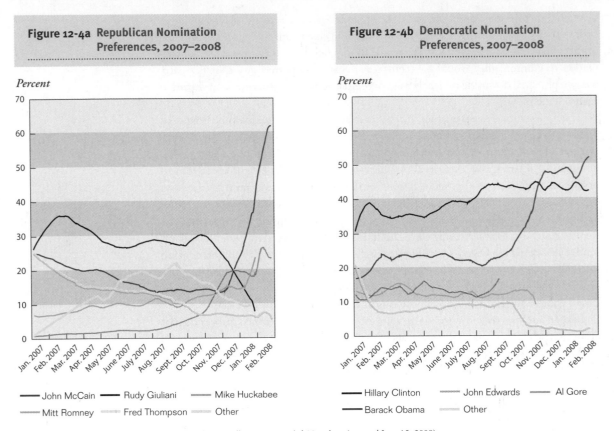

Figure 12-4a Republican Nomination Preferences, 2007–2008

Percent

— John McCain — Rudy Giuliani — Mike Huckabee
— Mitt Romney — Fred Thompson — Other

Figure 12-4b Democratic Nomination Preferences, 2007–2008

Percent

— Hillary Clinton — John Edwards — Al Gore
— Barack Obama — Other

Sources: www.pollingreport.com/wh08dem.htm and www.pollingreport.com/wh08rep.htm (accessed June 15, 2008).

Clinton came back in New Hampshire and did well in some later primaries, and ordinary Democrats remained almost evenly divided until the end of the primary season in June. Clinton's effort to overcome Obama's early delegate lead was seriously hampered by the party's proportionality rule. For example, she won 52 percent of the vote in California's primary to Obama's 43 percent, but she got only 55 percent of the delegates to his 45 percent.

The 2008 presidential nomination process in both parties left no doubt that party allocation rules matter. McCain won 46.7 percent of the votes cast in all Republican primaries and ended up with 72.9 percent of the delegates; Obama won a larger share of the votes cast in his primaries (47.3 percent) but a smaller share of his party's delegates (53.2 percent). Hillary Clinton actually won a larger share of total votes cast in all Democratic primaries than Obama (48.0 percent) but ended up with fewer delegates (44.6 percent) because of Obama's showing in the states holding caucuses.

THE CONVENTIONS EVOLVE. Now that primaries and caucuses effectively determine the parties' nominees, the purpose and meaning of national conventions have changed. Conventions were once venues for state and local party leaders to renegotiate their complex coalitions and to choose a torchbearer around whom the troops could rally. Now, delegates belong to candidates, not party officials. Conventions no longer choose the party's candidate; caucus activists and voters in primaries do. The focus is less on renewing the party coalition and rallying the faithful and more on presenting an attractive image and message to citizens watching the action at home on television. In 2000, for example, the Republicans sought to present a friendlier, more inclusive, and more moderate face than they had displayed in 1992 and 1996. In place of the hard-line conservatives who had defined the party's image in the 1990s, prime-time speakers included a stream of Republican African Americans, Hispanics, and women of all ethnic backgrounds. An openly gay Republican representative was even given the podium, although he was allowed to speak only on foreign policy. The message of moderation and inclusiveness and the nominee's espousal of a "compassionate conservatism" were designed to make the party more attractive to groups with whom it had been relatively unpopular in recent years—women, minorities, and moderate swing voters. In 2004 the Democratic convention that nominated John Kerry emphasized his heroic action as a young naval officer in Vietnam. Featured prominently were sailors who had served with him on the "swift boats" that patrolled the Mekong Delta. The idea was to convince voters that Kerry had the qualities of leadership and courage necessary to combat international terrorism, attempting to counter the inevitable Republican charge that a Democratic president would be insufficiently zealous in defending the nation.

In 2008, both parties' conventions became venues for patching up party divisions arising from the bruising primary season as well as for trumpeting the candidates' central campaign themes for the fall (see Chapter 11). Barack Obama sought to unite the Democrats behind his candidacy by giving his defeated rival Hillary Clinton a prominent speaking role in return for her enthusiastic endorsement, hoping to soften the disappointment of Democrats who had been eager to nominate and elect the first woman to the White House. John McCain sought to unite the Republicans by wooing social conservatives, most of whom had not supported his candidacy, by choosing one of them, Gov. Sarah Palin of Alaska, as his running mate. Both efforts were largely successful.

These efforts serve as a reminder that conventions are still crucially important to parties, reassembling the party coalitions for the fall campaign as well as showing voters what sorts of people make up the party and what groups and causes they champion. A display of party unity still matters, not merely to energize activists, its earlier purpose, but to convince the public that the party has its act together and can be trusted to govern.

A party's self-display at its national convention is not without risk, as both parties have had more than one occasion to discover. Party activists often hold more extreme views on the issues of the day than do ordinary party voters, who may question whether the party actually represents their values and interests. The problem is illustrated in the box "Voters versus Party Activists in 2008: Differences of Opinion," which compares the views of voters who identify themselves as Republicans or Democrats with the respective parties' convention delegates in 2008. On almost every question the opinions

Voters versus Party Activists in 2008
Differences of Opinion

	Democratic Delegates	Democratic Voters	Republican Voters	Republican Delegates
1. Ideology: Liberal	43%	48%	5%	0%
Moderate	50	34	30	26
Conservative	3	16	63	72
2. The United States did the right thing in taking military action in Iraq.	2	14	71	80
3. The Iraq War is going very or somewhat well.	22	28	82	95
4. The troop surge in Iraq has made things better.	36	28	67	96
5. Prefer health coverage for all and higher taxes to lower taxes leaving some without health coverage.	94	90	40	7
6. Protecting the environment is more important than developing new sources of energy.	25	30	9	3
7. Gun control laws should be made more strict.	62	71	32	8
8. Illegal immigration is a very serious issue.	15	36	63	58
9. Same-sex couples should be allowed to marry legally.	55	49	11	6
10. Abortion should be generally available to those who want it rather than under stricter limits or not permitted.	70	43	19	9
11. The condition of the economy is good.	2	7	40	57
12. The 2001 Bush tax cuts should be made permanent.	7	34	62	91

Source: CBS News/*New York Times* polls, July–August 2008, at www.cbsnews.com/htdocs/pdf/RNCDelegates_issues.pdf and www.cbsnews.com/htdocs/pdf/RNCDelegates_who_are_they.pdf, accessed September 2, 2008.

Note: Percentage indicates the proportion of each group that agreed with each numbered statement.

of convention delegates are more sharply divided than those of their parties' voters; on average, the respective delegations' responses differ by about sixty percentage points. On a few issues, delegates' views are also quite distinct from those of party supporters (Democrats on abortion; Republicans on health care policy). It is easy to understand why many voters would see the Republicans as too conservative and the Democrats as too liberal to represent their views reliably. However, the responses show that ordinary Democratic and Republican voters differ on many issues as well, particularly on the Iraq War, health care policy, and same-sex marriage. The average difference in responses among the parties' voters is about thirty-eight percentage points.

CONSEQUENCES OF FRACTURED ALIGNMENTS. When issues arise that split the existing party coalitions, partisan identities weaken and the party label may not provide the information voters want. The fracturing of the New Deal alignments in the 1960s and 1970s and the difficulty party politicians faced in reconstructing stable coalitions around new issues reduced the importance of party cues to voters, who became less certain about which political camp to identify with. The consequences of this breakdown were abundantly evident in election and polling results.

Party line voting declined, and ticket splitting increased. As we saw in Figure 11-2 (page 527), party-line voting in presidential elections declined between the 1950s and the 1970s. The same was true of House and Senate elections during this period: the proportion of voters who were party loyalists fell by more than ten percentage points. Ticket splitting increased sharply over the same period (see Figure 12-5). Clearly, party identification lost some of its influence on the vote as the New Deal coalition unraveled.

Voters became more indifferent to the parties. Political scientist Martin Wattenberg analyzed responses to four decades (1952–1992) of survey questions asking people what they liked and disliked about the parties. He found that, over time, the net sum of voters' comments about the parties became increasingly neutral (an even partisan balance of likes and dislikes) mainly because a growing share of respondents had nothing good *or* bad to say about either party (see Figure 12-6).[22] In 1952 far more voters gave responses that, when summed up, favored one of the parties than gave responses that were evenly balanced between the parties; by the 1970s neutrality was as common as partisan bias.

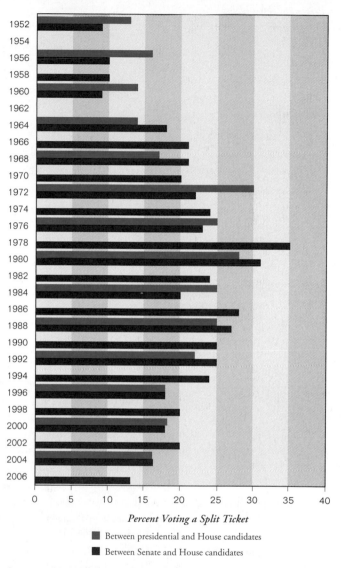

Figure 12-5 Split-Ticket Voting

Percent Voting a Split Ticket

■ Between presidential and House candidates
■ Between Senate and House candidates

Sources: For 1952–2004, American National Election Studies; for 2006, Cooperative Congressional Election Study.

Note: Data not available for 1954 and 1962.

Figure 12-6 Public Attitudes toward the Parties

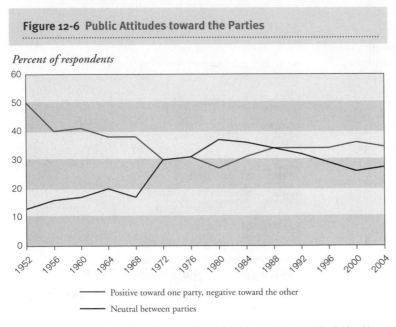

Percent of respondents

Positive toward one party, negative toward the other

Neutral between parties

Sources: Martin P. Wattenberg, *The Decline of American Political Parties, 1952–1992* (Cambridge: Harvard University Press, 1994), 174; personal communication, 1997; and American National Election Studies, 2000 and 2004.

With voters substituting personal cues for party cues, the electoral advantage enjoyed by congressional incumbents grew. Incumbents got greater mileage from their name recognition advantage and assiduous delivery of services to constituents when fewer voters automatically rejected them because of their party affiliation. (For details, see section "The Advantages of Incumbency" in Chapter 6, page 258.)

The electorate became more volatile. The Democrats' presidential vote dropped by twelve million between 1964 and 1968; the Republican vote dropped by fifteen million between 1984 and 1992. In House contests partisan vote swings became more variable across districts, making election results less predictable from one election to the next.[23]

Independent and third-party candidates increased their take. Between the beginning of the New Deal in 1932 and 1964, no minor party or independent candidate received more than 3 percent of the vote. Since then, three candidates in four races have exceeded that margin: George Wallace (14 percent in 1968), John Anderson (7 percent in 1980), and Ross Perot (19 percent in 1992, 8 percent in 1996).

Divided partisan control of governments became common. American voters now regularly divide control of the White House and Congress between the parties (see Table 7-2, page 339). Do they do it on purpose? Certainly, moderate voters might prefer **divided government** because it allows each party to block the other's more extreme proposals and forces both parties to compromise when making policy.[24] People who simply distrust politicians also might prefer to have the parties in a position to check one another. Despite this logic, there is little evidence that many people deliberately split their votes to achieve moderate policies or to make "ambition counteract ambition." Divided government is more likely a byproduct of voters applying different criteria for different offices, responding to the specific options in each contest, or making tradeoffs among their incompatible preferences (for low taxes but generous middle-class entitlements, for less regulation but more protection from environmental and market risks).[25] But even if few people deliberately vote for divided government, most are happy when they get it. In a survey taken early in 2007, 47 percent of voters preferred to have the presidency and Congress split between the parties, while only 33 percent preferred to have one party control both (the rest said it did not matter).[26]

MEDIA AND MONEY. The weakening of party influence on voters was hastened along by technological changes and the growing availability of campaign resources—money, skill, activists—from sources other than political parties. The most important technological innovation was the advent of television as a campaign medium, but newer technologies, such as computerized direct mail, mass-produced campaign videos, and now the Internet have contributed as well. The electronic media have made parties less essential to candidates and voters alike. Ross Perot was able to conduct a surprisingly successful campaign in 1992 with no party at all behind him. (He did not organize the Reform Party until 1995.) Voters informed by the news media as well as by the candidates' electronic campaigns are offered cheap cues other than party labels to guide their decisions. News coverage of elections, not to mention campaign advertising, focuses on individual candidates and largely ignores parties, thus inviting voters to do the same.

Multimillionaire Ross Perot demonstrated that, with enough money, a candidate does not need a party to mount a national campaign for president. Perot bought large chunks of television time to present his populist ideas with charts and folksy analogies. Here, he attacks Bill Clinton's job-creation record in Arkansas. Perot won 19 percent of the vote in the 1992 election, the best showing of any independent or third-party candidate since 1912.

The technology of modern campaigns is expensive, driving up the demand for campaign funds. The proliferation of candidate-centered campaigns also has driven up costs because such campaigns cannot operate with the economies of scale enjoyed by candidates working as a party team, communicating a common message, and sharing the cost of consultants, specialists, and advertising. But these changes would not have happened had the supply of money not risen to meet the demand. It did so because a growing economy provided the funds for people to invest in politics, and the expanding role of the government in their lives and businesses gave them more reasons to do so.

The Revival of the Parties: A Sixth Party System?

Despite the forces working against parties, and despite the public's doubts about the value of parties in general, the Democratic and Republican Parties continue to dominate electoral politics. Indeed, the evidence in Figures 12-5 and 12-6 indicates a revival of partisanship among voters over the past two decades. Ticket splitting has returned to its levels of the 1960s, and voters have become steadily less neutral toward the major parties since 1980. Parties have survived for the same reasons they came into being: elected officials, candidates, and voters still find them indispensable.

Partisanship Endures

Although fewer voters think of themselves as staunch partisans than was the case forty years ago, most people are still willing to call themselves Democrats or Republicans, and significantly, party affiliation remains the single best predictor of how people will vote. The distribution of partisan identities from 1952 through 2006, shown in

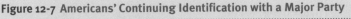

Figure 12-7 Americans' Continuing Identification with a Major Party

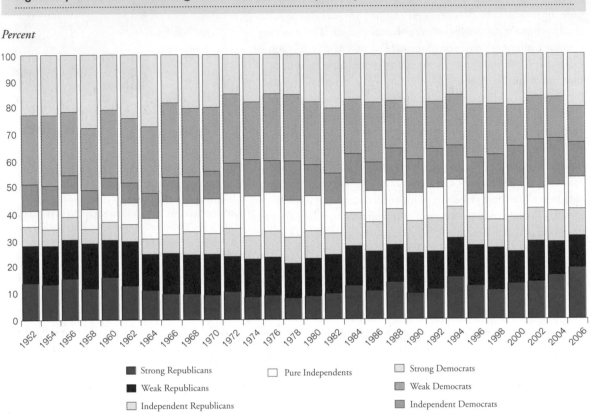

Percent

Legend:
- Strong Republicans
- Weak Republicans
- Independent Republicans
- Pure Independents
- Strong Democrats
- Weak Democrats
- Independent Democrats

Sources: For 1952–2004, American National Election Studies; for 2006, Cooperative Congressional Election Study.

Figure 12-7, is surprisingly stable despite the dramatic political events that occurred within that period. The proportion calling themselves independents has grown, but most independents are actually closet partisans leaning toward one of the parties and supporting its candidates as consistently as do weak partisans.[27] The proportion of "pure" independents grew from 6 percent in 1952 to 15 percent in 1976, but by the early part of this decade independent identifiers had fallen to about 10 percent. Because self-described independents are less likely to vote, their share of the electorate was actually closer to 5 percent. The proportion of strong partisans (of both parties) declined between the 1950s and the 1970s but has since rebounded.

Party Differences

Voters may not think much of parties, but large majorities still admit to a party preference and use parties to guide their voting decisions. They do so because, despite the divisions within the party coalitions and regardless of how they feel about the parties, the party labels still carry valuable information about candidates (see box "2008 Party Platforms"). That is, party labels continue to provide the cheap, shorthand cue so useful to rationally ignorant voters.

In general Republicans tend to favor a smaller, cheaper federal government; they advocate lower taxes, less regulation of business, and lower spending on social welfare. They would be more generous only to the Defense Department. Democrats are more inclined to regulate business in behalf of consumers and the environment and are more supportive of government programs designed to improve domestic welfare; they would spend less on national defense. Democrats are more concerned with "fairness" and equality, Republicans with letting free enterprise flourish. Republicans would ban abortion and gay marriage and allow official prayer in public schools; Democrats would not. Not all candidates adhere to their party's modal positions; some Republicans support freedom of choice on abortion, and some Democrats advocate large defense budgets. But the party label continues to distinguish candidates from one another on many issues with considerable accuracy. Indeed, in Congress party divisions are sharper and clearer now than they have been since the 1950s (see Chapter 6).* As the predictive accuracy of party labels has grown in recent decades, so has the usefulness—and therefore use—of party cues.

Changes in the Party Coalitions

The party coalitions of the early 2000s still retain strong traces of the New Deal alignment (for example, lower-income voters are still more likely to be Democrats; higher-income voters, Republicans), but they have undergone several crucial changes since the 1960s. In the 1950s white southerners were overwhelmingly Democratic, but they responded to the civil rights revolution—and the Republicans' "southern strategy" to exploit the discontent civil rights aroused—by moving gradually but steadily into the Republican camp. A solid majority of white southerners now identify themselves as Republicans. African Americans favored Democrats even before the 1960s, but the magnitude of the Democratic advantage more than doubled in the 1960s, has remained huge ever since, and was reinforced in 2008 by the Obama candidacy.

Men have become more Republican, while women have not, creating the famous "gender gap" between the parties.† The Democratic advantage among Catholics has shrunk, and regular religious service attendees of all religions have become relatively

---

*Even a national crisis as profound as 9/11 did not suppress partisanship for long. Although politicians and ordinary citizens rallied almost unanimously behind President George W. Bush's leadership in the war on terrorism, traditional ideological battle lines quickly re-formed when Congress turned to debating domestic policies intended to help the victims and revive the battered economy.

†The National Election Studies from 1964 through 1978 found women to be, on average, only about two percentage points more Democratic in their partisanship than men. In studies conducted from 1980 through 1990, however, women averaged six percentage points more Democratic; since then, the gender gap in party identification has grown to about eleven percentage points. These differences show up in presidential voting. In 2000 support for Al Gore was ten percentage points higher among women than among men; in 2004 support for John Kerry was about seven percentage points higher among women than among men. For a general discussion of the gender gap in party identification, see Warren E. Miller and J. Merrill Shanks, *The New American Voter* (Cambridge: Harvard University Press, 1996), 141–145.

2008 Party Platforms

These excerpts from the 2008 Democratic and Republican platforms reveal some of the differences between positions typically held by the parties. But few voters learn of these differences by reading the platforms. Rather, they learn about the parties' positions through political news and campaign advertising.

	Democrats	Republicans
Abortion	The Democratic Party strongly and unequivocally supports *Roe v. Wade* and a woman's right to choose a safe and legal abortion, regardless of ability to pay, and we oppose any and all efforts to weaken or undermine that right.	We support a human life amendment to the Constitution, and we endorse legislation to make clear that the Fourteenth Amendment's protections apply to unborn children. We oppose using public revenues to promote or perform abortion and will not fund organizations which advocate it.
Education— School Vouchers	We will fix the failures and broken promises of No Child Left Behind. . . . We will end the practice of labeling a school and its students as failures and then throwing our hands up and walking away from them without having provided the resources and supports these students need.	We support choice in education for all families . . . whether through charter schools, vouchers or tax credits for attending faith-based or other nonpublic schools, or the option of home schooling.
Energy	We know we can't drill our way to energy independence and so . . . we must invest in . . . forms of new energy— solar, wind, as well as technologies to store energy through advanced batteries and clean up our coal plants. . . . We'll double fuel efficiency standards and we'll help manufacturers convert to build the cars and trucks of the future and other green innovations. . . . We will . . . install a smarter grid, build more efficient buildings . . . We'll invest in advanced biofuels like cellulosic ethanol. . . . To lower the price of gasoline, we will crack down on speculators who are driving up prices beyond the natural market rate.	We support accelerated exploration, drilling and development in America, from new oilfields off the nation's coasts to onshore fields. . . . We will encourage refinery construction and modernization and . . . an expedited permitting process. We oppose any efforts that would permanently block access to the coastal plain of the Arctic National Wildlife Refuge. . . . Republicans will pursue dramatic increases in the use of . . . nuclear power.
Guns	We will preserve Americans' continued Second Amendment right to own and use firearms. We believe that the right to own firearms is subject to reasonable regulation, but we know that what works in Chicago may not work in Cheyenne. We can work together to enact and enforce common-sense laws and improvements, like closing the gun show loophole, improving our background check system and reinstating the assault weapons ban.	We uphold the right of individual Americans to own firearms. . . . We applaud the Supreme Court's decision in *[District of Columbia v.] Heller* affirming that right, and we assert the individual responsibility to safely use and store firearms. . . . Gun control only affects and penalizes law-abiding citizens, and that such proposals are ineffective at reducing violent crime.
Same-Sex Marriage	We support the full inclusion of all families in the life of our nation, and support equal responsibility, benefits, and protections. . . . We oppose the Defense of Marriage Act and all attempts to use this issue to divide us.	We call for a constitutional amendment that fully protects marriage as a union of a man and a woman, so that judges cannot make other arrangements equivalent to it.
Income Tax	We will shut down the corporate loopholes and tax havens and use the money so that we can provide an immediate middle-class tax cut. . . . We'll eliminate income taxes for millions of retirees. . . . We won't increase taxes on any family earning under $250,000 and we will offer additional tax cuts for middle class families. For families making more than $250,000, we'll ask them to give back a portion of the Bush tax cuts. . . . We will expand the Earned Income Tax Credit.	Along with making the 2001 and 2003 tax cuts permanent. . . . Republicans will lower their tax burden by doubling the exemption for dependents . . . [and] continue our fight against the federal death tax. The Alternative Minimum Tax . . . must be repealed. . . . We support a major reduction in the corporate tax rate. . . . We support giving all taxpayers the option of filing under current rules or under a two-rate flat tax.

	Democrats	Republicans
Global Warming	We will lead to defeat the epochal, man-made threat to the planet: climate change. Without dramatic changes, rising sea levels will flood coastal regions around the world. . . . Warmer temperatures and declining rainfall will reduce crop yields, increasing conflict, famine, disease, and poverty. . . . Never again will we sit on the sidelines, or stand in the way of collective action to tackle this global challenge.	While the scope and long-term consequences of [climate change] are the subject of ongoing scientific research, common sense dictates that the United States should take measured and reasonable steps today to reduce any impact on the environment. . . . Any policies should be global in nature, based on sound science and technology, and should not harm the economy.
Health Care	We . . . oppose . . . policies that would thrust millions of Americans out of their current private employer-based coverage without providing them access to an affordable, comprehensive alternative. . . . Families and individuals should have the option of keeping the coverage they have or choosing from a wide array of health insurance plans, including many private health insurance options and a public plan. Coverage should be made affordable for all Americans with direct financial assistance through tax credits and other means.	Republicans believe all Americans should be able to obtain an affordable health care plan, including a health savings account. . . . Republicans propose to correct inequities in the current tax code that drive up the number of uninsured and to level the playing field so that individuals who choose a health insurance plan in the individual market face no tax penalty.
Stem Cell Research	We will lift the current Administration's ban on using federal funding for embryonic stem cells—cells that would have otherwise have been discarded and lost forever—for research that could save lives.	We call for a major expansion of support for the stem-cell research . . . with adult stem cells, umbilical cord blood, and cells reprogrammed into pluripotent stem cells—without the destruction of embryonic human life.
Iraq	We must . . . bring the Iraq war to a responsible end. . . . Iraq was a diversion from the fight against the terrorists who struck us on 9/11, and incompetent prosecution of the war by civilian leaders compounded the strategic blunder of choosing to wage it in the first place. . . . We will be as careful getting out of Iraq as we were careless getting in. We can safely remove our combat brigades at the pace of one to two per month and expect to complete redeployment within 16 months.	A stable, unified, and democratic Iraqi nation is within reach. Our success in Iraq will deny al Qaeda a safe haven, limit Iranian influence in the Middle East, strengthen moderate forces there, and give us a strategic ally in the struggle against extremism. . . . To those who have sacrificed so much, we owe the commitment that American forces will leave that country in victory and with honor. That outcome is too critical to our own national security to be jeopardized by artificial or politically inspired timetables.
Social Security	We reject the notion of the presumptive Republican nominee that Social Security is a disgrace; we believe that it is indispensable. We will fulfill our obligation to strengthen Social Security and to make sure that it provides guaranteed benefits Americans can count on, now and in future generations. We will not privatize it. We will safeguard from discrimination those who choose to work past the age of 65.	We are committed to putting Social Security on a sound fiscal basis. . . . Under the current system, younger workers will not be able to depend on Social Security as part of their retirement plan. We believe the solution should give workers control over, and a fair return on, their contributions. . . . Comprehensive reform should include the opportunity to freely choose to create your own personal investment accounts which are distinct from and supplemental to the overall Social Security system.
Immigration	We support a system that requires undocumented immigrants . . . to pay a fine, pay taxes, learn English, and go to the back of the line for the opportunity to become citizens. . . . At the same time . . . we need to secure our borders, and support additional personnel, infrastructure and technology on the border and at our ports of entry. . . . We also need to do more to promote economic development in migrant-sending nations. . . . And we need to crack down on employers who hire undocumented immigrants.	Our determination to uphold the rule of law begins with more effective enforcement, giving our agents the tools and resources they need to protect our sovereignty, completing the border fence quickly and securing the borders, and employing complementary strategies to secure our ports of entry. . . . We oppose amnesty. . . . We support English as the official language in our nation.

Sources: Adapted from 2008 Democratic and Republican platforms at www.workinglife.org/storage/users/4/4/images/111/2008%20democratic%20 platform%20080808.pdf and www.gop.com/pdf/PlatformFINAL_WithCover.pdf, respectively.

more Republican. Indeed, during the Reagan years the electorate as a whole became more Republican, less Democratic. Since 2004, reflecting the unpopularity of the second G. W. Bush administration (2005–2008), the trend has moved in the opposite direction, with younger voters leading the way. Comparing the averages of all of their surveys taken in 2004 to those taken in 2008, the Pew Center found that the Democrats' advantage in party identification had grown from two to nine points, and among 18–29-year-old voters, from four to fourteen points, between the two years.[28] Not coincidentally, according to the 2008 exit poll, Barack Obama won this age group decisively, 66 percent to 32 percent for John McCain.[29]

The changes in the party coalitions have been extensive enough to suggest that a sixth party system is now in place. Because the changes occurred gradually and at different times, the new system's starting date is unclear: some analysts propose 1968, while others say 1980 or 1984. Whatever the timing, the most salient difference between the current and New Deal party systems is the Republican Party's increased strength, symbolized by its winning majorities in the House and Senate in six straight elections (1994–2004), unprecedented since the fourth party system. It is too early to say whether Republican setbacks since 2004 signal a durable enlargement of the Democrats' coalition. Although Democrats enjoy an edge in party identifiers, the Republican coalition includes more people with higher incomes and more formal education, so Republican identifiers tend to vote at higher rates than do Democrats. The Democrats' advantage therefore is typically smaller when the analysis is confined to voters. Because Republican voters also are somewhat more loyal to their party, electoral competition tends to be evenly balanced in the current party system.

Modern Party Organizations

On paper the modern Democratic and Republican parties might be depicted as pyramidal organizations. Each party's sovereign body is its national nominating convention, which officially elects the national party chair and ratifies the states' selections to the party's national committee (the Republican National Committee or the Democratic National Committee). The national committee, with at least two members from each state, is charged with conducting the party's affairs between national conventions and hiring and directing a large professional staff. Below the national committees are the state committees and chairs, which oversee the committees representing congressional and state legislative districts and counties. Further subdivisions would include diverse township, city, ward, and precinct committees, also with formal leaders, some chosen by caucuses, some in primary elections.*

CONTROL. In reality, however, the national parties are far from hierarchical organizations, and at most levels they are controlled by elected politicians, not party officials. The national party's chair is always the choice of the party's presidential nominee, and the national committee's primary task is to win or retain the presidency, although at-

---

* Party organization at the state and local levels is highly varied, reflecting differences in historical development, local custom, and state law. Moreover, in many places the formal party units are joined by a diverse set of party clubs, caucuses, factional organizations, and allied interest groups that also participate in party politics.

tention is given to other forms of party building between presidential contests. House and Senate candidates have their own separate national campaign organizations—all under the control of their respective party's congressional leaders (see Chapter 6).

Elected officials also usually control state parties, which are in no way subordinate to the national parties; governors are frequently the most powerful figures in their state parties, for example. State parties often have little influence over local organizations, and both state and local parties are sometimes split into personal, ideological, or regional factions. Local party offices sometimes go begging, and on occasion insurgent groups have been able to take over party committee and leadership posts just by getting their people to show up at the usually lightly attended caucuses or precinct conventions where such choices are made. That is how, for example, Christian conservatives came to control local Republican Party organizations in some places, including Texas, South Carolina, and Minnesota.[30]

Although they continue to display the organizational fragmentation that has always characterized them, the

The development of modern national party committees is expressed in bricks and mortar as well as organization charts and bank accounts. In 2004 the National Republican Senatorial Committee unveiled a Founders Wall, which lists engraved in granite the names of donors who contributed $300 or more to its programs.

American parties of today are in some ways more closely linked than ever. Both national parties and many state organizations have become modern, businesslike enterprises with permanent offices, professional staffs, and relatively stable budgets, producing a stronger institutional basis for ongoing coordination and cooperation.

ORGANIZATIONAL INNOVATIONS. Although both major parties have had permanent national committees since before the Civil War, only since the 1970s have national organizations played a significant role in party politics. The Democrats began to nationalize their party structure when the various post–1968 reform commissions operating out of national headquarters imposed rules on state and local parties. But the Republicans led the way after that.

As always, the "outs" did the major innovating. The Watergate scandal and the economic recession that beset the second Nixon administration devastated the Republicans in the 1974 congressional elections and helped defeat Gerald Ford in 1976. Party leaders William Brock, Guy Vander Jagt, and Robert Packwood—chairs, respectively, of the Republican National Committee and the party's House and Senate campaign committees—resolved to build their organizations into effective promoters of Republican candidates. The first thing they did was to raise money—lots of it. They perfected the new technique of computerized direct-mail fund-raising, developing lists of people who were willing to send modest checks in response to regular solicitations to create a steady source of income for the party. Their growing success during the early 1980s, when they were raising 80 percent of their money through the mail in checks averaging less than $30, is documented in Figure 12-8.

Figure 12-8 Growth of Party Spending in Federal Elections

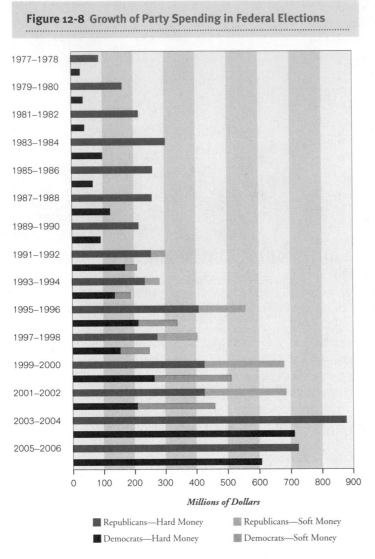

Millions of Dollars

■ Republicans—Hard Money   ■ Republicans—Soft Money
■ Democrats—Hard Money   ■ Democrats—Soft Money

Source: Federal Election Commission.

Note: Before 1991 the Federal Election Commission did not require parties to report soft money spending; after 2002 soft money was banned.

With the money coming in, the Republicans enlarged their organization staff and began to provide a host of services to their candidates. Today they help candidates for federal office raise money, comply with campaign finance regulations, design polls, set up Web sites, research opponents' records, put together lists of voters to contact, and design campaign strategy. They contribute a good deal of money directly to candidates' campaign war chests. In some years, they have conducted national campaigns for the entire party ticket. Republican candidates also are helped indirectly by the money and training the national party has contributed to state and local Republican organizations across the nation to strengthen the party at the grass roots. In addition, the campaign committees stepped up efforts to identify, recruit, and train effective candidates for Congress and, in some instances, for state offices as well.[31]

The Democrats were shocked into a similar effort to expand the services offered by their national party committees when in 1980 they lost both the White House (to Ronald Reagan) and their Senate majority. They are still playing catch-up in fundraising, although they have managed to close the gap (see Figure 12-8). Contrary to expectations, the ban on soft party money enacted in 2002 (see Chapter 11) did not put them at further disadvantage, as they were able to make up much of the difference by raising more hard dollars. Republicans, too, vastly increased their take of hard money, and between them, the parties raised more than $1.6 billion for the 2004 federal election campaigns, and more than $1.3 billion for the 2006 midterm campaigns. Instead of transferring soft money to state parties to help federal candidates as they had in the past, the Hill committees simply switched to spending hard money on independent campaigns (separate from the candidates' campaigns) in the most competitive congressional races. Spending of this sort exceeded $223 million in 2006, up from a mere $3.4 million in 2002.[32] The president remains the preeminent fund-raiser for his party, as both Bill Clinton and George W. Bush have so amply demonstrated (see box "The President as Party Coordinator").

STRATEGY AND CHOICE

The President as Party Coordinator

Political parties would like to allocate political contributions to those campaigns in which party money will have the greatest impact. So would many of the political action committees and individual contributors whose interests ride on which party controls the government. Despite their common goal, parties and their financial supporters face a formidable coordination problem. As a result, tens of millions of dollars in campaign contributions are allocated inefficiently in every election. That is, they are directed to campaigns in which the electoral bang for the buck is less than it might have been had the money been spent on some other candidate.

The problem arises because each party fields numerous challengers. All of them promote themselves as potential winners, but few have any realistic prospect of victory. Donors are left uncertain about whom to support. Presumably, party officials are better informed than are individual contributors, but they may be unable to guide potential donors effectively or prevent the inefficient distribution of resources produced by candidates busily trying to amass large campaign war chests. In the competition for donations, the most skilled fund-raisers are incumbent officeholders, precisely those politicians whose election is often least dependent on additional money. To the degree they succeed, they divert money from those who need it most—the party's competitive challengers. Yet a party official who intervenes to try to redirect money from the

(box continues on next page)

The President as Party Coordinator *(continued)*

party's incumbents to its challengers will soon join the ranks of the unemployed.

So what can parties do? Two things: first, they can raise as much money as possible for themselves by assuring donors that they will spend it wisely. As shown in Figure 12-8, both political parties have partially succeeded in these efforts. Another strategy is for the party to send its president to the campaign hustings, where the party's top fund-raiser can speak to local contributor groups and share the podium with (and thus enhance the credibility of) challengers. Besides helping to fill party coffers and candidates' pockets, the president's appearances show other donors where to invest their campaign dollars.

Bill Clinton demonstrated the president's unique drawing power during the 1999–2000 election cycle. He attended, by one count, 295 fund-raising events that harvested more than $160 million for Democratic congressional candidates. Over $100 million of these funds were divided among the Democratic National Committee, the Democratic Congressional Campaign Committee, and the Democratic Senatorial Campaign Committee. Not to be outdone, his successor, George W. Bush, attended fewer events (seventy-four) but raised even more money during the 2001–2002 election cycle, an estimated $193 million, including more than $72 million for the party's three main national campaign committees.[1] Nearing the end of his second term, Bush, during his tenure as a two-term president, had personally raised nearly $1 billion for his party, its candidates, and his own reelection.[2]

---

1. Mark Knoller of CBS Radio News kindly supplied these figures. For a fuller analysis of Clinton's financial signaling during the 2000 election cycle, see Gary C. Jacobson, Samuel Kernell, and Jeffrey Lazarus, "Assessing the President's Role as Party Agent in Congressional Elections," *Legislative Studies Quarterly* 29 (May 2004): 159–184.

2. Deb Riechmann, "Who Says George W. Isn't Popular," Associated Press, at http://cnews.canoe.ca/CNEWS/World/2008/08/15/6466061-ap.html.

Although modern parties continue to play a major financial and organizational role in electoral politics, they have clearly lost the near-monopoly they had on campaign resources until the mid-twentieth century. Candidates, rather than parties, are the focus of campaigns; the party's activities are aimed at helping individual candidates compete more effectively, not at promoting the party. According to political scientist John Aldrich, "A new form of party has emerged, one that is 'in service' to its ambitious politicians but not 'in control' of them as the mass party [of the past] sought to be."[33]

Expediency Persists

American parties developed and continue to endure because they have proven so useful to politicians and voters attempting to act collectively within the institutional framework established by the Constitution. The federal system offers powerful incentives for organizing and expanding both legislative and electoral coalitions—that is, political parties—to win and exercise political power. For one thing, it rewards political entrepreneurs who can organize collective action across government institutions and electoral arenas. For another, it prompts voters to use party labels to simplify their decisions, giving politicians a reason to cooperate with party leaders to maintain the value of the party's "brand name."

Although the party coalitions have shifted periodically in response to new national issues and conflicts, leaving five—perhaps six—identifiable party systems, the basic pattern of competition between two broad, usually fractious coalitions persists. The two-party system arises from strategic voting in the winner-take-all competition for the presidency (and for all other federal offices as well) and has been strengthened by laws (mandating, for example, primary elections) that treat the parties as official components of the electoral machinery. Party coalitions remain fractious because party entrepreneurs pursuing majorities must combine diverse groups that are neither natural allies nor disposed to pay high conformity costs for the sake of the party. But these coalitions persist because party organizations remain decentralized, mirroring the decentralized institutions of American federalism.

Progressive Era reforms, followed by the development of new technologies of communication after the Second World War, weakened traditional party organizations and ended their monopoly control of campaigns, but parties continue to play a central role in electoral politics. Despite their expressed disdain for parties, voters still rely heavily on party cues in making their decisions because party labels continue to provide useful, cheap information about candidates. Party entrepreneurs, for their part, have simply redesigned party organizations to operate more effectively in today's media-based, candidate-centered electoral arena. They are walking down the trail blazed by Jefferson and Van Buren, and for the same reason: to elect those who share their views so that they may shape public policy to their liking.

logic.cqpress.com

Key Terms

Australian ballot, 581

caucus, 572

divided government, 594

fusion tickets, 566

national party convention, 574

New Deal coalition, 584

party machine, 579

patronage, 568

political party, 559

primary election, 581

Progressive Era, 581

proportional representation, 566

split ticket, 581

superdelegate, 588

two-party system, 564

Suggested Readings

Aldrich, John H. *Why Parties? The Origin and Transformation of Party Politics in America.* Chicago: University of Chicago Press, 1995. An astute theoretical and historical analysis of American parties that deepens and extends the approach taken in this text.

Chambers, William Nesbit, and Walter Dean Burnham, eds. *The American Party Systems: Stages of Political Development.* 2nd ed. New York: Oxford University Press, 1975. Fascinating historical essays on American party development. The essay by Eric L. McKitrick explaining how partisan politics helped Abraham Lincoln and how its absence hurt Jefferson Davis during the Civil War is especially instructive.

Cohen, Jeffrey E., Richard Fleisher, and Paul Kantor, eds. *American Political Parties: Decline or Resurgence?* Washington, D.C.: CQ Press, 2001. Historical and contemporary material explore changes in American parties and analyze party weaknesses, the reasons for revitalization, and the responsibilities of parties in a democracy.

Mayhew, David R. *Placing Parties in American Politics.* Princeton: Princeton University Press, 1986. To understand why some states developed strong party organizations and others did not, read this book.

Polsby, Nelson W. *Consequences of Party Reform.* New York: Oxford University Press, 1983. According to Polsby, the consequences have not been good.

Riordan, William L., ed. *Plunkitt of Tammany Hall.* New York: Dutton, 1963. According to the subtitle, "a series of very plain talks on very practical politics, delivered by George Washington Plunkitt, the Tammany Philosopher, from his rostrum—the New York County Court House bootblack stand." Includes a good introductory essay on nineteenth-century party machine politics.

Sundquist, James L. *The Dynamics of the Party System,* rev. ed. Washington, D.C.: Brookings, 1983. Highly detailed study of historical party realignments; for those who prefer complex stories to simple ones.

Wattenberg, Martin P. *The Decline of American Political Parties, 1952–1994.* Cambridge: Harvard University Press, 1996. Based on analysis of public attitudes toward parties, this book is the strongest statement to date of the "party decline" thesis.

Review Questions

1. Why didn't the Framers of the Constitution want parties? How did the Constitution help promote the emergence of parties?

2. Where did U.S. parties first arise? Why did they prove necessary in this setting? Why did parties spread from there to other areas of politics?

3. What incentives did nineteenth-century parties provide to encourage prospective voters and party workers to participate in politics? What changed this system?

4. Why do third parties tend to do so poorly in U.S. elections? Why do such parties do so much better in other democracies?

5. How have the roles of national and state party organizations changed over time? Are these organizations more or less important than they were in the past?

6. How have rates of "ticket splitting" changed over time? How have public attitudes toward the parties changed over that same time? Are Americans more or less partisan in their views and behavior than they were in the 1970s?

7. How has the nomination process for party candidates changed over time? If national conventions no longer decide on the party's presidential nominee, why are they still held?

8. How do party activists differ from rank-and-file voters of their party? What consequences does this difference have for American politics?

9. How has the decline of the New Deal coalition affected recent developments in American politics?

10. How do parties affect the fund-raising of candidates? What limitations do they face in giving their members financial assistance?

Exercises

Counting Noses

Go to the National Election Studies' historical results for party identification at www.electionstudies.org/nesguide/toptable/tab2a_1.htm. Based on the results of this table, how would you describe the relative popularity of the Democratic and Republican Parties in each decade since the 1950s? What portion of the electorate regards itself as apolitical or independent of the two parties? Have such voters become more or less common over time?

Interest Groups

Do interest groups spawn government programs, or do government programs spawn interest groups?

Most lobbyists are paid advocates of special interests. Why should politicians believe anything they say?

Do political action committees buy policy with their campaign donations? If not, what do they buy?

As the number of interests represented in Washington has grown, have they become more or less powerful?

Free riding should doom "public interest" lobbies. Why do so many emerge and thrive nonetheless?

N o one responded more quickly to the September 11, 2001, terrorist attacks than Washington's **lobbyists.** The morning after, congressional offices began receiving calls from farm lobbyists, defense contractors, and representatives of the insurance, travel, telecommunications, computer, and pharmaceutical industries. Most did not ask for anything they had not already advocated, but all now framed their arguments to fit the radically altered political context. Rep. Edward Markey, D-Mass., noted wryly,

> No self-respecting lobbyist has not repackaged his position as a patriotic response to the tragedy:
>
> The challenge is terrorism. The answer is to re-establish telecommunications monopolies.
>
> The challenge is terrorism. The answer is to drill for oil in the Arctic Wildlife Refuge.
>
> The challenge is terrorism. The answer is a $15 billion retroactive tax break to scores of corporations.[1]

The insurance and airline industries, which suffered huge financial losses, could make the clearest cases for assistance. But they were joined by farm lobbyists promoting subsidies as a way to prevent wartime disruptions of the food supply, travel

The V-22 Osprey, the trouble-plagued experimental aircraft whose fortunes appeared to take off again after 9/11, a redesign, and a new $30 million plan to increase production from eleven a year to thirty a year.

industry advocates proposing a temporary $1,000 tax credit to help families offset vacation expenses, and Boeing Aircraft and the U.S. Marines, both of which pushed for revival of the V-22 Osprey, an experimental aircraft grounded because of fatal crashes.

Telecommunications giant Verizon sought to kill federal rules that gave smaller competitors access to its network, arguing that its quick restoration of telephone service in lower Manhattan had shown the need for large telecommunications companies. The American Traffic Safety Services Association, which represents makers of traffic signs, called for more federal money for road signs to prevent traffic jams as people fled terrorist attacks. California date growers sought to ensure that food packages dropped on Afghanistan contained dates as a treat for Afghans during the evenings of Ramadan, the Islamic holy month.[2]

In the ensuing months, lobbyists continued to link their usual pleas to the threat of terrorism. The private electric power industry justified its old wish list of tax breaks, higher rates of return, and eligibility for federal disaster insurance as necessary to protect the power grid against terrorist attacks. Drug companies sought exemption from antitrust laws to work together on drugs and vaccines against anthrax, smallpox, and germ warfare agents, and protection against lawsuits that might arise when the new drugs were used.[3] Governors sought federal money for transportation projects on the ground that they would speed evacuations following future disasters. The restaurant industry renewed its struggle to restore the full deductibility of business meals lost to tax reform back in 1986 by arguing that dining out was "the cornerstone of the economy" and thus essential to its revival after the disaster.[4] "What happened was a tragedy, certainly, but there are opportunities," said one unusually candid lobbyist. "We're in business. This is not a charity."[5]

And a thriving business it is. The changed political landscape wrought by September 11 did not so much galvanize Washington, D.C., interest group representatives as redirect their already formidable energies. For notwithstanding the national emergency, **interest groups** and **lobbying** are inevitable and, indeed, essential components of modern democratic politics. They also are a continual source of problems for democracy. The American political system could not function without the endlessly busy work of organized interests and their representatives trying to sway policy in their favor. Yet there has never been a time in American history when they have not been under attack from one quarter or another as threats to democracy itself. This chapter looks at why interest groups are both essential and problematic.

The Logic of Lobbying

The logic of lobbying is transparent. People who want to influence government decisions that affect their lives and welfare quickly recognize the advantages of banding together with others of like mind and asking astute and powerful friends to help out. Governments, for their part, have good reason to welcome lobbying, defined as appeals from citizens and groups for favorable policies and decisions. Even officials in blatantly nondemocratic governments find life considerably easier if they have the support, or at least the acquiescence, of the governed (as any parent knows). Such officials cannot estimate the costs and benefits of alternative actions without having some idea of how people will react to their initiatives. All governments also need the information, political as well as technical, that people and organizations outside the government are in the best position to provide—for a price. Elected officials, looking to keep their jobs, try to accommodate the people who command valuable electoral resources—votes, money, organizational structures, and skills. And always and everywhere, at least a few government officials have been willing to trade favors for personal "gifts" of every imaginable sort.

Lobbyists crowd the hallway waiting to enter a Senate Appropriations Committee markup session dealing with fiscal 2007 appropriations for the Departments of Defense, Labor, Health and Human Services, Veterans, Treasury, and Transportation.

Modern politics also breeds professional lobbyists. For the same reason they hire lawyers to represent them in court, people hire agents who are specialists to represent them before legislatures and executive agencies. Like courts, modern legislatures and bureaucracies are complex institutions bound by arcane rules, procedures, and customs. People wanting these institutions to act in their behalf are more likely to succeed if they are represented by agents who understand how the institutions work and enjoy warm personal friendships with the key institutional players.

Lobbying as a profession thus emerged with modern representative government and has flourished with the growing scope and complexity of government activities. But if interest groups and lobbyists arise naturally with the development of representative institutions, so do doubts about their legitimacy. Their very presence, not to mention any political success they may achieve, raises the suspicion that "special interests" win at the expense of the "public interest." Even people who deny that the public interest can be defined objectively—as do many modern political scientists—often argue that successful lobbying subverts the basic principles of democratic equality and majority rule. Groups vary widely in wealth and in how readily they can be organized for collective action, creating marked imbalances in the representation of social interests. Moreover, **policy gridlock** and political paralysis in the face of pressing national problems are commonly blamed on the cacophony of competing interests. For these reasons, organized political interests have been attacked and criticized as long as they have existed.

James Madison, with his usual cogency, captured the dilemma posed by politically active groups in his famous discussion of factions in *Federalist* No. 10. For Madison, factions were by definition pernicious, pursuing selfish aims contrary to the rights of others or to the public interest. As such, factions were, in Madison's view, a major threat to popular government: "The instability, injustice, and confusion introduced into the public councils" by the "dangerous vice" of faction "have, in truth, been the mortal diseases under which popular governments have everywhere perished." (The full text of *Federalist* No. 10 appears in the Appendix.)

Why then not just get rid of factions? Madison's answer was that factions could be eliminated only by "destroying the liberty which is essential to [their] existence . . . [or by] giving every citizen the same opinions, the same passions, and the same interests." He found the first cure "worse than the disease" because popular government is supposed to protect liberty; he found the second impossible: "as long as the reason of man continues to be fallible, and he is at liberty to exercise it, different opinions will be formed."

Practically speaking, then, to maintain the freedoms specified in the First Amendment—to speak, publish, assemble, and "petition the Government for a redress of grievances"—a political system must tolerate factions even though they may be, as by Madison's definition, opposed to the public good. Political parties, interest groups, lobbyists, and peaceful political organizations of all kinds are, in effect, licensed by the Constitution and can be suppressed only by violating its principles.

If factions cannot be suppressed without subverting the very purpose of popular government, how can they be prevented from destroying the polity? As we saw in Chapter 2, Madison's solution was to divide authority among federal institutions. This fragmentation of authority would prevent any single faction from dominating the others. The wide variety of competing interests could then use this institutional machinery to thwart each other's selfish designs. Madison's answer to the problem of faction was, in other words, institutional and social pluralism. It was, characteristically, a solution firmly grounded in American realities.

The Origins of Interest Group Politics in America

Madison's discussion of factions, though abstract, was anything but academic. Organized attempts to influence government decisions have been an integral part of American politics since the nation's earliest days.

The Colonial Era

Merchants, manufacturers, and ethnic and religious minorities during the colonial era actively sought favorable policies from the authorities in London as well as from colonial governors and assemblies. By the middle of the eighteenth century such groups had developed most of the techniques of persuasion still used today. Colonial interests submitted petitions to the government, hired agents to "handle the delicate work involved in extracting concessions from ministers and lesser bureaucrats," examined the voting records of legislators to identify prospective supporters, organized letter-writing campaigns, reminded legislators that a group's supporters were among their constituents, and formed logrolling coalitions with other interests.[6]

American interests and their British allies learned to cultivate parliamentary leaders, as well as draft legislation and slip it into an opportune spot on the parliamentary calendar. They also bombarded members of Parliament with information and arranged for expert testimony. Such insider lobbying—direct appeals to lawmakers for policy support by narrowly focused interests—has been a familiar part of legislative politics in Anglo-American democracies ever since.

The eighteenth century also witnessed the invention of the **public interest lobby** and the tactic of appealing to the general public for support of an outsider group's goals. The chief innovator was the English radical John Wilkes, whose Bill of Rights Society promoted a general cause—the expansion of suffrage—rather than defending any particular interest. Disdaining the customary methods of friendly persuasion, the Wilkesites attacked government officials.[7] Similar organizations appeared in the colonies, the best known of which was the Sons of Liberty. Among other subversive activities, this group threw the Boston Tea Party.

By the time of the American Revolution, a wide variety of politically active groups had emerged: merchants' societies, chambers of commerce, religious sects, organizations pushing radical causes, groups interested in local improvements, ethnic associations, insurance societies, clubs with social and intellectual aspirations, workers' organizations, and military and professional associations. Delegates to the Constitutional Convention were so accustomed to lobbying that they agreed to meet behind locked doors and to keep their deliberations secret until after the convention was over. No official record was kept "lest word of their intentions leak out and they become beset by a horde of citizens seeking to advance their own interests."[8] This was by no means the last time the public interest was best served by letting negotiations proceed out of the public eye.

The Early Republic

As Madison had anticipated, the American political system allowed "factions" to flourish. Political parties emerged almost immediately (see Chapter 12). Of the many coordinated efforts made to shape government decisions in the early decades of the Republic, most were directed at state and local governments, since at that time they made most of the decisions important to citizens. By the 1830s organizations of all kinds formed an integral part of American life. French visitor Alexis de Tocqueville noted with astonishment the abundance and variety of organized groups in the United States: "In no country in the world has the principle of association been more successfully used, or applied to a greater multitude of objects, than in America. . . . There is no end which the human will despairs of attaining through the combined power of individuals united into a society."[9]

Because most of these groups that Tocqueville observed sought to achieve their ends without involving the government, they were not what we would call political interest groups, but many did have explicit political aims. Examples were the American Anti-Slavery Society (founded in 1833); the National Trades Union (1834), which lobbied

Joseph Keppler, one of the most popular political cartoonists of his day, pays tribute to the "Bosses of the Senate." By 1889 the Senate was known as the millionaires' club. The presiding officer was a Wall Street banker and its principal members represented the oil, lumber, railroad, insurance, silver, gold, utility, and manufacturing interests. Note that the "People's Entrance" is "closed."

for a ten-hour workday;* and the American Temperance Union (1836), which lobbied for a halt to the sale of alcoholic beverages, or prohibition. Like Madison, Tocqueville thought that such associations could be dangerous to public order and good government, but his observations convinced him that voluntary groups were essential to an egalitarian social and political system.[10] Later observers were not so sure. During the years of national expansion—geographic and industrial—after the Civil War, the scope of the federal government's activities expanded enormously, and so did the activities aimed at shaping its decisions. Among the most visible were those undertaken by the newly emerging, large-scale industrial corporations and trusts. The methods of their political agents, exposed by a generation of journalists and social critics known collectively as "muckrakers," tainted lobbying with an evil reputation it has never fully lived down (see box "But Their Mothers Still Loved Them").

---

* Employers of this era could demand as much work time as their employees would tolerate. People desperate for employment put up with workdays of twelve to fourteen hours—sometimes even more during the lengthy days of summer.

But Their Mothers Still Loved Them

1841. Historian James Silk Buckingham defined *lobbyists* as "agents, selected for their skill in the arts of deluding, persuading, and bribing members of legislative bodies."

1856. Poet Walt Whitman dismissed "lobbyers" as "crawling serpentine men, the lousy combings and born freedom sellers of the earth."

1873. A reporter for *The Nation* depicted the professional lobbyist as "a man whom everybody suspects; who is generally during one half of the year without honest means of livelihood; and whose employment by those who have bills before a legislature is only resorted to as a disagreeable necessity."

1875. Novelist John William De Forest in his novel *Honest John Vane* let out all the stops: "Men of unwholesome skins, greasy garments, brutish manners, filthy minds, and sickening conversation; men who so reeked and drizzled with henbane tobacco and cockatrice whisky that a moderate drinker or smoker would recoil from them as from a cesspool; men whose stupid, shameless boasting of their briberies were enough to warn away from them all but the elect of Satan . . . [and] decayed statesmen, who were now, indeed, nothing but unfragrant corpses, breeding all manner of vermin and miasma."

1888. Everit Brown and Albert Strauss's *Dictionary of American Politics* offered this definition: "*Lobby, The,* is a term applied collectively to men that make a business of corruptly influencing legislators. The individuals are called lobbyists. Their object is usually accomplished by means of money paid to the members, but any other means that is considered feasible is employed."

Source: Margaret Susan Thompson, *The "Spider Web": Congress and Lobbying in the Age of Grant* (Ithaca, N.Y.: Cornell University Press, 1985), 54–57.

Citizens outraged by political corruption formed new associations to agitate for reform. Over time, these groups succeeded in reorganizing government at all levels and rewriting the rules of electoral and party politics (see Chapters 8 and 12). These changes were part of a larger collection of innovations—child labor and wages-and-hours laws, regulation of railroads and other large-scale business enterprises, women's suffrage, the income tax—that were adopted during the late nineteenth and early twentieth centuries, a period historians now label the Progressive Era (see Chapter 12). The impetus for these innovations, as well as a good deal of the resistance to them, came from interest groups of every description. One of the most remarkable, if temporary, successes was achieved by the Anti-Saloon League, which engineered the adoption of the Eighteenth Amendment. It prohibited the sale of alcoholic beverages in the United States from 1919 to 1933, when the amendment was repealed (see box "Punishing Wets at the Polls: The Success of the Anti-Saloon League").

The groups that had so impressed Tocqueville in the 1830s had been largely local and short-lived. By the last decades of the nineteenth century, however, a proliferation of large-scale organizations, fueled by an emerging industrial economy, was spawning the Industrial Revolution. Expanding national and international markets bred large corporations, trusts, and other complex financial structures, as well as numerous labor and farm organizations. Members of such groups were attracted mainly

POLITICS/POLICY

Punishing Wets at the Polls
The Success of the Anti-Saloon League

The Anti-Saloon League, the most successful single-issue lobbying group in U.S. history, was the leading force behind adoption of the Eighteenth Amendment, which from 1919 until its repeal in 1933 prohibited the sale and transportation of "intoxicating liquors" (including beer and wine) in the United States.

For decades before the Anti-Saloon League was founded in 1896, numerous groups had advocated abstinence from alcohol and opposed the liquor traffic, but they had come and gone. Even a political party—the eponymous Prohibition Party—was on the temperance bandwagon, but the movement's political achievements were limited until the Anti-Saloon League took root.

The league's leaders, Purley Baker and Wayne Wheeler, were among the most astute politicians of their day. They put together an organization led by paid professional staff and supported by monthly subscriptions as well as large donations from wealthy benefactors. Working through preexisting organizations—mainly churches, but also local temperance groups—the league operated as the central coordinator of the movement's many components.

It focused strategically on a single issue—stopping the liquor trade; it took no political stance on any other issue. Tactically, the league concentrated on electoral politics with the simple goal of defeating "wets" and electing "drys." It monitored legislative votes and demanded written pledges from aspiring candidates who wanted the league's support and did not have track records on the issue. The league did not care whether candidates themselves drank, only how they would vote on legislation restricting liquor sales. It established the value of its support by mobilizing sympathetic voters (largely through Protestant churches) and persuading them to cast votes based exclusively on the liquor issue: wets were punished at

the polls. When the movement for prohibition went national, the league rallied constituents to send mail and petitions to Congress demanding action and even staged a march on Washington, attended by four thousand temperance advocates, to lobby for a constitutional amendment establishing Prohibition.

Success, however, was the league's undoing. Because Prohibition lacked widespread public support in many areas, especially in the big cities, enforcement could be achieved only at great expense. But stringent enforcement would have made it even more unpopular. It finally fell victim to waning popular support and the Great Depression, which spurred demands for the jobs and taxes the liquor industry could offer. Prohibition was repealed on December 5, 1933, putting whiskey smugglers, like the one shown in the photo, out of business.

Source: Peter H. Odegard, *Pressure Politics: The Story of the Anti-Saloon League* (New York: Columbia University Press, 1928).

by the specialized services and enhanced status they offered, but once organized and staffed, with a steady income from membership dues, the groups formed a permanent institutional base for attending to the political interests of members.

The Pluralist Defense of Interest Groups

With the emergence of stable political associations as major players in national politics, scholars began to study interest groups. One result was the first systematic defense of their legitimate role in a modern democracy. The case was made most fully by political scientist David Truman in his influential book *The Governmental Process,* published in 1951.[11] Truman viewed the proliferation of political interest groups as a natural and largely benign consequence of economic development. These groups formed spontaneously whenever shared interests were threatened or could be enhanced by political action. Modern industrial society, characterized by an ever more elaborate division of labor, became awash in interests and therefore in interest groups. As society became progressively more fragmented and variegated, so did the universe of associations.

Because groups were free to organize and participate in an open political system, the political process balanced competing interests, just as James Madison had promised. If established groups advocated policies that threatened the interests of other citizens, the threatened would organize to defend themselves. Demands provoked counterdemands, and so policies embodied the numerous compromises and trade-offs necessary for building winning coalitions within and between political institutions. Aware that overreaching would stir opposition, established groups prudently moderated their demands. Thus unorganized interests constrained active groups even when they were not represented by lobbies of their own.

Truman and other pluralist scholars also emphasized that the American political system was particularly conducive to pluralist politics. Its decentralized structure offered numerous points of access—political parties, congressional committees and subcommittees, the courts, the enormous variety of federal, state, and local governing agencies—where groups could bid for favorable policies. It also provided a set of political actors—elected officials—whose purposes were served by building broad-based coalitions and defending widely shared values. In this idealized conception, pluralist politics created a policy balance that reflected both the distribution of interests in society and the intensity with which they were pursued. Widely shared interests weighed in heavily because elections make numbers count; intensity entered the equation because the people who care the most about an issue are those most inclined to organize and act.

Clearly, then, this view of American pluralism did not embrace the customary disdain of "special interests" or "pressure groups" or "lobbies." Rather, interest groups were regarded as essential and valuable participants in the democratic politics of a modern industrial society. Without their participation, policy would be made in far greater ignorance of what citizens actually wanted from their government.

As a description of reality, this sunny conception of pluralism was open to some obvious criticisms. No one doubted that organized groups often were important political players; this was not at issue. But it was also undeniable that the groups most visibly active in politics did not, by any stretch of the imagination, form a balanced cross-section of economic or social interests. Some interests, such as those of large industrial corporations, seemed to be vastly overrepresented; other interests, such as those of migrant laborers and the unemployed, were not represented at all. "The flaw in the pluralist heaven," as political scientist E. E. Schattschneider put it, "is that the heavenly chorus sings with a strong upper-class accent." [12] The readiest explanation for this bias is that organizational resources—money, information, access to authority, skill, bargaining power—are distributed very unequally across political interests. Thus when organizations invest in politics, the outcome will be biased in favor of groups supported by the affluent, informed, and powerful.

The Problem of Collective Action

A subtler but equally important explanation for the observed bias in group representation lies in the way the incentives for collective action and the barriers to organization vary across different types of groups. The explanation, developed by the economist Mancur Olson in *The Logic of Collective Action* (1965), begins by pointing out that classical pluralists such as Truman were mistaken in assuming that people would form interest groups spontaneously to promote or defend shared interests. [13] Someone has to take on the work of organizing the group and finding the resources to keep it going. And to succeed, organizers have to overcome a standard collective action problem: most political interest groups pursue collective goods that, by definition, all group members will enjoy whether or not they help to provide them. Rational self-interest leads to universal free riding, dooming the organization and the effort unless some way is found around this difficulty.

Some kinds of groups solve the free-rider problem far more easily than do others. Small groups are easier to organize than are large groups because transaction costs are lower and the free-rider problem less severe, since free riders are more readily detected and subject to scorn and other social sanctions. Moreover, interests with a great deal at stake in a policy domain are more readily organized for political action than are people with little at stake (see box "Minorities Rule"). When prospective costs or benefits are large, so are incentives to invest in political action.

Group size and stakes often are inversely related, compounding the bias. For a few fortunate groups, a single member might have enough at stake to justify paying the entire cost of pursuing the group's collective interests. Exxon-Mobil, for example, might find it profitable to invest in lobbying for repeal of price controls on gasoline even if it has to pay the entire cost of producing a benefit that would have to be shared with all gasoline producers (a small group—just ten companies control 79 percent of U.S. domestic refining capacity). By contrast, many widely shared, diffuse collective interests will be poorly represented if those who share them behave rationally and remain free riders.

This analysis may explain why lobbies representing narrow economic interests predominate in Washington, but it raises a new question: why are there nonetheless so many vigorous lobbies claiming to speak for widespread, diffuse interests? Indeed, one of the most striking changes in the interest group universe over the past three decades

LOGIC OF POLITICS

Minorities Rule

The "special interests" have had an unsavory reputation in American politics since the beginning of the Republic, when James Madison warned about the "violence of faction" in *Federalist* No. 10 (see Chapter 2). According to the prevailing view, when special interests influence public policy, democracy suffers. This is not necessarily so. Even when politicians focus on maximizing their votes in the next election and thereby stay responsive to majority rule, special interests have ample opportunity to lobby successfully for favored policies.

To understand why this is so, one needs simply to recognize that information is costly. Voters will monitor their representatives' actions only on issues that are important to them and only when such information might, consequently, alter their preference for candidate A or candidate B in the next election. A milk subsidy under consideration in Congress might, if it passes, add a penny or two to every milk consumer's bill at the checkout counter. However, the vast majority of voters will ignore this issue because the cost of learning about it and studying their representatives' voting records would exceed any expected benefit of having the information.

Although most voters will elect to remain ignorant about milk subsidies, dairy farmers most certainly will not. A small surcharge on milk could add up to a major improvement in their income. So these farmers will pay much higher costs to learn about the details of the policy and to track representatives' actions. Frequently these costs will include hiring lobbyists.

Just as information is costly to consume, it is costly to communicate. Few consumers who do happen to hear about the milk subsidy proposal will bother to register their opposition to it, while dairy farmers will spend significant amounts of time and money to communicate their preferences.

Politicians will notice that most citizens do not much care about the subsidy and are unlikely to vote on the issue. At the same time, they will recognize that a few others, the dairy farmers, care passionately and can be expected to base their votes and campaign contributions on the actions of their representatives on this one issue. So even politicians who are single-mindedly pursuing as many votes as possible will sometimes favor the preferences of a special interest over those of the far more numerous ordinary citizens.

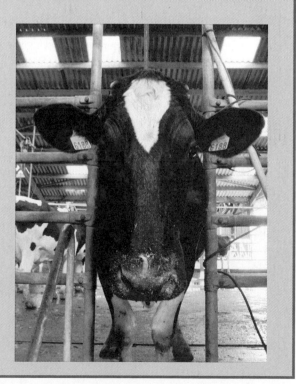

AARP: "Gray Power"

With its thirty-eight million members, AARP (originally the American Association of Retired Persons but now officially known by its acronym, which rhymes with *harp*) is the largest interest group in the United States. Nearly half of all Americans over fifty, or about one-fifth of the electorate, belong. AARP has more members than all the nation's labor unions combined; only the Roman Catholic Church has more.

Membership is attractive because for a mere $12.50 in annual dues members receive a bimonthly magazine plus discounts on rental cars, hotels, airlines, and travel packages, and access to attractively priced health insurance and prescription drugs. Its Washington, D.C., headquarters, housing a staff of more than eleven hundred, including forty-four policy specialists and twenty-two registered lobbyists, even has its own five-digit zip code. In 2006 AARP took in $1.04 billion in revenues and spent $683 million on programs and services, including $67 million on "legislation, research, and development," the lobbying expense category in its budget. AARP is the prime defender of Social Security and Medicare. The Bush administration's 2003 effort to overhaul Medicare, featuring a complicated new prescription drug benefit, got a major boost when it won AARP's endorsement; but in 2005 the organization strongly and successfully opposed the administration's proposal to divert a portion of Social Security taxes into private investment accounts. AARP's effectiveness as a lobby helps to explain why the proportion of federal dollars going to support retirees continues to grow even faster than their share of the population.

Logo of AARP's "Divided We Fail" campaign during the 2008 elections.

During the 2008 election season, AARP mounted its largest political campaign ever, named "Divided We Fail," aimed at mobilizing seniors to ask "our nation's leaders to commit to working in a bipartisan way to provide Americans with actions and answers on health and long-term financial security." According to AARP, as of October 2008, "360 Members of Congress have either signed the Divided We Fail congressional pledge or written a letter of approval supporting the Divided We Fail platform."[1]

Sources: Christopher Georges, "Old Money," *Washington Monthly* (June 1992): 16–21; Susan Levine, "AARP Hopes That Boom Times Are Ahead," *Washington Post,* June 2, 1998, A1; Bill McAllister, "AARP Alters Name to Reflect Reality," *Washington Post,* November 18, 1998, A25; *AARP Consolidated Financial Statements,* December 31, 2005 and 2006, 5.

1. AARP, "Divided We Fail Congressional Pledge," at www.aarp.org/issues/dividedwefail/about_issues/congressional_pledge.html, accessed October 7, 2008.

has been the proliferation of organizations claiming to represent millions of citizens devoted to some version of the public interest. This proliferation stems in part from the many people willing to contribute to groups espousing causes they care about without worrying about whether their contribution will make any appreciable difference. **Moral incentives,** the personal satisfactions of active self expression, trump the economist's concept of rationality for the countless concerned citizens who send checks to groups pursuing environmental protection, political reform, a ban on abortion, animal rights, and a host of other social causes. These groups did not arise spontaneously through the action of concerned citizens; most were put together by enterprising activists supported by charitable foundations, wealthy individuals, or the government itself. Yet many are sustained by dues and small contributions from a large number of private citizens.

Other large organizations circumvent the collective action problem by offering **selective incentives**—benefits that can be denied to individuals who do not join and contribute. Unions representing workers in firms with "closed shops" can compel union membership (and the payment of dues) as a condition of holding a job. Professional associations control licensing or offer useful assistance. Attorneys become members of state bar associations in order to practice law; physicians join the American Medical Association to qualify for malpractice insurance and to receive the association's journal; and farmers seek membership in the American Farm Bureau Federation to receive the assistance of county farm agents. Groups that initially attract members by providing them with individual benefits may invest some of their resources in pursuing collective benefits through political action. The largest interest group in the United States by far—AARP—was formed to market insurance to senior citizens and thrives by providing members with a variety of selective benefits (see box "AARP: 'Gray Power' "). Indeed, to a remarkable extent the interest groups that now throng the nation's capital are offshoots of organizations that exist for reasons other than political action.

Contemporary Interest Groups

The exact dimensions of the present-day interest group universe are unknown, but it is an expanding one. According to one estimate, the number of lobbying organizations more than tripled between the 1960s and the 1990s; a subsequent analysis indicated a further doubling between 2000 and 2005.[14] The 2007 edition of *Washington Representatives,* a directory of interest groups and lobbyists, listed approximately 18,000 lobbyists serving a host of corporations, labor unions, trade and professional associations, political action committees, and advocacy groups, including lawyers registered as lobbyists, public relations consultants, and think tank staff. In addition to the active lobbying organizations sponsored by private sector organizations, government entities—states, cities, counties, and their agencies—are behind much lobbying activity. No fewer than 168 California government bodies employ Washington, D.C., representatives. So do more than 300 colleges and universities, 148 Native American tribes, 16 ethnic groups, and more than 100 religious organizations.[15] More than 27,000 individuals are registered as lobbyists with Congress, and more than 100,000 Washingtonians are employed somewhere in the lobbying industry.[16]

Most advocacy groups also are the creatures of preexisting institutions. From abolition to temperance to civil rights to nuclear disarmament to the "right to life," churches and synagogues have provided a stable institutional base for organizing movements pursuing social and political change. Most of the self-designated public

From Consumer Advocate to Presidential Candidate
How Ralph Nader Got His Start

Ralph Nader, the most successful of all public interest entrepreneurs, got an initial boost from an unlikely source. In 1965 Nader published a bestselling book, *Unsafe at Any Speed*, charging that the Chevrolet Corvair, the first American entry of General Motors into the compact car market, was unsafe to drive. GM responded by hiring private investigators to pry into Nader's private life, presumably looking for dirt to discredit or silence him. When he discovered the spying, Nader sued GM, eventually settling out of court for $250,000. He used the publicity as well as the money garnered from the suit to set up the Center for the Study of Responsive Law, the first of his many consumer lobbies. Later he formed Public Citizen, a mass-membership organization that funded enterprises such as the Tax Reform Research Group; Congress Watch; Health Research Group; Citizen Action Group; Litigation Group; Critical Mass (for nuclear power issues); and the national Public Interest Research Group (PIRG), the inspiration for numerous state-level PIRGs now active in consumer issues. Nader was the Green Party's 2000 presidential can-

didate, taking enough votes away from Al Gore in Florida to give that state, and the election, to George W. Bush. Unrepentant, Nader ran again in 2004 and 2008.

Source: James Q. Wilson, *Political Organizations* (New York: Basic Books, 1973), 322–323.

interest groups that have proliferated in recent decades initially were financed by patrons—philanthropic foundations, corporations, wealthy individuals, or the government itself—and many depend on continuing subsidies for significant parts of their budgets. The interests of welfare recipients, the mentally ill, children, and the homeless do not lack advocates, even though such groups themselves are not organized for collective action. Their causes have been taken up by lobbies representing the social service professionals (mostly government employees) who run the programs that serve these groups. Even the flourishing public interest industry begun by longtime consumer advocate Ralph Nader got its start with the timely if unintended help of one of its initial targets (see box "From Consumer Advocate to Presidential Candidate").

Not every group depends on outside assistance for its resources. Prominent public interest groups such as Common Cause and Nader's various organizations are financed principally by membership dues and small donations, as are many of the large environmental lobbies, such as the Sierra Club, the National Audubon Society, and

STRATEGY AND CHOICE

The Blessings of Adversity

Voluntary organizations that survive on dues and small contributions from a mass membership often do best when the political climate is the most unfavorable. Such groups solicit most of their members and raise most of their money through direct-mail appeals, which are most effective when they invoke threats that make people angry or fearful enough to leave off free riding and join up or send another check. As one practitioner put it, "You've got to have a devil. If you don't have a devil, you're in trouble."[1] Devils are easier to find when power is in enemy hands. Thus, for example, membership in the National Rifle Association (NRA), a group adamantly opposed to any kind of gun control, grew rapidly during Democrat Jimmy Carter's administration (1977–1981), peaked in the early 1980s, then drifted downward from 1984 though 1991 when pro-gun Republicans Ronald Reagan (1981–1989) and then George H. W. Bush (1989–1993) sat in the White House. NRA growth revived with the election of gun control advocate Bill Clinton in 1992, then fell off again after the Republicans took control of Congress in 1995. But after the 1999 shootings at Columbine High School in Colorado (two students killed twelve schoolmates and a teacher and injured twenty-three other people before committing suicide), proposals for stricter gun laws gained momentum, and in response NRA membership rose sharply to reach its highest level ever in 2000. After George W. Bush defeated gun control advocate Al Gore that year, NRA membership began to tail off once again.[2]

For environmental groups the pattern was inverted. They received an enormous boost from the Reagan and Bush administrations. Their best (if unwitting) recruiters were James Watt, Reagan's first secretary of the interior, and Anne Gorsuch Burford, head of the Environmental Protection Agency, who made no apologies for putting private economic interests ahead of environmental protection. The Sierra Club's membership rose from 181,000 in 1980 to 364,000 in 1985 and to 650,000 in 1992, and its budget more than quadrupled (from $9 million to $40 million). The National Audubon Society grew by 50 percent, adding 200,000 members to its rolls during the Reagan-Bush years, and other major environmental groups also grew rapidly. After 1992, however, with an environmentalist safely in the White House, membership in most of these groups stabilized or fell off, and by 2000 the Sierra Club was down to 550,000 members. But George W. Bush's victory that year threw environmentalists on the defensive once again; rallying against what its publications portrayed as his administration's multipronged assault on environmental values. By 2004 the Sierra Club had raised its membership to 757,000 and its budget to more than $95 million.

---

1. Jeffrey M. Berry, *The Interest Group Society* (Boston: Little, Brown, 1984), 84.

2. Kelly Patterson and Matthew M. Singer, "The National Rifle Association in the Face of the Clinton Challenge," in *Interest Group Politics,* 6th ed., ed. Allan J. Cigler and Burdett A. Loomis (Washington, D.C.: CQ Press, 2002), 60–65; Kelly Patterson, personal communication, July 28, 2004.

the Wilderness Society. These and other organizations have taken advantage of modern computer technology to solicit and maintain a mass membership and donor base through direct-mail and Internet appeals to current and prospective supporters. Because they depend on moral or purposive incentives—persuading people to invest in collective goods despite the temptation to free ride on the efforts of others—their memberships and budgets fluctuate with circumstances. They tend to grow when opponents run the government and shrink when sympathetic politicians are in power (see box "The Blessings of Adversity").

Why Have Interest Groups Proliferated?

Several interacting factors have contributed to the rapid proliferation of interest groups since the 1960s. For one thing, the *social ferment* initiated by the civil rights movement inspired and instructed the stream of organizations that agitated for social change. Some led the opposition to the war in Vietnam; others asserted the rights of women, gays, Native Americans, Hispanics, Asians, and people with disabilities. Environmental and consumer groups emerged, along with the antiabortion and conservative Christian movements and animal rights organizations. The list could (and no doubt will) go on. Organizers of **social movements**—amorphous aggregates of people sharing general values and a desire for social change—quickly imitate successful innovations, and each new group has been able to draw on the experience of its predecessors.

The clientele for such groups has come from a *growing and increasingly well-educated and affluent middle class,* people with a surplus of money or time to invest in causes that excite their moral imaginations strongly enough to discourage free riding. *Technological innovations*—computerized mass mailings, toll-free 800 numbers, fax machines, the Internet—have made it easier and cheaper than ever before for entrepreneurial leaders to establish and maintain organizations that have a large number of geographically scattered and socially unconnected members.

Successful groups inspire *opponents* as well as imitators. Corporate and business leaders whose interests were threatened by the political gains of environmental and consumer groups organized to defend themselves. Legislation that added to their regulatory burden and threatened the bottom line was a powerful stimulus to political action by industries and firms. Business leaders sought as well to beef up the intellectual case for their side by financing think tanks* dedicated to promoting conservative ideas and policies—among them the Hoover Institution, the American Enterprise Institute, the Heritage Foundation, and the Cato Institute.[17]

The most important part of the dynamic behind the expanding interest group universe, however, has been the *encouragement of the federal government* itself. In addition to stimulating the organization of business interests, the growing scope of government activity has encouraged the proliferation of organizations in the nonprofit and public sectors:

---

* *Think tank* is the common term for an organization that employs or sponsors professional intellectuals to study issues of public policy and to prepare books, reports, newspaper essays and opinion pieces, magazine articles, and speeches promoting their conclusions. Most, though not all, adhere to some identifiable ideology that reflects the values and interests of their sponsors.

The growth, during the twentieth century, of public schools, parks and forest preserves, agricultural research stations, public hospitals, and social welfare agencies of all kinds stimulated the creation of numerous professional associations made up of the providers of these new public services. *These groups often were created at the suggestion of public officials who realized the political value of organized constituents working to promote their programs from outside of government* [emphasis added].[18]

Prominent examples include private business groups such as the U.S. Chamber of Commerce and the Business Roundtable, which were created under the leadership of secretaries of commerce in, respectively, the Taft and Nixon administrations; the American Farm Bureau Federation, which developed from a network of official advisory committees to the U.S. Department of Agriculture's county agents; and the National Organization for Women (NOW), a leading feminist organization. Indeed, the women's movement itself was jumpstarted by the government. In the early 1960s the Kennedy administration sponsored legislation that encouraged the creation of a Commission on the Status of Women in every state. Later, the state and federal governments funded a series of conferences on women's issues. In 1966 some delegates to the annual meeting of State Commissioners on the Status of Women, frustrated by how their position as government officials limited their ability to take political action, sought a voice by founding NOW, which could work outside government.[19]

The federal government also has contributed to the proliferation of interest groups through the tax code. Many groups qualify as nonprofit organizations, which are exempt from most taxes, and donors may deduct contributions to some kinds of nonprofit groups from their taxable income. The government also subsidizes the mass mailings of nonprofit groups through special postal rates. These organizations do face some restrictions on their political activity, however; they may educate, but they are not supposed to lobby openly or to engage in partisan electoral politics. The philanthropic foundations that fund many advocacy groups are themselves creatures of tax policy; rich people and families put their assets into foundations as a legal way to avoid income and inheritance taxes. Administrations also subsidize some politically favored organizations by hiring them to conduct studies or carry out specific projects. Groups thrive in good part because public policy has encouraged them to do so.

With the growth of federal programs and regulation, lobbying has thrived as a profession. Because so many lobbyists practice their profession on Washington's K Street, it has become synonymous with the whole industry, just as New York's Wall Street stands for the financial sector.

Finally, although discussions of pluralist politics commonly assume that government programs emerge in response to interest group demands, in reality it often is the other way around: interests (and interest groups) arise in *defense of government programs*. Typically, groups benefiting from government programs get organized and active only after the programs are in place. For example, most of the potent groups defending the interests of elderly people emerged after the enactment of Social Security (1935), Medicare (1965), and the Older Americans Act of 1965; AARP did not become the eight-hundred-pound gorilla of American politics until these programs were already in place to defend.

With or without the deliberate instigation of government officials, new policies create constituencies ripe for organization. People who adapt their plans to existing policies (on tax credits for capital investments, for example) develop a stake in continuation of the policies. And it is easier to mobilize people to defend what they already have than to pursue the more doubtful prospective benefits they do not yet enjoy—that is, the threat of loss is a more powerful spur to action than the hope of gain.[20] In general, the more the government does, the more incentives it creates for organized political action.

Fragmentation and Specialization

The expanding interest group universe also reflects the fragmentation of old interests and the growing division of labor among groups sharing the same broad goals. New organizations form when new issues pull old groups apart; increasingly complex issues and fragmented policy processes force groups to specialize to be effective. Meanwhile, as links between diverse problems have become more transparent, a wider range of organized interests has pushed into formerly isolated issue domains.

Farm policy, for example, was for many years the exclusive domain of the farm bloc, an alliance composed of a handful of interest groups (most notably the American Farm Bureau Federation), U.S. Department of Agriculture officials, and members of Congress from the farm states who sat on the agriculture and appropriations committees and subcommittees. Together, they formed a classic "iron triangle" that dominated federal agriculture policy (see Chapter 8). Today, more than two hundred organizations attempt to shape agricultural policy in a far more diffuse policy environment. Commodity groups (representing, for example, growers of wheat, cotton, corn, soybeans, rice, sugar beets, and peanuts, as well as producers of milk, honey, beef, chicken, and wool) have been joined by groups concerned with nutrition, food safety, international trade, food processing and distribution, environmental quality, farm credit, and the welfare of rural residents. A study of 130 of these groups found that only one in six pursued a broad agenda; the rest addressed only a narrow range of policy issues in their chosen niches.[21] The participants are far too many and diverse to form anything resembling the stable, exclusive iron triangle of old.

The growth of federally sponsored medical research has also spawned a variety of specialized lobbying organizations. Various bodily organs (heart, lungs, brain, kidneys, eyes) as well as diseases (HIV/AIDS, diabetes, epilepsy, cystic fibrosis, arthritis, lupus) have their own advocacy groups. Cancer research is promoted not only by the Ameri-

Lance Armstrong, Tour de France winner, cancer survivor, and founder and chair of the Lance Armstrong Foundation, speaks during a news conference following the Senate Health, Education, Labor, and Pensions Committee's hearing on cancer challenges and opportunities on Capitol Hill in Washington, D.C., on May 8, 2008. To his direct left is Sen. Kay Bailey Hutchison, R- Tex.; to his right is Sen. Edward Kennedy, D-Mass., who would be diagnosed with a brain tumor within weeks. Groups successfully pressuring Congress to devote more resources to combating "their" disease have inspired imitators, making this strategy increasingly common.

can Cancer Society, but by groups specializing in its various forms (breast, prostate, ovarian, leukemia, lymphoma). Associations lobby for more investment in curing birth and developmental diseases (spina bifida, cystic fibrosis), maladies of youth (sudden infant death syndrome) and age (osteoporosis), and mental as well as physical illnesses (manic depression, autism, alcoholism). All want the health research budget to grow, but each also works to expand the share devoted to its particular specialty.

Specialization responds not only to changes in the external environment but also to organizational imperatives. To survive, an interest group must convince its individual or institutional backers that their continued investment is worthwhile. To do so, it must distinguish itself from similar outfits competing for the same constituency by showing that its contribution is unique. Most groups survive by staking an exclusive claim to leadership and expertise on a particular subset of issues. To avoid mutually destructive poaching, potential competitors for the same constituency reach informal accommodations, deferring to each other's issue turf. Opponents do not threaten an interest group's health; indeed, as we saw earlier in this chapter, powerful opponents often invigorate a group. A group is in the greatest danger from similar groups appealing to the same supporters. This problem makes the formation of coalitions tricky. Groups often have to form alliances to succeed politically, but to be submerged in a coalition threatens the loss of a group's special identity. Thus many groups are reluctant to participate in coalitions and join them only on a temporary basis for specific purposes.[22] Nonetheless, groups with common interests—and no fear of losing their separate identities—do sometimes form new groups that are, in effect, standing coalitions. More than a few of the organizations listed in *Washington Representatives* are coalitions of other groups that are themselves representatives of institutions. There is even a National Association of Business Political Action Committees (NABPAC), representing 132 business political action committees (PACs) that themselves represent corporations and trade associations. NABPAC advises its members on PAC management, fund-raising, and candidates, and testifies in defense of PACs in congressional hearings on campaign finance legislation.

What Do Interest Groups Do?

What do all these interest groups spend their time doing? For most, the first objective is not political influence but simple survival. Interest group leaders keep their organizations in business by cultivating and retaining patrons willing to pay the bills or supply other essential resources. This activity not only absorbs a great deal of time and energy but also strongly shapes a group's political activity. Organizations that survive on small contributions from a mass membership, for example, have no choice but to focus on the issues that continue to generate contributions. Common Cause, which initially advocated a broad range of civic reforms, has spent much of its time in recent decades agitating for campaign finance reform because the issue always tops the list when members are surveyed at membership renewal time.

Lobbying groups that represent corporations and trade associations have to pass muster with executives or boards of directors who may have only a shaky understanding of political realities. As a result, group leaders may spend as much time explaining government to their patrons as they do explaining their patrons' interests to government officials. They also may spend more time engineering a consensus among patrons on what the group's policy goals should be than pursuing the goals themselves. For example, "representatives of the Peanut Growers Group . . . spent considerably more time agreeing on what they would contest in the 1985 farm bill than they did working to get it."[23] In short, interest group leaders and their constituents are involved in a principal-agent relationship, with all the familiar problems and challenges such relationships pose. On a more mundane level, group officials must manage their offices—hiring and firing, assigning work, keeping staff productive and content. All of this activity adds up; interest group officials spend a good deal of their time just keeping the organization going.

Insider Tactics: Trafficking in Information and Cultivating Access

Interest groups have proliferated in Washington, D.C., in part because the federal government's expanded activities affect almost everything that people care about deeply, giving them plenty of reasons to defend or extend their interests. But to do so they first must know when and how their interests are at stake, not always a simple matter in a world of complex issues and processes. Meanwhile, political decision makers, facing the same complex and uncertain world, are always hungry for information about the potential consequences of different courses of action. The informational needs of politicians and interest groups create a basis for mutually beneficial exchanges. The importance of these exchanges was confirmed when officials from a representative sample of 175 organizations with Washington offices were asked to specify their most important activities: exchanging and presenting information topped the list, shown in Table 13-1.[24]

The information provided by interest groups is inherently suspect, of course, for, as government officials realize, it is intended not merely to inform but also to persuade. Thus much of what goes on between lobbyists and government officials is aimed at establishing sufficient trust to permit mutually beneficial exchanges of information. For example, lobbyists spend a lot of their time just keeping in touch with the government officials—members of Congress, congressional staff, bureaucrats—who deal with their issues so they can know when their interests are at stake. Much of their work lies in responding to proposals or actions, and early warning of a proposed action often is essential to an effective response (see box "Sharp Eyes"). Lobbyists also gather intelligence by regularly reading newspapers and more specialized publications and talking to other lobbyists as well as to government officials. Keeping in touch facilitates cordial relations with the officials they might do business with someday. People are more inclined to listen to friends than to strangers, but even mere acquaintance makes it easier to interpret, and therefore take into account, a lobbyist's pitch. Indeed, just being visible is important: "*You have to be seen. Even if the legislators*

TABLE 13-1

What Lobbying Groups Say They Do

Activity	Percentage Engaging in Activity
1. Testifying at hearings	99
2. Contacting government officials directly to present the group's point of view	98
3. Engaging in informal contacts with officials—at conventions, over lunch, and so forth	95
4. Presenting research results or technical information	92
5. Sending letters to members of the group to inform them about its activities	92
6. Entering into coalitions with other groups	92
7. Attempting to shape the implementation of policies	90
8. Talking with people from the media	89
9. Consulting with government officials to plan legislative strategy	86
10. Helping to draft legislation	85
11. Inspiring letter-writing or telegram campaigns	84
12. Shaping the government's agenda by raising new issues and calling attention to ignored problems	84
13. Mounting grassroots lobbying efforts	80
14. Having influential constituents contact their members of Congress	80
15. Helping to draft regulations, rules, or guidelines	78
16. Serving on advisory commissions and boards	76
17. Alerting members of Congress about the effects of a bill on their districts	75
18. Filing suit or otherwise engaging in litigation	72
19. Making financial contributions to electoral campaigns	58
20. Doing favors for officials who need assistance	56
21. Attempting to influence appointments to public office	53
22. Publicizing candidates' voting records	44
23. Engaging in direct-mail fund-raising for the group	44
24. Running advertisements in the media about the group's position on issues	31
25. Contributing work or personnel to electoral campaigns	24
26. Making public endorsements of candidates for office	22
27. Engaging in protest demonstrations	20

Source: From a survey of interest groups reported in Kay Lehman Schlozman and John T. Tierney, *Organized Interests and American Democracy,* Copyright © 1986. Reprinted by permission of Pearson Education, Inc.

Sharp Eyes

The executive director of a major trade association representing the petroleum industry noticed an announcement buried in the fine print of the *Federal Register*. The Federal Aviation Administration (FAA) was intending to issue new regulations that would require the pilots of noncommercial aircraft to file detailed flight plans. The FAA was responding to recent events: several noncommercial aircraft had gone down, and search and rescue efforts had been hampered by lack of information on the pilots' intended routes. But for the trade association director, the FAA's remedy was the petroleum industry's headache. He frantically phoned his group's members, asking them to pressure the FAA to set aside the regulation. Why? Once detailed flight plans were on record with the FAA, anyone using the open disclosure provisions of the Freedom of Information Act could learn where his member companies' planes were exploring for oil, gas, and minerals. The director's sharp eyes and rapid mobilization of his member industries prevented the loss of possibly millions of dollars in secret data to their competitors.

Source: Edward Laumann and David Knoke, *The Organizational State: Social Choice in National Policy Domains* (Madison: University of Wisconsin Press, 1987), 3.

don't know who you are, if they see you often enough, they'll start to feel you belong." [25]

When an issue of concern to an interest group does arise, information is central to persuading government officials to act. Decision makers need two related types of information: technical and political. The Environmental Protection Agency cannot carry out its mandate, and Congress cannot legislate clean air or water, without a great deal of technical information on the dangers of, say, certain pesticides. Many important policy questions are fiendishly complex; government officials, wishing to avoid disastrous, costly mistakes, welcome any information that reduces uncertainty and the likelihood of nasty surprises. Knowing this, interest groups provide volumes of technical information designed to show that their preferred course of action will produce superior results and that policies they oppose will fail, cost too much, or produce new disasters.

Political information tells politicians how voters are likely to react to alternative policies. Lobbyists, not surprisingly, take pains to point out that the actions they favor will please a politician's supporters and the actions they oppose will have the opposite effect. Whenever possible, they carefully frame proposals in terms consistent with prevailing currents of public opinion. As we saw, their creativity in adapting messages to changing political circumstances was on full display following the terrorist attacks of September 11, 2001.

Since politicians know that lobbyists are advocates, when can they trust a lobbyist's information? Only when both sides expect to have a continuing relationship. A lobbyist who needs a politician's good offices on a continuing basis must maintain credibility or go out of business. If information turns out to be misleading or inflicts political damage, its source will never be heeded again.

Lobbyists do have ways of increasing the credibility of their messages. One reason they arrange for scientists or scholars to testify at congressional committee hearings is to back technical claims with evidence from more neutral sources. Testimony also allows groups to put their cases into the public record that will later guide the interpretation of laws by courts and administrative agencies. Because arranging testimony is costly for a lobbyist, it demonstrates to members of Congress that the group represented really does care about the issue under discussion. Testimony also is a way for lobbyists to show the people who pay their bills that they are doing their jobs. Often the same representatives of a group show up at the same subcommittee hearings and give the same testimony year after year, not because they expect to be effective but because the activity fits their job description. They are sustaining the organization, if not the cause.

The credibility of political information is enhanced when a group mobilizes its constituency as a part of the lobbying effort. Supportive letters, e-mails, phone calls, telegrams, and faxes from the districts of key members of Congress reinforce the impression that a favorable vote is in their best interests. A representative or senator who is skeptical of messages coming from some hired gun in Washington may be convinced by evidence that some constituents care enough to put time and effort into sending the same message. Opponents of Bill Clinton's 1994 health care reform proposals, for example, used hundreds of business groups to mobilize millions of ordinary citizens to express their opposition to the package. "The most effective tactic against our program," said chief architect Ira Magaziner after its defeat, "was grass roots mobilization and phone banks in swing districts." [26]

Lobbying by informing requires *access*, the professional lobbyist's indispensable stock in trade (see box "The Politics of Access"). Persuasive information does no good if it does not reach decision makers. Politicians grant access to people who can help them achieve their own goals. These people are the representatives of politically important interests in their constituencies, the supporters who help finance their campaigns, the men and women who have provided valuable information or assistance in the past—in other words, the people who can help them do what they want to do more effectively. Indeed, successful lobbying is political persuasion in its purest form: a lobbyist must get people to do what he or she wants them to do by convincing them that the action serves their goals.

Legislators and other government officials always have more things to do than they have time to do them. An interest group can encourage a sympathetic politician to spend time on its issue by making it cheaper (in time and staff resources) for the politician to do so. (See Table 13-1, page 629, for some of the things lobbying groups can do to help politicians.) By helping officials plan legislative strategy, assemble legislative coalitions, draft legislation, organize hearings, and write rules and regulations, lobbyists will not so much change minds as activate politicians already on their side by reducing the politicians' cost of getting involved.

Interest groups also can make the jobs of regulators and other bureaucrats easier. Congress usually writes general legislation, leaving decisions on the detailed rules and regulations up to the administrative agencies. The Administrative Procedure Act of 1946 requires that all such proposed rules and regulations be published in the *Federal Register* before they are promulgated and that public hearings be held on them if anyone objects (see Chapter 8). An important task of many group officials is to monitor the *Federal Register* for proposed rules that might affect their group's interests and to provide research and testimony in opposition or support.

For their part, regulators, hoping to avoid writing rules that get shot down by appeals to the courts or Congress, keep in touch with politically potent groups in the sectors they regulate. Often the relationship is formalized through the creation of advisory groups representing the relevant private interests, which can be consulted on a

The Politics of Access

Successful insider lobbying requires access, so it is no wonder that lobbying firms compete to hire former members of Congress as senior partners. Unlike other folks, former senators and representatives have the run of their old chamber, with floor, restaurant, gym, and parking privileges. They also enjoy personal ties from long association with members and staff, and they often have unmatched political and substantive expertise on issues they dealt with while in office. Although a 1989 ethics law forbids former members to lobby on Capitol Hill until they have been out of Congress for a year (extended to two years for senators in 2007), it has not slowed the migration to K Street. In 2006, 155 former members registered as lobbyists.[1] One-time congressional, White House, and agency staffers are also well represented in the lobbying profession. By moving from the public to the private political sector, they can multiply their incomes several times over, cashing in on the specialized knowledge and contacts acquired in their former jobs.

The problem, according to critics, is that people in government eyeing high-paying lobbying jobs will, to please prospective employers, put private ahead of public interests. In early 2004, for example, shortly after playing a key role in crafting a Medicare prescription drug law notably generous to the drug industry, retiring representative Billy Tauzin of Louisiana was offered a new job as head of the Pharmaceutical Research and Manufacturers of America at an annual salary reported to be more than $2 million. Pressure from Republican colleagues fearing a public backlash forced him to decline the offer.

Traditionally, K Street firms have welcomed politicians and staffers from both parties because they have needed friends on both sides of the aisle. But after winning Congress in 1994 and the White House in 2000, Republican leaders mounted an organized effort to stack them with Republicans. Sen. Rick Santorum, R-Penn., held weekly meetings with lobbyists to track job openings and to decide which loyal Republicans should fill them. According to a retired Republican representative and lobbyist who participated, "The underlying theme was [to] place Republicans in key positions on K Street. Everybody taking part was a Republican and understood that that was the purpose of what we were doing. It's been a very successful effort."[2] Indeed it was, because lobbying firms needing access to Republicans in Congress and the White House in order to represent their clients had little option but to comply. In 2003 a Republican National Committee

official bragged to a group of Republican lobbyists that thirty-three of the thirty-six top openings he had been tracking had gone to Republicans.[3]

That Republican advantage ended abruptly when the Democrats won House and Senate majorities in the 2006 election. Even before the election, lobbying firms and trade associations had begun hiring well-connected Democrats as a hedge against the growing possibility that the Democratic party would win control of one or both chambers, and the trend accelerated after the election:

> Gone in a matter of months was the years-long effort to build a permanent majority through an alliance with lobbying firms and trade groups, which supplied high-paid employment to Republicans. . . . Instead, as soon as Republicans lost control of Congress, even as they retained the presidency, lobby shops shook off the vestige of what was known as the "K Street Project." . . . "To coin a phrase, the K Street project has been consigned to the dustbin of history," said Craig Shirley, a Republican consultant.[4]

Firms for whom access to key congressional leaders is their stock in trade had little choice but to adjust the partisan coloring of their personnel to reflect the changed realities. Prudently, however, they did not shift as far toward the Democrats as the "K Street Project" had tilted toward the Republicans. The number of lobbyists with ties to the Democrats shot up in early 2007, but Republicans were not fired to make way for them.[5] The Democrats' Senate majority was exceedingly narrow, and their grip on the House was also quite tenuous, so most major lobbying firms sought a partisan balance that would keep their businesses healthy no matter who wound up in control after 2008.

---

1. "Former Members of Congress Who Were Registered Lobbyists in 2006," http://abcnews.go.com/Politics/BrianRoss/story?id=2822749&page=1 (February 2, 2008).

2. Howard Kurtz, "Republicans Rule," *Washington Post,* June 30, 2003, at www.washingtonpost.com/ac2/wp-dyn?pagename=article&contentId=A50600-2003Jun30.

3. Ibid.

4. Jonathan Salant, "Republicans' Lobbying Grip Crumbles after Congressional Shakeup," Bloomberg, March 16, 2007, at www.bloomberg.com/apps/news?pid=20601070&sid=a6VJFfn.kWHQ&refer=home, accessed April 20, 2007.

5. Jeffrey Birnbaum, "Lobbyists Profit from Power Shift in Congress," *Washington Post,* April 23, 2007, D01.

continuing basis. About one thousand such groups exist, including the Interagency Committee on Smoking and Health of the U.S. Department of Health and Human Services and the U.S. Department of Agriculture's Burley Tobacco Advisory Committee.[27] Again, the benefits are mutual. On the one hand, the interests represented on the advisory group have permanent access to decision makers, so their views are guaranteed a hearing. On the other hand, the regulators can get an early reading on the likely reaction to their proposals and maintain a conduit to the groups whose interests they affect. Interest group officials, sitting on the inside, develop a greater appreciation for technical, legal, and political grounds for regulatory decisions and may end up lobbying their own members to accept them.

Interest groups also can be valuable to bureaucrats as allies in dealing with the elected officials who control their budgets. During the Cold War, for example, all three branches of the military mobilized civilian support groups to help fight the battles in Congress and, more important, with each other, for a larger share of the defense pie. The Navy League, Air Force Association, and Association of the U.S. Army lobbied vigorously for the programs and weapon systems sought by their respective services and against those of rival services. Each organization enjoyed the financial support of the defense contractors who proposed to build the weapons systems they advocated.

Outsider Tactics: Altering the Political Forces

The **insider tactics** just described depend on personal access to government officials and work through mutually beneficial exchanges between lobbyists and politicians.

In pursuing insider influence, lobbyists do not always forgo illegal inducements, and politicians do not always resist the temptation to accept them. Bribery scandals are thus a recurring if relatively infrequent feature of political life in Washington, D.C. When exposed, the costs to participants can be high. One time high-powered lobbyist Jack Abramoff, pictured here preparing to testify before the Senate Committee on Indian Affairs, wound up in jail for fraud and corrupting public officials, and investigations of his dealings led to the convictions of two White House staffers, a U.S. representative, and nine other lobbyists and congressional aides. Several members of Congress also lost their seats in 2006 at least in part because of their association with Abramoff.

The **outsider tactics** employed by interest groups do not require any personal contact with politicians and may take the form of implicit or explicit threats—real pressure—rather than offers of reciprocally helpful exchanges. The strategy is to persuade politicians to act as the group desires by altering the political forces they feel obliged to heed.

One common tactic is use of the mass media to shape public opinion. The Center for Responsive Politics tries to generate support for its campaign finance reform proposals by assembling and publicizing reports on campaign contributions and spending. Think tanks regularly hold press conferences to bring attention to research reports on public issues. The Children's Defense Fund assembles and publicizes reports on childhood poverty to encourage public pressure on Congress to spend more on

Mass demonstrations are a staple tactic of groups trying to get government leaders to pay attention to their issue. In April 2006, an estimated one hundred thousand people assembled on the National Mall in Washington, D.C., as part of an ongoing campaign to pressure the Bush administration to take action to halt what they regarded as genocide in Sudan's Darfur region. The speakers included actor George Clooney, Nobel Prize winner and Holocaust survivor Elie Wiesel, and politicians Barack Obama and Nancy Pelosi.

programs for poor children. Other groups try to get the media to buy their version of the public interest on, for example, the danger from pesticides or the incidence of breast cancer so that the threat of bad publicity will hang over the heads of politicians who oppose their demands.

Demonstrations—picketing, marches, sit-ins—are another time-honored outsider device. The principal techniques, around for centuries, were used by antislavery groups, suffragists, and prohibitionists, but they were perfected in their contemporary form by civil rights groups in the 1950s and 1960s and have since been widely imitated by a host of social movements. Demonstrations are intended to focus public attention on the cause. Freedom marches in the South brought the issue of segregation—and the brutality of its defenders—into the homes of Americans everywhere through the then-fresh medium of television (see Chapter 4). Demonstrations also may show the breadth of support for a cause. In the early 1970s opponents of the Vietnam War amassed hundreds of thousands of demonstrators in Washington, D.C., for this purpose. Civil disobedience—sit-ins and other demonstrations that openly violate the law—dramatizes the intensity of commitment; it is difficult to ignore a cause for which large numbers of people are willing to go to jail. Finally, demonstrations foster group solidarity—shared work and risk are powerful bonding agents—and thus may strengthen the organization. Demonstrations are used most often by groups that do not enjoy insiders' access. They have become so familiar in Washington, D.C., that, unless they are extraordinary in some way, the news media pay little attention to them.

Reports, news conferences, and demonstrations aimed at putting issues on the agenda and compelling government officials to do something about them depend on media attention. If the news media ignore them, they fail. Private interests that wish to publicize their views without the uncertainties of relying on free coverage may, if they can afford the cost, buy advertising. Mobil Oil, for example, for many years bought a regular space on the op-ed page of the *New York Times* to express its views on public issues.

Insider and outsider strategies are not mutually exclusive, and groups may use either or both, depending on circumstances and opportunities. The health insurance industry employs top Washington professionals for its day-to-day insider lobbying, but in 1994 it adopted outsider tactics to fight Bill Clinton's health care reform package. Most organizations, however, tend to specialize in one strategy or the other. Groups with money and expertise whose issues are narrow or nonconflictual usually take the insider route. Large groups whose issues are conspicuous and contentious are more likely to operate from the outside, relying on **grassroots lobbying,** mobilizing members to send messages that reiterate the group's demands to their senators and representatives. For example, when the National Rifle Association wants to prevent new restrictions on firearms, its members shower Congress with letters, e-mails, faxes, and telegrams supporting its position. The intended message is that people who care enough to write on an issue care enough to vote for members of Congress according to their stance on the issue. Members of Congress discount patently stimulated mail—that is, hundreds of identically worded letters—that may count for less than a handful of spontaneous, original messages. Indeed, some supposedly grassroots efforts, particularly those run by firms specializing in the business, are so patently artificial that they are dismissed as "Astroturf campaigns."

This is not news to the organizations that use this tactic, so some contrive to make the process seem more personal and less mechanical. Some groups

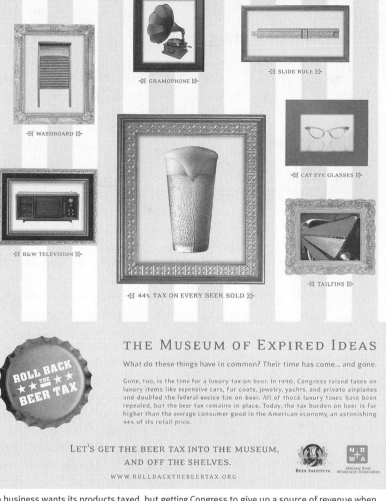

No business wants its products taxed, but getting Congress to give up a source of revenue when the federal budget is deeply in the red is an uphill battle. In addition, politicians find it easier to tax activities once considered "sinful," such as drinking alcohol, that at least some portion of the public wants the government to discourage. In this advertisement in a magazine read by Washington insiders, the beer industry tries to persuade members of Congress (notice the plea in the last line of the ad) that the federal excise tax on brews is out of date.

provide appropriate letters that vary in wording, typeface, and styles of stationery; others ask members to use their own words but to emphasize suggested themes. Members may be urged to write in longhand, even to use colloquial grammar, to make messages appear more authentic.

Outsider tactics differ from insider tactics because they impose real pressure, even threats—sometimes veiled, sometimes not—pushing politicians to act in ways they otherwise would prefer not to. Politicians, then, are far more resentful of outsider lobbying tactics than of insider ones. Indeed, such tactics can backfire when overdone; the pose of "standing up to pressure" has its political attractions, after all.

Litigation

One tactic that is equally available to insiders and outsiders is litigation. Interest groups snubbed by lawmakers or regulators may seek redress in court, challenging hostile laws or regulations. This strategy is especially attractive to groups that can rest claims on constitutional rights and that do not have the political clout to influence elected politicians. During the 1940s and 1950s, when many black citizens were effectively denied the right to vote and there was only limited public sympathy for their cause, civil rights groups used the courts extensively (see Chapter 4). People in jail or accused of crimes, unpopular religious minorities, and groups on the political fringe—none of whom is likely to be championed by officials who depend directly on voters for their jobs—have all found redress in court. But then so have General Motors, Philip Morris, and Microsoft. Despite the notable court victories of some groups on the margins of society, large corporations with deep pockets make the most frequent and effective political use of litigation.

Although about one-third of the Washington representatives of interest groups are lawyers, only a small proportion of interest groups list litigation as their predominant activity. Using the courts to good purpose often requires winning legislative battles in the first place. For example, environmental groups, notably the Environmental Defense Fund, have been able to use the courts effectively because the National Environmental Policy Act (1969) was deliberately designed to make it easy for private citizens to go to court to enforce environmental regulations (see the discussion of *standing* in Chapter 8).

In court cases where they do not participate directly, interest groups may attempt to influence judicial decisions by submitting *amicus curiae* or "friend of the court" briefs. Such briefs present evidence and arguments intended to strengthen one side under the guise of supplying judges with information on social facts relevant to the decision. Today, *amicus* briefs are filed in more than 90 percent of the cases heard by the Supreme Court.[28] Controversial cases generate the most *amicus* filings; *Webster v. Reproductive Health Services,* an important abortion rights case decided in 1989, attracted seventy-five *amicus* briefs signed by hundreds of organizations.[29] Court decisions seem to be affected by neither the numerical balance of *amicus* briefs nor the status of their sponsors, but the more briefs submitted with a case, the more likely the Court is to hear the case (see Chapter 9).

Organized interests also seek to shape court decisions indirectly by lobbying on judicial appointments. Nearly three hundred groups joined the battles over Senate approval of Supreme Court nominees Robert Bork (1987) and Clarence Thomas (1991), liberals winning the first by derailing Bork, conservatives the second by elevating Thomas.[30] Less extensive but still vigorous lobbying campaigns faced off over the nomination of Samuel A. Alito Jr. in 2006. Lower court appointments usually attract much less attention, but six of George W. Bush's circuit court nominees, noisily opposed by liberal groups for their positions on civil rights, abortion, and environmental regulation, were blocked by filibustering Senate Democrats in the 108th Congress (2003–2004).

Electoral Politics and Political Action Committees

Both outsiders and insiders use electoral politics to influence elected officials, but insiders offer electoral help, while outsiders more commonly threaten electoral harm. Groups unhappy with current policy always can try to replace the current decision makers with friendlier ones by recruiting and financing challengers, but this tactic is used mainly by partisan or ideological organizations. For example, GOPAC, chaired by Georgia Republican Newt Gingrich from 1986 to 1995, when he became House Speaker, nurtured the political careers of many of the Republican freshmen elected to the House in 1994. More typically, though, groups monitor and publicize the voting records of elected officials on their key issues. The idea is to identify friends and enemies so that campaign contributors and voters sympathetic to the group know which politicians to reward and which to punish (see box "The Return of the Dirty Dozen"). Interest groups act most conspicuously in electoral politics, however, through PACs.

As noted in Chapter 11, modern election campaigns are unavoidably expensive. Candidates who are not independently wealthy have to rely primarily on private individuals and PACs to pay the bills. In their modern form, PACs are a creation of the Federal Election Campaign Act (FECA) of 1971 (as amended in 1974). The FECA encouraged groups to form PACs by clarifying their legal status and specifying rules under which they could legitimately participate in financing campaigns; it also put the financial activities of PACs on the public record. To qualify as a *multicandidate committee* (the legal term for a political action committee), a PAC must raise money from at least fifty people and contribute to at least five candidates. The maximum contribution is $5,000 per candidate per campaign, which means, in effect, $10,000—$5,000 each for the primary and general election campaign (plus another $5,000 if there is a primary runoff in states where one is required when no candidate wins more than half the votes cast). By contrast, individuals may contribute only $2,300 per candidate per campaign.

GROWTH OF PACS. The number of PACs grew dramatically in the first decade after FECA was enacted but then leveled out at about four thousand in the mid-1980s and has remained near that level since then (see Figure 13-1). PAC contributions to candidates grew in a similar fashion, increasing by 375 percent between 1974 and 1986 (see Figure 13-2). Thereafter PAC contributions grew only modestly until 2000, when the bitter legacy of impeachment politics and the closely fought battle for control of both houses of Congress inspired a new surge of PAC spending, which continued to grow through 2006. The sharp increase in PAC activity during FECA's first decade and the continuing financial importance of PACs since then are at the center of a lively controversy, for PAC generosity raises an obvious question: what do PACs get in return for their contributions? Indeed, assaults on the legitimacy of interest groups now focus commonly on PACs.

The Return of the Dirty Dozen

During the 1970s an environmental lobby, Environmental Action (EA), compiled and publicized a list of the "Dirty Dozen," twelve members of Congress who supposedly had the worst environmental records (according to EA's standards). The group shrewdly targeted members who were vulnerable as well as objectionable. In elections from 1972 through 1980, twenty-four of the fifty-two who made the list (some more than once) were defeated—a striking record when compared with the greater-than-90-percent success rate of incumbents during the period. A consultant who worked on the campaigns claimed that the tactic "was very effective at making congressmen think twice about certain votes. There were numerous examples of members or their staff calling and saying, 'Is the congressman close to being on the list?' or 'Is this vote going to be used to determine the list?' "[1]

The group's later campaigns were less successful as it ran out of vulnerable targets, and it faded away. But another environmental alliance, the League of Conservation Voters (LCV), revived the tactic for the 1996 election and has since used it with considerable success. In elections from 1996 through 2006, thirty-nine of the eighty-one candidates targeted were eventually defeated, including twenty-nine incumbents and seven House members trying to move up to the Senate.[2] Like Environmental Action, LCV deliberately targeted close races where its investment—including $12.5 million in independent expenditures during this period[3]—had a reasonable chance of paying off. Its goals were both to

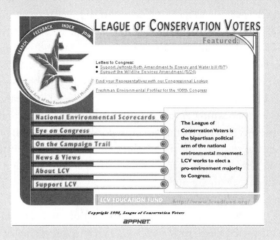

defeat objectionable candidates and to demonstrate the perils of opposing environmental interests. The tactic's potential was underlined by the reaction of Bob Dornan, a former representative trying in 1998 to recapture the California district he had lost in 1996, to being listed. The flamboyant conservative, with a career LCV environmental support score of about 10 on a 100-point scale, said, "In my heart, I'm a Greenpeace kind of guy."[4]

---

1. Bill Keller, "The Trail of the Dirty Dozen," *Congressional Quarterly Weekly Report,* March 21, 1981, 510.

2. *League of Conservation Voters,* www.lcv.org/Campaigns/Campaigns.cfm? ID=2236&c=1 (July 29, 2004).

3. *League of Conservation Voters,* www.lcv.org/campaigns/2006-campaigns.html (February 2, 2008).

4. *League of Conservation Voters,* http://lcv.org/dirtydozen/callahan_poststmt. htm (June 3, 1999).

The term PAC is applied to a diverse set of organizations. The categories of PACs used by the Federal Election Commission (FEC) in reporting financial activities—labor, corporate, corporation without stock, cooperative, trade/membership/health, and nonconnected—merely hint at the variety.* Some amount to little more than an entrepreneur with a mailing list; others are adjuncts of huge corporations or labor unions. Some pass out millions of dollars in every election cycle; others exist only on paper. Donations may be made at the sole discretion of the PAC director or only after extensive input from the PAC's contributors. The goals of some are immediate, narrow, and self-interested; others pursue long-term objectives based on broad ideological visions. Most PACs just give money, but a few also provide campaign workers, offer endorsements (who would not want to be regarded as a "friend of small business"?), produce advertising, advise on campaign strategies, get out the vote, and recruit and train candidates.

Although all PACs hope to influence public policy, they differ in how broadly or narrowly policy objectives are conceived and in strategies for reaching them. For many business corporations, labor unions, and trade associations, a PAC is simply an aid to traditional insider lobbying for narrowly focused economic interests. Money is given not so much to affect the outcome of the election as to gain access to and curry favor with the winner. PACs of this sort thus contribute to sure winners, to members of both parties sitting on committees dealing with legislation they care about, and to newly elected members after the election. Incumbents, already holding office and likely to retain it, naturally benefit.

At the other end of the spectrum are PACs with broad ideological agendas. Their goal is to maximize the number of seats held by people sympathetic to their views, changing policies by changing representatives rather than by persuading representatives to change policies. Thus they support promising nonincumbent candidates and concentrate their resources on close races, where the help is most likely to make a difference. Although such PACs may support friendly incumbents in tight races, they primarily adopt an outsider strategy. Examples are the Conservative Victory Committee on the right and the Women's Campaign Fund and EMILY's List (both of which support pro-choice women) on the left.

---

* The first two PAC categories, "labor" and "corporate," are self-explanatory, as is the minor category, "corporations without stock." "Cooperatives," another minor category, are special economic entities owned by their members, such as the dairy cooperatives run by groups of dairy farmers. The "trade/membership/health" category includes PACs representing trade, business, and professional associations. "Nonconnected" PACs have no separate organizational sponsor; the category includes a wide variety of ideological and single-issue groups.

Dirty Dozen
Election Results

Pennsylvania Senate
Bob Casey (D)* ☑ VICTORY!
Rick Santorum (R) ☒

Florida Senate
Bill Nelson (D) * ☑ VICTORY!
Katherine Harris (R) ☒

Missouri Senate
Jim Talent (R) ☒
Claire McCaskill (D)* ☑ VICTORY!

Montana Senate
John Tester (D)* ☑ VICTORY!
Conrad Burns (R) ☒

Virginia Senate
Jim Webb (D)* ☐ UNDECIDED
George Allen (R) ☐

California House
Jerry McNerney (D)* ☑ VICTORY!
Richard Pombo (R) ☒

Arizona House
J.D. Hayworth (R) ☒
Harry Mitchell (D)* ☑ VICTORY!

North Carolina House
Charles Taylor (R) ☒
Heath Schuler (D)* ☑ VICTORY!

Colorado Governor
Bill Ritter (D)* ☑ VICTORY!
Bob Beauprez (R) ☒

New Mexico House
Patricia Madrid (D)* ☐ UNDECIDED
Heather Wilson (R) ☐

Ohio House
Deborah Pryce (R) ☐ UNDECIDED
Mary Jo Kilroy (D)* ☐

Oklahoma House
Dan Boren (D) ☑
(no endorsed opponent)

Texas House
Henry Cuellar (D) ☑
(no endorsed opponent)

* LCV Action Fund endorsed candidate

Click For More Results ▸

LCV posted these results on election night to celebrate its victories; one of the three "undecided" contests eventually went to its candidate (James Webb), but Republican incumbents Heather Wilson and Deborah Pryce were narrowly reelected.

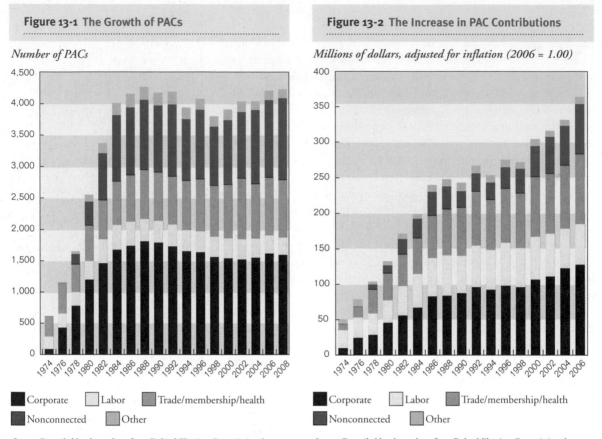

Figure 13-1 The Growth of PACs

Number of PACs

Corporate ■
Labor ▢
Trade/membership/health ■
Nonconnected ■
Other ▢

Source: Compiled by the authors from Federal Election Commission data.

Figure 13-2 The Increase in PAC Contributions

Millions of dollars, adjusted for inflation (2006 = 1.00)

Corporate ■
Labor ▢
Trade/membership/health ■
Nonconnected ■
Other ▢

Source: Compiled by the authors from Federal Election Commission data.

Between the extremes are PACs that pursue both short- and long-term goals. In the years before 1994, when the Democrats controlled Congress, many business-oriented PACs supported incumbent Democrats who seemed certain to be reelected, switching to Republican challengers only when their prospects looked extraordinarily promising. Although most business groups are closer to Republicans ideologically, they were reluctant to risk loss of access by offending Democratic incumbents when they ran Congress. When Republicans took control after 1994, the short- and long-term goals of business PACs were more easily reconciled. Republican leaders threatened retaliation against PACs that continued to support Democrats.[31] As New York representative Bill Paxon, chair of the National Republican Congressional Committee, put it,

> Our members have felt they were carrying the legislative water for many of these groups who then gave their money to the other side. It's very difficult for me to argue that people should open their arms to those who are embracing

their opponents. I certainly am not going to embrace someone who's constantly stabbing me in the back. We're making sure that the members know who's wielding the knife.[32]

Thus whereas in the four elections between 1988 and 1994 Democrats received an average of 54 percent of corporate PAC contributions to House candidates, in the four subsequent elections, Democrats received an average of only 34 percent. In 2007, the first year after the Democrats resumed control of the House, their share went back up to 49 percent.[33]

Some PACs also conduct independent campaigns for or against specific candidates, a practice that has become increasingly common in recent elections. For a campaign to be independent, it must not coordinate its activities with the candidate's campaign. The law does not limit independent expenditures, but they must be reported to the FEC. In 2006, for example, 146 PACs spent a total of $40 million on independent campaigns for or against particular House and Senate candidates. Interest groups also may conduct "voter education" campaigns, which are totally unregulated (their costs are not even reported to the FEC) so long as they do not explicitly recommend voting for or against a candidate. In 1996, for example, the AFL-CIO, the nation's leading labor organization, spent as much as $35 million on voter education drives aimed at defeating sixty-four House Republicans.[34] The campaign finance reform bill passed in 2002 tried to ban this kind of activity during the two months before a general election unless it is financed by hard money contributions, but a Supreme Court decision in June 2007 left the scope of this prohibition unclear (see Chapter 11).

Ellen Malcolm, president of EMILY's List (the acronym is derived from the group's slogan, "early money is like yeast, it makes the dough rise"), rallies supporters at the 2004 Democratic National Convention. The organization combines independent campaign activities of this sort with efforts to recruit, train, and help finance pro-choice women candidates.

PAC INFLUENCE. How does PAC activity affect public policy? According to one view, PACs corrupt the entire legislative process, giving citizens "the best Congress money can buy" because members vote with an eye more to the interests of their PAC donors than to those of their constituents or the nation. Proponents of this view say that PAC contributions buy votes and policy, period.[35] The evidence usually offered for this charge, however, is largely circumstantial or anecdotal. An investigative reporter or a campaign reform lobby such as the Center for Responsive Politics reveals that members supporting legislation desired by some interest group—milk producers, used car dealers, physicians, the banking industry, and the National Rifle Association are examples—got more campaign money from PACs representing the group than did members who opposed the legislation.

Such evidence is inconclusive, however. PAC officials counter that they are merely helping to elect legislators who share their own conception of the public interest. It would be bizarre indeed if PACs distributed money randomly to friend and foe alike; no one should expect them to be that careless. The fact is, no simple matching of contributions to roll-call votes (recorded votes cast on the floor of the House or Senate) or other activities can prove that PACs buy influence. More careful scholarly studies have found that PAC contributions exert, at most, only a modest effect on a legislator's decisions, most of which are shaped by party, ideology, and state or district interests. But on issues that attract little public attention and do not divide members along party or ideological lines, votes appear to reflect, in a modest way, prior PAC contributions. All things being equal, members of Congress favor interests that help finance their campaigns. But all things are not usually equal. Despite the many tales of members who vote to please financial backers or who demand money from lobbyists in return for help, there is little reliable evidence that policy is being bought wholesale by special interests.[36]

This is not to say, however, that PAC contributions do not have other effects on some members of Congress. Both members and PAC officials admit that, at minimum, contributions ensure access—a necessary if not sufficient condition for insider influence. Doors are open to lobbyists representing groups who have supported members' campaigns. Furthermore, roll-call votes are by no means the only important decisions shaping legislation. Crucial choices are made before bills reach the floor, but little is known about how PACs influence the preliminary stages of the legislative process. One study did find, however, that PAC contributions stimulated committee activity in behalf of the PACs' legislative goals.[37] Interest groups are not likely to put much time, energy, and money into PAC activities without some perceived legislative payoff.

Still, there are some formidable barriers to PAC influence. Many important issues generate conflicts among well-organized interests, giving members access to PAC money no matter which side they take and thus freeing them to take whatever side is consistent with their personal or district preferences. Given the variety of sources of campaign money available to incumbents—private individuals and parties as well as the thousands of PACs—most should have little difficulty financing campaigns without putting their principles on the block. Furthermore, the point of campaigns is to win elections, not raise money. Campaign contributions are a means to an end—winning votes and elections—not the end in themselves. For incumbents, the marginal return on campaign spending is small; the prospective value, in votes, of even the maximum PAC contribution ($10,000) is tiny. Thus it makes no sense for a member, to please a PAC, to take a stand that produces even a small net loss of voter support. The sentiments of a member's constituents, when they can be estimated, far outweigh campaign contributions in determining roll-call votes.

Finally, one fact, often overlooked, is that members of Congress are in a much stronger position to influence PACs than PACs are to influence them. Like other forms of lobbying, the activities undertaken by PACs are largely defensive. They ignore invitations to fund-raisers at their peril because they risk losing access and putting the interests they represent at a competitive disadvantage. Yet for politicians, granting access is relatively cheap; it does not promise action, merely the opportunity to be heard. Groups are thus "awash in access but often subordinate in influence." [38] PACs that cannot afford to say no or to offend members by funding their challengers are scarcely the powerhouses of legend.

It is important to remember that PACs are not themselves lobbying organizations, though lobbyists sometimes organize PACs to try to bolster the political clout of the interest groups they represent. In fact, PACs form a relatively small, quite specialized part of the interest group universe, and only a small portion of the money spent to influence politics passes through them. Most politically active interest groups do not form PACs at all. Rather, they use one or more of the other methods described in this chapter to influence politics. If PACs were to be abolished tomorrow, interest group politics would continue unabated.

Interest Group Politics: Controversial and Thriving

The charges levied against PACs are only the most recent variation on the enduring theme that special interest lobbies subvert democracy and trample the public interest. Scholarly critics of mid-twentieth century interest group politics emphasized two faults. The first was captured by Schattschneider's oft-quoted observation, noted earlier, that in the pluralist paradise, "the heavenly chorus sings with a strong upper-class accent"—that is, group representation is biased in favor of wealthy corporations and affluent individuals. The second was that rampant pluralism had let private interests hijack public authority. The mutually advantageous iron triangles formed by interest groups, agencies, and congressional subcommittees allowed special interests to dominate their policy domains. Agencies established to protect the public were soon captured by the very interests they were supposed to be regulating.

As we saw in Chapter 8, few observers today fret about iron triangles or captured agencies. The rise of public interest groups and the fragmentation of the interest group universe, as well as the ability of legislators to learn from past mistakes, broke up the iron triangles and liberated (or eliminated) the captured regulatory agencies. Public interest groups kept the spotlight on agencies and changed the political equation by promising political benefits (good publicity, a reputation as the defender of citizens) to elected officials who pursued the groups' versions of the public interest and by threatening political damage to those who did not. Organizational fragmentation undermined old accommodations: the more than two hundred organizations active in agricultural policy, for example, cannot form stable, autonomous alliances with agencies and legislators. [39] Changes in the way Congress operates also contributed to the breakup of iron triangles. During the 1970s, the legislative process became more open and permeable; committee and subcommittee autonomy declined, and influence over policy became more widely distributed. There were simply too many

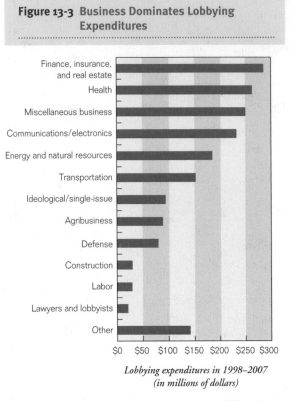

Figure 13-3 Business Dominates Lobbying Expenditures

Lobbying expenditures in 1998–2007 (in millions of dollars)

Source: Center for Responsive Politics at www.opensecrets.org/lobbyists/overview.asp?txtindextype=c, January 22, 2008.

potential players for stable subgovernments to persist. Since then, the growing legislative dominance of party leaders has proven equally inhospitable to them.

The demise of iron triangles, however, has not ended the criticism of pluralist politics. The charge of class bias remains plausible. Business organizations and other groups representing well-heeled interests still account for the largest share of lobbying expenditures by far (see Figure 13-3). The Enron Corporation's lobbying operation, if not the firm's fate, shows what this money can buy (see box "Enron's Matrix: The Limits of Lobbying"). Even public interest groups represent largely upper-middle-class clienteles—well-educated people with enough discretionary income to indulge in expressive contributions to causes they deem worthy. The interests of poor people, welfare mothers, and the homeless may be represented, but only through the good offices of middle-class people and organizations presuming to speak for them.[40]

Although iron triangles no longer reign, the proliferation of groups that contributed to their demise has created problems of its own. The clamor of competing groups is blamed for policy gridlock. With more active players, policy advocates find it harder to assemble winning coalitions. And with so many groups capable of vigorously defending themselves, some observers argue that it is impossible to initiate any change that imposes concentrated costs to achieve general benefits even if the benefits greatly outweigh the costs.[41]

Examples of policy gridlock are plentiful. The long battle to reduce the budget deficits during the 1980s and 1990s (and resumed in the 109th Congress [2005–2006]) is one. Although nearly everyone pays lip service to the ideal of a balanced budget, every spending program and every tax break is defended by organized beneficiaries, while deficit reduction, a diffuse collective good, inspires far less active organized support.

Yet if interest group politics produced only gridlock and maintenance of the status quo, then the airline, telecommunications, and trucking industries would never have been deregulated; tax reform would have failed in 1986; major deficit-reduction packages would not have been enacted in 1990, 1993, and 1997; and Medicare would not have been overhauled in 2003. The success of the 1986 tax bill surprised almost everyone. As we saw in Chapter 6, few thought that a bill eliminating tax breaks to finance a general reduction in income tax rates would stand a chance. Nonetheless, it passed because congressional leaders rigged the legislative game to ensure that political wisdom lay in voting for reform.

Enron's Matrix
The Limits of Lobbying

The financial collapse of Enron, once ranked seventh in annual revenues among American corporations, turned the spotlight on the company's audacious lobbying practices. Operating in sectors where government policies strongly influence profits—among them energy production and distribution, telecommunications, and commodity trading—Enron invested lavishly in trying to shape public policies to its corporate benefit. Best known for its generous support of George W. Bush's presidential aspirations (Enron's political action committees and employees contributed $114,000 to his campaign, and its former CEO, Kenneth Lay, was a top Bush fund-raiser) and large "soft money" gifts to the political parties, Enron was also heavily involved in financing congressional campaigns.

When Congress began in early 2002 to investigate charges of accounting irregularities, document shredding, and insider trading at the firm, it did so with embarrassment: 43 percent of representatives and 71 percent of senators had enjoyed Enron's financial support. Enron's generosity was bipartisan, though with a Republican slant. Sixty-two percent of the recipients were Republicans, who received about two-thirds of the total amount contributed to congressional candidates.

Campaign contributions were only a fraction of Enron's investment in politics, however. The firm also developed a state-of-the-art system for gathering and evaluating political intelligence. A computer program its designers dubbed "the matrix" tracked policy changes that might affect Enron's profits. Staffers in Washington, D.C., entered information on proposed regulations or statute changes into the matrix, which Enron economists back at the company's Houston headquarters then used to project future costs to the firm, carefully adjusting for growth and inflation. An economist who helped develop the program said, "I would tell [senior executives], 'This is your exposure. You decide whether it is worth it to use the lobbying machinery.' "[1] If it was worth it, executives cranked up "their vast influence machine, mobilizing lobbyists and dialing up politicians who had accepted some of Enron's millions in campaign contributions."[2]

The matrix evidently found much for Enron's lobbyists to do. By one count, in the first half of 2001 alone the company spent more than $2 million lobbying Congress on eighty-five different bills and issues. Subjects included taxes, foreign trade, energy, telecommunications, transportation, and budget issues.[3] Enron also sought friendly treatment in the media by inviting opinion leaders—journalists, commentators, and political activists—to join a select panel of advisers. Just for talking current events with Enron executives in Houston a couple of times a year, each adviser received a $50,000 annual stipend.[4]

Enron's lobbying juggernaut may have fostered a favorable regulatory and tax climate, enhancing the firm's apparent prosperity and enriching its top executives, but lobbying did nothing to protect the company or its leaders when Enron's shaky financial house began to collapse. Senior officials in the Treasury and Commerce Departments listened to its executives' pleas for help but evidently did nothing. Instead, the Justice Department, the Labor Department, and the Securities and Exchange Commission opened investigations into its activities. The company found nary a defender in Congress; members who had benefited from Enron's campaign contributions were sometimes especially critical to show that they had not been bought. President Bush had little to say about Enron or Lay, his family friend and most generous financial supporter, and the president's press secretary referred reporters who asked about the company's failure to the Treasury Department. Everyone involved took pains to show that they sympathized entirely with the thousands of employees and investors whose jobs, pensions, or investments had vanished with the company's insolvency. The Enron scandal also brought enough wavering House members to the side of campaign finance reform to pass a bill—over the vigorous objections of the House Republican leadership—that eliminated soft money from federal campaigns.

1. Joe Stephens, "Hard Money, Strong Arms, and 'Matrix'," *Washington Post,* February 10, 2002, A1.
2. Ibid.
3. Center for Responsive Politics, "Enron: A Look at the Company's Lobbying in 2001." www.opensecrets.org/alerts/v6/alertv6_37.asp, February 20, 2002.
4. Stephens, "Hard Money, Strong Arms," A1.

The tax bill example raises a crucial point: the proliferation of interest groups has actually strengthened the hand of elected officials. Specialized, fragmented groups are more dependent on members of Congress or White House officials to build and lead legislative coalitions. Legislators control access, an essential commodity that is in ever-greater demand because of the growing number of interest groups. As the real insiders, members of Congress are in the best position to know when particular interests are likely to be at stake—crucial information for lobbyists facing a political world fraught with uncertainty. Moreover, opposing groups often simply cancel one another out, leaving politicians free to pick and choose among interests according to their own personal or partisan beliefs. There are some obvious and important exceptions—not many elected officials are willing to cross AARP, for example—but most interest groups exercise little clout individually. Collectively, however, they remain enormously influential, for they are the main source of the technical and political information that shapes public policy.

Although James Madison would be astonished at the proliferation of organized "factions" in contemporary American politics, he also would be the first to acknowledge the logic behind this development. The rules and institutions established by the Constitution, adapted to a drastically transformed society and economy, have made interest groups both inevitable and essential. Government distributes scarce goods and values, creating incentives for citizens to influence its decisions. Acting on their First Amendment rights, citizens exercise their freedom to combine forces and act together to pursue their interests and values through politics. The wider and the greater the impact of government decisions, the more diverse and intense is the level of interest group activity. Moreover, the more government does, the more officials need to know about the potential consequences of their choices. Elections make political information essential; complexity makes technical information essential. Modern American government could not function without the information supplied by organized interests.

Yet Madison also would be the first to recognize that factions continue to raise serious problems for American democracy. The interest group universe, though remarkably large and diverse, favors some interests at the expense of others. The resources needed to gain influence—money, access, and expertise—are distributed very unevenly. And some groups are able to overcome the barriers to collective action more easily than others. Narrow private interests thus often enjoy an advantage over broader ones.

These problems are somewhat mitigated by electoral incentives; candidates for public office rationally champion widely shared values and interests whether or not these have wealthy or well-organized advocates. The advent of many lobbying groups dedicated to some moral vision of the public good also has mitigated the problems just described. The institutional and social pluralism Madison thought would cope adequately with the "mischiefs of faction" has grown ever more luxuriant, embracing more groups that are more highly specialized and linked in increasingly complex ways. This change has raised the specter of hyperpluralism and policy gridlock, but the fundamental source of policy stalemate is the public itself. Health care reform failed in 1994, not simply because interest groups lobbied it to death but also because no popular consensus emerged for any particular approach. Congress and the president find it difficult to balance the budget not simply because special interests defend every spending program and every tax break but also because there is no popular consensus on what combination of spending cuts and tax increases should be made to balance it (or, indeed, that balancing the budget is the most important goal of government). The conflicts among organized interests mirror, and sometimes crystallize, divisions and uncertainties prevalent among Americans. To paraphrase the comic strip character Pogo, we have met the special interests, and they are us.

logic.cqpress.com

Key Terms

grassroots lobbying, 635

insider tactics, 633

interest groups, 610

lobbying, 610

lobbyists, 609

moral incentives, 620

outsider tactics, 633

policy gridlock, 611

public interest lobby, 613

selective incentives, 621

social movements, 624

Suggested Readings

Browne, William P. *Private Interests, Public Policy, and American Agriculture.* Lawrence: University Press of Kansas, 1988. A thorough case study of modern interest group politics. It focuses on the agricultural sector and shows how the proliferation of interest groups has transformed the once-cozy politics shaping farm policies.

Cigler, Allan J., and Burdett A. Loomis. *Interest Group Politics.* 7th ed. Washington, D.C.: CQ Press, 2007. A collection of contemporary essays that examines the development of organized interests and recent changes in interest group politics. The book covers such topics as the Internet as an organizational tool, the political role of corporate lobbyists, and interest groups and gridlock.

Lowi, Theodore J. *The End of Liberalism: The Second Republic of the United States.* 2nd ed. New York: Norton, 1979. A vigorous scholarly polemic arguing that private interest groups have taken control of bureaucratic agencies, allowing special interests to dominate policymaking and thereby subvert democracy.

Moe, Terry M. *The Organization of Interests: Incentives and the Internal Dynamics of Interest Groups.* Chicago: University of Chicago Press, 1988. A critique and revision of Mancur Olson's seminal argument in *The Logic of Collective Action,* which asserts that political entrepreneurs and nonmaterial incentives often are able to solve the free-rider problem.

Olson, Mancur. *The Logic of Collective Action: Public Goods and the Theory of Groups.* Cambridge: Harvard University Press, 1965. A classic analysis of how the free-rider problem hampers organization for voluntary collective action and how the problem can be overcome.

Schlozman, Kay Lehman, and John T. Tierney. *Organized Interests and American Democracy.* New York: Harper and Row, 1986. A thorough account of Washington-based interest groups in the early 1980s. It concludes that the huge increase in the number of groups has not changed the balance of group power, for groups representing business interests still far outnumber their opponents.

Walker, Jack L., Jr. *Mobilizing Interest Groups in America: Patrons, Professions, and Social Movements.* Ann Arbor: University of Michigan Press, 1991. Emphasizes the role of patronage by government agencies and private foundations in organizing interests for collective political action.

Review Questions

1. What sorts of benefits do politicians receive from lobbyists? If these groups are so beneficial, why do citizens view them with such suspicion?

2. What actions has the government taken to foster interest groups? How do governmental policies themselves create potential interest groups?

3. How do "insider" and "outsider" lobbying tactics differ? What situations favor the use of each? When might an interest group choose to enlist litigation as it tries to influence policy?

4. What do political action committees (PACs) get in return for their donations to candidates? What evidence exists that such contributions are corrupting our political system?

5. Overall, how does PAC activity affect public policy? Has the proliferation of interest groups strengthened or weakened the influence of elected officials? Why?

Exercises

Membership Has Its Privileges
Go to the Web site of AARP (www.aarp.org). What legislative issues does AARP identify as being important to its members (www.aarp.org/issues/dividedwe fail/about_issues/)? What incentives does it provide to join the organization (www.aarp.org/sk/ awareness/)? How do the issues and incentives mentioned in its site compare with those mentioned in sites sponsored by the Republican National Committee (http://gop.com) and the Democratic National Committee (http://democrats.org)?

Pick a PAC of Pickled Peppers
Go to http://fec.gov/finance/disclosure/srssea.shtml to search Federal Election Commission (FEC) records of contributions by PACs for the most recent election cycles. Search for your favorite two PACs or interest groups (*note:* you might need to search for their full names, not their abbreviations) and answer the following questions:

- Where did the committees get their money (see the links under "Total Receipts")?

- Where did they spend their money (see the links under "Total Disbursements")?

- How did their spending and fund-raising activities change across election periods?

Next, go to the FEC's report on historical PAC activity (http://fec.gov/press/press2001/053101pacfund/ 053101pacfund.html). Did total contributions to candidates change a lot across elections? Did they seem to be higher in presidential versus midterm election years? Did the proportion of the PACs' contributions that went to Republicans increase after the 1994 election, in which Republicans seized majority control of Congress?

14

The News Media

What is the best source of news in the United States— newspapers, television, or the Internet?

A news "leak" is rarely inadvertent. What advantages do politicians and others gain by leaking information to the press?

How has the Internet altered the nature of news and its influence on politics?

Is political news a "mirror reflection" of politics in Washington, or is it better understood as a product of a political process?

In the United States news is the product of private, profit-seeking businesses. How does this weaken or strengthen its value to citizens in monitoring their elected officials?

In 1963 a father complained to parish authorities in Boston's Catholic archdiocese that a priest had sexually abused his son. Later he learned that his wife had also complained about another incident involving their son and the priest. Neither report appears to have elicited church action. Court records show that these were not isolated events. Yet, at the time the church either did not respond or did so quietly and, from the record of recidivism by some priests, ineffectively. Rather than launching an investigation, the diocese handled these incidents in an ad hoc fashion, either by transferring the priest to another parish or offering counseling. Most parishioners never learned of the charges, including other victims who lived with the misconception that they alone had suffered sexual abuse from a local priest.[1]

After a 1992 *Boston Globe* series investigating sexual abuse incidents in the church, a full-fledged scandal erupted. No longer isolated, former victims came forward to tell their story. Soon all the local news media were involved in rooting out an apparent pedophilia epidemic.* The cascade of stories and revelations culminated in an enterprising lawyer's highly publicized announcement that he was preparing a victims' "class action" suit against the church.[2] By year's end, ninety-nine parishioners had gone public with their long-repressed stories. Inexperienced in public relations,

---

*One local television station aired a priest's private recording in which he confessed to hundreds of incidents. This opening vignette closely follows Clay Shirky's narrative and insightful assessment in *Here Comes Everybody* (New York: Penguin Press, 2008), a fascinating book on the implications of the Internet on civic life.

Shortly before resigning, Cardinal Bernard Law briefed reporters on the efforts of the U.S. Conference of Catholic Bishops to formulate new policies to deal with sex abuse in the Roman Catholic Church.

the local diocese aggravated the situation by appealing for divine retribution against critics. From the pulpit the local bishop summoned the Lord: "By all means we call down God's power on the media, particularly the *Globe*." Over time, however, the church effectively weathered the ordeal. The hierarchically organized Roman Catholic Church had long experience—at least since the Reformation—in muting internal dissent. Eventually press coverage waned, the court case stalled, and the issue gradually receded from public view. Even at its crest, however, the scandal remained localized. It received sparse news coverage beyond New England, and national coverage treated the story as local to the Boston church rather than the first breakout of an eventual national epidemic.

Comparing the absence of a public outcry in 1963 to the steady tattoo of complaints and calls for reform that dogged the church for over six months in 1992 offers a lesson in how news may be vital to groups undertaking collective action. In 1963, with the church hushing up these incidents, parishioners were left in the dark. Thirty years later news coverage offered them an opportunity to escape from their collective ignorance and organize. The parishioners' informational problems may be an extreme instance, but it illustrates the importance of news in informing and coordinating the activities of unorganized constituencies.*

The sequel to the sex abuse story offers an additional lesson on the rapidly expanding impact of the media on modern civic life. In early 2002 yet another series of news reports of sexual abuse in the local diocese broke out, this time dwarfing the public's reaction a decade earlier. Based on recently unsealed court documents, the *Boston Globe* published a series documenting hundreds of instances of sexual abuse by Catholic clergy over the past four decades. Soon thereafter, several dozen frustrated parishioners met at a Wellesley, Massachusetts, church to address the chronic failure of church leaders to correct this problem, and the Voice of the Faithful (VOTF) was born. While not on par with Martin Luther's launching of the Reformation four hundred years earlier, the creation of VOTF was, in its own way, a revolutionary act. In claiming an independent role for the laity in church affairs, these parishioners directly challenged church authority. Had such a group formed in the 1960s and even in the early 1990s, it surely would have soon faded into oblivion. What, after all, could thirty or so parishioners, acting alone, expect to accomplish? Beyond press conferences, which would eventually tax the media's attention, how would they publicize their cause, attract members, raise funds, and coordinate a serious reform movement? When African American civil rights leaders found their efforts frozen out of news coverage from the white-controlled news media, they drew upon an extraordinary asset—hundreds of black clergy informing and mobilizing their congregations (see Chapter 4). VOTF had no such infrastructure, but by 2002 a new, extraordinary resource for coordinating the efforts of dispersed individuals was available—the Internet. VOTF's organizers promptly created a Web site. The Webmaster posted links to the *Boston*

---

*Recall the description in Chapter 1 (page 13) of how the huge 2006 Latino rights demonstration in Los Angeles grew beyond all expectations after Spanish-language radio disc jockeys began publicizing the event.

Globe's and others' news stories on its Web site, making the information easily available to readers throughout the world.* Over the next several months tens of thousands of individuals had visited the VOTF site, and many of them joined the organization.† VOTF's first convention, held in Boston just a few months after the group's inception, attracted four thousand participants.

Sensing the magnitude of the rebellion, Cardinal Bernard Law sent one of his bishops to pacify the group. Several days later, the church banned VOTF from church property and required that a priest preside over all lay meetings. It also issued a statement—myopic in this age of e-mail—directing parishioners to refrain from discussing these matters with fellow parishioners outside the diocese. Unsurprisingly, these local edicts proved ineffective. As the news revelations accumulated and VOTF mobilized an outraged constituency, the church haltingly initiated reforms in reporting abuse cases to authorities. After initially stonewalling VOTF, Cardinal Law in November finally met with its leaders. Nothing was resolved. A month later the Vatican summoned him; shortly after his return, Cardinal Law resigned. By the beginning of the next year, the scandal became a national issue and the Roman Catholic Church had begun systematic reforms to screen applicants for the priesthood and establish more stringent and transparent rules for reporting and disciplining sexual abusers.

Because of the Internet, the same, basic news stories in 2002 triggered a much different response than they had just a decade earlier. Almost spontaneously, a highly effective grassroots movement coalesced to reform church policy. This case offers a special lesson on the impact of technology on mass communication and the news media. Use of the Internet enabled this particular constituency—victims of sexual abuse, their families, and concerned parishioners—to become aware of their shared interest and to coordinate a far more effective collective response than would individuals' private appeals to parish fathers. In allowing the community to reverse the information flow, the Internet enabled the lay group, VOTF, to circumvent the church's barriers to collective action. It also largely liberated this latent collectivity from dependence on the traditional, *mediating* role of the news media, whose enterprise is based on selecting and framing the information provided to the public. Indeed, once the initial reports triggered a community response, the news organizations began taking their cues from VOTF's activities and the testimonials of abuse they elicited. In these ways, the development of the Internet has allowed latent groups to identify a common interest and mobilize collective action.

The Internet is only the most recent development in a long, steady stream of innovations in mass communications technology that has periodically transformed the news media. Each change made the news more widely available to more consumers. News has also become more engaging, with most technical advances enhancing the news report, first with engraved images, then photographs, sound, moving images,

---

*So many people followed the story, the *Globe's* parent company credited the scandal as the main reason for the paper's successful launch of its online edition.

†The Web site, www.votf.org, is still active and the organization is busier than ever, with over twenty-five thousand members and local chapters throughout the world.

and now an interactive relationship between news producer and consumer via the Internet. Marketplace competition for consumers' attention is a key driver of these innovations, prompting news providers to embrace new communications technologies as they try to get an edge on their competitors. The result is news that is cheaply and easily available to everyone.

Development of the News Business

The **news media** are the organizations that gather, package, and transmit the news through some proprietary communications technology. To characterize the news media as businesses does not discredit their integrity as suppliers of vital civic information. To the contrary, the influence of profit seeking has been in some respects highly democratic. Especially since the introduction of mass circulation and advertising, the news media have been in continual competition to increase the audiences for their product. The national broadcast networks, newspaper chains, public television and radio programs, twenty-four-hour cable news shows, and even news blogs all reflect the press's entrepreneurial tradition.

The following history explores the evolution of production technology, business organization and practices, audience characteristics, and regulatory environments that have continuously transformed America's news media.

The Economics of Early Newspapers

While editors of colonial newspapers shared the same desire to maximize profits that now drives modern media corporations, the constraints facing their businesses were quite different from what they are today. In colonial times almost no one earned a living solely by publishing the news. Instead, most early newspapers were run by people in related businesses, such as print shop owners and postmasters, who ventured into the news business because their marginal printing and delivery costs made newspaper publishing a viable sideline.[3] Still, producing newspapers in the colonial era was an extremely expensive undertaking. In fact, high **unit costs**—the costs of transmitting a news product to each consumer—characterized journalism in the United States until the mid-nineteenth century. Some of these costs stemmed from the nation's poor communications and transportation infrastructure. It was not unusual for newspapers to feature "breaking news" that had occurred two months earlier. (Compare that with the streaming news banners supplying viewers with instant poll responses to the 2008 presidential candidates' remarks during televised debates.)

Perhaps the main source of high unit costs was the time-consuming, labor-intensive printing process. Every page had to be composed (in reverse) from individual pieces of metal type. And the act of printing a single impression on paper with a wooden, hand-cranked press required thirteen separate steps. The best printers of the day could manage to print only 240 impressions an hour. The printing process itself was characterized as "physically demanding work, repetitive and often dreary, usually carried on in uninviting, foul-smelling (urine was the preferred substance for soaking the leather covers of inking balls), and poorly lighted surroundings."[4]

By the mid-1770s approximately twenty-five weekly newspapers were serving the colonies. Some, such as the *Massachusetts Spy,* helped to whip up public support for independence; others opposed the notion. But this era's most significant medium of political communication was the pamphlet. During the Revolution Thomas Paine's famous pamphlet, *Common Sense* (1776), became an instant best-seller: more than 120,000 copies were sold in its first three months. Eventually more than a half million copies were published.[5] The pamphlet was the preferred medium for good reason. More durable than newspapers, it could (much like used college textbooks) be passed easily from reader to reader. Where sufficient demand existed, in fact, commentaries or reporting that first appeared in a weekly paper—as with *The Federalist* essays—would be republished in pamphlet form to allow wider circulation.

With the emergence of the Federalist and Democratic-Republican parties in the 1790s, commercial concerns redirected newspapers toward politics. Almost immediately the parties launched newspapers wherever they competed in order to advance their particular vision for the Republic. Objective reporting had little place in these partisan organs. Instead, their pages advocated party platforms, promoted candidates, and attacked the opposition.[6] These party-sponsored newspapers did not attract large audiences. According to one estimate, during the first few decades of the Republic the number of subscribers held steady at approximately four thousand, most of whom were likely voters, already committed to a party.[7] The laws of supply and demand could not be defied for the long term, however; the papers had to be subsidized by the parties. And, when possible, party politicians turned to the government for subsidies in the form of printing contracts or appointment of newspaper editors as local postmasters.

The union of press and party politics was fully realized during the administration of Andrew Jackson (1829–1837). Three of the five members of Jackson's group of close advisers (identified in the press as his "kitchen cabinet") were seasoned journalists, including Postmaster General Amos Kendall, whom the opposition press dubbed "Jackson's lying machine." Jackson also developed a close relationship with Francis Blair, editor of the *Washington Globe,* with whom he exchanged government printing contracts for favorable news. In fact, Jackson appointed fifty-seven editors to patronage positions, primarily as postmasters or customs agents. This unrestrained use of the spoils of victory led even some of Jackson's supporters to worry that placing so many editors on the public payroll might compromise freedom of the press.

Thus, during the early days of the Republic, newspaper publishers came to serve as the agents of the party politicians who hired and fired them. Readers were more or less incidental to this relationship, except that publishers needed sufficient numbers of subscribers to justify the party's financial support. These publishers' real principals were the politicians who recruited and financed them. Publishers knew that if their papers lacked sufficient partisan fervor, their sponsor might withdraw its subsidy. Moreover, the government subsidy also might disappear if the party lost the election.

Baltimore artist Richard Caton Woodville's *War News from Mexico* (1848) depicts the singular role of newspapers in informing the citizenry during this era. Note that women and African Americans, neither of whom could vote, remain interested, if peripheral, participants in the scene.

Consequently, the newspapers championed their party as if their survival depended on it—because it did. In sum, within a couple of decades of ratification of the First Amendment, the notion that the "free press" would guard the citizenry's liberties against the designs of ambitious politicians had been replaced by dedicated partisan boosterism.

The changeable fortunes of political parties in election years provided a poor foundation for building a business. Many editors probably wanted to extricate themselves from the grip of their partisan principals, not so much to justify the Framers' faith in the press as to place their small businesses on a more secure financial footing. Somehow they would have to break their financial dependence on political parties.

The Rise of the Penny Press

While parties were generally interested in communicating only with the party faithful, businesses had an incentive to reach a mass audience, thereby generating revenue and attracting advertisers. But increasing market size depended on lowering prices, and that in turn depended on lowering unit costs. Until some cheaper, less labor-intensive way to print newspapers could be found, these small businesses would be locked into low readership and party subsidies.

Liberation began in the 1830s with the adaptation of steam power to printing and the development of faster, more reliable cylinder presses. These two technologies introduced dramatic economies of scale, allowing publishers to sell papers more cheaply, increase their audiences, and, in the process, split away from party sponsorship (see Figure 14-1). The *New York Sun* was the first paper to enlist this new technology, but not until several years later, when the *Sun's* competitor, the *New York Herald,* hit the newsstands, was the full potential for cultivating a mass readership realized.

The *Herald* sold for a penny, while most of the competition was still wedded to six-cent, limited editions. Soon the *Herald's* readership was twice that of its nearest competitor, and advertising revenues soared. The success of the "penny press" depended

Figure 14-1 The Rise and Decline of Newspapers

*Number of daily newspapers
in circulation*

*Circulation as a percentage
of total population*

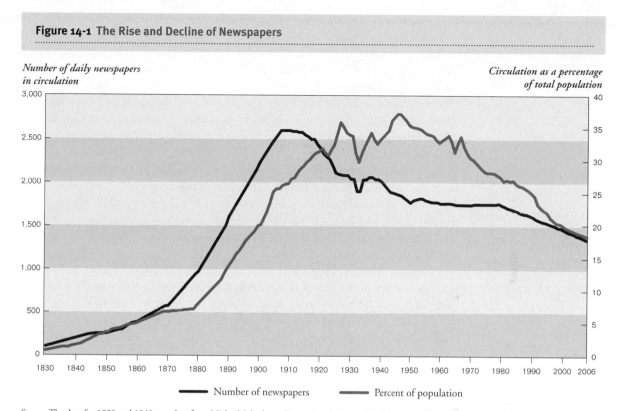

Number of newspapers   Percent of population

Sources: The data for 1830 and 1840 are taken from Michael Schudson, *Discovering the News: A Social History of American Newpapers* (New York: Basic Books, 1978), 13–14; for 1850–2000, Harold W. Stanley and Richard G. Niemi, *Vital Statistics on American Politics, 2005–2006* (Washington, D.C.: CQ Press, 2006); for 2006, "Survey of Statistics" online, Bureau of the Census, Table 1102.

on more than price, however.* To attract new readers, the *Herald* and the dozen imitators that soon surfaced in the nation's largest markets expanded the realm of the news to include human interest stories and coverage of crime, business, and social events. Not only did these topics squeeze out space devoted to party politics, but editors muted their partisan affiliations in order to appeal to a broader audience.† To supply copy for newspapers' expanded coverage—particularly coverage of the war with Mexico—*The Sun* joined with several dozen other papers to create the Associated Press (AP). It remains the dominant wire service today, and is increasingly enlisted as newspapers cut back their overseas and Washington news bureaus.

---

*Several contemporaneous social changes also aided the rise of the penny press. Sidney Kobre identifies these factors as the growth of cities, the modernization of transportation, the rise of a larger working class, the onset of mass production of consumer items, and increases in literacy, among others. Sidney Kobre, *The Development of American Journalism* (Dubuque, Iowa: William C. Brown, 1969), 208.

†In the first edition of the *Herald,* its publisher, John Gordon Bennett, a longtime Democratic Party functionary who had clashed with others in the party, denounced allegiances to all political parties and political principles. He claimed that the *Herald* would support no party or faction. Instead, he said, it would concentrate on reporting the news "stripped of verbiage and coloring." Michael Schudson, *Discovering the News: A Social History of American Newspapers* (New York: Basic Books, 1978), 22.

Competition for a mass readership became even more intense at the end of the nineteenth century. Screaming headlines and sensational stories tempted newsstand browsers. Critics of these devices, many of whom worked for competing papers, derided these papers as **"yellow journalism"**—a reference to the yellow ink in which the comic strips, especially the nightshirt-clad Yellow Kid in Joseph Pulitzer's *New York World,* were printed.[8] These criticisms impressed publishers around the country less than did the huge circulations and profits megapublishers like Pulitzer and William Randolph Hearst were accumulating (see box "The Megapublishers: Joseph Pulitzer and William Randolph Hearst"). From 1870 to 1900 the circulation of the nation's daily newspapers grew from roughly two and a half million to more than fifteen million. By 1904 there were twelve million readers of Sunday papers.

Publishers of established successful newspapers in one city often tried to repeat their success elsewhere. The result was the emergence of the great modern newspaper chain. Building on the success they enjoyed after launching the *Detroit Evening News* in 1873, the brothers James and E. W. Scripps owned nine daily newspapers in 1900, by 1910 twenty-two. But it was Hearst who built the largest chain. By 1935 he owned twenty-four dailies and sixteen Sunday newspapers from New York to Los Angeles. Indeed, at one point he could boast that nearly one in four Americans read one of his papers.[9]

Like Hearst, newspaper publishers and editors discovered that their freedom from party control enabled them to influence public opinion and, in turn, national politics. And few were reluctant to assume their weighty civic responsibility as opinion leaders. The transformation of newspapers into instruments of mass communication meant that politicians frequently found themselves genuflecting to powerful editors and publishers. Some rising stars in the news industry, in fact, tried to exploit their influence on public opinion by running for elective office. The most famous instance arose in 1872, when New York publisher Horace Greeley won the Democratic Party's nomination for president. The power of the media was not lost on incumbent Republican Ulysses S. Grant, who welcomed another newspaper publisher, Henry Wilson, to be his running mate.

In many ways the period between 1883 and 1925 was the golden age of newspapers. They essentially held a monopoly over mass communication in the growing urban markets; national political news was reported in their pages or not at all. Moreover, the publishers and editors who ran the chains relished the power their monopolies conferred. Reflecting the interests of a mass market, these newspapers took a decidedly populist slant on America's national civic life at a time when few other institutions did. Corporate greed, government abuse, and **muckraking** exposés of the rough edges of capitalism on the lives of ordinary Americans won the papers a large audience. Even cartoon protagonists—among others, the syndicated Happy Hooligan and the Katzenjammer Kids cartoon series—were lower class, immigrant urchins.[10] The most vivid demonstration of this medium's willingness to exercise its power came in 1898, when the Pulitzer and Hearst chains declared war on Spain. Shortly thereafter, Congress issued an official declaration of war. During the heat of jingoistic propaganda, the sales of the two New York papers soared to one and a half million copies a day. Citing the inflammatory rhetoric, one critic of the fighting dubbed the venture

The Megapublishers
Joseph Pulitzer and William Randolph Hearst

Via different routes, publishers Joseph Pulitzer and William Randolph Hearst came to New York and competed fiercely for readers. From the innovations their rivalry fostered, the modern mass-circulation newspaper was created. Joseph Pulitzer arrived first. He had begun as a reporter for a German-language newspaper in St. Louis. After a brief stint in the state legislature, he decided his calling was that of crusading publisher. He bought a couple of ailing dailies, merged them into the present-day *St. Louis Post-Dispatch,* and demonstrated that by expanding the market to the "common man," large dailies could be profitable. With the purchase of the *World* in 1883, Pulitzer took his strategy to the most important testing ground in the nation, New York City, with its millions of recent immigrants who were not being targeted for marketing by the mainstream dailies.

William Randolph Hearst was named managing editor of the *San Francisco Examiner* in 1887 when he was only twenty-four years old. His father, George Hearst, a wealthy California investor and U.S. senator, had owned the newspaper for seven years. Eight years later, in 1895, the younger Hearst bought the *New York Journal* and challenged the *World.*

For a while, Hearst (like Pulitzer) became infatuated with holding public office. He served in the House of Representatives for two terms but gave it up to dedicate himself to "yellow journalism." Hearst's insatiable political ambition and megalomania were captured by actor, writer, and producer Orson Welles in his 1941 classic film *Citizen Kane* (see photo).

Both men used their newspapers to promote causes. Hearst's paper, like the man, was more flamboyant and erratic in its commitments. His political views vacillated from the radical left to the radical right. When he boosted Franklin Roosevelt for the Democratic Party nomination in 1932, he did so vigorously and with hyperbolic praise; his ardor was repeated a few years later when he turned against Roosevelt. Pulitzer, by contrast, employed his editorial pages (as well as the news articles themselves) to promote consistently liberal causes. Freedom of speech, personal liberty, and the excesses of "money power" were the staples of his commentaries.

In 1912 Pulitzer, in a bequest to Columbia University, established annual awards for achievements in journalism and letters. The coveted Pulitzer Prize is awarded annually on the recommendations of an advisory board at the Columbia School of Journalism.

In 1898 William Randolph Hearst's *New York Journal* stirred war fever with its unsubstantiated charges that the Spanish had destroyed the U.S. battleship *Maine* in a Cuban harbor.

"Mr. Hearst's War." The prime minister of Spain echoed this sentiment when he ruefully remarked that newspapers in America apparently had more power than did the national government.[11]

Over the past half-century the extensive power of newspapers has eroded substantially. One need look no further than the declining circulation figures to appreciate the extent to which consumers have substituted first radio, then television, and more recently the Internet, for newspapers. In 1920, the year of the first commercial radio broadcast, about 2,400 daily newspapers dotted the nation with a circulation encompassing 31 percent of the population. By 2006 the number of dailies had declined by 60 percent and the daily news circulation shrank to almost half the 1920 share. With the loss of their monopoly on the news, the formidable publisher barons—the Pulitzers and Hearsts—disappeared from the political landscape.

The Emergence of Radio and Television

In 1920 Westinghouse launched the nation's first commercial radio station, KDKA, in Pittsburgh. Within a few years five hundred stations were broadcasting to an audience of two million. By 1930 just over 40 percent of all households owned radios.[12] Despite its advantages, radio initially had little to do with civic affairs. During its first decade, most radio news consisted of brief on-the-hour announcements, which the newspapers welcomed because they believed readers would then turn to them for the "whole story." By the early 1930s, however, radio was beginning to take advertising dollars away from the papers. In 1933 the newspaper association organized a news boycott of radio. No longer could radio networks draw news from the papers or the AP wire service, which the newspaper industry effectively controlled. The boycott collapsed quickly, however, under pressure from advertisers and independent broadcasters. Within several years, the print industry's efforts to keep radio broadcasting out of the news business was history.[13]

For several decades radio threatened to eclipse newspapers as the primary news medium. As early as 1940 *Fortune* magazine reported that most respondents to its reader survey claimed to get their news mainly from the radio. President Franklin D. Roosevelt noted the rapid growth of radios as a common household appliance and strategically used radio communication during his presidency. In 1933 shortly after his inauguration he went on the air nationwide to announce a brief "bank holiday" (closing) and emergency legislation to bolster the banks' solvency. The size of his audience and the outpouring of support prompted the president to deliver more national radio addresses. Altogether he delivered thirty "fireside chats." In Figure 14-2, which is taken from archival material found in Roosevelt's Oval Office files, we can see the extent to which the radio audience swelled over a five-year period, from 1936 to 1941. Of course, the last rating of 79 percent of all households came after Japan's attack on Pearl Harbor and the U.S. entry into the Second World War.*

By the turn of the century, the American public had a wealth of print news media available.

Throughout World War II Roosevelt's fireside chats and regular news broadcasts kept the American public informed about the war's progress. Today, radio remains a significant but distinctly secondary source of news. Rather, the medium has found a special niche in the talk radio format—particularly in syndicated and call-in programs with a conservative slant on public affairs. One 2004 study found national and local conservative talk programs totaled forty thousand broadcast hours a week throughout the country, compared to only three thousand for liberal talk shows.[14]

Although television technology was developed by the 1930s, the television broadcast industry did not take root until the close of the war in 1945 as national production turned from weapons to consumer goods. As shown in Figure 14-3 (see page 665), the 1950s witnessed astonishing growth as the public embraced television as an essential home appliance. From 1950 to 1960 the television audience exploded from six to sixty million viewers, more than 88 percent of U.S. households.[15] By the end of the 1960s the penetration of televisions into America's homes was nearly complete.

---

*Note the small discrepancies between the numbers of homes tuned into Roosevelt's addresses and the percentages of households actually owning radios in Figure 14-3. They suggest that everyone owning a radio listened to FDR's fireside chats. In fact, more households are reported listening than actually owning a radio. Although these small differences could easily reflect differences in measurement, they are consistent with the anecdotal evidence that neighbors gathered around the radio to hear the president.

Figure 14-2 FDR Radio Audience Ratings, 1936–1941

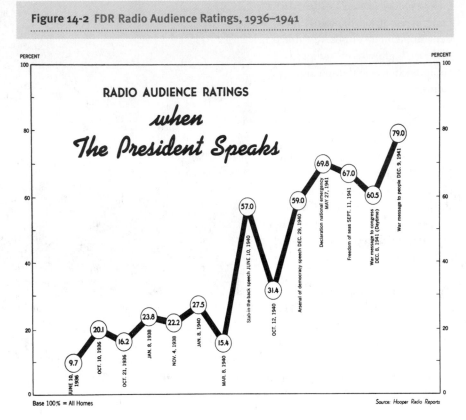

Note: This chart, found in President Roosevelt's office files, depicts the early development of mass audiences in presidential communications.

Households with television outnumbered those with indoor plumbing. Just as newspapers had to adapt to radio, so too did radio with the rise of television.

Contributing to the growth of the television audience was the rapid development of a broadcast infrastructure—locally owned stations affiliated with one of three national networks. Each major market also had an affiliate of the national public television network and one or two independent stations relegated mostly to showing network reruns and local sports. The early concentration of the television industry contained the essential ingredients of an oligopoly both nationally and locally. Nationally, the three major networks dominated audience shares and news programming. This was the era of network anchors as national celebrities. With nightly audience shares in the tens of millions, Walter Cronkite, Chet Huntley, David Brinkley, John Chancellor, and Howard K. Smith projected objectivity and authority as guides to current events. For many Americans the nightly evening network news became their chief source of news.

But as with every other news technology reviewed here, market dominance is never permanent. Even at the peak of network television in the early 1980s when 42 percent of the television audience regularly tuned into one of the three evening network news programs, cable was on the horizon. Over the next two decades cable and satellite, which initially served a largely rural niche market that lay beyond clear over-the-air broadcast signals, would take away a large chunk of the network's market share in all programming areas, including news. In 1970 less than 10 percent of viewers received cable. Over time as cable providers began to invest heavily in laying lines into urban and suburban markets, they began offering substantially more channels to lure new subscribers. Where in 1970 the average subscriber had seven channels available, by 2000 this subscriber enjoyed over sixty-three options.[16] Cable providers' strategy of innovation and marketing succeeded. Today, the share of television households subscribing to cable or comparable satellite services is just short of 90 percent.

Broadcast Technology Introduces Regulation

The advent of radio not only introduced a major new player to a news industry, broadcast technology also required government participation in the commercial enterprise for the first time. During the early 1920s hundreds of stations came on the air, creating massive congestion problems across the broadcasting spectrum. Stations overcrowded desirable spots on the radio dial, causing signal interference and threatening to reduce this new medium to an unintelligible Tower of Babel. Broadcasters acting individually could not solve this classic tragedy of the commons. Soon, they accepted that the air waves were a public good instead of their private property. The solution was to establish a government commission that could license stations to occupy a particular spot on the bandwidth. Since the air waves belonged to the public, the Communications Act of 1934 reasoned that in return for their exclusive licenses, broadcasters must "serve the public interest, convenience and necessity." Although the law explicitly prohibited government censorship, it did not precisely define what the mandate to serve the public interest entailed. Responsibility for interpreting and implementing Congress's legislative intent was given to a new independent agency (see Chapter 8), the Federal Communications Commission (FCC).

The 1934 law instituted the **equal time** provision, which required stations to provide equal access to candidates for office. And by lodging this authority in an

On location in Vietnam in the aftermath of the Tet offensive in 1968, CBS anchor Walter Cronkite broke from the standard of objective journalism when he concluded his report with the judgment that the war would end in a stalemate. At the same time, our military leaders were privately concluding that the severe casualties inflicted on the Vietcong and North Vietnamese forces constituted a decisive victory for the United States. Nonetheless, Cronkite's assessment confirmed the numerous news images, and one month later U.S. president Lyndon B. Johnson announced he would not seek reelection.

Millions of Americans—with RCA television—will see history as it is made at the two National Political Conventions.

Look _before_ you vote — with Television

As political leaders step up to speak, you're right with them on the platform. This year, television joins press and radio as a "political reporter" in Philadelphia at the Republican Convention, June 21, and the Democratic Convention, July 12.

The Candidate will be televised as he looks into the camera—talks to the people, face to face. His appearance, smile, gestures, combine with his voice to complete the transmission of personality. You have a new chance to know your man!

Important as any in history, the 1948 political conventions will be covered from start to finish by keen-eyed RCA Image Orthicon television cameras. Highlights and sidelights, all will be seen. And what the television camera catches will be sharp and clear on the screens of RCA Victor home television receivers...

Today, 40,000,000 Americans are within easy reach of daily television programs.

Television as an aid to good

citizenship and to the formation of an enlightened public opinion is only one way in which developments from RCA Laboratories serve the Nation and its people. Advanced research is part of any instrument bearing the name RCA or RCA Victor.

• • •

When in Radio City, New York, be sure to see the radio, television and electronic wonders at RCA Exhibition Hall, 36 West 49th Street. Free admission. Radio Corporation of America, RCA Building, Radio City, N. Y. 20.

This 1948 ad for RCA televisions promised a new day for democracy. We voters just need to see and size up the candidates for ourselves.

independent agency, they removed it as a resource for some future political party. Over the years, another prominent FCC policy, called the **fairness doctrine,** required that stations devote a share of their airtime to public affairs programming, and that they do so in a manner that is balanced and equitable. In 1987 the FCC dismantled this rule on the theory that it caused stations to shy away from examining political issues for fear of violating some regulator's view of fairness. This policy appears to have been correct, for shortly afterwards talk radio with a political slant blossomed across the nation. Much of the public and many members of Congress have recently expressed interest in restoring some form of the fairness doctrine, but with the rapid spread of broadband Internet as an alternative, wide-open source of political expression, the issue may soon become moot.

In local media markets many newspaper publishers frequently sought to recapture advertising revenue lost to television by buying a local station. They were, after all, already producing news copy and with over 40 percent of stations' profits typically coming from local news programming, newspaper publishers viewed acquisition of a local station as an easy extension of their business. In 1975 this strategy had become disturbing to an FCC concerned with reductions in the variety of available news sources. The agency adopted a regulation banning cross-ownership in markets where it had not already occurred. Under the new rules a newspaper could not control a local television station in the same market served by the newspaper.*

---

*Over the years, either Congress or the FCC itself has sought to soften these rules. But on each occasion, the legislature, the agency, or a district court has intervened to block it. In many communities the newspaper industry has fallen on hard times; adding a station, some publishers argue, is the only way they can keep the newspaper afloat.

The Internet

The Internet has not yet realized its full potential as an information medium, but the variety and volume of information the Internet makes available to the public are already profound. During the 2008 presidential campaign, for example, Obama's YouTube video had received over sixteen million hits by early October, nearly ten times that of McCain's; later in the month, even though McCain's received over twenty-two million views, Obama's still surpassed McCain's by far, having received over eighty-four million views (see Table 14-1). All of the top five political blogs averaged more than a million visits a month during the fall campaign.* What makes these numbers truly stunning is that the Internet is still in its infancy. As Figure 14-3 shows, barely half of America's households have a broadband connection. Moreover, virtually everyone's access is tethered to a personal computer or handheld device. In 2008 Intel announced development of computer chip technology that will allow interactive access to the Internet via television.[17] We will soon experience the Internet—and the information it contains—as a ubiquitous, ever-present part of our lives. Though it is not clear what these technological developments on the horizon will mean for the consumption and use of news, we can discern several ways in which this technology will continue the historical trend toward an ever-increasing volume of information more cheaply available to the public.

First, other news technologies are piggybacking onto the Internet to become more accessible to larger audiences. Almost all daily newspapers now have online sites, thus expanding their audiences beyond their locales.† Indexing these sources, the easily searched Google News continuously updates news stories from over 4,500 print sources.

Second, in addition to providing easy access to thousands of alternative sources, the Internet continues to develop its own news format—blogs. Blogging began as either

Figure 14-3 Households with Radios, Televisions, Cable or Satellite, or Broadband Internet Access

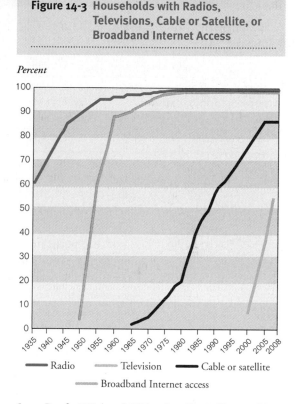

Percent

Radio   Television   Cable or satellite
Broadband Internet access

Sources: Data for 1935 through 1974 are from *Historical Statistics of the United States: Colonial Times to 1970*, Vols. 1 and 2 (Washington, D.C.: Government Printing Office, 1975), series R104, R105, and A335. Data for 1975 through 2005 are from *Vital Statistics on American Politics, 2005–2006* (Washington, D.C.: CQ Press, 2006). Data for Broadband Internet shares are from Journalism.org.

Note: For 1975 through 2005, data for cable televisions represent percentages of television households. Otherwise, data reflect percentages of all households.

---

*Topping the "hits" list is HuffingtonPost.com with 7.5 million visits. The others in order of visits are NewsMax.com, Salon.com, RealClearPolitics.com, and DrudgeReport.com. The figures were tallied by Quantcast in early October 2008.

†This development addresses one problem for newspapers experiencing steadily declining subscriptions, but so far they have not found a business model that translates this audience into revenue. Online viewers have proven highly resistant to paying access fees, and advertising rates for the Internet are too meager to support substitution of online audiences for daily newspaper readership as a viable business model.

TABLE 14-1

Social Networking Sites and the 2008 Candidates

Site	Barack Obama	John McCain
Facebook	2,228,508 supporters	591,412 supporters
MySpace	758,152 friends	191,615 friends
YouTube	84,637,742 video views	22,475,292 video views

Source: Compiled by the authors, as of 5:39 p.m., Wednesday, October 22, 2008.

---

the personal pages of Web-savvy individuals or as "news aggregators" providing links to news stories published elsewhere on the Internet. Early news blogs typically trafficked in political gossip—unconfirmed information that traditional news bureaus spurned. The major political blogs now include teams of writers and investigators and attract hundreds of thousands of visits a week. Over their brief history blogs have formed a symbiotic relationship with the mainstream print and broadcast news services. A blog publishes an unconfirmed story, the newspaper or network news bureau then reports factually that the blog reported the story. Soon, all of the media are in the hunt for new leads that allow them to write the next chapter. The 1998 story about President Clinton's affair with a White House intern, Monica Lewinsky, originated on a political exposé blog, the Drudge Report, after one or more mainline news organizations decided against breaking the story. Soon the intern story dominated the news and led eventually to the president's impeachment. More recently, a false blogosphere rumor flushed out an equally sensational story about the 2008 Republican vice presidential nominee, Sarah Palin. To quash rumors that her newborn son was actually the child of her seventeen-year-old daughter, Palin held a news conference to announce that her unwed daughter was pregnant. This revelation became the next day's headlines and remained so for the next couple of weeks. All the news media from the *New York Times* to the *National Enquirer* (and including the prominent blogs) feverishly investigated the identity of the father, the nuptial arrangements, and the like. During this period the presidential candidates' campaigns played second fiddle to this story, until it was taken over by dismal economic news.

Third, the Internet allows the public to participate in the news in a manner unimaginable with any other media format.* Without VOTF's ability in 2002 to set up a Web site disseminating information about the sex scandal and inviting Catholics everywhere to join in changing church policy, it is difficult to imagine how the outcome would have much differed from 1992. With the resources of the Internet available to all, public figures no longer catch a break from their constituents' collective action problems.

An Ever-Changing News Media

As a business the news industry has been continuously transformed by technological advances as competing producers have sought a greater share of their potential market. The trend is toward ever-expanding access to greater amounts of information. In this respect, market competition has provided a positive externality in offering more

---

*The only technology that comes remotely close to generating systematic feedback is the news bureau public opinion poll, of which there are a dozen or so that conduct national opinion surveys about current affairs.

people easier access to a greater variety of news. The history of the news in the United States has always been a story of change, which makes it especially instructive to present-day students, since the news media—indeed, the nature of news itself—continues to change rapidly. From the early days of the Republic when several dozen weekly and a few daily newspapers delivered the national news to today when news blogs routinely receive millions of visits, the history of the news media is essentially market responses to changing communications technology. As a new technology made mass communication easier and cheaper—that is, reduced the unit cost, the cost of distributing a news item to a consumer—those who produced the news either adapted, left the market, or assumed a subordinate rank. To a great degree the changes have been cumulative. The modern newspapers, themselves heirs of the penny press, are undoubtedly in decline because of the Internet, but they are likely to endure into the foreseeable future. New communications technology does not drive an old technology out of business, but instead forces these suppliers to more carefully target their audience and tailor their news accordingly. Television news scooped afternoon newspapers, leading the industry to consolidate around the morning daily. Radio lost its general news audience only to find a new, secure niche in talk radio. On the whole, innovation in mass communications has resulted in a dramatic expansion of news as a consumer product in a highly competitive marketplace.

Thinking of news as a product in a competitive market helps account for the alacrity with which this industry has embraced innovations in communications technology. As previously noted, in addition to reduced unit costs, most of the new technologies have presented consumers with news that comes in a more attractive, life-like package. Newspapers introduced photographs in the late nineteenth century; radio captivated the public with live sound; television initially offered anchors Edward R. Murrow and John Cameron Swayze reading news reports and interviewing public figures; the invention of Tri-X film in the 1950s allowed correspondents in the field to report on camera; the introduction of satellite technology allowed live reports from anywhere on earth (and beyond); and finally, cable brought viewers many more news options, including some—like C-SPAN and ESPN—that specialize in in-depth coverage of a narrow range of news. The Internet is capable of distributing news from anywhere, whatever its format, to every computer attached to the Web. Within hours the *Boston Herald*'s 2002 reports on the church's sexual abuse record were posted on the paper's Web site and made available to a worldwide audience. And the Internet empowers a new, broad class of consumers—namely, those motivated to set up a Web site—allowing them to join the news media.

News as a Consumer Product

One might think that easier access to news and information, combined with the population's steadily increasing educational attainment, would convert the United States into that elusive, ideal democratic polity in which fully informed citizens elect representatives who enact enlightened public policy. Not so. Students of journalism and communications are quick to point out troubling trends that accompany truly mass communications. The proliferation of alternative media gives viewers the opportunity to opt out of consuming political information altogether. Even for those who are attentive to news, the profusion of programming choices allows consumers to select those sources that they find most congenial with their political views.

Content and Form: Inherent Differences in News Media

A key consideration for news producers in selecting and scripting news reports is the preferences—in content and form—of their targeted audience. Because the television networks cater to a nationwide clientele, they devote proportionately far more space to national and international stories than do their local affiliates, which concentrate on local events and personalities. One 2000 study found that about half of local newspaper coverage and over 40 percent of local broadcast programming in Chicago were devoted to weather, sports, crime, entertainment, and obituaries, whereas about 10 percent of the national news broadcasts touched on these subjects. The national media, conversely, more than doubled local news sources in their coverage of national topics such as politics and the economy.[18]

Another important determinant of news content is a medium's **carrying capacity**—the amount of information a particular communication technology can economically provide its audience. The more restricted a medium's carrying capacity, the more selective it must be in the kinds of information it offers. The carrying capacity of newspapers is much greater than that of the evening news programs of the television networks. In fact, the front page alone of a typical daily newspaper contains more words than does the script of the average evening news broadcast from the networks.

Television news stories are kept brief in part because of the medium's limited carrying capacity, but also to minimize the cost to the marginally interested viewer in waiting for the next story. Television news editors select and present stories that are targeted to the tastes and sophistication of the "median viewer" and are framed in ways that make them more appealing and comprehensible. Along the way, abstractions and ambiguities give way to more concrete and simpler frameworks. Election campaigns are presented as "horse races" between two individuals rather than as contests between candidates committed to different policies. A failed public policy is attributed to the incompetence or malfeasance of individual officeholders rather than to the intractability of the problems the policy seeks to correct. News stories that do not have culprits tend to be ignored. The savings and loan crisis in the 1980s was arguably the most expensive domestic policy fiasco in American history, costing taxpayers nearly $150 billion. But it never achieved sustained network coverage. By contrast the $700 billion bailout of the financial industry in 2008 had a full cast of villains on Wall Street. Consequently, the bailout story, which some tried to reframe as a "rescue," easily outstripped all other issues in public opinion surveys as the nation's most important problem.

While television may be fairly criticized as presenting a superficial, stripped-down representation of reality, evidence indicates that for some news consumers, simpler is better. In one experiment, subjects who scored on pretests as relatively uninformed about apartheid in South Africa were found to learn more when exposed to television reports than when presented with newspaper accounts on the subject. The opposite pattern turned up for those subjects with high levels of prior information. For many of them, television only repeated what they already knew, whereas the newspaper coverage offered new information.[19] Apparently, in emphasizing new information rather than context, newspaper articles pose barriers to readers who do not already have a framework for acquiring and integrating information. This finding fits well with various survey research findings that better-educated respondents are more likely to rely on newspapers as their primary source of information.*

Television as a medium trumps all competing forms on one critical dimension—credibility. However sophisticated tape editors may be in selecting footage and thereby slanting the information a broadcast conveys, the fact remains that television (and, to a lesser degree, radio) appears to supply consumers with more direct, "primary" data than do newspapers. In offering sound and video images "straight from the source," television allows viewers to form their own interpretations of news events. This advantage probably explains why, despite providing comparatively skimpy and frequently contrived narrative scripts, the public finds television not only easier to consume but more credible than other news sources.[20] One comprehensive public opinion survey on news consumption in 2008 (see Figure 14-4) showed that the public continues to trust television—and its images—over all other news sources. Internet news sites are too recent to have comparable trends available. In 2008, most Internet sites had a credibility rating just above that for the *National Enquirer,* with Google News and Yahoo News scoring the highest believability rating of 13 and 11 percent, respectively.

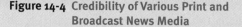

Figure 14-4 Credibility of Various Print and Broadcast News Media

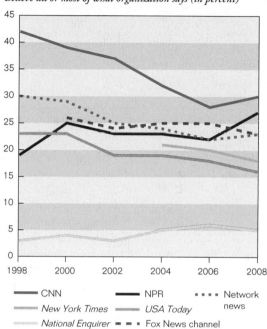

Believe all or most of what organization says (in percent)

Legend: CNN, NPR, Network news, New York Times, USA Today, National Enquirer, Fox News channel

Source: Pew Research Center for the People and the Press, "Key News Audiences Now Blend Online and Traditional Sources," August 17, 2008, http://peoplepress.org/report/444/news-media.

Note: Percentages based on those who could rate each organization.

The Dominance of Television and the Rise of the Internet

For now, television dominates as the preferred source for news. Despite the best efforts of newspaper publishers to juggle the mix of news content and alter a paper's

---

*A national survey during the 2000 presidential campaign found that 40 percent of the respondents who said they got their political news mainly from newspapers scored as very knowledgeable on the researchers' factual test. By comparison, 32 percent of those respondents relying mainly on network news and only 27 percent favoring TV news magazine programming did so. The Pew Research Center for the People and the Press, "The Tough Job of Communicating with Voters," http://people-press.org.

TABLE 14-2

Where the Public Gets Its News about Presidential Campaigns

Medium	1992	1996	2000	2004	2008
Television	55	54	59	50	60
Newspapers	32	31	24	26	12
Radio	9	10	10	11	8
Magazines	3	4	2	2	2
Internet	—	1	5	11	15

Source: The Pew Research Center, "Internet's Broader Role in Campaign 2008," http://people-press.org/report/384/internets-broader-role-in-campaign-2008.

Note: The numbers represent percentages of Americans who rely on the medium as their primary source.

format, the drift of news consumers to television from newspapers appears inexorable. As early as 1963 television had eclipsed newspapers as the preferred source of news, and since then the trend has continued steadily.[21] Since the early 1990s television has enjoyed a nearly two-to-one advantage over newspapers as the preferred medium for following presidential campaigns (see Table 14-2). But it is worth noting that in 2004 the Internet appears for the first time to be making inroads into televised news consumption.*

In part this shift away from newspapers reflects the changing composition of the news audience. Older respondents in national surveys (see Figure 14-5) consistently report a stronger preference for newspapers than do younger respondents who prefer television and, increasingly, the Internet. Age differences in attention to news have been a common finding for decades. Young adults are more mobile and have more claims on their time. As they age and settle into the routines of work and family, they pay more attention to civic affairs. This agrees with the trend reported in Chapter 11 that as individuals age they begin to vote more regularly.

Some evidence shows that past patterns may be changing and a permanent alteration of the news media is under way. First, young people today have a media option that was unavailable when their parents were young—the Internet. Marketing research shows that young people consume a greater share of the news from the Internet. They may form consumption habits now that will only increase their reliance on the Internet in the future. Second, older news consumers are also taking up the Internet. One recent study (see Figure 14-5) found, in fact, that overall news consumption on the Internet is increasing for all age groups.

The Emergence of Cable News

The continued domination of television may in part reflect the growth of cable as a readily available source for news and information. No longer does television news imply a network evening news program. Continuous news on several all-news channels is now a standard feature of cable subscriptions, and loyal viewers are tuning in daily. Just as we found for presidential addresses in Chapter 7, the networks' audience

---

*This is consistent with a variety of research reporting that time spent on the Internet tends to substitute for time watching television. A 2004 Pew Research Center survey found, "In terms of actual behavior, however, the Internet appears to have a significantly greater impact on online users' TV news time than on time spent on news from other sources. Only about a quarter of Internet users (27 percent) say they spent an hour or more watching TV news on a typical day, compared with 41 percent of those who do not go online. Both groups are equally likely to have read a newspaper the previous day." In *News Audiences Increasingly Politicized,* http://people-press.org/reports/display.php3?PageID=835.

Figure 14-5 News Consumption "Yesterday," by Age (in percent)

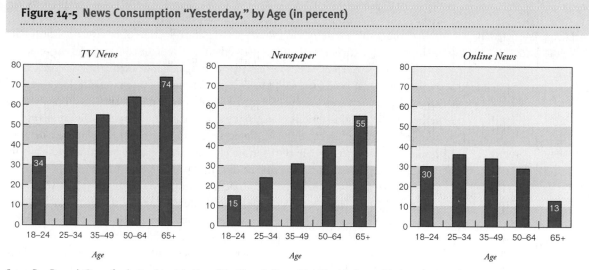

Source: Pew Research Center for the People and the Press, "Key News Audiences Now Blend Online and Traditional Sources," August 17, 2008, http://people-press.org/report/444/news-media.

shares are declining with the growth of cable. Many viewers appear to have shifted permanently to cable for their national news. For others, the launching of Cable News Network (CNN) in 1980 (and Fox and MSNBC in 1996) meant an opportunity to catch the news at more convenient times.* By 2007 the networks' combined audience shares had shrunk to less than 17 percent, and the figures continue to drop.[22] In the 1996 presidential election, one survey found 39 percent of respondents who rely principally on television for news said they learned about the campaign mostly from network news, compared with 23 percent for cable news. Eight years later these percentages had largely reversed to 32 percent and 44 percent, respectively.

With the creation of twenty-four-hour cable news channels and growing shares of the households connected via cable or satellite, it is not surprising to find cable and satellite television poaching viewers once controlled by the networks. In addition to the twenty-four-hour news format, cable programming is directed to sizable blocks of former network television viewers. Perhaps the most important of these innovations for changing news consumption is the development of **infotainment,** a neologism that took quick root in the media literature. It refers to a new genre of television programming that blends news with entertainment. Infotainment programming includes talk shows, celebrity gossip, and political comedy, which many young respondents report as a source of political information. Whenever international affairs heat up, political scandals erupt, and elections loom, *Entertainment Tonight, Access Hollywood, Extra,* and other infotainment programs pick up these subjects. Even as they sensationalize

---

*Consequently, younger survey respondents (under age 40) report watching cable news more frequently than network news. By comparison, viewers over age 54 say they divide their news time about evenly between the two sources.

coverage to prick audience interest, a lot of viewers—particularly those who normally avoid traditional news—learn about civic affairs this way.[23]

Another cable programming strategy is the introduction of an overt political slant to appeal to a particular segment of the audience. The slant comes out in the selection of which news to report and how it is reported. Charges of **media bias** go back as far as the era of the partisan press, but it is a fairly recent phenomenon for broadcast news. When the three broadcast networks dominated the market they bunched together in the political middle like car dealerships in auto row. If any of them had adopted a distinctly partisan or ideological slant on the news, the wayward network would have forfeited a share of the available audience placing it at a competitive disadvantage for viewers and advertising. So, they all delivered pretty much the same news and garnered roughly the same audience ratings.

With the proliferation of competitive cable news channels the situation changed. When Fox News channel started out, CNN already dominated this second-tier news market. Rather than match the product of its larger, more established competitor, Fox sought to appeal to a segment of the market that was dissatisfied with its news options. For years conservatives, especially conservative Republicans, had viewed the national media as biased in favor of liberal causes and points of view.* Discerning an opportunity to gain a profitable market niche by differentiating its product from that of CNN and the broadcast networks, Fox News introduced a conservative slant by hiring conservative news anchors and loosening traditional constraints on editorializing while presenting the news. And it created energetic, combative talk shows propounding conservative views. In 2008 a third of self-classified "conservative Republican" survey respondents said they wanted to see their viewpoints presented in the news rather than news with "no point of view." Only 15 percent of independents preferred a point of view in their news. The share of self-proclaimed "liberal Democrats" wanting news that expressed their views resembled the preferences of their polar opposites: 31 percent prefer news with a liberal slant. Unfortunately for this latter group, less than half as many Americans call themselves liberals. So conservatives but not liberals have been able to attract a cable news channel to cater to their tastes.†

Fox's business strategy worked. About half of conservative viewers say they regularly go to Fox for news, compared to less than a fifth of the self-identified liberal audience.[24] By 2002 Fox was winning larger audiences than its cable competitors. As President George W. Bush's public approval ratings and support for his party declined,

---

*Consequently, in 2008 it came easy for Republicans at their national convention to chant a refrain of "media bias" directed at the mainstream television news producers for questioning the credentials and preparation of Sarah Palin, the virtually unknown "hockey mom" governor of Alaska, when John McCain tapped her to be his running mate.

†Liberals have it a little better in their listening choices. Although swamped by the conservative programming on radio, surveys confirm that liberals tend to congregate at National Public Radio, which conservatives generally shun. In 2004 former vice president Al Gore led an investment team to create a national radio network, Air America, giving liberals their own call-in programming. Too few liberals were interested in talking and listening to Bush-bashing comedian Al Franken, however, and the network filed for bankruptcy two years later.

however, so too did Fox's audience shares. Emboldened, both CNN and MSNBC hired openly partisan, Democratic-boosting pundits to ride the new political crest and succeeded in regaining some of the market share lost to Fox.[25]

Going Newsless?

The plethora of available news products raises complex questions about the public's news consumption. In the past choices were much more limited. For most individuals, the news consisted of the morning newspaper and one of the network nightly news programs. Everyone received similar doses of information at the same time. Now that news is ubiquitous, the decision on what news to consume and when is more complex. Choices will reflect differences in lifestyles and interests, and citizens may consume more varied amounts and content than ever. Or, paradoxically, they may be consuming less. The same communications technologies that are broadening the availability of news are even more actively expanding the range of entertainment options. With so many choices, fewer citizens today may be tuning into news and current affairs programming than in the past.

In addition to providing comparative ratings of news producers, Figures 14-4 and 14-5 and Table 14-2 depict unfavorable trends for the news media generally. Over the past decade, most news suppliers have been judged less believable than they were a decade ago. Moreover, all, except for the Internet, appear to be attracting fewer consumers.* Numerous reasons have been offered to explain declining news consumption. Perhaps audiences are increasingly consuming news through entertainment programs—in addition to the infotainment programs listed above, *Oprah,* the *Daily Show,* the *Colbert Report,* and others frequently contain information about public affairs.[26] News consumption also appears to be changing from fixed routines—such as the evening network news and the morning paper—to what some media observers have labeled news "grazing." With information available seemingly everywhere (including screens at some gas pumps and elevators), consumers collect news in bits and pieces throughout the day.† Respondents are less likely to recall these incidental and even inadvertent consumption events in survey questions, but they are getting the news nonetheless.

We shift now from the consumption of news to its production. Specifically, we examine news as the product of the interaction between politicians and journalists. News producers, from journalism professors to corporate owners, fondly refer to themselves as occupying the "fourth branch of government." They feel that they merit this lofty status for providing an essential service of monitoring (and thereby "checking") the

---

*The same survey that asked respondents to name the source for yesterday's news followed the question by asking how much time the respondents spent with the source. Here, too, one finds a significant audience drop-off. In each age group respondents reported spending less time with the news than did their counterparts a decade earlier.

†This approach to news is much more common among younger consumers. Pew Research Center for the People and the Press, "Key News Audiences Now Blend Online and Traditional Sources," August 17, 2008, http://pewresearch.org/.

actions of officeholders with whom the public has entrusted authority to make its collective decisions. As with the Constitution's branches of government, the success of this "fourth branch" in conducting journalistic oversight requires sufficient independence and distance to perform credible oversight.

News Media as the "Fourth Branch"

News (or its absence) critically shaped Boston parishioners' response to the sexual abuse scandal. The collective action problems they experienced in learning about this problem (especially for the victims in finding others with similar experiences) and confronting church leaders who concealed information are similar to the challenges citizens face in monitoring their elected leaders. When citizens succeed, their politicians will be motivated to serve their constituency faithfully or they will run the risk of defeat in the next election. In other contexts (most notably in political control of the bureaucracy), gaining access to information is no small task. Agents, as we discovered with the dioceses officials, inherently enjoy an informational advantage over the principals they serve. They are quick to disclose information that places their performance in a favorable light and to conceal that which damages their reputations. We have already examined one solution the Framers devised to the information deficit—frequent elections. Presumably, the Framers expected that ambitious challengers coveting the incumbent's office would ferret out incompetence and malfeasance in office.* Parishioners cannot vote their priests out of office, but they had another oversight avenue available to them in an independent press.

The early appearance of a free press in the First Amendment, which occupied then as now a special status within the Bill of Rights, is not happenstance. Both proponents and opponents of the Constitution's ratification agreed that the press had been crucial in mobilizing public protests and boycotts and coordinating the colonies' efforts during the early days of the independence movement. Recognized as a bulwark against tyranny, no one objected to including freedom of the press alongside freedom of speech and religion. Thomas Jefferson explained to a friend his rationale for listing it at the beginning of his proposed Bill of Rights: "The basis of our government being the opinion of the people, the very first object should be to keep that right."† In sweeping language, the First Amendment constructs a wall between the government

---

*Even opponents of the Constitution's ratification endorsed frequent elections but charged that the Framers did only a half-hearted job in installing the safeguards of elections. With the campaign slogan, "Tyranny begins where annual elections end," Patrick Henry hammered ratification advocates on the grounds that elections were too infrequent.

†In a favorite, often-quoted passage of journalists, Jefferson added with customary rhetorical flare, "were it left to me to decide whether we should have a government without newspapers or newspapers without a government, I should not hesitate a moment to prefer the latter." But with the accumulated bruises that accompany public life, Jefferson came to despise the partisan press. During his long retirement at Monticello, Jefferson prided himself on never picking up a "putrid" newspaper and turning to poetry instead. Meanwhile, down the road at Montpelier, his longtime political partner James Madison spent his retirement (he outlived all of the Constitution's Framers) pouring over news from Washington and firing off letters to the editor to correct wrongheaded news and opinions.

and the press: "Congress shall make no law . . . abridging the freedom of speech, or of the press." Journalists are understandably inclined to see this provision as establishing a "fourth branch" of government charged with monitoring and reporting the self-interested actions of politicians in the other branches.

Despite the apparent consensus behind the principle of freedom of the press, the practices of the new government initially went in the opposite direction. The First Congress sent the Bill of Rights amendments to the states for ratification; the Fifth Congress passed the Sedition Act in 1798. It expressly forbade any criticism of the president and Congress, both controlled by the Federalist Party, that contained "any false, scandalous and malicious writing . . . to bring [government officials] . . . into contempt or disrepute or to excite against them . . . the hatred of the good people of the United States." After passage, the John Adams administration promptly arrested twenty-five people and convicted eleven, mostly newspaper editors aligned with the emerging Democratic-Republican opposition. The resulting political uproar contributed to the Federalist debacle in the 1800 election from which it never recovered. The newly installed President Jefferson pardoned all convicted under this act, and the new Democratic-Republican–controlled Congress passed resolutions of apology and compensation. The real lesson of this early test came with the disastrous political consequences of blatantly breaching press freedom.*

In the modern era public policy has buttressed the news media's independence. First, the idea that the press should be fair is left to the marketplace to address, at least where print journalism is concerned. Lawsuits by disgruntled candidates charging unfair treatment from the local press has always fallen on deaf ears in the courts. Anyone can start a newspaper, at least can hypothetically, and certainly, anyone can set up a Web site or open a blog. During the modern era the courts have extended the First Amendment's categorical language in two important areas of journalism that have served to insulate news producers from government censorship and intimidation. These concern government efforts at prior restraint and the press's exposure to libel and slander laws.

Prior Restraint

When a government seeks to *prevent* the publication and dissemination of written and recorded speech, it is exercising **prior restraint.** Beginning with a 1931 decision, the Supreme Court has consistently taken a dim view of this form of censorship.† Perhaps the most famous application of this doctrine occurred in 1971 when the *New York*

---

*The most famous of those arrested was Vermont newspaper editor Matthew Lyon, who won election to Congress while in jail awaiting trial. We encountered this contentious individual in the image on page 24, where he is wielding tongs against a Federalist colleague. In the deadlocked election of 1800 decided in the House of Representatives, Lyon casts the decisive vote for Thomas Jefferson.

†The case establishing this doctrine is *Near v. Minnesota* 283 U.S. 697 (1931). Jay Near was the editor of a small Minnesota newspaper who used his paper as a forum for vilifying Jews and politicians. After a state judge ordered him to stop publication, Near challenged the state law that allowed local courts and law enforcement to shut down a "malicious, scandalous, and defamatory newspaper, magazine, or other periodical." In enunciating new doctrine, the Court did acknowledge that national security might sometimes require government censorship.

Signaling a victory for the *Washington Post* and *New York Times,* a pleased pressman at the *Post* holds the first edition of the paper announcing the Supreme Court's 1971 decision in *New York Times Co. v. United States.* The papers had contended that the government's attempt to enjoin publication of the so-called *Pentagon Papers* amounted to nothing less than prior restraint.

Times and other newspapers announced their intent to publish the *Pentagon Papers,* an immense, top-secret compilation of U.S. government decisions and information about the Vietnam War.[27] The Nixon administration won an injunction against publication in a district court with the argument that publication would undermine national security at a moment when the war was still raging. In striking down the lower court's decision to suspend publication, the Supreme Court emphasized its four-decades-old precedent: "any system of prior restraints of expression comes to this Court bearing a heavy presumption against its constitutional validity." In other words, the government had to demonstrate—and in this case had failed to do so—that publication of the documents would damage national security. Today this presumption lives on, and prior restraint is rarely permitted, except in "troopship" circumstances, when a news report threatens to endanger the lives of American soldiers by publicly disclosing their position.

Slander and Libel

A similar strain of judicial reasoning crops up in libel doctrine. (This covers both written—**libel**—and spoken—**slander**—forms of false and malicious information that damages another person's reputation.) Civil litigation involving private citizens follows well-established standards of what constitutes libel and appropriate monetary damages, but when one party is a newspaper and the other a public figure—such as a politician, televangelist, or movie star—an altogether different doctrine kicks in. Simply stated, public figures largely forfeit legal recourse to protect their reputation. Not only must injured individuals prove that the story was false, they must also prove that the news producer acted with "malice" by publishing the damaging story it knew to be false. This test raises the bar of proof so high that politicians and other public figures stand little chance of winning in court.[28] Presumably, because the press is free from any real threat of being sued, it will feel less constrained in seeking and speaking truth to politics. Critics charge that such a high threshold of proof gives news media free rein to distort public figures' actions and motives.

News as the Product of Politics

From 1962 until his retirement in 1981, Walter Cronkite anchored the *CBS Evening News*. During his tenure, public opinion surveys repeatedly found him to be one of the most trusted persons in the country. When Cronkite matter-of-factly closed each broadcast with his signature statement, "And that's the way it is," the American public believed him. But is news reporting ever a simple, objective "mirror image" of reality? Americans are accustomed to thinking about news—especially television news—in this way. Perhaps it is more accurate and suggestive to think about news less as an objective record and more as a particular *representation* of facts and events.

Most political news does not actually claim to report events. One careful content analysis of two major newspapers found that barely 1 percent of politics-related news stories did so. Instead, almost all of the examined news derived from political talk intended to attract public notice. A quarter of all stories came from interviews and another 42 percent from press conferences and news releases. Altogether, individuals and organizations engaged in talk or discourse of some kind contributed two-thirds of all sources of political news.[29]

Political talk assumes many forms—from official declarations to press releases to "off the record" conversations with a reporter over lunch. Politicians undertake these activities because they are important to political success. As naturally garrulous as elected officeholders may appear on camera, political purpose lies behind all of their efforts to make news. They may be simply trying to garner favorable publicity or to build public support for their position on some issue. Frequently the ultimate target of their efforts is not the public but other politicians in Washington. But whatever the strategy underlying their public utterances, they must in every instance persuade a reporter that what they have to say is worth transmitting to an audience.

Earlier chapters noted some of the many news-making activities undertaken with specific purposes in mind—activities such as the publication of *The Federalist*, interest groups' creation of Web sites and newsletters for their members, the selection of Birmingham and Selma as sites for major civil rights demonstrations, campaign advertising, and the staging by presidents of bill-signing ceremonies in the White House Rose Garden. In each of these instances, someone—James Madison in one instance, the Reverend Martin Luther King Jr. in another—made news in order to influence the preferences of the public and, ultimately, the positions of other leaders.

The great majority of political news derives more from what people are *saying* than from what they are *doing*, but this does not necessarily diminish its status as news or its value to the audience. Much of what specialists and officials have to say is invaluable to a public trying to make sense of a particular set of facts or group of actions. For example, a scientist publishes a paper offering a new explanation for climate change; the chair of the Federal Reserve Board interprets the latest economic indicators at a congressional briefing; the head of a local housing agency announces a critical shortage of shelters for the homeless. In deciding to portray the gravity of a problem and in selecting the information to disclose—including whether to disclose it at all and when—these experts and officials are using the news media to achieve some political purpose.

Unlike television commercials produced by inspired Madison Avenue copywriters or academic journal articles hammered into submission by solitary professors, news does not spring forth as the product of a single actor or set of collaborators. Rather, it is the joint product of two independent actors—politicians and the news media—frequently competing with one another to define the story. As they engage each other in an enterprise of news making, they do so to achieve different and frequently incompatible goals. Politicians seek to influence the course of political events. Not surprisingly, they want news stories to cast them and their positions on the issues in the most favorable light. Those in the business of reporting and producing the news must keep a keen eye on their audience's interest in the proposed story and the willingness of their readers or viewers to rely on their coverage over that of a competitor. Reporters find it pays to demonstrate independence from their political sources and not simply pass along what politicians would like the public to know. The relationship between politicians and reporters, then, reflects a tension between reciprocity and competition. Occasionally unhappiness over the other side's performance erupts publicly in charges and countercharges. Politicians typically complain that the news media are biased and uninformed; reporters may charge that they, or the news, are being manipulated. When politicians participate in news making they usually have one or both of two audiences in mind: the public and fellow politicians. Although elected officeholders are always on the lookout for ways to improve the public's estimate of their service, much of their news-making activity is really an attempt to communicate with other politicians. The reason is simple: public statements often capture their colleagues' attention and force a response when a private communication will not. In 1993 the leader of the Congressional Black Caucus called a press conference to declare that just because almost all of its members were Democrats, President Bill Clinton should not take for granted the caucus's support for his proposed welfare reforms. Surely the caucus had said this repeatedly to the president and his staff, but by going public they placed him on notice that disregarding their views might damage his support with the African American community. Similarly, when a president threatens publicly to veto legislation nearing a floor vote in Congress, the threat gains credibility by having been publicized. If Congress were to pass the legislation anyway and a veto were not forthcoming, the president would damage his reputation both on Capitol Hill and with the public. Recognizing this to be the case, legislators regard public threats more seriously than threats conveyed privately.

Every elected politician in Washington has a press secretary on staff to generate favorable news about the boss. The president's press secretary probably has the biggest job of them all, befitting the importance of public opinion to modern presidential leadership. The institutions within which these politicians serve offer them numerous occasions to generate favorable news. Members of Congress can, among other things, conduct public hearings, publicly state their issue positions on the floor of their cham-

President Theodore Roosevelt has been generally credited with introducing the trial balloon to the presidency. He would try out an idea on a reporter, but if it backfired he would deny the story and denounce the reporter. In these early days of White House correspondents, the president held the advantage in the relationship.

ber in front of C-SPAN's cameras, and insert speeches and press releases into the *Congressional Record.* Every time a president steps outside the White House, he is trailed by the White House press corps, which looks for a story in a presidential speech, an appearance in an elementary school classroom, or even a foray into a department store to shop. In early 2005 President Bush lobbied Congress almost daily to pass his Social Security legislation, but his lobbying was not limited to phone calls, invitations to the White House, or instructions to his staff to work the corridors of Congress. The president devoted several days each week to traveling around the country and speaking on the need for Social Security reform. Bush and his advisers knew that presidential travel ensured the network television coverage required to keep this issue in the news and before a reluctant Congress.

One venerable news strategy employed by politicians to transact politics with one another is the **trial balloon.** A politician "floats" a policy or some other idea with a reporter on the condition that the source of the story remain anonymous. If the story containing the proposal elicits a favorable response from others in Washington, the politician then publicly announces the proposal. Presidents often float trial balloons by persuading a member of Congress to propose a policy, allowing the president to gauge the political breezes before committing to a course of action.

When Mark Felt revealed (and *Washington Post* reporter Bob Woodward confirmed) that he was Deep Throat in May 2005 it ended over three decades of continuous speculation. Felt was the second in command at the FBI and headed its day-to-day operations, which gave him direct access to hundreds of FBI interviews investigating the Watergate burglary. Suspecting complicity in the break-in and subsequent cover-up in the leadership of the Justice Department and White House, Felt claimed he had no alternative to spurring investigation through news leaks. Shortly before his tenure as Deep Throat Felt had become embittered with the Nixon administration after being passed over as J. Edgar Hoover's successor at the Bureau.

Another discreet, news-making strategy equally available to presidents, members of Congress, and lesser government officials is the news **leak.** This political term, first listed in Noah Webster's American dictionary in 1832, refers to giving strategically consequential information to the news media on the condition that its source not be identified by name. The "leaker" may be seeking to influence the public, other politicians, or both. The most common leaks involve a source revealing something good about themselves or bad about someone else.[30] More than simply scoring points, the most important leaks force an action or response from others in Washington. Arguably, the most famous leaker in American history was "Deep Throat," who continuously provided news reporters at the *Washington Post* leads for investigating the June 1972 break-in at Democratic headquarters at the Watergate Hotel.

Later, as revelations mounted, a special Senate committee began conducting a formal, nationally televised investigation. Deep Throat continued his news leaks, leading Senate investigators to new and productive avenues of inquiry into the Watergate scandal, ultimately ending in Richard Nixon's resignation from the presidency and the sentencing of numerous White House aides to federal prison.

An interesting variant that appeared more than once during the massive leaking that accompanied the Clinton White House sex scandal was the "inoculating" leak. Independent counsel Kenneth Starr, who was investigating the affair between the president and White House intern Monica Lewinsky, denied serving as the source of leaks and then blamed Clinton's staff. He chided White House aides for preemptorily releasing unfavorable information in order to minimize any future damage when the news became public. The president's lawyer, David Kendall, vigorously challenged Starr's assertions, arguing that the independent counsel's office had waged an ongoing campaign of leaks and then placed blame on the president.[31] Virtually every administration in recent decades has at one time or another become entangled in a major scandal or conflict that was begun or fueled by leaks. In its eight years, President Bush's administration had to deal with several major controversies based on leaked information. In the Valerie Plame scandal (see box "The Dicey Game of Leaks"), White House aides were finally exposed as leaking information that revealed the identity of a

CIA operative in a vendetta directed at her husband, a diplomat who had recently criticized the administration in a newspaper op-ed essay.

News Producers: Reporters and Their News Organizations

Both the broadcast and print news outlets rely heavily on the talents of their reporters and correspondents, who work directly with politicians and other sources in uncovering stories and following leads. Sometimes a close relationship with a source will allow the reporter to scoop a story for his or her news organization or gain an exclusive interview.

The role of reporter is so pivotal to making news that a professional creed has grown up around the job and sets its members apart from others who work in the news business. Reporters make the initial decisions about the newsworthiness of a story and may play the chief role in defining the context or framework within which the story will be eventually reported. Within their organizations, reporters may act as a story's sponsor; "selling" a story to the editor is a venerable challenge and a source of journalistic pride.

THE BEAT. Both newspapers and broadcast media cover the regular sources of important stories in a systematic fashion by permanently assigning reporters to certain venues, traditionally called **beats.** At the national level, regular news beats include the White House, Congress, the Supreme Court, the State Department, and the Pentagon. Moreover, during political campaigns reporters are assigned to cover each of the major candidates. Every campaign organization in turn assigns staff members to serve as the reporters' contacts. At the White House reporters receive much of their information at the daily briefings conducted by the president's press secretary. In fact, nearly all government agencies and senior officials have press staffs responsible for providing the media with information. More often than not, these are the agents who initiate "news" by issuing a statement or talking with a reporter.

The beat system has several important implications for news. Because news organizations rely on a continuous flow of stories, beat reporters routinely file dispatches every day or so, regardless of their newsworthiness. The president is a favorite subject for daily reporting; a national news broadcast almost always mentions the president, even if only to report what movie was screened over the weekend in the White House theater. Recognizing reporters' need for material, the office of the White House press secretary supplies them with self-serving stories and ample photo opportunities.

If a particular government agency is not on a beat, it is less likely to generate news. In the late 1980s a major scandal was uncovered at the Department of Housing and Urban Development in which an undersecretary awarded government subsidies and consulting contracts as political favors. Although the scandal involved many clear violations of the law and millions of dollars, the story first broke in an obscure trade journal devoted to housing issues. The national newspapers and networks had not assigned a correspondent to regularly monitor HUD, but this specialized journal had. Beats allow news organizations to work efficiently because their agents in the field can

The Dicey Game of Leaks

Spy: Valerie Plame

Ace reporter: Judith Miller

Protecting the anonymity of sources has long been a cherished right of the news industry. Some argue that extending such a guarantee to a source—say, a government official, such as Mark Felt (also known as Deep Throat), who is leaking information revealing the participation of other government officials in a lie—represents the highest service this "fourth branch of government" can perform for the public. Generally, leaks also make for great stories that attract large consumer interest. But leaks do not necessarily speak truth to politics. What happens when government officials anonymously leak information, including false information, in order to gain some political advantage over other politicians? Are news reporters being manipulated by government officials who benefit by remaining anonymous while spinning stories to their advantage or attacking those who disagree with them? Or are reporters—men and women who are proud of their savvy pursuit of a scoop—in cahoots with the politicians in order to break a stunning story?

All of these questions were raised by the Valerie Plame scandal, which showed that the use of "leaking" sources can be a very dangerous political game. In February 2002, the CIA sent former diplomat Joe Wilson to Africa to investigate whether Iraq had purchased uranium from Niger. Wilson's subsequent report back to the CIA concluded that the sources documenting such a purchase were not credible. Almost a year and a half later, Wilson wrote an op-ed piece in the *New York Times* in which he criticized President George W. Bush's continuing reference to the African uranium purchase to make his case for the invasion of Iraq. Eight days later Wilson's wife, Valerie Plame—a career CIA operative—was "outed" in the *Washington Post* by veteran syndicated columnist Robert Novak, who referred to his sources merely as "[t]wo senior administration officials."

White House leak: I. Lewis "Scooter" Libby

Another White House leak: Karl Rove

The firestorm that followed centered on two questions: who were these anonymous officials who leaked Plame's identity to the press—effectively ending her career, endangering field operatives, and possibly violating a criminal law in the process—and was the purpose of the leak to retaliate against her husband for criticizing the Bush administration?

It would take three years and the appointment of a special prosecutor, Patrick Fitzgerald, to answer the first question. Novak's sources included Karl Rove, President Bush's close friend and senior advisor, and Richard Armitage, then–assistant secretary of state. But the biggest controversy centered around special prosecutor Fitzgerald's questioning of Judith Miller, a reporter for the *New York Times* who researched but never actually wrote a story about Joe Wilson and the administration's response to his claims. In the end, Miller spent twelve weeks in jail for refusing to reveal her source—who turned out to be Vice President Dick Cheney's chief of staff, I. Lewis "Scooter" Libby, who was later convicted of perjury for his role in the Plame affair. Miller and her paper claimed that the "freedom of the press" allowed her to shield sources from revelation, even when crimes were involved. Federal courts recognize a vague, weak shield right by insisting the investigators first pursue other avenues to the information. But unlike many states that have passed strong **shield laws** that protect journalists from having to testify about their sources in court, the Supreme Court has never agreed that the "freedom of the press" implies this professional freedom. Eventually, the Miller case turned from a professional *cause célèbre* to a sordid instance of a journalist abetting a vengeful government official's effort to ruin someone's career.

Controversy attracts the press. Above, each day of the Clinton impeachment trial dozens of reporters filled the Senate Press Gallery, but six weeks later the room was almost vacant for a debate on a bill to give states latitude in spending federal school aid.

specialize in particular sectors of the government. But they also steer the news toward sometimes trivial events while missing more important ones.

Another implication of the beat system is that reporters for rival publications and networks tend to write about the same limited range of events. Moreover, while on the beat they are in daily contact with other correspondents from other news organizations whom they tend to regard more as colleagues than competitors. The White House press corps consists of members of an organized club that has been in continuous operation for over a half century. Given the close proximity in which reporters on the same beat work, news reports emanating from a particular beat tend to be similar across newspapers and even across the news media. Occasionally these social dynamics create a conspicuously narrow or skewed representation of an event. On such occasions, critics charge reporters with practicing **pack journalism,** in which journalists follow the same story in the same way because they read each other's copy for validation of their own reporting or interpretations.

SELECTING THE NEWS. To accommodate their various carrying capacities, the news media must exercise discretion in allocating time and space to news stories. The media employ various criteria in deciding which stories to include in their papers and broadcasts. The first criterion is the authority and status of the source. Like no other politicians, presidents command the front pages and lead stories. Far behind are the Senate and its members, who edge out their counterparts in the House of Representatives.[32] Another consideration, according to some media observers, is the number of "talking heads," which may help to explain why the Senate rates more highly than does the House. The rest of Washington is normally relegated to coverage by the wire services (Associated Press and Reuters) to which newspapers subscribe; these reports may or may not make the inside pages of the nation's newspapers.

A second criterion for running a story is its level of controversy: conflict and disagreement are preferable to consensus. As journalists attempt to sell stories to editors and news organizations compete with each other, the news media often create controversy where it does not exist. In early 1995 Speaker Newt Gingrich dressed down the press corps for refusing to cast a bipartisan meeting with President Clinton in a favorable light. After Gingrich announced that the recently elected Republican Congress looked forward to working constructively with the Democratic president, a reporter asked, "What do you think it [bipartisanship] will break down over?" Gingrich retorted, "You just heard the leaders of the Republican Party say that the Democratic president today had a wonderful meeting on behalf of America; we're trying to work together. Couldn't you try for twenty-four hours to have a positive, optimistic message as though it might work?"[33]

A third criterion, closely related to the second, is negativity—bad news is preferred to good news. Economic downturns attract greater coverage than does rising prosperity. Similarly, the news media find far more to criticize than to praise in politicians' performances. Presidents cry foul more than most, though Congress fares little better.[34] In 1993, when asked pointedly in a press conference why he thought his popularity had dropped fifteen percentage points in only two months, President Clinton quickly shot back, "I bet not five percent of the American people know that we passed a budget . . . and it passed by the most rapid point of any budget in 17 years. I bet not one in 20 American voters knows that because . . . success and the lack of discord are not as noteworthy as failure."[35] The systematic evidence on this issue suggests that presidents' complaints are not far off the mark. One study, which scored every evening network news statement about Presidents George H. W. Bush and Clinton during the first three years of each president's administration, found that both chief executives garnered mostly negative coverage. Only for four of the twenty-four quarters did they average as much favorable as unfavorable coverage on network news.*

To the extent that reporters and their editors actively filter and interpret messages in a way that favors conflict over consensus and bad news over good, the news media do not serve as a strictly neutral conduit for the flow of civic information to their intended audience. Some media critics charge that in selecting which messages to communicate and in slanting the content, news organizations inject a pernicious bias. Such charges are more abundant than is the evidence supporting them. Nonetheless, survey research finds respondents generally claiming to detect a media bias. Indeed, partisans on opposite sides of numerous issues believe that their views are not receiving fair coverage. In recent years "media watch" organizations have proliferated to keep a sharp eye out for press bias against their particular point of view. They are quick to sound an alarm, and in doing so they put pressure on news organizations to give their side more "balanced" (that is, more sympathetic) coverage. Organizations undertake these costly exercises because they believe that news influences voters and ultimately national policy.

---

*Even during the first quarter of 1991, when the Gulf War lifted George H. W. Bush's Gallup Poll approval rating to a record-setting 88 percent, the president still barely managed to win mostly favorable coverage. The network news sound-bite data for this analysis were generously provided by the Center for Media and Public Affairs.

Sen. Joseph McCarthy, the master of props, was effective at giving the media what they needed in their earlier days. Fistfuls of papers, pointers, and maps were among the many devices he used in the 1950s for his frequent "photo-ops."

Certainly the surplus of messages offered to the news media each day gives them great opportunity to favor some kinds of stories and points of view over others. But this latitude does not necessarily allow reporters to insinuate their political opinions into their stories or to use the news to serve the financial interests of their corporate sponsors. Unlike the bygone party press, modern print and broadcast media depend on readers and viewers for their livelihood. In addition to collecting direct payment for information—such as subscriptions for newspapers and Internet services—all news media sell advertising, and the fees they charge are directly related to the size of their audiences. In today's highly competitive marketplace, these commercial enterprises can ill afford to have their audiences view their product (the news) as contaminated by bias. In effect, the marketplace exercises a discipline that reins in any inclination of owners, editors, or reporters to exploit their control over news as a means to manipulate public opinion.

Strategic Relations between Politicians and Reporters

Politicians have long enlisted the cutting-edge communications technology of their age. The **franking privilege** gave nineteenth-century members of Congress free access to the postal system, and it is still embraced by their present-day counterparts. Rare is the modern congressional staff without a resident Webmaster. Democratic presidential nominee Barack Obama announced selection of his vice presidential running mate not at a press conference but via a cell phone text message to four million supporters.

The average politician has trouble getting their message to voters because he or she attracts too little news coverage and direct communication is far too expensive. To address this problem, most politicians "buy" as much direct communication as they can afford and chase as much news attention as their skills and positions of authority permit. To that end, many politicians have perfected techniques of generating favorable coverage. Presidents, for example, have appreciated for years that foreign travel and visits to disaster sites engender favorable news reports. And as President George W. Bush discovered after his sluggish response to Hurricane Katrina, failure to rush to the scene of disasters can engender the public's enmity. So, in 2007 when a Minnesota bridge buckled and plummeted thirteen motorists to their deaths and injured many dozens of others, few were surprised to find the president on the scene shortly thereafter.

Television viewers crave visual images, and savvy politicians have learned how to create irresistible ones. In the 1950s anticommunist witch hunter senator Joseph McCarthy always appeared with loose sheets of paper that he could wave at any live camera and claim they contained his list of 205 or 81 or 57 (the number changed daily) known communists in the State Department.[36] Civil rights leaders in the 1960s realized that by confronting southern segregation through often-violent television images of segregationists in action, they could validate their claims of racism to the rest of the nation. The movement's success with highly telegenic passive resistance continues to inspire the media strategies of those who protest to advance a cause.

Shortly after the 1962 California gubernatorial election, the defeated Richard Nixon held what was then termed his "last press conference." There he made bitter reference to his treatment by the press, saying they "would not have Nixon to kick around anymore."

In many respects, relations between politicians and reporters have not changed much since the early days of the Republic, when a newspaperwoman spotted President John Quincy Adams skinny-dipping in the Potomac and threatened to scream if he came out of the water before giving her an interview on his policy toward the state banks.[37] (Adams had been hiding in the White House, hoping to avoid public statements on the issue.) This amusing scene is a reminder of the tension inherent in the relationship between politicians and reporters. If they could, each side would exploit the other since each possesses (and would prefer not to surrender) something the other needs. The politician needs sympathetic access to voters, and the reporter requires information that makes for a good story. Both are, in some sense, costly to obtain. No working journalist wants to appear to be a publicist for some politician. And the conveyed information that best serves the politician's purpose will rarely coincide with that good story coveted by the reporter. President Adams clearly thought no story at all would best suit his purposes, but the intrepid reporter caught him in an unguarded moment. This obstacle to cooperation is precisely what the Framers had in mind when they placed protection for the press immediately after freedom of speech in the First Amendment. Anyone suspicious of the concentration of government authority should applaud the wariness with which the press and politicians deal with one another.

The "boys" on the bus? Women journalists occupy seats on the press bus as well (in this case former Vermont governor Howard Dean's plane over Michigan, February 1, 2004). The presidential hopeful was taking questions regarding criticism of his opponent, Sen. John Kerry.

Conclusion: Politician-Press Relations Then and Now

Veteran newspaper reporters sometimes wax nostalgically about the "good old days" when the print journalists ruled the news and worked closely with politicians on the basis of mutual trust and profit. The "good old days" probably never were as rosy as hindsight allows, but a look back at politician-press relations in an earlier era during the 1930s and 1940s does reveal much more relaxed and mutually satisfactory interactions than one finds today. It was an era in which news about national politics was dominated by a small number of Washington correspondents who had organized themselves professionally to reduce cutthroat competition. These Washington fixtures cultivated close, frequently chummy, relations with the comparatively few politicians who actively sought to influence the news.

Then as now, the president was at the center of the news media's attention. During his years in the White House, Franklin D. Roosevelt (1933–1945) conducted 998 biweekly press conferences with a regular group of White House correspondents. The president used these "family gatherings," as he called them, as occasions to make significant announcements. Reporters favored press conferences because they created a level playing field and limited competition for stories. They came to the Oval Office expecting hard news that would secure them a byline on the front page of the next day's paper. "[Roosevelt] never sent reporters away empty-handed," reminisced one veteran, adding that correspondents "are all for a man who can give them several laughs and a couple of top-head dispatches in a twenty-minute visit."[38] In return the correspondents gave Roosevelt and his New Deal full and generally sympathetic coverage.

Throughout our inquiry into the logic of American politics, we see that collective action generally involves two or more actors successfully solving a prisoner's dilemma. Each participant has to agree to forego some short-term advantage, pay some cost, or accept risk that the other side will break an agreement in order to secure a more attractive outcome through cooperation. Institutions create settings that bring these actors together and ensure that any agreements will be honored. Thus far, we have examined how governmental institutions allow politicians to engage in mutually profitable exchange by solving this dilemma. Here, a more informal institution, Roosevelt's biweekly, open press conferences, regulated by the ground rules of hard news and no

STRATEGY AND CHOICE

···

The Military's Media Strategy

During the Civil War, a newspaper correspondent tried to acquit himself with Union general William Tecumseh Sherman by saying that he simply sought to report the truth. Sherman instructed him to take the next train out of town: "The truth, eh? No sir! . . . We don't want the enemy any better informed than he is. Make no mistake about that train." Until recently military authorities could aspire to control news from the front. As long as the military could manage the news effectively, it could prevent useful information from falling into enemy hands, and it could bury failures and promote sympathetic coverage. The first Persian Gulf War, in 1991, was probably the last conflict in which the military could hope to "contain" news reports from the front.

The relations between the military and the news media during the Afghanistan and Iraq Wars displayed features similar to the relations between politicians and the news media. Advancing communications technology liberated journalists from transmission centers, removing them from military oversight and censorship. Hundreds of journalists roamed Afghanistan, unescorted and unconfined. At times, American soldiers found themselves approaching not the enemy but swarms of network and freelance reporters representing news media from all over the world. As one officer remembered ruefully, soon after a firefight with the Taliban forces in a remote village, reporters from al Jazeera, the Arab television news network, showed up to conduct live interviews and transmit graphic images of civilian casualties while the American soldiers looked on. As war approached in March 2003, a small army of print and broadcast journalists descended on Iraq equipped with satellite phones and video transmission backpacks. General Sherman's policy of banishing the news media from the front was simply no longer viable.

Communications technology in the field and news programming at home were combining to pull the public into the war as never before. One news editor summed up the military's emerging news dilemma: "[T]he Pentagon can't keep information from people, like it did so well in the first Persian Gulf War. That's clearly going to be a losing game now." The Pentagon realized, as it planned the invasion of Iraq, it would also need a media strategy. Its novel plan took the form of **embedding** more than six hundred journalists (as many as eight hundred, by one estimate) to military units. Within general guidelines requiring the withholding of information that might be useful to the Iraqi military commanders, who were reputed to be avid fans of U.S. cable news channels, re-

A soldier, with an entourage of photographers, stands sentry during a sandstorm in the Kuwaiti desert south of Iraq.

porters were free to interview soldiers and file reports from the field whenever they liked.[1] Moreover, embedded slots were not limited to American journalists; even al Jazeera was awarded a half-dozen positions. Most assessments have concluded that the military's strategy was a brilliant stroke of political generalship.

But soon rivalries broke out between the military services as each discovered that these embedded journalists were writing inspiring stories of heroism and success. Each service viewed favorable publicity as a key ingredient in their annual budget battles with the other services. Some of America's generals enjoyed candid on-camera interviews and did not hesitate to use their network appearances to disclaim responsibility for any failure. Jostling for reporters and the media limelight became intensely competitive. By most accounts, during the early days of the invasion the army was a big winner in numbers of both reporters and favorable stories filed with news bureaus. The navy attracted almost 150 embedded reporters, no small share of the total. But much to the chagrin of the admirals, the Pentagon instituted a news blackout as the ships launched their missile attacks. An undersecretary of defense tried to smooth over ruffled feelings: "The contributions of every service are going to be well known. We are a combined arms team nowadays."

---

1. The U.S. military was discovered in late 2004 to have planted a false story with CNN in order to fool the enemy. Mark Mazetti, "PR Meets Psy-Ops in War on Terror," *Los Angeles Times,* December 1, 2004.

The Shrinking Presidential Sound Bite

Politicians' survival depends on successful adaptation. Whereas in 1968 presidential candidates could speak on camera during news segments for an average of about forty seconds without interruption, today they should consider themselves lucky to achieve the average allotment of nine seconds.[1] How did they adapt to this change? For one thing, they stopped trying to present an argument (most of their sentences were too long). Instead, they developed **sound bites,** catchy phrases and slogans that encapsulated their appeal to viewers.

At a conference of former press secretaries and network news officials, participants debated the cause of the shrinking sound bite. Did politicians increasingly prefer to engage in empty sloganeering, or were they adapting to a news media less willing to give them airtime? These questions led to the following exchange between former *NBC Nightly News* anchor John Chancellor and President Jimmy Carter's press secretary, Jody Powell.

---

1. Daniel C. Hallin, "Sound Bite News: Television Coverage of Elections, 1968–1988," in *Do the Media Govern? Politicians, Voters, and Reporters in America,* ed. Shanto Iyengar and Richard Reeves (Thousand Oaks, Calif.: Sage, 1997), 57–65.

Chancellor: ... I think television reporters out in the field—when presented with pre-packaged, pre-digested, plastic-coated phrases and with no opportunity to question a president—want to get something that isn't just pre-packaged and pre-digested, and that's why you are getting a more contentious kind of reporting in the twenty seconds at the end of the spot. I had an argument with [CBS correspondent] Tom Pettit during the 1988 election, and I said, "Why is it that all of our correspondents end their pieces with some little snippy, nasty saying? Why don't they just say, 'And tomorrow the president goes to Cleveland.'" And Pettit says, "It wouldn't come out that way. They would say, 'Tomorrow the president goes to Cleveland and no one knows why.'"

... So you compress the political propaganda on the one hand, or increase the reactive hostility on the other hand, and that's what a minute-and-a-half television spot is today. I think both sides are probably equally responsible for it, but I think that the politicians started it.

Powell: I will just raise a logical question. Assuming that there are other things

favoritism, allowed the president and the press to cooperate to achieve their separate goals. Both sides, then, got what they needed from their long-standing relationship. Two key elements of the setting that allowed this relationship between the president and the press corps to succeed in overcoming each side's temptation to exploit the other was the community's stability and small size. The president served as an authoritative and routinely available source for more than a dozen years, a long enough time for a trust relationship to develop, where each party knew the other intimately.

to do in a White House . . . now and then, . . . why would you go to all of the trouble to [package the president's message] if you did not find yourself faced with a situation in which it's the way to deal with it? . . . Are we supposed to believe that one morning ten, fifteen years ago somebody in the Johnson White House or the Nixon White House . . . woke up and said, "We don't need to do this, but just for the hell of it, why don't we create this whole structure here about going out on the road and doing that sort of thing?" Or rather perhaps it was a reaction—maybe intelligent, maybe unwise, maybe in the public interest, maybe not— . . . to a set of circumstances which they saw and said, "We've got to do something."

Source: Daniel C. Hallin, *The Presidency, the Press and the People* (La Jolla; University of California Extension, 1993).

The Washington, D.C., of today contains a far larger, more diverse population of news producers (see Figure 14-6). They compete as much with each other as with politicians in ferreting out stories. One could sense this emerging reconfiguration as early as 1961, when President John F. Kennedy conducted his first press conference on live, prime-time television. Network news bureaus relished their newfound access to the press conference and quickly turned Roosevelt's "family gathering" into a media event. Veteran news reporters understandably despised the intrusion of network

Figure 14-6 Growth of Congressional Press Corps

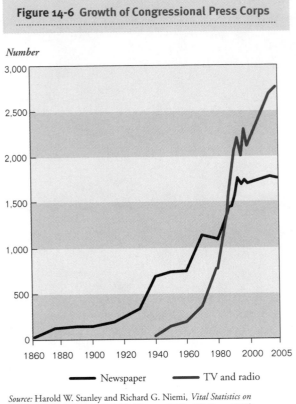

Number

Legend: Newspaper — TV and radio

Source: Harold W. Stanley and Richard G. Niemi, *Vital Statistics on American Politics, 2007–2008* (Washington, D.C.: CQ Press, 2007).

Notes: Press corps members are those correspondents entitled to admission to the Senate and House press galleries and radio and television galleries. Prior to 1986, the number of press corps members was recorded approximately every ten years.

cameras, likening it to "making love in Carnegie Hall."[39] Derision toward modern, television-based journalism remains commonplace (to learn why, see box "The Shrinking Presidential Sound Bite"). The problem print correspondents had with television journalism ran deeper, though. The television cameras reported stories instantly. With television, print coverage became nearly obsolete.

Today's freewheeling marketplace of politicians and reporters is a far cry from the cartel-like setting that permeated politician-press relations during Roosevelt's time. Today many more politicians engage in political talk, trying to attract the attention of an increasingly diverse news media. By one count, more than ten thousand government officials in Washington, D.C., alone are involved in press and public relations on a daily basis. The number of trade associations and other interest groups seeking to influence public opinion easily surpasses this number. The greatest barrier to successful media exposure is the sheer volume of competing news stories chasing media outlets on any given news day.

Television competed with newspapers for audiences and advertisers, and consequently, for the attention of presidents and other politicians. Now, the Internet potentially wields the same impact. "An item can emerge on an Internet Web site," complained a former network correspondent, "worm its way into a late-night comedian's act, appear as a topic on the morning radio show, and catapult onto the pages of the *New York Times*—all within the space of a few hours."[40] The new, still-evolving medium of Internet communication is ill-suited for the cultivation of cozy politician-press relations. Rather, it is conducive to the flourishing of a prisoner's dilemma between reporters and government officials, one that arises from competition and manipulation.

Some students of the news media attribute the modern era's strained relations between politicians and the press to the widespread suspicion among reporters that presidents will lie to them whenever it serves their interest and they think they can get away with it. Veteran journalists point to two specific events—Vietnam and Watergate—as critical in fostering a pervasive and enduring **credibility gap.** Charges of presidential manipulation became daily occurrences during the Vietnam War, which took place largely on Lyndon Johnson's watch. Before the credibility gap had much chance to dissipate, the Watergate scandal broke, and eventually, through the persistent efforts of reporters, President Nixon was forced to resign in 1974. The most recent rendition of Washington correspondents protesting that they were duped was the

Bush administration's campaign of false claims about the imminent threat of Saddam Hussein's chemical, biological, and nuclear weapons of mass destruction in order to justify an invasion of Iraq. In the aftermath of September 11, 2001, and with the United States at war in Afghanistan, the national press adopted a largely uncritical stance toward these claims. Vietnam, Watergate, and the Iraq War—all falling within the professional careers of many of today's news editors and senior reporters—have conditioned reporters to greet all White House claims with a suspicion of duplicity. Yet even without these major press failings, a credibility gap would probably still color the politician-press relationship. It is embedded in the tension between the preferred news story of reporters and that of politicians. In the absence of institutions designed for their mutual benefit, such as Roosevelt's "family gatherings," the news media's relationship with politicians is likely to remain one of mutual suspicion.

logic.cqpress.com

Key Terms

beat, 681

carrying capacity, 668

credibility gap, 692

embedding, 689

equal time, 663

fairness doctrine, 664

franking privilege, 686

infotainment, 671

leak, 680

libel, 676

media bias, 672

muckraking, 658

news media, 654

pack journalism, 684

prior restraint, 675

shield laws, 683

slander, 676

sound bite, 690

trial balloon, 679

unit cost, 654

"yellow journalism," 658

Suggested Readings

Ansolabehere, Stephen, Roy Behr, and Shanto Iyengar. *The Media Game: American Politics in the Television Age.* New York: Macmillan, 1993. A brief overview of news and politics, this book offers especially useful treatments of the news and information in election campaigns and reports experiments in media effects on public opinion.

Baum, Matthew A. *Soft News Goes to War.* Princeton: Princeton University Press, 2003. This book successfully resolves two inconsistent findings in public opinion research: a public expressing less interest in foreign affairs than in previous times but scoring as well informed as in the past. Baum presents persuasive evidence that many who shun formal news do, nonetheless, become informed via "soft" news, entertainment programs.

Davis, Richard, and Diana Owen. *New Media and American Politics.* New York: Oxford University Press, 1998. A thorough survey of the various "new media," this volume also compares modern communication technologies with traditional media, noting their respective effects on political knowledge and awareness.

Epstein, Edward Jay. *News from Nowhere.* New York: Vintage Books, 1973. An authoritative consideration of how the television medium dictates news production by the networks. One of the first books on the subject, it is well written and rich with observations and insights based on extensive field studies.

Hamilton, James T. *All the News That Is Fit to Sell.* Princeton: Princeton University Press, 2004. An economist examines modern television programming practices as a product of business strategies. A surprisingly readable book in which the author explains the decline of traditional news and the rise of infotainment.

Iyengar, Shanto, and Richard Reeves, eds. *Do the Media Govern? Politicians, Voters, and Reporters in America.* Thousand Oaks, Calif.: Sage, 1997. This fine anthology combines social science research with journalistic introspection. Taken together, these essays offer a comprehensive survey of scholarship on politics and the news media.

Review Questions

1. How do market forces make political news more "democratic"? Have market forces played the same role in press coverage throughout American history?

2. Why did newspaper editors accept party subsidies in the early Republic? What motivated these same editors to give up the subsidies later? Why didn't they give them up earlier?

3. How did the rise of newspaper chains affect the political influence of the press? What ultimately eroded the political power of these chains? How and why has the influence of newspapers continued to decline today?

4. How do differences in factors such as carrying capacity and target audiences lead to differences in the substance and style of news in different media?

5. How and why do politicians seek to manipulate the news? What strategies do they use to generate beneficial coverage?

6. What resources do politicians have that might allow them to "go around" the press and communicate with the public directly? In general, how successful are these attempts?

Exercises

In the Strictest of Conference

Go to the White House briefing room online (http://whitehouse.gov/news/briefings) and examine the content of the most recent press conference or briefing. What sorts of questions are asked? Do they all receive answers? Next, go to the online site of a major news outlet such as the *Washington Post* (http://washingtonpost.com) and try to find an article in which material from the press conference is cited. Generally speaking, what kind of information is selected? What information is not selected?

Find the Leak

Go to your local newspaper's front page and identify stories containing at least one unattributed piece of information. How many leaks can you find on the front page? In each case, how was the source identified? What point of view is the source advancing? If you had to guess, who do you think the source would be? Why do you think he or she chose to remain anonymous?

Headlined News

Google's news index (http://news.google.com) lists news stories from sources across the country. In many cases, these stories are taken from the same wire service story. Find a case where multiple news outlets have taken the same story. Then contrast the ways in which the story is presented. How do the headlines differ? What parts (if any) have been edited out? What illustrations are used?

15

The Prospects for Institutional Reform

Since Americans generally believe that the United States is the most successful democracy in history, why are there so many movements to reform it?

How does the power given to states in the U.S. federal system allow them to experiment with reforms, and how likely is it that successful innovations will spread to the national government?

Can citizens trust elected officials—who by definition have been winners at the game of politics—to set its rules in a way that will be fair to all players?

Is it too hard to change the structure of government in the United States, or too easy?

As the 105th session of Congress neared its end in 1998, the prospects of the campaign finance bill authored by Sens. John McCain and Russell Feingold—which aimed to be the furthest-reaching reform of federal elections in a generation—looked bleak. It was being debated to death in the Senate, while a parallel bill authored by Reps. Chris Shays and Marty Meehan was bottled up in the House. This impending defeat shocked and discouraged supporters of the legislation.

After all, the time seemed exactly right for a crackdown on "soft money," the unlimited contributions to political parties that had totaled $262 million in the 1996 elections. This figure had tripled since the last presidential election, raising the question of whether candidates were more interested in representing voters or the big-money donors who funneled contributions to their campaigns through party committees. When congressional investigations revealed that some of these donations were illegal, and that others had led to sleepovers in the White House's Lincoln Bedroom for some of President Clinton's most generous supporters, a bipartisan group of legislators appeared open to reform. With authors from both parties, the McCain-Feingold and Shays-Meehan bills were the perfect vehicles. Fine-tuned over many sessions with compromises designed to broaden their appeal, the measures seemed to have majority support in both houses of Congress.

As readers know by now, even such a confluence of favorable conditions and majority sentiment does not always secure victory. The many barriers that the American political system places in the way of major policy shifts killed the bills that session.

Senators John McCain, the maverick Republican from Arizona, and Russell Feingold, the liberal Democrat from Wisconsin, found common ground and shared fame through their pursuit over many sessions of the campaign finance reform legislation that came to be known as the McCain-Feingold bill.

697

Although fifty-two senators backed the Senate version, it did not have the sixty votes necessary to invoke cloture and shut down the filibuster led by Sen. Mitch McConnell, who argued that its limits on party soft money and issue advertising by interest groups violated First Amendment protections of political speech. In the House, Newt Gingrich used his power as Speaker to keep the bill off the floor agenda. The impediments to change that are built into U.S. institutions had seemed to trap this popular reform just when it appeared most needed.

Yet as the 1998 elections drew nearer, the political incentives faced by vulnerable legislators began to work against these institutional obstacles. The reform bills proved quite popular, making sympathetic legislators eager to voice their support for them before November. Democrats in the House allied with some Republicans to use a rare process—a discharge petition signed by enough members to bring the Shays-Meehan bill directly to the floor, over the Speaker's objections—during the summer. The legislation remained stalled in the Senate, but passed by a 252–179 margin when it reached the House floor in August.

Suddenly, campaign finance reform had political momentum. Rebellion on this issue became an almost annual ritual, with another discharge petition succeeding the next year. The Senate continued its filibuster, but the 2000 elections provided even more impetus for reform. Soft money fund-raising by both parties totaled $495 million in federal campaigns that year. John McCain, who earlier in his career had been tainted by allegations of corruption as a member of the "Keating Five," used his bill to wear the mantle of reform and ran an unexpectedly strong race for the Republican presidential nomination. When Congress came back into session, McCain and Feingold convinced their colleagues to engage in a real debate. With a few amendments, the bill gathered enough votes to end the filibuster and pass, and Congress sent it to President George W. Bush in March 2002. By this time, the president faced his own political pressures, as the misdeeds of Enron and other corporate scandals again fanned public outrage at the influence of big money in politics. He reluctantly signed the Bipartisan Campaign Reform Act (BCRA) in a quiet ceremony, declaring in a press release that "the American electorate will benefit from these measures to strengthen our democracy," but noting that "the bill does have flaws. Certain provisions present serious constitutional concerns."[1]

Senator McConnell agreed, and sued to overturn in the courts the legislation that he had blocked so long in the Senate. In their first look at BCRA in the 2003 *McConnell v. Federal Election Commission* case, a narrow majority of Supreme Court justices upheld both its ban on party soft money and its strict limits on issue advocacy during campaigns.[2] As the Court's membership changed, however, its view of the issue evolved. After John Roberts took over as chief justice, the Court issued a 2007 decision calling into question BCRA's ban on genuine issue advertisements funded with corporate or union money. The Court also invalidated a Vermont law placing tight contribution limits on state candidates, and in 2008 struck down the McCain-Feingold bill's "millionaire's amendment," which relaxed restrictions on candidates running against those financing their own campaigns. One leading campaign finance law expert judged that "[s]upporters of reasonable campaign finance regulation are now zero for three in the

Roberts Court,"[3] while another scholar observed that "[r]ecent campaign finance developments raise serious questions about the viability of the entire regime of campaign finance law."[4]

The commentator was referring not only to the Court's recent decisions, but also to the innovative (and, to some, illegitimate) methods that large contributors had used to stay influential in the 2004 presidential race. As Chapter 11 detailed, soft money found a new home in so-called 527 groups, such as the conservative "Swift Boat Veterans for Truth" and the liberal "Americans Coming Together," which raised unlimited funds to spend in-

As the sports analogy in this cartoon suggests, those who backed campaign finance reform may have scored a touchdown with the passage of the McCain-Feingold bill but did not win the game. The Supreme Court's recent decisions served as a goal-line stand for fans of free speech protections for political spending.

dependently of candidates. These groups, spending $405 million in the 2004 contests, quickly filled the vacuum left when BCRA stopped soft money contributions to parties. If politics is the relationship between principals (voters) and agents (politicians), this shifting flow of money in American elections is troubling. In the 1990s, reformers worried that candidates were paying more heed to soft-money contributors than to voters. The McCain-Feingold reforms may have succeeded in preventing this problem, but did not institute a perfect solution. The new set of principals who may unduly influence politicians includes contributors who give through 527 groups and the corporations and unions that the Supreme Court has allowed back into issue advocacy. It appears that the long, hard-fought battle over BCRA has been an incomplete victory for reform.

Casting campaign finance regulation and BCRA's journey in these terms ties them to the themes replayed throughout this book. All reforms are proposed solutions to some collective action problem, but they may themselves create new collective action problems, or move us too far on the continuum between imposing transaction costs (in this case, by opening the door to corruption) and conformity costs (by infringing upon free speech). Reforms may attempt to solve collective action problems, but the process of reform itself faces many of these same problems. Changing American political institutions, it should come as no surprise, is neither simple nor easy.

Toward a More Perfect Union?

Americans revere the Constitution, memorize its preamble, but often try to amend it. We salute the flag, yet debate whether we should require everyone to pledge allegiance to it or prevent anyone from burning it. Although the vast majority of our citizens view our leaders and government as legitimate—even after bitterly contested elections—few of us question the legitimacy of attempts to improve our governing institutions. It is a characteristic paradox of our political creed that we celebrate our nation's democracy as the greatest in world history, while constantly considering what reforms* might move us toward a more perfect Union.

Hard polling numbers demonstrate the exceptional patriotism of Americans as well as the reasons why efforts to change the nation are regarded as patriotic. In a recent international survey, 94 percent of Americans answered that they were proud of their country, a figure that easily surpassed the levels of national pride found in large European countries. Sixty-five percent of Americans would be willing to fight for their country in a war, which again rose far above the levels measured in France, Germany, Great Britain, Italy, and Spain. But when Americans were asked how satisfied they are with their democracy, 28 percent said they were "not very satisfied" and 7 percent were "not at all satisfied." [5] Many of those who are proud of the United States and willing to fight for it are not completely contented with the way the government works, a dissatisfaction that gives rise to many fervent, patriotic reform movements.

That does not mean, of course, that the American governmental system makes the process of reform easy. Satisfied with their work, the Framers constructed the Constitution so that a momentary flash of popular passion would not undo it. After the passage of the Bill of Rights, a mere seventeen amendments have been added to the Constitution, a testament more to the deliberate obstacles built into the amendment process than to a lack of reform ideas.

Worried that those unhappy with the new government would soon press for yet another constitutional reform, the Framers intentionally placed high transaction costs—the investments of time, effort, and resources needed to reach collective decisions—on attempts to change the American political system. In the states, where the Framers worried less about constitutional revisions, proponents of reform have faced fewer barriers, many reform experiments have been launched, and a few have spread across the country. Yet changing the rules of politics and policymaking at the federal level remains difficult. Perhaps this reflects the pride of Americans in their nation, but the resistance to change that is woven into American political institutions can also be viewed as a consequence of collective action dilemmas. The collective action problems that inspire reform efforts also confront campaigns for change with new problems. Before they begin their battles, disparate reform groups must settle on a single proposed solution, a dilemma in itself. Once the fight is joined, collective action problems pose further obstacles to organizing a movement, assembling a broad coalition, and winning in the multiple political arenas that have authority over the structure of government.

The strategic incentives that politicians face also play into the process of reform. Although not every change in the way U.S. government works is initiated by an elected

---

* We use the term "reform" here to denote any proposed change to U.S. governing institutions, while remaining agnostic about whether particular reforms would improve the operation of American politics or harm it.

official, it is nearly always necessary to secure the sponsorship or at least the grudging acquiescence of politicians for anything to happen. This inescapable fact could be an impenetrable barrier against changes to the status quo. After all, elected officials by definition succeeded under the old rules of the game. While those on the losing side of politics often want to change the rules, the winners generally have the power to set the rules. This logic does not, however, dictate stasis in American institutions.

Because democratic competition makes it uncertain who will hold power after the next elections, electoral pressures open three clear routes to reform. First, those in government often yield to calls for reform because they wish to maintain their popularity and win again. Politicians may even find future political advantage in reform. As Chapter 4 discussed, leaders opposing slavery in territories won widespread support from white voters worried about having to compete with slave labor. Some of the Republicans who promoted Reconstruction, the most ambitious constitutional reforms since Philadelphia in 1787, did so to stave off the specter of Democratic congressional majorities once the rebellious southern states were readmitted to the Union. In a second rationale for reform, elected officials who fear that they may soon lose their offices have an incentive to change the rules so that they will still have some influence once they are on the outside of the power centers. Third, when politicians fail to forecast the political tides and are swept out of office, new leaders brought in by the surge may want to secure reforms before their power also washes away. Even though the strategic incentives politicians face make changes to the system that elected them less likely and more complicated, they do not rule out reform entirely.

The logic of American politics, then, both creates problems that need to be solved and places profound obstacles in the way of any proposed solution. It is a formula for incrementalism, for continual skirmishing over the important narrow details of the political system within a lasting consensus over its broad shape. Revolutionary change is unlikely, while persistent tweaking is certain.

This chapter tells the stories of both successful and failed reforms, viewed through the lens of the collective action framework. It maps the path to change, highlighting the many roadblocks as well as a few opportunities to accelerate change. It then focuses on four areas of proposed reform, viewed as solutions to the four major collective action problems identified in the introduction. To solve their *coordination problems,* political parties have employed various methods—today, they have often settled on the direct primary—to focus the support of their adherents on a single candidate. When voters want more turnover among politicians, but hesitate to sacrifice the seniority that their representative has built up while other districts keep their incumbents, they deal with their *prisoner's dilemma* by supporting term limits. Because individual citizens are tempted to *free ride* in a democracy by not making the effort to cast a ballot, reformers have made various attempts to boost turnout. Finally, presidents have sought line-item veto powers in order to stop members of Congress from writing budgets that deliver spending to each of their districts while turning the overall budget into a *tragedy of the commons.*

Each story demonstrates the trade-offs between solving an old problem and creating a new one, as well as the strategic dilemmas faced by political actors who care both about reforming the political process and about advancing their own policy goals and political careers. Reformers often draw upon the toolkit of institutional design described in the introduction to this book, proposing changes that can be evaluated according to the transaction and conformity costs that they impose. When would-be reformers do settle on an idea, the narratives illustrate, their campaigns for change must overcome both collective action problems and the institutional impediments built in by the Framers. To implement change, reformers can harness the energy and ingenuity of a nation whose citizens are as engaged in the operation of their democracy as any people in the world. Combined, these obstacles and opportunities make changing American politics difficult yet not, as our rich history of reform shows, impossible.

The Barriers to Institutional Change

How difficult it is to reform U.S. institutions depends on how fundamental and broad an intended reform will be. The sturdiest barricades are built around the Constitution, which is amended only rarely and with great effort. Changing the statutes that govern the everyday operations of the national political system is less difficult, but still no easy task. Facing these daunting prospects, many reformers begin at the state level, pushing for change with a more limited geographic scope in the hope that their ideas will then spread across the country.

Amending the Constitution

Amending the Constitution may be the toughest task in American politics. It has been accomplished only seventeen times in the past two centuries, a rate of less than one amendment per decade. This is no accident. To ensure that their work at the Constitutional Convention not be undone quickly or foolishly, the Framers placed formidable barriers in the way of a proposed change. They required amendments to gain support from multiple layers of government so that neither the states nor the federal government could impose new rules upon each other. They used supermajority voting rules to prevent narrow coalitions from making broad changes. All in all, they stacked the deck against any faction that wished to rewrite the rules.

The obstacles that the Framers put in the way of reform can be thought of as transaction costs imposed on anyone attempting an amendment. The first impediment in the most viable path* toward amending the Constitution is the requirement that any proposal receive the support of two-thirds of the members of both houses of Congress. This means that a reform movement must first gain a congressional sponsor, a politician convinced that leading this difficult fight will be a wise use of time and political capital. The sponsor must then lobby committee and floor leaders in both houses to convince them that holding hearings and a vote on the proposal is worth

---

*As described in Chapter 2, an amendment can also be proposed if two-thirds of the states petition Congress to call a constitutional convention. The fact that this route has never been taken is testimony to the high transaction costs—and unclear payoffs—associated with it.

the investment of scarce time on their agendas. While it is difficult even to secure a vote on a proposed amendment, the supermajority rule makes this vote tougher still to win. Except in rare circumstances in American political history, getting two-thirds support in both houses requires bipartisan agreement and it has always necessitated building a coalition across much of the American ideological spectrum. Backers of an amendment may have to bargain with reluctant legislators, compromising on critical details of the language. It certainly entails a major organizational effort, backed by displays of public support that promise that the proposed amendment has a good chance of winning eventual ratification.

The recent history of a proposed constitutional ban on flag burning shows that even when an effort to amend the Constitution is well organized and popular, securing enough votes in Congress is no easy trick. As discussed in Chapter 5, the 1989 Supreme Court case that struck down a Texas ban on flag desecration led to a widely supported effort to place the ban in the Constitution. The proposed amendment soon gathered the necessary two-thirds majority in the House of Representatives. Yet senators, perhaps because their longer terms insulate them against electoral forces, have been less supportive. In the run up to the 2006 elections, the proposed amendment failed on a 66–34 vote, one short of the necessary Senate supermajority. A poll taken at the time showed that it was favored by a 56 to 40 percent margin among American adults, a level of support that is perhaps not high enough to ensure ratification by the states if and when it clears the hurdle of the U.S. Senate.[6]

This second stage of the process, ratification, also comes with high transaction costs. To ratify an amendment proposed by Congress, three-fourths of the state legislatures must support it (or, in the path taken only in Twenty-first Amendment's ratification, special conventions called by three-fourths of the states must back it). Essentially, the proponents of an amendment must surmount the hurdles that they overcame in Congress thirty-eight more times, winning majority votes in states with diverse political cultures and different forms of legislative organization. Broad national support is no guarantee of victory at this stage. As Chapter 4 details, the Equal Rights Amendment received overwhelming support in Congress and quickly won victories in many state legislatures across the country. But six years after its ratification drive began, the ERA stalled with support from thirty-five states, agonizingly close to victory but caught up in state political debates over abortion rights. Because constitutional amendments must succeed in varied political venues and often over an extended period of time, many reform campaigns that begin with overwhelming support eventually fail.

Yet the Framers' barriers are not the only roadblocks to reform; anyone wishing to change the U.S. political system must also solve collective action dilemmas. First, all those who agree that the old system is broken must coordinate on the way to fix it. If reform leaders can agree, motivating their followers becomes the next challenge. One clear problem that anyone trying to turn a popular idea into a well-organized movement needs to overcome is the incentive that sympathetic supporters have to free ride. Voters may be open to an idea, but unwilling to contribute money to a ratification campaign or spend their own time rallying support for it. They may simply sit on the sidelines and wait for someone else to exert the effort, because political reforms rarely

Enthusiasm about Arnold Schwarzenegger, who is not a "natural born citizen," prompted some supporters to call for a constitutional amendment that would allow immigrants who had become citizens to run for the nation's highest office (and perhaps take their place on Mt. Rushmore, as this political cartoon suggests). Yet because no organized group has a direct stake in pushing hard for this reform, it met the same quiet end as many other apparently popular ideas for amending the Constitution.

promise a huge payoff to all of their many backers. Various political entrepreneurs have organized membership groups to overcome this problem by gathering together citizens who care deeply about one area of reform, winning some notable successes. Direct Legislation Leagues in many states were key in importing the initiative process from Switzerland and spreading it across the United States in the early twentieth century. Today, groups like Common Cause and the League of Women Voters push for "good government" reforms such as campaign finance laws, and the contributors to U.S. Term Limits have successfully enacted and maintained term limits on many state legislators. Still, these groups face the constant challenge of keeping their members active and engaged on issues that have little concrete impact on most peoples' daily lives. If the support for change is a mile wide but an inch deep, we can expect little to happen.

This logic may have doomed the most recent attempt to remove the Constitution's requirement (Article II, Section 1) that the president be a "natural born" citizen. To most modern Americans, this provision adopted at the time of the Founding may seem anachronistic, and there are few apparent reasons to prevent naturalized citizens from running for the office. But while an amendment to eliminate this qualification for office might ultimately succeed, no organized group has a strong incentive to campaign for such an amendment. One moment of hope for this cause came after Arnold Schwarzenegger, who was born in Austria but became a U.S. citizen in 1983, was elected governor of California. A group of supporters capitalized on his early popularity by running a few television ads in his home state advocating the change, and Sen. Orrin Hatch introduced a constitutional amendment that would allow it.[7] Yet the movement quickly fizzled, and the proposed amendment has gone nowhere. No narrow group has an incentive to push for it, and the vast numbers of voters who might support it have every incentive to free ride.

A final barrier to change is erected by American voters, who often hesitate to take the fundamental and universal step of amending the Constitution, even when an idea seems personally appealing. Public opinion on the issue of gay marriage illustrates this tendency. In a 2004 national poll, 55 percent of Americans said that they felt same-sex marriage should be illegal. Yet when they were asked about a constitutional ban on gay marriage, only 38 percent said they would support it, while 58 percent preferred to leave the issue up to the states.[8] The American public can be reluctant to alter their foundational document even for momentarily popular causes.

Combined, these forces create a **status quo bias** in U.S. political institutions. The system fundamentally favors a continuation of its current design, making deviation from the basic blueprint difficult. Building stability into political institutions is reasonable, since they are intended, among other things, to stabilize power relationships and to make deals durable enough for people to make them in the first place. Much the same

appraisal can be made for other mature democracies, but this bias is abnormally strong for
the U.S. political system, with its separated
branches and comparatively weaker political
parties. It is not automatically a conservative
bias, placing as many obstacles in the path of efforts to enact term limits (usually favored by
conservative voters) as it does in the way of campaign finance reforms (backed most strongly
by liberals). Rather, it is a bias against adopting
new institutions and in favor of preserving old
ones, regardless of their ideological tenor.

Reforms That Stop Short of Constitutional Change

This status quo bias still exists, though not as
strongly, for the rules that govern American
politics but are not so fundamental as to be
enshrined in the Constitution. Changing a
statute, regulation, or an internal rule of Congress can be easier than amending the Constitution, with fewer steps required and less
reluctance expected from voters or legislators.
This does not mean, however, that reformers
can simply scale down their ambitions to ensure their success. The system's typical checks
and balances apply here, especially those possessed by the judicial branch. The fundamental
dilemma is that if reformers stop short of
amending the Constitution, those charged with
interpreting the Constitution can stop a reform in its tracks.

Although many barriers make it very difficult to amend the Constitution, one
issue in American history inflamed public passion so much that it led to two successful amendments. The Eighteenth Amendment imposed Prohibition in 1919,
blocking the sale of beer, wine, and liquor and leading to scenes like this one, in
which New York police officers poured liquor confiscated in a raid into the sew-
ers. When it was repealed by the Twenty-First Amendment in 1933, readers of
New York's *Daily Mirror* rejoiced.

As Part II of this book demonstrated, anyone who has an idea for a bill faces considerable difficulties convincing Congress to turn it into a law, pressuring the president to sign it, and lobbying the federal bureaucracy to implement it in a particular
way. Nothing in this process is simple, with the legislative and executive branches able
to put a check on radical policy change. Still, compared with amending the Constitution, the obstacles to passing a statute are much less imposing; Congressional vote
thresholds are lower, and states need not give their assent. The key difference, though,
is the additional check possessed by the judicial branch. Even if a law is passed by
Congress and signed by the president, federal judges may throw it out—or invalidate
some portion of it—by ruling that it is unconstitutional.

The intervention of the judicial branch occurs frequently in American politics. As
we have seen, two key parts of the BCRA reforms have been thrown out by the

Supreme Court. The underlying basis for these decisions was the reasoning, set forth in the 1976 *Buckley v. Valeo* Supreme Court decision, that political spending represents an exercise of constitutionally protected speech. This famous case not only established an important precedent, it also (as Chapter 11 shows) invalidated half of the victories that had seemed to be won by the major campaign finance reform law passed just two years before.

The 1974 amendments to the Federal Election Campaign Act together formed a comprehensive approach to constraining the influence of money on American politics by setting limits both on the amount of money that candidates could raise and on the sums that candidates and their allies could spend. In *Buckley*, the Supreme Court upheld the caps on contributions, but not on spending. Under the Court's interpretation, candidates were allowed to spend as much as they could raise, millionaire candidates were free to give their campaigns unlimited sums, and interest groups could spend money for or against candidates so long as they acted independently. In the words of a leading campaign finance expert, "Congress's grand scheme of regulation was savaged."[9] Although reformers appeared to win a major victory by passing the 1974 amendments in the wake of the Watergate scandal, half of their statutory changes disappeared as Supreme Court justices assumed their roles as interpreters and defenders of the Constitution.

Federalism as an Opportunity for Reform

One more avenue to reform—blocked by fewer obstacles, but reaching fewer people—is opened by America's federal system. The states serve as key **laboratories for reform.** States control their own governing structures, providing their citizens the opportunity to change politics on a smaller scale and giving everyone else the chance to observe the effects of a reform without risking it themselves. Activists have seized upon this opening just as political observers have celebrated the patchwork of policy that it can create. In a famous passage from his 1932 *New State Ice Co v. Liebmann* decision, Supreme Court Justice Louis Brandeis wrote, "It is one of the happy incidents of the Federal System that a single, courageous state may, if its citizens choose, serve as a laboratory and try novel social and economic experimentation without risk to the rest of the country."

Reformers have won many victories when they experiment first with the political system of one state, and then seek to spread their ideas across the country. As Chapter 4 noted, the national struggle to give women the right to vote won its first victories in the states. Suffragists, the well-organized groups led by women such as Elizabeth Cady Stanton and Susan B. Anthony, first secured the franchise in the territory of Wyoming in 1869. They found much success in the West, where women received the right to vote in Colorado (the first state success) in 1893, and in Utah, Idaho, and then Washington over the next two decades. This piecemeal approach to reform then spread eastward, putting ever more pressure on Congress to pass the women's suffrage amendment that had been introduced each session for decades. The House and Senate finally passed the proposal in 1918, and when the Nineteenth Amendment was ratified two years later, the national government had followed the states in allowing women to vote.

Not every reform that begins its journey in the states sees national success. In the early twentieth century, many western states and a few others began America's experiment with direct democracy by giving citizens the right to initiate legislation by petition, throw out laws written by legislators, and recall elected officials. These reforms have remained popular in the states that adopted them—and, as the box on the following page shows, served as springboards to further reform—but their spread slowed down greatly after 1918. Only five states have enacted direct democracy measures in the past ninety years, and the idea has never gained serious traction at the federal level. Legislative term limits are also an idea that, after an initial rapid proliferation across the country, have not been adopted widely and are clearly stalled at the national level. Not surprisingly the states can sometimes be a graveyard for reforms as well. In many ways, this makes sense. At the heart of Brandeis's reasoning is the idea that experiments can go awry, and that voters in other states and the nation as a whole can judge whether or not a vanguard reform is worth replicating in their government. Federalism provides an opportunity for reforms to succeed—and to fail.

Four Stories of Reform and Collection Action

Despite all the obstacles in the way of changing our political system, the American people have often fought to overcome them. Some of these reform movements have transformed our democracy, most have gone nowhere, and many have met with partial success. Nearly all of them can be thought of as attempts to draw upon the apparatus of the Framers' toolkit, described in Chapter 1, to solve collective action problems. Our introductory framework can also be used to evaluate the impact of these changes to determine whether or not they truly deserve to be judged "reforms."

Candidate Nominations: Parties Solving Their Coordination Problems

Whenever an office comes open that the parties compete for in American politics, there is no shortage of people willing to stand as their party's standard bearer. We live in—as one book on candidate emergence put it—*The United States of Ambition.*[10] But this abundance of volunteers creates a dilemma. How do the parties focus their electoral supporters on just one candidate, instead of seeing their coalition fracture into many small groups backing each ambitious contestant? In the language of collective action, parties and their members face a coordination problem. Even when all of the voters in a party want to see one of its candidates win office, they face the challenge of figuring out which one has the most support and cooperating with each other to cast all of their ballots for the chosen standard bearer. In a large-scale democracy such as the United States, party adherents cannot coordinate their action through personal communication; some sort of institutional solution is needed.

Over our nation's history, parties have experimented with three different solutions to this coordination problem. All of these methods of designating a formal party

Direct Democracy as a Springboard to Further Reform

After turn-of-the-century Progressive reformers pushed for direct democracy provisions to take power out of the hands of state legislatures, their victories eased the way to future reforms. One of these provisions, the citizen initiative now allowed in twenty-four states, gives anyone the power to propose new laws. Of course, successful initiatives are authored far more often by interest groups than by everyday citizens. It takes organizational might in order to collect enough signatures to put an initiative on the ballot and to fund the campaign for its passage. But even though initiatives do not simply amplify the "voice of the people," they offer someone other than current elected officials the chance to enact new laws.

This is especially helpful to reform causes when a new law directly threatens the interests of lawmakers. The path to legislative approval is quite difficult for laws like term limits, which throw officeholders out of office when their time is up, or campaign finance regulations that make it harder for politicians to raise money. By opening up another route for such proposals, the initiative process greatly improves their chances of becoming law. One example of a reform that was stifled in the legislature, but which succeeded through direct democracy, is Colorado's "Give

A Vote to Every Legislator (G.A.V.E.L.)" amendment. Before this initiative passed in 1988, the majority party ruled the state legislature with an iron fist, able to kill bills in committees without taking a vote and to keep them from reaching the floor of either house. Minority party members complained, but it should come as no surprise that majority leaders stifled their reform proposals in the legislature. Things did not change until a coalition of twenty-three interest groups—many of which were at odds with the Republican majority—put the G.A.V.E.L. initiative on the ballot. It passed by a 72 to 28 percent margin, stripping the majority party of its ability to control the legislative agenda.

Without the initiative process, such a change would have been next to impossible in Colorado. Across the states, recent research has shown, direct democracy has eased the way to the adoption of limits on how much anyone could contribute to legislative candidates or to parties. And as the map illustrates, states with initiative provisions have been much more likely to pass term limits on their legislators. Voters in nearly every state that allows initiatives backed term limits, although courts in four of these states later invalidated the measures. Where reform groups lacked the ability to go directly to the ballot, term

nominee are examples of "agenda control," one of the design mechanisms introduced in our first chapter's description of the Framers' toolkit (pages 26–34). In each of them, some portion of a party's membership helps set the agenda of options available to general election voters. This solves the coordination problem by focusing all of the party's electoral resources on one nominee, so that party members do not waste their

limits almost never succeeded. In only three states did legislators vote to limit their own terms. In two of these, Utah and Idaho, they did so facing the pressure of planned initiatives, and later repealed their term limits before they took effect. Louisiana's is the only legislature that has term limited itself in the absence of direct democracy provisions.

States That Have Imposed Term Limits and That Allow Citizen Initiatives

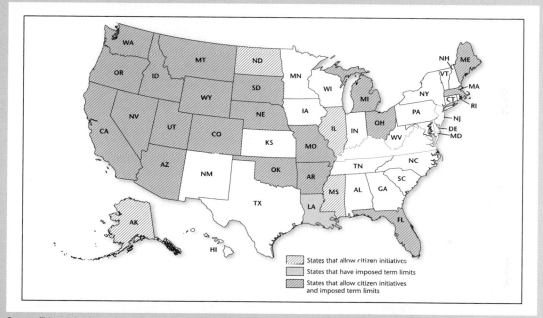

Sources: This map is adapted from the list of term limit laws compiled by the National Conference of State Legislatures and available at www.ncsl.org/programs/legismgt/about/states.htm. It includes all states that initially passed term limits, even if those limits have since been repealed by legislatures or invalidated by courts. It is also adapted from the list of states with citizen initiatives compiled by the Initiative and Referendum Institute and available at www.iandrinstitute.org/statewide_i&r.htm.

Sources: John Straayer, *The Colorado General Assembly,* 2nd ed. (Boulder: University Press of Colorado, 2000); John Pippen, Shaun Bowler, and Todd Donovan, "Election Reform and Direct Democracy: Campaign Finance Regulations in the American States," *American Politics Research* 30, no. 6 (2002): 559–585.

Notes: There are six states in which term limits passed but were subsequently either overturned by courts (Massachusetts, Oregon, Washington, and Wyoming) or repealed by legislatures (Idaho and Utah). Only in Oregon, from 1998 through 2001, did limits go into effect by removing veteran members before the limits were overturned. Term limits are due to go into effect in Nevada in the 2010 elections.

votes by working at cross-purposes. But it comes at the clear price of giving tremendous power to those with authority to set the agenda, and it imposes less obvious costs as well. This brief history of the various reforms made to the way that American parties choose their nominees—a story told more thoroughly in Chapter 12—considers the different types of costs brought by attempts to solve the coordination problem.

The first method devised to nominate presidential candidates, an innovation that the Federalist and the Democratic-Republican parties used in the early years of the republic, was the congressional caucus. To coordinate the behavior of their voters, party leaders elected to Congress would pick a presidential nominee. This imposition of elite authority over mass action comes quite close to being a command solution, one in which a single actor is given dictatorial power to command the actions of others. It leads to coordination, to be sure, but also imposes high conformity costs—the sacrifices that come with having to abide by the decisions of others—by forcing voters in a party to back a nominee whom they did not choose. By placing this crucial decision in the hands of a congressional caucus, party leaders also deprive themselves of the opportunity to test the mass appeal of potential nominees.

These twin flaws—the perceived illegitimacy of elite authority in the young democracy and the caucus's lack of responsiveness to public sentiment—contributed to the downfall of the caucus system after the presidential election of 1824. Since the Democratic-Republican Party had grown dominant by this time, securing the party's nomination appeared tantamount to being elected president. This gave members of Congress tremendous power, and seemed to hand the presidency to William Crawford, the caucus nominee that year. Yet the February 14, 1824, caucus was attended by only 66 members of Congress, with the remaining 195 representatives refusing to attend because they supported one of many other factional leaders who aspired to the presidency that year but lacked Crawford's plurality support.[11] In the end, four powerful Democratic-Republicans ran in the general election. The caucus nominee proved to be ordinary voters' least favored option as Crawford finished last in the popular vote. The plurality leader, in both popular and Electoral College voting, was the charismatic retired general Andrew Jackson. Congress misjudged popular sentiment, but because no candidate won a majority outright, the House of Representatives had the final say and coalesced behind second-place finisher John Quincy Adams.

With Jackson and his many followers enraged at the way that **"King Caucus"** denied him the nomination and the House denied him ultimate victory the Democratic-Republican coalition splintered and the shift toward a new method of nomination began. Jackson's ally, Martin Van Buren, channeled the anger of Old Hickory's supporters into the first true mass party organization, the Democratic Party. Its pyramid of state committees and local clubs helped elect Jackson in 1828 and came together in the first national party convention to nominate him again in 1832. Compared to the caucus, the **nominating convention** ostensibly broadened the group of party members who would set the agenda for everyone else. Local organizers attended these more democratic events, and their participation helped party leaders better gauge the public support for various candidates. Party conventions were soon established in nearly every state, completing the rebellion against King Caucus.

Yet while the convention system was initially "regarded as a great triumph for the plain people over the aristocracy," in the words of one contemporary scholar, soon "[c]onditions developed that were so intolerable as to arouse indignation and protest."[12] Put in terms of the collective action framework, as the century wore on and some parties transitioned from mass organizations to tightly controlled machines,

After losing the battle for the presidency in 1924, Gen. Andrew Jackson won his war against the caucus system of nomination and ultimately won the office that he felt "King Caucus" and Congress had denied him. In this contemporary cartoon, Jackson is shown battling the "caucus curs."

conventions veered toward again becoming "command" solutions to the coordination problem. This occurred because party conventions were private functions, initially unregulated by government. The seemingly democratic mechanism of the convention was open to manipulation by the party organizations that maintained complete control over its operation. For many decades, bribery at a state convention did not constitute a legal offense and the delegates, selected in local primaries or caucuses, were not guaranteed the right to vote by ballot. Party machines and bosses could dictate nominees and "[b]oth sneaks and sluggers were employed as the occasion dictated."

The current system of nomination used in the United States—choosing candidates through a primary election or, less frequently, a caucus attended by everyday voters—came as a result of the Progressive Era crusade against corrupt conventions. Turn-of-the-century Progressive leaders were sincerely outraged by the control that party

Presidential nominating conventions used to be dramatic, high-stakes events as the vote to pick the nominee stretched long into the night. Today, they are made-for-television spectacles planned to boost the campaign of a nominee chosen many months before, and they sometimes put even those attending them to sleep.

bosses exerted over conventions, but they also saw that the old system stifled their own political ambitions. They recognized that a direct vote by party members, organized and regulated by government, could clean up corrupted nominations while at the same time improving their own chances of winning a nomination. "Fighting Bob" LaFollette's Progressives led Wisconsin in jettisoning the convention and replacing it with the nation's first mandatory primary in 1903, which in turn helped nominate LaFollette and many of his allies. By the time that California adopted the primary in 1909, and then elected Progressive Hiram Johnson to office the next year, a total of fifteen states required primaries.[13] By midcentury, every state had adopted primaries or caucuses to nominate candidates for state and federal office, providing an infrastructure that became ever more important in nominating presidential candidates through the 1960s and 1970s.

Today, parties use primaries for nearly all state and national nominations. While the details of who can vote in them and how ballots are structured vary in critically important ways, the collective action implications of all these systems can be analyzed together. Compared with the congressional caucus, with conventions, or with the systems that most European nations use to give party leaders power over nominations, a primary is much further removed from a command solution. Party members, at least those who care to participate in a primary, set their own agenda for the general election. This democratization of the process also provides a useful gauge of all candidates' popularity. Still, primary elections do impose some conformity costs. In 2008, primary voters who were energized by Hillary Clinton's campaign had to support Barack Obama if they wanted a Democrat to win in November, just as followers of Mike Huckabee and Mitt Romney were forced to unite with John McCain's backers in hopes of securing a Republican victory.

The major challenges that primary campaigns create come through the transaction costs that they impose. State and local governments spend millions of dollars to administer primary and caucus elections, the financial cost of keeping them fair and open. Candidates themselves often spend far more to compete in these contests, and the "money primary" that this creates can tilt the system toward favoring those who are able to raise large sums or to fund their own campaigns. Finally, if party elites in conventions or legislative caucuses pick nominees with an eye toward winning in the general election, then selecting them instead through a primary imposes an ideological transaction cost on nominees. Primary candidates have to take positions outside of the political center to please the party faithful, while those seeking to please party leaders would have an incentive to position themselves as the most moderate, electable candidate. While none of these are convincing arguments to justify a return to the nominating systems of the past, they do point out that a party's current solution to its coordination problem brings with it collection action trade-offs.

Term Limits as a Way Out of the Prisoner's Dilemma

Legislative **term limits** are an ancient idea—practiced in Athenian democracy and advocated by Aristotle—that has been revived in modern America. Term limits mandate turnover in a legislature, preventing representatives from running for reelection after they have held office for a specified period of time, typically six or eight years. These limits universally enforce a preference that many voters have for a government run by temporary servants whose tenure is cut short, no matter how well or poorly they serve the public. Because they intentionally sever the electoral connection between voters and their representatives, term limits can be thought of as a solution to one collective action problem that leads to another dilemma.

For voters wishing to be represented by a series of new legislators who bring fresh perspectives into office but don't stay there long, term limits provide a way out of the prisoner's dilemma that they face. Suppose a voter in one district has this preference. He can voice it by voting against his incumbent legislator once she has served a few terms in office. But during her tenure, this legislator has probably built up seniority on a committee, a reputation within the legislature, and the lawmaking experience necessary to deliver policies that the voter desires and certainly some special projects for the district. Voting the incumbent out would sacrifice all of these advantages. Another voter in a neighboring district might also favor turnover in the abstract, but faces the same concrete quandary. Both voters would like to elect someone new to office, but each worries that the other will defect from this plan and continue to vote for the current legislator. If either voter stands on principle and votes against the incumbent, his neighbor could reap the rewards of reelecting the only legislator in the area with much seniority, who could then deliver the lion's share of special projects to the district. In the end, both will probably play it safe, keep their incumbents in office, and grumble.

This is the crux of a prisoner's dilemma; neither voter can risk choosing his most-preferred option because he will suffer when the other voter reaps the rewards of deviating from this strategy. The potential path out of it follows the common pattern of solutions to prisoner's dilemmas. Term limits use the power of governmental command to bind all voters together in regularly dumping their incumbents, ensuring that no district can defect to build up its legislator's seniority and influence. They coerce cooperation, once a majority of voters across the political system decide that they want turnover for turnover's sake.

Thinking about term limits this way provides a reasonable response to one argument often made against them. Politicians ranging from former California Assembly Speaker Antonio Villaraigosa to fictional *West Wing* President Josiah "Jed" Bartlet have asserted that "[w]e have term limits, and they are called elections."[14] Certainly, voters in a district can use elections to limit the terms of their own incumbents, but this amounts to unilateral disarmament if voters in other districts do not follow suit. Voters in some districts will use elections to maintain senior legislators in office and keep their interests influential, unless there is an enforceable agreement to limit everyone's term.

Of course, the language of collective action was rarely used by the modern campaign for term limits that began in the late 1980s. During this decade, dissatisfaction with Congress and state legislatures mounted in the wake of a number of scandals, but the voters—perhaps because they faced the prisoner's dilemma—kept reelecting their own incumbents at high rates. Groups of activists across the country saw an opportunity to take advantage of the public's momentary "throw the bums out!" mood to push for a reform that had been enacted in the Athenian legislature and in the first American Congress under the Articles of Confederation. Legislative term limit proposals came from a liberal group in the state of Washington, and from conservative activists everywhere else.

Initially, many of these were grassroots groups run by people like Oregon health club owner Frank Eisenzimmer, who led the drive to pass his state's "L.I.M.I.T.S.: Let Incumbents Mosey Into The Sunset" initiative in 1992 (see box "The Health Club Owners Who Changed Oregon Politics"). Very soon, however, a national group dubbed U.S. Term Limits professionalized the movement, spending money raised from conservative donors on initiative campaigns in many states. Their efforts met with considerable success. Twenty states imposed term limits on their legislators between 1990 and 1996. At the time, the movement seemed poised for national success as well. Some state laws contained provisions limiting the number of terms for which members of the U.S. Congress from these states could serve. George Will, a prominent national political commentator, published *Restoration: Congress, Term Limits, and the Recovery of Deliberative Democracy* in 1992, and the "Contract with America" that Republican congressional candidates pledged to in 1994 called for a vote on federal term limits.

Since that time of promise for term limit proponents, however, very little has gone right. When the constitutional amendment that Newt Gingrich and others had promised came to the House floor in March 1995, the vote split mostly along party lines and, with 227 votes for to 204 votes against, it fell far short of the two-thirds supermajority that amendments must capture. In May of that year, the Supreme Court ruled in *U.S. Term Limits, Inc. v. Thornton* that states did not have the authority to limit the terms of members of Congress, because doing so would create an inconsistent patchwork of qualifications for office. These twin blows effectively ended the drive for federal term limits. In the states, the movement stalled after its initial burst of victories, with some of these gains eroding through the check that state courts possess on their own governments. Four state supreme courts threw out term limit initiatives, primarily on the technical grounds that they should have been passed as state constitutional amendments rather than statutes. Two state legislatures that had enacted limits, Utah and Idaho, later decided that cutting short their own terms was not such an appealing idea, after all.[15]

While their spread across the nation appears to be halted, term limits are now in effect in fourteen states ranging from Florida to Maine to Ohio to California. This

The Health Club Owners Who Changed Oregon Politics

Although they owned competing gyms in the small town of Gresham, Oregon, Don McIntire and Frank Eisenzimmer cooperated to bring big changes to the structure of Oregon's government. In the early 1990s, each led a winning initiative drive that flexed the muscles of the potent anti-tax and anti-incumbent movements. Each demonstrated that everyday citizens with little record of political success could achieve big victories through smart, dedicated organizing efforts made at the right time and place.

McIntire's career had included stints as a disc jockey, an assistant city engineer, a health club owner, and a losing candidate for the Oregon state senate in 1980. When his personal candidacy failed, he became involved in initiative campaigns aimed at shrinking the size of government. After failed attempts at the state level and local successes, he ran into Eisenzimmer (who used to work out at McIntire's gym) when both were collecting signatures for ballot measures in 1990.

Oregon activist Don McIntire during an interview on Portland's KOIN-TV.

They worked together on what became Measure 5 on that year's ballot, an initiative that proposed cutting property taxes in half, saving residents billions of dollars a year but putting funding for schools and other programs in jeopardy. McIntire took the lead, and took the brunt of criticism from political opponents who called him "a ding-a-ling" who "knows school financing like my dead dog does," and compared his tactics to those of Bolshevik revolutionary Leon Trotsky. But McIntire relished his role, and had the last laugh when Measure 5 passed in November.

Following this victory, Don McIntire receded from the political scene in order to spend more time running his health club, allowing Frank Eisenzimmer to take charge of the movement Measure 5 had created. After giving up his dream of becoming the next Mr. Oregon bodybuilding champion, Eisenzimmer had worked in a grocery store, in a cabinet shop, as a firefighter, and finally by running his own gym. He seemed to get the same sort of adrenaline rush from politics that he did from weightlifting, and certainly was no pushover. When Oregon's legislature voted down a term limits proposal in 1991, Eisenzimmer was waiting in the wings with his own initiative, and declared "This is going to be a slam-dunk." He led the "L.I.M.I.T.S.: Let Incumbents Mosey Into The Sunset" campaign to victory the next year. After state legislators moved to repeal term limits five years later, Eisenzimmer reemerged to declare "They're not only hypocritical, they're not very bright, because they're not going to pass this." He turned out to be right. In the end,

(box continues on next page)

The Health Club Owners Who Changed Oregon Politics (continued)

Oregon's term limits law was overturned by the state Supreme Court, but not until after Eisenzimmer's initiative had gone into effect for two elections and ended the careers of many incumbent politicians.

On their face, these stories may seem at odds with this chapter's focus on the ways in which collective action problems can discourage individual action. That logic provides an explanation of how most people behave in the realm of politics, but gives no moral prescription for how everyone should act. Many citizens ignore their incentives to free ride, and instead put great efforts toward changing American government. A few of them succeed. Those who are passionately committed to a cause—whether or not it is one we all believe in—often provide the impetus for reforms that would otherwise be doomed by collective action dilemmas. The paradox of individual participation is that people can provide themselves with collective goods through politics only if they work for their provision for reasons other than enjoying the goods. This is why moral commitment was included as an asset in the earlier list of the advantages and disadvantages enjoyed by different groups. It is also why American politics is filled with colorful, potentially irrational, and often successful reformers such as Eisenzimmer and McIntire.

Sources: Barnes C. Ellis, "Measure 5 Triumph Converts Gadfly into Gad-Elephant," *The Oregonian,* November 8, 1990, C5, Phil Stanford, "Just Don't Call Him Late for Dinner," *The Oregonian,* November 5, 1990, Jeff Mapes, "Oregon Defeats Bid to Limit Congressional Terms, *The Oregonian,* March 19, 1991, B10, and Steve Suo, "State Senate Wants Voters to Ease Term Limits," *The Oregonian,* May 6, 1997, A1.

limited application has provided scholars and citizens alike the chance to observe and evaluate their effects. The limits did indeed bring the increased turnover that they promised, sometimes preventing as many as half of a house's members from running for reelection. Yet when they are "termed out," very few of these politicians simply disappear from politics. In every state, they run for other offices or seek other political jobs at surprisingly high rates. This fundamentally changes the relationship between voters as principals and legislators as agents. When politicians cannot run for reelection, they lose their incentive to serve the voters in their district, and instead have reason to please the next principal for whom they plan to work. Whether that principal is a new constituency, a governor from whom they want a job, or an interest group that they plan to lobby for, this shift in the incentives of legislators can hurt the interests of the voters who first elected them. Research shows that term limited legislators spend less time getting to know voters in their district, working for constituent interests, or responding to their preferences on tough votes.

The steep spikes in turnover brought by the implementation of term limit laws also impose transaction costs on legislatures. Much institutional knowledge is lost at once, and the deliberative processes that houses have worked out over generations are disrupted. The most costly disruption, many studies have shown, affects the legislature's interaction with the executive branch. Power shifts greatly toward the governor and state bureaucracies, as legislatures do less to scrutinize the governor's budget proposals and oversee the administration of laws by state agencies.[16] This jeopardizes the legislature's role as a check on the executive, the mechanism for maintaining the separation of powers that James Madison argued so forcefully for in *Federalist* No. 51. Whether it was intended or not, term limits in the states have threatened the legislature's role as a co-equal branch. Perhaps that is why the Framers, after observing that term limits had weakened Congress in the Articles of Confederation, kept them out of the Constitution.

Attempts to Fight Free Riding and Increase Voter Turnout

Because elections are meant to measure the desires of the electorate, and since accurately reflecting these desires is necessary for perfect representation to take place, the U.S. political system would work best if every eligible voter turned out on Election Day. Yet accomplishing this collective goal requires actions by individuals who face incentives to free ride. It is undeniably costly to take time out of one's day to cast a ballot, and the chances that any single vote swings an election are minute. Everyone certainly shares a stake in holding participatory

In an attempt at reforming American government through voluntary, individual actions rather than a mandatory law, some members of Congress took the "Term Limits Pledge" when they first ran for office during the 1990s, promising to step down after three or four terms. When U.S. representative George Nethercutt of Washington, a member of the "Republican Revolution" class of 1994, broke his pledge, U.S. Term Limits ran television ads attacking him as the "Weasel King." But he won reelection in 2000, demonstrating once again the ineffectiveness of voluntary reform efforts.

elections; if nobody turned out, government would cease to be representative and legitimate. But because a hesitant voter can rely on others who share his views to vote, he can get away with shirking his democratic duty. As Chapter 11 notes, it is perfectly logical for a single citizen to free ride on the democratic participation of others, leading to a classic collective action problem in which individuals enjoy the benefits of everyone else's effort while failing to contribute themselves.

The classic solution would be for the government to step in and enforce behavior, just as the government does in requiring everyone who meets certain criteria to pay taxes or to register for the draft. Some countries such as Australia, Belgium, and Italy make voter turnout mandatory. The United States has never seriously moved in that direction. In fact, as Chapter 4's coverage of the civil right movement shows, the most consequential steps taken by government for most of American history have been to suppress, rather than to increase, voter turnout. Why have there been no reform campaigns to make voting mandatory, or to offer a selective benefit by having election officials pay everyone who turns out?

At the level of theory, one might argue that this imposes high conformity costs on citizens who simply do not want to vote. But the more practical reason that these potential reforms have not been pursued with greater energy is that while full turnout might be good for the nation as a whole, it is never clearly in the interests of any faction with the organizational might to push for it. Unlike the collection of taxes, full turnout does not bring in trillions of dollars for Congress and the president to spend. Unlike the draft, full turnout does not provide the armed forces with soldiers in a time of large-scale war. Neither major party would likely benefit from full voter turnout: Research on political participation indicates that although nonvoters differ from voters in their demographic characteristics, they generally share the preferences of those who turn out in major elections. Since no narrow group would derive a discrete benefit from full participation in elections, none has a direct incentive to take up the fight. In effect, a collective action dilemma lies in the way of solving the free rider problem that plagues voter turnout.

Our national and state governments have taken some relatively minor steps toward increasing voter participation. Some, such as the federal Motor Voter Law described in Chapter 11, on page 523, and the vote-by-mail elections held in Oregon, aim to discourage free riding by making registration and voting as easy as possible. The "I Voted!" stickers that many local election officials hand out are a selective benefit akin to the coffee mugs and tote bags that PBS stations give out during pledge breaks, designed to reward their proud wearers individually for contributing to the collective good. While any effort to increase voter turnout is certainly laudable, American government has shied away from the sorts of larger steps, such as mandating turnout or automatically registering eligible voters, which help many European nations achieve much higher levels of participation than in the United States.

Instead, the American approach has largely been to delegate the task of turning out voters to political parties and interest groups. While none of these organizations has a stake in increasing the turnout rate overall, each has a profound incentive to bring its own supporters to the polls. The grassroots efforts of parties, labor unions, trade organizations, and ideological movements are all designed to stop their adherents from free riding. Get-out-the-vote drives decrease the costs of turnout by informing people about elections and offering rides to polls. They also increase the penalty for free riding when campaign volunteers, constantly checking the sign-in sheets at a polling place, knock on targeted voters' doors until they cast a ballot. Throughout our history, these faction-based turn-out drives have been extraordinarily successful, and new technologies allow groups to be even more focused on isolating and mobilizing their follow-ers. Major campaigns now routinely use **micro-targeting** databases that combine voter rolls with credit card purchase information and even gro-cery store savings club records in order to identify potential supporters, then send volunteers out with networked PDAs directing them straight to a tar-geted voter's doorstep.

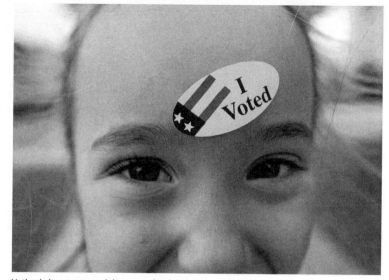

Voting is its own reward, but some local registrars provide an extra selective benefit by handing out stickers at the polls so that anyone who turns out can show off their demo-cratic participation to family, friends, coworkers, and neighbors. During the 2006 election in Rhode Island, this five-year-old girl accompanied her mother to the polling place and proudly wore her sticker.

America's decentralized approach to voter mobilization works for those allied with a well-organized party or interest group, but what about every-one else? When the task of turning out voters is delegated to a set of agents whose incentives are not aligned with those of voters overall, there is a risk that agency loss may result. No group has an incentive to mobilize truly independent voters, mak-ing it more likely that they will free ride. If the parties or interests are evenly balanced, then each will mobilize its own supporters in equal numbers. This fits with Madison's notion of setting faction against faction, but can create problems when one faction is locally dominant. In this case, a status quo bias will emerge because the party in power, which is better positioned to recruit volunteers and raise resources for a mobilization drive, can turn out its adherents at a higher rate and capture even more political power. The reliance on parties and interest groups to pay the price of discouraging free riding on Election Day comes with potential costs to electoral equity.

Seeking the Line-Item Veto to Avoid the Tragedy of the Commons

Members of Congress have authority over the entire nation's budget, but each member has a direct electoral incentive to guide as much of this money as possible to his or her home district. Constituents and local groups constantly come to their representatives with pleas to fund a new post office, to widen an interstate highway, to support a mu-seum, or to pay to advertise a crop grown in their district. If Congress **earmarks** money in the federal budget to pay for one of these projects, district voters receive a big benefit, while only paying a tiny share of the costs because the price tag is spread across all districts. The problem is that because this is such a great deal for each member of Congress, every member wants to make it happen for their own district.

The aggregate effect of 435 representatives' individual decisions is that total spending on earmarks rises dramatically, setting up a classic "tragedy of the commons." Just as herdsmen will overgraze a pasture because each pays hardly any costs for allowing one more cow to feed on it, Congress may overspend when its members are tempted to bring home one more project at little direct cost to their own districts.

Congress spent a total of $17.2 billion on 11,610 earmarked projects in the 2008 fiscal year, according to Citizens Against Government Waste, the leading group that has taken up the crusade against such spending. This includes $3 million for The First Tee, a program designed "[t]o impact the lives of young people by providing learning facilities and educational programs that promote character development and life enhancing values through the game of golf"; $2 million for the Charles B. Rangel Center for Public Service; and $188,000 for the Lobster Institute in Maine, which maintains the "Lobstercam" Web site.[17] Groups like Citizens Against Government Waste approach ending earmarks by publicizing this spending in an attempt to shame members of Congress into abstaining from it. While a handful of representatives and senators do refuse to pursue money for their districts, hoping for voluntary compliance has largely failed. The logic of the tragedy of the commons explains why. If one legislator alone abstains from spending a portion of the federal budget on his or her own district, the voters there lose out on valuable projects while only a small amount in overall spending has been saved.

A more rational solution is the mandatory, institutional approach of the **line-item veto.** This tool, also called an "item veto," gives a chief executive the authority to cut individual items out of the budget that a legislature passes, while signing the rest of the spending bill into law. A president could use it to veto earmarks, without derailing the entire federal budget. Not surprisingly, this is an example of a "veto" from the Framers' toolkit, a unilateral power to block new policy and preserve the status quo. In this way, it preserves the commons by giving one officeholder who is not tied to any particular district the ability to regulate how much money comes out of the federal treasury. To be sure, the line-item veto would increase the president's influence greatly. But it is also not a bad deal for members of Congress, especially compared to passing a self-imposed ban on earmarks or individually abstaining from them. When the president possesses final authority over each line of spending in appropriations bills, members of Congress are free to load them up with as many earmarks as they please, knowing that they can claim credit for fighting for their district but blame the president when he eventually vetoes the projects.

This may have been part of the strategy motivating Congress's passage, under Newt Gingrich's leadership and in fulfillment of a promise contained in the "Contract with America," of a statute giving the president the line-item veto. The politics of this bill made for strange bedfellows. As Chapter 7 details, when the Republican-led Congress passed the Line Item Veto Act of 1996, President Bill Clinton happily signed it. Over the next two years, Clinton used the new authority that the opposition party had given him to veto eighty-two of the items that they sent him in eleven spending bills. Because one of these items vetoed happened to promise more Medicaid funding for

A primary rationale for the line-item veto passed in 1996 was that it would allow presidents to eliminate spending on inefficient local projects championed by individual members of Congress. Because the Supreme Court struck down the item veto two years later, the federal budget still includes items like the $1.5 million won by Alabama senator Richard Shelby to refurbish the Vulcan Statue (left) in Birmingham, Alabama. Another earmark was the $2 million won by House Ways and Means Committee chair Charles B. Rangel for the "Charles B. Rangel Center for Public Service" (right), which Republican congressman John Campbell lampooned as Rangel's "Monument to Me."

New York City, Mayor Rudolph Giuliani initiated a lawsuit arguing that Congress did not have the authority to give up power in this way to presidents. The Supreme Court agreed in *Clinton v. City of New York* (1998) that because the line-item veto gave the executive branch powers not granted by the Constitution, a constitutional amendment was necessary in order to institute it. Democratic senator Robert Byrd, who had led an earlier suit against the line-item veto, joined Mayor Giuliani in celebrating the decision, while President Clinton and congressional Republicans bemoaned it.[18] These peculiar alignments demonstrate that neither party has a consistent ideological stance on the issue, with positions dictated mostly by every player's institutional role.

The fate of the line-item veto underscores that reform victories can be ephemeral when they stop short of amending the Constitution. But what if the line-item veto had survived judicial review? Would it have solved the tragedy of the commons, without causing any further problems? Some scholarly works[19] on the contribution of earmarks to the smooth operation of legislatures imply that a line-item veto would place high transaction costs on Congress. Including earmarks in a bill, these works argue, is a relatively cheap way to secure the support of hesitant legislators, in effect "greasing the wheels" of Congress. Earmarks serve as a selective benefit offered to members to support a bill containing policies that might cause them to take political heat in their districts. General spending bills could become even more difficult to pass if they were not loaded with concrete, district-specific projects, or if these projects were sure to be vetoed. This potential for an increase in gridlock makes it easier for Congress to ignore presidential requests—most recently made by President George W. Bush in his 2006 State of the Union Address—to try once again to pass a line-item veto in a way that passes constitutional muster.

The Tricky Business of Institutional Reform

All of these stories point out problems in the American political system, the trade-offs associated with proposed solutions to them, and the challenges that must be overcome by any attempt to enact major change. Institutional shortcomings inevitably become targets for reform; some people in every generation want to "reinvent government." Those who believe that particular rules and practices or the system as a whole slight their interests or thwart necessary changes naturally look for alternative arrangements that would redress these problems. But designing effective institutions—ones that accomplish what their designers intend—is tricky business. The political world is so densely interconnected and human beings are so clever at discovering and exploiting opportunities that the full impact of any significant institutional innovation is impossible to predict; every significant change is likely to have unintended and unwanted consequences.

What might happen if one of the reform proposals currently gaining attention comes to fruition? Getting rid of the Electoral College would ensure that whichever presidential candidate wins the popular vote is elected, and shift candidates' focus from a dozen or so "battleground states" to voters all across the nation. But note that in doing so, it would require candidates to raise vastly larger sums to run serious nationwide campaigns, all but dooming our system of voluntary public financing for presidential campaigns. And rather than conducting "retail politics" campaigns in swing states such as New Mexico, Wisconsin, and Virginia, candidates would be forced to market themselves wholesale, spreading their efforts broadly but making few deep connections. These potential side effects should be considered before backing an otherwise reasonable reform. Speculation about the potentially perverse consequences of well-intentioned reforms is important, even if perfect prediction is impossible.

Thinking hard about the logic of collective action can provide hints for anticipating some of the consequences of institutional innovations. Any reform that alters individual incentives changes behavior in predictable ways because in politics most people, most of the time, are engaged in the strategic pursuit of transparent interests—interests that can frustrate the capacity of the community to achieve desired collective goods. Yet those who design institutions can take the interests into account and structure participants' incentives so that the play of interests will yield successful collective action. Any institutional reform whose success requires political actors to routinely ignore their own interests is certain to disappoint. As James Madison observed in *Federalist* No. 51, connecting "the interest of the man . . . with the constitutional rights of the place" was an uppermost concern of the Framers as they fashioned new governmental institutions. Well-informed by both theory and experience, the Framers employed this logic well, an important reason why their work has lasted.

Thus the first task for anyone intent on redesigning institutions involves mapping out how proposed changes would alter incentives and therefore the strategic behavior of political actors. Do the revised rules and reformed institutions tempt politicians to renege on collective pursuits when citizens would want them to cooperate? Or conversely, do they invite their collusion when the citizenry's interests would be best served by healthy competition? Does the reform encourage agents to shirk or in other ways violate their responsibilities to their principals? Proposals for change that do not anticipate at least the obvious strategic responses of those who occupy new or reconfigured offices are thus fundamentally misguided and probably doomed.

Yet when reforms align the incentives of individuals with collective goals—as many have in American history, beginning with the work of the Framers—the benefits that they bring can clearly outweigh any flaws. Success is possible, even if it is not inevitable. The barriers to reform built into our system are designed to help distinguish between ideas that merely strive for laudable goals and plans that wisely harness human nature to achieve their ends. The winnowing process may not be perfect. Still, the overarching design of our political system, with its status quo bias, opportunities for state-level trials, and multiple checks and balances, seems to be suited for our national character. We can love our country and its institutions, but be unafraid of the endeavor to make it better. We can see reform ideas as worth pursuing, debating, often discarding, and sometimes deserving of an experiment. We have built enough obstacles into our political system to slow the pace of radical reforms, both bad ones and good ones, but never to stifle change completely. As long as America lasts, our brief, brilliant, and imperfect Constitution will remain the battlefield for our nation of energetic reformers.

logic.cqpress.com

Key Terms

earmarks, 719

King Caucus, 710

laboratories for reform, 706

line-item veto, 720

micro-targeting, 719

nominating convention, 710

status quo bias, 704

term limits, 713

Suggested Readings

Bernstein, Richard B., and Jerome Agel. *Amending America: If We Love the Constitution So Much, Why Do We Keep Trying to Change It?* Lawrence: University Press of Kansas, 1993. Lively discussion not only of the debates and politics that led to the twenty-seven successful constitutional amendments in American history but also of the thousands of failed attempts.

Farrar-Myers, Victoria A., and Diana Dwyre. *Limits and Loopholes: The Quest for Money, Free Speech, and Fair Elections.* Washington, D.C.: CQ Press, 2007. Two political scientists who have also served on congressional staffs discuss the goals and effects of campaign finance laws, with special attention given to the BCRA reforms.

Green, Donald P., and Alan S. Gerber. *Get Out the Vote! How to Increase Voter Turnout.* Washington, D.C.: Brookings Institution Press, 2004. This book applies rigorous scientific methods to discover how well voter mobilization techniques such as door-to-door canvassing, direct mail, and phone banking actually work.

Kurtz, Karl T., Bruce Cain, and Richard G. Niemi, eds. *Institutional Change in American Politics: The Case of Term Limits.* Ann Arbor: University of Michigan Press, 2007. Also Rick Farmer, Christopher Z. Mooney, Richard J. Powell, and John C. Green, eds. *Legislating Without Experience: Case Studies in State Legislative Term Limits.* Lanham, Md.: Lexington Books, 2007. These companion volumes present the result of a unique cooperative study conducted in nine states by scholars and staff organizations to evaluate the impact of term limits on state legislatures.

Thompson, Hunter S. *Fear and Loathing on the Campaign Trail '72.* New York: Warner Books, 1973. The inventor of "gonzo journalism" covers the race for the Democratic presidential nomination in 1972, the party conventions, and the general election, beginning with his chance meeting with eventual nominee George McGovern in a hotel restroom.

Review Questions

1. What are some basic principles of institutional design that have been used by the Framers and others to ensure that the interests of those who make political decisions are aligned with those affected by those decisions?

2. What are the benefits of making the U.S. Constitution difficult to change? What are the disadvantages? Do these rules enhance or inhibit democracy?

3. What collective action problems do political parties and voters face in elections where multiple candidates from each party are running? How are these problems addressed by the implementation of direct primaries? Are there any disadvantages to primaries?

4. Why do many reforms, such as campaign finance laws, fail to work as intended?

5. Is there a particular institution, law, or policy in American politics that currently is in desperate need of reform? What solutions or reforms would you propose to deal with this problem? Is your solution realistic politically?

6. What role can individuals play in efforts to reform American laws and institutions? What are the benefits of engaging in political activity—be it voting, donating to, or working for a candidate or party? Do such activities ever pay off?

7. What are some potential unintended consequences of giving the president a line-item veto? Can you think of another example of the tragedy of commons in American politics?

Reference
Material

Appendixes

Appendix 1

<table>
<tr><td>**Articles of Confederation**</td></tr>
</table>

To all to whom these Presents shall come, we the undersigned Delegates of the States affixed to our Names send greeting.

Articles of Confederation and perpetual Union between the states of New Hampshire, Massachusetts-bay Rhode Island and Providence Plantations, Connecticut, New York, New Jersey, Pennsylvania, Delaware, Maryland, Virginia, North Carolina, South Carolina and Georgia.

ARTICLE I

The Stile of this Confederacy shall be **"The United States of America".**

ARTICLE II

Each state retains its sovereignty, freedom, and independence, and every power, jurisdiction, and right, which is not by this Confederation expressly delegated to the United States, in Congress assembled.

ARTICLE III

The said States hereby severally enter into a firm league of friendship with each other, for their common defense, the security of their liberties, and their mutual and general welfare, binding themselves to assist each other, against all force offered to, or attacks made upon them, or any of them, on account of religion, sovereignty, trade, or any other pretense whatever.

ARTICLE IV

The better to secure and perpetuate mutual friendship and intercourse among the people of the different States in this Union, the free inhabitants of each of these States, paupers, vagabonds, and fugitives from justice excepted, shall be entitled to all privileges and immunities of free citizens in the several States; and the people of each State shall free ingress and regress to and from any other State, and shall enjoy therein all the privileges of trade and commerce, subject to the same duties, impositions, and restrictions as the inhabitants thereof respectively, provided that such restrictions shall not extend so far as to prevent the removal of property imported into any State, to any other State, of which the owner is an inhabitant; provided also that no imposition, duties or restriction shall be laid by any State, on the property of the United States, or either of them.

If any person guilty of, or charged with, treason, felony, or other high misdemeanor in any State, shall flee from justice, and be found in any of the United States, he shall, upon demand of the Governor or executive power of the State from which he fled, be delivered up and removed to the State having jurisdiction of his offense.

Full faith and credit shall be given in each of these States to the records, acts, and judicial proceedings of the courts and magistrates of every other State.

ARTICLE V

For the most convenient management of the general interests of the United States, delegates shall be annually appointed in such manner as the legislatures of each State shall direct, to meet in Congress on the first Monday in November, in every year, with a power reserved to each State to recall its delegates, or any of them, at any time within the year, and to send others in their stead for the remainder of the year.

No State shall be represented in Congress by less than two, nor more than seven members; and no person shall be capable of being a delegate for more than three years in any term of six years; nor shall any person, being a delegate, be capable of holding any office under the United States, for which he, or another for his benefit, receives any salary, fees or emolument of any kind.

Each State shall maintain its own delegates in a meeting of the States, and while they act as members of the committee of the States.

In determining questions in the United States in Congress assembled, each State shall have one vote.

Freedom of speech and debate in Congress shall not be impeached or questioned in any court or place out of Congress, and the members of Congress shall be protected in their persons from arrests or imprisonments, during the time of their going to and from, and attendence on Congress, except for treason, felony, or breach of the peace.

ARTICLE VI

No State, without the consent of the United States in Congress assembled, shall send any embassy to, or receive any embassy from, or enter into any conference, agreement, alliance or treaty with any King, Prince or State; nor shall any person holding any office of profit or trust under the United States, or any of them, accept any present, emolument, office or title of any kind whatever from any King, Prince or foreign State; nor shall the United States in Congress assembled, or any of them, grant any title of nobility.

No two or more States shall enter into any treaty, confederation or alliance whatever between them, without the consent of the United States in Congress assembled, specifying accurately the purposes for which the same is to be entered into, and how long it shall continue.

No State shall lay any imposts or duties, which may interfere with any stipulations in treaties, entered into by the United States in Congress assembled, with any King, Prince or State, in pursuance of any treaties already proposed by Congress, to the courts of France and Spain.

No vessel of war shall be kept up in time of peace by any State, except such number only, as shall be deemed necessary by the United States in Congress assembled, for the defense of such State, or its trade; nor shall any body of forces be kept up by any State in time of peace, except such number only, as in the judgement of the United States in Congress assembled, shall be deemed requisite to garrison the forts necessary for the defense of such State; but every State shall always keep up a well-regulated and disciplined militia, sufficiently armed and accoutered, and shall provide and constantly have ready for use, in public stores, a due number of filed pieces and tents, and a proper quantity of arms, ammunition and camp equipage.

No State shall engage in any war without the consent of the United States in Congress assembled, unless such State be actually invaded by enemies, or shall have received certain advice of a resolution being formed by some nation of Indians to invade such State, and the danger is so imminent as not to admit of a delay till the United States in Congress assembled can be consulted; nor shall any State grant commissions to any ships or vessels of war, nor letters of marque or reprisal, except it be after a declaration of war by the United States in Congress assembled, and then only against the Kingdom or State and the subjects thereof, against which war has been so declared, and under such regulations as shall be established by the United States in Congress assembled, unless such State be infested by pirates, in which case vessels of war may be fitted out for that occasion, and kept so long as the danger shall continue, or until the United States in Congress assembled shall determine otherwise.

ARTICLE VII

When land forces are raised by any State for the common defense, all officers of or under the rank of colonel, shall be appointed by the legislature of each State respectively, by whom such forces shall be raised, or in such manner as such State shall direct, and all vacancies shall be filled up by the State which first made the appointment.

ARTICLE VIII

All charges of war, and all other expenses that shall be incurred for the common defense or general welfare, and allowed by the United States in Congress assembled, shall be defrayed out of a common treasury, which shall be supplied by the several States in proportion to the value of all land within each State, granted or surveyed for any person, as such land and the buildings and improvements thereon shall be estimated according to such mode as the United States in Congress assembled, shall from time to time direct and appoint.

The taxes for paying that proportion shall be laid and levied by the authority and direction of the legislatures of the several States within the time agreed upon by the United States in Congress assembled.

ARTICLE IX

The United States in Congress assembled, shall have the sole and exclusive right and power of determining on peace and war, except in the cases mentioned in the sixth article—of sending and receiving ambassadors—entering into treaties and alliances, provided that no treaty of commerce shall be made whereby the legislative power of the respective States shall be restrained from imposing such imposts and duties on foreigners, as their own people are subjected to, or from prohibiting the exportation or importation of any species of goods or commodities whatsoever—of establishing rules for deciding in all cases, what captures on land or water shall be legal, and in what manner prizes taken by land or naval forces in the service of the United States shall be divided or appropriated—of granting letters of marque and reprisal in times of peace—appointing courts for the trial of piracies and felonies commited on the high seas and establishing courts for receiving and determining finally appeals in all cases of captures, provided that no member of Congress shall be appointed a judge of any of the said courts.

The United States in Congress assembled shall also be the last resort on appeal in all disputes and differences now subsisting or that hereafter may arise between two or more States concerning boundary, jurisdiction or any other causes whatever; which authority shall always be exercised in the manner following. Whenever the legislative or executive authority or lawful agent of any State in controversy with another shall present a petition to Congress stating the matter in question and praying for a hearing, notice thereof shall be given by order of Congress to the legislative or executive authority of the other State in controversy, and a day assigned for the appearance of the parties by their lawful agents, who shall then be directed to appoint by joint consent, commissioners or judges to constitute a court for hearing and determining the matter in question: but if they cannot agree, Congress shall name three persons out of each of the United States, and from the list of such persons each party shall alternately strike out one, the petitioners beginning, until the number shall be reduced to thirteen; and from that number not less than seven, nor more than nine names as Congress shall direct, shall in the presence of Congress be drawn out by lot, and the persons whose names shall be so drawn or any five of them, shall be commissioners or judges, to hear and finally determine the controversy, so always as a major part of the judges who shall hear the cause shall agree in the determination: and if either party shall neglect to attend at the day appointed, without showing reasons, which Congress shall judge sufficient, or being present shall refuse to strike, the Congress shall proceed to nominate three persons out of each State, and the secretary of Congress shall strike in behalf of such party absent or refusing; and the judgement and sentence of the court to be appointed, in the manner before prescribed, shall be final and conclusive; and if any of the parties shall refuse to submit to the authority of such court, or to appear or defend their claim or cause, the court shall nevertheless proceed to pronounce sentence, or judgement, which shall in like manner be final and decisive, the judgement or sentence and other proceedings being in either case transmitted to Congress, and lodged among the acts of Congress for the security of the parties concerned: provided that every commissioner, before he sits in judgement, shall take an oath to be administered by one of the judges of the supreme or superior court of the State, where the cause shall be tried, 'well and truly to hear and determine the matter in question, according to the best of his judgement, without favor, affection or hope of reward': provided also, that no State shall be deprived of territory for the benefit of the United States.

All controversies concerning the private right of soil claimed under different grants of two or more States, whose jurisdictions as they may respect such lands, and the States which passed such grants are adjusted, the said grants or either of them being at the same time claimed to have originated antecedent to such settlement of jurisdiction, shall on the petition of either party to the Congress of the United States, be finally determined as near as may be in the same manner as is before presecribed for deciding disputes respecting territorial jurisdiction between different States.

The United States in Congress assembled shall also have the sole and exclusive right and power of regulating the alloy and value of coin struck by their own authority, or by that of the respective States—fixing the standards of weights and measures throughout the United States—regulating the trade and managing all affairs with the Indians, not members of any of the States, provided that the legislative right of any State within its own limits be not infringed or violated—establishing or regulating post offices from one State to another, throughout all the United States, and exacting such postage on the papers passing through the same as may be requisite to defray the expenses of the said office—appointing all officers of the land forces, in the service of the United States, excepting regimental officers—appointing all the officers of the naval forces, and commissioning all officers whatever in the service of the United States—making rules for the government and regulation of the said land and naval forces, and directing their operations.

The United States in Congress assembled shall have authority to appoint a committee, to sit in the recess of Congress, to be denominated 'A Committee of the States', and to consist of one delegate from each State; and to appoint such other committees and civil officers as may be necessary for managing the general affairs of the United States under their direction—to appoint one of their members to preside, provided that no person be allowed to serve in the office of president more than one year in any term of three years; to ascertain the necessary sums of money to be raised for the service of the United States, and to appropriate and apply the same for defraying the public expenses—to borrow money, or emit bills on the credit of the United States, transmitting every half-year to the respective States an account of the sums of money so borrowed or emitted—to build and equip a navy—to agree upon the number of land forces, and to make requisitions from each State for its quota, in proportion to the number of white inhabitants in such State; which requisition shall be binding, and thereupon the legislature of each State shall appoint the regimental officers, raise the men and cloath, arm and equip them in a solid-like manner, at the expense of the United States; and the officers and men so cloathed, armed and equipped shall march to the place appointed, and within the time agreed on by the United States in Congress assembled. But if the United States in Congress assembled shall, on consideration of circumstances judge proper that any State should not raise men, or should raise a smaller number of men than the quota thereof, such extra number shall be raised, officered, cloathed, armed and equipped in the same manner as the quota of each State, unless the legislature of such State shall judge that such extra number cannot be safely spread out in the same, in which case they shall raise, officer, cloath, arm and equip as many of such extra number as they judge can be safely spared. And the officers and men so cloathed, armed, and equipped, shall march to the place appointed, and within the time agreed on by the United States in Congress assembled.

The United States in Congress assembled shall never engage in a war, nor grant letters of marque or reprisal in time of peace, nor enter into any treaties or alliances, nor coin money, nor regulate the value thereof, nor ascertain the sums and expenses necessary for the defense and welfare of the United States, or any of them, nor emit bills, nor borrow money on the credit of the United States, nor appropriate money, nor agree upon the number of vessels of war, to be built or purchased, or the number of land or sea forces to be raised, nor appoint a commander in chief of the army or navy, unless nine States assent to the same: nor shall a question on any other point, except for adjourning from day to day be determined, unless by the votes of the majority of the United States in Congress assembled.

The Congress of the United States shall have power to adjourn to any time within the year, and to any place within the United States, so that no period of adjournment be for a longer duration than the space of six months, and shall publish the journal of their proceedings monthly, except such parts thereof relating to treaties, alliances or military operations, as in their judgement require secrecy; and the yeas and nays of the delegates of each State on any question shall be entered on the journal, when it is desired by any delegates of a State, or any of them, at his or their request shall be furnished with a transcript of the said journal, except such parts as are above excepted, to lay before the legislatures of the several States.

ARTICLE X

The Committee of the States, or any nine of them, shall be authorized to execute, in the recess of Congress, such of the powers of Congress as the United States in Congress assembled, by the consent of the nine States, shall from time to time think expedient to vest them with; provided that no power be delegated to the said Committee, for the exercise of which, by the Articles of Confederation, the voice of nine States in the Congress of the United States assembled be requisite.

ARTICLE XI

Canada acceding to this confederation, and adjoining in the measures of the United States, shall be admitted into, and entitled to all the advantages of this Union; but no other colony shall be admitted into the same, unless such admission be agreed to by nine States.

ARTICLE XII

All bills of credit emitted, monies borrowed, and debts contracted by, or under the authority of Congress, before the assembling of the United States, in pursuance of the present confederation, shall be deemed and considered as a charge against the United States, for payment and satisfaction whereof the said United States, and the public faith are hereby solemnly pledged.

ARTICLE XIII

Every State shall abide by the determination of the United States in Congress assembled, on all questions which by this confederation are submitted to them. And the Articles of this Confederation shall be inviolably observed by every State, and the Union shall be perpetual; nor shall any alteration at any time hereafter be made in any of them; unless such alteration be agreed to in a Congress of the United States, and be afterwards confirmed by the legislatures of every State.

And Whereas it hath pleased the Great Governor of the World to incline the hearts of the legislatures we respectively represent in Congress, to approve of, and to authorize us to ratify the said Articles of Confederation and perpetual Union. Know Ye that we the undersigned delegates, by virtue of the power and authority to us given for that purpose, do by these presents, in the name and in behalf of our respective constituents, fully and entirely ratify and confirm each and every of the said Articles of Confederation and perpetual Union, and all and singular the matters and things therein contained: And we do further solemnly plight and engage the faith of our respective constituents, that they shall abide by the determinations of the United States in Congress assembled, on all questions, which by the said Confederation are submitted to them. And that the Articles thereof shall be inviolably observed by the States we respectively represent, and that the Union shall be perpetual.

In Witness whereof we have hereunto set our hands in Congress. Done at Philadelphia in the State of Pennsylvania the ninth day of July in the Year of our Lord One Thousand Seven Hundred and Seventy-Eight, and in the Third Year of the independence of America.

Agreed to by Congress 15 November 1777
In force after ratification by Maryland, 1 March 1781

Appendix 2

Declaration of Independence

On June 11, 1776, the responsibility to "prepare a declaration" of independence was assigned by the Continental Congress, meeting in Philadelphia, to five members: John Adams, Benjamin Franklin, Thomas Jefferson, Robert Livingston, and Roger Sherman. Impressed by his talents as a writer, the committee asked Jefferson to compose a draft. After modifying Jefferson's draft the committee turned it over to Congress on June 28. On July 2 Congress voted to declare independence; on the evening of July 4, it approved the Declaration of Independence.

In Congress, July 4, 1776,
The Unanimous Declaration of
the Thirteen United States of America,

When in the Course of human events, it becomes necessary for one people to dissolve the political bands which have connected them with another, and to assume among the Powers of the earth, the separate and equal station to which the Laws of Nature and of Nature's God entitle them, a decent respect to the opinions of mankind requires that they should declare the causes which impel them to the separation.

We hold these truths to be self-evident, that all men are created equal, that they are endowed by their Creator with certain unalienable Rights, that among these are Life, Liberty and the pursuit of Happiness. That to secure these rights, Governments are instituted among Men, deriving their just powers from the consent of the governed. That whenever any form of Government becomes destructive of these ends, it is the Right of the People to alter or to abolish it, and to institute new Government, laying its foundation on such principles and organizing its powers in such form, as to them shall seem most likely to effect their Safety and Happiness. Prudence, indeed, will dictate that Government long established should not be changed for light and transient causes; and accordingly all experience hath shown, that mankind are more disposed to suffer, while evils are sufferable, than to right themselves by abolishing the forms to which they are accustomed. But when a long train of abuses and usurpations, pursuing invariably the same Object evinces a design to reduce them under absolute Despotism, it is their right, it

is their duty, to throw off such Government, and to provide new Guards for their future security. Such has been the patient sufferance of these Colonies; and such is now the necessity which constrains them to alter their former Systems of Government. The history of the present King of Great Britain is a history of repeated injuries and usurpations, all having in direct object the establishment of an absolute Tyranny over these States. To prove this, let Facts be submitted to a candid world.

He has refused his Assent to Laws, the most wholesome and necessary for the public good.

He has forbidden his Governors to pass Laws of immediate and pressing importance, unless suspended in their operation till his Assent should be obtained; and when so suspended, he has utterly neglected to attend to them.

He has refused to pass other Laws for the accommodation of large districts of people, unless those people would relinquish the right of Representation in the Legislature, a right inestimable to them and formidable to tyrants only.

He has called together legislative bodies at places unusual, uncomfortable, and distant from the depository of their Public Records, for the sole purpose of fatiguing them into compliance with his measures.

He has dissolved Representative Houses repeatedly, for opposing with manly firmness his invasions on the rights of the people.

He has refused for a long time, after such dissolutions, to cause others to be elected; whereby the Legislative Powers, incapable of Annihilation, have returned to the People at large for their exercise; the State remaining in the mean time exposed to all the dangers of invasion from without, and convulsions within.

He has endeavored to prevent the population of these States; for that purpose obstructing the Laws of Naturalization of Foreigners; refusing to pass others to encourage their migration hither, and raising the conditions of new Appropriations of Lands.

He has obstructed the Administration of Justice, by refusing his Assent to Laws for establishing Judiciary Powers.

He has made Judges dependent on his Will alone, for the tenure of their offices, and the amount and payment of their salaries.

He has erected a multitude of New Offices, and sent hither swarms of Officers to harass our People, and eat out their substance.

He has kept among us, in times of peace, Standing Armies without the Consent of our legislature.

He has affected to render the Military independent of and superior to the Civil Power.

He has combined with others to subject us to a jurisdiction foreign to our constitution, and unacknowledged by our laws; giving his Assent to their acts of pretended legislation:

For quartering large bodies of armed troops among us:

For protecting them, by a mock Trial, from Punishment for any Murders which they should commit on the Inhabitants of these States:

For cutting off our Trade with all parts of the world:

For imposing taxes on us without our Consent:

For depriving us in many cases, of the benefits of Trial by Jury:

For transporting us beyond Seas to be tried for pretended offences:

For abolishing the free System of English Laws in a neighbouring Province, establishing therein an Arbitrary government, and enlarging its Boundaries so as to render it at once an example and fit instrument for introducing the same absolute rule into these Colonies:

For taking away our Charters, abolishing our most valuable Laws, and altering fundamentally the Forms of our Governments:

For suspending our own Legislature, and declaring themselves invested with Power to legislate for us in all cases whatsoever.

He has abdicated Government here, by declaring us out of his Protection and waging War against us.

He has plundered our seas, ravaged our Coasts, burnt our towns, and destroyed the lives of our people.

He is at this time transporting large armies of foreign mercenaries to compleat the works of death, desolation and tyranny, already begun with circumstances of Cruelty & perfidy scarcely parallel in the most barbarous ages, and totally unworthy the Head of a civilized nation.

He has constrained our fellow Citizens taken Captive on the high Seas to bear Arms against their Country, to become the executioners of their friends and Brethren, or to fall themselves by their Hands.

He has excited domestic insurrections amongst us, and has endeavoured to bring on the inhabitants of our frontiers, the merciless Indian Savages, whose known rule of warfare, is an undistinguished destruction of all ages, sexes and conditions.

In every stage of these Oppressions We have Petitioned for Redress in the most humble terms: Our repeated Petitions have been answered only by repeated injury. A Prince, whose character is thus marked by every act which may define a Tyrant, is unfit to be the ruler of a free People.

Nor have We been wanting in attention to our British brethren. We have warned them from time to time of attempts by their legislature to extend an unwarrantable jurisdiction over us. We have reminded them of the circumstances of our emigration and settlement here. We have appealed to their native justice and magnanimity, and we have conjured them by the ties of our common kindred to disavow these usurpations, which would inevitably interrupt our connections and correspondence. They too have been deaf to the voice of justice and of consanguinity. We must, therefore, acquiesce in the necessity, which denounces our Separation, and hold them, as we hold the rest of mankind, Enemies in War, in Peace Friends.

We, therefore, the Representatives of the United States of America, in General Congress, Assembled, appealing to the Supreme Judge of the world for the rectitude of our intentions, do, in the Name, and by Authority of the good People of these Colonies, solemnly publish and declare, That these United Colonies are, and of Right ought to be Free and Independent States; that they are Absolved from all Allegiance to the British Crown, and that all political connection between them and the State of Great Britain, is and ought to be totally dissolved; and that as Free and Independent States, they have full Power to levy War, conclude Peace, contract Alliances, establish Commerce, and to do all other Acts and Things which Independent States may of right do. And for the support of this Declaration, with a firm reliance on the Protection of Divine Providence, we mutually pledge to each other our Lives, our Fortunes and our sacred Honor.

John Hancock.

New Hampshire:
Josiah Bartlett,
William Whipple,
Matthew Thornton.

Massachusetts-Bay:
Samuel Adams,
John Adams,
Robert Treat Paine,
Elbridge Gerry.

Rhode Island:
Stephen Hopkins,
William Ellery.

Connecticut:
Roger Sherman,
Samuel Huntington,
William Williams,
Oliver Wolcott.

New York:
William Floyd,
Philip Livingston,
Francis Lewis,
Lewis Morris.

Pennsylvania:
Robert Morris,
Benjamin Harris,
Benjamin Franklin,
John Morton,
George Clymer,
James Smith,
George Taylor,
James Wilson,
George Ross.

Delaware:
Caesar Rodney,
George Read,
Thomas McKean.

Georgia:
Button Gwinnett,
Lyman Hall,
George Walton.

Maryland:
Samuel Chase,
William Paca,
Thomas Stone,
Charles Carroll of Carrollton.

Virginia:
George Wythe,
Richard Henry Lee,
Thomas Jefferson,
Benjamin Harrison,
Thomas Nelson Jr.,
Francis Lightfoot Lee,
Carter Braxton.

North Carolina:
William Hooper,
Joseph Hewes,
John Penn.

South Carolina:
Edward Rutledge,
Thomas Heyward Jr.,
Thomas Lynch Jr.,
Arthur Middleton.

New Jersey:
Richard Stockton,
John Witherspoon,
Francis Hopkinson,
John Hart,
Abraham Clark.

Appendix 3

Constitution of the United States

The United States Constitution was written at a convention that Congress called on February 21, 1787, for the purpose of recommending amendments to the Articles of Confederation. Every state but Rhode Island sent delegates to Philadelphia, where the convention met that summer. The delegates decided to write an entirely new constitution, completing their labors on September 17. Nine states (the number the Constitution itself stipulated as sufficient) ratified by June 21, 1788.

The Framers of the Constitution included only six paragraphs on the Supreme Court. Article III, Section 1, created the Supreme Court and the federal system of courts. It provided that "[t]he judicial power of the United States, shall be vested in one supreme Court," and whatever inferior courts Congress "from time to time" saw fit to establish. Article III, Section 2, delineated the types of cases and controversies that should be considered by a federal—rather than a state—court. But beyond this, the Constitution left many of the particulars of the Supreme Court and the federal court system for Congress to decide in later years in judiciary acts.

We the People of the United States, in Order to form a more perfect Union, establish Justice, insure domestic Tranquility, provide for the common defence, promote the general Welfare, and secure the Blessings of Liberty to ourselves and our Posterity, do ordain and establish this Constitution for the United States of America.

ARTICLE I

Section 1. All legislative Powers herein granted shall be vested in a Congress of the United States, which shall consist of a Senate and House of Representatives.

Section 2. The House of Representatives shall be composed of Members chosen every second Year by the People of the several States, and the Electors in each State shall have the Qualifications requisite for Electors of the most numerous Branch of the State Legislature.

No Person shall be a Representative who shall not have attained to the age of twenty five Years, and been seven Years a Citizen of the United States, and who shall not, when elected, be an Inhabitant of that State in which he shall be chosen.

[Representatives and direct Taxes shall be apportioned among the several States which may be included within this Union, according to their respective Numbers, which shall be determined by adding to the whole Number of free Persons, including those bound to Service for a Term of Years, and excluding Indians not taxed, three fifths of all other Persons.][1] The actual Enumeration shall be made within three Years after the first Meeting of the Congress of the United States, and within every subsequent Term of ten Years, in such Manner as they shall by Law direct. The Number of Representatives shall not exceed one for every thirty Thousand, but each State shall have at Least one Representative; and until such enumeration shall be made, the State of New Hampshire shall be entitled to chuse three, Massachusetts eight, Rhode-Island and Providence Plantations one, Connecticut five, New-York six, New Jersey four, Pennsylvania eight, Delaware one, Maryland six, Virginia ten, North Carolina five, South Carolina five, and Georgia three.

When vacancies happen in the Representation from any State, the Executive Authority thereof shall issue Writs of Election to fill such Vacancies.

The House of Representatives shall chuse their Speaker and other Officers; and shall have the sole Power of Impeachment.

Section 3. The Senate of the United States shall be composed of two Senators from each State, [chosen by the Legislature thereof,][2] for six Years; and each Senator shall have one Vote.

Immediately after they shall be assembled in Consequence of the first Election, they shall be divided as equally as may be into three Classes. The Seats of the

Senators of the first Class shall be vacated at the Expiration of the second Year, of the second Class at the Expiration of the fourth Year, and of the third Class at the Expiration of the sixth Year, so that one third may be chosen every second Year; [and if Vacancies happen by Resignation, or otherwise, during the Recess of the Legislature of any State, the Executive thereof may make temporary Appointments until the next Meeting of the Legislature, which shall then fill such Vacancies.]³

No Person shall be a Senator who shall not have attained to the Age of thirty Years, and been nine Years a Citizen of the United States, and who shall not, when elected, be an Inhabitant of that State for which he shall be chosen.

The Vice President of the United States shall be President of the Senate, but shall have no Vote, unless they be equally divided.

The Senate shall chuse their other Officers, and also a President pro tempore, in the Absence of the Vice President, or when he shall exercise the Office of President of the United States.

The Senate shall have the sole Power to try all Impeachments. When sitting for that Purpose, they shall be on Oath or Affirmation. When the President of the United States is tried, the Chief Justice shall preside: And no Person shall be convicted without the Concurrence of two thirds of the Members present.

Judgment in Cases of Impeachment shall not extend further than to removal from Office, and disqualification to hold and enjoy any Office of honor, Trust or Profit under the United States: but the Party convicted shall nevertheless be liable and subject to Indictment, Trial, Judgment and Punishment, according to Law.

Section 4. The Times, Places and Manner of holding Elections for Senators and Representatives, shall be prescribed in each State by the Legislature thereof; but the Congress may at any time by Law make or alter such Regulations, except as to the Places of chusing Senators.

The Congress shall assemble at least once in every Year, and such Meeting shall [be on the first Monday in December],⁴ unless they shall by Law appoint a different Day.

Section 5. Each House shall be the Judge of the Elections, Returns and Qualifications of its own Members, and a Majority of each shall constitute a Quorum to do Business; but a smaller Number may adjourn from day to day, and may be authorized to compel the Attendance of absent Members, in such Manner, and under such Penalties as each House may provide.

Each House may determine the Rules of its Proceedings, punish its Members for disorderly Behaviour, and, with the Concurrence of two thirds, expel a Member.

Each House shall keep a Journal of its Proceedings, and from time to time publish the same, excepting such Parts as may in their Judgment require Secrecy; and the Yeas and Nays of the Members of either House on any question shall, at the Desire of one fifth of those Present, be entered on the Journal.

Neither House, during the Session of Congress, shall, without the Consent of the other, adjourn for more than three days, nor to any other Place than that in which the two Houses shall be sitting.

Section 6. The Senators and Representatives shall receive a Compensation for their Services, to be ascertained by Law, and paid out of the Treasury of the United States. They shall in all Cases, except Treason, Felony and Breach of the Peace, be privileged from Arrest during their Attendance at the Session of their respective Houses, and in going to and returning from the same; and for any Speech or Debate in either House, they shall not be questioned in any other Place.

No Senator or Representative shall, during the Time for which he was elected, be appointed to any civil Office under the Authority of the United States, which shall have been created, or the Emoluments whereof shall have been encreased during such time; and no Person holding any Office under the United States, shall be a Member of either House during his Continuance in Office.

Section 7. All Bills for raising Revenue shall originate in the House of Representatives; but the Senate may propose or concur with Amendments as on other Bills.

Every Bill which shall have passed the House of Representatives and the Senate, shall, before it become a Law, be presented to the President of the United States; If he approve he shall sign it, but if not he shall return it, with his Objections to that House in which it shall have originated, who shall enter the Objections at large on their Journal, and proceed to reconsider it. If after such Reconsideration two thirds of that House shall agree to pass the Bill, it shall be sent, together with the Objections, to the other House, by which it shall likewise be reconsidered, and if approved by two thirds of that House, it shall become a Law. But in all such Cases the Votes of both Houses shall be determined by yeas and Nays, and the Names of the Persons voting for and against the Bill shall be entered on the Journal of each House respectively. If any Bill shall not be returned by the President within ten Days (Sundays excepted) after it shall have been presented to him, the Same shall be a Law, in like Manner as if he had signed it, unless the Congress by their Adjournment prevent its Return, in which Case it shall not be a Law.

Every Order, Resolution, or Vote to which the Concurrence of the Senate and House of Representatives may be necessary (except on a question of Adjournment) shall be presented to the President of the United States; and before the Same shall take Effect, shall be approved by him, or being disapproved by him, shall be repassed by two thirds of the Senate and House of Representatives, according to the Rules and Limitations prescribed in the Case of a Bill.

Section 8. The Congress shall have Power To lay and collect Taxes, Duties, Imposts and Excises, to pay the Debts and provide for the common Defence and general Welfare of the United States; but all Duties, Imposts and Excises shall be uniform throughout the United States;

To borrow Money on the credit of the United States;

To regulate Commerce with foreign Nations, and among the several States, and with the Indian Tribes;

To establish an uniform Rule of Naturalization, and uniform Laws on the subject of Bankruptcies throughout the United States;

To coin Money, regulate the Value thereof, and of foreign Coin, and fix the Standard of Weights and Measures;

To provide for the Punishment of counterfeiting the Securities and current Coin of the United States;

To establish Post Offices and post Roads;

To promote the Progress of Science and useful Arts, by securing for limited Times to Authors and Inventors the exclusive Right to their respective Writings and Discoveries;

To constitute Tribunals inferior to the supreme Court;

To define and punish Piracies and Felonies committed on the high Seas, and Offences against the Law of Nations;

To declare War, grant Letters of Marque and Reprisal, and make Rules concerning Captures on Land and Water;

To raise and support Armies, but no Appropriation of Money to that Use shall be for a longer Term than two Years;

To provide and maintain a Navy;

To make Rules for the Government and Regulation of the land and naval Forces;

To provide for calling forth the Militia to execute the Laws of the Union, suppress Insurrections and repel Invasions;

To provide for organizing, arming, and disciplining, the Militia, and for governing such Part of them as may be employed in the Service of the United States, reserving to the States respectively, the Appointment of the Officers, and the Authority of training the Militia according to the discipline prescribed by Congress;

To exercise exclusive Legislation in all Cases whatsoever, over such District (not exceeding ten Miles square) as may, by Cession of particular States, and the Acceptance of Congress, become the Seat of the Government of the United States, and to exercise like Authority over all Places purchased by the Consent of the Legislature of the State in which the Same shall be, for the Erection of Forts, Magazines, Arsenals, dock-Yards, and other needful Buildings;—And

To make all Laws which shall be necessary and proper for carrying into Execution the foregoing Powers, and all other Powers vested by this Constitution in the Government of the United States, or in any Department or Officer thereof.

Section 9. The Migration or Importation of such Persons as any of the States now existing shall think proper to admit, shall not be prohibited by the Congress prior to the Year one thousand eight hundred and eight, but a Tax or duty may be imposed on such Importation, not exceeding ten dollars for each Person.

The Privilege of the Writ of Habeas Corpus shall not be suspended, unless when in Cases of Rebellion or Invasion the public Safety may require it.

No Bill of Attainder or ex post facto Law shall be passed.

No Capitation, or other direct, Tax shall be laid, unless in Proportion to the Census or Enumeration herein before directed to be taken.[5]

No Tax or Duty shall be laid on Articles exported from any State.

No Preference shall be given by any Regulation of Commerce or Revenue to the Ports of one State over those of another; nor shall Vessels bound to, or from, one State, be obliged to enter, clear, or pay Duties in another.

No Money shall be drawn from the Treasury, but in Consequence of Appropriations made by Law; and a regular Statement and Account of the Receipts and Expenditures of all public Money shall be published from time to time.

No Title of Nobility shall be granted by the United States: And no Person holding any Office of Profit or Trust under them, shall, without the Consent of the Congress, accept of any present, Emolument, Office, or Title, of any kind whatever, from any King, Prince, or foreign State.

Section 10. No State shall enter into any Treaty, Alliance, or Confederation; grant Letters of Marque and Reprisal; coin Money; emit Bills of Credit; make any Thing but gold and silver Coin a Tender in Payment of Debts; pass any Bill of Attainder, ex post facto Law, or Law impairing the Obligation of Contracts, or grant any Title of Nobility.

No State shall, without the Consent of the Congress, lay any Imposts or Duties on Imports or Exports, except what may be absolutely necessary for executing its inspection Laws: and the net Produce of all Duties and Imposts, laid by any State on Imports or Exports, shall be for the Use of the Treasury of the United States; and all such Laws shall be subject to the Revision and Controul of the Congress.

No State shall, without the Consent of Congress, lay any Duty of Tonnage, keep Troops, or Ships of War in time of Peace, enter into any Agreement or Compact with another State, or with a foreign Power, or engage in War, unless actually invaded, or in such imminent Danger as will not admit of delay.

ARTICLE II

Section 1. The executive Power shall be vested in a President of the United States of America. He shall hold his Office during the Term of four Years, and, together with the Vice President, chosen for the same Term, be elected, as follows:

Each State shall appoint, in such Manner as the Legislature thereof may direct, a Number of Electors, equal to the whole Number of Senators and Representatives to which the State may be entitled in the Congress: but no Senator or Representative, or Person holding an Office of Trust or Profit under the United States, shall be appointed an Elector.

[The Electors shall meet in their respective States, and vote by Ballot for two Persons, of whom one at least shall not be an Inhabitant of the same State with themselves. And they shall make a List of all the Persons voted for, and of the Number of Votes for each; which List they shall sign and certify, and transmit sealed to the Seat of the Government of the United States, directed to the President of the Senate. The President of the Senate shall, in the Presence of the Senate and House of Representatives, open all the Certificates, and the Votes shall then be counted. The Person having the greatest Number of Votes shall be the President, if such Number be a Majority of the whole Number of Electors appointed; and if there be more than one who have such Majority, and have an equal Number of Votes, then the House of Representatives shall immediately chuse by Ballot one of them for President; and if no Person have a Majority, then from the five highest on the list the said House shall in like Manner chuse the President. But in chusing the President, the Votes shall be taken by States, the Representation from each State having one Vote; A quorum for this Purpose shall consist of a Member or Members from two thirds of the States, and a Majority of all the States shall be necessary to a Choice. In every Case, after the Choice of the President, the Person having the greatest Number of Votes of the Electors shall be the

Vice President. But if there should remain two or more who have equal Votes, the Senate shall chuse from them by Ballot the Vice President.][6]

The Congress may determine the Time of chusing the Electors, and the Day on which they shall give their Votes; which Day shall be the same throughout the United States.

No Person except a natural born Citizen, or a Citizen of the United States, at the time of the Adoption of this Constitution, shall be eligible to the Office of President; neither shall any Person be eligible to that Office who shall not have attained to the Age of thirty five Years, and been fourteen Years a Resident within the United States.

In Case of the Removal of the President from Office, or of his Death, Resignation, or Inability to discharge the Powers and Duties of the said Office,[7] the Same shall devolve on the Vice President, and the Congress may by Law provide for the Case of Removal, Death, Resignation or Inability, both of the President and Vice President, declaring what Officer shall then act as President, and such Officer shall act accordingly, until the Disability be removed, or a President shall be elected.

The President shall, at stated Times, receive for his Services, a Compensation, which shall neither be increased nor diminished during the Period for which he shall have been elected, and he shall not receive within that Period any other Emolument from the United States, or any of them.

Before he enter on the Execution of his Office, he shall take the following Oath or Affirmation:—"I do solemnly swear (or affirm) that I will faithfully execute the Office of President of the United States, and will to the best of my Ability, preserve, protect and defend the Constitution of the United States."

Section 2. The President shall be Commander in Chief of the Army and Navy of the United States, and of the Militia of the several States, when called into the actual Service of the United States; he may require the Opinion, in writing, of the principal Officer in each of the executive Departments, upon any Subject relating to the Duties of their respective Offices, and he shall have Power to grant Reprieves and Pardons for Offences against the United States, except in Cases of Impeachment.

He shall have Power, by and with the Advice and Consent of the Senate, to make Treaties, provided two thirds of the Senators present concur; and he shall nominate, and by and with the Advice and Consent of the Senate, shall appoint Ambassadors, other public Ministers and Consuls, Judges of the supreme Court, and all other Officers of the United States, whose Appointments are not herein otherwise provided for, and which shall be established by Law: but the Congress may by Law vest the Appointment of such inferior Officers, as they think proper, in the President alone, in the Courts of Law, or in the Heads of Departments.

The President shall have Power to fill up all Vacancies that may happen during the Recess of the Senate, by granting Commissions which shall expire at the End of their next Session.

Section 3. He shall from time to time give to the Congress Information of the State of the Union, and recommend to their Consideration such Measures as he shall judge necessary and expedient; he may, on extraordinary Occasions, convene both Houses, or either of them, and in Case of Disagreement between them, with Respect to the Time of Adjournment, he may adjourn them to such Time as he shall think proper; he shall receive Ambassadors and other public Ministers; he shall take Care that the Laws be faithfully executed, and shall Commission all the Officers of the United States.

Section 4. The President, Vice President and all civil Officers of the United States, shall be removed from Office on Impeachment for, and Conviction of, Treason, Bribery, or other high Crimes and Misdemeanors.

ARTICLE III

Section 1. The judicial Power of the United States, shall be vested in one supreme Court, and in such inferior Courts as the Congress may from time to time ordain and establish. The Judges, both of the supreme and inferior Courts, shall hold their Offices during good Behaviour, and shall, at stated Times, receive for their Services, a Compensation, which shall not be diminished during their Continuance in Office.

Section 2. The judicial Power shall extend to all Cases, in Law and Equity, arising under this Constitution, the Laws of the United States, and Treaties made, or which shall be made, under their Authority; —to all Cases affecting Ambassadors, other public Ministers and Consuls; —to all Cases of admiralty and maritime Jurisdiction; —to Controversies to which the United States shall be a Party; —to Controversies between two or more States; —between a State and Citizens of another State;[8] —between Citizens of different States; —between Citizens of the same State claiming Lands under Grants of different States, and between a State, or the Citizens thereof, and foreign States, Citizens or Subjects.[8]

In all Cases affecting Ambassadors, other public Ministers and Consuls, and those in which a State shall be Party, the supreme Court shall have original Jurisdiction. In all the other Cases before mentioned, the supreme Court shall have appellate Jurisdiction, both as to Law and Fact, with such Exceptions, and under such Regulations as the Congress shall make.

The Trial of all Crimes, except in Cases of Impeachment, shall be by Jury; and such Trial shall be held in the State where the said Crimes shall have been committed; but when not committed within any State, the Trial shall be at such Place or Places as the Congress may by Law have directed.

Section 3. Treason against the United States, shall consist only in levying War against them, or in adhering to their Enemies, giving them Aid and Comfort. No Person shall be convicted of Treason unless on the Testimony of two Witnesses to the same overt Act, or on Confession in open Court.

The Congress shall have Power to declare the Punishment of Treason, but no Attainder of Treason shall work Corruption of Blood, or Forfeiture except during the Life of the Person attainted.

ARTICLE IV

Section 1. Full Faith and Credit shall be given in each State to the public Acts, Records, and judicial Proceedings of every other State. And the Congress may by general Laws prescribe the Manner in which such Acts, Records and Proceedings shall be proved, and the Effect thereof.

Section 2. The Citizens of each State shall be entitled to all Privileges and Immunities of Citizens in the several States.

A Person charged in any State with Treason, Felony, or other Crime, who shall flee from Justice, and be found in another State, shall on Demand of the executive Authority of the State from which he fled, be delivered up, to be removed to the State having Jurisdiction of the Crime.

[No Person held to Service or Labour in one State, under the Laws thereof, escaping into another, shall, in Consequence of any Law or Regulation therein, be discharged from such Service or Labour, but shall be delivered up on Claim of the Party to whom such Service or Labour may be due.][9]

Section 3. New States may be admitted by the Congress into this Union; but no new State shall be formed or erected within the Jurisdiction of any other State; nor any State be formed by the Junction of two or more States, or Parts of States, without the Consent of the Legislatures of the States concerned as well as of the Congress.

The Congress shall have Power to dispose of and make all needful Rules and Regulations respecting the Territory or other Property belonging to the United States; and nothing in this Constitution shall be so construed as to Prejudice any Claims of the United States, or of any particular State.

Section 4. The United States shall guarantee to every State in this Union a Republican Form of Government, and shall protect each of them against Invasion; and on Application of the Legislature, or of the Executive (when the Legislature cannot be convened) against domestic Violence.

ARTICLE V

The Congress, whenever two thirds of both Houses shall deem it necessary, shall propose Amendments to this Constitution, or, on the Application of the Legislatures of two thirds of the several States, shall call a Convention for proposing Amendments, which, in either Case, shall be valid to all Intents and Purposes, as Part of this Constitution, when ratified by the Legislatures of three fourths of the several States, or by Conventions in three fourths thereof, as the one or the other Mode of Ratification may be proposed by the Congress; Provided [that no Amendment which may be made prior to the Year One thousand eight hundred and eight shall in any Manner affect the first and fourth Clauses in the Ninth Section of the first Article; and][10] that no State, without its Consent, shall be deprived of its equal Suffrage in the Senate.

ARTICLE VI

All Debts contracted and Engagements entered into, before the Adoption of this Constitution, shall be as valid against the United States under this Constitution, as under the Confederation.

This Constitution, and the Laws of the United States which shall be made in Pursuance thereof; and all Treaties made, or which shall be made, under the Authority of the United States, shall be the supreme Law of the Land; and the Judges in every State shall be bound thereby, any Thing in the Constitution or Laws of any State to the Contrary notwithstanding.

The Senators and Representatives before mentioned, and the Members of the several State Legislatures, and all executive and judicial Officers, both of the United States and of the several States, shall be bound by Oath or Affirmation, to support this Constitution; but no religious Test shall ever be required as a Qualification to any Office or public Trust under the United States.

ARTICLE VII

The Ratification of the Conventions of nine States, shall be sufficient for the Establishment of this Constitution between the States so ratifying the Same.

Done in Convention by the Unanimous Consent of the States present the Seventeenth Day of September in the Year of our Lord one thousand seven hundred and Eighty seven

and of the Independence of the United States of America the Twelfth. IN WITNESS whereof We have hereunto subscribed our Names,

George Washington, *President and deputy from Virginia, and thirty-eight other delegates.*

[The language of the original Constitution, not including the Amendments, was adopted by a convention of the states on September 17, 1787, and was subsequently ratified by the states on the following dates: Delaware, December 7, 1787; Pennsylvania, December 12, 1787; New Jersey, December 18, 1787; Georgia, January 2, 1788; Connecticut, January 9, 1788; Massachusetts, February 6, 1788; Maryland, April 28, 1788; South Carolina, May 23, 1788; New Hampshire, June 21, 1788.

Ratification was completed on June 21, 1788.

The Constitution subsequently was ratified by Virginia, June 25, 1788; New York, July 26, 1788; North Carolina, November 21, 1789; Rhode Island, May 29, 1790; and Vermont, January 10, 1791.]

Amendments

Amendment I

(First ten amendments ratified December 15, 1791.)

Congress shall make no law respecting an establishment of religion, or prohibiting the free exercise thereof; or abridging the freedom of speech, or of the press; or the right of the people peaceably to assemble, and to petition the Government for a redress of grievances.

Amendment II

A well regulated Militia, being necessary to the security of a free State, the right of the people to keep and bear Arms, shall not be infringed.

Amendment III

No Soldier shall, in time of peace be quartered in any house, without the consent of the Owner, nor in time of war, but in a manner to be prescribed by law.

Amendment IV

The right of the people to be secure in their persons, houses, papers, and effects, against unreasonable searches and seizures, shall not be violated, and no Warrants shall issue, but upon probable cause, supported by Oath or affirmation, and particularly describing the place to be searched, and the persons or things to be seized.

Amendment V

No person shall be held to answer for a capital, or otherwise infamous crime, unless on a presentment or indictment of a Grand Jury, except in cases arising in the land or naval forces, or in the Militia, when in actual service in time of War or public danger; nor shall any person be subject for the same offence to be twice put in jeopardy of life or limb; nor shall be compelled in any criminal case to be a witness against himself, nor be deprived of life, liberty, or property, without due process of law; nor shall private property be taken for public use, without just compensation.

Amendment VI

In all criminal prosecutions, the accused shall enjoy the right to a speedy and public trial, by an impartial jury of the State and district wherein the crime shall have been committed, which district shall have been previously ascertained by law, and to be informed of the nature and cause of the accusation; to be confronted with the witnesses against him; to have compulsory process for obtaining witnesses in his favor, and to have the Assistance of Counsel for his defence.

Amendment VII

In Suits at common law, where the value in controversy shall exceed twenty dollars, the right of trial by jury shall be preserved, and no fact tried by a jury, shall be otherwise re-examined in any Court of the United States, than according to the rules of the common law.

Amendment VIII

Excessive bail shall not be required, nor excessive fines imposed, nor cruel and unusual punishments inflicted.

Amendment IX

The enumeration in the Constitution, of certain rights, shall not be construed to deny or disparage others retained by the people.

Amendment X

The powers not delegated to the United States by the Constitution, nor prohibited by it to the States, are reserved to the States respectively, or to the people.

Amendment XI *(Ratified February 7, 1795)*

The Judicial power of the United States shall not be construed to extend to any suit in law or equity, commenced or prosecuted against one of the United States by Citizens of another State, or by Citizens or Subjects of any Foreign State.

Amendment XII *(Ratified June 15, 1804)*

The Electors shall meet in their respective states and vote by ballot for President and Vice-President, one of whom, at least, shall not be an inhabitant of the same state with themselves; they shall name in their ballots the person voted for as President, and in distinct ballots the person voted for as Vice-President, and they shall make distinct lists of all persons voted for as President, and of all persons voted for as Vice-President, and of the number of votes for each, which lists they shall sign and certify, and transmit sealed to the seat of the government of the United States, directed to the President of the Senate; — The President of the Senate shall, in the presence of the Senate and House of Representatives, open all the certificates and the votes shall then be counted; — The person having the greatest number of votes for President, shall be the President, if such number be a majority of the whole number of Electors appointed; and if no person have such majority, then from the persons having the highest numbers not exceeding three on the list of those voted for as President, the House of Representatives shall choose immediately, by ballot, the President. But in choosing the President, the votes shall be taken by states, the representation from each state having one vote; a quorum for this purpose shall consist of a member or members from two-thirds of the states, and a majority of all the states shall be necessary to a choice. [And if the House of Representatives shall not choose a President whenever the right of choice shall devolve upon them, before the fourth day of March next following, then the Vice-President shall act as President, as in the case of the death or other constitutional disability of the President. —][11] The person having the greatest number of votes as Vice-President, shall be the Vice-President, if such number be a majority of the whole number of Electors appointed, and if no person have a majority, then from the two highest numbers on the list, the Senate shall choose the Vice-President; a quorum for the purpose shall consist of two-thirds of the whole number of Senators, and a majority of the whole number shall be necessary to a choice. But no person constitutionally ineligible to the office of President shall be eligible to that of Vice-President of the United States.

Amendment XIII *(Ratified December 6, 1865)*

Section 1. Neither slavery nor involuntary servitude, except as a punishment for crime whereof the party shall have been duly convicted, shall exist within the United States, or any place subject to their jurisdiction.

Section 2. Congress shall have power to enforce this article by appropriate legislation.

Amendment XIV *(Ratified July 9, 1868)*

Section 1. All persons born or naturalized in the United States, and subject to the jurisdiction thereof, are citizens of the United States and of the State wherein they reside. No State shall make or enforce any law which shall abridge the privileges or immunities of citizens of the United States; nor shall any State deprive any person of life, liberty, or property, without due process of law; nor deny to any person within its jurisdiction the equal protection of the laws.

Section 2. Representatives shall be apportioned among the several States according to their respective numbers, counting the whole number of persons in each State, excluding Indians not taxed. But when the right to vote at any election for the choice of electors for President and Vice President of the United States, Representatives in Congress, the Executive and Judicial officers of a State, or the members of the Legislature thereof, is denied to any of the male inhabitants of such State, being twenty-one years of age,[12] and citizens of the United States, or in any way abridged, except for participation in rebellion, or other crime, the basis of representation therein shall be reduced in the proportion which the number of such male citizens shall bear to the whole number of male citizens twenty-one years of age in such State.

Section 3. No person shall be a Senator or Representative in Congress, or elector of President and Vice President, or hold any Office, civil or military, under the United States, or under any State, who, having previously taken an oath, as a member of Congress, or as an officer of the United States, or as a member of any State legislature, or as an executive or judicial officer of any State, to support the Constitution of the United States, shall have engaged in insurrection or rebellion against the same, or given aid or comfort to the enemies thereof. But Congress may by a vote of two-thirds of each House, remove such disability.

Section 4. The validity of the public debt of the United States, authorized by law, including debts incurred for payment of pensions and bounties for services in suppressing insurrection or rebellion, shall not be questioned. But neither the United States nor any State shall assume or pay any debt or obligation incurred in aid of insurrection or rebellion against the United States, or any claim for the loss or emancipation of any slave; but all such debts, obligations and claims shall be held illegal and void.

Section 5. The Congress shall have power to enforce, by appropriate legislation, the provisions of this article.

Amendment XV *(Ratified February 3, 1870)*

Section 1. The right of citizens of the United States to vote shall not be denied or abridged by the United States or by any State on account of race, color, or previous condition of servitude.

Section 2. The Congress shall have power to enforce this article by appropriate legislation.

Amendment XVI *(Ratified February 3, 1913)*

The Congress shall have power to lay and collect taxes on incomes, from whatever source derived, without apportionment among the several States, and without regard to any census or enumeration.

Amendment XVII *(Ratified April 8, 1913)*

The Senate of the United States shall be composed of two Senators from each State, elected by the people thereof, for six years; and each Senator shall have one vote. The electors in each State shall have the qualifications requisite for electors of the most numerous branch of the State legislatures.

When vacancies happen in the representation of any State in the Senate, the executive authority of such State shall issue writs of election to fill such vacancies: *Provided,* That the legislature of any State may empower the executive thereof to make temporary appointments until the people fill the vacancies by election as the legislature may direct.

This amendment shall not be so construed as to affect the election or term of any Senator chosen before it becomes valid as part of the Constitution.

Amendment XVIII *(Ratified January 16, 1919)*

Section 1. After one year from the ratification of this article the manufacture, sale, or transportation of intoxicating liquors within, the importation thereof into, or the exportation thereof from the United States and all territory subject to the jurisdiction thereof for beverage purposes is hereby prohibited.

Section 2. The Congress and the several States shall have concurrent power to enforce this article by appropriate legislation.

Section 3. This article shall be inoperative unless it shall have been ratified as an amendment to the Constitution by the legislatures of the several States, as provided in the Constitution, within seven years from the date of the submission hereof to the States by the Congress.][13]

Amendment XIX *(Ratified August 18, 1920)*

The right of citizens of the United States to vote shall not be denied or abridged by the United States or by any State on account of sex.

Congress shall have power to enforce this article by appropriate legislation.

Amendment XX *(Ratified January 23, 1933)*

Section 1. The terms of the President and Vice President shall end at noon on the 20th day of January, and the terms of Senators and Representatives at noon on the 3d day of January, of the years in which such terms would have ended if this article had not been ratified; and the terms of their successors shall then begin.

Section 2. The Congress shall assemble at least once in every year, and such meeting shall begin at noon on the 3d day of January, unless they shall by law appoint a different day.

Section 3.[14] If, at the time fixed for the beginning of the term of the President, the President elect shall have died, the Vice President elect shall become President. If a President shall not have been chosen before the time fixed for the beginning of his term, or if the President elect shall have failed to qualify, then the Vice President elect shall act as President until a President shall have qualified; and the Congress may by law provide for the case wherein neither a President elect nor a Vice President elect shall have qualified, declaring who shall then act as President, or the manner in which one who is to act shall be selected, and such person shall act accordingly until a President or Vice President shall have qualified.

Section 4. The Congress may by law provide for the case of the death of any of the persons from whom the House of Representatives may choose a President whenever the right of choice shall have devolved upon them, and for the case of the death of any of the persons from whom the Senate may choose a Vice President whenever the right of choice shall have devolved upon them.

Section 5. Sections 1 and 2 shall take effect on the 15th day of October following the ratification of this article.

Section 6. This article shall be inoperative unless it shall have been ratified as an amendment to the Constitution by the legislatures of three-fourths of the several States within seven years from the date of its submission.

Amendment XXI *(Ratified December 5, 1933)*

Section 1. The eighteenth article of amendment to the Constitution of the United States is hereby repealed.

Section 2. The transportation or importation into any State, Territory, or possession of the United States for delivery or use therein of intoxicating liquors, in violation of the laws thereof, is hereby prohibited.

Section 3. This article shall be inoperative unless it shall have been ratified as an amendment to the Constitution by conventions in the several States, as provided in the Constitution, within seven years from the date of the submission hereof to the States by the Congress.

Amendment XXII *(Ratified February 27, 1951)*

Section 1. No person shall be elected to the office of the President more than twice, and no person who has held the office of President, or acted as President, for more than two years of a term to which some other person was elected President shall be elected to the office of the President more than once. But this Article shall not apply to any person holding the office of President when this Article was proposed by the Congress, and shall not prevent any person who may be holding the office of President, or acting as President, during the term within which this Article becomes operative from holding the office of President or acting as President during the remainder of such term.

Section 2. This article shall be inoperative unless it shall have been ratified as an amendment to the Constitution by the legislatures of three-fourths of the several States within seven years from the date of its submission to the States by the Congress.

Amendment XXIII *(Ratified March 29, 1961)*

Section 1. The District constituting the seat of Government of the United States shall appoint in such manner as the Congress may direct:

A number of electors of President and Vice President equal to the whole number of Senators and Representatives in Congress to which the District would be entitled if it were a State, but in no event more than the least populous State; they shall be in addition to those appointed by the States, but they shall be considered, for the purposes of the election of President and Vice President, to be electors appointed by a State; and they shall meet in the District and perform such duties as provided by the twelfth article of amendment.

Section 2. The Congress shall have power to enforce this article by appropriate legislation.

Amendment XXIV *(Ratified January 23, 1964)*

Section 1. The right of citizens of the United States to vote in any primary or other election for President or Vice President, for electors for President or Vice President, or for Senator or Representative in Congress, shall not be denied or abridged by the United States or any State by reason of failure to pay any poll tax or other tax.

Section 2. The Congress shall have power to enforce this article by appropriate legislation.

Amendment XXV *(Ratified February 10, 1967)*

Section 1. In case of the removal of the President from office or of his death or resignation, the Vice President shall become President.

Section 2. Whenever there is a vacancy in the offie of the Vice President, the President shall nominate a Vice President who shall take office upon confirmation by a majority vote of both Houses of Congress.

Section 3. Whenever the President transmits to the President pro tempore of the Senate and the Speaker of the House of Representatives his written declaration that he is unable to discharge the powers and duties of his office, and until he transmits to them a written declaration to the contrary, such powers and duties shall be discharged by the Vice President as Acting President.

Section 4. Whenever the Vice President and a majority of either the principal officers of the executive departments or of such other body as Congress may by law provide, transmit to the President pro tempore of the Senate and the Speaker of the House of Representatives their written declaration that the President is unable to discharge the powers and duties of his office, the Vice President shall immediately assume the powers and duties of the office as Acting President.

Thereafter, when the President transmits to the President pro tempore of the Senate and the Speaker of the House of Representatives his written declaration that no inability exists, he shall resume the powers and duties of his office unless the Vice President and a majority of either the principal officers of the executive departments or of such other body as Congress may by law provide, transmit within four days to the President pro tempore of the Senate and the Speaker of the House of Representatives their written declaration that the President is unable to discharge the powers and duties of his office. Thereupon Congress shall decide the issue, assembling within forty-eight hours for that purpose if not in session. If the Congress, within twenty-one days after receipt of the latter written declaration, or, if Congress is not in session, within twenty-one days after Congress is required to assemble, determines by two-thirds vote of both Houses that the President is unable to discharge the powers and duties of his office, the Vice President shall continue to discharge the same as Acting President; otherwise, the President shall resume the powers and duties of his office.

Amendment XXVI *(Ratified July 1, 1971)*

Section 1. The right of citizens of the United States, who are eighteen years of age or older, to vote shall not be denied or abridged by the United States or by any State on account of age.

Section 2. The Congress shall have power to enforce this article by appropriate legislation.

Amendment XXVII *(Ratified May 7, 1992)*

No law varying the compensation for the services of the Senators and Representatives shall take effect, until an election of Representatives shall have intervened.

SOURCE: U.S. Congress, House, Committee on the Judiciary, *The Constitution of the United States of America, as Amended,* 100th Cong., 1st sess., 1987, H Doc 100–94.
NOTES: 1. The part in brackets was changed by section 2 of the Fourteenth Amendment.

2. The part in brackets was changed by the first paragraph of the Seventeenth Amendment.

3. The part in brackets was changed by the second paragraph of the Seventeenth Amendment.

4. The part in brackets was changed by section 2 of the Twentieth Amendment.

5. The Sixteenth Amendment gave Congress the power to tax incomes.

6. The material in brackets was superseded by the Twelfth Amendment.

7. This provision was affected by the Twenty-fifth Amendment.

8. These clauses were affected by the Eleventh Amendment.

9. This paragraph was superseded by the Thirteenth Amendment.

10. Obsolete.

11. The part in brackets was superseded by section 3 of the Twentieth Amendment.

12. See the Nineteenth and Twenty-sixth Amendments.

13. This amendment was repealed by section 1 of the Twenty-first Amendment.

14. See the Twenty-fifth Amendment.

Appendix 4

Federalist No. 10

The Same Subject Continued: The Union as a Safeguard Against Domestic Faction and Insurrection.

From the New York Packet
Friday, November 23, 1787.

Author: James Madison

To the People of the State of New York:

AMONG the numerous advantages promised by a well-constructed Union, none deserves to be more accurately developed than its tendency to break and control the violence of faction. The friend of popular governments never finds himself so much alarmed for their character and fate, as when he contemplates their propensity to this dangerous vice. He will not fail, therefore, to set a due value on any plan which, without violating the principles to which he is attached, provides a proper cure for it. The instability, injustice, and confusion introduced into the public councils, have, in truth, been the mortal diseases under which popular governments have everywhere perished; as they continue to be the favorite and fruitful topics from which the adversaries to liberty derive their most specious declamations. The valuable improvements made by the American constitutions on the popular models, both ancient and modern, cannot certainly be too much admired; but it would be an unwarrantable partiality, to contend that they have as effectually obviated the danger on this side, as was wished and expected. Complaints are everywhere heard from our most considerate and virtuous citizens, equally the friends of public and private faith, and of public and personal liberty, that our governments are too unstable, that the public good is disregarded in the conflicts of rival parties, and that measures are too often decided, not according to the rules of justice and the rights of the minor party, but by the superior force of an interested and overbearing majority. However anxiously we may wish that these complaints had no foundation, the evidence, of known facts will not permit us to deny that they are in some degree true. It will be found, indeed, on a candid review of our situation, that some of the distresses under which we labor have been erroneously charged on the operation of our governments; but it will be found, at the same time, that other causes will not alone account for many of our heaviest misfortunes; and, particularly, for that prevailing and increasing distrust of public engagements, and alarm for private rights, which are echoed from one end of the continent to the other. These must be chiefly, if not wholly, effects of the unsteadiness and injustice with which a factious spirit has tainted our public administrations.

By a faction, I understand a number of citizens, whether amounting to a majority or a minority of the whole, who are united and actuated by some common impulse of passion, or of interest, adversed to the rights of other citizens, or to the permanent and aggregate interests of the community.

There are two methods of curing the mischiefs of faction: the one, by removing its causes; the other, by controlling its effects.

There are again two methods of removing the causes of faction: the one, by destroying the liberty which is essential to its existence; the other, by giving to every citizen the same opinions, the same passions, and the same interests.

It could never be more truly said than of the first remedy, that it was worse than the disease. Liberty is to faction what air is to fire, an aliment without which it instantly expires. But it could not be less folly to abolish liberty, which is essential to political life, because it nourishes faction, than it would be to wish the annihilation of air, which is essential to animal life, because it imparts to fire its destructive agency.

The second expedient is as impracticable as the first would be unwise. As long as the reason of man continues fallible, and he is at liberty to exercise it, different opinions will be formed. As long as the connection subsists between his reason and his self-love, his opinions and his passions will have a reciprocal influence on each other; and the former will be objects to which the latter will attach themselves. The diversity in the faculties of men, from which the rights of property originate, is not less an insuperable obstacle to a uniformity of interests. The protection of these faculties is the first object of government. From the protection of different and unequal faculties of acquiring property, the possession of different degrees and kinds of property immediately results; and from the influence of these on the sentiments and views of the respective proprietors, ensues a division of the society into different interests and parties.

The latent causes of faction are thus sown in the nature of man; and we see them everywhere brought into different degrees of activity, according to the different circumstances of civil society. A zeal for different opinions concerning religion, concerning government, and many other points, as well of speculation as of practice; an attachment to different leaders ambitiously contending for pre-eminence and power; or to persons of other descriptions whose fortunes have been interesting to the human passions, have, in turn, divided mankind into parties, inflamed them with mutual animosity, and rendered them much more disposed to vex and oppress each other than to co-operate for their common good. So strong is this propensity of mankind to fall into mutual animosities, that where no substantial occasion presents itself, the most frivolous and fanciful distinctions have been sufficient to kindle their unfriendly passions and excite their most violent conflicts. But the most common and durable source of factions has been the various and unequal distribution of property. Those who hold and those who are without property have ever formed distinct interests in society. Those who are creditors, and those who are debtors, fall under a like discrimination. A landed interest, a manufacturing interest, a mercantile interest, a moneyed interest, with many lesser interests, grow up of necessity in civilized nations, and divide them into different classes, actuated by different sentiments and views. The regulation of these various and interfering interests forms the principal task of modern legislation, and involves the spirit of party and faction in the necessary and ordinary operations of the government.

No man is allowed to be a judge in his own cause, because his interest would certainly bias his judgment, and, not improbably, corrupt his integrity. With equal, nay with greater reason, a body of men are unfit to be both judges and parties at the same time; yet what are many of the most important acts of legislation, but so many judicial determinations, not indeed concerning the rights of single persons, but concerning the rights of large bodies of citizens? And what are the different classes of legislators but advocates and parties to the causes which they determine? Is a law proposed concerning private debts? It is a question to which the creditors are parties on one side and the debtors on the other. Justice ought to hold the balance between them. Yet the par-

ties are, and must be, themselves the judges; and the most numerous party, or, in other words, the most powerful faction must be expected to prevail. Shall domestic manufactures be encouraged, and in what degree, by restrictions on foreign manufactures? are questions which would be differently decided by the landed and the manufacturing classes, and probably by neither with a sole regard to justice and the public good. The apportionment of taxes on the various descriptions of property is an act which seems to require the most exact impartiality; yet there is, perhaps, no legislative act in which greater opportunity and temptation are given to a predominant party to trample on the rules of justice. Every shilling with which they overburden the inferior number, is a shilling saved to their own pockets.

It is in vain to say that enlightened statesmen will be able to adjust these clashing interests, and render them all subservient to the public good. Enlightened statesmen will not always be at the helm. Nor, in many cases, can such an adjustment be made at all without taking into view indirect and remote considerations, which will rarely prevail over the immediate interest which one party may find in disregarding the rights of another or the good of the whole.

The inference to which we are brought is, that the CAUSES of faction cannot be removed, and that relief is only to be sought in the means of controlling its EFFECTS.

If a faction consists of less than a majority, relief is supplied by the republican principle, which enables the majority to defeat its sinister views by regular vote. It may clog the administration, it may convulse the society; but it will be unable to execute and mask its violence under the forms of the Constitution. When a majority is included in a faction, the form of popular government, on the other hand, enables it to sacrifice to its ruling passion or interest both the public good and the rights of other citizens. To secure the public good and private rights against the danger of such a faction, and at the same time to preserve the spirit and the form of popular government, is then the great object to which our inquiries are directed. Let me add that it is the great desideratum by which this form of government can be rescued from the opprobrium under which it has so long labored, and be recommended to the esteem and adoption of mankind.

By what means is this object attainable? Evidently by one of two only. Either the existence of the same passion or interest in a majority at the same time must be prevented, or the majority, having such coexistent passion or interest, must be rendered, by their number and local situation, unable to concert and carry into effect schemes of oppression. If the impulse and the opportunity be suffered to coincide, we well know that neither moral nor religious motives can be relied on as an adequate control. They are not found to be such on the injustice and violence of individuals, and lose their efficacy in proportion to the number combined together, that is, in proportion as their efficacy becomes needful.

From this view of the subject it may be concluded that a pure democracy, by which I mean a society consisting of a small number of citizens, who assemble and administer the government in person, can admit of no cure for the mischiefs of faction. A common passion or interest will, in almost every case, be felt by a majority of the whole; a communication and concert result from the form of government itself; and there is nothing to check the inducements to sacrifice the weaker party or an obnoxious individual. Hence it is that such democracies have ever been spectacles of turbulence and contention; have ever been found incompatible with personal security or the rights of property; and have in general been as short in their lives as they have been violent in their deaths. Theoretic politicians, who have patronized this species of government, have erroneously supposed that by reducing mankind to a perfect equality in their political rights, they would, at the same time, be perfectly equalized and assimilated in their possessions, their opinions, and their passions.

A republic, by which I mean a government in which the scheme of representation takes place, opens a different prospect, and promises the cure for which we are seeking. Let us examine the points in which it varies from pure democracy, and we shall comprehend both the nature of the cure and the efficacy which it must derive from the Union.

The two great points of difference between a democracy and a republic are: first, the delegation of the government, in the latter, to a small number of citizens elected by the rest; secondly, the greater number of citizens, and greater sphere of country, over which the latter may be extended.

The effect of the first difference is, on the one hand, to refine and enlarge the public views, by passing them through the medium of a chosen body of citizens, whose wisdom may best discern the true interest of their country, and whose patriotism and love of justice will be least likely to sacrifice it to temporary or partial considerations. Under such a regulation, it may well happen that the public voice, pronounced by the representatives of the people, will be more consonant to the public good than if pronounced by the people themselves, convened for the purpose. On the other hand, the effect may be inverted. Men of factious tempers, of local prejudices, or of sinister designs, may, by intrigue, by corruption, or by other means, first obtain the suffrages, and then betray the interests, of the people. The question resulting is, whether small or extensive republics are more favorable to the election of

proper guardians of the public weal; and it is clearly decided in favor of the latter by two obvious considerations:

In the first place, it is to be remarked that, however small the republic may be, the representatives must be raised to a certain number, in order to guard against the cabals of a few; and that, however large it may be, they must be limited to a certain number, in order to guard against the confusion of a multitude. Hence, the number of representatives in the two cases not being in proportion to that of the two constituents, and being proportionally greater in the small republic, it follows that, if the proportion of fit characters be not less in the large than in the small republic, the former will present a greater option, and consequently a greater probability of a fit choice.

In the next place, as each representative will be chosen by a greater number of citizens in the large than in the small republic, it will be more difficult for unworthy candidates to practice with success the vicious arts by which elections are too often carried; and the suffrages of the people being more free, will be more likely to centre in men who possess the most attractive merit and the most diffusive and established characters.

It must be confessed that in this, as in most other cases, there is a mean, on both sides of which inconveniences will be found to lie. By enlarging too much the number of electors, you render the representatives too little acquainted with all their local circumstances and lesser interests; as by reducing it too much, you render him unduly attached to these, and too little fit to comprehend and pursue great and national objects. The federal Constitution forms a happy combination in this respect; the great and aggregate interests being referred to the national, the local and particular to the State legislatures.

The other point of difference is, the greater number of citizens and extent of territory which may be brought within the compass of republican than of democratic government; and it is this circumstance principally which renders factious combinations less to be dreaded in the former than in the latter. The smaller the society, the fewer probably will be the distinct parties and interests composing it; the fewer the distinct parties and interests, the more frequently will a majority be found of the same party; and the smaller the number of individuals composing a majority, and the smaller the compass within which they are placed, the more easily will they concert and execute their plans of oppression. Extend the sphere, and you take in a greater variety of parties and interests; you make it less probable that a majority of the whole will have a common motive to invade the rights of other citizens; or if such a common motive exists, it will be more difficult for all who feel it to discover their own strength, and to act in unison with each other. Besides other impediments, it may be remarked that, where there is a consciousness of unjust or dishonorable purposes, communication is always checked by distrust in proportion to the number whose concurrence is necessary.

Hence, it clearly appears, that the same advantage which a republic has over a democracy, in controlling the effects of faction, is enjoyed by a large over a small republic,—is enjoyed by the Union over the States composing it. Does the advantage consist in the substitution of representatives whose enlightened views and virtuous sentiments render them superior to local prejudices and schemes of injustice? It will not be denied that the representation of the Union will be most likely to possess these requisite endowments. Does it consist in the greater security afforded by a greater variety of parties, against the event of any one party being able to outnumber and oppress the rest? In an equal degree does the increased variety of parties comprised within the Union, increase this security. Does it, in fine, consist in the greater obstacles opposed to the concert and accomplishment of the secret wishes of an unjust and interested majority? Here, again, the extent of the Union gives it the most palpable advantage.

The influence of factious leaders may kindle a flame within their particular States, but will be unable to spread a general conflagration through the other States. A religious sect may degenerate into a political faction in a part of the Confederacy; but the variety of sects dispersed over the entire face of it must secure the national councils against any danger from that source. A rage for paper money, for an abolition of debts, for an equal division of property, or for any other improper or wicked project, will be less apt to pervade the whole body of the Union than a particular member of it; in the same proportion as such a malady is more likely to taint a particular county or district, than an entire State.

In the extent and proper structure of the Union, therefore, we behold a republican remedy for the diseases most incident to republican government. And according to the degree of pleasure and pride we feel in being republicans, ought to be our zeal in cherishing the spirit and supporting the character of Federalists.

PUBLIUS.

Federalist No. 51

The Structure of the Government Must Furnish the Proper Checks and Balances Between the Different Departments

From the New York Packet.
Friday, February 8, 1788.
Author: James Madison

To the People of the State of New York:

TO WHAT expedient, then, shall we finally resort, for maintaining in practice the necessary partition of power among the several departments, as laid down in the Constitution? The only answer that can be given is, that as all these exterior provisions are found to be inadequate, the defect must be supplied, by so contriving the interior structure of the government as that its several constituent parts may, by their mutual relations, be the means of keeping each other in their proper places. Without presuming to undertake a full development of this important idea, I will hazard a few general observations, which may perhaps place it in a clearer light, and enable us to form a more correct judgment of the principles and structure of the government planned by the convention.

In order to lay a due foundation for that separate and distinct exercise of the different powers of government, which to a certain extent is admitted on all hands to be essential to the preservation of liberty, it is evident that each department should have a will of its own; and consequently should be so constituted that the members of each should have as little agency as possible in the appointment of the members of the others. Were this principle rigorously adhered to, it would require that all the appointments for the supreme executive, legislative, and judiciary magistracies should be drawn from the same fountain of authority, the people, through channels having no communication whatever with one another. Perhaps such a plan of constructing the several departments would be less difficult in practice than it may in contemplation appear. Some difficulties, however, and some additional expense would attend the execution of it. Some deviations, therefore, from the principle must be admitted. In the constitution of the judiciary department in particular, it might be inexpedient to insist rigorously on the principle: first, because peculiar qualifications being essential in the members, the primary consideration ought to be to select that mode of choice which best secures these qualifications; secondly, because the permanent tenure by which the appointments are held in that department, must soon destroy all sense of dependence on the authority conferring them.

It is equally evident, that the members of each department should be as little dependent as possible on those of the others, for the emoluments annexed to their offices. Were the executive magistrate, or the judges, not independent of the legislature in this particular, their independence in every other would be merely nominal. But the great security against a gradual concentration of the several powers in the same department, consists in giving to those who administer each department the necessary constitutional means and personal motives to resist encroachments of the others. The provision for defense must in this, as in all other cases, be made commensurate to the danger of attack. Ambition must be made to counteract ambition. The interest of the man must be connected with the constitutional rights of the place. It may be a reflection on human nature, that such devices should be necessary to control the abuses of government. But what is government itself, but the greatest of all reflections on human nature? If men were angels, no government would be necessary. If angels were to govern men, neither external nor internal controls on government would be necessary. In framing a government which is to be administered by men over men, the great difficulty lies in this: you must first enable the government to control the governed; and in the next place oblige it to control itself.

A dependence on the people is, no doubt, the primary control on the government; but experience has taught mankind the necessity of auxiliary precautions. This policy of supplying, by opposite and rival interests, the defect of better motives, might be traced through the whole system of human affairs, private as well as public. We see it particularly displayed in all the subordinate distributions of power, where the constant aim is to divide and arrange the several offices in such a manner as that each may be a check on the other that the private interest of every individual may be a sentinel over the public rights. These inventions of prudence cannot be less requisite in the distribution of the supreme powers of the State. But it is not possible to give to each department an equal power of self-defense. In republican government, the legislative authority necessarily predominates. The remedy for this inconveniency is to divide the legislature into different branches; and to render them, by different modes of election and different principles of action, as little connected with each other as the nature of their common functions and their common dependence on the society will admit. It may even be necessary to guard against dangerous encroachments by still further precautions. As the weight of the legislative authority requires that it should be thus divided, the weakness of the executive may require, on the other hand, that it should be fortified.

An absolute negative on the legislature appears, at first view, to be the natural defense with which the executive magistrate should be armed. But perhaps it would be neither altogether safe nor alone sufficient. On ordinary occasions it might not be exerted with the requisite firmness, and on extraordinary occasions it might be perfidiously abused. May not this defect of an absolute negative be supplied by some qualified connection between this weaker department and the weaker branch of the stronger department, by which the latter may be led to support the constitutional rights of the former, without being too much detached from the rights of its own department? If the principles on which these observations are founded be just, as I persuade myself they are, and they be applied as a criterion to the several State constitutions, and to the federal Constitution it will be found that if the latter does not perfectly correspond with them, the former are infinitely less able to bear such a test.

There are, moreover, two considerations particularly applicable to the federal system of America, which place that system in a very interesting point of view. First. In a single republic, all the power surrendered by the people is submitted to the administration of a single government; and the usurpations are guarded against by a division of the government into distinct and separate departments. In the compound republic of America, the power surrendered by the people is first divided between two distinct governments, and then the portion allotted to each subdivided among distinct and separate departments. Hence a double security arises to the rights of the people. The different governments will control each other, at the same time that each will be controlled by itself. Second. It is of great importance in a republic not only to guard the society against the oppression of its rulers, but to guard one part of the society against the injustice of the other part. Different interests necessarily exist in different classes of citizens. If a majority be united by a common interest, the rights of the minority will be insecure.

There are but two methods of providing against this evil: the one by creating a will in the community independent of the majority that is, of the society itself; the other, by comprehending in the society so many separate descriptions of citizens as will render an unjust combination of a majority of the whole very improbable, if not impracticable. The first method prevails in all governments possessing an hereditary or self-appointed authority. This, at best, is but a precarious security; because a power independent of the society may as well espouse the unjust views of the major, as the rightful interests of the minor party, and may possibly be turned against both parties. The second method will be exemplified in the federal republic of the United States. Whilst all authority in it will be derived from and dependent on the society, the society itself will be broken into so many parts, interests, and classes of citizens, that the rights of individuals, or of the minority, will be in little danger from interested combinations of the majority.

In a free government the security for civil rights must be the same as that for religious rights. It consists in the one case in the multiplicity of interests, and in the other in the multiplicity of sects. The degree of security in both cases will depend on the number of interests and sects; and this may be presumed to depend on the extent of country and number of people comprehended under the same government. This view of the subject must particularly recommend a proper federal system to all the sincere and considerate friends of republican government, since it shows that in exact proportion as the territory of the Union may be formed into more circumscribed Confederacies, or States oppressive combinations of a majority will be facilitated: the best security, under the republican forms, for the rights of every class of citizens, will be diminished: and consequently the stability and independence of some member of the government, the only other security, must be proportionately increased. Justice is the end of government. It is the end of civil society. It ever has been and ever will be pursued until it be obtained, or until liberty be lost in the pursuit. In a society under the forms of which the stronger faction can readily unite and oppress the weaker, anarchy may as truly be said to reign as in a state of nature, where the weaker individual is not secured against the violence of the stronger; and as, in the latter state, even the stronger individuals are prompted, by the uncertainty of their condition, to submit to a government which may protect the weak as well as themselves; so, in the former state, will the more powerful factions or parties be gradually induced, by a like motive, to wish for a government which will protect all parties, the weaker as well as the more powerful.

It can be little doubted that if the State of Rhode Island was separated from the Confederacy and left to itself, the insecurity of rights under the popular form of government within such narrow limits would be displayed by such reiterated oppressions of factious majorities that some power altogether independent of the people would soon be called for by the voice of the very factions whose misrule had proved the necessity of it. In the extended republic of the United States, and among the great variety of interests, parties, and sects which it embraces, a coalition of a majority of the whole society could seldom take place on any other principles than those of justice and the general good; whilst there being thus less danger to a minor from the will of a major party, there must be less pretext, also, to provide for the security of the former, by introducing into the government a will not dependent on the latter, or, in other words, a will independent of the society itself. It is no less certain than it is important, notwithstanding the contrary opinions which have been entertained, that the larger the society, provided it lie within a practical sphere, the more duly capable it will be of self-government. And happily for the REPUBLICAN CAUSE, the practicable sphere may be carried to a very great extent, by a judicious modification and mixture of the FEDERAL PRINCIPLE.

PUBLIUS.

Appendix 6

Presidents, Vice Presidents, Speakers, and Chief Justices, 1789–2009

President/Vice President	Term	Congress	Speaker of the House	Chief Justice of the United States
George Washington[1]	(1789–1797)	1st	Frederick A.C. Muhlenberg, Pa.	John Jay (1789–1795)
John Adams		2nd	Jonathan Trumbull, F-Conn.	John Rutledge (1795)
		3rd	Muhlenberg	Oliver Ellsworth (1796–1800)
		4th	Jonathan Dayton, F-N.J.	
John Adams, F	(1797–1801)	5th	Dayton	Ellsworth
Thomas Jefferson, D-R		6th	Theodore Sedgwick, F-Mass.	John Marshall (1801–1835)
Thomas Jefferson, D-R	(1801–1809)	7th	Nathaniel Macon, D-N.C.	Marshall
Aaron Burr (1801–1805)		8th	Macon	
George Clinton (1805–1809)		9th	Macon	
		10th	Joseph B. Varnum, Mass.	
James Madison, D-R	(1809–1817)	11th	Varnum	Marshall
George Clinton[2] (1809–1812)		12th	Henry Clay, R-Ky.	
Elbridge Gerry[2] (1813–1814)		13th	Clay/Langdon Cheves, D-S.C.	
		14th	Clay	
James Monroe, D-R	(1817–1825)	15th	Clay	Marshall
Daniel D. Tompkins		16th	Clay/John W. Taylor, D-N.Y.	
		17th	Philip P. Barbour, D-Va.	
		18th	Clay	
John Quincy Adams, D-R	(1825–1829)	19th	Taylor	Marshall
John C. Calhoun		20th	Andrew Stevenson, D-Va.	
Andrew Jackson, D	(1829–1837)	21st	Stevenson	Marshall
John C. Calhoun[3] (1829–1832)		22nd	Stevenson	Roger B. Taney (1836–1864)
Martin Van Buren (1833–1837)		23rd	Stevenson/John Bell, W-Tenn.	
		24th	James K. Polk, D-Tenn.	
Martin Van Buren, D	(1837–1841)	25th	Polk	Taney
Richard M. Johnson		26th	Robert M.T. Hunter, D-Va.	
William Henry Harrison,[2] W	(1841)			Taney
John Tyler				
John Tyler, W	(1841–1845)	27th	John White, W-Ky.	Taney
		28th	John W. Jones, D-Va.	
James K. Polk, D	(1845–1849)	29th	John W. Davis, D-Ind.	Taney
George M. Dallas		30th	Robert C. Winthrop, W-Mass.	
Zachary Taylor,[2] W	(1849–1850)	31st	Howell Cobb, D-Ga.	Taney
Millard Fillmore				
Millard Fillmore, W	(1850–1853)	31st	Cobb	Taney
		32nd	Linn Boyd, D-Ky.	

(continued)

(continued)

President/Vice President	Term	Congress	Speaker of the House	Chief Justice of the United States
Franklin Pierce, D William R. King[2] (1853)	(1853–1857)	33rd 34th	Boyd Nathaniel P. Banks, R-Mass.	Taney
James Buchanan, D John C. Breckinridge	(1857–1861)	35th 36th	James L. Orr, D-S.C. William Pennington, R-N.J.	Taney
Abraham Lincoln,[2] R Hannibal Hamlin (1861–1865) Andrew Johnson,[4] D (1865)	(1861–1865)	37th 38th	Galusha A. Grow, R-Pa. Schuyler Colfax, R-Ind.	Taney Salmon P. Chase (1864–1873)
Andrew Johnson, D	(1865–1869)	39th 40th	Colfax Colfax/Theodore M. Pomeroy, R-N.Y.	Chase
Ulysses S. Grant, R Schuyler Colfax (1869–1873) Henry Wilson[2] (1873–1875)	(1869–1877)	41st 42nd 43rd 44th	James G. Blaine, R-Maine Blaine Blaine Michael C. Kerr, D-Ind./ Samuel J. Randall, D-Pa.	Chase Morrison R. Waite (1874–1888)
Rutherford B. Hayes, R William A. Wheeler	(1877–1881)	45th 46th	Randall Randall	Waite
James A. Garfield,[2] R Chester A. Arthur	(1881)			Waite
Chester A. Arthur, R	(1881–1885)	47th 48th	Joseph Warren Keifer, R-Ohio John G. Carlisle, D-Ky.	Waite
Grover Cleveland, D Thomas A. Hendricks[2] (1885)	(1885–1889)	49th 50th	Carlisle Carlisle	Waite Melville W. Fuller (1888–1910)
Benjamin Harrison, R Levi P. Morton	(1889–1893)	51st 52nd	Thomas Brackett Reed, R-Maine Charles F. Crisp, D-Ga.	Fuller
Grover Cleveland, D Adlai E. Stevenson	(1893–1897)	53rd 54th	Crisp Reed	Fuller
William McKinley,[2] R Garret A. Hobart[2] (1897–1899) Theodore Roosevelt (1901)	(1897–1901)	55th 56th	Reed David B. Henderson, R-Iowa	Fuller
Theodore Roosevelt, R Charles W. Fairbanks (1905–1909)	(1901–1909)	57th 58th 59th 60th	Henderson Joseph G. Cannon, R-Ill. Cannon Cannon	Fuller
William Howard Taft, R James S. Sherman[2] (1909–1912)	(1909–1913)	61st 62nd	Cannon James B. "Champ" Clark, D-Mo.	Fuller Edward D. White (1910–1921)
Woodrow Wilson, D Thomas R. Marshall	(1913–1921)	63rd 64th 65th 66th	Clark Clark Clark Frederick H. Gillett, R-Mass.	White
Warren G. Harding,[2] R Calvin Coolidge	(1921–1923)	67th	Gillett	William Howard Taft (1921–1930)
Calvin Coolidge, R Charles G. Dawes (1925–1929)	(1923–1929)	68th 69th 70th	Gillett Nicholas Longworth, R-Ohio Longworth	Taft
Herbert C. Hoover, R Charles Curtis	(1929–1933)	71st 72nd	Longworth John Nance Garner, D-Texas	Taft Charles Evans Hughes (1930–1941)

President/Vice President	Term	Congress	Speaker of the House	Chief Justice of the United States

Franklin D. Roosevelt,[2] D
  John Nance Garner (1933–1941)
 	
Henry A. Wallace (1941–1945)
  Harry S. Truman (1945)
	(1933–1945)	73rd
		74th
		
		75th
		76th
		77th
		78th
		79th
			Henry T. Rainey, D-Ill.
			Joseph W. Byrns, D-Tenn./
			  William B. Bankhead, D-Ala.
			Bankhead
			
			Bankhead/Sam Rayburn, D-Texas
			Rayburn
			Rayburn
			Rayburn
				Hughes
				Harlan F. Stone (1941–1946)

Harry S. Truman, D Alben W. Barkley (1949–1953)	(1945–1953)	79th 80th 81st 82nd	Rayburn Joseph W. Martin Jr., R-Mass. Rayburn Rayburn	Stone Frederick M. Vinson (1946–1953)
Dwight D. Eisenhower, R Richard Nixon	(1953–1961)	83rd 84th 85th 86th	Martin Rayburn Rayburn Rayburn	Vinson Earl Warren (1953–1969)

John F. Kennedy,[2] D
 	
  Lyndon B. Johnson
	(1961–1963)	87th
		
		88th
			Rayburn/John W. McCormack,
			  D-Mass.
			McCormack
				Warren

Lyndon B. Johnson, D Hubert H. Humphrey (1965–1969)	(1963–1969)	88th 89th 90th	McCormack McCormack McCormack	Warren

Richard Nixon,[3] R
  Spiro T. Agnew[3] (1969–1973)
  Gerald R. Ford[5] (1973–1974)
	(1969–1974)	91st
		92nd
		93rd
			McCormack
			Carl Albert, D-Okla.
			Albert
				Warren
				Warren E. Burger (1969–1986)

Gerald R. Ford, R Nelson A. Rockefeller[5]	(1974–1977)	93rd 94th	Albert Albert	Burger
Jimmy Carter, D Walter F. Mondale	(1977–1981)	95th 96th	Thomas P. O'Neill Jr., D-Mass. O'Neill	Burger
Ronald Reagan, R George Bush	(1981–1989)	97th 98th 99th 100th	O'Neill O'Neill O'Neill Jim Wright, D-Texas	Burger William Rehnquist (1986–2005)
George H. W. Bush, R Dan Quayle	(1989–1993)	101st 102nd	Wright/Thomas S. Foley, D-Wash. Foley	Rehnquist
Bill Clinton, D Al Gore	(1993–2001)	103rd 104th 105th 106th	Foley Newt Gingrich, R-Ga. Gingrich J. Dennis Hastert, R-Ill.	Rehnquist
George W. Bush, R Richard B. Cheney	(2001–2009)	107th 108th 109th 110th	J. Dennis Hastert, R-Ill. Nancy D. Pelosi, D-Ca.	Rehnquist John Roberts (2005–)
Barack Obama, D Joseph R. Biden Jr.	(2009–)	111th	Pelosi	Roberts

NOTES: The vice president's term or party is noted when it differs from that of the president. Key to abbreviations: D—Democrat; D-R—Democratic-Republican; F—Federalist; R—Republican; W—Whig.

1. Washington belonged to no formal party.   2. Died in office.   3. Resigned from office.
4. Democrat Johnson and Republican Lincoln ran under the Union Party banner in 1864.   5. Appointed to office.

Map of Congressional Districts

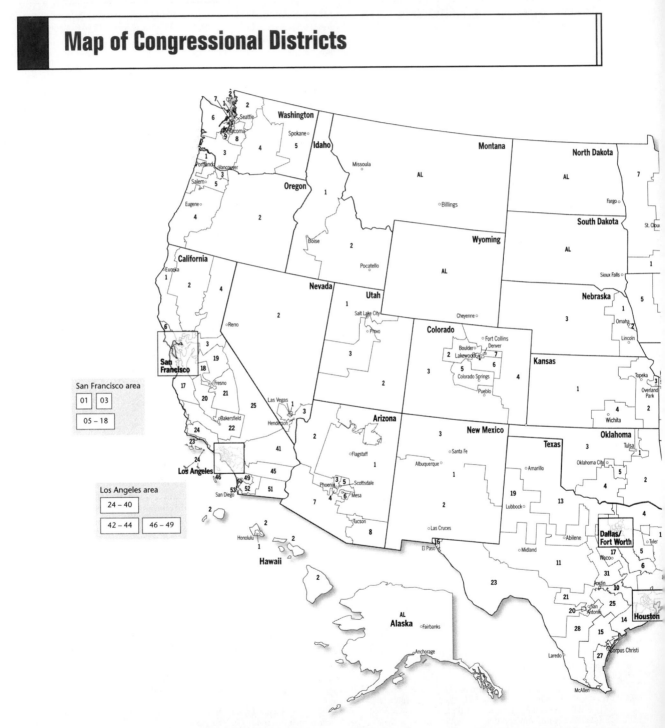

Source: *CQ Weekly*, November 10, 2008, 3017.

Note: District lines were those used in the 2008 general election.

Appendix 8

Political Party Affiliations in Congress and the Presidency, 1789–2009

Year	Congress	House Majority party	House Principal minority party	Senate Majority party	Senate Principal minority party	President
1789–1791	1st	AD-38	Op-26	AD-17	Op-9	F (Washington)
1791–1793	2nd	F-37	DR-33	F-16	DR-13	F (Washington)
1793–1795	3rd	DR-57	F-48	F-17	DR-13	F (Washington)
1795–1797	4th	F-54	DR-52	F-19	DR-13	F (Washington)
1797–1799	5th	F-58	DR-48	F-20	DR-12	F (John Adams)
1799–1801	6th	F-64	DR-42	F-19	DR-13	F (John Adams)
1801–1803	7th	DR-69	F-36	DR-18	F-13	DR (Jefferson)
1803–1805	8th	DR-102	F-39	DR-25	F-9	DR (Jefferson)
1805–1807	9th	DR-116	F-25	DR-27	F-7	DR (Jefferson)
1807–1809	10th	DR-118	F-24	DR-28	F-6	DR (Jefferson)
1809–1811	11th	DR-94	F-48	DR-28	F-6	DR (Madison)
1811–1813	12th	DR-108	F-36	DR-30	F-6	DR (Madison)
1813–1815	13th	DR-112	F-68	DR-27	F-9	DR (Madison)
1815–1817	14th	DR-117	F-65	DR-25	F-11	DR (Madison)
1817–1819	15th	DR-141	F-42	DR-34	F-10	DR (Monroe)
1819–1821	16th	DR-156	F-27	DR-35	F-7	DR (Monroe)
1821–1823	17th	DR-158	F-25	DR-44	F-4	DR (Monroe)
1823–1825	18th	DR-187	F-26	DR-44	F-4	DR (Monroe)
1825–1827	19th	AD-105	J-97	AD-26	J-20	DR (John Q. Adams)
1827–1829	20th	J-119	AD-94	J-28	AD-20	DR (John Q. Adams)
1829–1831	21st	D-139	NR-74	D-26	NR-22	DR (Jackson)
1831–1833	22nd	D-141	NR-58	D-25	NR-21	D (Jackson)
1833–1835	23rd	D-147	AM-53	D-20	NR-20	D (Jackson)
1835–1837	24th	D-145	W-98	D-27	W-25	D (Jackson)
1837–1839	25th	D-108	W-107	D-30	W-18	D (Van Buren)
1839–1841	26th	D-124	W-118	D-28	W-22	D (Van Buren)
1841–1843	27th	W-133	D-102	W-28	D-22	W (W. Harrison) W (Tyler)
1843–1845	28th	D-142	W-79	W-28	D-25	W (Tyler)
1845–1847	29th	D-143	W-77	D-31	W-25	D (Polk)
1847–1849	30th	W-115	D-108	D-36	W-21	D (Polk)
1849–1851	31st	D-112	W-109	D-35	W-25	W (Taylor) W (Fillmore)
1851–1853	32nd	D-140	W-88	D-35	W-24	W (Fillmore)
1853–1855	33rd	D-159	W-71	D-38	W-22	D (Pierce)

Year	Congress	House		Senate		President
		Majority party	Principal minority party	Majority party	Principal minority party	
1855–1857	34th	R-108	D-83	D-42	R-15	D (Pierce)
1857–1859	35th	D-131	R-92	D-35	R-20	D (Buchanan)
1859–1861	36th	R-113	D-101	D-38	R-26	D (Buchanan)
1861–1863	37th	R-106	D-42	R-31	D-11	R (Lincoln)
1863–1865	38th	R-103	D-80	R-39	D-12	R (Lincoln)
1865–1867[1]	39th	U-145	D-46	U-42	D-10	U (Lincoln)
						U (A. Johnson)
1867–1869	40th	R-143	D-49	R-42	D-11	R (A. Johnson)
1869–1871	41st	R-170	D-73	R-61	D-11	R (Grant)
1871–1873	42nd	R-139	D-104	R-57	D-17	R (Grant)
1873–1875	43rd	R-203	D-88	R-54	D-19	R (Grant)
1875–1877	44th	D-181	R-107	R-46	D-29	R (Grant)
1877–1879	45th	D-156	R-137	R-39	D-36	R (Hayes)
1879–1881	46th	D-150	R-128	D-43	R-33	R (Hayes)
1881–1883	47th	R-152	D-130	R-37	D-37	R (Garfield)
						R (Arthur)
1883–1885	48th	D-200	R-119	R-40	D-36	R (Arthur)
1885–1887	49th	D-182	R-140	R-41	D-34	D (Cleveland)
1887–1889	50th	D-170	R-151	R-39	D-37	D (Cleveland)
1889–1891	51st	R-173	D-159	R-37	D-37	R (B. Harrison)
1891–1893	52nd	D-231	R-88	R-47	D-39	R (B. Harrison)
1893–1895	53rd	D-220	R-126	D-44	R-38	D (Cleveland)
1895–1897	54th	R-246	D-104	R-43	D-39	D (Cleveland)
1897–1899	55th	R-206	D-134	R-46	D-34	R (McKinley)
1899–1901	56th	R-185	D-163	R-53	D-26	R (McKinley)
1901–1903	57th	R-198	D-153	R-56	D-29	R (McKinley)
						R (T. Roosevelt)
1903–1905	58th	R-207	D-178	R-58	D-32	R (T. Roosevelt)
1905–1907	59th	R-250	D-136	R-58	D-32	R (T. Roosevelt)
1907–1909	60th	R-222	D-164	R-61	D-29	R (T. Roosevelt)
1909–1911	61st	R-219	D-172	R-59	D-32	R (Taft)
1911–1913	62nd	D-228	R-162	R-49	D-42	R (Taft)
1913–1915	63rd	D-290	R-127	D-51	R-44	D (Wilson)
1915–1917	64th	D-231	R-193	D-56	R-39	D (Wilson)
1917–1919	65th	D-216	R-210	D-53	R-42	D (Wilson)
1919–1921	66th	R-237	D-191	R-48	D-47	D (Wilson)
1921–1923	67th	R-300	D-132	R-59	D-37	R (Harding)
1923–1925	68th	R-225	D-207	R-51	D-43	R (Coolidge)
1925–1927	69th	R-247	D-183	R-54	D-40	R (Coolidge)
1927–1929	70th	R-237	D-195	R-48	D-47	R (Coolidge)
1929–1931	71st	R-267	D-163	R-56	D-39	R (Hoover)
1931–1933	72nd	D-216	R-218	R-48	D-47	R (Hoover)
1933–1935	73rd	D-313	R-117	D-59	R-36	D (F. Roosevelt)
1935–1937	74th	D-322	R-103	D-69	R-25	D (F. Roosevelt)
1937–1939	75th	D-333	R-89	D-75	R-17	D (F. Roosevelt)
1939–1941	76th	D-262	R-169	D-69	R-23	D (F. Roosevelt)
1941–1943	77th	D-267	R-162	D-66	R-28	D (F. Roosevelt)
1943–1945	78th	D-222	R-209	D-57	R-38	D (F. Roosevelt)
1945–1947	79th	D-243	R-190	D-56	R-38	D (F. Roosevelt)
						D (Truman)

(continued)

(continued)

Year	Congress	House Majority party	House Principal minority party	Senate Majority party	Senate Principal minority party	President
1947–1949	80th	R-246	D-188	R-51	D-45	D (Truman)
1949–1951	81st	D-263	R-171	D-54	R-42	D (Truman)
1951–1953	82nd	D-234	R-199	D-48	R-47	D (Truman)
1953–1955	83rd	R-221	D-213	R-48	D-46	R (Eisenhower)
1955–1957	84th	D-234	R-201	D-48	R-47	R (Eisenhower)
1957–1959	85th	D-233	R-200	D-49	R-47	R (Eisenhower)
1959–1961	86th	D-283	R-153	D-64	R-34	R (Eisenhower)
1961–1963	87th	D-262	R-175	D-64	R-36	D (Kennedy)
1963–1965	88th	D-258	R-176	D-67	R-33	D (Kennedy) D (L. Johnson)
1965–1967	89th	D-295	R-140	D-68	R-32	D (L. Johnson)
1967–1969	90th	D-248	R-187	D-64	R-36	D (L. Johnson)
1969–1971	91st	D-243	R-192	D-58	R-42	R (Nixon)
1971–1973	92nd	D-255	R-180	D-54	R-44	R (Nixon)
1973–1975	93rd	D-242	R-192	D-56	R-42	R (Nixon) R (Ford)
1975–1977	94th	D-291	R-144	D-60	R-37	R (Ford)
1977–1979	95th	D-292	R-143	D-61	R-38	D (Carter)
1979–1981	96th	D-277	R-158	D-58	R-41	D (Carter)
1981–1983	97th	D-242	R-192	R-53	D-46	R (Reagan)
1983–1985	98th	D-269	R-166	R-54	D-46	R (Reagan)
1985–1987	99th	D-253	R-182	R-53	D-47	R (Reagan)
1987–1989	100th	D-258	R-177	D-55	R-45	R (Reagan)
1989–1991	101st	D-260	R-175	D-55	R-45	R (G.H.W. Bush)
1991–1993	102nd	D-267	R-167	D-56	R-44	R (G.H.W. Bush)
1993–1995	103rd	D-258	R-176	D-57	R-43	D (Clinton)
1995–1997	104th	R-230	D-204	R-52	D-48	D (Clinton)
1997–1999	105th	R-226	D-207	R-55	D-45	D (Clinton)
1999–2001	106th	R-223	D-211	R-55	D-45	D (Clinton)
2001–2003	107th	R-221	D-212	D-50	R-50	R (G. W. Bush)
2003–2005	108th	R-229	D-204	D-48	R-51	R (G. W. Bush)
2005–2007	109th	R-232	D-202	D-44	R-55	R (G. W. Bush)
2007–2009	110th	D-233	R-202	D-49	R-49	R (G. W. Bush)
**2009–	111th	D-254	R-175	D-57	R-40	D (Obama)

SOURCES: For data through the 33rd Congress, see U.S. Bureau of the Census, *Historical Statistics of the United States, Colonial Times to 1970* (Washington, D.C.: Government Printing Office, 1975), 1083–1084; for data after the 33rd Congress, see U.S. Congress, Joint Committee on Printing, *Official Congressional Directory* (Washington, D.C.: Government Printing Office, 2008), 553–554; for 2008 election data see *CQ Politics Election 2008*, www.cqpolitics.com/wmspage.cfn?parm1=2. See also http://innovation.cq.com/election_night08?tab2=f.

NOTES: Figures are for the beginning of the first session of each Congress. Key to abbreviations: AD—Administration; AM—Anti-Masonic; D—Democratic; DR—Democratic-Republican; F—Federalist; J—Jacksonian; NR—National Republican; Op—Opposition; R—Republican; U—Unionist; W—Whig.

1. The Republican Party ran under the Union Party banner in 1864.

**Numbers current as of time of publication. For the Senate, three races have not yet been called—Alaska, Georgia, and Minnesota. For the House, four races have not yet been called (1 in California-District 4, 1 in Ohio-District 15, 1 in Virginia-District 5, and 1 in Maryland-District 1). Two Louisiana races—Districts 2 and 4—will be decided after this book goes to press.

Appendix 9

Summary of Presidential Elections, 1789–2008

Year	No. of states	Candidates		Electoral vote		Popular vote	
1789[a]	10	*Fed.* George Washington		*Fed.* 69		———[b]	
1792[a]	15	*Fed.* George Washington		*Fed.* 132		———[b]	
1796[a]	16	*Dem.-Rep.* Thomas Jefferson	*Fed.* John Adams	*Dem.-Rep.* 68	*Fed.* 71	———[b]	
1800[a]	16	*Dem.-Rep.* Thomas Jefferson Aaron Burr	*Fed.* John Adams Charles Cotesworth Pinckney	*Dem.-Rep.* 73	*Fed.* 65	———[b]	
1804	17	*Dem.-Rep.* Thomas Jefferson George Clinton	*Fed.* Charles Cotesworth Pinckney Rufus King	*Dem.-Rep.* 162	*Fed.* 14	———[b]	
1808	17	*Dem.-Rep.* James Madison George Clinton	*Fed.* Charles Cotesworth Pinckney Rufus King	*Dem.-Rep.* 122	*Fed.* 47	———[b]	
1812	18	*Dem.-Rep.* James Madison Elbridge Gerry	*Fed.* George Clinton Jared Ingersoll	*Dem.-Rep.* 128	*Fed.* 89	———[b]	
1816	19	*Dem.-Rep.* James Monroe Daniel D. Tompkins	*Fed.* Rufus King John Howard	*Dem.-Rep.* 183	*Fed.* 34	———[b]	
1820	24	*Dem.-Rep* James Monroe Daniel D. Tompkins	———[c]	*Dem.-Rep* 231	———[c]	———[b]	
1824[d]	24	*Dem.-Rep* Andrew Jackson John C. Calhoun	*Dem.-Rep* John Q. Adams Nathan Sanford	*Dem.-Rep* 99	*Dem.-Rep.* 84	*Dem.-Rep* 151,271 41.3%	*Dem.-Rep* 113,122 30.9%
1828	24	*Dem.-Rep.* Andrew Jackson John C. Calhoun	*Nat.-Rep.* John Q. Adams Richard Rush	*Dem.-Rep.* 178	*Nat.-Rep.* 83	*Dem.-Rep.* 642,553 56.0%	*Nat.-Rep.* 500,897 43.6%
1832[e]	24	*Dem.* Andrew Jackson Martin Van Buren	*Nat.-Rep.* Henry Clay John Sergeant	*Dem.* 219	*Nat.-Rep.* 49 54.2%	*Dem.* 701,780	*Nat.-Rep.* 484,205 37.4%

(continued)

(continued)

Year	No. of states	Candidates		Electoral vote		Popular vote	
1836[f]	26	*Dem.* Martin Van Buren Richard M. Johnson	*Whig* William H. Harrison Francis Granger	*Dem.* 170	*Whig* 73	*Dem.* 764,176 50.8%	*Whig* 550,816 36.6%
1840	26	*Dem.* Martin Van Buren Richard M. Johnson	*Whig* William H. Harrison John Tyler	*Dem.* 60	*Whig* 234	*Dem.* 1,128,854 46.8%	*Whig* 1,275,390 52.9%
1844	26	*Dem.* James Polk George M. Dallas	*Whig* Henry Clay Theodore Frelinghuysen	*Dem.* 170	*Whig* 105	*Dem.* 1,339,494 49.5%	*Whig* 1,300,004 48.1%
1848	30	*Dem.* Lewis Cass William O. Butler	*Whig* Zachary Taylor Millard Fillmore	*Dem.* 127	*Whig* 163	*Dem.* 1,233,460 42.5%	*Whig* 1,361,393 47.3%
1852	31	*Dem.* Franklin Pierce William R. King	*Whig* Winfield Scott William A. Graham	*Dem.* 254	*Whig* 42	*Dem.* 1,607,510 50.8%	*Whig* 1,386,942 43.9%

Year	No. of states	Candidates		Electoral vote		Popular vote	
		Dem.	*Rep.*	*Dem.*	*Rep.*	*Dem.*	*Rep.*
1856[g]	31	James Buchanan John C. Breckinridge	John C. Fremont William L. Dayton	174	114	1,836,072 45.3%	1,342,345 33.1%
1860[h]	33	Stephen A. Douglas Herschel V. Johnson	Abraham Lincoln Hannibal Hamlin	12	180	1,380,202 29.5%	1,865,908 39.8%
1864[i]	36	George B. McClellan George H. Pendleton	Abraham Lincoln Andrew Johnson	21	212	1,812,807 45.0%	2,218,388 55.0%
1868[j]	37	Horatio Seymour Francis P. Blair, Jr.	Ulysses S. Grant Schuyler Colfax	80	214	2,708,744 47.3%	3,013,650 52.7%
1872[k]	37	Horace Greeley Benjamin Gratz Brown	Ulysses S. Grant Henry Wilson		286	2,834,761 43.8%	3,598,235 55.6%
1876	38	Samuel J. Tilden Thomas A. Hendricks	Rutherford B. Hayes William A. Wheeler	184	185	4,288,546 51.0%	4,034,311 47.9%
1880	38	Winfield S. Hancock William H. English	James A. Garfield Chester A. Arthur	155	214	4,444,260 48.2%	4,446,158 48.3%
1884	38	Grover Cleveland Thomas A. Hendricks	James G. Blaine John A. Logan	219	182	4,874,621 48.5%	4,848,936 48.2%
1888	38	Grover Cleveland Allen G. Thurman	Benjamin Harrison Levi P. Morton	168	233	5,534,488 48.6%	5,443,892 47.8%
1892[l]	44	Grover Cleveland Adlai E. Stevenson	Benjamin Harrison Whitelaw Reid	277	145	5,551,883 46.1%	5,179,244 43.0%
1896	45	William J. Bryan Arthur Sewall	William McKinley Garret A. Hobart	176	271	6,511,495 46.7%	7,108,480 51.0%

Year	No. of states	Candidates		Electoral vote		Popular vote	
		Dem.	Rep.	Dem.	Rep.	Dem.	Rep.
1900	45	William J. Bryan Adlai E. Stevenson	William McKinley Theodore Roosevelt	155	292	6,358,345 45.5%	7,218,039 51.7%
1904	45	Alton B. Parker Henry G. Davis	Theodore Roosevelt Charles W. Fairbanks	140	336	5,028,898 37.6%	7,626,593 56.4%
1908	46	William J. Bryan John W. Kern	William H. Taft James S. Sherman	162	321	6,406,801 43.0%	7,676,258 51.6%
1912[m]	48	Woodrow Wilson Thomas R. Marshall	William H. Taft James S. Sherman	435	8	6,293,152 41.8%	3,486,333 23.2%
1916	48	Woodrow Wilson Thomas R. Marshall	Charles E. Hughes Charles W. Fairbanks	277	254	9,126,300 49.2%	8,546,789 46.1%
1920	48	James M. Cox Franklin D. Roosevelt	Warren G. Harding Calvin Coolidge	127	404	9,140,884 34.2%	16,133,314 60.3%
1924[n]	48	John W. Davis Charles W. Bryant	Calvin Coolidge Charles G. Dawes	136	382	8,386,169 28.8%	15,717,553 54.1%
1928	48	Alfred E. Smith Joseph T. Robinson	Herbert C. Hoover Charles Curtis	87	444	15,000,185 40.8%	21,411,991 58.2%
1932	48	Franklin D. Roosevelt John N. Garner	Herbert C. Hoover Charles Curtis	472	59	22,825,016 57.4%	15,758,397 39.6%
1936	48	Franklin D. Roosevelt John N. Garner	Alfred M. Landon Frank Knox	523	8	27,747,636 60.8%	16,679,543 36.5%
1940	48	Franklin D. Roosevelt Henry A. Wallace	Wendell L. Willkie Charles L. McNary	449	82	27,263,448 54.7%	22,336,260 44.8%
1944	48	Franklin D. Roosevelt Harry S. Truman	Thomas E. Dewey John W. Bricker	432	99	25,611,936 53.4%	22,013,372 45.9%
1948[o]	48	Harry S. Truman Alben W. Barkley	Thomas E. Dewey Earl Warren	303	189	24,105,587 49.5%	21,970,017 45.1%
1952	48	Adlai E. Stevenson II John J. Sparkman	Dwight D. Eisenhower Richard M. Nixon	89	442	27,314,649 44.4%	33,936,137 55.1%
1956[p]	48	Adlai E. Stevenson II Estes Kefauver	Dwight D. Eisenhower Richard M. Nixon	73	457	26,030,172 42.0%	35,585,245 57.4%
1960[q]	50	John F. Kennedy Lyndon B. Johnson	Richard M. Nixon Henry Cabot Lodge	303	219	34,221,344 49.7%	34,106,671 49.5%
1964	50*	Lyndon B. Johnson Hubert H. Humphrey	Barry Goldwater William E. Miller	486	52	43,126,584 61.1%	27,177,838 38.5%
1968[r]	50*	Hubert H. Humphrey Edmund S. Muskie	Richard M. Nixon Spiro T. Agnew	191	301	31,274,503 42.7%	31,785,148 43.4%
1972[s]	50*	George McGovern Sargent Shriver	Richard M. Nixon Spiro T. Agnew	17	520	29,171,791 37.5%	47,170,179 60.7%
1976[t]	50*	Jimmy Carter Walter F. Mondale	Gerald R. Ford Robert Dole	297	240	40,830,763 50.1%	39,147,793 48.0%

(continued)

(continued)

Year	No. of states	Candidates Dem.	Candidates Rep.	Electoral vote Dem.	Electoral vote Rep.	Popular vote Dem.	Popular vote Rep.
1980	50*	Jimmy Carter Walter F. Mondale	Ronald Reagan George H.W. Bush	49	489	35,483,883 41.0%	43,904,153 50.7%
1984	50*	Walter F. Mondale Geraldine Ferraro	Ronald Reagan George H.W. Bush	13	525	37,577,185 40.6%	54,455,075 58.8%
1988[u]	50*	Michael S. Dukakis Lloyd Bentsen	George H.W. Bush Dan Quayle	111	426	41,809,074 45.6%	48,886,097 53.4%
1992	50*	William J. Clinton Albert Gore	George H.W. Bush Dan Quayle	370	168	44,909,326 43.0%	39,103,882 37.4%
1996	50*	William J. Clinton Albert Gore	Robert J. Dole Jack F. Kemp	379	159	47,402,357 49.2%	39,198,755 40.7%
2000	50*	Albert Gore Joseph I. Lieberman	George W. Bush Richard B. Cheney	266	271	50,992,335 48.4%	50,455,156 47.9%
2004	50*	John Kerry John Edwards	George W. Bush Richard B. Cheney	252	286	59,026,013 47.3%	62,025,554 50.7%
**2008	50*	Barack Obama Joe Biden	John McCain Sarah Palin	365	162	65,712,788 53.3%	57,620,818 46.7%

SOURCES: Harold W. Stanley and Richard G. Niemi, *Vital Statistics on American Politics, 2007–2008* (Washington, D.C.: CQ Press, 2008), 26–30; *CQ Press Guide to U.S. Elections*, 5th ed. (Washington, D.C.: CQ Press, 2006), 715–719; for the 2008 election: for presidential race electoral vote data, see *CQ Politics Election 2008*, http://innovation.cq.com/election_night08?tab2=f. For presidential race popular vote data, see the *New York Times*'s Presidential Big Board, http://elections .nytimes.com/2008/ results/president/votes.html.

NOTE: Dem.-Rep.—Democratic-Republican; Fed.—Federalist; Nat.-Rep.—National-Republican; Dem.—Democratic; Rep.—Republican.

a. Elections from 1789 through 1800 were held under rules that did not allow separate voting for president and vice president.

b. Popular vote returns are not shown before 1824 because consistent, reliable data are not available.

c. 1820: One electoral vote was cast for John Adams and Richard Stockton, who were not candidates.

d. 1824: All four candidates represented Democratic-Republican factions. William H. Crawford received 41 electoral votes and Henry Clay received 37 votes. Because no candidate received a majority, the election was decided (in Adams's favor) by the House of Representatives.

e. 1832: Two electoral votes were not cast.

f. 1836: Other Whig candidates receiving electoral votes were Hugh L. White, who received 26 votes, and Daniel Webster, who received 14 votes.

g. 1856: Millard Fillmore, Whig-American, received 8 electoral votes.

h. 1860: John C. Breckinridge, southern Democrat, received 72 electoral votes. John Bell, Constitutional Union, received 39 electoral votes.

i. 1864: Eighty-one electoral votes were not cast.

j. 1868: Twenty-three electoral votes were not cast.

k. 1872: Horace Greeley, Democrat, died after the election. In the electoral college, Democratic electoral votes went to Thomas Hendricks, 42 votes; Benjamin Gratz Brown, 18 votes; Charles J. Jenkins, 2 votes; and David Davis, 1 vote. Seventeen electoral votes were not cast.

l. 1892: James B. Weaver, People's party, received 22 electoral votes.

m. 1912: Theodore Roosevelt, Progressive party, received 88 electoral votes.

n. 1924: Robert M. La Follette, Progressive party, received 13 electoral votes.

o. 1948: J. Strom Thurmond, States' Rights party, received 39 electoral votes.

p. 1956: Walter B. Jones, Democrat, received 1 electoral vote.

q. 1960: Harry Flood Byrd, Democrat, received 15 electoral votes.

r. 1968: George C. Wallace, American Independent party, received 46 electoral votes.

s. 1972: John Hospers, Libertarian party, received 1 electoral vote.

t. 1976: Ronald Reagan, Republican, received 1 electoral vote.

u. 1988: Lloyd Bentsen, the Democratic vice-presidential nominee, received 1 electoral vote for president.

* Fifty states plus the District of Columbia.

**Numbers are current as of time of publication, with 11 electoral votes remaining undecided in Missouri. Please note that popular vote data is tentative and may vary after publication.

Appendix 10

The American Economy

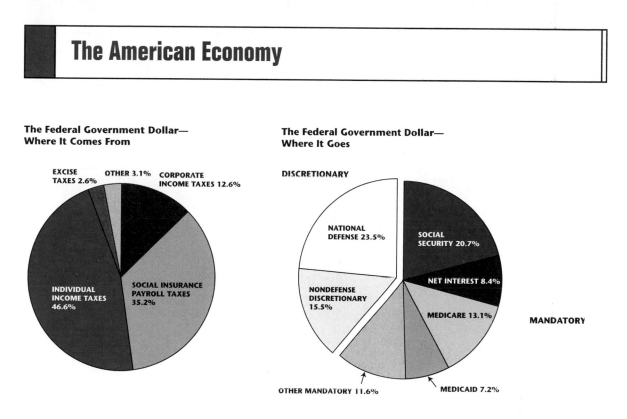

The Federal Government Dollar— Where It Comes From

EXCISE TAXES 2.6%
OTHER 3.1%
CORPORATE INCOME TAXES 12.6%
INDIVIDUAL INCOME TAXES 46.6%
SOCIAL INSURANCE PAYROLL TAXES 35.2%

The Federal Government Dollar— Where It Goes

DISCRETIONARY
NATIONAL DEFENSE 23.5%
SOCIAL SECURITY 20.7%
NET INTEREST 8.4%
NONDEFENSE DISCRETIONARY 15.5%
MEDICARE 13.1%
MANDATORY
OTHER MANDATORY 11.6%
MEDICAID 7.2%

Source: Office of Management and Budget, *Budget of the United States Government, Fiscal Year 2009* (Washington, D.C.: U.S. Government Printing Office, 2008).

Year	GDP (in constant 2000 dollars)	Federal Government Spending (billions) (in constant 2000 dollars)			National Debt (current dollars)	
		National Defense	Non-defense	Total	Debt held by the public (millions)	As a percentage of GDP
1940	1,034.1	$19.9	$88.9	$108.8	42,772	44.2
1941	1,211.1	64.7	82.4	147.1	48,223	42.3
1942	1,435.4	216.3	125.2	341.8	67,753	47.0
1943	1,670.9	526.0	173.8	700.1	127,766	70.9
1944	1,806.5	684.0	176.5	860.5	184,796	88.4
1945	1,786.3	774.6	115.6	890.6	235,182	106.3
1946	1,589.4	405.7	110.1	515.7	241,861	108.6
1947	1,574.5	112.6	184.3	296.9	224,339	95.6
1948	1,643.2	86.5	147.2	233.8	216,270	84.3
1949	1,634.6	123.8	187.9	311.7	214,322	78.9
1950	1,777.3	129.6	201.1	330.7	219,023	80.1
1951	1,915.0	211.7	144.1	355.9	214,326	66.8
1952	1,988.3	396.6	132.3	528.8	214,758	61.6
1953	2,079.5	416.1	140.3	556.3	218,383	58.5
1954	2,065.4	381.9	121.0	502.9	224,499	59.4
1955	2,212.8	320.1	150.5	470.4	226,616	57.3
1956	2,255.8	298.4	164.4	462.9	222,156	51.9
1957	2,301.1	303.5	175.0	478.3	219,320	48.7

(continued)

Year	GDP (in constant 2000 dollars)	Federal Government Spending (billions) (in constant 2000 dollars)			National Debt (current dollars)	
		National Defense	Non-defense	Total	Debt held by the public (millions)	As a percentage of GDP
1958	2,279.2	299.7	188.8	488.5	226,336	49.1
1959	2,441.3	297.6	229.8	527.5	234,701	47.7
1960	2,501.8	300.2	226.5	526.8	236,840	45.6
1961	2,560.0	301.5	242.9	544.4	238,357	44.8
1962	2,715.2	315.9	276.4	592.5	248,010	43.6
1963	2,834.0	309.4	284.7	594.3	253,978	42.4
1964	2,998.6	314.9	309.0	623.8	256,849	40.1
1965	3,191.1	291.8	321.6	613.2	260,778	37.9
1966	3,399.1	322.8	358.6	681.5	263,714	35.0
1967	3,484.6	383.3	393.8	777.2	266,626	32.8
1968	3,652.7	420.1	426.8	847.0	289,545	33.3
1969	3,765.4	400.1	423.2	823.5	278,108	29.3
1970	3,771.9	375.1	453.1	828.0	283,198	28.0
1971	3,898.6	340.8	493.4	834.3	303,037	28.0
1972	4,105.0	310.4	547.2	857.6	322,377	27.3
1973	4,341.5	278.6	588.5	867.3	340,910	26.1
1974	4,319.6	267.4	609.8	877.4	343,699	23.8
1975	4,311.2	262.7	719.2	982.1	394,700	25.3
1976	4,540.9	252.7	768.9	1,021.4	477,404	27.5
TQ[1]	n/a	61.0	194.7	255.8	495,509	27.1
1977	4,750.5	250.6	789.6	1,040.2	549,104	27.8
1978	5,015.0	251.1	842.7	1,093.6	607,126	27.4
1979	5,173.4	257.4	850.0	1,107.3	640,306	25.6
1980	5,161.7	267.1	907.9	1,175.1	711,923	26.1
1981	5,291.7	282.2	937.2	1,219.4	789,410	25.8
1982	5,189.3	307.0	944.8	1,251.7	924,575	28.6
1983	5,423.8	330.7	963.7	1,294.4	1,137,268	33.1
1984	5,813.6	334.0	965.6	1,299.5	1,306,975	34.0
1985	6,053.7	356.5	1,039.0	1,395.7	1,507,260	36.4
1986	6,263.6	380.7	1,045.1	1,425.7	1,740,623	39.4
1987	6,475.1	387.1	1,018.5	1,405.7	1,889,753	40.7
1988	6,742.7	393.1	1,053.4	1,446.5	2,051,616	41.0
1989	6,981.4	398.9	1,100.0	1,498.9	2,190,716	40.6
1990	7,112.5	382.7	1,207.0	1,589.8	2,411,558	42.0
1991	7,100.5	333.7	1,276.2	1,609.9	2,688,999	45.3
1992	7,336.6	354.3	1,269.8	1,623.9	2,999,737	48.1
1993	7,532.7	340.3	1,275.3	1,615.5	3,248,396	49.4
1994	7,835.5	322.8	1,319.3	1,642.2	3,433,065	49.3
1995	8,031.7	305.9	1,356.3	1,662.2	3,604,378	49.2
1996	8,328.9	289.2	1,384.0	1,673.0	3,734,073	48.5
1997	8,703.5	288.4	1,395.8	1,684.2	3,772,344	46.1
1998	9,066.9	282.4	1,438.7	1,721.0	3,721,099	43.1
1999	9,470.3	283.6	1,462.5	1,746.0	3,632,363	39.8
2000	9,817.0	294.4	1,494.8	1,789.2	3,409,804	35.1
2001	9,890.7	297.2	1,523.5	1,820.6	3,319,615	33.0
2002	10,048.8	329.3	1,599.8	1,929.2	3,540,427	34.1
2003	10,301.0	364.4	1,654.0	2,018.2	3,913,443	36.2
2004	10,675.8	394.3	1,686.7	2,081.9	4,295,544	37.4
2005	10,989.5	407.3	1,757.7	2,165.0	4,592,212	37.5
2006	11,294.8	412.4	1,836.8	2,249.2	4,828,972	37.1

Year	GDP (in constant 2000 dollars)	Federal Government Spending (billions) (in constant 2000 dollars)			National Debt (current dollars)	
		National Defense	Non-defense	Total	Debt held by the public (millions)	As a percentage of GDP
2007	11,523.9	426.4	1,836.9	2,263.1	5,035,129	36.8
2008 est.	n/a	463.9	1,901.6	2,365.6	5,428,619	37.9
2009 est.	n/a	504.7	1,947.2	2,451.8	5,856,153	39.0
2010 est.	n/a	432.7	1,959.3	2,391.9	6,031,101	38.2
2011 est.	n/a	402.9	2,001.3	2,404.3	6,139,655	37.0
2012 est.	n/a	391.1	1,993.2	2,390.3	6,109,503	35.1
2013 est.	n/a	395.2	2,073.5	2,468.7	6,097,433	33.4

[1]Transitional quarter when fiscal year start was shifted from July 1 to October 1.
SOURCE: Office of Management and Budget, *Budget of the United States Government, Fiscal Year 2009, Historical Tables* (Washington, D.C.: U.S. Government Printing Office, 2008), 119–128; U.S. Department of Commerce Bureau of Economic Analysis, *National Economic Accounts: National Income and Product Tables*, Table 1.1.5., 1955–2007 (2008).

Notes

Chapter 1. The Logic of American Politics

pages 2–43

1. Frank Bruni, "The President's Decision: Of Principles and Politics," *New York Times,* August 10, 2001.

2. James Harrington, *The Common-wealth of Oceana and a System of Politics* (1656; reprinted, ed. J G. Pocock, New York: Cambridge University Press, 1992).

3. C. R. Hallpike, "Functionalist Interpretations of Primitive Warfare," *Man* (September 1973). Cited in Russell Hardin, "Hobbesian Political Order," *Political Theory* (May 1991): 168.

4. Thomas Hobbes, *Leviathan, or The matter, forme, & power of a commonwealth ecclesiasticall and civill* (1651; reprint, Oxford: Clarendon Press, 1958).

5. Mark Kurlansky, *Cod: A Biography of the Fish That Changed the World* (New York: Walker, 1997).

6. Chris Den Hartog, "Limited Party Government and the Majority Party Revolution in the Nineteenth-Century House." PhD diss., University of California, San Diego, 2004.

7. Eric Schmitt, "Testing of a President: The Votes; Impeachment Doubts Erode Slim Republican Majority," *New York Times,* November, 19, 1998.

8. Michael Cooper, "So How Bad Is Albany? Well, Notorious," *New York Times,* July 22, 2004, B1 and B5.

9. We will examine the Electoral College more closely in Chapter 2.

10. James Madison, *Federalist* No. 51, in Alexander Hamilton, James Madison, and John Jay, *The Federalist Papers* (see Appendix).

11. They were, among others, the French philosopher Baron de Montesquieu (1689–1755) and the English philosopher John Locke (1632–1704).

Chapter 2. The Constitution   *pages 44–93*

1. Wayne Carp, *To Starve the Army at Pleasure: Continental Army Administration and American Political Culture, 1775–1783* (Chapel Hill: University of North Carolina Press, 1984), 197. During 1780 Washington frequently repeated this warning in correspondence with political leaders.

2. Letter from John Adams to Timothy Pickering, August 22, 1822, in John Adams, *Life and Works,* Vol. 2, ed. Charles Francis Adams (Boston: Little, Brown, 1850–1856).

3. This expression comes from Revolutionary War general Nathaniel Greene—see Carp, *To Starve the Army at Pleasure,* 196. Remarkably, although the field commanders showered Congress with contempt, none ever suggested that the military could do a better job of running the government.

4. Gordon S. Wood, *The Creation of the American Republic: 1776–1787* (New York: Norton, 1969), 405–410.

5. Letter to Thomas Jefferson, October 17, 1788, in William T. Hutchinson et al., eds., *The Papers of James Madison,* Vol. 9 (Chicago: University of Chicago Press, 1962).

6. This discussion follows David P. Szatmary's treatment in *Shays's Rebellion: The Making of an Agrarian Insurrection* (Amherst: University of Massachusetts Press, 1980), 120–134.

7. John Locke, *Essay Concerning the True Original Extent and End of Civil Government. Second Treatise of Government,* ed. C. B. Macpherson (Indianapolis: Hackett, 1980).

8. William Lee Miller, *The Business of May Next: James Madison and the Founding* (Charlottesville: University Press of Virginia, 1992), 87.

9. *Marbury v. Madison,* 1 Cr. 137 (1803).

10. Quoted in James MacGregor Burns, *The Vineyard of Liberty* (New York: Vintage, 1983), 28.

11. Catherine Drinker Bowen, *Miracle at Philadelphia: The Story of the Constitutional Convention, May to September 1787* (Boston: Atlantic–Little, Brown, 1966), 278.

12. See Locke, *Essay Concerning the True Original Extent and End of Civil Government*; and David Hume, "The Perfect Commonwealth," in *Essays, Moral, Political, and Literary,* ed. Eugene F. Miller (Indianapolis: Liberty Fund, 1987). In 1776 Madison had urged fellow members of the Virginia House of Burgesses to embrace a multitude of religious sects in promoting religious reform, proposing that "all men are equally entitled to enjoy the free exercise of religion, according to the dictates of conscience." Ralph Ketcham, *James Madison: A Biography* (Charlottesville: University Press of Virginia, 1990), 72. In an essay on the "vices" of republican governments, Madison fleshed out the argument more fully and applied it to political factions. Also see Douglas Adair, "'That Politics May Be Reduced to a Science,' David Hume, James Madison and the Tenth Federalist," *Huntington Library Quarterly* (1957), reprinted in Douglas Adair, *Fame and the Founding Fathers* (New York: Norton, 1974), 93–106.

13. This argument is developed more fully in Samuel Kernell, "'The True Principles of Republican Government': Reassessing James Madison's Political Science," in *James Madison: The Theory and Practice of Republican Government,* ed. Samuel Kernell (Stanford: Stanford University Press, 2003).

14. See Robert Dahl, *A Preface to Democratic Theory* (Chicago: University of Chicago Press, 1956); and E. E. Schattschneider, *Party Government* (New York: Holt, Rinehart and Winston, 1942), 18–21.

Chapter 3. Federalism   *pages 94–137*

1. Schwarzenegger's quote appeared in "Schwarzenegger, Sarkozy Meet to Talk About Global Warming," *The Associated Press,* June 25, 2007, and coverage of his agreement with Britain comes

from John Heilprin, "Blair, Schwarzenegger to Strike Global Warming Deal," *The Associated Press,* July 31, 2006.

2. Coverage of the EPA's decision and Johnson's statement are taken from Richard Simon and Janet Wilson, "California Emissions Law Rejected," *Los Angeles Times,* December 20, 2007, and Gov. Schwarzenegger's response is quoted in Margot Roosevelt, "Lawsuit Targets EPA's Refusal," *Los Angeles Times,* January 3, 2008.

3. For a record of the House debate over these exemptions, and for a critique of the exemptions themselves, see Valerie J. M. Brader, "Congress' Pet: Why the Clean Air Act's Favoritism of California is Unconstitutional Under the Equal Footing Doctrine," *Hastings West-Northwest Journal of Environmental Law & Policy* (Winter 2007). For a contemporary commentary on the states' rights issues involved, see Jeffrey Kessler, "The Clean Air Act Amendments of 1970: A Threat to Federalism?" *Columbia Law Review* 76(6):990–1028, October 1976.

4. This definition comes directly from Parris N. Glendening and Mavis Mann Reeves, *Pragmatic Federalism,* 2nd ed. (Pacific Palisades, Calif.: Pacific Palisades, 1984), 11.

5. This quotation is from Howard L. McBain, *The Law and the Practice of Municipal Home Rule* (New York: Columbia University Press, 1916), 15. Dillon was an Iowa Supreme Court justice who set forth the doctrine that local governments were fully subordinate to states in an 1868 decision (*Clinton v. Cedar Rapids and Missouri River R. R.,* 24 Iowa 455) and an 1872 book. It was the U.S. Supreme Court's 1907 decision in *Hunter v. Pittsburgh* (207 U.S. 161) that applied Dillon's Rule to local governments across the nation.

6. For a review of contemporary state-local relations, see Russell L. Hanson, *Governing Partners: State-Local Relations in the United States* (Boulder, Colo.: Westview, 1998).

7. William H. Riker, "The Senate and American Federalism," *American Political Science Review* 49 (1955): 452–469.

8. For a discussion of the Senate's special role in spawning presidential candidates, see Nelson W. Polsby, *Political Innovation in America* (New Haven: Yale University Press, 1984).

9. See Article I, Section 9.

10. It also is known as the necessary and proper clause.

11. *McCulloch v. Maryland,* 4 Wheat. 316 (1819).

12. *Gibbons v. Ogden,* 22 U.S. 1 (1824).

13. This history is well told by Robert H. Wiebe in *The Search for Order, 1877–1920* (New York: Hill and Wang, 1967).

14. The case was *United States v. F. W. Darby Lumber Co.,* 312 U.S. 100 (1941). Passage cited in Lee Epstein and Thomas G. Walker, *Constitutional Law for a Changing America: A Short Course,* 3rd ed. (Washington, D.C.: CQ Press, 2005), 192–193.

15. The "welfare magnets" idea and the initial evidence that states raced to the bottom in welfare payments was introduced in Paul E. Peterson and Mark C. Rom, *Welfare Magnets: The Case for a National Welfare Standard* (Washington, D.C.: Brookings, 1990). The findings of the literature that this book inspired have been critiqued by Craig Volden in "The Politics of Competitive Federalism: A Race to the Bottom in Welfare Benefits?" *American Journal of Political Science* 46(2):352–363.

16. Louis Uchitelle, "States Pay for Jobs, but It Doesn't Always Pay Off," *New York Times,* November 10, 2003.

17. MADD did meet some resistance in the low-drinking-age states that benefited economically from the commerce in alcohol.

18. *South Dakota v. Dole,* 483 U.S. 203 (1987).

19. These laws were compiled in the "2007 State Scorecard" produced by the Brady Campaign to Prevent Gun Violence, accessible at www.stategunlaws.org/xshare/pdf/scorecard/2007/2007_state_scorecard.pdf.

20. *Garcia v. San Antonio Metropolitan Transit Authority,* 469 U.S. 528 (1985).

21. Kenneth T. Palmer and Edward B. Laverty, "The Impact of *United States v. Lopez* on Intergovernmental Relations: A Preliminary Assessment," *Publius* 26 (Summer 1996): 109–126. This revisionism continued in a 1997 case in which the Court invalidated a provision of the 1993 Brady handgun law that required local law enforcement officials to run background checks on purchasers of handguns. Dan Carney, "Brady Decision Reflects Effort to Curb Congress' Authority," *Congressional Quarterly Weekly Report,* June 28, 1997, 1524–1525.

22. Elizabeth A. Palmer, "High Court Further Circumscribes Congress' Power in Ruling on Violence Against Women Act," *CQ Weekly,* May 20, 2000, 1188. The Court again invoked *Lopez* in 2001, ruling by a 5–4 vote that state employees could not use the federal Americans with Disabilities Act (see Chapter 4) to sue their employers.

23. John Kincaid, "Constitutional Federalism: Labor's Role in Displacing Places to Benefit Persons," *PS* (June 1993): 172.

24. The exact ratio for a matching grant varies across states, with poorer states receiving a higher matching rate in order to give financially strapped state governments an incentive to expand their services. While high-income states like New York, Massachusetts, and California receive one federal dollar for every state dollar that they spend on Medicaid, states with poorer residents such as Arkansas, West Virginia, and Louisiana receive more than two federal dollars.

25. L. Nye Stevens, "Unfunded Mandates—Reform Act Has Had Little Effect on Agencies' Rulemaking Actions, Report to the Committee on Governmental Affairs, U.S. Senate," General Accounting Office, Washington, D.C., 1998.

Chapter 4. **Civil Rights**   *pages 138–189*

1. Sam Howe Verhovek, "Americans Give in to Race Profiling," *New York Times,* September 23, 2001.

2. "Guidance for Screeners and Other Security Personnel," U.S. Department of Transportation, Federal Aviation Administration, www.dot.gov/airconsumer/ARPScreeners.htm.

3. Henry Weinstein et al., "After the Attack; Law Enforcement," *Los Angeles Times,* September 24, 2001.

4. Harold Sullivan proposes this distinction in *Civil Rights and Liberties: Provocative Questions and Evolving Answers* (New York: Prentice Hall, 2001), 1–2.

5. John M. Broder, "Clinton, Softening Slap at Senate, Names 'Acting' Civil Rights Chief," *New York Times,* December 16, 1997.

6. Mary B. Norton et al., *People and a Nation: A History of the United States,* Vol. 1, 5th ed. (Boston: Houghton Mifflin, 1987), 238.

7. Chaplain W. Morrison, *Democratic Politics and Sectionalism: The Wilmot Proviso Controversy* (Chapel Hill: University of North Carolina Press, 1967).

8. *Dred Scott v. Sandford,* 19 How. 393 (1857).

9. Quoted in C. Vann Woodward, *The Burden of Southern History* (Baton Rouge: Louisiana State University Press, 1968), 95.

10. Ibid.

11. C. Vann Woodward, *Reunion and Reaction: The Compromise of 1877 and the End of Reconstruction* (Boston: Little, Brown, 1966).

12. *Plessy v. Ferguson,* 163 U.S. 737 (1896).

13. Edward G. Carmines and James A. Stimson, *Issue Evolution: Race and the Transformation of American Politics* (Princeton: Princeton University Press, 1989).

14. *Brown v. Board of Education of Topeka,* 347 U.S. 483 (1954).

15. *Smith v. Allwright,* 321 U.S. 649 (1944).

16. *Sweatt v. Painter,* 339 U.S. 629 (1950).

17. *Brown v. Board of Education,* 349 U.S. 294 (1955).

18. David J. Garrow, *Bearing the Cross: Martin Luther King, Jr., and the Southern Christian Leadership Conference* (New York: Morrow, 1986), 91.

19. Dennis Chong elaborates on these issues in his *Collective Action and the Civil Rights Movement* (Chicago: University of Chicago Press, 1991).

20. Paul Burstein, "Public Opinion, Demonstrations, and the Passage of Antidiscrimination Legislation," *Public Opinion Quarterly* 43 (1979): 157–172.

21. Taylor Branch, *Parting the Waters: America in the King Years, 1954–1963* (New York: Simon and Schuster, 1988).

22. Ibid.

23. Robert M. Axelrod, "Where the Votes Come From: An Analysis of Electoral Coalitions, 1952–1958," *American Political Science Review* (March 1972).

24. From Gary Orfield, *Congressional Power: Congress and Social Change* (New York: Harcourt Brace Jovanovich, 1975), 102.

25. *Regents of the University of California v. Bakke,* 438 U.S. 265 (1978).

26. The 1987 case is *Johnson v. Transportation Agency of Santa Clara County*; the 1995 case, *Adarand Constructors, Inc. v. Peña,* 515 U.S. 200 (1995).

27. *Gratz v. Bollinger,* 539 U.S. 244 (2003), involved the undergraduate point system, while *Grutter v. Bollinger,* 539 U.S. 306 (2003), concerned the law school's consideration of race as a variable. Analysis of subsequent undergraduate admission rates at Michigan has found little difference under the revised formula. In 2006 the Court appeared to back away from "diversity" as providing an adequate rationale for affirmative action. *Parents v. Seattle* and *Meredith v. Jefferson* ruled (again, 5–4) such practices unconstitutional in Seattle, Wash., and Louisville, Ky.

28. Alexander Keyssar, *The Right to Vote* (New York: Basic Books, 2000); Judith Apter Klinghoffer and Lois Elkis, "The Petticoat Electors: Women's Suffrage in New Jersey, 1776–1807," *Journal of the Early Republic* 12 (1992): 159–193.

29. Keyssar, *The Right to Vote,* 177.

30. The rise of the abortion issue after the Supreme Court legalized abortions in its 1973 *Roe v. Wade* decision stalled the ERA. Jane Mansbridge, *Why We Lost the ERA* (Chicago: University of Chicago Press, 1986).

31. The case that triggered Congress's response was *Grove City College v. Bell,* 465 U.S. 555 (1984).

32. This estimate is based on "Charge Statistics" compiled by the EEOC and reported on its Web site: www.eeoc.gov/stats/charges.html.

33. *Lawrence v. Texas,* 539 U.S. 558 (2003); *Romer v. Evans,* 517 U.S. 620 (1996).

34. The list, updated in 2004, is contained in the General Accouting Office Report located at www.gao.gov/new.items/d04353r.pdf.

35. *Sutton v. United Airlines,* 527 U.S. 471 (1999), and *PGA Tour v. Martin,* 532 U.S. 661 (2001).

Chapter 5. **Civil Liberties**   *pages 190–245*

1. *Reno v. ACLU,* 117 S. Ct. 2329, 138 L. Ed. 2d 874 (1997).

2. From a speech to Congress, June 8, 1789. Quoted in *The Papers of James Madison,* ed. William T. Hutchinson et al. (Chicago: University of Chicago Press, 1962), 197–206.

3. *Employment Division, Department of Human Resources of Oregon v. Smith,* 494 U.S. 872 (1990). This case is described more fully in the section "Free Exercise and National Security."

4. *City of Boerne v. Flores,* 136 L. Ed. 2d 709 (1997).

5. Donald S. Lutz, "The State Constitutional Pedigree of the U.S. Bill of Rights," *Publius* 22 (Spring 1992): 19–45.

6. Quoted in Alpheus Thomas Mason, *The States' Rights Debate* (New York: Oxford University Press, 1972), 174. Madison informed the House of Representatives: "I will not propose a single alteration which I do not wish to see take place, as proper in itself, or proper because it is wished by a respectable number of my fellow citizens."

7. *Barron v. Baltimore,* 7 Pet. 243 (1833).

8. Andrew W. Young, *Introduction to the Science of Government,* 3rd ed. (Rochester, N.Y.: William Alling, 1843).

9. This discussion of incorporation follows the presentation in Lee Epstein and Thomas G. Walker, *Constitutional Law for a Changing America: Rights, Liberties, and Justice,* 5th ed. (Washington, D.C.: CQ Press, 2004), 75–97. Indeed, this text provides a thorough review and treatment of all issues described in this chapter.

10. *The Butchers' Benevolent Association of New Orleans v. The Crescent City Livestock Landing and Slaughterhouse Co.; Esteben v. Louisiana* (The Slaughterhouse Cases), 16 Wall. 36 (1873).

11. *Hutardo v. California,* 110 U.S. 516 (1884).

12. *Schenck v. United States,* 249 U.S. 47 (1919).

13. *Gitlow v. New York,* 268 U.S. 652 (1925).

14. *Dennis v. United States,* 341 U.S. 494 (1951).

15. *Tinker v. Des Moines,* 393 U.S. 503 (1969).

16. *Texas v. Johnson,* 491 U.S. 397 (1989).

17. *United States v. Eichman,* 496 U.S. 310 (1990).

18. "Support of Free Speech Faltering, Poll Finds," *San Diego Union Tribune,* August 30, 2002.

19. Leslie Eaton, "On New York's Streets and across the Nation, Protestors Speak Out," *New York Times,* March 23, 2003; Kate

Zernike and Dean E. Murphy, "Antiwar Effort Emphasizes Civility over Confrontation," *New York Times,* March 29, 2003.

20. Finally, the healthy condition of personal liberties was unwittingly confirmed by then–attorney general John Ashcroft's announced plan to set up neighborhood spies—the Terrorism Information and Prevention System, or TIPS—among government and private service workers (postal carriers, truckers, toll takers, and the like). The plan was greeted with derision on all fronts and quickly disappeared into the dustbin of ill-considered press releases. Rights groups had a field day and promptly seized the issue for their fundraising appeals. In an increasingly rare display of bipartisanship, Congress quickly drafted an addition to the pending Homeland Security bill that explicitly prohibited any federal funds being spent on Ashcroft's scheme. Dan Eggen, "Proposal to Enlist Citizen Spies Was Doomed from Start," *Washington Post,* November 24, 2002.

21. *Brandenburg v. Ohio,* 395 U.S. 444 (1969).

22. *National Socialist Party of America v. Village of Skokie,* 432 U.S. 43 (1977).

23. *Roth v. United States,* 354 U.S. 476 (1957).

24. Epstein and Walker, *Constitutional Law,* 371–372.

25. *Miller v. California,* 413 U.S. 15 (1973).

26. *Jacobellis v. Ohio,* 378 U.S. 184 (1964).

27. Epstein and Walker, *Constitutional Law,* 371–372.

28. *Reno v. ACLU.*

29. *Sheppard v. Maxwell,* 384 U.S. 333 (1966).

30. *Globe Newspaper Co. v. Superior Court,* 457 U.S. 596 (1982).

31. The Court first employed this doctrine in 1964 in *New York Times Co. v. Sullivan,* 376 U.S. 254 (1964).

32. Ralph Ketcham, *James Madison* (Charlottesville: University Press of Virginia, 1971), 166.

33. *Bradfield v. Roberts,* 175 U.S. 291 (1899).

34. *Everson v. Board of Education,* 330 U.S. 1 (1947).

35. Frank J. Sorauf, *The Wall of Separation* (Princeton: Princeton University Press, 1976), 257.

36. *Lemon v. Kurtzman, Earley v. DiCenso,* 403 U.S. 602 (1971).

37. *Lynch v. Donnelly,* 465 U.S. 668 (1984); *County of Allegheny v. ACLU, Greater Pittsburgh Chapter,* 492 U.S. 573 (1989).

38. Leonard W. Levy, *The Establishment Clause* (New York: Macmillan, 1986), 128.

39. *Board of Education of Kiryas Joel Village School District v. Grumet,* 512 U.S. 687 (1994).

40. *Agostini v. Felton,* 521 U.S. 203 (1997); *Mitchell v. Helms,* 530 U.S. 793 (2000); *Zelman v. Simmons-Harris,* 536 U.S. 639 (2002).

41. The case is *Locke v. Davey,* 000 U.S. 02-1315 (2004). Linda Greenhouse, "States Allowed to Avoid Subsidy of Divinity Study," *New York Times,* February 26, 2004.

42. Jeanne Cummings and Jim VandeHei, "Faith-Based Charity Initiative Takes Worldly, Rocky Path," *Wall Street Journal,* August 16, 2001, A16.

43. *Engel v. Vitale,* 370 U.S. 421 (1962).

44. *School District of Abington Township v. Schempp,* 374 U.S. 203 (1963).

45. Dan Carney, "With Barely a Prayer of Ratification, Religious Freedom Amendment Opens Perennial Election-Year Debate," *CQ Weekly,* June 6, 1998, 1530.

46. *Wallace v. Jaffree,* 472 U.S. 38 (1985).

47. *Lee v. Weisman,* 505 U.S. 577 (1992).

48. Robert Birkby, "The Supreme Court in the Bible Belt: Tennessee Reaction to the *Schempp* Decision," *American Journal of Political Science* 10 (1966): 304.

49. Kevin Sack, "In South, Prayer Is a Form of Protest: A Ruling Is Opposed in Classrooms, Courtroom and Statehouse," *New York Times,* November 8, 1997, A7.

50. *Employment Division, Department of Human Resources of Oregon v. Smith.*

51. *Church of the Lukumi Babalu Aye, Inc., et al. v. City of Hialeah,* 508 U.S. 502, 533 (1993).

52. Cited in Kenneth Janda, Jeffrey M. Berry, and Jerry Goldman, *The Challenge of Democracy,* 4th ed. (Boston: Houghton Mifflin, 1995), 537.

53. *Brown v. Mississippi,* 297 U.S. 278 (1936).

54. Harold W. Stanley and Richard G. Niemi, *Vital Statistics on American Politics, 2007–2008* (Washington, D.C.: CQ Press, 2007), 155.

55. *Katz v. United States,* 389 U.S. 347 (1967).

56. *Kyllo v. United States,* 533 U.S. 27 (2001).

57. For a full discussion of each of these conditions, see Epstein and Walker, *Constitutional Law,* 509–541.

58. *Brendlin v. California,* 551 U.S. ___ (2007), and *Georgia v. Randolph,* 547 U.S. 103 (2006).

59. *Mapp v. Ohio,* 367 U.S. 643 (1961).

60. *United States v. Leon,* 468 U.S. 897 (1984); *Massachusetts v. Sheppard,* 468 U.S. 981 (1984).

61. *Hudson v. Michigan,* 547 U.S. 586 (2006).

62. *Nix v. Williams,* 467 U.S. 431 (1984).

63. *Malloy v. Hogan,* 378 U.S. 1 (1964).

64. *Miranda v. Arizona,* 384 U.S. 436 (1966).

65. *Dickerson v. United States,* 530 U.S. 428 (2000).

66. *Gideon v. Wainwright,* 372 U.S. 335 (1963).

67. *Argersinger v. Hamlin,* 407 U.S. 25 (1972).

68. *Strickland v. Washington,* 466 U.S. 668 (1984).

69. Charles Lane, "Death Penalty of Md. Man Is Overturned," *Washington Post,* June 23, 2003.

70. Ten years after the legislation was enacted, the state had over seven thousand people incarcerated under the three-strikes law for twenty-five years or more. This number includes three hundred whose last conviction was for "petty theft." Linda Greenhouse, "Justices Uphold Long Prison Terms in Repeat Crimes," *New York Times,* March 6, 2004.

71. *Furman v. Georgia,* 408 U.S. 238 (1972). This description of the case is taken from Lee Epstein and Thomas G. Walker, *Constitutional Law for a Changing America: A Short Course,* 3rd ed. (Washington, D.C.: CQ Press, 2005), 573–574.

72. *Gregg v. Georgia,* 428 U.S. 153 (1976).

73. *Wiggins v. Smith,* 000 U.S. 02-311 (2003).

74. *Atkins v. Virginia,* 536 U.S. 304 (2002). For a detailed case study of *Atkins,* see Thomas G. Walker, *Eligible for Execution: The Story of the Daryl Atkins Case* (Washington D.C.: CQ Press, 2009).

75. *Baze v. Rees,* 553 U.S. ___ (2008) at 14.

76. *Kennedy v. Louisiana,* 554 U.S. ___ (2008) at 15.

77. Death Penalty Information Center, http://deathpenaltyinfo.org (August 27, 2008).

78. *Rasul v. Bush,* 542 U.S. 466 (2004).

79. See Linda Greenhouse, "Justices, 5-4, Back Detainee Appeals for Guantanamo," *New York Times,* June 13, 2008, www.nytimes.com/2008/06/13/washington/13scotus.html.

80. *Boumediene v. Bush,* 553 U.S. ___ (2008).

81. *Griswold v. Connecticut,* 381 U.S. 479 (1965).

82. Most efforts to protect privacy have emerged from the state legislatures and Congress. In 1988, perhaps to the comfort of Bork and others, Congress passed the Video Privacy Protection Act, which placed video rental records out of bounds. And lawmakers continue to deliberate more sweeping privacy legislation in the domain of medical records and the Internet.

83. *Eisenstadt v. Baird,* 410 U.S. 113 (1972), extended access to contraceptives to unmarried women.

84. *Planned Parenthood of Southeastern Pennsylvania v. Casey,* 505 U.S. 833 (1992).

85. *Gonzales v. Carhart,* 550 U.S. ___ (2007).

86. *Cruzan v. Director, Missouri Department of Health,* 497 U.S. 261 (1990).

87. *United States v. Miller,* 307 U.S. 174 (1939).

88. *Chicago, Burlington & Quincy Railroad Co. v. City of Chicago,* 166 U.S. 226 (1897).

89. *Kelo v. City of New London,* 545 U.S. 469 (2005).

90. Linda Greenhouse, "In New York Visit, O'Connor Foresees Limits on Freedom," *New York Times,* September 29, 2001.

Chapter 6. **Congress** *pages 246–313*

1. *Wesberry v. Sanders,* 376 U.S. 1 (1964).

2. *Thornburg v. Gingles,* 478 U.S. 30 (1986).

3. *Davis v. Bandemer,* 478 U.S. 109 (1986).

4. *Vieth v. Jubelirer,* 000 U.S. 02-1580 (2004).

5. *Thornburg v. Gingles.*

6. *Shaw v. Reno,* 590 U.S. 630 (1993).

7. *Miller v. Johnson,* 515 U.S. 900 (1995).

8. Frances E. Lee and Bruce I. Oppenheimer, "Senate Apportionment: Competitiveness and Partisan Advantage," *Legislative Studies Quarterly* 22 (February 1997): 3–24.

9. Alan I. Abramowitz and Jeffrey A. Segal, *Senate Elections* (Ann Arbor: University of Michigan Press, 1992), 18.

10. The Progressive Era and its effects on U.S. politics are described more fully in Chapter 12, Political Parties.

11. Richard F. Fenno Jr., *Home Style: House Members in Their Districts* (Boston: Little, Brown, 1978), chaps. 1–5.

12. Data collected and analyzed by the authors.

13. Jerrold G. Rusk, "The Effects of the Australian Ballot Reform on Split Ticket Voting, 1876–1908," in *Controversies in Voting Behavior,* ed. Richard G. Niemi and Herbert F. Weisberg (San Francisco: W. H. Freeman, 1976), 485–486.

14. Gary C. Jacobson, *The Politics of Congressional Elections,* 6th ed. (New York: Longman, 2004), 23–38.

15. Norman J. Ornstein, Thomas E. Mann, and Michael J. Malbin, *Vital Statistics on Congress, 2001–2002* (Washington, D.C.: AEI, 2002), Tables 5-11 and 5-12.

16. David R. Mayhew, *Congress: The Electoral Connection* (New Haven: Yale University Press, 1974), 37.

17. Gary C. Jacobson and Samuel Kernell, *Strategy and Choice in Congressional Elections,* 2nd ed. (New Haven: Yale University Press, 1983), chaps. 2–3.

18. Gary C. Jacobson and Michael A. Dimock, "Checking Out: The Effects of Bank Overdrafts on the 1992 House Elections," *American Journal of Political Science* 38 (August 1994): 601–624.

19. John Kingdon, *Congressmen's Voting Decisions,* 2nd ed. (New York: Harper and Row, 1981), 47–50.

20. John R. Johannes, *To Serve the People: Congress and Constituency Service* (Lincoln: University of Nebraska Press, 1984), 19.

21. Jacobson, *Politics of Congressional Elections,* 130–134.

22. Gary C. Jacobson, "The 105th Congress: Unprecedented and Unsurprising," in *The Elections of 1996,* ed. Michael Nelson (Washington, D.C.: CQ Press, 1997), 143–166.

23. Mike Christensen, "Congress's Cornucopia: A Sampler of Spending Add-Ons," *CQ Weekly,* October 7, 2000, 2322.

24. Roger H. Davidson, Walter J. Oleszek, and Frances E. Lee *Congress and Its Members,* 11th ed. (Washington, D.C.: CQ Press, 2008), 124.

25. Mayhew, *Congress,* 87–97.

26. Sarah A. Binder, *Minority Rights, Majority Rule: Partisanship and the Development of Congress* (Cambridge: Cambridge University Press, 1997).

27. Gary W. Cox and Mathew D. McCubbins, *Legislative Leviathan: Party Government in the House* (Berkeley: University of California Press, 1993), part 2.

28. David W. Rohde, *Parties and Leaders in the Postreform House* (Chicago: University of Chicago Press, 1991), chap. 3.

29. Ibid., 31–49.

30. Diana Evans, *Greasing the Wheels: Using Pork Barrel Projects to Build Majority Coalitions in Congress* (Cambridge: Cambridge University Press, 2004).

31. George B. Galloway, *The History of the House of Representatives* (New York: Crowell, 1961), 12.

32. Barbara Hinckley, *Stability and Change in Congress,* 4th ed. (New York: Harper and Row, 1988), 155.

33. Roger H. Davidson et al., *Congress and Its Members,* 213.

34. Richard E. Cohen, Siobhan Gorman, and Sydney J. Freedberg Jr., "National Security: The Ultimate Turf War," *National Journal,* January 4, 2003.

35. Ibid.

36. Ibid.

37. Garry Young and Joseph Cooper, "Multiple Referral and the Transformation of House Decision Making," in *Congress Reconsidered,* 5th ed., ed. Lawrence C. Dodd and Bruce I. Oppenheimer (Washington, D.C.: CQ Press, 1993), 212.

38. Barbara Sinclair, *Unorthodox Lawmaking: New Legislative Processes in the U.S. Congress,* 3rd ed. (Washington, D.C.: CQ Press, 2007).

39. John W. Ellwood and James A. Thurber, "The New Congressional Budget Process: The Hows and Whys of House-Senate Differences," in *Congress Reconsidered,* ed. Lawrence C. Dodd and Bruce I. Oppenheimer (New York: Praeger, 1977), 168.

40. Joseph White and Aaron Wildavsky, *The Deficit and the Public Interest: The Search for Responsible Budgeting in the 1980s* (Berkeley: University of California Press, 1989), chaps. 16–17.

41. Sinclair, *Unorthodox Lawmaking,* chaps. 2–3.

42. Mathew D. McCubbins and Thomas Schwartz, "Congressional Oversight Overlooked: Police Patrols vs. Fire Alarms," *American Journal of Political Science* 28 (February 1984): 165–179.

43. Barbara Sinclair, *Party Wars: Polarization and the Politics of National Policy Making* (Norman: University of Oklahoma Press, 2006), 191. Also see Sarah A. Binder and Steven S. Smith, *Politics or Principle? Filibustering in the United States Senate* (Washington, D.C.: Brookings, 1997).

44. Sinclair, *Unorthodox Lawmaking,* 126.

45. Kingdon, *Congressmen's Voting Decisions,* 47–54.

46. George Hager and David S. Cloud, "Democrats Tie Their Fate to Clinton's Budget Bill," *Congressional Quarterly Weekly Report,* August 7, 1993, 2212–2219.

47. Harold W. Stanley and Richard G. Niemi, *Vital Statistics on American Politics,* 6th ed. (Washington, D.C.: Congressional Quarterly, 1998), 252; http://en.wikipedia.org/wiki/List_of_United_States_presidential_vetoes, accessed May 15, 2008.

48. Sinclair, *Unorthodox Lawmaking,* 5.

49. John R. Hibbing and Elizabeth Theiss-Morse, *Congress as Public Enemy: Public Attitudes toward American Political Institutions* (New York: Cambridge University Press, 1995), 46–61.

Chapter 7. **The Presidency** *pages 314–361*

1. *Morrison v. Olson,* 487 U.S. 654, 705 (1988).

2. Jim Puzzanghera, "Financial Crisis: A Seesaw Day of Negotiations," *Los Angeles Times,* September 26, 2008.

3. Richard E. Neustadt, *Presidential Power and the Modern Presidents: The Politics of Power from Roosevelt to Reagan* (New York: Free Press, 1990), 34.

4. Marcus Cunliffe, *The Presidency* (Boston: Houghton Mifflin, 1968).

5. Quotation from David Herbert Donald, "Lincoln, the Politician," in *Lincoln Reconsidered: Essays on the Civil War Era* (New York: Random House, 1956).

6. Louis Fisher, *The Politics of Shared Power,* 3rd ed. (Washington, D.C.: CQ Press, 1993), 156–157.

7. Mark J. Rozell, *Executive Privilege: The Dilemma of Secrecy and Democratic Accountability* (Baltimore: Johns Hopkins University Press, 1994).

8. Theodore Roosevelt, *The Works of Theodore Roosevelt* (New York: Scribner, 1926), 347.

9. Ibid., 93; Glendon A. Schubert Jr., "Judicial Review of the Subdelegation of Presidential Power," *Journal of Politics* 12 (1950): 668.

10. Louis Fisher, *Constitutional Conflicts between Congress and the President,* 3rd ed. (Lawrence: University Press of Kansas, 1991), 103.

11. Sterling Denhard Spero, *Government as Employer* (Carbondale: Southern Illinois University Press, 1972), 117–143.

12. Richard E. Neustadt, "The Presidency and Legislation: The Growth of Central Clearance," *American Political Science Review* 48 (September 1954): 461–671.

13. Theodore J. Lowi and Benjamin Ginsberg, *American Government: Freedom and Power,* 4th ed. (New York: Norton, 1996), 625.

14. This figure covers presidential initiatives from 1935 through 1996. Jon R. Bond and Richard Fleisher, *Polarized Politics* (Washington, D.C.: CQ Press, 2000), 120.

15. Alexis de Tocqueville, *Democracy in America,* ed. J. P. Mayer (Garden City, N.Y.: Doubleday, 1969), 122.

16. Alison Mitchell, "Clinton Seems to Keep Running Though the Race Is Run and Won," *New York Times,* February 12, 1997, A1, A12.

17. Noble E. Cunningham Jr., *In Pursuit of Reason: The Life of Thomas Jefferson* (Baton Rouge: Louisiana State University Press, 1987).

18. John Hart, *The Presidential Branch: From Washington to Clinton,* 2nd ed. (Chatham, N.J.: Chatham House, 1995), 31.

19. Quoted in Samuel Kernell, "New and Old Lessons on White House Management," in *Executive Leadership in Anglo-American Systems,* ed. Colin Campbell and Margaret Jane Wyszomirski (Pittsburgh: University of Pittsburgh Press, 1991), 350.

20. Terence Smith, "Carter Liaison Aide with Jews to Quit White House," *New York Times,* March 9, 1978.

21. Neustadt, *Presidential Power.*

22. Bob Woodward, *The Agenda: Inside the Clinton White House* (New York: Simon and Schuster, 1994).

Chapter 8. **The Bureaucracy** *pages 362–411*

1. Sydney J. Freedberg Jr., quoted in Donald F. Kettl, *System under Stress: Homeland Security and American Politics* (Washington, D.C.: CQ Press, 2004), 36.

2. Michael Nelson, "A Short, Ironic History of Bureaucracy," *Journal of Politics* 44 (1982): 750.

3. Leonard D. White, *The Jeffersonians: A Study in Administrative History, 1801–1829* (New York: Macmillan, 1961), 139–140.

4. James Q. Wilson, "The Rise of the Bureaucratic State," in *The American Commonwealth, 1976,* ed. Nathan Glazer and Irving Kristol (New York: Basic Books, 1976), 78.

5. Nelson, "Short, Ironic History of Bureaucracy," 756.

6. Leonard D. White, *The Federalists: A Study in Administrative History* (New York: Macmillan, 1961), 427–431.

7. White, *Jeffersonians,* 357.

8. Quoted in Leonard D. White, *The Jacksonians: A Study in Administrative History, 1829–1861* (New York: Macmillan, 1963), 318.

9. Ibid., 320.

10. Max Weber, "Bureaucracy," in *Essays in Sociology,* translated by H. H. Gerth and C Wright Mills (New York: Oxford University Press, 1962), 196–244.

11. Matthew A. Crenson, *The Federal Machine: Beginnings of Bureaucracy in Jacksonian America* (Baltimore: Johns Hopkins University Press, 1975), 4.

12. House Ways and Means Committee, Report 641, 24th Cong., 1st sess., 1836, 2, quoted in Crenson, *The Federal Machine,* 137–138.

13. Paul P. Van Riper, *History of the United States Civil Service* (Evanston, Ill.: Row, Peterson, 1958), 74–75.

14. Nelson, "Short, Ironic History of Bureaucracy," 767.

15. In 1961 President John F. Kennedy, recognizing the politically sensitive nature of the office of attorney general, entrusted it to his brother Robert.

16. Donald R. Whitnah, ed., *Government Agencies* (Westport, Conn.: Greenwood, 1983).

17. Ibid., 152–172.

18. The Pentagon's symbolic status made it a target of al Qaeda terrorists, who crashed a hijacked airliner into its west wall on September 11, 2001. The terrorists' original objective was probably an even more potent symbol, the White House, with the Pentagon chosen as a secondary target when the pilot could not locate the presidential mansion. R. W. Apple Jr., "After the Attacks: The Trip Back; Aides Say Bush Was One Target of Hijacked Jet," *New York Times,* September 13, 2002, A1.

19. Terry M. Moe, "The Politics of Bureaucratic Structure," in *Can the Government Govern?* ed. John E. Chubb and Paul E. Peterson (Washington, D.C.: Brookings, 1989), 276.

20. Harold Seidman and Robert Gilmour, *Politics, Position, and Power: From the Positive to the Regulatory State* (New York: Oxford University Press, 1986), 316–319.

21. Paul C. Light, *The True Size of Government* (Washington, D.C.: Brookings, 1999), 24.

22. Martin Kady II and Joseph C. Anselmo, " 'Private Army' Blurs the Lines," *CQ Weekly,* May 8, 2004, 1067.

23. Paul C. Light, "The New True Size of Government," *Research Brief No. 2,* Robert F. Wagner Graduate School of Public Service, New York University, August, 2006, 11.

24. Paul C. Light, "Fact Sheet on the New True Size of Government," Center for Public Service, Brookings Institution (September 5, 2003), at www.brookings.edu/cps/light20030905.htm.

25. Charles T. Goodsell, *The Case for Bureaucracy: A Public Administration Polemic,* 4th ed. (Washington, D.C.: CQ Press, 2004), 141.

26. Ibid., 84–111.

27. James Q. Wilson, *Bureaucracy: What Government Agencies Do and Why They Do It* (New York: Basic Books, 1989), 91.

28. Martin Kady II, "Security's Swelling Price Tag," *CQ Weekly,* January 11, 2003, 75.

29. Just the opposite; for example, congressional outrage went into overdrive when, six months after the attacks of September 11, 2001, the Immigration and Naturalization Service (INS) sent word to the Florida flight school where two of the terrorists had been trained that the terrorists' student visas had been approved. The agency had granted approval the previous summer, before the at-

tacks, but "backlogs and antiquated computers" had delayed delivery, and the INS had failed to recheck what was in the pipeline. Elizabeth A. Palmer and John Godfrey, "Sensenbrenner Leading the Charge for Immediate INS Overhaul," *CQ Weekly,* March 16, 2002, 705.

30. Jack L. Walker, *Mobilizing Interest Groups in America: Patrons, Professions, and Social Movements* (Ann Arbor: University of Michigan Press, 1991), 30–33.

31. R. Douglas Arnold, *Congress and the Bureaucracy: A Theory of Influence* (New Haven: Yale University Press, 1979), 136–137.

32. Theodore J. Lowi, *The End of Liberalism: The Second Republic of the United States,* 2nd ed. (New York: Norton, 1979).

33. Nothing prevents Congress from passing legislation contrary to Supreme Court rulings, and Congress can have its way as long as it does not depend on the courts to enforce compliance. One scholar notes: "An agency might advise the committee: 'As you know, the requirement in this statute for committee prior-approval is unconstitutional under the Court's test.' Perhaps agency and committee staff will nod their heads in agreement—after which the agency will seek prior approval of the committee." Louis Fisher, in *Extensions,* a newsletter of the Carl Albert Congressional Research and Studies Center (Spring 1984): 2.

34. David Nather, "Congress as Watchdog: Asleep on the Job," *CQ Weekly,* May 22, 2004, 1193.

35. Wilson, *Bureaucracy,* 82–83.

36. Ibid., 235.

37. B. Dan Wood and Richard W. Waterman, "The Dynamics of Political Control of the Bureaucracy," *American Political Science Review* 85 (September 1991): 801–828.

38. Carl Hulse, "Mukasey Wins Vote in Senate, Despite Doubts," *New York Times,* November 9, 2007, A1.

39. Hugh Heclo, *Government of Strangers: Executive Politics in Washington* (Washington, D.C.: Brookings, 1977), 195–198.

40. Richard W. Waterman, *Presidential Influence and the Administrative State* (Knoxville: University of Tennessee Press, 1989), chap. 7.

41. This broad antiterrorism package (PL 107-56), enacted at the behest of the administration, passed 357-66 in the House, 98-1 in the Senate during the last week of October 2001.

42. Joseph J. Schatz, "Has Congress Given Bush Too Free a Spending Hand?" *CQ Weekly,* April 12, 2003, 858.

43. Martin Shapiro, *Who Guards the Guardians? Judicial Control of Administration* (Athens: University of Georgia Press, 1988), 57.

44. Douglas Cater, *Power in Washington* (New York: Vintage, 1964).

45. Hugh Heclo, "Issue Networks and the Executive Establishment," in *The New American Political System,* ed. Anthony King (Washington, D.C.: American Enterprise Institute, 1978), 87–124.

46. Joel D. Aberbach, "The Federal Executive under Clinton," in *The Clinton Presidency: First Appraisals,* ed. Colin Campbell and Bert A. Rockman (Chatham, N.J.: Chatham House, 1996), 179.

47. Goodsell, *The Case for Bureaucracy,* 146.

48. Ibid.

49. Donald F. Kettl, *System under Stress: Homeland Security and American Politics,* 2nd ed. (Washington, D.C.: CQ Press, 2006), 122.

Chapter 9. **The Federal Judiciary**
pages 412–457

1. Letter from Jefferson to John Dickinson, December 19, 1801, cited in Donald O. Dewey, *Marshall versus Jefferson: The Political Background of* Marbury v. Madison (New York: Knopf, 1970), 63.

2. *Stuart v. Laird,* 1 Cr. 299 (1803).

3. *Marbury v. Madison,* 1 Cr. (5 U.S.) 137 at 177–180 (1803); emphasis added.

4. *Pollock v. Farmers' Loan & Trust Co.* (157 U.S. 429) (1895).

5. *McCulloch v. Maryland,* 4 Wheat. 316 (1819).

6. *Dred Scott v. Sandford,* 19 How. (60 U.S.) 393 (1857).

7. Quoted by Paul Brest and Sanford Levinson in *Processes of Constitutional Decisionmaking,* 3rd ed. (Boston: Little, Brown, 1992), 75.

8. *Fletcher v. Peck,* 6 Cr. 87 (1810).

9. *Munn v. Illinois,* 94 U.S. 113 (1877); *Mugler v. Kansas,* 123 U.S. 623 (1887).

10. *Lochner v. New York,* 198 U.S. 45 (1905).

11. *Muller v. Oregon,* 208 U.S. 412 (1908). Nine years later still, the Court disregarded *Lochner* altogether to uphold an Oregon law limiting to ten hours the workday of any person working in a "mill, factory, or manufacturing establishment." *Bunting v. Oregon,* 243 U.S. 426 (1917).

12. Robert McCloskey and Sanford Levinson, eds., *The American Supreme Court,* 2nd ed. (Chicago: University of Chicago Press, 1994); and Lawrence Baum, *The Supreme Court,* 6th ed. (Washington, D.C.: CQ Press, 1998), 208.

13. *West Coast Hotel v. Parrish,* 300 U.S. 379 (1937).

14. David G. Savage, "IRAs Shielded in Bankruptcy, Justices Rule," *Los Angeles Times,* April 5, 2005; and "Justices to Decide if Social Security Can Be Seized," *Los Angeles Times,* April 26, 2005.

15. Lori Hausegger and Lawrence Baum, "Inviting Congressional Action: A Study of Supreme Court Motivations in Statutory Interpretation," *American Journal of Political Science* 43 (January 1999): 162–185.

16. *Jaffree v. Board of School Commissioners,* 554 F. Supp. 1104, 1128 (S.D. Ala. 1983).

17. *Brown v. Board of Education,* 347 U.S. 483 (1954).

18. "Chief Justice's 2007 Year-End Report" Public Information Office, U.S. Supreme Court

19. J. Woodford Howard Jr., *Courts of Appeals in the Federal Judicial System* (Princeton: Princeton University Press, 1981), 76.

20. Jeffrey R. Lax, "Certiorari and Compliance in the Judicial Hierarchy: Discretion, Reputation, and the Rule of Four," *Journal of Theoretical Politics* 15(1) 2003: 61–86.

21. Peter Linzer, "The Meaning of Certiorari Denials," *Columbia Law Review* 79 (1979): 1227–1305.

22. David O'Brien, *Storm Center: The Supreme Court in American Politics,* 4th ed. (New York: Norton, 1996).

23. Laurie P. Cohen, "Double Standard: In Wake of Ruling, Disarray Plagues Federal Sentencing," *Wall Street Journal,* December 28, 2004; Linda Greenhouse, "Justices, Revisiting Issue, Rule on Judges' Role in Sentences," *New York Times,* March 7, 2005.

24. Gregory A. Caldeira and John R. Wright, "Organized Interests and Agenda Setting in the U.S. Supreme Court," *American Political Science Review* 82 (1988): 1109–1127.

25. *United States v. Nixon,* 418 U.S. 683 (1974).

26. *Worcester v. Georgia,* 31 U.S. (6 Pet.) 515 (1832).

27. *Immigration and Naturalization Service v. Chadha,* 462 U.S. 919 (1983).

28. Louis Fisher, "The Legislative Veto: Invalidated, It Survives," *Law and Contemporary Problems* 56 (1993): 288.

29. Mathew McCubbins, Roger G. Knoll, and Barry R. Weingast, "Political Control of the Judiciary: A Positive Theory of Judicial Doctrine and the Rule of Law," *University of Southern California Law Review* (September 1995): 1631–1683.

30. See William N. Eskridge Jr., "Overriding Supreme Court Statutory Interpretation Decisions," *Yale Law Journal* 101 (1991): 331–455; James Meernik and Joseph Ignagni, "Judicial Review and Coordinate Construction of the Constitution," *American Journal of Political Science* 41 (April 1997): 446–467.

31. *Mobile v. Bolden,* 446 U.S. 55 (1980).

32. In 2001 the Supreme Court endorsed the federal government's authority to override a California law that allowed medicinal consumption of marijuana. Sabin Russell, "California Pot Clubs Targeted," *San Francisco Chronicle,* January 10, 1998. The 8–0 opinion overruled the decision of the Ninth Circuit in *United States v. The Oakland Cannabis Buyers' Cooperative,* No. 00-151.

33. Neil A. Lewis, "Republicans Seek Greater Influence in Naming Judges," *New York Times,* April 27, 1997.

34. Robert A. Carp and Ronald Stidham, *The Federal Courts,* 2nd ed. (Washington, D.C.: CQ Press, 1991), 102.

35. Baum, *Supreme Court,* 45. Eisenhower might not have used those exact words, but the story probably is an accurate reflection of his attitude toward these two justices.

36. Lee Epstein et al., *The Supreme Court Compendium: Data, Decisions and Developments,* 2nd ed. (Washington, D.C.: Congressional Quarterly, 1996).

Chapter 10. **Public Opinion** *pages 458–507*

1. In nineteen CBS News/*New York Times* polls taken between January 2002 and the beginning of the war, an average of 68 percent of respondents "approved" when asked, "Do you approve or disapprove of the United States taking military action against Iraq to try and remove Saddam Hussein from power?" In the five polls taken in the month after the war started, an average of 78 percent approved. Different polling questions produced different results, but every poll taken in the six months prior to the invasion found a majority of Americans in favor of going after Hussein. In five polls taken in the months before the war, 79 percent thought Hussein was hiding WMDs and 46 percent thought he was personally involved in the September 11 attacks. See http://pollingreport.com/iraq6.htm, August 17, 2004.

2. For examples, see Steven Kull, Clay Ramsay, and Evan Lewis, "Misperceptions, the Media, and the Iraq War," *Political Science Quarterly* 118 (Winter 2003–2004): 591–593.

3. Kirk Victor, "Congress: Congress in Eclipse," *National Journal,* April 5, 2003.

4. See the comprehensive selection of polling data at http://pollingreport.com /iraq.htm, August 17, 2004.

5. The trend in Figure 10-1 is estimated by lowess smoothing of responses in 865 polls to more than twenty differently worded questions designed to register support for the war. Responses varied systematically by question wording, but the overall trend appears regardless of wording. Data are from the CBS News/*New York Times* poll, the Gallup Poll, NBC News/*Wall Street Journal* poll, Pew Research Center for the People and the Press poll, *Newsweek* poll, ABC News/*Washington Post* poll, *Los Angeles Times* poll, *Time*/CNN poll reported at http://pollingreport.com/iraq.htm, October 17, 2008, and the National Annenberg election survey reported at http://annenbergpublicpolicycenter.org/naes/, September 23, 2004.

6. See http://pollingreport.com/wh.htm and http://pollingreport.com/iraq.htm, August 17, 2004.

7. The trends in Figure 10-2 are estimated by lowess smoothing of responses in 675 polls to seven differently worded questions designed to register support for the war. Responses varied systematically by question wording but the overall trend appears regardless of wording. Data are from the CBS News/*New York Times* poll, the Gallup Poll, Pew Research Center for the People and the Press poll, ABC News/*Washington Post* poll, *Los Angeles Times* poll, and the National Annenberg Election survey, collected at the Web sites of each of these sources.

8. See the CBS News/*New York Times* polls of April 23–27, 2004, and June 23–27, 2004, at http://pollingreport.com/iraq.htm, August 17, 2004.

9. CBS News/*New York Times* poll, March 15–18, 2008; Gary C. Jacobson, "Perception, Memory, and the Partisan Polarization of Opinion on the Iraq War," paper presented at the Annual Meeting of the American Political Science Association, Boston, August 28–31, 2008.

10. *Los Angeles Times,* national exit poll results, at www.latimesinteractive.com/pdfarchive/nationworld/la-110404 superchart-g.pdf, accessed March 11, 2005.

11. National exit poll, Edison, 2006 (Media Research/Mitofsky International.)

12. V. O. Key Jr., *Public Opinion and American Democracy* (New York: Knopf, 1967), 14.

13. Quoted in Susan Herbst, *Numbered Voices: How Opinion Polling Has Shaped American Politics* (Chicago: University of Chicago Press, 1993), 108.

14. George C. Edwards III, "Frustration and Folly: Bill Clinton and the Public Presidency," in *The Clinton Presidency: First Appraisals,* ed. Colin Campbell and Bert A. Rockman (Chatham, N.J.: Chatham House, 1996), 234.

15. Joshua Green, "The Other War Room," *Washington Monthly,* April 2002, at http://washingtonmonthly.com/features/2001/0204.green.html.

16. Alison Mitchell, "Clinton Seems to Keep Running Though the Race Is Run and Won," *New York Times,* February 2, 1997, A1.

17. Samuel Kernell, *Going Public: New Strategies of Presidential Leadership,* 3rd ed. (Washington, D.C.: CQ Press, 1997), 23.

18. "Survey Bolsters Global Warming Fight," *Los Angeles Times,* November 21, 1997, A4.

19. Rebecca Fairly Raney, "Flood of E-Mail Credited with Halting U.S. Bank Plan," *New York Times,* at http://nytimes.com, March 24, 1999.

20. William W. Lambert and Wallace E. Lambert, *Social Psychology* (Englewood Cliffs, N.J.: Prentice Hall, 1964), 50.

21. Warren E. Miller and Santa Traugott, *American National Election Studies Sourcebook, 1952–1986* (Cambridge: Harvard University Press, 1989), 94.

22. Robert S. Erikson and Kent L. Tedin, *American Public Opinion,* 5th ed. (Boston: Allyn and Bacon, 1995), 65–78.

23. Stanley Feldman and John Zaller, "The Political Culture of Ambivalence: Ideological Responses to the Welfare State," *American Journal of Political Science* 36 (1992): 268–307.

24. Angus Campbell et al., *The American Voter* (New York: Wiley, 1960), chaps. 6 and 7.

25. Morris P. Fiorina, *Retrospective Voting in American National Elections* (New Haven: Yale University Press, 1981), chap. 5.

26. The Gallup Poll at http://gallup.com/poll/releases/pr001220.asp, December 21, 2000.

27. Gary C. Jacobson, "Public Opinion and the Impeachment of Bill Clinton," in *British Elections and Parties Review,* Vol. 10, ed. Philip Cowley, David Denver, Andrew Russell, and Lisa Harrison (London: Frank Cass, 2000), 1–31.

28. Annenberg Public Policy Center, "*Fahrenheit 9/11* Viewers and Limbaugh Listeners About Equal in Size Even Though They Perceive Two Different Nations," press release, August 3, 2004.

29. An April 2004 CBS News/*New York Times* poll found that 73 percent of Republicans, but only 53 percent of Democrats, believed Iraq had possessed WMDs; a June 2004 poll from the same source found that 52 percent of Republicans, compared to 33 percent of Democrats, thought Hussein had been personally involved in the September 11, 2001, attacks. See http://pollingreport.com/iraq.htm, August 21, 2004.

30. George F. Bishop, Robert W. Oldendick, and Alfred J. Tuchfarber, "Pseudo-Opinion on Public Affairs," *Public Opinion Quarterly* (1980): 189–209.

31. John Zaller and Stanley Feldman, "A Simple Theory of Survey Response: Answering Questions versus Revealing Preferences," *American Journal of Political Science* 36 (1992): 581.

32. Support was about nine points higher if "removing Saddam Hussein" replaced "the result of the war" in the question that mentioned the loss of American lives.

33. Philip E. Converse, "The Nature of Belief Systems in Mass Publics," in *Ideology and Discontent,* ed. David Apter (New York: Free Press, 1964); and Christopher Achen, "Mass Political Attitudes and Survey Response," *American Political Science Review* 69 (1995): 1218–1231.

34. Zaller and Feldman, "Theory of Survey Response," 585–586.

35. Thomas E. Nelson, Rosalee A. Clawson, and Zoe M. Oxley, "Media Framing of a Civil Liberties Conflict and Its Effect on Tolerance," *American Political Science Review* 91 (September 1977): 567–583.

36. Shanto Iyengar and Donald R. Kinder, *News That Matters* (Chicago: University of Chicago Press, 1987), 63–72.

37. Benjamin I. Page and Robert Y. Shapiro, *The Rational Public* (Chicago: University of Chicago Press, 1992), 63.

38. Ibid., 130.

39. James A. Stimson, *Public Opinion in America: Moods, Cycles, and Swings* (Boulder, Colo.: Westview Press, 1991), 29–31.

40. Michael B. MacKuen, Robert S. Erikson, and James A. Stimson, "Macropartisanship," *American Political Science Review* 83 (1989): 1125–1142.

41. Stimson, *Public Opinion,* 125.

42. Arthur Lupia and Mathew D. McCubbins, *The Democratic Dilemma: Can Citizens Learn What They Really Need to Know?* (New York: Cambridge University Press, 1998).

43. Paul Burstein, "The Impact of Public Opinion on Public Policy: A Review and an Agenda," *Political Research Quarterly* 56 (March 2003): 29–40.

44. Herbert McClosky and John Zaller, *The American Ethos* (Cambridge: Harvard University Press, 1984), 38.

45. Pew Research Center for the People and Press survey, December 12, 2006–January 9, 2007, at www.pollingreport.com/terror.htm, accessed April 29, 2008.

46. Herbert McClosky and Ada Brill, *Dimensions of Tolerance* (New York: Basic Books, 1983).

47. McClosky and Zaller, *American Ethos,* 83.

48. Ibid., 84.

49. Page and Shapiro, *Rational Public,* 74; http://pollingreport.com/race.htm, August 20, 2004.

50. *American National Election Study, 2000,* variable 000694.

51. Barbara Hinkson Craig and David M. O'Brien, *Abortion and American Politics* (Chatham, N.J.: Chatham House, 1993), 266–270.

52. The Gallup Poll, June 23–27, 1999, at http://pollingreport.com/civil.htm, August 21, 2004.

53. See the polling data on these issues at http://pollingreport.com/civil.htm, August 20, 2004.

54. Richard A. Brody, *Assessing the President* (Stanford: Stanford University Press, 1991).

55. John E. Mueller, *War, Presidents, and Public Opinion* (New York: Wiley, 1973), 58–63.

56. Mark Peffley and Jon Hurwitz, "International Events and Foreign Policy Beliefs: Public Responses to Changing U.S.-Soviet Relations," *American Journal of Political Science* 36 (May 1992): 431–461.

57. See http://pollingreport.com/terror.htm, October 31, 2001.

58. Gallup Poll, June 12–15, 2003, at www.pollingreport.com/race.htm, accessed April 29, 2008

59. "Black Americans and the 2004 Vote," BET/CBS News poll, July 6–15, 2004, at http://cbsnews.com/stories/2004/07/21/opinion/polls/main630986.shtml, August 20, 2004.

60. Ibid., 210.

61. See www.cnn.com/ELECTION/2008/results/polls/#USP00p1 and www.gallup.com/poll/108058/Candidate-Support-Marital-Status-Gender, accessed November 5, 2008.

62. Voter News Service exit poll at http://cnn.com/ELECTION/epolls/US/P000.html, November 14, 2000.

Chapter 11. **Voting, Campaigns, and Elections** *pages 508–555*

1. "McCain Lambasts Bush Years," *Washington Times,* October 23, 2008, at www.washingtontimes.com/news/2008/oct/23/mccain-lambasts-bush-years/, accessed October 26, 2008.

2. More than 90 percent in some pre-election polls; see www.pollingreport.com, accessed October 29, 2008.

3. See www.pollingreport.com/wh08.htm, accessed November 6, 2008.

4. Chilton Williamson, *American Suffrage: From Property to Democracy 1760–1860* (Princeton: Princeton University Press, 1960), 49.

5. Alexis de Tocqueville, *Democracy in America,* Vol. 1 (New York: Vintage, 1990), 57.

6. Quoted by David Morgan in *Suffragists and Democrats: The Politics of Women's Suffrage in America* (East Lansing: Michigan State University Press, 1972), 84.

7. Ibid., 124.

8. See, for example, Americans for a Society Free from Age Restrictions, "ASFAR Position Paper on Voting," http://asfar.org/voting.

9. See http://elections.gmu.edu/preliminary_vote_2008.html.

10. Steven J. Rosenstone and John Mark Hansen, *Mobilization, Participation, and Democracy in America* (New York: Macmillan, 1993).

11. Ibid., 150.

12. Ibid., 241.

13. Ibid., 214–218.

14. Ruy A. Teixeira, *The Disappearing American Voter* (Washington, D.C.: Brookings, 1992), 86–101; Michael M. Gant and William Lyons, "Democratic Theory: Nonvoting and Public Policy: The 1972–1988 Presidential Elections," *American Politics Quarterly* 21 (April 1993): 194–195.

15. Martin P. Wattenberg, *The Decline of American Political Parties, 1952–1992* (Cambridge: Harvard University Press, 1994), 155–157, 171–180.

16. "Outlook: Kansas," *Congressional Quarterly Weekly Report,* October 11, 1989, 2432.

17. Samuel L. Popkin, *The Reasoning Voter: Communication and Persuasion in Presidential Campaigns,* 2nd ed. (Chicago: University of Chicago Press, 1994), 1.

18. Paul R. Abramson, John H. Aldrich, and David W. Rohde, *Continuity and Change in the 1992 Elections* (Washington, D.C.: CQ Press, 1994), 56–57.

19. Stephen J. Wayne, *The Road to the White House 1996: The Politics of Presidential Elections* (New York: St. Martin's, 1997), 260–261.

20. Paul S. Herrnson and Clyde Wilcox, "The 1996 Presidential Election: A Tale of a Campaign That Didn't Seem to Matter," in

Toward the Millennium: The Elections of 1996, ed. Larry J. Sabato (Boston: Allyn and Bacon, 1997), 136.

21. Alan Ehrenhalt, "Technology, Strategy Bring New Campaign Era," *Congressional Quarterly Weekly Report,* December 7, 1985, 2559.

22. Stephen Ansolabehere et al., "Does Attack Advertising Demobilize the Electorate?" *American Political Science Review* 88 (December 1994): 829–838.

23. Nelson W. Polsby and Aaron Wildavsky, *Presidential Elections,* 9th ed. (Chatham, N.J.: Chatham House, 1996), 215–216.

24. ABC News/*Washington Post* poll of likely voters taken October 17–19, 2008, at www.pollingreport.com/wh08.htm.

25. Joel Bradshaw, "Strategy, Theme, and Message" (paper presented at the Conference on Campaign Management, American University, Washington, D.C., December 10–11, 1992), 114.

26. *Buckley v. Valeo,* 424 U.S. 1 (1976).

27. *Colorado Republican Federal Campaign Committee v. Federal Election Commission,* 518 U.S. 604 (1996).

28. Gary C. Jacobson, *The Politics of Congressional Elections* 7th ed. (New York: Longman, 2009), 124–134.

Chapter 12. **Political Parties** *pages 556–607*

1. Larry Sabato, *The Party's Just Begun: Shaping Political Parties for America's Future* (Glenview, Ill.: Scott, Foresman, 1988), 133.

2. American National Election Study, 1980.

3. American National Election Study, 2000.

4. American National Election Study, 2004.

5. Martin P. Wattenberg, *The Decline of American Political Parties, 1952–1994* (Cambridge: Harvard University Press, 1996); Everett Carll Ladd, "1996 Vote: The 'No Majority' Realignment Continues," *Political Science Quarterly* 112 (Spring 1997): 1–23.

6. Gary C. Jacobson, *A Divider Not a Uniter: George W. Bush and the American People* (New York: Pearson Longman 2007), 62–63.

7. E. E. Schattschneider, *Party Government* (New York: Holt, Rinehart, Winston, 1942), 1.

8. Edmund Burke, *Thoughts on the Causes of the Present Discontents,* ed. W. Murison (Cambridge: The University Press, 1930).

9. Anthony Downs, *An Economic Theory of Democracy* (New York: Harper and Row, 1957), 25.

10. This conceptual trinity, originally proposed by V. O. Key Jr., is used routinely by political scientists who study parties. See *Politics, Parties, and Pressure Groups* (New York: Thomas Crowell, 1964), 163–165.

11. Maurice Duverger, *Political Parties* (New York: Wiley, 1954), 217.

12. John F. Hoadley, *The Origins of the American Party System* (Lexington: University of Kentucky Press, 1986), 51.

13. See Alexander Hamilton's discussion of the Electoral College in *Federalist* No. 68. This device is described in Chapter 7, "The Presidency."

14. Noble E. Cunningham Jr., "The Development of Parties," in *After the Constitution: Party Conflict in the New Republic,* ed. Lance Banning (Belmont, Calif.: Wadsworth, 1989), 104.

15. Paul Goodman, *The Democratic Republicans of Massachusetts: Politics in a Young Republic* (Cambridge: Harvard University Press, 1964), 204.

16. Quoted in Richard H. Brown, "The Missouri Crisis, Slavery, and the Politics of Jacksonianism," in Banning, *After the Constitution,* 446.

17. Michael F. Holt, *Political Parties and American Political Development from the Age of Jackson to the Age of Lincoln* (Baton Rouge: Louisiana State University Press, 1992), 41.

18. James S. Chase, *Emergence of the Presidential Nominating Convention, 1798–1832* (Urbana: University of Illinois Press, 1973), 85.

19. Richard P. McCormick, "Political Development and the Second Party System," in *The American Party Systems: Stages of Political Development,* 2nd ed., ed. William Nesbit Chambers and Walter Dean Burnham (New York: Oxford University Press, 1975), 108.

20. Ibid., 8.

21. Nelson W. Polsby, *Consequences of Party Reform* (New York: Oxford University Press, 1983), chaps. 2 and 3.

22. Martin P. Wattenberg, *The Decline of American Political Parties, 1952–1992* (Cambridge: Harvard University Press, 1994), 174.

23. Gary C. Jacobson, *The Electoral Origins of Divided Government: Competition in U.S. House Elections, 1946–1988* (Boulder, Colo.: Westview, 1990), 15–19.

24. Morris P. Fiorina, *Divided Government,* 2nd ed. (Boston: Allyn and Bacon, 1996), 72–81.

25. Jacobson, *Electoral Origins of Divided Government,* 105–120.

26. CBS News/New York Times poll, February 8–11, 2007.

27. Bruce E. Keith et al., *The Myth of the Independent Voter* (Berkeley: University of California Press, 1992), chap. 4.

28. Pew Research Center for the People and Press, "Convention Backgrounder: A Closer Look at the Parties in 2008,"August 22, 2008, at http://people-press.org/.

29. See www.cnn.com/ELECTION/2008/results/polls/#USP00p1, accessed November 5, 2008.

30. Mark Rozell and Clyde Wilcox, eds., *God at the Grass Roots: The Christian Right in the 1994 Elections* (Lanham, Md.: Rowman & Littlefield, 1995).

31. Paul S. Herrnson, *Party Campaigning in the 1980s* (Cambridge: Harvard University Press, 1988).

32. Federal Election Commission, "Congressional Campaigns Spend $912 Million Through Late November," news release, January 3, 2005.

33. John H. Aldrich, *Why Parties? The Origin and Transformation of Party Politics in America* (Chicago: University of Chicago Press, 1995), 273.

Chapter 13. **Interest Groups** *pages 608–649*

1. David E. Rosenbaum, "Since Sept. 11, Lobbyists Use New Pitches for Old Pleas," *New York Times on the Web,* www.nytimes.com, December 3, 2001.

2. Ibid.

3. Robert Pear, "Lobbyists Seek Special Spin on Federal Bioterrorism Bill," *New York Times,* December 10, 2001, 1.

4. Christopher H. Schmitt, Julian Barnes, and Douglas Pasternak, "Bellying Up to the Antiterror Bar," *U.S. News and World Report,* December 31, 2001, 18.

5. Rosenbaum, "New Pitches."

6. Alison Gilbert Olson, *Making the Empire Work: London and American Interest Groups, 1690–1790* (Cambridge: Harvard University Press, 1992), 56.

7. Ibid., 146.

8. Ibid., 3.

9. Alexis de Tocqueville, *Democracy in America,* ed. Andrew Hacker (New York: Washington Square, 1964), 71.

10. Ibid., 182.

11. David B. Truman, *The Governmental Process* (New York: Knopf, 1951).

12. E. E. Schattschneider, *The Semi-Sovereign People: A Realist's View of Democracy in America* (Hinsdale, Ill.: Dryden, 1960), 34–35.

13. Mancur Olson, *The Logic of Collective Action: Public Goods and the Theory of Groups* (Cambridge: Harvard University Press, 1965).

14. Jack L. Walker Jr., *Mobilizing Interest Groups In America: Patrons, Professions, and Social Movements* (Ann Arbor: University of Michigan Press, 1991), 1; Jeffrey Birnbaum, "The Road to Riches Is Called K Street," *Washington Post,* June 22, 2005, A01.

15. *Washington Representatives,* 31st ed. (Bethesda, MD: Columbia Books, 2007).

16. James A. Thurber, "Lobbying Reform: The Importance of Enforcement and Transparency," testimony before the Senate Committee on Rules and Administration, February 8, 2006, at http://spa.american.edu/ccpsfiles/File/Thurber%20Testimony%20for%20Senate%20Rules%20Committee2006.pdf, accessed February 12, 2008.

17. David Vogel, *Fluctuating Fortunes: The Political Power of Business in America* (New York: Basic Books, 1988), 220–227.

18. Walker, *Mobilizing Interest Groups,* 29.

19. Ibid., 31.

20. Daniel Kahneman and Amos Tversky, "Prospect Theory: An Analysis of Decision under Risk," *Econometrica* 47 (1979): 263–291.

21. William P. Browne, "Issue Niches and the Limits of Interest Group Influence," in *Interest Group Politics,* 3rd ed., ed. Allan J. Cigler and Burdett A. Loomis (Washington, D.C.: CQ Press, 1991), 348.

22. James Q. Wilson, *Political Organizations* (New York: Basic Books, 1973), chap. 13.

23. Browne, "Issue Niches and the Limits of Interest Group Influence," 356.

24. Kay Lehman Schlozman and John T. Tierney, *Organized Interests and American Democracy* (New York: Harper and Row, 1986), 150.

25. Unidentified lobbyist quoted in Jeffrey M. Berry, *The Interest Group Society* (Boston: Little, Brown, 1984), 117; emphasis in the original.

26. Kenneth M. Goldstein, *Interest Groups, Lobbying, and Participation in America* (Cambridge: Cambridge University Press, 1999), 73.

27. Schlozman and Tierney, *Organized Interests,* 333.

28. Kevin T. McGuire, *Understanding the U.S. Supreme Court* (Boston: McGraw-Hill, 2001), 151.

29. Karen O'Connor, "Lobbying the Justices or Lobbying for Justice?" in *The Interest Group Connection: Electioneering, Lobbying, and Policymaking in Washington,* 2nd ed., ed. Paul S. Herrnson, Ronald G. Shaiko, and Clyde Wilcox (Washington, D.C.: CQ Press, 2005), 319–340.

30. Gregory A. Caldeira and John R. Wright, "Lobbying for Justice: Organized Interests, Supreme Court Nominations, and the United States Senate," *American Journal of Political Science* 42 (April 1998): 510.

31. Andrew J. Polsky, "Giving Business the Business," *Dissent* (Winter 1996): 33–36.

32. Jonathan D. Salant and David S. Cloud, "To the '94 Election Victors Go the Fundraising Spoils," *Congressional Quarterly Weekly Report,* April 15, 1995, 1056.

33. Campaign Finance Institute, "PAC Fundraising Swings Democratic over the First Nine Months of 2007," November 8, 2007, at www.cfinst.org/pr/prRelease.aspx?ReleaseID=167, accessed February 1, 2008.

34. Jonathan D. Salant, "GOP Bumps Up against Court Precedent in Trying to Block AFL-CIO," *Congressional Quarterly Weekly Report,* April 13, 1996, 997.

35. See, for example, Philip Stern, *The Best Congress Money Can Buy* (New York: Pantheon, 1988); Brooks Jackson, *Honest Graft: Big Money and the American Political Process* (New York: Knopf, 1988); Elizabeth Drew, *Politics and Money: The New Road to Corruption* (New York: Macmillan, 1983).

36. John R. Wright, *Interest Groups and Congress* (Boston: Allyn and Bacon, 1996), 136–145; Frank J. Sorauf, *Inside Campaign Finance: Myths and Realities* (New Haven: Yale University Press, 1992), 163–174.

37. Richard L. Hall and Frank W. Wayman, "Buying Time: Monied Interests and the Mobilization of Bias in Congressional Committees," *American Political Science Review* 84 (1990): 797–820.

38. Robert S. Salisbury, *Institutions and Interests: Substance and Structure in American Politics* (Pittsburgh: University of Pittsburgh Press, 1992), 348.

39. William P. Browne, *Private Interests, Public Policy, and American Agriculture* (Lawrence: University Press of Kansas, 1988), 248–252.

40. Schlozman and Tierney, *Organized Interests,* 399–403.

41. Lester C. Thurow, *The Zero-Sum Society* (New York: Basic Books, 1980); Mancur Olson, *The Rise and Decline of Nations* (New Haven: Yale University Press, 1982).

Chapter 14. **The News Media** *pages 650–695*

1. Linda Matchan, Don Aucoin, and Stephen Kurkjian, "Anguished Cries Fell on Deaf Ears Despite Evidence, Church Muffled Charges that Rev. Porter Sexually Abused Children," *Boston Globe,* July 2, 1992.

2. Elizabeth Stankiewicz, "Group Criticizes Church Response to Sex Offenders," *Boston Globe,* July 26, 1992.

3. Timothy Cook, *Governing with the News: The News Media as a Political Institution* (Chicago: University of Chicago Press, 1998), 22.

4. Charles E. Clark, *The Public Prints: The Newspaper in Anglo-American Culture, 1665–1740* (New York: Oxford University Press, 1994), 195–196.

5. Edwin Emery, *The Press and America,* 2nd ed. (Englewood Cliffs, N.J.: Prentice Hall, 1962), 107–124.

6. Richard Hofstadter, *The Idea of the Party System* (Berkeley: University of California Press, 1969), 8.

7. Thomas C. Leonard, *The Power of the Press: The Birth of American Political Reporting* (New York: Oxford University Press, 1986), 57.

8. Willard Grosvenor Bleyer, *Main Currents of the History of American Journalism* (Boston: Houghton Mifflin, 1927), 377.

9. Alfred M. Lee, *The Daily Newspaper in America* (New York: Macmillan, 1937), 214–217.

10. Paul Starr, *The Creation of the Media* (New York: Basic Books, 2004), 258.

11. *New York Journal,* May 8, 1898, 1.

12. *Historical Statistics of the United States: Colonial Times to 1970,* Vols. 1 and 2 (Washington, D.C.: Government Printing Office, 1975), series R104–5.

13. Erik Barnouw, *The Golden Web,* Vol. 2 (New York: Oxford University Press, 1968), 18–22.

14. Julia Angwin and Sarah McBride, "Radio's Bush-Bashing Air America Is Back in Fighting Form," *Wall Street Journal,* January 28, 2005.

15. Emery, *Press and America,* 663.

16. Figures cited in James T. Hamilton, *All the News Fit to Print* (Princeton: Princeton University Press, 2004), 284.

17. Miguel Helft, "Yahoo and Intel to Bring Interactive Applications to TV Sets," *New York Times* August 20, 2008.

18. Figures calculated from Doris A. Graber, *Mass Media and American Politics,* 6th ed. (Washington, D.C.: CQ Press, 2002), Table 4-5, 110–111.

19. W. Russell Neuman, Marion R. Just, and Ann N. Crigler, *Common Knowledge* (Chicago: University of Chicago Press, 1992), 87–95.

20. See Stephen Ansolabehere, Roy Behr, and Shanto Iyengar, *The Media Game: American Politics in the Television Age* (New York: Macmillan, 1993), 45. These results were confirmed in a *Wall Street Journal*/NBC News poll, in which Americans expressed greater confidence in every broadcast news outlet over every other media outlet (except CNBC/MSNBC—the lowest-rated broadcaster listed—which tied with the top-rated print outlet, *Time* magazine). Albert R. Hunt, "Washington Events Fuel Disdain for Media, Politics," *Wall Street Journal,* September 17, 1998.

21. Ansolabehere, et al., *Media Game,* 42–46.

22. Much of the statistical information from this section can be found at Jounalism.org. For the downward trend in network audience shares see its url, www.stateofthenewsmedia.org/2008.

23. Matthew A. Baum, *Soft News Goes to War* (Princeton: Princeton University Press, 2003).

24. Pew Research Center for the People & the Press, "News Audiences Increasingly Politicized," June 8, 2004.

25. Brian Stetler and Richard Pérez-Peña, "Media Outlets Are Seeking a Campaign Bounce of Their Own," *New York Times,* August 4, 2008. Available at www.nytimes.com/2008/08/04/business/media/04ratings.html.

26. Markus Prior, *Post-Broadcast Democracy* (New York: Cambridge University Press, 2007).

27. *New York Times Co. v. United States,* 403 U.S. 713 (1971).

28. The Court first employed this doctrine in 1964 in *New York Times Co. v. Sullivan,* 376 U.S. 254 (1964).

29. Leon V. Sigal, *Reporters and Officials: The Organization and Politics of News Reporting* (Lexington, Mass.: D. C. Heath, 1973), 122.

30. Howard Kurtz of the *Washington Post,* interview on *Nightline,* ABC News, January 30, 1998.

31. John Donovan of ABC News. Howard Kurtz said, "The White House decided the way that it could inoculate itself was to do the leaking itself, to do what they called document dumps, to get this stuff out, take their hits early . . . [and when] Fred Thompson and other investigating senators came along, the White House could say, 'Well this is old news. This has all been in the papers. We already know all this stuff.'" Interview on *Nightline,* ABC News, March 11, 1998.

32. Stephen Hess, *Live from Capitol Hill* (Washington, D.C.: Brookings, 1991).

33. Joseph N. Cappella and Kathleen Hall Jamieson, *Spiral of Cynicism: The Press and the Public Good* (New York: Oxford University Press, 1997), 3–5.

34. Coverage of Congress is mostly neutral, but when it is not, it tends to be negative. Charles M. Tidmarch and John J. Pitney Jr., "Covering Congress," *Polity* 17 (1985): 463–483.

35. Transcript, presidential press conference, May 7, 1993, Washington, D.C.

36. Richard H. Rovere, *Senator Joe McCarthy* (Cleveland: Meridian, 1966), 124.

37. Paul F. Boller Jr., *Presidential Anecdotes* (New York: Penguin, 1982), 63–64.

38. James E. Pollard, *The Presidents and the Press* (New York: Macmillan, 1947), 775.

39. Cited in Worth Bingham and Ward S. Just, "The President and the Press," *Reporter* 26 (April 12, 1962): 20.

40. Marvin Kalb, "The Rise of the 'New' News: A Case Study of Two Root Causes of Modern Scandal Coverage" (discussion paper D-34, John F. Kennedy School of Government, Harvard University, October 1998).

Chapter 15. **The Prospects for Institutional Reform** *pages 696–726*

1. This quotation, as well as all of the specifics in the preceding discussion, are taken from Anthony Corrado, 2003, "The Legislative Odyssey of BCRA," in *Life After Reform: When the Bipartisan Campaign Reform Act Meets Politics,* edited by Michael J. Malbin (Lanham, Md.: Rowman and Littlefield Publishers, Inc.). The quotation appears on page 38.

2. 540 U.S. 93 (2003).

3. This statement was made by Richard L. Hasen and quoted in Adam Liptak, "Justices Strike Down Law That Aids Campaign Rivals of Rich Candidates," *New York Times,* June 27, 2008, A11.

4. This statement appears in Thomas E. Mann, 2008, "A Collapse of the Campaign Finance Regime?" *Forum,* Vol. 6, no. 1, Article 1.

5. These figures were compiled using the Online Data Analysis feature of the publicly accessible Web site, www.worldvaluessurvey.org/.

6. CNN, "Flag-burning Amendment Fails by a Vote," Wednesday, June 28, 2006, accessed at www.cnn.com/2006/POLITICS/06/27/flag.burning/index.html in July, 2008.

7. Associated Press, "Schwarzenegger: Let Foreign-Born Seek White House," February 22, 2004, accessed at www.cnn.com/2004/ALLPOLITICS/02/22/elec04.prez.schwarzenegger.ap/ in July, 2008.

8. ABC News/ *Washington Post* poll press release, "Most Oppose Same-Sex Marriage, but Balk at Amending the Constitution," January 21, 2004.

9. Frank J. Sorauf, *Inside Campaign Finance: Myths and Realities* (New Haven: Yale University Press, 1992), 11.

10. Alan Ehrenhalt, *The United States of Ambition: Politicians, Power, and the Pursuit of Office* (New York: Times Books, 1991).

11. Everett S. Brown, 1925, "The Presidential Election of 1824–1825," *Political Science Quarterly,* 40:384–403, 393.

12. All of the quotes in this paragraph are taken from pages 1, 5, and 6 of C. Edward Merriam's *Primary Elections* (Chicago, University of Chicago Press, 1908).

13. V. O. Key, *Parties, Politics, and Pressure Groups,* 5th ed. (New York: Crowell, 1964)

14. Villaraigosa made this statement on the July 13, 1998, broadcast of the PBS program *NewsHour with Jim Lehrer,* and President Bartlet uttered a similar statement on Episode 20 of the *West Wing*'s first season, according to Bartlet4America.org.

15. Our discussion of the growth of the term limits movement draws mostly upon Thad Kousser, *Term Limits and the Dismantling of State Legislative Professionalism* (Cambridge: Cambridge University Press, 2005), and from the National Conference of State Legislature's comprehensive record of term limit laws posted at www.ncsl.org/programs/legismgt/ABOUT/termlimit.htm.

16. Our discussion of the effects of term limits on the states draws from Thad Kousser, "Term Limits and State Legislatures," in Caroline Tolbert, Todd Donovan, and Bruce E. Cain, eds., *Democracy in the States: Experiments in Election Reform* (Washington, D.C.: Brookings, 2008), with the finding that term-limited legislators generally stay in government found in Richard J. Powell, "The Unintended Effects of Term Limits on the Career Paths of State Legislators," in Rick Farmer, John David Rausch Jr., and John C. Green, eds., *The Test of Time: Coping with Legislative Term Limits* (Lanham, Md.: Lexington Books, 2003).

17. These aggregate spending figures as well as colorful descriptions of individual projects can be found in the Citizens Against Government Waste's "2008 Congressional Pig Book Summary," available for download at www.cagw.org/site/PageServer.

18. CNN AllPolitics, "Supreme Court Deletes Line-Item Veto," June 25, 1998. Accessed at www.cnn.com/ALLPOLITICS/1998/06/25/scotus.lineitem/ in July, 2008.

19. See Diana Evans, *Greasing the Wheels: Using Pork Barrel Projects to Build Majority Coalitions in Congress* (New York: Cambridge University Press, 2004) and John Ellwood and Eric M. Patashnik, "In Praise of Pork," *Public Interest* 110 (1993): 19–33.

Glossary

access The ability of privileged outsiders, such as interest group representatives, to obtain a hearing from elected officials or bureaucrats. *(Page 548.)*

ad hoc committee A congressional committee appointed for a limited time to design and report a specific piece of legislation. *(Page 285.)*

activism When judges deliberately shape judicial doctrine to conform with their personal view of the Constitution and social policy. *(Page 437.)*

affirmative action Policies or programs designed to expand opportunities for minorities and women and usually requiring that an organization take measures to increase the number or proportion of minorities and women in its membership or employment. *(Page 174.)*

agenda control The capacity to set the choices available to others. *(Page 29.)*

agency loss The discrepancy between what citizens ideally would like their agents to do and how the agents actually behave. *(Page 32.)*

agent Someone who makes and implements decisions on behalf of someone else. *(Page 31.)*

aggregate partisanship The distribution, or percentage, of the electorate that identifies with each of the political parties. *(Page 482.)*

aggregate public opinion In a democracy, the sum of all individual opinions. *(Page 480.)*

ambivalence A state of mind produced when particular issues evoke attitudes and beliefs that pull in opposite directions. *(Page 477.)*

amicus curiae "Friend of the court." A brief filed in a lawsuit by an individual or group that is not party to the lawsuit but that has an interest in the outcome. *(Page 434.)*

Antifederalists A loosely organized group (never a formal political party) that opposed ratification of the Constitution, which the group believed would jeopardize individual freedom and states' rights. After ratification, the efforts of the Antifederalists led to adoption of the first ten amendments, the Bill of Rights. *(Page 81.)*

Articles of Confederation The compact among the thirteen original states that formed the basis of the first national government of the United States from 1777 to 1789, when it was supplanted by the Constitution. *(Page 47.)*

attitude An organized and consistent manner of thinking and feeling about people, groups, social issues, or, more generally, any event in one's environment. *(Page 467.)*

attorney general The head of the Justice Department. As the nation's chief legal officer, the attorney general of the United States represents the federal government's interests in law courts throughout the nation. The attorney general is also the chief law enforcement officer. *(Page 443.)*

Australian ballot A ballot prepared and distributed by government officials that places the names of all candidates on a single list and is filled out by voters in private. First adopted in the United States in 1888, the Australian ballot replaced oral voting and party-supplied ballots. *(Page 581.)*

authority The right to make and implement a decision. *(Page 9.)*

bargaining A form of negotiation in which two or more parties who disagree propose exchanges and concessions to find a course of acceptable collective action. *(Page 5.)*

beat A regularly assigned venue that a news reporter covers on an ongoing basis. *(Page 681.)*

bicameral legislature A legislature composed of two houses or chambers. The U.S. Congress (House and Senate) and every U.S. state legislature (with the exception of Nebraska's, which is unicameral) are bicameral legislatures. *(Page 52.)*

Bill of Rights The first ten amendments to the U.S. Constitution. *(Page 73.)*

black codes Laws enacted by southern legislatures after the Civil War that prevented former slaves from voting and holding certain jobs, among other prohibitions. *(Page 150.)*

block grant A broad grant of money given by the federal government to a state government. The grant specifies the general area (such as education or health services) in which the funds may be spent but leaves it to the state to determine the specific allocations. *(Page 129.)*

bureaucracy A complex structure of offices, tasks, and rules in which employees have specific responsibilities and work within a hierarchy of authority. Government bureaucracies are charged with implementing policies. *(Page 364.)*

bureaucratic culture The norms and regular patterns of behavior found within a bureaucratic organization. Different agencies often develop their own norms, which shape the behavior of those who work in the agency. *(Page 388.)*

cabinet The formal group of presidential advisers who head the major departments and agencies of the federal government. Cabinet members are chosen by the president and approved by the Senate. *(Page 35.)*

candidate A person who is running for elected office. *(Page 528.)*

carrying capacity The amount of information a communication technology can deliver to its audience. Newspapers, for example, have much higher carrying capacities than do television news programs. *(Page 668.)*

casework The activity undertaken by members of Congress and their staffs to solve constituents' problems with government agencies. *(Page 261.)*

caucus A closed meeting of a political or legislative group to choose candidates for office or to decide issues of policy. *(Page 572.)*

central clearance A presidential directive requiring that all executive agency proposals, reports, and recommendations to Congress—mostly in the form of annual reports and testimony at authorization and appropriations hearings—be certified by the Office of Management and Budget as consistent with the president's policy. *(Page 336.)*

checks and balances A constitutional mechanism giving each branch some oversight and control of the other branches. Examples are the presidential veto, Senate approval of presidential appointments, and judicial review of presidential and congressional actions. *(Page 69.)*

civil liberties Constitutional and legal protections from government interference with personal rights and freedoms such as freedom of assembly, speech, and religion. *(Page 141.)*

civil rights The powers or privileges that are conferred on citizens by the Constitution and the courts and that entitle them to make claims upon the government. Civil rights protect individuals from arbitrary or discriminatory treatment at the hands of the government. *(Page 141.)*

clear and present danger test A rule used by the Supreme Court to distinguish between speech protected and not protected by the First Amendment. Under this rule, the First Amendment does not protect speech aimed at inciting an illegal action. *(Page 205.)*

clear and probable danger test A rule introduced by Chief Justice Fred Vinson for the courts to enlist in free expression cases: "In each case [the courts] must ask whether the gravity of the 'evil,' discounted by its probability, justifies such invasion of free speech as is necessary to avoid the danger." *(Page 208.)*

clientele The category of people, or groups, served by a bureaucratic agency. *(Page 374.)*

closed rule An order from the House Rules Committee limiting floor debate on a particular bill and disallowing or limiting amendment. *(Page 298.)*

cloture A parliamentary procedure used to close debate. Cloture is used in the Senate to cut off filibusters. Under the current Senate rules, three-fifths of senators, or sixty, must vote for cloture to halt a filibuster. *(Page 299.)*

coalition An alliance of unlike-minded individuals or groups to achieve some common purpose such as lobbying, legislating, or campaigning for the election of public officials. *(Page 36.)*

cognitive shortcut A mental device allowing citizens to make complex decisions based on a small amount of information. For example, a candidate's party label serves as a shortcut by telling voters much about his or her positions on issues. *(Page 484.)*

collective action An action taken by a group of like-minded individuals to achieve a common goal. *(Page 12.)*

collective goods Goods that are collectively produced and freely available for anyone's consumption. *(Page 40.)*

commander in chief The title that is given to the president by the Constitution and that denotes the president's authority as the head of the national military. *(Page 326.)*

command The authority of one actor to dictate the actions of another. *(Page 27.)*

commerce clause The clause in Article I, Section 8, of the Constitution that gives Congress the authority to regulate commerce with other nations and among the states. *(Page 66.)*

committee and conference reports Documents submitted by committees that often instruct agencies how Congress expects them to use their "discretion." Though not legally binding, bureaucrats ignore such instructions at their peril. *(Page 396.)*

community standards The Supreme Court's 1973 ruling that a work is obscene if it is "utterly without redeeming social importance" and, "to the average person, applying contemporary 'community standards,' the dominant theme of the material, taken as a whole, appeals to prurient interests." *(Page 209.)*

compromise Settlement in which each side concedes some of its preferences in order to secure others. *(Page 5.)*

concurring opinion A written opinion by a Supreme Court justice who agrees with the decision of the Court but disagrees with the rationale for reaching that decision. *(Page 440.)*

conditional party government The degree of authority delegated to and exercised by congressional leaders; varies with and is conditioned by the extent of election-driven ideological consensus among members. *(Page 276.)*

confederation A political system in which states or regional governments retain ultimate authority except for those powers they expressly delegate to a central government. *(Page 55.)*

conference committee A temporary joint committee of the House and Senate appointed to reconcile the differences between the two chambers on a particular piece of legislation. *(Page 285.)*

conformity costs The difference between what a person ideally would prefer and what the group with which that person makes collective decisions actually does. Individuals pay conformity costs whenever collective decisions produce policy outcomes that do not best serve their interests. *(Page 22.)*

conservative In the United States, a proponent of a political ideology that favors small or limited government, an unfettered free market, self-reliance, and traditional social norms. *(Page 468.)*

constitution A document outlining the formal rules and institutions of government and the limits placed on its powers. *(Page 9.)*

constitutional courts Category of federal courts vested with the general judicial authority outlined in Article III of the Constitution. The most important are the Supreme Court, the courts of appeals, and the ninety-four district courts. Their authority derives from that of the Supreme Court, and they are supposed to conform to its decisions. *(Page 427.)*

coordinated spending Spending by the Democratic and Republican Party committees on behalf of individual congressional candidates. *(Page 540.)*

coordination The act of organizing a group to achieve a common goal. Coordination remains a prerequisite for effective collective action even after the disincentives to individual participation (that is, prisoner's dilemma problems) have been solved. *(Page 12.)*

core values Moral beliefs held by citizens that underlie their attitudes toward political and other issues. As integral parts of an individual's identity, these beliefs are stable and resistant to change. *(Page 469.)*

court of appeals The second tier of courts in the federal judicial system (between the Supreme Court and the district courts). One court of appeals serves each of eleven regions, or circuits, plus one for the District of Columbia. *(Page 429.)*

Court-packing plan An attempt by President Franklin Roosevelt, in 1937, to remodel the federal judiciary. Its purpose ostensibly was to alleviate the overcrowding of federal court dockets by allowing the president to appoint an additional Supreme Court justice for every sitting justice over the age of seventy. The legislation passed the House of Representatives but failed in the Senate by a single vote. If it had passed, Roosevelt could have added six new justices to the high bench, thereby installing a new Court majority sympathetic to his New Deal programs. *(Page 423.)*

credibility gap The widespread suspicion among reporters that presidents will lie to the media when doing so serves their interest and they think they can get away with it. *(Page 692.)*

cruel and unusual punishment Criminal penalties that are not considered appropriate by a society, that involve torture, or that could result in death when the death penalty had not been ordered. *(Page 227.)*

cutthroat competition Competition among states that involves adopting policies that each state would prefer to avoid. For example, states engage in cutthroat competition when they underbid one another on tax breaks to attract businesses relocating their facilities. *(Page 119.)*

Declaration of Independence The document drafted by Thomas Jefferson and adopted by the Second Continental Congress on July 4, 1776, declaring the independence of the thirteen colonies from Great Britain. *(Page 54.)*

de facto segregation Segregation that results from practice rather than from law. *(Page 172.)*

de jure segregation Segregation enacted into law and imposed by the government. *(Page 173.)*

delegation The act of one person or body authorizing another person or body to perform an action on its behalf. For example, Congress often delegates authority to the president or administrative agencies to decide the details of policy. *(Page 31.)*

direct democracy A system of government in which citizens make policy decisions by voting on legislation themselves rather than by delegating that authority to their representatives. *(Page 34.)*

discharge petition A petition that removes a measure from a committee to which it has been referred in order to make it available for floor consideration. In the House a discharge petition must be signed by a majority of House members (218). *(Page 298.)*

dissenting opinion The written opinion of one or more Supreme Court justices who disagree with the ruling of the Court's majority. The opinion outlines the rationale for their disagreement. *(Page 440.)*

district courts The trial courts of original jurisdiction in the federal judicial system. The ninety-four district courts are the third tier of the federal judicial system, below the Supreme Court and the courts of appeals. *(Page 429.)*

divided government A term used to describe government when one political party controls the executive branch and the other political party controls one or both houses of the legislature. *(Pages 338 and 594.)*

dual federalism A system of government in which the federal government and state governments each have mutually exclusive spheres of action. *(Page 101.)*

due process clause A clause found in both the Fifth and Fourteenth Amendments to the Constitution protecting citizens from arbitrary action by the national and state governments. *(Page 200.)*

earmarks Money set aside by Congress in the federal budget to pay for projects in the home district of a member of Congress. *(Page 719.)*

elastic clause Allows Congress to "make all Laws which shall be necessary and proper for carrying into Execution the foregoing Powers." *(Page 105.)*

Electoral College A body of electors in each state, chosen by voters, who formally elect the president and vice president of the United States. Each state's number of electoral votes equals its representation in Congress; the District of Columbia has three votes. An absolute majority of the total electoral vote is required to elect a president and vice president. *(Page 72.)*

embedding Military media strategy of putting journalists among military units in the field. *(Page 689.)*

enrolled bill A bill that has been passed by both the Senate and the House and has been sent to the president for approval. *(Page 352.)*

entitlement A benefit that every eligible person has a legal right to receive and that cannot be taken away without a change in legislation or due process in court. *(Page 289.)*

enumerated powers The explicit powers given to Congress by the Constitution in Article I, Section 8. These include the powers of taxation, coinage of money, regulation of commerce, and provision for the national defense. *(Page 105.)*

equal protection clause A Fourteenth Amendment clause guaranteeing all citizens equal protection of the laws. The courts have interpreted the clause to bar discrimination against minorities and women. *(Page 200.)*

equal time A "fairness" rule established by the Federal Communications Commission to ensure that broadcasters offer balanced coverage of controversial issues. If a radio or television station sells or gives airtime to one candidate for political office, it must provide other candidates with equal time. *(Page 663.)*

establishment of religion clause The first clause of the First Amendment. The establishment clause prohibits the national government from establishing a national religion. *(Page 214.)*

exclusionary rule A judicial rule prohibiting the police from using at trial evidence obtained through illegal search and seizure. *(Page 224.)*

executive agreement An agreement between the president and one or more other countries. An executive agreement is similar to a treaty, but unlike a treaty, it does not require the approval of the Senate. *(Page 328.)*

Executive Office of the President (EOP) A collection of agencies that help the president oversee department and agency activities, formulate budgets and monitor spending, craft legislation, and lobby Congress. The major components of the EOP, established in 1939 by President Franklin Roosevelt, include the White House Office, Office of Management and Budget, National Security Council, and Council of Economic Advisers, among other agencies. *(Page 351.)*

executive order A presidential directive to an executive agency establishing new policies or indicating how an existing policy is to be carried out. *(Page 331.)*

executive privilege The president's right to withhold information from Congress and the courts. Presidents assert that executive privilege, nowhere mentioned in the Constitution, is necessary to maintain separation of powers among the branches of government. *(Page 330.)*

externality Public goods or bads generated as a byproduct of private activity. For example, air pollution is an externality (public bad) because it is, in part, the byproduct of the private activity of driving a car. *(Pages 37 and 96.)*

faction A group of people sharing common interests who are opposed to other groups with competing interests. James Madison defined a faction as any group with objectives contrary to the general interests of society. *(Page 84.)*

fairness doctrine Rule that assures that different points of view on controversial issues have access to the airwaves. *(Page 664.)*

federalism A system of government in which power is divided between a central government and several regional governments. In the United States the division is between the national government and the states. *(Page 99.)*

Federalists Name given to two related, but not identical, groups in late-eighteenth-century American politics. The first group, led by Alexander Hamilton and James Madison, supported ratification of the Constitution in 1787 and 1788. Subsequently, Hamilton and John Adams led the second group, the Federalist Party, which dominated national politics during the administrations of George Washington (1789–1797) and Adams (1797–1801). *(Page 81.)*

Federal Register A government publication listing all proposed federal regulations. *(Page 382.)*

filibuster A tactic used in the Senate to halt action on a bill. It involves making long speeches until the majority retreats. Senators, once holding the floor, have unlimited time to speak unless a cloture vote is passed by three-fifths (sixty) of the members. *(Page 299.)*

focal point Focus identified by participants when coordinating their energies to achieve a common purpose. *(Page 13.)*

focus group A method of gauging public opinion by observing a small number of people brought together to discuss specific issues, usually under the guidance of a moderator. *(Page 530.)*

framing Providing a context that affects the criteria citizens use to evaluate candidates, campaigns, and political issues. *(Page 479.)*

franking privilege The legal right of each member of Congress to send official mail postage-free under his or her signature. *(Page 686.)*

free exercise clause The second clause of the First Amendment. The free exercise clause forbids the national government to interfere with the exercise of religion. *(Pages 214 and 686.)*

free-rider problem A situation in which individuals can receive the benefits from a collective activity whether or not they helped to pay for it, leaving them with no incentive to contribute. *(Page 19.)*

Fugitive Slave Law The 1850 law compelling northerners to honor southerners' property claims to slaves, passed in return for the South's agreeing to admit California as a free state (and hence lose its ability to block legislation in the Senate). *(Page 147.)*

fusion tickets Slates of candidates that "fused" the nominees of minor and major parties. Fusion tickets, eventually banned by state legislatures, allowed minor parties to boost their votes by nominating candidates also nominated by major parties. *(Page 566.)*

gag rule An executive order prohibiting federal employees from communicating directly with Congress. *(Page 336.)*

gerrymandering Drawing legislative districts in such a way as to give one political party a disproportionately large share of seats for the share of votes its candidates win. *(Page 253.)*

going public Presidents "go public" when they engage in intensive public relations to promote their policies to the voters and thereby induce cooperation from other elected officeholders in Washington. *(Page 344.)*

government The institutions and procedures through which people are ruled. *(Page 9.)*

Government Accountability Office Office with a staff of more than five thousand that audits programs and agencies and reports to Congress on their performance. *(Page 396.)*

grandfather clauses Statutes stating that only those people whose grandfather had voted before Reconstruction could vote, unless they passed a literacy or wealth test. After the Civil War this mechanism was used to disenfranchise African Americans. *(Page 153.)*

grants-in-aid Funds given by Congress to state or local governments for a specific purpose. *(Page 128.)*

grassroots lobbying Lobbying conducted by rank-and-file members of an interest group. *(Page 635.)*

Great Compromise The agreement between large and small states at the Constitutional Convention (1787) that decided the selection and composition of Congress. The compromise stipulated that the lower chamber (House of Representatives) be chosen by direct popular vote and that the upper chamber (Senate) be selected by the state legislatures. Representation in the House would be proportional to a state's population; in the Senate each state would have two members. *(Page 71.)*

gridlock A legislative "traffic jam" often precipitated by divided government. Gridlock occurs when presidents confront opposition-controlled Congresses with policy preferences and political stakes that are in direct competition with their own and those of their party. Neither side is willing to compromise, the government accomplishes little, and federal operations may even come to a halt. *(Page 339.)*

hate crime A violent crime directed against individuals, property, or organizations solely because of the victims' race, gender, national origin, or sexual orientation. *(Page 184.)*

hearings and investigations Meetings in which bureaucrats are called before subcommittees to explain and defend their decisions, and outsiders are sometimes invited to criticize them. Most agencies must testify annually about their activities before the House Appropriations subcommittee that has jurisdiction over their budgets. *(Page 396.)*

home rule Power given by a state to a locality to enact legislation and manage its own affairs locally. Home rule also applies to Britain's administration of the American colonies. *(Page 48.)*

ideology A comprehensive, integrated set of views about government and politics. *(Page 468.)*

imperial presidency Refers to a presidency in which the president and the executive staff try to extend executive power and influence through unilateral actions. *(Page 319.)*

incorporation The Supreme Court's extension of the guarantees of the Bill of Rights to state and local governments through its various interpretations of the Fourteenth Amendment. *(Page 198.)*

independent spending Campaign spending—by a person or organization for or against a political candidate—that is not controlled by or coordinated with any candidate's campaign. *(Page 540.)*

infotainment Increasingly popular, nontraditional source of political information that combines news and entertainment. Examples include talk shows and political comedy programs. *(Page 671.)*

initiative An approach to direct democracy in which a proposal is placed on an election ballot when the requisite number of registered voters have signed petitions. *(Page 34.)*

insider tactics Interest group activity that includes normal lobbying on Capitol Hill, working closely with members of Congress, and contributing money to incumbents' campaigns. Contrasts with *outsider tactics. (Page 633.)*

inspectors general Positions with independent offices (outside the normal bureaucratic chain of command) in virtually every government agency, who audit agency books and investigate activities on Congress's behalf. *(Page 396.)*

institution In a democracy, an organization that manages potential conflicts between political rivals, helps them to find mutually acceptable solutions, and makes and enforces the society's collective agreements. Among the prominent federal political institutions in the United States are Congress, the presidency, and the Supreme Court. *(Page 7.)*

interest groups Organized groups of people seeking to influence public policy. *(Page 610.)*

iron triangle A stable, mutually beneficial political relationship among a congressional committee (or subcommittee), administrative agency, and organized interests concerned with a particular policy domain. *(Page 403.)*

issue network A loose, informal, and highly variable web of relationships among representatives of various interests who are involved in a particular area of public policy. *(Page 404.)*

issue publics Groups of citizens who are more attentive to particular areas of public policy than average citizens because such groups have some special stake in the issues. *(Page 484.)*

issue voting Voting for candidates based on their positions on specific issues, as opposed to their party or personal characteristics. *(Page 526.)*

Jim Crow laws A series of laws enacted in the late nineteenth century by southern states to institute segregation. These laws created "whites only" public accommodations such as schools, hotels, and restaurants. *(Page 153.)*

joint committee Permanent congressional committees made up of members of both the House and the Senate. Joint committees do not have any legislative authority; they monitor specific activities and compile reports. *(Page 284.)*

judicial doctrine The practice of prescribing in a decision a set of rules that are to guide future decisions on similar cases. Used by the Supreme Court to guide the lower courts in making decisions. *(Page 435.)*

judicial review The authority of a court to declare legislative and executive acts unconstitutional and therefore invalid. *(Pages 72 and 415.)*

King Caucus A pejorative term used to refer to the first method of nominating presidential candidates in which party leaders elected to Congress would pick a presidential nominee. More generally, refers to the imposition of elite authority over mass action. This method of presidential nomination was retired after the presidential election of 1824. *(Page 710.)*

laboratories for reform The idea that states provide their citizens with opportunities to change politics on a smaller scale, giving everyone else the chance to observe the effects of a reform without risking it themselves. *(Page 706.)*

leak Strategically consequential information given to reporters on the condition that its source not be identified by name. *(Page 680.)*

legislative veto A procedure that allows one or both houses of Congress to reject an action taken by the president or an executive agency. In 1983 the Supreme Court declared legislative vetoes unconstitutional, but Congress continues to enact legislation incorporating the veto. *(Page 396.)*

***Lemon* test** The most far-reaching of the controversial cases in which the Supreme Court specified three conditions every state law must satisfy to avoid running afoul of the establishment of religion prohibition: the statute in question "must have a secular legislative purpose," such as remedial education; the statute's "primary effect must be one that neither advances nor inhibits religion"; and the statute must not foster "an excessive government entanglement with religion." *(Page 215.)*

libel A published falsehood or statement resulting in the defamation of someone's character. The First Amendment does not protect libelous statements. *(Pages 213 and 676.)*

liberal In the United States, a proponent of a political ideology that favors extensive government action to redress social and economic inequalities and tolerates social behaviors that conservatives view as deviant. Present-day liberals advocate policies benefiting the poor, minority groups, labor unions, women, and the environment and oppose government imposition of traditional social norms. *(Page 468.)*

line-item veto A procedure, available in 1997 for the first time, permitting a president to cancel amounts of new discretionary appropriations (budget authority), as well as new items of direct spending (entitlements) and certain limited tax benefits, unless Congress disapproves by law within a specified period of time. It was declared unconstitutional in 1998. *(Pages 341 and 720.)*

literacy test A legal barrier used to exclude African Americans from voting. Local white registrars would require prospective black voters to read and interpret arcane passages of the state's constitution. Since few satisfied these registrars' rigorous demands, by 1910 fewer than 10 percent of black males were voting in the South. *(Page 153.)*

lobbying Activities through which individuals, interest groups, and other institutions seek to influence public policy by persuading government officials to support their groups' position. *(Page 610.)*

lobbyists Professionals who work to influence public policy in favor of their clients' interests. *(Page 609.)*

logroll The result of legislative vote trading. For example, legislators representing urban districts may vote for an agricultural bill provided that legislators from rural districts vote for a mass transit bill. *(Page 78.)*

majority leader The formal leader of the party controlling a majority of the seats in the House or the Senate. In the Senate the majority leader is the head of the majority party. In the House the majority leader ranks second in the party hierarchy behind the Speaker. *(Page 278.)*

majority rule The principle that decisions should reflect the preferences of more than half of those voting. Decision making by majority rule is one of the fundamental procedures of democracy. *(Page 30.)*

mandatory reports Method by which Congress keeps its bureaucratic agents in line, in this case requiring executive agencies—even the president—to report on programs. *(Page 396.)*

matching grant A grant of money given by the federal government to a state government for which the federal government provides matching funds, usually between one and two dollars, for every dollar the state spends in some area. *(Page 129).*

measurement error Uncertainties in public opinion, as revealed by responses to polls, that arise from the imperfect connection between the wording of survey questions and the terms in which people understand and think about political objects. *(Page 483.)*

media bias Bias or slant in the selection of which news to report and how the news is reported. *(Page 672.)*

message In a political campaign, the central thematic statement of why voters ought to prefer one candidate over others. *(Page 530.)*

micro-targeting The process of targeting very specific groups of potential voters. For example, using databases that combine voter rolls with credit card purchase information or grocery store savings club records to identify potential supporters. *(Page 719.)*

minority leader The formal leader of the party controlling a minority of the seats in the House or the Senate. *(Page 278.)*

***Miranda* rule** Requirement that police inform suspects that they have a right to remain silent and a right to have counsel while being interrogated. Failure to inform suspects of their rights will result in any confession or evidence thus obtained being inadmissable against them at trial. *(Page 225.)*

mobilization Also known as "getting out the vote." Mobilization occurs when activists working for parties, candidates, or interest groups ask members of the electorate to vote. *(Page 521.)*

moral incentives The personal satisfactions of active self-expression through contribution or other involvement to social causes. *(Page 620.)*

muckraking Journalistic investigation and exposure of scandals, corruption, and injustices, pioneered during the late nineteenth century Progressive Era. *(Page 658.)*

multiple referral The act of sending a proposed piece of legislation to more than one committee in the same chamber. *(Page 288.)*

nationalists Constitutional reformers led by James Madison and Alexander Hamilton who sought to replace the Articles of Confederation. Opposed at the Constitutional Convention (1787) by states' rights proponents, the nationalists favored a strong national legislature elected directly by the citizenry rather than the states and a national government that could veto any state laws it deemed unfit. *(Page 61.)*

nationalization Shifting to the national government responsibilities traditionally exercised by the states. *(Page 101.)*

national party convention A gathering of delegates to select a party's presidential and vice-presidential ticket and to adopt its national platform. *(Page 574.)*

National Security Council (NSC) The highest advisory body to the president on military and diplomatic issues. Established in 1947, this agency in the Executive Office of the President helps the president coordinate the actions of government agencies, including the State and Defense Departments and the Joint Chiefs of Staff, into a single cohesive policy for dealing with other nations. *(Page 352.)*

necessary and proper clause The last clause of Article I, Section 8, of the Constitution. This clause grants Congress the authority to make all laws that are "necessary and proper" and to execute those laws. *(Pages 66 and 251.)*

negative campaigning The act of attacking an opposing candidate's platform, past political performance, or personal characteristics. *(Page 534.)*

neutrality test Policy favored by justices in establishment of religion decisions. The justices used the neutrality test not so much to prevent favoritism among religious groups as to root out policies that preferred religious groups generally over nonreligious groups engaged in a similar activity. *(Page 216.)*

New Deal coalition An electoral alliance that was the basis of Democratic dominance from the 1930s to the early 1970s. The alliance consisted of Catholics, Jews, racial minorities, urban residents, organized labor, and white southerners. *(Page 584.)*

New Jersey Plan New Jersey delegate William Patterson's proposal for reforming the Articles of Confederation. Introduced at the Constitutional Convention (1787), the New Jersey Plan was favored by delegates who supported states' rights. *(Page 64.)*

news media The organizations that gather, package, and transmit the news through some proprietary communications technology. *(Page 654.)*

nominating convention A political convention used to select a candidate to run in an upcoming election *(Page 710.)*

obscenity Defined as publicly offensive acts or language, usually of a sexual nature, with no redeeming social value. The Supreme Court has offered varying definitions in its rulings over the years. *(Page 209.)*

office Subdivision of some government departments that confers on its occupants specific authority and responsibilities. *(Page 9.)*

Office of Management and Budget (OMB) Previously known as the Bureau of the Budget, OMB is the most important agency in the Executive Office of the President. The budget bureau, created in 1921 to act as a central clearinghouse for all budget requests, was renamed and given increased responsibilities in 1970. OMB advises the president on fiscal and economic policies, creates the annual federal budget, and monitors agency performance, among other duties. *(Page 351.)*

open rule A provision governing debate of a pending bill and permitting any germane amendment to be offered on the floor of the House. *(Page 298.)*

open seat A seat in a state or district being contested by candidates, none of whom none currently holds the office. Congressional seats become "open" when the incumbent dies or does not run for reelection. *(Page 541.)*

opinion leader A citizen who is highly attentive to and involved in politics or some related area and to whom other citizens turn for political information and cues. *(Page 483.)*

outsider tactics Interest group activities designed to influence elected officials by threatening to impose political costs on them if they do not respond. Tactics include marches, demonstrations, campaign contributions to opponents, and electoral mobilization. *(Page 633.)*

pack journalism A method of news gathering in which news reporters all follow the same story in the same way because they read each other's copy for validation of their own. *(Page 684.)*

parliamentary government A form of government in which the chief executive is chosen by the majority party or by a coalition of parties in the legislature. *(Page 35.)*

party identification An individual's enduring affective or instrumental attachment to one of the political parties; the most accurate single predictor of voting behavior. *(Page 526.)*

party label A label carrying the party's "brand name," incorporating the policy positions and past performance voters attribute to it. *(Page 526.)*

party machines State or local party organizations based on patronage. They work to elect candidates to public offices that control government jobs and contracts, which, in turn, are used by party leaders (often denigrated as "bosses") to reward the subleaders and activists who mobilize voters for the party on election day. *(Page 579.)*

patronage The practice of awarding jobs, grants, licenses, or other special favors in exchange for political support. *(Page 568.)*

penumbras Judicially created rights based on various guarantees of the Bill of Rights. The right to privacy is not explicitly stated in the Constitution, but the Supreme Court has argued that this right is implicit in various clauses found throughout the Bill of Rights. *(Page 233.)*

performance voting Basing votes for a candidate or party on how successfully the candidate or party performed while in office. *(Page 526.)*

pluralism A theory describing a political system in which all significant social interests freely compete with one another for influence over the government's policy decisions. *(Page 86.)*

plurality A vote in which the winning candidate receives the greatest number of votes (but not necessarily a majority—over 50 percent). *(Page 31.)*

pocket veto A method by which the president vetoes a bill passed by both houses of Congress by failing to act on it within ten days of Congress's adjournment. *(Page 306.)*

policy gridlock Political paralysis in the face of pressing national problems. *(Page 611.)*

political action committee (PAC) A federally registered fund-raising group that pools money from individuals to give to political candidates and parties. *(Page 257.)*

political party A coalition of people who seek to control the machinery of government by winning elections. Not specifically mentioned in the Constitution, political parties make mass democracy possible by, among other functions, coordinating the group activities necessary to translate public preferences into public policy. *(Page 559.)*

political socialization The process by which citizens acquire their political beliefs and values. *(Page 473.)*

politician Elected professional who specializes in providing compelling reasons for people with different values and interests to join in a common action. *(Page 36.)*

politics The process by which individuals and groups reach agreement on a common course of action even as they continue to disagree on the goals that action is intended to achieve. *(Page 5.)*

poll tax A tax imposed on people when they register to vote. In the decades after the Civil War this tax was used primarily to disenfranchise black voters. With passage of the Twenty-fourth Amendment, in 1964, it became unconstitutional. *(Page 153.)*

popular sovereignty Citizens' delegation of authority to their agents in government, with the ability to rescind that authority. *(Page 61.)*

pork barrel legislation Legislation that provides members of Congress with federal projects and programs for their individual districts. *(Page 264.)*

power An officeholder's actual influence with other officeholders, and, as a consequence, over the government's actions. *(Page 10.)*

preemption legislation Laws passed by Congress that override or preempt state or local policies. The power of preemption derives from the supremacy clause (Article VI) of the Constitution. (See also *supremacy clause*.) *(Page 128.)*

preferences Individuals' choices, reflecting economic situation, religious values, ethnic identity, or other valued interests. *(Page 6.)*

presidential coattails Common metaphor for the capacity of a successful presidential candidate to generate votes for other candidates further down the ticket and pull fellow partisans into office. *(Page 262.)*

president pro tempore In the absence of the vice president, the formal presiding officer of the Senate. The honor is usually conferred on the senior member of the majority party, but the post is sometimes rotated among senators of the majority party. *(Page 281.)*

primary election An election held before the general election in which voters decide which of a party's candidates will be the party's nominee for the general election. *(Page 581.)*

prime The news media's influence on how citizens make political judgments, through emphasis on particular stories. *(Page 479.)*

principal An individual with the authority to make some decision. This authority may be delegated to an agent who is supposed to act on the principal's behalf. *(Page 31.)*

prior restraint A government agency's act to prohibit the publication of material or speech before the fact. The courts forbid prior restraint except under extraordinary conditions. *(Page 675.)*

prisoner's dilemma A situation in which two (or more) actors cannot agree to cooperate for fear that the other will find its interest best served by reneging on an agreement. *(Page 12.)*

private goods Benefits and services over which the owner has full control of their use. *(Page 37.)*

privatize Prevent a common resource from being overexploited by tying the benefit of its consumption to its cost. *(Page 21.)*

privileges and immunities clause The clause in Section 1 of the Fourteenth Amendment stipulating that "no State shall make or enforce any law which shall abridge the privileges or immunities of citizens of the United States." *(Page 200.)*

procedural doctrine Principle of law that governs how the lower courts do their work. *(Page 435.)*

Progressive Era A period of American history extending roughly from 1880 to 1920 and associated with the reform of government and electoral institutions in an attempt to reduce corruption and weaken parties. *(Page 581.)*

proportional representation An electoral system in which legislative seats are awarded to candidates or parties in proportion to the percentage of votes received. *(Pages 252 and 566.)*

public goods Goods that are collectively produced and freely available for anyone's consumption. *(Page 37.)*

public interest lobby A group that promotes some conception of the public interest rather than the narrowly defined economic or other special interests of its members. *(Page 613.)*

public opinion "Those opinions held by private persons which governments find it prudent to heed." *(Page 462.)*

quorum The minimum number of congressional members who must be present for the transaction of business. Under the Constitution, a quorum in each house is a majority of its members: 218 in the House and 51 in the Senate when there are no vacancies. *(Page 300.)*

quotas Specific shares of college admissions, government contracts, and jobs set aside for population groups that have suffered from past discrimination. The Supreme Court has rejected the use of quotas wherever it has encountered them. *(Page 174.)*

racial profiling Identifying the suspects of a crime solely on the basis of their race or ethnicity. *(Page 139.)*

race to the bottom When states "race," or compete, to provide a minimum level of services (such as welfare spending) or regulation (such as tax incentives for corporations). There remains much debate over whether or not states do indeed race toward the bottom. *(Page 119.)*

red tape Excessive paperwork leading to bureaucratic delay. The term originated in the seventeenth century, when English legal and governmental documents were bound with red-colored tape. *(Page 369.)*

referendum An approach to direct democracy in which a state legislature proposes a change to the state's laws or constitution which all the voters subsequently vote on. *(Page 34.)*

representative government A political system in which citizens select government officials who, acting as their agents, deliberate and commit the citizenry to a course of collective action. *(Page 34.)*

republic A form of democracy in which power is vested in elected representatives. *(Page 34.)*

restraint The judicial action of deferring to the policies emanating from the elected branches in the absence of a clear violation of the Constitution or established doctrine. *(Page 437.)*

restricted rule A provision that governs consideration of a bill and that specifies and limits the kinds of amendments that may be made on the floor of the House of Representatives. *(Page 298.)*

rider An amendment to a bill that is not germane to the legislation. *(Page 300.)*

roll-call vote Vote taken by a call of the roll to determine whether a quorum is present, to establish a quorum, or to vote on a question. Usually the House uses its electronic voting system for a roll call, but when the system is malfunctioning the Speaker directs the clerk to read the names. The Senate does not have an electronic voting system; its roll is always called by a clerk. *(Page 304.)*

rotation in office The practice of citizens serving in public office for a limited term and then returning to private life. *(Page 367.)*

rule A provision that governs consideration of a bill by the House of Representatives by specifying how the bill is to be debated and amended. *(Page 298.)*

rule of four A rule employed by the Supreme Court's stating that when four justices support hearing a case the certiorari petition is granted. *(Page 432.)*

scientific polling Tool developed in the twentieth century for systematically investigating the opinions of ordinary people, based on random samples. *(Page 464.)*

segregation The political and social practice of separating whites and blacks into dual and highly unequal schools, hospitals, prisons, public parks, housing, and public transportation. *(Page 153.)*

select committee A temporary legislative committee created for a specific purpose and dissolved after its tasks are completed. *(Page 284.)*

selective incentives Private goods or benefits that induce rational actors to participate in a collective effort to provide a collective good. *(Page 621.)*

selective incorporation The Supreme Court's gradual process of assuming guardianship of civil liberties by applying piecemeal the various provisions of the Bill of Rights to state laws and practices. *(Page 201.)*

senatorial courtesy An informal practice in which senators are given veto power over federal judicial appointments in their home states. *(Page 446.)*

seniority rule The congressional practice of appointing as committee or subcommittee chairs the members of the majority with the most years of committee service. *(Page 271.)*

separate but equal doctrine The Supreme Court–initiated doctrine that separate but equivalent facilities for

African Americans and whites are constitutional under the equal protection clause of the Fourteenth Amendment. *(Page 154.)*

separation of powers The distribution of government powers among several political institutions. In the United States, at the national level power is divided between the three branches: Congress, the president, and the Supreme Court. *(Page 35.)*

shared federalism A system in which the national and state governments share in providing citizens with a set of goods. *(Page 101.)*

Shays's Rebellion Uprising of 1786 led by Daniel Shays, a former captain in the Continental army and a bankrupt Massachusetts farmer, to protest the state's high taxes and aggressive debt collection policies. The rebellion demonstrated a fundamental weakness of the Articles of Confederation—its inability to keep the peace—and stimulated interest in strengthening the national government, leading to the Philadelphia convention that framed the Constitution. *(Page 59.)*

shield laws Laws that protect journalists from having to testify about their sources in court. *(Page 683.)*

signing statements A statement issued by the president that is intended to modify implementation or ignore altogether provisions of a new law. *(Page 316.)*

simple majority A majority of fifty percent plus one. *(Page 30.)*

single-issue voters People who base their votes on candidates' or parties' positions on one particular issue of public policy, regardless of the candidates' or parties' positions on other issues. *(Page 524.)*

slander Forms of false and malicious information that damage another person's reputation. *(Pages 213 and 676.)*

social movements Amorphous aggregates of people sharing general values and a desire for social change. *(Page 624.)*

soft money Money used by political parties for voter registration, public education, and voter mobilization. Until 2002, when Congress passed legislation outlawing soft money, the government had imposed no limits on contributions or expenditures for such purposes. *(Page 538.)*

solicitor general The official responsible for representing the U.S. government before the Supreme Court. The solicitor general is a ranking member of the U.S. Department of Justice. *(Page 434.)*

sound bite A catchy phrase or slogan that encapsulates a politician's message, broadcast especially on television news programs. *(Page 690.)*

Speaker of the House The presiding officer of the House of Representatives. The Speaker is elected at the beginning of each congressional session on a party-line vote. As head of the majority party the Speaker has substantial control over the legislative agenda of the House. *(Page 274.)*

special committee A temporary legislative committee, usually lacking legislative authority. *(Page 284.)*

split ticket The act of voting for candidates from different political parties for different offices—for example, voting for a Republican for president and a Democrat for senator. *(Page 581.)*

spoils system A system in which newly elected officeholders award government jobs to political supporters and members of the same political party. The term originated in the saying "to the victor go the spoils." *(Page 367.)*

standing The right to bring legal action. *(Pages 397 and 436.)*

standing committee A permanent legislative committee specializing in a particular legislative area. Standing committees have stable memberships and stable jurisdictions. *(Pages 283.)*

stare decisis "Let the decision stand." In court rulings, a reliance on precedents, or previous rulings, in formulating decisions in new cases. *(Page 435.)*

State of the Union address A presidential message to Congress under the constitutional directive that he shall "from time to time give to the Congress Information of the State of the Union, and recommend to their Consideration such Measures as he shall judge necessary and expedient." *(Page 344.)*

states' rights Safeguards against a too-powerful national government that were favored by one group of delegates to the Constitutional Convention (1787). States' rights advocates supported retaining those features of the Articles of Confederation that guarded state prerogatives, such as state participation in the selection of national officeholders and equal representation for each state regardless of population. *(Pages 64 and 96.)*

status quo bias Institutional bias that fundamentally favors continuation of current public policy. *(Page 704.)*

substantive doctrine Principle that guides judges on which party in a case should prevail—akin to policymaking. *(Page 435.)*

suffragists Women who campaigned in the early twentieth century for the right of women to vote. *(Page 176.)*

superdelegate A delegate to the Democratic National Convention who is eligible to attend because he or she is an elected party official. The Democrats reserve a specific set of delegate slots for party officials. *(Page 588.)*

supermajority A majority larger than a simple 51 percent majority, which is required for extraordinary legislative actions such as amending the Constitution or certain congressional procedures. For example, in the Senate sixty votes are required to stop a filibuster. *(Page 31.)*

supremacy clause A clause in Article VI of the Constitution declaring that national laws are the "supreme" law of the land and therefore take precedence over any laws adopted by states or localities. *(Page 72.)*

"take care" clause The provision in Article II, Section 3, of the Constitution instructing the president to "take Care that the Laws be faithfully executed." *(Pages 70 and 331.)*

takings clause The Fifth Amendment's provision on property rights: "private property [shall not] be taken for public use, without just compensation." *(Page 237.)*

Tenth Amendment The amendment that offers the most explicit endorsement of federalism to be found in the Constitution: "The powers not delegated to the United States by the Constitution, nor prohibited by it to the States, are reserved to the States respectively, or to the people." *(Page 106.)*

term limits A movement begun during the 1980s to limit the number of terms both state legislators and members of Congress can serve. *(Page 713.)*

ticket-splitting (See *split ticket*.) *(Page 258.)*

tragedy of the commons A situation in which group members overexploit a common resource, causing its destruction. *(Page 20.)*

transaction costs The costs of doing political business reflected in the time and effort required to compare preferences and negotiate compromises in making collective decisions. *(Page 22.)*

trial balloon Policy announced by the president in order to test public opinion and floated either by members of Congress or the media. *(Page 679.)*

two-party system A political system in which only two major parties compete for all of the elective offices. Third-party candidates usually have few, if any, chances of winning elective office. *(Page 564.)*

tyranny A form of government in which the ruling power exploits its authority and permits little popular control. *(Page 30.)*

unanimous consent agreement A unanimous resolution in the Senate restricting debate and limiting amendments to bills on the floor. *(Page 281.)*

unit cost The cost of transmitting a news product to a consumer. *(Page 654.)*

unitary executive When a president claims prerogative to attach signing statements to bills and asserts his/her right to modify implementation or ignore altogether provisions of a new law that encroaches on his/her constitutional prerogatives as "the chief executive" or as commander in chief. *(Page 316.)*

unitary government A system of government in which a single government unit holds the power to govern the nation (in contrast to a federal system, in which power is shared among many governing units). (See also *federalism*.) *(Page 99.)*

veto The formal power of the president to reject bills passed by both houses of Congress. A veto can be overridden by a two-thirds vote in each house. *(Pages 28 and 71.)*

Virginia Plan Constitutional blueprint drafted by James Madison that sought to reform the Articles of Confederation. Introduced at the Constitutional Convention (1787), the plan proposed a tripartite national government, but unlike the subsequent Constitution, it provided for a popularly elected legislature that would dominate national policymaking. Moreover, the national government would possess the authority to veto any state laws. *(Page 63.)*

War Powers Act Law that requires the president to inform Congress within forty-eight hours of committing troops abroad in a military action. *(Page 327.)*

whip A member of a legislative party who acts as the communicator between the party leadership and the rank and file. The whip polls members on their voting intentions, prepares bill summaries, and assists the leadership in various other tasks. *(Page 278.)*

White House Office Agency in the Executive Office of the President (EOP) that serves as the president's personal staff system. Although the entire EOP does the president's business, the White House staff consists of the president's personal advisers, who oversee the political and policy interests of the administration. *(Page 351.)*

white primary A practice that permitted political parties to exclude African Americans from voting in primary elections. Because historically in the South winning the Democratic primary was tantamount to winning the general election, this law in effect disenfranchised black voters in southern states. *(Page 153.)*

writ of certiorari An order that is given by a superior court to an appellate court and that directs the lower court to send up a case the superior court has chosen to review. This is the central means by which the Supreme Court determines what cases it will hear. *(Page 432.)*

writ of mandamus "We command." A court-issued writ commanding a public official to carry out a specific act or duty. *(Page 416.)*

"yellow journalism" Style of journalism born of intense competition and characterized by screaming headlines and sensational stories. Coined at the end of the nineteenth century, the term referred to the yellow ink in which the *New York World's* comic strips were printed. *(Page 658.)*

zero sum Issues for which mutual gains through cooperation are not possible. *(Page 18.)*

Index

Note: Page references in italics indicate photographs or illustrations. Page references with *f, m, n,* or *t* refer to figures, maps, notes, and tables respectively.

Photo Credits

1 The Logic of American Politics
2 AP Images
6 Library of Congress
14 AP Images (left, right, below)/Getty Images (center)
16 Courtesy of Photofest for 20th Century Fox (left, right)
18 North Wind Picture Archives
21 AP Images
24 Library of Congress
25 Andrew Winning/Reuters/Landov
28 Library of Congress
30 © The New Yorker Cartoon Collection 1997 Frank Cotham from cartoonbank.com. All Rights Reserved.
33 Los Angeles Times
36 Warren J. Samuels Portrait Collection at Duke University

2 The Constitution
44 Library of Congress
47 Library of Congress
49 Library of Congress
51 Library of Congress
54 Library of Congress
60 CQ File Photo
66 AP Images
70 Library of Congress (left)/AP Images (right)
74 Library of Congress
76 Corbis/Bettmann
81 North Wind Picture Archives
84 CQ File Photo
86 AP Images

3 Federalism
94 AP Images
101 Artizans
112 Getty Images
114 Library of Congress
116 AP Images
118 Corbis/Bettmann
120 Georgia Department of Economic Development (left)/Getty Images (right)
122 AP Images
126 AP Images
127 AP Images
130 Getty Images
132 Getty Images
134 AP Images

4 Civil Rights
138 Lyndon B. Johnson Library Collection
140 Farm Security Administration, Office of War Information Photograph Collection/Library of Congress
141 Courtesy of the ACLU
144 Photographs and Prints Division/Schomberg Center for Research in Black Culture/The New York Public Library/Astor, Lenox, Tilden Foundations
147 The Granger Collection, New York
148 Courtesy of the Lincoln Museum
152 Photofest
154 Library of Congress

156 Franklin D. Roosevelt Presidential Library
161 Will Counts (left, right)
164 AP Images
165 AP Images
167 AP Images
168 Lyndon B. Johnson Library Collection
174 AP Images
178 Chicago History Museum
181 Corbis/Bettmann
185 © 2004 The New Yorker Cartoon Collection from cartoonbank.com

5 Civil Liberties
190 Getty Images
193 Missouri Eminent Domain Abuse Coalition
206 AP Images
207 Academy Foundation/Margaret Herrick Library
212 Corbis/Bettmann
215 AP Images
216 AP Images
219 Steve Latham/The Gadsden Times
238 Courtesy of Anthony Palazzolo

6 Congress
246 Larry Downing/Reuters/Landov
248 R. Michael Jenkins/Congressional Quarterly
250 Library of Congress
254 Library of Congress
258 Jay Mallin/Bloomberg News/Landov
260 Sam Kernell
264 AP Images
269 AP Images
272 Scott J. Ferrell/Congressional Quarterly
275 Library of Congress
278 © 2007 Matt Wuerker/Cartoonist Group
281 Office of Sen. Robert Byrd
282 AP Images
286 AP Images
289 Jason Reed/Reuters/Landov
292 © The Birmingham News 2002. All Rights Reserved. Reprinted with permission.
297 AP Images
300 Strom Thurmond Institute
304 Scott J. Ferrell/Congressional Quarterly

7 The Presidency
314 AP Images
316 Reuters/Landov
320 © 2005 Nick Anderson/Washington Post Writers Group/Cartoonist Group
322 Library of Congress
323 Library of Congress
327 Kevin Lamarque/Reuters/Landov
329 Christer Weyant, The Hill
330 Courtesy of the Harry S. Truman Library
345 AP Images
346 Courtesy of the Ronald Reagan Presidential Library
353 AP Images

About the Authors

Left to right: Samuel Kernell, Thad Kousser, and Gary C. Jacobson.

Samuel Kernell is professor of political science at the University of California, San Diego, where he has taught since 1977. Previously, he taught at the University of Mississippi and the University of Minnesota. Kernell's research interests focus on the presidency and American political history. His books include *Going Public: New Strategies of Presidential Leadership,* 4th Edition; an edited collection of essays, *James Madison: The Theory and Practice of Republican Government;* and, also with Gary C. Jacobson, *Strategy and Choice in Congressional Elections,* 2nd Edition.

Gary C. Jacobson is professor of political science at the University of California, San Diego, where he has taught since 1979. He previously taught at Trinity College, the University of California at Riverside, Yale University, and Stanford University. Jacobson specializes in the study of U.S. elections, parties, interest groups, and Congress. He is the author of *Money in Congressional Elections; The Politics of Congressional Elections,* 7th Edition; *The Electoral Origins of Divided Government: Com-*

petition in the U.S. House Elections, 1946–1988; and *A Divider, Not a Uniter: George W. Bush and the American People;* and is coauthor with Samuel Kernell of *Strategy and Choice in Congressional Elections,* 2nd Edition. Jacobson is a Fellow of the American Academy of Arts and Sciences.

Thad Kousser is associate professor of political science at the University of California, San Diego. He has served as a legislative aide in the California, New Mexico, and U.S. Senates. His publications include work on term limits, the initiative process, voting by mail, reapportionment, campaign finance laws, the blanket primary, health care policy, and European Parliament elections. He is the author of *Term Limits and the Dismantling of State Legislative Professionalism,* which won the APSA Legislative Studies Section's Alan Rosenthal Prize, and the coeditor of *The New Political Geography of California.* Kousser has been awarded the UCSD Academic Senate's Distinguished Teaching Award, and he serves as coeditor of *State Politics and Policy Quarterly.*